Business
Plans
Handbook

Highlights

Business Plans Handbook, Volume 3 (BPH -3) is a collection of actual business plans compiled by entrepreneurs seeking funding for small businesses throughout North America. For those looking for examples of how to approach, structure, and compose their own business plans, *BPH-3* presents 25 sample plans, including plans for the following businesses:

- Auto Accessories and Detailing
- Carpet Cleaning Service
- Computer Matchmaking Service
- Dial-It Service
- Fast Food
- Indoor Playground
- Internet Consultant

- Mailing List Service
- Manufacturing Business
- Marketing Consultant
- Multilevel Marketing
- Pharmaceutical Company
- Refrigerant Recovery
- Video Service

FEATURES AND BENEFITS

BPH-3 offers many features not provided by other business planning references including:

○ Twenty-five business plans, with a focus on the uses and effects of the Internet and various online services within the small business sector, and the explosion of franchising opportunities. Each of these real business plans represents an owner's successful attempt at clarifying (for themselves and others) the reasons that the business should exist or expand and why a lender should fund the enterprise.

○ Two fictional plans that are used by business counselors at a prominent small business development organization as examples for their clients. (You will find these in the Business Plan Template Appendix.)

○ An expanded directory section that includes: listings for venture capital and finance companies, which specialize in funding start-up and second-stage small business ventures, and a comprehensive listing of Service Corps of Retired Executives (SCORE) offices. In addition, the Appendix also contains updated listings of all Small Business Development Centers (SBDCs); associations of interest to entrepreneurs; Small Business Administration (SBA) Regional Offices; and consultants specializing in small business planning and advice. It is strongly advised that you consult supporting organizations while planning your business, as they can provide a wealth of useful information.

○ An enhanced Glossary, including over 100 new small business terms, to help you decipher the sometimes confusing terminology used by lenders and others in the financial and small business communities.

○ An expanded bibliography, arranged by subject, containing citations from over 1,500 small business reference publications and trade periodicals.

○ A Business Plan Template which serves as a model to help you construct your own business plan. This generic outline lists all the essential elements of a complete business plan and their components, including the Summary, Business History and Industry Outlook, Market Examination, Competition, Marketing, Administration and Management, Financial Information, and other key sections. Use this guide as a starting point for compiling your plan. Also in this section are two fictional plans used as examples by professional business counselors.

○ Extensive financial documentation required to solicit funding from small business lenders. *BPH-3* contains the most comprehensive financial data within the series to date. You will find examples of: Cash Flows, Balance Sheets, Income Projections, and other financial information included with the textual portions of the plan.

Business Plans Handbook

A COMPILATION OF ACTUAL BUSINESS PLANS DEVELOPED BY SMALL BUSINESSES THROUGHOUT NORTH AMERICA

VOLUME 3

Amy Lynn Park,
Editor

Virgil L. Burton, III,
Eva M. Felts,
Angela M. Shupe,
Associate Editors

GALE

DETROIT • NEW YORK • TORONTO • LONDON

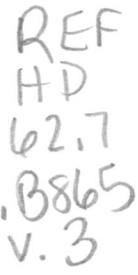
Editor: Amy Lynn Park

Contributing Editors: Kelly Hill, Jennifer Arnold Mast, Holly M. Selden, Deborah J. Untener
Associate Editors: Virgil L. Burton III, Eva M. Felts, Angela M. Shupe
Assistant Editors: Kimberly N. Hunt, Cynthia R. Parker

Managing Editor: Deborah M. Burek

Production Director: Mary Beth Trimper
Assistant Production Manager: Evi Seoud
Production Assistant: Deborah Milliken

Product Design Manager: Cynthia Baldwin
Desktop Publisher: CJ Jonik

Data Entry Supervisor: Gwendolyn S. Tucker

ISBN 0-7876-0952-8
ISSN 1084-4473

The paper used in this publication meets the minimum requirements of American National Standard for Information Sciences—Permanence Paper for Printed Library Materials, ANSI Z39.48-1984.

Printed in the United States of America

Gale Research
Detroit * New York * Toronto * London

Contents

Appendixes

Introduction

METHODS OF COMPILATION

In order to provide our readers with the most timely business plan information, we corresponded with over 400 small business consultants and monitored small business bulletin boards on the Internet. The explosion of online and electronic mediums has unleashed a plethora of small business opportunities and entrepreneurial ventures. By utilizing these resources while compiling the third volume of *Business Plans Handbook (BPH-3),* we believe that we have captured the current trends, identified the fastest growing industries, and witnessed the future possibilities available to visionary entrepreneurs.

This third volume, like each volume of the series, offers genuine business plans used by real people. *BPH-3* provides 25 business plans used by actual entrepreneurs to gain funding support for their new businesses. Only the business and personal names have been changed to protect the privacy of the plan authors.

NEW BUSINESS OPPORTUNITIES

There are 25 genuine business plans in the third volume of *BPH,* including several examples of business plans for new and growing business opportunities. Examples of such business opportunities can be found within the evolving world of Internet/Online services and in the expanding franchise industry. We have included numerous plans detailing the exploitation of the Internet and various online services to develop and expand fledgling businesses. Entrepreneurs have identified new markets, creating global avenues for marketing and selling products/services; gained accessibility to customers by utilizing e-mail and electronic surveys; and created support networks with fellow entrepreneurs to obtain essential industry statistics, resources, and advice. We have also included two plans for businesses that were developed as a result of the introduction of the Internet into the mainstream business community. These businesses can be found in the Internet Consultant chapter of *BPH-3.* The Internet Consultant business plans include profiles of the emerging electronic industry; marketing strategies; competition; and financial data, including Projected Income Statements and Balance Sheets.

The franchise plans we have collected detail the specific strategies and goals necessary to establish a successful franchise venture. Common topics found in the franchise plans include: market analysis; competitive strategies; operation and management plans; and extensive financial data. In an attempt to cover all aspects of the franchise industry, we also include a pair of business plans which illustrate the relationship between a franchising organization and a prospective franchisee. The inclusion of these two plans provides valuable how-to instruction for expanding a business by franchising, as well as initial start-up and operating strategies for a newly acquired franchise business. You can find these plans, Pasta Express and Pasta Now!, in the Fast Food chapter of *BPH-3.*

The business plans in *BPH-3* contain the most extensive financial data in the series. Comprehensive financial documentation has become increasingly important as today's entrepreneurs compete for the finite resources of business lenders. Our plans illustrate the financial data generally required of loan applicants, including Income Statements, Financial Projections, Cash Flows, and Balance Sheets.

ENHANCED APPENDIXES

In an effort to provide the most relevant and valuable information for our readers, we have further expanded the coverage of small business resources. For instance, you will find: an enlarged directory section, which now includes a listing of all of the Service Corps of Retired Executives (SCORE) offices; venture capital and finance companies, which specialize in funding start-up and second-stage small business enterprises; an expanded glossary, which includes over 100 new small business terms; and an expanded bibliography, which includes reference titles essential to starting and operating a business venture in all 50 states. In addition we have updated the list of Small Business Development Centers (SBDCs); associations of interest to entrepreneurs; and consultants, specializing in small business advice and planning. For your reference, we have also reprinted the business plan template, which provides a comprehensive overview of the essential components of a business plan and two fictional plans used by small business counselors.

NEW FORMAT

We have once again revised the page layout of *BPH* to include more text and financial tables per page. Several of the Appendix sections have also been revised to accommodate a three-column format, which allows us to increase the coverage of associations, organizations, and publications of interest to entrepreneurs.

SERIES INFORMATION

If you already have the first two volumes of *BPH*, with this third volume, you will now have a collection of 81 real business plans (not including the one plan reprinted in the second volume from the first, or the two fictional plans in the Business Plan Template Appendix section of the second and third volumes); contact information for hundreds of organizations and agencies offering business expertise; a helpful business plan template; a foreword providing advice and instruction to entrepreneurs on how to begin their research; more than 1,500 citations to valuable small business development material; and a comprehensive glossary of terms to help the business planner navigate the sometimes confusing language of entrepreneurship.

ACKNOWLEDGEMENTS

The Editor wishes to thank all of the members of the Small Business Resources and Technology team, especially Angela M. Shupe, Virgil L. Burton III, Eva M. Felts, Kelly Hill, Kimberly N. Hunt, Jennifer Arnold Mast, Cynthia R. Parker, and Deborah J. Untener all of whom contributed to this project in unique and valuable ways.

Thanks are also in order for the many contributors to *BPH-3*, a number of whom have very good timing and whose business plans will serve as examples to future generations of entrepreneurs: the users of the title who called with their helpful suggestions; and World Franchise Consultants, for their shared knowledge and contributions regarding the franchise industry. Your help was greatly appreciated.

COMMENTS WELCOME

Your comments on *BPH-3* are appreciated. Please direct all correspondence, suggestions for future volumes of *BPH*, and other recommendations to the following:

Business Plans Handbook, Volume 3
Gale Research
835 Penobscot Bldg.
Detroit MI 48226-4094
Phone: (313)961-2242
Fax: 800-339-3374
Toll-Free: 800-347-GALE
Telex: 810 221 7087
E-mail: SmallBus@gale.com@galesmtp

Business Plans

Auto Accessories and Detailing

BUSINESS PLAN

AUTO ACCESSORIES UNLIMITED

1012 Lafayette Blvd.
Allen Park, MI 48101

This business plan for an auto accessories and detailing facility contains a comprehensive list of the physical needs of the business, as well as a detailed account of the financial status of the business.

- BUSINESS DESCRIPTION

- MARKET ANALYSIS

- PRODUCTS AND SERVICES

- MARKETING STRATEGY

BUSINESS DESCRIPTION	Auto Accessories Unlimited provides automotive aftermarket accessories, electronics, and glass repair and replacement.
Name	Auto Accessories Unlimited's corporate experience includes 29 stores in the Michigan tri-state area. Franchises for the stores have been offered since 1984. The Allen Park location has approximately 4,800 square feet, consisting of a 2,000 sqare foot retail showroom, 500 square feet in office space, and a 2,300 square foot on-site installation service area divided into six bays.

Products and Services

Auto Accessories Unlimited's products and services consist of:

- Auto security
- Car audio systems
- Cellular
- Car and truck accessories
- Auto care protection
- Glass repair and replacement
- Classic car parts

Market and Competition

Nationally: steady continuous growth for the last ten years
Regionally: very popular, some areas fairly unexposed but continuous growth
Locally: untapped, virtually no advertising done. Not a single company in area offering even half as much. Very few of those companies even offer such products or services.
Competition:
Auto security - three players in town. No advertising.
Car audio systems - same three players. One major advertiser.
Cellular - many players. Both GTE and Cellular One. Very little advertising. Some newspaper, very little radio.
Auto accessories - almost non-existent. No advertising.
Truck accessories - no real competition.
Auto care protection - one major player; little advertising.
Glass replacement - three major players; one well established.
Classic car parts - no competition.

Management Expertise

Auto Accessories Unlimited is a partnership between Jane De Vries and Mike Hansen. As co-owner, Jane will be the sales manager, with nine years of increased responsibilities in automotive aftermarket and cellular sales, including management of Car Tunes of Grand Rapids, Michigan. Mike will be the service shop manager, with more than five years of aftermarket installation experience. Both will be responsible for customer service in the overall operations of the business.

Business Goals

- To establish and maintain the number one market position of the automotive after-market accessories business in the local market, opening two additional stores within the next five years.
- To strive for 100% customer satisfaction by establishing a loyal and repeat customer base.
- To provide consistent services and affordable quality products.

Summary of Financial Needs and Applications of Funds

The following table lists the top-level approximate investment needed to provide the resources to build, establish, and maintain a successful business. The second table lists business collateral along with a proforma with estimated annual sales of $500,000 for the first year.

Application of Funds and Financial Need

Franchise	$24,000
Shop Equipment	17,900
Office and Showroom Equipment	21,000
Inventory	28,000
Store Awning	5,000
Signage	3,500
Neon Lighting	3,000
Working Capital	25,000
Set-up Costs	1,500
Interior Development	2,500
Training	1,000
Rent Deposit	3,800
Other Deposits	2,000
Insurance	2,000
CPA/Attorney	2,500
Grand Opening	5,500
Miscellaneous	2,000
TOTAL	**$150,000**

Funds Breakdown

Shop Equipment

100 gallon air compressor
Heavy-duty pressure washer
Gold/chrome plating machine
Drive-on auto lift (7000 lb.)
Large tool chest with complete set of tools (approx. $2,500)
Makita cordless drills
Electric Makita drill
Assorted air drills
Makita air snips
Makita electric snips
Two shampoo interior extractors
Wet/dry heavy-duty vacuums
Two buffers
Two polishers
Heavy-duty jig saws
Impact air tools
Air ratchets
Heavy duty washer and dryer
Battery charger
Jumper cables
Dremel tool
Solder guns
Heat guns
Die grinders
Vice
Bench grinder
Fender covers
File set
Blow guns
Drop-cord lights

Tube lights
Extension cords
Air hoses
Multi-meters
Heavy-duty drill bit set
Punch and chisels
Tape measures
Rubber mallets
Utility knives
Large supply of electrical connectors
Various nuts and bolts
Ozone machine (odor remover)
Metal storage cabinets
Large metal bins
Heavy-duty folding tables
Numerous detailing accessories
Miscellaneous

Office Equipment
Fax machine
Copier
Phone system
Computers
486x100 pentium services
CD ROM drive
1 grey scale scanner
1 laser printer
1 dot matrix printer
3 14" color VGA monitors
Software
3 large desks and 6 chairs
Assorted filing cabinets
Credit-card terminal and printer
Metal storage cabinets
Large deluxe customer counter (to be built)
Office supplies

Showroom Equipment
Large audio display and comparator/sound room (to be built)
Waiting room seating
Small TV for waiting room
Water cooler
Display racks
232 square feet of slatwall and hangers
Tint display

NOTE: Numbered items below correspond to items listed in the table - "Applications of Funds"

Collateral

Shop equipment	$17,900	
Office and showroom equipment	21,000	
Inventory	28,000	
Rent deposit	3,800	
Other deposits	2,000	48%
Total	**72,700**	

Additional Collateral (to sell at one-half value)

Franchise	$12,000	56%
Total	**84,700**	

Additional Collateral (to sell to other locations at 75% of cost)

Awnings	5,000	
Signage	3,500	
Neon lighting	3,000	62%
	$11,500 x .75 = 8,625	
Total	**$93,325**	

Working capital of .5 of original figure ($25,000)	12,500	70%
Total	**$105,825**	

Operations Budget	**500,000**

Proforma 1996/1997

Income	May 96	Jun 96	Jul 96	Aug 96	Sep 96	Oct 96	Nov 96	Dec 96	Jan 97	Feb 97	Mar 97	Apr 97	Total	YTD
Sales-Auto Glass	5000	4000	4500	4000	4500	4500	3500	4000	3500	3500	4500	4500	50000	10%
Sales-Cellular	6000	4800	5400	4800	5400	5400	4200	4800	4200	4200	5400	5400	60000	12%
Sales-Security	13500	10800	12150	10800	12150	12150	9450	10800	9450	9450	12150	12150	135000	27%
Sales-Accessories	11500	9200	10350	9200	10350	10350	8050	9200	8050	8050	10350	10350	115000	23%
Sales-Detailing	6500	5200	5850	5200	5850	5850	4550	5200	4550	4550	5850	5850	65000	13%
Sales-Classic Parts	2500	2000	2250	2000	2250	2250	1750	2000	1750	1750	2250	2250	25000	5%
Sales-Audio	5000	4000	4500	4000	4500	4500	3500	4000	3500	3500	4500	4500	50000	10%
Net Income %	50000	40000	45000	40000	45000	45000	35000	40000	35000	35000	45000	45000	500000	100%
Cost of Sales														
Cost-Auto Glass	2000	1600	1800	1600	1800	1800	1400	1600	1400	1400	1800	1800	20000	
Cost-Cellular	300	240	270	240	270	270	210	240	210	210	270	270	3000	
Cost-Security	4725	3780	4253	3780	4253	4253	3308	3780	3308	3308	4253	4253	47250	
Cost-Accessories	4600	3680	4140	3680	4140	4140	3220	3680	3220	3220	4140	4140	46000	
Cost-Detailing	325	260	293	260	293	293	228	260	228	228	293	293	3250	
Cost-Classic Parts	1250	1000	1125	1000	1125	1125	875	1000	875	875	1125	1125	12500	
Cost-Audio	2000	1600	1800	1600	1800	1800	1400	1600	1400	1400	1800	1800	20000	
Direct Labor	4000	3200	3600	3200	3600	3600	2800	3200	2800	2800	3600	3600	40000	
Total Cost of Sales	19200	15360	17280	15360	17280	17280	13440	15360	13440	13440	17280	17280	192000	
Gross Profit Margin	30800	24640	27720	24640	27720	27720	21560	24640	21560	21560	27720	27720	308000	
G&A Expenses														
Salaries-Office														
Salaries-Sales	2426	2426	2426	2426	2426	2426	2426	2426	2426	2426	2426	2426	29112	
Sales-Management	6000	6000	6000	6000	6000	6000	6000	6000	6000	6000	6000	6000	72000	
Casual Labor	45	45	45	45	45	45	45	45	45	45	45	45	540	
Subcontract Labor	150	150	150	150	150	150	150	150	150	150	150	150	1800	
Payroll Taxes	994	930	962	930	962	962	898	930	898	898	962	962	11289	
Outside Services	50	50	50	50	50	50	50	50	50	50	50	50	600	
Royalties	1500	1500	1500	1500	1500	1500	1500	1500	1500	1500	1500	1500	18000	
Rent	3500	3500	3500	3500	3500	3500	3500	3500	3500	3500	3500	3500	42000	
Office Supplies	125	125	125	125	125	125	125	125	125	125	125	125	1500	
Repairs & Maintenance	0	0	0	0	0	0	0	0	0	0	0	0	0	
Uniforms	100	100	100	100	100	100	100	100	100	100	100	100	1200	
Utilities	400	400	400	400	400	400	400	400	400	400	400	400	4800	

Bldg & Grds Maintenance	0	0	0	0	0	0	0	0	0	0	0	0	0
Automobile Lease	0	0	0	0	0	0	0	0	0	0	0	0	0
Automobile Expense	150	150	150	150	150	150	150	150	150	150	150	150	1800
Postage	200	200	200	200	200	200	200	200	200	200	200	200	2400
Printing	125	125	125	125	125	125	125	125	125	125	125	125	1500
Forms & Stationery	100	100	100	100	100	100	100	100	100	100	100	100	1200
Telephone	333	333	333	333	333	333	333	333	333	333	333	333	3996
Advertising	3333	3333	3333	3333	3333	3333	3333	3333	3333	3333	3333	3333	39996
Membership	20	20	20	20	20	20	20	20	20	20	20	20	240
Dues & Subscriptions	20	20	20	20	20	20	20	20	20	20	20	20	240
Office Equipment Rental	25	25	25	25	25	25	25	25	25	25	25	25	300
Contributions	10	10	10	10	10	10	10	10	10	10	10	10	120
Training/Education	100	100	100	100	100	100	100	100	100	100	100	100	1200
Entertainment	250	250	250	250	250	250	250	250	250	250	250	250	3000
Legal & Accounting	350	350	350	350	350	350	350	350	350	350	350	350	4200
Bank Charges	250	250	250	250	250	250	250	250	250	250	250	250	3000
Bank Business Loan	1983	1983	1983	1983	1983	1983	1983	1983	1983	1983	1983	1983	23796
Interest Expense	10	10	10	10	10	10	10	10	10	10	10	10	120
License & Fees	30	30	30	30	30	30	30	30	30	30	30	30	360
Property Tax	0	0	0	0	0	0	0	0	0	0	0	0	0
Property Tax-Personal	50	50	50	50	50	50	50	50	50	50	50	50	600
Insurance-General	70	70	70	70	70	70	70	70	70	70	70	70	840
Insurance-Medical	70	70	70	70	70	70	70	70	70	70	70	70	840
Insurance-Workers Comp.	70	70	70	70	70	70	70	70	70	70	70	70	840
Employee Benefits	40	40	40	40	40	40	40	40	40	40	40	40	480
Equipment Lease	0	0	0	0	0	0	0	0	0	0	0	0	0
Total G&A Expenses	22879	22815	22847	22815	22847	22847	22783	22815	22783	22783	22847	22847	273909
Operating Profit/Loss	7921	1825	4873	1825	4873	4873	-1223	1825	-1223	4873	-1223	4873	34091

Operations Budget

550,000 10% increase from previous year

Proforma 1997/1998

Income	May 97	Jun 97	Jul 97	Aug 97	Sep 97	Oct 97	Nov 97	Dec 97	Jan 98	Feb 98	Mar 98	Apr 98	Total	YTD
Sales-Auto Glass	5500	4400	4950	4400	4950	4950	3850	4400	3850	3850	4950	4950	55000	10%
Sales-Cellular	6600	5280	5940	5280	5940	5940	4620	5280	4620	4620	5940	5940	66000	12%
Sales-Security	14850	11880	13365	11880	13365	13365	10395	11880	10395	10395	13365	13365	148500	27%
Sales-Accessories	12650	10120	11385	11880	10120	11385	8855	10120	8855	8855	11385	11385	126500	23%
Sales-Detailing	7150	5720	6435	5720	6435	6435	5005	5720	5005	5005	6435	6435	71500	13%
Sales-Classic Parts	2750	2200	2475	2200	2475	2475	1925	2200	1925	1925	2475	2475	27500	5%
Sales-Audio	5500	4400	4950	4400	4950	4950	3850	4400	3850	3850	4950	4950	55000	10%
Net Income %	55000	44000	49500	44000	49500	49500	38500	44000	38500	38500	49500	49500	550000	100%
Cost of Sales														
Cost-Auto Glass	2200	1760	1980	1760	1980	1980	1540	1760	1540	1540	1980	1980	22000	
Cost-Cellular	330	264	297	264	297	297	231	264	231	231	297	297	3300	
Cost-Security	5198	4158	4678	4158	4678	4678	3638	4158	3638	3638	4678	4678	51975	
Cost-Accessories	5060	4048	4554	4048	4554	4554	3542	4048	3542	3542	4554	4554	50600	
Cost-Detailing	358	286	322	286	322	322	250	286	250	250	322	322	3575	

Cost-Classic Parts	1375	1100	1238	1100	1238	1238	963	1100	963	963	1238	1238	13750
Cost-Audio	2200	1760	1980	1760	1980	1980	1540	1760	1540	1540	1980	1980	22000
Direct Labor	4400	3520	3960	3520	3960	3960	3080	3520	3080	3080	3960	3960	44000
Total Cost of Sales	21120	16896	19008	16896	19008	19008	14784	16896	14784	14784	19008	19008	211200
Gross Profit Margin	33880	27104	30492	27104	30492	30492	23716	27104	23716	23716	30492	30492	338800

G&A Expenses
Salaries-Office

Salaries-Sales	2426	2426	2426	2426	2426	2426	2426	2426	2426	2426	2426	2426	29112
Sales-Management	6000	6000	6000	6000	6000	6000	6000	6000	6000	6000	6000	6000	72000
Casual Labor	45	45	45	45	45	45	45	45	45	45	45	45	540
Subcontract Labor	150	150	150	150	150	150	150	150	150	150	150	150	1800
Payroll Taxes	1026	956	991	956	991	991	920	956	920	920	991	991	11609
Outside Services	50	50	50	50	50	50	50	50	50	50	50	50	600
Royalties	1500	1500	1500	1500	1500	1500	1500	1500	1500	1500	1500	1500	18000
Rent	3500	3500	3500	3500	3500	3500	3500	3500	3500	3500	3500	3500	42000
Office Supplies	125	125	125	125	125	125	125	125	125	125	125	125	1500
Repairs & Maintenance	0	0	0	0	0	0	0	0	0	0	0	0	0
Uniforms	100	100	100	100	100	100	100	100	100	100	100	100	1200
Utilities	400	400	400	400	400	400	400	400	400	400	400	400	4800
Bldg & Grds Maintenance	0	0	0	0	0	0	0	0	0	0	0	0	0
Automobile Lease	0	0	0	0	0	0	0	0	0	0	0	0	0
Automobile Expense	150	150	150	150	150	150	150	150	150	150	150	150	1800
Postage	200	200	200	200	200	200	200	200	200	200	200	200	2400
Printing	125	125	125	125	125	125	125	125	125	125	125	125	1500
Forms & Stationery	100	100	100	100	100	100	100	100	100	100	100	100	1200
Telephone	333	333	333	333	333	333	333	333	333	333	333	333	3996
Advertising	3333	3333	3333	3333	3333	3333	3333	3333	3333	3333	3333	3333	39996
Membership	20	20	20	20	20	20	20	20	20	20	20	20	240
Dues & Subscriptions	20	20	20	20	20	20	20	20	20	20	20	20	240
Office Equipment Rental	25	25	25	25	25	25	25	25	25	25	25	25	300
Contributions	10	10	10	10	10	10	10	10	10	10	10	10	120
Training/Educations	100	100	100	100	100	100	100	100	100	100	100	100	1200
Entertainment	250	250	250	250	250	250	250	250	250	250	250	250	3000
Legal & Accounting	350	350	350	350	350	350	350	350	350	350	350	350	4200
Bank Charges	250	250	250	250	250	250	250	250	250	250	250	250	3000
Bank Business Loan	1983	1983	1983	1983	1983	1983	1983	1983	1983	1983	1983	1983	23796
Interest Expense	10	10	10	10	10	10	10	10	10	10	10	10	120
License & Fees	30	30	30	30	30	30	30	30	30	30	30	30	360
Property Tax	0	0	0	0	0	0	0	0	0	0	0	0	0
Property Tax-Personal	50	50	50	50	50	50	50	50	50	50	50	50	600
Insurance-General	70	70	70	70	70	70	70	70	70	70	70	70	840
Insurance-Medical	70	70	70	70	70	70	70	70	70	70	70	70	840
Insurance-Workers Comp.	70	70	70	70	70	70	70	70	70	70	70	70	840
Employee Benefits	40	40	40	40	40	40	40	40	40	40	40	40	480
Equipment Lease	0	0	0	0	0	0	0	0	0	0	0	0	0
Total G&A Expenses	22911	22841	22876	22841	22876	22876	22805	22841	22805	22805	22876	22876	274229
Operating Profit/Loss	10969	4263	7616	4263	7616	7616	911	4263	911	911	7616	7616	64571

Operations Budget
605,000 10% increase from previous year

Proforma 1998/1999

Income	May 98	Jun 98	Jul 98	Aug 98	Sept 98	Oct 98	Nov 98	Dec 98	Jan 99	Feb 99	Mar 99	Apr 99	Total	YTD
Sales-Auto Glass	6050	4840	5445	4840	5445	5445	4235	4840	4235	4235	5445	55445	60500	10%
Sales-Cellular	7260	5808	6534	5808	6534	6534	5082	5808	5082	5082	6534	6534	72600	12%
Sales-Security	16335	13068	14702	13068	14702	14702	11435	13068	11435	11435	14702	14702	163350	27%
Sales-Accessories	13915	11132	12524	11132	12524	22524	9741	11132	9741	9741	12524	12524	139150	23%
Sales-Detailing	7865	6292	7079	6292	7079	7079	5506	6292	5506	5506	7079	7079	78650	13%
Sales-Classic Parts	3025	2420	2723	2420	2723	2723	2118	2420	2118	2118	2723	2723	30250	5%
Sales-Audio	6050	4840	5445	4840	5445	5445	4235	4840	4235	4235	5445	5445	60500	10%
Net Income %	60500	48400	54450	48400	54450	54450	42350	48400	42350	42350	54450	54450	605000	100%
Cost of Sales														
Cost-Auto Glass	2420	1936	2178	1936	2178	2178	1694	1936	1694	1694	2178	2178	24200	
Cost-Cellular	363	290	327	290	327	327	254	290	254	254	327	327	3630	
Cost-Security	5717	4574	5146	4574	5146	5146	4002	5474	4002	4002	5146	5146	57173	
Cost-Accessories	5566	4453	5009	4453	5009	5009	3896	4453	3896	3896	5009	5009	55660	
Cost-Detailing	393	315	354	315	354	354	275	315	275	275	354	354	3933	
Cost-Classic Parts	1513	1210	1361	1210	1361	1361	1059	1210	1059	1059	1361	1361	15125	
Cost-Audio	2420	1936	2178	1936	2178	2178	1694	1936	1694	1694	2178	2178	24200	
Direct Labor	4840	3872	4356	3872	4356	4356	3388	3872	3388	3388	4356	4356	48400	
Total Cost of Sales	23232	18586	20909	18586	20909	20909	16262	18586	16262	16262	20909	20909	232320	
Gross Profit Margin	37268	29814	33541	29814	33541	33541	26088	29814	26088	26088	33541	33541	372680	
G&A Expenses														
Salaries-Office														
Salaries-Sales	2547	2547	2547	2547	2547	2547	2547	2547	2547	2547	2547	2547	30568	
Sales-Management	6300	6300	6300	6300	6300	6300	6300	6300	6300	6300	6300	6300	75600	
Casual Labor	45	45	45	45	45	45	45	45	45	45	45	45	540	
Subcontract Labor	150	150	150	150	150	150	150	150	150	150	150	150	1800	
Payroll Taxes	1095	1018	1056	1018	1056	1058	979	1018	979	979	1056	1056	12365	
Outside Services	50	50	50	50	50	50	50	50	50	50	50	50	600	
Royalties	1500	1500	1500	1500	1500	1500	1500	1500	1500	1500	1500	1500	18000	
Rent	3500	3500	3500	3500	3500	3500	3500	3500	3500	3500	3500	3500	42000	
Office Supplies	125	125	125	125	125	125	125	125	125	125	125	125	1500	
Repairs & Maintenance	0	0	0	0	0	0	0	0	0	0	0	0	0	
Uniforms	100	100	100	100	100	100	100	100	100	100	100	100	1200	
Utilities	400	400	400	400	400	400	400	400	400	400	400	400	4800	
Bldg & Grds Maintenance	0	0	0	0	0	0	0	0	0	0	0	0	0	
Automobile Lease	0	0	0	0	0	0	0	0	0	0	0	0	0	
Automobile Expense	150	150	150	150	150	150	150	150	150	150	150	150	1800	
Postage	200	200	200	200	200	200	200	200	200	200	200	200	2400	
Printing	125	125	125	125	125	125	125	125	125	125	125	125	1500	
Forms & Stationery	100	100	100	100	100	100	100	100	100	100	100	100	1200	
Telephone	333	333	333	333	333	333	333	333	333	333	333	333	3996	
Advertising	3333	3333	3333	3333	3333	3333	3333	3333	3333	3333	3333	3333	39996	
Membership	20	20	20	20	20	20	20	20	20	20	20	20	240	
Dues & Subscriptions	20	20	20	20	20	20	20	20	20	20	20	20	240	
Office Equipment Rental	25	25	25	25	25	25	25	25	25	25	25	25	300	
Contributions	10	10	10	10	10	10	10	10	10	10	10	10	120	
Training/Education	100	100	100	100	100	100	100	100	100	100	100	100	1200	
Entertainment	250	250	250	250	250	250	250	250	250	250	250	250	3000	
Legal & Accounting	350	350	350	350	350	350	350	350	350	350	350	350	4200	

Bank Charges	250	250	250	250	250	250	250	250	250	250	250	250	3000
Bank Business Loan	1983	1983	1983	1983	1983	1983	1983	1983	1983	1983	1983	1983	23796
Interest Expense	10	10	10	10	10	10	10	10	10	10	10	10	120
License & Fees	30	30	30	30	30	30	30	30	30	30	30	30	360
Property Tax	0	0	0	0	0	0	0	0	0	0	0	0	0
Property Tax-Personal	50	50	50	50	50	50	50	50	50	50	50	50	600
Insurance-General	70	70	70	70	70	70	70	70	70	70	70	70	840
Insurance-Medical	70	70	70	70	70	70	70	70	70	70	70	70	840
Insurance-Workers Comp.	70	70	70	70	70	70	70	70	70	70	70	70	840
Employee Benefits	40	40	40	40	40	40	40	40	40	40	40	40	480
Equipment Lease	0	0	0	0	0	0	0	0	0	0	0	0	0
Total G&A Expenses	23401	23324	23363	23324	23363	23363	23285	23324	23285	23285	23363	23363	280041
Operating Profit/Loss	13867	6491	10179	6491	10179	10179	2802	6491	2802	2802	10179	10179	92639

Operating Profit by Year

Year	Operating Profit
96-97	34091
97-98	64571
98-99	92639
99-00	129520
00-01	158623
01-02	158623
02-03	158623
03-04	158623
04-05	158623
05-06	158623
06-07	182419
Total (10 Years)	**1454975**

MARKET ANALYSIS

Auto Accessories Unlimited covers the retail, wholesale, commercial fleet, insurance and business-to-business markets.

Description of Total Market

The primary market consist of females between the ages of 18-50 and males between the ages of 16-55. We will target high-school graduates with an annual income of at least $15,000.

The county-wide market (population) to be targeted is 78,000+ of 130,000. The eight-county market targeted is 203,000 of 290,000. Market ratio of men to women is 50/50.

Average income of the target market is $27,500 with roughly 22% of income going toward automobile purchase and improvements. Eleven percent of additional income is used toward vehicle maintenance and insurance.

- Average number of cars per household is 2.
- Average amount paid for new vehicles is $17,000.
- Average amount paid for used vehicles is $7,100.
- Average finance time for new vehicles is 4+ years
- Average age of vehicles on road today is 7+ years.
- Average mileage per year is 13,000-18,000.
- Average daily amount of time spent in vehicles is 60 minutes.

Industry Trends

Economic

In good times—more cars are purchased (in turn providing more miles to be driven). Steady production of new cars and a very high trend toward leasing. Usually spend more money on service and appearance work. Costs for service is greater. Increased number of cars on the road. Trade-in market becomes healthier but much more inexpensive, thus allowing owners to spend more money on extras.

In poor times—people keep cars longer, thus requiring more service and care of cars. Owners try to make cars look better and last longer. The market keeps resale value higher. People like to feel good about their older cars being in such good shape.

Vehicles

The number-one selling vehicle in America is the truck. With that comes the need for a number of accessories and vehicle protection. Trucks and sports cars have the highest theft rate of all stolen vehicles, thus a need for auto security (insurance) increases.

Because today's vehicles have more glass than earlier models, the need has increased for glass repair and replacement. Today's vehicles also have thinner paint and more clearcoat than before, requiring more outside attention and care.

Vehicle owners today feel more secure with the help of cellular phones and security systems.

These trends develop almost as fast as a new model or design arrives on the market.

Market Segments

Retail (Primary Target Market)

Retail sales are generated in three ways: 1) walk-in traffic; 2) advertising traffic; 3) phone inquiries and orders. Retail sales payment methods include cash, check, special financing (90 days same as cash), and major charge credits. Specific areas defining sales terms are shown later in this document.

Wholesale

Wholesale accounts consist of auto accessories, window tinting, rust-proofing, and sunroofs. These accounts are subject to net-thirty sales terms and are usually automobile dealerships within the eight-county market.

Insurance

These accounts are set up on an as-needed basis. They are for the recovery of stolen or vandalize property, interior damage due to fire or water damage, exterior reconditioning and rustproofing, and after-collision repair, etc.

Commercial Fleet and Business-to-Business

This includes communications equipment and car care products for large businesses (blanket protection), employee discount programs, incentives, bonuses and additional auto security for large business fleets.

Competition

Auto Security
Good Vibes Sound
Pro Audio
Soundlab

Car Audio Systems
Same three listed above.

Cellular
Cellular Express
Cellular One

Car and Truck Accessories
Zeibart Tidy Car
Unique Auto Options

Auto Care Protection
Zeibart Tidy Car
Two or three small detail shops (wash and wax)

Glass Repair and Replacement
Lafayette Glass
Magie Glass
Safe Lite Autoglass

Classic Car Parts
None

PRODUCTS AND SERVICES

Description of Products and Services

Auto Security

Complete security systems including remote car starters, power windows and door locks, trunk releases, sunroof closers, and complete keyless entry systems. State-of-the-art vehicle recovery systems.

Car Audio Systems

From the most basic to the most exotic, including all installations and a wide range of audio name brands. Interactive radar systems that interface with stereo components.

Cellular

The most complete line of cellular phones including name brands and a complete line of cellular accessories in the eight-county area. Service provided by Cellular One.

Car Accessories

Sunroofs, ground effects, spoilers, luggage racks, trim molding, light covers, driving lights, rear wings, splash guards, interior woodgrain kits, body side moldings, bras, louvres, etc.

Truck Accessories

Running boards, tonneau covers, brush guards, bed liners, roll bars, driving lights, lift kits, lowering kits, tailgate nets, bumpers, bug shields, hitches, grills, light covers, rear sliding windows, etc.

Auto Care Protection

Rustproofing, electronic rustproofing, undercoating, paint protection, scotchguarding, buff and shine, washing, detailing, ozoning (odor removal), steam cleaning, engine cleaning, waxing, pinstriping, leather and vinyl protection. Rustproofing, paint protection, and scotchguarding are exclusive service and guarantees.

Glass Repair and Replacement

Complete autoglass replacement and minor chip repair; the area's most complete auto window tinting, shades, and colors.

Classic Car Parts

The most extensive classic car parts catalog center in the Midwest.

MARKETING STRATEGY

Auto Accessories Unlimited is a retail store. Sixty percent of the business base will be store-generated customers. Thirty percent of the business will be wholesale/dealership generated business. The remaining ten percent will be commercial and business-to-business. All retail business will be generated by incoming phone inquiries and sales and over-the-counter product purchase, service, and installation.

The retail sales will be generated through advertising media such as newspaper, radio, and direct mail. Wholesale sales will be generated through dealership and business-to-business outside sales personnel. Commercial and business-to-business sales will be generated through phone contact and direct contact from the owners.

Pricing Policy

Auto Accessories Unlimited will maintain a 50-60% price margin on all in-store products. A basic shop labor rate of $35 per hour will be charged on all service and non-warranty work. Electronics, bench-testing work rate of $25 per hour (with a one hour minimum) will be assessed on all electronics out-of-warranty date or being purchased from outside sources.

Sales Terms

Retail services and products carry a limited lifetime product and labor warranty. This warranty covers all workmanship and/or product to be free from defect. All over-the-counter electronics will have an exchange only policy. These products must be returned within 15 of purchase. After 15 days have lapsed, customers may receive in-store credits for the amount of purchase.

Any problems or discrepancies of products or services not reported within 48 hours of installation are subject to void warranty.

Wholesale terms will consist of general business practices, net 30 days. 30-on will carry APR interest rate of 2% per month.

Method of Selling, Distributing, and Servicing Products

All products sold by Auto Accessories Unlimited will be purchased from industry distributors.

Auto Accessories Unlimited offers monthly sales. These sales change every month, providing better customer awareness for different products.

January	New Year Super Cellular Sale
February	2 Presidents Sale
March	Shape Up for Spring Sale
April	Auto Accessories Unlimited Summer Audio Tune-Up
May	Super 7 Sunroof Spectacular
June	Auto Security Super Saver
July	Beat the Heat Sunroof and Tint Sale
August	Back to Business Cellular Blowout
September	Super 7 Sunroof Spectacular (twice-a-year event)
October	Watch Out for Winter Auto Care Sale
November	Neat Tricks for Trucks Clearance
December	Car Care—Christmas for Cars

Hours of Operation

Monday through Friday 7:30 a.m. to 7:00 p.m.
Saturday 8:00 a.m. to 3:00 p.m.

Closed for all national holidays.

Auto Accessories and Detailing

BUSINESS PLAN J.E.M. VENTURES, INC.

342 Eastwind
Newport, MI 48299

The purpose of this business plan is to secure funding for opening an automobile accessories franchise. The franchise will offer a wide range of products and services for the care and protection of automobiles and for the convenience of their owners. The franchiser provides full training and support to franchisees in order to ensure a successful business venture.

- EXECUTIVE SUMMARY

- INITIAL COSTS

- THE PRINCIPALS

- MANAGEMENT PLAN

- MARKETING PLAN

- HISTORY

- THE PRODUCT

- FINANCIALS

- SUPPORTING INFORMATION

AUTO ACCESSORIES AND DETAILING
BUSINESS PLAN

EXECUTIVE SUMMARY

J.E.M. Ventures, Inc., is seeking a loan and investment of $50,000,00 to be used toward the purchase of an Auto Extras franchise. This would include the franchise fee, inventory, equipment, and working capital. This money, in addition to the $30,000 to be invested by J.E.M. Ventures, will be sufficient financing through the growing phase so that the business can operate as an ongoing profitable enterprise.

The goal of an Auto Extras franchise is to take advantage of the concept that almost everyone has a vehicle and most people like to keep their vehicles clean and neat. Auto Extras is among the leading auto accessory and detailing franchisers in two states, with a very strong track record of supporting franchisees.

INITIAL COSTS

(per J.E.M. Ventures, Inc.)

Franchise Fee	$20,000.00
Inventory	7,500.00
Equipment	8,000.00
Furniture	1,000.00
Signs	3,000.00
Training	3,000.00
Grand Opening Advertising	3,500.00
Insurance	2,000.00
Leasehold Improvements	5,000.00
Security Deposit	2,000.00
Legal and Accounting	1,000.00
Working Capital	24,000.00
Total	**$80,000.00**

INITIAL COSTS

(per Auto Extras)

Franchise Fee	$20,000.00
Inventory	7,500.00
Equipment	10,000.00
Furniture	3,000.00
Signs	5,000.00
Training	3,000.00
Grand Opening Advertising	5,500.00
Insurance	2,000.00
Leasehold Improvements	12,000.00
Security Deposit	2,000.00
Legal and Accounting	2,000.00
Working Capital	24,000.00
Total	**$96,000.00**

THE PRINCIPALS

Ely Masters is presently employed as a warehouse manager for a large produce wholesaler in Newport. He oversees the shipping and receiving department, as well as doing the computerized inventory and billing for all production of the company.

Ely has also attended classes at Newport Business College. Course studies include Business Communications, Small Business Management, and Marketing.

Jeff Masters is presently employed at Cel-Phone, where he has been the Senior Maintenance Technician for the past three years. Jeff has attended Newport Institute of Technology and is certified in the field of H.V.A.C.

Both Ely's and Jeff's work ethic and past experience in the managing of personnel, scheduling, and budgeting will prove beneficial to this endeavor.

MANAGEMENT PLAN

In order to manage the business as an owner-operator, Ely Masters is going to resign from his position with Homefresh Foods. He will attend the 15-day training class held by Auto Extras before the opening of the store.

Jeff Masters will be an owner-operator also, but will only work at the store on a part-time basis. He will keep his employment at Cel-Phone in order to support his family and also to assist Ely with his personal financial needs.

One full-time employee will be hired prior to the opening of the store so that said employee may also attend the training class. Additional employees will be added as needed.

MARKETING PLAN

The location of the store and its visibility to the general public is a very important consideration in planning a marketing strategy. Therefore, site selection must be a priority. Additionally, traffic flow and traffic mix is also an important consideration in developing a plan.

Auto Extras franchisees share an established name and an aggressive advertising plan that includes radio and television advertisement, as well as advertising at many major sporting events. Ads are also placed in a number of major and community newspapers.

Franchisees also take advantage of the use of window and building signs. Many also send out direct mailings that include self-promotional materials to households in the community.

HISTORY

Auto Extras is in the business of automobile aftermarket, accessories, electronics, and glass replacement.

Auto Extras started in 1974 with 6 stores; currently, there are 33 franchises in Michigan and 2 franchises in Ohio. The company is projecting a total of 60 stores by Fall, 1996.

Auto Extras is a franchise system designed to put entrepreneurs in business with a moderate amount of up-front capital.

Franchisees have been successful in starting with basics and expanding as their sales and knowledge of their particular markets have increased. This reduced overhead has translated into a shorter, more direct route to profit.

The franchiser has also found it helpful to provide the following types of assistance:

- Site location and store layout assistance;
- fifteen days of training before store opening, and one or more weeks of training after store opening;
- ongoing technical support;
- marketing assistance;
- advertising support;
- equipment and inventory vendors.

THE PRODUCT

Auto Extras presents a diversified and well-balanced product mix to effectively respond to automotive customers' "wants and needs." Five products and services are the backbone of the business:

Glass Replacement: Auto glass is a product that customers always need, from a replacement windshield to a quick chip repair.

Security Systems: In today's world, car prices average around $20,000.00, and a car is stolen approximately every 28 seconds. Therefore, an auto security system is a necessary and in-demand product.

Cellular Phones: With just over 5% subscriber penetration, the cellular market is expected to triple by the end of the 1990s. Also, with phones and cellular service becoming more affordable, these are no longer only for the upscale customer.

Detailing: Auto Extras offers interior and exterior cleaning and protection products. These products and services are aimed at increasing a vehicle's value and protecting the vehicle's finish.

Accessories: Auto Extras offers a number of auto accessories, from running boards, tonneau covers, and sunroofs to a wide range of electronics, including remote car starters, car stereo systems, and personal pagers.

FINANCIALS

Personal Financials

Jeff Masters

Assets:	Newport Bank 300 Mariner Square Newport, MI 48299	
	State Bank One Main Square St. George, MI 48290	
401K	Cel-Phone retirement	$5,389.00
	One Touch Teleservice	$748.06
Real Estate Value		$110,000.00
Liabilities:	Liens on Real Estate: Newport Bank Note on Automobile: GMAC Mortgage: Blue Lake Mortgage Life Insurance: Cel-Phone: 3 times base salary Transamerica $100,000- Whole Life	
Income:	Salary: Base $34,519.16 + overtime Bonus: 10% of base salary & overtime	

Ely Masters

Assets:	First Commercial Bank 250 Sterling Dr. St. George, MI 48290	
Real Estate Value		$85,000.00
Liabilities:	Mortgage: Hillwood Mortgage P.O. Box 100 Indianapolis, IN 46240	
	Automobile: National Bank of Newport P.O. Box 330 Newport, MI 48299	

Life Insurance:	Central Life	$15,000
	Travelers Insurance (MMH)	$10,000
Income:		
	Salary: Base $26,000	
	Bonus: $1,000	
	Spouse Income: $20,000	

Sample Operations Budgets

360K Sales

	Jan	Feb	March	April	May	June	July	August	Sept	Oct	Nov	Dec	Total	YTD %
Income														
Sales-Auto Glass	6,300	6,300	8,100	8,100	8,880	7,200	8,100	7,200	8,100	8,100	6,300	7,200	90,000	0.25
Sales-Cellular	3,024	3,024	3,888	3,888	4,320	3,456	3,888	3,456	3,888	3,888	3,024	3,456	43,200	0.12
Sales-Security	6,804	6,804	8,748	8,748	9,720	7,776	8,748	7,776	8,748	8,748	6,804	7,776	97,200	0.27
Sales-Accessories	5,544	5,544	7,128	7,128	7,920	6,336	7,128	6,336	7,128	7,128	5,544	6,336	79,200	0.22
Sales-Detailing	3,276	3,276	4,212	4,212	4,680	3,744	4,212	3,744	4,212	4,212	3,276	3,744	46,800	0.13
Miscellaneous Income	0	0	0	0	0	0	0	0	0	0	0	0	0	0
Net Income %	25,200	25,200	32,400	32,400	36,000	28,800	32,400	28,800	32,400	32,400	25,200	28,800	360,000	
Cost of Sales														
Cost - Auto Glass	2,520	2,520	3,240	3,240	3,552	2,880	3,240	2,880	3,240	3,240	2,520	2,880	36,000	0.40
Cost - Cellular	151	151	194	194	216	173	194	173	194	194	151	173	2,160	0.05
Cost - Security	2,381	2,381	3,062	3,062	3,402	2,722	3,062	2,722	3,062	3,062	2,381	2,722	34,020	0.35
Cost - Accessories	2,495	2,495	3,208	3,208	3,564	2,851	3,208	2,851	3,208	3,208	2,495	2,851	35,640	0.45
Cost - Detailing	164	164	211	211	234	187	211	187	211	211	164	187	2,340	0.05
Direct Labor	3,024	3,024	3,888	3,888	4,320	3,456	3,888	3,456	3,888	3,888	3,024	3,456	43,200	0.12
Total Cost of Sales	10,735	10,735	13,802	13,802	15,288	12,269	13,802	12,269	13,802	13,802	10,735	12,269	153,360	0.43
Gross Profit Margin	14,465	14,465	18,598	18,598	20,712	16,531	18,598	16,531	18,598	18,598	14,465	16,531	206,640	0.57
G & A Expenses														
Salaries - Office	0	0	0	0	0	0	0	0	0	0	0	0	0	0.00
Salaries - Sales	0	0	0	0	0	0	0	0	0	0	0	0	0	0.00
Salaries - Management	2,167	2,167	2,167	2,167	2,167	2,167	2,167	2,167	2,167	2,167	2,167	2,167	26,000	0.07

Casual Labor	42	42	42	42	42	42	42	42	42	42	42	42	500	0.00
Payroll Taxes	577	577	577	577	577	577	577	577	577	577	577	577	6,920	0.02
Outside services	0	0	0	0	0	0	0	0	0	0	0	0	0	0.00
Royalties	1,500	1,500	1,500	1,500	1,500	1,500	1,500	1,500	1,500	1,500	1,500	1,500	18,000	0.05
Office supplies	125	125	125	125	125	125	125	125	125	125	125	125	1,500	0.00
Rent	3,000	3,000	3,000	3,000	3,000	3,000	3,000	3,000	3,000	3,000	3,000	3,000	36,000	0.10
Repairs & Maintenance	417	417	417	417	417	417	417	417	417	417	417	417	5,000	0.01
Uniforms	125	125	125	125	125	125	125	125	125	125	125	125	1,500	0.00
Utilities	375	375	375	375	375	375	375	375	375	375	375	375	4,500	0.01
Bldg & Grds Maintenance	250	250	250	250	250	250	250	250	250	250	250	250	3,000	0.01
Automobile lease	0	0	0	0	0	0	0	0	0	0	0	0	0	0.00
Automobile expense	167	167	167	167	167	167	167	167	167	167	167	167	2,000	0.01
Postage	200	200	200	200	200	200	200	200	200	200	200	200	2,400	0.01
Printing	100	100	100	100	100	100	100	100	100	100	100	100	1,200	0.00
Forms & Stationery	75	75	75	75	75	75	75	75	75	75	75	75	900	0.00
Telephone	333	333	333	333	333	333	333	333	333	333	333	333	4,000	0.01
Advertising	2,500	2,500	2,500	2,500	2,500	2,500	2,500	2,500	2,500	2,500	2,500	2,500	30,000	0.08
Membership	42	42	42	42	42	42	42	42	42	42	42	42	500	0.00
Dues & Subscriptions	17	17	17	17	17	17	17	17	17	17	17	17	200	0.00
Office Equipment Rental	25	25	25	25	25	25	25	25	25	25	25	25	300	0.00
Contributions	17	17	17	17	17	17	17	17	17	17	17	17	200	0.00
Educational	125	125	125	125	125	125	125	125	125	125	125	125	1,500	0.00
Entertainment	250	250	250	250	250	250	250	250	250	250	250	250	3,000	0.01
Legal & Accounting	333	333	333	333	333	333	333	333	333	333	333	333	4,000	0.01
Bank Charges	267	267	267	267	267	267	267	267	267	267	267	267	3,200	0.01
Interest expense	8	8	8	8	8	8	8	8	8	8	8	8	100	0.00

												Total	
Licenses & fees													
33	33	33	33	33	33	33	33	33	33	33	33	400	0.00
Property tax													
333	333	333	333	333	333	333	333	333	333	333	333	4,000	0.01
Property tax - personal													
83	83	83	83	83	83	83	83	83	83	83	83	1,000	0.00
Insurance - general													
250	250	250	250	250	250	250	250	250	250	250	250	3,000	0.01
Insurance - Medical													
208	208	208	208	208	208	208	208	208	208	208	208	2,500	0.01
Insurance - Workers Comp.													
208	208	208	208	208	208	208	208	208	208	208	208	2,500	0.01
Employee Benefits													
42	42	42	42	42	42	42	42	42	42	42	42	500	0.00
Equipment lease													
1,046	1,046	1,046	1,046	1,046	1,046	1,046	1,046	1,046	1,046	1,046	1,046	12,552	0.03
Total G & A Expenses													
15,239	15,239	15,239	15,239	15,239	15,239	15,239	15,239	15,239	15,239	15,239	15,239	182,872	0.51
Operating Profit (Loss)													
(775)	(775)	3,358	3,358	5,473	1,292	3,358	1,292	3,358	3,358	(775)	1,292	23,768	0.07

Break Even Point for:
Fixed Cost in Dollars
Total G & A Exp.

Break Even=1-Variable Costs in %
Break Even=1-Total Operating Exp in %

	182,872	182,872
Break Even =	1 - .43	0.574
	182,872	182,872
Break Even =	1 - .43	0.574
	182,872	182,872
Break Even =	1 - .43	0.574

Break Even $318,592.33 per year

Break Even $26,549.36 per month

Break Even $6,126.78 per week

460K Sales

	Jan	Feb	March	April	May	June	July	August	Sept	Oct	Nov	Dec	Total	YTD %
Income														
Sales-Auto Glass														
	8,050	8,050	10,350	10,350	11,347	9,200	10,350	9,200	10,350	10,350	8,050	9,200	115,000	0.25
Sales-Cellular														
	3,864	3,864	4,968	4,968	5,520	4,416	4,968	4,416	4,968	4,968	3,864	4,416	55,200	0.12
Sales-Security														
	8,694	8,694	11,178	11,178	12,420	9,936	11,178	9,936	11,178	11,178	8,694	9,936	124,200	0.27
Sales-Accessories														
	7,084	7,084	9,108	9,108	10,120	8,096	9,108	8,096	9,108	9,108	7,084	8,096	101,200	0.22
Sales-Detailing														
	4,186	4,186	5,382	5,382	5,980	4,784	5,382	4,784	5,382	5,382	4,186	4,784	59,800	0.13
Miscellaneous Income														
	0	0	0	0	0	0	0	0	0	0	0	0	0	0.00
Net Income %														
	32,200	32,200	41,400	41,400	46,000	36,800	11,400	36,800	41,400	41,400	32,200	36,800	460,000	

Cost of Sales

Cost - Auto Glass	3,220	3,220	4,140	4,140	4,539	3,680	4,140	3,680	4,140	4,140	3,220	3,680	46,000	0.40
Cost - Cellular	193	193	248	248	276	221	248	221	248	248	193	221	2,760	0.05
Cost - Security	3,043	3,043	3,912	3,912	4,347	3,478	3,912	3,478	3,912	3,912	3,043	3,478	43,470	0.35
Cost - Accessories	3,188	3,188	4,099	4,099	4,554	3,643	4,099	3,643	4,099	4,099	3,188	3,643	45,540	0.45
Cost - Detailing	209	209	269	269	299	239	269	239	269	269	209	239	2,990	0.05
Direct Labor	3,864	3,864	4,968	4,968	5,520	4,416	4,968	4,416	4,968	4,968	3,864	4,416	55,200	0.12
Total Cost of Sales	13,717	13,717	17,636	17,636	19,535	15,677	17,636	15,677	17,636	17,636	13,717	15,677	195,960	0.43
Gross Profit Margin	18,483	18,483	23,764	23,764	26,465	21,123	23,764	21,123	23,764	23,764	18,483	21,123	264,040	0.57

G & A Expenses

Salaries - Office	0	0	0	0	0	0	0	0	0	0	0	0	0	0.00
Salaries - Sales	2,167	2,167	2,167	2,167	2,167	2,167	2,167	2,167	2,167	2,167	2,167	2,167	26,000	0.06
Salaries - Management	2,167	2,167	2,167	2,167	2,167	2,167	2,167	2,167	2,167	2,167	2,167	2,167	26,000	0.06
Casual Labor	42	42	42	42	42	42	42	42	42	42	42	42	500	0.00
Payroll Taxes	893	893	893	893	893	893	893	893	893	893	893	893	10,720	0.02
Subcontract labor	333	333	333	333	333	333	333	333	333	333	333	333	4,000	0.01
Outside services	83	83	83	83	83	83	83	83	83	83	83	83	1,000	0.00
Royalties	1,500	1,500	1,500	1,500	1,500	1,500	1,500	1,500	1,500	1,500	1,500	1,500	18,000	0.04
Office supplies	175	175	175	175	175	175	175	175	175	175	175	175	2,100	0.00
Rent	3,000	3,000	3,000	3,000	3,000	3,000	3,000	3,000	3,000	3,000	3,000	3,000	36,000	0.08
Repairs & Maintenance	417	417	417	417	417	417	417	417	417	417	417	417	5,000	0.01
Uniforms	200	200	200	200	200	200	200	200	200	200	200	200	2,400	0.01
Utilities	500	500	500	500	500	500	500	500	500	500	500	500	6,000	0.01
Bldg & Grds Maintenance	500	500	500	500	500	500	500	500	500	500	500	500	6,000	0.01
Automobile lease	125	125	125	125	125	125	125	125	125	125	125	125	1,000	0.00
Automobile expense	333	333	333	333	333	333	333	333	333	333	333	333	4,000	0.01
Postage	250	250	250	250	250	250	250	250	250	250	250	250	3,000	0.01

													Total	%
Printing	167	167	167	167	167	167	167	167	167	167	167	167	2,000	0.00
Forms & Stationery	92	92	92	92	92	92	92	92	92	92	92	92	1,100	0.00
Telephone	381	381	381	381	381	381	381	381	381	381	381	381	4,572	0.01
Advertising	3,333	3,333	3,333	3,333	3,333	3,333	3,333	3,333	3,333	3,333	3,333	3,333	40,000	0.09
Membership	42	42	42	42	42	42	42	42	42	42	42	42	500	0.00
Dues & Subscriptions	17	17	17	17	17	17	17	17	17	17	17	17	200	0.00
Office Equipment Rental	25	25	25	25	25	25	25	25	25	25	25	25	300	0.00
Contributions	17	17	17	17	17	17	17	17	17	17	17	17	200	0.00
Educational	125	125	125	125	125	125	125	125	125	125	125	125	1,500	0.00
Entertainment	250	250	250	250	250	250	250	250	250	250	250	250	3,000	0.01
Legal & Accounting	333	333	333	333	333	333	333	333	333	333	333	333	4,000	0.01
Bank Charges	267	267	267	267	267	267	267	267	267	267	267	267	3,200	0.01
Interest expense	8	8	8	8	8	8	8	8	8	8	8	8	100	0.00
Licenses & fees	33	33	33	33	33	33	33	33	33	33	33	33	400	0.00
Property tax	333	333	333	333	333	333	333	333	333	333	333	333	4,000	0.01
Property tax - personal	83	83	83	83	83	83	83	83	83	83	83	83	1,000	0.00
Insurance - general	250	250	250	250	250	250	250	250	250	250	250	250	3,000	0.01
Insurance - Medical	208	208	208	208	208	208	208	208	208	208	208	208	2,500	0.01
Insurance - Workers Comp.	208	208	208	208	208	208	208	208	208	208	208	208	2,500	0.01
Employee Benefits	42	42	42	42	42	42	42	42	42	42	42	42	500	0.00
Equipment lease	1,046	1,046	1,046	1,046	1,046	1,046	1,046	1,046	1,046	1,046	1,046	1,046	12,552	0.03
Total G & A Expenses	19,945	19,945	19,945	19,945	19,945	19,945	19,945	19,945	19,945	19,945	19,945	19,945	239,344	0.52
Operating Profit (Loss)	(1,463)	(1,463)	3,818	3,818	6,520	1,178	3,818	1,178	3,818	3,818	(1,463)	1,178	24,696	0.05

Break Even Point for:
Fixed Cost in Dollars
Total G & A Exp.

Break Even=1-Variable Costs in %
Break Even=1-Total Operating Exp in %

	239,344		239,344
Break Even =	1 - .43		0.574
	239,344		239,344

Break Even $416,975.61 per year

Break Even =	1 - .43		0.574		Break Even $34,747.97 per month	
	239,344		239,344			
Break Even =	1 - .43		0.574		Break Even $8,018.76 per week	

600K Sales

	Jan	Feb	March	April	May	June	July	August	Sept	Oct	Nov	Dec	Total	YTD %
Income														
Sales-Auto Glass	10,500	10,500	13,500	13,500	14,799	12,000	13,500	12,000	13,500	13,500	10,500	12,000	150,000	0.25
Sales-Cellular	5,040	5,040	6,480	6,480	7,200	5,760	6,480	5,760	6,480	6,480	5,040	5,760	72,000	0.12
Sales-Security	11,340	11,340	14,580	14,580	16,200	12,960	14,580	12,960	14,580	14,580	11,340	12,960	162,000	0.27
Sales-Accessories	9,240	9,240	11,880	11,880	13,200	10,560	11,880	10,560	11,880	11,880	9,240	10,560	132,000	0.22
Sales-Detailing	5,460	5,460	7,020	7,020	7,800	6,240	7,020	6,240	7,020	7,020	5,460	6,240	78,000	0.13
Miscellaneous Income	0	0	0	0	0	0	0	0	0	0	0	0	0	0
Net Income %	42,000	42,000	54,000	54,000	60,000	48,000	54,000	48,000	54,000	54,000	42,000	48,000	600,000	
Cost of Sales														
Cost - Auto Glass	4,200	4,200	5,400	5,400	5,920	4,800	5,400	4,800	5,400	5,400	4,200	4,800	60,000	0.40
Cost - Cellular	252	252	324	324	360	288	324	288	324	324	252	288	3,600	0.05
Cost - Security	3,969	3,969	5,103	5,103	5,670	4,536	5,103	4,536	5,103	5,103	3,969	4,536	56,700	0.35
Cost - Accessories	4,158	4,158	5,346	5,346	5,940	4,752	5,346	4,752	5,346	5,346	4,158	4,752	59,400	0.45
Cost - Detailing	273	273	351	351	390	312	351	312	351	351	273	312	3,900	0.05
Direct Labor	5,040	5,040	6,480	6,480	7,200	5,760	6,480	5,760	6,480	6,480	5,040	5,760	72,000	0.12
Total Cost of Sales	17,892	17,892	23,004	23,004	25,480	20,448	23,004	20,448	23,004	23,004	17,892	20,448	255,600	0.43
Gross Profit Margin	24,108	24,108	30,996	30,996	34,520	27,552	30,996	27,552	30,996	30,996	24,108	27,552	344,400	0.57
G & A Expenses														
Salaries - Office	500	500	500	500	500	500	500	500	500	500	500	500	6,000	0.01
Salaries - Sales	2,167	2,167	2,167	2,167	2,167	2,167	2,167	2,167	2,167	2,167	2,167	2,167	26,000	0.04
Salaries - Management	2,167	2,167	2,167	2,167	2,167	2,167	2,167	2,167	2,167	2,167	2,167	2,167	26,000	0.04
Casual Labor	42	42	42	42	42	42	42	42	42	42	42	42	500	0.00
Payroll Taxes	1,083	1,083	1,083	1,083	1,083	1,083	1,083	1,083	1,083	1,083	1,083	1,083	13,000	0.02

Subcontract labor	417	417	417	417	417	417	417	417	417	417	417	417	5,000	0.01
Outside services	83	83	83	83	83	83	83	83	83	83	83	83	1,000	0.00
Royalties	1,500	1,500	1,500	1,500	1,500	1,500	1,500	1,500	1,500	1,500	1,500	1,500	18,000	0.03
Office supplies	250	250	250	250	250	250	250	250	250	250	250	250	3,000	0.01
Rent	3,000	3,000	3,000	3,000	3,000	3,000	3,000	3,000	3,000	3,000	3,000	3,000	36,000	0.06
Repairs & Maintenance	417	417	417	417	417	417	417	417	417	417	417	417	5,000	0.01
Uniforms	200	200	200	200	200	200	200	200	200	200	200	200	2,400	0.00
Utilities	542	542	542	542	542	542	542	542	542	542	542	542	6,500	0.01
Bldg & Grds Maintenance	500	500	500	500	500	500	500	500	500	500	500	500	6,000	0.01
Automobile lease	125	125	125	125	125	125	125	125	125	125	125	125	1,500	0.00
Automobile expense	417	417	417	417	417	417	417	417	417	417	417	417	5,000	0.01
Postage	250	250	250	250	250	250	250	250	250	250	250	250	3,000	0.01
Printing	167	167	167	167	167	167	167	167	167	167	167	167	2,000	0.00
Forms & Stationery	92	92	92	92	92	92	92	92	92	92	92	92	1,100	0.00
Telephone	381	381	381	381	381	381	381	381	381	381	381	381	4,572	0.01
Advertising	3,333	3,333	3,333	3,333	3,333	3,333	3,333	3,333	3,333	3,333	3,333	3,333	40,000	0.07
Membership	42	42	42	42	42	42	42	42	42	42	42	42	500	0.00
Dues & Subscriptions	17	17	17	17	17	17	17	17	17	17	17	17	200	0.00
Office Equipment Rental	25	25	25	25	25	25	25	25	25	25	25	25	300	0.00
Contributions	17	17	17	17	17	17	17	17	17	17	17	17	200	0.00
Educational	167	167	167	167	167	167	167	167	167	167	167	167	2,000	0.00
Entertainment	333	333	333	333	333	333	333	333	333	333	333	333	4,000	0.01
Legal & Accounting	333	333	333	333	333	333	333	333	333	333	333	333	4,000	0.01
Bank Charges	267	267	267	267	267	267	267	267	267	267	267	267	3,200	0.01
Interest expense	8	8	8	8	8	8	8	8	8	8	8	8	100	0.00
Licenses & fees	33	33	33	33	33	33	33	33	33	33	33	33	400	0.00

Property tax													
333	333	333	333	333	333	333	333	333	333	333	333	4,000	0.01
Property tax - personal													
83	83	83	83	83	83	83	83	83	83	83	83	1,000	0.00
Insurance - general													
250	250	250	250	250	250	250	250	250	250	250	250	3,000	0.01
Insurance - Medical													
208	208	208	208	208	208	208	208	208	208	208	208	2,500	0.00
Insurance - Workers Comp.													
208	208	208	208	208	208	208	208	208	208	208	208	2,500	0.00
Employee Benefits													
42	42	42	42	42	42	42	42	42	42	42	42	500	0.00
Equipment lease													
1,046	1,046	1,046	1,046	1,046	1,046	1,046	1,046	1,046	1,046	1,046	1,046	12,552	0.02
Total G & A Expenses													
21,044	21,044	21,044	21,044	21,044	21,044	21,044	21,044	21,044	21,044	21,044	21,044	252,524	0.42
Operating Profit (Loss)													
3,064	3,064	9,952	9,952	13,477	6,508	9,952	6,508	9,952	9,952	3,064	6,508	91,876	0.15

Break Even Point for:
Fixed Cost in Dollars
Total G & A Exp.

Break Even = 1 - Variable Costs In %
Break Even = 1 - Total Operating Exp in %

	252524	252524
Break Even =	1 - .00	0.574
	252524	252524
Break Even =	1 - .00	0.574
	252524	252524
Break Even =	1 - .00	0.574

Break Even $439,937.28 per year

Break Even $36,661.44 per month

Break Even $8,460.33 per week

SUPPORTING INFORMATION

Technical & Financial Training Schedule

Week 1

Monday	Tuesday	Wednesday	Thursday	Friday
Intro to Auto Extras Products/Services "What do we sell?"	Auto Glass Sales	Auto Glass Tech Windshield	Security Tech Install 2 Alarms 950 and Hawk?	Auto Extras Financial Royalty Reports
Detailing Sales	Insurance Claims Quoting Manual Look-up	Door Glass Chip Repair	Basics	Forms Necessary Info
Protection Chemicals Procedures, etc.				
		Discuss warranty Prep Alarm Tech	Security Sales	Financial planning
Perform an environmental package on a car	Computer Look-up Price Quoting	Tools Differences Parts	Product Knowledge Basic Features Comparisons	I Can Plan
	Tooling Urethane			

Monday	Tuesday	Wednesday	Thursday	Friday
Discuss Warranty Quiz	General Procedure Quiz	Quiz	Quiz	Quiz

Week 2

Monday	Tuesday	Wednesday	Thursday	Friday
Security Sales	Communication Sales	Communication Sales	Accessories Tech	Computer
Keyless Starters			Install Sunroof	Invoicing
	Cellular Product Knowledge	Cellular Other		
More Product Knowledge		Fraud	Running Boards	
	Service			
	Current Promo	Pagers - PK Pricing Contracts		
Security Tech	Service Aps	Communication	Accessories Tech Install: Tonneau Cover	Computer
Install loaded alarm and a remote start	Instant Credit	Install phone if possible	Mud Flaps	A/R A/P
	Programming Handset		Bedliner	G/L
	Chip	Activate 1 phone	DEG	Checkbook
	Book	Activate 1 pager		
			Review Tech Work	Review
Quiz	Quiz	Quiz	Quiz	Quiz

Week 3

Monday	Tuesday	Wednesday	Thursday	Friday
Accessory Sales Sunroofs Running Bds Tonneau Covers Bedliners	Merchandising Showroom Displays Pricing Set-up, etc.	Install Your Choice Class picks product to install and participates directly in installation	Sales Your Choice Class picks product to discuss and get more product knowledge/features and benefits	Course Test 60 minutes 75-100 questions
Accessory Sales	Advertising	Install Your Choice	Financial/Computer Your Choice	Review Test Open Discussion
	Review current	Class picks product to install and		
Any Sales Review	Auto One Local Direct Mail	participates directly in installation	Class picks area in financial/computer study to practice or learn more about	Course Evaluation

Certificates/Awards |
| Quiz | Quiz | | | |

Carpet Cleaning Service

BUSINESS PLAN

CARPET CHEM CORPORATION

585 Linberg
Salt Lake City, Utah 84116

Carpet Chem Corporation began as a family-owned and operated business venture. The owners identified a need for a quality carpet and upholstery cleaning system, and their son developed the formula for success. Today, the business has been franchised 21 times in 16 different states. Carpet Chem Corporation attributes its steady growth and financial achievements to a quality product line, through market research and an effective price strategy.

- EXECUTIVE SUMMARY

- COMPANY INFORMATION

- MARKET ANALYSIS

- MARKET STRATEGY AND IMPLEMENTATION

- MANAGEMENT SUMMARY

- FINANCIAL PLAN AND INFORMATION

CARPET CLEANING SERVICE
BUSINESS PLAN

EXECUTIVE SUMMARY

Carpet Chem Corporation (CCC) formulates, manufactures, and re-labels special high quality carpet and upholstery cleaning solutions for use by its network of franchises and customers nation-wide. We sell these products to these franchises, and provide them with specific support services, including marketing and technical support. Our products are developed, packaged, and sold out of our headquarters located in Salt Lake City, Utah.

Objectives

- To give CCC the market presence needed to support marketing and sales goals.
- To continue to provide quality products and support to our franchises.
- To develop consistent quality standards for our products and provide a guarantee to all those purchasing our products.
- To continue research and development efforts to produce the best products on the market.
- To grow sales to $25,000 monthly by the end of 1996, and $100,000 monthly by the end of 2000.

Mission

Carpet Chem Corporation is a support company dedicated to developing and selling the highest quality, and most productive, carpet solutions at competitive prices. We combined this with the best method of cleaning carpets known as The Carpet Chem Advanced Drycleaning System. We intend to make enough profit to generate a fair return for our investors, and to finance continued growth and development in a quality product. We also maintain a friendly, fair, and creative work environment, which respects diversity, new ideas, hard work, and unity.

Keys to Success

The keys to success in this business are:

- Marketing: by dealing with channel problems and barriers to entry, or solving problems with major advertising and promoting budgets.
- Product quality.
- Management: products delivered on time, costs controlled, marketing budgets managed. There is a temptation to fixate to growth, at the expense of profits.

COMPANY INFORMATION

Carpet Chem supports franchises, hospitals, hotels, schools, carpet cleaning companies and janitorial cleaning companies with proven methods of carpet cleaning and upholstery cleaning designed to help them provide quality service to their customers and facilities. Its customers are intelligent business people who want a practical and high quality method of cleaning carpets to accomplish their needs and/or their customer's needs, with as little expenditure of time and money as possible. The company was incorporated in Utah in 1993, after twenty-two years of previous operation under different names.

Company Ownership

Carpet Chem Corporation is a privately held Utah corporation. Samantha Berns is the majority owner. Dave and Alex Berns are the other owners.

Company History

Carpet Chem Corporation (CCC) was incorporated on December 16, 1993 by Samantha, Dave, and Alex Berns. The corporation was formed by liquidating the assets of Builders Basics Cleaning (BBC), a predecessor of CCC. BBC operated two franchise programs, Carpet Chem Cleaning Corp. and Builders Basics Commercial Cleaning. Both franchise programs started between 1990 and 1992. Previous to this, Samantha and Dave had ownership in nine other commercial cleaning companies. Samantha and Dave started their own janitorial company in 1972 because they identified a need for a quality cleaning company in a building where Dave was employed. After they started their business, they found that there was money to be made in the commercial cleaning industry. From 1972 until 1990, they operated commercial cleaning companies in several states with great success. During this time, one of the services that they offered was carpet cleaning. Many methods were tried, but none of them satisfied the owners or the customers. Finally, after much research, development, and trial and error, Alex Berns, their son, developed a carpet cleaning system that effectively satisfied their high standards for quality. This system cleans the entire fiber of the carpet without getting any moisture below the primary backing, dries quickly, and leaves no residue. This system was so incredible that they decided to franchise it nationwide. Today, this system is known as the Carpet Chem Total DryCleaning System.

CCC provides high-quality solutions, equipment, and supplies, along with a complete support program for its franchisees. In July of 1995, Samantha and Dave recognized the success of the Carpet Chem System, as they reviewed the increasing list of satisfied customers. They introduced a new idea that will open up the Carpet Chem System to everyone, releasing it from franchise restrictions. Now, hospitals, hotels, schools, carpet cleaning companies, janitorial cleaning companies, and entrepreneurs can enjoy the benefits of a franchise without paying for one.

The new program was researched using a survey during the beginning of September 1995. Recently, it has been marketed locally, and in the surrounding states of Utah, with great interest and success.

Currently, there are 21 Carpet Chem franchises in 16 different states. As of November 1st, one hotel and one school district in Salt Lake City are using the new program, and many more clients have expressed interest in the program.

The following table illustrates past performance over the last three years, including sales, gross margin, net revenue, and cash flow. The plan also includes financial statements for the last three years.

	1993	1994	1995	
				Past Financial
Sales	$0	$103,490	$186,085	**Performance**
Gross Margin	$0	$69,814	$115,671	
Gross % (calculated)	0.00%	67.46%	62.16%	
Operating expenses	$0	$76,973	$119,888	
Collection period (days)	0	47	45	
Inventory turnover	0	126	66	
Balance Sheet	–	–	1995	
Short-term Assets	–	–	–	
Cash	–	–	$11,694	
Accounts receivable	–	–	$7,679	
Inventory	–	–	$6,583	
Other Short-term Assets	–	–	$2,596	
Total Short-term Assets	–	–	$28,552	
Long-term Assets	–	–	–	
Capital Assets	–	–	$42,854	
Accumulated Depreciation	–	–	$9,732	
Total Long-Term Assets	–	–	$33,122	
Total Assets	–	–	$61,674	
Debt and Equity	–	–	–	
Accounts Payable	–	–	$14,664	
Short-term Notes	–	–	$0	

Other ST Liabilities	–	–	$0
Subtotal Short-term Liabilities	–	–	$14,664
Long-term Liabilities	–	–	$45,218
Total Liabilities	–	–	$59,882
Paid in Capital	–	–	$12,969
Retained Earnings	–	–	($6,960)
Earnings	$0	($7,159)	($4,217)
Total Equity	–	–	$1,792
Total Debt and Equity	–	–	$61,674
Other Inputs	–	–	1995
Payment Days	–	–	45
Sales on credit	–	–	$150,000
Receivables turnover	–	–	19.53

Company Products

The Carpet Chem products go through a series of testing and development to insure quality and to make sure they are safe for stain-resistant carpets. CCC performs tests similar to those used by Smithson flooring systems.

Company Locations and Facilities

Headquarters are located in office space of approximately 900 square feet and warehouse space of approximately 1200 square feet at 585 Linberg, Salt Lake City, Utah 84116.

We have first rights of refusal for both office and warehouse space of equal size on each side of our current location for easy expansion. We already have all of the furniture and shelving needed to expand to twice our current size.

MARKET ANALYSIS

We have researched the national market and found the following results:

- 96.4% of people would like to have their carpets dry within less than 1 hour of cleaning.
- 98.2% of people want a cleaning solution that removes stains during cleaning, eliminating pre-spraying.
- 94.5% of people want a toll-free number to answer technical questions about cleaning and spotting.
- 3.6% of people nationwide are currently acquainted with Carpet Chem.
- 58.2% of people want to see a free demonstration of Carpet Chem.
- 85.5% of people spend $0 - $500 on carpet cleaning in a month.
- 14.5% of people spend $500 - $1000 in a month,
- 0% spend over $1000 in a month.
- 78.2% of people currently use a wet carpet cleaning system.
- 9.1% of people currently use a dry carpet cleaning system.
- 10.9% of people currently use both wet and dry types of carpet cleaning systems.
- 52.7% of people would pay $100-$150 to learn how to be fully trained and certified on how to use Carpet Chem System.
- 3.6% of people would pay $150-$200 to become educated about the Carpet Chem System.

According to our market research, conducted in 5 different areas of the United States with 25 different companies, there is a need for our services and products.

Main Competitors

Our main competitors are other supply houses that are specific to the carpet cleaning industry.

Market Analysis

The chart below compares the percentage of each of our target markets. We are currently targeting carpet cleaning companies and janitorial cleaning companies because they have the most experience with cleaning carpets. We have had little success with hospitals, hotels, or schools.

Analysis of Potential Market

Potential Customers	Customers	Growth rate
Carpet Cleaning Companies	170	0%
Janitorial Cleaning Companies	120	13%
New Business Owners-Service Industry	150	4%
Hospitals	32	-11%
Hotels	105	11%
Schools	250	14%
Other	–	0%
Total	**827**	**N\A**

We will attend trade shows and send advertisements to cleaning companies, offering them the same supplies, support, and solutions that we provide to our franchises.

We have decided to offer prices a bit lower than the average to acquire new customers.

Yearly	Total Sales
1996	270,000
1997	410,000
1998	620,000

Sales Forecast

Sales	1996	1997	1998
Supply Sales	$176,621	$300,000	$500,000
Seminar Training	$2,725	$5,000	$10,000
Video Training	$2,098	$3,000	$3,500
Carpet Cleaning Revenue	$47,548	$58,000	$65,000
Franchise Royalties	$23,683	$20,000	$20,000
Misc. Income	$1,197	$1,100	$2,000
Other	$12,672	$15,100	$16,600
Total Sales	$266,544	$402,200	$617,100
Cost of sales			
Supply Sales	$94,290	$140,000	$200,000
Seminar Training	$606	$500	$1,000
Video Training	$80	$125	$200
Carpet Cleaning Revenue	$7,344	$8,700	$9,750
Franchise Royalties	$0	$0	$0
Misc. Income	$0	$0	$0
Other	$0	$0	$0
Total Cost of Sales	**$102,320**	**$149,325**	**$210,950**

Alex Jenkins, President of CCC, has several years experience in management. His objective is to provide a comfortable work environment.

Dave and Samantha Berns consult with Alex on many decisions. Alex then organizes them, delegates them, and carries on the day-to-day operations.

MARKET STRATEGY IMPLEMENTATION

Marketing Strategy

Pricing strategy

Sales Strategy

MANAGEMENT SUMMARY

Organizational Structure

Personnel Plan

	1996	1997	1998
Payroll	$56,981	$69,000	$75,000

FINANCIAL PLAN AND INFORMATION

We plan to market our idea nationwide while maintaining our carpet cleaning revenue and franchises.

Important Assumptions

General Assumptions
1996 1997 1998

	1996	1997	1998
Short Term Interest Rate	12.00%	12.00%	12.00%
Long Term Interest Rate	14.00%	14.00%	14.00%
Collection days	45	40	37
Payment days	40	30	30
Inventory Turnover	7.00	6.00	5.00
Tax Rate Percent	0.00%	0.00%	0.00%
Expenses in cash%	7.25%	7.00%	7.00%
Sales on credit	52.83%	70.00%	75.00%
Personnel Burden %	10.28%	11.00%	11.25%

Projected Profit and Loss
1996 1997 1998

	1996	1997	1998
Sales	$266,544	$402,200	$617,100
Cost of Sales	$102,320	$149,325	$210,950
Other	$0	$0	$0
Total Cost of Sales	$102,320	$149,325	$210,950
Gross margin	$164,224	$252,875	$406,150
Gross margin percent	61.61%	62.87%	65.82%
Operating expenses:			
Advertising/Promotion	$19,800	$20,000	$25,000
Auto Expense	$3,310	$8,000	$12,000
Bank Service Charges	$520	$650	$750
Printing Expense	$366	$500	$1,000
Legal Fees/Licenses $ Other Fees			
	$262	$200	$500
Miscellaneous	$956	$1,500	$2,500
Entertainment	$242	$0	$0
Payroll Expense	$56,981	$69,000	$75,000
Office Expense	$3,767	$4,000	$5,000
Postage	$5,426	$6,000	$10,000
Professional Fees	$444	$750	$1,000
Taxes - Property and Other	$277	$300	$350
Utilities	$2,350	$2,500	$3,000
Insurance	$2,773	$3,500	$5,000
Rent	$6,350	$6,500	$7,200
Depreciation	$4,524	$3,500	$4,000
Telephone	$4,444	$4,700	$5,000
Pagers	$616	$750	$800
Travel	$1,789	$3,000	$5,000
Total Operating Expenses	$115,197	$135,350	$163,100
Profit Before Interest\Taxes	$49,027	$117,525	$243,050
Interest Expense ST	$0	$0	$0
Interest Expense LT	$7,614	$7,731	$7,731

Taxes Incurred	$0	$0	$0
Net Profit	$41,413	$109,794	$235,319
Net Profit/Sales	15.54%	27.30%	38.13%

Projected Cash Flow

	1996	1997	1998
Net Profit:	$41,413	$109,794	$235,319
Plus:	—	—	—
Depreciation	$4,524	$3,500	$4,000
Change in Accts Payable	$2,846	($1,590)	$14,513
Current Borrowing	$0	$0	$0
Increase (decrease) Other Liabilities			
	$0	$0	$0
Long-term Borrowing	$10,000	$0	$0
Capital input	$0	$0	$0
Subtotal	$58,783	$111,704	$253,833
Less:			
Change in Accts Rec	$16,725	$596	$19,000
Change in Inventory	$7,943	$20,723	$13,882
Change in Other ST Assets	$0	$0	$0
Capital Expenditure	$0	$0	$0
Dividends	$0	$0	$0
Subtotal	$24,668	$21,319	$32,882
Net Cash Flow	$34,115	$90,385	$220,951
Cash balance	$45,809	$136,195	$357,145

Projected Balance Sheet
1996 1997 1998

Short-term Assets

Cash	$45,809	$136,195	$357,145
Accounts receivable	$24,404	$25,000	$44,000
Inventory	$14,526	$35,249	$49,131
Other Short-term Assets	$2,596	$2,596	$2,596
Total Short-term Assets	$87,335	$199,040	$452,872
Long-term Assets	—	—	—
Capital Assets	$42,854	$42,854	$42,854
Accumulated Depreciation	$14,256	$17,756	$21,756
Total Long-Term Assets	$28,598	$25,098	$21,098
Total Assets	$115,933	$224,138	$473,970

Debt and Equity

	1996	1997	1998
Accounts Payable	$17,510	$15,920	$30,433
Short-term Notes	$0	$0	$0
Other ST Liabilities	$0	$0	$0
Subtotal Short-term Liab.	$17,510	$15,920	$30,433
Long-term Liabilities	$55,218	$55,218	$55,218
Total Liabilities	$72,728	$71,138	$85,651
Paid in Capital	$12,969	$12,969	$12,969
Retained Earnings	($11,177)	$30,236	$140,031
Earnings	$41,413	$109,794	$235,319
Total Equity	$43,205	$153,000	$388,319
Total Debt and Equity	$115,933	$224,138	$473,970
Net Worth	$43,205	$153,000	$388,319

Projected Business Ratios

Profitability Ratios 1996 1997 1998

Gross margin	61.61%	62.87%	65.82%
Net profit margin	15.54%	27.30%	38.13%
Return on Assets	35.72%	48.99%	49.65%
Return on Equity	95.85%	71.76%	60.60%
Activity Ratios			
AR Turnover	5.68	11.26	10.52
Collection days	42	32	27
Inventory Turnover	9.69	6.00	5.00
Accts payable turnover	8.50	12.60	9.14
Total asset turnover	2.30	1.79	1.30

Debt Ratios	**1996**	**1997**	**1998**
Debt to Net Worth	1.68	0.46	0.22
Short-term Debt to Liab.	0.24	0.22	0.36
Liquidity ratios			
Current Ratio	4.99	12.50	14.88
Quick Ratio	4.16	10.29	13.27
Net Working Capital	$69,825	$183,120	$422,439
Interest Coverage	6.44	15.20	31.44

Additional ratios	**1996**	**1997**	**1998**
Assets to sales	0.43	0.56	0.77
Debt/Assets	63%	32%	18%
Current debt/Total Assets	15%	7%	6%
Acid Test	2.76	8.72	11.82
Asset Turnover	2.30	1.79	1.30
Sales/Net Worth	6.17	2.63	1.59

Projected Balance Sheet

	Jan-96	Feb-96	Mar-96	Apr-96	May-96	Jun-96	Jul-96
Short-term Assets							
Cash	$7,233	$4,126	$2,265	$6,169	$7,861	$14,855	$19,056
Accounts receivable	$11,488	$13,592	$15,818	$14,787	$17,016	$16,339	$17,772
Inventory	$7,070	$10,431	$11,751	$12,585	$13,222	$13,451	$13,521
Other S-term Assets	$2,596	$2,596	$2,596	$2,596	$2,596	$2,596	$2,596
Total S-term Assets	$28,388	$30,746	$32,430	$36,136	$40,695	$47,241	$52,945
Long-term Assets							
Capital Assets	$42,854	$42,854	$42,854	$42,854	$42,854	$42,854	$42,854
Accum Depreciation	$10,109	$10,486	$10,863	$11,240	$11,617	$11,994	$12,371
Total Long-term Assets							
	$32,745	$32,368	$31,991	$31,614	$31,237	$30,860	$30,483
Total Assets	$61,133	$63,114	$64,421	$67,750	$71,932	$78,101	$83,428
Debt and Equity							
Accounts Payable	$18,171	$19,000	$19,522	$19,584	$18,584	$17,521	$16,529
Short-term Notes	$0	$0	$0	$0	$0	$0	$0
Other ST Liabilities	$0	$0	$0	$0	$0	$0	$0
Subtotal Short-term Liabilities							
	$18,171	$19,000	$19,522	$19,584	$18,584	$17,521	$16,529
Long-term Liabilities	$45,218	$55,218	$55,218	$55,218	$55,218	$55,218	$55,218

Aug-96	Sep-96	Oct-96	Nov-96	Dec-96	1996	1997	1998
$28,451	$31,769	$39,847	$42,754	$45,809	$45,809	$136,195	$357,145
$15,822	$18,578	$18,196	$21,274	$24,404	$24,404	$25,000	$44,000
$13,259	$14,526	$14,500	$14,500	$14,526	$14,526	$35,249	$49,131
$2,596	$2,596	$2,596	$2,596	$2,596	$2,596	$2,596	$2,596
$60,127	$67,469	$75,139	$81,124	$87,335	$87,335	$199,040	$452,872
$42,854	$42,854	$42,854	$42,854	$42,854	$42,854	$42,854	$42,854
$12,748	$12,13,125	$13,125	$13,502	$13,879	$14,256	$17,756	$21,756
$30,106	$29,729	$29,352	$28,975	$28,598	$28,598	$25,098	$21,098
$90,233	$97,198	$104,491	$110,099	$115,933	$115,933	$224,138	$473,970
$16,524	$15,754	$17,333	$16,746	$17,510	$17,510	$15,920	$30,433
$0	$0	$0	$0	$0	$0	$0	$0
$0	$0	$0	$0	$0	$0	$0	$0
$16,524	$15,754	$17,333	$16,746	$17,510	$17,510	$15,920	$30,433
$55,218	$55,218	$55,218	$55,218	$55,218	$55,218	$55,218	$55,218

...continued

	Jan-96	Feb-96	Mar-96	Apr-96	May-96	Jun-96	Jul-96
Total Liabilities	$63,389	$74,218	$74,740	$74,802	$73,802	$72,739	$71,747
Paid in Capital	$12,969	$12,969	$12,969	$12,969	$12,969	$12,969	$12,969
Retained Earnings	($11,177)	($11,177)	($11,177)	($11,177)	($11,177)	($11,177)	($11,177)
Earnings	($4,049)	($12,897)	($12,111)	($8,844)	($3,663)	$3,569	$9,889
Total Equity	($2,256)	($11,104)	($10,319)	($7,052)	($1,870)	$5,362	$11,681
Total Debt & Equity	$61,133	$63,114	$64,421	$67,750	$71,932	$78,101	$83,428
Net Worth	($2,256)	($11,104)	($10,319)	($7,052)	($1,870)	$5,362	$11,681

Projected Cash Flow

	Jan-96	Feb-96	Mar-96	Apr-96	May-96	Jun-96	Jul-96
Net Profit:	($4,049)	($8,848)	$786	$3,267	$5,182	$7,232	$6,320
Plus:							
Depreciation	$377	$377	$377	$377	$377	$377	$377
Change in Accts Payable							
	$3,507	$829	$522	$62	($1,000)	($1,063)	($992)
Current Borrowing (repayment)							
	$0	$0	$0	$0	$0	$0	$0
Increase (decrease) Other Liabilities							
	$0	$0	$0	$0	$0	$0	$0
Long-term Borrowing (repayment)							
	$0	$10,000	$0	$0	$0	$0	$0
Capital input	$0	$0	$0	$0	$0	$0	$0
Subtotal	($165)	$2,358	$1,685	$3,706	$4,559	$6,546	$5,705
Less:							
Change in Accounts Receivable							
	$3,809	$2,104	$2,226	($1,032)	$2,230	($677)	$1,433
Change in Inventory	$487	$3,361	$1,320	$834	$637	$229	$70
Change in Other ST Assets							
	$0	$0	$0	$0	$0	$0	$0
Capital Expenditure	$0	$0	$0	$0	$0	$0	$0
Dividends	$0	$0	$0	$0	$0	$0	$0
Subtotal	$4,296	$5,465	$3,546	($198)	$2,867	($448)	$1,503
Net Cash Flow	($4,461)	($3,107)	($1,861)	$3,904	$1,692	$6,994	$4,202
Cash Balance	$7,233	$4,126	$2,265	$6,169	$7,861	$14,855	$19,056

General Assumptions

Short Term Interest Rate

	12.00%	12.00%	12.00%	12.00%	12.00%	12.00%	12.00%
Long Term Interest Rate							
	14.00%	14.00%	14.00%	14.00%	14.00%	14.00%	14.00%
Collection Days	45	45	45	45	45	45	45
Payment Days	40	40	40	40	40	40	40
Inventory Turnover	6.00	7.00	7.00	7.00	7.00	7.00	7.00
Tax Rate Percent	0.00%	0.00%	0.00%	0.00%	0.00%	0.00%	0.00%
Expenses in Cash%	8.00%	8.00%	8.00%	7.00%	7.00%	7.00%	7.00%
Sales on Credit	55.00%	64.00%	64.00%	44.00%	55.00%	41.00%	51.00%
Personnel Burden%	10.15%	10.15%	10.15%	10.15%	10.15%	10.35%	10.35%

Personnel Plan

Payroll	$1,766	$4,943	$4,943	$4,943	$4,943	$4,943	$5,000

Aug-96	Sep-96	Oct-96	Nov-96	Dec-96	1996	1997	1998
$71,742	$70,972	$72,551	$71,964	$72,728	$72,728	$71,138	$85,651
$12,969	$12,969	$12,969	$12,969	$12,969	$12,969	$12,969	$12,969
($11,177)	($11,177)	($11,177)	($11,177)	($11,177)	($11,177)	$30,236	$140,031
$16,699	$24,434	$30,148	$36,343	$41,413	$41,413	$109,794	$235,319
$18,491	$26,226	$31,941	$38,136	$43,205	$43,205	$153,000	$388,319
$90,233	$97,198	$104,491	$110,099	$115,933	$115,933	$224,138	$473,970
$18,491	$26,226	$31,941	$38,136	$43,205	$43,205	$153,000	$388,319

Aug-96	Sep-96	Oct-96	Nov-96	Dec-96	1996	1997	1998
$6,810	$7,735	$5,715	$6,195	$5,070	$41,413	$109,794	$235,319
$377	$377	$377	$377	$377	$4,524	$3,500	$4,000
($5)	($770)	$1,579	($587)	$764	$2,846	($1,590)	$14,513
$0	$0	$0	$0	$0	$0	$0	$0
$0	$0	$0	$0	$0	$0	$0	$0
$0	$0	$0	$0	$0	$10,000	$0	$0
$0	$0	$0	$0	$0	$0	$0	$0
$7,182	$7,342	$7,670	$5,985	$6,211	$58,783	$111,704	$253,833
($1,950)	$2,757	($382)	$3,078	$3,130	$16,725	$596	$19,000
($262)	$1,267	($26)	$0	$26	$7,943	$20,723	$13,882
$0	$0	$0	$0	$0	$0	$0	$0
$0	$0	$0	$0	$0	$0	$0	$0
$0	$0	$0	$0	$0	$0	$0	$0
($2,212)	$4,024	($408)	$3,078	$3,156	$24,668	$21,319	$32,882
$9,394	$3,318	$8,079	$2,907	$3,055	$34,115	$90,385	$220,951
$28,451	$31,769	$39,847	$42,754	$45,809	$45,809	$136,195	$357,145
12.00%	12.00%	12.00%	12.00%	12.00%	12.00%	12.00%	12.00%
14.00%	14.00%	14.00%	14.00%	14.00%	14.00%	14.00%	14.00%
45	45	45	45	45	45	40	37
40	40	40	40	40	40	30	30
7.00	7.00	7.00	7.00	7.00	7.00	6.00	5.00
0.00%	0.00%	0.00%	0.00%	0.00%	0.00%	0.00%	0.00%
7.00%	7.00%	7.00%	7.00%	7.00%	7.25%	7.00%	7.00%
38.00%	51.00%	44.00%	61.00%	66.00%	52.83%	70.00%	75.00%
10.35%	10.35%	10.35%	10.35%	10.50%	10.28%	11.00%	11.25%
$5,100	$5,100	$5,100	$5,100	$5,100	$56,981	$69,000	$75,000

...continued

Projected Profit and Loss

	Jan-96	Feb-96	Mar-96	Apr-96	May-96	Jun-96	Jul-96
Sales	$13,479	$14,355	$16,706	$21,456	$22,356	$24,856	$24,856
Cost of Sales	$6,535	$6,085	$6,855	$8,435	$8,570	$9,020	$8,975
Other	$0	$0	$0	$0	$0	$0	$0
Total Cost of Sales	$6,535	$6,085	$6,855	$8,435	$8,570	$9,020	$8,975
Gross Margin	$6,944	$8,270	$9,851	$13,021	$13,786	$15,836	$15,881
Gross Margin %	51.52%	57.61%	58.97%	60.69%	61.67%	63.71%	63.89%
Operating expenses:							
Advertising/Promotion							
	$3,824	$8,000	$126	$500	$500	$500	$700
Auto Expense	$185	$100	$175	$250	$250	$250	$300
Bank Service Charges	$0	$40	$40	$40	$40	$40	$40
Printing Expense	$356	$0	$10	$0	$0	$0	$0
Legal Fees/Licenses and Other Fees							
	$212	$50	$0	$0	$0	$0	$0
Miscellaneous	$56	$50	$50	$50	$50	$50	$100
Entertainment	$142	$100	$0	$0	$0	$0	$0
Payroll Expense	$1,766	$4,943	$4,943	$4,943	$4,943	$4,943	$5,000
Office Expense	$517	$300	$250	$300	$300	$300	$300
Postage	$526	$800	$300	$800	$200	$200	$800
Professional Fees	$194	$100	$50	$0	$0	$0	$0
Taxes - Property and Other							
	$13	$264	$0	$0	$0	$0	$0
Utilities	$225	$225	$225	$225	$175	$175	$175
Insurance	$473	$200	$200	$200	$200	$200	$200
Rent	$525	$525	$525	$525	$525	$525	$525
Depreciation	$377	$377	$377	$377	$377	$377	$377
Telephone	$469	$350	$350	$350	$350	$350	$350
Pagers	$66	$50	$50	$50	$50	$50	$50
Travel	$539	$0	$750	$500	$0	$0	$0
Total Operating Expenses							
	$10,465	$16,474	$8,421	$9,110	$7,960	$7,960	$8,917
Profit Before Interest and Taxes							
	($3,521)	($8,204)	$1,430	$3,911	$5,826	$7,876	$6,964
Interest Expense ST	$0	$0	$0	$0	$0	$0	$0
Interest Expense LT	$528	$644	$644	$644	$644	$644	$644
Taxes Incurred	$0	$0	$0	$0	$0	$0	$0
Net Profit	($4,049)	($8,848)	$786	$3,267	$5,182	$7,232	$6,320
Net Profit/Sales	-30.04%	-61.64%	4.70%	15.23%	23.18%	29.09%	25.43%

Sales Forecast

	Jan-96	Feb-96	Mar-96	Apr-96	May-96	Jun-96	Jul-96
Supply Sales	$7,871	$9,000	$10,250	$14,000	$14,000	$16,500	$16,500
Seminar Training	$625	$600	$0	$500	$0	$0	$500
Video Training	$99	$99	$300	$300	$200	$200	$200
Carpet Cleaning Revenue							
	$1,548	$1,500	$3,000	$3,500	$5,000	$5,000	$4,500
Franchise Royalties	$2,183	$2,000	$2,000	$2,000	$2,000	$2,000	$2,000
Misc. Income	$97	$100	$100	$100	$100	$100	$100
Other	$1,056	$1,056	$1,056	$1,056	$1,056	$1,056	$1,056
Total Sales	$13,479	$14,355	$16,706	$21,456	$22,356	$24,856	$24,856

Aug-96	Sep-96	Oct-96	Nov-96	Dec-96	1996	1997	1998
$24,956	$27,131	$25,631	$25,631	$25,131	$266,544	$402,200	$617,100
$9,000	$9,900	$9,670	$9,675	$9,600	$102,320	$149,325	$210,950
$0	$0	$0	$0	$0	$0	$0	$0
$9,000	$9,900	$9,670	$9,675	$9,600	$102,320	$149,325	$210,950
$15,956	$17,231	$15,961	$15,956	$15,531	$164,224	$252,875	$406,150
63.94%	63.51%	62.27%	62.25%	61.80%	61.61%	62.87%	65.82%
$750	$1,000	$1,200	$1,200	$1,500	$19,800	$20,000	$25,000
$300	$350	$350	$350	$450	$3,310	$8,000	$12,000
$50	$50	$50	$65	$65	$520	$650	$750
$0	$0	$0	$0	$0	$366	$500	$1,000
$0	$0	$0	$0	$0	$262	$200	$500
$100	$100	$100	$100	$150	$956	$1,500	$2,500
$0	$0	$0	$0	$0	$242	$0	$0
$5,100	$5,100	$5,100	$5,100	$5,100	$56,981	$69,000	$75,000
$300	$300	$300	$300	$300	$3,767	$4,000	$5,000
$200	$250	$800	$250	$300	$5,426	$6,000	$10,000
$0	$0	$0	$0	$100	$444	$750	$1,000
$0	$0	$0	$0	$0	$277	$300	$350
$175	$175	$175	$200	$200	$2,350	$2,500	$3,000
$200	$200	$200	$200	$300	$2,773	$3,500	$5,000
$525	$525	$525	$55	0$550	$6,350	$6,500	$7,200
$377	$377	$377	$377	$377	$4,524	$3,500	$4,000
$375	$375	$375	$375	$375	$4,444	$4,700	$5,000
$50	$50	$50	$50	$50	$616	$750	$800
$0	$0	$0	$0	$0	$1,789	$3,000	$5,000
$8,502	$8,852	$9,602	$9,117	$9,817	$115,197	$135,350	$163,100
$7,454	$8,379	$6,359	$6,839	$5,714	$49,027	$117,525	$243,050
$0	$0	$0	$0	$0	$0	$0	$0
$644	$644	$644	$644	$644	$7,614	$7,731	$7,731
$0	$0	$0	$0	$0	$0	$0	$0
$6,810	$7,735	$5,715	$6,195	$5,070	$41,413	$109,794	$235,319
27.29%	28.51%	22.30%	24.17%	20.17%	15.54%	27.30%	38.13%
$16,500	$18,000	$18,000	$18,000	$18,000	$176,621	$300,000	$500,000
$0	$0	$500	$0	$0	$2,725	$5,000	$10,000
$300	$100	$100	$100	$100	$2,098	$3,000	$3,500
$5,000	$6,000	$4,000	$4,500	$4,000	$47,548	$58,000	$65,000
$2,000	$1,875	$1,875	$1,875	$1,875	$23,683	$20,000	$20,000
$100	$100	$100	$100	$100	$1,197	$1,100	$2,000
$1,056	$1,056	$1,056	$1,056	$1,056	$12,672	$15,100	$16,600
$24,956	$27,131	$25,631	$25,631	$25,131	$266,544	$402,200	$617,000

...*continued*

Cost of Sales	Jan-96	Feb-96	Mar-96	Apr-96	May-96	Jun-96	Jul-96
Supply Sales	$5,810	$5,735	$6,355	$7,840	$7,800	$8,250	$8,250
Seminar Training	$406	$50	$0	$50	$0	$0	$50
Video Training	$0	$0	$0	$20	$20	$20	$0
Carpet Cleaning Revenue	$319	$300	$500	$525	$750	$750	$675
Franchise Royalties	$0	$0	$0	$0	$0	$0	$0
Misc. Income	$0	$0	$0	$0	$0	$0	$0
Other	$0	$0	$0	$0	$0	$0	$0
Total Cost of Sales	$6,535	$6,085	$6,855	$8,435	$8,570	$9,020	$8,975

Aug-96	Sep-96	Oct-96	Nov-96	Dec-96	1996	1997	1998
$8,250	$9,000	$9,000	$9,000	$9,000	$94,290	$140,000	$200,000
$0	$0	$50	$0	$0	$606	$500	$1,000
$0	$0	$20	$0	$0	$80	$125	$200
$750	$900	$600	$675	$600	$7,344	$8,700	$9,750
$0	$0	$0	$0	$0	$0	$0	$0
$0	$0	$0	$0	$0	$0	$0	$0
$0	$0	$0	$0	$0	$0	$0	$0
$9,000	$9,900	$9,670	$9,675	$9,600	$102,320	$149,325	$210,950

Computer Matchmaking Service

BUSINESS PLAN   MATCHMATE, INC.

200 Elm St.
Boston, MA 02290
February 28, 1996

The authors of this plan are attempting to diversify their business by offering matchmaking franchises to others. This plan illustrates the franchisor side of planning and preparation, and serves as a counterpoint to the franchisee plans that appear elsewhere in this volume.

- DESCRIPTION OF COMPANY

- LEGAL STATUS

- MISSION STATEMENT/PURPOSE

- STAGE OF DEVELOPMENT

- PRODUCT/SERVICES

- TARGET MARKETS/MARKET ANALYSIS

- MARKETING/ADVERTISING/SALES STRATEGIES

- COMPETITORS' MARKET DISTRIBUTION

- COMPETITORS' ADVANTAGES/DISADVANTAGES

- MANAGEMENT

- LONG-TERM GOALS

- MILESTONES

- FINANCIAL STATEMENTS

DESCRIPTION OF COMPANY

MatchMate is a custom designed, home-based, computer matchmaking service created by a marriage counselor and Fortune 100 software designer. The company provides local matchmaking services to Boston-area singles; national and international matchmaking services to singles worldwide via the Internet; and exclusive licenses to other entrepreneurs to own and operate MatchMate software using the MatchMate name and system within geographic boundaries around the world. To date, 110 local MatchMates operate in the USA and a dozen more operate internationally.

The MatchMate Internet world wide web site, in addition to offering matchmaking services, hosts a singles' mall replete with photo gallery listings in a variety of geographic locations, and markets other singles-related services and products.

The company employs three full-time staff, three outside sales representatives, and several contract programmers who maintain and develop the web site presence.

LEGAL STATUS

MatchMate, Inc., headquartered in Boston, Massachusetts, is a limited Massachusetts company incorporated in June of 1993. From its inception in December of 1988 until incorporation, MatchMate operated as a D.B.A./Proprietorship.

MISSION STATEMENT/ PURPOSE

MatchMate's explicit purpose is to help singles find compatible long-term or life partners by offering psycho-social screening through the sale of memberships to the service. The unique matchmaking system matches and cross-matches each client for 350 items of compatibility that are deemed by university researchers to be the most compelling elements in long-lasting relationships. The internal scoring system, based on surveys of how singles rank various categories, declares only those who score at 60% percent or higher.

The implicit purpose of the system is to educate and raise awareness about one's individual dating patterns and needs in terms of romantic partnership. In completing the application form, singles evaluate themselves and potential partners in terms of race, religion, education, personality traits, physical description, health, interests, lifestyle, sexual orientation, children, personal habits, and relationship goals. In the course of both completing the application and experiencing the results, singles gain valuable self-awareness and self-esteem.

The MatchMate system was designed by a marriage counselor and former social worker who believes that the pattern of dating in America is backwards. Too much emphasis is placed on chemistry, which is an undefinable component, and not enough is placed on compatibility, which is a definable component. The result is a 52% divorce rate, and that rate climbs each decade. While the service uses photos, pictures are not viewed until the after the matchmaking has occurred. Over a seven-year period, singles who met and married using the MatchMate system report only a 1% divorce rate, implying that matching for compatibility first is a more accurate method for predicting long-term relationship success.

STAGE OF DEVELOPMENT

MatchMate began as a small, local matchmaking service in Marlborough, Massachusetts. Matches were made manually while software specifications were developed and the software designed. The original client base grew the first year to 200 clients. The owners moved to Springfield, Massachusetts, where the first automated system was offered. Western Massachusetts was added as a second base of operations. Within three years the service grew to offering data base matching in all of Massachusetts and Rhode Island. The total client base in 1994 comprised 1,800 singles.

In March of 1993, MatchMate began offering licensed copies of its software as a business opportunity. The United States was divided into 150 geographic zones based on population demographics. By April of 1996, 110 units were sold in the USA.

The international territory was divided into 220 zones, and 13 have been sold since March of 1993. Since December of 1994, visibility on the Internet has increased sales to potential buyers in foreign countries by 40%.

In December of 1994, MatchMate launched an Internet Web site with several pages of information and an on-line application for local and national bases. International bases were added in the summer of 1994. By the first anniversary, the MatchMate home page was recording 40,000 hits a month. By early 1996, that figure had doubled.

In the spring of 1995, MatchMate sold its interest in Western Massachusetts as an existing base and moved its headquarters to Boston, Massachusetts. A new Boston-area base serving the metropolitan area was developed. To date, it is the only local database that the corporation owns. The corporation also exclusively owns and operates the national and international databases.

In January of 1996, MatchMate added singles' mall features to its home page. This included a photo gallery and biographical data about singles who posted in a special section called American Ads (listed by state). That section grew in the second month to include Canadian and Asian photo personals and will be further expanded to include Russian and Brazilian personals. As more international sites are sold, personals pages will be added as a service to singles who do not wish to undergo matchmaking. While this portion of the service does not match-make, it accommodates those singles who wish only to view photos and contact other singles. In February of 1996, the advice feature was added to the home page. This page allows singles to ask founder Susan Hamilton, M.S.W., questions on relationships, marriage, and dating. Initially, it is a free service. Eventually, there will be a nominal charge and the pages will become interactive. Ms. Hamilton intends this section to have an educational format in which guided discussions occur. She will monitor the discussion group at specific times, answering and posing questions. Singles' mall pages also include other products and services for singles to purchase. To date, vendors include those who provide books, tapes, newsletters, videos, gifts, and other singles-related services.

Future development goals include multi-media capabilities so that singles can see videos and hear the voices of singles with whom they have been matched. While the technology is available to offer these value-added services, the average user does not have the equipment to receive the presentation. Media experts project that it will be another year or two before the average computer will come fully equipped with the necessary tools for reception.

PRODUCT/ SERVICES

Matchmaking: 123 local databases. Available on and off the Internet.

Enhanced Services: One-on-one, personalized services for singles who have more complicated needs. Involves personal interviews and more detailed screening of matches. Fees vary. Availability of enhanced services is at owner's discretion. Not available in all locations.

Matchmaking: National and international databases. Available on and off the Internet.

Worldwide Photo Ads: Browse a photo gallery and leave E-mail for singles. Available only on the Internet.

Licensed business opportunities in the USA and internationally.

Advice Forum, a question-and-answer page for free; professional advice on life's pressing romantic/relationship issues.

"Myths about Love," a video seminar presentation in three chapters, based on common myths about love, romance, and finding a soulmate. The video features Susan Hamilton, marriage counselor and founder of the MatchMate system.

TARGET MARKETS/ MARKET ANALYSIS

According to National Demographics magazine, 42% of the population in the USA between the ages of 18 and 75 is single. Many wish to meet other singles for companionship, a relationship, and marriage. Due to the pressures of daily life in America, that goal is becoming more and more complex. Many singles have limited income, as they are single parents and cannot afford expensive services estimated at two to three thousand dollars per year.

A vast number of singles surveyed in the past seven years report that they no longer find meeting people in bars an acceptable method for enhancing their social lives. Fear of meeting someone with a criminal background or criminal intent, fear of meeting someone who is an alcoholic, and fear of being viewed as politically incorrect are all reasons why singles' bars no longer hold the fascination they did in the 1980s.

Singles also express concerns about dating people they meet at work. Women are particularly sensitive to the possibility that today's lover could be tomorrow's ex-lover/supervisor. Research suggests that women are more negatively affected by work-place romances, and many corporate policies discourage these liaisons.

MatchMate conducts ongoing polls each year asking singles what they are looking for, what they have tried, and what they hope to find. The responses indicate that the singles population is not just looking for a date. What they especially want is best described as a soulmate. They seek not only a suitable partner, but one who shares interests, goals, habits, and personality. Many have tried 900-number voice personals and found them to be too general and ineffective. As the minutes add up quickly, singles have come to realize that 900 lines can be insidiously expensive. The concept of screening people for highly desirable elements is appealing, modern, and cost-effective. Using services to find a romantic partner is no longer viewed as an act of desperation or for the "lonely heart." Services have become not only acceptable, but a welcome convenience in a frantic age.

As the singles population increases, the opportunity to meet others decreases, leaving a void filled by matchmaking services. If the service is reasonably priced and matches specific traits and characteristics, the inclination of today's single is to join, rather than be increasingly shut out of social contact.

MARKETING/ ADVERTISING/ SALES STRATEGIES

To reach this segment of the population, the ideal method is to place display advertising in daily newspapers, especially the weekend entertainment sections. These entertainment pages draw the attention of singles who are looking for weekend activities. One ad placed in a "weekender" has a shelf-life of the entire weekend, providing maximum exposure for the dollar.

Singles newspapers also produce strong response and further target the market share each MatchMate owner seeks. The presence of other services does not pose competition problems. Actually, MatchMate is more of a threat to the competition than vice-versa. 900-number voice personals, ever part of the singles scene, are not competitive with the matchmaking service concept. They merely serve as another alternative for the single who wants to diversify the search. Ad placement near the 900-number pages is beneficial and productive.

Arts and entertainment publications also draw the single reader and provide a format for MatchMate ads. These publications are usually weeklies, providing seven days of exposure for one placement, and costs are often below that of the daily paper. Arts and entertainment ads are not a replacement for the major daily, but a supplement to the main form of advertising.

Direct mail is a prime form of marketing the MatchMate name and service. Inexpensive post cards outlining the advantages of this unique form of matchmaking are sent to singles in a targeted community. Mail lists can be obtained from list brokers or lists can be cross-referenced from business or client lists the owner has accumulated. Lists can be developed by driving through upscale apartment complexes, recording apartment building numbers and individual apartment numbers, then sending a mailer marked "resident" to each person. It isn't necessary to know the name of the occupant. Since 42% of any given population is single, the average apartment complex holds an ideal market. Some indicators suggest that upper-end town homes and apartments actually hold the bulk of the singles population in most communities.

Distribution of door-hanger direct marketing materials provides inexpensive exposure in upscale apartment/town home communities where singles dwell. The marketing pieces go directly to the occupant and can be passed along to family and friends. Discount coupons are incorporated so occupants feel they are getting a better price and are more apt to join. Each piece is marked with a two-week coupon mandating an immediate response.

Pundits of advertising report that the wise advertiser "hits" the prospect with material three times. The MatchMate business plan includes second and third mailers to prospects who did not join the service after requesting information. The second mailer, sent three to four weeks after the initial inquiry, offers the service at a moderate 10% discount. The third mailer, sent annually in June or July, offers a significant 30% discount. (The "Summer Special" compensates for the slower registration rate that traditionally occurs during summer months, when singles are either on vacation or more socially active).

The name and address of every single who inquired about the service is entered into a master mailing list for future use. No lead is considered "dead" until that person has received at least three "hits."

Telemarketing is another technique for contacting prospects. The format used is partially a survey to determine how and where singles connect and partially an information builder. The script asks five questions and leads the prospect to agree to receive information.

Owners are encouraged to contact singles groups, like Parents Without Partners, church singles, and activity/interest groups to make presentations about the service. Informal presentations provide valuable information and encourage singles to participate without sales pressure.

Informational form letters are sent to local counselors/therapists/psychologists outlining the benefits of the MatchMate system to professionals who traditionally endorse compatibility matching. The letter explains how the service operates—by matching key, holistic elements of compatibility—and that it was designed by a certified professional. Many referrals come from therapists who have urged their clients to pursue relationships in a more realistic and logical manner than random dating offers.

Free or nominally-priced educational seminars offered to the public using the video "Myths about Love," by founder Susan Hamilton, is also an effective marketing tool. Corporate research indicates that singles are hungry for specific information on how to meet and how to select the appropriate partner. This 90-minute video answers the most frequently asked questions and, although generic, is a subtle promotion of the MatchMate system. Ms. Hamilton is available by phone for a question-and-answer period following the presentation. If the owner is using a hotel meeting room for the seminar, it is suggested that a speaker phone be placed in the room for Ms. Hamilton to address the audience.

A 45-minute audio tape is provided to all owners. This master can be duplicated at the owner's expense and mailed to prospective clients along with the brochure and application form. The tape answers the most frequently asked questions about the service and provides background information on how and why it functions so accurately. The advantage to the tape is that if the prospect isn't interested, perhaps they will give the tape to another single friend, making it an automatic distribution tool.

A marketing packet of successful ads, direct-mail post cards, telemarketing scripts, video/audio tapes, and door hangers is provided to all owners as part of the purchase price.

COMPETITORS' MARKET DISTRIBUTION

Knowing a competitor's product, how and where they distribute, and the efficacy of their plan is important to each new owner. Owners are instructed to shop the competition by researching local Yellow Pages. In most cities, the research will reveal a collection of "Ma & Pa" services, most of which are not computerized and therefore will only be able to serve a finite number of clients, and the more well-known companies like Dream Mates, Couples Alone, and Singles Syndicate. By calling these companies and requesting printed information and speaking to sales staff, owners can get an overview of services and costs. The competition will not quote prices over the phone, which is a disadvantage to the wise arm-chair shopper. To get prices from these companies you must schedule an appointment, visit a local office, and sit through a long sales presentation. Your credit card information, occupation, social security number, salary, assets, and other personal data will be reviewed. Many singles complain about the high-pressure sales tactics that these companies use to sell memberships, and the inconvenience of having to stop by the office to see photos/videos of new clients each month. MatchMate clients relish the fact that they can participate by mail, fax, or E-mail, saving them valuable time and producing equal or better results at a fraction of the price.

The major competition relies primarily on direct-mail advertising to reach clients. Their return ratio is only 2%. They also use TV infomercials and radio advertising at a considerable expense, and often these costs are not absorbed by the sale of memberships. The trend for these companies is more and more toward direct-mail, where the profit margin is greater.

COMPETITORS' ADVANTAGES/ DISADVANTAGES

The competitors each have a unique approach to offsetting the MatchMate system in their pitch to clients. Dream Mates uses the approach that the computer is not a personalized method for finding romance. They claim their approach is done by manual screening. Our rebuttal is that they make mistakes due to human error or deliberate oversight of data when they match clients by hand. The use of manual labor also requires more staff hours and that expense is passed on to the consumer.

Couples Alone claims to use a computer, but the software is nothing more than a data base catalog program that doesn't have internal weighting systems, nor does it match and cross-match. Many clients who have joined Couples Alone report that they were mismatched in critical areas, implying that the company either does not use its computer system or its system is highly inaccurate.

Singles Syndicate does not use computer matching, but offers a three-tiered membership plan of social gatherings of varying degrees of frequency, depending on which plan a member selects. Their fees are less than the other companies, but they have few locations nationally. Rather than formal matchmaking, the matches are made informally at social gatherings.

MatchMate's research indicates that these social gatherings have limited appeal to the average client over time. Members are less likely to rejoin after their initial membership. They feel like they've met everyone and renewal is pointless. With the MatchMate system, volume registration is the key. Each member meets so many new matches each month that renewal is a favored option. MatchMate has also determined that these social functions, if presented properly, are expensive affairs that cut into profits. Our theory is to do one thing and to do it the best. Leave the social gatherings to other types of singles businesses. It has been our experience that social functions do not make for high profits, take considerable time to develop, cost many dollars in organizational manpower, and lead to going out of business faster than other services do.

These three competitors have all made the news due to lawsuits filed by disgruntled members of franchisees. One was sued for price gouging. The suit is pending. Another is currently fighting multiple-member suits for violation of trade regulations and by its franchisees for fraud. The other has been sued by the family of a woman who was murdered by a client she met via the service. Former members of one service were so outraged that they formed an organization for the purpose of class action suits and mutual support. Clearly, these companies are doing something wrong to incur this much legal action.

Neither MatchMate nor any of its licensees have ever been sued, nor was a lawsuit ever attempted. All issues of dissatisfaction, some of which are inevitable in any business, have been resolved satisfactorily. The MatchMate reputation for reasonably-priced service, fair resolution of disputes, and quality service remains unblemished.

MatchMate, Inc., the parent company, is owned and operated by Susan Hamilton, M.S.W., and Lawrence Hamilton, M.ED.

MANAGEMENT

Ms. Hamilton is a relationship counselor, free-lance writer, and lecturer. She received her Master's in Social Work from Central University. She has held numerous administrative social work positions with charitable agencies in Massachusetts and California. She is a recipient of a Commissioner's award for Excellence in Community Service.

She is the author of feature articles in numerous national magazines, a frequent radio and TV talk show guest, and is recognized as a leading expert of computer matchmaking by industry associations.

She is the president of MatchMate, Inc., and functions as the Marketing and Sales Director for services and licensees. She also provides Enhanced Services to members who desire the personalized, one-to-one matchmaking service.

Mr. Hamilton is a computer and Internet consultant and a free-lance technical writer. He holds a Master's in Education from Dalhousie University. He taught mathematics for several years before being recruited by a major computer firm to teach computer programming. Mr. Hamilton has held positions in Fortune 500 and 1000 companies. His software design of the MatchMate system is technically unparalleled.

He is the vice president of MatchMate, Inc., and functions as Technical Support Director and Chief Financial Officer. He is also responsible for Internet Marketing and Development.

Cheryl Smith is Executive Administrative Assistant. She is in charge of data processing, employees, outside sales representatives, and client support.

MatchMate's primary goals are two-fold. First, to continue the growth of local, national, and international memberships on and off the Internet and to experience no less than the current annual 30%-40% growth rate. Second, to continue to sell licensed business opportunities to entrepreneurs around the globe. We fully expect to hold and continue our growth as the world's largest matchmaking service. As the availability of zones in the USA and Canada diminishes, the corporate goals will focus on the sale of international zones and the addition of personals for individual countries.

LONG-TERM GOALS

In addition to growth-oriented goals, MatchMate, Inc. has a commitment to fostering the development and passage of state legislation governing the regulation of trade practices in the dating/matchmaking service industry. Due to the rising number of complaints from singles in this state who have been defrauded by other services, we feel that we are the obvious change agents in this state. We hope to be able to start a grass-roots movement that will result in the passage of similar bills in other states, or federally mandated guidelines. Given the current trend toward both federal and state deregulation, this goal may require more singles to speak out against the companies who have mistreated and defrauded them. Efforts to achieve this goal are currently underway.

On the technical front, our goals include the development and addition of interactive multi-media capabilities so that singles can see videos and hear the voices of those with whom they have been matched on the Internet. While the technology is available, very few users have the necessary equipment to enjoy these more advanced services. MatchMate projects that within two years, 30% of Internet users will have the more advanced equipment to view these enhanced services. At that time, we will make them available.

MatchMate's future plans also include making the Advice Forum pages interactive and presenting seminars on topics of interest to singles. These topics will include issues on single parenting, health, investments, travel, and romantic relations, and will be delivered by other esteemed professionals. This service will be available by the end of 1996.

For licensees, MatchMate plans to coordinate singles' fairs in major cities in the USA. A singles' exhibition organizer has been hired to deliver these one-day events, which draw thousands of singles to a full day of exhibits, seminars, games, and a dance. The prototype was developed in the Boston market in November of 1995. The event, the first ever held in the Boston area, drew 800 singles and was considered a huge success. Similar events are planned for major cities as licensees develop their local singles lists and gain knowledge of other singles-related organizations in their communities. Not only does this marketing format produce on-the-spot registrations, the end result is a community-wide mailing list garnered from competitors who also attract attendees.

MatchMate fully expects to produce national infomercials and to produce two additional videos, each containing three more chapters of "Myths about Love." As promotion for the videos and the matchmaking service, Susan Hamilton will appear on various national talk shows.

MILESTONES

1993 MatchMate was voted the number 1 matchmaking service by the New England Singles Association.

1994/1995 MatchMate was rated by Entrepreneur magazine as one of the top 500 business opportunities in America and listed in their July "Business 500" edition. MatchMate will also be included in the July 1996 edition.

1995 Susan Hamilton was selected as a member of the U.S. Society of Ethical Dating Services and appointed the nation's expert on computer matchmaking. Membership to this organization is not purchased, but given for outstanding merit.

1996 MatchMate joined the Worldwide Association of Matchmaking and was appointed the northeastern USA expert on computer matchmaking. Membership is purchased, but expert status is voted.

1996 MatchMate's Internet home page was selected for a Magellan Three Star award for home page content and design.

Balance Sheet

December 31, 1995

Assets

Current Assets

Cash Clearing	22,378.85
Total Current Assets	22,378.85

Fixed Assets

Computer/Equipment	5,708.50
Depr/Computer/Equipment	(3,597.50)
Total Fixed Assets	2,111.00

Other Assets

Organization Expense	226.00
Amortization/Organization	(116.00)
Security Deposit	600.00
Total Other Assets	710.00

Total Assets	$25,199.85

Liabilities and Equity

Current Liabilities

Visa Payable	1,589.66
Total Current Liabilities	1,589.66

Long Term Liabilities

L/P - Lawrence Hamilton	19,484.00
Total Long-term Liabilities	19,484.00

Equity

Capital	(5,295.00)
Current Income (Loss)	9,421.19
Total Equity	4,126.19

Total Liabilities & Equity	$25,199.85

Income Statement

For the Period Ended December 31, 1995

	1 Month Ended Dec. 31, 1995	Pct	12 Months Ended Dec. 31, 1995	Pct
Revenue				
Sales/License Softwares	88,454.00	78.98	88,454.00	78.98
Sales/Profiles	4,561.00	4.07	4,561.00	4.07
Sales/Programming	5.00	0.00	5.00	0.00
Sales/Registration	18,974.00	16.94	18,974.00	16.94
Total Revenue	111,994.00	100.00	111,994.00	100.00
Cost of Sales				
Returns & Allowance	3,683.80	3.29	3,683.80	3.29
Total Cost of Sales	3,683.80	3.29	3,683.80	3.29
Gross Profit	108,310.20	96.71	108,310.20	96.71

Operating Expenses

Contract Labor	7,332.91	6.55	7,332.91	6.55
Advertising	23,019.50	20.55	23,019.50	20.55
Accounting	504.51	0.45	504.51	0.45
Amortization Expense	45.00	0.04	45.00	0.04
Auto Expense	12,506.24	11.17	12,506.24	11.17
Bank Charges	263.40	0.24	263.40	0.24
Commission Expense	3,266.53	2.92	3,266.53	2.92
Contributions	1,396.45	1.25	1,396.45	1.25
Depreciation Expense	3,240.50	2.89	3,240.50	2.89
Dues & Subscriptions	729.29	0.65	729.29	0.65
Entertainment (50%)	230.00	0.21	230.00	0.21
Insurance Expense	1,162.50	1.04	1,162.50	1.04
Legal Expense	804.72	0.72	804.72	0.72
Licenses	33.88	0.03	33.88	0.03
Office Expense	2,699.66	2.41	2,699.66	2.41
Office Supplies	1,529.90	1.37	1,529.90	1.37
Office/Computer Expense	643.90	0.57	643.90	0.57
Office/Computer Supplies	270.12	0.24	270.12	0.24
Operation Expenses	4,168.54	3.72	4,168.54	3.72
Postage	7,093.85	6.33	7,093.85	6.33
Rent	13,649.12	12.19	13,649.12	12.19
Tax/Other	436.00	0.39	436.00	0.39
Telephone	12,035.21	10.75	12,035.21	10.75
Travel Expense	49.00	0.04	49.00	0.04
Utilities/Other	1,778.28	1.59	1,778.28	1.59
Total Expenses	98,889.01	88.30	98,889.01	88.30
Operating Income	9,421.19	8.41	9,421.19	8.41
Net Income (Loss)	9,421.19	8.41	9,421.19	8.41

General Ledger

Period Ending 12/31/95

Date	Mt	Ref #	Account	Description	Current	Year-To-Date
Beginning Balance			115	Cash Clearing		0.00
12/31/95	12	2	115	1995 Sales	111,994.00	
12/31/95	12	3	115	1995 Refunds/Rebates	3,683.80	
12/31/95	12	4	115	Cheryl Smith	-7,332.91	
12/31/95	12	5	115	1995 Advertising	-23,019.50	
12/31/95	12	7	115	1995/Accounting	-504.51	
12/31/95	12	8	115	1995 Auto	-12,506.24	
12/31/95	12	9	115	1995/Bank Chge	-263.40	
12/31/95	12	10	115	1995/Commission	-3,266.53	
12/31/95	12	11	115	1995/Contributions	-1,396.45	
12/31/95	12	12	115	1995/Subscriptions	-729.29	
12/31/95	12	13	115	1995/Entertainment	-230.00	
12/31/95	12	14	115	1995/Insurance	-1,162.50	
12/31/95	12	15	115	1995/Legal	-804.72	
12/31/95	12	16	115	1995/Licenses	-33.88	

Date	Mt	Ref#	Account	Description	Current	Year-To-Date
12/31/95	12	17	115	1995/Office Exp	-2,699.66	
12/31/95	12	18	115	1995/Office Sup	-1,529.90	
12/31/95	12	19	115	1995/Computer Exp	-643.90	
12/31/95	12	20	115	1995/Computer Sup	-270.12	
12/31/95	12	21	115	1995/Operation Exp	-4,168.54	
12/31/95	12	22	115	1995/Postage	-7,093.85	
12/31/95	12	23	115	1995/Rent	-13,649.12	
12/31/95	12	24	115	1995/Taxes	-436.00	
12/31/95	12	25	115	1995/Telephone	-12,035.21	
12/31/95	12	26	115	1995/Travel	-49.00	
12/31/95	12	27	115	1995/Utilities	-1,778.28	
12/31/95	12	28	115	Lawrence Hamilton	13,000.00	
12/31/95	12	29	115	Laptop Computer	-2,702.00	
12/31/95	12	30	115	Software	-220.50	
12/31/95	12	35	115	Reverse 1994 Visa	-2,395.00	
12/31/95	12	36	115	1995 Visa Balance	1,589.66	
12/31/95	12	37	115	1994 Balance	400.00	
				Ending Balances =	**22,378.85**	**22,378.85**
Beginning Balance			142	Computer/Equipment		0.00
12/31/95	12	29	142	Laptop Computer	2,702.00	
12/31/95	12	30	142	Software	220.50	
12/31/95	12	37	142	1994 Balance	2,786.00	
				Ending Balances =	**5,708.50**	**5,708.50**
Beginning Balance			152	Depr/Computer/Equipment		0.00
12/31/95	12	31	152	1995 Depr	-240.00	
12/31/95	12	32	152	1995 Depr Sec 179	-2,922.50	
12/31/95	12	33	152	1995 Depr	-78.00	
12/31/95	12	37	152	1994 Balance	-357.00	
				Ending Balances =	**-3,597.50**	**-3,597.50**
Beginning Balance			162	Organization Expense		0.00
12/31/95	12	37	162	1994 Balance	226.00	
				Ending Balances =	**226.00**	**226.00**
Beginning Balance			172	Amorization / Organization	0.00	
12/31/95	12	34	172	1995 Amoriz Exp	-45.00	
12/31/95	12	37	172	1994 Balance	-71.00	
				Ending Balances =	**-116.00**	**-116.00**
Beginning Balance			198	Security Deposit	0.00	
12/31/95	12	37	198	1994 Balance	600.00	
				Ending Balances =	**600.00**	**600.00**
Beginning Balance			220	Visa Payable		0.00
12/31/95	12	35	220	Reverse 1994 Visa	2,395.00	
12/31/95	12	36	220	1995 Visa Balance	-1,589.66	
12/31/95	12	37	220	1994 Balance	-2,395.00	
				Ending Balances =	**-1,589.66**	**-1,589.66**
Beginning Balance			275	L/P - Lawrence Hamilton		0.00
12/31/95	12	28	275	Lawrence Hamilton	-13,000.00	
12/31/95	12	37	275	1994 Balance	-6,484.00	
				Ending Balances =	**-19,484.00**	**19,484.00**
Beginning Balance			295	Capital		0.00
12/31/95	12	37	295	1994 Balance	5,295.00	
				Ending Balances =	**5,295.00**	**5,295.00**

Date	Mt	Ref #	Account	Description	Current	Year-To-Date
Beginning Balance			310	Sales / License Software		0.00
12/31/95	12	2	310	1995 Sales	-88,454.00	
				Ending Balances =	**-88,454.00**	**-88,454.00**
Beginning Balance			311	Sales / Profiles	0.00	
12/31/95	12	2	311	1995 Sales	-4,561.00	
				Ending Balances = -	**4,561.00**	**-4,561.00**
Beginning Balance			312	Sales / Programming		0.00
12/31/95	12	2	312	1995 Sales	-5.00	
				Ending Balances =	**-5.00**	**-5.00**
Beginning Balance			313	Sales / Registration	0.00	
12/31/95	12	2	313	1995 Sales	-18,974.00	
				Ending Balances =	**-18,974.00**	**-18,974.00**
Beginning Balance			490	Returns & Allowance		0.00
12/31/95	12	3	490	1995 Refunds	3,504.00	
12/31/95	12	3	490	1995 Rebates	179.80	
				Ending Balances =	**3,683.80**	**3,683.80**
Beginning Balance			506	Contract Labor		0.00
12/31/95	12	4	506	Cheryl Smith	7,332.91	
				Ending Balances =	**7,332.91**	**7,332.91**
Beginning Balance			510	Advertising		0.00
12/31/95	12	5	510	Adv/Billboard	300.00	
12/31/95	12	5	510	Adv/Direct Mail	744.10	
12/31/95	12	5	510	Adv/Electronic	2,833.18	
12/31/95	12	5	510	Adv/Pr	11,646.24	
12/31/95	12	5	510	Adv/Printing	5,555.71	
12/31/95	12	5	510	Adv/Cheryl/Printing	1,940.27	
				Ending Balances =	**23,019.50**	**23,019.50**
Beginning Balance			512	Accounting		0.00
12/31/95	12	7	512	1995/Accounting	504.51	
				Ending Balances =	**504.51**	**504.51**
Beginning Balance			515	Amortization Expense		0.00
12/31/95	12	34	515	1995 Amoriz Exp	45.00	
				Ending Balances =	**45.00**	**45.00**
Beginning Balance			520	Auto Expense		0.00
12/31/95	12	8	520	Auto/Fees	78.60	
12/31/95	12	8	520	Auto/Insurance	1,426.92	
12/31/95	12	8	520	Auto/Lease	10,056.07	
12/31/95	12	8	520	Auto/Repair	944.65	
				Ending Balances =	**12,506.24**	**12,506.24**
Beginning Balance			528	Bank Charges		0.00
12/31/95	12	9	528	1995/Bank Chge	263.40	
				Ending Balances =	**263.40**	**263.40**
Beginning Balance			537	Commission Expense		0.00
12/31/95	12	10	537	1995/Commission	3,266.53	
				Ending Balances =	**3,266.53**	**3,266.53**
Beginning Balance			540	Contributions		0.00
12/31/95	12	11	540	1995/Contributions	1,396.45	
				Ending Balances =	**1,396.45**	**1,396.45**
Beginning Balance			545	Depreciation Expense		0.00
12/31/95	12	31	545	1995 Depr	240.00	
12/31/95	12	32	545	1995 Depr Sec 179	2,702.00	
12/31/95	12	32	545	1995 Depr Sec 179	220.50	

Date	Mt	Ref#	Account	Description	Current	Year-To-Date
12/31/95	12	33	545	1995 Depr	78.00	
				Ending Balances =	**3,240.50**	**3,240.50**
Beginning Balance			550	Dues & Subscriptions		0.00
12/31/95	12	12	550	1995/Subscriptions	729.29	
				Ending Balances =	**729.29**	**729.29**
Beginning Balance			555	Entertainment (50%)		0.00
12/31/95	12	13	555	1995/Entertainment	230.00	
				Ending Balances =	**230.00**	**230.00**
Beginning Balance			570	Insurance Expense		0.00
12/31/95	12	14	570	1995/Insurance	1,162.50	
				Ending Balances =	**1,162.50**	**1,162.50**
Beginning Balance			585	Legal Expense		0.00
12/31/95	12	15	585	1995/Legal	804.72	
				Ending Balances =	**804.72**	**804.72**
Beginning Balance			590	Licenses		0.00
12/31/95	12	16	590	1995/Licenses	33.88	
				Ending Balances =	**33.88**	**33.88**
Beginning Balance			605	Office Expense		0.00
12/31/95	12	17	605	1995/Office Exp	2,699.66	
				Ending Balances =	**2,699.66**	**2,699.66**
Beginning Balance			606	Office Supplies		0.00
12/31/95	12	18	606	1995/Office Sup	1,529.90	
				Ending Balances =	**1,529.90**	**1,529.90**
Beginning Balance			607	Office/Computer Expense		0.00
12/31/95	12	19	607	Computer/Prog Fee	462.60	
12/31/95	12	19	607	Computer/Software	181.30	
				Ending Balances =	**643.90**	**643.90**
Beginning Balance			608	Office/Computer Supplies		0.00
12/31/95	12	20	608	1995/Computer Sup	270.12	
				Ending Balances =	**270.12**	**270.12**
Beginning Balance			615	Operation Expenses		0.00
12/31/95	12	21	615	Oper/Fees	765.30	
12/31/95	12	21	615	Oper/Moving	1,126.74	
12/31/95	12	21	615	Oper/Consulting	320.00	
12/31/95	12	21	615	Oper/Gifts	591.70	
12/31/95	12	21	615	Oper/Membership	150.00	
12/31/95	12	21	615	Oper/Vis Serv Chge	59.80	
12/31/95	12	21	615	Oper/Loan	1,155.00	
				Ending Balances =	**4,168.54**	**4,168.54**
Beginning Balance			620	Postage		0.00
12/31/95	12	22	620	Post/Federal Exp	2,849.09	
12/31/95	12	22	620	Post/Equip Lease	314.61	
12/31/95	12	22	620	Post/Mail Box Rent	124.00	
12/31/95	12	22	620	Post/Postmaster	3,733.17	
12/31/95	12	22	620	Post/Supplies	72.98	
				Ending Balances =	**7,093.85**	**7,093.85**
Beginning Balance			640	Rent		0.00
12/31/95	12	23	640	1995/Rent	13,649.12	
				Ending Balances =	**13,649.12**	**13,649.12**
Beginning Balance			660	Tax/Other		0.00
12/31/95	12	24	660	1995/Taxes	436.00	
				Ending Balances =	**436.00**	**436.00**

Date	Mt	Ref#	Account	Description	Current	Year-To-Date
Beginning Balance			670	Telephone		0.00
12/31/95	12	25	670	Tele/Centel	59.92	
12/31/95	12	25	670	Tele/Centel	179.11	
12/31/95	12	25	670	Tele/Fax Options	134.46	
12/31/95	12	25	670	Tele/Misc	124.61	
12/31/95	12	25	670	Tele/Sprint 800	6,066.90	
12/31/95	12	25	670	Tele/Sprint Cellular	389.83	
12/31/95	12	25	670	Tele/Sprint	533.23	
12/31/95	12	25	670	Tele/GTE	1,097.38	
12/31/95	12	25	670	Tele/GTE	1,754.78	
12/31/95	12	25	670	Tele/Voice Store	187.11	
12/31/95	12	25	670	Tele/GTE Cellular	1,507.88	
				Ending Balances =	**12,035.21**	**12,035.21**
Beginning Balance			675	Travel Expense		0.00
12/31/95	12	26	675	1995/Travel	49.00	
				Ending Balances =	**49.00**	**49.00**
Beginning Balance			682	Utilities / Other		0.00
12/31/95	12	27	682	1995/Utilities	1,778.28	
				Ending Balances =	**1,778.28**	**1,778.28**

This is a partial G/L. General Ledger is in balance.   0.00
111 Transactions
Current Profit   9,421.19   Y-T-D Profit   9,421.19

Journal Entries

Period Ending: 12/31/95

Date	Mt	Ref #	Account	Description	Item Amt	Ref Amt
12/31/95	12	2	115	1995 Sales	111,994.00	
12/31/95	12	2	310	1995 Sales	-88,454.00	
12/31/95	12	2	311	1995 Sales	-4,561.00	
12/31/95	12	2	312	1995 Sales	-5.00	
12/31/95	12	2	313	1995 Sales	-18,974.00	
12/31/95	12	3	115	1995 Refunds/Rebates	-3,683.80	
12/31/95	12	3	490	1995 Refunds	3,504.00	
12/31/95	12	3	490	1995 Rebates	179.80	
12/31/95	12	4	115	Cheryl Smith	-7,332.91	
12/31/95	12	4	506	Cheryl Smith	7,332.91	
12/31/95	12	5	115	1995 Advertising	-23,019.50	
12/31/95	12	5	510	Adv/Billboard	300.00	
12/31/95	12	5	510	Adv/Direct Mail	744.10	
12/31/95	12	5	510	Adv/Electronic	2,833.18	
12/31/95	12	5	510	Adv/Pr	11,646.24	
12/31/95	12	5	510	Adv/Printing	5,555.71	
12/31/95	12	5	510	Adv/Cheryl/Printing	1,940.27	
12/31/95	12	7	115	1995/Accounting	-504.51	
12/31/95	12	7	512	1995/Accounting	504.51	
12/31/95	12	8	115	1995 Auto	-12,506.24	
12/31/95	12	8	520	Auto/Fees	78.60	
12/31/95	12	8	520	Auto/Insurance	1,426.92	
12/31/95	12	8	520	Auto/Lease	10,056.07	

12/31/95	12	8	520	Auto/Repair	944.65
12/31/95	12	9	115	1995/Bank Chge	-263.40
12/31/95	12	9	528	1995/Bank Chge	263.40
12/31/95	12	10	115	1995/Commission	-3,266.53
12/31/95	12	10	537	1995/Commission	3,266.53
12/31/95	12	11	115	1995/Contributions	-1,396.45
12/31/95	12	11	540	1995/Contributions	1,396.45
12/31/95	12	12	115	1995/Subscriptions	-729.29
12/31/95	12	12	550	1995/Subscriptions	729.29
12/31/95	12	13	115	1995/Entertainment	-230.00
12/31/95	12	13	555	1995/Entertainment	230.00
12/31/95	12	14	115	1995/Insurance	-1,162.50
12/31/95	12	14	570	1995/Insurance	1,162.50
12/31/95	12	15	115	1995/Legal	-804.72
12/31/95	12	15	585	1995/Legal	804.72
12/31/95	12	16	115	1995/Licenses	-33.88
12/31/95	12	16	590	1995/Licenses	33.88
12/31/95	12	17	115	1995/Office Exp	-2,699.66
12/31/95	12	17	605	1995/Office Exp	2,699.66
12/31/95	12	18	115	1995/Office Sup	-1,529.90
12/31/95	12	18	606	1995/Office Sup	1,529.90
12/31/95	12	19	115	1995/Computer Exp	-643.90
12/31/95	12	19	607	Computer/Prog Fee	462.60
12/31/95	12	19	607	Computer/Software	181.30
12/31/95	12	20	115	1995/Computer Sup	-270.12
12/31/95	12	20	608	1995/Computer Sup	270.12
12/31/95	12	21	115	1995/Operation Exp	-4,168.54
12/31/95	12	21	615	Oper/Fees	765.30
12/31/95	12	21	615	Oper/Moving	1,126.74
12/31/95	12	21	615	Oper/Consulting	320.00
12/31/95	12	21	615	Oper/Gifts	591.70
12/31/95	12	21	615	Oper/Membership	150.00
12/31/95	12	21	615	Oper/Vis Serv Chge	59.80
12/31/95	12	21	615	Oper/Loan	1,155.00
12/31/95	12	22	115	1995/Postage	-7,093.85
12/31/95	12	22	620	Post/Federal Exp	2,849.09
12/31/95	12	22	620	Post/Equip Lease	314.61
12/31/95	12	22	620	Post/Mail Box Rent	124.00
12/31/95	12	22	620	Post/Postmaster	3,733.17
12/31/95	12	22	620	Post/Supplies	72.98
12/31/95	12	23	115	1995/Rent	-13,649.12
12/31/95	12	23	640	1995/Rent	13,649.12
12/31/95	12	24	115	1995/Taxes	-436.00
12/31/95	12	24	660	1995/Taxes	436.00
12/31/95	12	25	115	1995/Telephone	-12,035.21
12/31/95	12	25	670	Tele/Centel	59.92
12/31/95	12	25	670	Tele/Centel	179.11
12/31/95	12	25	670	Tele/Fax Options	134.46
12/31/95	12	25	670	Tele/Misc	124.61
12/31/95	12	25	670	Tele/Sprint 800	6,066.90
12/31/95	12	25	670	Tele/Sprint Cellular	389.83
12/31/95	12	25	670	Tele/Sprint	533.23

12/31/95	12	25	670	Tele/GTE	1,097.38
12/31/95	12	25	670	Tele/GTE	1,754.78
12/31/95	12	25	670	Tele/Voice Store	187.11
12/31/95	12	25	670	Tele/GTE Cellular	1,507.88
12/31/95	12	26	115	1995/Travel	-49.00
12/31/95	12	26	675	1995/Travel	49.00
12/31/95	12	27	115	1995/Utilities	-1,778.28
12/31/95	12	27	682	1995/Utilities	1,778.28
12/31/95	12	28	115	Lawrence Hamilton	13,000.00
12/31/95	12	28	275	Lawrence Hamilton	-13,000.00
12/31/95	12	29	115	Laptop Computer	-2,702.00
12/31/95	12	29	142	Laptop Computer	2,702.00
12/31/95	12	30	115	Software	-220.50
12/31/95	12	30	142	Software	220.50
12/31/95	12	31	152	1995 Depr	-240.00
12/31/95	12	31	545	1995 Depr	240.00
12/31/95	12	32	152	1995 Depr Sec 179	-2,922.50
12/31/95	12	32	545	1995 Depr Sec 179	2,702.00
12/31/95	12	32	545	1995 Depr Sec 179	220.50
12/31/95	12	33	152	1995 Depr	-78.00
12/31/95	12	33	545	1995 Depr	78.00
12/31/95	12	34	172	1995 Amoriz Exp	-45.00
12/31/95	12	34	515	1995 Amoriz Exp	45.00
12/31/95	12	35	115	Reverse 1994 Visa	-2,395.00
12/31/95	12	35	220	Reverse 1994 Visa	2,395.00
12/31/95	12	36	115	1995 Visa Balance	1,589.66
12/31/95	12	36	220	1995 Visa Balance	-1,589.66
12/31/95	12	37	115	1994 Balance	400.00
12/31/95	12	37	142	1994 Balance	2,786.00
12/31/95	12	37	152	1994 Balance	-357.00
12/31/95	12	37	162	1994 Balance	226.00
12/31/95	12	37	172	1994 Balance	-71.00
12/31/95	12	37	198	1994 Balance	600.00
12/31/95	12	37	220	1994 Balance	-2,395.00
12/31/95	12	37	275	1994 Balance	-6,484.00
12/31/95	12	37	295	1994 Balance	5,295.00

111 Transactions For The Period   **Journal Balance**   **0.00**

Dance & Skate Outfitter

BUSINESS PLAN

ARABESQUE DANCE & SKATE SHOP

5005 Main Street
Plymouth, Michigan 48170

The purpose of this business plan is to outline and summarize the plans of the partners regarding: financial resources, needs and uses; marketing, advertising, and promotions strategies; inventory resources and requirements; demographics of the community and customer; and the backgrounds and roles of Arabesque's partners.

- STATEMENT OF PURPOSE & GOALS

- EXECUTIVE SUMMARY

- BRIEF BUSINESS DESCRIPTION

- MARKET ANALYSIS

- MANAGEMENT

- CUSTOMER DEMOGRAPHICS

- TEACHER AND STUDENT SURVEYS

- CHECKLIST OF RESOURCES

- BUILDING/FIXTURE SOURCES

- FINANCIAL PROJECTIONS

STATEMENT OF PURPOSE & GOALS

The purpose of Arabesque Dance & Skate Shop is to meet a need in the rapidly growing Plymouth community for high-quality, reasonably priced dance, skate, and exercise wear. Recognizing that currently residents of the Plymouth community must drive to other cities for supplies or must order through catalogs and not be certain of what they will receive, Arabesque will provide these products locally.

The goal of Arabesque Dance & Skate Shop is to provide high-quality, reasonably priced dance, skate, and exercise apparel to dancers, skaters, and exercise enthusiasts. Inherent in this goal is the desire to provide excellent service to every customer.

The goal of this business plan is to outline and summarize how the goals of Arabesque will be accomplished.

EXECUTIVE SUMMARY

Arabesque Dance & Skate Shop is a family owned and operated retail business specializing in dance, skate, and exercise wear.

The decision to establish a business in Plymouth was based on a market analysis that showed no existing retail dance or skate wear shops within the city limits, and few shops in nearby cities. The nearest store, in Novi, is owned by a woman who is ready to retire and is considering selling her store to an employee. Currently, dancers must drive to Ann Arbor, Livonia, or Dearborn. Because dance wear and dance shoes are required by studios, students have no choice but to drive great distances for their attire.

Prior to making the decision to open in the Plymouth area, the principals conducted a market analysis that included:

- Studying the population and economic demographics of the area;
- Surveying dance studios and students;
- Researching the competition, including their strengths and weaknesses, and
- Meeting with supplier representatives.

The population includes about 377,700 potential customers within a 20-mile radius of Plymouth with an average household income of $42,267. A survey of the studios showed roughly 1,500 students in the area, taking ballet, tap and/or jazz. Each type of dance requires a different type of shoe. Ballet students report going through two pair of ballet shoes, four to ten pair of pointe shoes each year. They also need tap and jazz shoes and leotards and tights in a variety of styles each year.

In meeting with potential suppliers, the principals have narrowed their choice of suppliers to Danzier, Emmet, and Performance attire. The range of shoe suppliers would be broader to include Brien and Korkov.

The principals have developed a marketing action plan that includes news releases, fact sheets, advertising, direct mail, visits to dance studios and skating clubs, discounts, gift certificates, give-aways, a Grand Opening celebration. The target date for opening is early January.

The store would be managed by Sarah Harper, Carol Simmons, and Elizabeth Alexander with assistance from the other principals. Two principals would be present weekdays; three would be in the store on Saturdays. Hours are Monday - Wednesday, 10 am - 7 pm; Thursday -Friday, 10 am - 9 pm; Saturday, 10 am - 5 pm.

Of the seven principals, two are in finance, two are in marketing, two have danced a number of years and are familiar with the merchandise, and one has the technical ability to maintain the building.

Products to be offered include name-brand dance, skate and exercise wear; a small selection of costume props, and miscellaneous dance-related keepsake or statement products. These include:

- •Tap and jazz shoes
- •Ballet and point shoes
- •Leotards
- •Skate Leotards
- •Tights
- •Skirts
- •Sweaters
- •Warmup suits and leg warmers
- •Statement items: "Dance" T-shirts, sweatshirts, boxers,
- •Miscellaneous: ribbons, combs, keychains, picture frames, calendars, how-to books, snoods, belts, and other dance related keepsakes.

Arabesque Dance & Skate Shop is a family-owned partnership comprised of seven principals: John Harper; his wife, Sarah Harper; their son, Matt Harper; their daughter Carol Simmons and her husband, Steve Simmons; and their daughter Elizabeth Alexander and her husband, Paul Alexander.

Each partner brings to the business varying areas of expertise and is responsible for the area of the company that best utilizes his or her skills. All will assist in other areas where needed.

Arabesque is slated to open for business in January 1996, if not sooner. Hours are:

10:00 a.m. to 7:00 p.m. Monday through Wednesday
10:00 a.m. to 9:00 p.m. Thursday and Friday
10:00 a.m. to 5:00 p.m. Saturday

Initially, the store will be staffed by two employees, at least one a principal, at all times. Three employees will work on Saturdays. Additional principals would come in as needed to handle customer service, inventory, and maintenance. With expansion, additional customer service representatives would be employed.

Arabesque Dance & Skate Shop will offer for purchase dance, skate and exercise wear, including ballet, jazz and tap shoes, tights, leotards, and warmup wear. It will also offer "dance" statement clothing and items, such as T-shirts, carry-all bags, and boxers, as well as miscellaneous impulse items, such as keychains, picture frames, calendars, and how-to books. With expansion, it will offer performance-related props and costumes.

Dance, skate, and exercise students and enthusiasts must currently purchase through limited supplies dance teachers carry, order through a catalog, or drive to Ann Arbor, Livonia or Dearborn for a complete line of ballet, tap, jazz and skating apparel and shoes. One or two studios try to stock their own apparel, but to date, this method has not been reliable. Their stock is old, outdated, and limited. Arabesque Dance & Skate Shop will meet the needs of students by offering a complete line of high-quality, reasonably priced dance and skate apparel and shoes.

The target audience of Arabesque Dance & Skate Shop includes dancers, skaters, and exercise enthusiasts within a 20 mile radius of the city of Plymouth. This radius encompasses residents of Livingston, Washtenaw, western Oakland, western Wayne, and southern Shiawassee counties. Cities in these counties include Ann Arbor, Brighton, Dexter, Hartland, Highland, Howell, Milford, Novi, Northville, Pinckney, Plymouth, South Lyon, Wixom, and Ypsilanti.

General Population

Roughly 377,690 potential customers live within a 20 mile radius of Plymouth with an average household income of $42,267 and an average per capita income of $17,930.

Demographics for the city of Plymouth indicate a population of 5,686, with an average household income of $35,551 and average per capita income of $17,019. The population of Plymouth is 14,815 with an average household income of $56,009 and average per capita income of $20,360.

Within a 10 mile radius of Plymouth is another 92,240 potential customers with an average household income of $43,943 and an average per capita income of $16,991. Within the next 10 mile radius are 264,949 more potential customers with an average household income of $40,566 and an average per capita income of $18,463. For a breakdown of potential customers by city, please reference the section titled Demographics.

Dancers, Skaters, and Exercisers

Potential customers would be drawn from dance studios, skate clubs, fitness centers, community education programs, YMCA classes, and public and private schools. The following demographics for dance studio teachers and students were obtained through a survey. Skate clubs were not surveyed because we assumed the results would be similar to those of dance studios. Fitness centers, the YMCA, and community/public school programs were not surveyed because they are considered transient customers who are unreliable, yet still with customer potential.

Dance Studios

A survey of dance studios in the Plymouth area shows the following:

Brighton Institute of Dance which is located at 800 Marnier, Brighton, MI. Ariel Lyndstrom is the teacher. There are approximately 200 students, ages 3-18 years. Of the students, 200 are in ballet; 30 on pointe. The Institute offers ballet, jazz, and tap. For ballet, black leotard & pink tights are required. Students can wear skirts and a different color once a week. Danzier and Korkov shoes are used for beginning students.

Amy Scott School of Dance is located at 20534 Lyon Drive, Lyon Twp., MI. Amy Scott, the owner, is the primary teacher.

Located at Howell is the *Centre for the Art of Dance*. Rachel Hathaway is the primary teacher. The center has 250-300 students, most of which are between the ages of 3-11 years old. Approximately 300 students participate in ballet, 100 in tap, and 100 in jazz. The Centre's requirements are for ballet--pink leotard, powder blue for intermediate students; black leotard for teens and adults. Most ballet students are required to use Danzier shoes. For tap, black leotards are required.

Alex's School of Dance is located at 482 Indian Trail in Howell, Michigan. The primary teacher is the owner, Alex Sanchez.

The House of Dance is located at 1350 S. Main St. in Brighton with approximately 230 students of all ages, most are in ballet and tap. Approximately 10 students are on pointe. Alex's offers ballet, jazz, and tap. Alex's requires ballet students to wear pink ballet shoes, whatever brand fits the best. Tap students wear black taps, Reba, Tones or Harver. No jazz shoes are required until students are 10 years old.

Jesse's Studio of Dance located at 10 Sullivan Street in Brighton has an even distribution of students between ballet, jazz, and tap. Jesse's requires ballet students to wear black leotards, pink seamed tights, as well as Danzier or Korkov shoes. For tap, Jesse requires Danzier and Tones shoes.

Kim's School of Dance found at 946 Highland, MI has approximately 560 students, with an even distribution of ages. Kim offers ballet, jazz, and tap. She requires ballet students to wear black leotards, pink tights, pink skirts with elastic waistbands and Danzier or Korkov shoes with a split sole for company; others can wear anything. Kim requires Danzier and Tones tap shoes for tap students.

The *Plymouth Dance Theatre* has approximately 150 students, ages 3-18 years. There is an even distribution of students in the classes, but 10 are on pointe. The Theatre offers ballet, jazz, tap, and acrobatics. Uniforms are not required, but ballet students wear leotards, and tights. Also ballet shoes must be either Danzier and pointe shoes must be Danzier or Korkov to start, then students have their own choice. For tap, students must wear Danzier or Tones taps.

Skate Clubs

Discussion with individuals whose children take skating lessons in Plymouth showed that students were lined around the block to sign up for lessons this September. All indications are that figure skating is growing rapidly as an alternative for girls, especially with the Olympics emphasizing it. A three-rink ice arena is slated to open soon in Ann Arbor; and a large skating arena, Amber Oaks Ice Arena, currently exists in Howell. Competitive roller skating also requires the appropriate skating attire.

Community and Public School Dance Programs

Although requiring dance apparel and shoes, students in these programs are considered by Arabesque to be "gravy" customers. We would not rely on them, but would welcome their purchases.

Fitness Centers

Exercise and physical fitness programs in the area requiring apparel include:

- Aerobic House in Highland, MI
- Gym Dandy in Plymouth, MI
- Jazzy's in Howell, MI
- Orlando Fitness Center in Brighton, MI
- The Nutrition Center in Howell, MI

Buying Decisions

Peak buying times for dancers and skaters are September when classes start up and March through May when studios are preparing for recitals and performances. Sales increase during the holiday season in December, but not substantially. The slow months are January and February.

Dancers and skaters tend to devote their lives to dancing and skating, practicing long hours. A child between the ages of 4 and 12 years of age needs ballet shoes, two leotards, and two pair of tights each year for ballet. If the child chooses to learn tap dancing, she needs tap shoes.

A survey of students at studios in the Plymouth area shows that a ballet student between the ages of 12 and 18 goes through four to ten pairs of pointe shoes a year, two pairs of ballet shoes, two leotards, and three or four pairs of tights, and warmup attire. Students almost always branch into tap and jazz in their teens, requiring tap shoes, jazz shoes and jazz outfits. Additionally, they purchase almost any products related to their passion, including T-shirts, carry-all bags, key chains, and calendars. (Please see the Teacher and Student Surveys section.)

Adult students are not quite as passionate as teenagers about their buying; they tend to buy attire that is as "artsy-looking" as possible. Exercise enthusiasts like the variety of exercise wear, changing "costumes" often for the sake of wearing the latest fashions.

Purchasing Criteria

Purchases are based on need and quality; name brands are important only to the extent that they connote high quality, especially for ballet students. Teens want state-of-the-art pointe shoes; and parents pay what is necessary to help them be the best in their class. The survey of students in Plymouth showed that they stick to Danzier, Emmet and Performance for apparel; shoes are a different matter. Students start with Danzier or Korkov and then go on to whatever is comfortable. The survey indicates that many go into Emmet, Brien or Krisnov.

Competitors

The active lifestyle of teens and parents, combined with the lack of existing nearby stores, requires that parents look at price last. Few stores exist in the area, forcing students, dancers and skaters to take what is available at the nearest store, which may be a great distance away. If parents and students do not find what they need at small, high-priced, sometimes unreliable stores in Ann Arbor, Novi, or Howell, they must drive to Livonia, an estimated 75 mile round trip, or Dearborn, an estimated 100 mile round trip.

With their busy schedules, parents simply do not have the time to drive great distances for the sake of cheaper prices. Arabesque Dance & Skate Shop would like to change that by offering high-quality merchandise at a fair price that does not take advantage of the customer or the situation. No parent should have to pay $55 for a simple skating leotard.

No dance or skate wear stores exist in Plymouth. A survey of dance studios in the Plymouth area was met with enthusiasm by several studios. Dancers at these studios must currently drive great distances for apparel. The nearest store is in Howell, and it is small and open mostly to service the students of the owner. Due to a lack of proper organization, marketing, and management, the store offers little competition. Many dancers living in Howell drive to Novi rather than purchase apparel from the store. The owners of the store are ready to leave the business; currently, a woman working at the store is considering purchasing it. Only one dance studio said it tries to have tights and leotards available for purchase. The rest of the studios do not. It appears that doing so is often a hassle and done only out of necessity. Most studios surveyed said they would welcome a store in the area. Competitors and their strengths and weaknesses include:

Dance Station - Novi

Located in a strip mall at a busy intersection. Hours: 10 am -7 pm Monday-Friday; 10 am -6 pm Saturday.

Strengths

The store offers a pleasant, modern decor that would appeal to customers who like bright colors, plastic, and metal fixtures. It stocks a variety of products, including a large supply of keepsakes, carry-all bags, and boxer shorts. It has two dressing rooms for trying on leotards and a seating area for trying on shoes. It is carpeted. It has a large selection of jazz and tap shoes and jazz leotards. Shoes are on a rack, making self-service easy.

Weaknesses

Area for trying on shoes is carpeted, making it difficult to try on pointe, tap and jazz shoes. Upon visiting the store, we found that the customer service representative was not very service oriented. Merchandise is glitzy and impractical for most dancers, appealing to small children who like lots of cute ruffles. Very few basic leotards were available, just those with ruffles--fun-type wear, but not for the serious dancer. The selection of pointe shoes is limited. The store tends to specialize in jazz wear. Leotards are difficult to sort through. No T-shirts were available; no warmup attire was available. The store is about 20 miles from Plymouth.

Bravo

Store is located in Livonia, Michigan and is open from 11 am - 7 pm Monday to Thursday, and 12 pm - 4 pm on Saturday.

Strengths

It is the only dance wear supply store in Livonia and it is established.

Weaknesses

Store is closed on Fridays. Store is frequently closed regardless of the hours posted. It is very small and offers a small inventory. Products are outdated. Shoes offered were only made five years ago.

Positions

Store is located in Howell, Michigan. Hours: 10 am - 6 pm Monday - Thursday, 10 am - 9 pm Friday, 10 am - 6 pm Saturday, 12 pm - 5 pm Sunday.

Strengths

Enjoys a captive audience with college students who take dance and exercise classes. Students do not always have cars and must buy supplies in Howell. Leotards are displayed by color. Store carries two largest brand names: Performance and Danzier. Warmups can be found in one area, and they are high-quality brands. Children have their own section. There is a seating area for trying on shoes. It has a professional atmosphere for the serious dancer--not glitsy impractical junk. It has a wide selection of shoes. It makes good use of sales, special offers and packaged deals. They are negotiable on damaged merchandise. They offer a wide selection of shoes.

Weaknesses

There is no place to park except on the street at a meter. The streets are congested. Store is in the basement of a T-shirt shop. The only signage is in a 3 foot wide window. Store is difficult to find. Store moved from a larger store to a smaller one. There are no lyrical outfits, no skating outfits and no jazz or exercise clothes. The skirt selection is limited, and the color selection is limited. Merchandise is basic shoes, tights, leotards and warmups. It charges customer $5 just to try on pointe shoes. Rumor has it that the store is not doing well due to poor management.

Rhythmic Movements

Store is located in Novi, Michigan. Hours: 10 am - 7 pm Monday - Friday; 10 am - 5 pm Saturday.

Strengths

The store has an established reputation. Although it looks like it is going out of business, it is doing well. It was packed with customers patiently waiting for their daughters' turn to try on shoes. It is the only store servicing the Northville, and Novi area. It stocks a large supply of pointe, tap, and jazz shoes. It has a raised wooden floor for trying on shoes. It has a large inventory of skating leotards and tights. It is packed in September with students getting shoes for lessons. They sell costume props, such as batons and boas, and trim for costumes.

Weaknesses

The store is in the back of a swimwear store and looks like everything was shoved into a storage room. Customers have to climb steps and walk over the wooden floor used for trying on shoes. Customers have to sign in for service. Not enough customer service representatives are available. No evening hours. The store is dirty.

Howard's Dance Center

Howard's is located in Dearborn, Michigan. Open six days a week. A second and third store are located in Warren and Wyandotte, MI.

Strengths

Offers many brands, including Performance, Danzier, Emmet, Halley's and Tones taps, body wear and shoes. Offers theatrical costumes, wigs, masks, magic supplies, costume accessories, sequins, beads, trims, costume fabric, appliques, fringe. Stocks skating dresses, jazz outfits, a variety of skirt lengths and types, a variety of leotards and tights. It is very service oriented, willing to call around and get what the customer needs. Very helpful and accommodating. It has two floors and encourages customer to browse. Store has a large inventory.

Weaknesses

It is 75 to 100 miles from the Plymouth area. Customer has to drive into the metropolitan Detroit area.

Strides

Strides is located in Canton, Michigan.

Strengths

Convenient for parents of children.

Weaknesses

It is a shoe store that carries the basic ballet shoe and basic tap shoe for children only. It orders only once a year, in September.

Gurnecky's Dance Outlet

Gurnecky's is located in Farmington, Michigan. Store hours are: 10 am - 6 pm Monday - Wednesday, Friday; 10 am - 8 pm Thursday; 10 am - 6 pm, Saturday.

Strengths

One of the few stores serving the Farmington area.

Weaknesses

It is a shoe store that carries dance shoes and some dance wear. It does not specialize in dance and skate apparel.

Halley's Studio Goods

Halley's is located in Brighton, Michigan. Hours: 10 am - 6 pm Monday - Friday; 10 am - 5 pm, Saturday.

Strengths

The only store in Brighton providing dance shoes.

Weaknesses

It is a children's shoe store that carries dance shoes and some tights and leotards for children and adults. It does not specialize in dance and skate apparel.

Marketing Action Plan

The marketing plan for Arabesque is twofold, encompassing marketing Arabesque itself and marketing the merchandise.

Marketing the Business

A major effort to market Arabesque involves sending news releases and fact sheets to local newspapers, distributing brochures and gift certificates to all dance studios, featuring promotional events at the store, and participating in local community events. The following schedule would be used to publicize Arabesque. The goal is to get name recognition, store awareness, and customers into the store.

Early Oct. Develop a logo.
Cost: $100 for the graphic designer.

Late Nov. Develop business cards and letterhead with the store logo, address, telephone and hours on them.
Cost: $100

Late Nov. Develop and print two-color brochure on how we can work with studios.
Cost: $100

Late Nov. Develop and print $10 gift certificate for teachers.
Cost: $20

Late Nov. Purchase keepsake with our logo to give out at studios we visit: carry-all bags with logo.
Cost: $150

Early Dec. Possibly purchase dance T-shirts with the Arabesque Dance & Skate Shop logo. These would be worn by sales staff and given away at the Grand Opening.
Cost: T-shirts with logo

Early Dec. Print invitations for Grand Opening Eve Party for Teachers focusing on dance, skate, and fitness center proprietors and their guest and offering 15% discount for everyone.
Cost: Paper and printing and postage--$100.

Early Dec. Send fact sheet and photo to the Hometown Papers about the family joining forces to open their dream store. This is a unique event because seven family members (father and mother, daughters and their husbands, and son) are willing to invest in the store, work in it, and become involved in the community. Four of the family members have moved to the Brighton area, and two more are looking to move there. All children took dance lessons, some for as many as 10 years. All have degrees and work in another field, but like the idea of working together. All believe in making a difference in the community.
Cost: $2.00 for telephone call and postage.

Early Jan. Send news release to newspapers within a 20 mile radius, the Ann Arbor News, and the Detroit Free Press, announcing the Grand Opening Celebration for the store, the festivities involved, and how Arabesque is meeting a need in this rapidly growing community.
Cost: $5.00 postage and paper.

Early Jan. A representative from Arabesque will:
- Deliver to each studio business cards from Arabesque, a brochure detailing our hours.
- Check to see if they got their invitation to the Grand Opening Eve Party for Teachers and again invite teachers and a guest to attend.
- If they cannot attend, give them a $10 gift certificate toward anything in the store and invite them to attend the Grand Opening Celebration the next day for the general public.
  Cost: gas to visit each studio.

Jan 20 Grand Opening Celebration for Teachers.
- Survey any who have not completed a survey to what they want in a store: what products, what service, what hours, etc.
- Give them 15% off for the day.
- Give teachers a card entitling them to 10% off future purchases.
- Tell them about our Teachers Bulletin Board and display area.
- Tell them about our plans for monthly information events--updating students and teachers on the latest shoes and other merchandise.
- Tell them about plans, and get suggestions for, a "Meet the Teachers from Your Local

Dance Studios Day" for parents to meet proprietors of local dance studios. Teachers would make short presentations about their studios, the number of students they have, the types of dance lessons they offer, etc.

Jan. Opening Day--Grand Opening Celebration.
- Every hour, we will give away gift items (possibly carry-all bags or T-shirts) between 10 am and 4 pm for persons 12 years and over.
- We will give a free helium balloon to each child under 12.
- We will have a bunch of helium balloons marking the event.
- Have someone dressed like a ballerina in the children's area, reading stories to small children.

Feb. Visit studios of anyone who didn't come to Grand Opening. Offer our Teachers' Bulletin Board for them to post a notice about their recital. Also mention that we want to know when their recital is so that we can place our order for tights, shoes, and whatever else their students may need to purchase; for example, if they will need a certain color of tights, we will go ahead and order a supply. Mention that we would like to attend the recital.

Mar. Compile a list of recitals. Try to have at least one person attend. Then after each, send a handwritten card congratulating them on a fine recital, mentioning something specific to their recital. Get a copy of their program for our files.
Cost: $10.-- Ticket to the recital; stamp and paper.

June/July Participate in any community events, giving away balloons.

August Sponsor a "Meet the Teachers from Your Local Dance Studios Day" for parents to meet proprietors of local dance studios. Teachers could make short presentations about their studios, the number of students they have, the types of dance lessons they offer, etc.

Marketing Merchandise

The goal should be to move merchandise off the shelf. We do not want anything to stay in the store; we will move it out through clearance sales if necessary. In the Fall, when classes start up, we would:

- Offer a package for children--tights, leotard, and ballet shoes, all for a discount.
- Offer a 10% discount off all tap, jazz and ballet leotards and tights.
- Have a sidewalk sale.
- Offer special promotions: buy one, get one at half off, etc.

MANAGEMENT

Skills Needed

To be successful in a retail operation in the dance, skate and exercise field requires a wide array of skills including: the ability to be proactive in management, organization, finance, marketing, and inventory control skills. Rarely does one individual possess all these skills. In Arabesque Dance & Skate Shop each partner brings to the corporation a set of skills developed through years of education, training, and work experience.

Briefly, John Harper works in investment sales for a local bank; Matt Harper works for the same bank as a real estate lender. They will handle the accounting and finance. Sarah Harper has worked in the promotions and marketing fields for about 10 years. Paul Alexander works in marketing and is pursuing an MBA in Marketing. They will handle the marketing and outside sales. Carol Simmons is a former teacher and youth worker. A dancer for more than 15 years, she knows dance wear. She will serve as buyer and as contact person for studios. Elizabeth Alexander is a speech pathologist and a former dancer. Her organizational skills will enable her to track inventory and do much of the clerical work. Steve Simmons, a designer, is skilled at fine carpentry and building. He will handle any problems related to fixtures and maintenance.

Each principal brings to Arabesque his or her own area of expertise. In addition, he or she will assume secondary responsibilities. They are:

Partner & Title	Expertise	Responsibilities
John Harper, CFP Accounting Manager	Finance Organization	Management Customer service Building Inventory
Sarah Harper Manager	Organization Management Marketing	Customer service Inventory Building Finances
Matt Harper Controller	Finance Organization	Management Customer service Building Inventory Marketing
Steve Simmons Building & Maintenance Manager	Technical Design	Inventory Customer Service Building Management Finances
Carol Simmons Asst. Mgr - Buyer	Inventory Management Customer Service	Marketing Organization Building Finances
Paul Alexander Marketing Manager	Marketing Outside sales Inventory procurement	Customer Service Management Building Finances Inventory
Elizabeth Alexander Asst. Mgr - Cust. Service	Inventory Customer service Management	Building Organization Marketing Finances

In addition to financial resources (see section on Financing), two other types of resources are required: those needed to conduct business, including the building, fixtures, and equipment and additional staff, and the inventory itself.

Resources to Conduct Business

A building will be leased, preferably in a strip mall. A small oak "stage" will be installed to allow students to try on pointe and tap shoes on the same type of surface they will be dancing. An area will be set aside in the store for small children visiting with parents and another area for teacher notices and brochures. (Please reference Checklist of Resources to Do Business, for a list of items necessary to conduct business and Building/Fixture Sources for a partial list of potential sources.)

The need for human resources will be met through the principals and possibly one part-time employee. Two individuals will be available at all times during the week. On Saturday, three persons will be on hand. The remaining principals will be on call to come in and assist during overloads.

Inventory

Roughly $20,000 in inventory will be carried. Meetings with the Danzier representative were helpful in narrowing down sources. The representative is delighted that we will be in the Plymouth area. She had been looking for someone to open a store for over a year. A meeting with the representative from Emmet brought similar results, and it is expected that the meeting to take place October 10 with Performance will do likewise. These are the three most sought-after suppliers of dancing apparel. A wide array of shoes will be carried, including Danzier, Emmet, Korkov, Reflex and Krisnov.

CUSTOMER DEMOGRAPHICS

A study of the demographics of the Plymouth and surrounding communities suggests that the area is rapidly growing as residents of the metropolitan Detroit area seek a countrylike environment to raise families. In 1995, the population, average household income and per capita income by 10 and 20 mile radii are:

	Average Population	Average Household Income	Per Capita Income
City of Plymouth	5,686	$35,551	$17,019
Plymouth Township	14,815	$56,009	$20,360
10 mile radius	92,240	$43,943	$16,991
Green Oak Township	11,604	$47,421	17,272
Hamburg Township	13,083	48,481	18,058
Hartland	6,860	50,627	17,690
Howell	8,184	31,674	15,268
Howell Township	4,298	47,784	16,725
Independence Township	24,722	53,233	21,271
Milford	5,511	37,323	14,814
Milford Township	12,121	45,938	17,745
South Lyon	5,857	33,095	14,075
Next 10 mile radius	264,949	40,566	18,463
Ann Arbor	109,592	33,344	17,786
Ann Arbor Township	3,793	56,359	35,387
Fenton	8,444	33,998	13,327
Fenton Township	10,055	48,425	19,555
Highland	17,941	42,157	15,716
Holly	5,595	28,995	12,766
Holly Township	8,852	32,895	13,828
Northville	6,226	49,282	24,568
Northville Township	17,313	55,465	23,917
Salem Township	3,734	51,948	19,936
Whitmore Lake	3,251	39,128	17,605
Ypsilanti	24,846	21,219	10,655
Ypsilanti Township	45,307	34,140	14,977
Total 20 Mile Radius including Brighton	377,690	$42,267	$17,930

Teacher Survey

Thank you for taking the time to complete this survey. You are helping us to better serve you and your students. We carry a variety of dance and skate apparel, shoes and accessories; and we want to pay special attention to your needs and preferences. As a means of saying "thank you," we will present you with a token of our appreciation when Arabesque opens.

How many students are currently enrolled at your studio?

　25-50　　　51-75　　　76-100　　　100-150　　　151-250　　　250-350　　　350+

How many students do you have in each age group?

　3-5　　　6-7　　　8-9　　　10-11　　　12-13　　　14-18　　　18+

How many students participate in each of the following classes?

　　　Ballet　　　　　　　Tap　　　　　　　　Jazz

　　　Lyrical　　　Modern　　　Acrobatics　　　　Other

Do you require a uniform for your classes? If so, please indicate the color and style.

Ballet:　　　yes　　　　　no

If yes, what is your uniform preference for each age group?

Tap:　　　yes　　　　　no

If yes, what is your uniform preference for each age group?

Jazz:　　　yes　　　　　no

If yes, what is your uniform preference for each age group?

Do you prefer that your beginning pointe students wear a specific brand or style of pointe shoe?

　　　yes　　　　　no

If yes, please indicate brand and style.

Name: _____

Address: _____

Student Survey

Thank you for taking the time to complete this survey. In doing so, you are helping us to better serve you. We carry a variety of dance and skate apparel, shoes and accessories; and we want to pay special attention to your preferences and needs.

What style and size dancing shoe do you wear?

Ballet: Brand (Danzier, Emmet, etc.) _____ Size (length/width) _____

Style (split sole, canvas, whole sole, etc.)_____

Pointe: Brand (Korkov, Grisnov, etc.)_____ Size (length/width) _____

Style (Feather, Pavlova, etc.) _____

Special Needs (extra long vamp, double shank, etc.) _____

Tap: Brand (Lyndon, Tones, etc.) _____ Size (length/width)_____

Style (low heel, mid heel, buckle etc.) _____ Color_____

Jazz: Brand (Danzier, Grisnov, etc.)_____ Size (length/width)_____

Style (sneaker shoe, boot, traditional etc.)_____ Color_____

Other: Brand_____ Size (length/width)_____

Style_____ Color_____

How many pairs of shoes do you purchase per year?

Ballet_____ Pointe_____ Jazz_____ Tap_____ Other_____

How many performances, competitions or recitals do you participate in per year?

What are your preferences/needs in tights? Brand_____

Style (seamed, unseamed, footless, etc.)_____ Size_____ Color_____

What type dance apparel do you purchase most? (leotard, unitard, shorts, sport tanks, long-sleeved, short-sleeved, tank, thin strapped, high back, scoop back, etc.) Warm-ups?(yes/no) Ballet Skirts (yes/no)

For Ballet _____

For Tap _____

For Jazz _____

Where do you currently get most of your dance or skate wear and shoes?

Please tell us about some of your past frustrations with other dance retail stores? (i.e., unfriendly personnel, inconvenient hours, didn't carry your size, didn't have what you wanted, etc.)

Name: _____

CHECKLIST OF RESOURCES NEEDED TO DO BUSINESS

The material resources needed to conduct business include the following.

A large mirror and dance bar for the stage.

Carpeting for the remainder of the building

Shelving

Racks, circular, free standing, and hanging

Metal storage racks for warehouse

Benches for trying on shoes--available

Tables, cabinets--available

Hangers: shirt and clip

Bags and tissue

Cash register, paper tape, ribbon, etc.

Credit card forms and machines

Typewriter and tapes--available

Office supplies: tape, push pins, straight pins, scissors, rubber bands, pens, pencils, markers, note pads, ruler, tape measure

Letterhead, white bond, envelopes, business cards, post cards

Postage

Telephone

Burglar alarm system

Inventory software

Iron, ironing board, steamer--available

Building cleaning supplies: vacuum, duster, toilet cleaner, furniture polish, toilet cleaning brush, sponges, window cleaner, push broom, shovel.

Paper towels and toilet paper, Kleenex, paper plates, plasticware, paper cups

Coffee maker, filters and coffee.

Following companies will be contacted for materials:

Store Fixtures--New

The Fixture Co. -- Detroit

Marlow, Inc. -- Westland

Millworks -- Wixom

Blackville & Assoc. -- Southfield

Alpine Fixtures -- Plymouth

Store Fixtures--Used

Alpine Fixtures -- Plymouth

Retail Again -- Warren

Madison, Inc. -- Madison Heights

Shelving

ABC Shelves -- Detroit

Lenox, Inc. -- Troy

Rack Supply Shop -- Walled Lake

Mirrors

Glassworks -- Livonia

Carpeting

Carpets-R-Us -- Detroit

BUILDING/FIXTURE SOURCES

Signs

Sign On -- Farmington Hills

Sign World -- Livonia

National Signs -- Livonia

Cash Register & Supplies

Register Supplies Company -- Redford

Ohio Register Corp. -- Monroe

Credit card machine comes from bank. Quoted:

$569 -- Basic cash register with receipt, breakdown of depts, figures change

$4000 -- Cash register with scanner for credit cards

Bags--Paper

Almond Bag Warehouse -- Garden City

Recycled Papers, Inc. -- Auburn Hills

Paper Distributors -- Farmington

6 ½ x 9 ½ - 1000 @ $13.05

8 ½ x 11 - 1000 @ $19.35

10 x 13 - 1000 @ $24.75

15 x 18 - 1000 @ $47.75

17 X 4 X 24 - 500 @ $44.20

Total = $149.10

Bags--Plastic

Waterford Bags -- Waterford

Rayman Plastics -- Sterling Hgts.

FINANCIAL PROJECTIONS

Opening Sources and Uses

Uses	Projected
Inventory	$23,060
Prepaid Expenses	
One Year Rent	$11,761
Employee (8 months)	3,617
Telephone (8 months)	300
Utility Expenses (8 months)	1,700
Security (8 months)	340
Yellow Pages (8 months)	462
Miscellaneous (8 months)	800

One Time Start-Up Costs

Cash Register	$650
Sign	1,000
Credit Card Machine	400
Fixtures	1,000
Four Mirrors	510
Carpeting	2,800
Benches	100
Accounting Software	100
Logo Design	100
One Year Supply of Bags	150
Telephone	100
One Time Advertising	500
Hangers	100
Construction	0
Business Insurance	450
Total Prepaid and One Time	
Start-up Expenses	**$26,940**
Total Uses of Cash	50,000

Sources of Cash

Partners	50,000

Breakeven Projected Operations

	OCT	NOV	DEC	JAN	FEB	MAR	APR	MAY	JUN	JUL	AUG	SEP	TOTAL
Sales:													
Pointe Shoes	0	0	958	958	958	958	958	958	958	958	958	958	9580
Slippers	0	0	3410	3410	3410	3410	3410	3410	3410	3410	3410	3410	34104
Leotards	0	0	3979	3979	3979	3979	3979	3979	3979	3979	3979	3979	39788
Tap Shoes	0	0	550	550	550	550	550	550	550	550	550	550	5502
Jazz Shoes	0	0	1111	1111	1111	1111	1111	1111	1111	1111	1111	1111	11107
Tights	0	0	2984	2984	2984	2984	2984	2984	2984	2984	2984	2984	29841
Miscellaneous	0	0	0	0	0	0	0	0	0	0	0	0	0
Gross Sales	0	0	12992	12992	12992	12992	12992	12992	12992	12992	12992	12992	129921
Less: Credit Card Service Charge (5% of 50% of sales)													
	0	0	-325	-325	-325	-325	-325	-325	-325	-325	-325	-325	-3248
Less: 1st & 2nd Month Discounts (10% Discount)													
	0	0	-1299	-1299	0	0	0	0	0	0	0	0	-2598
Net Sales	0	0	12667	12667	12667	12667	12667	12667	12667	12667	12667	12667	126673
Cost of Goods Sold (50%):													
Pointe Shoes	0	0	479	479	479	479	479	479	479	479	479	479	4790
Slippers	0	0	1705	1705	1705	1705	1705	1705	1705	1705	1705	1705	17052
Leotards	0	0	1989	1989	1989	1989	1989	1989	1989	1989	1989	1989	19894
Tap Shoes	0	0	275	275	275	275	275	275	275	275	275	275	2751
Jazz Shoes	0	0	555	555	555	555	555	555	555	555	555	555	5553
Tights	0	0	1492	1492	1492	1492	1492	1492	1492	1492	1492	1492	14920
Miscellaneous	0	0	0	0	0	0	0	0	0	0	0	0	0
Total Cost of Good Sold	0	0	6496	6496	6496	6496	6496	6496	6496	6496	6496	6496	64961
Gross Margin	0	0	6496	6496	6496	6496	6496	6496	6496	6496	6496	6496	64961
Less Costs:													

*Base Rent (1,200 SQF @ $11.50/SQF + $2/SQF CAM)

	1350	0	0	1350	1350	1350	1350	1350	1350	1350	1350	1350	13500
*Part Time Employee	0	0	646	646	646	646	646	646	646	646	646	646	6460
*Telephone	0	0	50	50	50	50	50	50	50	50	50	50	500
*Utilities	100	100	250	250	250	250	250	250	250	250	250	200	2650
*Security	200	20	20	20	20	20	20	20	20	20	20	20	420
*Advertising (Yellow Pages)	0	0	77	77	77	77	77	77	77	77	77	77	770
*Miscellaneous	100	100	100	100	100	100	100	100	100	100	100	100	1200
Shipping(H)	0	0	98	98	98	98	98	98	98	98	98	98	984
Manager Salary	0	0	2000	2000	2000	2000	2000	2000	2000	2000	2000	2000	20000
Social Security Withholding	0	0	153	153	153	153	153	153	153	153	153	153	1530
Sales Tax (6% of Sales)	0	0	780	780	780	780	780	780	780	780	780	780	7795
Start-up Costs(I)	7960	0	0	0	0	0	0	0	0	0	0	0	7960
Total Operating Expenses	9710	220	4174	5524	5524	5524	5524	5524	5524	5524	5524	5574	63,769
Pretax Income	-9710	-220	2322	972	972	972	972	972	972	972	972	1022	1191

(H) Assumes $8.20 to ship a 25 lb box from NYC to Detroit - Shipment received every other day

(I) Includes all items noted as one time start-up costs on sources and uses page

* Accounts which have been prepaid

Dial-It Service

BUSINESS PLAN

CALLMASTER, INC.

1003 Marina Way
Long Beach, CA 90803

January 22, 1996

In the competitive pay-per call industry, Callmaster, Inc. succeeds by creating new and unique programs, and by utilizing the latest high-tech telecommunication and computer equipment. Callmaster, Inc. seeks to maintain their position as an industry leader by securing additional capital for growth and development. This plan details the company's vision for the future, including new program offerings and financial projections.

- COMPANY PRINCIPALS

- NEW PROGRAMS

- PROJECTIONS

- COMPANY ORGANIZATION

- COMPANY OVERVIEW

- PRODUCT LIST AND PAYOUT DESCRIPTION

COMPANY PRINCIPALS

Callmaster, Inc.'s two directors, Leslie New and Scott Smith are both at the top of their respective areas of expertise. Both individuals are veterans of the audio text industry with many years of experience collectively. After having worked together successfully for years, a partnership was formed. This dynamic combination, coupled with their expertise and professional contacts has positioned Callmaster, Inc. as a much sought after commodity. This is indeed the "Dream Team" of the Pay-Per-Call Industry.

Leslie New, an aggressive, goal-oriented individual, heads the west coast operation in Long Beach, California. This is where she applies her specialties in sales, multi-media marketing and customer relations. A successful audio text business owner for over four years, she is considered by many to be a guru in the marketing of audio text. Leslie's background is in advertising, film broadcasting and marketing. After attending college, she worked in radio broadcasting.

Scott Smith supervises the east coast offices in Miami, Florida. He has been a successful audio text business owner for over 11 years and is considered one of the pioneers of this industry. Scott's background is in broadcasting and direct marketing. Scott works with many broadcasters, and also handles the technological aspects of audio text. Most of Callmaster's pay-per-calls are serviced within the Miami communications facility.

In today's competitive industry, to run a successful service bureau, it takes both technical and marketing experience. To start your own bureau, you would of course need equipment. You would have to determine what programs on the market you wish to either run yourself or market to other businesses or individuals. Equipment such as computers, T1's, PBX's, etc. are very expensive. Normally, starting in this industry, one would start small. However, given today's market a small bureau will not have the opportunity to establish key relationships with phone companies, or accrue the amount of minutes necessary to offer competitive payouts and competitive programs. Many smaller companies, resellers and small bureaus, have gone out of business, due to the stiff competition. The pay-per-call business is, not very accepting of new bureaus.

The combined costs for equipment, facilities and staff to create a service bureau, utilizing 900, 800, and international numbers, are approximately $300,000 - $400,000. Marketing will increase these costs depending on which programs the starting bureau would like to offer. For instance, a bureau may decide to invest a small amount into equipment and only offer short custom programs with the audio recorded off location. This is fine, however, industry trends show the demand for custom programs is a small niche market with very little to be made on the back end minutes. To succeed in such a closed, competitive industry, the bureau must offer competitive, profitable and technically elaborate programs. One technical glitch and clients will go on to another service provider.

This is a highly technical field and because the industry is very new, the technicians can be difficult to find. We, at Callmaster, Inc. have assembled an expert panel of technicians who have been with us for quite some time. Scott continues to be a leader in this area. His vast technical expertise is unparalleled. Callmaster, Inc. is the only registered retail service bureau in the industry that has the ability to offer 800, 900 and 011 international numbers. Callmaster, Inc.'s product list is included at the end of this plan. As you will see, Callmaster's offerings are unparalleled.

NEW PROGRAMS

Dream Sense

Dream Sense was launched January 25, 1996. This program will initially be offered and sold as a pay-per-call line. Once the purchases and set-up of the program is complete, advertising must be implemented. Callers responding to the ads will be able to call a fully staffed phone room of trained dream interpreters. The caller will be charged for this information on a per minute basis. These calls will be handled from the Miami facility of Callmaster, Inc.

Callmaster, Inc. will be the only service bureau in the country to offer this turn-key line. Dream Sense addresses virtually the same target market as the psychic lines. The proven success of the psychic program in such publications as Metro magazine paves the way for the marketing of the Dream Sense line. The main advantage of this new program is that there is absolutely no competition. The production of radio and television advertising, including an infomercial, will certainly help propel this new information source to the top of the pay-per-call field.

The rapid growth of technology in the computer industry, coupled with the on-line services of the Internet, has made a new pay-per-call program possible. Until now, to have a visual conversation with an individual, you had to be physically face to face. Today, we can have a similar visual conversation over our personal computers.

Interactive Video Conferencing

Interactive Video Conferencing, for the adult entertainment market, as introduced by Callmaster, Inc. will enable an individual or group to access a software program, provided to them either on the Internet or through the purchase of a 3.5 inch floppy disk. Once the access is made, the computer user (caller) will now be able to interact with an individual(s) on-line. The main difference between IVC and current on-line communication, is that when the caller is communicating with the individual (recipient of the call) with keyboard strokes, they will also view that individual in full color on their personal computer. The recipient of the call, however, cannot see the caller.

An additional option that will be offered is the ability to use a telephone line (other than that used by the computer's modem) to call and communicate with the individual they are viewing on their computer screen. The participants now have audio and visual interaction without having to type in dialogue on the keyboard.

We have contracted to use, Hollywood star, Sonya Daniels. This program will be marketed as "Sonya's Dreams." The program will also be offered and sold as a pay-per-call line in a similar manner to our other successful pay-per-call lines. Advertising for this service over the Internet can also be a dynamic source of revenue in addition to traditional methods of exposure.

One of the great loves in this world is sports and the competition surrounding sports. Let's face it, every news program must have a sports segment, and almost every newspaper a sports section in order to meet the demand for sports information. Previous programs in the pay-per-call industry have limited themselves to recorded sports information such as scores, lines, over and unders, betting picks or handicap horse racing tips.

Sports: Nothing But Sports

Sport talk shows on radio and television have also been very successful. The main drawback to most of these shows is that most callers who wait on hold never get on the air. In addition, callers end up debating the biased opinion of the talk show host(s).

Callmaster, Inc.'s Nothing But Sports will allow callers from all over the country to talk with each other and discuss their personal reviews, opinions and predictions. For example, a Pittsburgh Steeler fan might have some comments for a Dallas Cowboy fan regarding the Super Bowl before, during and after the game. This type of interaction exists all throughout the year in a wide variety of sports and related topics.

This program is being considered for exclusive ownership by Callmaster, Inc. for its investors profit center.

In February, Callmaster, Inc. will be the first to launch both Sonya Daniel's video teleconferencing and the Dream Sense line. Callmaster's most recent program, offering the first three minutes free or a free reading in conjunction with The Halley Psychic Network, has done well in many markets. We are confident of it's continued success in 1996.

Through the years, both Scott Smith and Leslie New have together accumulated many key industry relationships, as well as many clients. As of January, 1996, Callmaster, Inc. has over 1000 lines on the market and over 260 clients. Many service bureaus who have been in the industry five years can not boast these incredible statistics. Here is what these numbers mean:

With 280 clients:

> Up front fees paid
> $2500 each (approx.) = $700,000 monthly gross revenue

> Monthly fees paid
> $75/month = $21,000/month

> Approximate minutes
> 40,000 x .30/minute (service bureau)
> ($12,000)/month

PROJECTIONS

Callmaster's costs are minimal. We have kept our overhead low. With our diligence, expertise and hard work we expect our new 1996 products to bring us in excess of two million dollars in revenue. We plan to increase our marketing campaign by finishing our infomercial. In 1995, we filmed an infomercial that has remained unedited. We are now ready to finish production.

We are currently expanding into other countries. We will have an additional office open by March 1, 1996. We have expansion plans for other viable countries on, or before, November of 1996. We plan to take our new products; video teleconferencing, dream interpretation and sports lines to an all time high in terms of profits. We feel that with all of our existing products, and with our new ventures, our minutes per month have the potential to grow from 40,000 to over 4,000,000. We have some very wealthy investors interested in our psychic product as well as our three new products. Through all of our growth Callmaster, Inc. intends to keep its reputation for always being on the cutting edge.

**1996 - 1998
Projections**

Number of clients set up fees Gross profit

1200 clients $2900 = $3,480,000
1200 $75/per month = $90,000

Number of minutes per month

900,000 x .40/min. = $360,000
$3,930,000/month

We plan on doubling our client base from 300 clients to 600 clients without P.P. Call Enterprises money. With P.P. Call Enterprises money, we expect our client base to grow to 1,200 clients over the next three years. We, of course, would expect our customer service department to expand with our client growth. Our equipment expansion costs would run approximately $10,000 - $20,000 per month and our customer service payroll would increase by approximately $15,000 per month.

Using P.P. Call Enterprises monies to increase our marketing campaign, the following would be the three year estimated projection:

3 Office Location Totals

<u>Cost/Month (approx.)</u>	<u>Profit/Month</u>
Payroll - $150,000/mo.	Set-up fees - $3,480,000/mo.
T1 access - $20,000/mo.	Monthly fees -
Misc. expenses:	1500 clients x 75/Mo. - $112,500
Mail, rent, $70,000/mo.	minutes/mo.
phones, etc.	900,000 x .40 = 360,000/mo (min/mo.)
$290,000/cost/mo.	$3,953,500/gross profit/mo.
Net Profit/Month	$3,732,500

<table>
<tr><td></td><td>**COMPANY ORGANIZATION**</td></tr>
</table>

The company's internal functions are divided between the California and Florida locations. In California, initial customer contact and sales activity is conducted. Once the sale has closed, it is serviced by the Florida staff, which performs all service and back office functions. All call accounting is completed in Florida. Accounting services are augmented by a staff of seven programmers, who have automated most of the back office functions of the company. The Florida staff is also responsible for interfacing with clients and providing clients with technical assistance.

COMPANY OVERVIEW

The legal name of the company is Callmaster, Inc.

Legal Business Description

The company is currently incorporated in the State of Florida. Within the near-term, it will be re-domiciled within the State of California and converted from an S-Corporation to C-Corporation.

Legal Form of Business

Current shareholders are Leslie New and Scott Smith, equally. Both New and Smith are directors. There are no other shareholders or directors

Shareholders/ Directors

	Charge to Caller Guaranteed	**Payout to Client***
Adult Menu (900/800)		
Live One on One	$3.99 min	$1.25 min

PRODUCT LIST AND PAYOUT DESCRIPTION

Live One on One $3.99 min $1.25 min
Caller engages in a two-way conversation with a live operator/telephone actress.

Live Two on One $4.99 min $1.40 min
Caller engages in a two-way conversation with 2 live operators/telephone actresses.

Live Party Line $2.99 min $1.00 min
Engages in a group conversation with up to 8 callers, monitored by a live operator who directs the conversation.

Dateline/Voice Personals $2.99 min $1.30 min

Fully automated dating system. Callers can place, browse or respond to recorded personal ads with intentions of connecting with other singles.

Adult Fantasy Line $2.50 min $1.00 min

Caller listens to a fully recorded fantasy message narrated by a sexy female voice.

Live Psychic (900/800) $3.99 min $1.25 min

Caller talks with an individual psychic in a question/answer method or in a free-flowing conversation. Services include tarot card readings, numerology, clairvoyance and birth (natal) chart readings.

900/800 Adult-Gay Line

Live 1 on 1	$3.99 min	$1.25 min
Dateline	$2.99 min	$1.30 min
Group Party Line	$2.50 min	$1.00 min
Fantasy Line	$2.50 min	$1.00 min
900 Sports Line:	$2.99 min	$1.25 min

Caller receives the Hottest Tips & Scores for sporting events from experts.

International Lines* (long distance charges apply)

011 - (Unrestricted) - 809, Canadian Lines, plus our new Exclusive 011 International Psychic Number's   Long Distance   as high as $1.30 min

305 Collect Call Back $3.99 min $1.12 min

Fully automated system allowing callers with call blocking and/or no credit card for billing to receive a collect call back.

500 Numbers $3.99 min $1.00 min

Similar to 900 #'s with no call blocking.

Custom Lines/Re-directs

You may use your own ideas to design your custom programs. There are no guaranteed payouts on custom lines.

* All guaranteed payouts are less 7% for guarantee fee

Dry Cleaner
BUSINESS PLAN

**A.Z. VENTURES, INC.
DBA EXPERT CLEANING**

*1000 Major Blvd.
Albuquerque, NM 81234*

This business plan is for an expanding dry cleaning business. The business has been franchised in numerous locations. The owners feel that there is room for even more expansion, as the plan indicates. The risk analysis section of the plan contains an interesting discussion of the environmental issues faced by the dry cleaning industry.

- EXECUTIVE SUMMARY

- COMPANY HISTORY

- OPERATIONS

- MARKETING PLAN

- MANAGEMENT TEAM

- FINANCIAL PLAN

- RISK ANALYSIS

- SUMMARY

EXECUTIVE SUMMARY

Introduction

A.Z. Ventures, Inc., dba Expert Cleaning, a New Mexico corporation, has been in business since 1986 and was incorporated in November, 1988. The sole purpose of the business at that time was to operate a full-service dry cleaning plant, with quality and customer service playing key roles in the plan of success. This proved to be a successful formula as within two years the business grew into the #1 Expert Cleaning franchise location in the country. In 1988, a second full-service plant was opened. Expansion continued in 1992 as A.Z. Ventures purchased the rights to the state of New Mexico from the Expert Cleaning Franchise Company. The contract gives A.Z. Ventures the right to further develop the market through franchise sales. In June of 1992, the business expanded once again when Felgen's Shop 'n Save offered A.Z. Ventures the contract to develop satellite locations within Albuquerque metro area Felgen's Shop 'n Save stores. These sites are excellent as they provide high foot traffic and visibility in one of the area's largest supermarket chains. Expert Cleaning is dynamic, on-the-move, growing, and in position to become a market leader in retail dry cleaning the Albuquerque metro area within the next decade.

Expansion Continues in 1996

Three years of networking with shopping center developers and real estate brokers is paying large dividends. Expert Cleaning has been offered a lease at perhaps the most sought-after retail development to be built in Albuquerque this year. The company's 1996 expansion is based upon a location at the NW corner of Major & Campbell. The demographics and trade area for this site are nothing short of spectacular. The aforementioned location is scheduled to be opened in the second quarter of 1996.

Experienced Management Team

LeRoy and Monica Arnold are the co-founders and owners of the company (A.Z. Ventures, Inc.), as well as the Master Franchisers for the state of New Mexico. Furthermore, their son, Alan A. Arnold, joined the management of the company subsequent to graduation from the University of New Mexico in 1993. Over the past eight years, management has nurtured and expanded the business by focusing on high-quality dry cleaning and superior customer service. Furthermore, management has created an enjoyable and challenging workplace for their employees, which has greatly assisted in minimizing employee turnover and training expenses. Currently, the company is training and nurturing several individuals for positions as managers and supervisors at the new location.

Brand Name Creates Advantages

The company enjoys several sustainable advantages through the use of the Expert Cleaning brand name. Within the past ten years, franchises have become dominant players in all types of retail industries. A well-known brand name, such as Expert Cleaning, creates a high level of trust among the public. This not only helps bring more customers into the store, but the company's outstanding reputation "opens doors" with shopping center and land developers. Currently, the company is the only national dry cleaning franchise in New Mexico and is being considered for several sites based solely on the brand name and reputation of Expert Cleaning in New Mexico.

Capital Requirements

Management is seeking debt financing to fund the company's expansion. The total cost of the expansion has been calculated at approximately $166,000. It is important to note that a large portion of the funds needed will be used to purchase equipment. Consequently, financing can be secured with these assets. The planned locations are scheduled to be built and opened in the 2nd quarter of 1996. From past experience, management realizes that construction delays are reasonably possible, thus slowing expansion and the timing for financing.

The company has conservatively projected sales of $930,000 for 1996. Despite large expansion costs, the company anticipates a net profit of approximately $140,000. Projected sales revenue of $1.1 million in 1997 will result in $180,000 of net profit.

Expert Cleaning and Expert Cleaning Franchise Company were incorporated in Florida in 1977. In 1988, American Partners, Inc. (API), a Nevada corporation and wholly-owned subsidiary of American Partners Cleaners (a corporation organized under the laws of the United Kingdom), acquired both divisions of the company. Currently, Expert Cleaning internally operates 105 locations in the Los Angeles metro area and Expert Cleaning Franchise Company has 250 operating franchisees in states including New Mexico, California, Florida, Maryland, New York, Ohio, Pennsylvania, Texas, Virginia, Washington, Wisconsin, and Massachusetts. Furthermore, Expert Cleaning Franchise Company has embarked on a program to expand Expert Cleaning internationally, beginning with Mexico and South America. Currently, plants operate in Mexico, Puerto Rico, and other Latin American countries.

A.Z. Ventures, dba Expert Cleaning, opened its first location in Albuquerque in late 1986. A carefully prepared demographic, customer, and competitor study highlighted the need for a high-quality, competitively-priced dry cleaning establishment in this area. The results of the research were quickly confirmed as the store made an immediate impact. Within one year, Expert Cleaning was the market share leader of the four dry cleaners on the corner of Major Blvd. and Ottawa. First-year sales of $260,000 increased 20% in each of the next two years, finally reaching $500,000. Since that time sales revenues have increased approximately 5% each year. These outstanding results propelled A.Z. Ventures's location to the top of the Expert Cleaning franchise system.

In 1992, Expert Cleaning Franchise Company introduced the Master Franchise Program. Moving away from company-employed franchise sales agents, specific territories and regions were made available for sale to private interests. Because of the outstanding success of A.Z. Ventures in New Mexico, the first Master Franchise in the United States was offered to A.Z. Ventures. As a part of this agreement, A.Z. Ventures shares both one-half of the $25,000 franchise fee and one-half of the commission on equipment (exact amount varies) with the Expert Cleaning Franchise Company. Furthermore, A.Z. Ventures is entitled to one-half of the monthly royalty paid by franchisees to the Expert Cleaning Franchise Company. The Master Franchise Agreement qualifies A.Z. Ventures for distributor status and entitles the company to substantial price discounts (30% off list price) for all equipment purchased. The distributor discount provides a cost savings of $32,500 from the current equipment list price of $125,000.

The Master Franchise Agreement was signed in 1992, and since that time A.Z. Ventures has been actively seeking locations which exceed the demographic requirements of the Expert Cleaning Franchise Company. Briefly, the minimum demographic requirements are: a median household income of $42,000 within a one-mile radius, 2,000 households within a one-mile radius, and a traffic count of 30,000 per day in the intersection of the store. Locations under consideration include in-line spaces in strip centers, preferably anchored by a grocery store. In addition, stand-alone buildings, either on a pad in the parking lot of a shopping center or on a separate piece of land, are acceptable. The business is location-driven, and the above-mentioned criteria are strictly followed when selecting potential locations.

A.Z. Ventures has established relationships with several commercial real estate agents in the Albuquerque metro area, as well as Santa Fe. These individuals work closely with real estate developers and keep A.Z. Ventures apprised of future development and construction plans.

Although there are several expanding dry cleaners in the Albuquerque metro area, real estate agents and developers are eager to speak with A.Z. Ventures about future sites for the following reasons:

First, Expert Cleaning is the only national brand-name dry cleaner in New Mexico. The idea of a "brand name" in dry cleaning is an attractive prospect to developers, especially because the industry is composed mainly of one-location "mom & pop" operations. National brand names attract more people to the shopping center and ensure the developing company successful tenants.

Second, Expert Cleaning offers a $10 million environmental insurance package that protects the landlord from any environmental concerns. Within the past few years, landlords have become very sensitive to environmental liability issues, and in some cases have refused to allow dry cleaners to rent space in shopping centers. In an effort to curb these apprehensions, the environmental package was created. Beyond the liability concerns, the package details the safety features and test results of the equipment to be used within an Expert Cleaning store. The developers who have been introduced to the environmental package are very impressed with the proactive policy that Expert Cleaning is taking. Moreover, it is a noteworthy competitive advantage as no other companies in this industry have developed a comprehensive environmental policy.

Duties of the Master Franchiser

Locating qualified franchisees is chief among A.Z. Ventures's responsibilities. Leads are accumulated through the use of advertisements that run each Sunday in the business opportunity section of the classified advertisements. Additionally, A.Z. Ventures hosts a booth at franchise shows in Albuquerque and Santa Fe. Furthermore, avenues such as contacting out-placement and personnel offices for large corporations are being explored.

Financial qualification is among the early topics discussed with the potential franchisee. The size of the investment (about $225,000, depending on equipment) is clearly presented to the franchise candidate. If the individual is financially capable of making such an investment and remains interested in the dry-cleaning business, the information process continues and the potential franchisee is disclosed and receives the Expert Cleaning Uniform Franchise Offering Circular (UFOC).

A.Z. Ventures's company-owned locations have become successful due mainly to the high level of quality and customer service. To be successful in these two areas, it is crucial to understand and be able to relate to the customers needs and wants. In order to keep Expert Cleaning positioned as a company dedicated to quality and customer service it is important that every Expert Cleaning franchisee is committed to surpassing the customer's expectations. Therefore, the candidate's attitude, values, and enthusiasm are carefully evaluated.

Felgen's Shop 'n Save Offers Convenient Locations

In early 1992, Felgen's Shop 'n Save, Inc., one of the largest supermarket chains in the Albuquerque metro area, contacted A.Z. Ventures in regards to opening Expert Cleaning outlets in specific Felgen's Shop 'n Save locations. In an effort to draw more customers and increase its share of the grocery market, Felgen's Shop 'n Save undertook a campaign to remodel its stores. Bank of America, along with national franchisers such as Taco Bell and Kentucky Fried Chicken, and Expert Cleaning were invited to join the Felgen's Shop 'n Save team.

The Felgen's opportunity provides a challenging and exciting opportunity for A.Z. Ventures dba Expert Cleaning to expand within the Albuquerque area. In recent years, new sites are rarely developed and always accompanied by "bidding wars" and fierce competition among local dry cleaners. The Felgen's Shop 'n Save contract enables A.Z. Ventures to open locations in high-traffic environments shielded from the aforementioned competition. Moreover, these sites are considered to be of the highest convenience, presenting A.Z. Ventures with a notable competitive advantage in an industry where "convenience is king." Felgen's Shop 'n Save has provided highly visible store placements near the front doors of the supermarkets. Signage (neon) has been made available on the front facade of the building and within the store. Additionally, in-store advertising is available via advertisements and coupons placed in several aisle locations within the supermarket.

The company's operations strategy is designed to efficiently turn out quality garments that exceed the customer's expectations. The Expert Cleaning Operating System (EC-OS), a proven and tested system, outlines operational procedures and processes and serves as the backbone of the operation. The EC-OS will be fully applied to all franchised locations as well as stores opened internally through the company.

A.Z. Ventures consists of two divisions: internally operated plants, and Master Franchiser responsibilities. The operations responsibilities of the Master Franchiser are split into two sections: franchise sales and franchisee support. Procedures for each of these areas have been established and utilized by the Expert Cleaning Franchising Company. Briefly, franchise sales include such areas as lead generation, candidate qualification, real estate, lease negotiations, and demographic analysis. Additionally, as the Master Franchiser, A.Z. Ventures will act as a liaison in regards to financing issues, equipment procurement, and installation.

The company is willing to assist its franchisees in any way possible as operational and financial success of the franchise system directly affects the success of the company. After a franchise location is opened, A.Z. Ventures will offer ongoing operational support, beginning with the grand opening "festivities." Monica Arnold, Vice President of Operations and Training, will assist the new franchisee with operations for the first two weeks. Although all franchisees spend three weeks in a comprehensive training program (required and provided by the Expert Cleaning Franchising Company), the expertise of a knowledgeable trainer is crucial in the start-up phase. Furthermore, A.Z. Ventures will provide ongoing training that is either requested or necessary, and will remain available to assist with issues involving production and equipment maintenance.

Equipment used in an Expert Cleaning production plant is strictly automated and state-of-the-art. In order to maximize production throughput and efficiency, utilization of equipment on the "cutting edge" is specified. Furthermore, all equipment is environmentally safe and exceeds Environmental Protection Agency and OSHA requirements.

The equipment layout in each production plant varies depending on the size and shape of the space. Facilities of 1800–2000 sq. ft. allow adequate space to properly place and operate equipment. Efficiency and convenience are key issues in this process. Currently, this duty is subcontracted to a knowledgeable and experienced individual in the industry. Eventually, however, floor plan layouts for franchised plants, as well as A.Z. Ventures plants, will be handled internally by the company. Floor plans for satellite locations are easily constructed due to the absence of equipment. The Felgen's Shop 'n Save satellite locations are approximately 600 sq. ft. and consist of counters, a finishing station (bagging station), and stationary storage railings.

Equipment is the largest expenditure involved with opening a plant location. With the discount of 30% off list price that A.Z. Ventures receives, equipment for a full-service plant will cost approximately $100,000. The dry-cleaning machine is the most important and also the most expensive single item of equipment, costing $27,500. The particular machine to be used by the company is a 50 lb. Columbia 1050 Dry-to-Dry, with spin disc filters. This machine is highly efficient and minimizes waste. Other important equipment includes shirt pressing equipment, a boiler, and standard utility presses.

The company performs preventative equipment maintenance on a regular basis. However, this does not prevent all equipment breakdowns. Most often, the malfunction is caused by a relatively inexpensive component. When this happens, one of several equipment mechanics in the Albuquerque metro area will be called to fix the machine. Maintenance expenses average approximately $250 per month, per plant. The equipment is very durable and the initial equipment purchased in 1986 is still in operation. The manufacturer's estimated useful life for equipment ranges between 12-15 years.

MARKETING PLAN

In a competitive environment like the dry-cleaning industry, a well structured marketing strategy is crucial to long-term success. Simply stated, the Expert Cleaning marketing plan centers around a complete understanding of the customer. Store location, service alternatives, advertising, and pricing are designed to attract and meet the needs of the Expert Cleaning target market.

Target Market

The target market is composed of several important facets. In general terms, the customer can be classified as an upwardly mobile, "white collar" individual with a dual household income. The customer is price-conscious but strongly values quality and is willing to pay for it, within reason. Furthermore, convenience plays a chief role in the target customer's decision process.

The company allocates valuable resources towards the selection of locations and works closely with real estate agents and developers to determine potential sites. Several important factors compose the location "formula." Among them are such elements as: income level, traffic counts in the intersection, real estate prices, average age of residents, an evaluation of other types of businesses in close proximity to the location, housing construction, and nearby dry-cleaning competition.

A minimum median household income of $42,000 is required for residences within a 1-mile radius of the location. Furthermore, income trends from the past three years are evaluated to ascertain future levels. The daily traffic count in the intersection or street is also an important issue. In some instances heavy traffic can be a deterrent to a successful location. Because of this, traffic patterns and ease of access are viewed and charted.

Brand Name & Advertising Create Customer Loyalty

Expert Cleaning is positioned within the market as a quality and competitively-priced dry cleaner. In addition to excellent service and quality, the strength of a national brand name has greatly assisted in drawing customers to the locations. The public has grown very accustomed to dealing with national franchises in all areas of retail business. Franchises are dominating the retail scene because people know and trust that they will receive a similar experience each time. This is very important from the company's standpoint. Customers have spent a lot of time and money selecting their clothes and expect their "investment" to be returned in perfect condition. The company strives to not only meet the customer's expectations, but surpass them.

Advertising is one of the dominant and perennial strengths of Expert Cleaning The company has won several national advertising awards based on artwork and themes used in advertising campaigns. The creativity involved effectively positions, distinguishes, and separates the company from competing dry cleaners. Direct mail (utilizing zip codes) is the most effective medium to reach the designated target market. Several times during the year, advertisements and coupons will be sent to residences within a three-mile radius of each retail location. Approximately two percent of sales is devoted to advertising each year. Furthermore, other creative types of advertising will be considered on a city-wide basis as more locations are opened.

Competition is a strong force in the dry-cleaning industry and is considered location-specific. In a general sense, each dry cleaner in the Albuquerque metro area is a competitor, but direct competition is considered to be only those operations in close proximity to a given location. In addition to the many "mom & pop" operations, several non-franchised chains exist in the market. Marshall's, Presto-Clean, Southwest, Janet's, and Finer are among the most noteworthy. Within the next three years of expansion, competitive encounters with all of the aforementioned may occur. In light of this, these operations have been scouted and evaluated in regards to competitive criteria. The company is confident that its formula of high quality and competitive prices will spell success against any competitor.

Competitor Evaluation

The founders of A.Z. Ventures, LeRoy and Monica Arnold, have and continue to nurture and support this growing business. With a mutual understanding of the multiple facets of a service-oriented operation, LeRoy and Monica have used their strengths to make A.Z. Ventures a success. The energy, excitement, and experience of the team increased in January 1994, when their son, Alan A. Arnold, graduated from the University of New Mexico and joined the business. The roles of each of these individuals within A.Z. Ventures will be clearly distinguished and defined.

MANAGEMENT TEAM

LeRoy Arnold is the president and co-founder of A.Z. Ventures. Born and raised in Marine City, Michigan, Mr. Arnold pursued and completed a Bachelor of Science Degree in Accounting from Wayne State University in Detroit. For the next four years, LeRoy honed his financial skills working as a Senior Staff Accountant for two CPA firms. In 1971, Mr. Arnold joined the Air Force and was assigned to the Air Force Academy in Colorado Springs. He attained the rank of Staff Sergeant (E-5), the highest grade possible in four years. In 1975, LeRoy joined a *Fortune* 500 company as Chief Accountant for its automotive subsidiary. Over the next thirteen years, LeRoy diligently served the company in a variety of roles and steadily climbed the corporate ladder. In 1985 his hard work paid off as he was promoted to Controller of the Western Division. Growing weary of corporate life after several relocations, he made the decision to become self-employed. After a year of researching small business alternatives, Monica and he decided that Expert Cleaning was their future.

Key Managers Provide Experience and Dedication

Over the past eight years, Mr. Arnold has used his accounting background to oversee the financial, expansion, and strategic planning responsibilities for A.Z. Ventures. Furthermore, management skills and techniques previously acquired have been useful in organizing and leading employees.

In 1992, when A.Z. Ventures became the Master Franchiser for the state of New Mexico, LeRoy quickly began the franchise sales effort. Creating and maintaining relationships with commercial real estate agents, advertising, candidate presentations, and close communication with Expert Cleaning Franchise Company in Los Angeles are among a few of his current responsibilities.

Monica Arnold, co-founder of A.Z. Ventures, was also born in Marine City, Michigan, and is a graduate of Holy Cross High School. Immediately after graduation she attended Wayne County Community College with emphasis on retail management. During the last two years of high school and while attending college, Mrs. Arnold broadened her retail experience by working for J.L. Hudson's, a major Detroit-area department store, and National Bank of Detroit. The Arnolds had their first child in 1971 and Monica geared her efforts to raising the family. Three children later, she returned to the workforce in a position with the McDonald's Corporation. As a store manager, Monica was able to sharpen her customer service and personnel and operations management skills.

Monica currently serves A.Z. Ventures as the Vice President of Operations and Training. In addition to the experience gained from everyday involvement, she has expanded her expertise in these areas by completing several seminars offered by the International Fabricare Institute. With a thorough understanding of the dry-cleaning industry, Monica has tailored her management style to fully utilize the skills of A.Z. Ventures employees. She creates a positive and enjoyable work-place which emphasizes mutual respect and customer satisfaction. Using her experience from previous employers in service-oriented industries, Monica deals with patrons very effectively. Always striving to exceed the customer's expectations, Mrs. Arnold leads by example. By employing an even blend of patience and firmness, employees are effectively trained and re-trained. The low turnover rate enjoyed by A.Z. Ventures is partially attributed to the impressive and complete training program. Presently, Monica holds a position on the Expert Cleaning Presidents Council, and is a board member of the New Mexico Drycleaners and Laundry Association.

Currently, both Mr. and Mrs. Arnold are overextended in their job responsibilities. An expanding business requires attention to both the growing areas as well as to the original entity. Reluctant to take attention away from the profit center of the current operation, expansion areas such as franchise sales have not been fully developed. In light of this, the Arnolds welcomed the addition of their son to the management team.

Alan A. Arnold graduated with Bachelor of Science Degrees in Entrepreneurship and Accounting from the University of New Mexico in December, 1993. Admitted to the graduate level Entrepreneurship Program as an undergraduate, Mr. Arnold excelled. While within the program, he and a partner authored a business plan which was used to successfully attract over $200,000 in start-up financing. Additionally, Mr. Arnold was a finalist in the business plan competition at the University of New Mexico and invited to participate in the prestigious International Business Plans Challenge. This was the first time in the twelve-year history of the contest that an undergraduate student earned the chance to participate. Furthermore, Alan was invited to join an international business consulting team traveling to developing countries. In addition to leading a two-day business seminar, Mr. Arnold assisted three companies in adapting their business strategies to be competitive within a free market economy.

Over the course of the past six years, Mr. A.A. Arnold has actively participated in the operations of A.Z. Ventures. Involved in such areas as personnel management, quality control, and customer satisfaction, he has gained a considerable amount of experience. Mr. A.A. Arnold has worked on both daily operations and franchise sales over the past year. Management of at least one of the production centers and multiple satellite locations falls under his responsibility. Furthermore, Alan has joined LeRoy on the A.Z. Ventures franchise sales team, taking over such duties as lead investigations, candidate qualification, and sales presentations. LeRoy handles franchise real estate, franchisee financing issues, equipment, and most importantly, "closing the deal." Furthermore, as president, he is accountable for marketing, advertising, legal, and financial issues. Monica continues her operational and training duties on an expanded basis to include franchise locations.

Employee Training and Retention are Keys to Future Success

In order to remain cost effective, the organizational structure of the company will remain streamlined and lean. In addition to the key personnel aforementioned, each plant will be under the direct supervision of a plant manager responsible for production (employees, throughput, quality control) and retail operations at the location. In addition, each plant will have an afternoon (non-production) supervisor. Accountable to the plant manager, this individual will be responsible for supervising employees, customer relations, and all closing duties (generating computerized reports, cash drawers, bank transmissions, and general clean-up).

Currently, the company is cultivating several individuals for management and supervisory positions. Plant managers will lead employees by example. In light of this, training strongly emphasizes the importance of becoming sufficient in all facets of the operation. Furthermore, ongoing training and education is strongly advocated by management. The plant manager (along with key production employees) will be required to attend quarterly trade seminars.

Attracting and retaining qualified and talented employees is chief among the company's responsibilities and objectives. In order to accomplish this, management is in the process of establishing employee incentive programs. In addition to monetary compensation (above the industry average), health insurance (not commonly offered), paid holidays, paid vacation (one week), and a bonus plan based upon a combination of sales and net income will be offered.

The company's ability to retain production employees has been a key factor in its success. Beyond financial compensation, job enrichment and multi-tasking create and sustain morale and interest. Employees are required to train and become sufficient in several production areas within the plant. This removes the monotony of performing the same task each day and provides a high level of personnel flexibility for daily operations. Moreover, training expense is minimized and consistency, in regards to quality and performance, is achieved.

In closing, the management team is healthy, energetic, and determined to make this company flourish. Profitable companies do not achieve their success without successful people; Expert Cleaning is no different.

FINANCIAL PLAN

The projected financial statements will attempt to provide an informative and clear view of the projected financial status of the company for the next three years. It is important to note that all financial models are based on conservative estimates and assumptions.

Management is interested in seeking debt financing to fund the proposed expansion. Currently management's personal resources, as well as the company's retained earnings, are being completely utilized to fund this growth strategy. As aforementioned, equipment purchases comprise a large proportion of the costs of the expansion. Hence, debt financing can be secured with these assets. Maintaining equity and the controlling interest of the company are important considerations of management.

The projected financial statements are derived through the use of actual expense amounts and cost percentages from previous years of operation. An allowance for inflation and an increase in costs is included in these figures.

Revenues

The stream of sales revenues in the Projected Statement of Profit and Loss is considered by management to be very conservative. The estimates for projected revenues are based upon the performance of locations recently opened by the company and franchisees.

Similar to the satellite locations, revenue projections for plant locations are based upon a combination of past sales performance of the company and national averages. According to the International Fabricare Institute, the largest dry-cleaning association in the world, the average revenue for 30,000 dry cleaning operations in the United States is $191,000. Expert Cleaning company-operated stores across the country average sales revenues of $309,000. Expert Cleaning plants in New Mexico exceed both of the aforementioned, with average yearly revenues of $325,000. Management has estimated first-year sales revenues for the two new plants to be approximately $300,000. Second-year and third-year revenues are forecasted to be $350,000 and $385,000 respectively.

Exit Strategy

The nature, demand, and longevity of the dry-cleaning industry, coupled with the expertise of the company and a qualified management team, will minimize risk and bring financial success to the endeavor. In the case that a chain of unforeseeable events should force the company to cease ongoing operations, the assets will be liquidated and distributed in the normal order of priority.

Management is confident that the tools necessary to build a foundation for short- and long-term success with this business are present. This business plan is built around several assumptions (such as interest rates) which have been adequately noted and explained. Despite this, there are several inherent risks associated with dry cleaning operations, as well as franchising, that are addressed below.

Financial Rationale

Cost of Sales

Production Supplies	6.5% of sales revenue (not including revenues from royalties) hangers, cleaning products, plastic
Labor	35% of sales revenue (not including revenues from royalties)
Overhead	2.5% of sales revenue (not including revenues from royalties)
Payroll Taxes	12.5% of labor and management salary, workmen's comp (3%), FICA (7.65%), State Unemployment (1.5%), Federal Unemployment (.075%)

Operating Expenses
Sales and Marketing

Advertising	2% of sales revenue	direct mail, classified advertisements
Entertainment	1% of sales revenue	meetings with developers, brokers, franchisees
Literature	$300 yearly	industry trade magazines, manuals
Salaries	5% of sales revenue	salary for key management
Trade/Franchise Shows	$2,150 yearly	booth rental, freight, admission, dues
Travel	.05% of sales revenue	travel related to franchise/trade shows, meetings

General & Administrative Costs

Bank Service Charges	.06% of sales revenue	expense related to credit, debit cards
Customer Claims	.025% of sales revenue	based upon historical records
Depreciation	10 year SL method	—
Dues/Subscriptions	$175/month	trade associations, IFI, ICSC, ADLA
Equipment Repairs	$150 per location/month	general repairs
Gas & Oil	$350 per month	company vehicles and vans
Hazardous Waste Removal	$100/month	removal of by-product waste
Franchise Fee	2.5% of sales revenue	—
Insurance (General)	$250 per location	general insurance
Insurance (Officer / Life)	$1,080 per year	life insurance for key management
Insurance (Auto)	$670 per month	insurance for company vehicles, vans
Insurance (Medical)	$500 per plant	approx. $55 per full-time employee
Legal & Accounting	$575 per month	$175 per plant, $50 per drop store
Lease Auto	$1,343 per month	company vehicles for key management
License & Permits	$540 per plant/year	business, environmental, employment permits
Office Expense	$100 per plant/month	photocopies, answering service, etc.
Postage	$15 per plant/month	Federal Express, general mail, etc.
Rent	$3,200 month	Major & Ottawa 1350 sq. ft. @ $20 per sq. ft.

	$2,000 month	Forest & Merrick 750 sq. ft. (in Felgen's Shop 'n Save)
	$4,333 month	Major & Campbell 2000 sq.ft. @ $26 per sq.ft.
Repairs/Maintenance	$4,200 per year	Major & Ottawa equipment repairs, parts
	$1,800/year 1	Major & Campbell equipment repairs, parts
	$2,500/year 2	Major & Campbell equipment repairs, parts
Supplies, Computer	$350 month per plant	maintenance, paper, ribbons, invoices
Taxes (Personal Property)	$1,500 per year	Major & Ottawa
	$150 per year	Forest & Merrick
	$2,000 per year	Major & Campbell
Telephone	$225/plant/month	—
	$60 per month	Merrick
	$250 per month	yellow pages
	$200 per month	cellular phones
	$20 per month	beepers
Utilities	$1,100/plant/month	electric, water, gas
Vehicle Expense	$40/vehicle/month	repairs, maintenance, etc.

1996 Consolidated Statement of Projected Profit and Loss

	Jan	Feb	Mar	Apr	May	Jun	Jul	Aug	Sep	Oct	Nov	Dec	Total	%
Sales Revenue														
Major & Ottawa	$41,000	40,000	46,000	44,000	43,500	41,000	39,000	41,000	43,800	46,000	46,400	47,200	518,900	55.83
Forest & Merrick	11,000	11,000	11,000	11,000	11,000	11,000	10,500	10,000	10,500	10,500	11,000	11,000	129,500	13.93
Major & Campbell	0	0	0	21,000	23,000	25,000	27,000	28,000	29,000	31,000	32,000	33,000	249,000	26.79
Royalty Revenue	2,139	2,139	2,189	2,664	2,714	2,814	2,801	2,814	2,901	2,901	2,939	3,014	32,027	3.45
Total Sales	$54,139	53,139	59,189	78,664	80,214	79,814	79,301	81,814	86,201	90,401	92,339	94,214	$929,427	
Cost of Sales														
Production Supplies	$3,380	3,315	3,705	4,940	5,038	5,005	4,973	5,135	5,415	5,688	5,811	5,928	$58,331	6.28
Labor	18,200	17,850	19,950	26,600	27,125	26,950	26,775	27,650	29,155	30,625	31,290	31,920	314,090	33.79
Overhead	1,300	1,275	1,425	1,900	1,938	1,925	1,913	1,975	2,083	2,188	2,235	2,280	22,435	2.41
Payroll Tax	2,613	2,563	2,864	3,817	3,892	3,868	3,843	3,968	4,183	4,393	4,488	4,579	45,070	4.85
Total Cost of Sales	25,493	25,003	27,944	37,257	37,992	37,748	37,503	38,728	40,835	42,893	43,824	44,707	439,9264	7.33
Gross Profit	28,645	28,135	31,245	41,407	42,222	42,066	41,799	43,086	45,366	47,508	48,514	49,507	489,500	
Gross Margin	52.91%	52.95	52.79	52.64	52.64	52.71	52.71	52.66	52.63	52.55	52.54	52.55	52.67%	

Operating Expenses

Sales and Marketing

Advertising

0	0	1,100	3,200	0	0	3,500	0	0	0	3,500	0	11,300	1.22

Entertainment

500	500	500	500	500	500	500	500	500	500	500	500	6,000	0.65

Literature

25	25	25	25	25	25	25	25	25	25	25	25	300	0.03

Salaries

2,707	2,657	2,959	3,933	4,011	3,991	3,965	4,091	4,310	4,520	4,617	4,711	46,471	5.0

Trade/Franchise Shows

0	1,650	0	0	0	500	0	0	0	0	0	0	2,150	0.23

Travel

550	550	550	550	550	550	550	550	550	550	550	550	6,600	0.71

Total Sales/Marketing Costs

3,782	5,382	5,134	8,208	5,086	5,566	8,540	5,166	5,385	5,595	9,192	5,786	72,821	7.84

General & Admin. Costs

Bank Service Charges

271	265	301	415	424	421	421	439	462	487	495	506	4,907	0.53

Customer Claims

130	128	143	190	194	193	191	198	208	219	224	228	2,244	0.24

Depreciation

1,756	1,756	1,756	3,137	3,137	3,137	3,137	3,137	3,137	3,137	3,137	3,137	33,502	3.60

Dues/Subscriptions

125	125	125	150	150	150	150	150	150	150	150	150	1,725	0.19

Equipment Repairs

180	180	180	330	330	330	330	330	330	330	330	330	3,510	0.38

Gas & Oil

182	179	200	266	271	270	268	277	292	306	313	319	3,141	0.34

Hazardous Waste Removal

72	72	72	144	144	144	144	144	144	144	144	144	1,512	0.16

Franchise Fee

922	922	922	1,972	2,072	2,172	2,247	2,272	2,347	2,447	2,522	2,572	23,389	2.52

Insurance (General)

290	290	290	540	540	540	540	540	540	540	540	540	5,730	0.62

Insurance (Officer/Life)

90	90	90	90	90	90	90	90	90	90	90	90	1,080	0.12

Insurance (Auto)

669	669	669	669	669	669	669	669	669	669	669	669	8,028	0.86

Insurance (Employee Med)

250	250	250	500	500	500	500	500	500	500	500	500	5,250	0.56

Legal & Accounting

225	225	225	400	400	400	400	400	400	400	400	400	4,275	0.46

Lease Auto

848	848	848	848	848	848	848	848	848	848	848	848	10,172	1.09

License & Permits

45	45	45	90	90	90	90	90	90	90	90	90	945	0.10

Office Expense

110	110	110	210	210	210	210	210	210	210	210	210	2,220	0.24

Postage

25	25	25	40	40	40	40	40	40	40	40	40	435	0.05

Rent

5,300	5,300	5,300	9,633	9,633	9,633	9,633	9,633	9,633	9,633	9,633	9,633	102,600	11.04

	Jan	Feb	Mar	Apr	May	June	July	Aug	Sept	Oct	Nov	Dec	Total	%
Repairs/Maintenance	350	350	350	500	500	500	500	500	500	500	500	500	5,550	0.60
Supplies, Computer	350	350	350	700	700	700	700	700	700	700	700	700	7,350	0.79
Taxes (Personal Property)	130	130	290	290	290	290	290	290	290	290	290	3,000	5,870	0.63
Telephone	561	561	561	786	786	786	786	786	786	786	786	786	8,757	0.94
Utilities	1,100	1,100	1,100	2,200	2,200	2,200	2,200	2,200	2,200	2,200	2,200	2,200	23,100	2.49
Vehicle Expense	110	110	110	110	110	110	110	110	110	110	110	110	1,320	0.14
Total G&A Costs	12,320	12,308	12,540	21,114	21,232	21,326	21,398	21,456	21,580	21,730	21,825	24,607	233,436	25.12
TotalOperating Exp.	16,102	17,690	17,674	29,322	26,318	26,892	29,938	26,622	26,965	27,325	31,017	30,392	306,257	32.95
Income from Operations	12,544	10,446	13,571	12,085	15,904	15,174	11,860	16,464	18,401	20,183	17,497	19,115	183,243	19.72
Interest Income 0.00%														
Interest Expense	0	0	0	1,884	1,884	1,884	1,884	1,884	1,884	1,884	1,884	1,884	16,956	1.82
Income before Taxes	12,544	10,446	13,571	10,201	14,020	13,290	9,976	14,580	16,517	18,299	15,613	17,231	166,287	17.89
Taxes on Income	2,258	1,880	2,443	1,836	2,524	2,392	1,796	2,624	2,973	3,294	2,810	3,102	24,943	2.68
Net Income after Taxes	10,286	8,565	11,128	8,365	11,496	10,898	8,181	11,956	13,544	15,005	12,803	14,129	141,344	
% of Total Sales	19.00	16.12	18.80	10.63	14.33	13.65	10.32	14.61	15.71	16.60	13.87	15.00	15.21	

1997 Consolidated Statement of Projected Profit and Loss

	Jan	Feb	Mar	Apr	May	June	July	Aug	Sept	Oct	Nov	Dec	Total	%
Sales Revenue														
Major & Ottawa	41,000	40,000	46,000	44,000	43,500	41,000	39,000	41,000	43,800	46,000	46,400	47,200	518,900	46.74
Forest & Merrick	11,000	11,000	11,000	11,000	11,000	11,000	10,500	10,000	10,500	10,500	11,000	11,000	129,500	11.67
Major & Campbell	34,000	33,000	34,000	35,000	36,000	35,000	34,000	33,000	34,000	36,000	37,000	37,000	418,000	37.65
Franchise Sales	0	0	0	0	0	0	0	0	0	0	0	0	---	0.00
Royalty Revenue	3,614	3,589	3,664	3,639	3,664	3,689	3,601	3,564	3,651	3,651	3,689	3,739	43,752	3.94
Total Sales	89,614	87,589	94,664	93,639	94,164	90,689	87,101	87,564	91,951	96,151	98,089	98,939	1,110,152	
Cost of Sales														
Production Supplies	5,590	5,460	5,915	5,850	5,883	5,655	5,428	5,460	5,740	6,013	6,136	6,188	69,316	6.24

Labor													
30,100	29,400	31,850	31,500	31,675	30,450	29,225	29,400	30,905	32,375	33,040	33,320	373,240	33.62
Overhead													
2,150	2,100	2,275	2,250	2,263	2,175	2,088	2,100	2,208	2,313	2,360	2,380	26,660	2.40
Payroll Tax													
4,323	4,222	4,573	4,523	4,548	4,373	4,198	4,222	4,438	4,648	4,743	4,783	53,593	4.83
Total Cost of Sales													
42,163	41,182	44,613	44,123	44,368	42,653	40,938	41,182	43,290	45,348	46,279	46,671	522,809	47.09
Gross Profit													
47,451	46,406	50,051	49,516	49,796	48,036	46,164	46,381	48,661	50,803	51,810	52,267	587,342	
Gross Margin %													
52.95	52.98	52.87	52.88	52.88	52.97	53.00	52.97	52.92	52.84	52.82	52.83	52.91	

Operating Expenses

Sales and Marketing

Advertising													
0	0	3,500	0	0	0	3,500	0	0	0	3,500	0	10,500	0.95
Entertainment													
500	500	500	500	500	500	500	500	500	500	500	500	6,000	0.54
Literature													
25	25	25	25	25	25	25	25	25	25	25	25	300	0.03
Salaries													
4,481	4,379	4,733	4,682	4,708	4,534	4,355	4,378	4,598	4,808	4,904	4,947	55,508	5.00
Trade/Franchise Shows													
0	1,650	0	0	0	500	0	0	0	0	0	0	2,150	0.19
Travel													
550	550	550	550	550	550	550	550	550	550	550	550	6,600	0.59
Total Sales/Marketing Costs													
5,556	7,104	9,308	5,757	5,783	6,109	8,930	5,453	5,673	5,883	9,479	6,022	81,058	7.30

General & Admin. Costs

Bank Service Charges													
475	463	505	499	502	481	463	469	492	517	525	530	5,921	0.53
Customer Claims													
215	210	228	225	226	218	209	210	221	231	236	238	2,666	0.24
Depreciation													
3,298	3,298	3,298	3,298	3,298	3,298	3,298	3,298	3,298	3,298	3,298	3,298	39,573	3.56
Dues/Subscriptions													
148	145	163	157	156	148	142	148	156	163	164	167	1,857	0.17
Equipment Repairs													
400	400	400	400	400	400	400	400	400	400	400	400	4,800	0.43
Gas & Oil													
301	294	319	315	317	305	292	294	309	324	330	333	3,732	0.34
Hazardous Waste Removal													
144	144	144	144	144	144	144	144	144	144	144	144	1,728	0.16
Franchise Fee													
2,622	2,572	2,622	2,672	2,722	2,672	2,597	2,522	2,597	2,697	2,772	2,772	31,839	2.87
Insurance (General)													
540	540	540	540	540	540	540	540	540	540	540	540	6,480	0.58
Insurance (Officer/Life)													
90	90	90	90	90	90	90	90	90	90	90	90	1,080	0.10
Insurance (Auto)													
446	446	446	446	446	446	446	446	446	446	446	446	5,352	0.48
Insurance (Employee Med)													
500	500	500	500	500	500	500	500	500	500	500	500	6,000	0.54

Legal & Accounting													
400	400	400	400	400	400	400	400	400	400	400	400	4,800	0.43
Lease Auto													
848	848	848	848	848	848	848	848	848	848	848	848	10,172	0.92
License & Permits													
90	90	90	90	90	90	90	90	90	90	90	90	1,080	0.10
Office Expense													
210	110	110	210	210	210	210	210	210	210	210	210	2,320	0.21
Postage													
25	25	25	40	40	40	40	40	40	40	40	40	435	0.04
Rent													
9,633	9,200	9,200	9,200	9,200	9,200	9,200	9,200	9,200	9,200	9,200	9,200	110,833	9.98
Repairs/Maintenance													
770	770	770	770	770	770	770	770	770	770	770	770	9,240	0.83
Supplies, Computer													
700	700	700	700	700	700	700	700	700	700	700	700	8,400	0.76
Taxes (Personal Property)													
290	290	290	290	290	290	290	290	290	290	290	3,000	6,190	0.56
Telephone													
786	786	786	786	786	786	786	786	786	786	786	786	9,432	0.85
Utilities													
2,200	2,200	2,200	2,200	2,200	2,200	2,200	2,200	2,200	2,200	2,200	2,200	26,400	2.38
Vehicle Expense													
110	110	110	110	110	110	110	110	110	110	110	110	1,320	0.12
Total G&A Costs													
22,145	21,534	21,686	21,833	21,888	21,788	21,668	21,608	21,740	21,897	21,993	24,715	264,499	23.83
Total Operating Exp.													
27,700	28,639	30,995	27,590	27,671	27,898	30,598	27,062	27,413	27,780	31,473	30,737	345,557	31.13
Income from Operations													
19,751	17,767	19,056	21,926	22,125	20,138	15,565	19,320	21,248	23,023	20,337	21,530	241,786	21.78
Interest Income	0.00%												
Interest Expense													
1,720	1,680	1,820	1,800	1,810	1,740	1,670	1,680	1,766	1,850	1,888	1,904	21,328	1.92
Income before Taxes													
18,031	16,087	17,236	20,126	20,315	18,398	13,895	17,640	19,482	21,173	18,449	19,626	220,458	19.86
Taxes on Income													
3,246	2,896	3,103	3,623	3,657	3,312	2,501	3,175	3,507	3,811	3,321	3,533	39,682	3.57
Net Income after Taxes													
14,785	13,192	14,134	16,503	16,658	15,086	11,394	14,465	15,976	17,362	15,128	16,093	180,775	
% of Total Sales													
16.50	15.06	14.93	17.62	17.69	16.64	13.08	16.52	17.37	18.06	15.42	16.27	16.28	

1996 Statement of Projected Profit and Loss

	Jan	Feb	Mar	Apr	May	June	July	Aug	Sept	Oct	Nov	Dec	Total	%
Sales Revenue														
Major & Campbell														
	0	0	0	21,000	23,000	25,000	27,000	28,000	29,000	31,000	32,000	33,000	249,000	100
Total Sales														
	0	0	0	21,000	23,000	25,000	27,000	28,000	29,000	31,000	32,000	33,000	249,000	

Cost of Sales

Production Supplies														
0	0	0	1,365	1,495	1,625	1,755	1,820	1,885	2,015	2,080	2,145	16,185	6.5

Labor														
0	0	0	7,140	7,820	8,500	9,180	9,520	9,860	10,540	10,880	11,220	84,660	34

Overhead														
0	0	0	525	575	625	675	700	725	775	800	825	6,225	2.5

Payroll Tax														
0	0	0	893	978	1,063	1,148	1,190	1,233	1,318	1,360	1,403	10,583	4.3

Total Cost of Sales														
0	0	0	9,923	10,868	11,813	12,758	13,230	13,703	14,648	15,120	15,593	117,653	47

Gross Profit														
0	0	0	11,078	12,133	13,188	14,243	14,770	15,298	16,353	16,880	17,408	131,348	

Gross Margin														
0	0	0	52.75	52.75	52.75	52.75	52.75	52.75	52.75	52.75	52.75	52.75	

Operating Expenses

Sales and Marketing

Advertising														
0	0	0	2,000	0	0	1,200	0	0	0	1,200	0	4,400	1.77

Entertainment														
0	0	0	0	0	0	0	0	0	0	0	0	---	0.00

Literature														
0	0	0	0	0	0	0	0	0	0	0	0	---	0.00

Salaries														
0	0	0	0	0	0	0	0	0	0	0	0	---	0.00

Trade/Franchise Shows														
0	0	0	0	0	0	0	0	0	0	0	0	---	0.00

Travel														
0	0	0	0	0	0	0	0	0	0	0	0	---	0.00

Total Sales/Marketing Costs														
0	0	0	2,000	0	0	1,200	0	0	0	1,200	0	4,400	1.77

General & Admin. Costs

Bank Service Charges														
0	0	0	126	138	150	162	168	174	186	192	198	1,494	0.60

Customer Claims														
0	0	0	53	58	63	68	70	73	78	80	83	623	0.25

Depreciation														
0	0	0	1,381	1,381	1,381	1,381	1,381	1,381	1,381	1,381	1,381	12,430	4.99

Dues/Subscriptions														
0	0	0	25	25	25	25	25	25	25	25	25	225	0.09

Equipment Repairs														
0	0	0	150	150	150	150	150	150	150	150	150	1,350	0.54

Gas & Oil														
0	0	0	74	81	88	95	98	102	109	112	116	872	0.35

Hazardous Waste Removal														
0	0	0	72	72	72	72	72	72	72	72	72	648	0.26

Franchise Fee														
0	0	0	525	575	625	675	700	725	775	800	825	6,225	2.50

Insurance (General)														
0	0	0	250	250	250	250	250	250	250	250	250	2,250	0.90

Insurance (Officer/Life)														
0	0	0	0	0	0	0	0	0	0	0	0	---	0.00

Insurance (Auto)

												Total	%
0	0	0	0	0	0	0	0	0	0	0	0	---	0.00

Insurance (Employee Med)

| 0 | 0 | 0 | 250 | 250 | 250 | 250 | 250 | 250 | 250 | 250 | 250 | 2,250 | 0.90 |

Legal & Accounting

| 0 | 0 | 0 | 175 | 175 | 175 | 175 | 175 | 175 | 175 | 175 | 175 | 1,575 | 0.63 |

Lease Auto

| 0 | 0 | 0 | 0 | 0 | 0 | 0 | 0 | 0 | 0 | 0 | 0 | --- | 0.00 |

License & Permits

| 0 | 0 | 0 | 45 | 45 | 45 | 45 | 45 | 45 | 45 | 45 | 45 | 405 | 0.16 |

Office Expense

| 0 | 0 | 0 | 100 | 100 | 100 | 100 | 100 | 100 | 100 | 100 | 100 | 900 | 0.36 |

Postage

| 0 | 0 | 0 | 15 | 15 | 15 | 15 | 15 | 15 | 15 | 15 | 15 | 135 | 0.05 |

Rent

| 0 | 0 | 0 | 4,333 | 4,333 | 4,333 | 4,333 | 4,333 | 4,333 | 4,333 | 4,333 | 4,333 | 39,000 | 15.7 |

Repairs/Maintenance

| 0 | 0 | 0 | 150 | 150 | 150 | 150 | 150 | 150 | 150 | 150 | 150 | 1,350 | 0.54 |

Supplies, Computer

| 0 | 0 | 0 | 350 | 350 | 350 | 350 | 350 | 350 | 350 | 350 | 350 | 3,150 | 1.27 |

Taxes (Personal Property)

| 0 | 0 | 0 | 160 | 160 | 160 | 160 | 160 | 160 | 160 | 160 | 160 | 1,440 | 0.58 |

Telephone

| 0 | 0 | 0 | 225 | 225 | 225 | 225 | 225 | 225 | 225 | 225 | 225 | 2,025 | 0.81 |

Utilities

| 0 | 0 | 0 | 1,100 | 1,100 | 1,100 | 1,100 | 1,100 | 1,100 | 1,100 | 1,100 | 1,100 | 9,900 | 3.98 |

Vehicle Expense

| 0 | 0 | 0 | 0 | 0 | 0 | 0 | 0 | 0 | 0 | 0 | 0 | --- | 0.00 |

Total G&A Costs

| 0 | 0 | 0 | 8,233 | 8,307 | 8,381 | 8,455 | 8,492 | 8,529 | 8,603 | 8677 | 8,677 | 76,321 | 30.65 |

Total Operating Exp.

| 0 | 0 | 0 | 10,233 | 8,307 | 8,381 | 9,655 | 8,492 | 8,529 | 8,603 | 9,840 | 8,677 | 80,721 | 32.4 |

Income from Operations

| 0 | 0 | 0 | 844 | 3,825 | 4,806 | 4,587 | 6,278 | 6,768 | 7,749 | 7,040 | 8,730 | 50,627 | 20.3 |

Interest Income

| | | 0.00 | | | | | | | | | | | |

Interest Expense

| 0 | 0 | 0 | 1,884 | 1,884 | 1,884 | 1,884 | 1,884 | 1,884 | 1,884 | 1,884 | 1,884 | 16,956 | 6.81 |

Income before Taxes

| 0 | 0 | 0 | (1,040) | 1,941 | 2,922 | 2,703 | 4,394 | 4,884 | 5,865 | 5,156 | 6,846 | 33,671 | 13.5 |

Taxes on Income

| 0 | 0 | 0 | (187) | 349 | 526 | 487 | 791 | 879 | 1,056 | 928 | 1,232 | 5,051 | 2.03 |

Net Income after Taxes

| 0 | 0 | 0 | (853) | 1,592 | 2,396 | 2,217 | 3,603 | 4,005 | 4,809 | 4,228 | 5,614 | 27,610 | |

% of Total Sales

| 0 | 0 | 0 | (4.06) | 6.92 | 9.58 | 8.21 | 12.87 | 13.81 | 15.51 | 13.21 | 17.01 | 11.09 | |

USE OF FUNDS

Major & Campbell

Equipment Total	$80,728
Equipment Installation	21,000
Initial Stock of Supplies	3,000
Leasehold Improvements	*30,000
Working Capital	5,500
Deposits	5,000
Grand Opening	4,000
Initial Marketing	2,000
Floor Safe	500
POS Computer System	10,000
Counters	3,000
Misc.	1,000
Total	**$165,728**

* This figure will probably be much lower due to the fact that the building is build-to-suit.

RISK ANALYSIS

Environmental Issues

In the past few years environmental issues have become a serious concern. Increased legislation and social concern have led to new requirements and practices that must be followed. The dry-cleaning industry is not an exception. Fortunately, however, the company is in an excellent position to deal with these issues. Equipment purchased for new locations is state-of-the-art and exceeds the minimum requirements of the Environmental Protection Agency. An example of this is the spill tank that sits underneath the dry-cleaning machine. If solvent (perchloroetheylene) is accidentally released from the process, the spill pan will catch and contain it. After the leak is repaired, the solvent can be automatically pumped back into the operational tanks. Furthermore, other add-on components that minimize risk are regularly used.

Environmental issues have also affected the expansion and franchising. Fearing a potentially dangerous and costly accident, developers and landlords are apprehensive about allowing a dry-cleaning plant to operate on their property. Recognizing this as an impediment to future expansion, Expert Cleaning established a $10 million environmental insurance policy. This holds the developer and land owner harmless in the event of a mishap. The policy has been very effective and distinguishes Expert Cleaning from local dry-cleaning chains which cannot afford to offer a policy of this magnitude.

SUMMARY

The preparation of this business plan serves several purposes for the company. In addition to adding a high level of internal organization and planning to management's efforts, the document is designed to attract financing to support upcoming expansion.

The location that A.Z. Ventures is proposing to open is at the NW corner of Major Blvd. and Campbell Blvd. Management has been working to obtain this excellent site for over a year. The most important aspect of our business is location, and the demographics of this site are in the top echelon of new sites in the Albuquerque metro area. The new store will undoubtedly prove to be a great performer for A.Z. Ventures, Inc.

The contract with Felgen's Shop 'n Save allows the company to operate highly convenient and extremely busy locations, an environment which is integral to success in the dry-cleaning industry. Furthermore, this contract has opened new doors and led to the cultivation of business relationships with members of the real estate and development communities in Albuquerque. Incidentally, several of the prospective plant sites currently under management's consideration are products of aforementioned relationships. A.Z. Ventures has no immediate plans to open Felgen's Shop 'n Save satellite stores in 1995 due to the upcoming renovations of several of the potential Felgen's stores. However, it is possible that a Felgen's satellite location could be sold to a franchisee.

The company possesses several strengths which will play an instrumental role in its upcoming ventures. Assets, such as a tested and proven concept, the Expert Cleaning brand name, its operating system, and award-winning marketing program will assist in making Expert Cleaning the market leader in retail dry-cleaning in the Albuquerque metro area. In conclusion, an investment in A.Z. Ventures, Inc., is an investment in qualified and determined individuals— a dedicated team that is striving and working together to achieve the stated goals and objectives of the company.

Fast Food

PASTA EXPRESS

1018 Southwestern Highway
Farmington Hills, MI 48151

This business plan for a fast food pasta restaurant describes how the owners have built and plan to continue building their worldwide fast food pasta franchise. The owners explain in the plan how the fast food pasta industry is a newly developing industry. By taking advantage of this opportunity now, while the concept is new and hot, the owners plan to continue expanding their pasta empire.

- EXECUTIVE SUMMARY

- PROJECT DESCRIPTION AND FINANCIALS

- COMPANY DESCRIPTION

- INDUSTRY ANALYSIS

- COMPETITIVE ANALYSIS

- HISTORY

- CURRENT STATUS

- MANAGEMENT PROFILE

- ADVISORY BOARD

- COMPILED FINANCIAL STATEMENTS

EXECUTIVE SUMMARY

Pasta Express specializes in quick serve pasta. The originator of the fast-food pasta concept, it began franchising in 1992, and has grown from one company-owned location to 62 franchises.

The fast-food pasta concept allows the customer to enjoy a high-quality, great tasting meal within minutes of placing the order. A typical consumer is a middle- to upper middle-income adult, age 25 to 55 who is tired of fried fast food and has chosen to eat a nutritious pasta meal instead.

Pasta Express has grown substantially in the past two years. In 1995, Pasta Express sold the rights for twenty franchise units in the state of Wisconsin and for thirty units in the Corpus Christ-Houston, Texas area. Several other franchises in Missouri, Florida, California, and Colorado are in various stages of the sales process.

Pasta Express has experienced a 500% increase in franchise leads over the past two years for the following reasons:

Immediate Profitability: Because of our expertise in site selection, the effective Grand Opening, and ongoing advertising, franchisees can often become profitable in the first month of operation.

Mass Appeal: The large and diverse menu gives Pasta Express the strength and flexibility to appeal to every kind of consumer. The Italian food lover, the health conscious eater, the pizza lover, the salad eater, children and adults, and families or couples can all find items to enjoy on the menu.

Ease of Replication: A good chef can help increase sales, and a good business operator can help up to six restaurants perform well, but only a food concept that can be easily replicated can become a national and international sensation. Ease of operation is what separates Pasta Express from other dynamic food concepts. One does not need any experience in the food industry to make the system work successfully. All that matters is that one follow the franchise program.

With so many advantages, the only downside is lack of capital. With or without financing, Pasta Express will continue to grow. The question is whether it can grow quickly enough to seize the opening available in the marketplace. With additional financing, Pasta Express can easily become the next dominant trend in the quick serve food market.

PROJECT DESCRIPTION

Pasta Express is currently looking for investment capital of $250,000. This investment will be taken in two installments—one installment of $175,000 to be paid immediately, and another $75,000 to be paid in six months.

Use of Investment Capital

Phase I--Investment Capital	Investment	Expense
	175,000	
Expenditures		
Marketing		75,000
Working Capital		75,000
Systems Upgrade		25,000

Phase 2—Investment Capital	75,000	
Marketing Expense		75,000
Totals	250,000	250,000

Due to expansion, we are in need of additional operations employees, marketing, and office support. Funds in this category will be used to add and upgrade computer hardware and software, phone systems, and to purchase a booth for franchise shows.

1996 Projected income

Income												Category
Jan	**Feb**	**Mar**	**Apr**	**May**	**June**	**July**	**Aug**	**Sept**	**Oct**	**Nov**	**Dec**	**Totals**
Royalties												
1,750	2,550	5,200	5,200	5,300	7,700	8,200	8,700	9,200	9,700	10,200	10,700	84,400
Rochester												
-	400	600	600	600	600	600	600	600	600	600	600	64,000
Taylor												
400	400	400	400	400	500	500	600	500	500	500	500	5,500
Lansing												
350	350	400	400	400	500	500	500	500	500	500	500	5,400
E. Lansing												
300	300	400	400	400	500	500	500	500	500	500	500	5,300
Troy												
-	-	-	-	-	-	-	-	-	-	-	-	-
Southgate												
-	-	600	600	600	700	700	700	700	700	700	700	6,700
Ann Arbor												
-	-	600	600	600	700	700	700	700	700	700	700	6,700
Farmington Hills												
-	-	600	600	600	700	700	700	700	700	700	700	6,700
Milwaukee												
700	700	700	700	700	800	800	800	800	800	800	800	9,100
Sterling Heights												
-	400	300	300	400	500	500	500	500	500	500	500	4,900
Milwaukee #2												
-	400	300	300	400	500	500	500	500	500	500	500	3,500
Texas #1												
-	-	-	-	500	500	500	500	500	500	500	500	3,500
New Stores												
-	-	-	-	-	500	1,000	1,500	2,000	2,500	3,000	3,500	14,000
Product Sales												
Spice Bags												
-	200	400	500	600	700	800	900	1,000	1,100	1,200	1,300	8,700
Franchise Sales												
-	15,000	-	15,000	-	15,000	-	15,000	-	15,000	-	15,000	90,000
Territory Sales												
-	-	-	100,000	-	-	-	-	-	100,000	-	-	90,000
Totals												
1,750	17,750	5,600	120,700	5,900	23,400	9,000	24,000	10,200	125,800	11,400	27,000	383,100

Individual Store Sales Volume

	1992	1993	1994	1995	1996
(Projections)					
Troy	138,000	155,000	187,360	231,000	258,000
Lansing	11,000	140,000	152,000	187,000	200,000
East Lansing	-	-	-	166,900	220,000
Taylor	-	115,000	154,000	161,000	175,000
Milwaukee	-	-	-	45,000	260,000
Ann Arbor	-	-	-	-	200,000
Southgate	-	-	-	-	140,000
Southfield	-	-	-	-	150,000
Farmington Hills	-	-	-	-	150,000
Livonia	-	-	-	-	50,000
Milwaukee #2	-	-	-	-	-
Texas #1	-	-	-	-	200,000
Ann Arbor #2	-	-	-	-	-
Rochester	-	141,000	91,000	-	150,000
Sterling Heights	75,000	110,000	128,000	131,000	150,000
Totals	224,000	661,000	712,360	921,900	2,303,000

•**1992** Lansing opened in mid-December
    Sterling Heights opened in June

•**1993** Taylor opened in April
    Rochester opened in March

•**1994** Rochester closed. A Main Street location was sought.

•**1995** East Lansing opened in April
    Milwaukee opened in November
    Main Street location was found for Rochester. It should re-open in 1996.

Food Truck Revenue

	1996	1997	1998	1999	2000
Income					
20 Festivals	300,000	400,000	450,000	500,000	550,000
Expenses					
Cost of Sales	75,00	100,000	112,500	125,000	137,500
Cost of Labor	90,000	120,000	125,000	150,000	165,000
Insurance	3,000	3,200	3,400	3,600	3,800
Lease Payments	18,000	18,000	18,000	18,000	18,000,
Maintenance	1,800	2,400	3,000	3,600	4,200
Fees for Festivals	10,000	15,000	20,000	25,000	30,000
Fuel	2,000	3,000	4,000	5,000	6,000
Small Wares	1,500	-	-	-	-
Total Expenses	201,300	261,600	295,900	330,200	364,500
Net Profit	98,700	138,400	154,100	169,800	185,500

Five Year Projected Income

	1996	1997	1998	1999	2000
Royalties	84,400	94,600	130,830	184,620	256,850
New	-	107,500	112,500	225,000	375,000
Operations	8,700	9,800	11,300	13,300	15,800
Food Truck	300,000	400,000	450,000	500,000	700,000
New Stores	90,000	250,000	300,000	500,000	700,000
New Territories	200,000	300,000	450,000	600,000	750,000
Totals	683,100	1,161,900	1,454,630	2,022,920	2,647,650

Revenue

Revenue					
Royalties	-	-	-	-	-
Old Stores	84,400	94,600	130,830	184,620	256,850
New Stores	-	107,500	112,500	225,000	375,000
Operations	8,700	9,800	11,300	13,300	15,800
Truck Revenue	300,000	400,000	450,000	500,000	550,000
New Stores	90,000	250,000	300,000	500,000	700,000
New Territories	200,000	300,000	450,000	600,000	750,000
Total Revenue	683,100	1,161,900	1,454,630	2,022,920	2,647,650

Expenses					
Advertising	8,000	62,000	75,000	140,00	160,000
Labor	85,000	128,000	180,000	328,000	563,000
Rent	4,000	9,500	12,000	36,000	36,000
Phone	20,000	25,000	27,000	33,000	36,000
Insurance	1,000	1,000	1,900	3,000	4,000
Supplies	1,500	2,400	3,000	36,000	38,000
Utilities	1,500	1,500	2,000	2,800	3,000
Travel Expenses	4,000	8,000	10,000	11,000	13,000
Postage	2,000	3,000	3,000	4,000	5,000
Vehicle Expense	5,000	5,000	5,000	5,000	7,000
Sales Expense	120,000	180,000	225,000	240,000	520,000
Miscellaneous	700	1,000	-	-	-
Office	5,000	4,000	2,500	3,000	4,000

Professional Services					
Accounting	25,000	20,000	20,000	30,000	40,000
Legal	25,000	10,000	15,000	30,000	50,000
Marketing	25,000	10,000	20,000	60,000	70,000
Truck Expenses	201,300	261,400	295,800	329,600	364,500
Interest	15,000	15,000	15,000	15,000	15,000
Total Expenses	549,000	746,800	912,200	1,306,400	1,928,500
Profit/Loss	134,100	415,100	542,430	716,520	719,150

Equity and Debt Positions

In exchange for the $250,000 investment, Pasta Express is offering an equity position of $150,000 and a note for the remaining $100,000.

Terms

Pasta Express will pay 10% interest for three years on the note of $100,000. Pasta Express will give a 25% stock position in exchange for the remaining $150,000 investment. Pasta Express will buy out the 25% stock position at 2.5 times the initial investment, or the investor may choose to remain a stockholder in anticipation of a public stock offering. If a buyout is chosen, it will occur in late 1997 or 1998.

COMPANY DESCRIPTION

Mission Statement

Pasta Express provides the best-tasting and most nutritious meal in the fast food industry at a reasonable cost. Our customers may take this meal home with them or can enjoy it in an upbeat, comfortable atmosphere.

Services

Pasta Express is committed to the development of our restaurants through company-owned units, single-unit franchises, and Master Franchise territories. The concept is a turnkey system wherein the franchisor handles every step of the development process, beginning with the signing of the franchise or Master Franchise agreement, and proceeding to site selection, site design, layout, and blueprints, securing local government approvals and permits, store buildout, signage, ordering and installing food equipment, training, and grand opening. Pasta Express provides everything a franchise owner needs to develop and successfully operate a store. All the franchisee needs to supply is the funding.

Development

Founded in 1989, Pasta Express was designed to be franchised and developed into a national chain. The concept began with one company-owned location, and by 1995 the chain had expanded to six locations. All of those locations remain open and profitable. Four new locations will open in 1996.

Immediate development goals include increasing the number of local and national locations through franchise and Master Franchise sales, designing and building a company-owned freestanding prototype unit, increasing profitability at all locations, and further developing the corporate infrastructure to support national expansion.

Legal Name, Status, and Ownership

Pasta Express is incorporated under the laws of Michigan as an "S" Corporation. 90,000 shares of Pasta Express are outstanding and 53,500 have been issued. 36,000 shares are owned by Lynn Ott, the founder, president, and CEO. 17,500 shares are owned by David Huff. Shares have been selling for $20 per share. Your purchase will give you a 25% equity position, with 22,500 shares at a price of $6.70 per share.

INDUSTRY ANALYSIS

According to Maria Stevens, president of Stevens Consulting, the largest franchise consulting firm in the United States, "The pasta market . . . is very hot. There are a number of new franchisors, but nobody has established themselves as a runaway success." One of the greatest reasons that makes Pasta Express a great investment at this time is the fact that the pasta market is still in the development stage, providing a window of opportunity for us.

Fast Food Pasta— A Developing Industry

With the exception of Sbarro, which began in 1959 and started franchising in 1977, the fast food Italian pasta industry is brand new Sbarro is confined mainly to regional shopping malls. Among more traditional fast food locations, the first company to open a fast food Italian pasta store was Spaghetti Shoppe in 1985.

Open Competitive Market

In an emerging market, the goal of all industry competitors is to gain a foothold in the new market, create a brand identity within the market, and establish themselves as the clear leader. The players in this market are still in the "foothold" stage, with each trying to put as many stores in the best locations as quickly as possible all over the nation. Each of three industry leaders is developing their own brand identity within the market. However, no one has established itself as the clear industry leader. The opportunity to open the market nationwide is available to the company that is able to move most quickly into the major population and growth centers.

Long-Term Opportunities

Since the fast Italian market is still emerging, the long-term opportunities for Pasta Express are enormous. The national trend toward eating out has increased over the last five year. In 1993, the amount of money spent on restaurant food was equal to what was spent in homes for "homemade meals." 1993 was the first year that Americans spent as much on food outside the home as they did for meals inside the home. According to American Demographics Magazine, 1996 will be the first year that spending on restaurants and take-out food will exceed the nation's grocery bill. Since Americans are spending more on restaurant food than ever, these consumers are looking for more eating alternatives. The market demand for healthy, great-tasting menu items as an alternative to hamburgers, steaks, tacos, chicken, and pizza has never been greater. National chains such as Taco Bell and McDonald's have experimented with healthy menu items because they realize an enormous market is developing for healthy tasty food. Other chains like Boston Market are servicing an enormous market for homestyle meals in an upscale environment. Pasta Express is one of the best alternatives in the market to meet the demands of this new market segment.

The restaurant industry in the United States has been characterized by rapid change. During the 1950s and '60s, dining out was a new experience to people who were just getting used to enjoying the post-war affluence. Local diners spread across the country and soon evolved into restaurant "chains" owned by local and regional corporations. Hamburger stands began to evolve into a new restaurant concept known as "fast food." In the '70s and '80s hamburger and pizza operations created a whole new market for menus alternatives such as chicken, fish, and tacos. Now the new restaurant trend is affordable fast food that has the home-cooked taste. The runaway success story of the early- to mid-1990s, Boston Chicken (Market) shows the untapped potential market. Rather than having to wait thirty minutes to an hour in a sit-down or casual dining restaurant, most consumers want a tasty fast food meal which families and single persons alike can enjoy. Pasta Express is on the cutting edge of this new restaurant trend. As the late 1990s empty into the next century, Pasta Express has poised itself to be the leader in the new concept.

Pasta Express—Poised to Dominate the Market

There are five major competitors:

- Fazoli's
- Spaghetti Shoppe
- Little Caesar's Italian Kitchen
- Sbarro, the Italian Eatery
- Papa Romano's Pizza and Pasta

COMPETITIVE ANALYSIS

Fazoli's currently operates 104 units. Eighty of these are company-owned and operated, and 24 are franchised units. The strength of the Fazoli's concept is its stress on opening free-standing units, which offers immediate visibility and credibility to the consumer. Despite their adequate funding, rapid growth, and free-standing store concept, they are vulnerable to the competition on three fronts. (1) Food Quality. The menu items and prices listed are nearly identical to ours, but the portions are smaller. (2) Start-Up Costs. The start-up costs for Fazoli's are projected between $400,000 and $795,000 per store, as opposed to $80,000 to $100,000 for Pasta Express. This enables us to qualify more potential franchisees, which enable faster development. (3) Name Recognition. One of the most important factors in establishing a company as a leader in any new industry is developing brand name and brand identity among potential customers. While it is not impossible to use an unfamiliar brand name, establishing the brand name and linking it to the product identity takes a significant amount of marketing funds. Companies that have been able to use a brand name to automatically link them to the target market (Coca-Cola, Boston Chicken, Subway, Burger King, Taco Bell, Pizza Hut, etc.) have a leg up on the competition in establishing brand identity. This is why Pasta Express has chosen its name. The name instantly informs the consumer that we are a fast food Italian enterprise. Fazoli's does not have this advantage. Fazoli's is leading the fast food Italian trend, but has not established itself as the runaway leader.

Fazoli's

With the exception of Sbarro, Spaghetti Shoppe has been in the fast food Italian franchising business the longest. Its menu is similar to Pasta Express, but the prices are a little higher. Spaghetti Shoppe, with both inline and free-standing stores, has 40 franchised units and one

Spaghetti Shoppe

company store. The company has struggled recently, selling no franchises and closing one company store. This stagnation seems to be related to the high cost of opening a Spaghetti Shoppe. The projected opening costs are between $200,000 and $800,000. If a franchisee spent even the minimum $200,000 on an inline store, it would be difficult to operated profitably for the first 3-5 years. Unless they can trim costs, strengthen their brand, and step up expansion, Spaghetti Shoppe will have difficulty becoming a market leader.

Little Caesar's Italian Kitchen

Although nationally known as a pizza chain, Little Caesar's has shifted its focus toward the pasta market in the last 12-16 months. This new concept is called Little Caesar's Italian Kitchen. The Little Caesar's Pizza chain currently operates 4,500 units in all 50 states and several foreign countries. Unlike Pasta Express, Little Caesar's does not offer the customer a made-to-order option for pasta; the pasta is pre-cooked, pre-sauced, and sitting under a food warmer waiting for the customer to order. The menu offers only limited kinds of noodles and sauces, and very few of the locations offer dine-in options. The strategy and placement of the Italian Kitchen within Little Caesars's Enterprises is extremely limited at this point. With the Little Caesar's Pizza chain adding delivery (in an attempt to cannibalize the market share of Domino's Pizza) and adding new menu items (i.e., stuffed crust pizza) to compete with Pizza Hut, marketing and strategy has focused on strengthening the position of Little Caesar's Pizza in the pizza market. This renewed focus has come at the expense of research, development, and marketing of Little Caesar's newest concepts, especially Italian Kitchen. Although the pizza market has been flooded for years, competitors continue to pour into this lucrative segment. Unfortunately, this market is beginning to mature and all parties are positioning themselves to compete with each other for a stagnant number of consumers. This does not bode well for the Italian Kitchen concept, which still faces major developmental and marketing challenges and needs capital to strengthen their competitive position. Little Caesar's Italian Kitchen has two enormous strengths but, as with many mature companies, its greatest strengths can also be their major weaknesses: (1) Brand Recognition. Millions of consumers already know and love Little Caesar's Pizza Pizza. A decision to offer pasta in every location will make Little Caesar's a major competitive force. However, having to live down a reputation as a "pizza" restaurant is a major competitive disadvantage for the Little Caesar's Italian Kitchen concept. The brand identification with the pizza is so strong that an enormous amount of marketing would be needed to make pasta a major contributor to their sales revenue. At this point in development, the revenue generated from pasta is so small that the franchisees are less likely to invest in food equipment, remodeling costs, marketing, and food and labor costs to change to the Italian Kitchen. Focusing on the pizza customer is the option franchisees will most likely choose. (2) Financial Resources. Given their success in the pizza and franchising business, Little Caesar's Enterprises has an enormous resource pool which could be dedicated to becoming a major player in the fast food pasta industry. However, given the enormous amount of capital already spent to establish Little Caesar's as a major pizza brand name and the intense competition Little Caesar's faces in the pizza market with Pizza Hut Delivery and Domino's it seems unlikely that Little Caesar's Italian Kitchen will ever be a major factor in the pasta market.

Sbarro, the Italian Eatery

Sbarro, the grandfather of the fast Italian pasta business, has been in business since 1959 and began franchising in 1977. It has 578 company owned units and 146 franchised units in the United States alone. In Canada and other countries, Sbarro maintains 36 franchised units. Although it bills itself as "The Italian Eatery" and is well-capitalized, Sbarro is not in the same class as Pasta Express. It offers mainly pizza and Italian pies, along with baked ziti and garlic bread. Such items as lasagna, spaghetti, mostaccoli, linguini, fettucini, and marinara and alfredo sauces are not often on the menu. In addition, the prices are often significantly higher than ours and the market is much different, since Sbarro has dedicated itself almost exclusively to food courts in shopping malls. Finding Sbarro in a free-standing unit or an inline store is very rare, and any such units do not carry the staple menu items of a Pasta Express. If Sbarro attempted to establish itself as our competitor, it would have the advantages of capitalization and brand recognition. In addition, high start-up costs ($179,000 to $723,000) and the highest franchise fees ($35,000 and 5% royalties) make Sbarro an expensive option for would-be franchisees. Someone interested in competing with Pasta Express is more likely to choose Fazoli's or Spaghetti Shoppe. Thus Pasta Express regards Sbarro as only a peripheral competitor at this time.

With 66 franchises and five company-owned units, Papa Romano's Pizza and Pasta has established itself as a developing player in the pizza market. Although it has strong brand recognition in the Detroit, Michigan area, its development outside Michigan is still in its infancy. While a limited amount of pasta products are available, Papa Romano's overwhelming source of revenue is pizza. All of the marketing currently conducted is targeted toward the pizza consumer. Their commitment to pasta appears to be only as a menu alternative. Because of their commitment to the pizza enterprise, they face an even greater challenge than Little Caesar's --they have fewer financial resources and have not established themselves as a major player nationally. If they were to switch focus mid-stream to compete in the fast Italian market, they would face a number of developmental hurdles which Pasta Express, Fazoli's, and Spaghetti Shoppe have already conquered. Additionally, they would have to scrap all their advertising and start fresh in an attempt to develop a brand identity in the fast Italian pasta market. This makes Papa Romano's an unlikely competitor.

Papa Romano's

Several other major chains, including Olive Garden and Salvatore Scaloppini, sell pasta, but they are not directly competitive since the venues and pricing differ dramatically from Pasta Express. These restaurants were designed for sit-down consumption of pasta in a more formal atmosphere. They are not easily accommodating to carry-out customers, nor can they handle the volume that a Pasta Express handles. In addition, the prices are often twice what a customer at Pasta Express would pay for a comparable meal.

Pasta Express differs from other quick serve operations in three ways. Some of our competitors may combine one or two of the following ideas, but none have all three in their favor.

Pasta Express offers more delicious menu options than any other quick serve restaurant:

   • Pasta noodle: spaghetti, fettucini, linguini, mostaccioli, lasagna and many more
   • Gourmet sauces: meat sauce, meat sauce with fresh mushrooms, alfredo sauce, marinara sauce, and pesto sauce
   • Chicken dishes: chicken cacciatore, chicken caesar salad, chicken alfredo, chicken broccoli alfredo, chicken parmesan, chicken parmesan sandwich, and chicken primavera
   • Fresh salads: garden salad, tossed salad, pasta salad, greek salad, antipasto salad, and caesar salad
   • Hot sandwiches: meatball, Italian, ham & cheese, and vegetarian
   • Soup: vegetable, minestrone, and chicken noodle
   • Cheesecake

Pasta Express is the only quick serve restaurant offering healthy menu alternatives.
In addition to providing a low-fat marinara sauce and salads, Pasta Express has retained the services of a nutritionist to aid us in the development of a healthy alternatives menu for all locations.

Pasta Express is one of the few quick serve restaurants to offer a party menu.
We provide gourmet food at reasonable prices. Pasta Express is by far the most cost available of all the major competitors, making the pool of potential franchisees and area developers much larger that for the other competitors.

Pasta Express was created to fill an obvious opening in the fast food market. William Grumman, the founder, was operating a very successful local pizzeria. Since he was not satisfied with a local-only concept, he had only one option: find a market that is just opening and prepare to capitalize

HISTORY

on it. Although hamburgers, chicken, pizza, and Mexican food markets were already saturated with intense competition, Mr. Grumman's vision was to satisfy a desire for high quality Italian food. Some pizzerias were offering pasta as a menu alternative, the quality was poorer and the selection limited to spaghetti or lasagna. The only other alternative was to eat in a casual or fine dining restaurant where pasta meals were not designed for people on the move and the average cost was $10-$12.

The popularity of pasta increased at a tremendous rate in the mid-1980s and the USDA included pasta as one of the seven food groups in the Food Pyramid. After realizing this, Mr. Grumman formed the vision that governs Pasta Express to this day. He wanted to design a company similar to Pizza Hut, Domino's and Little Caesar's. In 1987, Pasta Express was launched. The first three years were spent developing the concept in one company owned store, preparing the operations manual and completing the legal requirements for franchising. In 1991, he sold one franchised unit. By 1994, 8 franchises were sold. In 1995, two stores were sold locally and the first two Master Franchise territories were sold in Milwaukee, Wisconsin and Houston, Texas. The concept of the third generation store was also introduced in 1995.

CURRENT STATUS

As of January 1996, eight stores are operating and three more will be operational by March. Four other stores are in development and scheduled to open this year. In addition, several franchise and Master Franchise territories are in negotiations. We project selling at least three Master Franchise territories this year and opening at least ten individual units. With the proper financing, we will begin development of our first free-standing store, a company-owned unit.

MANAGEMENT PROFILE

Lynn Ott

- President and Secretary/Treasurer of Pasta Express since it incorporation
- Sixteen years in the food industry
- Expert in restaurant management, business administration, real estate, and marketing
- Owned a succesful sit-down pizza and pasta restaurant
- Ten years of experience with the Pizza Hut chain of restaurants, attaining the role of General Manager, Assistant Area Manager, and Turn Around Specialist
- B.A. in Accounting and a brokers license in real estate

David Huff

- Mr. Huff is the Vice President and Director of Pasta Express
- Works closely with the franchise attorney to ensure that the Uniform Franchise Offering Circular (UFOC) is current
- Responsible for organizing and implementing the food truck program
- Vice President and CFO of a successful retail sportswear company
- Responsible for all financial consideration of day-to-day operations as well as personnel manager for all employees. He has developed and coordinated all accounting procedures for the management of multiple locations
- Has several years in the food service industry where he was responsible for food management, ordering and inventory control, and implementing new food products and promotions
- Expert in retail sales, multiple location mangement, and finance

Samuel Smith

- Mr. Smith is the General Manager.
- Experience in management and administration
- Head of research and development, marketing strategy, operational improvement, and franchise expansion

•Coordinates franchise support efforts between the stores
•Responsible for qualifying and developing franchise candidates
•Regarded nationwide as an expert in the field of franchise sales
•Twenty years of experience in the franchise industry
•Also owns his own franchise consulting firm which has been profiled in The Detroit News and The Detroit Free Press, Crain's Detroit Business, and Franchise Buyer
•Has been interviewed on national TV and radio and is a major source in the franchise industry for all media outlets, including The Wall Street Journal
•Advisory board member and quarterly article writer for Franchise Handbook

Jodi Jones

•Marketing Director
•Produces all electronic and print media material used for advertising and store promotion
•Manages the advertising message and ensures that Pasta Express is successful in reaching its target market
•Former Broadcast Supervisor for Campbell-Ewald Company, where she handled advertising for Magnavox, Goodyear, A.C. Delco, Delco Electronics, National Car Rental, GMAC, and others
•Twenty years in the advertising business
•Owns and operates her own advertising firm

Kathleen Olivera

•Chief Financial Officer
•Handles the financial reports
•Accredited Business Accountant
•Owns and operates her own accounting and tax prepartion firm, Olivera and Asso ciates
•Enrolled to practice before the Internal Revenue Service
•Member of the Independent Accountants Association of Michigan

Cameron Powers

•Operations Manager and Training Manager
•Fourteen years of experience in the restaurant business
•Expert in the operational areas
•Authored major sections of the Pasta Express Operations Manual

William Stewart

•Buildout Manager
•Proposed manager of food truck operations
•Six years of experience in food truck management for Ernesto's Pizza and Pasta
•Twenty years of restaurant management experience with Pizza Hut and Big Boy Restaurants

COMPILED FINANCIAL STATEMENTS

Statement of Income and Retained Earnings

For the year ended December 31, 1995

Revenue

Franchise sales	225000
Franchise royalties	34620
Build out revenue	180034
Operations	11240
	450894

Operating Expenses

Advertising	51486
Amortization	0
Bank Charges	179
Build out costs	158630
Contributions	200
Due & License	250
Equipment & supplies cost	0
Franchise package and resale	0
Franchise fees	0
Labor	28450
Legal & Professional	10650
Meals & Entertainment	2095
Maintenance & Repairs	853
Office & general	367
Rent	2300
Sales commission	145000
Telephone	264459
Travel	2780
Utilities	0
Vehicle Expense	1854
Total Operating Expenses	431553

Other Income & Expense

Interest expense	
Net income (loss)	19341
Retained earnings - January 1, 1995	4403.79
Retained earnings - December 31, 1995	23744.79

Statement of Assets and Liabilities— Accrual Basis

As of December 31, 1995

Assets

Current Assets

Cash	18360
Accounts receivable—royalties	2490
Accounts receivable—franchise fee	80000
Notes receivable	48063
Equipment	2100
Total Current Assets	151013

Non-Current Assets

Deferred development costs	5820
Advances recoverable	9467
Total Non-Current Assets	15287
Total Assets	166300

Liabilities and Stockholders Equity

Current Liabilities	0
Accounts payable	19150
Note Payable	0
Total Current Liablilities	19150
Long Term Liabilities	0
Note Payable	53418
Total Long Term Liablities	53418
Total Liabilities	72568
Stockholders Equity	0
Common Stock $1 Par Value	70874
Retained Earnings	22858
Total Stockholders Equity	93732
Total Liabilities and Stockholders Equity	166300

Fast Food

BUSINESS PLAN

PASTA NOW!

74250 Mainline Rd.
Las Vegas, NV 89101

January, 1995

Franchises continue to be the most secure form of small business start-up, requiring less money and less risk than a brand new venture. The franchiser often supplies assistance, ranging from financing to hiring and training staff. This plan details a fastfood franchise that specializes in quick and healthy pasta dishes.

- EXECUTIVE SUMMARY

- DESCRIPTION OF BUSINESS

- MARKET ANALYSIS

- COMPETITIVE ANALYSIS

- DESIGN & DEVELOPMENT PLANS

- OPERATIONS & MANAGEMENT PLANS

- FINANCIAL COMPONENTS

EXECUTIVE SUMMARY

The market demand has never been greater for food that is healthy, economically priced, and great tasting. This is the last market with wide open potential for growth. Traditionally, pasta has been consumed in fine restaurants, usually in a more formal or sit-down atmosphere at high prices. As pasta has moved to the center stage as a product that both tastes good and is good for you, Pasta Now! has positioned itself to provide the services in demand by the American consumer: a variety of healthy pastas, moderately priced and with very good taste. The basic focus is to provide the consumer with a healthy, quality meal which is economically priced. This is a concept that will never grow old.

Pasta Now! is a franchise system with ongoing support from the national franchisor. National assistance includes site selection, restaurant design, comprehensive training, and support of ongoing operations through marketing assistance, quality control programs, research and development.

Pasta Now! of Las Vegas will require a total financial commitment of $100,000. The franchise fee for the Las Vegas store will be $10,000, with an additional $12,500 to purchase the rights for all of Nevada. The remaining money will be used in opening the first Nevada store in Las Vegas. The Miller's equity contribution will be $15,000 in cash. Additionally, the Millers have $60,000 of equity in their residence.

Pasta Now! of Las Vegas will have the right to sell stores throughout Nevada. As these additional franchises are sold, Pasta Now! will retain $7,500 of each franchise fee paid. Monthly royalties from each of these Nevada stores will be 3% of gross.

DESCRIPTION OF BUSINESS

History

Pasta Now! of Las Vegas is being structured to operate franchises of the national chain Pasta Now! Additionally, we will sell a limited number of franchises of the national chain. Pasta Now! is headquartered in the Cleveland, OH area. Pasta Now! of Las Vegas has the exclusive right to operate and sell franchises in Nevada.

The national Pasta Now! chain was established in 1987 with the opening of the original Pasta Now! The company has been franchising since 1991. Recent growth has been in the Cleveland metro area, where there are currently eight stores in operation. Pasta Now! has recently signed a master franchise agreement to open ten additional stores in the state of Michigan in the next five years.

Ownership Structure

Ownership of the business is in the form of a Nevada corporation with 51% of the stock owned by Roland Miller and the remaining 49% owned by Sheila Miller. This Nevada corporation will in turn own Pasta Now! of Las Vegas.

Sheila Miller has prior business experience in the ownership of a mobile Ice Cream/Catering business. Mrs. Miller has also acquired human resource experience while employed as a Human Resources Assistant for St. Mary's Hospital.

Roland Miller has gained management and budget experience through his work as a Captain with the Las Vegas Fire Department.

Both Mr. & Mrs. Miller have been educated in the Total Quality Management concept used by many of today's successful major corporations.

Pasta Now! is a fast food pasta chain that focuses on the drawing power of an Italian restaurant that meets the needs of people on the go who still want a healthy product at reasonable prices.

For many years, the only place you could get a variety of quality pasta was at sit-down Italian restaurants that were expensive and did not meet the needs of the customer in a hurry.

Products/Services

The Pasta Now! menu is centered around a variety of pasta dishes with a variety of sauces. The majority of sauces are cooked on site. For diversity, Pasta Now! also offers individual pizzas, a line of Italian sandwiches and a selection of salads. Pasta Now! menu items are available for eat-in or take-out. Pasta Now! also features a complete party menu. Catering for any size occasion is available.

The service will be exceptional. The #1 goal of each employee will be customer satisfaction. Pasta Now! believes in the old fashioned motto, "the customer is always right." In today's society, where customer service is often lacking (or nonexistent), we will structure our business to provide the best service possible in a friendly, helpful atmosphere.

Geographical Area

Pasta Now! will draw customers primarily from Las Vegas, with some penetration in to neighboring counties.

Pasta Now! will draw on the Las Vegas community's growing reputation as a regional shopping hub. Pasta Now! franchises are structured to operate in areas with populations between 25,000 and 30,000 people.

There are no physical limitations to the market area since the Las Vegas location is well served by several state highways. There are many competing, well-established fast food outlets in the area; however, none of them are currently providing a similar product.

Major Customers

Pasta Now! relies on customer volume with no identifiable major customers. However, the customers can be categorized as:

- baby boomers and their children
- state employees
- adults age 50 and above
- tourists

Facilities/Equipment

Pasta Now! is structured to operate in strip mall-type locations. The corporate headquarters provides detailed site selection assistance, including lease negotiations.

Pasta Now! is designed to function in a 1500 to 2000 square-foot store. A drive-up window can be utilized if a suitable site for such is located.

Prospective sites which have been preliminarily identified include; the Bryson's shopping center in south Las Vegas, the Forest center in Northern Las Vegas or the Daly shopping center on Highway 12.

The equipment necessary for the operation of Pasta Now! will be purchased from any of the several restaurant supply companies located in the area.

Organization

Pasta Now's staff will be divided into two functional areas, Operations and Administration. Each division will he headed by one of the principals.

MARKET ANALYSIS

Geography/ Demographics

The national trend toward eating out has increased over the last 5 years. In 1993, the amount of money spent on eating out was equal to what was spent for consumption inside the home. This is the first time that consumers spent as much for "eat out" food as they did for "at home" food. According to American Demographics magazine, by the year 1996, spending on restaurants and take-out food will overtake the nation's grocery bill. The market demand has never been greater for food that is healthy, economically priced, and great tasting. The recent health-oriented menu options added to national chains like Taco Hut and even Smith's, point to the nation's desire for healthy food. In an analysis of casual dining, Restaurant Business Magazine noted that baby boomers, and others, are coming face-to-face with the realization that youth is ephemeral. With that realization has come more emphasis on healthy dining alternatives like pasta.

Customers

The customers for restaurants in the geographical area served by Pasta Now! can be categorized as follows:

- Baby boomers and their children
- State employees
- Adults age 50 and above
- Tourists

There are several identifiable characteristics of the market area that determine the segmentation as listed. Since this area is rapidly growing, as opposed to mature, there are new home buyers who tend to have families and dine out often. According to American Demographics Magazine, baby boomers and their families eat out an average four times per week.

Since Las Vegas is such a busy area, there are a large number of tourists and state employees who are looking for a place to take lunch. During a recent, non-scientific, interview session, state employees from the Department of Transportation and the Department of Motor Vehicles were asked at random how many times per week they dine out for lunch. The average number of times the respondents dined out for lunch was 2.7 days per week.

Adults over 50 dine out an average of 2.4 times per week. Recent trends indicate that adults age 50+ are dining out less often, but they are more attracted to restaurants that offer food to be eaten at home. Pasta Now! can satisfy their needs.

Assumptions

The strategic goals and plans for Pasta Now! are based on the following assumptions:

The national and local trends toward consumption of healthy food will continue. All indications from national publications consulted agree that healthy food which is reasonably priced will continue its popularity well into the next century.

The trend toward dining out will remain steady. Indications are that dining out will actually increase over the next five to seven years.

Supply & Demand

The restaurant industry in the U.S. has been characterized by rapid change. During the 50's and 60's, dining out was a new experience for a country feeling the effects of post-war affluence. Also, the various wars have increased the awareness of many Americans with foods from different cultures. This has spawned a trend toward restaurants featuring food from Europe and Asia.

An American original, the diner, spread across the country and soon evolved into chain restaurants operated by local and regional corporations. During this period, a new restaurant concept grew up from the corner hamburger stand. The fast food restaurant was started from such humble beginnings and quickly multiplied.

Over the next two decades fast food matured and changed at the same time to meet the changing tastes of the public.

While fast food chains experienced significant growth, restaurants evolved also. During the late 60's and 70's, "natural" food restaurants became popular, only to give way to nouvelle cuisine in the 80's. The trend in the 90's is to healthy food low in fat, cholesterol and sugar.

The national restaurant industry includes approximately 125,000 restaurants plus 235,000 fast food restaurants, according to the National Restaurant Owners Association (NROA). NROA estimates that combined restaurant sales reached 4.5 billion dollars last year.

The local market reflects the national trends. As pasta has moved to the center stage as a product that both tastes good and is good for you, Pasta Now! has positioned itself to provide the services in demand by the American consumer: a variety of healthy pastas, moderate price, and very good taste.

Growth Factors

The number of restaurants will grow at an annual rate of 7.3% for the next five years according to the latest report from the U.S. Department of Agriculture.

The growth can be attributed to many factors, such as a continued trend toward two income families, thus eating out more for lunches and having little time to prepare a meal after work. The biggest potential for growth involves food prepared for consumption, or take-out food. As the name Pasta Now! implies, we are positioned to take advantage of either market segment.

The local area will experience a growth rate above the national average due to the rapid growth of the population throughout Nevada.

Product Lifecycle

The restaurant industry is in a rapidly growing phase. Although this growth trend means opportunities for increased sales volume and higher profit margins, overhead must be closely monitored. The importance of quality control, purchasing, low overhead, advertising and marketing cannot be overstated.

At all of the Pasta Now! franchise locations, customer loyalty has been developed through its excellent service and popular menu. Attention must be paid to trends, however, and changes should be made early in both the menu and the decor before customers become bored and move on to a newer experience.

Price Structure

Pasta Now! is structured to present good food and reasonable prices. As such, Pasta Now! operates with food costs at 34% of gross. This figure is somewhat higher than industry standards for the same type of menu; however, Pasta Now! strives to maintain affordable prices. Pasta Now! will keep menu prices at reasonable levels to attract the largest share possible from its demographic base.

Marketing Process

Pasta Now! will market the food and service of its restaurant using a custom designed campaign by the Jules Advertising agency in Cleveland.

Advertising campaigns will utilize newspaper, radio, and direct mail coupon marketing. Pasta Now! also markets its catering services through fax advertising to local businesses.

The ad agency has developed several creative direct mail promotions for use throughout the Pasta Now! system.

COMPETITIVE ANALYSIS

Pasta Now! will have no direct competition in the Las Vegas market. City records show that there are a total of 89 businesses listed in the broad category of restaurants. Of these, 12 feature some form of pasta as a menu item. Additionally 4 Italian restaurants are listed, each with several pasta items. None of the local restaurants specializes in quality pasta at affordable prices in a fast food setting.

Disadvantages	**Name recognition**
	As a fast food outlet, Pasta Now! does not have the name recognition of other national chains.
	New food concept
	Italian food in general, and more specifically pasta, are new concepts in fast food.
	Rental costs
	Prime rental locations are extremely costly.
Advantages	**Healthy food**
	The current fast food market does not provide for fast healthy food. Pasta Now! fills that void by allowing customers to obtain fast food which is healthy for them and their children.
	Price
	Pasta Now! offers Italian food at lower prices than typical sit-down Italian restaurants.
	Service
	Pasta Now! will operate with the motto "the customer is always right." In today's busy world, the customer service aspect of the restaurant business is often overlooked.
	Untapped market
	Pasta Now! will offer an alternative not currently available in the Las Vegas area.

DESIGN & DEVELOPMENT PLANS

Goals	**Goal 1**
	Opening of first Pasta Now! in Las Vegas by October 1 of 1995.
	Goal 2
	Achieve $250,000 - $300,000 in gross sales in the first year of operation.
	Goal 3
	Sell 5 additional franchises within the first 7 years of operation.
Risk Analysis	The following risks are inherent in the pursuit of the stated goals:
	• The lack of name recognition in our area will impede sales potential. • Attracting potential franchise owners will be difficult. • Opening of our first store will be dependent on receiving financial assistance through loans.
Evaluation Methods	Pasta Now! will evaluate the achievement of its stated goals by measuring financial factors.
	Pasta Now! will monitor monthly sales volume as compared to monthly operating costs. Monthly increases will be expected in the gross sales category.
	Sales of additional franchises will be measured by the actual opening of new stores in Nevada.

Contacts with potential franchisees will be measured in terms of the number of inquiries obtained on a monthly basis.

Strategy 1

The goal is to open the first Pasta Now! in Las Vegas by October 1, 1995. The area is growing rapidly and presents many opportunities to take advantage of the shopping market.

Strategy 1 calls for finding financing to the level necessary to satisfy our needs. The estimated level necessary to accomplish this goal is $65,000 to $100,000.

Additionally, a location will need to be secured. Location assistance is provided by the corporate headquarters. Location considerations include traffic patterns and counts, immediate area demographics, and location of a suitable strip mall facility.

Strategy 2

The goal is to achieve $250,000 - $300,000 in gross sales in the first year of operation. This will be accomplished through a marketing plan which is constructed by the corporate office. The franchisor requires that 4% of the monthly gross be spent on advertising. 2% of this goes directly to a local marketing campaign. The remaining 2% goes to the corporate headquarters to be used to develop radio and print material for our local franchise stores. The plan includes advertising, direct mail marketing and promotional activities. In addition, corporate headquarters structures food preparation and management styles to maximize profit while keeping the overhead to a minimum.

Strategy 3

The goal is to sell 5 additional franchises within a five-year period. This will be accomplished through an extensive training program provided to Mr. & Mrs. Miller by the president of the corporation. In addition to the sales assistance provided by the corporate headquarters, a franchise consultant has been retained.

Schedule for Goal 1 - Opening of first Pasta Now! in Las Vegas.

Develop a business plan for presentation to bank/investors by April 14.

Finalize franchise and master franchise agreement with corporate headquarters by April 17.

Await approval of financing and obtaining of funds. Deadline is May 15.

Complete all preliminary administrative work, such as incorporating, etc. by May 15.

Review traffic studies and demographic information. Consult with corporate headquarters regarding site selection. Site selection committee from corporate headquarters to visit area. Negotiate lease and leasehold improvements. Deadline by June 30.

Remodeling of site location to specification of Pasta Now! by August 15.

Obtain bids for supply of inventory and equipment (including signage) from various local restaurant supply companies. Select best company and set delivery date by September 1.

Receive delivery of equipment by September 10.

Obtain marketing package from corporate headquarters advertising agency and customize to our local by September 1.

Printing of all menus, forms, and promotional items by September 15.

Arrange local advertising for grand opening celebration by September 15.

Hire and train employees during soft opening period from September 15 to September 30.

Grand opening on Monday, October 1, 1995.

Schedule for Goal 2 - Achieve $250,000 - $300,000 gross sales in first year.

Evaluate monthly sales to provide for increases on a monthly basis, allow for seasonal adjustments.

Meet with president of Pasta Now! who will review entire operation and make recommendations for improving sales. Deadline January 5, 1996.

Review menu for items which are popular and unpopular, make adjustments accordingly. Deadline February 15, 1996.

Implement new PTA marketing plan by end of February, 1996.

Schedule for Goal 3 - Sell 5 additional franchises within five years.

Obtain training in the sale and finalization of franchise selling by March 30, 1996.

Develop advertising material for the sale of franchises for use in local and regional publications by April 15, 1996.

Provide for immediate response to inquiries for interest in franchise purchase.

Make a minimum of five presentations on a quarterly basis for individuals or corporations interested in purchasing a Pasta Now! franchise.

OPERATIONS & MANAGEMENT PLANS

Key Individuals

Sheila Miller - President

Mrs. Miller graduated from high school in Hartford, Connecticut in 1981. Employment out of high school was with Rocklin Corporation as a Senior Data Entry Operator. After moving to Nevada in 1983, Mrs. Miller served in various capacities with the State of Nevada - Department of Motor Vehicles.

Mrs. Miller's past business experience includes operation of her own mobile ice cream/catering truck. She was entirely responsible for the complete operation of the business. This included day-to-day operations, accounting, advertising and marketing, personnel matters, and equipment maintenance.

Mrs. Miller has experience in the personnel field having worked as a Human Resource Assistant for St. Mary's Hospital. Her responsibilities included compliance with state and federal Equal Employment Opportunity mandates, processing and training of all new employees, recruitment, advertising, insurance and benefits coordination, and payroll accounting. Mrs. Miller is currently employed with the Nevada Department of Transportation. She will resign her position upon the opening of the first store.

Roland Miller - Vice President

Mr. Miller graduated from Las Vegas High School in 1980. Mr. Miller is pursuing an education at Nevada Community College, and has earned 54 credits towards a fire science degree.

Mr. Miller has worked in the broadcasting industry since 1980, having functioned as operations manager for a local radio station. Mr. Miller currently works as a freelance radio broadcaster, covering sporting events throughout Nevada for radio stations throughout the United States. Mr. Miller has been employed by the Las Vegas Fire Department since 1984, currently holding the rank of Captain. His duties include supervising the operations of one of three city fire stations, commanding equipment and personnel at the scene of various types of emergencies, responding with a regional hazardous material team to mitigate hazardous materials incidents, and providing training and instruction to department members. In addition, Mr. Miller serves as the Department's Public Information Officer. Mr. Miller also serves in the information Officer role for the Fire Management team, responding to major emergencies. Mr. Miller's fire department work schedule, which is ten 24-hour shifts per month, allows him the freedom to pursue outside employment.

Andrew Kline - Assistant Manager

Mr. Kline is currently in retirement. His previous experience includes ownership and operation of Guido's Italian Delicatessen. The deli was located in Redwood City, California. Mr. Kline first opened his deli in 1972. In 1976, Mr. Kline moved to Las Vegas. He was completely responsible for all aspects of the store's operation. He had direct responsibility for all operations, including food preparation, customer relations, personnel relations, marketing, catering, etc.

Lynn Sher - Assistant Manager

Mrs. Sher is Andrew Kline's mother. Mrs. Sher was involved in the previously mentioned deli. Mrs. Sher's involvement was centered around direct assistance to Mr. Kline. Mrs. Sher had the added responsibility of handling all accounting activities, relations with state/city agencies, payroll, and like administrative functions.

Staff Positions

Sheila Miller will be responsible for the functions within the operations department. Including supervision of day-to-day operations & food preparations. Mrs. Miller will also be responsible for personnel relations. Mrs. Sher will assist within the operations department as necessary.

Mrs. Sher will be responsible for the administrative department. Including marketing, advertising, franchise sales, and franchise operations. Mrs. Sher will assist in the administrative department by handling all accounting responsibilities.

Mr. Miller & Mr. Kline will have responsibility for assisting with day-to-day operations, food preparation, and bookkeeping advice and support.

FINANCIAL COMPONENTS

Sources & Uses

Financial requirements are as follows:

Franchise fee and purchase of area agreement	$22,000
Equipment package and signage	$35,500
Initial inventory	$4,000
Leasehold improvements	$13,000
Pre-opening expenses, travel and lodging for training	$7,500
Grand Opening	$5,000
Working Capital	$13,000
Total Financial Requirement	**$100,000**

Financing to be obtained through local bank loans, secured through the Small Business Association or USDA if necessary. Equity of property owned in Las Vegas will be used as partial collateral. Loan term to be discussed.

Income/Cash Flow Statement

The following income and cash flow statements are based on information supplied by Pasta Now's corporate headquarters. Figures used are pro-forma; however, they reflect results obtained at other Pasta Now! franchise locations.

The statement is based on a fiscal year which begins with the opening date of the business.

Projected Income Statements — Best Case

	Oct	Nov	Dec	Jan	Feb	Mar	Apr	May
Gross Sales								
Sales	36,000	30,000	33,000	15,000	19,500	24,000	28,500	33,000
Total Sales	36,000	30,000	33,000	15,000	19,500	24,000	28,500	33,000
Cost of Sales:								
Food/Drink/Spoilage								
	12,240	10,200	11,220	5,100	6,630	8,160	9,690	11,220
Total Cost of Sales								
	12,240	10,200	11,220	5,100	6,630	8,160	9,690	11,220
Gross Profit	23,760	19,800	21,780	9,900	12,870	15,840	18,810	21,780
Expenses:								
Accounting	100	100	100	100	100	100	100	100
Advertising Local	720	600	660	300	390	480	570	660
Advertising National								
	720	600	660	300	390	480	570	660
Bank Charges	15	15	15	15	15	15	15	15
Depreciation	292	292	292	292	292	292	292	292
Franchise Fee	83	83	83	83	83	83	83	83
Insurance	188	188	188	188	188	188	188	188
Interest	636	632	627	622	616	611	606	601
Legal and Pro.	100	100	100	100	100	100	100	100
Licenses & Permits	15	15	15	15	15	15	15	15
Office Expense	50	50	50	50	50	50	50	50
Outside Services	200	200	200	200	200	200	200	200
Rent - Property	2,673	2,673	2,673	2,673	2,673	2,673	2,673	2,673
Repairs & Maint.	100	100	100	100	100	100	100	100
Royalties	1,440	1,200	1,320	600	780	960	1,140	1,320
Telephone	300	300	300	300	300	300	300	300
Travel	250	250	250	250	250	250	250	250
Utilities	558	558	558	558	558	558	558	558
Wages	5,760	4,800	5,280	2,400	3,120	3,840	4,560	5,280
Employer's Burden								
	1,319	1,156	1,238	748	870	993	1,115	1,238
Manager Salary	2,000	2,000	2,000	2,000	2,000	2,000	2,000	2,000
Misc.	720	600	660	300	390	480	570	660
Total Expenses	18,239	16,511	17,368	12,193	13,481	14,768	16,055	17,342
Net Operating Income								
	5,521	3,289	4,412	(2,293)	(611)	1,072	2,755	4,438
Other Income	0	0	0	0	0	0	0	0
Other Expenses	0	0	0	0	0	0	0	0
Net Profit (Loss) Before Tax								
	5,521	3,289	4,412	(2,293)	(611)	1,072	2,755	4,438

Jun	Jul	Aug	Sep	Year 1	%	Year 2	%	Year 3	%
36,000	37,500	34,500	33,000	360,000	100.00%	450,000	100.00%	495,000	100.00%
36,000	37,500	34,500	33,000	360,000		450,000		495,000	
12,240	12,750	11,730	11,220	122,400	34.00%	153,000	34.00%	168,300	34.00%
12,240	12,750	11,730	11,220	122,400	34.00%	153,000	34.00%	168,300	34.00%
23,760	24,750	22,770	21,780	237,600	66.00%	297,000	66.00%	326,700	66.00%
100	100	100	100	1,200	0.33%	1,500	0.33%	1,650	0.33%
720	750	690	660	7,200	2.00%	9,000	2.00%	9,900	2.00%
720	750	690	660	7,200	2.00%	9,000	2.00%	9,900	2.00%
15	15	15	15	180	0.05%	225	0.05%	248	0.05%
292	292	292	292	3,500	0.97%	4,375	0.97%	4,813	0.97%
83	83	83	83	1,000	0.28%	1,000	0.22%	1,000	0.20%
188	188	188	188	2,250	0.63%	2,813	0.63%	3,094	0.63%
596	590	585	580	7,302	2.03%	6,513	1.45%	5,626	1.14%
100	100	100	100	1,200	0.33%	1,500	0.33%	1,650	0.33%
15	15	15	15	180	0.05%	200	0.04%	220	0.04%
50	50	50	50	600	0.17%	750	0.17%	825	0.17%
200	200	200	200	2,400	0.67%	3,000	0.67%	3,300	0.67%
2,673	2,673	2,673	2,673	32,076	8.91%	33,680	7.48%	37,048	7.48%
100	100	100	100	1,200	0.33%	1,500	0.33%	1,650	0.33%
1,440	1,500	1,380	1,320	14,400	4.00%	18,000	4.00%	19,800	4.00%
300	300	300	300	3,600	1.00%	4,500	1.00%	4,950	1.00%
250	250	250	250	3,000	0.83%	3,750	0.83%	4,125	0.83%
558	558	558	558	6,700	1.86%	8,375	1.86%	9,213	1.86%
5,760	6,000	5,520	5,280	57,600	16.00%	72,000	16.00%	79,200	16.00%
1,319	1,360	1,278	1,238	13,872	3.85%	16,660	3.70%	18,564	3.75%
2,000	2,000	2,000	2,000	24,000	6.67%	26,000	5.78%	30,000	6.06%
720	750	690	660	7,200	2.00%	9,000	2.00%	9,900	2.00%
18,199	18,624	17,757	17,321	197,860	54.96%	233,340	51.85%	256,674	51.85%
5,561	6,126	5,013	4,459	39,740	11.04%	63,660	14.15%	70,026	14.15%
0	0	0	0	0	0.00%	0	0.00%	0	0.00%
0	0	0	0	0	0.00%	0	0.00%	0	0.00%
5,561	6,126	5,013	4,459	39,740	11.04%	63,660	14.15%	70,026	14.15%

Statement of Cash Flows — Best Case

	Oct	Nov	Dec	Jan	Feb	Mar	Apr	May
Sales	36,000	30,000	33,000	15,000	19,500	24,000	28,500	33,000
Expenses	30,479	26,711	28,588	17,293	20,111	22,928	25,745	28,562
Depreciation	292	292	292	292	292	292	292	292
Principal	502	507	512	517	522	527	533	538
Net Cash Position								
	5,310	3,073	4,191	(2,519)	(841)	836	2,514	4,191
Previous Cash Position								
	13,000	18,310	21,383	25,574	23,056	22,214	23,050	25,564
Cumulative Cash Position								
	18,310	21,383	25,574	23,056	22,214	23,050	25,564	29,756

Projected Income Statements - Worst Case

	Oct	Nov	Dec	Jan	Feb	Mar	Apr	May
Gross Sales								
Sales	22,000	18,333	20,167	9,167	11,917	14,667	17,417	20,167
Total Sales	22,000	18,333	20,167	9,167	11,917	14,667	17,417	20,167
Cost of Sales:								
Food/Drink/Spoilage								
	7,480	6,233	6,857	3,117	4,052	4,987	5,922	6,857
Total Cost of Sales								
	7,480	6,233	6,857	3,117	4,052	4,987	5,922	6,857
Gross Profit	14,520	12,100	13,310	6,050	7,865	9,680	11,495	13,310
Expenses:								
Accounting	100	100	100	100	100	100	100	100
Advertising Local	440	367	403	183	238	293	348	403
Advertising - National								
	440	367	403	183	238	293	348	403
Bank Service Charges								
	15	15	15	15	15	15	15	15
Depreciation	292	292	292	292	292	292	292	292
Franchise Fee	83	83	83	83	83	83	83	83
Insurance	188	188	188	188	188	188	188	188
Interest Loan	636	632	627	622	616	611	606	601
Legal and Pro.	100	100	100	100	100	100	100	100
Licenses & Permits	15	15	15	15	15	15	15	15
Office Expense	50	50	50	50	50	50	50	50
Outside Services	200	200	200	200	200	200	200	200
Rent - Property	2,673	2,673	2,673	2,673	2,673	2,673	2,673	2,673
Repairs & Maint.	100	100	100	100	100	100	100	100
Royalties	880	733	807	367	477	587	697	807
Telephone	125	125	125	125	125	125	125	125
Travel	83	83	83	83	83	83	83	83
Utilities	458	458	458	458	458	458	458	458
Wages	3,520	2,933	3,227	1,467	1,907	2,347	2,787	3,227
Employer Burden	938	839	889	589	664	739	814	889
Manager Salary	2,000	2,000	2,000	2,000	2,000	2,000	2,000	2,000
Misc.	440	367	403	183	238	293	348	403
Total Expenses	13,777	12,719	13,241	10,076	10,861	11,646	12,430	13,215

Jun	Jul	Aug	Sep		Year 2	Year 3
36,000	37,500	34,500	33,000		450,000	495,000
30,439	31,374	29,487	28,541		386,340	424,974
292	292	292	292		4,375	4,813
543	548	554	559		7,152	8,039
5,310	5,869	4,751	4,191		60,883	66,799
29,756	35,066	40,935	45,685		49,877	110,760
35,066	40,935	45,685	49,877		110,760	177,559

Jun	Jul	Aug	Sep	Year 1	%	Year 2	%	Year 3	%
22,000	22,917	21,083	20,167	220,000	100.00%	275,000	100.00%	302,500	100.00%
22,000	22,917	21,083	20,167	220,000		275,000		302,500	
7,480	7,792	7,168	6,857	74,800	34.00%	93,500	34.00%	102,850	34.00%
7,480	7,792	7,168	6,857	74,800	34.00%	93,500	34.00%	102,850	34.00%
14,520	15,125	13,915	13,310	145,200	66.00%	181,500	66.00%	199,650	66.00%
100	100	100	100	1,200	0.55%	1,500	0.55%	1,650	0.55%
440	458	422	403	4,400	2.00%	5,500	2.00%	6,050	2.00%
440	458	422	403	4,400	2.00%	5,500	2.00%	6,050	2.00%
15	15	15	15	180	0.08%	225	0.08%	248	0.08%
292	292	292	292	3,500	1.59%	4,375	1.59%	4,813	1.59%
83	83	83	83	1,000	0.45%	1,000	0.36%	1,000	0.33%
188	188	188	188	2,25 0	1.02%	2,813	1.02%	3,094	1.02%
596	590	585	580	7,302	3.32%	6,513	2.2%	5,626	1.86%
100	100	100	100	1,200	0.55%	1,500	0.55%	1,650	0.55%
15	15	15	15	180	0.08%	200	0.07%	220	0.07%
50	50	50	50	600	0.27%	750	0.27%	825	0.27%
200	200	200	200	2,400	1.09%	3,000	1.09%	3,300	1.09%
2,673	2,673	2,673	2,673	32,076	14.58%	33,680	12.25%	37,048	12.25%
100	100	100	100	1,200	0.55%	1,500	0.55%	1,650	0.55%
880	917	843	807	8,800	4.00%	11,000	4.00%	12,100	4.00%
125	125	125	125	1,500	0.68%	1,875	0.68%	2,063	0.68%
83	83	83	83	1,000	0.45%	1,250	0.45%	1,375	0.45%
458	458	458	458	5,500	2.50%	6,875	2.50%	7,563	2.50%
3,520	3,667	3,373	3,227	35,200	16.00%	44,000	16.00%	48,400	16.00%
938	963	913	889	10,064	4.57%	11,900	4.33%	13,328	4.41%
2,000	2,000	2,000	2,000	24,000	10.91%	26,000	9.45%	30,000	9.92%
440	458	422	403	4,400	2.00%	5,500	2.00%	6,050	2.00%
13,736	13,994	13,462	13,194	152,352	69.25%	176,455	64.17%	194,100	64.17%

	Oct	Nov	Dec	Jan	Feb	Mar	Apr	May
Net Opr Income	743	(619)	69	(4,026)	(2,996)	(1,966)	(935)	95
Other Income	0	0	0	0	0	0	0	0
Other Expenses	0	0	0	0	0	0	0	0
Net Profit (Loss) Before Tax								
	743	(619)	69	(4,026)	(2,996)	(1,966)	(935)	95

Statement of Cash Flows - Worst Case

	Oct	Nov	Dec	Jan	Feb	Mar	Apr	May
Sales	22,000	18,333	20,167	9,167	11,917	14,667	17,417	20,167
Expenses	21,257	18,952	20,097	13,193	14,913	16,632	18,352	20,072
Depreciation	292	292	292	292	292	292	292	292
Principal	502	507	512	517	522	527	533	538
Net Cash Position	532	(835)	(151)	(4,252)	(3,227)	(2,202)	(1,176)	(151)
Prev Cash Pos	13,000	13,532	12,698	12,547	8,295	5,068	2,866	1,690
Cum Cash Pos	13,532	12,698	12,547	8,295	5,068	2,866	1,690	1,539

Projected Income Statements — Most Likely Case

	Oct	Nov	Dec	Jan	Feb	Mar	Apr	May
Gross Sales								
Sales	27,500	22,917	25,208	11,458	14,896	18,333	21,771	25,208
Total Sales	27,500	22,917	25,208	11,458	14,896	18,333	21,771	25,208
Cost of Sales:								
Food/Drink/Spoilage								
	9,350	7,792	8,571	3,896	5,065	6,233	7,402	8,571
Total Cost of Sales								
	9,350	7,792	8,571	3,896	5,065	6,233	7,402	8,571
Gross Profit	18,150	15,125	16,638	7,563	9,831	12,100	14,369	16,638
Expenses:								
Accounting	100	100	100	100	100	100	100	100
Advertising Local	550	458	504	229	298	367	435	504
Advertising - National								
	550	458	504	229	298	367	435	504
Bank Service Charges								
	15	15	15	15	15	15	15	15
Depreciation	292	292	292	292	292	292	292	292
Franchise Fee	83	83	83	83	83	83	83	83
Insurance	188	188	188	188	188	188	188	188
Interest	636	632	627	622	616	611	606	601
Legal & Pro.	100	100	100	100	100	100	100	100
Licenses & Permits	15	15	15	15	15	15	15	15
Office Expense	50	50	50	50	50	50	50	50
Outside Services	200	200	200	200	200	200	200	200
Rent - Property	2,673	2,673	2,673	2,673	2,673	2,673	2,673	2,673
Repairs & Maint	100	100	100	100	100	100	100	100
Royalties	1,100	917	1,008	458	596	733	871	1,008
Telephone	167	167	167	167	167	167	167	167
Travel	167	167	167	167	167	167	167	167
Utilities	517	517	517	517	517	517	517	517
Wages	4,400	3,667	4,033	1,833	2,383	2,933	3,483	4,033
Employer Burden	1,088	963	1,026	652	745	839	932	1,026
Manager Salary	2,000	2,000	2,000	2,000	2,000	2,000	2,000	2,000

Jun	Jul	Aug	Sep	Year 1	%	Year 2	%	Year 3	%
784	1,131	453	116	(7,152)	-3.25%	5,045	1.83%	5,550	1.83%
0	0	0	0	0	0.00%	0	0.00%	0	0.00%
0	0	0	0	0	0.00%	0	0.00%	0	0.00%
784	1,131	453	116	(7,152)	-3.25%	5,045	1.83%	5,550	1.83%

Jun	Jul	Aug	Sep			Year 2		Year 3	
22,000	22,917	21,083	20,167			275,000		302,500	
21,216	21,786	20,611	20,050			269,955		296,950	
292	292	292	292			4,375		4,813	
543	548	554	559			7,152		8,019	
532	874	191	(151)			2,268		2,323	
1,539	2,071	2,945	3,136			2,985		5,253	
2,071	2,945	3,136	2,985			5,253		7,575	

Jun	Jul	Aug	Sep	Year 1	%	Year 2	%	Year 3	%
27,500	28,646	26,354	25,208	275,000	100.00%	343,750	100.00%	378,125	100.00%
27,500	28,646	26,354	25,208	275,000		343,750		378,125	
9,350	9,740	8,960	8,571	93,500	34.00%	116,875	34.00%	128,563	34.00%
9,350	9,740	8,960	8,571	93,500	34.00%	116,875	34.00%	128,563	34.00%
18,150	18,906	17,394	16,638	181,500	66.00%	226,875	66.00%	249,563	66.00%
100	100	100	100	1,200	0.44%	1,500	0.44%	1,650	0.44%
550	573	527	504	5,500	2.00%	6,875	2.00%	7,563	2.00%
550	573	527	504	5,500	2.00%	6,875	2.00%	7,563	2.00%
15	15	15	15	180	0.07%	225	0.07%	248	0.07%
292	292	292	292	3,500	1.27%	4,375	1.27%	4,813	1.27%
83	83	83	83	1,000	0.36%	1,000	0.29%	1,000	0.26%
188	188	188	188	2,250	0.82%	2,813	0.82%	3,094	0.82%
596	590	585	580	7,302	2.66%	6,513	1.89%	5,626	1.49%
100	100	100	100	1,200	0.44%	1,500	0.44%	1,650	0.44%
15	15	15	15	180	0.07%	200	0.06%	220	0.06%
50	50	50	50	600	0.22%	750	0.22%	825	0.22%
200	200	200	200	2,400	0.87%	3,000	0.87%	3,300	0.87%
2,673	2,673	2,673	2,673	32,076	11.66%	33,680	9.80%	37,048	9.80%
100	100	100	100	1,200	0.44%	1,500	0.44%	1,650	0.44%
1,100	1,146	1,054	1,008	11,000	4.00%	13,750	4.00%	15,125	4.00%
167	167	167	167	2,000	0.73%	2,500	0.73%	2,750	0.73%
167	167	167	167	2,000	0.73%	2,500	0.73%	2,750	0.73%
517	517	517	517	6,200	2.25%	7,750	2.25%	8,525	2.25%
4,400	4,583	4,217	4,033	44,000	16.00%	55,000	16.00%	60,500	16.00%
1,088	1,119	1,057	1,026	11,560	4.20%	13,770	4.01%	15,385	4.07%
2,000	2,000	2,000	2,000	24,000	8.73%	26,000	7.56%	30,000	7.93%

Food Processor

BUSINESS PLAN

RIO GRANDE

12659 San Ablo Blvd.
Santa Fe, New Mexico

This business plan is for a food processor within the specialty foods industry who will be using various marketing strategies to reposition their product and become a reknowned manufacturer of high quality foods. The following plan will outline the products history, competition, potential new markets, and promotional opportunities.

- EXECUTIVE SUMMARY

- SITUATIONAL ANALYSIS

- STRATEGIC PLAN

- TACTICAL PLAN

- CONTROL

- BIBLIOGRAPHY

- APPENDICES

**EXECUTIVE
SUMMARY**

Rio Grande Foods is a food processor in the specialty foods industry (SIC 2033) and sells its products on a wholesale basis to brokers, distributors, and retailers. The present product mix is one product wide and the line is two products deep. The product is Rio Grande Salsa Picante, which can be found in a 16 oz. Paragon jar in both mild and medium heat levels. The salsa is a rich-textured, home style salsa which sustains the individual flavors of the all-natural ingredients. The ingredients are as follows: diced tomatoes, garlic, cilantro, onions, jalapeno peppers, salt, and a trace of organic vinegar.

Rio Grande Foods utilizes a co-packer for processing purposes. A co-packer is a company that has the facilities to process foods for public consumption. In order to be an acceptable and legitimate co-packer, the company must be certified by the Food and Drug Administration and the New Mexico Department of Health. Rio Grande Foods' co-packer is C & D Mexican Foods. Taking marginal costs and operating expenses into consideration along with primary competition prices, Rio Grande Salsa Picante's wholesale cost is $2.25. The company's primary competition has its product priced at $2.50 on the wholesale level. Rio Grande Salsa Picante can be found at three different concept stores - grade "A" grocery stores, specialty food stores, and gift shops. Rio Grande Foods utilizes mostly push strategy efforts through the use of guerrilla warfare tactics. The type of sale promotions utilized are trade oriented in the form of credit terms, discount offers, and occasional volume discounts. Consumer oriented sales promotions will be through the print media, such as point of purchase recipes and some couponing (premiums). Rio Grande Foods mission is to earn a position in consumers minds as a manufacturer of high quality Mexican foods in the specialty foods industry. The company will do this by producing products that have an authentic texture and flavor by using the highest quality ingredients possible. Objectives are to be positioned in the specialty foods market throughout New Mexico by 1998 with sales volume increasing 9% on an annual basis. These figures will be based on the number of case units sold annually (12/16 oz. Pack). The company has a .03% market share at the present time and has goals of attaining a .0316% hold on the market by the end of the third quarter in 1995.

**SITUATIONAL
ANALYSIS**

**Business and
Product Service
Description**

The Industry

Rio Grande Foods is in the processed foods industry. The Standard Identification Classification code for this industry is 2033. More specifically, Rio Grande Foods is in the specialty foods industry procession and wholesaling Mexican salsa picante. Specialty products are foods, beverages or confections meant for human use that are of the highest grade, style and/or quality in their category. The specialty food nature derives from a combination of some or all of the following qualities: their uniqueness, exotic origin, particular processing, design, limited supply, unusual application or use, extraordinary packaging or channel of distribution has been growing strong since the 1950's and is now beginning to stabilize the rate of growth. This specialty foods segment is small compared to the highly commercialized market in which Pace foods and Old El Paso venture. Being that this is a relatively small industry the composition of it consists of several small independent processors and wholesalers. Even though the niche of the specialty foods industry is small, it was worth $30 billion in 1993. The condiment segment itself is worth $13 billion. Rio Grande Foods' products are aimed at middle aged consumers with high disposable incomes. However, prices are much lower than most competitors that other income brackets can afford to purchase a specialty Mexican salsa. Rio Grande Foods has had great success thus far in its start up period. The high quality and fancy packaging go hand in hand with the authentic flavor of Mexican salsa picante. The availability of two heat levels allow for access into other consumers tastes. Larger product mixes of other companies are forcing Rio Grande Foods to develop other products in the future.

Mission and Objectives

Rio Grande Foods' mission is to earn a position in consumers minds as a manufacturer of high quality foods in the specialty foods industry. This will be done by producing food products that have an authentic texture and flavor by using only the highest quality ingredients. Objectives are to be positioned in the specialty foods market throughout New Mexico by 1988 with sales volume increasing 9% on an annual basis. These figures will be based on the number of case units sold annually (12/16 oz. Pack).

The Product

Rio Grande Salsa Picante is a rich-textured, home style salsa which sustains the individual flavors of 100% all-natural ingredients. The ingredients consist of diced tomatoes, garlic, cilantro, onions, jalapeno peppers, salt, and a trace of vinegar. They combine to yield a product that has no fat, 2 grams of carbohydrates, 2% vitamin A, and 10% vitamin C. Rio Grande Salsa Picante has no artificial preservatives, fillers, oil, water, or sugars. This is what distinguishes it from other brands and qualifies it as a specialty food. The packaging is also very attractive. It has a very "classy" and conservative look at the same time. The trademark is a ristra of chiles and the name Rio Grande written in a vibrant red. The background is a chipped stucco wall that exposes bricks. It helps amplify the authenticity of the product.

Market Potential

Market Environment

Market potential for the condiment segment is very high. The two highest ranking condiments are Mexican salsa and ketchup, first and second respectively. Since Mexican salsa is out selling ketchup it is apparent that there is a lot of room for growth within this segment. Recently, there has been some growth within minority ethnic populations and sales are expected to increase in the specialty food industry as a whole. The Hispanic population has seen a 38% increase since 1980 along with a 71% income increase. Also, several cooks have developed recipes which contain Mexican salsa, for example, chile con queso and salad dressings.

Market size

The current market size of Rio Grande Foods is held within Santa Fe, NM. The customer base on the wholesale level is made up of 10 companies for a total of 16 retail store locations. All of these accounts handle a vast variety of specialty foods. The market size is expected to grow steadily.

Demand Trend for Product

Mexican salsa picante has reached a point of saturation in the southern part of the United States. A shake out is presently occurring, large wealthy processors are riding out losses for long periods at a time by offering sales promotions and price savings. They are trying to keep customers from buying the competitions brands so that their competitors might go out of business. However, this is going on in the high volume commercial market. In the specialty foods industry, prices are not going down, the product mixes are going up per company. All sorts of varieties are beginning to appear. J. Jose's has a Mexican salsa, a salsa verde, chile con queso, spices, candies, hot sauces (Tabasco style), mayonnaise, tartar sauce, and gift boxes. End consumers like to be different and daring. Mexican fruit salsa is the latest in the market, with variations such as peach, strawberry, pineapple, and other strange and exciting flavors. Rio Grande Foods plans to diversify its product line offerings so that it might be able to increase revenues and consumer interest.

Current Market Segments

Rio Grande Foods' is only supplying retail stores in three categories. They are grade A grocery stores, specialty food stores, and gift shops. An example of a grade A grocery store is J.E.B.

Marketplace in Santa Fe, NM. These are the larger grocery stores that large grocery chains, such as J.E.B. open in locations near large upper income locations. They carry all of the highly commercialized grocery and general merchandise, but they also carry some specialty food items. About 24% of their total merchandise is specialty food items. These stores are normally close to several small populations with access from several different locations. Specialty food stores are generally small in size yet very fancy or unique in design. They are located in or near wealthy neighborhoods. They only carry specialty food products. The average cost for a 16 oz of Mexican salsa at these stores is $3.75. An example of a specialty food store would be Farm To Market on Taylor Hwy. in Santa Fe, NM. Products found in these stores' gift shops are normally products that are indigenous to the city or state in which it is located. The reason for this is that the majority of the customers are tourists. They are located near tourist attractions in cities or in major malls. An example of a tourist gift shop is Toddies in Franklin Mall located in downtown Santa Fe, NM. All of these stores have one thing in common, they all attract specialty food enthusiasts.

Market Segment Currently Targeted

The market segment currently targeted are individuals that fall into the following categories:

- 35-44 years old
- married
- home rented (not owned)
- income of $50,000 and over
- dual income household

Of the people who will fit in above, these are the top ten lifestyles ranked by index:

Wines	328
Fine Arts/Antiques	223
Attend Cultural Arts Events	201
Fashion Clothing	199
Foreign travel	199
Real Estate Investment	192
Health Foods/Vitamins	181
Home Furnishing/Decorating	179
Money Making Opportunities	173
Science/New Technology	169

Immediate Competitors

Rio Grande Foods' immediate competitor is J. Jose's. J. Jose's has a product mix of 11 products with an average depth of 3. They have Mexican salsa (red), salsa verde, chile con queso, mayonnaise, tartar sauces, Tabasco style hot sauce, spices candies, olives, mustard, and chips. Other competitors are New Canyon Farms, Don Jovencio's, Rio Diablo, Truly Texas, Guiltless Gourmet, and Rose's. These all process specialty salsa in the same market segments, however, they are priced slightly higher.

Different Advantage(s) by Segment

Rio Grande Foods has an overall lower cost throughout the channels. On the wholesale Rio Grande Salsa Picante is priced lower, thus allowing the retailer to still meet their pricing margins and at the same time the product has a lower retail price. Rio Grande Salsa has a fancy package in a competitive container. The label also reveal nutritional facts about the product unlike the competitor's products.

Product Usage

Members of the targeted market enjoy Rio Grande Salsa Picante on an occasional basis. A consumer can expect to pay anywhere from $1.99 to $3.50 for a 16 oz. jar of Rio Grande Salsa Picante. The consumer is beginning to be inventive by using salsa on almost anything that has cheese, vegetables, or meats, along with several other dishes.

Comparison of Competitive Players

This year Rio Grande Foods saw sales increase by 200% by the end of the second quarter as it began establishing and broadening its customer base. In terms of volume, sales increased from 1993 sales of 82 cases to 1994 third quarter sales of 244 cases. In terms of market share, some difficulty is encountered because of the fragmented and small specialty Mexican salsa market. In the specialty Mexican salsa market, the market leaders J. Jose's and New Haven Farms who hold 34% and 27% respectively when the 23.8% allocated below will show how small the specialty food market is compared to the entire Mexican salsa market as a whole.

Mexican Sauce Top Brands

	Sales ($mil.)	Market Share
Pace	$153.0	28.2%
Old El Paso	120.8	22.3%
Frito-Lay	55.8	10.3%
Chi-Chi's	45.6	8.4%
Ortega	37.9	7.0%
Other (specialty/private label)	129.5	23.8%

The category titled other does not only consist of specialty food processors in the specialty food industry, but countless other small private label companies selling in mom and pop convenience stores, grocery stores, and even to friends.

Comparison of Competitor's Resources/Willingness

After having viewed the breakdown of market share and Rio Grande Foods' sales volume, it is plain to see that this company is only a pebble in a quarry when compared to J. Jose's. Jose's has a larger flow of capital and has a higher inventory turnover rate compared to Rio Grande Foods. Rio Grande Foods has a lot of growing up to do before it even becomes a contended or an actual threat to Jose's. Jose's has a large product mix with great adequate depth in each line. They have consumer recognition due to the large amount of shelve space they occupy in the stores. Jose's know the tricks of the trade in production, distribution, and direct marketing, because they have been in the game longer than Rio Grande Foods. There is a new contender in the market that could pose a threat for Rio Grande Foods in the future. The name of the Mexican salsa is Chili's. Chili's utilizes the same 16 oz. container as Rio Grande Foods and has a mild, medium, and hot Mexican salsa picante. They are small players like Rio Grande foods with potential to grow and increase market share.

Additional Segments to Target

Rio Grande Foods would also do very well to expand into other large metropolitan cities, such as Albuquerque, Las Cruces, Roswell, etc.. Other very strong cities where the National Association for the Specialty Food Trade, Inc. is headquartered in New York along with the entire east cost region of the United States. Mexican salsa has just begun to make its mark in this region. Specialty food stores can be found all over in these areas. The larger the city in most cases the larger the standard of living thus yielding higher incomes. Being that Rio Grande Salsa Picante is from Santa Fe, NM, people of these eastern regions would be very excited to try an authentic Mexican salsa like Rio Grande.

Potential Competition

A primary competitor in the un-targeted segments would be J. Jose's. Jose's is the leader of Mexican salsa in the specialty foods market. They have surplus resources to venture and test other potential markets. Being that Rio Grande Foods is fighting as a guerrilla, it has to put all of its resources into one attack and only one. It does not have the resources to fight a flanking battle. The assets that Rio Grande Foods does have are creativity and enthusiasm. Another restaurant that might pose a threat in the future is Chili's. It is based in Santa Fe, NM and is competing in the current segment of Rio Grande Foods. It is important that Rio Grande Foods eats up all of the available market share possible before Chili's does, because it can not afford another competitor.

Macro Environment

Impact of Economic Trends

Food processors and retail food store operators approach 1995 with some concern. While inflation is expected to remain under control, processors and retailers are concerned about the pace of domestic and international recovery and the expected growth of non-traditional retail outlets. Processors of brand name products will strive to stem the flow of less costly generic goods while retailers will attempt to offset the effects of new, non-traditional competition. Adjusted for inflation, the value of shipments of the food and beverage sector is forecasted to rise about 1 percent in 1995. Processors are also concerned about NAFTA, it has brought great export opportunities and will continue to bring opportunity in the future years. However, some processors fear backlash, which would have adverse effect on 1995 U.S. export sales. Processors are also concerned about the rate of recovery worldwide. For 1995, the value of processed foods and beverage exports is forecasted to rise about 5% to more than $25 billion. Over the next five years, the processed food and beverage industries are likely to grow slowly; adjusted for inflation, the value of aggregate industry shipments is forecasted to grow 1% a year. The industry growth in the beginning of the year will not be large, but will improve as the U.S. and international economies improve.

Impact of Social/Cultural Trends

Aside from the presently targeted consumers for a specialty Mexican salsa like Rio Grande Salsa Picante, other ethnic markets are beginning to emerge in the 1990's. For example, the Hispanic population in the United States has increased by 38% since 1980. But not only is the population growing, so is their annual income. More and more Hispanics are seeking an education past high school, which has led to a 71% increase in their income. At the present time, Rio Grande Salsa Picante is appealing to the Hispanic market, in terms of flavor and authenticity. The only problem is that the portion of this population that can afford to purchase specialty items has remained very small. Now, in the 90's it is beginning to reach a point where the Hispanic purchasing power cannot continue going on without notice by small and large processors.

Impact of Political/Legal Trends

As specialty food and retailers know, many consumers are reading food labels. Interest in the nutrition label and claims such as "no cholesterol" are examples of this phenomenon. So, just around the corner is another marketing tool for specialty food processors. It is known as organic labeling. In 1995, the Department of Agriculture (USDA) is expected to finalize its rules on organic food production, processing and labeling. This federal program will go side-by-side with state organic certification programs, which may contain additional or more restrictive that the federal program. However, the state programs must be approved by USDA, the state labeling must be consistent with federal labeling. Labeling cannot say that the particular state's products are of superior quality, and the state may not discriminate against out of state foods that bear the USDA label. A food which contains at least 95% ingredients which meet the farm-to-table requirements may use an organic claim, such as, "100% organic". It may also bear the USDA shield to show that the product meets USDA standards for organic production, and also bear the logo of the certifying agent. This is something that Rio Grande Foods can concern itself with in the future, it is not something that is mandatory. Rio Grande Foods needs to allocate all of its capital resources to what it is trying to accomplish in the marketplace. This organic logo is just another point of purchase tool that Rio Grande Salsa Picante has already used. The latest law that has been already ratified since May 1993 is the Nutrition Labeling and Education Act. This law was developed and ratified by the Food and Drug Administration (FDA) as the consumer market demanded. This law simply requires food products for public consumption to reveal nutritional facts on the package itself. Rio Grande Foods has already complied with this required law. The reason Rio Grande Foods did not have to comply with the law immediately is because there is a low volume item exemption. If a processor does not have volumes sales that generate $60,000 or more on an annual basis or sell 600,000 individual units, it is not required to comply.

Impact of Related Technology

In the grade A grocery stores like J.E.B. Marketplace mentioned above, Efficient Consumer Response is beginning to be utilized by large grocery store suppliers. This service is being used by processors and distributors alike. This service is offered by the Uniform Code Council (U.C.C.), which is located in Dayton, Ohio. This is the same company that makes the service of Uniform Product Code symbols (U.P.C.) on most retail items these days. The Efficient Consumer Response service allows processors to be directly in touch with their customers, be it distributors or retailers. The information they receive is scan movement information, this means that each time a related product of the processor is sold at a particular retail location, they are made aware of it electronically. This scan/product movement allows processors to operate on the efficient Just In Time method. Present primary competitors are not using this service, however, it is a thing of the future. Pace Foods is already utilizing this service. The reason they are is because they move such high volumes of product and their processing material requirement planning depends on it. Rio Grande Foods is only utilizing the U.P.C. symbols for efficient retail handling of the products. It also allows the retailers to know if the product is moving good enough to make them a profit with the shelf space Rio Grande Salsa Picante is occupying.

Capabilities and Responsibilities

Rio Grande Foods is a very small company in the start up stages of a business venture. The product itself is in the growth stage at the present time. Rio Grande foods will continue to look for an additional customer base outside of Santa Fe, NM and will aim for larger and wealthier markets such as the ones mentioned above in the opportunities section. Rio Grande Foods has a lot of potential in terms of growth if it can successfully launch a product that is unique into the specialty foods market. Customers are already testifying that it is truly an authentic experience and they are asking for a list of other products the company has to offer. Rio Grande Foods is led by a young, creative and talented management team. The primary product has surprisingly gotten off the ground in a market which was said to be super saturated by the Wall Street Journal in 1993. The credit goes to the quality of the product and the management team which consisted of one individual and later expanded to two in the summer of 1994.

Organizational Support/Willingness

Rio Grande Foods is very committed to maintaining their mission statement of authenticity. The company will not put a product on the market just to have a diverse product mix. If the products that they try to develop do not abide by the mission statement they will be discontinued. Management works hard to maintain the authentic reputation from the stationery their presentations are presented on to the products themselves. Management knows that without profits the company will no longer exist, but profit is not the only reason for the company's existence. Management puts employee and customer satisfaction above everything else. They

Organizational Environment

feel that if the consumer is happy so are the employees, because they are directly related. If the consumer is happy, profits will take care of themselves.

THREATS AND OPPORTUNITIES

Threat Statements

- Consumer preference of non-traditional salsa, such as the fruit salsa discussed above over authentic salsa picante like Rio Grande brand
- Target market becomes more interested in Tabasco style hot sauces
- Constant entry of new competitors with more capital may win any potential market share
- Food processing plant may be brought out by a large successful processor who is ready to handle its own production
- The economy stumbles and the Hispanic population is unable to flourish the way it has been into the specialty foods market
- Communicating wrong message to consumers about the product/company
- Company is unable to keep up with changing factors in the targeted segments
- Sales are not good enough to sustain growth

Opportunity Statements

- Consumers of other types of salsa and sauces prefer a more authentic experience
- Growth in consumer awareness is directly related to word of mouth advertising
- The growth segment of the products life cycle will show consumers that Rio Grande Salsa
- Picante is preferred over the others
- Changes in market segmentation will be a new path for new markets (restaurants)
- Current targeted consumers become brand loyal to Rio Grande Salsa Picante
- Increased product diversity can make the company more noticeable for its brand name and quality
- A more diversified product mix can open the doors to new consumer segments and markets
- Rio Grande Foods product will set a new standard for specialty Mexican salsa
- Rio Grande Foods' can prosper while large competitors rival amongst themselves
- Ability to stay ahead of the competition by complying with new packaging and product laws even though it is not required to do so

STRENGTHS AND WEAKNESSES

Strength Statements

- Young motivated, creative, and educated management
- High quality product
- Lower wholesale cost due to cost savings on packaging: three color label
- High volume jar and lid make for lower costs, and low miscellaneous expenses
- Financed only through family equity
- Good relationship with co-packer (C&D Mexican Foods)
- Competitive packaging
- Located near larger consumer markets, such as Albuquerque, Las Cruces, and Santa Fe
- Appropriate packaging for the specialty food market
- Experienced independent sales representative
- Nutritional facts table
- Development of new recipes
- Member of the National association for the Specialty Food Trade, Inc. (NASFT)
- Aware of primary competitor (J. Jose)

Weakness Statements

- Limited time to allocate 100% effort by management
- One product-product mix

- Small distribution established
- Low inventory turnover rate
- Limited consumer awareness
- Small budget for print media (direct marketing)

Assumptions for Threat and Opportunity Statements

- Consumers will continue to purchase traditional authentic salsa picante
- Tabasco style hot sauces already have their own share of the "hot sauce market" as a whole, but there is plenty of room for both styles of salsa
- Rio Grande Foods will have to continue with Guerrilla warfare tactics in order to stay ahead of the big player's advertising campaigns
- Food processing plant co-packer is committed to several large private label companies that will not allow it to sell out
- Rio Grande Foods will not lose its focus and communicate the wrong message to its consumers
- Sales will pick up in the future when the product line becomes more diversified with product categories that are not nearly as competitive as the Mexican salsa product category

STRATEGIC PLAN

Objectives of Marketing Plan

Marketing Objectives

The company's objectives are to earn a position in the marketplace as a manufacturer of high quality Mexican food products in the specialty foods industry. Committed to supplying grade "A" grocery stores, specialty food stores, and gift shops, on a wholesale basis only, throughout Texas by 1998. At the same time the company wants to diversify its product mix steadily with products of the same quality standards as Rio Grande Salsa Picante. Sales for 1 year from 1994 up to the present have increased by 300%. The reason for the big surge is because it wasn't until the beginning of 1994 that the company started to push its products. Revenues were $2,200 in 1993, they have grown to $6,600 by the end of the third quarter in 1994. However, the company needs to reach revenues of $7,500 before it can break even. The company is sure to do this by the third quarter of 1995 if it can meet its goal of a 9% increase in sales per year up to 1998, once account growth stabilizes by the end of the second quarter in 1995. By the third quarter in 1995 with all goals met, market share should be .0316% up from .03% at the end of the third quarter in 1994. The company is planning on accomplishing its goals by doing what is written in the mission/objective statement, which is to position the company and the product in the client and consumers mind as a processor of high quality products and nothing less. Packaging will assist in the positioning of the product by revealing nutritional facts and by reinforcing the idea of authenticity.

Product Positioning

Marketing Strategies

The national marketplace for the condiment segment of the specialty foods industry is worth $13 billion. Rio Grande Foods has just begun its hike in terms of growth. It has only tapped into the Santa Fe, NM market at the present time. The beginning of 1994 marked the beginning of the company's intial effort to establish its customer base, at which time it saw an increase of 200% by the second quarter and 300% by the end of the third. When growth begins to stabilize the company expects growth of 9% per annum. The company will continue to target the high income educated individuals originally discussed in the "Market Segment Currently Targeted" section of this plan. Any promotional efforts will be prepared and implemented with that type of individual in mind. Rio Grande Foods will also have to remember the flourishing Hispanic market in the near future who will be very capable of purchasing specialty foods. In order to achieve the company's print media marketing objectives, sales will have to be in the $7,500 plus (+) category overall. The company will have to keep enlarging its customer base and must also maintain a 9% annual growth rate once growth has been stabilized. Other important factors to consider are consumer taste/preferences and trends.

Perceptual Positioning

The target market that the company will need to satisfy is one that is looking for specialty food items. Products are considered specialty food items because of their unusually high product quality due to ingredients and not for unusual packaging. The consumer in the specialty food industry is just as concerned about value as the consumer in the highly commercialized industry. The specialty foods consumer is not simply interested in spending his/her money on more expensive food products to make a fashion status statement. This is why Rio Grande Salsa Picante can be found a few cents cheaper, to a few dollars cheaper in some cases, in the market place. The company wants to be perceived as a "quality leader" in the specialty foods industry.

Product/Service

Current Product Fit per Segment - The current products of Rio Grande Foods satisfies the very active, health conscious consumers in the specialty food industry, because of the better quality products that can be found in terms of ingredients. This consumer pays more for a specialty food item only because the quality of the ingredients justify the higher price. The nutritional factors are also very important to them and that is why Rio Grande Foods has nutritional facts on its packaging. *Required Product Additions/Modifications -* In order for the company to stay in operation it will have to increase its distribution to cities outside of Santa Fe, NM to increase the inventory turn over rate. It will also need to increase its product mix to a more diverse mix so that it can please a lot more consumers and to increase point of purchase visibility/awareness. *Additional Product Strategies -* Utilize all of the company's strengths to make itself a strong preference to consumers and position itself as a "quality leader." To assist in accomplishing its goals the company will utilize a push strategy to get retailers to carry their product. Credit terms of 2/10 Net 30 are offered and occasional volume discounts will be offered.

Distribution

Due to the nature of the product (Mexican salsa) and the specialty food industry itself, volume per store delivery is low. To elaborate, a delivery destination outside a 5 mile radius of the company is not cost effective if done by a company truck. Therefore, the company utilizes a parcel delivery company to distribute its products. United Parcel Services (UPS) is the company utilized for all deliveries to specialty food stores and gift shops. When orders need to be filled and product distributed, a phone call is all it takes to get a delivery truck over to the company to pick up the product. A $5.00 pick-up fee is charged per visit and the cost per package varies from $4.85 on up depending on the destination. Distribution to the higher volume grade "A" grocery stores are handled by the company itself. Not only is it cost effective, but it also helps increase product freshness and all merchandising activities as well. Quality and dependability is important in large stores, such as J.E.B Market Place, because without it the company risks loosing customers and eventually loosing the account. The reason UPS delivery is accepted in the other two segments is because those stores are not as competitive and busy as grade "A" grocery stores. They have someone to unpack and stock low volume items every day. *Additional/Modified Distribution per Segment -* The only thing that can be improved is the number of accounts being serviced at the present time. The reason for this is not only to improve sales and profits, however, it is a factor that will assist in the process. If distribution could be increased to the point where there was a shipment every day, an account could be set up with UPS. This would eliminate the $5.00 pick up fee they have on sporadic pick up calls.

Distribution for Efficiency/Effectiveness - A larger customer base and a higher consumer awareness over other products will be needed to gain sales, market share, and to reduce marginal costs. Increased sales will increase inventory turnover rates, which means higher volume manufacturing will bring fixed manufacturing costs down. This will make the net profit margin larger if all expenses remain fixed. This will allow the company to allocate more funds to promotional efforts and product development.

Price

Pricing Fit per Segment - The company is trying to position itself as a processor of highly valuable products in the specialty foods industry. It wants to be a "quality leader" and at the same time a "price leader". On the following page a breakdown of the company's specialty foods pricing practices can be seen on Table 1 in the appendices. The price will adjust through the years up to 1998 to compensate for an average inflation rate of 4%, this can also be seen at the bottom of Table 1. Table 1.5, is a pricing schedule that has been developed to show the average competitor's pricing practices for comparison. After comparing the two tables, the differences can be seen in the wholesale cost per unit and the cost of goods sold. Most competitors are using not so fresh ingredients while maintaining a higher wholesale cost. Rio Grande Foods is trying to do the opposite within a relevant range so that the company is making a suitable profit that is consistent with corporate objectives.

Required Pricing Modifications per Segment - The company needs to reduce the cost of goods sold through increased volumes and not through cheaper ingredients. Also, more funds need to be allocated to point of purchase advertisements, such as recipe books. Recipe books will present new ways to use Rio Grande Salsa Picante, which will increase the rate of consumption - increasing turn over.

Promotion

Refined Messages - The niche of Rio Grande Foods is accented by its products' packaging that represents authenticity from the name to the graphic trade mark and label scheme complete with nutritional facts. There is also plenty of clear glass that allows for easy view of the sauces authentic texture and appearance. It "tells" the consumer that there is no need to eat out or to make they're own salsa, that home style texture and flavor can now be found in a jar at a valuable price that is not only good for my pocket book, but also for my health.

Optimal Promotional Mix - Targeting the consumer at his/her favorite events and bringing that appeal to them in the form of pure eating satisfaction at a price that will not be taking advantage of them. Formulating a memorable slogan that will remind the consumer of authenticity, value, quality, and satisfaction.

TACTICAL PLAN

Tactical Product Objectives

Product

Rio Grande Foods will continue to grow with the original product, because it has proven to be satisfactory since the beginning. The packaging and the ingredients help the company as it tries to reach its positioning objectives. Being that Rio Grande Foods is fighting guerrilla warfare tactics, it cannot not afford to launch another product because all of its resources are pushing the Mexican salsa in 1995.

Tactical Objectives for Channel Distribution

Marketing Channels

In 1995, Rio Grande Foods will continue to satisfy its current accounts while continuing to increase its consumer base/distribution. The company will keep servicing its present accounts the same reliable way it has been from the beginning. It will try to increase consumer awareness at the present stores by increasing shelf space. Some success has been seen at the J.E.B. grade "A" grocery stores where shelf space went from four-facings/two cases to eight-facings/four cases. The company will have to continue pushing the product through the marketing channels on a wholesale basis to the targeted segments. There is a great need to prove to the retail customers that the product does move and that it could do even better with increased exposure on the shelf.

Physical Distribution

Tactical Objectives for Physical Distribution

For 1995, the company will continue to service the grade "A" grocery stores through direct store delivery (DSD) methods. The specialty food stores and gift shops will continue to be supplied via UPS. The objective is to have a broad enough distribution to establish an account with UPS so that the $5.00 pick up fee can be eliminated, thus making distribution more cost effective. The company will have to continue pushing the product as explained above so that it can reach a level where an account with UPS can be established. If the company can establish approximately 35 separate accounts this goal can be met. The accounts will have to be staggered carefully for delivery according to demand so that a daily pick up will be possible.

Price

Tactical Pricing Objectives

For 1995, the price on a wholesale basis will remain the same as it was in 1994 ($2.25/unit - $27.00/case). However, there will be price increases in the future years as seen in the situational analysis on table 2. The only thing the company hopes to do is increase volume so that the cost of goods sold can go down allowing more funds to be allocated to the promotional margin. These funds can be used to meet the marketing objectives.

Advertising

Tactical Objectives for Advertising

In 1995, advertising will equal $300.00 due to the low amount of money available. These funds will be used to make consumers notice Rio Grande brand salsa picante in the market place. Funds will be spent on print media only. The company must continue with steady growth of sales so that the margin allocated to advertising can generate the required funds to meet objectives.

Personal Selling

Tactical Objectives for Sales Promotions

The company will continue approaching new customers on the retail level in hopes of meeting growth objectives so that all other factors discussed will fall into place. The company will do this by setting up appointments for presentations to grocery buyers. It is important to only target those consumers listed in its target segments - grade "A" grocery stores, specialty food stores, and gift shops. The company will also continue to sell itself and its product to its present customers in hopes of increasing shelf-facings and shelf-space in the same manner. The company will have to begin compiling a list of potential customers that can be screened for accuracy. Once the list has been narrowed down, the company can begin setting appointments on an efficient schedule so that it is not in conflict with other company operations.

Sales Promotions

Tactical Objectives for Sales Promotions

The company will use allocated promotional funds to conduct samplings and to produce point of purchase advertisements, such as recipes. Samplings can be held on the weekends inside some of the busier stores, between 9:00 a.m. to 11:00 a.m. in the mornings and 4:00 p.m. to 9:00 p.m. in the evenings. At the same time the company can distribute recipes that require Rio Grande Salsa Picante as one of the ingredients. These new food ideas will help stimulate a more frequent use of the product thus increasing consumer consumption while causing the same effect all the way up to higher volume production runs. These recipes can also be used as a point of purchase marketing tool. They have proven more successful at the privately owned specialty food stores and gift shops, because the employees have more time to discuss the products and ideas to customers. This helps to answer any questions and make the customer aware of the recipes. This promotion proved to be successful at Toddie's in downtown Santa Fe, NM, where the recipes were placed on hooks directly below the product for better visibility to the consumer. The company will also offer occasional business to business promotional allowances to retailers in terms of lower wholesale costs. In order for these sales promotions to be feasible, the company will have to maintain sales growth as mentioned above.

CONTROL

Operational Budgets

On table 2, the cost of goods sold will be dropping steadily if growth of 9% per annum can be sustained after account growth has stabilized at the end of the second quarter in 1995 with revenues of $7,500. From that point on to 1998, the 4% inflation rate is taken into consideration along with the 9% annual growth rate, the result is what is seen on Table 2 in the appendices. The expenses margin will remain at 30% because as other expenses are reduced, the advertising margin will grow accordingly. These extra funds will help the company become more recognized through the use of print media as it tries to establish itself in the specialty foods industry as a "price" and "quality leader".

FINANCIAL INFORMATION

Rio Grande Foods Fiscal Year 1994-95

Inventory Order (160 cases @ $1,971.20)	$12.32
Cost per case (12/16 oz.)	$12.32
Cost per unit	$1.03
Cost per label	$0.08
Total Unit Cost	$1.11
Gross Margin	50.81%
Revenue	$2.25
Cost	$1.11
Revenue Per Case	$27.00

	Suggested Retail Price	Rev. Per Case
25%	$3.00	
27%	$3.08	$36.99
30%	$3.21	$38.57
33%	$3.36	$4030
35%	$3.46	$41.54
50%	$4.50	$54.00
Revenue	$2.25	100%
Cost of Goods Sold	$1.11	0.49%
Gross Revenue	$1.14	0.51%
Expenses		
Broker	$0.23	10%
Distributor	$0.00	0%
Other	$0.45	20%
Total Expenses	$0.68	0.3%
Net Profit	$0.47	0.21%
Net Profit per Inventory purchase	$899.20	
Return	$2,870.40	
Turnover	$1,072.00	

Prices adjustments to compensate for inflation through 1998: Year Adjusted Price

Average inflation 4%	1996	$2.34
1994-95 wholesale price $2.25	1997	$2.43
	1998	$2.53

Average Competitor's Price Fiscal Year 1994-95

Inventory Order (160 cases @ $1,840.00)	$11.50
Cost per case (12/16 oz.)	$11.50
Cost per unit	$0.96
Cost per label	$0.08
Total Unit Cost	$1.04
Gross Margin	58.47%
Revenue	$2.50
Cost	$1.11
Revenue Per Case	$30.00

	Suggested Retail Price	Rev. Per Case
25%	$3.33	$40.00
27%	$3.42	$41.10
30%	$3.57	$42.86
33%	$3.73	$44.78
35%	$3.85	$46.15
50%	$5.00	$60.00
Revenue	$2.50	100%
Cost of Goods Sold	$1.04	0.42%
Gross Revenue	$1.46	0.58%

Expenses

Broker	$0.25	10%
Distributor	$0.00	0%
Other	$0.50	20%
Total Expenses	$0.75	0.3%
Net Profit	$0.71	0.28%
Net Profit per Inventory purchase	$1,366.40	
Return	$3,206.40	
Turnover	$473.60	

Price adjustments to compensate for inflation through 1998: Year Adjusted Price

Average inflation 4%	1996	$2.34
1994-95 wholesale price $2.25	1997	$2.43
	1998	$2.53

	1995	%	1996	%	1997	%	1998	%
Revenue	8,100	100	9,098	100	10,219	100	11,478	100
Costs of Goods Sold								
	3,969	49	4,095	45	4,394	43	4,591	40
Gross Profit	4,131	51	5,004	55	5,825	57	6,887	60
Less Expenses								
	2,430	30	2,729	30	3,066	30	3,443	30
Net Profit	1,701	21	2,274	25	2,759	27	3,443	30

Operational Budgets 1995-1998

Graffiti Removal Service

BUSINESS PLAN

GRAFFITI, USA

8100 Los Ablos Blvd.
Boulder City, Nevada, 89700

Written for a graffiti cleaning business, this plan details the research and preparation that are required by both the franchisor and franchisee when opening franchises in a new territory, area, or city.

- EXECUTIVE SUMMARY

- THE CONCEPT

- MARKET ANALYSIS

- MANAGEMENT

- CUSTOMERS

- FORECASTING REVENUE

- UTILIZATION OF FUNDS

- CONCLUSION

- APPENDIX

GRAFFITI REMOVAL SERVICE
BUSINESS PLAN

EXECUTIVE SUMMARY

Graffiti, USA is a sole proprietorship business in formation. Our licensing agreement is with Hodan Enterprises, Incorporated dba Graffiti, USA, Houston, Texas. Our company offers various cleaning and stripping services using modified baking soda under pressure of water or air and a protective wall coating service. The company's primary goal is to establish premier graffiti removal, abrasive cleaning and coatings service in the Boulder City and Las Vegas areas.

To open Graffiti, USA, we are asking for a revolving line of credit of $ 30,000 to purchase capital equipment and a business supplies package including materials, stationery, and incidentals.

The company plans a phased opening beginning with the purchase and outfitting of the service van and the training of key personnel. Then, our marketing efforts will be streamlined to target our carry-over client base and to capture the Boulder City and Las Vegas graffiti removal market. Conceptually, the baking soda cleaning method will be combined with a waterproofing and protective coating service for walls to provide a complete graffiti and grime removal and prevention system.

Our market does not fully exist in these areas yet, but pressure washing and sandblasting customers closely resemble our clients. Applications for our services include graffiti removal, auto and aircraft paint removal, commercial kitchen and industrial plant cleaning, pressure washing or blasting of sidewalks and hotel valet areas, waterproofing residential development walls, and more. Based on our research, and from detailed information from Graffiti, USA in Houston, Texas, we predict this market will reach $ 200,000 or more in sales within the next two years.

Direct competition does not exist for our combined services. Individually, graffiti removal, pressure washing, wall restoration and coating, and soda blasting companies account for over $ 1.3 million dollars in annual sales in Boulder City and the Las Vegas valley. Our ability to remove with baking soda, coat and waterproof with environmentally safe products, and benefit the community by graffiti removal are unique in these areas.

The Graffiti, USA system has been a successful business opportunity for over three years in Houston, Texas. We will tap into their knowledge base and use the unique atmosphere of Nevada to force rapid growth and a competitive edge. Graffiti, USA's versatility and innovation will generate high-volume sales and a rapid return on investment.

THE CONCEPT

The science of graffiti removal can be considered to be in its "grass roots" developmental stage. Certain techniques of removal, such as muriatic acid treatments or "hydroblasting" with sand and water and using hydrochloric acid to clean concrete walkways, are common in Nevada. This old technology is not only ineffective but dangerous.

Product/Service Description

The principal method of operation and revenue generation for Graffiti, USA is abrasive cleaning and paint stripping through graffiti removal and abatement contracts. In theory and method, the systems and procedures offered will not only fill many current voids but will develop an industry altogether. Our combination of unique and effective services will attract statewide publicity, benefit the environment, and place Graffiti, USA in its own niche market.

Graffiti, USA uses the Harly Accustrip soda blaster as the principal means of abrasive cleaning and stripping. Complimenting the blaster is the Wand attachment for the Hydroblaster 3000 psi hot water pressure washer. This battery of soda blasting methods and the graffiti and grime abatement contract, developed by Graffiti, USA over two years ago, is more effective than conventional pressure washing and safer than sandblasting.

Once the cleaning and blasting are finished, Graffiti, USA completes the job by spraying a superficial coating on the application to make subsequent removal faster and significantly less expensive. Graffiti or tagging can be called in, or a long-term abatement contract will guarantee the property to be free of graffiti and grime with minimum participation from the client for a year or more. Under the contract, a weekly patrol is set up for the property and, when required, removal is scheduled and documented. The philosophy of the abatement contract is to be as relentless and determined as the problem, eliminating the high cost of repeated "reactive" removal.

Abatement Contract

In Nevada, the process of maintaining any size property involves heavy watering of the plants and landscaping. Consequently, overwatering, translocation, and effluorescence reach and eventually destroy retaining walls, sidewalks, and other masonry. Protection through coatings and sealants has thus become a $ 300,000.00 annual industry.

Protective Coatings

As part of Graffiti, USA's versatility, we'll use current assets and knowledge to bid and provide waterproofing and protective coatings services under contract. A commonality of equipment and service exists, and minimum training is required for our technicians to perform virtually any coating job.

Graffiti, USA's equipment assets include a powerful Hydroblaster 3000 psi hot or cold water pressure washer which allows for rapid and aggressive cleaning of cement, asphalt, and other applications. Pressure washing and steam cleaning account for nearly $ 500,000.00 in annual sales in the Boulder City and Las Vegas markets and are growing rapidly. Graffiti, USA will use pressure washing as a performance multiplier and to round out our current services.

Pressure Washing

Using the input of the three existing licensees in Texas, net profit margins of 15 to 20% can be expected beginning the first year. Ideally, Graffiti, USA will service the kitchens, schools, common walkways, parking areas, walls, frontages, and other areas of the many hotel/casinos and increasing industrial properties in the Las Vegas and Boulder City areas. In addition, our services will be involved in auto and boat prep and stripping, food plants, construction sub-contracting, and residential property maintenance.

Potential

As two of the fastest growing cities in the nation, both cities' graffiti abatement market, about 30% of our estimated business, is poised for immediate expansion. Versatility, depth of coverage, and focus give Graffiti, USA excellent potential as a money-making opportunity.

For most customers, the Graffiti, USA method of service will pay for itself in terms of a quality clean never before demonstrated or known to be available. Other benefits include the fact that our method won't impact the underlying paint of the application or the substrate, overall abatement costs will be far less than continual removal services because of the superficial coating, and Graffiti, USA technicians will be on the property for less time than the nearest comparable method because of the greater aggressiveness of baking soda blasting. All Graffiti, USA products are safe, benign, and are friendly to the environment, which means no possibility of costly EPA or local fines and restrictions.

Pay Back

Graffiti, USA will be in greater touch with the needs and desires of the community. We promise a strong orientation on product and service improvement to meet the needs and desires of both markets. New products on the drawing board include citrus-based solvents and cleaners, wider bands of baking soda media, and numerous non-chemical coatings and pre-treatments.

Planned Products/ Services

Monthly cash flow from sales will be used to service bank debt. The line of credit will be guaranteed by personal and company assets and receivables. Graffiti, USA will maintain a business checking account through the same institution and provide detailed financial statements on a recurrent basis.

Financial Management

Based on a 40% market share for our service, we estimate our return on investment measured in gross profits to be as high as 250% for the first year. The current indicators show the average monthly sales will involve approximate gross profits of 37% due to the low labor and material costs (cost of sales). Cash flow management, budget, payroll, and job cost control will be closely monitored and balanced.

All Graffiti, USA financial statements, budget, payroll, expenses, and other functions will be handled on computer spreadsheets and text programs. Financial data will be organized on a Lotus-style spreadsheet and contact management, accounting, and collections will utilize the ACT for Windows program. In the future, Graffiti, USA also plans to establish a networking "on-line" database and communication system for faster and more efficient corporate communication.

Estimated Annual Sales

Year 1	$170,000
Year 2	$240,000
Year 3	$270,000
Year 4	$320,000
Year 5	$330,000

Concept for Growth

Graffiti, USA performs all service functions from a full-size van, referred to by the company as a mobile unit. Each complete van system, including the technician and a helper, generates $1,000.00 in daily sales. Service volume/sales increase can reach as high as 80% in just the first two years from multi-shift, multi-crew utilization and the addition of one service van.

We also plan a strong publicity campaign to earn the endorsements and support of the local police, scouting organizations, and community clean-up/awareness groups. Community volunteer work and special projects will earn high-quality free publicity from TV stations, newspapers, awareness groups, and other media.

Position for Growth

•Understand customers, competition and industry.
•Product/service/customer congruency.
•Service versatility.
•Balance people/management/business goals.
•Community orientation.
•Operate at 5 vs. 1 employees.
•Hire the best people.

Other objectives we have set for ourselves include expanding into other western cities as a future regional franchise distributor.

MARKET ANALYSIS

Marketing Concept

Since 1991, Las Vegas has been the fastest growing city in America and the second most popular tourist destination in the U.S., next to Disney World. Construction, tourism, conventions, and population growth in Las Vegas breed some of the most successful companies in America. Companies that bring sound ideas and new or better technology to this market experience minimum competition and high rewards.

Boulder City has also been expanding consistently since 1991, but not at the same rate as Las Vegas. Yet, the market here is untapped. Residential areas, schools and businesses all would benefit from our successful removal systems.

Users of cleaning and pressure washer services in Las Vegas and Boulder City are looking for quality and productivity improvements. The complete lack of development of the pressure washer and steam cleaning industry leaves the door wide open for new and better methods. Graffiti removal is another field that has suffered because of primitive methods and lack of dedicated services in both areas.

Our marketing concept is threefold: show how and why the baking soda blasting technology outcleans pressure washers and scrubbers, explain and sell the concept of a superficial wall coating for easy graffiti removal, and show how and why waterproofing and coating walls adds life and improves their overall appearance.

The overall market for abrasive cleaning is projected to skyrocket by the year 2000. The area of greatest sustained growth in the soda blasting market is in the service of stripping and removing paint and surface coatings from various applications. This could be from automobiles, construction equipment, flooring, roads, structures, or other surfaces. Additionally, removal of fats, oils, and greases (FOG) in food serving and processing and certain construction applications will account for roughly 20-50% of the market.

The major national market segments are:

- Industrial manufacturing plants
- Industrial/commercial/residential properties
- Industrial/commercial kitchens
- Automotive paint and body services
- Graffiti and paint removal
- Construction and demolition

Our own local research shows that there are about 10 - 18 steam cleaning/pressure washing services in Boulder City & Las Vegas, some calling themselves auto detailing services. There are also approximately 4 companies owning soda blasters and providing cleaning and stripping as their primary or peripheral service. The growth potential for soda blasting/graffiti removal specialty companies is high because of greater system reliability, continuity in method, focus, technology improvement, and dedication to the industry.

Business owners, school administrators, hotel engineers, painting contractors, property managers, bar and restaurant owners, and other professionals, polled unofficially, agree that the safe and effective baking soda blasting technology is a viable alternative to their current methods and resources. The growth and existence of large public access and commercial properties in both communities mean a greater market and increased concern for aesthetics, preservation, and cleanliness of walls, floors, machinery, and other assets.

Anticipated local applications include:

•Graffiti removal	30%
•Industrial properties	20%
•Commercial kitchens	15%
•School and commercial properties	15%
•Auto/aviation	10%
•Residential	10%

This segment of the market is generally based on the more effective removal of graffiti and the application of superficial coatings under contract. The vast majority of sales in this category will be handled by "patrolling" client properties weekly and subsequent abatement under long-term contracts. The minority of sales will be through direct on-call channels.

Over the past three years, graffiti removal performances have shown that there is extensive need for improvement. These "competitive" companies have primarily focused on the use of chemicals, sandblasting, power washing, and over-painting to remove the graffiti. The sales potential for a service with a guaranteed removal and abatement package, which is what Graffiti, USA will offer, is approximately 150-300 thousand dollars annually.

This segment is based on the efficiency and effectiveness of blasting with FDA food grade, chemical-free baking soda in industrial applications. The majority of sales in this category will be handled by controlled blasting of kitchens, frontages, and other areas of hotels/casinos, industrial properties, and processing plants. The focus of sales and marketing efforts for these services is the establishment of long-term (1 or more years) contracts. The minority of sales in this segment will be on-call services or unique applications such as large boilers, items or property for repainting, and protective/preservative coatings.

The kitchen or restaurant owner will find greater convenience in soda blasting the parking lot and kitchen areas than the messy and slow pressure washer or elbow grease methods. The baking soda blasting method in the food service environment saves time and man hours and covers more than simple hand cleaning. There is less effort spent under and over the fryer, greater cutting power on cooked-in grease, and the baking soda media carries the fats, oils, and grease away instead of moving it aside (translocation).

School and Commercial Properties

Schools and large commercial property management and development companies have set high property cleanliness standards. Their sidewalks, common areas, and walls are coated and cleaned on a regular basis by subcontractors. We hope to capitalize heavily on our ability to accomplish these cleaning and coating contracts better than their current methods and services.

Auto/Aviation

Several companies in Boulder City & Las Vegas offer auto and/or aircraft stripping, detailing, and painting. Successful companies such as Sunset, Now Auto Paint, and Neil Rawls are currently using acid treatments, hand sanding, and wet sandblasting to prepare and strip the targeted surface. The baking soda blasting method will be marketed to these and other services, providing greater removal capabilities, less taping and preparation, increased user friendliness and safety, and easier clean-up.

Overall Strategy

As part of our package, Graffiti, USA will operate on a multi-shift service rotation. We plan to have the ability to work on regular applications during the daylight hours and provide a "swing" shift to fill the off-hours. The schools, construction, casino, industrial, and other industries will benefit significantly from a flexible multi-shift service operation.

Graffiti, USA will also exploit versatility as a competitive edge and customer benefit. By offering graffiti, grime, and mineral/alkaline removal, repainting, sacrificial, waterproofing, protective coatings and sealants, and concrete/asphalt cleaning, we'll fulfill many needs of our customers under one company name.

Graffiti, USA will advertise as the first dedicated graffiti abatement service company. We'll also be a strong volunteer and sponsor in the community, bringing a much-needed service for "tagged" neighborhoods and quality publicity. Our multi-state orientation as a national franchise will also allow us a sense of corporate affiliation and strength, as well as an open line to the techniques and markets that are hot and expanding nationally.

Marketing our system will be relatively easy. Our most powerful asset is a far greater variety of functions and programs designed around customer needs. We provide a graffiti abatement system, a property cleaning program, and coatings to preserve and extend the life of brick, cement, tile, marble, etc. Graffiti, USA is Nevada's first dedicated graffiti removal specialty service company with a commitment to the community and the environment.

MANAGEMENT

Graffiti, USA, a business opportunity, is sold by Hodan Enterprises, Incorporated of Houston, Texas. Essentially, our Boulder City and Las Vegas operations will be known as licensees of Graffiti, USA, allowing us to use the trademarked name and logo and allowing management unlimited training and assistance from the parent company.

Support Structure

Gerry Evans, President of Graffiti, USA in Houston, Texas, will play a significant role in assisting with marketing, operations, personnel, and virtually every other aspect of operations. Mr. Evans, as co-licensor of Graffiti, USA, will provide invaluable guidance and advise in the early stages of development.

Norm Collins, the Baking Soda, Inc. distributor in Houston and co-founder of Hodan Enterprises, Inc., the licensing entity for Graffiti, USA, will assist in forming, maintaining, and implementing a solid business and financial strategy.

The leadership and organization of Graffiti, USA, Boulder City and Las Vegas, is managed by Steve Rocklin. Together with Gerry Evans, Norm Collins, and the advice and guidance of other Graffiti, USA licensees, the Boulder City and Las Vegas offices will have a strong head start on success.

Our Las Vegas operation will be staffed by a principal manager/salesman, an office person, and a technician. Daily duties place the manager/salesman in a comprehensive mobile marketing capacity. The office person will handle telephone inquiries, manage inventory flow, budgeting, basic accounting, bidding, and other clerical functions. The technician will drive the service van and provide primary on-call and scheduled removals, coatings, and consultations/demonstrations. Through time, the technician will gain the assistance of a "helper" and the office and sales staff will increase as the company grows.

Staffing

The sources of income for Mr. Rocklin leading into and in addition to Graffiti, USA include the Army Reserves and Sunlight Helicopters of Las Vegas. Mr. Rocklin has been a member of the Army Reserves actively for the past fourteen years as a flight officer and intends to maintain this status until eligible for retirement at age 60. Additionally, he has continued his civilian flying career as an on-call pilot for Sunlight Helicopters for the past three years.

Secondary Source of Loan Repayment

Both methods of secondary employment have the potential of becoming full-time employment opportunities with estimated combined earnings of $45,000 annually. If required, these income sources could successfully continue servicing the debt with little adjustment or difficulty.

Monthly Payment Computation

$30,000 over 84 months @ 11% interest = $514.00 mo.
Army Reserve Average Monthly Salary = $660.00 mo.

There is no typical Graffiti, USA customer. The variety of services and capabilities of the product line is limitless. In general, the Graffiti, USA customer base will follow closely to that of the pressure washing/steam cleaning, graffiti removal/masonry services, asbestos and lead-based paint abatement contractors, highway, road, and building service companies, and sub-contractors services, especially painters, pavers and concrete contractors.

CUSTOMERS

The most typical customer for our services is someone who has used cleaning or washing services for their property either on a regular basis or to remedy some immediate situation. It is likely that our future customers are going to be familiar with pressure washing, stripping and steam cleaning and that they will readily accept our new methods and supplemental services.

A test was recently conducted at the local gas utility main offices. The area in question was a brick wall frontage where customers would pass enroute to the service entrance. This area not only served as a 4' high retaining wall for a grassy knoll, but was battered by sprinkler overflow several times a day. As a result of effluorescence and translocation, a rock hard white mineral residue was left on the red brick wall.

Case Study

In an effort to remedy the situation, the facility manager for the multi-million dollar property asked several different contractors to perform a demonstration on a small sample area, with the winner gaining a contract for the entire property. After two years and twelve separate attempts using different methods, the management still had no safe, reliable, cost effective method to clean and restore the wall to its original red brick look.

Then the Hanly Soda Blaster was used on a small area of the wall by the local distributor. The baking soda media not only cut through the alkaline deposits that were previously attempted with other methods but cut rapidly and without any damage to the brick substrate. Blasting an area 10' by 10' took only three minutes compared to twenty minutes with the wet sand blasting technique.

Additionally, the soda blasting method was able to force the media further into the affected pores of the brick, where it pulverized and cleaned the previously inaccessible trapped alkaline and mineral deposits. After cleaning the wall and a thirty-minute drying period the wall was ready to be coated and treated with a protective waterproofing or the graffiti superficial coating.

Needless to say, the property manager was pleased to learn of the effectiveness and speed with which the Hanly safely cleaned the wall. He was also impressed with the limited clean-up involved and the complete absence of acids or chemicals which would have required recovery and proper disposal. Through this demonstration, the Hanly earned the waterproofing company a long-term preventive maintenance contract for all of the gas utility's properties.

Future Customers

The following list combines verbally-committed customers and carry-over clients from preliminary marketing surveys and ongoing feasibility studies. Initial marketing studies were conducted by introducing the Graffiti, USA system through video and on-site demonstrations, product brochures and industry articles and testimony. This list shows those prospects who have issued verbal commitments and permission to perform services and/or render demonstrations pursuant to awarding contracts.

Customer	Application	Contact
University of Boulder City Arena and Bowl	Frontages	Ron Livingston
World Hotel and Theme Park	Frontages and Walls	Trevor Houston
Genie Hotel	Frontages and Walls	Don Alexis
Grovestand Hotel	Frontages and Walls	Tim Johnson
Lancelot Hotel	Frontages, Walls, Kitchens	Marian Brown
Cool Weather Water Park	Walks, Pools and Walls	Steve Hamel
Sands Property Management	Walks and Graffiti	Rachel Enright
Lake Front Marina	Boat Hulls	Joe Canducci
Indian Painting	Graffiti and Paint Prep	Selene Victor
National Beverage Plant	Walks and Prep Areas	Keith Niles
Allen Property Management Group	Walks and Walls	Oliver Holmes
World Resorts	Walks, Walls and Pools	John Holmes

FORECASTING REVENUE

Graffiti, USA's revenue will be based on sales of contract services, on-call services, and peripheral services such as coatings, consultations, and product sales.

Graffiti Removal Pricing

Wand service costs $ 75.00 for the first 10 square feet (minimum), then $ 1.50 each additional foot.

The Maximum Strip costs $ 250.00 for the first 25 square feet (minimum), then $ 1.50 for each additional foot.

Sample graffiti removal bid:

Actual graffiti covered: 40 square feet of a 4000 square foot masonry wall.

Option 1. Wand Removal $=$ $ 75.00
$+ 15 \times $ 1.50$ $=$ $ 22.50

Option 2. Soda coating
$4000 \times $ .40$ $=$ $ 1,600.00

Option 3. Service option: 1 scheduled patrol per week plus any additional call outs for graffiti removal at no additional charge at a rate of $ 150.00 per month.

Option 4. Individual call outs for graffiti removal at a rate of $ 75.00 (minimum) per call out. Includes 25' section, $ 1.50 each additional foot.

First Year

	Month 1	Month 2	Month 3	Month 4	Month 5	Month 6	Semi-Total
Sales	2,200	4,500	8,500	14,000	17,000	19,000	65,200
Cash Sales	500	700	2,100	2,500	2,300	3,000	11,100
Less Rec.	(1,800)	(3,800)	(6,300)	11,250	(15,000)	(16,000)	(31,650)
Plus Collections	0	1,800	3,800	6,300	11,500	15,000	38,400
Less Bad Debts	0	0	0	(300)	(200)	0	(500)
Cash From Sales	500	2,500	5,900	8,500	13,600	18,000	49,000

	Month 7	Month 8	Month 9	Month 10	Month 11	Month 12	Year Total
Sales	21,000	22,000	20,000	18,000	17,000	19,000	182,200
Cash Sales	4,000	3,000	2,000	2,000	1,500	1,800	25,400
Less Rec.	(17,000)	(19,000)	(18,000)	(16,000)	(15,500)	(17,200)	(134,350)
Plus Collections	16,000	17,000	19,000	18,000	15,800	15,300	139,500
Less Bad Debts	(300)	(200)	(300)	(500)	(200)	(200)	(2,200)
Cash From Sales	19,700	19,800	20,700	19,500	17,100	16,900	162,700

Second Year

	Month 1	Month 2	Month 3	Month 4	Month 5	Month 6	Semi-Total
Sales	17,000	17,000	18,000	20,000	22,000	23,000	117,000
Cash Sales	3,000	2,500	3,500	3,000	3,000	3,000	18,000
Less Receivables	(15,000)	(14,500)	(14,500)	(17,000)	(19,000)	(20,000)	(100,000)
Plus Collections	15,000	15,000	14,500	14,500	17,000	19,000	95,000
Less Bad Debts	(300)	(300)	(200)	(300)	(500)	(700)	(2,300)
Cash From Sales	17,700	17,200	17,800	17,200	19,500	21,300	110,700

	Month 7	Month 8	Month 9	Month 10	Month 11	Month 12	Year Total
Sales	22,000	19,000	19,000	20,000	22,500	23,000	242,500
Cash Sales	2,000	2,000	2,000	2,000	2,500	2,000	30,500
Less Rec.	(20,000)	(17,000)	(17,000)	(18,000)	(20,000)	(21,000)	(213,000)
Plus Collections	20,000	20,000	17,000	17,000	18,000	20,000	207,000
Less Bad Debts	(300)	(300)	(500)	(200)	(300)	(500)	(4,400)
Cash From Sales	21,700	21,700	18,500	18,800	20,200	21,500	233,100

Materials include the Hanly Blast Media, the Hanly Hydroflex Media, superficial coatings, and Terminator removal assist treatment, as well as freight costs.

Equipment includes rental of a 250 cfm or greater air compressor and a Hanly Maximum Strip soda blaster.

Equipment maintenance covers the preventive maintenance of the equipment and the van.

Van lease covers the monthly payment of a leased or purchased 1-ton new or used utility van.

Labor is the hourly wage(s) of a technician and helper and, when necessary, an office person.

Vehicle and washer gas are the monthly cost of fuels.

Phone includes the cost of the office phone and a field cellular phone service.

Mailbox is the monthly cost of a PO Box and business license posting fee at a private mailbox service.

Advertising covers a 1" local Yellow Pages ad with three other single listings.

Loan covers repayment of the line of credit.

License/Bond/Insurance covers business licenses, a bid or performance bond when necessary, and general liability/auto/life insurance premiums.

Office supplies combine the costs of business stationery, cards, fax paper, supplies, and processing fees.

Credit purchases are accounts payable on credit for materials and equipment rentals.

Credit payments will be made within 30-day terms covering the preceding calendar month's credit purchases.

Sales and Expenses

Forecast Expenses

Month:	1	2	3	4	5	6	7	8	9	10	11	12	Total
Materials	440	900	1,700	2,800	3,400	3,800	4,200	4,400	4,000	3,600	3,400	3,800	36,440
Equipment	300	500	500	500	1,000	1,000	1,000	1,000	1,000	1,000	1,000	1,000	9,800
Equip. Maint.	20	50	100	100	100	100	100	100	100	100	100	100	1,070
Van Lease	400	400	400	400	400	400	400	400	400	400	400	400	4,800
Labor	0	500	1,000	2,000	2,200	2,500	2,700	2,700	2,700	2,500	2,500	2,500	23,800
Veh gas	150	150	300	300	350	350	350	350	250	250	250	250	3,300
Washer gas	75	100	75	75	75	100	100	100	100	100	100	100	1,100
Phone	250	250	250	250	250	250	250	250	250	250	250	250	3,000
Mailbox	30	30	30	30	30	30	30	30	30	30	30	30	360
Advertising	207	207	207	207	207	207	207	207	207	207	207	207	2,484
Loan	1,000	1,000	1,000	1,000	1,000	1,000	1,000	1,000	1,000	1,000	1,000	1,000	12,000
Lic/Bond/Ins	300	300	300	300	300	300	300	300	300	300	300	300	3,600
Office supplies	50	150	200	200	200	250	250	250	250	200	250	250	2,500
Total	3,222	4,537	6,062	8,162	9,512	10,287	10,887	11,487	11,187	10,337	10,187	10,587	106,454
Less credit prch	(225)	(250)	(375)	(375)	(425)	(450)	(450)	(450)	(350)	(350)	(350)	(350)	(4,400)
Plus credit pymt	0	225	250	375	375	425	450	450	450	350	350	350	4,050
Expenses	2,997	4,512	5,937	8,162	9,462	10,262	10,887	11,487	11,287	10,337	10,187	10,587	**106,104**
Monthly CFS	500	2,500	5,900	8,500	13,600	18,000	19,700	19,800	20,700	19,500	17,100	16,900	**162,700**
Cash Flow	**2,497**	**2,012**	**37**	**338**	**4,138**	**7,738**	**8,813**	**8,313**	**9,413**	**9,163**	**6,913**	**6,313**	**56,596**

Assumptions

Pressure washing jobs are billed competitively for .05 cents per square foot

Hydroblasting (washer and sand pot attachment) is billed at .50 cents per square foot

Superficial coatings are billed at .40 cents per square foot

Wand and Hanly soda blasting are billed at $1.30 per square foot

Labor is calculated at 40 hours a week at $10.00 per technician, beginning in the 5th month

First month includes securing 1 job, second month 2 jobs, thereafter 4 per month

Industry standard of 97% collection of receivables within 30 days

UTILIZATION OF FUNDS

Initial expenditures and purchases cover the equipment and basic supplies and operating capital necessary to support operations for at least four to six months.

Equipment and Supplies Package	$14,000
Used 1-Ton Utility Van	$10,000
Computer and Laser Printer	$ 3,000
Initial Baking Soda Inventory	$ 2,000
Cellular Phone	$ 500
Beeper ·	$ 100
Sub-Total	$29,600
Plus 4 months Operating Costs	$10,000
Total Project Requirement	**$39,600**

Availability of Funds

Provided From Loan	$30,000
Funds Committed by Applicant (= 32%)	$12,600
Total Funds	**$42,600**

Equipment and Supplies

Hydroblaster Pressure Washer	$ 6,000
Airless Paint Sprayer	$ 3,000
Wand System	$ 500
55 Gallons Graffiti Avenger	$ 1,500
55 Gallons Americoat	$ 1,500
Miscellaneous Supplies	$ 1,500
Total	**$14,000**

CONCLUSION

Graffiti, USA is a new and much-needed enterprise in Boulder City and Las Vegas valley. We'll seek a niche market for graffiti removal and abatement, capitalize on service diversity and new baking soda cleaning technology, benefit the community, and be environmentally oriented.

To start Graffiti, USA in Boulder City and Las Vegas, we're asking for a bank line of credit of $30,000.00. These funds will help buy our capital equipment and vehicle assets, and help provide a working capital "buffer" for the first six months of business.

Our profit expectations are the results of a detailed analysis of the two markets and the actual financial reports of Graffiti, USA franchises in Houston. Our first year is expected to produce gross sales of $162,700 with costs of sales and expenses expected to be $106,104 leaving a net profit before interest and taxes of $56,596.

The starting schedule for Graffiti, USA is set for January 1, 1995. Our first two weeks will be occupied by capital equipment and materials acquisitions, training and installation, initial press releases and canvass marketing, and other events.

Graffiti, USA Boulder City and Las Vegas has been carefully researched, planned, and studied. We believe that our efforts and hard work will pay off better than our numbers indicate and will take less time to realize a positive cash flow. We look forward to establishing a long-term business relationship with an institution willing to accept our low risk and strong earning potential.

APPENDIX

Terms and Definitions

Abatement - For the purposes of this plan, this term refers to consistent removal and subsequent elimination of graffiti and alkalinity by a dedicated source or means. Technically speaking, true abatement would be catching the tagger in the act and ultimately arresting him.

Baking Soda Blasting - A process similar in theory and operation to sandblasting whereby a special machine (Hanly Accustrip System and or the Wand pressure washer attachment) is used to meter and distribute baking soda under air or water pressure. Either method uses about 50-100 psi pressure and propels the soda mixture towards the application where it explodes or is pulverized.

Media - A special mixture of baking soda four times the size of normal soda and sold in 50 lb bags by a local distributor. These mixtures include various biodegradable detergents, varying viscosities, or the basic pure mixture. The WAND system uses the Hydro formula and the Accustrip uses Hanly Blast Media. All forms of media are environmentally safe, non-toxic, USDA grade, and emulsify with fats, oils, grease, lead, and other chemicals.

Pressure Washing - Also called steam cleaning (230 degrees F or higher), water jetting, or power washing; any process or system using pressurized water (1000-5000 psi) for cleaning, demolition, paint and grime removal, and other applications. Graffiti, USA will use a 3000 psi hot water (up to 275 degrees F) pressure washer.

Superficial Coating - A safe, non-toxic wall sealer/coating often referred to as a micro-wax, applied by hand sprayer or paint sprayer. The coating is sprayed on a clean or recently blasted surface to form an easily removable barrier between new graffiti and the wall.

Tagger - A person who creates graffiti in any form illegally. Taggers could be considered "artists" because they are known more for their creativity in selecting locations and techniques than their gang affiliation. This is not to say that a gang member is not a tagger, more so it's to say that a tagger is not always a gang member. Taggers can be highly prolific and are often very persistent in a certain territory.

WAND - A pressure washer attachment which uses the Venturi effect to inject media into the water path. It was specifically designed for baking soda media.

Waterproofing - The process by which protective sealants and coatings are applied on cement and masonry to repel water and its harmful effects. All coatings and treatments use clear, environmentally safe, water-based, and non-toxic ingredients.

Ice Cream Shop

BUSINESS PLAN

FRAN'S ICE

Davis Plaza Regional Mall
19 Orchard Avenue
Davis, CA 95616

January 1996

This business plan details a franchise ice cream shop located in a California shopping center. Fran's Ice anticipates continued success due to its superb location, diverse menu, and well-known quality product.

ICE CREAM SHOP
BUSINESS PLAN

INTRODUCTION

The purpose of this business plan is to outline the parameters under which the principals will pursue the construction, development and operation of a franchised Fran's Ice Cream Shoppe in a key location at the mall entrance to the food court of Davis Plaza, a successful, dominant, super regional shopping center in metropolitan Woodland - Sacramento.

Davis Plaza's management company, Martin Richardson and the franchisor, the Fran's Ice Shoppe Company, Inc., are optimistic and enthusiastic about locating a high-volume shop within Davis Plaza.

Martin Richardson, The Fran's Ice Shoppe Company, Inc., and the franchisees, Augustus and Cheryl Dwyer, are all confident that this Fran's shop will be successful among the other national stores already committed to doing business in Davis Plaza.

EXECUTIVE SUMMARY

The Fran's Ice Shoppe of Davis (franchisee), will construct, develop and operate a licensed franchised ice cream dipping shop of The Fran's Ice Shoppe Company, Inc. (franchisor). This single retail dipping shop will sell Fran's ice cream and related products, all manufactured by the franchisor under its name.

Revenue will be primarily from the sale of hand-dipped ice cream and related products consumed within Davis Plaza. Franchisees will also sell ice cream cakes, traditional gourmet cakes, birthday cakes and Cola products. Sales are anticipated to be $360,000 in the first year and to increase at an average annual rate of 4% per year in the first five years of operation.

The franchise will be located in Davis Plaza in Davis, California. Because of its location in the center of the Woodland - Sacramento areas, Davis Plaza serves many communities and is commonly considered the Tri-Cities' premier retail facility. Davis Plaza, which opened in 1968, is a two-level, enclosed regional shopping center containing a total of 1.2 million square feet and 200 stores, shops and food service establishments. The Plaza is anchored by Hank's, B.P.'s, and Westbury's. Fran's Ice Shoppe of Davis will be located in "The Outdoorum" which is Davis Plaza's 40,000 square foot food court containing 17 food service establishments including Cheese Pleese, Beefeaters, and Sweet Dreams.

Franchisee's primary customers will be drawn from Davis Plaza's 1994 trade area population of over 853,000 people, which is projected to reach 940,000 people by 1999. Customers shopping The Plaza will purchase Fran's handdipped ice cream and other products on an impulse basis during their shopping trip, or as a dessert treat upon completing a meal at The Outdoorum. Franchisee also anticipates that many patrons will make the shop their primary destination due to name recognition and product quality. Except for a small Earl's Ice Cream Shop and a Frozen Treat selling soft serve vanilla only, there is no other competition within Davis Plaza, and no outside competition within 2 miles of The Plaza.

The principals will be managing their own shop. Augustus Dwyer will be the hands-on manager for daily operations. Cheryl Dwyer will retain her present position as a nurse clinician for J. Landers, but will assist with her employee management and accounting skills. In addition, approximately six to ten school and/or college students will be hired to work shifts during peak sales periods. Other part-time employees may be hired on an "as needed" basis for special projects such as cake decorating, preparing large orders for caterers and servicing of other special functions.

Project costs are projected to be $250,000 which includes leasehold improvements (buildout of the shop), equipment purchases, opening inventory, and working capital needs. This amount does not include the $35,000 franchise fee, $3500 Fran's grand opening contribution, or $7870 cost of architect's plans for the store which Gus and Cheryl Dwyer have already invested in this business from their own funds. The principals are seeking to finance the remainder of this project through a local lending institution using the assistance of a Small Business Administration (SBA) guarantee, with an agreement that allows for loan repayment over 10 years.

Based on a preliminary timetable it is anticipated that the shop will be operational for business no later than April, 1, 1996.

FACT SHEET

Requested Loan:	$250,000
Cash Invested:	$50,000
Business Type:	Fran's Ice Franchise Ice Cream Shop
Location:	In the food court of Davis Plaza Regional Mall Davis, California
Size:	556 Sq. Ft.
Rent:	$3,487 gross (includes all CAM charges) $6.27/sq. ft.
Projected Sales - Year 1:	$360,000
Sales Break-even:	$295,650
Loan Collateral Available:	$91,000 Equipment Value $30,000 Equity in home $12,000 Opening Inventory
Principals:	Augustus and Cheryl Dwyer 37 Huckleberry Lane Fair Oaks 95628

Other Noteworthy Facts:

- A 2.5 gallon tub of ice cream from Fran's costs $29.00 ($11.60 gal.)
- From a 2.5 gallon tub come 72 4 oz. scoops which sell for from $1.50 to $1.95 a scoop. Therefore a tub will sell for $108 to $140.
- Average ticket for a Fran's shop runs around $2.30.

DESCRIPTION OF THE BUSINESS/ OBJECTIVES

The Fran's Ice Shoppe of Montclair (Shoppe), will be a franchised operation of The Fran's Ice Shoppe Company, Inc. licensed to sell Fran's ice cream and related products. The Fran's name has been associated with the ice cream business since 1961. The Company manufactures a large and growing volume of Fran's products which it distributes through a variety of channels. The ice cream ordinarily is not sold for retail dipping except to franchised dipping shops.

The Franchisor is Connecticut Corporation, with principal offices in New Haven, C.T. The ultimate parent of the company is Drake PLC, a public corporation listed on the London Stock Exchange, via ownership of The Harley Company.

Franchisees have been granted a license to sell certain ice cream products under the Fran's name since 1977, although the franchisor has been conducting a business of the type operated by the franchisee since 1983. Affiliates of the franchisor are actively engaged in various other sectors of the food service industry, including fast service restaurants, theme restaurants, food service supply business, institutional and retail food production, distribution and sales and food commodity transactions.

The main items for sale will be hand dipped ice cream and yogurt cups/cones, sundaes finished with a variety of toppings such as hot fudge, caramel, butterscotch or fruit, banana splits shakes malts, and ice cream sodas and floats. Most of these items will be consumed immediately on the premises. Davis Plaza provides extensive indoor seating for the food court customers.

In addition to hand-dipped ice cream sales, the Shoppe anticipates doing a material business in the sale of both ice cream cakes and gourmet traditional cakes and birthday cakes. These cakes will be displayed for immediate sale at all times during business hours and can also be produced in quantity on a special order basis for caterers and parties. Phenomenal foot traffic in the plaza and employees from the 200 shops in the mall can support a lucrative cake business for the Shoppe.

The goals and objectives of The Fran's Ice Shoppe of Davis are as follows:

"To deliver a quality product in a consistent, courteous and timely manner in order to have the customer return again for another satisfying, flavorsome treat, while at the same time earning a reasonable return on the initial investment"

The principals believe that for an organization to be successful, the organization must ensure that the customer continues to return to purchase the product, again and again. One way to ensure repeat business is to provide consistency in both the product and service. Fran's product speaks for itself; the service our Shoppe provides will be a function of training, evaluation, and retraining in order to deliver it courteously and in a timely manner.

In order to earn a reasonable return on the investment, along with the ability to repay debt, strict cost-control measures will be implemented. These measures will include, among others, proper and prudent purchasing practices, maximization of product distribution through strict adherence to weights, amounts and recipes (portion control), effective utilization of personnel, and the constant search for ways to reduce the cost of sales of our products without sacrificing quality and service.

In summary, the principals are committed to ensuring that this operation is successful.

THE MARKET

The purchase of hand-dipped ice cream and related products is basically an impulse-type purchase by a consumer relating to one of the following stimuli:

- Passing by the Shoppe on the way to another destination,
- Visual contact with the Shoppe's signs,
- Observing someone else consuming one of the Shoppe's products,
- The final course (dessert) after a meal has been consumed elsewhere.

Locating the Shoppe in Davis Plaza gives the business the opportunity to take advantage of all of the above mentioned ways which motivate the consumer to purchase the products offered.

Passing by on the Way to Another Destination

Davis Plaza is comprised of the best known, nationally recognized retail stores and outlets. The unique blend of these operations draws a large cross section of the population to the Plaza to shop for a variety of goods and services. The Fran's Ice Shoppe of Davis will be a 556 square foot store located at the entrance to the food court of the mall. It is on the second level, right across from the main escalators carrying shoppers from the lower to the second level. It is between the main parking structure and B.P.'s, requiring all B.P.'s patrons entering from the main parking structure to pass directly in from of the Shoppe on their way to B.P.'s. The Shoppe is well within walking distance from anywhere in Davis Plaza in five minutes or less. Because of its location, many patrons of the Plaza will pass by the Shoppe on the way to and from another store, making it convenient for an impulse purchase.

Signage is planned for the Shoppe in two locations. Large, colorful neon signs will be located over the dipping cabinets, making them visible from both the food court and from down the mall. Since the Shoppe will be in a corner location, the Shoppe will be visible from several directions in the "I" shaped mall. There is also an opening to below directly in front of the Shoppe, allowing visibility to patrons on the lower level. The location for the Shoppe has the greatest amount of foot traffic in front of it than any other food service in Davis Plaza.

Visual Contact from the Shoppe's Sign

As previously mentioned, the Shop's products more than likely will be consumed on or nearby the premises. The fact that Davis Plaza is enclosed and self-contained will make Fran's products very visible to many shoppers, particularly since all products will be served in containers that display the Fran's logo.

Observing Someone Else Consuming One of the Products

In addition to the tremendous foot traffic generated by the major department stores and numerous nationally renowned shops surrounding The Fran's Ice Shoppe of Davis, the Shoppe is to be located at the entrance to The Outdoorum, the Plaza's food court. The food court houses 17 places to eat. The Shoppe can be seen from anywhere in the food court, making it a likely destination for a dessert treat following a meal for the entire family. The Shoppe will have two 3-foot wide, 4-shelf display cases for cakes. One 3-foot display will be for frozen ice cream cakes, and the other will be refrigerated for display of traditional gourmet cakes and gourmet birthday cakes. The principals believe that tremendous potential exists for the sale of birthday cakes in the Plaza since many gifts are purchased there and no competition exists for these items in the Plaza.

The Final Course (Dessert) After a Meal has been Consumed Elsewhere

An additional marketing strategy of the Shoppe will be sales generated from freezer carts bearing the Fran's logo and colors off site from Davis Plaza. There are many fairs, festivals and parties within the Shoppe's geographic service area (including the Sacramento County Fair, and Renaissance Days) where significant additional sales may be generated on ice cream bars and other novelties. Most importantly, these outside sales will give the Shoppe name recognition which will help make it a primary destination for an expanded segment of the market.

Additional methods of enhancing the Shoppe's name recognition will be local newspaper advertising with coupons, special promotions and discounts to employees of Davis Plaza, companion promotions and discounts with other merchants in the Plaza, and offers to local schools for discounts to students with good grades.

Lastly, additional sales revenue and name recognition for the Shoppe will be generated by sponsoring sports, social, educational and fund-raising activities within the communities served by Davis Plaza. The principals have numerous fund-raising idea and plans for community involvement that will help make the Shoppe a money-maker.

The primary competitors of The Fran's Ice Shoppe of Davis are within the Davis Plaza itself. The principals have done a detailed analysis of the existing ice cream and yogurt shops outside Davis Plaza, and this study is available upon request. The principals believe that the two ice cream and yogurt related businesses inside Davis Plaza are the Shoppe's main competition. They are:

COMPETITIVE ANALYSIS

Located across The Outdoorum from the Shoppe. Frozen Treat does not serve real ice cream at all. They serve only one flavor of soft serve, vanilla. They make cones, cups, sundaes and shakes and, according to Davis Plaza management, enjoyed $550,000 in sales volume in 1994 and approximately the same sales volume in 1995.

Frozen Treat

Located in the Westbury wing of Davis Plaza. This is a small shop with extremely limited visibility. It is not located in The Outdoorum but is on the outskirts of the heavy traffic area of the Plaza.

Earl's Ice Cream and Yogurt

Earl's serves 24 flavors of real ice cream and 2 flavors of frozen yogurt. No cakes are offered for sale. According to Davis Plaza management Earl's enjoyed $303,000 in sales volume in 1994 and approximately the same sales volume in 1995.

The principals believe that there is outstanding potential for the sale of Fran's super premium quality ice cream, yogurt and related products in Davis Plaza. As just noted, in 1994 and 1995 the sales volume generated for ice cream, frozen yogurt and soft serve in Montclair Plaza was $852,000. The Fran's Ice Shoppe of Davis will be located in the most visible food service location in Davis Plaza. The principals feel that Frozen Treat will not hinder the Shoppe's sales because Frozen Treat serves only average quality soft serve vanilla products. The Shoppe will have 32 flavors of the finest quality ice cream and 6 flavors of frozen yogurt and sorbet ready for sale at all times...as well as ice cream cakes, birthday cakes, gourmet traditional cakes by the slice or whole, and shakes, malts, sundaes, ice cream bars, frozen yogurt and sorbet bars, and sodas.

Other ice cream and frozen yogurt stores exist within a three-mile radius of Davis Plaza. There are four small independent stores and three Scoops stores in this three-mile circle. The closest independent to the Plaza is approximately 2 miles away. As stated previously the principals strongly believe that the Shop's main and most important competitors are inside Davis Plaza. The principals also firmly believe that the quality and selection of Fran's products they will offer, coupled with a superior location within the Davis Plaza, will help them achieve the success they anticipate and will work toward. The principals are also actively engaged in negotiations with the landlord to exclude any new competition from The Plaza during the term of their lease.

MANAGEMENT

The principals, themselves, will manage this business. Augustus Dwyer will be the hands-on manager for the daily operation of the Shoppe, assisted by Cheryl Dwyer. Gus Dwyer shall have the following responsibilities and perform the following duties:

- Oversee the design, development and construction of the Shoppe

- Collect competitive bids for the buildout of the Shoppe and for the equipment needed for the Shoppe. Select contractors and equipment suppliers to complete the Shoppe.

- Seek and obtain the necessary financing for this project.

- Attend and successfully complete Fran's Ice Basic Management Training Course # 318 at The Fran's Ice Shoppe Company, Inc. corporate offices in New Haven Connecticut. This is an eleven day training course which will prepare Gus to successfully operate a Fran's ice cream shop. Gus is registered to attend this course from 1-16-96 to 1-26-96.

- Plan, coordinate and execute merchandising and promotion of the Shoppe, including Grand Opening activities, and a year round calendar of holidays, special events and numerous other promotional activities.

- Prepare all products to be sold, sourcing the most cost effective suppliers on goods not purchased from Fran's directly. Maintain adequate levels of inventory, while maximizing inventory turns and losing no sales due to out-of-stocks.

- Ensure that standards of product quality control and shop cleanliness required by the franchisor are maintained on a daily basis.

- Recruit, select, interview and hire all Shoppe personnel.

- Perform orientation, training and re-training of all Shoppe personnel.

- Perform all required accounting functions for the Shoppe.

- Personally make a commitment to give 100% best effort and a personal full-time commitment to operating the Shoppe to its greatest potential. Gus will demonstrate the leadership necessary to operate the Shoppe successfully on a daily basis, and to ensure an acceptable return on the initial investment and repayment of debt.

The principals will designate certain properly trained personnel who will coordinate the activities of the other employees during periods when Augustus Dwyer is not on the premises. Those employees will be trained to make prudent decisions in the absence of Gus Dwyer and to carry out the duties of the Manager on an as-needed basis. In the event of an emergency, the principals can be contacted by phone or paged by remote pager and be on-site within 15 minutes.

Six to eight high school and/or college students will be hired to work at the Shoppe on a part-time basis. There will be no full-time employees of the Shoppe other than management.

PERSONNEL

The principals are developing a program of orientation and training which all Shoppe employees must complete prior to starting work. A written policies and procedures manual will be the foundation for that that training. All Shoppe employees will be trained to perform all customer service, quality control, and cleanliness and sanitation procedures utilized by the Shoppe, and will know exactly what is expected of them as a Fran's Ice Shoppe employee.

The principals have worked for many different supervisors in their 37 years of combined work experience, and have seen many different management techniques and styles. Augustus Dwyer has extensive management experience in both retail and wholesale sales and customer service. Cheryl Dwyer brings to Fran's a wealth of experience as house supervisor in a 205 bed J. Landers Hospital, supervising 60 or more nurses at a time. The combined management experience which the principals have will be an asset to them in training and managing a productive team of Shoppe employees.

The proposed timetable for the project is as follows:

DEVELOPMENT TIMETABLE

Activity	Target Timetable
• Site selection approved by Fran's	May 11, 1995
• Franchise Agreement signed and franchise fee/grand opening contribution paid to Fran's by principals	Nov. 26, 1995
• Submitted lease proposal to Martin Richardson (Davis Plaza management firm)	Nov. 28, 1995
• Received draft lease from attorneys for Martin Richardson and forwarded lease to principals lease attorney, Chip Barker of Burns, Webster, Paquette, Walton, and Weigand	Dec. 20, 1995
• Submit business plan and loan application to financing institution for review and approval of loan request	Jan. 8, 1996
• Receive loan approval from lender and SBA	Jan. 15, 1996
• Receive complete Blueprints and drawings of leasehold improvements for the Shoppe from Lee Freemont Architecture & Design, Detroit, MI	Jan 15, 1995
• Attend and successfully complete all courses offered at Fran's Ice Basic Management Training Course # 318 in New Haven, C.T.	Jan. 16-26, 1996

- Perform competitive bid process for leasehold improvements (buildout of Shoppe), purchase all Shoppe equipment   Jan. 27, 1996

- Award contracts and commence buildout of Shoppe   Feb. 1, 1996

- Grand Opening   April 1, 1996

PRINCIPALS' PROFILES

Augustus Herman Dwyer

A strong, responsible businessman and manager, Augustus Dwyer has over 21 years experience in retailing, wholesaling and customer service Gus' roots are in the grocery industry, where he was employed for 14 years. The first 5 years Gus spent working at store level as a boxboy, grocery clerk, produce clerk, and produce department manager. He was elevated by Division Corporate Personnel who felt that his talents would be best utilized at the division level and promoted to Division Produce and Floral Buyer.

During this 9 year period, Gus' hands-on approach to his work greatly benefitted his company. Gus planned, researched and implemented a program of fresh fruit, soup and salad bars for the company and personally assisted in the set-up of 41 new salad bars divisionwide.

Gus was also responsible for planning the division's floral program and purchased cut flowers and plants for 110 stores for 4 years.

Utilizing his knowledge and experience in the floral trade, Gus now works as National Sales Manager for a flower wholesaling company in San Francisco. He has an outstanding record in high volume sales and increasing sales revenues. He has expanded the customer base, sourced new suppliers, and increased the variety of product his company sells, resulting in a 30% increase in sales since coming on board with the company.

Gus' strengths include the ability to plan, organize, achieve results quickly, and evaluate and implement winning marketing strategies. He has significant influence with other employees and positively motivates his subordinated and peers. He is an experienced buyer, merchandiser, salesman, and customer satisfaction specialist.

Cheryl Lynn Dwyer

An experienced nurse manager, Cheryl's nursing background involves a total of 10 years as a Registered Nurse, all employed with J. Landers. Seven of the years have been dedicated towards the Management Of Medical-Surgical And Maternal Child Health Nursing Services. Accountabilities include yearly performance evaluations of approximately 45 employees and the general supervision of J. Landers Florin on the evening shift of the entire hospital, which averages 120 employees. All problems unresolved are directed to her for her successful resolution and follow-up.

Cheryl is responsible for the successful planning and implementation of the Medical-Surgical Department Quality Management Program, which encompasses directing nurses in data collection, action plans and evaluation on a monthly basis. She has completed a 12 week, total quality management course and participated in two task forces utilizing Total Quality Management (TQM).

Cheryl's strengths include effective organization and leadership abilities and extensive interpersonal skills. Cheryl has seven years experience hiring successful employees, coaching, counseling and motivating them to deliver the best nursing care to J. Landers members.

Note: Please see attached career/work histories of Augustus and Cheryl for details.

Sales Break-Even Point

A common question business owners have when considering new business opportunities is this: "How much do I have to sell just to break even?" In other words, "How much revenue do I need to pay all my expenses?"

The question is not as difficult to answer as it might seem. Only three pieces of information is needed to make the calculation.

- The *average price* of whatever you sell.

- The *average cost* of whatever you sell.

- The total *fixed costs* your have to pay no matter what you sell.

Formula

Breakeven $ amount in Sales   = $\dfrac{\text{Fixed Costs}}{\text{1 - average cost/average price}}$

or to state it another way...

Breakeven $ Amount in Sales   = $\dfrac{\text{Fixed Costs}}{\text{Gross Profit Margin}}$

In the case of The Fran's Ice Shoppe of Davis the Sales break-even is computed as follows:

Breakeven $ Amount in Sales   = $\dfrac{141{,}912}{68\%\,(\text{gross margin}) - 20\%\,(\text{variable payroll expenses})}$

$= \dfrac{141{,}912}{48\%}$ **= $295,650**

Build out of leased space (tenant improvements)	110,000
Equipment Costs	91,000
Architect Plans	7,870
Opening Inventory (product & paper supplies)	12,000
Working Capital & Misc.	30,000
Total	**$250,870**

Summary of Build-Out and Start-Up Costs

Investment by franchisees, Augustus and Cheryl Dwyer

Franchise Fee	35,000
Grand Opening Contribution	3,500
Architect Plans	7,870
Misc. costs, fees and licenses	4,000
Total	**$50,370**

FINANCIAL INFORMATION
Projected Income & Expense

Year 1	Apr	May	Jun	Jul	Aug	Sep	Oct	Nov	Dec	Jan	Feb	Mar		
INCOME Month:	1	2	3	4	5	6	7	8	9	10	11	12	Total	%
Sales														
Ice Cream														
Beverages														
Cakes & Pastries														
Other														
Total Sales	25,213	26,497	29,749	34,679	33,818	32,000	26,000	27,000	44,000	27,044	26,000	28,000	360,000	100
Cost of Goods Sold	8,068	8,479	9,520	11,097	10,822	10,240	8,320	8,640	14,080	8,654	8,620	8,960	115,200	32
Ice Cream														
Beverages														
Cakes & Pastries														
Other														
Labor Cost	5,043	5,299	5,950	6,936	6,764	6,400	5,200	5,400	8,800	5,409	5,200	5,600	72,000	20
Total Cost of Goods	13,111	13,778	15,470	18,033	17,586	16,640	13,520	14,040	22,880	14,063	13,820	14,560	187,200	52
Gross Profit	12,102	12,719	14,279	16,646	16,232	15,360	12,480	12,960	21,120	12,981	12,180	13,440	172,800	48
EXPENSES														
Advertising & H-D Marketing Fee														
	254	254	254	254	254	254	254	254	254	254	254	254	3,048	
Accounting & Legal	420	420	420	420	420	420	420	420	420	420	420	420	5,040	
Auto Expense														
Bank Service Charges														
Contributions														
Depreciation Expense														
Dues & Subscriptions														
Equipment Rental														
Freight Expense														
Insurance	585	585	585	585	585	585	585	585	585	585	585	585	7,020	
Interest Expense (SBA Guar. Loan) (1)														
	1,375	1,375	1,375	1,375	1,375	1,375	1,375	1,375	1,375	1,375	1,375	1,375	16,500	
Licenses & Permits														
Miscellaneous														
Payroll (2)														
Payroll Taxes														
Postage														
Printing & Reproduction														
Rent	3,487	3,487	3,487	3,487	3,487	3,487	3,487	3,487	3,487	3,487	3,487	3,487	41,844	12
Repairs & Maintenance														
Supplies														
Taxes														
Property														
Sales	205	205	205	205	205	205	205	205	205	205	205	205	2,460	
Telephone	100	100	100	100	100	100	100	100	100	100	100	100	1,200	
Travel & Entertainment														
Uniforms														
Utilities	900	900	900	900	900	900	900	900	900	900	900	900	10,800	
Owner Draw	2,500	2,500	2,500	2,500	2,500	2,500	2,500	2,500	2,500	2,500	2,500	2,500	30,000	
Total Expenses	9,826	9,826	9,826	9,826	9,826	9,826	9,826	9,826	9,826	9,826	9,826	9,826	117,912	33
Net Income Before Taxes														
	2,276	2,893	4,453	6,820	6,406	5,534	2,654	3,134	11,294	3,155	2,354	3,614	54,587	15

Notes:

(1) Principal reduction on the SBA loan (in the amount of approx. $24,000 is not shown as an expense on the Inc. & Exp. Statement.

(2) Payroll expenses are listed under "Labor" under cost of goods sold.

Cash Flow Projection - First Year

Income	Apr 1st	May 2nd	Jun 3rd	Jul 4th	Aug 5th	Sep 6th	Oct 7th	Nov 8th	Dec 9th	Jan 10th	Feb 11th	Mar 12th	Total	%
Sales-Cash(1)	25,213	26,497	29,749	34,679	33,818	32,000	26,000	27,000	44,000	27,044	26,000	28,000	360,000	100
Purchases (32%)	8,068	8,479	9,520	11,097	10,822	10,240	8,320	8,640	14,080	8,654	8,320	8,960	115,200	32
Gross Profit	17,145	18,018	20,229	23,582	22,996	21,760	17,680	18,360	29,920	18,390	17,680	19,040	244,800	68
Expenses - Variable														
Payroll Expense (16%)	4,034	4,240	4,760	5,549	5,411	5,120	4,160	4,320	7,040	4,327	4,160	4,480	57,600	16
Payroll Taxes (20% of payroll)	807	848	952	1,110	1,082	1,024	832	864	1,408	865	832	896	11,520	3
Related Fringe Benefits(2)	202	212	238	277	271	256	208	216	352	216	208	224	2,880	1
Sub-total	5,043	5,299	5,950	6,936	6,764	6,400	5,200	5,400	8,800	5,409	5,200	5,600	72,000	20
Expenses - Fixed														
Advertising (includes Mo.H-D Fee)	254	254	254	254	254	254	254	254	254	254	254	254	3,048	1
Accounting & Legal	420	420	420	420	420	420	420	420	420	420	420	420	5,040	1
Rent	3,487	3,487	3,487	3,487	3,487	3,487	3,487	3,487	3,487	3,487	3,487	3,487	41,844	12
Utilities/Telephone	1,000	1,000	1,000	1,000	1,000	1,000	1,000	1,000	1,000	1,000	1,000	1,000	12,000	3
Insurance	585	585	585	585	585	585	585	585	585	585	585	585	7,020	2
Loan Payments(3)	3,375	3,375	3,375	3,375	3,375	3,375	3,375	3,375	3,375	3,375	3,375	3,375	40,500	11
Owner Draw	2,500	2,500	2,500	2,500	2,500	2,500	2,500	2,500	2,500	2,500	2,500	2,500	30,000	8
Sales Tax(4)	205	205	205	205	205	205	205	205	205	205	205	205	2,460	1
Sub-total	11,826	11,826	11,826	11,826	11,826	11,826	11,826	11,826	11,826	11,826	11,826	11,826	141,912	39
Total Cash Paid Out	16,869	17,125	17,776	18,762	18,590	18,226	17,026	17,226	20,626	17,235	17,026	17,426	213,912	59
Monthly Cash Surplus (deficit)	276	893	2,454	4,820	4,407	3,534	654	1,134	9,294	1,155	654	1,614	30,888	9
Beginning Cash(5)	10,000	10,276	11,169	13,622	18,442	22,849	26,383	27,037	28,171	37,465	38,620	39,274		
Cash Flow Monthly	276	893	2,454	4,820	4,407	3,534	654	1,134	9,294	1,155	654	1,614		
Cash Flow Cumulative	10,276	11,169	13,622	18,442	22,849	26,383	27,037	28,171	37,465	38,620	39,274	40,888		

Notes:

(1) Sales figures taken from actual first year revenue figures of the North Point Plaza Fran's Ice Shoppe adjusted down to 81% for size and location and with seasonal adjustment for month of the year. North Point Plaza Fran's Ice Shoppe did $444,176 in sales in the first year. Principals feel that $360,000 (81% of $444,176 = $360,000 rounded) is a conservative figure based on extensive research with four other Fran's locations in malls in California.

(2) Related Fringe Benefits is computed at 5% of payroll expense

(3) $250,000 @10.5% for 10 years (P&I) = $3375/mo.

(4) Food consumed on premises is subject to sales tax. This expense will vary but we assumed a fixed amount each month.

(5) Working capital of $30,000 less $20,000 for pre-opening supplies, expenses, labor, training, etc. = $10,000 beginning cash.

Proforma Balance Sheet

Loan Amount:	$250,000
Term:	10 years
Interest Rate:	10.5%
Payment:	$3,375/mo.

	Capital Contribution	Debit	Credit	Proforma
Assets				
Cash	5,000	25,000		30,000
Prepaid Expenses (Incl. architect Plans)	10,000	12,000		22,000
Grand Opening Contribution	3,500			3,500
Inventory		12,000		21,000
Total Current Assets	**18,500**	**49,000**		**76,500**
Equipment		91,000		91,000
Equipment Installation				
Leasehold Improvements		110,000		110,000
Signage (included in equipment)				
Franchise Fee	35,000			35,000
TOTAL ASSETS	**53,500**	**250,000**		**303,500**
Liabilities & Net Worth				
SBA Loan (Current Portion)			24,000	24,000
Total Current Liabilities				24,000
Long Term Debt (SBA)			226,000	226,000
Total Liabilities			250,000	250,000
Net Worth				**53,500**
Total Liabilities & Net Worth				303,500
Working Capital				$52,500
Net Worth				53,500
Debt to Worth Ratio				4.8 :1
Current Ratio				3:1

ProForma Statements

Years 1-5

Assumptions	Year 1	Year 2	Year 3	Year 4	Year 5
Revenue Rate Increases		4.00%	4.00%	4.00%	4.00%
Volume Increases		4.00%	4.00%	4.00%	4.00%
Inflation Increases		4.00%	4.50%	5.00%	5.50%
Revenue %					
Ice Cream					
Other					
Cost of Sales as % of Revenue					
Ice Cream					
Other					
Direct Expenses as % of Revenues					
Salaries	17.00%	17.00%	17.00%	17.00%	17.00%
Salary Related	3.40%	3.40%	3.40%	3.40%	3.40%
Controllable Expense as % of Revenue	12.00%	12.00%	12.00%	12.00%	12.00%
Interest Rate on Borrowings	10.50%	10.50%	10.50%	10.50%	10.50%

Cash Receipts as % of Revenue	99.50%	99.50%	99.50%	99.50%	99.50%
Lease Expense/Sq. Ft. (incl. CAM chg.)	$6.27	$6.52	$6.78	$7.05	$7.34
Square Footage	556	556	556	556	556
Advertising Fees/Year	3048	3048	3048	3048	3048
Royalty Fees as % of Revenue	2%	2%	2%	2%	2%

Years 1 - 5

Financial Summary

	Year 1	Year 2	Year 3	Year 4	Year 5
Gross Sales (increase 4%/yr)	360,000	374,400	389,376	404,951	421,149
Gross Profit	244,800	254,592	264,776	275,367	286,381
Gross Margin	68%	68%	68%	68%	68%
Expenses	213,912	219,180	226,512	229,733	230,823
Net Profit	25,620	28,080	35,043	44,544	54,749
Net Profit Margin	7.00%	7.50%	9.00%	11.00%	13.00%
Net Cash Flow(1)	30,888				

Notes:

Cash flow based on owner monthly draw of $2500

Equipment Schedule

Item #	Description	Cost from Lowest Bid Vendor
1	16 Can Illuminated Dipping Cabinet	3,208
2	8 Can Illuminated Dipping Cabinet - 2 units	3,950
3	Dipper Well - 4 units	440
4	Upright Pie & Freezer Display Case	5,817
5	Refrigerated Pastry Display Case	4,663
6	27" Fountainette Cabinet	1,731
7	Drop-in Ice Cream Bar Freezer	1,238
8	Single Door Reach-in Freezer	1,903
9	Single Door Reach-in Flash Freezer	3,219
10	Single Door Reach-in Refrigerator	1,593
11	6 X 8 ft - 15 degree Walk-in Freezer	4,310
12	Medium Capacity (1 phase-air cooled) Ice Machine	2,360
13	Soft-serve (3 Phase-AC) Machine w/ Faucet - 2 units	17,360

Dispensing & Topping Units

14	Dip-Coat Warmer - 2 units	242
15	Butterscotch & Fudge Warmet with Pump - 3 units	587
16	Milk Shake Machine	525
17	5-quart Mixer	384
18	Spoon Dispenser - 4 units	33

Sink Units

19	2-Compartment Sink	1,472
20	Counter MTD 2-Comp Hand Sink	295
21	Wall Mounted Hand Sink	252

Beverage Dispensing Equipment

22	Soft Drink Dispenser with Ice Bin (supplied by Coca-Cola at no charge)	0
23	Carbonator with Double Check Valve (supplied by Coca-Cola at no charge)	0
24	Wall Mounted Syrup Pumps (supplied by Coca-Cola at no charge)	0

	Item #	Description	Cost From Lowest Bid Vendor
Equipment Schedule *...continued*			
	25	CO-2 Tanks (supplied by Coca-Cola at not charge	0
	26	Automatic Coffee Maker	472
	27	Coffee Grinder	534
	28	Cup Dispensers - 10 units required	388
	29	Lid Organizer	57

Storage Equipment Units

Item #	Description	Cost
30	6 x 8 Freezer Storage Shelving Set	628
31	18" x 36" Storage Shelf Unit - 4 units required	685
32	18" x 38" Storage Shelf Unit - 4 units required	774
33	42" Overshelves - 2 units required	292
34	Electric Can Opener	47

Sales & Display Equipment

Item #	Description	Cost
35	Cash Register - 2 units required	5,500
36	Menu Board - 1 8-panel unit and 1 4-panel unit required	5,000
37	Quality Statement Panel	90
38	36" x 33" Topping Unit (Cabinet work by gen. contr.-includ. in his quote)	0
39	Dry Topping Bowls with covers - 8 units required	70
40	1/9th S/S Insert Pan - 4 units required	19
41	36" Sneeze Guard Assembly	1,410

Miscellaneous Equipment

Item #	Description	Cost
42	Work Table	797
43	File Cabinet	250
44	7-Person Locker	174
45	Safe	1,000
46	Tackboard	150
47	Mop & Broom Holder	16
48	Acrylic Cone/Bowl Holders - 18 units required various sizes	500
49	Personal Computer, Printer and Software	3,000
50	2 Haagen-Dazs Logo Neon Signs (Incl. freight)	1,250
51	Translites (pictures/ads) for Menu Boards - 12 units incl. freight	750
52	Freight and Sales Tax for Major Equipment Purchased	6,670

Total $86,105

Indoor Playground

BUSINESS PLAN

KID'S WORLD

5568 Inkster Rd.
Livonia, MI 48150

This plan is for a franchised indoor children's playground. The plan provides a good description of possible competitors and the methods that will be used to achieve a competitive advantage in this industry.

- EXECUTIVE SUMMARY

- MISSION AND STRATEGY

- MARKET

- COMPETITIVE ANALYSIS

- PRICING, PROFITABILITY, AND BREAK EVEN

- OPERATIONS

- MANAGEMENT AND STAFFING

- CONTINGENCY PLANNING

- FINANCIAL PROJECTIONS

EXECUTIVE SUMMARY

Market

A market opportunity exists in the Western Detroit area to service children aged 13 and under with a supervised indoor exercise and recreation facility. Market research shows that children often do not get the required amount of exercise to maintain a healthy lifestyle. Indoor playgrounds provide an outlet for active children during inclement weather or when the temperature is too hot or cold for outdoor play. Furthermore, parents want an environment for their children to play without harsh language and an arcade atmosphere.

Proposed Business

Kid's World will provide a safe, clean, and stimulating environment for physically active children aged 13 and under to play in and explore. Kid's World's supervised, visually open play area will ensure children's safety, while challenging them to reach, think, interact, explore, and have fun. The store will require approximately 14,000 square feet, consisting of a giant 5,000 square foot play structure for children over the age of 4, a smaller play area for toddlers under the age of 4, an area with several interactive skill games, a snack bar with seating to accommodate 100 to 125 persons at a time, and a merchandise and souvenir stand. Both play areas have soft indoor playpark equipment with extensive padding and no sharp edges. Furthermore, the game area will not offer video games, pinball-type games or games with a violent theme. For family celebrations, such as birthdays and special occasions, Kid's World will offer private party rooms hosted by trained staff to provide a child everything he/she would want in a birthday - several hours of supervised fun on the play structures, cake and ice cream, prizes, food and beverage, and game tokens. Kid's World desires playtime to be as rewarding for the parents as it is for the children, as they spend time together.

Location

Kid's World will be located in a strip shopping center on the west side of Livonia. Within a twenty-five mile drive from this location, there are at least 49,000 children at or under the age of 14, living in a household with average annual income exceeding $45,000. Furthermore, the Census Bureau expects the communities of Canton, Plymouth and South Lyon to be the fastest growing regions of Wayne and Washtenaw Counties over the next decade.

Management

The business will be operated on a full-time basis by a manager, Alice Cushaw, who has had over 3 years of restaurant management experience. In addition, all member-managers will actively assist in the management of the business on a part-time basis.

Loan Request

The owners are requesting a loan to fund a portion of the start-up costs and inventory. They are also requesting a line of credit in the amount of $500,000. The owners are contributing $35,000 to the business venture and various investors are contributing another $40,000. The money will be needed in equal monthly installments commencing three months prior to opening and will be repaid in a steady manner from available operating cash flows. The loan will be entirely repaid within five years after opening with payments beginning three months after opening.

MISSION AND STRATEGY

Kid's World is a diversified destination family entertainment center combining recreation, entertainment, and restaurant facilities that creates substantial drawing power. Kid's World's basic focus is children's play and fitness for 1 to 13 year old children. At Kid's World, these activities have been packaged into a safe, clean, climate-controlled, supervised environment for children aged 13 and under to exercise and have fun while stimulating their imagination and challenging them physically. The indoor playpark is based on the premise that if you set a large number of children inside a safe, yet challenging, imaginative soft playground area, they are going to have fun. They are also going to develop basic motor skills, social skills, muscle tone, and self-confidence. Furthermore, the parents can enjoy hours of close interaction with their children in a safe, secure, and stimulating environment.

Currently, there are no other indoor children playgrounds in the Western Detroit area. In addition, there are relatively few alternatives for children's birthday parties. Kid's World will be able to immediately fill this void in the market by providing extensive recreation, entertainment, and restaurant facilities for children to play in and explore. Within 1 year, Kid's World will be known as the primary recreation facility for children aged 1 to 13 and the destination of choice for children to enjoy birthday parties with friends. Kid's World's safe, secure, and clean environment will assure parents while providing opportunities for their children to have fun in a stimulating environment.

Kid's World will base its appeal on providing a stimulating indoor environment for children to play in, while adhering to the strictest quality control standards emphasizing excellence in service, safety, security, food quality and value, sanitation, cleanliness, and creativity. Furthermore, Kid's World is dedicated to the continual development of creative themes and interactive designs that have entertainment and educational value that will ensure Kid's World's competitiveness and success in the family entertainment market years into the future.

MARKET

Background

Indoor playgrounds serve an increasing need in our society. Studies show that American children are less active and less fit than they were even five years ago, probably due to increasing time in front of television sets and high calorie-high fat diets. Studies have also shown that less active children are more likely to be overweight, and overweight children have a greater propensity to become overweight adults. As people have become more aware of the healthy aspects of their lifestyles, enrollment in adult health clubs, aerobic exercise, recreational activities, and attention to nutrition has increased dramatically. This trend will continue as parents attempt to provide a healthier lifestyle for their children. Another area of parental concern is their children's safety. Nationally, as well as locally, concern for the physical well-being of children has created a further need for a safe play environment. This concern shows no sign of diminishing.

While it is difficult to determine the size of the indoor playground industry, there are currently about 49 million children 12 years old or younger in the United States and this figure is expected to rise to 51 million by the year 2000, according to the Bureau of Census. There are approximately 26 million households with children younger than 18 years of age, who spend about $1,800 per year on family entertainment or $46 billion annually. Per-capita expenditures on children's activities are likely to rise as families with children spend a larger percentage of their income on recreation. Children aged 4-12 spent, from their own income, $6 billion in 1989, up 41% from 1984. This increase in discretionary income is coming from several factors. First, the increase in dual income families has provided for more discretionary income to be spent on children. Second, women are having children later as evidenced by the rising birth rate among women in their thirties. Third, per-capita family income is increasing and families are choosing to take wealth increases in the form of leisure. Last, grandparents are living longer and spending more on their grandchildren. Based on these demographics, industry analysts believe that there is room for about 600 store locations in primary markets throughout the United States and an additional 200-300 in secondary markets.

The Customer Need and the Target Customer

With the recent concerns over child safety on outdoor playground equipment, many schools have elected to remove their playground equipment entirely. Parents are more aware than ever before over the safety and security of their children's play areas. Consequently, a safe, supervised indoor play area will enable parents to relax while their children enjoy playing in and exploring the soft indoor playpark.

Kid's World will target children aged 13 and under within a 25 minute drive of Western Livonia, comprising about 250,000 people of which at least 49,000 are under the age of 13. Within a five-mile radius of Livonia, census information indicates there are approximately 23,000 children aged 13 and under, living in a household with an average annual income exceeding $55,000. These customers will form Kid's World's primary market base. Kid's World will also target children in the outlying regions of Oakland County.

Product Description

Kid's World is geared for children 13 years old or younger who desire an imaginative, challenging, and fun environment in which to exercise, play, and explore. For safety, children must be accompanied by an adult in order to be admitted and adults are not permitted to enter without a child. Furthermore, each person admitted to the playpark will receive a color-coded wristband identifying him/her with rest of the party. To further promote security, each person's wristband will only be removed when the entire party is present together at the exit desk. Trained staff will supervise the play areas at all times to ensure adherence to the playpark rules while assisting the children to maximize their enjoyment of the facilities.

There will be several play areas within Kid's World; the largest, a 5,000 square foot structure targeting children aged 4 and over, will be comprised of a series of colorful tubes, slides, ball baths, climbing structures, air and water trampolines, obstacle courses, ramps, and stairs. A smaller play area will cater to toddlers and consist of cushions, ramps, a small ball bin, and toys. To encourage active participation by parents, all play areas will have a visually open design with comfortable rest areas in full view of the play structures.

Kid's World will also be equipped with a smaller area of interactive games designed to promote eye and hand coordination. This area will include the "Magic Keyboard", a unique piece of musical play equipment specifically designed for Kid's World. Parents and children can also play several games of skill to win tickets redeemable for prizes. There will also be a snack bar with seating for 100 to 125 customers at a time. It will serve food and beverages that appeal to children and parents such as pizza, hot dogs, salads, sandwiches, popcorn, pop, fruit juice, cappuccino, cake, and ice cream. In addition, Kid's World will have a merchandise counter with small souvenirs emblazoned with the Kid's World logo such as T-shirts, sweaters, and hats.

Kid's World will have six private party rooms and will offer packages for birthdays and other special occasions hosted by staff members, significantly reducing the hassle and mess for parents. The design of the rooms will allow for groups as large as 30 children at a time. For family celebrations, Kid's World will offer three birthday packages for parties of 8 of more, consisting of a two hour limited time of play, birthday cake and ice cream, free game tokens, and, depending on the type of package, pizza or hot dogs, party favors for the guests, and a special gift for the birthday child.

Strategy and Approach to the Market

Kid's World will strive to appeal to value-oriented customers who desire hours of entertainment for their children at reasonable prices. Kid's World will be competitively priced at $4.95 for unlimited play which is comparable to other forms of entertainment. However, the distinguishing feature of Kid's World will be its clean, safe, secure environment for children to play in while parents can either relax or participate in their child's activities.

Advertising

Kid's World will reach its target customers through such advertising media as local newspapers, local television, and direct mail campaigns. Local television advertising has been found to be very effective in reaching the target market segment of children 13 and under, so we will focus our efforts here. The advertising and promotion campaign will be funded through operating cash flows and will build upon the close proximity of the store to the corporate location. In addition, the franchisor will assist its franchisees through regional advertising programs to obtain synergy among all franchisees within the region. Kid's World will initially promote its concept through a Grand Opening advertisement campaign employing an invitation-only free evening for local business and government leaders and their children as well as local radio coverage. The franchisor will assist in the preparation of initial advertising and scheduling of promotions.

Location Characteristics

The nature and location of Kid World's business will support both destination and walk-in shopping. Since the majority of birthday parties are pre-planned events, the exact location of Kid's World with respect to major shopping centers is not as critical as it is in other retail businesses. However, parents shopping with their children may desire an outlet for their children in the form of indoor exercise and recreation. Once customers are aware of Kid's World's location, they will return again and again. Figures from the corporate store indicate an average return rate of seven times per child per year. Our financial forecasts conservatively project 1/3 less. The awareness of our location will develop over several months due to advertising, word of mouth, and simple observation by shoppers in the area.

Kid's World will locate in Livonia on Inkster Road in the Heights Shopping Center. This shopping center consists of two separate buildings totaling 73,480 square feet of rental space and contains both destination and walk-by businesses. The center is primarily focused on providing family related services to the local community. Within three miles of this location, census data indicates there are 9,854 children under the age of 14. Within five miles of this location, census data indicates there are 23,061 children under the age of 14. In addition, there are several elementary schools located in the proximity, a day care center directly behind the shopping center, and many other child-related businesses within a few blocks along Inkster Rd. in either direction.

To better ensure Kid's World's success, the franchisor, Kid's World, Inc., must approve the final location and subject it to their proprietary location requirements.

Weekly Usage Patterns

With 60 to 65% of the costs fixed and only 35 to 40% variable, even small increases in capacity utilization can have a major impact on profitability. With a projected 60% of revenue coming from Friday through Sunday, it will be important to effectively utilize capacity on weekdays. Kid's World will provide the following services to increase customer usage during this period: group discounts to day care centers, churches, community groups, schools, etc., a frequent user card to encourage repeat customer visits, nutritious food to attract health-conscious families, and promoting birthday parties during the week.

Seasonality

The winter months are usually the strongest, and the beginning of spring and the beginning of the school year are usually the weakest periods. On a quarterly basis, Kid's World's best quarter should be the first, followed by the third, second, and fourth quarters. To manage this seasonal variation in customer demand, management will actively monitor weekly sales volume and maintain a flexible staffing arrangement.

Threat of a Fad Product

There is a risk that children may tire of the concept of indoor padded playgrounds. To keep the concept fresh, Kid's World will strive to introduce new play equipment, skill games, and/or new marketing concepts annually. In addition, the franchisor is committed to ongoing research and

Unique Market Characteristics

development in the area of child interaction and stimulation through consultation with staff child psychologists.

Safety/Liability Concerns

To reduce the potential for injuries and lawsuits, Kid's World will employ every means possible to protect children from hurting themselves on the play equipment. Kid's World will only utilize the softest and most extensively-padded equipment in the industry. Furthermore, Kid's World will employ trained staff to continuously monitor each play area and enforce the rules of the playpark. The playpark will be designed to provide parental viewing on all sides and at all times. Parents will also be encouraged to play in the equipment with their children (knee pads will be available for a nominal charge.) In addition, security wristbands will be issued to each person upon entering to ensure the child's safety and prohibit stranger abduction of children. Strict security measures will be observed at all times. Kid's World will carry a $1 million per occurrence liability insurance policy in the event of lawsuit.

COMPETITIVE ANALYSIS

Nature of Competition

Competition in the children's recreation and entertainment industry consists of a highly diverse group of children's activities, including television, libraries, YMCA's, health clubs, parks and other recreation centers, movies, the zoo, and related activities. All of these activities provide for enjoyment by both the parents and the children. However, an indoor playground offers a safe, clean indoor environment for physical activity that is specifically designed for children. It provides children with the security and the skill development opportunities that parents desire.

The indoor playground industry is relatively new. Among the existing players in the indoor playground industry, competition is fragmented. The only company with a strong national presence is Surprise Land, possessing over 250 store locations across the United States, Canada, Mexico, and Europe. A significant threat also exists from Connell Corporation, which has started an indoor playground concept of its own, Jungle Play. Although Jungle Play is still in a testing phase, Connell's has the resources and experience to expand its concept rapidly. In addition, there are numerous regional players with fewer than 10 stores across the nation, although relatively few of them are actively seeking franchisees.

Presently, there are no indoor children's playgrounds operating in the Livonia area. Within a 25 minute drive from Livonia are the following primary competitors to Kid's World:

Competitor	Major Strength	Major Weakness
Captain Sam's Pizza	Video games	Restaurant focus
Surprise Land	Large play structure	Congested/chaotic
Jungle Play	Name recognition	—
Kidville	Separate toddler area	—

Competitive Advantage

After reviewing the characteristics and environment of each of the above competitors, we believe that Kid's World offers several advantages over the existing competitors. First, Kid's World offers the lowest admission price, charging $4.95 per child, of any establishment dedicated to providing an extensive indoor playground. Second, Kid's World encourages parents to participate in their children's recreational activities through a careful layout of the playpark which ensures high-visibility of the play areas and close proximity for the parents. Third, Kid's World is the only indoor playground operator that provides such unique play equipment as the Magic Keyboard, an air mattress, and games of skill that are specifically designed to promote child development. Fourth, Kid's World goes to extra lengths to ensure the safety and security of the environment by providing such extras as CPR certification for all employees of a certain level, video monitors of the entire playpark, and strictly controlling the entrances and exits to Kid's World. Last, with the corporate Kid's World location being so close to Michigan, name recognition should be high, as many of the potential customers have already been to the existing Kid's World location.

The following section briefly discusses each competitor's market position, strategy, and unique operating characteristics.

Captain Sam's

Captain Sam's primary focus is on an extensive array of video games, mini-rides, interactive skill games, a puppet show, and food. Although it has a small playpark area for toddlers, Captain Sam's is primarily dedicated to food service and games. Consequently, it serves as a destination business for pre-planned visits, centered around its food service for family outings and birthday parties. It is an open layout with more windows than other children's entertainment centers and has the atmosphere of a large noisy cafeteria. It charges no entry fee, but maintains high prices for its pizza, ice cream, and beverages. Catering more to parents, the Ypsilanti location allows smoking and serves alcoholic beverages along with pizza, hot dogs, and nachos. It does not instill a sense of security for the parents, nor does it provide the challenging and stimulating environment that children desire.

Surprise Land

With over 250 fun centers in operation as of April 1994, Surprise Land is the largest operator of indoor playgrounds for children. The company was founded in 1990 and began its early growth through franchising. In 1993, Reeves Entertainment acquired 20.1% of Surprise Land's shares with an option to purchase additional shares up to a 51% interest in the company. In order to sustain market leadership and pre-empt competitive threats, Surprise Land has adopted an aggressive expansion campaign with the goal of securing what they feel are the best locations across the country. Specifically, Surprise Land plans on opening 90-100 domestic fun centers a year and franchisees are expected to open another 100 in 1994, the majority of which will be opened by Reeves Entertainment. At this rate, they will have an estimated 360-400 stores by the end of this year and 600 by 1996. This rapid expansion is evidence of the acceptance of this concept by both children and adults. To complete this aggressive plan, Surprise Land has adopted a regional organizational structure and invested in systems to operate and maintain a chain with hundreds of stores in many markets.

In October, 1993, Surprise Land entered the Detroit market by opening its first store location in Warren (east side of Detroit), followed by additional locations in Taylor (downriver area), Plymouth (western suburb), Farmington Hills (northern suburb). Surprise Land has future plans for an additional locations in the metro-Detroit area, including Troy, Novi, and Ann Arbor. In addition, Surprise Land is planning to locate in such outstate areas as Flint, Lansing, Traverse City and Saginaw.

Surprise Land is similar in concept to Kid's World in that it provides a controlled environment for children to play in and explore with their parents. It consists of the Menster-Zone, a 3,000 to 4,000 square foot play area for children aged 4 to 12, the Tiny-Zone, a smaller play area for toddlers, an area of interactive skill games, five or six party rooms, and a snack bar serving foods such as pizza, hot dogs, popcorn, and ice cream. In addition, Surprise Land provides a quiet room for parents who wish to let their children enjoy the play areas unattended.

The primary difference between Surprise Land and Kid's World is the emphasis on a safe, clean, secure atmosphere as well as the level of encouraged interaction between child and parent. While Surprise Land promotes the safety and security aspects of its play areas, it's easier for children to leave the premises unnoticed and it allows adults to tour the facilities unescorted. Furthermore, the snack bar seating is usually located in the center of the play space, leading to sticky floors, congested walkways, and visible food wrappers next to trash dispensers in every interior corner of the playpark. The play structure at Surprise Land is contained in a smaller area than Kid's World and is typically placed in a corner of the facility. This can lead to heavy congestion in the play area during peak hours, a restriction of airflow throughout the playpark, and a general lack of incentive for parents to interact with their children. Kid's World's play structure is located in the center of the room with benches provided on the walls surrounding the structure, promoting visibility at all times by the parents and staff monitors and encouraging parent/child interaction.

Jungle Play

A subsidiary of Connell Corporation, Jungle Play started in 1991 and has since grown to approximately 40 locations nationwide. Connell's plans for Jungle Play include a steady but cautious introduction of new stores located primarily in major market areas. In the Detroit area, Jungle Play outlets are located in Southfield, Dearborn Heights, and Redford Township. Connell's usually builds free-standing structures on land located adjacent to major shopping malls. Therefore, it is likely that Jungle Play may be looking at the available real estate on the exterior of Novi Mall for future expansion. If Jungle Play were to locate in Novi they could represent formidable competition for Kid's World. However, the strong demographics of this area suggest that it could support 3 or more children's indoor play facilities.

Jungle Play is similar in concept to Kid's World and Surprise Land in that it provides a safe, secure, clean, and stimulating environment for children to play in. Jungle Play is somewhat larger in size than Kid's World. Unlike Surprise Land, Jungle Play's play structure is designed to promote parent/child interaction. Jungle Play is particularly adept at providing birthday services by including such extras as a name board to alert all customers of the day's birthday children, a cart for transporting birthday gifts, and extremely friendly and courteous staff. Jungle Play obtains additional business by giving discounts during non-peak hours, allowing groups to rent the facility after-hours, and promoting such activities as overnight lock-ins, fund raisers, and school field-trips.

Kidville

Kidville opened its first and only location this past March in Garden City and has since expressed interest in franchising its concept. Similar in size and appearance to Surprise Land, Kidville offers a multi-level play-park complete with treeforts and slides for children over 4 and a separate play area for children under the age of 4. It is similar in concept to Surprise Land, Jungle Play, and Kid's World, but it does not represent a formidable threat since it has not yet decided to expand via franchising or additional corporate locations.

**PRICING,
PROFITABILITY,
AND BREAK
EVEN**

Kid's World will derive its sales revenues from admissions, games of skill, restaurant/snack bar operations, birthday party packages, and gift shop and souvenir sales. A detailed description of each component of revenue is provided below.

Admissions/Games

Admission fees will be $4.95 per child (ages 1-17) which includes unlimited play in all of the play areas. Adults will be admitted free of charge and encouraged to play in the play areas with their children. This price compares favorably to other forms of family entertainment such as movies where both adults and children must pay admission. The goal of Kid's World is for a visit to the playpark to become a regular family event. Reflecting this goal, a frequent user card will enable a customer to receive discounts off future admissions to Kid's World after a specified number of paid admissions to the playpark. Statistics from the corporate location show the average child returning seven times per year. In addition, Kid's World will offer group discounts for groups of 12 or more at $3.95 per person to encourage day care centers, youth group activities, and summer camps to visit the playpark. For larger groups of 30 or more children, Kid's World offers a special package at $5.00 per child that includes unlimited play in the playpark, two game tokens per child, a slice of pizza or a hot dog, and a beverage.

Snack Bar

The 125 person capacity snack bar will offer food products that appeal to both children and parents alike. It will offer traditional children's favorites such as pizza, hot dogs, and popcorn as shown below on a sample menu:

Traditional Pizza

10" Small Pizza with 1 Item	$4.99
14" Large Pizza with 1 Item	$7.99

Pan Pizza

18" by 12" Pan Pizza with 1 Item	$9.99

Specials

#1: 2 Small 10" Pizzas with 1 Item and 2 Large Beverages	$10.99
#2: 1 18" by 12" Party Pan Pizza with 1 Item and	
2 Large Beverages	$11.49
#3: 2 Large 14" Pizzas with 1 Item and 4 Large Beverages	$16.99

Salads

Garden Salad	$2.50
Chef Salad	$3.00

Miscellaneous

Hot Dogs	$1.30
Popcorn	$0.50
Chips	$0.70
Ice Cream Bars	$0.70

Beverages

Pepsi Products, Root Beer, Fruit Punch, Lemonade, Milk, Juice, Coffee, Cappuccino

Birthday Party Packages

For family celebrations Kid Kingdom will offer three birthday packages for parties of 8 of more, consisting of a two hour limited time of play, birthday cake and ice cream, free game tokens, and, depending on the type of package, pizza or hot dogs and a special gift for the birthday child. The three birthday packages offered include the following:

é Regal Celebration

    $7.95 per child

    Three game tokens per child

    Invitations/Balloons

    Nine-inch double layer cake

    Pop/punch

    Ice cream

é Supreme Celebration

    $8.95 per child

    Three game tokens per child

    Invitations/Balloons

    Half-sheet cake

    Pop/punch

    Ice cream

    Pizza or hot dogs

    Special Kid Kingdom gift for the birthday child

é *Supreme "Theme" Celebration*
$10.95-$12.95 per child
Includes all items in Supreme Celebration, plus:
Special theme gifts for all children in the party
Custom decorated half-sheet cake

Gift Shop/Souvenirs

The gift shop will contain various souvenir merchandise available for sale such as T-shirts, hats, sweaters, and wristbands with the Kid Kingdom logo. The gift shop will also provide various prizes and gifts for children to redeem with tickets received from completing the games of skill.

Projected Revenue Breakdown

Source	Revenue	% of Total
Admissions	279,002	28%
Games	225,456	23%
Snack Bar	300,608	30%
Birthday Parties	131,240	14%
Gifts/Souvenirs	39,455	4%
Misc.	10,800	1%
Total Revenue	$986,561	100%
	or $82,213/month	

Break-Even Analysis

Projected fixed costs for an average month include the following:

Rent	8,750
Utilities	2,083
Insurance	1,400
Maintenance	2,060
Taxes	1,458
Depreciation	6,700
Advertising	3,335
Interest	1,000
Salaries	24,133
Total Fixed Costs	$50,919

Hence, at a projected gross margin of 78% (contribution margin of 83% less franchise fees of 5% of sales) monthly break-even volume is:

$$\$50,919/.78 = \$65,281 \text{ or } 4,340 \text{ visits per month}$$

Per the attached financial projections, break-even is projected to be achieved at a monthly revenue level of $65,281. Given our revenue forecasts of $82,213 per month, it appears that we will be able to exceed break-even revenue levels at significantly less volume. Competitive assessment suggests that indoor playgrounds of comparable size and scope typically exceed the break-even monthly sales level within the first month after opening.

OPERATIONS

Hours of Operation

Initially, store operating hours will be from 10 AM to 9 PM Monday through Thursday, 10 AM to 10 PM Friday and Saturday, and 12 PM to 6 PM on Sunday.

Vendor	Item	**Sources of Inputs**
ParkPlay, Inc.	Playpark equipment/toddler equipment	
Simmons, Inc.	Playpark equipment	
Nisco, Inc.	Gaming equipment	
Liveball, Inc.	Gaming equipment	
Springwall, Inc.	Gaming equipment	
Lyons & Associates	Magic Keyboard	
Okemos Food Equipment Co.	Restaurant equipment, furniture, party rooms	
Symtec	Restaurant supplies (includes pizza ingredients)	
Best Cola	Soft drinks, punches, juices	
Livewire Computers	Computer software package	
TNB	Computer hardware	

Costs

Projected Initial Investment

Equipment	397,000
Leasehold Improvements	30,000
Lease—first month's rent	8,750
Lease—security deposit	8,750
Insurance (6 mos.)	7,500
Legal/accounting fees	2,000
Licenses and permits	1,500
Training	2,500
Architect	3,500
Uniforms	1,500
Misc. (unanticipated)	14,000
Subtotal	$475,000
Franchise fee	30,000
Inventory	7,500
Working Capital	50,000
Total Initial Investment	$564,500

Rent

Description of Cost Items

We have identified a prospective rental location of 14,000 square feet and have negotiated a ten-year lease with one ten-year optional extension. The rental payment schedule is as follows:

Years 1 & 2: $7.50/sq.ft.	**Year 3:** $8.00/sq.ft.
Years 4 & 5: $8.50/sq.ft.	**Years 6 & 7:** $9.00/sq.ft.
Year 8: $9.50/sq.ft.	**Years 9 & 10:** $10.00/sq.ft.

The terms of this lease call for a one month's rent security deposit. Per agreement with the prospective landlord, our first ninety days of occupancy will be free of rent. We anticipate the first thirty days of that period will be devoted to equipment set-up and staff training, hence we estimate approximately sixty days after opening as the date the first rental payment will be due. The lease does not contain a percentage rent clause based on achievement of certain sales levels.

Leasehold Improvements

The majority of leasehold improvements will be completed by the landlord prior to our occupancy. These include painted outer walls, carpeted and/or tiled flooring, acoustical tile drop ceiling with recessed flourescent lighting, two restrooms, and a manager's office. Items we have budgeted for include: party room construction (estimated by landlord at $10,000), signage - an exterior facade sign, an interior neon sign, and an exterior sign for the shopping center's pylon sign (estimated at $15,000), front entry desk and counter-tops (estimated by franchisor at $9,000), and wall decorations, decorative lighting, party room decoration, storage room shelving and lockers, workshop/game repair room, and miscellaneous items (total budget of $11,000).

Fixtures and Equipment

In addition to the leasehold improvements, we have budgeted $50,000 for restaurant fixtures and furnishings. These include pizza ovens, refrigeration units, beverage dispensers, sinks, counter-tops, tables and bench seats, and storage shelving. The two most significant equipment expenditures are the main playpark structure (including the toddler play structure) and the various games of skill. The total cost of the playpark structure has been budgeted at $220,000 and depends on many factors, including its overall size, configuration, and complexity. The franchisor has developed several playpark layouts to accomodate the unique characteristics of our rental space. Preliminary estimates from two indoor playground manufacturers have been in the range of $175,000 - $200,000 for the entire playpark structure. Typically, 50% of the total purchase price is due upon ordering the equipment and the remaining 50% is due upon shipment. Lead-time for playpark equipment has been estimated at 7-8 weeks. The total cost of the games of skill has been budgeted at $75,000. The franchisor has developed an extensive list of pre-approved games of skill to select from, most individual games priced between $2,000 and $5,000 each. Most game equipment companies also require 50% down when ordering and the remaining 50% upon shipment with an estimated lead-time of 4-6 weeks. We have also budgeted $15,000 for computer hardware, $5,000 for the franchisor's software programs, and $5,000 for miscellaneous office equipment, such as a copy machine, fax machine, public address system, and telephones.

Depreciable Total and Method

The depreciable costs listed above are summarized as follows:

Depreciable Cost	Cost	Length
Play Equipment	220,000	5 years
Restaurant Equipment	50,000	7 years
Leasehold Improvements	30,000	31 1/2 years
Office/Computer Equipment	27,000	5 years
Games	75,000	7 years
Furniture/Signs/Misc.	25,000	7 years
	$427,000	

These capital expenditures will be depreciated using the Modified Accelerated Costs Recovery System (MACRS) over various lengths depending on the useful lifes of the assets as mentioned above.

Utilities

Utilities include electricity, gas, and water/sewer. Our estimates of electricity, gas, and water/sewer costs (based on franchisor estimates and contact with Detroit Edison, MichCon, and the City water department), suggest annual utilities will cost approximately $25,000.

Insurance

Kids World will carry extensive insurance policies protecting it in the event of lawsuit. The insurance policies carried include: $1,000,000 per incident premises liability insurance covering bodily injury, property damage, and non-owned autos; $1,000,000 product liability insurance coverage; 100% replacement coverage on building contents and leasehold improvements; three month business interruption insurance, and worker's compensation insurance as required by law. These insurance policies have been estimated at $15,000 on an annual basis.

Inventory

Inventory will consist of redemption items, game tokens, tickets, identification bracelets, paper products, food ingredients, restaurant supplies, and gift shop sale items. The budgeted initial investment in inventory is $7,500 based on franchisor estimates.

Working Capital

Based on franchisor estimates, Kid's World will require $50,000 of available cash, line of credit, or other liquid reserves to cover operating expenses for wages, utilities, rent, and similar expenses.

The business will be organized as a partnership under the name of Kid's World. Thomas Jones and Alice Cushaw will serve as Registered Agents.

Employee	Monday-Thursday 10AM-6PM/5-9PM		Friday 10AM-6PM/6-10PM		Saturday 10AM-6PM/5-10PM		Sunday 12-6PM
Mgr-owner	as needed	1	as needed	1	1	1	1
Mgr-employee	1		1		1		1
Ass't Mgr	1	1	1	1	1	1	1
Party Coord	1	1	1	1	1	1	1
Restaurant Staff	2	2	2	4	4	4	4
Play Monitors	2	2	2	3	3	3	3
Front Desk	1	2	2	2	3	3	3
Misc.	0	0	0	1	1	1	1
Total	**8**	**9**	**9**	**13**	**15**	**14**	**15**

In the event Kid's World's acceptance is slower than anticipated, expenses can be reduced as follows:

Certain games and planned playpark additions can be leased, reducing up-front cash expenditures by $20,000 - $50,000.

The Secretary position can be eliminated and its job responsibilities performed by the two Assistant Managers. This can reduce salary expenditures by $20,000 annually.

Since the majority of Kid's World's employees are part-time and only scheduled to work up to two weeks in advance, the employment level can quickly and easily be adjusted to operating conditions.

Management fees can be reduced or eliminated entirely, as the member-managers do not depend on the business as their main source of income. This can reduce expenditures by up to 5.0% of sales, or up to $50,000.

These savings can significantly reduce operating expenses in the event of unforseen circumstances, lowering the break-even volume of the store.

Business Organization

MANAGEMENT AND STAFFING

Staffing Plan

CONTINGENCY PLANNING

FINANCIAL PROJECTIONS

Projected Revenue Buildup

Market Size

Region	Miles from store	Population aged 0-13	Avg household income
A	5	23,061	$55,000
B	10	38,869	$52,748
C	25	49,121	$45,861

Projected Market Penetration

Miles from store	Market penetration	No. of initial visits	Percentage returning	No. of return trips (7x per child)
0-5	30%	6,918	67%	32,447
5-10	25%	3,952	67%	18,535
10-25	15%	1,538	50%	5,382
Total		**12,408**		**56,364**

Projected Revenues by Source

		Revenues	Percent of Revenues

Admissions

Number of visits per year	56,364		
Average admission revenue per visitor	$4.95		
Total admission revenue		$279,002	28%

Games

Number of visits per year	56,364		
Average game revenue per visitor	$4.00		
Total game revenue		$225,456	23%

Food

Number of visits (children) per year	56,364		
Average number of children per parent	3		
Percentage of total visitors purchasing food	80%		
Total number of visitors purchasing food	60,122		
Average food revenue per visitor	$5.00		
Total food revenue		$300,608	30%

Birthday Parties

Regal Celebration Package

Number of parties per year	800		
Average number of children per party	12		
Average revenue per party	$95.40		
Total Regal Celebration revenues	$76,320		

Supreme Celebration Package

Number of parties per year	400		
Average number of children per party	10		
Average revenue per party	$89.50		
Total Supreme Celebration revenues	$35,800		

Supreme Theme Celebration Package

Number of parties per year	200		
Average number of children per party	8		
Average revenue per party	$95.60		
Total Supreme Theme revenues	$19,120		
Total party revenue		$131,240	13%

Gift/Souvenier Shop

Number of visits per year	56,364		
Percentage of visitors purchasing souveniers	5%		
Average souvenier revenue per visitor	$14.00		
Total gift/souvenier revenue		$39,455	4%

Special Events, Sleep Overs, etc.

Number of events per year	36		
Average number of children per event	30		
Average revenue per visitor	$10.00		
Total special events revenue		$10,800	1%

Total Projected Annual Revenues		**$986,561**	**100%**

Leasehold improvements			$30,000
Lease: first month's rent (two months free)			$8,750
Square footage	14,000		
Cost/sq.ft.	$7.50		
Lease: security deposit			$8,750

Projected Start-up Costs

Equipment

Play structure	$220,000	
Games	$75,000	
Furniture and fixtures	$10,000	
Restaurant equipment	$50,000	
Signs	$15,000	
Computer hardware	$15,000	
Computer software	$5,000	
Telephone system	$2,000	
Misc. office equipment	$5,000	
Total Equipment		$397,000

Other start-up costs

Franchise fee	$30,000
Insurance (6 mos.)	$7,500
Licenses and permits	$1,500
Training costs	$2,500
Architect	$3,500
Legal and accounting fees	$2,000
Uniforms	$1,500
Inventory	$7,500
Working Capital	$50,000
Misc. (unanticipated costs)	$14,000

Total Initial Investment	**$564,500**

Full-time employees

Projected Salary and Wage Expense

	Number	Annual Salary	Total
Manager	1	$32,000	$32,000
Assistant Managers	2	$20,000	$40,000
Secretary	1	$20,000	$20,000
Total full-time	4		$92,000

Part-time employees

	Number	Average Rate/hr	Average Hrs/wk	Total
Restaurant workers	12	$5.00	20	$62,400
Monitors	12	$5.00	20	$62,400
Front desk	10	$5.00	20	$52,000
Misc.	4	$5.00	20	$20,800
Total part-time	34			$197,600
Total	**38**			**$289,600**

Management Fee Schedule

Net Income before Management Fee			Management Fee as % of Sales
$0	-	$50,000	0.0%
$50,000	-	$100,000	2.0%
$100,000	-	$150,000	4.0%
$150,000	+		5.0%

Projected Capital Contributions by Source

	Amount	Percentage
Equity		
Contribution of Owners	$200,000	
Contribution of Investors	$200,000	
Total Equity	$400,000	70.9%
Debt		
Bank Loan - 5 yr. term	$114,500	
Line of Credit	$50,000	
Total Debt	$164,500	29.1%
Total Initial Investment	$564,500	

Debt - Equity Ratio: **41.1%**

Proforma Income Statement - by year

	Year 1	Year 2	Year 3	Year 4	Year 5	Assumptions
Net Sales	$986,561	$1,035,889	$1,087,683	$1,142,067	$1,199,171	5.0% sales growth
Cost of goods sold	137,033	143,885	151,079	158,633	166,565	13.9% of sales
Gross Profit	$849,527	$892,004	$936,604	$983,434	$1,032,606	
Operating Expenses						
Rent	87,500	105,000	112,000	119,000	119,000	per lease
Utilities	25,000	25,750	26,523	27,318	28,138	3.0% inflation
Repairs and maintenance	20,833	22,660	23,340	24,040	24,761	3.0% inflation
General taxes	17,500	21,630	22,279	22,947	23,636	3.0% inflation
Telephone expense	10,000	10,300	10,609	10,927	11,255	3.0% inflation
Salaries and wages	289,600	298,288	307,237	316,454	325,947	3.0% wage growth
Insurance - general	17,333	18,334	18,884	19,451	20,034	3.0% inflation
Insurance - health	1,800	1,800	1,800	1,800	1,800	manager only
Permits and licenses	1,500	0	0	0	0	one-time expense
Bank service charge	1,424	1,424	1,424	1,424	1,424	ongoing
Legal and accounting	8,000	4,000	4,000	4,000	4,000	ongoing
Depreciation	85,400	85,400	95,400	95,400	109,400	SL 5 yrs
Amortization	3,000	3,000	3,000	3,000	3,000	amort 10 yrs
Office expense	9,866	10,359	10,877	11,421	11,992	1.0% of sales
Supplies	58,207	61,117	64,173	67,382	70,751	5.9% of sales
Franchise fees	49,328	51,794	54,384	57,103	59,959	5.0% of sales
Training	2,500	2,500	2,500	2,500	2,500	ongoing
Security and alarm expense	280	280	280	280	280	ongoing
Bad checks	1,000	1,000	1,000	1,000	1,000	$1,000 allowance
Payroll taxes	28,960	29,829	30,724	31,645	32,595	10.0% of salary
Sales tax expense	20,404	21,424	22,495	23,620	24,801	food sales
Operating supplies	19,731	20,718	21,754	22,841	23,983	2.0% of sales
Advertising	39,731	40,718	41,754	42,841	43,983	2.0% of sales + regional
Entertainment, promotion and meals	400	0	0	0	0	one-time expense
Michigan single business tax	392	392	392	392	392	provision
Interest expense	7,312	8,214	6,309	4,225	1,946	9.0% interest rate
Management fees	0	0	21,754	22,841	23,983	per schedule
Total Operating Expense	$807,001	$845,931	$904,890	$933,853	$970,560	
Net Income	$42,526	$46,073	$31,714	$49,581	$62,046	

Proforma Balance Sheet - by year

	Opening	Year 1	Year 2	Year 3	Year 4	Year 5	Assumes
Current Assets							
Cash	$50,000	$154,577	$206,196	$301,580	$342,784	$478,224	
Prepaid insurance	0	0	0	0	0	0	
Prepaid taxes	0	0	0	0	0	0	
Inventories	7,500	7,500	7,500	7,500	7,500	7,500	
Other	0	0	0	0	0	0	
Total current assets	57,500	162,077	213,696	309,080	350,284	485,724	
Property, Plant and Equipment							
Furniture and fixtures	10,000	10,000	10,000	10,000	15,000	15,000	
Playground equipment	220,000	220,000	260,000	260,000	290,000	290,000	
Games	75,000	75,000	85,000	85,000	95,000	95,000	
Leasehold improvements	30,000	30,000	30,000	30,000	50,000	50,000	
Office equipment	7,000	7,000	7,000	7,000	7,000	7,000	
Signs	15,000	15,000	15,000	15,000	15,000	15,000	
Computer equipment	20,000	20,000	20,000	20,000	20,000	20,000	
Kitchen equipment	50,000	50,000	50,000	50,000	55,000	55,000	
Total PPE	427,000	427,000	477,000	477,000	547,000	547,000	
Less: Accumulated Depreciation	0	85,400	170,800	266,200	361,600	471,000	SL Depr
Total Property, Plant and Equipment	427,000	341,600	306,200	210,800	185,400	76,000	
Other Assets							
Franchise cost - net	30,000	27,000	24,000	21,000	18,000	15,000	10-yr amort
Total Assets	$514,500	$530,677	$543,896	$540,880	$553,684	$576,724	
Current Liabilities							
Accounts payable	0	0	0	0	0	0	
Notes payable	0	0	0	0	0	0	
Total Current Liabilities	0	0	0	0	0	0	
Intermediate-term Debt	114,500	100,151	79,297	56,566	31,790	4,783	5-yr payback
Stockholder's Equity							
Paid-in Capital	400,000	400,000	400,000	400,000	400,000	400,000	
Accumulated Adjustments Account							
Opening Balance	0	0	30,526	64,599	84,314	121,895	
Net income	0	42,526	46,073	31,714	49,581	62,046	
Distributions	0	12,000	12,000	12,000	12,000	12,000	3% payout
Closing Balance	0	30,526	64,599	84,314	121,895	171,941	
Total Stockholder's Equity	400,000	430,526	464,599	484,314	521,895	571,941	
Total Liabilities and Stock Equity	$514,500	$530,677	$543,896	$540,880	$553,684	$576,724	

Proforma Statement of Cash Flows - by year

	Year 1	Year 2	Year 3	Year 4	Year 5
Cash Flow from Operations					
Net income	$42,526	$46,073	$31,714	$49,581	$62,046
Depreciation	85,400	85,400	95,400	95,400	109,400
Amortization	3,000	3,000	3,000	3,000	3,000
Increase in current liabilities	0	0	0	0	0
Decrease in current assets	0	0	0	0	0
Net Cash Provided by Operations	130,926	134,473	130,114	147,981	174,446
Cash Flow from Investments					
Purchase of equipment	0	50,000	0	50,000	0
Addition to leasehold improvements	0	0	0	20,000	0
Net Cash Used by Investing Activities	0	50,000	0	70,000	0
Cash Flows from Financing Activities					
Loan Proceeds	0	0	0	0	0
Repayment of Debt	14,349	20,854	22,731	24,777	27,007
Distributions to shareholders	12,000	12,000	12,000	12,000	12,000
Net Cash Provided by Financing Activities	(26,349)	(32,854)	(34,731)	(36,777)	(39,007)
Net Increase (Decr) in cash	104,577	51,619	95,384	41,204	135,440
Cash at beginning of year	50,000	154,577	206,196	301,580	342,784
Cash at end of year	$154,577	$206,196	$301,580	$342,784	$478,224

Proforma Income Statement - Year 1

	Nov	Dec	Jan	Feb	Mar
Net Sales	$73,992	$90,435	$98,656	$106,877	$98,656
Cost of goods sold	10,277	12,561	13,703	14,845	13,703
Gross Profit	$63,715	$77,873	$84,953	$92,032	$84,953
Operating Expenses					
Rent	0	0	8,750	8,750	8,750
Utilities	2,083	2,083	2,083	2,083	2,083
Repairs and maintenance	1,250	1,250	1,833	1,833	1,833
General taxes	0	0	1,750	1,750	1,750
Telephone expense	833	833	833	833	833
Salaries and wages	21,720	26,547	28,960	31,373	28,960
Insurance - general	1,444	1,444	1,444	1,444	1,444
Insurance - health	150	150	150	150	150
Permits and licenses	1,500	0	0	0	0
Bank service charge	119	119	119	119	119
Legal and accounting	4,333	333	333	333	333
Depreciation	7,117	7,117	7,117	7,117	7,117
Amortization	250	250	250	250	250
Office expense	740	904	987	1,069	987
Supplies	4,366	5,336	5,821	6,306	5,821
Franchise fees	3,700	4,522	4,933	5,344	4,933
Training	2,500	0	0	0	0
Security and alarm expense	280	0	0	0	0
Bad checks	83	83	83	83	83
Payroll taxes	2,172	2,655	2,896	3,137	2,896
Sales tax expense	1,530	1,870	2,040	2,210	2,040
Operating supplies	1,480	1,809	1,973	2,138	1,973
Advertising	3,147	3,475	3,640	3,804	3,640
Entertainment, promotion and meals	400	0	0	0	0
Michigan single business tax	0	0	0	0	0
Interest expense	0	0	0	859	847
Management fees	0	0	0	0	0
Total Operating Expense	$61,196	$60,781	$75,996	$80,986	$76,843
Net Income	$2,518	$17,093	$8,957	$11,046	$8,110

Apr	May	Jun	Jul	Aug	Sept	Oct	Total	**Proforma Income**
$90,435	$61,660	$57,549	$61,660	$78,103	$73,992	$94,545	$986,561	**Statement - Year 1**
								...continued
12,561	8,565	7,994	8,565	10,848	10,277	13,132	137,033	
$77,873	$53,095	$49,556	$53,095	$67,254	$63,715	$81,413	$849,527	
8,750	8,750	8,750	8,750	8,750	8,750	8,750	87,500	
2,083	2,083	2,083	2,083	2,083	2,083	2,083	25,000	
1,833	1,833	1,833	1,833	1,833	1,833	1,833	20,833	
1,750	1,750	1,750	1,750	1,750	1,750	1,750	17,500	
833	833	833	833	833	833	833	10,000	
26,547	18,100	16,893	18,100	22,927	21,720	27,753	289,600	
1,444	1,444	1,444	1,444	1,444	1,444	1,444	17,333	
150	150	150	150	150	150	150	1,800	
0	0	0	0	0	0	0	1,500	
119	119	119	119	119	119	119	1,424	
333	333	333	333	333	333	333	8,000	
7,117	7,117	7,117	7,117	7,117	7,117	7,117	85,400	
250	250	250	250	250	250	250	3,000	
904	617	575	617	781	740	945	9,866	
5,336	3,638	3,395	3,638	4,608	4,366	5,578	58,207	
4,522	3,083	2,877	3,083	3,905	3,700	4,727	49,328	
0	0	0	0	0	0	0	2,500	
0	0	0	0	0	0	0	280	
83	83	83	83	83	83	83	1,000	
2,655	1,810	1,689	1,810	2,293	2,172	2,775	28,960	
1,870	1,275	1,190	1,275	1,615	1,530	1,955	20,404	
1,809	1,233	1,151	1,233	1,562	1,480	1,891	19,731	
3,475	2,900	2,818	2,900	3,229	3,147	3,558	39,731	
0	0	0	0	0	0	0	400	
0	0	0	0	0	0	392	392	
836	824	813	801	789	777	765	7,312	
0	0	0	0	0	0	0	0	
$72,700	$58,227	$56,149	$58,203	$66,455	$64,377	$75,087	$807,001	
$5,174	($5,131)	($6,593)	($5,108)	$799	($663)	$6,326	$42,527	

Proforma Balance Sheet - Year 1

	Oct	Nov	Dec	Jan	Feb
Current Assets					
Cash	$50,000	$59,885	$84,344	$100,668	$117,486
Prepaid insurance	0	0	0	0	0
Prepaid taxes	0	0	0	0	0
Inventories	7,500	7,500	7,500	7,500	7,500
Other	0	0	0	0	0
Total current assets	57,500	67,385	91,844	108,168	124,986
Property, Plant and Equipment					
Furniture and fixtures	10,000	10,000	10,000	10,000	10,000
Playground equipment	220,000	220,000	220,000	220,000	220,000
Games	75,000	75,000	75,000	75,000	75,000
Leasehold improvements	30,000	30,000	30,000	30,000	30,000
Office equipment	7,000	7,000	7,000	7,000	7,000
Signs	15,000	15,000	15,000	15,000	15,000
Computer equipment	20,000	20,000	20,000	20,000	20,000
Kitchen equipment	50,000	50,000	50,000	50,000	50,000
Total PPE	427,000	427,000	427,000	427,000	427,000
Less: Accum. Depreciation	0	7,117	14,233	21,350	28,467
Total PPE	427,000	419,883	412,767	405,650	398,533
Other Assets					
Franchise cost - net	30,000	29,750	29,500	29,250	29,000
Total Assets	$514,500	$517,018	$534,111	$543,068	$552,519
Current Liabilities					
Accounts payable	0	0	0	0	0
Notes payable	0	0	0	0	0
Total Current Liabilities	0	0	0	0	0
Intermediate-term Debt	114,500	114,500	114,500	114,500	112,906
Stockholder's Equity					
Paid-in Capital	400,000	400,000	400,000	400,000	400,000
Accumulated Adjustments Account					
Opening Balance	0	0	2,518	19,611	28,568
Net income	0	2,518	17,093	8,957	11,046
Distributions	0	0	0	0	0
Closing Balance	0	2,518	19,611	28,568	39,613
Total Stockholder's Equity	400,000	402,518	419,611	428,568	439,613
Total Liabilities & Stock, Equity	$514,500	$517,018	$534,111	$543,068	$552,519

	Mar	Apr	May	Jun	Jul	Aug	Sept	Oct	Proforma Balance Sheet - Year 1 *...continued*
	$131,368	$142,314	$142,955	$142,134	$142,798	$149,370	$154,479	$154,577	
	0	0	0	0	0	0	0	0	
	0	0	0	0	0	0	0	0	
	7,500	7,500	7,500	7,500	7,500	7,500	7,500	7,500	
	0	0	0	0	0	0	0	0	
	138,868	149,814	150,455	149,634	150,298	156,870	161,979	162,077	
	10,000	10,000	10,000	10,000	10,000	10,000	10,000	10,000	
	220,000	220,000	220,000	220,000	220,000	220,000	220,000	220,000	
	75,000	75,000	75,000	75,000	75,000	75,000	75,000	75,000	
	30,000	30,000	30,000	30,000	30,000	30,000	30,000	30,000	
	7,000	7,000	7,000	7,000	7,000	7,000	7,000	7,000	
	15,000	15,000	15,000	15,000	15,000	15,000	15,000	15,000	
	20,000	20,000	20,000	20,000	20,000	20,000	20,000	20,000	
	50,000	50,000	50,000	50,000	50,000	50,000	50,000	50,000	
	427,000	427,000	427,000	427,000	427,000	427,000	427,000	427,000	
	35,583	42,700	49,817	56,933	64,050	71,167	78,283	85,400	
	391,417	384,300	377,183	370,067	362,950	355,833	348,717	341,600	
	28,750	28,500	28,250	28,000	27,750	27,500	27,250	27,000	
	$559,034	$562,614	$555,888	$547,700	$540,998	$540,203	$537,946	$530,677	
	0	0	0	0	0	0	0	0	
	0	0	0	0	0	0	0	0	
	0	0	0	0	0	0	0	0	
	111,311	109,717	108,123	106,528	104,934	103,340	101,745	100,151	
	400,000	400,000	400,000	400,000	400,000	400,000	400,000	400,000	
	39,613	47,723	52,897	47,765	41,172	36,064	36,863	36,201	
	8,110	5,174	(5,131)	(6,593)	(5,108)	799	(663)	6,326	
	0	0	0	0	0	0	0	12,000	
	47,723	52,897	47,765	41,172	36,064	36,863	36,201	30,527	
	447,723	452,897	447,765	441,172	436,064	436,863	436,201	430,527	
	$559,034	$562,614	$555,888	$547,700	$540,998	$540,203	$537,946	$530,677	

Proforma Statement of Cash Flows - Year 1

	Nov	Dec	Jan	Feb	Mar
Cash Flow from Operations					
Net income	$2,518	$17,093	$8,957	$11,046	$8,110
Depreciation	7,117	7,117	7,117	7,117	7,117
Amortization	250	250	250	250	250
Increase in current liabilities	0	0	0	0	0
Decrease in current assets	0	0	0	0	0
Net Cash Provided by Operations	9,885	24,459	16,324	18,412	15,476
Cash Flow from Investments					
Purchase of equipment	0	0	0	0	0
Addition to leasehold improvements	0	0	0	0	0
Net Cash Used by Investing Activities	0	0	0	0	0
Cash Flows from Financing Activities					
Loan Proceeds	0	0	0	0	0
Repayment of Debt	0	0	0	1,594	1,594
Distributions to shareholders	0	0	0	0	0
Net Cash Provided by Financing Activities	0	0	0	(1,594)	(1,594)
Net Increase (Decr) in cash	9,885	24,459	16,324	16,818	13,882
Cash at beginning of month	50,000	59,885	84,344	100,668	117,486
Cash at end of month	59,885	84,344	100,668	117,486	131,368

Apr	May	Jun	Jul	Aug	Sept	Oct	Total
$5,174	($5,131)	($6,593)	($5,108)	$799	($663)	$6,326	$42,527
7,117	7,117	7,117	7,117	7,117	7,117	7,117	85,400
250	250	250	250	250	250	250	3,000
0	0	0	0	0	0	0	0
0	0	0	0	0	0	0	0
12,540	2,236	773	2,259	8,166	6,704	13,693	130,927
0	0	0	0	0	0	0	0
0	0	0	0	0	0	0	0
0	0	0	0	0	0	0	0
0	0	0	0	0	0	0	0
1,594	1,594	1,594	1,594	1,594	1,594	1,594	14,349
0	0	0	0	0	0	12,000	12,000
(1,594)	(1,594)	(1,594)	(1,594)	(1,594)	(1,594)	(13,594)	(26,349)
10,946	641	(821)	665	6,571	5,110	98	104,577
131,368	142,314	142,955	142,134	142,798	149,370	154,479	
142,314	142,955	142,134	142,798	149,370	154,479	154,577	

Proforma Statement of Cash Flows - Year 1

...continued

Proforma Income Statement - Year 2

	Dec	Jan	Feb	Mar	Apr
Net Sales	$77,692	$94,956	$103,589	$112,221	$103,589
Cost of goods sold	10,791	13,189	14,388	15,588	14,388
Gross Profit	$66,900	$81,767	$89,200	$96,634	$89,200
Operating Expenses					
Rent	8,750	8,750	8,750	8,750	8,750
Utilities	2,146	2,146	2,146	2,146	2,146
Repairs and maintenance	1,888	1,888	1,888	1,888	1,888
General taxes	1,803	1,803	1,803	1,803	1,803
Telephone expense	858	858	858	858	858
Salaries and wages	22,372	27,343	29,829	32,315	29,829
Insurance - general	1,528	1,528	1,528	1,528	1,528
Insurance - health	150	150	150	150	150
Permits and licenses	0	0	0	0	0
Bank service charge	119	119	119	119	119
Legal and accounting	333	333	333	333	333
Depreciation	7,117	7,117	7,117	7,117	7,117
Amortization	250	250	250	250	250
Office expense	777	950	1,036	1,122	1,036
Supplies	4,584	5,602	6,112	6,621	6,112
Franchise fees	3,885	4,748	5,179	5,611	5,179
Training	2,500	0	0	0	0
Security and alarm expense	280	0	0	0	0
Bad checks	83	83	83	83	83
Payroll taxes	2,237	2,734	2,983	3,231	2,983
Sales tax expense	1,607	1,964	2,142	2,321	2,142
Operating supplies	1,554	1,899	2,072	2,244	2,072
Advertising	3,220	3,566	3,738	3,911	3,738
Entertainment, promotion and meals	0	0	0	0	0
Michigan single business tax	0	0	0	0	0
Interest expense	753	741	729	716	704
Management fees	0	0	0	0	0
Total Operating Expense	$68,793	$74,572	$78,845	$83,118	$78,820
Net Income	(1,893)	7,195	10,355	13,516	10,380

May	Jun	Jul	Aug	Sept	Oct	Total	
$94,956	$64,743	$60,427	$64,743	$82,008	$77,692	$99,273	$1,035,889
13,189	8,993	8,393	8,993	11,391	10,791	13,789	143,885
$81,767	$55,750	$52,034	$55,750	$70,617	$66,900	$85,484	$892,004
8,750	8,750	8,750	8,750	8,750	8,750	8,750	105,000
2,146	2,146	2,146	2,146	2,146	2,146	2,146	25,750
1,888	1,888	1,888	1,888	1,888	1,888	1,888	22,660
1,803	1,803	1,803	1,803	1,803	1,803	1,803	21,630
858	858	858	858	858	858	858	10,300
27,343	18,643	17,400	18,643	23,614	22,372	28,586	298,288
1,528	1,528	1,528	1,528	1,528	1,528	1,528	18,334
150	150	150	150	150	150	150	1,800
0	0	0	0	0	0	0	0
119	119	119	119	119	119	119	1,424
333	333	333	333	333	333	333	4,000
7,117	7,117	7,117	7,117	7,117	7,117	7,117	85,400
250	250	250	250	250	250	250	3,000
950	647	604	647	820	777	993	10,359
5,602	3,820	3,565	3,820	4,838	4,584	5,857	61,117
4,748	3,237	3,021	3,237	4,100	3,885	4,964	51,794
0	0	0	0	0	0	0	2,500
0	0	0	0	0	0	0	280
83	83	83	83	83	83	83	1,000
2,734	1,864	1,740	1,864	2,361	2,237	2,859	29,829
1,964	1,339	1,250	1,339	1,696	1,607	2,053	21,424
1,899	1,295	1,209	1,295	1,640	1,554	1,985	20,718
3,566	2,962	2,875	2,962	3,307	3,220	3,652	40,718
0	0	0	0	0	0	0	0
0	0	0	0	0	0	392	392
691	679	666	653	640	627	614	8,214
0	0	0	0	0	0	0	0
$74,522	$59,511	$57,355	$59,485	$68,043	$65,887	$76,980	$845,931
7,245	(3,760)	(5,322)	(3,735)	2,574	1,013	8,504	$46,073

Proforma Income Statement - Year 2
...continued

Proforma Balance Sheet - Year 2

	Nov	Dec	Jan	Feb	Mar
Current Assets					
Cash	$158,313	$171,137	$187,122	$206,266	$222,276
Prepaid insurance	0	0	0	0	0
Prepaid taxes	0	0	0	0	0
Inventories	7,500	7,500	7,500	7,500	7,500
Other	0	0	0	0	0
Total current assets	165,813	178,637	194,622	213,766	229,776
Property, Plant and Equipment					
Furniture and fixtures	10,000	10,000	10,000	10,000	10,000
Playground equipment	220,000	220,000	220,000	220,000	220,000
Games	75,000	75,000	75,000	75,000	75,000
Leasehold improvements	30,000	30,000	30,000	30,000	30,000
Office equipment	7,000	7,000	7,000	7,000	7,000
Signs	15,000	15,000	15,000	15,000	15,000
Computer equipment	20,000	20,000	20,000	20,000	20,000
Kitchen equipment	50,000	50,000	50,000	50,000	50,000
Total PPE	427,000	427,000	427,000	427,000	427,000
Less: Accum. Depreciation	92,517	99,633	106,750	113,867	120,983
Total PPE	334,483	327,367	320,250	313,133	306,017
Other Assets					
Franchise cost - net	26,750	26,500	26,250	26,000	25,750
Total Assets	$527,047	$532,504	$541,122	$552,900	$561,542
Current Liabilities		-			
Accounts payable	0	0	0	0	0
Notes payable	0	0	0	0	0
Total Current Liabilities	0	0	0	0	0
Intermediate-term Debt	98,413	96,675	94,937	93,200	91,462
Stockholder's Equity					
Paid-in Capital	400,000	400,000	400,000	400,000	400,000
Accumulated Adjustments Account					
Opening Balance	30,527	28,634	35,829	46,184	59,700
Net income	(1,893)	7,195	10,355	13,516	10,380
Distributions	0	0	0	0	0
Closing Balance	28,634	35,829	46,184	59,700	70,080
Total Stockholder's Equity	428,634	435,829	446,184	459,700	470,080
Total Liabilities & Stock. Equity	$527,047	$532,504	$541,122	$552,900	$561,542

Apr	May	Jun	Jul	Aug	Sept	Oct	Proforma Balance
							Sheet - Year 2
							...continued
$235,149	$237,018	$237,325	$239,219	$247,422	$254,064	$206,197	
0	0	0	0	0	0	0	
0	0	0	0	0	0	0	
7,500	7,500	7,500	7,500	7,500	7,500	7,500	
0	0	0	0	0	0	0	
242,649	244,518	244,825	246,719	254,922	261,564	213,697	
10,000	10,000	10,000	10,000	10,000	10,000	10,000	
220,000	220,000	220,000	220,000	220,000	220,000	260,000	
75,000	75,000	75,000	75,000	75,000	75,000	85,000	
30,000	30,000	30,000	30,000	30,000	30,000	30,000	
7,000	7,000	7,000	7,000	7,000	7,000	7,000	
15,000	15,000	15,000	15,000	15,000	15,000	15,000	
20,000	20,000	20,000	20,000	20,000	20,000	20,000	
50,000	50,000	50,000	50,000	50,000	50,000	50,000	
427,000	427,000	427,000	427,000	427,000	427,000	477,000	
128,100	135,217	142,333	149,450	156,567	163,683	170,800	
298,900	291,783	284,667	277,550	270,433	263,317	306,200	
25,500	25,250	25,000	24,750	24,500	24,250	24,000	
$567,049	$561,551	$554,492	$549,019	$549,855	$549,130	$543,897	
0	0	0	0	0	0	0	
0	0	0	0	0	0	0	
0	0	0	0	0	0	0	
89,724	87,986	86,248	84,510	82,773	81,035	79,297	
400,000	400,000	400,000	400,000	400,000	400,000	400,000	
70,080	77,325	73,565	68,243	64,508	67,082	68,095	
7,245	(3,760)	(5,322)	(3,735)	2,574	1,013	8,504	
0	0	0	0	0	0	12,000	
77,325	73,565	68,243	64,508	67,082	68,095	64,600	
477,325	473,565	468,243	464,508	467,082	468,095	464,600	
$567,049	$561,551	$554,492	$549,019	$549,855	$549,130	$543,897	

Proforma Statement of Cash Flows - Year 2

	Nov	Dec	Jan	Feb	Mar
Cash Flow from Operations					
Net income	($1,893)	$7,195	$10,355	$13,516	$10,380
Depreciation	7,117	7,117	7,117	7,117	7,117
Amortization	250	250	250	250	250
Increase in current liabilities	0	0	0	0	0
Decrease in current assets	0	0	0	0	0
Net Cash Provided by Operations	5,474	14,562	17,722	20,882	17,747
Cash Flow from Investments					
Purchase of equipment	0	0	0	0	0
Addition to leasehold improvements	0	0	0	0	0
Net Cash Used by Investing Activities	0	0	0	0	0
Cash Flows from Financing Activities					
Loan Proceeds	0	0	0	0	0
Repayment of Debt	1,738	1,738	1,738	1,738	1,738
Distributions to shareholders	0	0	0	0	0
Net Cash from Financing Activities	(1,738)	(1,738)	(1,738)	(1,738)	(1,738)
Net Increase (Decr) in cash	3,736	12,824	15,984	19,145	16,009
Cash at beginning of month	154,577	158,313	171,137	187,122	206,266
Cash at end of month	158,313	171,137	187,122	206,266	222,276

Apr	May	Jun	Jul	Aug	Sept	Oct	Total	**Proforma Statement of Cash Flows - Year 2**
								...continued
$7,245	($3,760)	($5,322)	($3,735)	$2,574	$1,013	$8,504	$46,073	
7,117	7,117	7,117	7,117	7,117	7,117	7,117	85,400	
250	250	250	250	250	250	250	3,000	
0	0	0	0	0	0	0	0	
0	0	0	0	0	0	0	0	
14,612	3,606	2,045	3,632	9,941	8,380	15,871	134,473	
0	0	0	0	0	0	50,000	50,000	
0	0	0	0	0	0	0	0	
0	0	0	0	0	0	50,000	50,000	
0	0	0	0	0	0	0	0	
1,738	1,738	1,738	1,738	1,738	1,738	1,738	20,854	
0	0	0	0	0	0	12,000	12,000	
(1,738)	(1,738)	(1,738)	(1,738)	(1,738)	(1,738)	(13,738)	(32,854)	
12,874	1,868	307	1,894	8,203	6,642	(47,867)	51,619	
222,276	235,149	237,018	237,325	239,219	247,422	254,064		
235,149	237,018	237,325	239,219	247,422	254,064	206,197		

Internet Consultant

BUSINESS PLAN

ALLEN CONSULTING

8201 Annapolis Drive, Suite 60
Taylor, Michigan 48180

This business plan for a web consulting firm contains interesting information regarding the possibilities available for businesses through the internet. Look for a discussion in the executive summary regarding the current state of business on the Internet.

- EXECUTIVE SUMMARY

- BACKGROUND

- ALLEN BUSINESS CONCEPT

- MARKETING STRATEGY

- COMPETITIVE STRATEGY

- SELLING STRATEGY

- STRATEGIC PLANNING

- ORGANIZATION

- FINANCIAL DATA

EXECUTIVE SUMMARY

The World Wide Web as an advertising medium for the business community has experienced phenomenal growth. Since its inception, the Web has expanded to contain sites for over 17,000 businesses. The popularity of the Web has led corporate firms to include their World Wide Web site address on commercials, newspapers and magazine ads. This trend is understandable; of the 18 million users of the Web, 2.5 million users make purchases from the vendors who have Web home pages. The World Wide Web will form the foundation of the Virtual Economy, which is anticipated to be an increasingly popular way for savvy consumers to make purchases.

The Web's global presence allows companies to offer their products to consumers worldwide as well as build a corporate identity through their Web sites. Companies such as Marx and Babcock have taken the potential of the Web seriously enough to contract small, cutting edge Web site developing firms to create their Web sites. Often times, Web developing firms have stolen contracts from multi-million dollar ad agencies simply because they know the Web better than their huge, and somewhat staid, competitors. The mantra now is jump aboard or be left behind. Since the average Web browser earns close to $80,000 and has a college degree, those companies dragging their heels will be missing out on the new era of consumer commerce.

However, those businesses wishing to develop a professional web site are being forced to swallow considerable costs. While the cost of developing a site over the long run is considerably less than traditional media strategy, they are often still prohibitive to small and medium-sized businesses. On Jump, a Web site developer for Babcock International, charges fees from $10,000 to $15,000 to create a Web site, and from $5,000 to $150,000 per month to maintain it. While Babcock and Marx consider these numbers to be affordable, the local wedding photographer down the street would find these numbers slightly out of his/her price range. As the World Wide Web grows, small businesses that have Web pages are finding that they are generating few sales because their site is getting grouped with 700,000 other sites. Many of these other sites aren't even business related, as the baby's first picture and the favorite family pet are frequently finding their way onto the Web.

Furthermore, the ease of finding the site desired is becoming increasingly more burdensome. Browsing software programs that simplify "surfing" on the Web are making searches much easier, but the sheer volume of Web pages still ensures a lengthy on-line session to find the information needed. For a user wishing to make a purchase, the delays can be infuriating. Large companies use their financial strength to market their site, so a person wanting to visit Marx's site need only find their address on the bottom of their advertisement and jump on-line. The local dressmaker doesn't have this advantage.

Allen Consulting has been founded to address the issues of cost and visibility for the small to medium- sized business. Allen will enable the small business to create a Web presence that is exciting, affordable, and easy to find. By utilizing geography and combining it with easy-to-recognize topographical clues, a Web user will be able to make purchases from a local business easily and conveniently. In addition, Allen's fees are considerably lower than other competitors. Our innovative geographical/topographical search strategies, low fees, and hands-on customer support will set the standard for providing Web services. This document is the business plan for Allen Consulting.

BACKGROUND

The convergence of several factors created the opportunity for Allen Consulting to enter and dominate Web service providing for the small to medium business market. These factors include:

- The phenomenal growth of the World Wide Web as a center for commerce
- Increased usage of the Internet and the World Wide Web
- Increased familiarity with the benefits of the Web by businesses and individuals

- Continued improvement in providing secure on-line transactions
- Continued development of user-friendly Web Navigation Aides by Microsoft and Netscape
- Escalating sales of personal computers with on-line capabilities

These factors provide a clear picture of Allen's market. Currently, the average consumer appears to have a rapidly increasing knowledge of the Internet and the World Wide Web. This consumer understands the benefits of shopping from the home and has recognized the increased ease of navigating and making purchases on the Web. Similarly, companies are increasingly making their computers an essential business tool. The need to develop competitive advantages is motivating owners to investigate how they can use their computers to better respond to their customers, as well as increasing their market.

Allen Consulting will step into this scenario and provide services that will benefit consumers by making it considerably easier for them to find the products they desire. We will also aid small businesses in developing sites that will entice on-line users to purchase their products. While it is possible for businesses to develop their own Web pages, they typically cannot spend the significant time needed to constantly update and market their site to the public.

Allen Consulting will offer the following services to our clients:

Pix will be our main service offering. Pix directly answers the needs of the small business wishing to develop a Web Site. Pix will be a virtual commerce avenue that will have sites developed around a central categories. An example of this concept would be WeddingPix. This site will be exclusively devoted to the advertising of local wedding services. Since subscribers will be located in the greater Detroit area, a Web user can retain their services and, if need be, jump in the car and visit their business when time allows. WeddingPix will allow the bride-to-be to plan her wedding from her computer. In addition to WeddingPix, we will be building the following sites on Pix:

THE ALLEN BUSINESS CONCEPT

- **PetPix** - Lists everything from the perfect pet to the perfect vet.
- **CarPix** - Find the ideal vehicle and services to keep it running and looking great.
- **HealthPix** - Identifies health care providers including doctors, dentists, hospitals, HMOs, pharmacies, and medical supplies that are across the street, not across the country.
- **AttorneyPix** - Directory of convenient legal counsel with specializations such as malpractice, accidents, and business.
- **HomePix** - Not only can we find a prospective buyer the perfect place to live, we can locate someone to furnish it, landscape it, and maintain it as well!

Allen Consulting will market Pix to the greater Detroit area as an essential resource to the community. Our goal is to generate sales for our clients. We will be adding new sites on a steady basis. Compensation incentives will be offered to our employees for the development and successful marketing of new sites.

In addition to marketing Pix, we will develop the Web sites that will be listed on each Pix site. We will create the site, maintain it, and provide our clients with monthly Marketing Reports that will provide statistics on how their site is performing.

Allen Consulting will provide standard business Web consulting at a reasonable price. We will offer our Premium Services with graduated levels of service to help our clients better target their consulting needs. Based on their budget, businesses can retain our services for a single consultation, or negotiate an on-going service contract, essentially hiring our Web developing team.

Premium Services

MARKETING STRATEGY

Objective

Develop a recognizable and respected corporate identity within our target market while aggressively marketing Pix and our Premium Services.

Our Business

Allen Consulting will be headquartered at 8201 Annapolis Drive, Suite 60, Taylor, Michigan 48180.

Our Target Market

Our potential clients are business' employing 1-100 employees. We have not set a criteria for revenue expectations for our target market. Our clients will be initially located in the Detroit metropolitan area. However, due to lack of specific data for this area, our numbers will reflect our long-term strategy of marketing our services to the entire state of Michigan.

We will initially target businesses that have a unique service that they are providing to the community. These businesses will have the largest need of an interactive Web site to further promote their service or product to the residents of the Detroit metropolitan area. In addition, Pix will be a promotion tool for businesses in easily defined service/product categories, such as Wedding Services, Attorneys, and Health Care Providers. Therefore, our Marketing Strategy will encompass our efforts to gain the business of the general market of small companies, with specific targeting of those that fit the marketing criteria for Pix.

Target Market Statistics

> Number of potential clients in metropolitan Detroit: 7,371 businesses
> Average size of businesses by employment: 18 employees
> Number of potential clients in state of Michigan: 134,296 businesses
> Major business concentrations: Detroit, Grand Rapids, Lansing, Ann Arbor

Web User Demographics

According to a study conducted by the Nielsen Corporation, the average Web user has obtained a college degree and earns approximately $80,000. Along with our research of our potential client base, we have included statistics that reflect the number of potential users of our Pix service. These numbers show that our initial promotion of the Pix service in the greater Detroit area takes advantage of the exceptional demographic characteristics of this area.

> Number of consumers earning $35,000 - 50,000: (metro Detroit): 22,906
> Number of consumers earning $35,000-50,000: (Michigan): 1,246,162
> Number of affluent professionals (Michigan): 34,015

COMPETITIVE STRATEGY

Our Competitors

Due to our specific target market focus and business concept, Allen doesn't have any direct competitors. However, there are two consulting firms in the Detroit area that provide Web development services to the corporate community similar to our Premium Service offering. However, these firms are pursuing these clients according to standard consulting marketing practices, namely informal networking and referrals. These competitors are Maxwell, Inc. and Caravan Consulting. Lynn Strom is the President of Maxwell, Inc. Maxwell's services include:

- •Comprehensive planning to identify all appropriate Internet audiences and channels
- •Design and implementation of a World Wide Web site, including graphical and interactive elements
- •Registration of the Internet site with appropriate pointer and index sites
- •Coordination of Internet activities with existing marketing programs
- •Promotion of Internet presence to on-line and traditional media
- •Periodic reports documenting the number of visits to the Internet site
- •Ongoing maintenance and updates

Maxwell's fees are $3750 for a ten page site and $200 per month for maintenance. Maxwell's strategic alliances are Caravan Associates in information research and Connections, Inc. in web design. Strom states, "Our approach combines the best of traditional marketing with the global reach and advances communication capabilities of the Internet."

Caravan Consulting's President, Donald Alexander provides clients with mission development for Web sites, audience and content analysis and the design of interactive Web site elements that ease Web site navigation. Caravan's fees are negotiated based upon each project. Caravan's strategic alliances are with Maxwell, Inc. for integrated marketing utilizing Internet tools, Connection for web site design and Web Concepts for editorial design and production. According to Alexander, "Caravan specializes in specializes in strategy consulting and information architecture design for complex Web sites."

Competitor Analysis

Strengths
•Established businesses in their market niche
•Financial resources

Weaknesses
•Focus on large corporate customers
•Lack of strong traditional media marketing strategy
•Lack of business concept to capitalize on World Wide Web weaknesses
 (topography, Web site development costs for small businesses)

The key to any competitive strategy is to capitalize on our competitors weaknesses while matching and eventually surpassing their strengths. Allen Consulting will immediately work to protect our market niche by rapidly developing our proficiency in the areas where our competition is weak. At the same time, we will strive to keep these sleeping giants resting soundly. We plan to operate our business under their nose by sticking to the small-to-medium-sized market. We anticipate that this strategy will allow us to strengthen our market presence while our competitors considers us a non-player.

Our business concept takes into account the weaknesses inherent in our competitors target market focuses. The addition of a marketing department allows us to create a strong presence which we anticipate will stall new entrants until we are able to develop our identity and financial resources. The execution of our strategic plan will integrate the functional areas of Allen Consulting into one functional unit. We believe our focus and our small size will allow us to innovate faster than any potential competitors.

Also, by being first on the block, our business concept will prevent new players from jumping on board. By aggressively marketing our services to our target market, we will effectively freeze out competitors. A small business owner who has already paid $400 to get on the Web is less likely to go with a competitor who provides a similar service. If a competitor wants to go head to head with us, they will need to develop alternative services, hire a sales staff, and convince business owners that their present service isn't meeting their needs. We are anticipating that the cost of breaking into our market will be prohibitive, therefore barring their entry.

Competitor's Selling Strategies

Our indirect competitors primarily sell through networking strategies such as referrals and executive selling. Each has an ad in the Yellow Pages. Due to their focus on large corporate customers, their need for print-media advertising is minimal.

Both of our competitors, Maxwell, Inc. and Caravan Consulting have benefited from articles written about their services in the Detroit Times. Each of these articles focused on their service offerings. Due to the detail of each article, we have speculated that these articles were written as a result of press releases.

Competitive Statistics

In order to provide perspective, we have included statistics that will describe the general characteristics of the computer consulting industry in the greater Detroit area. This data will be used to provide a benchmark by which to gauge our size and growth. The data compiled here was taken from the Dun Consulting Directory.

- Avg. size by employees: 15
- Avg. sales: $1,287,500
- Most common business focus: Commercial and governmental concerns
- Number of firms listed in directory from metropolitan Detroit: 6

SELLING STRATEGY

The growth of the Internet and its commercial commerce component, the World Wide Web, has been astronomical. The World Wide Web has 17 million users from all over the world. Over 17,000 businesses have rushed to the Web to set up Web home pages to advertise and sell a myriad of products and services. Overall, the Internet is expected to double in size, and the Web is expected to match the Internet's growth rate. Already the Internet and the World Wide Web have attracted more browsers than America Online or CompuServe.

Currently the majority of businesses on the Web are corporations who have spent thousands of dollars to develop and market their sites. While individual users and small businesses have participated on the Web, they are quickly pushed out of the mainstream, and their sites are largely ignored. This occurs because of the large volume of Web sites (700,000 by last count) that may or may not have any practical use. Therefore, unless the business has spent a substantial amount of money to hire experts to market their sites, they are simply left out.

Allen Consulting has focused its selling strategy on reaching small businesses. They represent the largest growth sector of Web participants. Providing these businesses with an effective presence on the Web is the essence of our selling strategy. Our selling approach will be motivated by four principles:

- Meet the client's needs
- Show the client the benefits of a Web site
- Paint a picture of the clients investment
- Simplify the complex

All of our promotional literature will incorporate these principles. The success of each sale will be judged by our ability to perform each principle flawlessly and convincingly.

Short-term Tactics

Print Advertising

Print advertising is the most effective way to reach the population of greater Detroit. While many consulting firms rely solely on networking, the nature of our business differs substantially enough from the standard to merit a consistent a print-media presence. We intend this advertising to : 1) Alert small businesses of our ability to put them on the Web, and 2) Create price and name recognition. We want to convince the community that we are a cost-effective choice.

Executive Selling

The Sales Director will be responsible for all sales calls. This arrangement is based upon need and has strategic advantages. Executive selling will allow the company to stay very close to the market and enable us to set reasonable objectives and sales goals.

Once the firm has a client base that will support a full-time sales person, one will be hired to initiate and close selling contacts. Our strategic plan calls for a substantial sales department. Our hiring will reflect our execution of that strategy. Once a sales force is hired the Sales Director will concentrate on management and operational areas of the firm.

Direct Mail

We will increasingly use more targeted direct mail campaigns. These mailings will be followed up by sales calls by our sales personnel. We will extensively use mailing lists targeted to small- to medium-sized businesses (1-100) employees. With Pix advertising, our mailings will be designed exclusively for each category to add a sense of personalization, so that a customer will receive a hard-copy demo of what their site may potentially look like.

Promotional Props and Literature

We will be developing materials that will constantly advertise our services. For example, we will leave counter signs that advertise a company's Web address as well as the phrase "created by Allen Consulting." These materials will build name recognition and a presence in our niche.
Inside Sales

Our in-house sales team will handle the execution of the sales strategy. Executive sells will be concentrated on negotiated contract agreements for Premium Services. Our sales people will have the title of Account Executives. Training of the full-time Account Executives will be an on-gong concern focusing on such topics as product knowledge, Web marketing, and sales techniques. Supervision and training will be the responsibility of the Sales Director.
Account Executive Compensation

Each Account Executive will be compensated according to a base salary plus commission. Account Executives will also be eligible for bonuses based on sales performance. In order to create a performance based compensation strategy an Account Executive will be paid a small base salary and given proportionately larger commissions for each completed sales call.

Each client will have continual access to their Web site. If clients wish to modify their sites after initial activation, we will promptly provide an estimate of the time needed to design the change. In addition, monthly site Activity Reports will be sent to each client. Twice a year, the Marketing Team will distribute a newsletter keeping our clients up-to-date on the latest advances and company offerings that will improve their site. Finally, the Marketing Team will routinely distribute press releases announcing new clients and will be conducting client surveys to ensure that we are meeting customer needs.

Client Support will serve as our primary way of solidifying our relationship and securing our market influence. Responsibility for our client support initiatives will fall to the Marketing Team.

Be the leader in the providing of Web support services to small-and medium-sized businesses. Our niche will be the small to medium sized business market. We will not try to take on corporate customers until we have achieved the remainder of our objectives. This niche will allow us the time to grow and mature without having to go head-to-head with larger firms. While there are several competitors that provide Web support services, none are exclusively focused on our market niche. Our goal is to keep it that way.

Allen Consulting plans to attain leadership in our market niche with a double edged strategy. The advantages we will develop to dominate our market will also provide us with the competitive muscle needed to assault the market niche of our competitors.

Be technologically self-sufficient. In the computer industry, competitiveness is often gauged according to a company's ability to assimilate new technological advances and the subsequent marketing of these advances to its clients. We must be able to develop technological competence in-house and market our research and development successfully without the need

Long-Term Tactics

Client Support

STRATEGIC PLANNING

Objectives

to rely on out-of-house resources. This strategy will yield a competitive advantage throughout every functional area of the company.

Pioneer Web competitive strategies that will continually expand our market penetration and depth. Allen understands the highly competitive nature of Internet services. In order to attain and keep our competitive advantage it will be crucial for us to be pioneers within our market niche. We will actively cultivate and enhance our ability to develop new service offerings.

In each of the functional areas of the firm, we will encourage and compensate initiatives that expose and take advantage of competitive weaknesses. Our focus will be to defend our market by maintaining our ability to threaten the market of other Internet consultants. This strategy of defending by attacking will be the foundation of our competitive strategy.

Objective Implementation

Outlined below are our action plans for implementing these objectives throughout the firm's functional teams.

Sales

The key to our market dominance will be our sales force. The Sales Team will be responsible for hiring and developing top-notch, proficient sales professionals who will act as the firm's representatives to our clients. Our sales goals are to achieve solid name and reputation recognition among area businesses and market saturation -- all potential clients have been approached and offered our consulting services.

Sales Goal Measurement

From start-up through December 1998 we will have achieved the following goals:

- In the second fiscal year, Allen Consulting will commission a market research study to gauge name recognition and market penetration.
- Quarterly review of sales figures in comparison with Business Plan benchmarks, will be done.
- Weekly sales meetings focused on individual performance and goal attainment will be held.

Between December 1998 - December 2001, these goals will be accomplished:

- Continuation of initial evaluation procedures
- Improvement of compensation and benefits package for sales staff
- Headhunting key personnel to develop long-range capability of Sales Department.

Financial

The financial strength of Allen Consulting will be the most carefully scrutinized functional area. The ability of the company to increase its technological and human resource muscle will be important for the continued dominance of our market.

Financial Goals

- Increase funds for technological research and development
- Increase funds for compensation and benefits packaging

Financial Goals Measurement

From Start-Up - December 2001
- Weekly financial auditing of business receipts
- Monthly evaluation of key business ratios
- Quarterly drafting of income statement, changes in financial position and balance sheet
- Six-month technological and human resource review with the goal of continually improving the firm's capability and depth in these areas

Promotion of Pix and Allen's Premium Services will be undertaken by our Marketing Team. In addition, positioning our firm as a leader in our market niche will encompass the vision of the team. Our strategy will be to aggressively saturate our niche by successfully integrating our firm's competitive strengths according to our strategic plan.

Marketing

Marketing Goals

•Development of comprehensive company identity through traditional media
•Design nationally recognized Web site through Pix

Marketing Goals Measurement

Start-Up - December 2001
•Revise promotional materials every six months
•Cross-train the Marketing Team with technicians from Technology Team
•Develop on-going marketing plan in print and broadcast media

The ability of the Technology team to reinvent itself and expand its service offering will be crucial to our competitiveness. The Technology Team will be our front-line to the Internet community. Their expertise must continually be refined and they must research innovative methods to market the Internet to business customers.

Technology

Technology Goals

•Develop five new service offerings in the next five years
•Develop two new technological advances by December 2001

Technology Goal Measurement

Start-Up - December 2001
•A qualifiable new service offering must net the company $25,000 in revenues for the fiscal year introduced
•A new technological advance must be patentable and/or net the company $25,000 in revenues for the fiscal year introduced

Allen will maintain a relatively flat hierarchical management structure. The organization's operating units: Operations, Technology, Marketing, and Sales will be centered on team units. Each team unit will fall under the supervision of the Team Director. The Team Directors will form the Executive Council. The Executive Council will be responsible for planning company policies and developing long range plans for company growth. The Chairperson of the Executive Council will be elected for two year terms by anonymous vote by the Executive Council membership. This organizational structure was selected because it provides an informal team atmosphere where creativity and efficiency can be cultivated. We will strive to keep the company's hierarchy as flat as possible to encourage direct communication between company personnel and members of the Executive Council.

ORGANIZATION

Operations Team

Connie Harris is the Director of Operations. The operations team is responsible for the administrative tasks needed to keep the company operating smoothly. The Operations Team will include the VP of Finance, VP of Human Resources, and the Office Manager. Together these team members will provide support services to the rest of the company. The Director of Operations will be directly responsible for ensuring compliance with Executive Council directives throughout the company.

Executive Council and Management Teams

Marketing Team

Dan Bell is the Director of the Marketing team. This team is responsible for the execution of Allen Consulting's marketing strategy. They will design and distribute all company literature, handle all public relations contacts, and handle print and broadcast media advertisements. As part of the Strategic Plan, this team will be cross-trained with the Technology team to develop their knowledge of the Web and its applications for our business clients. The Marketing Director will recruit and hire the Marketing team as well as design their cross-training schedule with the Technology Team.

Technology Team

Linda Roten is the Director of the Technology team. This team will design the Web sites for our clients as well as handle monthly maintenance duties on each of our accounts. This team will be responsible for increasing the firm's hardware capabilities and accomplishing the goals set out in our Strategic Plan. In accordance with the Strategic Plan, the Technology Team will be cross-trained with the Marketing Team. The Technology Director is responsible for the recruiting and hiring of the technicians for the Technology team, as well as coordinating cross-training with the Marketing Team.

Sales Team

Steve Smith is the Director of the Sales team. The Sales team will initiate and close all sales contacts with the business community. They will also handle all contacts with the firm's clients in an effort to present a consistent professional image to the community. The Director is responsible for on-going training and hiring of the Account Executives. Also, the Sales Director will organize the Sales Team to effectively service the Account Units existing on Pix.

Management Needs

Within the first six months of operation we will seek to fill the position of VP of Finance. This position will be responsible for insuring compliance with our strategic initiatives as well as administering the company's finances. In addition to the VP, we will be searching for an additional WebMaster for the Technology Team to increase our Web design capabilities and improve our profitability. The compensation package for these positions shall be salaried and set at a later point by the Executive Committee.

After these two vacancies are filled we will begin to recruit our Sales Team in order to saturate our target market. The Sales Team will be formed in accordance with the Sales Strategy outlined in this Business Plan. Our Sales Team will add a member with each new increment of $100,000 in sales. This allows for a minimum $10,000 base salary. This compensation/recruitment package is in agreement with our sales strategy.

Personnel Review and Evaluation

Evaluation and review reports will be conducted by each Team Director on a six month cycle. The criteria for these reviews will be drafted by each Team Director and submitted to the Executive Council for review and final consideration. This procedure will be followed to insure consistency and compliance with long-term strategic considerations. The Director of Operations will develop a grievance procedure to be explained to each new hire. All compensation increases will be tied to these evaluations.

Legal Organization

Allen Consulting is a Limited Liability Company (LLC) organized in Ohio and registered in Ohio and Michigan. This legal entity was identified as the best way to provide options for capital infusions in the future by the addition of partners, while protecting those partners from liability beyond their initial investment. The LLC is considered the most sophisticated method of taking advantage of the benefits of a partnership while restricting unnecessary risks. We anticipate that our form of organization will provide us with better capitalization options in the future.

Web page development as a business service has only recently begun to be offered by computer consultants specializing in Internet service. Due to the relative infancy of the service, financial benchmarks are still being set. As a result, Allen Consulting financial calculations will be made using standard benchmarks for the consulting industry. Where appropriate, we have adjusted our calculations to take into account the unique nature of the World Wide Web's business service climate.

The Web itself is setting record numbers for growth, and its popularity is spreading rapidly throughout the business community. While we would be justified in assuming optimistic growth number, we have used conservative numbers in every segment of our financial statements.

Financial Benchmarks

Allen Consulting has two service categories that it will extend to its clients. Accordingly each of these categories has its own pricing scale.

Service Pricing

Pix - Web Real Estate
Standard Cybersite:
- •Site Activation Fee: $200.00
- •Site storage charge: $35.00/month
- •Includes storage fees and linking

Custom Cybersite Development:
- •Site Activation Fee: $300.00
- •Site Service Charge: $35.00/month
- •Includes storage fees and linking
- •Hourly Fee: $50.00

Pix Linking:
- •$20.00/month (Pix Link)
- •Site Activation: $50.00

Premium Services
Silver:
- •Activation Fee: $50.00
- •Hourly Billing: $50.00
- •Monthly Storage Charge: $30.00

Gold:
- •Flat Retainer Fee: $200.00
- •Includes 5 hours consultation per month
- •Monthly Storage Charge: $30.00

Platinum:
- •Site Design and Activation: Fee set upon Consultation
- •Includes on-going site design and modification
- •Includes training and on-going consultation of Web developments

FINANCIAL DATA

Preliminary Assumptions for Income Statement and Balance Sheet

The monthly income figure was calculated using an estimate of how many Web sites could be developed and implemented on a monthly basis by our Technical Director. The calculation is very conservative due to our marketing strategy of producing a quality product rather than compromising our standards for sales volume.

A Web site will be marketed for the price of $200 plus a monthly fee. This is our baseline for all calculation. The activation fee of $200.00 will be due upon signing of the business contract.

Pay scale for full time employees is $14.00 per hour. Part-Time employees will earn a wage commensurate with their experience and duties. The business plan does not include plans for hiring part-time employees.

Internet domain registration and storage space charges are calculated using figures negotiated with Salvador College who will be our Internet service provider.

Hardware upgrade costs incorporate our plans to upgrade our computing ability and speed on a yearly basis. The figure assumes performance upgrades that will equal the cost of one new computer system a year.

Prepaid expense will consist of advance charges for computer server storage.

Accounts Payable will be paid within 30 days. We will take advantage of any discounts offered.

Accounts Receivable represent monthly service charges.

Financial Assumptions for Monthly Statement of Income

Revenues will flow evenly throughout the year because 70% of revenues are obtained through monthly service charges.

Operating expenses are incurred uniformly on a monthly basis.

Breakdown Revenues were calculated using the following equation:

(Actual Revenues x Fixed Costs) / (Actual Revenues - Direct Costs).

Income taxes will be paid according to IRS regulation for the taxation of partnership income. Each partner will be responsible for their individual reporting of partnership income.

Forecasted Statement of Income Forecasted

For the years ending December 15th

	Year 1	Year 2	Year 3	Year 4	Year 5
Revenues					
Sales					
	88,400.00	153,600.00	165,888.00	179,159.04	193,491.76
Billables	-		-		-
	-		-		-
Total Income					
	88,400.00	153,600.00	165,888.00	179,159.04	193,491.76
Direct Expenses					
Salaries					
	50,000.00	100,000.00	100,000.00	100,000.00	100,000.00
Domain Registration					
	300.00		-		150.00
	150.00		150.00		
Storage Space					
	600.00		600.00		600.00
	600.00		600.00		
Computer Hardware Upgrade					
	2,200.00	2,200.00	2,200.00	2,200.00	2,200.00

Personnel

1,200.00	1,200.00	1,200.00	1,200.00	1,200.00

Cash Balance Beginning of Year

800.00	800.00	800.00	800.00	800.00

General & Administrative

1,152.00	1,152.00	1,152.00	1,152.00	1,152.00

Total Direct Expenses

56,252.00	105,952.00	106,102.00	106,102.00	106,102.00

Income Before Indirect Expenses and Fixed Charges

32,148.00	47,648.00	59,766.00	73,057.04	87,389.76

Indirect Expenses

Internet Connect Time

900.00	972.00	1,049.76	1,133.74	1,224.44

Communications Charges

350.00	378.28	408.24	440.90	473.17

Total Indirect Expenses

1,250.00	1,350.00	1,458.00	1,574.64	1,700.61

Income Before Fixed Charges

30,898.00	46,298.00	58,328.00	71,482.40	85,689.15

Fixed Charges

Business and Property Insurance

10,000.00	10,800.00	11,644.00	12,597.12	13,604.89

Total Fixed Charges

10,000.00	10,800.00	11,644.00	12,597.12	13,604.89

Income Before Interest, Depreciation and Taxes

20,898.00	35,498.00	46,664.00	58,885.28	72,084.26

Net Income

20,898.00	35,498.00	46,664.00	58,885.28	72,084.26

For Years ending December 15th   **Statement of Changes in Financial Position**

Year 1	Year 2	Year 3	Year 4	Year 5
Cash Provided				
Net Income (Loss)				
20,898.00	35.496.00	46,664.00	58,885.28	72,084.26
Depreciation				
-	-	-	-	-
Changes in Working Capital Components				
Accounts Receivable				
-	-	-	-	-
Prepaid Expenses				
(900.00)	(600.00)	(750.00)	(750.00)	(750.00)
Net Cash Provided by Operations				
19,998.00	34,898.00	45,914.00	58,135.28	71,334.26

Net Increase (Decrease) in Cash

19,998.00	34,898.00	45,914.00	58,135.28	71,334.26

Cash Balance Beginning of Year

19,998.00	54,896.00	100,810.00	158,945.28	-

Cash Balance End of Year

19,998.00	54,896.00	100,810.00	158,945.28	230,279.54

Projected Net Income Breakeven Analysis

For the Year Ending December 15th

__1995-1996__	__1996-1997__	__1997-1998__	__1998-1999__	__1999-2000__
Revenues				
88,400.00	153,600.00	165,888.00	179,159.04	193,491.76
Direct Costs				
0	0	0	0	0
Salaries				
50,000.00	100,000.00	100,000.00	100,000.00	100,000.00
Domain Registration				
300.00	-	150.00	150.00	150.00
Storage Space				
600.00	600.00	600.00	600.00	600.00
Computer Hardware Upgrade				
2,200.00	2,200.00	2,200.00	2,200.00	2,200.00
Personnel				
1,200.00	1,200.00	1,200.00	1,200.00	1,200.00
Printing				
800.00	800.00	800.00	800.00	800.00
Total Direct Costs				
55,100.00	104,800.00	104,950.00	104,950.00	104,950.00

Cash Balance Beginning of Year

General Administrative				
1,152.00	1,152.00	1,152.00	1,152.00	1,152.00
Business & Property Insurance				
10,000.00	10,800.00	11,664.00	12,597.12	13,604.89
Interest				
-	-	-	-	-
Depreciation				
-	-	-	-	-
Total Fixed Costs				
11,152.00	11,952.00	12,816.00	13,749.12	14,756.89
Breakeven Revenues				
66,252.00	116,752.00	117,766.00	118,699.12	119,706.89

Forecasted Monthly Statement of Changes in Financial Position 1995-1996

	APR	MAY	JUN	JUL	AUG	SEP	OCT	NOV	DEC	TOTAL
Cash Provided										
Net Income (Loss)	-	-	-	-	-	5,200.00	12,800.00	12,800.00	12,800.00	43,600.00
Depreciation	36.67	36.67	36.67	36.67	36.67	36.67	36.67	36.67	36.67	330.03
Changes in Working Capital Components										
Accounts Receivable	-	-	-	-	-	-	(2,400.00)	(2,400.00)	(2,400.00)	(7,200.00)
Prepaid Expenses	(75.00)	(75.00)	(75.00)	(75.00)	(75.00)	(75.00)	(75.00)	(75.00)	(75.00)	(675.00)
Net Cash Provided by Operations	(38.33)	(38.33)	(38.33)	(38.33)	(38.33)	5,161.67	10,361.67	10,361.67	10,361.67	36,055.03
Net Increase (Decrease) in Cash	(38.33)	(38.33)	(38.33)	(38.33)	(38.33)	5,161.67	10,361.67	10,361.67	10,361.67	36,055.03
Cash Balance Beginning of Year	-	(38.33)	(38.33)	(38.33)	(38.33)	(38.33)	5,161.67	10,361.67	10,361.67	-
Cash Balance End of Year	(38.33)	(76.66)	(114.99)	(153.32)	(191.65)	(229.98)	4,931.69	15,293.36	25,655.03	19,998.00

Forecasted Balance Sheet

	1995-1996	1996-1997	1997-1998	1998-1999	1999-2000
Current Assets					
Cash	19,998.00	54,896.00	100,810.00	158,945.28	230,279.54
Receivables	-	-	-	-	-
Prepaid Expenses	900.00	600.00	750.00	750.00	750.00
Total Current Assets	20,898.00	55,496.00	101,560.00	159,695.28	231,029.54
Fixed Assets					
Equipment	-	-	-	-	-
Less Acc. Depreciation	-	-	-	-	-
Total Assets	20,898.00	55,496.00	101,560.00	159,695.28	231,029.54
Liabilities					
Current Liabilities	-	-	-	-	-
Total Current Liabilities	-	-	-	-	-
Long Term Debt	-	-	-	-	-
Retained Earnings	20,898.00	55,496.00	101,560.00	159,695.28	231,029.54
Total Liabilities & Net Worth	20,898.00	55,496.00	101,560.00	159,695.28	231,029.54

Forecasted Monthly Statement of Changes in Financial Position 1995-1996

	APR	MAY	JUN	JUL	AUG	SEP	OCT	NOV	DEC	TOTAL
Revenues	10,400	10,400	10,400	10,400	10,400	5,200	10,400	10,400	10,400	88,400
Billables	-	-	-	-	-	-	2,400	2,400	2,400	7,200
Total Income	10,400	10,400	10,400	10,400	10,400	5,200	12,800	12,800	12,800	95,600
Direct Expenses										
Salaries	4,167	4,167	4,167	4,167	4,167	4,167	4,167	4,167	4,167	37,500
Domain Registration	300	-	-	-	-	-	-	-	-	300
Storage Space	300	-	-	-	-	-	300	-	-	600
Computer Hardware Upgrade	2,200	-	-	-	-	-	-	-	-	2,200
Personnel	100	100	100	100	100	100	100	100	100	1,200
Printing	60.00	-	60.00	-	60.00	-	60.00	-	60.00	800.00
General & Administrative	96.00	96.00	96.00	96.00	96.00	96.00	96.00	96.00	96.00	1,152.00
Total Direct Expenses	7,223	4,363	4,423	4,363	4,423	4,363	4,723	4,363	4,423	43,752
Income Before Indirect Expenses & Fixed Charges	3,177	6,037	5,977	6,037	5,977	837	8,077	8,437	8,377	52,935
Indirect Expenses										
Internet Connect Time	75.00	75.00	75.00	75.00	75.00	75.00	75.00	75.00	75.00	900.00
Communications Charges	29.00	29.00	29.00	29.00	29.00	29.00	29.00	29.00	29.00	350.00
Total Indirect Expenses	104	104	104	104	104	104	104	104	104	1,250
Income Before Fixed Charges	3,073	5,933	5,873	5,933	5,873	733	7,973	8,333	8,273	51,686
Fixed Charges										
Business & Property Insurance	833	833	833	833	833	833	833	833	833	10,000
Total Fixed Charges	833	833	833	833	833	833	833	833	833	10,000
Income Before Interest, Depreciation and Taxes	2,240	5,100	5,040	5,040	(100)	7,140	7,500	7,500	7,440	41,686
Depreciation	37.00	37.00	37.00	37.00	37.00	37.00	37.00	37.00	37.00	330.00
Income Before Taxes	2,203	5,063	5,003	5,063	5,003	(137)	7,103	4,463	4,403	41,356
Net Income	2,203	5,063	5,003	5,063	5,003	(137)	7,103	4,463	4,403	41,356

Internet Consultant

BUSINESS PLAN

WORLDWIDE INTERNET MARKETING SERVICES

18765 Industrial Turnpike
Denver, CO 80903

February 1996

This plan details an Internet consulting service that offers web page design and other services for businesses. The plan discusses at length the worldwide nature of the Internet and how the corporation will exploit this feature to gain market share and revenue across the U.S. and around the world. The plan includes the corporation's 90-day action plan, the purpose of which is to demonstrate their readiness to undertake this venture immediately, before the market is saturated. The principals take into account the fact that investors may not be familiar with the Internet or with computer terminology, and therefore take care to explain them within their plan.

- EXECUTIVE SUMMARY

- BUSINESS OVERVIEW

- COMPETITION

- PERSONNEL

- OPERATIONS

- FINANCIAL DATA

- APPENDIX

INTERNET CONSULTANT
BUSINESS PLAN

EXECUTIVE SUMMARY

No other marketplace in world history has exploded with the force of the global computer network known as the Internet. Meeting the challenges associated with conducting business online, which include concerns over transaction security, developing a successful service delivery mechanism, and overcoming issues associated with international commerce, requires a well-thought, systemic approach to doing business as a whole.

Worldwide Internet Marketing Services, a new Internet service provider with target markets in Montana, Texas and Colorado, is just such a company.

By competing directly with traditional print and broadcast media such as television, radio, and newspapers, Worldwide Internet Marketing Services will offer its clients a superior product to these traditional forms, both in content and price. The nature of the service allows Worldwide Internet Marketing Services to serve clients ranging in size from the individual Internet enthusiast to the largest of corporations.

Key strengths of Worldwide Internet Marketing Services are as follows:

- A driven, committed staff of professionals with experience in sales and marketing, business management, and information systems management;

- A process-centered approach to business management that combines complex information systems with the due diligence of the Worldwide Internet Marketing Services team to achieve a streamlined sales system that delivers quality services to clients, online customers, and employees;

- Ability to expand in four major cities immediately;

- A developing worldwide online market. Worldwide Internet Marketing Services is entering a brand new global marketplace with a potential audience measured in the tens of millions. Most of the Internet is made up of networks located within the United States, but the rest of the world is catching up quickly. This potential marketplace then becomes hundreds of millions. By entering the arena now, Worldwide Internet Marketing Services will become well-entrenched and ready to meet this explosive growth.

BUSINESS OVERVIEW

Worldwide Internet Marketing Services is an enterprise created to exploit the business opportunities within the global computer network known as the Internet. In recent history, no other marketplace has opened with the ferocity of the Internet. With a potential worldwide audience measured in the tens of millions, the Internet far outreaches traditional advertising media readership, including television, radio, and printed media such as newspapers and magazines. In fact, the key to the success of Worldwide Internet Marketing Services is to demonstrate not only the benefits of increasing readership on a worldwide scale, but to offer the service at greatly reduced rates when compared to traditional media.

The ability of Worldwide Internet Marketing Services to offer competitive rates against not only traditional media, but other local Internet service providers, lies in the construction of the business itself. By creating a streamlined organization that concentrates on employee satisfaction first, Worldwide Internet Marketing Services will offer an environment where individual talent is allowed to flourish. We believe that employee satisfaction results in customer satisfaction, the key to success in any business.

Another aspect of Worldwide Internet Marketing Services that sets it ahead of its competition is the caliber of its technical staff. Most of the businesses we surveyed that are offering online Internet services lease the use of hardware and software resources from an Internet access provider. In contrast, Worldwide Internet Marketing Services will own and operate all hardware and software needed to deliver its services. This allows greater flexibility regarding purchase, maintenance, and configuration than a lease arrangement. And, because Worldwide Internet Marketing Services employs two professional computer network engineers, the delivery system itself can be streamlined to further reduce the company's expenses.

In order to compete in a marketplace that is open 24 hours per day, 7 days per week, our sales staff must be equipped with tools that make them independent of the corporation's physical location. Using advanced database technology, Worldwide Internet Marketing Services account representatives will be able to access the corporation's central database from virtually anywhere in the world. This is accomplished using notebook computers and the public telephone network. Instead of distributing printed marketing materials, account representatives can show potential clients live systems that are doing business on the Internet today. Once an order is finalized, it can be processed immediately by entering it into the company's accounting system. This not only results in fast delivery of services, but also eliminates waste of corporate resources.

Proprietorship

Worldwide Internet Marketing Services is currently a D.B.A. (doing business as) of Shark Corporation. Shark Corporation itself is a venture capital firm founded to stimulate and develop online businesses. We expect Worldwide Internet Marketing Services to spin off into its own corporation once the business is established and begins to turn a profit. The board of directors for Shark Corporation are as follows:

Michael Bonelli, President
Richard McFeely, Vice President
Victor Gold, Treasurer
Leonard Morgan, Secretary

Target Markets

Worldwide Internet Marketing Services will target individuals and businesses who wish to establish and/or enhance their presence on the Internet. We will immediately begin marketing activities in the following cities:

Dallas, Texas
Houston, Texas
Billings, Montana
Denver, Colorado

The very nature of the Internet, being a global network, allows us to operate with equal efficiency in each of these target markets, as we have sales representatives located in each of the cities listed above. Combined with state-of-the-art contact management and accounting systems, delivery of professional services to our clients will be possible from virtually anywhere in the world.

Selling a Presence on the Internet

The main goal of Worldwide Internet Marketing Services is to assist its clients, ranging from private individuals to large corporations, in furthering their presence on the Internet. The primary media that Worldwide Internet Marketing Services will use to accomplish this goal is the Internet's World Wide Web (WWW). Three years ago, there were less than 10,000 Web pages on the Internet (we think of a Web page as a single, full-page color advertisement). Today, there are over 16 million. As of December, 1995, 4% of the U.S. population (9.5 million) had direct access to the Internet, spending an average of 6.6 hours per week online. The average Internet user is 36 years old, college educated, with an average yearly income of $62,000. The rapid emergence of advanced networking technologies and innovative software solutions has contributed to the Internet's staggering 30% annual growth rate since 1990.

We will present the Internet to our clients as a superior form of advertising in terms of the value of service per advertising dollar. By integrating Worldwide Internet Marketing Services into our client's existing marketing plans, we will establish ourselves quickly in this growing worldwide market. The following table indicates average rates for yellow pages, newsprint, radio and television (samples taken from the Denver, Colorado-area media markets), and demonstrates our ability to compete directly with these traditional forms.

Sample Media	Service Offering	Average Audience	Average Rates
Yellow Pages	Full page, color	250,000+ homes and businesses	$823 monthly
Newsprint	Full page, black/white	110,000 (Sundays only)	$6,000 monthly
Radio	30 seconds	500,000+	$150-$2,000
Television	30 seconds	2.5+ million (prime time)	$3,000-$5,000
Worldwide Internet Marketing Services	*Commercial web page*	*30+ million, 24 hrs./day, 7 days/wk.*	*$500 setup, $1,000 monthly*

Advantages

Unlike traditional media, information within the Web is cross-referenced. For example, a business may list additional resources that are related to the topic of one of its Web pages. In traditional media, this is usually some sort of citation or bibliography. On the WWW, these cross-references are live, meaning that a simple click of the mouse on a particular citation will take you there immediately. This mechanism will also be used to weave a client's pages into the fabric of the WWW. For example, when a new page is placed online, we will register the page and its contents with the various search engines (similar to indexes) within the Internet. Future search results matching the new page's contents will be presented to the online user.

This weaving mechanism is far more effective at increasing readership than simply increasing publication rates. Because search facilities within the Internet use a weighted average method of determining whether a page meets specific search criteria, our client's pages could come up even if they are only somewhat related to the purpose of the search. For example, searching for pages on the topic of "kitchen knives" will yield results from companies that manufacture knives, kitchen knife wholesalers and retailers, knife sharpeners, kitchen knife interest groups, and so on. For the user who is really interested in kitchen knife interest groups, he or she may actually end up visiting a kitchen knife wholesaler's page, and find a real bargain. This sort of "incidental readership" is simply not possible with traditional media.

Another edge the Web possesses over traditional media is the ability to display color, graphics, sound and even animation within each Web page. Otherwise static advertisements can be brought to life using state-of-the-art multimedia tools. Our professional graphic artists will work closely with clients to achieve effective results, at a cost significantly lower than traditional media publication rates.

Advanced readership data collection is another area where traditional media cannot compete with a Web-based publication. For example, one of the standard measures collected for each of our clients is the so-called "hit rate" of the client's Web pages. This represents the number of times the page was accessed by an online user. Newspaper can guess at their readership by their circulation, but targeting readership statistics on a single advertisement is nearly impossible. Television and radio likewise suffer from this dilemma. By evaluating hit rates over time, we can work with our clients to streamline their messages to increase readership.

Web page hit rates are just one kind of measure available to our clients. Because Worldwide Internet Marketing Services employs two professional database programmers, virtually any kind of demographic data can be collected from readers who choose to fill out a form online. The data can then be presented to our clients in a format that allows them to continue to refine both their Web pages and their actual business processes to target this new kind of customer base.

The ultimate platform for commerce on the Internet is online sales. By integrating advanced database technology with Web page delivery systems, we can create virtual "malls" to distribute the products and services our clients have to offer. Online sales represent our largest profit potential, made possible only because Worldwide Internet Marketing Services employs two full-time computer professionals. The challenges of such a system include resolving legal issues associated with international commerce, building a sound and efficient delivery system, resolving concerns over the security of online transactions, and making it profitable for our clients. For these reasons, online sales must follow after the successful creation of a Web page delivery system.

The services Worldwide Internet Marketing Services will provide are based on two general billing categories: setup and maintenance. Setup describes the processes and resources needed to put a series of Web pages online. This fee is collected at the beginning of the order process, and can include the billable hours of various Worldwide Internet Marketing Services staff members. Maintenance represents the processes and resources needed to maintain the pages within the corporation's data processing resources, and can include client change requests.

Service Offerings

The service groups Worldwide Internet Marketing Services will offer are as follows:

Electronic Mailboxes

Electronic mail represents the personal correspondence medium of the Internet. Rates are set to compete with existing Internet service providers, and group rates are available for businesses wishing to establish e-mail boxes for their employees.

Personal Web Pages

A personal Web page allows a private individual to create and maintain a presence on the Internet. Setup and maintenance rates are set for the home-user's budget, and content and scope are left entirely to the individual.

Commercial Web Pages

Advertisers, manufacturers, wholesalers, retailers...any commercial enterprise that is expanding into the Internet can set up customized Web pages to get their messages out. By using the professional layout and design staff resources of Worldwide Internet Marketing Services, clients can expect a polished look for their online customers. Rates are set to easily compete with traditional print and broadcast media, and can be scaled to meet any advertising budget. Content and layout are at the complete discretion of the client.

Online Sales

This service takes the commercial Web page to the ultimate Internet presence: online transaction processing. By providing Worldwide Internet Marketing Services with a list of items to sell, a collection of pictures to scan and digitize, and specifying the online price of each item, our clients can open their businesses to the entire world. Worldwide Internet Marketing Services acts as the storefront, collecting funds and distributing them along with sales orders to our clients, who must then fill the orders. Once the system is set up, no additional sales and marketing resources are needed to keep the orders coming. The demographics of each buyer can be meticulously collected, such that our clients can continue to hone their approach to online sales. Again, content and layout--as well as the final price paid by an online buyer--are at the complete discretion of the client.

Web Design and Publishing Services

While Worldwide Internet Marketing Services will offer complete service packages, which includes a number of pages, a boilerplate layout, and maintenance fees, client projects will often require additional customization. Our professional publishing staff can assist our clients in achieving the exact look and feel they desire to reach their online customers.

Network Design Services

As the Internet itself expands into businesses, knowledge of how and why the Internet works will reach our clients. Because Worldwide Internet Marketing Services employs network design professionals, we can offer our clients complete solutions for creating and expanding existing premise network services, or even troubleshoot complex network problems. The goal of this service is to enhance the integration of our client's businesses into our own--to form a seamless partnership for continuous, mutual growth.

COMPETITION

To understand the boundaries of the business, a discussion of what Worldwide Internet Marketing Services will not offer is as valuable as the previous discussion on service offerings. Biting off more than one can chew is often as dangerous as not biting enough. Setting the scope of the business--and, therefore, the expectations of all involved--will help us avoid feast/famine situations that disrupt cash flow and lead to unnecessary stress.

Indeed, each of our business processes is designed using this approach: specifying ahead of time what will be done and what will not. Such specificity will allow us to close business with clients much more effectively, and will allow us to measure and tune client satisfaction with precision.

Setting scope also allows us to fine-tune our position within this growing marketplace. In all instances, our services overlap with our local competitor's offerings to the extent of providing a presence online. Of the three Internet Web page provider companies we evaluated in the Denver, Colorado area, the following statements can be made:

- One is run by University of Colorado college students, and could not be contacted professionally. Their services cater to creating Web pages for businesses simply to get them online. No professional design services are available. They do not own their computing resources.

- Another offers much the same service, but is not scheduled to go online until March 1, 1996. Again, no professional contact was available to answer our questions. They do not own their computing resources.

- The third offers professional Web design services, and targets state and local government, schools and hospitals. They also offer connections to the Internet via large pools of modems (a modem is the computing device used to access the Internet using the public telephone network). Additionally, because of their relationship with a local cable TV provider, they commit resources to coordinating cable TV simulcasts with area educational institutions. Their biggest expense by far is the maintenance of the physical points of presence they have located in cities throughout Colorado. Since Worldwide Internet Marketing Services is focused simply on Web page delivery and not actual access to the Internet, we avoid these costs and their associated liabilities.

- None of the three offers online sales processing systems.

- None of the three offers network design and troubleshooting services.

- None of the three employ computer science professionals. Worldwide Internet Marketing Services employs two graduates from the Denver Technological University with a combined knowledge of networks, database systems, and application programming that spans more than 25 years.

During our research, it became clear that this is a new marketplace, with a huge amount of potential, but rife with potential obstacles as well. We believe the plan we have devised for this business fills the gaps we knew existed ahead of time, and effectively addresses the current competition. We firmly believe that breaking into this arena now will allow us to be entrenched and ready to meet the explosive growth the Internet will continue to see in the future.

One of the key strengths of Worldwide Internet Marketing Services is the people who make it possible. In addition to personal relationships that exist within the group--some that extend as far back as 18 years--each brings to Worldwide Internet Marketing Services a sense of professionalism and drive that has been consistently successful for them in past endeavors. We all understand how important a tool the Internet can be to the success of our clients, and are committed to being not only financially strong, but well-respected among our clients and our competition. We will achieve this goal by producing win-win situations between Worldwide Internet Marketing Services and its clients using tools such as effective project scoping, personal contact, and highly flexible information systems.

PERSONNEL

Introducing the Worldwide Internet Marketing Services team!

Michael Bonelli, Controller

Michael brings to Worldwide Internet Marketing Services a business management and sales background that includes establishing successful corporations. Michael's primary duties with Worldwide Internet Marketing Services include managing cash flow, acting as the corporation's primary non-client external contact, market analysis, and the day-to-day operation of Worldwide Internet Marketing Services as a business entity. Michael will also act as the Worldwide Internet Marketing Services account representative for the Denver, Colorado area.

Richard McFeely, Sales/Marketing Manager

Richard's experiences as a professional stage manager and technical director for area theater groups, where coordination of human and physical resources to form both technically and artistically sound performances is essential, make him ideal as the corporation's Sales/ Marketing Manager. Serving as the primary external client contact, Richard's duties include managing the sales process within Worldwide Internet Marketing Services, and ensuring orders are completed to client satisfaction. Richard is also the Worldwide Internet Marketing Services account representative for the Dallas, Texas area.

Charles Raschke, Artistic Director

Screenplay author, school teacher, professional graphic artist, accomplished actor...all skills that Charles will use in his role as the corporation's Artistic Director. Charles' primary responsibilities include establishing standards for online publication, designing custom services for Worldwide Internet Marketing Services clients, and ensuring that the online "look and feel" of Worldwide Internet Marketing Services Web pages are professional and easy to use. Charles is also the Worldwide Internet Marketing Services account representative for Houston, Texas, by far our largest target market.

Glen Harper, Publisher

We elected to ask Glen to join us in this venture primarily because of his limitless imagination and his skill with computers. As Web page publisher, Glen will transform client requests into Web pages using his graphic artistry and ability to invent realities where none existed before. Glen will also serve as the Worldwide Internet Marketing Services account representative for Billings, Montana.

Victor Gold, Database Administrator

One of two computer science professionals on the Worldwide Internet Marketing Services team, Victor's primary responsibility is the integrity of the corporation's central store of data. His other duties include application design and programming, timely response to client service issues, in-house user support, and assisting with the design and implementation of the corporation's information systems.

Leonard Morgan, Network Operations Manager

Leonard will use his extensive experiences with data networks and database systems to design, install and maintain the corporation's Network Operations Center, located in Denver, Colorado. Leonard's duties include application design and programming, training of in-house staff, and day-to-day operations of the corporation's hardware and software resources. Additionally, Leonard will contract his time out to clients needing network design and/or troubleshooting services.

Because the information system is key to the success of Worldwide Internet Marketing Services, Victor and Leonard will possess completely redundant knowledge of how the system operates, such that the corporation is protected from the untimely loss of either person.

Work Environment

The design of our work environment was driven primarily by the environment of the Internet itself--a 24 hours per day, 7 days per week marketplace. As such, distinctions such as 8:00 a.m. to 5:00 p.m., Monday through Friday, quickly lose meaning. Without exception, all members of the Worldwide Internet Marketing Services team believe such distinctions harm productivity in what must be a self-motivated, self-managed environment. While we appreciate that most of our clients will conduct their business using standard business hours, we also know that the real business--the delivery of our client's messages--goes on constantly.

Our work environment consists of company-provided mobile computing equipment installed in the home of each principle team member. Using the public telephone network, Worldwide Internet Marketing Services team members have complete access to the corporation's central data store 24 hours a day, 7 days a week. Actual work time will be scheduled around client availability and operating hours, allowing team members to integrate Worldwide Internet Marketing Services into their lives based on their own schedules. The result will be a much higher per-hour productivity rate than the traditional 8:00 to 5:00, Monday to Friday regimen.

This is made possible in part due to our order-entry system. Each request from a client is treated as a self-contained project with well-defined scope. As stated previously, setting project scope and expectations effectively on the front-end of the sales process will benefit both the client and Worldwide Internet Marketing Services. Any requests outside this pre-defined scope are considered new projects, and documented accordingly. Not only is this an effective change-control system, but it allows projects to be handed to Worldwide Internet Marketing Services employees to work on within their own schedules. Later, at the touch of a button, a customer's complete project history can be obtained and analyzed for areas where our relationship with the client can be enhanced.

Also, with such a system, we can normalize salaries across the board, and throw out a great deal of inter-office politics and "bad blood" from the very beginning. We feel these barriers are artificial, and only hurt the business. Our clients, we feel, will expect and appreciate that such a forward-looking company would have such a futuristic method of conducting business.

Finally, our work environment could not exist without the full support and commitment of each Worldwide Internet Marketing Services team member.

This section describes the operating procedures designed by the Worldwide Internet Market- ing Services team to meet the challenges of delivering consistent, quality services to our clients and their online customers.

OPERATIONS

Every new business faces similar challenges on the road to long-term financial health, and Worldwide Internet Marketing Services is certainly no exception. Meeting a payroll, establish- ing and maintaining relationships with both clients and vendors, the endless filing of forms both internally and externally...all these areas can threaten even the most seasoned business professionals if a key element is missing: due diligence.

The Challenges

To understand the complexities of a business operation, one must first address each of the components that make up the processes the business uses to carry on day-to-day activities. Using flowcharting and other analysis tools, each process can then be examined for potential waste and streamlined. The combined processes--the essence of the business--will become collectively more efficient.

Due diligence comes into play when one recognizes that this process-by-process analysis is an ongoing, never-ending task that must be shared by all of the company's participants. Two Worldwide Internet Marketing Services staff members, Victor and Leonard, are ready to meet this challenge immediately; they both have received training from a previous employer on Total Quality Management techniques, which stress process analysis through due diligence as a key to long-term success.

Identifying and setting scope, whether for client projects or process streamlining, will become the business management tool of choice for Worldwide Internet Marketing Services. The main purpose of effective scoping is to break a complex task into manageable pieces such that all involved parties gain a clear understanding of first what will be done, and second what will not be done.

Scope Revisited

For client relationships, the challenge becomes building an effective order-entry management system that not only provides flexible alternatives to the client, but one that guarantees a profit for the corporation as well. For employee relationships, it means building an infrastructure that allows individual talent to flourish within a home office environment while still maintaining immediacy with both the company and its clients.

For existing businesses, such an embrace of process analysis has traditionally been an arduous task, as many habits, such as sales commissions, departmental boundaries--anything that serves as a wedge between employees--must first be broken. Worldwide Internet Marketing Services has two distinct advantages in this regard. First, a new company has few, if any, bad habits to break. Second, being prepared for process analysis on the front end allows us to build key quality measurements into our information systems from the start. In this fashion, most of the process analysis can be done by computer.

Over time, what will develop is a business system that can react immediately to changes within the business environment, whether the forces of change come from internal or external sources. But even with such a complex business system, it must be made aware of the changes to its environment, and that is where due diligence on the part of the Worldwide Internet Marketing Services team is essential.

Most of the business management tools will be accessed using the corporation's computer information systems. One of the strengths of the Worldwide Internet Marketing Services team

Information Management Tools

is that it employs two professional trainers experienced with getting people quickly up to speed with complex software applications. The information system itself was designed to be accessible from remote mobile workstations using the public telephone network. What follows is a list of the tools available to each Worldwide Internet Marketing Services employee to carry on the business of the corporation.

Mobile Workstation

Each remote employee will use a color notebook computer with a docking station located within the home office environment. A docking station is a device that allows the notebook computer to be inserted when the employee is at home. This turns the notebook computer into a full-featured workstation, complete with full-sized keyboard and video display, mouse, and other peripherals. When the employee travels onsite to a client's place of business, the notebook can be detached from the docking station. The notebook contains a high-speed modem for attachment to the public telephone network while the employee is at a client's place of business.

The benefit of the mobile workstation to the client is instant access to the Internet during meetings with the client. This means that not only are Worldwide Internet Marketing Services resources available for access, but the entire Internet as well. In this fashion, our clients can receive instant answers to their questions and concerns, browse Worldwide Internet Marketing Services pages to get a feel for the kind of services we offer, and scan the Internet itself for ideas and additional information. As a sales tool, the mobile remote workstation conveys professionalism and competence to the client.

For the employee, the docking station solves the ergonomic problem of long-term use of small keyboards and small display screens. By turning the notebook into a high-powered workstation, the value of the notebook computer is enhanced, and the employee gains a much friendlier work environment.

Operating System

Each Worldwide Internet Marketing Services workstation will run the Microsoft Windows/NT operating system. Windows/NT represents the cutting edge of high-performance operating systems for personal computers, particularly in a business environment.

Accounting Software

Worldwide Internet Marketing Services will use a software package from Intuit called QuickBooks Pro, which is designed specifically for small businesses. It features bank account management, printed checks, payroll, accounts payable/receivable, invoices, statements, inventory, audit trails, job costing, budgeting, and many others. It also features data import and export features that will be used to exchange accounting information with a custom project control application written by the Worldwide Internet Marketing Services information services staff.

Project Management

Written specifically for Worldwide Internet Marketing Services, ProManager takes the entire process of doing business, combines it with quality management measurements, adds data shared with the accounting system, and produces a robust project management tool that is easy to use and understand. Worldwide Internet Marketing Services account representatives can create custom quotes, call up project information and history, and print custom contracts ready for client signature, all while the representative is on-site with the client. Change-orders, back steps (a quality management term used to describe inefficiencies within a business process), work history, and client satisfaction will all be documented within ProManager's history-tracking mechanism.

Web Browser

The World Wide Web browser software of choice for Worldwide Internet Marketing Services is NetScape Navigator. This award-winning package is actually a control center for a variety of Internet services, including the Web, file transfers (FTP), electronic mail, and network news (the Usenet). NetScape also contains a "helper application" feature that allows NetScape to be seamlessly integrated into the desktop environment. As particular resources on the Internet are accessed, NetScape evaluates the contents of the information and executes the appropriate "helper application" to actually view the information. For Worldwide Internet Marketing Services clients already using the Internet, NetScape offers a consistent interface for evaluating Worldwide Internet Marketing Services-created pages.

NetScape also supports a wide variety of forms control features so that Web pages can be constructed to retrieve data entered by online users. Another feature of Worldwide Internet Marketing Services ProManager is the ability to create and maintain customized databases to track this input. Examples include demographic information, product preferences, suggestion boxes, and of course, the ultimate in Internet commerce, online sales.

Mail and Scheduling

A benefit to the Windows/NT operating system is that it contains Microsoft Mail and Microsoft Schedule+. In an age of information, electronic mail is an indispensable business tool, and will be the primary form of internal correspondence. for clients already possessing electronic mail boxes, e-mail becomes a very useful tool to maintain client relationships. Microsoft Schedule+ is a calendering and scheduling package that allows appointments to be scheduled online for groups of both human and physical resources. Both tools drastically reduce the amount of paper necessary to operate a business, and have built-in searching features that allow historical data to be accessed with ease.

Office Automation

Office automation applications include word processing, spreadsheets, presentation managers, desktop publishers, and facsimile management. While complete suites of products exist to meet all these needs, Worldwide Internet Marketing Services will be using a customized suite of office automation tools designed to maximize productivity.

Document Management

One of the goals of the Worldwide Internet Marketing Services information systems design is a paper less office environment. Both computing professionals on the Worldwide Internet Marketing Services team have worked in paper less offices in the past, and know the mechanics--and the pitfalls--of installing such a system. The key to a successful document management system is to first understand how processes actually flow within the corporation, and then design a system that fits these processes. Too often, the system is installed first, and only later is it discovered that inefficiencies such as dual-entry, slow response times on archival searches, and poor document indexing methods are a necessary part of the document management process. Worldwide Internet Marketing Services has chosen instead to define and refine its business processes first. Given the system we will be implementing, a document management system could very well end up as an application written in-house; current document management applications available commercially are very new, and rife with potential pitfalls.

Software Development

One of the many advantages Worldwide Internet Marketing Services has over its competitors is two computer science professionals fluent in powerful programming languages. The ability to create robust applications on the fly will allow Worldwide Internet Marketing Services to be very flexible with regards to meeting both client and employee need. We think of application development as the "glue" holding the information systems design together.

Central Database

All of the corporation's data and application software will be centrally located and spread over three physical server-class computers. One server will act as the central repository for all data relating to clients, and Worldwide Internet Marketing Services as a business entity. Using high-end database server technology, Worldwide Internet Marketing Services will share, distribute, and secure its electronic data among clients and employees.

Network Operating System

The role of a network operating system is to provide secure access to shared resources such as files, printers, storage devices (hard disks, CD-ROMs, tape drives, etc.), and software applications. Worldwide Internet Marketing Services has selected the Microsoft Windows NT Advanced Server operating system to fill this important role. Windows NTAS, a network server edition of Windows NT, was designed for advanced networking within business environments, and is a perfect complement to our existing equipment.

Network Operations Center

The basis of the Worldwide Internet Marketing Services information system is the Network Operations Center to be installed at 18765 Industrial Turnpike in Denver, Colorado. The design for the Center includes hardware, software, and cabling necessary to support the applications described above, as well as provide a sound delivery system for Web pages to online customers. Many of the features of this network design set Worldwide Internet Marketing Services well ahead of its competition, both in terms of knowledge of how complex networks are designed and implemented, and in terms of the tremendous processing power of the system itself. The key areas of the design are as follows:

Internet Access

Direct Internet access from the Network Operations Center will be accomplished using Denver Cablevision's Netline Service. Traditionally, connections to the Internet have been made using dedicated digital service lines leased through a service provider, such as the local telephone company. This type of service contributes to one of the current problems associated with using the Internet: bandwidth shortage.

Bandwidth describes how much data can be moved through a network over a period of time. Because the Internet has grown in size so quickly, many older networks are struggling to keep up with the increasing demand for data. This is likely to be a temporary situation, however, as elements such as the United States Communications Act of 1996, which allows open competition between local phone, long-distance phone and cable companies, combined with ever-emerging, faster networking technologies, will help reduce bandwidth as a constraint to conducting business on the Internet.

Denver Cablevision has met the challenge of bandwidth consumption through their Netline service. If we assume that a Web page consists of two kilobytes of information (a byte is a basic unit of measure for data, and can be thought of as a single letter of the alphabet; a kilobyte is a collection of 1,024 bytes), then the following table indicates the differences between Denver Cablevision's offering and traditional Internet connection methods:

Service	Installation Cost	Per Month Fee	Max Web Pages per Second
64kbs Digital Circuit	$800-$1200	$400-$600	32
1.55Mbps Digital Circuit	$2500-$5000	$1500-$3000	794
Denver Cablevision 10Mbps Netline Service	$900 (waived for signing a 3-year contract)	$450	5120

Clearly, Denver Cablevision's offering is the most cost-effective method of connecting to the Internet. And, other than Fort Collins and Denver, Colorado, this service is unavailable in virtually every other part of the United States. This means Worldwide Internet Marketing Services can deliver its services at speeds its competitors can only dream about.

Another benefit Denver Cablevision brings to the table is that the first two services listed above establish the physical connection to the Internet only; additional costs would be incurred to contract with an Internet service provider to actually begin the delivery of network data. Denver Cablevision's offering includes these costs.

The signal is brought to the Network Operation Center through Denver Cablevision's existing cable TV system. Connecting the entry point of this cable into the building to the Worldwide Internet Marketing Services network is the only network infrastructure installation task required for Internet access.

Remote Internet Access

For each home office employee, the corporation will maintain an account with a nationwide Internet service provider that will allow them to access the Worldwide Internet Marketing Services network, as well as the rest of the Internet, from virtually any point in the public telephone network.

Premise Network

The infrastructure for the Network Operation Center consists of two physical networks. One network is connected to Denver Cablevision's Netline service, and is therefore exposed to the Internet. All premise workstations are attached to this network, which serves as the primary office automation delivery system. A second, private network is based on high-speed (100Mbps) technology to offer very high bandwidth between the corporation's server computers. This network will allow inter-server communications to remain separate and secure from the Internet, as well as provide enough bandwidth to scale easily as Worldwide Internet Marketing Services grows.

Cabling for the public data network will be distributed to most locations within the Network Operations Center. When employees come to the Center to work, they will be able to attach their notebook computers directly to the premise network. Groups of cables are located in key areas to facilitate employee work sessions.

Network Management

Managing a successful network installation typically means avoiding productivity back steps such as network downtime, loss of data, application failure, and gaps in employee knowledge of the system. Consistent notification and analysis of network problems, coupled with a fault-tolerant network design, are the keys to a successful network implementation.

Some of the management features of the Worldwide Internet Marketing Services corporate network are as follows:

- Modular component design. This means that hardware components can be easily swapped among all network devices.

- Hot, standby power supply. An uninterruptable power supply will be installed that is capable of supplying power to network servers and hubs for approximately one hour, providing ample time for a controlled shutdown of all network devices if a prolonged power outage is expected. Backup power duration can be increased by simply adding batteries.

- Dual, mirrored fixed disks and disk controllers within the database server. Data is written to multiple physical disk drives. Should a disk fail, a mirror copy of the data prevents data loss and server downtime.

- Interchangeable servers. Each server-class computer within the Worldwide Internet Marketing Services network will be configured such that it can perform all of the tasks of all other servers. This method allows periodic maintenance to be scheduled so that delivery of services is not interrupted.

- Backup and retrieval system. Every 24 hours, a complete copy of the corporation's data is written to data tapes. A tape rotation process ensures that multiple copies of the corporation's data are stored in secure locations to guard against catastrophic loss of the Network Operations Center. This is actually part of a larger disaster recovery plan covering the entire corporation.

- Windows NT Advanced Server. The network operating system itself contains a wealth of network management tools for monitoring the current health of the system. Notification of important network events is delivered by audible alarm, printed notification, electronic mail, and personal paging device. A management process that includes regular analysis of network activity logs will ensure stable network operation.

- Victor Gold and Leonard Morgan. The benefits of employing two computer science professionals means that Worldwide Internet Marketing Services will have much more intimate knowledge of its information systems than its competitors, who generally lease these services. This immediacy will result in a well-thought collection of network management processes designed to deliver consistent, quality services to Worldwide Internet Marketing Services employees, clients, and online customers.

FINANCIAL DATA

Note: Please see the Balance Sheet and Profit Analysis tables located at the end of this section for additional detail.

This section covers in detail the components that make up our financial plan. For the first year, we have detailed our forecast Balance Sheet and Profit Analysis by month. For years two and three, we have compiled the same information by quarter. A key assumption in this process was to select the most conservative numbers possible, based primarily on our competition within both traditional print and broadcast media, and other online service providers. Even though our forecasts indicate strong financial health in the first year, given our position both professionally and technically, we believe we will do much better than the forecasts suggest.

Income

In order to quantify each service rate, we constructed a series of spreadsheets that allowed us to break each service offering into its component parts. What followed were a series of formulas that we will integrate into ProManager, the project management software we will use. The main purpose of creating the formulas was to build a framework so that if the inputs into the formulas remain constant, the corporation will always earn revenue.

An ideal world consists of constant, predictable input into these formulas. However, meeting specific client's needs will almost certainly demand some flexibility with regard to actual billings. ProManager was designed to allow each Worldwide Internet Marketing Services account representative to modify the construction of these formulas in an easy-to-use fashion using both hypothetical and live client scenarios as guidelines. The deviation from the formulas can be recorded and later analyzed for possible streamlining of the entire sales process. The account representative can then look for patterns of sale, allowing the creation of an effective, ever-evolving sales presentation.

The key point to remember is that the mechanics of the business drive the formulas, not the reverse.

Service Points

A service point is the basic unit of measure in the Worldwide Internet Marketing Services business process, and represents a single project with well-defined scope and costs. On the attached Balance Sheet and Profit Analysis spreadsheet, the Service Acquisition Rate indicates how many service points within each service offering we expect to accumulate over a one-month period. This is a key measurement, as it indicates how much business we must conduct to meet our financial goals.

Setup fees

Setup costs represent the amount of time needed by various Worldwide Internet Marketing Services team members to create the essence of the service offering. For Web pages, this means the costs of the Worldwide Internet Marketing Services resources needed to design the layout, place and test the pages online, and scan any items to appear within the pages, all to the ultimate satisfaction of the client. Contracts will be constructed to include an agreed-upon number of changes, beyond which the client must pay for change-orders (such entities become new service points in this model).

Template Web page layouts will be available in package form. We expect, however, that most clients will want additional customization. The Design Services line item includes forecast costs for these add-on service points, and includes unscheduled change-orders. Similarly, the Network Services line item covers service points associated with consulting time for network design and troubleshooting services.

For consulting services, a service point is defined as a 10-hour block of time billed at $120 per hour. The worksheet forecasts the acquisition rate for consulting services as a single service point per month each for design and network services.

Maintenance Fees

Maintenance is defined as the per-month costs associated with storing and maintaining the integrity of client Internet resource information, and includes Web pages, database entries, and any other piece of information kept by Worldwide Internet Marketing Services on behalf of its clients. The maintenance fee formulas use the following criteria to evaluate maintenance costs:

- Amount of information stored, measured in bytes;
- Database transaction collection, measured in number of data item per form (clients receive at no cost the hit rate, which is the number of times a page is loaded, for all their Web pages);
- Web page "dead link" maintenance, measured in number of links per Web page (a link is defined as an item on a Web page that, when clicked, loads another Web page. Links can load pages from anywhere in the Internet. Ensuring that these links actually load something is part of regular Web system maintenance. This process is almost completely automated).

Online Sales

Because online sales represent the natural evolution of fully-interactive Web pages, it will be the last service point offering to become available. The forecast worksheet includes no revenue from this source for the first two months, and a modest acquisition rate of one service point every other month. Likewise, the elements that make up the online sales formulas are very conservative, and use the following assumptions:

- Setup and maintenance fees are identical to Commercial Web Page service points
- The per item cost of scanning and digitizing online sale items is $10
- Worldwide Internet Marketing Services collects 7.5% of the online price from each transaction
- The formula assumes 25 items are for sale, and each one is scanned
- The formula assumes it requires 10 Web pages to sell these 25 items
- The formula assumes the average price of each item is $10
- The formula assumes, in total, 30 items sold in one month

We believe that online sales will be a tremendous source of revenue for large-volume clients. Even using the numbers described above, the worksheet indicates and additional $500 of revenue per month over the maintenance costs of a commercial web client.

Non-profit Organizations

Community involvement is one way to build a company's reputation, and Worldwide Internet Marketing Services believes it can offer a tremendous service to non-profit organizations, who must deal with limited budgets. We expect to sign per-client contracts that specifically address these needs, and will, in many cases, offer pro bono services where the team feels it is warranted.

Expenses

Another strength of Worldwide Internet Marketing Services will be its ability to conduct business with minimal ongoing expense. Every element of our business process design has had the goal of reducing expense wherever possible. Our business management system will allow us to react instantly to changes in our cash flow. Our work environment seeks to maximize productivity and minimize stress. In all, Worldwide Internet Marketing Services will become a streamlined business entity that will require comparatively little resources for the services it intends to deliver.

Salary/Wages

The Worldwide Internet Marketing Services business philosophy allows us to normalize salaries for the six principle team members to $25,000 annually over the first three years. A tight belt is easily loosened, and since salaries make up the biggest portion of our ongoing expenses, we chose a salary that would allow the company to grow as quickly as possible, while still meeting individual need.

Employee benefits will be one of the first challenges we will face as a new corporation. We intend to provide a comprehensive set of benefits to all our employees. In fact, using Glen Harper, the Worldwide Internet Marketing Services Publisher, as an example (Glen has a wife and a new son; as such, they represent the greatest needs among all Worldwide Internet Marketing Services employees with regards to medical benefits), we intend to construct a package that is at once affordable to the corporation and meets the needs of all involved.

The percentage used to calculate the FICA line item was 6.2%.

Lease

Because the Network Operations Center is located within the residence of the Network Operations Manager, we can greatly reduce our leasehold expense. The number appearing in this line item was calculated as a percentage of total square footage the network will occupy, and then multiplied by the monthly lease amount: 30% of 1350 sq. ft. costing $850 per month is approximately $250.

Network Installation/Operation

By far the biggest start-up cost, network installation includes installing and testing the Network Operations Center, installing mobile workstations and testing remote connectivity, and designing and implementing the management processes needed to maintain network resources. A $6000 per year operating budget covers equipment malfunction, media (disks and tapes), printer resources (paper, toner and ink cartridges), and other expenses associated with operating a network of this size.

During our design, we looked at leasing the equipment we would need for this operation. The primary advantage of a lease arrangement is much lower start-up costs, and potentially less monthly maintenance. A secondary attraction to leases is that much less technical skill is required to operate the equipment, since a service agreement is generally part of the overall lease.

However, a lease can be a disadvantage when something actually goes wrong with the system. In our business, we lose revenue for every minute our network is down. Even the best service contracts still have 4-8 hour response times, and the service generally comes at a stiff premium. With two network professionals on staff, this disadvantage disappears, as most network problems can be solved immediately with the resources available.

Another advantage to purchasing lies in the structure of Worldwide Internet Marketing Services itself. We expect Worldwide Internet Marketing Services to become a separate, wholly-owned corporation in time. For the present, it is a D.B.A. of Shark Corporation. Shark Corporation will actually own the network resources. When Worldwide Internet Marketing Services incorporates, it will lease the use of these resources from Shark Corporation. The advantages come at tax time, when a combination of depreciation and leasehold write-offs reduces the real cost of ownership. The result is a fault-tolerant information delivery system that can react instantly to changes within its operating environment.

Marketing

To increase our own name recognition, we have budgeted $500 per month for year one, $750 per month for year two, and $1000 per month for year three. This amount covers not only marketing activities, but includes $280 per year for membership in the Denver Regional Chamber of Commerce. The Denver Regional Chamber of Commerce offers many services to small businesses, particularly new firms, and includes market analysis, resources for capital equipment acquisition, and member databases containing detailed information about Denver businesses.

Our first advertising activity will consist of a direct mail piece targeting audiences gathered from our research at the Denver Regional Chamber of Commerce. We will also target local radio early in our marketing campaign.

Utilities

Denver Cablevision's Netline service costs $450 per month for 8 Internet (IP) addresses. This means eight physical Worldwide Internet Marketing Services network devices can join the Internet community using Denver Cablevision's offering. For signing a three-year contract, they will waive their $1400 installation fee.

Power consumption is based on the specifications for the hardware as specified in the network design. We increase the cost $5 every two months to reflect the power consumption costs of a growing network.

A toll-free (800) phone service line will be necessary to ensure that the Network Operations Center can be easily reached by both employees and clients. It will also act as the initial primary phone contact point for the entire corporation. The cost increases $25 every six months to reflect increased usage over time.

Remote access costs are based on services available from one of the largest Internet service providers in the world. The cost of the service is $29.95 per month per remote employee. This will allow each remote employee to attach to the Internet at virtually any point within the public telephone system. Though this cost stays constant, we expect the actual cost to reduce over time as competition between service providers increases.

Loan Payments

This line item was included to show the monthly cost of a small business loan of $200,000 at 8.5% paid over three years. This amount would pay for the initial capital investment, and cover our expenses for six months.

Net Profits

The final section of the forecast spreadsheet indicates net profits before taxes. We expect this amount to be reduced at year-end by payments to shareholders and company reinvestment such that our revised net before taxes will place us in a strong tax situation.

Using the data from the entire forecast worksheet, we were able to create the enclosed cash flow analysis chart. Two elements of this chart worth noting are as follows:

- The corporation begins to turn a profit after month two.
- The start-up costs for the network are essentially paid for by month nine.

Even with the most conservative numbers, the financial outlook for Worldwide Internet Marketing Services is undeniably strong. Online sales, which we expect to be the biggest source of long-term revenue, do not figure significantly into our income projections due to our consistently conservative approach to the model itself. In short, we believe we are going to earn profits.

Balance Sheet and Profit Analysis (Year One)

Income

								Month						
Service Acq. Rate	Setup	Monthly Income	1	2	3	4	5	6	7	8	9	10	11	12
Personal WEB Service														
8.00	96	36	768	1,056	1,344	1,632	1,920	2,208	2,496	2,784	3,072	3,360	3,648	3,936
Commercial WEB Services														
12.00	500	1,000	6,000	18,001	30,003	42,004	54,006	66,007	78,009	90,010	102,012	114,013	126,014	138,016
Online Sales 0.50	500	1,565	0	0	1,815	2,597	3,379	4,161	4,944	5,726	6,508	7,290	8,073	8,855
E-Mail Svcs. 10.00	45	15	450	600	750	900	1,050	1,200	1,350	1,500	1,650	1,800	1,950	2,100
Design Svcs. 2.0	1,200	0	2,400	2,400	2,400	2,400	2,400	2,400	2,400	2,400	2,400	2,400	2,400	2,400
Network Svcs. 1.00	1,200	0	1,200	1,200	1,200	1,200	1,200	1,200	1,200	1,200	1,200	1,200	1,200	1,200
TOTALS			**10,818**	**23,257**	**37,511**	**50,733**	**63,955**	**77,177**	**90,398**	**103,620**	**116,842**	**130,063**	**143,285**	**156,507**
SERVICE POINTS			34	67	101	134	168	201	235	268	302	335	369	402

Six Month's Sales: 263,452   First Year Sales: 104,166

Expenses

	Startup	1	2	3	4	MONTH 5	6	7	8	9	10	11	12
Salary/Wages													
1. Controller	2,100	2,100	2,100	2,100	2,100	2,100	2,100	2,100	2,100	2,100	2,100	2,100	2,100
2. Sales/Mktg. Mgr.	2,100	2,100	2,100	2,100	2,100	2,100	2,100	2,100	2,100	2,100	2,100	2,100	2,100
3. Database Mgr.	2,100	2,100	2,100	2,100	2,100	2,100	2,100	2,100	2,100	2,100	2,100	2,100	2,100
4. Network Operations Mgr.	2,100	2,100	2,100	2,100	2,100	2,100	2,100	2,100	2,100	2,100	2,100	2,100	2,100
5. Artistic Dir.	2,100	2,100	2,100	2,100	2,100	2,100	2,100	2,100	2,100	2,100	2,100	2,100	2,100
6. Publisher	2,100	2,100	2,100	2,100	2,100	2,100	2,100	2,100	2,100	2,100	2,100	2,100	2,100
7. FICA	--	781	781	781	781	781	781	781	781	781	781	781	781
B. Lease	--	250	250	250	250	250	250	250	250	250	250	250	250
C. Network Installation/Operation	78,184	500	500	500	500	500	500	750	750	750	750	750	750
D. Marketing	--	500	500	500	500	500	500	500	500	500	500	500	500
E. Utilities	--	--	--	--	--	--	--	--	--	--	--	--	--
1. Denver Cablevision (Internet)	--	450	450	450	450	450	450	450	450	450	450	450	450
2. Power	--	50	50	55	55	60	60	65	65	70	70	75	75
3. (800 number)	100	100	100	100	100	100	100	125	125	125	125	125	125
4. Remote Access	--	599	749	749	749	749	749	749	749	749	1,048	1,048	1,048
F. Loan Payments (200,000 over 3 years @ 8.5%)	--	6,500	6,500	6,500	6,500	6,500	6,500	6,500	6,500	6,500	6,500	6,500	6,500
TOTALS	90,884	22,330	22,480	22,485	22,485	22,490	22,490	22,770	22,770	22,775	23,074	23,079	23,079

Six month's Expenses: 134,759 **First Year Expenses: 363,191**

Net

Month:	1	2	3	4	5	6	7	8	9	10	11	12
Net Before Taxes	(11,512)	778	15,027	28,248	41,465	54,687	67,628	80,850	94,067	106,989	120,206	133,427

Six month's Profits: 128,692 **First Year Profits: 731,860**

Profit Analysis (Years Two and Three)

Income

	Service Acq. Rate	Setup	Maint	Y2,Q1	Y2,Q2	Y2,Q3	Y2,Q4	Y3,Q1	Y3,Q2	Y3,Q3	Y3, Q4
Personal WEB Svcs.	8.00	96	36	4,800	5,664	6,528	7,392	8,256	9,120	9,984	10,848
Commercial WEB Svcs.	12.00	500	1,000	174,020	210,024	246,029	282,033	318,037	354,042	390,046	426,050
Online Sales	0.50	500	1,565	11,202	13,548	15,895	18,242	20,589	22,935	25,282	27,629
E-Mail Services	10.00	45	15	2,550	3,000	3,450	3,900	4,350	4,800	5,250	5,700
Design Services	2.00	1,200	0	2,400	2,400	2,400	2,400	2,400	2,400	2,400	2,400
Network Services	1.00	1,200	0	1,200	1,200	1,200	1,200	1,200	1,200	1,200	1,200
TOTALS:				196,172	235,837	275,502	315,167	354,832	394,497	434,162	473,827
SERVICE POINTS:				503	603	704	804	905	1005	1106	1206

Second Year Sales: 1,022,677 **Third Year Sales: 1,657,319**

Expenses

	Y2,Q1	Y2,Q2	Y2,Q3	Y2,Q4	Y3,Q1	Y3,Q2	Y3,Q3	Y3,Q4
A. Salary/Wages								
1. Controller	6,300	6,300	6,300	6,300	6,300	6,300	6,300	6,300
2. Sales/Marketing Mgr.	6,300	6,300	6,300	6,300	6,300	6,300	6,300	6,300
3. Database Manager	6,300	6,300	6,300	6,300	6,300	6,300	6,300	6,300
4. Network Operations Mgr.	6,300	6,300	6,300	6,300	6,300	6,300	6,300	6,300
5. Artistic Director	6,300	6,300	6,300	6,300	6,300	6,300	6,300	6,300
6. Publisher	6,300	6,300	6,300	6,300	6,300	6,300	6,300	6,300
7. FICA	2,343	2,343	2,343	2,343	2,343	2,343	2,343	2,343
B. Lease	750	750	750	750	750	750	750	750
C. Network Installation/Operation	2,250	2,250	2,250	3,000	3,000	3,000	3,000	4,500
D. Marketing	2,250	2,250	2,250	2,250	3,000	3,000	3,000	3,000
E. Utilities	--	--	--	--	--	---	--	--
1. Denver Cablevision (Internet)	1,350	1,350	1,350	1,350	1,350	1,350	1,350	1,350
2. Power	150	165	180	195	200	205	210	300
3. (800 Number)	375	375	375	375	400	400	400	400
4. Remote Access	1,048	1,048	1,048	1,498	1,498	1,498	1,498	1,498
F. Loan Payments (200,000 over 3 years @ 8.5%)								
	19,500	19,500	19,500	19,500	19,500	19,500	19,500	19,500
TOTALS:	67,816	67,831	67,846	69,061	69,841	69,846	69,851	71,441

2nd Year Expenses: 272,554   3rd Year Expenses: 280,977

Net

	Y2,Q1	Y2,Q2	Y2,Q3	Y2,Q4	Y3,Q1	Y3,Q2	Y3,Q3	Y3,Q4
Net Before Taxes	128,356	168,006	207,656	246,106	284,992	324,652	364,312	402,387

2nd Year Profits: 750,123   Third Year Profits: 1,376,342

Three-Year Profits: 2,858,324

Internetwork Component Cost Schedule

Network Infrastructure

Qty.	Description	Vendor	Cost	Total
1	100BASETXHub (8 100Mbps ports)	DCW,p 13	1,449.00	1,449.00
1	10BASET Hub (16 10Mbps ports)	DCW,p 13	259.00	259.00
1	Equipment rack 60"W x 24"D x 74"H	Global,p 215	222.95	222.95
1	Category Install Kit (1000ft cable, tester)	DCW,p 75	279.00	279.00
1	Universal Coaxial Installation Kit	DCW,p 70	299.00	299.00
6	Cat 5 patch cable, 25', 3 red, 3 green	DCW,p 82	15.95	95.70
6	Cat 5 patch cable, 14', 3 red, 3 green	DCW,p 82	11.95	71.70
2	SMC EtherPower PCI 10/100 NIC	DCW,p 24	529.00	1,058.00
1	SMC EtherPower EISA 10/100 NICs, 5pak	DCW,p 24	1,119.00	1,119.00
1	SMC EtherPower EISA 10/100 NIC	DCW,p 24	239.00	239.00
3	SMC EtherEZ 10Mbps NIC	DCW,p 24	94.95	284.85
1	APC Smart-UPS 2200 w/PowerChute	DCW,p 15	1,229.95	1,229.95
4	Megahertz PCMCIA Ethernet Modem 28.8	DCW,p 41	350.00	350.00
			Total:	6,957.15

Database Server

Qty.	Description	Vendor	Cost	Total
1	Dual Pentium 133, 32MB, 2GB, PCI/EISA	Gateway	5,135.00	5,135.00
1	32MB Memory upgrade	Gateway	1,200.00	1,200.00
1	Upgrade 2GB disk to 4GB	Gateway	500.00	500.00
2	GB disk	Gateway	1,200.00	2,400.00
1	ExeByte 7GB 8mm tape w/SCSI, external	Insight,p 28	1,999.00	1,999.00
			Total:	11,234.00

Process Servers

Qty.	Description	Vendor	Cost	Total
2	Pentium 133, 32MB, 2GB, PCI/EISA	Gateway	4,735.00	9,470.00
2	32MB Memory Upgrade	Gateway	1,200.00	2,400.00
			Total:	11,870.00

Workstations

Qty.	Description	Vendor	Cost	Total
2	Pentium 120, 16MB, 1.2GB, PCI/ISA	Net Computers	1,929.00	3,858.00
2	16MB memory upgrades	Net Computers	519.00	1,038.00
3	KFC 15" SVGA color display	Net Computers	335.00	1,005.00
3	KFC 17" SVGA color display	Net Computers	669.00	2,007.00
1	1MB video adapter upgrades	Net Computers	100.00	200.00
4	Compaq LTE 5000/810 notebook	Net Computers	4,700.00	18,800.00
4	Compaq Docking Stations for LTE 5000	Net Computers	2,000.00	8,000.00
4	Carrying cases for LTE 5000	Net Computers	150.00	600.00
4	8MB memory upgrades for LTE 5000	Net Computers	400.00	1,600.00
			Total:	37,108.00

Printing

Qty.	Description	Vendor	Cost	Total
1	Hewlett-Packard DeskJet 660c color Total	Insight, p 37	389.00	389.00
1	Color ink cartridge for HP 660c	Insight, p 37	29.00	29.00
1	Black ink cartridge for HP 660c	Insight, p 37	29.00	29.00
1	HP ScanJet Color Scanner	Insight, p 40	800.00	800.00
			Total:	1,247.00

Software

Qty.	Description	Vendor	Cost	Total
1	Windows/NTAS, 10 Win/NT client pak	DCW,p 10	949.95	949.95
2	Windows/NTAS server licenses	DCW,p 10	579.95	1,159.90
1	Borland Interbase for NT, 20 licenses	Borland	5,000.00	5,000.00
1	Borland delphi Client/Server	Borland	595.00	595.00

1	QuickBooks Pro	Intuit	200.00	200.00
1	Microsoft Excel 5.0	Global,p 54	289.95	289.95
1	WordPerfect 6.1	Global, p 56	279.00	279.00
1	Microsoft Mail Server	CS, p 380	299.00	299.00
1	Director 4.0 (desktop/WEB publishing)	CS, p 380	500.00	500.00
1	Purveyor WEB Server for Windows/NT	OTEC,p 86	495.00	495.00

Total:9,767.80

Subtotal:78,183.95

Services

Qty.	Description	Vendor	Cost	Total
1	TCI MET Service Installation	TCI	900.00	WAIVED
20	Systems Assured Network Design, hourly rate	L. Morgan	150.00	3,000.00
160	Newtwork Installation and Testing, hourly rate	Shark IS Staff	150.00	WAIVED

Total: 3,000.00

First-Year Expenses

Qty.	Description	Vendor	Cost	Total
12	TCI Met Service	TCI	450.00	5,400.00
12	Electric Utility	CPC	50.00	600.00
12	INTERNET Service Providers, 5 people	Interramp	149.75	1,797.00
1	Operating budget	Shark	6,000.00	6,000.00

Total: 13,797.00

First Year Cash Flow Analysis

Month:	1	2	3	4	5	6
Startup Equipment Costs	93,000	93,000	93,000	93,000	93,000	93,000
Expenses	22,000	22,000	22,000	22,000	22,000	22,000
Income	10,000	22,000	39,000	53,000	61,000	77,000
Profits	(10,000)	0	15,000	26,000	40,000	52,000

Month:	7	8	9	10	11	12
Startup Equipment Costs	93,000	93,000	93,000	93,000	93,000	93,000
Expenses	22,000	22,000	22,000	22,000	22,000	22,000
Income	93,000	104,000	120,000	137,000	142,000	157,000
Profits	70,000	77,000	93,000	110,000	120,000	130,000

This section includes an implementation plan outline that covers the first 90 days of operation, once financing is secured. We include this section to demonstrate our readiness to undertake this task immediately. For purposes of this outline, Month Zero represents the 30-day period just prior to where Month 1 starts within the forecast spreadsheet.

- Month Zero Goal - Ready to go live by beginning of Month 1
    - Begin client acquisition
    - Begin capital equipment purchases
    - Install Network Operation Center
    - Design all Worldwide Internet Marketing Services business processes. For each process:
        - Define each team member's operational scope
        - Define each business process, produce task list
        - Assign tasks to each team member. Tasks are ongoing
    - Begin test runs of accounting system processes
    - Begin test runs of Pro Manager integration
    - Train Worldwide Internet Marketing Services team on software applications

- Month One Goal - Demonstrate delivery System
    - Put first client Web pages online
    - Complete test runs on accounting system processes
    - Complete test runs on Pro Manager Integration
    - Complete training of Worldwide Internet Marketing Services team
    - Begin design of online sales delivery process
    - Continue test runs on all other Worldwide Internet Marketing Services business processes

- Month Two Goal - Systems Assurance
    - Continue to build client base
    - Complete test runs on business processes. Begin ongoing analysis and improvement.
    - Begin test runs of online sales delivery system
    - Begin to examine historical client data on a regular basis

- Month Three goal - Online Sales
    - Continue to build client base
    - Select first online sales client
    - Continue test runs of online sales delivery system
    - Continue business process analysis and improvement

Mailing List Service

BUSINESS PLAN

FOREST MAIL SERVICE

8380 Prospect Blvd.
Seattle, WA 98102

Forest Mail Service is a mailing list service business designed to assist small business owners with managing their direct mail efforts. Forest Mail Service provides database management of a business customer base to include list verification, merge/purge services, and lettershop services. Additionally, Forest Mail Service assists the business owner with direct marketing consultation in conducting a direct marketing campaign. This plan reviews the current market, competition, skills, and financing required to successfully build a mailing list service.

- EXECUTIVE SUMMARY

- DESCRIPTION OF BUSINESS

- PRODUCT OR SERVICE

- THE MARKET

- PRODUCTION & OPERATION

- ENTREPRENEURS

- FINANCING REQUIRED

- MAJOR RISKS & PROBLEMS

- FINANCIAL STATEMENTS

EXECUTIVE SUMMARY

Business Overview

Forest Mail Service is a home based sole proprietorship mailing list service business designed to assist small business owners in the Columbia Basin with managing their direct mail (or marketing) efforts. Forest Mail Service will provide database management of a business customer base to include list verification, merge/purge, and also provide lettershop services. Additionally, Forest Mail Service will assist the business owner with direct marketing consultation in conducting a direct marketing campaign.

Market Analysis

A data search reveals there are over 1100 small to medium businesses in the Columbia Basin region of Washington State. Currently, there isn't a business devoted to providing mailing list services in this region. One local firm does provide some mailing list services, but this service is an off-shoot of their printing business. They are viewed almost universally by other businesses as extremely expensive. Many firms will not deal with them due to their costs.

Preliminary analysis indicates that there is a market potential of approximately $100,000 in potential mailing list services. That market is expected to mirror the growth rate of the region at 5% per year.

The Five year goal would be to capture at least 45% of this market while keeping expenses approximately 22% of sales. Sales would be expected to achieve at least $54,000 after five years. Initial expectations would be to remain as a home based business to minimize expenses and maximize owner equity and salary.

Initial Financing

Initial financing will come from redemption of owners mutual funds. Start up costs and cash reserve are projected to total slightly over $17,000 with additional capital purchases in year one of $4,000.

Marketing Tactics

My business will adopt a three prong marketing strategy. One will be advertising in the local Yellow Pages under Mailing List Services.

The second part will be conducting a direct mail campaign to prospective businesses in the region followed up with telephonic contact. All direct mail products will focus on letting the business owner know that it is cheaper to keep an existing customer and track his purchases than it is to solicit a new customer. Additionally, I'll explain the advantages to the owner of having my firm provide them the mailing list and lettershop services at a cheaper cost than they can do it for themselves. This becomes especially important given there are expected dramatic changes in the next year on direct mail procedures and costs.

Lastly, through my marketing efforts and customer support, I'll establish myself as the local expert for mailing list services and direct marketing consultation. This will be accomplished by conducting training seminars for local businesses and continuous networking with other business owners at various local functions/meetings.

DESCRIPTION OF THE BUSINESS

Exactly what products and/or services will be sold? Forest Mail Service will provide mailing list services including: a) mailing list or customer database maintenance, b) merge/purging of existing or acquired mailing lists, c) list broker services, d) lettershop services, and e) direct marketing consultation focusing on cost analysis, mail design and conduct of a direct marketing advertising campaign.

Who will be the primary customer groups (market segments) for your product or service? Small business owners located in Seattle, WA. Any business owner who tracks his existing customer base or desires to target new or potential customers through direct mail advertising is a potential customer. Potential customers could include (but not limited to) those operating the following businesses: insurance companies, software companies, dry cleaners, non-profit groups, magazine publishers, janitorial and house cleaning services, beeper and paging services, answering services, doctors, dentists, chiropractors, opticians, gardening and landscaping services, accountants, chimney sweeps, plumbers, video stores, local grocery stores, dog grooming services, veterinarians, hotels, motels, caterers, public relations agencies, real estate agents, newsletter publishers, and stock brokers.

What are the uses of your product or service by the customer groups? The principle use of my service is to maintain an accurate, up-to-date customer database that may be used by a business owner. This database may also be used to track customer purchases, trends, etc. for direct marketing to people in the database. My service will ensure that there are no duplicates in the mailing (reducing costs of printed materials and postage costs), that the addresses are deliverable by the United States Post Service (USPS), and that the postage for the mailings is as inexpensive as possible using discounts offered by the USPS. I would produce mailing labels for the customer that would include delivery point bar coding in order to take advantage of existing or future postal discounts. I'd also be able to generate the mailing in carrier route sequence (assuming there are sufficient mail pieces to qualify for the discounts). If desired, I could affix the mailing labels to the mailing piece and/or insert contents into the envelopes to be mailed. I would be able to apply postage to the mailing piece at the correct amount, minimizing costs to the customer. I'd prepare the mailing for processing by the USPS, to include preparation of all applicable forms and records. Lastly, I'd deliver the mailing to the USPS for the customer. A side product of this database would be printing for the customer, lists or rosters or contact sheets that could be used for a multitude of things within the business.

Additionally, I could provide assistance to the customer who desires to expand his database by assisting them in acquiring or renting specific mailing lists and then merging those lists with the other lists the owner may desire to use. I'd ensure that there are no duplicates in the final product, by purging any duplicates. Again, I'd be able to verify that all addresses are deliverable by the USPS.

If a business owner desired to market his existing mailing list, I could serve as his list broker and help market that list so others would rent it from him. As a minimum, I'd ensure his list was placed in the Standard Rate and Data Services Mailing List directory.

Lastly, I could serve as a consultant to a business and help them determine the cost of doing a direct mail advertising campaign and whether it would be profitable to use direct marketing based on their profit margins. I could assist him in identifying all relevant costs and projecting his revenues from the mailing. I could assist him in locating a printer to design a mailing piece that will minimize his mailing costs based on guidelines established by the USPS. Additionally, I could assist the owner in advising them how to conduct the direct marketing campaign in terms of content, timing, follow-up, and statistical tracking of their customer response. As a part of this campaign, I would assist in testing their mailing effort so they don't spend any more than is necessary on their direct marketing effort. By testing the mailing, the customer would have a high confidence level that the direct mail campaign will achieve the desired results when a full rollout direct marketing effort is made.

Why will customers want to buy your product or service? Customers of Forest Mail Service would be taking advantage of my continuing knowledge of the USPS mailing regulations and how to maximize the amount of mailing they can do at the minimum cost. I would stay abreast of all changes to mail regulations and be able to capture the lowest possible postage costs for my customer. My knowledge would also save the customer the need to understand the USPS regulations and procedures for preparing and delivering a mailing to the USPS for mailing.

I would be able to save my customers time that they are spending on maintaining their customer lists. I'd be able to do the data entry, maintenance, and address verification for them, ensuring that accuracy of data and removal of any duplicates in their data. By saving them time, I would allow them to have their employees focusing on other priorities within their business and not having to concern themselves with this routine but critical and costly function.

I can provide accuracy in their mailing addresses by ensuring the mailing has deliverable addresses. I would accomplish this by checking their mailing list against a software program that has a listing of all of the deliverable addresses in the United States. The program has been certified (Coding Accuracy Support System or CASS) by the USPS and has greater than 98% accuracy on all addresses. I would then be able to correct almost all of those undeliverable addresses for the customer prior to the mailing. For these addresses not corrected, I would be able to provide a list with explanation(s) why the address was not deliverable.

My business will be able to provide the necessary output for the customer in whatever form he desires. From the existing database, I can provide mailing labels, reports, rosters, etc. for the customer for their use.

I would be able to provide the customer security and safeguarding of his data information. As the sole proprietor (and only employee), only I would have access to his data. Additionally, I'd ensure a backup copy of his data is maintained at another location, off of my business premises. If he rented his mailing list, I would monitor his data for unauthorized use. I would ensure that the data is tracked during and after the authorized rental period to preclude theft of their data.

Lastly, a very significant reason customers would want to use my service is: I can save them money while increasing their income. By achieving the lowest possible postage costs (through use of discounts), I am assisting them in getting their advertising message to their customers for the lowest price possible via direct marketing. Through the use of my bulk mailing permits, I have saved them that cost ($180 per year for First Class PreSort and Bulk mail permits). I will also save them mileage costs by providing free pickup and delivery of their mailing list information and mailing pieces. I will prepare the mailing as necessary and then deliver that product to the USPS for processing or back to the business if they desire. Through effective direct marketing assistance, I will be able to increase their sales and incomes assisting them in more effectively targeting their customers with their advertising campaigns.

Give the names of such customers and summarize their reactions to your product/service.

Halley's Landscaping: Seemed very interested, looking for someone to do complete DM effort, mailing, printing, database management. Owner stated that his time is worth $65/hr, needs someone to help out in this area. Has looked at Seattle firms, but prices were too high. Won't go out of region for service (e.g. Wenatchee, Spokane, etc.) Spoke of need for computer instruction services (specifically CAD and accounting programs). Stated there were other firms that needed assistance with computer instruction. Potential for spin off business if mailing services doesn't take off initially.

Sunshine Carpet Cleaning: Been in business for five years. Would be interested in increasing advertising and ability to target customers. Also seemed interested in ability to send reminder notices using customer database. Not very familiar with direct marketing aspect. Seemed positive towards the business.

Seattle Chamber of Commerce: Has heard of a couple of people discussing similar business, but hasn't seen anyone definitely providing the service. Stated I would need to educate the business owners in the region to convince them about the service. Most businesses don't advertise, if they do it is in the local paper.

Ephrata Chamber of Commerce: Acknowledged there is no similar service in the region. PK Printing is too pricey and doesn't readily advertise. Chamber has directed/advised a couple of people to check them out. They believe that there is a need for the service. When asked about member listing and they said that the listing is only given out to Chamber members, for myself that would be $50/year. Good feedback, also indicated that they would be willing to set up a presentation to the Chamber. They meet first Tues. each month at 7:00 AM. Need to lock in the presentation several months before hand. They indicated I'd be able to get positive feedback from the Chamber and be able to give/get education with the members. Could also join at that time and get the list for future use.

Pat Evans Tire: Parent company provides invoices and does the mailing preparation. Local office stuffs envelopes with promotions and sends them out. Not seeing good results from that effort. Willing to look at other advertising methods, currently using paper, radio, TV. Seemed interested in testing DM approach. Discussed using postcards as initial testing of DM trials to gain attention from recipient. Won't use any advertising not based in Ephrata.

Smith's Realty: Believes that with the right marketing approach, it could be a go. The need to educate businesses concerning DM is necessary. Didn't believe his business would benefit from it, but did see potential for other businesses (cited Gilligan's Men's Store for example).

How will you overcome any negative customer reactions? Unfamiliarity with the use of database management for mailing list services and the subsequent use of bulk mailing as a part of a direct marketing effort seemed to be the single greatest concern voiced by the business owners. My plan to overcome this in the market would consist of the following efforts:

Offer a free consultation to entice the owner to hear about the advantages of using mailing list services for direct marketing and how it could be used to increase their advertising effort for their business. Would also have cost breakouts to show what profits the business would need based on the success of the direct mail in order for the direct marketing effort to be profitable (include all costs broken down by mailing, printing, etc.)

Offer to provide seminars or serve as guest speaker to various local businesses' breakfasts and luncheons (e.g. Chamber of Commerce, Rotary, etc.) Another possibility is to advertise and host a 45-60 minute presentation as a seminar to business owners.

Because the majority of this small sample didn't currently use mailing list services and direct marketing (except for Pat Evans), I would need to show how DM will favorably compare (in terms of cost and resultant sales) as opposed to radio and local print media. Halley's Landscaping did desire to use DM but the cost was too prohibitive as quoted by the only firm in the area. The most positive aspect was that I didn't get any rejections from any of the owners as to the potential of the business. They did seem to acknowledge this is a niche business that would take some time for positive results to emerge and word of mouth would be important to reinforce the success of the business.

THE PRODUCT OR SERVICE

To be the basis of a business, the product or service offered must be technically feasible, it must have some competitive advantage, and its cost and time of development must not be prohibitive compared to its potential. This section is designed to evaluate these issues in a preliminary way.

Status

What is the current stage of development of the venture's product or service? The mailing list service offered by Forest Mail Service is in the preliminary stage. The only restriction from actually beginning the service is my relocation into the Seattle Area (specifically) and the initial set up of the business (administrative and purchase of business resources). The necessary technical skills I would need to operate the business follow:

Lettershop operations. To gain proficiency in bulk mail operations, I will take USPS bulk mailing classes in Syracuse NY in Oct 95 and then some refresher training in spring 96.

Mailing List software (PreSort Pro with CASS option). I will purchase this program after beginning of 1996. Will practice with the program prior to arriving in Seattle in Jul. 96. Expect to be proficient in the use of the program by the time the business is operational.

Data base management. Have necessary skills now to build a database, conduct necessary merge/purge, queries and reports. Will use either Access 2.0 or Foxpro 2.6 as database program (or the Windows 95 variants once they are released and bugs are corrected).

What remains to be done to get the product or service ready for sale? The earliest I could begin the service would be August 1, 1996. I will retire from the Army effective July 1, 1996 and then have to relocate to Seattle. Additionally, I will need to establish local business contacts and contract for business related materials (e.g. business cards, stationary, etc.) Various technical issues will have to be completed also, establishing phone lines, etc. Deliveries of equipment cannot take place until I have moved into our residence (which is expected to be completed by the time we arrive in mid July 96). The most difficult timing issue might be the establishment of yellow page ads for the business. I'll have to coordinate for business phone in Mar/Apr 96 when we come out to WA for home purchase. At that time, I'll have to reserve the phone number and order the yellow page ad(s) so that it will be in the current year's directory. Initial talks with the local phone company says I'll need to order the ad by May 96 to have it listed in the July 96 directory. For dollar estimate, see enclosed spreadsheet, titled "Start Up Costs For Forest Mail Service" (See Exhibit A). Currently I'm using the comfortable amount as my target figure for start up dollars. Some equipment is already on hand (such as laser printer, some office supplies, etc.)

Strengths and Weaknesses

The strengths of the service focus on the increased use (nationwide) of mail for direct marketing efforts. As the USPS continues to revise postal rates for bulk mailing and the Domestic Mail Manual procedures remains complex, these factors increase the reliance of small businesses to look for a mailing list service if they choose to spend their advertising dollars on mailing list and direct marketing efforts. In order to use mail for marketing efforts and capitalize on postal discounts the business person needs to master the bulk mail regulations or have someone else to it for them. Future pricing initiatives by the USPS are rewarding the mailer that incorporates bar coding with Zip+4. To achieve these price reductions, software specifically designed to do this is required. My service will have the necessary hardware and software to achieve the lowest possible rates. Additionally, use of computers and databases for data searches or queries to target the marketing effort requires the business owner to master the necessary programs. Some business owners are doing this, but for others they are short the time and are looking for someone else to take care of that need. Even with the rise of the Internet, the foreseeable future still holds that the USPS will continue delivering mail at increasing volumes.

What features of your product or service may put it at some disadvantage in the market place? For the small town business person, use of direct mail and mailing list services is not typically used. A significant number of businesses may not be very familiar with use of the mailing list services or direct marketing (as evidenced by lack of any established mailing list services in the region). An additional problem would be for some businesses who may rely on only a relatively small number of clientele (less than 200). In order to qualify for postal discounts, a business would need to send a minimum of 200 pieces in their mailing (10 pieces per zip code) for First Class PreSort or 500 pieces for Third Class Bulk. Consequently, they would not only have to have a sufficient profit margin to warrant using direct mail, but they would also need to target a large enough population of present and potential customers to meet the USPS minimum amounts for postal discounts.

Are there possibilities of rapid obsolescence because of technical and manufacturing developments, style changes, marketing fads, or other reasons? For the next five years, I would not rate this as likely. Even with the rise of computer communications via e-mail and the Internet, the USPS mail volume continues to climb. 1995 use is up over 3.3% as compared to the previous year. Also the increase of direct mail and firms supporting direct mail efforts indicates that the public is responding to direct mail to make their shopping decisions.

THE MARKET

Total Market Size and Trends

A data search of businesses located in Seattle and in surrounding areas identified approximately 1100 businesses that would be potential customers for Forest Mail Service. The database was extracted from 1st Qtr Edition of Select Phone Telephone Directory. This is an extract of Yellow Page listings from area phone books. The information was current as of early 1994. In all reality, there has been some changes to the specific businesses, but based on growth figures from the Chamber of Commerce, the baseline population of businesses should remain constant or in all probability increase since 1994. This 1100 market size covers all varieties of business, some with greater probability of need for the mailing services than others. The data extraction was conducted by myself. The current accuracy of data information is approximately 80-90% correct. I've derived that figure based on the data being one year old data with 10-15% of the existing businesses going out of business or moving within the last year. Additionally, there are some businesses that are now present in the area that were not listed in this data base (either because of new start ups or because they have chosen not to have a Yellow Page listing).

Assessment of the Competition

Are there several kinds of products or services that compete for the same business with the same customer? The number of local competitors in the area appear to be very limited. In the local Seattle Yellow Pages, the only advertised mailing list services is the Listings, 100 N. 94 Ave. Omaha NE 68129. Conversations with several businesses identified AAA Printers Inc., 30 W Marina Dr., Seattle WA, as a local business that does mailing list services, but AAA doesn't advertise in the Yellow Pages or in any local media. The only other mailing list service organization is Linden Mailing Service, 101 Westlane Wenatchee WA. Their add in the Wenatchee Yellow Pages states they have been serving customers for 12 years. Lastly, a potential competitor is the United States Post Service.

List your major competitors in order of their reputed share of the market. Comment as to who is the pricing leader, quality leader, most innovative, growing most rapidly, most aggressive, having problems, etc.

Competitor	Comments	
AAA Printers, Inc. 80 West Marina Dr. Seattle, WA	No advertising, word of mouth, several comments said they were very expensive.	**Competition**
Linden Mailing Service 101 Westlane Wenatchee. WA	Prices very similar to my pricing structure. They charge for permit use ($10), my use is free.	
Listings 100 N. 94th Ave. Omaha, NE 68129	$75 M company, provides 4K+ lists, provides mailing labels, prospect lists, sales leads cards, data on disk or on line retrieval. `National focus	
United States Postal Service, Washington, DC	New proposal by USPS. Still in test stages, no expectation when service would be available nationwide—if ever. Strong op position by national mailers.	

Competitor	Comments
Unknown parties who had voiced interest in starting service to Moses Lake Chamber of Commerce	Unknown, haven't entered the business to date as far as anyone knows

Dun and Bradstreet reports are unavailable for all three companies. There should be one on American Business Lists, but a search on CompuServe did not produce a match for a report.

What is the profitability as a percent of sales of the competition, and what is their profit trend in recent years? At present, this information is unknown.

What information do you have on your competitors' operations?

AAA Printers, Inc. Mailing list services is an off shoot of their main printing business. Company doesn't perform mailing services unless they are included as a part of a printing job. Only will quote based on combined work order. They don't advertise their mailing services, but work word of mouth. Several businesses stated AAA seemed to be very pricey. They were too expensive for one firm to even consider when that owner did want to conduct direct marketing.

Linden Mailing Service. Their pricing structure is very similar to mine. Didn't state whether they have a combined service rate or not. Use of permit is a charged fee, my usage is free to customer. Doesn't appear to be marketing in the Seattle area. Their services appear to be very similar to that I'm proposing for Forest Mail Service. Some businesses I spoke with would not use them because they aren't local and these owners won't deal with anyone unless they are local services.

Listings. National mailing list services bureau. Business compiles lists from variety of sources and then sells or rents the lists. Does have a refund policy for undeliverable mail. They will refund 5 cents per piece. If undeliverable mail exceeds 8%, the company will refund 30 cents per piece over 8%. Doesn't perform lettershop operations, nor does it work with firms and compile their existing lists. Also doesn't support merge/purge services for firms that have a list and want to rent/buy a list of merge with their list for a mailing. They do provide lists on magnetic media. List rentals vary by list, but industry rental rates are $50-75/M depending on the additional needs of the requester (e.g. gummed label, other data elements, etc.).

Northern Mailings. The firm is located in Omaha, NE. The services are primarily mailing list services and data input. His high volume rates (>1000 addresses) are less expensive than my rates. His rate for printing labels is $.03 per label (compared to my rate at $.04 per label) unless the data isn't maintained by Northern, then he will charge .10 per label to print them. The impression I have is his business has more volume than I could reasonably expect in Seattle. Additionally, he is one of 4-6 local mailing list services in the Omaha area along with all national mailing list services that advertise in the Omaha Yellow Pages.

United States Postal Service. The USPS intends to test market (in four locations in the United States) a proposal to provide a discount mailing rate for small business owners. The business owner would be able to send out a minimum of 200 mail pieces without requiring any address on the envelope (but the owner must send them to all businesses or deliverable addresses in the targeted area.) While a pricing structure hasn't been released, some analysts have indicated the mailing rate per piece may be as little as 11-13 cents per piece (much less than bulk mailing rates).

a. What makes you think it will be possible to compete successfully with them? What are their weaknesses? None of these businesses are committed to supporting the small business owner in the Seattle area. While AAA is located in Seattle, their limited operations in mailing services coupled with their high pricing structure don't pose a significant threat. The lack of local representation and limited services minimizes the impact of Listings. Lindens's lack of marketing efforts in the region restricts their penetration into the Seattle market. As long as I can price my services below AAA and provide quality service, I can capture the market in the Seattle area. The United States Post Office's proposal has some weaknesses in that it doesn't allow the business owner to target his mailings. It is an all or none proposition. For the mailer who wants to focus on a specific market segment, this program would have him mailing out materials to people who would be unlikely to accept his offer. Figuring a minimum of 40-50 cents per mail out piece, the savings from lower postal rates are soon negated by mailing out pieces with no expectation of a response. If the mailer wants to target his own customer base then this program would not be cost effective and the business owner would need to use another method of sending out presort or bulk mail.

What will make it difficult to compete with them? What are their strengths? AAA is established and has built in printing services for a customer who wants the company to provide not just mailing services, but to also handle the mailing piece design and printing. While their more expensive prices may shy away some customers, the convenience of one stop shopping is worth something. Forest Mail Service will need to enter into a referral partnership with a local (or several local) printers to provide the graphic design and printing for those customers that want a printing support option and don't want to have to do the work themselves. I can't compete with Listings on compiling lists for the vast majority of lists. However, I can create some locally compiled lists (new property owners, newly and existing registered voters, new businesses, etc.) that may have a market with local businesses. In order to compete with the United States Post Service, I'd need to explain the total costs of the mailing campaign to the business owner and show them how the USPS is costing them money or saving them money in the long run.

What is the price spread among your competitors for services that would compete with yours? Stated above, also see enclosed price listing (See Exhibit B) for basic services.

Do you think you can be price competitive and make a profit? Why? Based on my forecast of expenses, along with market potential in the area, I do believe I can remain below the costs of AAA and still make a profit.

What is your <u>first estimate</u> of your:

Product/Service Selling Price:	See enclosed price sheet.
Production Cost:	N/A
Overhead Cost - G & A:	$570 (See Exhibit 4 for detailed breakdown)
Marketing:	$230/month
Profitability as % of Sales:	22% (Includes owner salary, but doesn't include capital improvements.)

What marketing and promotion channels are used by your competitors to distribute their services? The only method I've come across is the Yellow Pages for Listings and Linden Mailing Services, and word of mouth/networking for AAA. I'm unaware of any efforts to use direct mail or cold calling (telemarketing) to promote their services.

Based upon your evaluation of the market, the competition, and apparent sales trends, make a preliminary, approximate estimate of the share of the market you feel you can obtain in each of the next five years.

Preliminary Estimate of Market Share and Sales

Market Share

	1996	1997	1998	1999	2000
Estimated Total Market,$ (1)	$100,000	$105,000	$110,000	$115,000	$120,000
Your Estimated Market Share, %	3.7	28	30	40	45
Your Estimated Sales, $'s	$3,700	$29,000	$33,000	$46,000	$54,000

(1) Total Market derived from determination that the local businesses would spend at least $1000 annually for mailing list services. Total market in region is more than 1100 businesses of all kinds. Estimating 10% of the businesses would participate in direct mail and mailing list services. Also estimate 5% annual growth in total market based on 5% growth of the region through the year 2000.

Marketing Tactics

What sort of service and warranty must you offer with your product/service?

The following items would be offered as special service incentives for customers: a) Free pickup and delivery in the region. b) No charge to customers that are using bulk mailing and desire to use my postal permit. c) Free consultation and cost benefits analysis for their business and applicability for using mailing list services and direct mail/marketing. d) Free archive back-up of their mailing data kept at my site in case of their data becoming corrupt or damaged. e) Customer satisfaction on the finished product (mailing list creation, CASS certification of data, duplicate removal, etc.) or their money back. f) Mailing data tracking and statistical analysis assistance on all mailings prepared and sent out. g) Total confidentiality of all data. h) Integrity and professionalism at all times.

What type of packaging is needed either for protection or for point of sale promotion? All PreSort and bulk mail will be protected from the elements to minimize any water damage and increased weight due to mailing pieces absorbing water. Mail will be kept indoors until time of mailing and then will be transported in a vehicle to the bulk mail postal clerk in Seattle, WA.

What methods do you plan to use to distribute your product or service? Will you use direct selling, sales reps, distributors? How will you "recruit" them? I will use a combination of telemarketing for high potential sales leads with regular use of direct mail post cards and brochures/newsletters.

How will you bring your product or service to the attention of potential customers? Customers for mail list services include both new and established small businesses. Some of these businesses operate with no computers (identified by hand addressed mailings), while there are other businesses or organizations that have the need to advertise but don't have the personnel or time to do the mailing list management and direct marketing.

My marketing plan will be built around the following campaign strategies:

Yellow Page Advertisements: I will place an ad in the yellow page directories that service Seattle & the surrounding areas that would focus on the following services for Forest Mail Service: free pick up and delivery, accuracy, promptness, service, speed, mail permit, total service, letter shop, free consultation available.

My direct marketing plan will be a two prong approach:

(1) I would target businesses in Seattle and the surrounding areas by using post card (folded over) mailers that incorporate my phone number, similar information as in my yellow page ad and I'd mail it using first class presort with address correction (initial mailing to get name out and focus on service in area). My goal would be to target specific industries in region based on created mailing list from ProPhone CD; estimate of approx. 1500 post cards at .15 mailing cost per card, plus printing cost, approx. $325 to $425 for initial mailing. I would follow up with this mailing approximately every quarter with similar post cards pointing out advantages to tracking a business's existing customer base, mailing list services and time and money savings, etc.

(2) My other primary strategy is to make telephone contact with high potential business: I will explain the purpose of my business and strive to set up a free consultation with the business to examine their customer tracking systems and their business's suitability for direct marketing. The objective of the consultation would be a follow up visit with price quotes for data entry, maintenance and preparation of a direct marketing mailing.

1Whether initial customer contact is made by phone or by direct mail response, I want to ensure I explain the advantages of my service, stressing these three key things: (1) Why should the customer let me manage the mailing? (2) Why should the customer start direct mailing? (3) Why should the customer let Forest Mail Service handle their mailings?

In answering these questions for the client, my answers will target the owner's business concerns and how he/she can use my mailing list service or direct marketing. I will analyze their business objectives and show them how my mailing service will benefit them. Included in this analysis: (1) How I will take care of the processing of their mail with the USPS including sorting, postal discounts, postal permits, and the need to stay on top of the USPS mailing regulations. (2) Maintenance of their mailing list and production of mailing labels and other reports thus allowing them time to manage their business. If one of their employees is doing this, my service would allow that person to focus on other aspects of the business and have more time to serve their own customers. (3) I would be able to verify their mailing addresses and ensure that they meet postal standards and incorporate barcoding into the address. (4) CASS certify and check their mailing list and cull out undeliverable names. This reduces their costs both in postage and in materials that never gets into the hands of their customer. (5) I would also be able to provide a design service in conjunction with a local print shop. This would allow the business owner to not only have the mailing list management handled by my firm, but also allow for a total direct marketing effort to be created in support of their advertising objectives. (6) Additionally, I'd see if the company is tracking customers and determine what they are doing with that information. If they are doing nothing, then I can help them get their data under control and incorporate it into a marketing plan for their business. This service would allow the owner to foster targeted direct marketing and allow him to provide directed offers to those 20% who provide him with 80% of his sales.

My bottom line is to focus on What's in it for the Customer!

A business's key advantages to using my service are: a) Save time on preparing and maintaining customer lists. I do the data entry, file manipulation, data base maintenance, publish customer listing based on owners report format, and safeguard the information. b) Save postage costs on their direct mail by using my bulk permit, my computer programs to verify, address, sort the mailing in carrier sequence for delivery to the USPS, and metering. The costs to use my service are less than the business trying to get the information out of a phone book or running the service themselves—Especially in terms of cost of time, equipment, training, software, permits, etc. c) Frees up the business to devote their time to their business and not learn how the post office is changing their mailing regulations. d) I can provide them access to thousands of lists that the customer can rent/buy for their use in targeting their marketing efforts. Also I can help them create their own lists from their existing customer base. e) I will offer free pick up and delivery (Seattle area). f) Free consultation on how to improve and/or use direct mail in their marketing efforts. g) I will show the customer what the costs of using direct mail are and how they can calculate their break even point in terms of gross sales to pay for the direct mailing effort. h) My integrity and professionalism as demonstrated by over twenty years of service to the US Army. h) Lastly, I'd provide a money back guarantee on the service aspect of my business. The guarantee wouldn't cover return rates on mail outs, but I'd have a broader guarantee that if the business owner was unsatisfied with my service, I'd refund the cost of all services provided (I'd not refund the cost of postage, materials, etc.)

Another key aspect of marketing to the Seattle area merchants will be to provide education to the business owners. I would educate the local business leaders by providing short (10-15 minute) presentations to the local Chambers of Commerce outlining what mailing list services are and how they can be used for cost effective direct marketing. In educating the client on why they need mailing services, I'd show them the advantages of maintaining a customer database for direct marketing efforts. One example I could use would show how a clothing store owner could track their customer preferences and sizes. They then could use that information to send direct marketing information to the customer, informing them about any special sales/offers that match their personal preferences. A variation of the seminar would be to present an hour to hour and half seminar explaining the use of mailing list services, what they can do and how a customer can focus direct marketing techniques on their advertising efforts. I'd also include how a direct mail effort is tracked to make sure it is effective and what are reasonable expectations for a direct marketing campaign.

In the first three months (Aug-Oct 96), I will target the following customers as ones who may have an immediate need for mailing list services and/or direct marketing assistance:

- All candidates for elected office in Seattle and nearby cities.

- Target restaurants who do weekly drawings for lunches, etc. Establish mailing list for specials, birthday clubs, etc.

- If there are any catalog mailers in the region, target them in the fall.

As special enhancements to my mailing list services, these following services would be available:

- Ability to customize labels—include logo on mailing labels or special information.

- Merge documents/letters for customers and also do special envelopes.

- Offer clear labels or colored labels for special effect.

- Advise customers about address correction and update of database with returned mail.

Networking will also be key. I will join as a minimum the Seattle and other Chambers of Commerce to take advantage of networking opportunities that their monthly meetings will offer. Additionally, I will look at serving with one of the local civic organizations (Kiwanis, Lions, etc.) I will attempt to meet with business clients for breakfast or lunch and discuss their current concerns and interests. Finally, I will provide assistance to the local Red Cross office for Grant County and help with disaster relief efforts and planning (utilizing my previous Red Cross experience and military logistics background).

i) The final piece of my marketing effort will be to send my current customers and strong potential customers a quarterly newsletter that will focus on mailing tips, news about postal regulations and change, how to take advantage of their internal mailing list information and customer data, etc. The newsletter would replace the post card mailings once I've established an initial customer base. The newsletter would then serve as a reminder to the business about my service and reinforce the need for future repeat business.

5. What pricing and discount structure do you envision? My pricing structure is a tiered approach allowing for quantity discounts. See enclosed Forest Mail Service Price List (Exhibit B).

PRODUCTION AND OPERATION

What do you anticipate will be the major difficulties (equipment, labor skills, special operations, suppliers, etc.) in the manufacture of the product or delivery of the service? The two principal areas of concern for my business are the initial set up of the business and my learning curve in mastering the internal aspects of the business.

Initial Set-up. Ordering, delivery, and set-up of all equipment and support materials will be a difficult operation. Due to my retirement from the Army on June 30, 1996, becoming operational by August 1, 1996 will require intensive tracking and coordination to get all of the necessary supplies and equipment to arrive at my office in time for me to begin setup. During the preceding months I will need to be able to determine the order ship time for the various supplies and equipment and then order the materials at the requisite date so the necessary materials arrive near July 15, 1996. This will allow me time to establish my residence and prepare to begin set-up of the business.

Learning Curve. There are three principal areas that I will need to focus on: the mailing software, USPS regulations and procedures, and lettershop equipment. All three areas can be studied and mastered during the time between now and when I retire. The mailing software will be ordered after the first of the year and I will then practice and gain proficiency with the software prior to my arrival in the Seattle area. The USPS regulations can be studied by getting a copy of the Domestic Mailing Manual and taking some USPS training seminars that are offered at Syracuse NY between now and my retirement date. I will also do some follow-up training with the bulk mail clerk and Postal Council in the Seattle area. Lastly, my familiarity with lettershop equipment will have to be accomplished by having a local New York business allow me to get exposure to the equipment and gain the necessary proficiency prior to my retirement.

Why do you think you can manufacture the product or deliver the service at competitive cost levels?

My overhead is much lower than other similar businesses. My business will be a small home office set up. My office space will be deductible and my rent for it is wrapped up in my home payment. The same applies to my utility bills. I will be the sole proprietor and employee in the business. Consequently my wages will be limited to paying myself. Additionally, my supplies and consumables are relatively inexpensive performing this service. Most of my supplies are standard office supplies used in the daily office administration chores. Mailing labels and printer ribbons are the principal consummables in the performance of producing my mailing labels for the customer. To keep these costs down, I'll order sufficient quantities of consummables via mail order from discount office supply stores or check with local dealers and see if they will provide similar discounts.

The majority of costs in the data input or mailing label delivery is time costs and setup of the computer program to produce the output or accept the input. As my business grows and I begin to gain repeat customers, my setup time will decrease because the unique requirements for that business will have already been met during the previous job(s). Also, once the setup has been accomplished, the greater volume contracted for, the higher the profit margin. Based on my competitor survey, my pricing structure is in line with their pricing structure. Also, based on my estimate of costs and production requirements I am confident I can achieve the necessary level of sales to remain a viable business. Using the information gathered from a very limited market survey, there appeared to be sufficient interest in the area for the business to become established. As a fall back, during my start up period, I am not totally dependent on the business for my personal income. Due to my military retirement, my essential needs are covered for myself and my family. Therefore, I can forego my own paycheck from the business, if necessary, until the business has enough sales to begin paying my salary. I am expecting to be able to begin paying myself after 4-6 months in the business.

Give the name and principal skill (finance, manufacturing, engineering, marketing, general management) of both the lead entrepreneur and co-founders.

ENTREPRENEURS

Name	Principal Skill
Harry N. Neilson-Lead Entrepreneur, Owner	General Management and Service Production

Why have you chosen the proposed venture? What experience has each of you had which gives you a knowledge of the venture's markets and technology and qualifies you to start such a business?

I chose this particular business because it uses personal skills that I possess. My knowledge and skills with computers and database management programs are very necessary. Also, assisting customers in conducting their bulk mailing and tracking the results of the mailing requires knowledge of statistical processes and set up a tracking system(s). Through personal study and many years of supervisory management where I have monitored organizations conducting both supply and service functions, I have gained the necessary personal and managerial skills to accomplish these skills. Secondly, my familiarity with government regulations and procedures will help me in dealing with the USPS personnel and their regulations. Additionally, my last five years in the Army have been in charge of organizations that are primarily focused on providing a logistical service to their customers. Throughout this time period, I have developed the necessary skills and attitudes to gauge my accomplishment in meeting the needs of my customers and how to make adjustments in my service procedures to refine my support and services. Lastly, I have spent the last two years studying the mailing list service business and have been conducting my own research to prepare for opening the business. Through that study, I have taught myself the necessary background information to begin the business. I have a proven history in entering a field and mastering the necessary skills to meet my customer's needs. I am confident of my abilities to be able to accomplish that again in starting Forest Mail Service.

As the development of the venture proceeds, it will be necessary to develop a balanced and experienced management team. If such a team does not now exist, how will you develop one? That will not be necessary in the first five years. My business goal is to achieve an acceptable sales level that will generate a personal income of approximately $24,000-36,000 per year. Based on my initial marketing information, I believe the limit of the local market will restrict any greater profits than this range (unless there is a dramatic growth rate in the local economy.) As long as I do not attempt to expand the scope of the business beyond my current estimates, I should be able to manage and run the business without requiring any outside support or help from other managers.

FINANCING REQUIRED

How much initial capital will be required to start up the company? Indicate amounts for:

	Range of Funds
Plant and Equipment	$9823.37
One-time Licensing Fees	220
Complete Development of Service	N/A
Market Research and Sales Planning (included in monthly expenses)	N/A
Other Organizational Expense	682.68
Additional cash for monthly expenses	6500
Grand Total	$17226.05

These funds will last 8-9 months.

How much additional capital will be required until your venture can support itself? This estimate should consider such items as: increases in manpower, working capital requirements, etc.

First Estimate - Capital Requirements

Year	Range of Funds
1	$4000
2	0
3	0
4	0
Total Capital Required	$4000

Indicate who prepared the preceding data:

Name: Harry N. Neilson Phone: (509) 321-5485

Name any financial or business who may have been consulted:

None at the present, do plan on discussing with a couple of banks in Seattle Spring 1996. Can any of this capital be obtained from bank loans (secured by fixed assets, receivable, inventory, etc.)? If so, give a rough estimate of this loan amount. $17,000 secured by personal assets (mutual funds) owned by Harry N. Neilson.

1. What are the major risks and problems that you see in the proposed business? List them in order of importance. Consider things like: reliability of market and sales projections; ability to manufacture at competitive cost levels; availability of trained labor; ability of competitors to underprice or make your product obsolete; ability to get the product exposed and sold, etc.

MAJOR RISKS AND PROBLEMS

a. Market area may not be of sufficient size to support projected sales.

b. Projected expenses may be too low and marketing efforts may require greater cash flow to achieve penetration into market place.

c. Increased penetration of computers and databases into the business place may make it easier for owners to establish their own mailing lists and manage their mailings using in house personnel.

d. Injury or illness to myself which will not allow me to operate the business.

e. Expansion of the Internet and reduction of mailed literature with increase of electronic literature.

2. What could you do to minimize the four most serious risks?

a. Market area may not be of sufficient size to support projected sales. If the market area proves to be too small to develop sufficient sales for the mailing service, I will have to expand the service into other areas in Central Washington. By expanding the service, my variable expenses will go up directly due to increased long distance charges, travel costs, and mailing (overnight and parcel). If such is the case, than the volume of the increased area will have to make up the increase. I won't be able to increase the prices of the service due to Linden Mailing Service, located in Wenatchee WA, which has very similar pricing structure. The second option would be to focus exclusively on the mailing list management aspect and begin targeting customers in other urban areas in Washington State (Spokane, etc.). This service doesn't require as great as much travel to deliver the product to the customer (data and mailing labels, etc.) consequently I could use UPS or FEDEX to provide overnight deliver of the data product. Lastly, if this proved unsuccessful, then I could branch out into other home businesses and merge two part time businesses into one full time business (examples would be: performing a computer data back up service to companies with data stored on their computers, event and meeting planner, inventory control services, computer instruction on software packages, part time instructor at community colleges, etc.)

b. Projected expenses may be too low and marketing efforts may require greater cash flow to achieve penetration into market place. Based on projected cash for expenses, if my marketing budget is inadequate for the proposed marketing plan, then I will have to expand in other marketing areas that require less money but may require more time (both cold calling and net working). Recognizing this may occur, it will be critical for me to track my cash flow from day one and also make forecasts of my available cash for the initial six-nine month period. It will take at least a quarter to establish some base line, but based on those figures, I will then have to evaluate the entire marketing plan against my cash flow and make sure it is still reasonable. If the marketing costs using direct mail are not achieving results due to insufficient penetration and volume, then I will have to spend more time on the phone talking to potential customers. Additionally, I will continue to network to increase awareness of the service. Lastly, conducting free seminars for business leaders and showing them how mailing services can increase their sales by focusing their marketing efforts on their existing customers should help by increasing my sales. I will either volunteer to different organizations to give these presentations, or be forced to pay the necessary rental fees for meeting rooms to carry out this aspect of the plan.

c. Increased penetration of computers and databases into the business place may make it easier for owners to establish their own mailing lists and manage their mailings using in house personnel. In the event that some businesses say they can't afford the service because they say they can do it cheaper in house, I will show them their incidental and hidden costs in managing their own lists and mailing their letters are higher than what I can do it for them. In making this argument, several conditions do need to exist: 1) The owner is using direct mail or will be working with a mailing list in some database format. 2) Owner must agree that time is money. 3) The amount of time he would spend to have himself keep up with postal regulations, software changes for both data management and postal certification, and time spend performing data entry and maintenance is not effective for the mail volume that most businesses in the region would have. Businesses who manage over 10,000 names can justify doing the work in house, but they also may be agreeable to outsourcing this work to Forest Mail Service.

d. Injury or illness to myself which will not allow me to operate the business. Because this business is a sole proprietor business with no employees other than myself, if I were to become ill or injured for more than a short period of time, the business could quickly suffer disastrous consequences. For the foreseeable future there would not be anyone else I could rely on to run the business until I recovered. Obviously the immediate impact of such a scenario would be loss of any positive cash flow the business had. Depending on the amount of loans and other liabilities in place, the negative cash flow could range from major to relatively minor. Besides the inability to pay off any liabilities, I would not be generating any income for myself. To counter this scenario, the most prudent course of action would be to secure a personal health insurance policy that would cover my income that would be lost due to the illness or injury. Because of my military retirement, my immediate cash requirements for my family and lodging will be met my that income. However, that income will not be sufficient to cover my liabilities in the business. Therefore the health insurance would come into play. This requirement could be lessened by liquidating some of my mutual funds to pay off the balance of any liabilities if necessary.

3. How would you rate the overall risk of the venture—high, medium, or low?

I would rate the overall risk of the venture between medium and low. I feel the low side is relevant due to the positive reaction I had from the initial market survey that there is a need in the region for mailing list services. The true test will be whether those same individuals are willing to pay a reasonable price for the service as offered. In order to convince them, I'll need to be able to show them that with a certain expected mailing list response results, they can expect a reasonable profit margin on these sales. Using those variables, I will assist them in determining whether the service will be cost effective for them or not. The medium risk is based on the minimum size for a service of this nature in the Seattle area. Consequently, I'll need to capture the market as much as I can.

Start Up Costs

Items/Supplies	Unit Cost	Survival Qty	Comfortable Qty	Ideal Qty	Survival Cost	Comfortable Cost	Ideal Cost
Office Supplies							
Stapler	2.5	1	1	1	2.5	2.5	2.5
Pens	0.3	10	15	15	3	4.5	4.5
Pencils	1.25	5	5	5	6.25	6.25	6.25
(inserts to mechanical pencils)							
Ruler	1.5	0	1	0	1	0	1.5
Hole Punch	10	0	1	1	0	10	10
Laser Paper	28	1	1	2	28	28	56
Post Its	5	2	2	2	10	10	10
Dry Erase Board and Pen	50	0	1	1	0	50	50
Stamps	.31	0	0	100	0	0	31
Return Address	15	1	1	1	15	15	15
Files/Labels	20	1	1	1	20	20	20
Various Self-Inking Stamps	3.5	5	10	10	17.5	35	35
In Baskets (4 ea. per bundle)	6.79	1	1	1	6.79	6.79	6.79
Message Pads	—	0	5	10	0	0	0
Memo Pads/ Tablets	1.5	5	10	15	7.5	15	22.5
Calendar	10	1	1	1	10	10	10
Binders/Folders	3.5	3	6	6	10.5	21	21
Wire File Orrganizer	5.49	1	2	3	5.49	10.98	16.47
AZ Desk File	7.99	1	1	1	7.99	7.99	7.99
Scissors	4.19	0	1	1	0	4.19	4.19
Pencil Palace	6.99	0	1	1	0	6.99	6.99
Tabs (various types)	15	1	1	1	15	15	15
Manila File Folders	2.69	1	1	2	2.69	2.69	5.38
Hanging Files	5.99	4	4	6	23.96	23.96	35.94
Index Cards	1.98	3	3	4	5.94	5.94	7.92
Business Cards	65	1	1	2	65	65	130
Brochures (Printed Professionally)	100	0	1	2	0	100	200
Envelopes (with logo)	50	0	1	2	0	50	100
Stationary (with logo)	50	1	2	3	50	100	150
Brochures (75 blank brochures/box)	27.95	1	2	4	27.95	55.9	111.8
Sub Total					**2677.9**	**4610.37**	**5696.85**
Office Equipment							
Telephone (2 or 3 line)	125	1	1	1	125	125	125

Brother 4500 ML Multi-Function	950	1	0	0	950	0	0
Fax/Voice Mail Program (Voice Fx)	199	0	0	1	0	0	199
Fax Machine	550	0	1	1	0	550	550
Copier	600	0	1	1	0	600	600
Scanner	350	0	1	1	0	350	350
Laser Printer (use current printer on hand)	600	0	0	0	0	0	0
Cordless Phone	100	0	0	1	0	0	100
Envelope Sealer (from Direct Paper)	35	1	1	1	35	35	35
Letter Folding Machine (Quill)	480	0	1	1	0	480	480
File Cabinet	250	1	1	1	250	250	250
Table	39.99	1	1	2	39.99	39.99	79.98
Postage Meter	150	0	0	0	0	0	0
Desk/wall lamps	35	2	3	3	70	105	105
Guest Chair	75	1	2	3	75	150	225
Book Shelf (5 shelves)	99.99	1	2	3	99.99	199.98	299.97
Book Shelf (3 shelves)	59.99	1	2	2	59.99	119.98	119.98
Office Desk	799.95	1	1	1	799.95	799.95	799.95
Label Machine	400	0	1	1	0	400	400
Matrix Printer (with print sharing device)	275	0	0	1	0	0	275
Postage Programmable Scale (2 lb)	99.99	1	1	1	99.99	99.99	99.99
Fire Sentry Safe	134.99	134.99	1	1	134.99	134.99	134.99
Copy Holder	10.49	1	1	1	10.49	10.49	10.49
Extra Floor Lamp	35	0	1	1	0	35	35
Coffee Pot	35	0	0	1	0	0	35
Typewriter	200	0	0	1	0	0	200
Floppy Disks	.45	50	100	150	22.5	45	67.5
Tape Backup	20	2	4	6	40	80	120
Sub Total					**2677.9**	**4610.37**	**5696.85**
Software & Reference Material							
Select Phone	49	1	1	1	49	49	49
Street Atlas Program	70	0	0	0	0	0	0
Mailing Label Program (PreSort Pro or Mailers +4)	690	1	1	1	690	690	690
Zip Code Processing Program--Zip +4 (CASS option)	0	1	1	1	0	0	0
DMM (Electronic Version)	150	0	0	1	0	0	150
Windows Program w/all US addresses	125	0	0	0	0	0	0
DMM	35	1	1	0	35	35	0
Winfax Pro	80	0	1	1	80	0	80
Sub Total					**774**	**854**	**969**

Computer Equipment

Pentium 133	4200	1	1	1	4200	4200	4200
Lap Top	3500	0	0	1	0	0	3500
Back Up Power	125	0	1	1	0	125	125
Toner Cartridge	125	0	1	1	0	125	125
Xerox Cartridge	125	0	0	1	0	0	125
Sub Total					**4200**	**4450**	**8075**
Mailing Permits	85	2	2	2	170	170	170
Sub Total					**170**	**170**	**170**
Business License	50	1	1	1	50	50	50
Sub Total					**50**	**50**	**50**
Grand Total					**8212.96**	**10817.05**	**16054.57**

Mailing List Data Base Services	Base Price	Discount Price	
Data Entry (based on 3 lines of input, per 100 names)	$20	>1000	$15
Verification of delivery address and correcting address (per 100)	$2	>1000	1.50/100
Duplicate name screen/removal (per 100 names screened)	$2	>1000	1.50/100
Merge/purge service (per 100 names screened)	$2	>1000	1.50/100

Price List

Output Services from Mailing Data Base

	Base Price	Discount Price	
Printing of mailing labels (gummed backed)* (per 100) (Includes preparation of mailing to qualify at lowest possible postage based on number and type of mailer, printing of USPS forms, etc.)	$4	>1000	$3/100
Printing of rosters/prospect listing (first page)	$2		$1/addl page

Lettershop Services

Applying labels to mailing piece, and stamp or meter (per 100 labels)	$1
Folding, stuffing envelopes and sealing envelope (per 100 pages)	$1
Delivery to post office	n/c
Use of bulk mail permit	n/c

Combined Service

Initial database input (standard 3 line record), maintain (includes duplicate check, zip code and address verification quarterly), update, print and affix gummed labels 4 times per year (per 100 records)	$60

Mailing List Rental Services

Research and rental of list from list owner/broker	Retail Cost of List Rental

* Specialty labels (clear, logo design, etc.) can be used, cost available on request.

Price Comparison

Forest Mail Service Price List vs AAA Printers, Inc.

Mailing List Data Base Services	Base Price	AAA* Price
Data Entry (based on 3 lines of input, per 100 names)	$20	unk
Verification of delivery address and correcting address (per 100)	$2	unk
Duplicate name screen/removal (per 100 names screened)	$2	unk
Merge/purge service (per 100 names screened)	$2	unk

Output Services from Mailing Data Base

	Base Price	AAA* Price
Printing of mailing labels (gummed backed)** (per 100) (Includes preparation of mailing to qualify at lowest possible postage based on number and type of mailer, printing of USPS forms, etc.)	$4	$25+ .03/label based on 500 count
Printing of rosters/prospect listing (first page)	$2	unk

Lettershop Services	Base Price	AAA1 Price
Applying labels to mailing piece, and stamp or meter (per 100 labels)	$1	$2.50
Folding, stuffing envelopes and sealing envelope (per 100 pages)	$1	unk
Delivery to post office	n/c	incl in $2.50 cost
Use of bulk mail permit	n/c	incl in cost of job

Combined Service

	Base Price	AAA1 Price
Initial database input (standard 3 line record), maintain (includes duplicate check, zip code and address verification quarterly), update, print and affix gummed labels 4 times per year (per 100 records)	$60	unk

Mailing List Rental Services

Research and rental of list from list owner/broker	Retail Cost of List Rental

* Quote was based on combined job to make mail piece and prepare it for mailing ($65 charge of printing of the postcard—500 count, single color on both sides of postcard) Job cost comparison of AAA vs. my charges for same job follows: They quoted a mailing piece rate of .226 per piece which is 3d class bulk, basic letter vice post card rate first class which if used without any presort, etc is .20 per piece. With bar-coding, this mailing could be done at .163 per piece (a savings of $18.42). Total savings I could have achieved would have been $55.42 less on a job costed at $165.50. My bill for this same job would have been $110.08.

** Specialty labels (clear, logo design, etc.) can be used, cost available on request.

Forest Mail Service Price List vs Linden Mailing Service

Mailing List Data Base Services	Base Price	Linden Price
Data Entry (based on 3 lines of input, per 100 names)	$20	$20
Verification of delivery address and correcting address (per 100)	$2	unk
Duplicate name screen/removal (per 100 names screened)	$2	unk
Merge/purge service (per 100 names screened)	$2	unk
Output Services from Mailing Data Base		
Printing of mailing labels (gummed backed)* (per 100) (Includes preparation of mailing to qualify at lowest possible postage based on number and type of mailer, printing of USPS forms, etc.)	$4	$4
Printing of rosters/prospect listing (first page)	$2	unk
Lettershop Services		
Applying labels to mailing piece, and stamp or meter (per 100 labels)	$1	$1
Folding, stuffing envelopes and sealing envelope (per 100 pages) pieces	$1	$1/100
Delivery to post office	n/c	unk
Use of bulk mail permit	n/c	$10

Combined Service

	Base Price	Linden Price
Initial database input (standard 3 line record), maintain (includes duplicate check, zip code and address verification quarterly), update, print and affix gummed labels 4 times per year (per 100 records)	$60	unk

Mailing List Rental Services

Research and rental of list from list owner/broker	Retail Cost of List Rental	

* Specialty labels (clear, logo design, etc.) can be used, cost available on request.

As of: July 30, 1995

Forest Mail Service vs Northern Mailings, Omaha, NE

Mailing List Data Base Services	Base Price	Northern Price
Data Entry (based on 3 lines of input, per 100 names)	$20	$20 $10/100
Verification of delivery address and correcting address (per 100)	$2	incl
Duplicate name screen/removal (per 100 names screened)	$2	unk
Merge/purge service (per 100 names screened)	$2	unk

Output Services from Mailing Data Base

Printing of mailing labels (gummed backed)* (per 100) (Includes preparation of mailing to qualify at lowest possible postage based on number and type of mailer, printing of USPS forms, etc.)	$4	$3
		$10 if they don't maintain database
Printing of rosters/prospect listing (first page)	$2	unk

Lettershop Services

Applying labels to mailing piece, and stamp or meter (per 100 labels)	$1	n/a
Folding, stuffing envelopes and sealing envelope (per 100 pages)	$1	n/a
Delivery to post office	n/c	n/a
Use of bulk mail permit	n/c	n/a

Combined Service	**Base Price**	**Northern Price**
Initial database input (standard 3 line record), maintain (includes duplicate check, zip code and address verification quarterly), update, print and affix gummed labels 4 times per year (per 100 records)	$60	unk

Mailing List Rental Services

Research and rental of list from list owner/broker	Retail Cost of List Rental

* Specialty labels (clear, logo design, etc.) can be used, cost available on request.

As of: July 30, 1995

Monthly Expenses Worksheet

Office Expenses	Amount
Yellow Page Ad	50
Business Line	40
800 line charges	36
Long Distance Charges	60
Voice Mail Cost	15
Supplies Office	30
Compuserve Charges	35
Insurance (office)	20
Insurance (health)	100
Auto expenses	100
Postage meter rental	18
Membership dues	15
Professional Magazines	15
Software Costs/Programs	50
Attorney/Tax Charges	25
Rent	0
Utilities	0
Sub Total	**609**

Marketing Charges

Postage Charges	100
Advertising charges	100
Sub Total	200
Salary	**2000**
Grand Total	**2809**

	Aug	Sept	Oct	Nov	Dec
Fixed Costs	$125	$125	$125	$125	$125
Variable Costs	500	700	700	700	700
Income	0	500	1,000	1,000	1,200

Breakeven Analysis - 1996

	Jan	Feb	Mar	Apr	May	Jun	Jul	Aug	Sep	Oct	Nov	Dec
Fixed Costs	$125	$125	$125	$125	$125	$125	$125	$125	$125	$125	$125	$125
Variable Costs	500	1,200	1,200	1,200	1,200	1,400	2,500	2,725	2,800	2,800	2,900	2,900
Income	1,200	1,400	1,500	2,000	2,375	2,500	2,700	2,900	3,000	3,125	3,125	3,125

Breakeven Analysis - 1997

	Jan	Feb	Mar	Apr	May	Jun	Jul
Fixed Costs	$125	$125	$125	$125	$125	$125	$125
Variable Costs	3,000	3,000	3,125	3,125	3,250	3,250	3,250
Income	3,250	3,350	3,350	3,400	3,400	3,500	3,500

As of: Nov 6, 1995

Breakeven Analysis - 1998

Estimated Pre-Start Up Position 1996-1997

Year 1 Cash Flow Worksheet

	Jul 96	Aug 96	Sep 96	Oct 96	Nov 96	Dec 96
1. Cash on Hand	17230	6381	5672	5313	5454	5595
2. Cash Receipts						
(a) Cash Sales	0	0	500	1000	1000	1200
(b) Collections from Credit Accounts	0	0	0	0	0	0
(c) Loan or Other Cash Injection	0	0	0	0	0	0
3. Total Cash Receipts	0	0	500	1000	1000	1200
4. Total Cash Avble	17230	6381	6172	6313	6454	6795
5. Cash Paid Out						
(a) Purchases (Merchandise)	0	0	0	0	0	0
(b) Gross Wages	0	0	0	0	0	0
(c) Payroll Expenses	0	0	0	0	0	0
(d) Outside Services	0	35	35	35	35	35
(e) Supplies (office and operating)	683	30	30	30	30	30
(f) Maintenance	0	0	50	50	50	50
(g) Advertising	0	250	250	250	250	250
(h) Delivery & Travel	0	100	100	100	100	100
(i) Accounting & Legal	0	25	25	25	25	25

...continued

(j) Rent	0	0	0	0	0	0
(k) Telephone	48	151	151	151	151	151
(l) Utilities	0	0	0	0	0	0
(m) Insurance (Office)	0	20	20	20	20	20
(n) Taxes (Real estate, etc.)	0	0	0	0	0	0
(o) Interest	0	0	0	0	0	0
(p) Other Expenses (specify each)						
Permits	220	0	0	0	0	0
Insurance health	0	0	100	100	100	100
(q) Miscellaneous (Unspecified)	0	48	48	48	48	48
(r) Subtotal	951	659	809	809	809	809
(s) Loan Principal Payment	0	0	0	0	0	0
(t) Capital Purchases (specify)	9898	50	50	50	50	50
(u) Other Start up Costs (Lap top)	0	0	0	0	0	0
(v) Reserve and/or Escrow	0	0	0	0	0	0
(w) Owner's Withdrawl	0	0	0	0	0	0
6. Total Cash Paid Out	10849	709	859	859	859	859
7. Cash Position	6381	5672	5313	5454	5595	5936
Essential Operating Data						
A. Sales Volume (Dollars)	0	0	500	1000	1000	1200
B. Accounts Receivable (EOM)	0	0	0	0	0	0
C. Bad Debt (EOM)	0	0	0	0	0	0
D. Inventory on Hand (EOM)	0	0	0	0	0	0
E. Accounts Payable (EOM)	0	0	0	0	0	0
F. Depreciation	0	140	140	140	140	140

	Jan 97	Feb 97	Mar 97	Apr 97	May 97	Jun 97	Jul 97	Totals
1. Cash on Hand	5936	6277	6318	6459	7100	4541	5432	70478
2. Cash Receipts	0	0	0	0	0	0	0	0
(a) Cash Sales	1200	4000	1500	2000	2300	2500	2800	17400
(b) Collections from Credit Accounts								
	0	0	0	0	0	0	0	0
(c) Loan or Other Cash Injection								
	0	0	0	0	0	0	0	0
3. Total Cash Receipts	1200	1400	1500	2000	2300	2500	2800	17400
4. Total Cash Available	7136	7677	7818	8459	9400	7041	8232	87878
5. Cash Paid Out	0	0	0	0	0	0	0	0
(a) Purchases (Merchandise)	0	0	0	0	0	0	0	0
(b) Gross Wages	0	500	500	500	500	750	1200	3950
(c) Payroll Expenses	0	0	0	0	0	0	0	0
(d) Outside Services	35	35	35	35	35	35	35	420
(e) Supplies (office and operating)								
	30	30	30	30	30	30	30	360
(f) Repairs and Maintenance	50	50	50	50	50	50	50	550
(g) Advertising	250	250	250	250	250	250	250	3000
(h) Car, Delivery & Travel	100	100	100	100	100	100	100	1200
(i) Accounting and Legal	25	25	25	25	25	25	25	300
j) Rent	0	0	0	0	0	0	0	0
(k) Telephone	151	151	151	151	151	151	151	1812
(l) Utilities	0	0	0	0	0	0	0	0
(m) Insurance (Office)	20	20	20	20	20	20	20	240
(n) Taxes (Real estate, etc.)	0	0	0	0	0	0	0	0

(o) Interest	0	0	0	0	0	0	0	0	*...continued*
(p) Other Expenses									
Permits	0	0	0	0	0	0	220	220	
Insurance health	100	100	100	100	100	100	100	1100	
(q) Miscellaneous	48	48	48	48	48	48	48	576	
(r) Subtotal	809	1309	1309	1309	1309	1559	2229	13728	
(s) Loan Principal Payment	0	0	0	0	0	0	0	0	
(t) Capital Purchases	50	50	50	50	50	50	425	975	
(u) Other Start up Costs	0	0	0	0	3500	0	0	3500	
(v) Reserve and/or Escrow	0	0	0	0	0	0	0	0	
(w) Owner's Withdrawl	0	0	0	0	0	0	0	0	
6. Total Cash Paid Out	859	1359	1359	1359	4859	1609	2654	18203	
7. Cash Position	6277	6318	6459	7100	4541	5432	5578	69675	
Essential Operating Data									
A. Sales Volume (Dollars)	1200	1400	1500	2000	2300	2500	2800	17400	
B. Accts Receivable (EOM)	0	0	0	0	0	0	0	0	
C. Bad Debt (EOM)	0	0	0	0	0	0	0	0	
D. Inventory on Hand (EOM)	0	0	0	0	0	0	0	0	
E. Accounts Payable (EOM)	0	0	0	0	0	0	0	0	
F. Depreciation	140	140	140	140	200	200	200	1860	

Management Consulting Firm

BUSINESS PLAN

SALMON & SALMON

38260 Lake Superior Dr., Ste. 222
Philadelphia, PA 35008

This business plan is for a management consulting firm which intends to operate as a "virtual corporation." This will allow the firm to engage independent contractors with various skills and experience to meet the changing needs of their clientele.

- EXECUTIVE SUMMARY

- OBJECTIVES

- PRESENT SITUATION

- MANAGEMENT

- SERVICE DESCRIPTION

- MARKET ANALYSIS

- MARKETING STRATEGY

- FINANCIAL INFORMATION

- AMERICAN CONSULTANTS LEAGUE CODE OF ETHICS

EXECUTIVE SUMMARY

Salmon & Salmon (S&S) is a privately owned for profit management consulting business, and a sole proprietorship. Consulting services are concentrated primarily in the services industry focusing on industrial, commercial, and governmental products in the Washington, D.C. metropolitan area.

Mission

Salmon & Salmon formulate strategies and facilitate change to clarify client objectives and goals. They provide a quantitative measurement of change based upon analysis integrity and special expertise.

Long Range Vision

Our primary service in five years will continue to be management consulting services. Our primary market will include industrial, commercial, trade, professional associations, political organizations and advocacy groups. Our competitive position will be as a niche specialist and virtual corporation that can easily adapt to rapid changes in the marketplace. Total sales will exceed $100,000 and administrative services will be out-sourced.

Core Values

Salmon & Salmon believe:

- Integrity and honesty guide all phases of the client and consultant relationship from the exploratory meeting to final delivery.
- Special expertise insures our clients attain cost effective, results oriented solutions.
- Excellence is the hallmark in all of our business associations with suppliers, independent consultants and most importantly our clients.

Management

Salmon & Salmon is a member in good standing with the American Consultants League and subscribes to their Code of Ethics. Our management team consists of the principal and owner, Pinky L. Salmon.

OBJECTIVES

The primary objectives of our organization are:

- To satisfy a market need to offer a full-time consulting product.
- To develop a client base requiring a team effort, versus a sole practitioner, to satisfy client requirements.

Business Goals

Compared to past performance offering strategy formulation and business planning in the consulting industry, we intend to form a virtual corporation whereby skilled consultants will match performance expectations to industry realities. As a virtual corporation, other sole practitioners can be brought onto a project as independent contractors, thereby preserving the consultant's desire to maintain independence.

Rationale

Considering our experience within the marketplace, we believe our clients demand more diverse services, especially small to medium size businesses. These companies typically do not have the financial resources to hire full-time professional staffs. They frequently look to "out-sourcing" or contracting for services focused on short-term task specific projects or on-going, less than full-time professional services.

All of our consultants come from environments where they managed large organizations, conducted comprehensive consultations in a variety of industries, and have proven records of obtaining results for their clients.

Position for Growth

Our position for growth is to understand our customers, competition, and industry. We intend to employ ethical and results driven consultants who are willing to remain independent and intent upon expanding their business development efforts.

We will jointly (principal and independent consultant) focus our business development efforts on companies with revenues exceeding $1.0 million, companies who are prime contractors to the federal government, national and international trade associations, and other businesses in the service sector.

The marketplace in Southern Pennsylvania is undergoing changes because of downsizing within the federal government. Currently, services to the federal government are concentrated within the telecommunications, computer and other high technology businesses.

PRESENT SITUATION

Market Environment

The second level of service is to those companies who are the prime contractors on government contracts or companies other than those providing government services. This secondary level is where Salmon & Salmon has focused its efforts.

The present stage of services is in the test market stage.

Services

Clients using our services are small businesses obtaining financing, negotiating leases, purchasing other businesses or starting a new enterprise. They have requested an expansion of our services to include a full-service package of consulting services.

Customers

Most of our management is in place, however, we require a Human Resource, Marketing and Technology, and Computer consultant to complete our team.

Management

Financial resources are based upon the personal assets of Pinky L. Salmon. Current cash available is $8000.00.

Financial Resources

Pinky L. Salmon is a certified professional consultant. For more than 20 years, she has provided management consulting services to private and public sector clients. Ms. Salmon's expertise includes: strategic formulation, business planning, system analysis and operational audits. Ms. Salmon was a Senior Analyst for a management and engineering firm in Washington, D.C. subsequent to establishing Salmon & Salmon. She frequently contributes articles to local business publications and magazines.

MANAGEMENT

Ms. Salmon is also a public speaker for a variety of business associations such as Rotary Clubs, the Association of Part Time Professionals, Tennessee Women in Business, etc.

She holds a B.A. degree in Business Administration from Northwestern University in Chicago, IL. She is certified in Total Quality Management principles. Ms. Salmon is a member of the American Consultants League, Sarasota, Florida and is an Executive Director the Business Advisory Council of Southern Pennsylvania.

In August 1993, Salmon & Salmon became licensed to do business in Pennsylvania. Salmon & Salmon conducted its market research throughout 1994 while simultaneously setting up operations. In January 1995, Salmon & Salmon positioned itself to offer management consulting services to medium size companies and trade associations.

Pinky L. Salmon is the principal and owner of the company. She is responsible for daily operations and performing the client's requirements within the scope of individual contracts. She is also responsible for business development including planning, advertising, public relations and identifying new markets.

Management Team

Outside Support

The services of an outside certified public accountant is required for income tax returns and financial statement preparation. A marketing professional assists the principal to make appropriate decisions related to marketing strategy. A transition management consultant assists the principal to make appropriate decisions related to the company's goals and vision.

People/Talent We Require

Pinky L. Salmon recognized that additional project support professionals are required to properly support clients' expanding requirements. Initial negotiations are underway with established consultants to market and collaborate on joint projects.

SERVICE DESCRIPTION

Salmon & Salmon's consulting service consists of strategic formulation and business planning. The service is used by enterprises (clients) who need to identify long term goals, get a new idea or venture "off the ground" or expand, acquire or refinance a project.

Development of other services is in progress and future services are planned using a network of other consultants. For example, when developing a business plan or strategy with a client, emerging requirements and/or deficiencies are often identified. Having the capability to offer services such as human resources, marketing and telecommunications will be a unique feature of Salmon & Salmon.

Useful Purpose and Benefits

Benefits that Salmon & Salmon offers are:

- A fresh perspective on a problem or business - an unbiased point of view.
- An objective assessment of the situation and help to define possible problems.
- A critique on how well a business is doing in such areas as strategy, executive compensation, marketing, production, point of sale effectiveness, and customer satisfaction.
- A project done faster and more skillfully at a lower cost (up to 40%) than in-house staff.

Outside management advisors provide tremendous support for management decisions and creativity. Outside advisors are:

- Tory Littman, C.P.A.
- Judith Walker, Livingston Communications, Marketing Consultant
- Caroline Smith, Transition Management Consultant
- Marcus Douglas, Attorney and Counselor at Law

Marketing

The fundamental thrust of our marketing strategy consists of attracting executives and business owners by personal contact and through conducting one hour seminars. We intend to reach management and business owners by conducting seminars on business planning strategies, and publishing "How To" reports at no cost to the prospective client. Advertising will be placed in the classified ads of leading business publications and through earned media.

Finance

Financial expectations for 1996 and 1997 are very conservative. By 1998, we expect to collect a return on investment.

Conclusion

Salmon & Salmon enjoys an established track record for excellent service for our customers. Their expressions of satisfaction and encouragement are numerous. We intend to continue our advances in the marketplace with a more comprehensive package of consulting services.

Key points in defining market segment for consulting services is based on 1989-1994 Statistical Summary Areas of Business concentration in Northern Tennessee. Listed in order of priority, these segments are as follows:

Major Market Segments

- •Government services, especially technical services and research and development.
- •National and international trade and professional associations.
- •Other business services, such as financial, personnel, office supply, public relations, etc.

Note: Businesses with 5-99 employees represent 39% of the small businesses in the state of Pennsylvania. Micro businesses with 0-4 employees represent 59%.

The stability of the first market segment is uncertain. Government downsizing and reductions planned for the next two years will have a direct impact on the ability of this segment to remain viable. Industry has been in a downsizing trend since 1985 and government has been slow to implement similar changes. Consequently, the need for technology to replace personnel should remain constant for firms providing R&D and technical services.

Technical Services and R&D Segment

This segment of the market should remain fairly stable in spite of government downsizing. The proximity to Washington, D.C. and the rapid transmission of information relating to public policy and legislation is essential to this market segment.

National and International Trade Associations

The market potential for consulting services for small businesses and start up enterprises is infinite. Two years of market research has revealed that this market segment has limitations. Unless the particular enterprise generates revenues of at least $1.0 million, the company typically is not in a financial position to pay consulting fees. Start ups, as a rule, are under financed and considered high risk clients.

Other Business Services

In terms of consulting services provided by Salmon & Salmon, the company has several distinct advantages over the competition. First, all independent consultants have established reputations in a variety of industries including telecommunications, trade associations and government services. Consultants are computer literate and continually update their skills.

Strengths

The breadth of options offered to clients is different from the competition. Salmon & Salmon is set up as a virtual corporation and can readily draw upon the resources of other independent consultants without maintaining a full-time staff of consultants.

In marketing, our most powerful assets are awareness, image and pricing. All independent consultants are well versed in business development techniques and fully understand the expertise of the other independent consultants. Should a client signal a need for services not directly related to the consultant's skills, the requirement will be passed on to the owner who in turn will take appropriate action.

Integrity, personal presentation skills and communicating product knowledge are paramount to carrying across quality and reliability to the client. Consultant's working under Salmon & Salmon's contract, exemplify these characteristics.

Pricing is far more competitive than larger consulting firms, simply because overhead is minimal and no full-time staff consultants will be used. Independent consultants will be sub-contracted on a per project basis. Consultants will be responsible for preparing their reports and deliverables using criteria set down by Salmon & Salmon.

There are two limitations inherent in our service. First, if an independent consultant does not complete a project because of unforeseen circumstances, Salmon & Salmon will have to develop

Vulnerabilities

a contingency plan acceptable to the client. A termination clause in the contract or letter of agreement will address such situations and should alleviate this problem and minimize the risk to the client.

Secondly, retaining a consultant who does not share the company's vision and method of operation is a weakness. Salmon & Salmon will employ only those independent consultants that have previously been contracted with S&S, or those who have a close personal relationship with S&S thereby reducing this potential weakness.

Unexploited Opportunities

An altogether new application for this service would be "spreading a wider net" when developing new business and tapping into new markets to identify opportunities for other consultants. Little risk is incurred by any consultant.

MARKETING STRATEGY

Salmon & Salmon's marketing strategy is to enhance, promote and support the fact that our services increase our clients' productivity and profit margins. Our consultants have the necessary "hands-on" expertise required to perform and in-depth, logical, practical and critical analysis of a client's needs, business strategies, goals, and short and long-term objectives at each stage of development and implementation.

To prove the value of our service, we involve the client in the entire consulting process from the conceptual stage to the finished product. Getting the client involved in every functional area of the business, is necessary so he/she will understand that these areas must be given equal attention in formulating short and long-term goals and objectives. The measurable benefit of this approach is a definite competitive edge and improvement of the client's chances of a prospective lender or investor funding the venture. It also ensures continued success, viability, profitability and growth.

Pricing and Profitability

Fees are set high enough to give Salmon & Salmon credibility in the eyes of the prospective client. Fees are charged on an hourly or daily rate, fixed fee, or on a retainer basis depending upon the client's needs. The hourly or daily fee applies to very short-term assignments - a few days or one week at most. Fixed fees are preferred by clients, because they serve to establish a total dollar commitment risk on the part of Salmon & Salmon. This makes the marketing task of Salmon & Salmon easier. Annual retainer fees are acceptable when a client, who has used our services frequently want consultants "on-tap" which can be called upon whenever the need arises without paying the hourly or daily fee. Salmon & Salmon will not accept contingency fees.

Selling Tactics

Current selling tactics include advertising, seminars, direct calling, mail and networking through professional and business associations.

Advertising and Promotion

The company advertises in Market Monthly, a business magazine with over 2,000 subscribers. Pinky Salmon is a frequent featured writer for this publication.

The primary objectives are to increase Salmon & Salmon awareness and name recognition among business managers and generate qualified sales leads.

In 1994, the company participated in one Chamber of Commerce trade show. No sales were generated.

Research indicates that the best way to reach potential clients is to conduct one hour "How To" seminars and publish a "How To" booklet at no cost to prospective clients on topics of specific interest. Salmon & Salmon conducted seminars and presentations in the area of total customer service and effective business planning. The purpose was to establish company image and generate leads.

Advertising is costly and has not been successful in generating revenues. Referral business and direct contact with executives and centers of influence has been the primary source of business for Salmon & Salmon.

The company will arrange for interviews on business talk radio and local cable programs.

Direct Mail

The company has no plans for using direct mail.

Sales Support Collateral Materials

Sales support materials consist of a company portfolio, which includes magazine article reprints. Business cards, presentations, proposals and stationery are coordinated to reflect the company's message and image.

Investment in Advertising and Promotion

In 1994, advertising expenses represented 34% of revenues. In 1995, advertising expenses represented 10% of revenues. Revenues increased 54% in 1995.

Salmon & Salmon is investing in promoting more seminars and publishing "How To" pamphlets. Local banks and Chambers of Commerce have expressed interest in sponsoring "How To" seminars charging a minimal fee.

Business Relationships

Salmon & Salmon has formed valuable business relationships with management, computer and marketing consultants. Built upon this foundation, the company is moving forward with its virtual corporation concept. Forming strategic alliances and collaborating with established consultants will produce stable revenues, credibility, and increase market presence.

The company is pursuing a marketing strategic alliance with consultants in Human Resources, Marketing and Computer specialists. Our plans include those consultants marketing our services within their product line. In turn, Salmon & Salmon will offer the independent consultants' services to augment S&S' product lines.

FINANCIAL INFORMATION

1996 Budget

	JAN	FEB	MAR	APR	MAY	JUN	JUL	AUG	SEP	OCT	NOV	DEC
Sales												
Consulting Services	0	0	0	1000	1000	2500	2500	3000	1500	1500	1000	1000
Total Sales	0	0	0	1000	1000	2500	2500	3000	1500	1500	1000	1000
Cost of Goods Sold (n/a)	0	0	0	0	0	0	0	0	0	0	0	0
Gross Profit												
Operating Expenses												
Sales & Marketing												
Advertising	0	0	100	0	0	100	0	0	0	100	100	100
Commissions	0	0	0	0	0	0	0	0	0	0	0	0
Entertainment	100	100	100	100	100	100	100	100	100	100	100	100
Literature	50	50	50	50	50	50	50	50	50	50	50	50
Promotions	0	0	0	0	0	0	0	0	0	0	0	0
Salaries	0	0	0	0	0	0	0	0	0	0	0	0
Trade Shows	0	0	0	0	0	0	0	0	0	0	0	0
Travel	0	0	0	0	0	0	0	0	0	0	0	0
Total Sales & Marketing Costs	150	150	250	150	150	250	150	150	150	250	250	250

Research & Development (n/a)

General & Administrative

Accounting	0	0	0	0	0	0	0	0	0	0	0	0
Admin Salaries	0	0	0	0	0	0	0	0	0	0	0	0
Bad Debts	0	0	0	0	0	0	0	0	0	0	0	0
Depreciation	0	0	0	0	0	0	0	0	0	0	0	0
Education	100	100	100	100	100	100	100	100	100	100	100	100
Equipment Lease	0	0	0	0	0	0	0	0	0	0	0	0
Insurance	0	0	0	0	0	0	0	300	0	0	0	0
Legal Fees	300	150	150	150	150	150	150	150	150	150	150	150
Licenses and Permits	25	0	0	0	0	0	0	0	0	0	0	0
Office Expenses	25	100	100	100	100	100	100	100	100	100	100	100
Office Rental or Lease	0	0	0	0	0	0	0	0	0	0	0	0
Taxes (non-income)	0	0	0	0	0	0	0	0	0	0	0	0
Telephone	150	150	150	150	150	150	150	150	150	150	150	150
Utilities	0	0	0	0	0	0	0	0	0	0	0	0
Total G&A Cost	675	500	500	500	500	500	500	800	500	500	500	500
Total Opr Expenses	825	650	750	650	650	750	650	950	650	750	750	750
Operations Income	-825	-650	-750	350	350	1750	1850	2050	850	750	250	250
Taxes on Income	0	0	0	120	120	603	638	705	293	603	86	86
Net Inc After Taxes	-825	-650	-750	230	230	1147	1212	1343	557	147	164	164

Cash Flow Forecast

	Last Year 1995	This Year 1996	Next Year 1997
Beginning Cash Balance	2,500	7,131	9,602
Cash Receipts	8,500	15,000	21,000
Collection of Receivables			
Interest Income	0	0	0
Total Cash Receipts	11,000	22,131	30,602
Cash Disbursements			
Accounts	2,264	6,475	12,000
Payments of Other Expenses	1,867	2,300	3,200
Income Tax Payments	0	3,254	7,200
Total Cash Disbursements	4,131	12,029	22,400
Net Cash from (Used for Operations)	1,131	10,102	8,202
Sale of Stock	N/A	N/A	N/A
Purchase of Equipment	0	500	0
Decrease (Increase in Funds Invested)	0	0	0
Short-term Borrowings (Repayments)	0	0	0
Ending Cash Balance	7,131	9,602	8,202

Start-Up Costs

Cash	2500
Business License & Permit	51
Education (books, tapes, courses)	1200
Initial Accounts Receivable	0
Inventory	0
Equipment	7500
Fixtures	N/A
Insurance (liability)	300

Rent Deposits	N/A
Remodeling	N/A
Utilities (telephones, fax)	750
Legal & Professional Fees	1200
Miscellaneous	500
Office Supplies	1100
Opening Advertising & Promotion	3000
TOTAL	**18,101**

Start-up cost were financed from personal assets of Pinky L. Salmon. Salmon & Salmon conducts business from a home office appropriately equipped for business activity. Therefore, rent deposits, fixtures and remodeling costs are not applicable. S&S plans to move from a home office to a commercial office in 1997, as part of a business "incubation" arrangement.

I, Pinky L. Salmon hereby certify that:

I am a member in good standing of the ACL.

I am competent in my field.

I will always make every attempt to identify the client's real problem.

I will always specify my role in the client's project or assignment.

I will adapt to the individuality of my client's problems.

My recommendations will be feasible.

I will at all times avoid a conflict of interest.

I will never deceive my client.

I will never fail to perform my services.

I will never be negligent.

I will always inform my client of the risks of any undertaking.

I will always inform my client of my basic approach to his problem.

The matter of my fee will always be presented forthrightly so that my client will always know what his or her money will buy.

I will maintain total confidentiality with regard to my client's business.

I will always work to the best of my ability to insure the quick success of my client's project.

Charges for expenses over and above my regular fee will always be fair and accurate.

I will never accept fees or commissions from others for recommending equipment, supplies or services to my client.

I understand that proven infraction to any of the above rules will cause immediate revocation of my CC accreditation as well as loss of membership in The American Consultants League.

AMERICAN CONSULTANTS LEAGUE CODE OF ETHICS

Manufacturing Business

BUSINESS PLAN

FIBER OPTIC AUTOMATION, INC.

141 S. Main St.
Boston, MA 02120

The authors of this plan have developed an innovative monitoring system for underground cables, wires, and storage tanks. They are seeking financing to expand their reach into consumer markets, while increasing their industrial market.

- EXECUTIVE SUMMARY

- DESCRIPTION OF BUSINESS

- SALES AND MARKETING

- COMPETITION

- MANAGEMENT

- FUNDING REQUIREMENTS

- FINANCIAL PROJECTIONS

EXECUTIVE SUMMARY

Overview

Fiber Optic Automation, Inc. ("FOA" or the "Company") was founded in 1986 and is based in Boston, Massachusetts. In September 1995, FOA was merged into Optech Inc. The Company has obtained the exclusive right to manufacture and market a patented monitoring and fault locating technology. The primary focus of the Company is in the telecommunications industry, telephone operating companies, ("Telco's"), Cable TV (CATV) and Local Area Network (LAN) fiber optic markets.

To date, the Company has raised approximately $6.0 million to support research and development, product introduction to the Telco market and initial sales. The Company seeks to raise an additional $5.0 million to fund its growth. The funds will be used for general corporate purposes, including working capital and expansion of the sales and marketing efforts. FOA's business plan projects that annual sales will reach the $34.0 million level by the fifth year with net after-tax profits of approximately $10.8 million.

The Company's monitoring system, Cablewatch, facilitates the continuous monitoring of fiber optic and copper cables. By providing "early warning" and by identifying and locating faults before an outage can occur, the system can save telephone companies as much as $1.0 million per minute in lost revenue and repair costs. This system can also extend the useful life of telephone cable network (outside plant) significantly. The outdoor telephone cable, splices, and repeater sites are generally known as outside plant. Management believes there is no other product currently available which can directly monitor and locate long-range faults on fiber optic cable. Most other competing technologies and products in this regard are more complementary to the Company's products than competitive.

The Company's technology was originally developed in Canada and has been in operation on the Canadian fiber optic network since 1988. Since the acquisition of the basic technology and a basic patent in late 1986, the Company has developed several important products and been awarded several new patents. In addition, several more patent disclosures are being processed for the Company's latest innovations dealing with automated monitoring and fault locating of both optical fiber copper cable and for solving one of the industry's major obstacles in bringing fiber to the home or fiber to the curb.

Customers for Cablewatch and related Telco telephone products include telephone companies worldwide. Product development has been completed and many of the products have already been approved and are now awaiting standardization. Product improvements, however, are an ongoing activity in the ever-changing market, as well as modifications in order to meet customer-specific requirements. The company has been developing sales of its products over the years since the business was established. Sales have fluctuated from year-to-year, from a low of $233,000 to a high of $700,000 during the period from 1990 to 1995. This was due to minimal sales and marketing efforts put forth during the early years, when we concentrated our efforts on development of products and partnership agreements. Cutbacks in customer's capital budgets and changes/cuts in personnel have partly contributed to the delays in Company growth and sales goal achievement. The Company has experienced a continued shortage of capital, and therefore has been unable to take itself to the next step of its growth cycle. The Company has been focusing its efforts on the fiber optic segment of the telephone market, which is growing rapidly (in excess of 20% a year) on a worldwide basis. The total market for Cablewatch application on fiber optic cables is estimated by management to grow from $156 million annually in 1993 to approximately $363 million by 1997. This has been limited due to manufacturing limitations. These numbers are based on the market size for fiber optic cables as projected by Kimbrough Marketing Inc. ("KMI") as shown in the accompanying charts and graphs that follow. That we have only addressed the fiber cable market in our plan, and that these products can also be utilized for copper cable, reduces cost justification for the Telco.

The same technology used in the Telco market has been applied to the industrial market for the development of a continuous monitoring system to detect spills and leaks of hazardous substances for use at factories, industrial storage facilities, high rise condominium complexes, and gasoline storage tanks, either above or below ground. FOA has sold an initial system to a major ammunition plant in Texas and is in the process of implementing an upgrade for automation of the monitoring system. Management estimates the market potential for products in this market to be hundreds of millions of dollars per year. However, limited resources preclude FOA from marketing this product line at this time.

FOA has also developed inexpensive monitoring devices to detect water or gas leaks, as well as basement flooding, in the home. Primary customers include mass merchandisers of all kinds. The current size of this market is estimated to be in excess of $100 million. Again, due to limited resources, marketing of these consumer products may be done through royalty arrangements.

It is possible that the non-fiber optic related market could be funded as separate business segments. Each product offers the potential to be the industry leader in its respective market. Management believes it has distinct competitive advantages in all three products. Additionally, the monitoring technology can be applied to other markets such as building security and secured communications, among others applications.

Telco Products Only
($000's)

	YR1	YR2	YR3	YR4	YR5
Sales	1,025	2,735	8,050	17,185	34,150
Gross Profit (Loss)	474	1,323	4,049	8,804	17,809
Operating Income		494	2,274	5,367	10,442
Income (loss) before Tax Provision		334	2,124	5,580	10,803

Selected Financial Projection

MANAGEMENT

Officers/Directors

Lyle Kasdan, 49 years old is Chairman of Optech, the parent, and President, CEO & Director and co-founder of FOA. At FOA, he was responsible for developing the Company's business strategy and raising approximately $5.0 million in equity financing through private & institutional sources. He oversaw the development of several new products & patents for application in the telecommunication, industrial & consumer markets.

Mr. Kasdan was also a co-founder of a leading publicly traded optical fiber manufacturer. He served as a Director, Treasurer and Executive Vice-President of Manufacturing & Engineering. He was responsible for all engineering and manufacturing including equipment technology, process technology, product development, quality assurance, plant engineering, plant automation and purchasing. He supervised the growth of manufacturing and engineering capabilities to become the third-largest manufacturer of optical fiber in the U.S. through installation of state-of-the-art manufacturing facilities and factory automation systems.

Dr. Aslami received his B.S. degree in Chemical Engineering, and his Ph.D. in Chemical Engineering. He has published several articles, taught at several universities, and has patented a unique vapor delivery system for fiber preform manufacture that increased productivity, reproducibility and yields of high-performance communication optical fiber.

Investment Merits

Proven Management Team

The principals of FOA, Lyle Kasdan and Roger Knight, have collectively over forty years of experience in the fiber optic field. Both executives were co-founders of Optech Inc., a leading optical fiber manufacturer.

Mr. Kasdan has developed and managed three different fiber optic manufacturing operations in addition to Optech. He is also the coauthor of several industry patents. Mr. Knight's management experience includes executive marketing roles in addition to his Optech experience.

Patented Technology

The Company has acquired exclusive rights to the initial electronic monitoring technology; all patents, products and know-how to manufacture and market Cablewatch worldwide (except Canada). Patent protection extends from the U.S. and Canada to the European Common Market countries and the Far East. The Company has also conducted patent searches, including a detailed infringement search, with positive results.

This proven technology was originally developed to meet the needs of the Canadian telephone system. It has been in operation on the Canadian fiber optic network since 1988 and is now used across that country. Penetration and acceptance in the U.S. Telco market has been slow over the last three years due to the Company's lack of capital. The company has received several new patents, with others in the process of being issued.

Management believes there is no similar competing technology which can monitor and locate long range faults on fiber optic cable and jel-filled copper cables. However, there are systems in place for the monitoring of old pressurized copper cables. Pressurization, however, is not practical for use on fiber optic and modern jel-filled copper cables.

Compatible Technologies

Although there is no direct competitive product in the market today, there are, however, several alternative technologies available:

Line Walker

This product has been around for over 30 years and works on the principle of sending an audio signal on the cable sheath and monitoring the leakage of this signal from the damaged site via a portable receiver. In order to do this, however, one must "walk the line," since the receiver has to be near the damaged site. Management believes this technology is more complementary than competitive. Several large companies are manufacturing this product.

Pressurization

This technology was developed and used on copper telephone cable for over 30 years. It is simply not practical and/or economical on small fiber optic cable.

ORD (Optical Reflectometer Device)

This instrument has also been used for approximately 10 years. It works on the principle of sending an optical signal on the individual fiber and measuring the elapsed reflection time of the signal from the damaged or broken fiber. This is a delicate and expensive instrument that is manufactured by several large and small companies. Again, because of the fact that this instrument works on the individual fiber and not the entire cable, it can be considered a complementary technology. This instrument is not capable of identifying the cable sheath damage that will in most cases result in fiber damage. There may be as many as 144 fibers in a fiber optic cable. FOA's instruments, on the other hand, provide early warning, identify and locate damage to the entire cable, and more importantly, prior to the fiber(s) being damaged. In most cases such sheath damage can be repaired through preventive maintenance before the full degradation and/or outage can occur. FOA's 1996 plan, once funded, is to build this instrument into our Long Range Cablewatch and thus provide the most powerful, useful, versatile, and economical instrument that is available to the industry.

Fiber Monitoring

In those cases where the fiber optic cable does not have a metallic armor to allow the company's Cablewatch to be implemented, an ORD monitoring approach must be used. This technique is costly and dependent on the number of fibers that must be monitored. There are a number of companies that offer ORD types for non-active fibers (dark fibers) monitoring. This is a "hit or miss" type of random monitoring. The Company has signed an agreement to offer its product, which is an active approach to 100% of the fibers being monitored. The Company believes that its product and that of their agreement partner makes for the offering of a unique package. It is working on a number of opportunities using both types of technology.

Large Potential Market

The total worldwide market for FOA's products has grown from approximately $156 million in 1993, and is expected to grow to $363 million annually by 1997. This growth in the fiber optic market is partially due to the development of the "Information Super Highway and The New Telecommunication Bill". The Company is in discussions with certain developers to consider the use of FOA's cable monitoring systems on these networks.

Customers for Cablewatch and related Telco products include telephone companies worldwide. The Cable TV (CATV) industry has recently started deploying large amounts of fiber optic cables from the distribution office to the end-user distribution panels in an attempt to meet tougher transmission quality standards as well as participate in the growing multi media market. These CATV networks, as well, will require the Company's products to maintain their network integrity. The company has sold a trial system for use on one cable company's fiber optic network in the California Area.

Wide Application of Technology

The Company's monitoring technology may have significant applications in other fields such as security, secured communications, building management/environmental control, and railroad tankcar monitoring. Although there are no official market size estimates for these fields and no current FOA products, management is continually evaluating applications beyond the core telecommunications market.

Management believes there will be a multi-million dollar market for its hazardous chemical leak detection system. Growth in this market will be spurred by recently passed federal legislation mandating chemical leak monitoring for gasoline storage tanks and other chemical storage facilities. The management, however, is not actively marketing in this area due to limited resources.

Current estimates for the consumer market for FOA's home flood detection equipment are approximately $100 million.

Due to limited resources, the primary focus of the company is the fiber optic portion of the telecommunication market and not the hazardous chemical leak detection or the consumer market.

Fiber Optic Trend

The telephone commercial and industrial marketplaces worldwide have made a commitment to fiber optic technology. A significant portion of their capital expenditures are dedicated to fiber optic installation. Fiber optic lines have supplanted copper line as the optimal cable medium, due to its higher transmission capacity, quality and greater price/performance characteristics. Telecommunications providers worldwide continue to invest heavily in fiber optic technology as most carriers plan to fully adopt optical transmission networks in the next century. The Clinton administration strongly supports the "Information Super Highway". The Company's patented technology is the only passive monitoring system available to support the integrity of the outside plant network. FOA is well positioned to profit from this trend by offering patented products that provide increased reliability, easier maintenance and lower systems maintenance costs for these industries.

FOA Financial Characteristics

As a marketing and light assembly operation, FOA believes it will operate as a high-margin, low-overhead firm with minimal needs for heavy capital investment. Accordingly, the greatest use of funds will be directed toward corporate purposes, including working capital, sales and marketing, and new product development and product improvements.

Fortune 1000 Customer Base

FOA's monitoring technology is directed toward Fortune 1000 customers that are reliable payers with ample resources and high profiles. Major current and potential customers for the Company's product lines include the long distance carriers the RBOC's (Regional Bell Operating Companies) and major independent utilities. Customers for the industrial product lines include chemical, petroleum and industrial companies, as well as nuclear contractors. Consumer products would be sold through mass merchandisers and hardware/home center stores.

DESCRIPTION OF BUSINESS

Corporate Overview

The Company was formed in September 1986, was merged into Optech in September 1995, and is engaged in the design, manufacturing and marketing of cable monitoring and automated long-range fault locating systems. These systems are used primarily for monitoring and fault locating of communication cables. By using the Company's patented electronic monitoring technology, the user has an early warning monitoring system which facilitates preventive maintenance, provides system integrity and long life, and offers substantial cost savings.

While the initial technology was designed for the detection of moisture and/or sheath penetration in fiber optic and/or electrical (copper) cables for the telecommunications industry, the Company has expanded the scope of applications by adapting the technology to meet all utility company needs (e.g. water, electric, gas, and telecommunication) such as automated fault locating, as well as to serve the industrial and consumer marketplace. In that regard, a hazardous leak and spill detection system, including leak monitoring of underground storage tanks (i.e. gas stations) was pioneered for the industrial market, and a home water leak detection alarm was developed for the consumer market.

The Company acquired the exclusive rights to the initial technology, patents, products and know-how to manufacture and market cablewatch worldwide (except Canada).

Since the issuance of the basic patents in 1984, several successful patent searches have been conducted by outside counsel, including a detailed infringement search. To further protect and enhance the Company's position, four new patents have been received with respect to concept upgrade and several new products and applications.

Cablewatch

Given the almost universal acceptance (anticipated market penetration of 80%) of the Cablewatch technology throughout the Canadian telecommunications industry where it was first introduced, the Company, since its inception, has concentrated its energies and resources primarily on marketing Cablewatch to the telecommunications industry, both in the United States and in certain overseas markets. Product development has essentially been completed and many of the products have already been approved and are now awaiting standardization. As such, the size of the sales orders have increased. In addition to the fiber optic installations, the system can also be used on copper cables. The Company expects that the application of Cablewatch technology to new and existing copper cable installations, given the size of these markets, represents a significant growth opportunity.

To date, Cablewatch and ancillary products have been sold primarily by the Company's sales force and independent sales representatives. To a lesser extent, distributors are also involved in sales of the product line. The distributor sales effort is expected to grow as the company supports these accounts in the future. The Company has entered into several distributor agreements, covering the U.S. and foreign markets.

Other Markets

Due to limited resources, the primary focus of the company is the fiber optic portion of the telecommunications market. With respect to the marketing of the home water leak detection system, the Company's consumer product, the Company previously marketed this product primarily through sales representative organizations.

For the hazardous chemical leak detection system, the Company has done most of the initial development activities and will begin marketing efforts through a licensing and/or marketing joint venture with an appropriate party.

No efforts are being made in either of the above market areas due to the Company's limited resources and focus.

Manufacturing

The Company's Cablewatch and related products are manufactured by subcontracting through outside vendors. Final assembly and testing are done at FOA prior to shipment. Manufacturing and packaging of the home water leak detection system were conducted in Mainland China, but no further manufacturing has occurred for this product since its initial run due to the Company's decision to focus on the Telco market.

Facilities

FOA is located in Optech's shared 20,000 sq ft. leased facility in Boston, MA. It is ideally suited for light manufacturing and assembly.

Employees

The Company presently has a limited number of full time employees. Candidates for various positions have been identified. Upon completion of this financing, additional employees will be hired to support the Company's efforts in sales, marketing, and product development to meet market needs.

Markets and Opportunities

Numerous applications for automated long-range fault locating and cable monitoring technologies exist today. The Company's annualized estimates of the market size for these technologies are as follows:

	Market Size (in $ millions/yr.)		
	1993	1994	1997
Telco - Fiber Optic Applications	156	191	363

Industrial - Hazardous Chemical Leak Detection
$1,000+/Year

Consumer - Water Leak Alarm, Gas Leak Alarm
$100+/Year

Source: (1) Kimbrough Marketing Inc. (2) EPA; (3) Management assumptions and interpretation of the data.

The foregoing is an estimate of market size and is not a prediction of sales. The Company does not have the capital or other resources to service more than a small fraction of the estimated market size. It should be noted that the fiber optic cable for the independent cable TV market sector is not included. The Company is focusing its efforts, due to limited resources, on the Telco market sector only.

Telco

Prior to the advent of petroleum jel-filled copper cables in the 1970's and, more recently, fiber optic cables in the early 1980's, pressurization was the telephone companies' standard approach for monitoring conventional (air-filled) copper cable. This was the case, despite the fact that for a small central office, the cost of installing and maintaining a pressurization system over the cable life is a multi-million dollar commitment.

However, with the introduction of smaller jel-filled (a water blocking agent) copper and fiber optic cables, pressurization is no longer feasible. The concept of monitoring via air pressure, given the high resistance levels associated with the smaller cables, proved to be no longer a viable approach.

As a result, an immediate demand was created for an approach that would provide an effective preventive maintenance program for the smaller (newer) cable designs. Without such a monitoring system, the telephone companies face significant cost exposure. Depending upon the extent of trunkline damage, major telephone companies have estimated downtime to run between $78,000 and $1,000,000 in loss of revenues per minute, excluding the labor cost associated with maintenance and repair.

A redundant system with a 100% alternate route backup allows for traffic to be rerouted in minutes. However, there are several major trunk routes across the U.S. which either have no back-up or only limited alternate rerouting capability. Therefore, until the line is repaired, the affected telephone companies must redirect traffic to either another in-house line or piggy-back onto the line of another telephone company under pre-existing arrangements. Restoration time is usually 4 to 8 hours at a cost of $50,000 to $100,000, excluding the significant loss of revenue discussed above. With the utilization of the Company's early warning system, the telephone companies are warned at the onset of cable deterioration, and thereby have adequate time to locate and repair the damage long before the cable system degrades to a state whereby a catastrophic outage may occur. As a result, the telephone companies avoid loss of revenues by way of downtime and/or sharing arrangements, as well as costly emergency repairs.

The Company believes that its products represent a proven solution for the monitoring of both fiber optic and conventional copper cables. Not only does the Company's product provide for early warning, positive feedback and continuous cable monitoring, but it also can locate the fault to within 0.5% of the line distance or a few hundred feet, by way of the Long Range Fault Locator. The company is able to provide monitoring of all (100%) of the fibers in an optical cable and cable monitoring system. Other providers of this type of equipment only provide 1-2 optical fibers, thereby providing only limited monitoring capability to the network.

Telephone Outages

One of the first major telephone outages occurred in the fall of 1991 in the New York and New Jersey areas. It was not clear at that time how frequently telephone outages occur and whether or not the situation is getting worse. The general feelings were that the outages were getting worse and more frequent due to greater penetration of fiber cable in FTTC, FTTH, and FTTL (Fiber to the Curb, Home, Loop). In order to determine the scope of this problem, the U.S. General Accounting Office (GAO) was directed by Congress to determine the frequency and causes of telephone outages. Data was received from 15 holding companies controlling over 83% of the local telephone service and 3 major long distance companies representing 89% of the long distance market. Outages that affected at least 10,000 customers and lasted 15 minutes or longer were reported in the GAO report that was published in March 1993.

An outline of the GAO results have been prepared from the GAO/RCED-93-79FS Telecommunication document. This report highlights cable cuts as the number one problem for telephone outages for the long distance carriers as shown in the accompanying charts and graphs. It also points out that cable failure nearly doubled during the one-year time frame.

From the results of the data, it can be concluded that a cable monitoring system could be useful in providing early warning of cable damage. This early warning can provide the time in certain cases to reduce the impact of an outage, and in certain other cases prevent a potential outage altogether.

In the case of local telephone companies, cable cuts were cited as one of the top four problems, and the only one in the top four that nearly doubled from 1990 to 1991. Since the local telephone companies are behind the long distance carriers in the deployment of fiber optic cables, this situation can get a lot worse for the local telephone companies in the future as they deploy more and more fiber optic cables, unless of course they choose to reduce such risks of cable related problems through utilizing FOA's cable monitoring system.

Industrial

The Company's hazardous chemical leak detection system helps solve a problem faced by businesses ranging from gas stations to major chemical complexes: the unintentional leakage and spilling of hazardous material. FOA offers an added measure of dependable protection and early warning at a cost which is slight in comparison with the potential liability of the user if the leaks and spills go undetected. Recently, additional regulatory authority was granted to the U.S. Environmental Protection Agency (EPA) in the area of managing and monitoring underground hazardous material stored in these tanks. The new requirements establish guidelines for underground tank monitoring and leak detection, and impose financial responsibility standards for tank owners. These standards will most likely include the posting of a bond or obtaining insurance coverage for an amount sufficient to provide for estimated tank replacement and cleanup costs. The EPA estimates that there are approximately 1.4 million underground tanks, and that the costs associated with decontamination and disposal can range from $30,000 to more than $250,000 for a cleanup of contaminated groundwater. Given the advantages of the Company's system, implementation of the new EPA regulations would place the Company in a strong position to compete in this market. In addition, a series of expensive cleanups in recent years relating to leakage from underground gasoline tanks has caused insurance premiums to rise sharply and has forced owners of such tanks to seek out detection systems. While the Company's initial product strategy was being directed toward the owners of petroleum storage tanks, the product has widespread applications beyond this market, including nuclear power plants, chemical plants and containment vaults. No marketing effort, however, has been applied to this area. The primary focus, as mentioned earlier, has been in the Telco application.

Consumer

The Company's consumer products provide homeowners with inexpensive, easily installed early warning system devices that greatly reduce the extent of water damage, fire, and asphyxiation. An enhanced version of the home water leak protection alarm contains a shut-off feature which is especially valuable for unattended homes. Again, no marketing effort, because of the Company's primary focus in the Telco market.

Technology and Patents

Telco-Cablewatch

Telecommunications companies face considerable cost from failures and disruptions of their cable installations. For both copper and fiber optic cable, the most common cause of disruption is moisture infiltration. Moisture entry can be caused by damage to the outside sheath during installation or by subsequent activity around the cable or at splice points. For fiber optic cable, contact of the optical fiber with water can change the chemical and surface characteristics of the fiber and thereby reduce transmission because of increased microbending sensitivity of the fiber. In addition, cable life can be reduced significantly by accelerating the deterioration rate caused by stress within the splice closure in the presence of water.

Historically, pressurization systems have been used on copper cables to detect and prevent water penetration inside of the copper cable that causes disruption of service. However, pressurization does not directly detect water, is costly to implement and maintain, and is ineffective for fiber optic cable. Moreover, if water penetration occurs, a pressurization system cannot pinpoint the location of the fault.

Cablewatch was designed for use with fiber optic cable installations, but also can be used with other metallic telephone cable and electric power lines. Cablewatch employs remote moisture sensors placed in splice closures, repeater housing, and other locations along the cable. When moisture activates a sensor, it triggers a digitally encoded alarm system to a terminal located in a central monitoring office. The terminal equipment intercepts, decodes and displays the exact location of the moisture penetration in the splice closure. In addition, the Company's automated Long Range Cablewatch can locate the fault within the cable from the central office to within 0.5% of the line distance or a few hundred feet.

Cablewatch operates by continuously monitoring a DC line current along the metallic sheath of a fiber optic cable. A decrease, increase or pulsating in the detection line current from set limits will activate an alarm. The detection current can flow through any conductor. Typically, the protective metallic cable outer and/or inner armor or sheath is used as the detection line. With this configuration, the metallic sheath forms a sensor in the system and is continuously monitored for physical damage. Thus, early detection of cable deterioration is provided allowing the crucial time to locate and repair the damage before costly cable failure occurs.

A cable monitoring system can monitor up to 99 sensors at splice closures, repeater sites, or control equipment vaults (CEV's). One system is capable of servicing approximately 100 kilometers of installed cable. However, because of boundary and jurisdictional limitations, users will typically employ one system to cover approximately thirty kilometers.

Industrial-Hazardous Leak Detection

The Company's hazardous chemical leak detection system uses the same patented technology as the Company's Cablewatch. Sensors are located at the most likely sources of leaks or spills. When a leak occurs, an alarm signal as well as a digital code are sent to a central monitoring station. The alarm and code not only signal that a leak has occurred, but also locate the source, a capability not available with any other competing system or monitoring approach known to exist. The system offers continuous monitoring, a high degree of reliability, and low maintenance.

Consumer-Water/Gas Detection

The home water leak detection device is based on the patented telecommunication cable monitoring technology previously described. Any water coming in contact with the detection leads or extended sensors is immediately sensed and alarmed by the solid state circuits.

Further enhancements and modifications of the device for marine applications and unattended homes (with auto shut-off feature) have been developed. This product will be marketed through licensing or an appropriate marketing joint venture.

The home gas detection device is designed to sound an alarm if a natural gas and/or propane gas leak occurs at home from either a gas heating system, a gas stove or similar gas appliances. A production prototype has been made for demonstration; however, manufacturing and marketing are awaiting financing and identification of a marketing partner or licensee.

Patents

The Company has acquired an exclusive right (except in Canada) to the technology, patents, products and know-how to manufacture and market the cable monitoring system. U.S. Patent #4480251 (issued October 30, 1984); Canadian Patent #1168707 (issued June 5, 1984); and United Kingdom Patent #2082406B (issued June 13, 1984) permit the Company to market and manufacture the product worldwide (except Canada).

New Patents

Since the acquisition of the basic technology, the Company has developed several new products and has filed for patent applications in the U.S., Canada and twelve countries in the European Common Market.

Two new US patents have been issued, which protect FOA's Long Range Cablewatch products.

A new patent recently issued has to do with solving one of the industry's major problems of how to power a telephone at the home using a fiber optic cable in power shutdown emergencies. This problem does not exist with copper cables, since copper lines carry 48 VDC from the telephone office. Fiber optic cables do not typically have copper lines, thus the problem.

The European patent filings have been approved and are in the process of being issued.

Products

At present, the Company is engaged in the manufacturing and marketing of products to three distinct customer markets: telecommunications, datacommunications and CATV. These products are derived from the same patented technology. In view of the fact that the Company's patent position is strongest in the Telco market, with practically no competition, and that the products are customer-driven and are receiving wide acceptance in the industry, the Company's primary focus has been in the these markets. The Company's other products for the industrial and consumer markets are well-positioned but, to date, because of a lack of resources, marketing has been limited.

Products for the Telecommunications Industry

The Company's telecommunications products ("Telco products") for use by telephone companies are based on patented concepts using the protective metal "armor or sheath" of both fiber optic and copper cables to provide a number of very useful functions.

Telco products ensure more reliable cable installation and provide continuous monitoring and protection of outdoor cables, splice points and other vital components of the communication circuits. Telco products provide for a more secure and easily maintained communications network.

The design of these products makes them unique to the Telco industry. The reliability and wide acceptance of the several of the Company's systems has been proven during years of "in service" use covering thousands of miles of fiber optic cables with several major telephone companies in North America. In the event of trouble, a patented concept is used to locate the faults quickly and effectively.

The following product descriptions provide a brief summary of the Company's current Telco products.

Fault Locating Products

FOA's Long Range Cablewatch is a unique instrument for the outside plant engineer. Based on patented technology, the Long Range Cablewatch can locate damage to the cable sheath from a distance of up to 60 miles. This can be done without walking the line with an A frame or other locating device. The unit is simply connected to each end of the cable being analyzed. The Long Range Fault Locator will display the results of the analysis, which includes, the location and size of any fault damage, in a matter of minutes.

The Long Range Cablewatch works in pairs. One unit is placed at one end of the cable being analyzed, and the second unit is then placed at the other end. The operator only has to provide the distance between the two units. The Long Range Fault Locator does the rest.

Cable Monitoring Products

The cables that are installed by telephone companies are called their "outside plant".

Outside plant cable is subjected to many forms of mechanical abuse and damage as well as normal wear and tear. Damage can occur during initial installation, subsequent rock settlement, or by digging or plowing and sabotage. Additionally, chewing rodents, gophers, termites, and the like cause serious damage to cables left to the environment. The FOA Cablewatch with reliable, low-cost, solid state circuitry, is designed to continuously monitor the integrity of outside cable plant and provide protection against these intrusions from end to end.

Using a central office terminal and remote sensors, Cablewatch continuously monitors the integrity of cables, splice closures, repeater sites and other critical locations for the presence of moisture and other mechanical intrusions. Operating over any metal circuit or a single conductor, such as metal "armor or sheath," and ground return, the system will sense and signal the damage of the cable sheath and the location of any water ingress allowing the crucial time for repair, before outages occur. In the alarm mode, the system provides cathodic protection of the sheath damage site, thus inhibiting corrosion of the protective "armor or sheath" until a repair can be carried out.

Communications Products

FOA's Hands-Off TalkSets are unique in the area of field communications. All units have the ability to operate on either the fiber, protective metal "armor or sheath" or other available conductor. They offer extremely long range and high power. All units allow for hands-free communication.

These talk sets are designed for outside plant maintenance personnel who need a reliable, rugged, long range communications tool when installing, splicing or restoring fiber optic cables under adverse conditions. The ability to communicate on the sheath as well as the fiber is unique, and provides a level of flexibility that is extremely important in restoration situations. The unit is packaged in a durable, water tight case and operates off of long-life rechargeable batteries. It can also be used as an optical or electrical repeater device to achieve even greater range of operation.

FOA has recently upgraded the design of the talk sets to allow the user to be able to "dial out" on a network called the "order wire." This is a unique and desirable feature in an outage/crisis situation. The user can dial out to advise alarm center personnel the status at the cable cut or damage site. A cut cable, depending on the number of fibers, could cost from $100,000 to $1 million per minute, so down time is expensive. The dial out can be done over the cable metallic sheath, twisted pair or over an optical fiber.

Cable Protection Devices

Cable protection devices are attached to the cable sheath at splices and regens to provide lightning and voltage protection. The units are designed to allow the sheath to be used for locating, fault locating, and communications, without entering splice closures. If a dangerous voltage appears on the sheath, the protection devices immediately provide a low impedance path to ground. Once the voltage has passed, the sheath is restored to its original state. If a power-cross or other condition results in an excess current flow for an extended period, a thermal fail-safe system grounds the line safely and permanently. The impact resistant polycarbonate enclosure is watertight and dust-tight. Other potential areas of use exist at the customer premise for CATV and datacomm users.

Products for the Industrial Market

Hazardous Chemical Leak Detection System

The system is used for the detection of hazardous chemicals, liquid waste leaks, and spills. The liquids detected by this system may be either organic or inorganic, and either acidic, basic, or neutral.

The hazardous chemical leak detection system uses the same patented technology as the Company's Cablewatch. This system is intended to be used for monitoring multiple points or zones within a factory, chemical plant or storage site. The sensors are strategically located at the most likely sources of leaks and spills of hazardous and toxic materials. Should a leak occur, an instant alarm signal as well as a digital code indicating the exact location are sent back to the central monitoring station alerting the security officer or alarm center that a spill or leak has occurred. Through such early detection of leaks and spills, expensive clean-up, repairs, injuries, and related liabilities could be reduced.

A smaller system has been developed for gas station use to monitor leaks in underground storage tanks. The system can also be adapted to monitor water leaks in unattended apartment and condominium complexes. Further engineering work is required to complete this package for marketing.

Products for the Consumer Market

Currently, the Company is engaged in the marketing and manufacturing of a home water detection device, and is ready to manufacture and market a home gas detection device. A device sensor for use with sump pumps and marine applications is also ready for product introduction.

Manufacturing

The Company uses several U.S. subcontractors to manufacture various components, PC boards, PC board assemblies, sheet metal work and the like. The final assembly and testing of these components are being done at the Company's facility.

The Company currently shares office and assembly space at Optech's leased building in Boston, MA.

Employees

The projected number of employees in the manufacturing, sales and marketing, and general and administrative areas is expected to increase over the next five years as follows:

	1 Mil	3 Mil	8 Mil	17 Mil	34 Mil
	YR1	YR2	YR3	YR4	YR5
MFG*	5	8	30	58	74
S&M	4	6	12	18	24
G&A	2	4	7	12	12
Total:	11	18	49	88	110

* These numbers are based on the Company essentially doing final assembly and testing on products in house, and continuing our current methodology where the bulk of the manufacturing is done by sub-contractors. This strategy will allow us to continue to reduce cost with increased volume and maintain low overhead.

SALES AND MARKETING

Telecommunication

Direct Sales

Cablewatch is a relatively new technology, and as such, requires that the market be developed. A direct sales approach is not a cost-effective means for this product line. However, due to the technical nature of the products, a direct customer contact needs to be made through the stages of product evaluation, qualification and field trials. The associated cost of direct sales will limit our sales efforts to targeted key accounts. Direct sales will be used increasingly to support agents and representatives in each respective territory.

Sales Representatives

The Company plans to continue to use independent sales representatives. The firms we are presently using sell products from other manufacturers to the same customer base. They are located in strategic areas across the country. While most of the individuals have some technical knowledge, factory support is required.

Distributors

Because of the number and location of the potential customer base, sales and marketing can be more effective on certain of FOA's products with the use of distributors. The distributor typically has direct salespeople calling on accounts selling many different items, thereby reducing their overall selling cost. Typically, these sales people are not technically knowledgeable about the products they sell. It is a challenge to find organizations that could promote the sale of the FOA system. As the products become qualified with more customers, the use of distributors becomes more appropriate.

Distributors can provide access to certain U.S. and foreign business opportunities. The distributor has qualified mailing lists and contacts which can be used to provide information about the company's products. These channels of distribution reach various telephone companies and contractors in the growing fiber optic telecommunications and data communications market place. Field sales people that the distributor uses are competent in outside plant practices to address field personnel needs. Inside sales personnel of the distributor handle the administrative functions required to support the field's efforts.

Advertising, Promotion & Trade Shows

As with any new product or technology, the user must be made aware of its existence. A continuous advertising program is used in trade journals to make potential users aware of the product and its ability to provide solutions to existing problems. This advertising helps achieve brand name recognition by management personnel. In addition, the ads generate "Bingo" leads for sale representatives to follow up on.

Promotional literature is provided to describe the system's operation. Application notes are provided upon request. A no-cost "postage pre-paid" card is available for the potential customer to use.

Trade shows are attended for industry visibility. A booth and equipment demonstration is used to promote the system.

International Sales and Marketing

The international market is no longer a "dumping grounds" for used telephone equipment and technology. They are focusing on the deployment of optical fiber. Even the Third World countries are looking to deployment of state-of-the-art fiber optic technology.

The international Telecom market is 1 to 1.5 times the size of the United States market. Because of the size, distance and politics involved, a totally direct sales approach is not effective; however, due to the technical nature of the product, a certain level of direct customer contact will be required. Local representatives/agents who are approved to sell to the government-owned telephone companies will be used to start the selling process. Direct contact will be made at appropriate stages of product evaluation, qualification and field trials.

Sales & Marketing Strategy

With mandated EPA regulations, as well as OSHA and corporate awareness as to liability costs associated with hazardous leaks, a heightened need to use monitoring systems for leak detection has been developed. At this time, however, the Company is not focusing on selling to this market. An appropriate marketing and distribution partner may be the best way to enter into this market.

Industrial - Hazardous Chemical Leak Detection Systems

Consumer Products

Sales and Marketing Strategy

There are 88 million single-family dwellings in the U.S. A viable market exists for water and gas leak detection in multiple family/condominium structures. At this time, however, the Company does not anticipate selling to the consumer market. An appropriate marketing, joint venture partner or licensing may be the best way to market these products.

COMPETITION

Telco

Non-Direct Competitors

Trojan Meter Industries and Notch Products offer air pressurized cable monitoring systems (not suited for fiber optic or other filled cable). Water or moisture penetration into any outside cable plant can cause communication circuits to fail. In copper cables, water causes short circuits, conductor corrosion and immediate loss of communication circuits. In fiber optic cables, water causes swelling and degradation of the protective coatings, stress corrosion of the glass fiber and deterioration of surrounding cable and splice components. These problems often cause outages which result in interrupted service, loss of revenue, added cost to locate and repair, and significant reduction in useful life of the outside plant.

A wide range of materials and methods have been tried, with varying degrees of success, in the battle to maintain outside plant. Pressurization, a common means to monitor and protect large air core copper cables, is difficult to place and maintain on small compact cables and cannot be used at all on modern filled designs (e.g., fiber optic cables). In an attempt to protect fiber optic splice closures, encapsulated double closure systems are sometimes used.

Fiber optic cables currently are not monitored for damage. Optical Reflectometer Devices (ORD's) are used to measure optical fibers for degradation. ORD's are used when a fiber break or cable has been cut. Manufacturers are: Bend Corporation, Yamagi Ltd., Faser, Laser Optics Corp., Cove Corp., and Amsterdam Technology.

Prior to the FOA products, cable faults could only be found by placing a tone signal on the cable's metallic sheath. An operator must then walk over the entire length of the cable to determine the location of the fault. There are four major manufacturers of this type of device: Faser, Fibertech, Cableco, and Applied Detection Inc. This product and technique does not directly complete with FOA's product. In fact it is considered more complementary than competitive.

All of the above methods have been used in an attempt to maintain the integrity of outside cable plant. While providing a degree of protection, these methods nevertheless all suffer from the same deficiency. None of the previous methods provide early detection and warning of developing cable trouble. The first signs are often outages. In addition, none of the above methods can locate long range faults.

Industrial

Mandated EPA regulations, OSHA requirements and environmental groups have exerted pressure on corporations to be environmentally responsive.

There are currently several companies with different types of products and techniques for use in the monitoring of leaks. It is also expected that many more will enter into this market. A few of the companies that are presently offering products include: Chemtech, Applied Detection, and Chemical Instruments.

The FOA device is derived from its patented technology. It allows for leak detection over great distance using a single or pair of copper conductors. The underground storage tank monitor provides three methods to monitor for leaks. These methods provide for the detection of gasoline vapor and liquid outside the tanks and gasoline liquid between the walls of a double wall tank. All three detection methods are expected to be required to meet final EPA regulations. The system could provide the owner with reduced cost for insurance coverage and payback in as little as one year. It is believed that FOA's approach, could compete effectively in this multi-billion dollar marketplace. The Company is not considering dilution of its effort in this area.

There are several lower-priced, but lower quality, products on the market.

FOA's advantages are:
- •Product quality
- •Low level battery alarm
- •Warranty
- •Attractive design, packaging & POP display
- •Remote sensor
- •Interchangeable sensor

The Company is not considering dilution of its effort in this area.

Consumer

MANAGEMENT

Roger Knight, 57 years old, is a Vice-President and Director of Optech Inc. and is Executive Vice-President of Sales & Marketing, Director and co-founder of FOA. Mr. Knight has assisted in the development of FOA's business plan & fund raising. He has been primarily responsible for the market & customer development activities for FOA's products. Mr. Knight successfully completed several product evaluation programs with major Telcos & has set up sales representative organizations in the US and abroad.

Mr. Knight has an excellent knowledge of the product scope proposed for the Company and its potential customer base. Mr. Knight has a B.S. in Economics, an M.B.A. in Management and Marketing, and has co-published several articles.

Harvey Winslow, 47 years old, is a Director of and Financial Advisor to FOA. Mr. Winslow is President of Financial Services Incorporated, a registered investment advisor, which is engaged in a diversity of financial activities, including establishing and/or managing security-related trading partnerships and other investment vehicles, and locating, structuring, and negotiating investment opportunities for business entities and financially sophisticated individuals. As a result, Mr. Winslow has become a director and/or officer of several of the companies associated with these activities. Prior to 1985, he spent seventeen years on Wall Street, fifteen of which were spent as Chief Financial Officer of a government and money market securities firm and two of which were spent as operations manager of a New York Stock Exchange Member Firm.

James Sullivan, 36 years old, is Manager of Product Development and Engineering, with extensive analog, digital and fiber optic communication system design expertise. Mr. Lavallee joined FOA in July 1988. He has been the principal developer of both the Long Range Cablewatch and Hands Off TalkSet which operate on the outer armor of fiber optic cables.

From 1976 to 1988, Mr. Sullivan held various positions with other fiber optic systems companies in product development and design.

He is licensed by the Federal Communications Commission and is a member of both the Society of Motion Picture and Television Engineers (SMPTE) and the Audio Engineering Society (AES).

William Fenkell, Director, is 51 years old, and from October 1969 to December 1987 held various positions at the Union Bank. In his latest position, he served as a Senior Loan Officer for South Asia programs. His responsibilities have included design and administration of the Bank's assistance to the countries for which he was responsible. He has conducted economic policy and operational discussions with senior foreign government officials and has led the

Bank's team to negotiate loans and credits with client governments for projects costing in excess of four billion dollars. He has also helped arrange financing packages for a number of these projects.

Hugh McDonald, is 49 years old. He has been retained by FOA as an independent telecommunication consultant and will assume the position of Vice President of Sales and Marketing upon completion of funding.

Mr. McDonald has an extremely broad background in Sales, Marketing, and Operation, with over twenty years of experience in telephony and cable industry. He was most recently employed by Fiber Cable Co. to develop a new sales and marketing organization for the telecommunications industry. He completed his task recently, where in less than twenty-four months the department was in place and generated more than $23 million in revenue with extremely handsome gross margins. Mr. McDonald has a B.A. in Business. He is a member of numerous industry organizations and associations.

FUNDING REQUIREMENT

Funding to Date

The Company has raised approximately $6 million to date in the form of equity and debt as outlined below. These funds have been invested toward the development of a unique and patented technology that has widespread application possibilities. The Company's main emphasis, however, has been in the Telco market. It plans on entering the datacommunications and CATV markets as well. Most of the funds have been used to finance R&D, patents, product development, field trials and market development for the telecommunications market place.

Funding to Date ($000)

Equity*(1)*	$ 5,371
Secured Debt	$ 600
Total	$ 5,971

(1) Includes equity from:

Officers/Directors	$ 957
Outside Directors	$ 857

Current Requirement

The Company seeks to raise $5 million to finance its anticipated growth over the next two years. The bulk of the new funds will be used to expand sales and marketing efforts worldwide.

Once the funds are raised, the Company would invest $500,000 to continue developing certain new products that can be marketed to the same Telco customer base. A breakdown of the uses for all the funds raised are outlined below.

Sources and Uses of Funds ($000)

Sources	
Equity &/or debt *(1)*	$5,000
Uses of Proceeds	
Sales & Marketing	$3,000
Manufacturing	750
Product Engineering	750
Research & Development *(2)*	500

(1) Preferably equity
(2) Consisting of new products for the same telco customer base

Sales, average price and margins by existing product line for specific years are as follows:

Income Statement

Sales ($000)		Avg Price ($)	Gross Margin (%)	
YR3	YR5		YR3	YR5
8050	34,150	36,000	51	55

Represents a market share of approximately 10.0% for fiber optic applications. Average prices shown represent initial pricing for purposes of market penetration and approximately 3% of the total network cost for a new fiber optic installation. Thereafter, it is anticipated that product pricing will bear a closer relationship to customer savings. This price is also subject to change, depending on the number of splices and number of cables monitored.

Sales are net of selling commission, estimated at between 5 - 7.5%

Cablewatch sales are attributable to new fiber optic installations and fiber optic retrofit markets. No sale amounts have been projected for the copper, fiber to home markets, CATV and security markets.

Industrial sales are derived from hazardous chemical leak detection system for underground gasoline station tanks only. These monitoring systems are estimated at $5,000 each. No sale amounts have been projected for aboveground and other underground applications.

The provision for income taxes reflects application of net operating loss carry forwards and an effective federal, state, and local tax rate of 38%.

The Company is currently negotiating with its creditors to convert most of the outstanding loans and accompanying warrants to stock. It is hoped to occur as of March 31, 1994. It is expected, however, the actual conversion may take place in the June quarter as opposed to March, and therefore the numbers may change slightly. For this reason, balance sheets are not included in this plan.

Pro-Forma Balance Sheet

The Company is authorized to issue 10,000,000 shares of common stock, par value $.01. As of December 31, 1993, the Company had 3,839,236 shares outstanding, allocated as follows:

Stockholders' Ownership

Name	Title	Shares Owned	% of Ownership
Lyle Kasdan	Chairman, Pres., Treasurer, Director	993,000	25.87
Roger Knight	Exec VP Mktg/Sales, Sec., Director	993,000	25.87
William Fenkell	Director	30,000	

Marketing Consultant

BUSINESS PLAN

SIMMONS MARKETING ASSOCIATES

4001 W. Main Street
Trenton, NJ 07720

This plan serves as a guide to Simmons Marketing Associates to grow the firm to its fullest potential. It includes goals, both tangible and intangible, as well as descriptions of all areas of the business. The document is structured in such a way that it will be easy for relevant areas to be extracted for submission to financial officers or investors should the need for additional funding become necessary.

- DESCRIPTION OF BUSINESS

- LOCATION OF BUSINESS

- ADVANTAGES OF THE FIRM

- TARGET MARKET

- COMPETITION

- MANAGEMENT

- PERSONNEL

- SUMMARY

- FINANCIAL DATA

- ANALYSIS OF FINANCIAL DATA

MISSION STATEMENT

Simmons Marketing Associates partners with its clients to provide comprehensive marketing services. The firm is dedicated to achieving the highest quality in its work while maintaining an environment that fosters creativity, dedication and the constant pursuit of new ideas by its employees. Maintaining a strong civic commitment, the firm regularly initiates programs that serve the common good.

BUSINESS AND SERVICE DESCRIPTION

Simmons Marketing Associates specializes in integrated marketing services. Because any marketing effort is stronger when a cohesive message is communicated through all channels of outside communication including public relations, advertising, direct mail, collateral development, electronic communication and promotion, the firm works with a variety of businesses to help them grow their businesses.

The firm is a sole proprietorship that has been in business since October 1992. Hours of operation are Monday through Friday 8:30 a.m. to 5:00 p.m. In its first three years, the agency has sustained steady yet controlled growth with little self-promotion. Through word-of-mouth marketing, the firm has obtained clients like Reynolds Publishing, The National Dairy Council, The New Jersey Gardening Show, Jersey Hospitals and others. With such a roster of success stories and an expanded in-house staff, the firm is now poised for an aggressive growth campaign. By developing lists of prospects, preparing presentations, advertising and initiating publicity efforts, including creating awareness of the five significant industry awards the firm has recently won.

At this point, the firm's business is approximately 60 percent public relations and event promotion, 20 percent collateral development including newsletters, brochures and direct mail campaigns, 10 percent advertising and 10 percent marketing consulting. The firm is best known for its public relations and collateral development services and has won a number of awards for its work in these arenas. Area businesses are attracted to the firm's national client list and the firm continues to capture the attention of large corporations because of its track record, ability to execute projects for tens of thousands of dollars less than other firms and flexibility in working with in-house marketing staffs. The firm has recently developed an Internet consulting service which will include creating World Wide Web pages for businesses, associations and other commercial ventures. This is a critical move for the firm. The future of public relations will be drastically affected by Internet activities. By joining the information revolution now, we have an advantage over firms that are still focusing on traditional venues. This addition also expands the roster of services that we are able to provide to our clients.

DESCRIPTION OF THE LOCATION

Simmons Marketing Associates shares leased space with one of its clients as it has done for the past two and a half years. The present location is near many major freeways. Since the business is conducted primarily through telephone, fax and overnight mail, location is a secondary concern.

ADVANTAGES OF SIMMONS MARKETING ASSOCIATES

There are several distinct advantages of contracting Simmons Marketing Associates. First, the firm works to contain its overhead, assembling work groups that are a combination of staff and independent consultants appropriate for each client. The expanse of experience of the principal and in-house staff as well as the diversity of the network of on-call talent makes the firm a one-stop center for all marketing communications needs. Simmons Marketing prides itself on assembling exactly the right group of professionals for each project and client. This network of on-call talent includes professionals in graphic design, direct mail, publicity, copywriting and other marketing disciplines.

Another distinct advantage is that Simmons Marketing works more closely with its clients than many firms. We keep them apprised of activities and progress every step of the way and value client input. For many clients, the firm acts as an adjunct marketing services department, as accountable to the contractor as an employee is to a supervisor. Through regular update memoranda and reports, we leave the door open for clients to share their vision and expertise. This often results in a heightened awareness of potential opportunities as a result of client input.

THE MARKET

The firm's market is businesses, associations and agencies with revenues of at least $3 million annually that have a need for public relations, advertising, collateral development and marketing services. Although the firm has, in the past, worked with firms with less than $3 million annually, that market has not proven to be open to ongoing marketing practices.

At this time, our client industries are broken down as follows:

•Expos and consumer shows	35 percent
•Consumer products businesses and associations	30 percent
•Health care facilities and associations	20 percent
•Service businesses	10 percent
•Arts	5 percent

There is a heavy concentration in the consumer and expo category at this time. This is a market that will continue to be important for Simmons Marketing Associates, because these types of events yield a wealth of client prospects within the industry. Over the next 12 months, Simmons Marketing Associates will embark on an aggressive self-promotion campaign that will include: direct mail, cold calling, publicity of industry awards, Internet services and advertising. The firm's goal in 1996 is to sign $120,000 worth of new client contracts. As of October 1995, we have signed or have strong prospects for over $90,000. Additional prospects of $39,000 also exist. Again, all of these prospects contacted Simmons Marketing through word-of-mouth marketing. The firm should be able to easily exceed its goals with the concentrated marketing effort that is planned. Our secondary goal is to achieve a 20% profit margin by 1998. Our 3-year income and expense report shows that we will be able to achieve a 16% profit margin by the end of 1997, even with the addition of two employees. We will be able to reach our goal by increasing our profit by a mere 4% in 1998.

DESCRIPTION OF COMPETITION

There are several firms in the area that offer services similar to those of Simmons Marketing Associates.

Stately Marketing: Handles primarily real estate and shopping malls. Produces a great number of collateral pieces. Industry sources state, however, that the firm is not financially solid and has questionable internal practices.

Expert Image Associates: Expert has five employees. The firm provides public relations services and are structured much like Simmons Marketing Associates. However, the firm does not offer Internet service. The firm is also focused on the local market, whereas Simmons Marketing Associates has been pitching and getting large regional and national clients. Expert also has a very visible staff in the local market.

Local freelance talent: There are many area freelancers that provide graphic design, writing and other services. Very few, however, provide public relations and certainly none have the client list or expertise of Simmons Marketing Associates.

DESCRIPTION OF MANAGEMENT

Terry Simmons is president of Simmons Marketing Associates. A former manager in sales promotion and marketing for New Book and Nostalgic Patterns Company, she graduated from the Newhouse School of Communications at Syracuse University with a Bachelor of Science degree in Advertising.

Simmon's experience in advertising and marketing includes planning and executing campaigns for New Book's Merchandise division. Among the products she promoted were juvenile books, audio books, videos, toys and games for adult and juvenile markets. After heading the promotion department of the division, Simmons moved to Nostalgic Pattern Company where she supervised promotion, advertising and marketing activities.

Simmons also worked in the marketing department of the Newspaper Advertising Bureau (now the Newspaper Association of America). During that time, she was responsible for initiating national newspaper buy strategies and pitching them to such companies as Lesco. Now, Simmons works with clients both on a regional and national level. From art direction to copywriting, she manages projects for clients with budgets that range from four to seven digits.

Recording secretary of the Jersey Public Relations Association, Simmons was also selected as a judge for the 1993 POPAI awards in Chicago and the 1995 Southwest Florida. She is a member of the International Association of Business Communicators, the Monmouth Ocean Development Council and the National Association of Female Executives. She has received a number of awards for her innovative marketing programs including the 1995 Jersey Shore Public Relations and Advertising Association's Helen Hoffman Best in Show Award.

DESCRIPTION OF PERSONNEL

Angela Moore has been hired as an account coordinator. She has assumed a heavy responsibility in overseeing independent contractors, facilitating projects, copywriting and Internet activities. Moore is a graduate of Rowan College and previously worked for the Educational Press Association of America where she handled public relations activities including a literary tour.

Keith Johnson is a graphic designer who handles most of the design services for Simmons Marketing Associates as an independent contractor. Johnson was previously with Phoneline International and Reese Consulting where he handled clients such as Carl Winslong and others. Johnson also handles Fairweather Parks, Jersey Hospitals and others.

Jean McDonald is a part-time publicist and writer. McDonald has achieved the status of Fellow and has been honored nationally by the Public Relations Society of America. She is a former associate with Novell in New York and handled accounts such as Woodsburn's. McDonald works with Simmons Marketing and has achieved placements for key clients such as the National Dairy Council.

Simmons Marketing Associates is a full-service marketing services firm based in Trenton, New Jersey. Headed by marketing specialist Terry Simmons and staffed by knowledgeable professionals overseeing a pool of top-notch freelance talent, the firm is poised for aggressive growth in 1996.

SUMMARY

The firm, a sole proprietorship, will market its services to events, businesses and associations on the East coast and nationally with annual revenues in excess of $3 million. The firm offers several advantages over other marketing services firms including its wide range of services, its roster of national and local clients, its media contacts and its ability to save clients money. Competitors in this market either lack the range of services or the vision to pitch national clients. This leaves the door open for Simmons Marketing Associates to use its prestigious list of clients to attract both regional and more national clients.

With four staff members in place in addition to a pool of twelve exceptionally talented freelance professionals, the firm can consistently sustain growth, continue to add members to its staff and provide high quality marketing services to its clients.

FINANCIAL DATA

1996 Sources of Revenue

New Jersey Gardening Show	$15,000.00
Antique Marketing	14,000.00
Interior Decor Shows	8,000.00
Colonial Festival	6,000.00
O'Brien's Consulting	6,000.00
Biotech	2,500.00
Jersey Hospitals	2,000.00
Gaze Communications	20,000.00
Shorebank Hospital	4,000.00
Evergood	2,500.00
St. Mary's Parish	900.00
New Jersey Nostalgia	1,200.00
Misc. Projects	8,000.00
(brochures, newsletters, etc.)	
TOTAL	**$90,100.00**

Additional prospects:

Reynolds Value Center	$15,000.00
Galleria Theater	12,000.00
National Dairy Council	8,000.00
National Gardener Association	4,000.00
TOTAL	**$39,000.00**

Capital Equipment List

Major Equipment	**Cost**
Computers	
IBM-compatible 486/33 mhz; 540 mb hard drive;	
modem; sound card	$1,600.00
IBM-compatible laptop 486/33; 210 mb hard drive	1,400.00
HP LaserJet 4P Printer	400.00
Software	
Windows '95	86.00
Windows Plus	45.00
Microsoft Office	250.00
Microsoft Publisher	80.00
Quickbooks	100.00
Timeslips	200.00
Telephones	
2 Two-line speaker phones (80.00 each)	160.00

1 One-line speaker phone	20.00

Furniture

Desk	100.00
3 Tables ($40.00 each)	120.00
3 chairs ($25.00 each)	75.00
2 Two-drawer filing cabinets ($25.00 each)	50.00
1 Four-drawer filing cabinets ($85.00 each)	85.00
1 Supply cabinet	100.00
1 Book case	40.00

Automobile

1995 Chrysler Sebring	$17,700.00

Electronic Equipment

Television	199.00
VCR	179.00
Radio/CD/Cassette Player	90.00

Minor equipment

Paper trays, disks, supplies, etc.	500.00
Library/reference	2,200.00
2 Calculators ($10.00 each)	20.00
TOTAL	**$25,799.00**

Balance Sheet

CURRENT ASSETS

Cash	$7,000.00
Accts. Receivable	11,618.00
Supplies	600.00
Total Assets	$17,218.00

CURRENT LIABILITIES

Accounts Payable	$6,100.00
Current Portion-Long-Term Debt	310.00
Total Liabilities	$6,410.00

FIXED ASSETS

Major Equipment	$8,099.00
Automobile	17,700.00
Total Assets	$25,799.00

LONG-TERM LIABILITIES

Loan payable (car)	$13,000.00
Total Long-Term Debt	$13,000.00

TOTAL ASSETS $43,017.00

TOTAL LIABILITIES $19,410.00

NET WORTH $23,607.00

Two-Year Projected Profit Loss Statement

		1996	1997
Revenue		$120,000	$185,000
Operating Expenses			
F	Rent/Utilities	6,600	6,600
F	Salaries	60,000	90,000
F	Advertising	3,000	6,500
F	Directories/Subscriptions	1,200	1,200
F	Telephone	4,600	4,800

F	Postage	6,400	6,700
F	Equipment	4,000	4,000
F	Professional Services	1,200	1,800
F	Professional Groups	1,000	1,500
F	Auto	9,900	9,900
F/V	Entertainment	2,200	2,400
F	Depreciation	1,200	2,200
F	Supplies	2,500	2,700
V	Seminars/luncheons	1,500	1,700
V	Miscellaneous	2,600	2,800
F	Insurance	2,500	2,800
V	Taxes	7,000	9,000
	Total Expenses	**$117,400**	**$156,600**
	Net Profit	**$2,600**	**$28,400**

F=Fixed   V=Variable

Note: 1996 profits decrease reflects new employee salaries. These new employees will have responsibilities that will include new business development and producing billable hours. Therefore, this investment will reflect in significantly increased profit in 1997.

ANALYSIS OF INCOME AND EXPENSE REPORT

Simmons Marketing Associates has operated at a profit since its beginning. We charge service fees that cover staff time and office overhead and bill separately for the cost of goods sold. These expenses include additional graphic design, printing, postage, telephone expenses, etc.

We fully expect to exceed our goal of $120,000 in service fees for 1996. Most of that business has been secured at this time and, with the aggressive advertising and public relations campaign starting this week, our momentum will carry us well into 1997.

In 1996, our rent and utility expenses will increase. We will be moving into a larger office space, most likely a shared space arrangement again. We expect to remain at this location for at least three years.

Salaries will increase as a result of increased staff and increased revenue. At Simmons Marketing Associates, we strive to reward employees for good work both financially and professionally. As a result, paid memberships to professional groups as well as seminars and luncheons will also increase. Advertising expenses will continue to increase as we strive to become more visible and aggressive in our own external marketing campaigns. Increased postage also reflects an increase in direct mail efforts. Other increases in expenses reflect an increase in business and staff.

Multilevel Marketing Business

BUSINESS PLAN

RFM ENTERPRISES

1842 Devon Lane
St. Cloud, MN 55123
October 1995

This plan describes one of the many different types of multilevel marketing businesses. In this type of arrangement, a business recruits individuals to sell its products or services for a cut of their profits. These individuals, in turn, recruit others to do the same thing, also for a cut of their profits. The process usually continues, in a pyramidal fashion, for 4 to 10 levels, with higher-level individuals earning more money as the lower levels fill with new recruits.

- EXECUTIVE SUMMARY

- COMPANY OVERVIEW

- PRODUCT STRATEGY

- MARKET ANALYSIS

- FINANCIAL PLAN

- CONCLUSION

EXECUTIVE SUMMARY

Vision/Mission

RFM Enterprises was created in 1994 and is currently in the start-up phase. Our company can be described as being in the long distance business. Our key strengths have been thorough planning & organization while taking advantage of the latest technology.

We are a family-owned business, so for the moment our management team is in place. As we expand and diversify, additional members will be brought on-board to meet our changing needs. Also, we are considering the addition of one partner.

We are both Independent Representatives with Advance Telecommunications, which is a solid professional corporation with a top management team. Jerry Bass, the chief executive officer, started Advance in Dallas, Texas in 1988. Today, Advance has thousands of Independent Representatives across the country. Advance is a national corporation, one of only a handful of nationally licensed long distance carriers in America, and offers the highest quality service at competitive rates. Advance offers immediate cash income, serious income potential, long term residual income and the opportunity to get paid, again and again, for the work we do today, because Advance Representatives receive a percentage of every customer's long distance phone bill in their down-line. Advance provides the finest long distance programs in America today. In addition to all the standard services offered by other major long distance companies, Advance offers the opportunity for our customers to save up to 50% on their long distance calls. Advance also offers a personal 800 service that can't be beat, and all of our customers, just for trying our service, receive the most attractive incentives in the industry.

A Few Facts About Advance

- Solid, professional corporation
- Digital, fiber-optic network
- $155 million dollar company
- Competitive rates and impressive discounts
- Nationally licensed
- Over 400% growth in 1994
- Highest quality service
- FCC and state regulated as a public utility

Marketing & Sales Environment

The long distance industry is controlled by US Telecommunications, who currently has 70% of the market. Advance currently has .0001% of the market and is shooting for 17% market share by 1998.

Vision & Mission Statements

The long range vision of RFM Enterprises is that by 1998, we will become a highly visible, diversified international corporation known for our customer service, sound management, profitability, and flexible working environment. By that time, we will have become Executive Directors for Advance Telecommunications & profits from services will exceed $300,000,000.00 annually as we actively grow our long distance customer base.

In order to achieve this vision, RFM Enterprises commits to the following mission statement:

We exist to provide cost-effective alternatives to our customers seeking quality long distance services. We believe our first responsibility is to our customers. We will strive to establish and maintain a strong financial position that enables us to expand as Advance grows. In conducting our day to day operations, we will strive to:

- Treat all colleagues and co-workers with respect & fairness.
- Follow a philosophy that says, "The customers are the business."
- Make positive contributions to the communities with which we do business and the community in which we live.
- Develop and enhance the skills of our down-line associates with the intention of providing promotional opportunities.

Through a long-term commitment to this mission statement, we will be known as a company that is committed to its customers, associates, and communities. Our profits, in part, will be derived from the intangible benefits received from making a positive impact through charitable donations to the "Just Say No" anti-drug program.

Strategic Goals

In order for RFM Enterprises to attain the vision described in our mission statement, the following primary strategic goals need to be achieved:

Products

By then end of 1995, we will have achieved a customer base and down-line to include:

- 40 personal customers.
- 6 personally sponsored representatives, all of which will be Area Coordinators.
- More than 12 people in the down-line of each business

Market

We will expand our marketing efforts to ensure our customer base is always 33% beyond the minimum of 20 required by Advance.

Sales

Independent studies show long distance sales will continue to grow by $500 million per month. We intend to capture a very small portion of that market.

Finance

Through the year 1995, RFM Enterprises will carefully evaluate & plan investments & budget expenses to generate a consistent pre-tax profit. Based on a 1% market share, we estimate our net profits will exceed 800% annually from our initial investment.

We feel very confident that the goals listed above are realistic and achievable. The driving force behind the written goal is our desire to be financially independent so we can spend more time together as a family. The reason why we are doing this is much more important than how. Since we understand why, the remainder of the business plan explains how we will achieve our goals.

COMPANY OVERVIEW

Legal Business Description

The legal form of RFM Enterprises is sole proprietorship located in St. Cloud, MN.

Management Team

The RFM management team is as diverse as the operation and our combined experience spans more than 35 years of sales, technical, financial analysis, and customer service with North American Airlines and the Industrial Film Corporation.

In-House Management

Rosalind Mathis, President

Rosalind will develop & maintain the vision of the company while managing marketing, product development, production, finance, and customer service operations. Rosalind has final approval of all financial obligations and initiates all new business opportunities. Rosalind provides direction for the financial programs to provide funding for new & continuing operations in an effort to maximize return on investments and increase productivity.

Franklin Mathis, Vice President

Frank manages market planning, research & development, advertising, sales promotion, merchandising and staffing. Frank identifies & oversees new market research and competitive research, directs training and sets performance standards for the staff, and develops performance evaluations to develop and control sales programs.

Outside Management Support

Dave Sweeney, Financial Planner

Christopher Davis, Corporate Attorney

Len Dart, Marketing Logo Designer

By January of 1996, an outside Board of Directors, including 3 highly qualified business and industry professionals, will assist our management team in making appropriate decisions that will result in effective action. They will not, however, be responsible for management decisions.

PRODUCT STRATEGY

Our long distance service offers the following:

- Discounted residential long distance service (Advance Bonus)
- Discounted commercial long distance services (Advance Bonus II, Charter Gold, Founders Club)
- Major national and international carriers & crystal clear digital fiber optic network
- 1 + dialing & fax, computer and voice carriage
- Residential incoming 800 service (Personal 800) & commercial incoming 800 service (Charter 800)
- Free Advance calling cards & account and project codes
- Commercial account 6-second billing & no minimum usage charges
- Full detailed billing by local phone companies and other LECs of Advance
- Unsurpassed customer incentives

The long distance division has several business advantages in this area which include:

- No inventory
- No deliveries
- No collections
- No customer risk
- No employees
- No quotas
- No products to purchase
- No complicated math or paperwork
- No experience necessary
- We are building our business nationally
- We gather customers nationally
- Our customers gather customers for us
- We have seen immediate weekly income
- We are working towards long-term residual income
- Advance provides training for us

In the long distance division, our target is the "warm" market of residential customers that consists of friends and family. We expand our business by recruiting other ambitious people like ourselves that want to earn additional cash. We became Independent Representatives with Advance by purchasing the Management Services Program for $195. This program included all the materials needed to successfully start our business. We were trained by a certified trainer, who is paid by Advance. Advance tracks our organization, provides us with a home office support system, monthly statements, newsletters, and most importantly, much of our bookkeeping is done by Advance. We will look at a separate or an additional opportunity to become an Area Coordinator in the near future. Area Coordinators train new Managing Representatives and are paid $40 for each. The cost is $395, which covers the cost of the training and the training tools used as an Area Coordinator.

Advance's compensation plan is quite extensive and I will provide some highlights in the financial section of this business plan. It is explained in detail in the Management Representative training.

Our target customer in the long distance industry is the residential customer.

Companies that compete in the long distance industry have not attempted to sell their services via network marketing and, therefore, the market is wide open and untapped at this time. Our prices are lower than US Telecommunications and our service is identical, since we utilize the same digital communications lines.

The following key factors have resulted in the present competitive position in the vending industry:

- Ease of entry into the market.
- Low overhead (i.e., labor),
- Relatively little knowledge is required for entry & operation.

Our strategy for holding our place in this competitive market is better customer service. It is our opinion that an individual could start any business in the United States, and if that business were to focus on customer service and satisfaction, the venture would certainly enjoy the lion's share of the market. This is because majority of the competition is not customer-driven but market & financial driven. In essence, you would stand alone if your service continually meets and exceeds the customer's expectations.

Risk

We see no risk in the long distance industry.

Sales Strategy

In the long distance division, we plan to approach friends and family who will switch their service in order to help us out. They are not concerned about rates: in fact, we could be as expensive as US Telecommunications and they would still be our customers because they are friends or family. Since we are lower than US Telecommunications, they will not switch when US Telecommunications calls them and asks for their business back.

When we sign additional people as Managing Representatives, we earn $100 as soon as each of them has 3 customers! We earn $5-$15 for new Managing Representatives on levels 2-7.

We earn varying commissions on the long distance usage of all the customers in our down-line 7 levels deep! We earn an annual retention bonus of $50 for each level 1 Managing Representative on their annual renewal date and smaller amounts for Managing Representatives on levels 2-7.

When we become Senior Representatives, instead of earning $100 for each new Managing Representative we sign up, we earn $190. We also receive $90 for each new Managing Representative signed up by representatives in our down-line to unlimited depth! When we become Regional Directors, we receive $240 for each new Managing Representative we sign up and $140 for new Managing Representatives in our down-line to unlimited depth! When we become Executive Directors, we receive $265 for each new Managing Representative we sign up and $165 for new Managing Representatives in our down-line to unlimited depth! The power of Advance's 7-level marketing plan is amazing.

As mentioned earlier in the Market Analysis, RFM Enterprises is of the opinion that any organization that is truly customer-driven will be successful in any marketplace because so few companies focus on this area. It costs nothing to be a customer-driven organization and the benefits are so great, they cannot be quantified.

Capital Requirements

According to the opportunities and requirements for RFM Enterprises described in this business plan, and based on what we feel are sound business assumptions, our initial capital requirements are complete.

We do not anticipate additional investment requirements in the future.

FINANCIAL PLAN

Detailed Financial Analysis

The following analysis was accomplished making the following assumptions:

- Rosalind & Frank will expend 10 hours each per week towards the business.
- We will recruit an average of 1 representative per month.
- Our representatives will each recruit 1 representative every 4 months.

Income Statement (Year 1 by Month)

	Apr	May	Jun	Jul	Aug	Sep	Oct	Nov	Dec	Jan	Feb	Mar	Year 1
Sales													
Filtered Water Services													
Div.	--	--	187.5	230.3	330.8	347.3	410.2	478.6	552.8	633.2	720.2	814.5	4,711.3
LDU	--	--	--	--	--	--	--	--	10	20	40	80	150
Training	--	--	--	--	--	--	120	240	320	400	400	520	2,000
FastStart Commis-													
sions	--	--	--	--	--	--	300	600	800	1,000	1,200	1,300	5,200
Bonuses	--	--	--	--	--	--	--	--	--	--	--	--	--
Total Sales	--	--	--	--	--	--	830.2	1,318.6	1,682.8	2,053.2	2,440.3	2,714.5	12,141.3
Variable COGS	--	--	--	--	--	--	--	--	--	--	--	--	--
% of Sales	0	0	0	0	0	0	0	0	0	0	0	0	0
Total COGS	--	--	--	--	--	--	--	--	--	--	--	--	--
Gross Profit	--	--	--	--	--	--	830.2	1,318.6	1,682.8	2,053.2	2,440.3	2,714.5	11,039.5
% of Sales	0	0	0	0	0	0	100	100	100	100	100	100	91
Operating Expenses													
Sales & Mktg.	--	--	--	--	--	--	83	13.2	16.8	20.5	24.4	27.2	110.4
R & D	--	--	--	--	--	--	83	13.2	16.8	20.5	24.4	27.1	110.4
G & A (w/o Deprecia-													
tion)	--	--	--	--	--	--	--	--	--	--	--	--	--
Depreciation	--	--	--	--	--	--	--	--	--	--	--	--	--
Total Operating													
Expenses	--	--	--	--	--	--	16.6	26.4	33.7	41.1	48.8	54.3	220.8
% of Sales	0	0	0	0	0	0	2	2	2	2	2	2	2
Income From													
Operations	--	--	--	--	--	--	813.6	1,292.2	1,649.1	2,012.1	2,391.5	2,660.2	10,818.7
% of Sales	0	0	0	0	0	0	98	98	98	98	98	98	89
Income before													
Taxes	--	--	--	--	--	--	813.6	1,292.2	1,649.1	2,012.1	2,391.2	2,660.16	10,818.74
Taxes on													
Income	--	--	--	--	--	--	--	--	--	--	--	--	--
Net Income After													
Taxes	--	--	--	--	--	--	813.6	1,292.2	1,649.1	2,012.1	2,391.5	2,660.2	10,818.7
% of Sales	0	0	0	0	0	0	98	98	98	98	98	98	89

Break-Even Analysis (Year 1 by Month)

	Oct	Nov	Dec	Jan	Feb	Mar	Apr	May	Jun	Jul	Aug	Sep	Year 1	% Total Sales
Sales	533	877	11237	11439	11641	11844	21046	21248	21450	21653	21855	31057	221881	
Fixed Costs														
Fixed Cost of Goods & Services	0	0	0	0	0	0	0	0	0	0	0	0	0	0.00%
Sales & Marketing (w/o Commissions)	300	0	100	100	0	0	0	0	0	0	0	0	500	2.19%
R & D	0	0	0	0	0	0	0	0	0	0	0	0	0	0.00%
G & A (w/o Depreciation)	0	0	0	0	0	0	0	0	0	0	0	0	0	0.00%
Depreciation	0	0	0	0	0	0	0	0	0	0	0	0	0	0.00%
Less Reclassified Fixed Costs	0	0	0	0	0	0	0	0	0	0	0	0	0	0.00%
Total Fixed Costs	300	0	100	100	0	0	0	0	0	0	0	0	500	2.19%
Variable Costs														
Material and Labor	0	0	0	0	0	0	0	0	0	0	0	0	0	0.00%
Commissions	0	0	0	0	0	0	0	0	0	0	0	0	0	0.00%
Plus Reclassified Fixed Costs	0	0	0	0	0	0	0	0	0	0	0	0	0	0.00%
Total Variable Costs	0	0	0	0	0	0	0	0	0	0	0	0	0	0.00%
Income from Operations	233	877	11137	11339	11611	11811	21046	21248	21150	21653	21855	31057	221381	97.81%
Interest Income (Expense) - "Fixed"	(900)	(881)	(862)	(843)	(824)	(806)	(788)	(770)	(752)	(734)	(716)	(698)	(91674)	-41.84%
Income Taxes "Variable"	(461)	(156)	149	750	11674	11368	148	147	146	145	144	140	41203	18.37%
Net Income After Taxes	(206)	152	126	(263)	(857)	(330)	11110	11331	11552	11774	11995	21219	81804	37.60%
Income from Operations Analysis														
Contribution Margin	100%	100%	100%	100%	100%	100%	100%	100%	100%	100%	100%	100%	100%	
Break-Even Sales Volume	300	0	100	100	0	0	0	0	0	0	0	0	500	2.19%
Sales Volume Above Break-Even	233	877	11137	11339	11641	11844	21046	21248	21450	21653	21855	31057	221381	97.81%
Net Income After Taxes Analysis														
Contribution Margin %	186.46	117.78	87.95	47.26	-1.98	25.80	92.77	93.46	94.04	94.53	94.96	95.42	81.63	
Break-Even Sales Volume	322	748	866	11572	411537	31124	849	824	800	776	754	731	111116	-48.58%
Sales Volume Above Break-Even	855	11625	21103	31011	391896	41968	21896	31072	31250	31429	31609	31788	331997	148.58%

Income Statement (Year 1 by Month)

	Oct	Nov	Dec	Jan	Feb	Mar	Apr	May	Jun	Jul	Aug	Sep	Year 1	% Total Sales
Sales														
Training	185	305	365	425	485	545	605	665	725	785	845	905	6840	29.89%
LDU	22	30	34	39	43	47	51	56	60	64	68	73	588	2.57%
Fast Start Commis-														
sion	326	542	650	758	866	974	1082	1190	1298	1406	1514	1622	12228	53.44%
Bonuses	0	0	188	218	248	278	308	338	368	398	428	458	3225	14.09%
Total Sales	533	877	1287	1439	1641	1844	2046	2248	2450	2653	2855	3057	22881	100.00%
Cost of Goods Sold														
Material	0	0	0	0	0	0	0	0	0	0	0	0	0	0.00%
Labor	0	0	0	0	0	0	0	0	0	0	0	0	0	0.00%
Variable COGS	0	0	0	0	0	0	0	0	0	0	0	0	0	0.00%
% of Total Sales	0	0	0	0	0	0	0	0	0	0	0	0	0	
Total Fixed Cost of Goods														
& Services	0	0	0	0	0	0	0	0	0	0	0	0	0	0.00%
Total COGS	0	0	0	0	0	0	0	0	0	0	0	0	0	0.00%
Gross Profit	533	877	1287	1439	1641	1844	2046	2248	2450	2653	2855	3057	22881	100.00%
% of Total Sales	100	100	100	100	100	100	100	100	100	100	100	100	100%	
Operating Expenses														
Sales & Mktg.	300	200	100	100	100	100	100	100	100	100	100	100	1500	6.56%
R & D	0	0	0	0	0	0	0	0	0	0	0	0	0	0.00%
G & A (w/o Deprecia-														
tion)	0	0	0	0	0	0	0	0	0	0	0	0	0	0.00%
Depreciation	0	0	0	0	0	0	0	0	0	0	0	0	0	0.00%
Total Operating														
Expenses	300	200	100	100	100	100	100	100	100	100	100	100	1500	6.56%
% of Total Sales	56.3	22.8	8.1	6.9	6.1	5.4	4.8	4.5	4.1	3.7	3.5	3.3	6.6	
Income From														
Operations	233	677	1167	1889	1641	1744	1946	2148	2850	2653	2765	2967	21881	93.44%
% of Total Sales	43.7	77.2	91.9	93.1	93.9	94.6	95.1	95.5	95.9	96.2	96.5	96.7	93.4	
Interest Income	100	110	120	130	140	150	160	170	180	190	200	210	1860	8.13%
Interest Expense	1000	991	982	973	964	956	948	940	932	924	916	908	11184	49.97%
Income before														
Taxes	(667)	(204)	275	496	717	938	1168	1878	1598	1819	2089	2259	11807	51.60%
Taxes on														
Income	(461)	(156)	149	759	1674	1868	148	147	146	145	144	140	4203	18.37%
Net Income After														
Taxes	(206)	(48)	126	(263)	(957)	(430)	1010	1281	1052	1674	1895	2019	7601	33.23%
% Total Sales	-38.6	-5.5	10.2	-18.3	-58.3	-23.3	49.4	54.8	59.3	63.1	66.4	69.3	33.2	

Income Statement (Years 1 - 5)

	Year 1	% Total Sales	Year 2	% Total Sales	Year 3	% Total Sales	Year 4	% Total Sales	Year 5	% Total Sales
Sales										
Training	6810	29.89	82080	29.89	1067010	29.89	14968560	29.89	224078100	29.89
LDU	588	2.57	7056	2.57	91728	2.57	1284192	2.57	19262880	2.57
Fast Start Commis-										
sions	12228	53.44	146736	53.44	1907568	53.44	26705052	53.44	400589280	53.44
Bonuses	3225	14.09	38700	14.09	503100	14.09	7043400	14.09	105651000	14.09
Total Sales	22881	100.00	274572	100.00	3569436	100.00	49972104	100.00	749501560	100.00
Cost of Goods Sold										
Material	0	0.00	0	0.00	0	0.00	0	0.00	0	0.00
Labor	0	0.00	0	0.00	0	0.00	0	0.00	0	0.00
Total Variable										
COGS	0	0.00	0	0.00	0	0.00	0	0.00	0	0.00
Total Fixed Cost of Goods										
& Services	0	0.00	0	0.00	0	0.00	0	0.00	0	0.00
Total COGS	0	0.00	0	0.00	0	0.00	0	0.00	0	0.00
Gross Profit	22881	100.00	274572	100.00	3569436	100.00	49972104	100.00	749501560	100.00
Operating Expenses										
Sales & Marketing	1500	6.56	4500	1.64	9000	0.25	18000	0.04	72000	0.01
R&D	0	0.00	0	0.00	0	0.00	0	0.00	0	0.00
G & A (without Deprecia-										
tion)	0	0.00	0	0.00	0	0.00	0	0.00	0	0.00
Depreciation	0	0.00	0	0.00	0	0.00	0	0.00	0	0.00
Total Operating										
Expenses	1500	6.56	4500	1.64	9000	0.25	18000	0.04	72000	0.01
Income From										
Operations	21881	93.44	270072	98.36	3560436	99.75	49954104	99.96	749509560	99.99
Interest										
Income	1860	8.13	2046	0.75	2292	0.06	2613	0.01	3031	0.00
Interest										
Expense	11464	49.97	11464	4.16	11464	0.32	11464	0.02	11464	0.00
Income before										
Taxes	11807	51.60	260684	94.94	3551294	99.49	49945283	99.95	749501157	99.99
Taxes on										
Income	4203	18.37	13492	4.91	18650	0.52	23861	0.05	37213	0.00
Net Income										
After Taxes	7604	33.23	247192	90.03	3562644	98.97	49921422	99.90	749463944	99.98

Cash Flows

Statement of Changes in Financial Position: Year 1 by Month

SOURCES OF CASH	Oct	Nov	Dec	Jan	Feb	Mar	Apr	May	Jun	Jul	Aug	Sep	Year 1
Operations during the year													
Net Income After Taxes	206	152	126	263	857	330	1110	1331	1552	1774	1995	2219	8604
Add items not decreasing cash													
Depreciation	$	$	$	$	$	$	$	$	$	$	$	$	$
Increase in Accounts Payable	$	$	$	$	$	$	$	$	$	$	$	$	$
Increase in Other Payables	$	$	$	$	$	$	$	$	$	$	$	$	$
Increase in Accrued Liabilities	$	$	$	$	$	$	$	$	$	$	$	$	$
Deduct items not increasing cash													
Increase in Accounts Receivable	$	$	$	$	$	$	$	$	$	$	$	$	$
Increase jn Inventory	$	$	$	$	$	$	$	$	$	$	$	$	$
Cash from Operations	-206	152	126	-263	-857	-330	1110	1331	1552	1774	1995	2219	8604
Cash from Operations & Financing	$	152	126	-263	-857	-330	1110	1331	1552	1774	1995	2219	8810
Increase/(Decrease) in Cash	$	152	126	-263	-857	-330	1110	1331	1552	1774	1995	2219	8810
Change in Cash Balance													
Beginning Cash Balance	$	$	152	278	15	-841	-1172	-62	1270	2822	4596	6591	$
Increase/(Decrease) in Cash	$	152	126	-263	-857	-330	1110	1331	1552	1774	1995	2219	8810
Ending Cash Balance	$	152	278	15	811	1172	62	1270	2822	1596	6591	8810	8810

Statement of Changes in Financial Position: Years 1 - 5

SOURCES OF CASH	Year 1	Year 2	Year 3	Year 4	Year 5
Operations during the year					
Net Income After Taxes	8,604	103,248	1,238,976	14,867,712	178,412,544
Cash from Operations	8,604	103,248	1,238,976	14,867,712	178,412,544
Financing & Other					
Sale of Stock	$	$	$	$	$
Proceeds from Short Term Loans	$	$	$	$	$
Proceeds from Long Term Loans	$	$	$	$	$
Sale of Investments	$	$	$	$	$
Collection of Notes Receivable	$	$	$	$	$
Reduction of Other Current Assets	$	$	$	$	$
Reduction of Other Assets	$	$	$	$	$
Cash from Operations & Financing	8,604	103,248	1,238,976	14,867,712	178,412,544
Increase/(Decrease) in Cash	8,604	103,248	1,238,976	14,867,712	178,412,544
Change in Cash Balance					
Beginning Cash Balance	40,000	48,604	151,852	1,390,828	16,258,540
Increase/(Decrease) in Cash	8,604	103,248	1,238,976	14,867,712	178,412,544
Ending Cash Balance	48,604	151,852	1,390,828	16,258,540	194,671,084

CONCLUSION

RFM Enterprises enjoys an established track-record of excellent service for our customers in a very short existence. Their expressions of satisfaction and encouragement are numerous, and we intend to continue our advances and growth in the long distance market with more unique and effective products and services.

Pharmaceutical Company

BUSINESS PLAN

PAIN AWAY LTD.

1117 High St.
Poughkeepsie, NY 13495

The company described in this plan has moved beyond the initial start-up phase and is now seeking investors to finance its growth. Much of the plan, therefore, is geared toward persuading, explaining, and reassuring potential investors that the company (which produces a therapeutic, topical pain cream), is well-managed and stable. The in-depth analysis of the company's competitors is an outstanding feature of this plan, as is its market research.

- EXECUTIVE SUMMARY/OVERVIEW

- MARKET

- COMPETITION

- MARKETING

- PRODUCTION

- PROPERTY & FACILITIES

- PATENTS & TRADEMARKS

- RESEARCH & DEVELOPMENT

- GOVERNMENT REGULATIONS

- INSURANCE AND TAXES

- CORPORATE STRUCTURE

- RISK FACTORS

- RETURN ON INVESTMENT AND EXIT

- ANALYSIS OF OPERATIONS & PROJECTIONS

- FINANCIAL STATEMENTS

PHARMACEUTICAL COMPANY
BUSINESS PLAN

EXECUTIVE SUMMARY/ OVERVIEW

Type of Business

Non-prescription drug wholesalers; US SIC Code - 2834 Pharmaceutical Preparations.

Company Summary

Pain Away Ltd. is a going concern, a Delaware corporation formed in January 1995 to manufacture and sell its premier launch product Pain Away, a topical pain remedy using FDA-approved homeopathic ingredients developed for the simple purpose of relieving pain. The company was formed by its parent S-corporation, Peale, Inc. in order to market products nationally and internationally. Peale, Inc. was formed in February 1994 to complete the development of the launch product. The formation of the company was a significant step in a 9-year process of refining and testing a homeopathic formula first used by company founder and CEO Robert Peale to alleviate his pain from carpal tunnel syndrome. The R&D phase of this product began when Mr. Peale purchased the original formula, did a thorough study of homeopathy, and refined the formula to its present marketable state. From the beginning of R&D, Mr. Peale worked within FDA guidelines in order to secure FDA registration. Then, in February 1994, the company was formed to finally manufacture and sell the product. Starting with only a handful of customers, including some professionals, chiropractors, physical therapists, etc., only 19 months of operation have yielded 12,000 individual customers with an 80% reorder rate. The current customer base now includes medical doctors from different specialties, sports trainers, and athletes, both professional and amateur. The company expects to show a profit in 1996 and estimates that it will be very profitable in 3 years.

Management

Mr. Peale is 49 years old and has a 25-year history in sales, sales management, and marketing for a tool distribution company. His deep study of homeopathic medicines started in 1985 and included studies in nutritional supplements. Mr. Peale has been invited to sit on a newly-formed FDA committee addressing the growing national interest in natural medicines.

Curtis Company president, Ms. Alana has 25 years of experience in retail and direct sales. She has been a senior sales director and sales trainer for Beautiful You Cosmetics, has owned and operated a retail sporting goods store, and has managed a 15 person, $1 million department for a major chain retailer. She also has some banking experience.

Vice-president of marketing, Ryan Lemon has 32 years of experience as production manager, buyer, sales manager, and marketing manager. He was director of marketing for Pilgrim Health and was responsible for their first launch into New Jersey which led to their first $18MM in sales (in 3 years). He has a BS degree in textile engineering and has also done independent marketing consulting.

Product and Competition

The R&D mission was to develop a greaseless, odorless, topical cream which was measurably more effective at relieving pain than any other OTC (over the counter) topical product. This mission has been accomplished. The company has collected anecdotal, testimonial, and uncontrolled medical study evidence that Pain Away is more effective than the leading topical analgesics such as Arthritin and others. The product's effectiveness in relieving pain is its most powerful benefit, besides the added benefits of it being greaseless and odorless. What distinguishes Pain Away from any other topical analgesic in this still-growing $402.1MM market is its advanced homeopathic formula - a refined blend of 11 FDA approved pure and natural ingredients. The typical OTC topical analgesic works to either block the sensation of pain or distract perception of deep pain by "counterirritating" another localized area near the pain. Pain Away's formula is different. Pain Away treats pain at its source. It stimulates improved circulation in the micro-capillary system in the ligaments and tendons, where most pain is felt. Pain-relief from Pain Away is the result of the body's own self-healing. It also can be applied several times a day because it is odorless and greaseless.

The US pain management market ($15.2 billion by 1997) is a mature market with intense, established competition ("The Market for Pain Management Products in the US - Introduction, Drugs, Devices, Trends, and Market Structure," in FIND-SVP). With future pharmaceutical market growth dependent upon new and innovative product additions, Pain Away is entering the field at the right time. The company will distinguish itself and its market position by dedication to the development of only natural-ingredient products. Since its unique formula of ingredients already has FDA approval, the company aims to penetrate the OTC pharmaceutical market, where new products traditionally find success. Here Pain Away will compete with topical as well as internal analgesics, including aspirin, acetaminophin and ibuprofen. An estimated 4,000 people a year die from aspirin overdose. A condition known as "analgesic neuropathy" can result from extended or inappropriate use of analgesics. Medical studies linking heavy usage to health problems have affected aspirin, acetaminophin, and ibuprofen. Pain Away can be marketed as a substitute for (reducing overdose risk with internal analgesics), or as a supplement to (using Pain Away can reduce needed dosage of internal analgesics) internal analgesics when used for certain pain relief. Furthermore, Pain Away is not contraindicated for use with any other medication. This broad-based appeal is built upon the reliability of Pain Away's effectiveness in relieving pain, inflammation, and spasm associated with arthritis, bursitis, sciatic spasm, neck/back pain, tendonitis, tennis elbow, tension headache, achilles tendonitis, and carpal tunnel syndrome.

A second product, a natural anti-inflammatory nutritional support system formula known as "Pain Away Plus," will soon be marketed as a companion product to Pain Away. This multi-staged formula is a combination of trace minerals, herbs, and a natural cartilage-derived substance. The company has long-term plans to develop more health-related products.

Company principals have invested all available personal assets into the product development and operations to date. The need for capital is in the context of the readiness of the product for mass marketing. Management is seeking a $1,500,000 equity investment in exchange for a suggested 30% ownership of the company. All terms of financing are negotiable in order to meet the financial requirements of the investor.

Funds Requested

Advertising & promotion campaign - $1,200,000 (see below); Market research - $300,000. The company anticipates the need for follow-on financing after 24 months of business.

Use of Proceeds

Advertising & Promotion	Projected Cost
Magazines	$330,000
Radio	$200,000
Shows & Conventions	$140,000
TV	$400,000
Retail Shops	$70,000
Sample - POP Display	$60,000
Total	**$1,200,000**

From 5/94-12/31/95	
Sales	543,633
Net Income	(226,600)
Assets	56,987
Liabilities	224,253
Net Worth	**(167,266)**

Financial History

Sales were first made in 5/94 under Peale Inc. ($143,881). As sales expanded nationally, Pain Away Ltd was formed in January 1995. All sales since then have been under Pain Away Ltd.

Financial Projections

	1996	1997	1998	1999	2000
Sales	3,000,000	8,000,000	18,000,000	32,000,000	50,000,000
Net Inc.	360,000	2,160,000	4,860,000	8,640,000	13,500,000

With capital request accomodated, the company believes that Pain Away will jump in sales starting in 1996.

Exit

The company will attempt a public offering based on year 2000 earnings. If there is no public market and no prospect for a public market in the near future, then the company will offer to buy back the stock owned by the venture capitalist. A predetermined price could be set ahead of time, if desired by the venture capitalist.

PRODUCT

The product effectiveness, evidenced largely through anecdotal evidence, personal testimonials, and repeat sales, has formed the basis for the future growth of the company. Together with a second, complementary product (nearly ready for market), the launch product will be aggressively mass marketed as a pain management system for the next five to ten years. Past and current sales have been to end-users, health professionals, and to some retail chains. The company and product are now poised for first stage expansion. Over 30 target wholesale markets have been identified. While the company uses its marketing strategy to enter these wholesale markets, simultaneous efforts will be made to develop research protocols. Management is confident that the anecdotal evidence and personal testimonials will be strengthened by controlled studies, designed to test the effectiveness of the product and demonstrate the physiological healing activity stimulated by the formula. With scientific credibility, the product will not only build its position in the $150 million homeopathic product category but will also strengthen its transition into the formidable mainstream topical analgesic category.

Future research is planned, based upon inquiry, in order to adapt the formula for animal use (Pain Away currently being tested on thoroughbred horses).

At the end of five years, the company intends to have at least one additional health product and should be able to go public off its revenues. The long-term goal for the company is to become an entrepreneurial leader in the development of natural products for various segments of the health care market. The company plans to capture enough share of the topical analgesic market to become either a viable joint venture partner or an acquisition candidate.

Uniqueness

The product formula and delivery system are proprietary. The formula is uniquely advanced and is nearly immediately effective in relieving pain. Homeopathy and immunization have much in common, namely the principle of similars, which states that whatever a substance causes in a large dose, it can stimulate an immune response to defend against it in a small dose. It works by the principles of stimulation to the body's own self-healing mechanism and by the scientific balancing of its natural active ingredients through a dilution process called micro-dosing. Micro-dosing has given homeopathy its 200-year history of safety with no known side effects or toxicity. This self-healing process is in contrast to the majority of commercially successful topical analgesics, which contain counter-irritants, including the newer capsaicin-based products. These ingredients cause a superficial inflammation on the skin which masks pain by deadening the sensation of pain in the epidermal nerve endings only, or by distracting from the perception of pain by irritating an area near the pain source. The Pain Away formula has been developed with precision and balance and is a product that is effective and safe for use on all skin types. Pain Away's eleven active ingredients stimulate improved circulation in the micro-capillary system to ligaments and tendons, where most pain is felt. Pain relief is the result of the body's self-healing.

The manufacturing is sub-contracted out to a highly respected FDA-licensed manufacturer of homeopathic products.

An important unique feature of Pain Away which distinguishes it from other homeopathic remedies is that Pain Away is a topical treatment and is not a systemic treatment. As such, it requires little knowledge to use and is conducive to cross-merchandising in the mainstream analgesic category. Furthermore, since Pain Away is a formula of ingredients, it provides a broad spectrum of effects as compared to single remedies.

The personal commitment of the founder to relieve his own pain also adds a unique value to the story of this product - a story which can enhance marketability - to anyone who is in pain or anyone who knows someone in pain.

Although Pain Away is an homeopathic product, the company will position itself as a natural ingredients company - not necessarily homeopathic. All the company principals plan to engage both septics and advocates of complementary medicine by applying rigorous scientific standards equally across the board, for both conventional and unconventional treatments. Contacts have already been made with the National Institute of Health regarding future research.

Product Description

The product is a specialty consumer good carrying a suggested retail price of $19.95 for a 3.7 oz. jar (1.9 oz. jar also available at $12.95). The jar is designed with a medical appearance. The jar is easy to ship in multiples, is easy to stack on a shelf, is aesthetically pleasing, and has an easy-to-handle screw cap. The actual cream is greaseless, easy and pleasant to apply, and is odorless. Pain Away has, to date, largely been sold directly to end-users, and wholesale to retailers, distributors, and catalogues. The markets have supported the suggested retail price, which was arrived at by surveying market research supporting the $19.95 price along with the perceived value of the product compared to similar products at about the same price. This price also yielded a gross profit of $3.75 per jar and allowed for 100% markup from wholesale.

The eleven ingredients are readily available through top-quality labs which control for purity and authenticity. The cream is compatible with any medication being taken. The product carries a money-back 30-day guarantee.

Purchasers of the Product

Preliminary studies done by independent treatment professionals (no control group used) have shown that Pain Away has been effective for relieving the pain, inflammation, and spasm associated with arthritis, bursitis, sciatic spasm, neck and back pain, tendonitis, tennis elbow, tension headache, achilles tendonitis, and carpal tunnel syndrome. Anyone suffering these ailments, treating these ailments, or caring about anyone suffering these ailments is a potential purchaser of the product. A New Jersey hockey team uses Pain Away prior to workouts, competition, and for pain relief. The head trainer for the team says, "There's no product better for contusion of the quadriceps." He has reported shorter recovery times as a result of using Pain Away. Reports from athletes are that using Pain Away before and after workouts yields less cramping, fatigue, and soreness.

Top purchasers of TPR to date:

Customer	Dollar Sales	Unit Sales
Mall Booth Marketing	$11,000/month	800/month
Direct Selling - Retail	$16,000/month	1200/month

MARKET

The total market for OTC internal and topical analgesics is estimated at $3.6 billion for 1995 and is projected to be $4 billion by 1997. With over 400 brands saturating this mature market, growth is still occurring through new products and product innovations. Driving this growth are:

- increasing use of pain management products for the over-50 population segment, whose numbers are increasing
- increasing awareness that pain does not have to be tolerated and can be treated
- price increases

**Body/Muscle
Pain Market**

The market is dominated by internal analgesics:

(In millions of dollars)	1994	1995	1996	1997
Internal OTC analgesics:	3,001.6	3151.7	3,282.5	3,340.2
Aspirin	840.4	819.4	787.8	756.8
Acetaminophen	1260.7	1339.5	1411.5	1496.5
Ibuprofen	900.5	992.8	1,083.2	1/086.9
Topical OTC analgesics	315.4	402.1	522.7	692.6

Pain Away is a new product to this sizable OTC pain-relief market. It will enter this large arena riding on its effectiveness and coming from the new and growing alternative health care market segment. As a new OTC product, Pain Away has such a broad-based appeal that it will be sold to a large portion of the total OTC pain-relief market (both internal & topical), estimated to be 84% of all US adults and growing as the baby boom population ages and concerns regarding age-related ailments, such as arthritis, increase. Of this 84%, about 25% alone use pain-relief products for body/ muscle pain for which Pain Away is especially suited. Just this one type of ailment offers a substantial market potential:

Population size	% need product	Frequency Use	=	Mkt. Potential
161.3 Million X	40.3 Million X	156x/year	=	6.3 Billion uses

If only 40.3 million Americans (25% of 84% of adults) use an OTC pain-relief product three times a week for body/muscle pain alone, then the market potential is 6.3 billion uses of a pain-relieving product per year. Past use of Pain Away has indicated that a minimum of 3 applications per week would use about one 3.7 oz. jar per month. A conservative yearly estimate would be 10 jars per year, with consistent use. In order to reach a five-year sales goal of $50 million (6.7 MM jars), 667 MM consistent purchasers (10 jars/yr.) are needed. Product history has indicated a consistent 80% re-order rate, so at this rate, 833,000 original purchasers are required. This figure is 2.07% of just this one market segment. The company is very confident that it can capture 2.07% of this market segment within five years, especially considering that the roughly 40 million Americans who exercise on a regular basis, and who are aging, are included in this segment. Anecdotal reports from athletes who use Pain Away are that it can prevent injuries by "warming up" vulnerable muscles and joints prior to a workout. The product has wide applicability within this segment. The table below shows the percentage of the body/muscle pain market segment required to meet the next 5 years of sales projections.

Year	Sales Goal (in millions)	Initial Purchasers	Needed % of Market (with 80% reorder rate)
1996	$3	50,000	.12%
1997	$8	133,000	.33%
1998	$18	300,000	.74%
1999	$32	533,000	1.32%
2000	$50	833,000	2.07%

These numbers are based upon a wholesale price of $7.50 per jar and a usage rate of 10 jars/year with a segment population of 40.3 million potential purchasers.

The prescription pain relief market is a distinct market which Pain Away will not attempt to penetrate. Pain Away can, however, compete directly with nearly all pain-relief products because of its unique identity of being both a substitute and a supplement to all competing products. This uniqueness fits a projected market shift from internal to topical analgesic use as the population ages, and derives from 2 factors: 1) Use of Pain Away can reduce the needed dosage of any pain-relieving medication and 2) Pain Away is already part of a rapidly growing segment (25%-30%/year) of consumers who use alternative health care because of a disenchantment with OTC drugs and a concern about side effects with adverse reactions.

Use of Pain Away can reduce needed dosage of other pain-relieving medications. As stated earlier, Pain Away's effectiveness is based upon the homeopathic principle of microdosing. While it promotes self-healing by stimulating blood flow to micro-capillaries, it remains safe for all skin types and with use of any other medication. Anecdotal evidence (from hospitals, some doctors, and occupational rehab center) has indicated that use of Pain Away alone has yielded positive results and use of Pain Away, along with other treatments, has seemed to accelerate recovery. As always, this kind of evidence will be scientifically studied. The salient point is that Pain Away can be a substitute and/or a supplement in pain management, and thereby reduce needed dosages of other medications.

Homeopathy, being an established (officially recognized by UK National Health Service) and significant alternative mode of treatment, is gaining increasing acceptance in mainstream American health care. The National Institute of Health has even awarded grant money for research in alternative treatments, including homeopathy. Drug retailers report that homeopathy may be the fastest-growing category in the trade class of drug chains. Since homeopathy is gaining acceptance as an alternative treatment, the market segments which are already embracing these alternatives will continue to be targeted in the company's initial expansion. These segments include people ages 25-elderly, who seek improved quality in life, and whose lifestyle values involve "newness." This segment includes most of the "baby-boomer" population, estimated at over 75 million. The market of alternative health care seekers is characterized by patients who can and will pay for their own care. As much as 70% of alternative medical treatments are still paid for by patients themselves rather than insurers. This kind of purchasing indicates a willingness to try an alternative product and continue purchasing based upon perceived value of the product's effectiveness. Company management has been encouraged by the consistent 80% reorder rate and knows sales will be sustained once initial purchases are made. The alternative health care market is of respectable proportion. According to the New England Journal of Medicine (1/28/93), 34% of Americans spend $13 billion/year on alternative treatments such as chiropractic, acupuncture, massage, and homeopathy. Pain Away is already marketed to all of these treatment specialties so it will reach the spectrum of alternative treatment. This 34% of Americans are familiar with the term "homeopathic," so there's a consumer predisposition to being further educated about homeopathy as a value-added natural ingredient alternative.

Alternative Health Care Segment

The company will build an early market position on the alternative health-care market and will join the growth of the homeopathic segment as it moves from the fringes to the mainstream of the OTC pharmaceutical market.

Alternative Market Potential:

Population size	% need product	Frequency Use	=	Mkt. Potential
262 Million X	89.1 M (34%) X	24x/Yr.	=	2,000 Billion

If only about one third of Americans use an an alternative pain-reliever just twice per month, then the market potential is 2 trillion uses of an alternative pain-relieving product per year. Market indicators are that both the number of users and the frequency of use will increase as the population ages. The use rate of 2 times per month converts to 2 jars of Pain Away per year with consistent use. Again, in order to reach the 6.7 million jar sales goal ($50 MM), at the re-order rate of 80%, Pain Away would have to make 4.2 million initial sales in order to sustain 3.3 million consistent purchasers. This size customer base comprises 4.71% of the growing alternative health care market. The company believes that this sales goal is attainable within the next five years. The table below shows the percentage of the alternative health care market segment required to meet projected sales.

Alternative Health Care Market

Year (in millions)	Sales Goal (with 80% reorder rate)	Initial Purchasers	Needed % of Market
1996	$3	250,000	.28%
1997	$8	667,000	.75%
1998	$18	1,500,000	1.68%
1999	$32	2,700,000	3.03%
2000	$50	4,200,000	4.71%

These numbers are based upon a wholesale price of $7.50 per jar and a usage rate of 2 jars/year with a segment population of 89.1 million potential purchasers.

Narrowing the Market Focus 2X

The market potential for pain relief products is huge. By narrowing the focus to product category sales, the potential becomes more exact. Pain Away's product category is within the topical analgesic market, estimated at $402.1 MM annually with a projected $522.7 MM market in 1996 (30% growth) and $692.6 in 1997 (32.5% growth). Starting with $522.7 as the base market volume, and with 30% growth per year for the next 5 years, Pain Away would have to capture 3.33% of the year 2000 market volume to make its sales goal of $50MM. Management believes that these goals are attainable.

The table below shows what percentage of the topical analgesic market will meet Pain Away's sales projections.

Topical Analgesic Market

Market Volume Projections (in millions)

Sales Goal (in millions)	1996	1997	1998	1999	2000
	$522.7	$692.6	$900.3	$1,170	$1,521
$3	.57%				
$8		1.16%			
$18			2.00%		
$32				2.73%	
$50					3.29%

The focus can be narrowed further to the homeopathic product category, which is growing at a rapid rate at this time. The dollar volume of this segment is estimated at present to be between $150 million and $215 million and expected to grow at a rate of 25% to 30% a year. Some market-trackers say that retail sales haven't grown enough to support the existing number of homeopathic manufacturers and that a shakeout will consolidate sales in the hands of fewer manufacturers. The forseeable trend, however, is progressive growth from the fringes to mainstream markets, and at a rapid rate. The table below again shows percentages of this dollar volume required to meet sales projections.

Homeopathic Products

Market Volume Projections (in millions)

Sales Goal (in millions)	1996	1997	1998	1999	2000
	$182.5	$228.1	285.2	356.5	445.6
$3	1.64%				
$8		3.51%			
$18			6.31%		
$32				8.98%	
$50					11.22%

These numbers are based upon a 1996 volume mid-point between the projected volume range of $150 MM and $215 MM. Growth rate is 25% a year. At first glance these percentages may seem daunting. However, the manufacturers supplying this niche are relatively few in number and therefore hold significant market shares A new player can get a reasonable market share with the right product and marketing plan. The mainstream merchandising of homeopathic products started in the early '90's and has been tested as a lucrative direction. Company management is very confident that Pain Away will gain enough share points to capitalize on the rapid growth of this product category. Pain Away will not remain in the homeopathic niche. Its effectiveness will make it competitive with mainstream topical angalgesics.

The company will also develop an international market. A 10,000-unit order has already been received from a distribution company in Hungary and is awaiting final approval from the Hungarian State Department of Pharmacy. A small order was also sent to well-known sports figure in Spain. Discussions are underway for this individual to start large-scale distribution. The homeopathy market in the UK is estimated at 18M pounds and in Germany at 120M pounds, so European marketing could be strengthened by the homeopathic identity alone. In Germany, an independent division of the German Federal Health Agency publishes monographs on the safety and efficacy of herbal medicines. The company believes that Pain Away would fare excellently under such review and will carefully research and plan when and how to reach such markets.

International Markets

There are many companies competing for shares of the 3.6 billion dollar OTC analgesic market. The major players are the internal analgesic manufacturers:

COMPETITION

Company	Product	Analgesic Sales-$	Mkt. %
Reynolds	Aspernol	1.2 B	34%
Pharmacorp	Aspiril	612 MM	17%
American Pharmacy	Anaprin	180 MM	5%
Oxford Co.	Maraprin	180 MM	5%
Jones-Smythe Benton	Aspirin	144 MM	4%

The balance of the OTC internal analgesic market is held by private label companies and "others." The major strengths of this level of competition are obvious in comparison to Pain Away's present market position. The major players have:

- a manufacturing cost advantage,
- sophisticated market knowledge and access,
- established sales capability,
- strong R&D capacity,
- and of course, brand name loyalty.

An important competitive strength of Pain Away is that it is topical - pain relief is accomplished without risk of overdose and consequent risk of serious side effects. This competitive strength derives from a previously noted shift in the market from internal to topical analgesic use. This shift in consumer preference, along with Pain Away's effectiveness, can position the product as a substitute/supplement among these large competitors. Management is ever mindful that mainstream pharmaceutical companies are watchful of the homeopathic market and will act accordingly should market share be lost to homeopathic remedies. Becoming a viable acquisition candidate to any one of its major competitors is a realistic goal. Pain Away management is committed to quality product development and is also open to strategic alliances which would enhance its market capability.

The competition in the topical analgesic market is head-to-head. The top competitors are:

Company	Product	Ingredients	Sales	% Share
Pepper Co.	Pepperub	Menthol	60.3 MM	15%
Athens	Vapol	Menthol	47.9 MM	11.9%
Lucia	Menthol Plus	Menthol	35.8 MM	8.9%
Skin Care Corp.	Zanprin	Capsaicin	44.2 MM	8.7%
Bioderm	Aspratin	Salycin	18.8 MM	5%
Capcreme	Capsaicin	NA		
Men-Thol Co.	Menthoflex	Menthol	NA	
Capthol	Capsaicin	Menthol	NA	
Bianco-Picard	Salicreme	Methylsalicilate	86 MM	
Synergy	Lyptum	Eucalyptus	NA	

The basis for the competitive analysis is Pain Away's most competitive feature:

- It doesn't have any of the aforementioned advantages held by the major, well-known players in this market - yet.
- It doesn't have widespread brand name recognition - yet.
- It doesn't have appreciable market share in topical analgesics, alternative health, or homeopathy - yet.
- It does have a unique formula of safe and effective ingredients which none of the above products have.

All topical analgesics contain counter-irritants, including camphor, menthol, methyl salicylate, eucalyptus, wintergreen, and even the popular capsaicin. These ingredients, even when blended, act primarily to cause a superficial inflammation on the skin. This inflammation serves to hide the pain by deadening pain receptors in the skin.

What distinguishes Pain Away from all of the above products is that the eleven active homeopathic ingredients stimulate the blood flow in the body's micro-capillaries and act synergistically with the body tissue. This stimulates the body's own self-healing. Pain is treated at its source. Company management believes that the unique effectiveness of Pain Away will give it competitive clout. The issue then becomes how to compete.

Although Pepperub (Pepper) and Vapol (Athens) enjoy the largest market share, they are vulnerable to new product introductions. Menthol Plus (Lucia) held the top position in this category last year until Pepperub was re-packaged and relaunched with line extensions. That relaunch along with a relaunch of Zanprin boosted sales of both brands and put Pepperub back on top. Pepperub, Vapol, and Mentholplus are all menthol-based products. Zanprin is a capsaicin-based product and has boosted usage of its relatively new ingredient. Other relatively new capsaicin products are Capcreme (Bioderm) and Capthol (Men-Thol Co.).

Company management believes that Pain Away is generally more effective than Pepperub and Vapol. However, these venerated brand names, large advertising budgets, and consumer loyalty are formidable competitive advantages. Pain Away will focus on other competitors in order to gain a market position.

The key competitors are Menthol Plus, made by Lucia and Zanprin, made by Skin Care Corp.. Menthol Plus is a menthol-based product which Pain Away has encountered head to head in the sports market. Menthol Plus has a retail price advantage in the mass market, selling for $4 for a 2 oz. tube. This price difference is of little concern because Pain Away will promote itself as a high value product. The topical analgesic, alternative health, and homeopathic markets all support pricing based on perceived product value. Menthol Plus' manufacturer has reduced the advertising budget for this product (about $2 million) recognizing from a 21% decrease in 1994 sales that the product has matured. The company plans to acquire other brands (no topical analgesics) and extend its other lines in order to generate sales growth. The company sells another topical analgesic which is doing well in sales but has not reached the same position as Menthol Plus. Pain Away will monitor the life cycle of Menthol Plus and move to gain any market share it might lose.

Zanprin, made by Skin Care Corp., is gaining market share because Zanprin (.025%) and Zanprin-X (.075%) are capsaicin-based products. Capsaicin, derived from cayenne peppers, has created a new segment in the market and is very popular. Other companies are making capsaicin products but Skin Care Corp. attracted market attention by relaunching Zanprin as an OTC consumer product. It had been marketed for seven years to physicians and kept behind the counter, carrying the credibility of a prescription product. In early 1995, the product was re-packaged for shelf space and supported by TV ads. Despite commanding premium prices ($19.95/2oz of Zanprin-X), the product has done dramatically well.

Skin Care Corp. claims that Zanprin is the "only brand with physician endorsement and specific clinical support." This is a credible claim, cultivated for seven years, and obviously contributing to sales of the product.

Skin Care claims to be the first in the industry to develop their highly purified version of capsaicin for a pharmaceutical base. Zanprin distinguishes itself by promoting controlled clinical studies which have supported its effectiveness. Skin Care claims that such clinical trials don't apply to other, less pure, capsaicin formulas. This scientific feature enhances product credibility among physicians and pharmacists.

The management of Pain Away Ltd. recognizes the effective marketing strategy used by Skin Care because it is similar to their own strategy. Advertising and promotion expense is critical. With proper capitalization, Pain Away can compete because the Pain Away homeopathic formula is unique and effective. Many capsaicin users, including Zanprin users, have complained about the burning sensation caused by capsaicin. Pain Away will stand up to any topical analgesic on the market and do very well with comfort, safety, and effectiveness. The company needs to get this message out. The seven-year product life of Zanprin, supported by unique and heavy TV advertising, gives Zanprin quite an edge. Zanprin is now a "new" growth product and Pain Away can grow behind it, by comparing ingredients and effectiveness at every turn. Pain Away is also in the same price range as Zanprin, doing slightly better with $19.95 for a 3.7 oz. jar or $12.95 for a 1.9 oz. jar.

Zanprin is not the "only brand with physician endorsement and specific clinical support." Pain Away has been cultivating health professional support since the R&D phase. The product is heavily endorsed, and more medical support is developing. Many of Pain Away's sales to date have been to health professionals. Regarding clinical support, Skin Care's success with this strategy underscores the strategic importance of Pain Away's plans for controlled clinical studies.

Speaking of "highly purified" formulas, Pain Away can compete strongly with any formula on the market, especially capsaicin-based. The company wants to discuss purity of ingredients and formula and will do so in all promotional efforts.

The remainder of the products listed in the top competitor list have of course the same advantages that any established company with significant market share has. Beyond these immediate competitive advantages, Pain Away can compete, again, on the ingredient effectiveness basis.

Aspratin, an odorless rub which contains Salycin, sold well when it was introduced in 1992. It held third place among topical analgesics at the end of 1993. It has since been surpassed by capsaicin-based Zanprin. Bioderm developed Capcreme and lowered its price when Zanprin was relaunched.

Capthol was recently developed by the long-established Men-Thol Co. and is a capsaicin-menthol blend designed to compensate for the sometimes delayed pain relief when using capsaicin alone.

Salicreme is a methylsalicylate product which has shown flat growth and has lost market share.

Lyptum was a rapid-growth product in 1990-1991 but has since lost market share. Besides the well-established brands like Pepperub, the products which are gaining in this market are the capsaicin-based. This product category is known to be affected by product innovation and development. With proper support, Pain Away will take a respectable market share.

Homeopathic Competition

The competition takes place in the drug chain arena. Homeopathy may well be the fastest-growing category in the trade class of drug chains (20% of all homeopathic product sales). Among the growing number of drug chains which are giving shelf space to homeopathic products are: Walgreens, Medicine Shoppes International, Thrifty Payless, Eckerd Corp., Edgehill Drugs, Genovese and FEDCO, a California supermarket chain. Research published in the Journal of Clinical Pharmacy and Therapeutics states that 27% of US pharmacists consider homeopathic medicines helpful while only 18% consider them useless. The crossover of homeopathy from health food stores, where sales are still strong, to mass markets is gaining momentum.

As mentioned earlier, there are relatively few companies supplying homeopathic products to the mass market. There are five major producers/distributors of homeopathic products.

Company	Product
Health System Products	Full line of products
Homeopathic Co.	Full line under brand name Organa
Life-Right Corp.	Full line
Del Sol Inc.	Full line
Scandinavian Co.	Full line
Bio Health	Full line

Health System, Homeopathic Co., and Life-Right pioneered the distribution of homeopathic products to chain drug stores in the early 1990's and are now market leaders, although more companies are entering this lucrative market. Health System Products now has about 40% market share. Homeopathic Co. and Del Sol are aggressively developing the crossover into mass marketing with line development and heavy TV advertising.

All the topical analgesics listed above are arnica-based, with few other ingredients. Arnica Montana is the premier homeopathic medicine for the treatment of shock and trauma to the muscle. These formulas come the closest to Pain Away's because they contain some of the essential homeopathic pain-reducing ingredients. Pain Away's formula, however, blends more ingredients than any other homeopathic topical analgesic on the market. This more inclusive formula gives the product wider applicability. Price-wise, Pain Away is more expensive than most of the competing homeopathic products, where prices are in the $5-$10 range for 2oz.-4oz. sizes. But, this is a value-priced market, so price is not a critical variable. Since Pain Away is very competitive on an ingredient/effectiveness basis, the critical factor is having the resources to promote the product.

Future Competition

As has been noted, the topical analgesic category, including natural ingredient, is rapidly influenced by new clinical studies and product innovations. There are three main sources of new competition:

1) New ingredients and/or new innovations of existing ingredients. Examples are new products which employ the medicinal benefits of ammonium compounds. These products are designed to provide pain relief without the objectionable training room smells, burning sensations and stinging

of abraded skin that are often caused by the majority of topical analgesics that contain menthol, methyl salicylate or capsaicin as active ingredients. Pain Away's formula has solved this sensation problem and is a less "high-tech" product, for which consumers are showing a preference.

2) Companies currently in this market who could increase market share and become major players. Pain Away Ltd. is in this category.

3) Chain drug companies may produce their own private label homeopathic products and corral a significant share of this growing market - much as they did in the non-homeopathic analgesic market. This scenario is more likely to happen as homeopathic companies expand the sales volume in this market and there are share points to be taken away by private labeling.

Pain Away Ltd. can be very competitive with the right promotional support.

MARKETING

Marketing Strategies

Increase market share by reducing market share of competitors. This strategy will capitalize on the market development to date and capture a share of markets held by existing pain-relieving topical applications. The key benefit is that conventional pain-relievers mask pain while Pain Away stimulates the body's own healing ability to directly battle an ailment. Another benefit is that homeopathic remedies have no known side effects while many pain-relievers, especially those ingested, have side effects. Neither will Pain Away interfere with any medication. This strategy requires extensive advertising in mainstream media, including infomercial, QVC (Pain Away already under review), 60 second commercial, cable TV, interactive TV, direct mail, independent sales reps, POP displays, and educational inserts/newsletters. One objective of planned controlled studies on the effectiveness of Pain Away is to use scientific evidence to help bridge the narrowing gap between natural and conventional medicine. Product studies will support this marketing strategy. In this context, the company will pursue preliminary inquiries from a favored vendor to use Pain Away in the workplace to study any reduction of lost work time and/or medical costs precipitated by repetitive stress injuries.

Expand a growing new market for alternative health care by positioning to lead this growing market. This strategy involves specialty catalogues (placed in 5 currently), placement on retail shelves of health food stores, educational product inserts/newsletters, media appearances discussing product, and independent sales reps. This strategy addresses the 89.1 million users of alternative health care.

The company has already been approached by two large Multi-Level Marketing companies. This strategy would involve creating private labels for a large customer. Of utmost consideration with this strategy is product identity and how this channel of distribution would affect it. This channel of distribution usually requires more price mark-up than the product would tolerate.

The company will create its own "competition" by developing private labels and/or separate companies to market to different niches.

Keep capital outlay to a minimum by licensing/franchising Pain Away to a brand-name company. This strategy would add value to the product in the form of brand name loyalty, manufacturing strength, and a strong sales/service force already in place. The company envisions its role in this type of strategic alliance as conducting scientific studies to increase the credibility of TPR and in developing new products. This strategy remains an option which could preclude other strategies under mutually acceptable terms.

Building on an initial order from a health product distribution company in Hungary, Pain Away Ltd. will penetrate the European market by targeting England and Germany, where homeopathy is an accepted form of treatment. This strategy would be developed only after a US market position was established.

Marketing Plan

The company is moving from start-up stage into its first growth stage. Market strategy to date can be succinctly described as selling "one jar at a time." Direct personal selling has been the mainstay in sales growth. This strategy has targeted any end-user willing to try the product. These early customers were reached through health care professionals and direct selling through state/county fairs, shopping mall space, health food store chains, and most recently lifestyle catalogues. As the company moves away from direct selling, a strategy which proved to be an excellent market test, into mass-marketing, identified market segments are being matched with appropriate distribution channels. The plan now is to expand and concentrate more on helping the consumer develop product preference by heavy advertising of the brand name, the benefits of the product, the ease of use, and the guarantee. Company expectations are that all advertising will be enhanced by results of controlled studies of product effectiveness.

The company intends to expand regionally, based on existing markets and consumer profiles (e.g., households from the South are likely heavy users of analgesics). The national market will only be tested by placement in catalogues with a distribution of 200 million. As regional sales grow and as the product gains recognition, then a national marketing strategy will take shape. Company management have begun discussions with a major marketing communications agency (Fortune 500 client list) who themselves approached Pain Away. The marketing and sales outline is as follows.

Marketing Function

Research

1) A complete review and analysis of the topical analgesic market.

2) Utilization of Triad Groups conducted with the professional community and general consumers. Purpose is to identify professional and consumer preferences.

3) Based on research, create a product identity.

4) From product identity, establish professional and consumer strategic directions, which would affect product design, packaging, advertising, consumer promotion, and product publicity.

5) Test both professional and consumer strategic direction via two more Triad Groups.

6) Develop launch marketing plan with all elements and budget for both professional and consumer.

7) Actual implementation of the plan to include product design changes, packaging, advertising, consumer promotion, display, and product publicity.

Sales Function

Retail

Utilize a sales organization enabling direct-call coverage on the top 25 customers, which generally account for 80% of retail sales, and broker-managed coverage for the remainder. Launch plan would include a national sales meeting and all necessary materials.

Professional

Concentrate on the pharmacist community via co-op direct mail. Pharmacist recommendation at the purchase counter does affect sales.

PRODUCTION

The production process takes place in a standard homeopathic laboratory where raw materials are blended. There are no significant health or safety risks involved. Production orders are processed by purchase order for finished product. Some raw materials are usually on hand but more are ordered against purchase order requirements. Jars are ordered from a separate manufacturer and sent to the homeopathic laboratory to be filled, packaged, and shipped to Pain Away Ltd., where fulfillment is done.

The homeopathic laboratory has the capacity to fill all projected orders. As orders increase, Pain Away management will consider using a fulfillment service and more drop-shipping to wholesale customers. Cost of goods is estimated at 18% of gross sales. This figure has been consistent throughout production to date and is based on the complete production cycle.

There is no backlog.

The production process does not require any specialized or proprietary machinery. The critical factors in the production process are the highest quality of raw materials and the incubation process, which assures a stable finished product. Water is added to a base of vegetable/plant emollients. The eleven active ingredients are then mixed into the emulsion, which incubates for about 48 hours in large vats, while monitored for any fungal invasion. The finished product is then lab-tested for potency, which is done by lot number (the company gets lot samples). Filling is currently done by gravity-feed. The manufacturer might advance to computerized filling. One batch is 500 gallons. Lead time from order to packaged product is 4 weeks. Only a skilled and experienced manufacturer can produce the formula. Even other homeopathic manufacturers not familiar with a cream-based product would have difficulty with the production process. General topical analgesic manufacturers would need to become familiar with the raw materials and the production process in order to blend Pain Away's eleven active and ten inert ingredients. The company currently has one back-up manufacturer, which has never been used.

Production Characteristics

The company administrative staff consists of 5 people (recently reduced by 3) including the 3 officers. The two employees are paid an hourly wage. The staff are not unionized and there is no expectation of such. The labor supply in the region is more than sufficient to meet all future staffing needs. The sales force is comprised of independent agents who are paid on commission.

Labor Force and Employees

Supplier	*Volume*	*Product*
Herbal Laboratories	35,000 jars	all raw materials
Portland, Oregon		jars & caps
		labels
		packaging
		shipping boxes

Suppliers

Currently, the laboratory procures all production materials. There are no shortages of key components, and multiple sources are available.

All production is sub contracted out. Only fulfillment and shipping are done in-house. The company has formed a strong working relationship with Herbal Laboratories, which is the key subcontractor. Although management has selected a back-up manufacturer, the existing relationship with Herbal Labs has been more than satisfactory, so no change is foreseen. Other subcontractors supplying jars, labels, and boxes are used based upon price and service and can be replaced.

Subcontractors

Standard office equipment is used for administrative functions. All production equipment at Herbal Laboratories is new and there is nothing that would cause production to be stopped for any appreciable time.

Equipment

The company facility is a single-story 1,950 square foot, cement block structure on about a two-acre cleared lot that is leased in one-year increments. The facility is located in northern Dutchess County, NY. All necessary commercial and industrial infrastructure is in place. The facility is

PROPERTY AND FACILITIES

easily accessible from major thoroughfares. The general area has been and is recovering from the closing of 2 large industrial facilities, so there's been a noticeable decline in property values. There is, however, a regional effort to re-direct the area to rely more upon small and entrepreneurial business. Management plans to purchase the building in order to add an appreciable fixed asset and to reduce expenses. The structure is easily expandable, so the company will not have to move during its critical growth stage.

PATENTS AND TRADEMARKS

Active homeopathics are not patentable. Management is exploring establishing a trademark and a formula patent.

RESEARCH AND DEVELOPMENT

The three principals have invested collectively $100,000, which has been capitalized. Plans for the immediate future include forming a research alliance with a university, hospital, or research group in order to develop a protocol for applying the "rigorous scientific standards" against which the effectiveness of Pain Away can be proven. Management has projected R&D expenses at $30,000 for the next 12-month period. These expenditures are intended for controlled studies proving effectiveness, and for continuation of developing applications for animals. Management is sales-marketing oriented and does not want to develop only a research lab. Any R&D will be designed to enhance sales and profits. Company management is currently investigating an SBIR grant.

GOVERNMENT REGULATIONS

There are no particular federal, state or local laws/regulations that affect the conduct of business. The manufacturer meets OSHA requirements, as does the Pain Away administrative facility. The FDA regulates homeopathy as an OTC non-prescription medicine. Pain Away's ingredients are in total compliance with FDA standards. Mr. Peale cultivated a working relationship with FDA representatives during the initial research and wisely intends to sustain such.

INSURANCE AND TAXES

Product liability insurance is underwritten. A buy-sell agreement among officers exists but is not yet backed by insurance. Key employee insurance is also yet to be written.

All taxes are current. The company pays standard payroll, Social Security, and corporate taxes. The product is sales tax exempt in many states.

CORPORATE STRUCTURE

Company principals first formed an S-corporation under the name Peale Inc. The realization of the likelihood of international sales prompted management to form Pain Away Ltd. as the operational company. Peale Inc. serves a limited partnership which was formed to attract investors. Both companies are run by the same management team. All R&D is done through Peale Inc. There is co-mingling of funds. This proposal seeks financing for Pain Away Ltd. Return on the investment will derive from the sale of the product Pain Away itself and any other products which the company sells.

Pain Away Ltd. is a member of the Homeopathic Manufacturers Association. The officers were invited to participate in an annual meeting of the newly formed FDA committee on natural medicines. This committee works on the bases for regulations, compliance, and claims for the natural ingredient industry, covering vitamins, herbs, and homeopathy.

Management subscribes to the following publications:

- *Homeopathy Today*
- *Natural Foods Merchandiser*
- *American Health*
- *Prevention Magazine*
- *Let's Live*
- *New England Journal of Medicine letter*

A board of directors will be developed in the near future. There is interest from the medical, nutritional, and professional sports communities, as well as from a local bank. Officers are:

Directors and Officers

Robert Peale - CEO
Alana Curtis - President
Ryan Lemon - Vice-President, Marketing

Profit and loss responsibilities are shared by the officers.

The officers are primary key employees (backgrounds in executive summary). Other key employees include:

Leslie Ottaviani - bookkeeper and office manager - known by management for 5 years and described as "a dedicated innovator with a true grasp for details." She has experience supervising 20 employees in the accounting department of Worldwide Airlines and has worked as an independent bookkeeper for several companies in Hudson Valley, NY.

Key Employees

Julia Allen - administrative assistant - known by management for 6 years and described as "having people and problem-solving skills and works incredibly well under pressure." Her background includes sales in a successful business which included business consulting.

Name	Capacity	Remuneration
Robert Peale	CEO	$1,600/mo.
Alana Curtis	President	$1,600/mo.
Ryan Lemon	Vice-President	$1,600/mo.
Leslie Ottaviani	Bookkeeper	$12/hr.-35 hrs/wk.
Julia Allen	Admin. Ass't	$8/hr.-20 hrs/wk.
Davis Associates	Marketing Consultant	$5,000/mo. eff. 1/96
Public Communications Inc.	Public Rel. Consultant	$2,500/mo. eff. 1/96
Dr. Jeff Beck	Radio host sponsor	$2,000/mo.
Cecil O'Connor	Finance Consultant	$80/hr. prepare bus. plan 3% fee for securing funds
Limited Partners (20)	Early investors	$.01/jar per $1,000 invested
Jonathan Wainwright	Accountant	no retainer\ fee for service only
Arnold Lee	Banker	no remuneration

Remuneration

Accountant and Banker

All other fees paid on an ad hoc basis. Different attorneys have been used on an ad hoc basis (finance closing fees will be paid by the company).

Name	# Shares	%Pre-financing	%Post-financing
Robert Peale	67 (1/3 of 200)	33 1/3%	23 1/3%
Alana Curtis	67 (1/3 of 200)	33 1/3%	23 1/3%
Ryan Lemon	67 (1/3 of 200)	33 1/3%	23 1/3%
Investor	0	0%	30%

Principal Shareholders

FINANCING

**Proposed
Financing**

Management is willing to negotiate any structure which suits the investor. The company is seeking an equity investor. Management will provide a seat on the company's board of directors. Ongoing reports of key ratios, profit-loss statements, balance sheets, and annual audits would be provided to the investor. It is management's intent that the investor will enjoy returns on investment in excess of that of alternative investments, as a privately held company, while providing investor liquidity of his investment by taking the company public at its earliest opportunity.

Capital Structure

The existing capital structure includes a $50,000 unsecured line of credit with Poughkeepsie National Savings Bank. This line of credit was just brought to maturity in 1/96 for a 30-day period, at which time the line was renewed. If the current financing proposal is accomodated, then the line of credit can be increased.

Additional financing to date has derived from the sale of limited partnerships offering $.01 per 3.7 oz. jar royalty for every $1,000 invested. Each limited partner has been given the right to convert his/her capital investment into common stock when the company goes public, or, to receive back his/her original capital investment when the company goes public. Total amount of financing raised through the limited partnership is $100,000.

As mentioned earlier, officers have collectively invested about $100,000 in the company, mostly through the R&D phase. Officers' "sweat equity" is immeasurable.

Use of Proceeds

As stated in the executive summary: Advertising & promotion campaign - $1,200,000 (see below); Market research - $300,000. The company anticipates the need for follow-on financing after 24 months of business.

Advertising & Promotion	Projected Cost
Magazines	$330,000
Radio	$200,000
Shows & Conventions	$140,000
TV	$400,000
Retail Shops	$70,000
Sample-POP Display	$60,000
Total	**$1,200,000**

Management intends to preserve cash flow by factoring much of the receivables. With the current lead time of 4 weeks, however, some capital may be used to increase merchandising inventory in order to fulfill initial large orders. It is hoped that any follow-on financing can and will be debt financing, serviced by cash flow.

The following table sets forth the capitalization of Pain Away Ltd. as of 12/31/95 and as adjusted to reflect the proposed sale of common stock.

Dilution

Stockholders' Equity	Before sale Actual	After sale As Adjusted
Common Stock, no par value,	(167,268)	1,332,732
200 shares authorized;		
0 outstanding		
Additional Paid-in Capital		1,500,000
Accumulated Earnings (deficit)	(167,268)	(167,268)
Total Stockholders' Equity	(334,536)	1,165,464

Dilution: The net tangible book value of the company as of 12/31/95 was minus $1,673 per share. Without taking into account any other changes in such net tangible book value after 12/31/96, other than to give effect to the sale of 60 shares (proposed 30% equity share) hereby, the pro forma net tangible book value of the company on 12/31/95 will be $5,827 per share, representing an immediate dilution of $13,597 per share to new investors.

Price per share to Investor	19,424
Net tangible book value before the sale	(1,673)
Increase attributable to new investor	7,500
Pro forma net tangible book value after the purchase	5,827
Dilution to new investor	**$13,597**

Management recognizes that this proposed financing implies a large premium value on the existing equity and so will negotiate any other conditions which would induce the investor to make the investment.

At the time of the company's IPO, limited partners who opt for common stock will receive their shares from the officers' share of owned stock. The negotiated ownership held by the investor will not be further diluted.

Management seeks a close working relationship with the investor. The investor will be given one seat on the board of directors. Management would solicit consultations (for a fee) on financial matters, or any other area of investor expertise (e.g., planning, management development), but voting power is not an option. Fees will also be paid for any future financing and/ or profitable business connections arranged by the investor.

Investor Involvement

RISK FACTORS

Limited Operating History

Even though management feels that the company is at first-stage expansion, it is definitely still an early-stage company. Two obvious risks inherent in early-stage companies are undercapitalization and poor liquidity. Management has capitalized the business operations to date well enough to have developed the product and identified penetrable market segments. The current proposed financing will provide enough capital to handle the anticipated growth.

Limited Resources

Management believes that it has the resources to continue at the present pace of business. An anticipated increase in sales through advertising media such as QVC, regional/national catalogues, retail outlets, and some European distribution can be financed by factoring. These "bootstrapping" approaches have sustained the company to date and will accommodate slow growth. Management believes, however, that more rapid expansion is desirable in order to penetrate its identified market segments. More rapid expansion requires more resources.

Limited Management Experience

All officers have successful backgrounds in marketing. Additional experience in manufacturing/ distribution has been gained in the past nine years of product development. Management has consistently shown a willingness to leverage themselves with accomplished professional consulting relationships. The company culture is one which reinforces sharing of expertise with mutual benefit to all concerned.

Market Uncertainties

Any consumer product business is subject to the changing preferences of the marketplace. As presented in the marketing section of this proposal, the target markets are showing substantial growth, which limits uncertainty. There is currently a growing consumer preference for homeopathic topical remedies. More uncertainty is evident when considering competition, but can be made tolerable by on-going research and analysis.

Production Uncertainties

The only uncertainty at present is whether or not the lead time (4 weeks) from purchase order to finished product can consistently be reduced. This uncertainty is of material concern as sales increase. Herbal Laboratories is a sound company with a promising long-term future and has always been customer-friendly, so no more serious uncertainties exist at present. Management believes that vertical integration of manufacturing is feasible in the long-term but is not practical in the near-term.

Liquidation

In the event that liquidation becomes necessary, management believes that the most value could be realized from the sale of the product formula itself. The formula is not patented, so valuation remains uncertain. However, the sales history, along with the testimonials attesting to the effectiveness of this "ready-made" product, should determine value. Office equipment would yield limited value, and unless the company building was purchased prior to liquidation, no value would be realized. Management believes that the company can and will generate increasing value in the near future, evidenced by increasing sales.

Dependence on Key Management

At present, CEO Robert Peale is considered the primary key manager/officer. His knowledge of the product ingredients, his history of public appearances promoting the product, his increasing recognition by the health community as an expert in natural medicine, and his charisma as a business professional highlight his key role. Managerially, the other officers are thoroughly competent and could manage the company and market its products without Mr. Peale. At this critical early stage, however, the product needs an identity and a market position before the loss of any key managers could be overcome. Once the premier product is securely launched and the product line is expanded, the loss of any officer could be absorbed by continued proper management of the company. Management believes that such a development is not far off, once the company is properly capitalized. Until such time, key person life insurance will be purchased.

What Could Go Wrong?

Upgraded advertising campaigns could not lead to any substantial increase in sales. This problem can be avoided by using experienced advertising/marketing consultants who have familiarity with the targeted markets. Furthermore, properly designed test runs on any advertising campaign would provide objective indicators of expected returns. Capital investment in advertising should be gradual and progressively based upon certain expected levels of return.

Stronger competition could capitalize on and stall Pain Away's early success by replicating the product and its marketing strategy. This problem can be solved in two ways: First, with proper capitalization, Pain Away can make an entry into targeted markets rapidly and with enough strength to grab market share. Keeping market share can be easier than getting it. This market requires extensive advertising. Increasing market share could mean an increasing advertising budget. An increasing advertising budget can easily reduce profit margin, so strategic planning is required. The second way to solve the competition problem is in the formula itself. Management will seek to patent the formula. The nature of the homeopathic ingredients is likely to inhibit any mainstream non-homeopathic company from replicating the product. Acquisition of a homeopathic company would make more sense. Narrowing the competition, then, to other homeopathic companies gives Pain Away more of a fighting chance, since its formula is more sophisticated and user-friendly than any homeopathic topical analgesic on the market.

Governmental controls could conceivably impede sales. This problem is unlikely because the ingredients are already FDA-approved. Furthermore, management's participation in the FDA committee to develop regulatory standards for the natural medicine field would provide early warnings of any such prohibitory controls.

The company could be controlled by non-investor stockholders. This problem is not likely to develop because the management team would hold a majority. Management is dedicated to the principles of increasing value and profits and is confident that its efforts will be in concert with those of the investor.

RETURN ON INVESTMENT AND EXIT

Public Offering

Management plans for an IPO in 5-7 years. The investor's shares would be sold to provide the targeted return on investment. Should there be no public market, then a buyback would occur.

Management will negotiate a buyback formula with the investor and will target milestones in planning for this possibility. Management aims for returning 6 times the original investment in five years.

The business has not shown a profit since sales activity began in May 1994. This lack of profit is not unusual for an early-stage company. Losses were incurred in the start-up phase, where the objective was to get consumers to try the product. Gross profit margins have remained stable, however. Management focus was targeted on getting professionals and consumers to try the product in order to collect anecdotal evidence and testimonials of its effectiveness. Not enough focus was on asset management, as evidenced by a low return on assets ratio (p.32). Now that the product has gotten some recognition, especially in professional circles, the focus will shift toward mass marketing. Management intends to improve inventory management by using factoring of receivables in conjunction with JIT inventory control. As sales volume increases, drop-shipping from plant to wholesale customer, will also be arranged.

Buyback

ANALYSIS OF OPERATIONS AND PROJECTIONS

FINANCIAL STATEMENTS

Balance Sheet

Assets as of 12/31/95

Current Assets		
Cash	690.89	1.21%
Accounts Receivable	10,119.48	17.76%
Allowance for Bad Debt	-3,662.25	-6.43%
Deposits	100.00	0.18%
Inventory	20,089.97	35.25%
Prepaid Expenses	13,339.06	23.41%
Total Current Assets	40,677.15	71.38%
Property & Equipment		
Furniture & Fixtures	13,644.79	23.94%
Total Prop & Equip	13,644.79	23.94%
Other Assets:		
Officers Loan Receivables	100.00	0.18%
Start Up	2,564.75	4.50%
Total Other Assets	2,664.75	4.68%
Total Assets	56,986.69	100.00%
Liabilities & Equity		
Current Liabilities		
Accounts Payable	77,960.80	136.81%
Performance Plus	47,937.46	84.12%
PPI Ltd Partnership Payable	24,281.73	42.61%
Notes Payable Short-term	7,000.00	12.28%
Total Current Liabilities	**157,179.99**	**275.82%**
Long-term Liabilities		
Note Payable	53,265.00	93.47%
RSB Loan - Computer	12,000.00	21.06%
Note Payable - Officers	1,809.93	3.18%
Total Long-term Liabilities	**67,074.93**	**117.70%**
Total Liabilities	**224,254.92**	**393.52%**
Equity		
Net Income (Loss)	(167,268.24)	-293.5%
Total Equity	**(167,268)**	**-293.52%**
Total Liabilities & Equity	**56,986.68**	**100.00%**

Monthly Income Statements 1995

	Jan 95	Feb 95	Mar 95	Apr 95	May 95	Jun 95
Sales	20,194	46,942	53,320	49,955	46,701	33,865
Cost of Goods	4,362	10,139	11,517	10,790	10,087	7,315
Gross Profit	15,832	36,803	41,803	39,165	36,614	26,550
Selling Expenses	15,549	36,078	29,754	36,564	30,178	10,381
General & Administrative	12,483	19,051	22,784	28,488	27,851	27,821
Total Operating Expenses	28,032	55,129	52,538	65,052	58,029	38,202
Net Income before Taxes	(12,200)	(18,326)	(10,735)	(25,887)	(21,415)	(11,652)
Provision for Taxes	—	—	—	—	—	—
Net Income after Taxes	(12,200)	(18,326)	(10,735)	(25,887)	(21,415)	(11,652)
Gross Profit Percentage	78.4%	78.4%	78.4%	78.4%	78.4%	78.4%
Cost of Goods as % of Sales	21.6%	21.6%	21.6%	21.6%	21.6%	21.6%
Selling Expenses as % of Sales						
	77.00%	76.86%	55.80%	73.19%	64.62%	30.65%
G&A as % of Sales	61.82%	40.58%	42.73%	57.03%	59.64%	82.15%
# Jars Sold						
Large	711	1,652	1,877	2,215	2,070	1,501
Small	627	1,457	1,656	1,071	1,001	726
Total Jars Sold	1,338	3,109	3,533	3,286	3,071	2,227

Income Statement - 12/31/95

Revenues: FYE 1995		
Sales - cash/checks	282,501.65	70.67%
Sales - MC, Visa	109,709.27	27.44%
Sales - American Express	8,371.88	2.09%
Sales - Discover/Novus	11,884.02	2.97%
Discounts	(4,710.34)	-1.18%
Returns	(7,468.74)	-1.87%
Short/Over	(535.39)	-0.13%
Total Revenues	399,752.35	100.00%
Cost of Sales		
Cost of Goods	66,453.96	16.62%
Total Cost of Sales	66,453.96	16.62%
Gross Profit	333,298.39	83.38%
Expenses:		
Salaries - Sales	59,734.52	14.94%
Commissions - Sales	18,754.35	4.69%
Commissions - Outside sales	69.93	0.02%
Bonus - Sales	3,218.75	0.81%
Advertising	46,721.87	11.69%
Printing	9,079.10	2.27%
Brochures & Catalogs	835.15	0.21%
Trade Show	10,501.98	2.63%
Travel	21,520.88	5.38%
Entertainment	777.22	0.19%
Miscellaneous Sales Exp.	1,811.78	0.45%
Rent - Carts	29,810.61	7.46%
Salaries - Officers	51,155.00	12.80%
Salaries & Wages - Employees	61,156.85	15.30%
Payrol Tax Exp.	20,816.36	5.21%
Rent	12,400.00	3.10%
Utilities	1,692.12	0.42%
Insurance - General	40.00	0.01%

Jul 95	Aug 95	Sep 95	Oct 95	Nov 95	Dec 95	YTD	% of Sales
22,948	34,256	13,998	24,431	27,168	25,969	399,747	100.00%
4,957	7,409	3,023	4,526	5,868	(13,541)	66,452	16.62%
17,991	26,847	10,975	19,905	21,300	39,510	333,295	83.38%
9,369	10,839	1,370	4,925	9,934	7,895	202,836	50.74%
26,230	37,979	20,405	18,887	15,101	40,282	297,362	74.39%
35,599	48,818	21,775	23,812	25,035	48,177	500,198	125.13%
(17,608)	(21,971)	(10,800)	(3,907)	(3,735)	(8,667)	(166,903)	-41.75%
—	—	—		—	362	362	
(17,608)	(21,971)	(10,800)	(3,907)	(3,735)	(9,029)	(167,265)	-41.84%
78.4%	78.4%	78.4%	81.5%	78.4%	152.1%	83.4%	
21.6%	21.6%	21.6%	18.5%	21.6%	-52.1%	16.6%	
40.83%	31.64%	9.79%	20.16%	36.57%	30.40%	50.74%	
114.30%	110.87%	145.77%	77.31%	55.58%	155.12%	74.39%	
1,302	1,410	775	871	871	871	16,126	
737	1,070	1,098	790	790	790	11,813	
2,039	2,480	1,873	1,661	1,661	1,661	27,939	

Telephone	36,265,64	9.07%
Professional Fees	6,241.95	1.56%
Outside Services	3,869.01	0.97%
Management Fees	24,441.68	6.11%
UPS Exp.	16,608.55	4.15%
Postage Exp.	10,116.10	2.53%
Auto Exp.	9,735.58	2.44%
Equip. Rental/Leasing	2,260.21	0.57%
Office Exp.	5,690.86	1.42%
Supplies	9,035.21	2.26%
Contributions	650.00	0.16%
Dues & Subscriptions	538.70	0.13%
Repairs & Maintenance	2,899.86	0.73%
Bank Charges	2,323.66	0.58%
MC/Visa Service Chg.	4,300.13	1.08%
Amexco Service Chg.	231.70	0.06%
Discover Service Chg.	275.05	0.07%
Miscellanious	1,035.90	0.26%
Interest Expense	10,141.79	2.54%
Filing Fees	10.00	0.00%
Taxes - Other	361.64	0.09%
Travel & Entertainment	119.87	0.03%
Bad Debt Exp.	3,281.10	0.82%
Fines & Penalties	93.92	0.02%
Interest Income	(62.95)	-0.02%
Total Expenses	**500,561.63**	**125.22%**
Net Income	**(167,263.24)**	**-41.84%**

Key Ratio Analysis

Statement Dated: 12/31/95
Industry Ratios-
RMA 1995 St. Studies

Total Current Assets	40,677	Current Ratio		Upper	Q 2.2
Total Current Liabilities	157,180 = Ratio		0.26:1	Median	1.9
				Lower Q	1.2
Cash + A/R + N. Receivable	10,810	Quick Ratio			1.6
Total Current Liabilities	157,180 = Ratio		0.07:1 1		0.5
Net Fixed Assets	13,645	Fixed/Net Worth			0.1
Tangible Net Worth	(167,268) = Ratio		-0.08:1		0.7
					1.1
Total Liabilities	224,255	Debt/Equity			0.7
Tangible Net Worth	(167,268) = Ratio		-1.34:1		1.1
					3.2
Total Liabilities	224,255	Overall Leverage			
Total Assets	56,987 = Ratio		3.94:1		
Net Sales	399,747	Sales/Receivables			32
Account & Notes Receivables	10,119 = Ratio		39.50:1		40
					39
Days in Year, 365	365	Day's Receivable			
Sales/Receivables Ratio		39.50 = Ratio	9.24 days		
Cost of Sales	66,454	Inventory Turnover			
Inventory		20,090 = Ratio	3.31x		
Days in Year, 365	365	Days Inventory			

Cost of Goods/Inventory Ratio	3.31 = Ratio		110.34 days
Net Sales	399,747	Sales to Working Capital	
Curr. Assets - Curr. Liabilities	(116,503) = Ratio	-3.43 x RMA Ratios NA	
Net Profit + Depr. + Amort.	(167,268)	Cash Flow/Long Term Debt	
Current Portion L T Debt	7,000 = Ratio	-23.90 x	
Profit, before Tax	(167,268)	Return on Equity	
Tangible Net Worth (Equity)	(167,268) = Ratio		1.00%
Profit, before Tax	(167,268)	Return on Assets	
Total Assets	**59,987 = Ratio -2.79**		

**THIS PORTION OF PAGE INTENTIONALLY LEFT BLANK
SEE NEXT PAGE FOR PROJECTED CASH FLOW TABLE**

Projected Cash Flow

12 Months - 1996

	Jan-96	Feb-96	Mar-96	Apr-96	May-96	Jun-96
Cash On Hand	700	(78,316)	(38,066)	(5,092)	46,819	178,117
Cash Receipts:						
Current month sales	48,750	53,625	48,400	64,886	158,564	174,420
Prior accts receivables	8,334	50,535	54,875	60,363	66,399	71,864
Investment proceeds	0	0	0	0	0	0
Total Cash Receipts	57,084	104,160	103,275	125,249	224,963	246,284
Cash Available	57,784	25,844	65,209	120,157	271,781	424,401
Cash disbursements:						
Cost of product	10,800	11,880	13,068	14,375	15,552	16,200
Advertising	6,000	6,600	7,260	7,986	8,640	9,000
Promotions	0	0	0	10,000	10,000	10,000
Selling expenses	8,300	9,130	10,043	11,047	11,952	12,450
General & admin	33,000	36,300	39,930	39,930	47,520	49,500
Research & Development	0	0	0	0	0	20,000
Income taxes	0	0	0	0	0	36,000
Prior accounts payable	78,000	—	—	—	—	—
Total Disbursements	136,100	63,910	70,301	73,338	93,664	153,150
Cash End of Month	(78,316)	(38,066)	(5,092)	46,819	178,117	271,251
Operating Data						
Sales per Month	50,000	55,000	60,500	66,550	72,000	75,000
Cost of Goods	10,800	11,880	13,068	11,979	12,960	13,500
Curr Mth collections	48,750	53,625	58,988	64,886	70,200	73,125
Factor Fees*	0	0	0	0	0	0
Collection of A/R						

*Factor fee 4% of sales.

Projected Annual Financial Statements

For Years 1996-2000
In Thousands

	FYE 1996	FYE 1997	FYE 1998	FYE 1999	FYE 2000
Sales	2,730	8,000	18,000	32,000	50,000
Cost of Goods sold	497	1,440	3,240	5,760	9,000
Gross Profit	2,233	6,560	14,760	26,240	41,000
Advertising	986	2,000	4,500	8,000	12,500
Selling Expenses	345	960	2,160	3,840	6,000
General & Administrative	669	1,440	3,240	5,760	9,000
Total Opr Expenses	2,000	4,400	9,900	17,600	27,500
Net Income Before Taxes	233	2,160	4,860	8,640	13,500
Provision for Taxes	93	864	1,944	3,456	5,400
Net Income After Taxes	140	1,296	2,916	5,184	8,100
Dividend Distributions	70	648	1,458	2,592	4,050
Retained Earnings	70	648	1,458	2,592	4,050

Assumptions

% Cost of Goods Sold	18%
% Selling Expenses	12%
% General & Administrative	18%
% Tax Provision	40%
Dividends - of NATP	50%
Advertising - 1996	40%
Advertising - all other years	25%

Jul-96	Aug-96	Sep-96	Oct-96	Nov-96	Dec-96	FYE -96
271,251	1,735,989	1,747,574	1,736,317	1,761,974	1,790,876	1,788,843
191,862	211,049	320,154	349,288	381,073	427,951	2,430,022
0	38,372	42,210	64,031	69,857	76,215	603,054
1,500,000						1,500,000
1,691,862	249,421	362,364	413,319	450,930	504,166	4,533,076
1,963,113	1,985,410	2,109,938	2,149,636	2,212,905	2,295,042	6,321,919
39,245	43,169	47,486	72,035	78,590	85,741	448,141
95,931	105,524	160,077	174,644	190,536	213,976	986,174
10,000	10,000	10,000	10,000	10,000	10,000	80,000
28,779	31,657	48,023	52,393	57,161	64,193	345,128
43,169	47,486	72,035	78,590	85,741	96,289	669,490
10,000	0	0	0	0	0	30,000
0	0	36,000	0	0	36,000	108,000
—	—	—	—	—	—	78,000
227,124	237,836	373,621	387,662	422,028	506,199	2,744,933
1,735,989	1,747,574	1,736,317	1,761,974	1,790,876	1,788,843	3,576,986
239,828	263,811	400,192	436,609	476,341	534,939	2,730,770
43,169	47,486	72,035	78,590	85,741	96,289	497,497
191,862	211,049	320,154	349,287	381,073	427,951	2,250,950
9,593	10,552	16,008	17,464	19,054	21,398	109,231
38,372	42,210	64,031	69,857	76,215	85,590	

Plumbing Shop

BUSINESS PLAN

JAX PLUMBING

5101 Bell Street
Toledo, OH 44027

Jax Plumbing of Northern Ohio is a professional plumbing service franchise. The owners of this franchise attribute their growth and financial success to an established reputation for excellent customer service, state of the art equipment, and a unique networking opportunity. As a member of a worldwide franchise organization, Jax Plumbing receives support, training, marketing, and accounting services from other group franchisees.

- LETTER FROM THE PRESIDENT
- MISSION STATEMENTS
- ORGANIZATION
- PRODUCTS AND SERVICES
- MARKETING STRATEGY
- FINANCIAL DATA

**LETTER FROM
THE PRESIDENT**

Mr. Rooter Plumbing of Northern Ohio is located at 5101 Bell Street, Toledo, Ohio 44027. This location allows us to reach any customer in need of service in 30 minutes or less. The company, a franchise, was started in 1983. The principal owners are Harry Smith and Eric Lane.

Jax Plumbing of Northern Ohio is a professional plumbing company that has no equal in the areas we service. Our company believes the primary focus of the business should be on the customer. We fully realize that the customer is really our employer and that we need them much more than they need us. All field employees are trained how to keep customers for life. They realize the importance of our customers and the value of retaining them.

We are able to offer our customer the latest in technology. This includes high pressure water jetting equipment which enables grease problems to be a thing of the past for restaurants and other light commercial customers. We have line locators and cameras which allow our company to locate and view exactly where and what the problem is and solve the problem faster and less expensively than in the past. We also have the latest in bacteria products that have been approved in areas where most chemical products are now banned. All our products carry a private label, giving us a marketing edge over most of our competitors.

Of our fifteen technicians, seven have a state journeymans license and three others have earned a state masters license. The other five technicians are currently in state approved courses that will allow them to become licensed plumbers as well. This lends to our credibility in the communities we serve. We have always made education a priority, and we have a tuition reimbursement program available for all employees.

Jax Plumbing of Northern Ohio had sales of $2,838,465 with a net profit of 16.48% in 1995. In 1996 we expect to increase sales 19.29%, to $3,386,000 with net profit of about 19%. How this will be accomplished is explained in the marketing strategy and financial data sections of this business plan.

Jax Plumbing is part of the Disson Group, a worldwide franchise organization operating in more than 2,800 locations across 29 countries. In addition to Jax Plumbing, the Disson Group also franchises Sun Carpet Cleaning and Dying, Clean Aire HVAC, Electric Solver, Levitt Accounting, Business Services for Today, Universal Refinishing, Kitchen Giants, and beginning in June 1996, Appliance Solver. The Disson Group is a publically traded company. It appears on the NASDAQ market under the stock symbol, DSSN.

By being a member of the Disson Group we are able to facilitate growth. They support the franchises from the home office and through four national conferences throughout the nation. Larry Samson, our regional director, is located in Columbus, Ohio. We also use other Disson Group franchisees for networking of customer bases and use their Levitt Accounting franchise for our accounting needs.

**MISSION
STATEMENTS**

**Mission Statement
for the Disson
Group**

To be a world class company admired for the excellence that customers, franchisees and associates experience with The Disson Group.

**Mission Statement
for Jax Plumbing
Corporation**

The mission of Jax Plumbing is to be known as the world leader in the plumbing services industries. We are committed to the selection, development and support of individuals who are dedicated to excellence with their customers, their communities and themselves.

We are committed to provide our organization with superior service and continuous education as we recognize that growth only comes through applied knowledge.

The mission of Jax Plumbing services is to be known as Northern Ohio's leader in the plumbing, sewer and drain cleaning industry. We are committed to provide our customers with the highest quality of workmanship and service possible. We are dedicated to providing our personnel with continuous education, training, and support.

Mission Statement for Jax Plumbing of Northern Ohio

ORGANIZATION

Jax Plumbing of Northern Ohio consists of two (2) partners.

- Eric Lane (75%)
- Harry Smith (25%)

The organizational key employees are:

Eric Lane is president and has 22 years in the industry. He started his career with Plumbing World, a regional, privately owned company, in 1973 as a sewer and drain trainee. While working full time, he also attended Pinehurst College and earned an Associate Degree in Business Management in 1976 and a Bachelor of Business Administration in 1980. In 1983, Mr. Lane purchased the Jax Plumbing franchise for Pinehurst, Creston, and Benning Counties. In the 13 years since Mr. Lane started the franchise, sales have gone from $110,000 in 1983 to record sales of $2,838,465 with a net profit of 16.48% in 1995. As testimony to the success of the Jax Plumbing franchise, it was named Jax Plumbing Corporation Franchise of the Year both in 1994 and 1995. The franchise has won numeruous awards in the 13 years of its existence.

Harry Smith came to Jax Plumbing in 1981. He holds a Master Plumbers license in 2 states and his knowledge in this area is unsurpassed. In 1985, Mr. Smith bought 25% of the Jax Plumbing of Northern Ohio franchise. It was his desire to be a part of the expected growth and management team that Mr. Lane was putting together.

Ellen Lane, Eric's wife, is also a graduate of Pinehurst College with a Bachelor of Business Administration. She has been with the business since its inception. She has experience with two major corporations as an executive assistant and as an office manager.

Jax Plumbing of Northern Ohio will conduct daily operations by utilizing a four tier reporting structure. The organizational flow begins with the President, Eric Lane, who will oversee three upper level managers: the Operations Manager, Harry Smith, the Sales Manager, Eric Lane (as acting manager), and the Office Manager, Ellen Lane.

The Operations Manager performs all the duties essential to maintaining the daily operations at the facility. Two managers report directly to the Operations Manager, the Warehouse Manager and the Field Manager.

The Field Manager oversees the work crew, which consists of a Master Plumber and fifteen technicians. The technicians report directly to the Master Plumber.

As Eric Lane is performing the duties of both the President and the (acting) Sales Manager, the chain of command is nonexistent at this time.

The Office Manager coordinates all the office procedures, guidelines, and miscellaneous tasks of the front office with a staff of eight individuals. The Office Manager oversees two clerical personnel, three dispatchers, and three customer service representatives.

PRODUCTS AND SERVICES

Jax Plumbing of Northern Ohio does full service plumbing as well as sewer and drain cleaning. The company is able to do any plumbing related job, from clearing an obstruction in a kitchen sink to installing a high efficient water heater to digging and installing a new septic system. We are equipped with state of the art machines, high pressure water jetters, cameras and line locaters.

Jax Plumbing of Northern Ohio is unique to the plumbing industry in regard to it's ability to keep their customers. We offer homeowners a service agreement program that is unparalleled in Northern Ohio. The service agreement is sold for one, two or three year periods, or customers can purchase a lifetime guarantee. These agreements allow our customers to benefit from discounted pricing, a complete home inspection twice a year, quarterly specials on products and services, preferred treatment, and peace of mind. To date, we have over 4,500 homeowners that have purchased service agreements representing 9,300 years and 1,100 of these are lifetime guarantees. This is a customer base that will use our services an average of once every 11 months, spending an average of $258 each time. This represents a total service agreement base of $1,161,000 in sales in 1996. We also have preventative maintenance contracts with 138 commercial accounts that are expected to generate $118,000 in sales in 1996.

MARKETING STRATEGY

What we are selling the customer is our exceptional service. We give our customers the type of service that no other company is providing for them. Service that will never inconvenience them. We provide service 24 hours a day, 7 days a week, 365 days a year. We never charge extra for evening calls, weekends or holidays.

Currently our market is undergoing significant changes. The population in 1995 rose to an all time high of 418,000. In 1983, the population was 245,000. This growth, according to the Northern Ohio Chamber of Commerce, is expected to continue at 8% annually into the next century.

Our jobs are menu priced, meaning that all jobs have a predetermined price that the customer sees in a book before we start the job. They are aware of the charges before we start. This has resulted in 65% fewer complaints on pricing, since we began menu pricing in 1991. The menu pricing book has a standard price and a value price for all jobs. The value price is for service agreement customers only and is approximately 25% lower than the standard price. In 1995, 58% of our residential customers either had, or purchased, a service agreement. Service agreement customers will have no need to look for another plumbing company, as we offer the most competitive price. An additional benefit this system is that it is possible to actually lower our Yellow Page advertising costs if we chose to do so. It is less expensive to retain customers than it is to gain new customers.

According to latest National Association of Plumbing, Heating, Cooling Contractors, $30 will be spent on plumbing products and services by each person in this country. With 418,000 people in Pinehurst, Creston, and Benning Counties, $12,540,000 will be spent locally. We were able to achieve a 22.6% share of the market. In 1996, we expect to reach a 25% share of market, with sales of $3,386,000. This translates to a profit of 19%. By the year 2000, we expect our market share to reach 33%, with sales of $6,081,042. This will increase our profit to 22%.

This will be our 13th year in business in Northern Ohio and our name recognition is second to none. The Jax Plumbing national TV campaign is currently in the third year of a five year plan that will triple the amount of ads each year. During the 1995/1996 ad campaign, Jax Plumbing ads will air 153 times on all major networks. In addition, we will run 388 ads on local cable channels, including the local weather channel.

Even though we could cut Yellow Page advertising, due to the success of our service agreement sales, we chose to retain this advertising. We will remain in the premiere advertising position with a full page ad in our local directory, and with well-placed 1/2 page ads, in six other community directories.

We will continue direct marketing efforts in a number of different ways. Our technicians will place door hanger advertising materials, offering discounts on our products and services, to neighbors by all jobs they do. We will continue with a program that targets businesses, explaining what we have to offer. We will also continue with coupons mailers. Over the years we have been utilizing coupon services we have continually had a 2 to 3% return on mailings. In 1996, we will mail out 100,000 coupon mailers.

We use a wide variety of promotional literature on the job site, such as disposal, water heater, furnace, stack line stickers, door hangers, valve identification tags and other items that have our name and phone number on them.

We will continue to network our customer base with the five other Disson Group franchises in our area.

We will market to our customer to ensure we do not forget them, but more importantly, they do not forget us.

FINANCIAL DATA

Jax of Northern Ohio

1996 Budget

Amounts to be recorded in whole dollars - A = Actual, B = Budget, F = Forecast

Job Count Summary - 1996

# of Jobs	1995A	Jan	Feb	Mar	Apr	May	Jun	Jul	Aug	Sep	Oct	Nov	Dec
Sew/Drain	6388	550	550	550	600	600	575	575	575	575	600	625	625
Jetting	220	15	15	19	28	28	24	24	24	24	24	24	28
Plumbing	4288	400	400	425	450	450	425	425	425	425	499	500	500
Pumping	305	27	27	31	31	35	35	35	35	35	35	35	35
Video Scan	47	5	5	6	7	7	6	6	6	6	6	6	7
Misc	61	3	3	4	4	5	5	5	5	5	5	5	5
TOTAL	11309	1000	1000	1035	1120	1125	1070	1070	1070	1070	1169	1195	1200
Con Prod	5000	500	500	518	660	662	535	535	535	535	584	597	600
Serv Agr	2439	210	210	220	225	225	230	230	230	230	250	255	260

%VAR 1996B

# of Jobs	1996B	VS1995A	1997F	1998F	1999F	2000F
Sew\Drain	7000	9.58%	7500	8100	8750	9450
Jetting	277	25.91%	350	425	525	725
Plumbing	5324	24.16%	6400	7500	8500	10000
Pumping	396	29.84%	485	575	665	750
Video Scan	73	55.32%	100	125	150	175
Misc	54	-11.48%	65	75	85	100
TOTAL	13124	16.05%	14900	16800	18675	21200
Con Prod	6761	35.22%	7350	8400	9438	10600
Serv Agr	2775	13.78%	3000	3100	3200	3300

Sales Summary - 1996

Sales	1995A	Jan	Feb	Mar	Apr	May	Jun	Jul	Aug	Sep	Oct	Nov	Dec
Sew/Drain	1117900	96250	96250	96250	105000	105000	100625	100625	100625	101200	105000	109375	109375
Jetting	93720	6450	6450	8170	12040	12040	10320	10320	10320	10320	10320	10320	12040
Plumb Lab	886830	84000	84000	89250	94500	94500	89250	89250	89250	89250	104790	105000	105000
Plumb Mat	305234	28000	28000	29750	31500	31500	29750	29750	29750	29750	34930	35000	35000
Pumping	42890	3915	3915	4495	4495	5075	5075	5075	5075	5075	5075	5075	5075
Con Prod	195000	20000	20000	20700	22400	22500	21400	21400	21400	21400	23380	23900	24000

	1995A	Jan	Feb	Mar	Apr	May	Jun	Jul	Aug	Sep	Oct	Nov	Dec
Video Scan	20022	2150	2150	2580	3010	3010	2580	2580	2580	2580	2580	2580	3010
Misc	8578	435	435	580	580	725	725	725	725	725	725	725	725
Serv Agr	168291	14490	14490	15180	15525	15525	15870	15870	15870	15870	17250	17595	17940
TOTAL	2838465	255690	255690	266955	289050	289875	275595	275595	275595	276170	304050	309570	312165

%VAR
1996B

Sales	1996B	VS1995A	1997F	1998F	1999F	2000F
Sew\Drain	1225575	9.63%	1380000	1498500	1645000	1795500
Jetting	119110	27.09%	152250	187000	236250	326250
Plumb Lab	1118040	26.07%	1344000	1664322	2000500	2347500
Plumb Mat	372680	22.10%	442206	528750	631646	750967
Pumping	57420	33.88%	72750	86825	102410	116250
Con Prod	262480	34.61%	298000	336000	373500	424000
Video Scan	31390	56.78%	43500	54750	66000	77875
Misc	7830	-8.72%	9490	11025	12665	15000
Serv Agr	191475	13.78%	207000	213900	220800	22770
TOTAL	3386000	19.29%	3949196	4581072	5288771	6081042

# of Employees	1995A	Jan	Feb	Mar	Apr	May	Jun	Jul	Aug	Sep	Oct	Nov	Dec
Techs	15	15	15	15	15	16	16	16	16	17	17	17	17
Office	8	8	8	8	8	9	9	9	9	9	9	9	9
Mgmt	6	6	6	6	6	6	6	6	6	6	6	6	6
TOTAL	29	29	29	29	29	31	31	31	31	32	32	32	32

	1997F	1998F	1999F	2000F
Techs	19	21	23	26
Office	10	11	12	13
Mgmt	6	7	7	7
TOTAL	35	39	42	46

Average Price/Job	1995A	1996B	1997F	1998F	1999F	2000F
Sew/Drain	175.00	175.08	184.00	185.00	188.00	190.00
Jetting	426.00	430.00	435.00	440.00	450.00	450.00
Plumbing	278.00	280.00	279.09	292.41	309.66	309.85
Pumping	140.62	145.00	150.00	151.00	154.00	155.00
Video Scan	426.00	430.00	435.00	438.00	440.00	445.00
Con Prod	17.24	20.00	20.00	20.00	20.00	20.00
Misc	140.62	145.00	146.00	147.00	149.00	150.00
Serv Agr	14.88	14.59	13.89	12.73	11.82	10.74
TOTAL	250.99	258.00	265.05	272.68	283.20	286.84

Average Per Year	1995A	1996A	1997B	1998F	1999F	2000F
Per Tech Jobs	754	772	784	800	812	815
Per Tech Sales	189231	199176	207852	218146	229947	233886
Per Office Jobs	1414	1458	1490	1527	1556	1631
Per Office Sales	354808	376222	394920	416461	440731	467772
Per Mgmt Jobs	1885	2187	2483	2400	2668	3029
Mgmt Sales	473078	564333	658199	654439	755539	868720
Total Jobs	390	410	426	431	445	461
Total Sales	97878	105813	112834	117463	125923	132197

Date Prepared: Jan. 14, 1996 Year End 1995

Sales	$	%
Sewer and Drain	1117900	39.38%
Jet Work	93720	3.30%
Plumbing Labor	886830	31.24%
Plumbing Materials	305234	10.75%
Gre/Sep Pumping	42890	1.51%
Consumer Products	118560	4.18%
Video Scan	20022	0.71%
Bacteria Systems	76440	2.69%
Miscellaneous	8578	0.30%
Service Agreements	168291	5.93%
Gross Sales	2838465	100%
(minus) Cost of Materials	102300	3.60%
(minus) Variable Costs	1045123	38.41%
(minus) Per/Ren/Subs	18655	0.66%
Gross Profit	1672387	57.33%
(minus) Fixed Costs	1159513	40.85%
Net Profit	512874	16.48%

Profit & Loss Statement

Variable Costs	$	%
Franchise Fees	85154	3.00%
Advertising Fees	56769	2.00%
Payroll - Technicians	667607	23.52%
Taxes - Federal	85154	3.00%
Taxes - State	0	0.00%
Taxes - Local	0	0.00%
Taxes - FICA	46267	1.63%
Taxes - Unemploy	12205	0.43%
Insurance - Work Comp	45132	1.59%
Fuel	91966	3.24%
Miscellaneous	0	0.00%
Total Variable Costs	1045123	38.41%

Variable Costs and Percentages

Fixed Costs	$	%
Salaries-Owner	127731	4.50%
Salaries-Office	175417	6.18%
Employee Benefits	1135	0.04%
Taxes - Federal	12773	0.45%
Taxes - State	0	0.00%
Taxes - Local	0	0.00%
Taxes - FICA	16179	0.57%
Taxes - Unemploy	3122	0.11%
Taxes-Property	0	0.00%
Utilities	14476	0.51%
Rent/Mortgage	14760	0.52%
Bad Debt	1703	0.06%
Bank Charges	24978	0.88%
Loan Interest	10786	0.38%

Fixed Costs and Percentages

Credit Card Fees	1419	0.05%
Legal/Accounting	38035	1.34%
Depreciation	91115	3.21%
Auto/Truck/Lease	70962	2.50%
Repair/Maint-Vehicle	44280	1.56%
Repair/Maint-Equip	26965	0.95%
Repair/Maint-Property	2838	0.10%
Equipment Rental	29520	1.04%
Licenses	16463	0.58%
Insurance - Health	11922	0.42%
Insurance - Liability	19018	0.67%
Insurance - Property	17315	0.61%
Insurance - Vehicle	17315	0.61%
Insurance - Work Comp	3690	0.13%
Advert - Yellow Page	166902	5.88%
Advert - General	30939	1.09%
Office Supplies	22992	0.81%
Postage	6245	0.22%
Outside Services	1703	0.06%
Educational	5109	0.18%
Uniforms	9935	0.35%
Telephone-Office	70678	2.49%
Telephone-Cellular	5109	0.18%
Pagers/Radios	7096	0.25%
Travel/Entertainment	40306	1.42%
Miscellaneous	7096	0.25%
Refunds	-568	-0.02%
Discounts/Coupons	-7948	-0.28%
Total Fixed Costs	1159513	40.85%

Balance Sheet

Date Prepared: Jan. 14, 1996 Year: Year End 1995

Assets

Cash on Hand	200
Cash in Bank	-5914
Accounts Receivable	58518
Inventory	38692
Total Current Assets	$91496
Equipment/Furniture	22752
Accumulated Depreciation	-4993
Vehicles	152680
Accumulated Depreciation	-49566
Leasehold Improvements	19877
Accumulated Depreciation	-499
Total Fixed Assets	140251
Goodwill	285000
Accumulated Amortization	-28665
Franchise Fee	141935
Accumulated Amortization	-12465
Organization Expense	19334
Accumulated Amortization	-2453
Total Long-Term Assets	$402686
Total Assets	$634433

Liabilities

Sales Tax	495
Federal Withholding - FICA	163987
Accounts Payable	188350
Total Current Liabilities	**$352832**
Note Payable - Bank	98799
Note Payable - Jim Brown	21976
Note Payable - John David	8314
Total Long-Term Liabilities	129089
Total Liabilities	**$481921**

Capital

Common Stock	158000
Returned Earnings Current	-5488
Total Capital	152512
Total Liabilities & Capital	**$634433**

Refrigerant Recovery

BUSINESS PLAN

ROAD RUNNER REFRIGERANT
RECOVERY SYSTEM

757 N. 22nd Dr.
Tucson, AZ 85028

Road Runner is an ecological manufacturing firm dedicated to providing refrigerant recovery systems to enterprises specializing in refrigeration. Refrigerant recovery systems are designed to retain refrigerants from refrigeration systems to avoid its illegal and dangerous release into the atmosphere.

- •MISSION STATEMENT

- •INDUSTRY BACKGROUND

- •PRODUCT OFFERING

- •MARKETING PLAN

- •OPERATIONS

- •MANAGEMENT TEAM

- •FINANCIAL PLAN

- •RISK AND CONTINGENCY

- •SUMMARY

**MISSION
STATEMENT**

ROAD RUNNER. We are an environmental manufacturing firm committed to providing product, service, and support of the highest quality. We will provide refrigerant recovery systems to the refrigeration industry, currently regulated by government law. Our product, designed for refrigeration service technicians, will be distributed throughout the entire United States. By creating a business environment built upon integrity, honesty, and ambition, ROAD RUNNER will help to revitalize the manufacturing industry and return it to the infrastructure of America. As we seek future challenges, we will continually embrace the passion of goodwill for our employees, our customers, our environment and our country.

Core Philosophies

• Ensure our continuing existence by satisfying the customer.

• Strive to manufacture products and provide service that maximizes value and minimizes cost.

• Create a corporate culture that emphasizes teamwork, integrity, honesty, and leadership.

**INDUSTRY
BACKGROUND**

Technology has changed our lives in many ways. It has enhanced nearly every activity that we undertake. Although technology has played a tremendous role in making our lives better, more efficient, and easier, it has played a role in endangering the safety of our earth. One such technology is refrigeration. Refrigeration uses gasses (such as freon) which contain chloroflourocarbons (CFCs) and hydrochloroflourocarbons (HCFCs). CFCs and HCFCs have been determined to deplete the ozone layer of our atmosphere, creating a large problem for our environment. In response to this, the United States government passed the Clean Air Act, regulating the handling and use of refrigerants.

On July 1, 1992, the United States Government and the Environmental Protection Agency established the Clean Air Act. Section 608 of the Act contains the following prohibition.

"Effective July 1, 1992, it shall be unlawful for any person, in the course of maintaining, servicing, and repairing, or disposing of any appliance or industrial process refrigerant, to knowingly vent or otherwise knowingly release or dispose of any class I or class II substance used as a refrigerant in such appliance (or industrial process refrigeration) in a manner which permits such substance to enter the environment. De minimis releases associated with good faith attempts to recapture and recycle or safely dispose of any such substance shall not be subject to the prohibition set forth."

The penalty for those technicians caught venting refrigerant into the atmosphere is as follows:

"With respect to enforcement, civil penalties of not more than $25,000 per day for each violation may be assessed. Criminal penalties for persons knowingly violating (after having been notified by the Administrator) a requirement or prohibition shall, upon conviction, be punished by a fine pursuant to Title 18 of the United States Code or by imprisonment not to exceed five years, or both."

This new law, along with the increasing pressure to uphold environmental standards, has created a dynamic market for refrigerant recovery systems. As the rules and regulations took effect in July of 1992, orders for refrigerant recovery systems greatly outnumbered available supply. Service technicians purchased approximately 132,000 recovery systems (research estimates that 18-20% of service technicians purchased units). This accounts for approximately $206 million in sales. However, many service technicians attempted to comply with the law, but could not do so.

Manufacturers granted these individuals "rain checks" since they could not meet the demand. At the same time, a large percentage of technicians felt reluctant to purchase a system.

To further compound the arduous start for this industry, service technicians were not satisfied with the refrigerant recovery systems on the market. These systems: operated slowly due to inferior compressors, could not operate efficiently during extreme summer temperatures, and were too heavy. (These problems are explained further in the Product Offering.) Furthermore, manufacturers failed to provide adequate service and attention to the problems that occurred in the field.

In addition to the Clean Air Act and the penalty, two additional forces will propel the sales and popularity of refrigerant recovery systems. The Clean Air Act served as the initial catalyst by creating immense public interest and publicity. However, the economic aspects of this situation will begin to outweigh the regulatory. First, since the inception of the Clean Air Act, prices of all varieties of refrigerant (R12, R22, R500, R502, R114, R60/40) have increased approximately 130% (as of March 1993), due to heavy government taxes. Taxes are currently $1.67/lb., and over the next six years will increase to $4.90/lb. Furthermore, refrigeration wholesalers are forecasting an increase in the manufacturers' price, which drive the retail prices even higher.

Economic Incentives Propel Industry

Second, environmentally safe refrigerant currently costs $17/lb. and is referred to in the industry as "liquid gold." At this exorbitant cost, twice the amount of non-environmental refrigerant technicians have a financial incentive to save as much of this "liquid gold" as possible. Thus, this creates an on-going market for the refrigerant recovery industry into the 21st century.

In order to understand the logic behind ROAD RUNNER's design strategy, it is essential to understand the process of capturing refrigerants. Before an air-conditioning system can be serviced, the refrigerant inside the system must be removed. Before the Clean Air Act passed, service technicians would generally detach a hose and allow the refrigerant to release into the atmosphere. As explained, current refrigerants contain chloroflourocarbons (CFCs) and hydrochloroflourocarbons (HCFCs). These refrigerants can no longer by legally vented into the atmosphere. ROAD RUNNER assures rapid recovery of all types of refrigerants (in both liquid and gaseous states) from refrigeration systems containing refrigerant (refrigerators, walk-in coolers, air conditioners, automobiles, etc.).

The Refrigerant Recovery Process

Liquid Recovery

Liquid recovery occurs faster than any other type of refrigerant recovery possible. During this process, liquid refrigerant gets extracted from the air conditioning unit, and moves directly into the storage tank. It does not pass through the recovery unit, as compressors are only designed to pump vapor. The ROAD RUNNER will recover liquid refrigerant by utilizing a push-pull method. A vacuum is drawn on the storage tank to assist the liquid flow from the higher pressure area of the A/C unit into the low pressure area established in the storage tank. After the liquid refrigerant has been recovered, vapor recovery can commence.

Vapor Recovery

During vapor recovery, an additional hose must be attached between the storage tank and the recovery unit. Vapor is drawn from the A/C unit into the recovery system. It passes through the compressor to the condenser, where cooling occurs. Once cooled to a sufficient temperature, the gas turns to liquid and proceeds into the storage tank. Refrigerant recovery systems operate on a temperature pressure relationship. A lower temperature facilitates a lower pressure, therefore allowing for faster and more efficient operation.

PRODUCT OFFERING

Technicians faced many design and performance problems with the recovery systems they purchased to fulfill the requirements of the Clean Air Act. Therefore, ROAD RUNNER faced a great opportunity to design a recovery system that would completely fulfill the needs of the refrigeration service technicians. ROAD RUNNER's product strategy centers around a second mover position and the ability to design a recovery system based upon the difficulties technicians encountered with competitors' systems.

ROAD RUNNER - Designing Archetype 2000

ROAD RUNNER's triple benefit positioning strategy (detailed explanation in the Marketing section) centers around the results of primary market research. This research indicated that the service technicians have a great need for a recovery unit with powerful and durable compression, rapid operation, and light weight. Taking this into consideration, the design engineer carefully chose components and system design in an effort to completely satisfy the needs of the service technician. Technicians faced big problems when it came to refrigerant recovery, but ROAD RUNNER solves them all.

Problems faced by technicians
• Damage to compressors caused by liquid
• Inadequate compressor strength
• Poor recovery rate in extreme temperatures
• Excessive weight for portable use

ROAD RUNNER provides solutions

• ROAD RUNNER contains a rotary compressor.

The first of several complaints focused on the situation of accidentally pulling liquid into the compressor. If liquid gets pulled into the compression chamber of a reciprocating piston compressor (similar to the piston and chamber in an automobile engine), the compressor will lock up and render the system useless. If the service technician works haphazardly, this can easily happen. Rotary compressors are much more durable and less vulnerable to damage if liquid is encountered.

• ROAD RUNNER utilizes a high capacity, one (1) horsepower compressor.

Secondly, service technicians complained that the recovery systems did not work quickly enough. What should have taken them minutes took several hours to capture the refrigerant from an A/C unit. This compressor nearly doubles the power of most competitors.

• ROAD RUNNER contains a tank cool down system.

Refrigerant recovery systems operate based on a direct temperature/pressure relationship. In order for a recovery system to work quickly and efficiently, it is crucial to minimize both temperature and pressure. Many of the current systems are unable to do this, thus slowing the refrigerant recovery process greatly. This became such a big problem during the summer of 1992, that service technicians were forced to submerge the refrigerant storage tank in ice in order to keep the temperature to a minimum. ROAD RUNNER's oversized condenser (300 cfm, three times the cooling capacity of competitors) coupled with a tank cool down system will enable the service technicians to recover refrigerants quickly and efficiently.

• ROAD RUNNER weighs only 41 lbs. and comes complete with a shoulder harness.

Finally, service technicians found that recovery systems weighed too much for portable use. Most commercial systems with the same recovery capabilities as ROAD RUNNER range from 60-100 lbs. Imagine climbing up a ladder onto a roof carrying a 100 pound machine. It is nearly impossible unless one has unbelievable balance and incredible strength. Technicians said they actually had to use pulley systems and ropes to bring their refrigerant recovery systems onto the roof!

ROAD RUNNER Archetype 2000 includes:

- ROAD RUNNER refrigerant recovery system
- Connection hoses (3)
- Float valve (controls automatic shut-off function)
- Inlet vapor filter (O52 dryer, liquid filter)
- ROAD RUNNER utility bag (to carry hoses and filter), shoulder harness, and 2 ROAD RUNNER baseball caps

Once Archetype 2000 becomes established in the marketplace, Archetype 250 will be introduced. This refrigerant recovery system will have orientation toward the more price-conscious service technician. Initial market research indicates that a unit with a smaller compressor and condenser and a lower price will serve the needs of this portion of the refrigeration industry much more adequately.

Additionally, ROAD RUNNER Archetype 3000 is currently under development. This system will have dual uses. It will serve as a recovery system (just like Archetype 2000) and a refrigerant recycler. Archetype 3000 will re-charge and clean old refrigerant on location. This will save the service technician time and the consumer money.

ROAD RUNNER Builds for the Future

MARKETING PLAN

Goals and Objectives

¨ *Create product awareness and a positive reputation for ROAD RUNNER Archetype 2000, ensuring a successful market introduction for future ROAD RUNNER products.*

- Establish feedback channels that will allow ROAD RUNNER to determine purchaser satisfaction and opinions.

- Use creative advertising (baseball caps, T-shirts, bumper stickers)

¨ *Utilize promotional activities to persuade our customers (wholesalers) to purchase ROAD RUNNER. Determine market demand for further ROAD RUNNER products.*

- Institute a three phase promotional strategy consisting of sales promotion, education, and advertising.

- Survey the market and determine potential demand for a smaller, less expensive recovery system, and a refrigerant recycling system.

- Provide demonstration and educational seminars with wholesalers and technicians.

ROAD RUNNER's marketing strategy is based upon in-depth interviews, surveys and information provided by the company's sales representatives. This provided ROAD RUNNER with concise knowledge of the refrigeration industry. Each of these sources was extremely helpful as the information was used as validation for the product design and concept. This continual validation prompted ROAD RUNNER to switch from prototype production to full scale operations late in the winter of 1992.

Experts Provide Information

The initial phase of our research consisted of a series of ten (10) in-depth interviews with wholesalers and service technicians. As the first phase of the research effort, ROAD RUNNER gathered information on trends in the industry, current manufacturers of refrigerant recovery systems, and consumer product preference. Both the wholesalers and technicians concurred that recovery systems on the market at that time were of poor quality. Another frequent complaint centered around the lack of service and assistance provided by the manufacturers.

Additionally, wholesalers indicated that many technicians planned on postponing a recovery system purchase until the Environmental Protection Agency began stringent enforcement of the law, and the quality standards of the recovery systems increased to acceptable levels. The information from these interviews served as the foundation for the marketing strategy and product development for ROAD RUNNER. Although the government drives the demand for refrigerant recovery systems, the consumer must also demand the unit in order to ensure product sales and success. The service technician must purchase a recovery system, but has several product options. Hence, by incorporating several useful product features, service technicians will choose the ROAD RUNNER over existing competitors.

Service Technician Survey Shows Viability

A survey of 114 residential and commercial air conditioning service technicians took place. The results of this survey provided an abundance of information that served as an integral tool in the product design of the ROAD RUNNER. This information helped to determine the wants and needs of service technicians in refrigerant recovery. Additionally, the survey provided an outlook on industry market share and extent of demand within the recovery industry.

Key Competitors and Market Share

The survey of 114 technicians also provided ROAD RUNNER with and estimate of the market share each of our competitors has captured. These numbers were validated at the International Refrigeration Industry Trade Show (Evanston, IL) in June 1994. Although minor discrepancies occurred as to the exact percentage captured by each competitor, ROAD RUNNER survey results were fairly accurate. The discrepancies are due mainly as a result of fluctuating sales intensity of different refrigerant recovery systems in different regions of the country.

ROAD RUNNER Targets Enormous Market

ROAD RUNNER's overall target market focuses on residential and commercial air conditioning service technicians governed by the Clean Air Act. More specifically, ROAD RUNNER targets residential and commercial technicians in need of a portable recovery system. Secondary research estimates this target to be $724,000,000. Within this target, ROAD RUNNER directs its efforts at the informed purchaser. This includes technicians who have learned about refrigerant recovery systems through trade shows, product literature, personal use, and the "grapevine." The largest portion of this segment, seventy percent, consists of technicians who have not purchased a refrigerant recovery system. The smaller portion of this segment, ten percent (10%), centers around technicians who purchased an inferior refrigerant recovery system that malfunctioned in the field. Victims of product failure, these individuals know exactly what features they require in a recovery system for optimal field performance. The remaining twenty percent (20%) of the informed segment is composed of technicians who purchased a competitor's system and technicians who will avoid the requirements of the Clean Air Act.

ROAD RUNNER's target market and segmentation scheme were selected based on several factors. The impact of the Clean Air Act focuses its attention at commercial and residential technicians. Before the legislation, the presence of refrigerant recovery systems in the field appeared scarce. According to sources within the industry (trade magazines, wholesalers, and manufacturers) it is estimated that approximately 132,311 registered refrigeration service contractors operate in the United States. Each of these individuals employs between 3-7 service technicians, on average. This presents ROAD RUNNER with an opportunity to initially sell 661,500 units to our specific target market. Additional sales opportunities will be available in the replacement market (exact numbers will depend on product breakdown and obsolescence).

The ROAD RUNNER will be sold to service technicians through refrigeration supply wholesalers. Wholesalers, as an industry standard, act as intermediaries between manufacturers and technicians. ROAD RUNNER will position itself as the highest quality and performance system in the light-weight niche of the market. ROAD RUNNER's positioning strategy also places great emphasis on a comprehensive service and support program that will solidify the ROAD RUNNER as the premiere refrigerant recovery system.

ROAD RUNNER's triple benefit positioning strategy centers around the results of market research. This research indicated that service technicians need a recovery unit with powerful and durable compression, rapid operation, and light weight. Taking this into consideration, the components and system design were carefully chosen and assembled in an effort to satisfy the needs of the service technician.

There are thirteen thousand (13,000) wholesaler/distributor (w/d) outlets in the United States which sell a variety of refrigeration related products in their stores. The geographic distribution area for ROAD RUNNER will encompass the entire United States. The ROAD RUNNER is designed to fit the demanding needs of the Southwest technician who will operate the machine in extreme temperatures. Because of this durable design structure, the ROAD RUNNER will, without question, serve technicians in other parts of the country with cooler climates.

The composition of the w/d portion of the refrigeration industry consists of four tiers:

National Wholesalers - This tier is composed of large companies who have outlet stores located all around the country. Because they have such immense size they enjoy economy of scale advantage. They account for over sixty percent (60%) of w/d sales. A few major players on this level include: Palmetto Air (270 stores), Rhinestone Supply, Ashby, and Burton.

Regional Wholesalers - These businesses typically consist of five (5) to fifteen (15) stores in two or three different states within the same geographic region. This portion of the industry has fifteen percent (15%) to twenty percent (20%) of the sales. Companies such as Frozen Stock Distributors (FSD), Williams Engineering and Nevada Refrigeration Company are regional wholesalers that operate in the Southwest.

Statewide - This tier is composed of companies that operate two (2) to five (5) stores within the same state. Wholesalers such as this account for eight percent (8%) to thirteen percent (13%) of sales. Faulkner Refrigeration Supply, McAdoo, and Moultrie's act as examples of w/ds who operate on the third tier.

Sole Proprietorships - Sole Proprietorships account for approximately four percent (4%) to eight percent (8%) of industry sales. Often times they find it difficult to compete as their larger competitors dominate the market and have more bargaining power with suppliers. Consequently they can obtain inventory at a lower cost.

Because of the highly concentrated (national w/d) make-up of the w/d structure, ROAD RUNNER's distribution strategy will place an emphasis on national and regional wholesalers. The majority of these companies have an established purchasing department that makes the inventory selection for all of its stores. A sale to the purchasing team will directly translate into a sale to each of the company stores nationwide. It has been determined that over seventy-five percent (75%) of ROAD RUNNER's recovery system sales will involve national and regional w/ds.

**ROAD RUNNER:
The High Quality
System**

**ROAD RUNNER
Utilizes National
Distribution Strategy**

ROAD RUNNER Attracts Experienced Sales Reps

The Production Workers National Association (PWNA) will represent ROAD RUNNER. John Caleb, Vice President of Marketing, selected sales agents who are specialized in the air conditioning industry and have established rapport with key members in distribution channels. Because of this, ROAD RUNNER will gain tremendous exposure. The sales representatives were selected on a basis of:

- Knowledge of the refrigerant recovery industry
- Number of products currently represented
- Past sales record
- Access to distribution channels

Currently ROAD RUNNER has twenty (20) sales representatives working for the company. These individuals are strategically placed in specific geographic regions across the entire United States. PWNA representatives will receive seven percent (7%) commission of ROAD RUNNER sales. These sales representatives handle a large portion of promotion, as they provide direct contact to the wholesalers. Furthermore, they will educate and attract the wholesalers who will, in turn, pass information on to service technicians. This develops an efficient "push through" marketing and promotion strategy for ROAD RUNNER.

Promotion Strategy Creates Awareness

The promotion strategy for ROAD RUNNER has two main goals. The first goal focuses on building consumer awareness for the ROAD RUNNER Archetype 2000. The second orients itself on creating extensive awareness and recognition for the company throughout the industry.

ROAD RUNNER's promotional strategy utilizes three phases: personal selling, product emonstrations, and advertisements.

The first phase of our promotional strategy centers around personal selling. Our sales representatives will make an appointment to meet with the wholesaler's purchasing agent. The first sales call lasts approximately an hour and includes a product demonstration. The second phase, advertising, will take the form of brochures, point-of-sale advertisements and wholesaler initiated mailers to technicians. All promotional activities will be implemented and monitored by John Caleb, Vice-President of Marketing. The third phase, product demonstrations and sales seminars, occurs after the wholesaler has purchased the ROAD RUNNER. At this point, ROAD RUNNER's service and support team will hold all-day demonstrations of the system in the wholesaler's showroom. The service and support team will consist of Real Manufacturing staff, along with the sales representative responsible for the sale. The support team will teach the wholesaler's sales staff how to use and sell the ROAD RUNNER. This adds value, as ROAD RUNNER's competitors do not offer this service.

Promotional Budget (Year 1)

Advertising		
	Brochures (36,000 at .35 per)	$12,600
	Point of Sale Displays (1200 at $1 per)	1,200
	ROAD RUNNER Baseball Caps (4800 at $1.50 per)	7,200
	Trade Magazine	2,000
Demonstrations		
	140 at $60 (set-up cost) per	8,400
	Travel expenses	19,000
Trade Shows		
	2 shows at $2000 per	4,000
TOTAL EXPENSES (year 1)		**$54,400**

Goals and Objectives

¨ *Produce and sell the premier refrigerant recovery system at a competitive price.*

- Determine the operational and design problems with recovery systems currently on the market and design a unit based on suggestions and input from service technicians and wholesalers/distributors.

- Utilize a forty six (46) point quality control system during manufacturing which will rigorously test each completed unit and ensure the highest quality and performance.

¨ *Establish an open channel of feedback between customers and the company.*

- Establish a customer "hot-line" to provide on-the-spot assistance and information.

- Send out follow-up questionnaires and conduct in-depth interviews with ROAD RUNNER users.

¨ *Keep employees enthusiastic, productive, and informed.*

- Provide job enrichment and job enlargement programs for employees (including cross-training, rotation, shift leadership, and educational seminars).

- Encourage a healthy social climate in the workplace (social outings, contests, theme days).

ROAD RUNNER's operations strategy is designed to efficiently manufacture the premier refrigerant recovery system. This will be achieved through the use of quality control checklists, time motion studies, and employee training. Furthermore, an ongoing research and development department along with established relations with suppliers, will enable ROAD RUNNER to stay at the forefront of its industry.

Efficient and High Quality Production

The operations of ROAD RUNNER will initially take place at the Real Manufacturing Co. plant in Phoenix, Arizona. This facility encompasses 12,000 square feet and has ample resources available for ROAD RUNNER's use. As sales and the distribution network grow, production of the ROAD RUNNER will expand to RMC's plant in Dallas, Texas (15,000 square feet). This facility will provide ROAD RUNNER extra manufacturing space and will serve as distribution center to the Midwest and east coast.

The assembly process includes eleven (11) different production stations. Through time motion studies, data pertaining to time-per-station was gathered and calculated. This resulted in an a highly efficient and organized operation flow. Moreover, ROAD RUNNER employees work as a team and are trained to participate in all phases of the manufacturing process. Through job enrichment and job enlargement practices, the cohesiveness and flexibility of the team have resulted in rapid and high quality production. Through the following manufacturing analysis, maximum production with current resources has been estimated at 13,360 units per year.

Assumptions:
- Two 7.5 hour shifts per day (8.5 hour shift less .5 hour lunch and two 15 minute breaks)
- 14 line employees per shift
- 37.5 hours per week per employee (7.5 hours x 5 days)
- 1050 production hours per week (2 shifts x 14 employees x 7.5 hours x 5 days)
- 4 hours to complete each unit
- 1050 production-hours/4 hours per unit = 262 per week
- 262 per week x 51 manufacturing weeks = 13,360 units/year

To ensure a defect free product, ROAD RUNNER utilizes a forty six (46) point quality control checklist. This checklist concentrates on such areas as structural integrity, pressure tests, electrical tests and packaging requirements. Through the first six months of production this system has ensured a virtually defect free product (less than 1%).

R&D Provides Quality Products

All product design and technical writing are completed by ROAD RUNNER's design engineer, Antoine Walker. The R&D period for the ROAD RUNNER elapsed over a four month period, by which ample in-depth research of all aspects of refrigerant recovery systems and the refrigeration industry took place. A thorough investigation of technician's needs, competitor's systems, and the components that comprise the ROAD RUNNER, has resulted in a recovery system that surpasses all others in quality and performance.

Perhaps the most noteworthy portion of the research and development of the ROAD RUNNER occurred upon the system's designing, building, and implementation. Through follow up interviews and customer surveys, an evaluation of the ROAD RUNNER's performance in the field took place. This provided the engineer with technician's opinions and actual field data, which have proven extremely valuable in making minor adjustments and in the design phase for future products.

ROAD RUNNER Carefully Selects Suppliers

To maintain control over cost and schedule, ROAD RUNNER will manage the purchasing of components, scheduling, and inventory control. Special order arrangements were negotiated with suppliers, allow ROAD RUNNER the advantage of purchasing assembly parts and components within one month of production. This will assist ROAD RUNNER in managing cash flow as well as storage concerns. Inventory will be purchased from a variety of suppliers. The suppliers were chosen based on a criterion composed of: quality, shipment flexibility, parts availability, location, payment terms, and price. *Choosing suppliers became a critical function of our initial operations as ROAD RUNNER views its suppliers as an integral part of the team.*

Only Minimal Capital Equipment Required

Although the assembly and production of the ROAD RUNNER will occur in-house, the capital equipment requirements are not immense. The manufacturing procedure is not "high-tech" since its composition consists mainly of a series of labor intensive tasks including: brazing, soldering, and fastening. As sales grow, further equipment investment will take place. A list of necessary capital equipment is provided below:

Capital Equipment

Tube bending machine ($1000/shape, 10 shapes)	$10,000
Welding equipment ($300/set, 3 sets)	900
Tube cutting machine	170
Misc. tools (sockets, screw drivers, wrenches, etc.)	700
Misc. equipment (safety gear, solders, packaging equip.)	520
Wire cutting machine	400
Lugging machine (Leased month-to-month, $195 per month)	
Electronic test equipment	2000
Total *	**$15,440**

*Total does not include leased machinery.
    Listed equipment is sufficient to produce 13,360 units

" Attract individuals who are experienced and will be capable of interacting with the other key personnel.

- Implement a well-rounded interviewing process including both personal and group interviews.

- Hire only those individuals the entire ROAD RUNNER team feels they can work with.

" Obtain skilled individuals at all levels of the organization.

- Hire personnel who understand organizational relationships.

- Hire personnel who have skills necessary to make informed decisions.

The management team of ROAD RUNNER is healthy, energetic, and very excited about the company. The strength of ROAD RUNNER's management team is derived from the blend of much needed experience and youthful ideas. Companies do not become profitable without successful employees. ROAD RUNNER is no different.

Goals and Objectives

Mr. Joseph Purdue currently serves as President and Chief Executive Officer of Real Manufacturing Company, Inc. He has held this position since he founded the company in 1987. As president and CEO, Mr. Purdue is responsible for strategic and financial planning. Furthermore, he oversees the personnel responsible for operating both of the company's divisions.

Previous to his current position, Mr. Purdue served as Executive Vice President of U.S. Chair Company, Inc. In his capacity as Vice President, he was directly responsible for returning his company to profitability one year after Chapter 11 proceedings. Mr. J. Purdue gained his twenty five years (25) of manufacturing background while being employed as Director of Materials with Computerized Supplies Inc.

Mr. Roger Burton was born in Denver, Colorado in 1971. He has been a resident of Arizona for the past twelve (12) years, having lived in Tucson and Phoenix. He is currently a senior at Arizona State University, pursuing dual degrees in Entrepreneurship and Accounting. Mr. Burton will be the Vice President of Operations for Road Runner. This position entails management of daily operations and research and development. Additionally, Mr. Burton will be responsible for the accounting function of ROAD RUNNER's operation. Mr. R. Burton is qualified for these responsibilities as he played a crucial role in the operations of a dry-cleaning franchise. Through this experience, Mr.Burton honed his skills in such areas as personnel management, operations management, customer satisfaction and franchise sales. Most importantly however, Mr. Burton has developed a great understanding of the intangibles necessary to operate a business.

Mr. Gary Purdue was born in San Francisco, California, in 1971. He has lived throughout the United States including Colorado, Pennsylvania, and Arizona. He is currently a senior at Arizona State University, pursuing dual degrees in Entrepreneurship and Finance.

Mr. Purdue will operate in the capacity of Vice President of Marketing for ROAD RUNNER. His main responsibility includes management of sales representatives. However, Mr. G. Purdue will also be responsible for the ROAD RUNNER's marketing and customer service programs. As the executive assistant for Real Manufacturing Co. for the past three years, Mr. Purdue has

Key Personnel Provide Experience and Energy

acquired a considerable amount of managerial and communication skills necessary to be successful in the world of business.

Mr. James Watson, ROAD RUNNER's design engineer, is a graduate of Northwestern University, with a B.S. in Manufacturing Engineering and Operations Management. Since his graduation in 1980, Mr. Watson has accumulated over 10 years experience in product design as he served a Chief Design Engineer with such companies as MRIP Inc. and Richard Spas. Mr. Watson is responsible for all research and development of future products. Furthermore, his responsibilities include designing the manufacturing process as well as conducting time motion studies.

FINANCIAL PLAN

Goals and Objectives

" *Achieve positive cash flow by the end of year 1.*

- Obtain needed financing ($230,000).

- Accurately forecast sales with the help of wholesalers and sales representatives.

" *Maintain at least a 40% gross margin throughout years 1, 2, and 3.*

- Keep raw material waste to .05%

- Maintain excellent relationships with suppliers.

- Continuously improve production efficiency.

" *Provide a 250% return on investment (ROI) by December 1994.*

- Pay back half of shareholders investment in December, 1996, and double the investment in December, 1997.

ROAD RUNNER is a division of Real Manufacturing Company, Inc. RMC has been in business for the past six years, and a historical record of actual expense amounts is available. Many of the forecasted general and administration expenses in ROAD RUNNER's business plan are approximations based on amounts that RMC incurred. However, the ROAD RUNNER division is of a different nature than RMC's other interests, and the expense structure will be different. Furthermore, in constructing the financials for ROAD RUNNER, the *conservative principle* was utilized.

Financial Rationale

- **Direct Materials** $450 per unit
- **Administrative Salaries** - During the inception of the ROAD RUNNER division, RMC instituted a "pool system" to manage salaries. Administrators will be responsible for overall operations at Real Manufacturing. Therefore, salaries are distributed equally between Real Manufacturing overhead and ROAD RUNNER overhead.
- **Commissions** - Based on the existing commission structure in the refrigeration industry, ROAD RUNNER is forecasting 7% commission for all sales representatives of ROAD RUNNER.
- **Payroll Taxes**   Estimated to be 14% of salaries.
- **Employee Fringe Benefits** - Employee fringe benefits include such items as contests, employee social functions, and employee bonuses. Fringe Benefits will average at $500 per employee per year.
- **Trade Shows** $2000 per show (Includes booth rental and freight.)
- **Travel**   Airfare: $550 avg./trip
                      Lodging: $70/ day avg.
                      Meals: $75/ day avg.
                      Car Rental: $50/ day avg.

- **Rent**   .44/ square foot per month
- **Utilities**   .16/ square foot per month
- **General Business Insurance** $850 per month
- **Telephone** $450 per month
- **Freight** $3450 per month
- **Office Expense** $590 per month
- **Dues and Subscriptions** $25 per month
- **Legal and Accounting** $3200 per year
- **Licensees and Fees** $108 per month
- **Bad Debt Expense**   2% of sales
- **Returns and Allowances**   2% of sales
- **Selling Price** - All prices are based on an average from a regressive cost structure

> Year 1: $950 average per unit
>
> Year 2: $910 average per unit
>
> Year 3: $870 average per unit

- **Unit Sales**   Year 1: 2,471 units

> Year 2: 11,950 units
>
> Year 3: 27,850 units

- **Product Warranties**   1% of overall sales per year
- **Accounts Receivable**   Collection terms - 2/10, net 30
- **Inventory Purchases**   31-60 days prior to sale: 50% of materials

> Month of sale: 50% of materials

- **Research & Development**   Year 1: 2% of sales

> Year 2: 4% of sales
>
> Year 3: 5% of sales

Established Financing Structure

Due to the fact that ROAD RUNNER is a division of Real Manufacturing Company (RMC), a closely held corporation, maintaining a substantial equity position has proven an important consideration. In the initial stages of the formation of ROAD RUNNER, the company secured both debt and equity financing.

Debt - Loans from Family Bank in Tucson, Arizona ($15,000) and the Bank of Dallas, Texas, ($15,000) were obtained. These moneys proved to be critical in maintaining adequate cash flow for the first few months of research and development and production. Furthermore, ROAD RUNNER received a $100,000 line-of-credit from Marble Industries. Interest on the line-of-credit will be three (3) points above the prime interest rate. Marble Industries currently stands as the primary customer of RMC.

Equity - 100,000 shares (common stock, par $1) have been distributed. Shareholders include: Real Manufacturing Corporation, 65,000 shares, Spring Inc. (outside investor), 35,000 shares.

Exit Strategies Protect Shareholders

ROAD RUNNER will utilize a "front-loaded" dividend structure to provide quick return on investment for shareholders. Shareholders will obtain dividends at the end of fiscal year 1996. Planned dividend payment structure is as follows. In December of 1996, shareholders will receive one-half of their original investment. In the subsequent year (1997) shareholders will obtain dividends in the amount of twice the original investment, bringing the total return on investment to 250%, after two years.

Shareholders have the option of holding onto their shares or selling them back to the company any time after 1997. A sell-back price for outstanding shares will be negotiated with the shareholders when the issue arises.

If an unforeseeable reason should force ROAD RUNNER to cease ongoing operations, very little risk will be encountered. ROAD RUNNER is a labor intensive operation that does not require large costs of capital equipment. Furthermore, at most, two months of inventory will remain in stock at all times. In the case of ROAD RUNNER liquidation, unused inventory would be sold back to the original suppliers, capital equipment (approximately $15,000) and other business assets will be sold. The proceeds of the liquidation will be distributed in the order of priority: debt holders, outside shareholders, Real Manufacturing Company, Inc. Furthermore, Real Manufacturing Company has agreed to provide financial protection for outside shareholders, in this situation.

Key Financial Data

	1993	1994	1995
Units Sold	2,471	11,950	27,850
Sales	$2,300,501	$10,657,010	$23,744,910
Net Profit (Loss) After Tax	$223,268	$1,330,240	$2,631,594
Gross Margin	41.1%	41.4%	39.0%
Break Even Point (Units)	864	3,331	7,154
Cash Flow (End of Year)	$158,249	$1,101,199	$2,947,265
Dividend Payout (paid in Dec.)	$50,000	$200,000	$400,000
Asset Turnover Ratio	3.06	3.76	3.20
Increase in Sales	—	463.2%	222.8%
Current Ratio	1.76	2.37	2.33
Debt-to-Equity Ratio	0.05	0.01	0.00

THIS PAGE INTENTIONALLY LEFT BLANK
SEE NEXT PAGE FOR PROJECTED BALANCE SHEET

Projected Balance Sheet: Year 1

	Oct 1992	Nov	Dec	Jan 1993
ASSETS				
Current Assets				
Cash	9,588	11,423	7,842	54,021
Accts Rcvable	6,783	18,169	28,682	57,268
Inventory	2,250	4,050	10,125	25,425
Total Current Assets	18,621	33,642	46,650	136,714
Property and Equipment - net of accumulated depreciation	10,817	10,633	10,450	14,178
TOTAL ASSETS	29,438	44,275	57,100	150,892
LIABILITIES AND STOCKHOLDERS' EQUITY				
Current Liabilities				
Accts Payable	16,400	25,850	26,775	60,025
Payroll Taxes Payable	958	1,949	0	1,106
Income Taxes Payable	0	0	0	0
Curr. Portion of Long-Term Debt	3,750	3,750	3,750	7,500
Line of Credit Balance	8,800	18,800	43,800	78,800
Total Current Liabilities	29,908	50,349	74,325	147,431
Long-Term Debt	10,938	10,625	10,313	20,938
Total Liabilities	40,846	60,974	84,638	168,369
Stockholders' Equity				
Common Stock	10,000	50,000	65,000	100,000
Retained Earnings	(21,408)	(66,699)	(92,538)	(117,477)
Total Stockholders' Equity	(11,408)	(16,699)	(27,538)	(17,477)
TOTAL LIABILITIES & STOCKHOLDER'S EQUITY	29,438	44,275	57,100	150,892
BALANCE CHECK	OK	OK	OK	OK
ASSETS VS. LIABILITIES	0	0	(0)	0

Feb	Mar	Apr	May	June	July	Aug	Sept	**Projected Balance Sheet: Year 1** *...continued*
29,449	13,738	24,837	51,487	67,992	96,095	121,748	158,249	
130,088	225,389	296,514	360,953	423,938	438,473	489,345	501,458	
43,425	54,675	65,925	77,175	77,175	88,425	88,425	65,925	
202,962	293,802	387,276	489,614	569,105	622,992	699,518	725,631	
13,906	13,633	15,819	19,417	19,014	21,069	22,569	25,019	
216,868	307,436	403,096	509,031	588,118	644,062	722,088	750,650	
114,700	173,250	227,500	276,500	307,750	328,750	353,250	342,500	
2,467	0	1,788	3,741	0	2,117	4,399	0	
0	0	0	19,383	35,898	34,914	42,585	42,645	
7,500	7,500	7,500	7,500	7,500	7,500	7,500	7,500	
78,800	78,800	68,800	58,800	48,800	38,800	28,800	18,800	
203,467	259,550	305,588	365,924	399,948	412,081	436,533	411,445	
20,313	19,688	19,063	18,438	17,813	17,188	16,563	15,938	
223,779	279,238	324,651	384,361	417,761	429,268	453,096	427,383	
100,000	100,000	100,000	100,000	100,000	100,000	100,000	100,000	
(106,911)	(71,802)	(21,555)	24,669	70,358	114,793	168,992	223,268	
(6,911)	28,198	78,445	124,669	170,358	214,793	268,992	323,268	
216,868	307,436	403,096	509,031	588,118	644,062	722,088	750,650	
OK	OK	OK	OK	OK	OK	OK	OK	
0	(0)	0	0	0	0	0	0	

Projected Balance Sheet: Years 2-5

	————————— YEAR 2 —————————			
	Dec 1993	**Mar 94**	**June 94**	**Sept 94**
ASSETS				
Current Assets				
Cash	228,806	185,680	274,615	1,101,199
Accts Rcvable	269,178	819,137	2,329,782	1,452,633
Inventory	88,425	268,425	403,425	223,425
Total Current Assets	586,409	1,273,242	3,007,822	2,777,257
Property and Equipment - net of				
accumulated depreciation	32,039	39,981	48,247	55,839
TOTAL ASSETS	618,448	1,313,222	3,056,069	2,833,096
LIABILITIES AND STOCKHOLDERS' EQUITY				
Current Liabilities				
Accts Payable	254,000	739,250	1,718,000	1,065,500
Payroll Taxes Payable	0	0	0	0
Income Taxes Payable	0	53,688	199,596	98,151
Curr. Portion of Long-Term Debt	7,500	7,500	7,500	7,500
Line of Credit Balance	0	0	0	0
Total Current Liabilities	261,500	800,438	1,925,096	1,171,151
Long-Term Debt	14,063	12,188	10,313	8,438
Total Liabilities	275,563	812,625	1,935,409	1,179,589
Stockholders' Equity				
Common Stock	100,000	100,000	100,000	100,000
Retained Earnings	242,886	400,597	1,020,661	1,553,508
Total Stockholders' Equity	342,886	500,597	1,120,661	1,653,508
TOTAL LIABILITIES & STOCKHOLDERS'				
EQUITY	618,448	1,313,222	3,056,069	2,833,096
BALANCE CHECK	OK	OK	OK	OK
ASSETS VS. LIABILITIES	0	0	(0)	0

	YEAR 3			YEAR 4	YEAR 5	Projected Balance
Dec 1994	**Mar 95**	**June 95**	**Sept 95**	**Sept 1996**	**Sept1997**	**Sheet: Years 2-5** *...continued*
1,441,193	1,330,034	1,472,878	2,947,265	5,695,546	8,544,868	
798,660	1,899,036	4,623,354	3,700,458	3,294,860	3,522,188	
178,425	605,925	988,425	673,425	720,450	720,450	
2,418,278	3,834,995	7,084,657	7,321,148	9,710,856	12,084,381	
66,158	75,639	85,203	107,289	193,689	236,511	
2,484,437	3,910,634	7,169,860	7,428,436	9,904,545	12,320,892	
664,000	1,699,000	3,680,000	2,901,000	2,698,475	2,125,375	
0	0	0	0	0	0	
19,502	124,237	344,889	233,897	150,324	143,127	
7,500	7,500	7,500	7,500	0	0	
0	0	0	0	0	0	
691,002	1,830,737	4,032,389	3,142,397	2,848,799	2,268,502	
6,563	4,688	2,813	938	0	0	
697,564	1,835,425	4,035,201	3,143,335	2,848,799	2,268,502	
100,000	100,000	100,000	100,000	100,000	100,000	
1,686,872	1,975,209	3,034,658	4,185,102	6,955,746	9,952,390	
1,786,872	2,075,209	3,134,658	4,285,102	7,055,746	10,052,390	
2,484,437	3,910,634	7,169,860	7,428,436	9,904,545	12,320,892	
OK	OK	OK	OK	OK	OK	
0	0	0	0	0	0	

Projected Statement of Profit and Loss: Year 1

	Oct 1992	Nov 92	Dec 92	Jan 1993	Feb 93	Mar 93
REVENUES						
Gross Sales	6,650	16,150	23,750	49,400	114,000	190,000
Less: Returns and Allowances	133	323	475	988	2,280	3,800
NET REVENUES	6,517	15,827	23,275	48,412	111,720	186,200
COST OF GOODS SOLD						
Direct Materials	3,150	30,600	19,800	34,200	54,000	90,000
Direct Labor	161	1,369	886	1,530	2,415	4,025
Manufacturing Overhead	2,440	5,276	4,149	5,652	8,183	11,941
TOTAL COST OF GOODS SOLD	5,751	37,245	24,835	41,382	64,598	105,966
GROSS MARGIN	766	(21,418)	(1,560)	7,030	47,122	80,234
GROSS MARGIN %	11.8%	-135.3%	-6.7%	14.5%	42.2%	43.1%
OPERATING EXPENSES						
Admin Salaries & Wages	5,567	5,567	5,567	5,567	5,567	5,567
Sales/Mktg Salaries & Wages	0	0	0	0	0	0
Sales Commissions	475	1,153	1,696	3,527	8,140	13,566
Payroll Taxes	796	796	796	796	796	796
Employee Fringe Benefits	750	750	750	750	750	750
Employee Training	320	320	320	320	320	320
Trade Shows	0	0	0	2,000	0	0
Advertising	850	822	1,005	3,460	3,285	3,346
Travel	4,150	4,150	4,150	4,150	4,150	4,150
Entertainment	500	500	500	500	500	500
Product R & D	470	1,331	861	1,487	2,348	3,914
Rent	1,056	1,056	1,056	1,056	1,056	1,056
Utilities	384	384	384	384	384	384
General Business Insurance	849	849	849	849	849	849
Telephone	450	450	450	450	450	450
Postage and Freight	3,450	3,450	3,450	3,450	3,450	3,450
Office Expense	590	590	590	590	590	590
Dues and Subscriptions	25	25	25	25	25	25
Legal and Accounting	417	417	417	417	417	417
Licenses and Fees	108	108	108	108	108	108
Depreciation	183	183	183	272	272	272
Equipment Maintenance	220	220	220	300	300	300
Vehicle Expense	400	400	400	400	400	400
Bad Debts	133	323	475	988	2,280	3,800
TOTAL OPERATING EXPENSES	22,142	23,844	24,252	31,846	36,437	45,010
OPERATING INCOME (LOSS)	(21,376)	(45,261)	(25,811)	(24,816)	10,685	35,224
INTEREST EXPENSE	(32)	(30)	(28)	(124)	(119)	(115)
INCOME BEFORE INCOME TAXES	(21,408)	(45,291)	(25,839)	(24,939)	10,566	35,109
INCOME TAXES	0	0	0	0	0	0
NET INCOME (LOSS)	(21,408)	(45,291)	(25,839)	(24,939)	10,566	35,109
NET INCOME (LOSS) %	-328.5%	-286.2%	-111.0%	-51.5%	9.5%	18.9%
RETAINED EARNINGS, BEGINNING	0	(21,408)	(66,699)	(92,538)	(117,477)	(106,911)
RETAINED EARNINGS, END	(21,408)	(66,699)	(92,538)	(117,477)	(106,911)	(71,802)

Apr 93	May 93	June 93	July 93	Aug 93	Sept 93	Total	%Total	
								Projected Statement of Profit and Loss: Year 1...*continued*
237,500	285,000	332,500	332,500	380,000	380,000	2,347,450	100.0%	
4,750	5,700	6,650	6,650	7,600	7,600	49,949	2.0%	
232,750	279,300	325,850	325,850	372,400	372,400	2,300,501	98.0%	
112,500	135,000	157,500	157,500	180,000	180,000	1,154,250	49.2%	
5,013	6,038	7,044	7,044	8,050	8,050	51,641	2.2%	
14,290	16,638	18,987	18,987	21,335	21,335	149,213	6.4%	
131,821	157,676	183,530	183,530	209,385	209,385	1,355,103	57.7%	
100,929	121,624	142,320	142,320	163,015	163,015	945,398	40.3%	
43.4%	43.5%	43.7%	43.7%	43.8%	43.8%	231.3%	0.0%	
5,567	5,567	5,567	5,567	5,567	5,567	66,800	2.8%	
0	0	0	0	0	0	0	0.0%	
16,958	20,349	23,741	23,741	27,132	27,132	167,608	7.1%	
796	796	796	796	796	796	9,552	0.4%	
750	750	750	750	750	750	9,000	0.4%	
320	320	320	320	320	320	3,840	0.2%	
0	0	0	2,000	0	0	4,000	0.2%	
3,496	3,346	2,746	2,896	2,746	2,502	30,500	1.3%	
4,150	4,150	4,150	4,150	4,150	4,150	49,800	2.1%	
500	500	500	500	500	500	6,000	0.3%	
4,893	5,871	6,850	6,850	7,828	7,828	50,530	2.2%	
1,056	1,056	1,056	1,056	1,056	1,056	12,672	0.5%	
384	384	384	384	384	384	4,608	0.2%	
849	849	849	849	849	849	10,188	0.4%	
450	450	450	450	450	450	5,400	0.2%	
3,450	3,450	3,450	3,450	3,450	3,450	41,400	1.8%	
590	590	590	590	590	590	7,080	0.3%	
25	25	25	25	25	25	300	0.0%	
417	417	417	417	417	417	5,000	0.2%	
108	108	108	108	108	108	1,296	0.1%	
314	403	403	444	500	550	3,981	0.2%	
350	430	430	480	520	580	4,350	0.2%	
400	400	400	400	400	400	4,800	0.2%	
4,750	5,700	6,650	6,650	7,600	7,600	46,949	2.0%	
50,571	55,910	60,630	62,872	66,137	66,003	545,654	23.2%	
50,358	65,714	81,689	79,448	96,877	97,011	399,744	17.0%	
(111)	(107)	(103)	(99)	(94)	(90)	(1,052)	0.0%	
50,247	65,607	81,587	79,349	96,783	96,921	398,692	17.0%	
0	19,383	35,898	34,914	42,585	42,645	175,425	7.5%	
50,247	46,689	45,689	44,436	54,198	54,276	223,268	9.5%	
21.6%	16.6%	14.0%	13.6%	14.6%	14.6%	9.5%		
(71,802)	(21,555)	24,669	70,358	114,793	168,992			
(21,555)	24,669	70,358	114,793	168,992	223,268			

Projected Statement of Profit and Loss: Year 2

	Qtr 1	Qtr 2	Qtr 3	Qtr 4	Total	% Total
REVENUES						
Gross Sales	455,000	1,001,000	2,912,000	2,639,000	7,007,000	100.0%
Less: Returns & Allowances	9,100	20,020	58,240	52,780	140,140	2.0%
NET REVENUES	445,900	980,980	2,853,760	2,586,220	6,866,860	98.0%
COST OF GOODS SOLD						
Direct Materials	225,000	495,000	1,440,000	1,305,000	3,465,000	49.5%
Direct Labor	10,063	22,138	64,400	58,363	154,963	2.2%
Manufacturing Overhead	34,076	62,169	160,494	146,448	403,186	5.8%
TOTAL COST OF GOODS SOLD	269,138	579,306	1,664,894	1,509,810	4,023,149	57.4%
GROSS MARGIN	176,762	401,674	1,188,866	1,076,410	2,843,711	40.6%
GROSS MARGIN %	79.1%	81.7%	83.3%	83.2%	327.3%	0.0%
OPERATING EXPENSES						
Admin Salaries & Wages	19,967	19,967	19,967	19,967	79,867	1.1%
Sales/Mktg Salaries & Wages	4,000	4,000	9,000	9,000	26,000	0.4%
Sales Commissions	32,487	71,471	207,917	188,425	500,300	7.1%
Payroll Taxes	3,427	3,427	4,142	4,142	15,139	0.2%
Employee Fringe Benefits	3,000	3,000	3,500	3,500	13,000	0.2%
Employee Training	1,300	1,300	1,300	1,300	5,200	0.1%
Trade Shows	0	2,000	0	2,000	4,000	0.1%
Advertising and Promotions	6,522	9,071	9,132	6,949	31,674	0.5%
Travel	12,450	12,450	12,450	12,450	49,800	0.7%
Entertainment	3,250	3,250	3,250	3,250	12,999	0.2%
Product R & D	16,853	37,077	107,862	97,750	259,542	3.7%
Rent	5,720	5,720	5,720	5,720	22,880	0.3%
Utilities	2,080	2,080	2,080	2,080	8,320	0.1%
General Business Insurance	5,518	5,518	5,518	5,518	22,072	0.3%
Telephone	2,925	2,925	2,925	2,925	11,699	0.2%
Postage and Freight	22,423	22,423	22,423	22,423	89,693	1.3%
Office Expense	2,360	2,360	2,753	2,753	10,227	0.1%
Dues and Subscriptions	100	100	117	117	433	0.0%
Legal and Accounting	2,354	2,000	2,000	2,000	8,354	0.1%
Licenses and Fees	216	216	216	216	864	0.0%
Depreciation	1,319	1,706	2,156	2,606	11,700	0.2%
Equipment Maintenance	1,390	1,780	2,240	2,700	12,100	0.2%
Vehicle Expense	1,200	1,200	1,200	1,200	4,800	0.1%
Bad Debts	9,100	20,020	58,240	52,780	140,140	2.0%
TOTAL OPERATING EXPENSES	159,562	234,661	485,707	451,370	1,331,299	19.0%
OPERATING INCOME (LOSS)	17,200	167,013	703,159	625,040	1,512,412	21.6%
INTEREST EXPENSE	(164)	(139)	(114)	(89)	(505)	0.0%
INCOME BEFORE INCOME TAXES	17,036	166,874	703,045	624,951	1,511,907	21.6%
INCOME TAXES	9,396	71,524	309,340	274,979	665,239	9.5%
NET INCOME (LOSS)	7,640	95,349	393,705	349,973	846,668	12.1%
NET INCOME (LOSS) %	1.7%	9.5%	13.5%	13.3%	12.1%	
RETAINED EARNINGS, BEGINNING	223,268	230,908	326,257	719,963		
RETAINED EARNINGS, END	230,908	326,257	719,963	1,069,935		

	Qtr 1	Qtr 2	Qtr 3	Qtr 4	Total	%Total
REVENUES						
Gross Sales	1,435,500	2,262,000	6,003,000	6,438,000	16,138,500	100.0%
Less: Returns & Allowances	28,710	45,240	120,060	128,760	322,770	2.0%
NET REVENUES	1,406,790	2,216,760	5,882,940	6,309,240	15,815,730	98.0%
COST OF GOODS SOLD						
Direct Materials	742,500	1,170,000	3,105,000	3,330,000	8,347,500	51.7%
Direct Labor	33,206	52,325	138,863	148,925	373,319	2.3%
Manufacturing Overhead	91,755	136,046	336,519	359,830	924,149	5.7%
TOTAL COST OF GOODS SOLD	867,461	1,358,371	3,580,381	3,838,755	9,644,968	59.8%
GROSS MARGIN	539,329	858,389	2,302,559	2,470,485	6,170,762	38.2%
GROSS MARGIN %	76.6%	77.2%	78.3%	78.3%	310.3%	0.0%
OPERATING EXPENSES						
Admin Salaries & Wages	22,175	22,175	22,175	22,175	88,700	0.5%
Sales/Mktg Salaries & Wages	13,593	13,593	13,593	13,593	54,373	0.3%
Sales Commissions	102,495	161,507	428,614	459,673	1,152,289	7.1%
Payroll Taxes	5,115	5,115	5,115	5,115	20,459	0.1%
Employee Fringe Benefits	4,500	4,500	4,500	4,500	18,000	0.1%
Employee Training	1,500	1,500	1,500	1,500	6,000	0.0%
Trade Shows	0	2,000	0	2,000	4,000	0.0%
Advertising and Promotions	7,610	9,610	11,610	11,610	40,440	0.3%
Travel	19,090	19,090	19,090	19,090	76,360	0.5%
Entertainment	9,086	9,086	9,086	9,086	36,346	0.2%
Product R & D	77,752	122,519	325,145	348,707	874,122	5.4%
Rent	11,000	11,000	11,000	11,000	44,000	0.3%
Utilities	4,000	4,000	4,000	4,000	16,000	0.1%
General Business Insurance	15,429	15,429	15,429	15,429	61,715	0.4%
Telephone	4,400	4,400	4,400	4,400	17,600	0.1%
Postage and Freight	32,000	32,000	32,000	32,000	128,000	0.8%
Office Expense	3,540	3,540	3,540	3,540	14,160	0.1%
Dues and Subscriptions	150	150	150	150	600	0.0%
Legal and Accounting	7,572	7,572	7,572	7,572	30,288	0.2%
Licenses and Fees	216	216	216	216	864	0.0%
Depreciation	3,125	3,692	4,286	5,367	16,469	0.1%
Equipment Maintenance	3,230	3,830	4,450	5,480	16,990	0.1%
Vehicle Expense	1,200	1,200	1,200	1,200	4,800	0.0%
Bad Debts	28,710	45,240	120,060	128,760	-	0.0%
TOTAL OPERATING EXPENSES	377,088	502,563	1,048,332	1,115,763	3,043,746	18.9%
OPERATING INCOME (LOSS)	162,240	355,826	1,254,227	1,354,723	3,127,016	19.4%
INTEREST EXPENSE	(64)	(39)	(14)	11	(105)	0.0%
INCOME BEFORE INCOME TAXES	162,177	355,787	1,254,213	1,354,734	3,126,911	19.4%
INCOME TAXES	71,358	156,546	551,854	596,083	1,375,841	8.5%
NET INCOME (LOSS)	90,819	199,241	702,359	758,651	1,751,070	10.9%
NET INCOME (LOSS) %	6.3%	8.8%	11.7%	11.8%	10.9%	
RETAINED EARNINGS, BEGINNING	1,069,935	1,160,754	1,359,995	2,062,354		
RETAINED EARNINGS, END	1,160,754	1,359,995	2,062,354	2,821,005		

Projected Statement of Profit and Loss: Year 3

Projected Statement of Profit and Loss: Years 4 & 5

	Year 4 Total	%Total	Year 5 Total	%Total
REVENUES				
Gross Sales	29,750,000	100.0%	31,875,000	100.0%
Less: Returns & Allowances	595,000	2.0%	638,000	2.0%
NET REVENUES	29,155,000	98.0%	31,238,000	98.0%
COST OF GOODS SOLD				
Direct Materials	15,750,000	52.9%	16,875,000	52.9%
Direct Labor	910,000	3.1%	975,000	3.1%
Manufacturing Overhead	1,984,000	6.7%	2,118,000	6.6%
TOTAL COST OF GOODS SOLD	18,644,000	62.7%	19,968,000	62.6%
GROSS MARGIN	10,511,000	35.3%	11,270,000	35.4%
OPERATING EXPENSES				
Admin Salaries & Wages	184,000	0.6%	221,000	0.7%
Sales/Mktg Salaries & Wages	94,000	0.3%	94,000	0.3%
Sales Commissions	2,124,000	7.1%	2,276,000	7.1%
Payroll Taxes	40,000	0.1%	45,000	0.1%
Employee Fringe Benefits	30,000	0.1%	36,000	0.1%
Employee Training	9,000	0.0%	10,000	0.0%
Trade Shows	4,000	0.0%	4,000	0.0%
Advertising and Promotions	90,000	0.3%	130,000	0.4%
Travel	123,000	0.4%	134,000	0.4%
Entertainment	60,000	0.2%	60,000	0.2%
Product R & D	1,488,000	5.0%	1,594,000	5.0%
Rent	84,000	0.3%	95,000	0.3%
Utilities	48,000	0.2%	54,000	0.2%
General Business Insurance	102,000	0.3%	117,000	0.4%
Telephone	30,000	0.1%	35,000	0.1%
Postage and Freight	210,000	0.7%	242,000	0.8%
Office Expense	22,000	0.1%	24,000	0.1%
Dues and Subscriptions	2,000	0.0%	2,000	0.0%
Legal and Accounting	30,000	0.1%	30,000	0.1%
Licenses and Fees	4,000	0.0%	4,000	0.0%
Depreciation	16,000	0.1%	34,000	0.1%
Equipment Maintenance	23,000	0.1%	30,000	0.1%
Vehicle Expense	12,000	0.0%	12,000	0.0%
Bad Debts	595,000	2.0%	638,000	2.0%
TOTAL OPERATING EXPENSES	5,422,000	18.2%	5,918,000	18.6%
OPERATING INCOME (LOSS)	5,089,000	17.1%	5,351,000	16.8%
INTEREST EXPENSE	0	0.0%	0	0.0%
INCOME BEFORE INCOME TAXES	5,089,000	17.1%	5,351,000	16.8%
INCOME TAXES	2,239,000	7.5%	2,355,000	7.4%
NET INCOME (LOSS)	2,850,000	9.6%	2,997,000	9.4%
RETAINED EARNINGS, BEGINNING	4,186,083		6,955,746	
RETAINED EARNINGS, END	6,955,746		9,952,390	

THIS PAGE INTENTIONALLY LEFT BLANK
SEE NEXT PAGE FOR PROJECTED CASH FLOWS

Projected Statement of Cash Flows: Part 1

	Oct 1992	Oct 92	Nov 92	Dec 92	Jan 1993	Feb 93
CASH FLOWS FROM OPERATIONS						
Net Income	(21,408)	(45,291)	(25,839)	(24,939)	10,566	35,109
Adjustments to reconcile net income to cash flows from operations:						
Depreciation & Amortization	183	183	183	272	272	272
Changes in certain assets and liabilities:						
Accounts Receivable	(6,783)	(11,386)	(10,514)	(28,586)	(72,820)	(95,301)
Inventory	(2,250)	(1,800)	(6,075)	(15,300)	(18,000)	(11,250)
Accounts Payable	16,400	9,450	925	33,250	54,675	58,550
Payroll Taxes Payable	958	991	(1,949)	1,106	1,361	(2,467)
Income Taxes Payable	0	0	0	0	0	0
Revolving Line of Credit	8,800	10,000	25,000	35,000	0	0
TOTAL FROM OPERATIONS	(4,099)	(37,853)	(18,268)	803	(23,947)	(15,086)
CASH FLOWS FROM INVESTING ACTIVITIES						
Purchase of Equipment	(11,000)	0	0	(4,000)	0	0
Pmnt of Patent Costs	0	0	0	0	0	0
Pmnt of Long-Term Deposits	0	0	0	0	0	0
TOTAL FROM INVESTING	(11,000)	0	0	(4,000)	0	0
CASH FLOWS FROM FINANCING ACTIVITIES						
Borrowing on Long-Term Debt	15,000	0	0	15,000	0	0
Pmnts on Long-Term Debts	(313)	(313)	(313)	(625)	(625)	(625)
Sales of Common Stock	10,000	40,000	15,000	35,000	0	0
Repayment of Line of Credit	0	0	0	0	0	0
TOTAL FROM FINANCING	24,688	39,688	14,688	49,375	(625)	(625)
NET CASH FLOWS	9,588	1,835	(3,581)	46,178	(24,572)	(15,711)
CASH, BEGINNING OF PERIOD	0	9,588	11,423	7,842	54,021	29,449
CASH, END OF PERIOD	9,588	11,423	7,842	54,021	29,449	13,738

Mar 93	Apr 93	May 93	Jun 93	Jul 93	Aug 93	Sept 93	Oct 93	Projected Statement of Cash Flows: Part 1 ...continued
50,2247	46,224	45,689	44,436	54,198	54,276	11,959	11,978	
314	403	403	444	500	550	592	661	
(71,125)	(64,439)	(62,985)	(14,535)	(50,873)	(12,113)	106,718	27,285	
(11,250)	(11,250)	0	(11,250)	0	22,500	0	22,500	
54,250	49,000	31,250	21,000	24,500	(10,750)	(44,500)	(45,500)	
1,788	1,953	(3,741)	2,117	2,282	(4,399)	3,056	3,056	
0	19,383	16,515	(985)	7,671	61	(33,249)	15	
0	0	0	0	0	0	0	0	
24,224	41,274	27,131	41,228	38,278	50,125	44,575	19,996	
(2,500)	(4,000)	0	(2,500)	(2,000)	(3,000)	(2,500)	(2,500)	
0	0	0	0	0	0	0	0	
0	0	0	0	0	0	0	0	
(2,500)	(4,000)	0	(2,500)	(2,000)	(3,000)	(2,500)	(2,500)	
0	0	0	0	0	0	0	0	
(625)	(625)	(625)	(625)	(625)	(625)	(625)	(625)	
0	0	0	0	0	0	0	0	
(10,000)	(10,000)	(10,000)	(10,000)	(10,000)	(10,000)	(10,000)	(8,800)	
(10,625)	(10,625)	(10,625)	(10,625)	(10,625)	(10,625)	(10,625)	(9,425)	
11,099	26,649	16,506	28,103	25,653	36,500	31,450	8,071	
13,738	24,837	51,487	67,992	96,095	121,748	158,249	189,698	
24,837	51,487	67,992	96,095	121,748	158,249	189,698	197,769	

Projected Statement of Cash Flows: Part 2

	Nov 1993	Dec 93	Jan 1994	Feb 94	Mar 94
CASH FLOWS FROM OPERATIONS					
Net Income	(4,318)	27,019	62,361	68,330	139,674
Adjustments to reconcile net income to cash flows from operations:					
Depreciation & Amortization	728	769	853	936	994
Changes in certain assets and liabilities:					
Accounts Receivable	98,277	(162,435)	(273,819)	(113,705)	(487,305)
Inventory	(45,000)	(56,250)	(11,250)	(112,500)	(135,000)
Accounts Payable	1,500	123,750	167,750	193,750	371,750
Payroll Taxes Payable	(6,112)	3,385	4,207	(7,592)	6,374
Income Taxes Payable	(9,411)	17,836	31,162	4,690	56,056
Revolving Line of Credit	0	0	0	0	0
TOTAL FROM OPERATIONS	35,663	(45,925)	(18,736)	33,909	(47,457)
CASH FLOWS FROM INVESTING ACTIVITIES					
Purchase of Equipment	(4,000)	(2,500)	(3,000)	(5,000)	(3,500)
Pmnt of Patent Costs	0	0	0	0	0
Pmnt of Long-term Deposits	0	0	0	0	0
TOTAL FROM INVESTING	(4,000)	(2,500)	(3,000)	(5,000)	(3,500)
CASH FLOWS FROM FINANCING ACTIVITIES					
Borrowings on Long-Term Debt	0	0	0	0	0
Pmnts on Long-Term Debts	(625)	(625)	(625)	(625)	(625)
Sales of Common Stock	0	0	0	0	0
Repayment of Line of Credit	0	0	0	0	0
TOTAL FROM FINANCING	(625)	(625)	(625)	(625)	(625)
NET CASH FLOWS	31,038	(49,050)	(22,361)	28,284	(51,582)
CASH, BEGINNING OF PERIOD	197,769	228,806	179,757	157,396	185,680
CASH, END OF PERIOD	228,806	179,757	157,396	185,680	134,098

Apr 94	May 94	Jun 94	Jul 94	Aug 94	Sept 94	Oct 94	Nov 94	Projected Statement
								of Cash Flows: Part 2
								...continued
226,359	254,031	225,053	182,874	124,920	65,998	42,546	24,820	
1,078	1,161	1,219	1,303	1,386	1,444	1,556	1,681	
(675,266)	(348,075)	111,384	315,588	450,177	240,363	229,449	184,161	
(45,000)	45,000	67,500	90,000	22,500	45,000	33,750	(33,750)	
425,500	181,500	(112,000)	(272,000)	(268,500)	(179,500)	(147,250)	(74,750)	
8,347	(14,721)	8,347	7,360	(15,708)	6,341	5,683	(12,025)	
68,110	21,743	(22,769)	(33,141)	(45,536)	(46,295)	(18,427)	(13,927)	
0	0	0	0	0	0	0	0	
9,128	140,639	278,735	291,985	269,239	133,352	147,307	76,210	
(3,000)	(5,000)	(3,500)	(3,000)	(5,000)	(3,500)	(4,000)	(7,500)	
0	0	0	0	0	0	0	0	
0	0	0	0	0	0	0	0	
(3,000)	(5,000)	(3,500)	(3,000)	(5,000)	(3,500)	(4,000)	(7,500)	
0	0	0	0	0	0	0	0	
(625)	(625)	(625)	(625)	(625)	(625)	(625)	(625)	
0	0	0	0	0	0	0	0	
0	0	0	0	0	0	0	0	
(625)	(625)	(625)	(625)	(625)	(625)	(625)	(625)	
5,503	135,014	274,610	288,360	263,614	129,227	142,682	68,085	
134,098	139,601	274,615	549,225	837,585	1,101,199	1,230,426	1,373,108	
139,601	274,615	549,225	837,585	1,101,199	1,230,426	1,373,108	1,441,193	

Projected Statement of Cash Flows: Part 3

	Dec 1994	**Jan 1995**	**Feb 95**
CASH FLOWS FROM OPERATIONS			
Net Income	41,121	89,096	158,120
Adjustments to reconcile net income to cash flows from operations:			
Depreciation & Amortization	1,739	1,828	1,953
Changes in certain assets and liabilities:			
Accounts Receivable	(90,959)	(381,582)	(627,836)
Inventory	(90,000)	(135,000)	(202,500)
Accounts Payable	123,250	354,250	566,500
Payroll Taxes Payable	5,683	6,999	(12,682)
Income Taxes Payable	12,807	37,695	54,233
Revolving Line of Credit	0	0	0
TOTAL FROM OPERATIONS	3,642	(35,714)	(62,212)
CASH FLOWS FROM INVESTING ACTIVITIES			
Purchase of Equipment	(3,500)	(4,000)	(7,500)
Purchase of Patent Costs	0	0	0
Pmnt of Long-Term Deposits	0	0	0
TOTAL FROM INVESTING	(3,500)	(4,000)	(7,500)
CASH FLOWS FROM FINANCING ACTIVITIES			
Borrowings on Long-Term Debt	0	0	0
Pmnts on Long-Term Debt	(625)	(625)	(625)
Sales of Common Stock	0	0	0
Repayment of Line of Credit	0	0	0
TOTAL FROM FINANCING	(625)	(625)	(625)
NET CASH FLOWS	(483)	(40,339)	(70,337)
CASH, BEGINNING OF PERIOD	1,441,193	1,440,710	1,400,371
CASH, END OF PERIOD	1,440,710	1,400,371	1,330,034

Mar 95	Apr 95	May 95	Jun 95	Jul 95	Aug 95	**Projected Statement of Cash Flows: Part 3** *...continued*
263,410	357,090	438,950	460,964	391,792	297,687	
2,011	2,150	2,275	2,481	2,547	2,886	
(949,518)	(936,207)	(838,593)	(368,271)	457,011	834,156	
(180,000)	(157,500)	(45,000)	135,000	180,000	0	
719,500	717,500	544,000	116,500	(408,500)	(487,000)	
11,933	14,564	(26,496)	17,524	15,550	(33,074)	
82,728	73,606	64,318	17,297	(54,349)	(73,940)	
0	0	0	0	0	0	
(49,937)	71,202	139,454	381,494	584,052	540,715	
(3,500)	(5,000)	(7,500)	(9,000)	(4,000)	(17,000)	
0	0	0	0	0	0	
0	0	0	0	0	0	
(3,500)	(5,000)	(7,500)	(9,000)	(4,000)	(17,000)	
0	0	0	0	0	0	
(625)	(625)	(625)	(625)	(625)	(625)	
0	0	0	0	0	0	
0	0	0	0	0	0	
(625)	(625)	(625)	(625)	(625)	(625)	
(54,062)	65,577	131,329	371,869	579,427	523,090	
1,330,034	1,275,972	1,341,549	1,472,878	1,844,747	2,424,174	
1,275,972	1,341,549	1,472,878	1,844,747	2,424,174	2,947,265	

RISK AND CONTINGENCY

ROAD RUNNER Refrigerant Recovery Systems will undoubtedly face many obstacles within the first months of operations. ROAD RUNNER has attempted to forecast these potential problems in an effort to ensure the minimization of potential detrimental surprises. Several of these potential risks and ROAD RUNNER's solution have been provided below.

Sales Representatives

A risk that faces ROAD RUNNER focuses reliability on its sales representatives. ROAD RUNNER does not solely employ these agents. By this, they also sell other company's products simultaneously (although no other recovery systems). Because sales rely heavily on these agents, the amount of sales drive they give to ROAD RUNNER will help to determine the amount of success in the marketplace. This problem will be circumvented by educating the sales representatives and making them part of the ROAD RUNNER team. *The education process will include: step-by-step analysis of the product design, a detailed explanation of the forces that drive the industry, and formation of strategy and methods that will be effective in selling the ROAD RUNNER.*

Barriers to Entry: Distribution Channels

A formidable risk facing entrants into the refrigeration industry stems from possible barriers to entry. One such barrier concerns accessibility to the established distribution network. Service technicians purchase equipment through wholesalers. Therefore, a manufacturer wishing to sell his product to the industry, must do it through the wholesalers. In order to penetrate these distribution channels, a manufacturer must have a quality system and properly timed entry, in accordance with industry "norms." For example, wholesalers make inventory and purchasing decisions during the winter (the off season for the industry). A manufacturer trying to sell his product during the summer will not have much success. *This risk has been greatly minimized as ROAD RUNNER has attracted twenty (20) experienced sales representatives. Many of these individuals have represented other refrigerant recovery systems, thus providing access to distribution channels across the entire United States.*

Political Environment

Due to the previous experience of key personnel many of the operational risks typically associated with a manufacturing firm have been circumvented. Despite past experience, possible risks in this area of the business still remain. The probable risk that faces ROAD RUNNER centers around the Environmental Protection Agency. This government organization has wavered from time to time in regards to its policy decisions. As a prime example, the EPA lacked stringent enforcement of the Clean Air Act during the summer of 1992. Furthermore, the EPA recently announced its decision to require the use of electronic testing equipment during the production of refrigerant recovery systems. This forced ROAD RUNNER to purchase this machinery at a cost of $2000. The uncertainty of the Environmental Protection Agency does not threaten the existence of ROAD RUNNER. It merely has created an inconvenience. ROAD RUNNER will deal with the Environmental Protection Agency by maintaining regular contact with a representative from the agency.

SUMMARY

Many new industries have been created as the result of government regulations over the past thirty years. In the early 1970's, "automobile safety" legislation was the hot topic. Soon thereafter, many new firms began manufacturing seat belts and automobile safety equipment. Today, this industry is larger than ever and moving ahead with new and safer equipment. The government's effect on the refrigeration industry will be just as profound. This industry is presented with an opportunity not often encountered in the business world. *Service technicians are required by law to purchase a refrigerant recovery system.* Therefore, presenting the refrigeration industry with an incredible need for a recovery system that will stand up to the everyday rigors of refrigeration recovery.

ROAD RUNNER will satisfy this need with Archetype 2000. A complete recovery system, designed from the input of service technicians for service technicians, this system surpasses its competition as the most complete refrigerant recovery system on the market.

However, ROAD RUNNER's product offering is not the only strength of the company. Great companies are built by great people. ROAD RUNNER will thrive in the future on a management team possessing much needed business experience and youthful excitement.

Although the industry was created based on government legislation, the economic benefits of refrigerant recovery use, is the force which will carry this industry into the future. Because of heavy government taxes, current refrigerant prices have increased over 130% in the past year. Current prices for "environmentally safe" refrigerants exceed standard refrigerants by twice the cost. Moreover, as the phase-out of standard refrigerants takes place in early 1997, the price of "environmentally safe" refrigerants are expected to increase. In this situation, refrigerant recovery systems are no longer viewed by service technicians as regulatory.

Through the use of refrigerant recovery systems, service technicians and the consumer will realize the short term benefit of economic savings. But more importantly, through the use of refrigerant recovery systems, the ultimate dream of our society, preserving our endangered world for future generations, will be one step closer to becoming reality.

Sandwich Shop

BUSINESS PLAN

ROMASTRANO INCORPORATED

705 Waltham Blvd.
Rutland, VT 05701

This business plan demonstrates how a franchise sandwich shop can compete with large fast-food chains by developing unique relationships with other established businesses.

- EXECUTIVE SUMMARY

- MISSION

- STRATEGY

- THE COMPANY

- CONCEPT

- ROMA'S MANAGEMENT TEAM

- THE ROMA'S FRANCHISE PROGRAM

- ROMA'S TRAINING PROGRAMS

- ON-GOING SUPPORT PROGRAM

- ROMA'S NON-TRADITIONAL STORE

- INDUSTRY AND COMPETITION

- ADVERTISING PROGRAM

- FUNDS REQUIRED AND THEIR USES

- FINANCIAL INFORMATION

EXECUTIVE SUMMARY

This business plan has been developed to present Romastrano Incorporated (hereinafter referred to as "Romastrano" or "Roma's") to perspective investors and to assist in raising a minimum of $500,000 in capital needed to expand the Franchise System of Roma's Delis from the present 14 units to 50 units over the next 12 to 18 months, thereby providing the foundation for the continued expansion of a nationwide sandwich chain.

The original Roma's Deli opened for business in 1958 in Burlington, Vermont, serving one specialty italian sandwich. This shop continues to do business within approximately 500 square feet at 15 Oak Street in Burlington, Vermont, serving a very limited menu consisting of its cold specialty italian sandwiches, soups, beverages and gelati. The sandwich, which over the years has become famous well beyond the border of Vermont, is made on its own special bread with Roma's mild cooked salami, provolene cheese, thinly sliced onions, peppers, pickles, tomatoes, and olives, and served with Roma's secret sauce or other toppings. The store grosses in excess of $500,000 annually. This shop is owned and operated by Roma's of Burlington, Inc. Henry Malogne, President. Romastrano Inc. does not derive any income from this store.

Romastrano Inc. was formed in July, 1993 for the purpose of franchising Roma's Deli. In the first 18 months, Romastrano Inc. sold fourteen (14) franchises, of which ten (10) are open and currently operating. The remaining four (4) franchises are scheduled to open over the next few months. In addition, Romastrano Inc. recently reached an agreement with Barrows to put two (2) Corporate non-traditional stores inside the Barrows stores in North Adams, MA and Rutland, VT. These stores opened in June, 1995 and May, 1995, respectively. Furthermore, a franchised store is going in at a Gas Max mini-mart in Barre, Vermont on August 15, 1995. The potential exists to expand rapidly within Barrows stores and other non-traditional channels, such as convenience stores, coffee shops (i.e. Baker's Cap), gasoline stations, university cafeterias, ball parks and arenas.

Roma's is uniquely situated since it offers a quality product at a competitive price point ($3.25 for a 12-inch sandwich) with excellent margins which can be served within very efficient space requirements in both a traditional (sit-down and take-out) and non-traditional sites.

Market Potential

Romastrano's market research shows that there is tremendous potential for a high-quality fast food sandwich shop which can operate efficiently in both traditional and non-traditional settings. The Fun Bun experience and its continued rapid growth demonstrates the demand for a low-cost entry into the fast food business. Romastrano offers the opportunity to enter into the food business for as low as $35,000 for a fully-equipped non-traditional store, including the $10,000 franchise fee. The franchise fee for a traditional location is $12,500 with an initial investment of $41,000 to $77,000. The entry cost together with the 5% royalty structure provide Roma's with a competitive edge over similarly structured companies.

One of the fastest growing segments in the fast food industry is the distribution of product through non-traditional locations. The Roma's System, with limited cooking and food preparation requirements, has an advantage over the competition in adapting to the minimum space requirement of many non-traditional sites. The opportunity for Roma's rapid expansion in the market is tremendous since many of the larger chains face encroachment problems at many potential locations. Barrows alone has approximately 1,000 stores. Roma's will be serving a limited breakfast menu of fresh bagels and muffins together with its famous sandwiches, soup, fountain soda and private label chips at its Cumberland Farms non-traditional shops.

The Company

The original Roma's Deli has for the past 36 years solely targeted the italian sandwich customer. The italian sandwich is the most frequently ordered submarine sandwich in the industry. Roma's prides itself in delivering the freshest, most delicious sandwich on the market. In order to provide the consumer with an alternative and thereby capture more of the market, Roma's is introducing a honey-smoked turkey to its menu. Roma's philosophy continues to center around providing a limited menu which satisfies the needs of the majority of fast food sandwich eaters but guarantees freshness and quality of product. The Roma's bread is baked daily and all of the vegetables are cut daily on the premises. The sandwich is made to the customer's specific specifications.

Marketing Strategy

The primary focus of the marketing strategy at the Roma's shops will be point of purchase promotional pieces, such as a Roma's Card, discount coupons, and special promotions. Marketing strategies for both traditional and non-traditional sites include radio, newspaper advertising and inserts, direct mail and billboards. If the company receives the required funding, it will engage in an aggressive advertising campaign which would also include cable television. This would expand the name recognition of Roma's Deli and develop new franchise sales.

Sales Activities

Romastrano currently receives in excess of ten (10) inquiries per week from potential franchisees. These inquiries are generated solely through word of mouth and in-store inquiry cards. Romastrano will utilize some of its funding to promote franchise sales through discovery nights and newspaper and periodical advertisements.

Romastrano Incorporated is uniquely positioned to take advantage of the market opportunity due to the managerial and field expertise of its officers and its superior product. Henry Malogne, Beatrice Philmont, Arthur Philmont, and Sandi Malogne all possess several years of experience in the food and/or business industry. Mr. Malogne has been the owner of the original Roma's Deli for the past 25 years, succeeding his father in the business. Beatrice Philmont has been a practicing attorney for the past 18 years with special focus on business, corporate, franchise and real estate law. Arthur Philmont has been managing Romastrano Incorporated since its inception and has had prior management experience. Sandi Malogne has been working with the original Roma's Deli since 1985 and currently acts as the trainer for Romastrano Incorporated.

Romastrano has operated profitably since its inception in July, 1993. If the company receives the requested minimum $500,000, it will be utilized for four (4) primary purposes:

- Marketing the Roma's image and concept to expand the franchise base to 40 units within 12 to 18 months and generate more product sales.

- To support the building of 8 additional corporate non-traditional locations within 12 to 18 months.

- To hire a veteran fast food executive as chief executive officer.

- To expand the corporate infrastructure to support the expansion of the Roma's System.

The Roma's financial model with 30 additional franchises and 10 company owned stores based on existing store volumes would be projected as follows (all figures are calculated on an annual basis):

	Present	**Jul 1995**	**Sep 1996**
	10 Franchises	13 Franchises & 2 Corp. Stores	40 Franchises & 10 Corp. Stores
Royalty Revenue	$77,400.00	$100,620.00	$309,600.00
Corporate Stores	$0.00	$53,424.00	$267,120.00

Marketing and Sales Activities

Organization and Personnel

Financial Summary

	Present	**Jul 1995**	**Sep 1996**
Product Sales	$9,000.00	$10,000.00	$36,000.00
Franchise Fees	$0.00	$0.00	$300,000.00
Gross Revenues	$86,400.00	$164,044.00	$912,720.00
Gross Expenses	$57,300.00	$107,300.00	$612,000.00
Net Profit: (Pre Tax)	$29,100	$56,744.00	$300,720.00

MISSION

To be a National Sandwich Shop Company with a total commitment to quality of product and customer service and to develop a company structure with a design to maximize economic efficiencies and to provide unsurpassed store support.

STRATEGY

The management team of Romastrano Incorporated believes that our mission can be achieved following the five (5) phase plan as shown below:

Phase	Dates	Objective & Status
I	Jan. 1992 - Jul. 1993	Design, develop and open prototype store conveying the Romastrano Concept - Completed.
II	Jul. 1993 - Dec. 1994	Sell ten franchises within VT, NH and MA to qualified buyers - Completed. 11 franchises sold by December, 1994.
III	Jan. 1995 - Dec. 1995	Expand development with Corporate and franchised units, in both traditional & non-traditional settings - As of July 1, 1995, 2 non-traditional company stores developed; 3 new non-traditional franchises to open by fall of 1995.
IV	Jan. 1996 - Jan. 1997	Expand the number of existing stores by adding 8 company stores and 30 franchises - To be completed.
V	Jan. 1997 forward	To continue the expansion of Romastrano Stores to 400+ units - To be completed.

THE COMPANY

Romastrano Incorporated ("the company") operates and franchises Roma's Delis. The company was formed in July, 1993 to acquire the trade name, recipes and concepts of Roma's of Burlington, Inc. which operated two stores in Burlington, and Newport, Vermont. Since 1959, Roma's of Burlington, Inc., operated by the Malogne Family, has become an institution in the Vermont region. Roma's has been exceptionally successful by offering specialty italian sandwiches, featuring Roma's mild salami, specially baked bread, fresh vegetables and oil blended from secret ingredients, and has been consistently voted as the number one sandwich in the region.

The Roma's concept was put through a franchise feasibility test in which it received exceptionally high ratings based in part on the ability to provide a consistent product, the simplicity of its operation, ease of training and duplication, low food costs, as well as the low-entry costs. A Roma's franchise offers the opportunity to enter the rapidly expanding fast food business for one of the most economical investments in the industry. The total investment for a traditional store ranges from $41,000 to $71,000, including a franchise fee of $12,500 and capital reserves of $10,000 to $20,000. The total investment for a non-traditional store starts as low as $35,000, including a $10,000 franchise fee.

In the first 18 months of the company's existence, Romastrano Incorporated sold 14 traditional franchise units. The company's remarkable growth and unique concept has been featured in several periodicals and newspapers throughout the region. In addition, the company was the subject of a case study by Montpelier School.

Of the 14 franchises sold in the first 18 months, 10 units have opened and are operating in Brattleboro, Middlebury, Windsor, Bellows Falls, Bennington, St. Albans, Burlington, and St. Johnsbury, Vermont and Glens Falls and Plattsburgh, New York. The company receives a weekly royalty of 5% of gross sales from each franchise, which totals approximately $1,500 per week. Romastrano recently opened 2 non-traditional stores inside Barrows stores in Rutland, Vermont and North Adams, Massachusetts, which have been in operation for two months and one month, respectively. In addition, franchised non-traditional shops are scheduled to open inside a Gas Max Mini-Mart in Barre, Vermont, and a convenience store in Windsor, Vermont by the fall of 1996. Both Barrows and Gas Max USA have informed the company that they desire to expand this non-traditional food concept throughout New England and beyond.

The success to date of the traditional franchised stores and the non-traditional company stores has led the company's management to the conclusion that it would be advantageous to open a substantial number of additional company stores and to expand franchised traditional and non-traditional units. The company, therefore, desires to obtain venture capital funding of $500,000. The new capital will be used to expand the business through the opening of non-traditional company owned stores, to promote the sale of franchised traditional and non-traditional stores, to build a brand equity of the Roma's products through a regional advertising campaign, and to hire an experienced CEO in the fast food business.

CONCEPT

Roma's Deli's represent a unique concept that combines total quality and unsurpassed freshness based on a limited menu selection. The units are bright and attractive and make maximum utilization of space. A traditional Roma's location can be operated in as little as 500 square feet, while a non-traditional shop can be comfortably operated within 110 square feet. The company has a variety of floor plans ranging from traditional stores with seating, traditional stores for take-out only, and non-traditional shops.

The Roma's concept originated in Burlington, Vermont with a single sandwich menu. The growth of our system has also led to the expansion of our menu line. Roma's recently introduced a honey-smoked turkey breast sandwich to go along with its original italian and vegetarian sandwiches. The original italian sandwich consists of Roma's own proprietary mild cooked salami, provolone cheese, thinly sliced onions, peppers, pickles and olives on a fresh baked roll made only for Roma's. The shops serve chips and a variety of beverages year-round, and also serve hot soup in the winter and gelati in the summer. All of the company's suppliers are positioned to meet the company's demands in all of its growth potential areas.

In 1992, there were approximately 120,000 fast-food, ready-to-serve and take-out convenience food restaurants in the U.S. Of these, approximately 70% are operated by franchisees. The market for a new, unique, high-quality italian sandwich is tremendous. The potential for a well-planned entry into this market by an aggressive operator with vision and experience couldn't be stronger and the timing couldn't be better.

Roma's competition is apparent in the big-named chains (i.e. Tony's, Fun Bun, Mama Mia's, etc.). The fastest growth area for all of the competition is in non-traditional settings. Roma's has a unique advantage over the competition in that it can locate in non-traditional settings without risk of encroaching on other traditional stores.

The Roma's non-traditional store is a full service shop which can be operated within 110 square feet. This provides a special advantage over the competition because most of them require a minimum of 200 square feet. This allows the anchor store (i.e. Barrows, Gas Max, Baker's Cap, etc.) to have more space for their own needs. Many of the non-traditional stores will also offer a limited breakfast menu of fresh bagels and muffins to complement the anchor stores' coffee sales during the morning hours. It is projected that a non-traditional store will gross in excess of $150,000 annually, which is based on the sales volumes presently experienced in the North Adams, MA and Rutland, VT stores. This, combined with the fact that the equipment and leasehold improvement cost is substantially less than a traditional store, make this an attractive investment from both the company and franchisee standpoints.

As the Roma's system expands, it is anticipated that area developers will supplement traditional stores with non-traditional locations which would allow them to centralize the preparation of the products (e.g. daily slicing of fresh vegetables). All of the Roma's locations are required to become actively involved with their communities, as is evidenced by the introduction of the Roma's Neighborhood Club in the fall of 1985.

ROMA'S MANAGEMENT TEAM

The current Romastrano Incorporated management team, responsible for all aspects of the training, opening and ongoing support of Roma's stores, is profiled below:

Henry Malogne President/Director

Mr. Malogne serves as president of the company and has held this position since July, 1993. Mr. Malogne is also president of Roma's of Burlington, Inc. Roma's of Burlington, Inc. has owned and operated Roma's Delis in Burlington, Vermont since 1958. Mr. Malogne is also a director of the company.

Beatrice Philmont General Counsel/Director

Ms. Philmont began Romastrano Incorporated in 1993 and serves as general counsel to the company. Ms. Philmont is an attorney with the law firm Johnston, Philmont & O'Connell, P.A. in Burlington, Vermont and has been a partner since 1981. Ms. Philmont is also a director of the company.

Arthur Philmont Vice President/Treasurer

Mr. Philmont serves as Vice President and Treasurer of the franchisor and has held these positions since July, 1993. Mr. Philmont is responsible for the day-to-day management of the company and provides the field support to the existing franchisees. Prior to this time, Mr. Philmont was general manager of Wesley Real Estate Company of Burlington, Vermont. Mr. Philmont is a shareholder of the company.

Sandi Malogne Director of Training

Ms. Malogne serves as Director of Training for the company and has held that position since July, 1993. Prior to this time, Ms. Malogne was employed as manager of Roma's Delis in Burlington, Vermont. Ms. Malogne is also a shareholder of the company.

THE ROMA'S FRANCHISE PROGRAM

The Roma's franchise program centers around the "business format" category of franchising, in which a proven concept is streamlined and is then developed or "packaged" into a legal, viable and marketable investment opportunity. Franchising is a strictly regulated area of business involving federal and state laws and agencies. The Roma's franchise program provides for diligent adherence to all such regulations and shall, at all times, continue to do so.

In order to be successful, a franchise opportunity must offer three basic benefits to the franchisee. First, the business concept must be appealing to a broad segment of the population. Second, the business must not be a "fad" or a short-term enterprise with short-term appeal. Third, the concept must have a strong possibility of being successful and offer a reasonable return on investment. The 35 year history of the Roma's store in Burlington, Vermont and the success of our existing franchisees demonstrates that these three basic benefits are present in the Roma's program. The

Burlington Roma's store, from which the company does not derive any royalties, has annualized net sales after discounts of in excess of $500,000. The Windsor franchisee, which is our oldest franchised store, now celebrating its second anniversary, will have annual net sales after discounts of approximately $250,000, while the Middlebury store's sales will exceed $300,000.

The franchises are in effect for a period of ten (10) years with five (5) year renewal options. An initial franchise fee is required for a single store. The initial fee is $12,500 for a traditional store and $10,000 for a non-traditional store, and is payable in full upon signing of the franchise agreement. The initial fee is in consideration for the rights to use the company's name and business format, its recipes, the operations and other manuals, real estate evaluation and selection assistance, and all initial training and management operations of the shop.

After the franchisee opens for business, the franchise agreement provides for payment of an ongoing business development fee or royalty of five percent (5%), based upon the gross sales of the franchised business. In addition, an advertising expenditure is required of each franchisee, as well as a modest contribution of one percent (1%) to a corporate ad fund, again based upon the gross sales of the franchised business.

Certain proprietary ingredients and products are purchased from Romastrano Inc. or a designated supplier, and the company realizes a reasonable mark-up on these items.

The ever increasing buying power of the growing Roma's network will be reflected in lower prices on all goods and services that the corporate and franchised shop purchase.

ROMA'S TRAINING PROGRAMS

Roma's provides a comprehensive training program which uses elements of classroom, hands-on and in-store training. The initial program is three (3) weeks in duration (depending on individual needs) and consists of on-site training in other Roma's locations. The subjects covered include: General Business Management, Budgeting, Retail Marketing and Merchandising, Purchasing, Negotiating, Point of Sale System Training, Use of Operations Manual, Sales Training, Store Operations, and Personnel.

Through observation and actual involvement, the franchisee is guided through the entire operating process, from shop opening to food handling, handling customers, sales techniques, and shop closing.

At least one member of the Romastrano corporate staff spends a week with each franchisee at his or her location, during the actual opening (approximately 2 to 3 days prior to opening and 2 to 3 days after opening). This is to insure that the franchisee is knowledgeable and comfortable with the day to day operations and the shop is properly set up and functioning smoothly.

Ongoing seminars and/or training sessions are held as needs are identified. Daily support is provided by answering questions and/or discussing problems via telephone with corporate headquarters.

Training is an essential, ongoing process at Roma's and will continue throughout the life of the business. Ongoing communications are maintained through newsletters, bulletins, quarterly meetings and seminars.

ON-GOING SUPPORT PROGRAM

Roma's provides a series of essential, on-going support programs, including the following:

Audits

Shop results are audited on a current and on-going basis to assist the franchisee and identify any weak spots or potential problems. In-store audits are performed to assist the franchisee with his or her maintenance of the standards of operations set forth in the Roma's confidential operations manual.

Bulletins

Special information of immediate importance is transmitted via telephone, facsimile or mail. Such information may be a change in products, procedures, special purchases, prices, etc.

Operations Manual Updates

The Roma's system is a dynamic system that requires revisions, updates and changes from time to time. As new and better methods are developed, they are incorporated into the system and transmitted to the franchisee via operations manual updates.

Accessible 800 Number

A hot line is maintained at headquarters to answer all franchisee inquiries and assist them with any problems.

On-site Assistance

On-site assistance is provided on a regular basis.

Incentive Programs

Roma's believes in recognition and incentive programs for its franchisees. These programs, which vary in approach, serve to build and maintain a friendly, competitive spirit and to generate enthusiasm among the entire franchise network.

ROMA'S NON-TRADITIONAL STORE

Roma's non-traditional shops are defined as Roma's locations which are co-branding with other fast food chains (e.g. Baker's Cap or other coffee shops, specialty ice cream shops, pizza chains) or Roma's stores located within existing convenience stores (e.g. Barrows, Dirks, Quik In, etc.), department stores (e.g. Helmot, Buddy's, Waltons, etc.), ballparks, airports, bus terminals and truck stops. This concept has been defined as the fastest growing segment of the food industry. For example, Fun Bun anticipates having 2,000 non-traditional franchise stores by the year 2000.

Roma's first venture into the non-traditional fast-food market has been inside a Barrows store in Rutland, Vermont (opened May 1, 1995) and a shop inside a Barrows store in North Adams, Massachusetts (opened June 1, 1995). These two stores were opened as company stores by Romastrano Incorporated. The company leases approximately 110 square feet of space in a high visibility section of the store. The North Adams, MA location is already under contract to a franchisee who will purchase this shop September 1, 1995. The company also has a franchisee who is constructing a non-traditional shop inside a Gas Max Mini-Mart in Barre, Vermont, scheduled to open by August 15, 1995.

All non-traditional shops offer the same menu as a traditional Roma's Deli, with the addition of fresh bagels and muffins. Under Roma's non-traditional concept, the Roma's store leases its space on a percent of gross basis which ranges from six percent (6%) to ten percent (10%) which includes rent, heat, air conditioning and electricity.

The non-traditional stores will be able to take advantage of the existing customer base of Barrows and Gas Max, which exceeds 750 customers per day. Roma's operating hours are from 7:00 am to 8:00 pm, plus extended hours depending upon customer demand.

The non-traditional stores will be afforded signage on the street sign and on the outside of the building. In addition, Roma's will place its menus and speakers on the Barrows and Gas Max gas pumps so the customer may order while filling up their automobile. Point of purchase coupons and promotional materials will be distributed by Barrows and Gas Max, and the companies engage in joint advertising.

The management of the Roma's corporate non-traditional stores will be under the direction of Romastrano Incorporated. Each shop will have a designated manager who will be directly responsible for the operation and staffing of the non-traditional store. Part-time sandwich makers will be employed at a base pay and all employees will be on an incentive bonus program. This will provide assurance of having a pleasant, motivated sales force. As the non-traditional corporate system expands, one full-time manager will be able to oversee three (3) non-traditional locations with part-time help filling the balance of the operating hours, minimizing the labor costs.

The sandwich business is a rapidly growing segment of the fast-food industry as demonstrated by the growth of Fun Bun, Tony's, Mama Mia's, etc. The most popular sandwich menu item is the traditional italian sandwich which, in many instances, comprises up to 70% of sandwich sales. Roma's limited menu has targeted the italian sandwich customer and built its reputation on selling the freshest, best italian sandwich anywhere. The introduction of the honey-roasted smoked turkey sandwich was designed to address the low-fat, no cholesterol customer demand and to provide variety to larger customer groups.

INDUSTRY AND COMPETITION

Roma's has always been a product driven company whose growth has been realized through word of mouth with virtually no advertising for many years. The Roma's customer has been known to travel several hours in search of Roma's sandwich. The Roma's customer service cards attest to the fact that Roma's customers are repeat customers who rate the quality and service at the highest levels.

The Roma's competition, especially Fun Bun and Tony's, relies heavily on an extensive marketing campaign to drive their sales. The competition also has extensive menu selections with which Roma's does not attempt to compete. The limited menu at Roma's guarantees freshness of product each and every time. The growth opportunities for a fresh, quality product, combined with an aggressive marketing campaign, are tremendous.

Roma's employs a comprehensive public relations, advertising and promotional program for its new stores that includes a pre-opening, grand-opening and on-going strategies campaigns. The overall plan includes an initial public relations effort through press releases developed to generate valuable publicity for the shop and its owner. At least three weeks prior to opening, Roma's displays "Yumming Soon" signs at the new location.

ADVERTISING PROGRAM

All ad copies are professionally developed at Roma's corporate headquarters and provided to the franchisees. All of the media and the target customer area are identified and a plan is developed for each of those selected. The program begins approximately three weeks prior to the shop opening with press releases sent to all area media profiling the Roma's franchisee.

A special campaign is used for the grand-opening (which usually takes place about a month or so after a quiet opening) and it includes a multiplicity of approaches. Included in the plan are print and visual ads, give aways, public relations releases, contests, invited dignitaries, etc.

It is the company's intent to develop an extensive and ongoing regional marketing campaign through cable television, free-standing color flyers, radio, print and point of sale purchase materials. The Roma's success has been astounding, especially in light of the fact that in some of the company's markets, Roma's name recognition does not exceed ten percent (10%). This has been determined by market surveys in some of Roma's franchised store areas. If the required funding is obtained, the company plans on spending upwards of $175,000 in regional advertising over the next six months which will provide continuous market recognition in Vermont, New York Massachusetts. This will help to develop the Roma's "brand equity" which will increase store sales and royalty revenues and greatly increase franchising inquiries.

FUNDS REQUIRED AND THEIR USES

Romastrano Incorporated has tremendous upside potential. In order to achieve that potential, the company needs to seek out and employ a chief executive officer who has a background and experience in the growth of franchised and company owned fast food restaurants. The company further needs to engage in an aggressive marketing campaign to increase its brand equity and to construct additional company stores to expand its system. If the company receives the requested $500,000, it will be utilized to fulfill those objectives as follows:

1. To seek out and employ an experienced chief executive officer with a solid track record in franchising fast food businesses. (Anticipated first year cost would be $100,000 salary plus a small equity position in the company.)

2. To engage in a consistent advertising program over the next six to eight months which would increase awareness of Roma's products and the value for the money, and place Roma's at "top of mind" with the consumer. This advertising campaign would consist of colored flyers, newspaper advertisements, point of sale advertising, radio ads, cable t.v. ads and direct community marketing. Direct marketing to companies, schools, bingo halls, etc. has proven to generate large orders and substantially increase a store's profitability. The effect of the advertising campaign would be two-fold in that it will expand Roma's name recognition and it will increase sales and royalty revenues in the existing Roma's stores. In addition, a portion of these funds will be utilized to engage a continuous advertising campaign for the sale of franchises which has never been done by the company.

As stated before, the company currently receives approximately ten inquiries per week from perspective franchisees and an advertising campaign in industry publications and regional newspapers would substantially increase those inquiries. (Advertising expenditures over the next 6 to 8 months would consist of $175,000 for direct advertising and $25,000 directed for the targeting of new franchisees.)

3. To support and build out an additional eight (8) corporate non-traditional shops within 12 to 18 months. The company built out and equipped the North Adams, MA and Rutland, VT stores for $15,000 per store (estimated cost for constructing 8 new stores would be $120,000).

The company's goals with this funding is to bring in an experienced CEO who can coordinate the rapid growth of the Roma's system and increase sales volumes in all of the existing stores. The company has the unique opportunity with Barrows, Gas Max, and other national companies, to rapidly expand its units. In order to do so, funding is essential to make Roma's a major player in the fast food industry.

If the requested funding is obtained, it will allow Roma's to grow to 40 franchised shops and 10 corporate shops within the next 24 months. The minimum net pre-tax profit is projected to be $300,720 annually, upon achieving the 40 franchises and 10 corporate stores. This is projected at the present franchised store sales volumes. These sales, however, are steadily increasing. Therefore, it is not expected that the company would need any additional funding unless or until there was a major expansion beyond 100 stores. The company expects that many of the corporate, non-traditional locations that are built will be sold out to franchisees at a profit. The company would reevaluate its need for additional capital only in the event that the company determined that it wanted to substantially increase its ratio between corporate and franchised stores.

Romastrano Incorporated is a C corporation and the stock is currently held by Arthur Philmont (50%) and Sandi Malogne (50%). The company proposes offering its funding provider with either equity in the form of common stock, preferred stock or convertible-preferred stock or a combination of debt and equity. The long-term goal of the company is to grow the company to an excess of 100 stores during the next five years and to position the company for acquisition or sale in five to seven years.

FINANCIAL INFORMATION

Romastrano Incorporated has operated profitably since its inception in July, 1993. The company has operated with minimum overhead and $30,000 in annual executive salaries during this period. During the initial phases of the company, a subsidiary company, Carters Inc., was formed for the purposes of delivering bread, produce, potato chips and other products to the franchised shops. This resulted in the hiring of one and one-half full-time employees, the purchasing of a truck, and other substantial expenses. It was determined that the delivery system was inadequate and too costly. The company has since made arrangements for direct shipment of all product by the suppliers to individual shops. The company receives a small mark-up for Romastrano product sales, which averages approximately $1,000 per month currently. Carters, Inc. was liquidated in 1994 and incurred a loss of approximately $25,000 during its first and only operating year, which loss was covered by Romastrano Incorporated.

The company has financial reports prepared by an independent CPA. Attached hereto is the balance sheet as of January 31, 1995. An updated balance sheet will be forthcoming within the next 30 days. Also attached are present and projected revenues and copies of disclosures from our offering circular that estimate the investment of a traditional and non-traditional store.

The Roma's financial model with 30 additional franchises and 10 company owned stores based on existing store volumes would be projected as follows (all figures are calculated on an annual basis):

Cash Flow Projections

	Present 10 Franchises	July, 1995 13 Franchises & 2 Corp. Stores	Sept. 1996 40 Franchises & 10 Corp. Stores
Royalty Revenue:	77,400.00	100,620.00	309,600.00
Corporate Stores: (Net Profit)	0.00	53,424.00	267,120.00
Product Sales:	9,000.00	10,000.00	36,000.00
Franchise Fees:	0.00	0.00	300,000.00
Gross Revenues:	86,400.00	164,044.00	912,720.00
Gross Expenses:	57,300.00	107,300.00	612,000.00
Net Profit: (Pre Tax)	29,100	56,744.00	300,720.00

Annual Expenses

	Present	Projected 40 Fran. & 10 Corp. Stores
Rent:	0.00	21,000.00
Salaries:	34,800.00	250,000.00
Insurance:	1,200.00	4,800.00
Utilities:	1,200.00	4,800.00
Equipment Leases:	1,620.00	5,000.00

	Present	Projected
Accounting:	1,200.00	4,800.00
Auto Loans:	3,480.00	10,200.00
Legal:	0.00	20,000.00
Telephone:	7,200.00	14,000.00
Dues:	1,500.00	3,000.00
Office Supplies:	2,400.00	10,000.00
Travel Expenses:	2,400.00	15,000.00
Marketing:	0.00	150,000.00
Subscription:	300.00	500.00
Totals:	**$ 57,300.00**	**$612,000.00**

Video Service

BUSINESS PLAN

EXPRESS VIDEO SERVICE

P.O. Box 1223
24 Stevens St.
Newark, NJ 08540
July 14, 1989

Express Video Service fulfills a unique niche in the competitive video rental market by specializing in corporate training videos, as well as special interest videos. Express Video Service further distinguishes itself from the competition by offering a delivery service. This plan highlights market analysis and strategy by identifying unfulfilled customer needs and providing exceptional customer service.

INTRODUCTION

Express Video Service will distribute pre-packaged videotape programming to the corporate and residential market. Our videotape programming inventory will consist of corporate management, training, sales, personal self-improvement and special interest titles.

Rentals of our tapes will be made available through on-site delivery and pick-up to the customer's office complex or condo/townhouse residential community. All titles will also be made available for purchase utilizing the same on-site delivery service.

Selling Points

Express Video Service brings to the consumer an exceptional collection of videotape programming; products especially selected by Express Video Service to satisfy the special lifestyle of the Madison and Arnold county corporate employee and community residents.

Express Video Service stands for quality service and convenience. Our customers will find that we've assembled not only a unique and wide variety of titles, but we feature the first tape delivery service in the area.

Quality and service underlies everything offered at Express Video Service. Every videotape in our inventory has been carefully selected with the customer's lifestyle in mind. The customer will find an answer to almost every need, for both corporate performance and personal value.

MARKET ANALYSIS

Market Definition

The key market segments for Express Video Service are corporate office complexes and townhouse/condominium developments within the Madison/Arnold County area. According to the U.S. Department of Commerce, business establishments in Madison County alone exceed 8,000, with close to 3,000 firms being service oriented and over 700 involved with finance, insurance and real estate. The New Jersey Department of Transportation has concluded in their Regional Forum that if the present land development trends continue, commercial development along the Main Street Corridor will increase by 214 percent from 20 million square feet in 1980 to 62.8 million square feet in 2005. Jobs will grow by 240 percent from 56,600 to 192,300.

Overall, Madison County's residential population has shown steady growth in the past twenty-five years. NJDOT estimates that housing units will increase by 165 percent, from 30,149 in 1980 to 79,957 in 2005. State projections from the Department Of Labor indicate a surge in population between 1980 and the year 2000, from 307,000 to approximately 362,000.

Currently, the market distribution is shared by several participants on the retail store-front level. With the stability and growth of the corporate and residential market segment in the Madison/Arnold County area, videotape rental performance, over the past two years, has generated substantial revenues for area suppliers. However, retail customers are looking for greater inventory variety and availability.

The lack of distribution of corporate and special interest programming has resulted in the need to change the way the average consumer views videotape rental as a "movie-only" business. This new outlook to videotape availability allows Express Video Service to step into the market and operate efficiently by catering to a new market niche. Express Video Service has the ability to provide educational and learning tapes to the corporate community, with on-site delivery and pick-up of inventory being unique to the videotape rental market.

Market Penetration

The videotape rental market continues to grow at a rapid rate. Currently, there is a 70% penetration of video recorders in American homes. Over the last 5 years, compared to homes receiving Cable

TV and the number of independent commercial television stations, VCR penetration has shown the largest growth over the period, increasing by a factor of 30. In 1988, figures published by A.C. Nielsen ratings showed a 9.5% decline in viewership. The trend away from network viewing will continue, and while VCR penetration may not grow as quickly as in the past, the rate at which new home video releases come out will increase.

An estimated 135 million prerecorded videos were sold to dealers in the consumer market in 1988. The top 70 golf instruction tapes, a prime tape category for the corporate market, have sold approximately 680,000 units, grossing wholesale revenues of over $50 million in the past 12 months.

Initial Start-Up Phase (First 3 Months):

Targeted Consumer Outlets Include:

Corporate Total

Davis Complex	2,000 employees
Park Industries	8,500 employees

Residential

Forest Trails	2,900 units
Strawberry Fields	621 units
Total	**14,021**

Secondary Phase (Second 3 Months):

Corporate Total

Sullivan Center	2,500 employees
Emerson Business Center	10,000 employees

Residential

Canton	1,500 units
Plymouth	2,000 units
Pine Forest	2,700 units
Total	**32,700**

(Initial & Secondary Phase Combined)

Of the 14,000 customers in our initial start-up phase, approximately 70% own VCRs. Of this 70%, we expect a 10% share of the market for the first month of operation, 15% for the second month, and 25% for the remainder of our first year:

	MKT Size	VCR Penetration	Mkt Share Sept. (10%)	Mkt Share Oct. (15%)	Mkt Share Nov. (25%)
Davis Complex	2000	1400	140	210	350
Park Industries	8500	5950	595	892.5	1487.5
Forest Trails	2900	2030	203	304.5	507.5
Strawberry Fields	621	434.7	43.47	65.205	108.675
Totals	**14021**	**9815**	**981**	**1472**	**2454**

The market potential for Express Video Service, based on a conservative average rental of one (1) videotape per month, per customer, totalling 4900 weekday and weekend rentals for the first quarter — with a current rental price of $5 per weekday and $7.50 per weekend rental — is approximately $14,600 in gross receipts for the first three months. Additionally, special weekly rentals of our corporate series tapes, available at $100 per week will generate an additional 300% annualized profit:

Revenues (1st Qtr)	
Weekday Rentals	$8183.01
Weekend Rentals	$6128.05
Corporate Rentals	$300.00
Gross Rental Revenue (1st Qtr)	**$14611.06**

Strengths

In terms of product/service strength, Express Video Service's tape inventory and delivery service has several distinct advantages over the competition. First, it has marked differentiation in product inventory offering training, management, sales and special interest videos, as opposed to a limited scope of blockbuster movies. Also, our service is favorably differentiated from the competition with our unique delivery and pickup service to the area's corporate office complexes and condo/townhouse residential communities.

Weaknesses

The only notable marketplace disadvantage is rental pricing, with most consumers used to paying between $1.50 and $3.50 per videotape rental. But, Express Video Service should be able to position itself as a service-oriented company with an unmatched inventory of very special titles in order to charge a premium for rentals and thereby reduce this weakness considerably.

Corporate weaknesses, at this time, consist only of a lack of awareness, on the employees part, to programming that is readily available for their use. However, we will take steps to educate and inform the consumer about the availability of product and its resulting benefits which we feel should alleviate this problem.

CUSTOMERS

The most typical customer for our product/service is someone who is in the corporate office environment, and who currently uses management training and sales tapes for seminars, training and overall corporate knowledge. We also appeal to those employees who rent entertainment and special interest titles for viewing pleasure in the privacy of their own homes.

It is highly likely that our potential customers are going to be familiar with VHS videotape as an entertainment medium, and that they will readily accept our unique inventory list of management training and special interest tapes, provided that we make the potential customer aware of the availability of Express Video Service's vast array of titles.

Complimentary products/services already in use by our customers are corporate training manuals and audio cassettes. These current products are seen as a tremendous help in compelling customers to acquire our product and to use our service.

The principal buying motive of corporate executives, managers and employees is education. Learning the various aspects of the corporate world enables them to better their performance, and thus, their company's profits. Their personal income may also increase as a result of these informative manuals and audio cassettes. The principal motive of action will be the availability of various titles through Express Video Service's on-site delivery service.

Key Market Consumers

Corporate Executive
Title: CEO, President, VP Finance, H.R. Director, Personnel Administrator, Office Manager.
Power: Permitter, Decision Maker, Influencer, Technical Consultant, Initiator

Young Professionals
Age: 25-35
Income: Medium to high
Sex: Male or Female
Family: Bachelor or married
Geographic: Suburban
Occupation: White collar

Housewife
Age: 35-55
Income: Fixed
Sex: Female
Family: Full nest
Geographic: Suburban
Occupation: White collar/Blue collar family

Young Married Couples
Age: 35-55
Income: Medium to high
Sex: Male or Female
Family: Married or no children
Geographic: Suburban
Occupation: White collar

Older Couple
Age: 55-70
Income: High or fixed
Sex: Male or Female
Family: Empty nest
Geographic: Suburban
Occupation: White collar or none

COMPETITION

Express Video Service's line of videotape programming offers important information and education to today's corporate managers and employees in everyday managerial and employment situations. Competitive threats today come from consultants who perform "live" for the company in training seminars.

Express Video Service's products/services perform in virtually every corporate environment where business managers and employees are well educated and informed on the uses of video in today's world. The ability to be informed, educated and entertained by your television set is nothing new in the world of video. What is new, however, is Express Video Service's full capability to develop a vast inventory of titles on a variety of topics and special interests as opposed to concentrating on blockbuster movie titles. These corporate training, management, sales and special interest titles, along with their on-site delivery to the corporate and residential markets is unique to Express Video Service's products/services. Our research indicates that the performance of our product line and titles is superior to anything else on the market today.

By all comparisons, Express Video Service's products/services provide a greater inventory, with a wider variety of titles, and have superior production values and product content than the local retail video outlets. Our delivery service is unmatched by anyone in our market area.

Videotape Product/Service

Companies that compete in this market are local retail outlets (for entertainment titles) and mail order catalogues (for management and special interest video). The home or office delivery feature of Express Video Service is not shared with any competitors. Competition does exist, however, in the residential market in relation to inventory of entertainment titles. Competitors in this area are American Video, Sunshine Video Production, and Jackson Video. While they stock a large inventory of titles, the diversity is lacking and delivery is non-existent. All companies charge competitive prices.

All of our competitors' products only operate in a limited way: the customer has to order through a catalogue and wait for delivery, or the customer has to go out of his way to a retail outlet to pick up a tape. Our competitor's product/service does not provide the same service that Express Video Service is offering: on-site delivery and pick-up of videotape programming, either on a rental or purchase basis.

Observations & Conclusions

It appears, from the above information, that Express Video Service has secured a specific market niche opportunity.

MARKETING STRATEGY

Express Video Service's marketing strategy is to enhance, promote and support the fact that our product and services are unique in the marketplace. Our inventory of videotape titles emphasizes corporate training, management, sales and special interest entertainment, rather than our competitors' strict adherence to blockbuster movie titles. Our service features on-site delivery to the office or home rather than our competitors' non-deliverable goods sold or rented through a retail outlet/storefront or mail order catalogue.

Comprehensive Plan

The overall marketing plan for our product/service is based on the following fundamentals:

Express Video Service is in the business of distributing pre-recorded videocassette programming.

We plan on reaching the company executives, office managers and employees located within the twenty largest office complexes in the Madison/Arnold County area, with a secondary market consisting of all the townhouse and condo residents located within the twenty largest residential complexes in the Madison/Arnold County area.

Express Video Service's channel of distribution will be door to door delivery of catalogues and inventory.

Express Video Service will be catering to an existing market of corporate trainers, consultants and personnel administrators familiar with video as a means of information. Specifically, Express Video Service will be establishing an entirely new attitude, with all employees, in the corporate use of video programming. Thus, we plan on a 10% share of the market upon upstart, increasing to a 25% share during the second quarter of operation. As the concept catches on and competitors enter the arena, Express Video Service expects to maintain a substantial share of the market through pre-established contacts, product knowledge, superior service and inventory. Additionally, following our corporate market introduction Express Video Service will also seek to capture a significant share of the consumer market with its unique delivery service to the home.

Positioning

Our products will be seen by the consumer as very professional in production value and content. Our service will be seen by the consumer as very professional, upscale, and second to none with its unique on-site delivery feature.

Our most unique advantage, being the on-site delivery and pick-up of videotape programming, can be exploited to achieve a winning position in the consumer's mind.

In terms of market segmentation advantages, we can use corporate managers, employees and upscale "yuppie" suburbanite consumers to arrive at a winning position.

We will reposition the videotape product as a training and learning tool in addition to an entertainment medium. We will reposition the service of the product as a deliverable item rather than an item which needs to be shopped for and picked up at a retail outlet or purchased only through the mail.

Reposition the Competition

We can reposition our competitors by showing their limitations of product line (only entertainment titles) and the limitations in service (you must go to them for a tape... Express Video Service comes to you!).

Express Video Service's marketing strategy incorporates plans to sell our line of products/ services through a catalogue of titles, with rental and sales implemented by a direct sales force.

SELLING TACTICS

Direct Sales

We have chosen to use a direct sales force because our products/services require considerable customer education and post sales support directly from the company. Express Video Service anticipates hiring one sales representative for the corporate community in each county of coverage.

Manufacturers' Representatives

Because various videotape distributors carry several product lines compatible with ours, in keeping with our upscale and professional corporate image, we feel that it would be appropriate to select production representatives carrying those titles containing high production values and professional content, regardless of cost. We will also establish business relationships with distributors selling entertainment titles appropriate to the companies' employees for take-home entertainment.

Distributors

One of the key elements designed into the Express Video Service marketing plan is the targeting of our distributors. It is important to select distribution channels already in existence and staffed with professionals possessing appropriate backgrounds and expertise.

The distributors' products are pertinent to the nature of Express Video Service's business and to the well-being of our customer base. It is not difficult for us to reach distributors who are educated as to the benefits available in using certain management and special interest tapes.

Express Video Service will also develop sales agreements directly with independent video producers, publishers and production companies who are involved with the actual production of special interest videos. This strategic marketing approach takes full advantage of the fact that these professionals are intimately involved with the content of the tape and its desired effect on the viewer. They already have expertise and have been practicing in their field for a length of time.

By operating within these distribution channels, in this manner, we feel that we can maintain control of our market. In addition, we can generate growth at a reasonable pace and obtain excellent sales results.

Ordering Structure

To place an order, the customer will call Express Video Service's local phone number or Fax Express Video Service's pre-printed order form to our corporate offices. All office rentals placed before noon will be delivered that same day to the customer's office by 4PM. Express Video Service will pick up returns from the office the following day. For residential delivery, tapes will be delivered door-to-door early that evening at a designated time for each particular community.

Pricing Structure

Daily weekday rentals to office complexes cost $5 per special interest title rental if ordered and delivered before 4 PM to an office. Daily weekday rentals to residential complexes cost $5 per special interest title. Customers will be charged $7.50 for weekend rental.

Corporate series rental titles are priced at $100 per weekly rental.

Payment is simple: Upon registering with Express Video Service, each interested customer (CEOs, Presidents, Managers, condo/townhouse residents) will receive a Free membership card. Our advertisements must address the following guidelines: all customers must be pre-approved to receive a special free membership card in their name, prior to issuing the customer's membership card. Express Video Service will make an imprint of each customer's major credit card along with registering any pertinent information necessary to establish credit. All rentals will then be billed to the credit cards—no checks written, no cash or exact change needed, no handling hassles with corporate offices or leasing agents. Monthly statements to customers will show all rentals and billings with order forms on file at Express Video Service's office should any discrepancy arise.

BUSINESS RELATIONSHIPS

Express Video Service, through contacts and past business relationships with AMY-TV's Julia Anderson, has formed some very important relationships with major teleproduction companies and independent producers in the industry. The following is a list of existing relationships:

Joint Marketing Agreements

Joint marketing with established companies will produce revenues, credibility, and market presence. Express Video Service is pursuing joint marketing agreements with other area businesses, management associations and residential communities to further the name of Express Video Service's products/services in the corporate and residential market. Our plans include having them market our videotape products/services within their office and community developments.

Express Video Service currently has a joint marketing relationship with Video Center, Inc., Manning Enterprises, and Techno Imagery. We are in the process of engaging in agreements with Water Springs residential community, Davis Complex Associates (Davis Complex), USA Business Parks (Park Industries), Young-Lynn Associates (Forest Trails) and several other large corporate and residential communities in the Madison and Arnold County area.

We feel that we require a substantial inventory of a large variety of management and special interest videotape titles to enhance the attractiveness of Express Video Service's product line to customers.

Third Party Supplier

Because we do not have the resources to acquire the rights to these titles for exclusive distribution, we rely on independent producers, publishers, professional associations, government agencies and established corporate telecommunication facilities for the development of many types of management, training and sales videotapes. Express Video Service will establish a Third Party Supplier relationship with several videotape distributors, independent producers, production facilities, management associations and corporate A/V coordinators.

Agreements Joint Development Efforts

Express Video Service, through AMY-TV's Julia Anderson, has been involved with joint development efforts with Techno Imagery, Manning Enterprises, Samuels Productions, Taz Enterprises, and Video Center, Inc.

A joint development project with Emily Ray Cosmetics and Tireman Videos has been discussed, but has not yet begun.

ADVERTISING & PROMOTION

Express Video Service recognizes that the key to success at this time requires extensive promotion. This must be done aggressively, but on a specifically concentrated scale within our initial target market area. To accomplish our sales goals, we require an extremely capable advertising agency and public relations firm. Express Video Service plans to advertise in the Madison County area's major business magazines and journals such as "Central Jersey Business", "Madison Business", "World Business News" and "Targeted Publications". Upon funding, an agency selection shall be made, and with their assistance, a comprehensive advertising and promotion plan will be drafted. Advertising will be done independently and cooperatively with distributors, publishers, producers and companies with whom Express Video Service has joint marketing/sales relationships.

Media Advertising and Promotion Objectives

Position Express Video Service as an upscale, service oriented firm for the business and residential community and as the leading supplier of corporate and special interest videotape programming to the corporate employee and community resident.

Increase company awareness and name recognition among company executives, business managers, and all company employees, with secondary consideration given to residential customers in condo/townhouse communities.

Develop, through Express Video Service's video marketing survey, significant information to develop immediate and long-term marketing plans and inventory control.

Create product advertising programs supporting Express Video Service's office and community delivery and pick-up service.

Coordinate sales literature, demonstration materials, telemarketing programs, and direct response promotions in order to boost the Express Video Service name and videotape programming inventory to the forefront of the corporate environment (from the executive's desk to the employee's cafeteria).

Maximize efficiency in selection and scheduling of publications to cover the Madison and Arnold County corporate and residential markets.

Because Express Video Service's tape distribution is so innovative and unique, it is important to develop a promotional campaign that is consistent and easy to understand. The best way to reach our potential customers is to develop an intense advertising campaign promoting our basic premise - on-site delivery of corporate management and special interest tapes for use, in office, by all corporate employees. This will be complimented by an inventory of entertainment and special interest titles for employee "take-home" and residential delivery.

Media Strategy/ Advertising Campaign

Position Express Video Service in a quality editorial environment consistent with creative objectives.

Select primary business publications and office newsletters with high specific market penetration.

Schedule adequate frequency to impact market with corporate image and product /service messages.

Where possible, position advertising in, or near, video reviews, video technology articles, training seminar ads and appropriate editorials.

To get the most out of our promotional budget, our media coverage will be to focus on the corporate executives, business managers and employees located within the twenty largest office complexes in Madison and Arnold County. The condo/townhouse owners/residents located within the twenty largest residential complexes in the area will be addressed as a secondary market.

We will develop an advertising campaign built around door-to-door delivery of videotape programming to the corporate and residential market with a specialized, demographically-controlled inventory list. Beginning with a "who we are" position, we'll support our position with ads that reinforce the Express Video Service message. Importantly, we will develop a consistent reach and frequency throughout the year.

For the greatest impact and recognition, it is necessary to run full page ads for the first quarter of advertising, with back page placement in business magazines preferable.

To maintain/establish our up-scale company image, the delivery and tone of our advertising must convey the excellence of the titles in our inventory, including quality content and production.

Ads will convey the look and feel of a professional, up-scale, corporate company.

Research indicates that door-to-door networking has not yet been used by any of our competitors. Express Video Service will offer that door-to-door personal touch!

Preliminary Media Schedule

| Targeted Publications | 94,000 households |
| | 23 communities |

World Business News	2500 business locations
	17,000 circulation
	50,000 working professionals
	Full page: $435-$695
	Half page: $220-$400

Central Jersey Business	15,000 circulation
	Full page: $1050-1500
	Half page: $575-$825

Madison Business	6,500 circulation
	Full page: $520-$650
	Half page: $300-$370

In regard to competitor's advertising, it is necessary to prioritize the corporate and special interest videos above the market-saturated entertainment titles, and the delivery and pick-up of these titles at the customer's place of employment or residential community.

Promotion

In addition to standard advertising practices, we will gain considerable recognition through:

- Corporate contact receptions and networking functions (sponsored year-round by the area's Chamber of Commerce and independent associations).
- Press releases
- Joint Sponsorship of corporate events and functions

Corporate videotape programming is already being utilized throughout the Madison County business community. Many of these products/titles are distributed internally from corporate headquarters to the satellite offices for internal use only. These tapes may only appear yearly or semi-annually. Our products/services will consist of a substantially larger inventory, not limited to only one company's internal library, and will be offered on a daily basis at a substantial cost savings, with rental availability, as well as purchase option.

The number of national trade shows attended will be approximately 4 each year, primarily Video Rental Association Conference, VRO, The New York Video Conference, and Corporate Video Show. We will also exhibit at approximately 5 local shows each year, both independently and with companies with which Express Video Service has joint marketing/sales agreements. Reports and papers will be published for trade journals.

Incentives

A select group of prospective clients (area firms with more than 50 employees or smaller firms with current high tape purchase/rental patterns) will receive a complimentary calendar/planner, custom designed with Express Video Service's sales promotion programs, products and services (available from Contemporary Graphics, 123 Main St., Simpson, OH 43812). A select group of prospective clients (area firms with more than 10 employees) will receive a complimentary blank T-120 videocassette, packaged in a custom designed Express Video Service sleeve.

For the corporate employee living in a local residential community, flyers introducing the Express Video Service concept and service will be mailed to select condo/townhouse complexes. These flyers will offer a coupon for a free membership or blank videocassette. When the potential customer calls for more information, an Express Video Service representative will make an appointment to go to the customer's home, set up an account, and personally deliver the Express Video Service catalogue.

Direct Mail

For the first annual quarter of our project, advertising and promotion will require about 20% of projected sales. After the first quarter, we feel that we can budget our advertising investment as 10% of total sales.

Investment in Advertising and Promotion

Compared to industry average we are investing more in trade promotion because Express Video Service is introducing an entirely new concept to the corporate market. Office delivery of videotape programming is new to the area, and we have to introduce the concept to the market and keep the Express Video Service name and service concept in front of the office managers and employees.

Compared to industry average we are investing more in consumer promotion because the "heavy spenders" perform better. The consumer is bombarded from every direction with video stores, inventory of movies, free memberships, etc. Express Video Service must establish a special niche in the market with a unique inventory list and an even more unique service: on-site delivery! We must stand out from, and above, the competition with our uniqueness!

PUBLIC RELATIONS

Position Express Video Service on the leading edge in providing management, training, sales and special interest videotape programming to, the corporate community and the residential community.

Objectives

Increase Express Video Service awareness and name recognition among buyers and customers in both the corporate and residential markets.

Communicate on a regular basis with three target publics:

- Major trade, business, and local publication editorial staffs
- Key management personnel in the existing customer companies
- Management/consultant organizations

Develop a sustaining public relations effort, with ongoing contact between key publication editors and Express Video Service personnel.

Strategies

Develop a regular and consistent product/service update program for the major target medias, keeping key editors abreast of inventory development, new territorial coverage and new product/service introductions.

Develop an internal newsletter which can cover key sales successes, significant marketing events, technical support and product/inventory development stories. Externally, the piece would be targeted to key customers and prospects.

Develop a minimum of four technical articles written by key management and production executives to be placed in "Madison Business" and "Central Jersey Business" within the next 12 months.

Establish contact with editorial staffs for the purpose of being included in product "round-ups". This exposure builds credibility and market acceptance.

**Corporate
Capabilities
Brochure**

Objective

Produce a complete company profile on Express Video Service to be used as the primary public relations tool for all target media editorial contact. This is also effective for inclusion in press kits and sales packages.

Portray Express Video Service as the leading supplier of quality special interest videotape programming; our product line is especially designed and selected by the Express Video Service staff to satisfy the corporate market's business needs and the employees' personal lifestyles. Express Video Service has assembled not only a tremendous selection of tapes, but a specialized list of titles that take videotape distribution and rental to a new level. The distinction between our product line of special interest video titles will be made over the competition's selection of only blockbuster movies. Importantly, a distinction between Express Video Service's "new and unique" office and home delivery service will be made over other store-front retailers.

Recommended Contents

The profile will include sections on the following broad subjects:

- Overview of the Market; size; characteristics
- The Market need in 1990, present & future
- The Company
  - History
  - Management Philosophy
  - Brief sketches of Top Executives
- The Products/Services
  - Market niches

Company Profile

Sales - portray Express Video Service's executives and full selling team, including representatives and distributors, as a savvy, dedicated support group with one overriding mission: customer satisfaction. We know our product line and the benefits that your company and employee can get from any one of our management/training and special interest tapes.

Marketing - present marketing department in their role of market research, tape and title selection, new product discovery/inventory, etc. Providing an updated and improved product line to the user.

Technical Support/Quality Assurance - portray the QA and technical support staff as a highly competent and dedicated group of individuals concerned with customer satisfaction.

Product Development - present high-tech image of the R&D group. The selection of top quality tapes, both in production level and content is critical.

Items that will assist the communications process:

•Ads	•Post Cards
•Brochures	•Presentations
•Bulletins	•Price Lists
•Business Cards	•Promotions
•Catalogs	•Stationery Forms
•Questionnaires	•Direct Mail
•Newsletters	

Major membership agreements with companies representing 100 or more employees should be written up and released to selected media, as soon as practical, after the signing of papers.

Develop a series of press releases on the entire Express Video Service product line and service area. Prepare press releases for each new inventory introduction/service area expansion, participation in a major event, recognition for product, etc.

Use local trade shows as a method for maintaining a high profile with the editors of key target media. Over the next 6 months invite the most influential reporters and editors from Madison Business, Central Jersey Business, Corporate Business Magazine, New Jersey Commerce, and the Targeted Publications to visit with Express Video Service's executives at the local trade shows and Chamber Of Commerce networking functions. During the visit, each of the editors would receive a product briefing, and an opportunity to interview the CEO and President. If logistics or timing is a problem with the interviews, then these could possibly be arranged at Express Video Service's corporate office.

If a major product/service announcement is feasible at one of the shows, care should be taken to plan the announcement well in advance. However, since the major publications send their editors to these shows, an opportunity exists to schedule, in advance, key personnel with selected reporters and editors. These mini-interviews can be used as opportunities to give editors a company or product update from a chief executive's point of view.

Produce a thirty-page, 2-color brochure/catalogue to serve both as an inventory list and as an informational piece for internal personnel, the sales force, and all corporate and residential customers. Include, sections covering each major department or inventory category within Express Video Service and a message from the executive staff. Highlight Express Video Service's major programming categories with a listing of all available titles. Prepare write-ups on key sales stories, successful customer applications and uses of our videotape line.

The income and expense schedule was developed in order to compare our forecasted revenues against our forecasted expenses. Since this is a new venture, our projections are not based upon any historical data, therefore certain assumptions were made to arrive at these figures. These assumptions will be explained below.

We determined a market potential by using a base figure of the total population of our targeted office and residential complexes. This figure was then multiplied by the average VCR penetration of the total U.S. population (70%) to arrive at the actual market potential for our product. From this market potential we set the following objective: within three months, we could achieve a 25% market penetration of this population and maintain it:

Total Population

Oct.	Nov.	Dec.	Jan.	Feb.	March	April	May	June	July	Aug.
1,500	2,400	4,250	4,600	5,750	5,750	5,750	5,750	5,750	5,750	5,750

Express Video Service's projections are based on a very conservative estimate of only one (1) video rental per month per potential client. We also assumed that 2/3 of all rentals would be weekday rentals with the remainder being weekend rentals. Weekly corporate series rentals were conservatively calculated therefore these revenue projections are negligible and do not affect our outcome negatively. As this business grows, it can only improve our projections:

- Weekday Rentals 56.8%
- Weekend Rentals 42.6%
- Corporate Rentals 0.6%

Weekday/Weekend Rentals

Revenues are based on a price structure which is untested in the market place. As part of our revenue projections we assumed all inventory (tape cost) as a part of cost of goods sold and therefore expensed the complete cost against gross revenues. At present the IRS has not made it clear whether, and on what basis, our inventory of tapes would become capital equipment and depreciated based on a useful life. There is presently a large market for used tapes and we have not calculated the resale value of our projected inventory, therefore our final net income calculations do not represent this hidden value and are therefore underestimated.

Finally, we have not included in our projections any revenue based on purchased product. We do not have any concrete data on what the potential ratio of sales to rentals may be, therefore we are assuming all revenues are based on a rental business only. We are still studying the dynamics of the business and will constantly update our projections as we proceed.

Assumptions Used in Calculating Expenses

As our method of sales collection will be through credit card debits, 2.5% of gross rental revenues expense is calculated as the cost of all sales.

Interest expense has been calculated on a financing arrangement of two (2) seperate $50,000 loans or lines of credit with a three year payout at 13%.

Payroll taxes have not yet been calculated, but are covered under miscellaneous expenses.

There has not been any provision made for income taxes since we figure to break even on the year or report a loss.

All expenses have been budgeted on current cost in the marketplace multiplied by our anticipated needs. Expenses have been generously calculated and therefore we do not anticipate excessive overruns.

Expense Breakdown

Credit Card Expense	1.5%
Employee Benefits	2.4%
Insurance	1.1%
Dividend Expense	1.6%
Loan Repayment	11.5%
Leasing Expense	3.0%
Marketing Expense	29.4%
Miscellaneous Expense	2.7%
Office Expense	1.9%
Professional Fees	1.5%
Rent	3.5%
Telephone	1.7%
Travel and Entertainment	5.5%
Wages	32.7%

Revenue & Expense Comparison - First Year

Our first year rental revenue projections amount to $156,258.25 less anticipated expenses of $263,438.36. Coupled with our anticipated start-up capital of $155,200.00, we arrive at a modest positive net income of $9,719.87. Overall, our third and fourth quarters represent a move to profitability as most major tape cost and marketing expenses have been covered in the previous quarters. In the third and fourth quarters, the marketing and tape expenses are only maintenance expenses. Following our initial marketing expenses for the our start-up and second phase expansion, we have assumed no further growth in order to determine whether, in six months time, we can cover our normal operating costs:

	Start-Up	1st Qtr	2nd Qtr	3rd Qtr	4th Qtr	Total
Start-up Capital	55200.00	49999.98	31250.00	9375.00	9375.00	155200.00
Revenues						
Weekday Rentals		8183.01	23188.30	28645.19	28645.19	88661.68
Weekend Rentals		6128.05	17365.15	21451.68	21451.68	66396.57
Corporate Rentals		300.00	300.00	300.00	300.00	1200.00
Gross Rental Revenue		14611.06	40853.45	50396.87	50396.87	156258.25
Total Revenue	55200.00	64611.04	72103.45	59771.87	59771.87	311458.23
Cost of Goods Sold						
Tape Purchases	18000.00		18000.00			36000.00
Tape Packaging	1100.00		1200.00			2300.00
Net Cost	19100.00		19200.00			38300.00
Net Rental Revenue	(19100.00)	14611.06	21653.45	50396.87	50396.87	117958.25
Total Net Revenue	36100.00	64611.04	52903.45	59771.87	59771.87	273158.23
Expenses						
Credit Card Expense		365.28	1021.34	1259.92	1259.92	3906.46
Dues and Subscriptions	1000.00				1000.00	2000.00
Employee Benefits	400.00	1200.00	1500.00	1500.00	1500.00	6100.00
Insurance		2200.00	600.00			2800.00
Dividend Expense			2125.00		2125.00	4250.00
Loan Repayment		3369.42	7897.05	8844.66	9792.27	29903.40
Leasing Expense	350.00	1500.00	1950.00	1950.00	1950.00	7700.00
Marketing Expense	22750.00	16750.00	20250.00	8250.00	8250.00	76250.00
Miscellaneous Expense	1000.00	1500.00	1500.00	1500.00	1500.00	7000.00
Office Expense	680.00	1640.00	840.00	840.00	840.00	4840.00
Payroll Expense						
Professional Fees	2000.00	1250.00	250.00	250.00	250.00	4000.00
Repairs and Maintainance		450.00	600.00	600.00	600.00	2250.00
Rent	868.00	1302.00	2034.00	2400.00	2400.00	9004.00
Telephone	500.00	1250.00	1250.00	750.00	750.00	4500.00
Travel and Entertainment	2250.00	3000.00	3000.00	3000.00	3000.00	14250.00
Wages	1437.50	13875.00	23124.00	23124.00	23124.00	84684.50
Total Expenses	33235.50	49651.70	67941.39	54268.58	58341.19	263438.36
Net Income	2864.50	14959.34	(15037.94)	5503.29	1430.68	9719.88

Revenue and Expense Comparison - First Year

The table below is designed to illustrate our revenue growth beginning in September (July and August represent start up months, with September being planned as the first month to generate income). Our revenue increases monthly before stabilizing in March when we assumed no further growth. Our expenses show large increases in September due to initial start-up expenses and further expansion expenses in December. From then on, our expenses are assumed as stabilize

July	Aug.	Sept.	Oct.	Nov.	Dec.	Jan.	Feb.	March	April	May	June	July	Aug.
Net Rental Revenue													
	-20,000	3,000	4,500	7,500	5,000	6,000	10,000	17,500	17,500	17,500	17,500	17,500	17,500
Total Expenses													
3,000	25,000	18,000	13,500	13,500	24,500	17,000	16,700	15,000	15,000	15,100	15,000	16,000	15,000

Revenue & Expense Comparison - Phase One

The following table will illustrate our revenue and expense projection for initial start-up of operations and phase one of our marketing efforts:

	July	Aug.	Sept.	Oct.	Nov.
Net Rental Revenue		-20,000	3000	4,500	7,500
Total Expenses	3,000	25,000	18,000	13,500	13,500

Revenue & Expense Comparison - Phase Two

The following table will illustrate our revenue and expense projections for our second quarter in which we plan our expansion phase:

	Dec.	Jan.	Feb.
Net Rental Revenue	5,000	6,000	10,000
Total Expenses	24,500	17,000	16,700

Revenue & Expense Comparison - Phase Three

This last table illustrates the constant revenue and expense projections we are forecasting for our third and fourth quarters. While Express Video Service does expect further revenue growth, we have not projected it into our calculations, thereby retaining conservative estimates at first:

	March	April	May	June	July	Aug.
Net Rental Revenue	17,500	17,500	17,500	17,500	17,500	17,500
Total Expenses	15,000	15,000	15,100	15,000	16,000	15,000

Conclusion

While we have maintained a conservative forecast of our revenues, we have also made sure that our expenses have not been underestimated. The dynamics of the business are new to us and at this time it is not viable to project a balance sheet or a cash flow statement. However, we will be constantly updating our projections as we become more familiar with the business and within the first quarter we should be able to project more definitively our financial statements.

Our initial costs are mainly the fixed costs of purchasing an inventory, which is an asset of the business with an undetermined resale value, and the initial variable cost such as marketing which can be easily controlled. From our forecast, if we wish to increase our total return on equity, we will need to closely monitor all expenses and make sure we reach our initial number of projected rentals. Finally, we believe if we do initially monitor the trends of the business closely in the beginning, we have allowed ourselves enough flexibility to adjust to any findings that will allow us to increase our profitability, and therefore, total return on investment.

SUMMARY

Rentals and sales of pre-packaged videotape programming is a booming business. The Electronic Industries Association estimates that 200 million prerecorded videocassettes will be sold by manufacturers in 1989 - a 48% increase over last year's record sales of 135 million units. The EIA also expects double digit growth in 1990, with video sales soaring 30% to 260 million units. Program suppliers' revenues, which approached $3 billion last year, are expected to rise to $4.2 billion in 1989 and $5.5 billion in 1990.

Express Video Service brings forth a new and unique marketing concept to videotape programming through inventory concentration of corporate management, training and sales tapes, complimented by special interest videos, including excercise, travel and classic movie titles. Our delivery and pick-up service is a first in our market and brings to the consumer a new era of quality service and convenience along with the selection, value and affordability of our inventory line.

Express Video Service will have an initial inventory selection completed by the second week of August with all videotapes shelved and available by the beginning of September. Actual start-up of order fulfillment and delivery will begin following Labor Day 1989.

Initial seed investment by the corporate officers, totalling $5200.00, has been expensed toward market analysis and business plan development.

Start-up capital required is $50,000.00. Additional working capital of $50,000.00 is projected.

Express Video Service has received a commitment of investment for $50,000.00 from a private investor.

A loan or line of credit for $50,000.00 is required for initial operating expenses, with an additional line of credit of up to $50,000.00 to be established for 2nd quarter expansion. Complete resumes for the Directors of Express Video Service are available upon request.

APPENDICES

Projected Inventory

A comprehensive listing of the videos available for rental and/or purchase at Express Video Service is available upon request. The alphabetic list includes the following information for each video: title, producer, length of play time, broad subject category, and specific sub category.

	July	August	September	October	November	December	January
Start-up Capital	$5200.00	$50000.00	$16666.66	$16666.66	$16666.66	$25000.00	$3125.00
Revenues							
Weekday Rentals	—	—	$1636.60	$2454.90	$4091.50	$6274.26	$7365.64
Weekend Rentals	—	—	$1225.61	$1838.42	$3064.03	$4698.64	$5515.95
Corporate Rentals	—	—	$100.00	$100.00	$100.00	$100.00	$100.00
Gross Rental Revenue	—	—	$2962.21	$4396.32	$7255.53	$11072.90	$12901.59
Total Revenue	$5200.00	$50000.00	$19628.87	$21059.98	$23922.19	$36072.90	$16106.59
Cost of Goods Sold							
Tape Purchases	—	—	$18000.00	—	—	—	$6000.00
Tape Packaging	—	—	$1100.00	—	—	—	$400.00
Net Cost	—	—	$19100.00	—	—	—	$6400.00
Net Rental Revenue	—	($19100.00)	$2962.21	$4393.32	$7255.53	$4672.90	$6581.59
Total Net Revenue	$5200.00	$30900.00	$19628.87	$21059.98	$23922.19	$29672.90	$9706.59
Expenses							
Credit Card Expense	—	—	$74.06	$109.83	$181.39	$276.82	$324.54
Dues & Subscriptions	$1000.00	—	—	—	—	—	—
Employee Benefits	—	$400.00	$400.00	$400.00	$400.00	$500.00	$500.00
Insurance	—	—	$2200.00	—	—	$600.00	—
Dividend Expense	—	—	—	—	—	$2125.00	—
Loan Repayment	—	—	$561.57	$1123.14	$1684.71	$2527.06	$2632.35
Leasing Expense	—	$350.00	$500.00	$500.00	$500.00	$650.00	$650.00
Marketing Expense	—	$22750.00	$6250.00	$5250.00	$5250.00	$11750.00	$4250.00
Misc. Expense	$500.00	$500.00	$500.00	$500.00	$500.00	$500.00	$500.00
Office Expense	—	$680.00	$680.00	$680.00	$280.00	$280.00	$280.00
Payroll Expense							
Professional Fees	$500.00	$1500.00	$1000.00	—	$250.00	—	—
Repairs and Maintenance	—	—	$150.00	$150.00	$150.00	$200.00	$200.00
Rent	$434.00	$434.00	$434.00	$434.00	$434.00	$434.00	$800.00
Telephone	$250.00	$250.00	$750.00	$250.00	$250.00	$250.00	$750.00
Travel and Entertainment	$2250.00	—	$1000.00	$1000.00	$1000.00	$1000.00	$1000.00
Wages	$250.00	$1187.50	$4625.00	$4625.00	$4625.00	$7708.00	$7708.00
Total Expenses	$5184.00	$28051.50	$19124.63	$15021.97	$15505.10	$28800.68	$19594.89
Net Income Before Tax	$16.00	$2848.50	$504.25	$6038.00	$9417.09	$872.02	($9888.30)
Provision for Taxes							
Net Income	$16.00	$2948.50	$504.25	$6038.00	$9417.09	$872.02	($9888.30)
Cum Cash Deficit/Surplus	$16.00	$2864.50	$3368.75	$9406.75	$17823.94	$18695.86	$8807.56

Expense Breakdown Schedule

	July	August	September	October	November	December	January
Dues and Subscriptions	$1000.00	—	—	—	—	—	—

Leasing Expense

	July	August	September	October	November	December	January
CEO's Lease	—	$350.00	$350.00	$350.00	$350.00	$350.00	$350.00
First Delivery Vehicle	—	—	$150.00	$150.00	$150.00	$150.00	$150.00
Second Delivery Vehicle	—	—	—	—	—	$150.00	$150.00
Total	—	—	$500.00	$500.00	$500.00	$650.00	$650.00

February	March	April	May	June	July	August	Total
$3125.00	$3125.00	$3125.00	$3125.00	$3125.00	$3125.00	$3125.00	$155200.00
$9548.40	$9548.40	$9548.40	$9548.40	$9548.40	$9548.40	$9548.40	$88661.68
$7150.56	$7150.56	$7150.56	$7150.56	$7150.56	$7150.56	$7150.56	$66396.57
$100.00	$100.00	$100.00	$100.00	$100.00	$100.00	$100.00	$1200.00
$16798.96	$16798.96	$16798.96	$16798.96	$16798.96	$16798.96	$16798.96	$156258.25
$19923.96	$19923.96	$19923.96	$19923.96	$19923.96	$19923.96	$19923.96	$311458.23
$6000.00	$6000.00	—	—	—	—	—	$36000.00
$400.00	$400.00	—	—	—	—	—	$2300.00
$6400.00	$6400.00	—	—	—	—	—	$38300.00
$10398.96	$16798.96	$16798.96	$16798.96	$16798.96	$16798.96	$16798.96	$117958.25
$13523.96	$19923.96	$19923.96	$19923.96	$19923.96	$19923.96	$19923.96	$273158.23
$419.97	$419.97	$419.97	$419.97	$419.97	$419.97	$419.97	$3906.46
—	—	—	—	—	$1000.00	—	$2000.00
$500.00	$500.00	$500.00	$500.00	$500.00	$500.00	$500.00	$6100.00
—	—	—	—	—	—	—	$2800.00
—	—	—	—	—	$2125.00	—	$4250.00
$2737.64	$2842.93	$2940.22	$3053.51	$3158.80	$3264.09	$3369.38	$29903.40
$650.00	$650.00	$650.00	$650.00	$650.00	$650.00	$650.00	$7700.00
$4250.00	$2750.00	$2750.00	$2750.00	$2750.00	$2750.00	$2750.00	$76250.00
$500.00	$500.00	$500.00	$500.00	$500.00	$500.00	$500.00	$7000.00
$280.00	$280.00	$280.00	$280.00	$280.00	$280.00	$280.00	$4840.00
—	—	$250.00	—	—	$250.00	$250.00	$4000.00
$200.00	$200.00	$200.00	$200.00	$200.00	$200.00	$200.00	$2250.00
$800.00	$800.00	$800.00	$800.00	$900.00	$800.00	$800.00	$9004.00
$250.00	$250.00	$250.00	$250.00	$250.00	$250.00	$250.00	$4500.00
$1000.00	$1000.00	$1000.00	$1000.00	$1000.00	$1000.00	$1000.00	$14250.00
$7708.00	$7708.00	$7708.00	$7708.00	$7708.00	$7708.00	$7708.00	$84684.50
$19545.61	$17900.90	$18006.19	$18361.48	$20341.77	$19322.06	$18677.35	$263438.36
($6021.66)	$2023.05	$1917.76	$1562.47	($417.82)	$601.89	$1246.60	$9719.88
($6021.66)	$2023.05	$1917.76	$1562.47	($417.82)	$601.89	$1246.60	$9719.88
$2785.90	$4808.96	$6726.72	$8289.19	$7871.30	$8473.27	$9719.88	$9719.88
—	—	—	—	—	$1000.00	—	$2000.00
$350.00	$350.00	$350.00	$350.00	$350.00	$350.00	$350.00	$4550.00
$150.00	$150.00	$150.00	$150.00	$150.00	$150.00	$150.00	$1800.00
$150.00	$150.00	$150.00	$150.00	$150.00	$150.00	$150.00	$1350.00
$650.00	$650.00	$650.00	$650.00	$650.00	$650.00	$650.00	$7350.00

	Jul	Aug	Sept	Oct	Nov	Dec	Jan
Marketing Expense							
Corporate Cap. Brochure							
	—	$2500.00	—	—	—	—	—
Printed Adv.	—	—	$2000.00	$2000.00	$2000.00	$2000.00	$2000.00
Catalogue	—	$15000.00	—	—	—	$7500.00	—
Public Relations	—	$750.00	$750.00	$750.00	$750.00	$100.00	$100.00
Trade Shows	—	$2500.00	$1000.00	—	—	—	—
Direct Mail	—	$500.00	$500.00	$500.00	$500.00	$150.00	$150.00
Planning	—	$1500.00	$1500.00	$1500.00	$1500.00	$1500.00	$1500.00
Misc.	—	—	$500.00	$500.00	$500.00	$500.00	$500.00
Total	—	$22750.00	$6250.00	$5250.00	$5250.00	$11750.00	$4250.00
Office Expense							
Fax Lease	—	$100.00	$100.00	$100.00	$100.00	$100.00	$100.00
Copy Machine Lease	—	$80.00	$80.00	$80.00	$80.00	$80.00	$80.00
Office Supplies	—	$500.00	$500.00	$500.00	$100.00	$100.00	$100.00
Total	—	$680.00	$680.00	$680.00	$280.00	$280.00	$280.00
Professional Fees							
Accounting	—	$500.00	—	—	$250.00	—	—
Legal	$500.00	$1000.00	$1000.00	—	—	—	—
Total	$500.00	$1500.00	$1000.00	—	$250.00	—	—
Repairs and Maintenance							
Gas and Maintenance for DV							
	—	—	$150.00	$150.00	$150.00	$200.00	$200.00
Telephone							
Monthly Telephone Bill							
	$250.00	$250.00	$250.00	$250.00	$250.00	$250.00	$250.00
Additional Phones	—	—	$200.00	—	—	—	—
Additional Lines	—	—	$300.00	—	—	—	$500.00
Total	$250.00	$250.00	$750.00	$250.00	$250.00	$250.00	$750.00
Wages							
CEO	—	$1187.50	$2375.00	$2375.00	$2375.00	$2375.00	$2375.00
Exec Assist. & Salesman							
	—	—	$1250.00	$1250.00	$1250.00	$3333.00	$3333.00
Delivery People	—	—	$1000.00	$1000.00	$1000.00	$2000.00	$2000.00
Total	$250.00	$1187.50	$4625.00	$4625.00	$4625.00	$7708.00	$7708.00
Insurance							
Auto Insurance	—	—	$1200.00	—	—	$600.00	—
Office Insurance	—	—	$1000.00	—	—	$0.00	—
Total	—	—	$2200.00	—	—	$600.00	—
Employee Benefits							
CEO	—	$300.00	$300.00	$300.00	$300.00	$300.00	$300.00
Employees	—	$100.00	$100.00	$100.00	$100.00	$200.00	$200.00
Total	—	$400.00	$400.00	$400.00	$400.00	$500.00	$500.00
Tape Costs							
Actual Purchase	—	$18000.00	—	—	—	$6000.00	$6000.00
Packaging Costs	—	$1100.00	—	—	—	$400.00	$400.00
Total	—	$19100.00	—	—	—	$6400.00	$6400.00

Feb	Mar	Apr	May	June	Jul	Aug	Total
—	—	—	—	—	—	—	$2500.00
$2000.00	$2000.00	$2000.00	$2000.00	$2000.00	$2000.00	$2000.00	$24000.00
—	—	—	—	—	—	—	$22500.00
$100.00	$100.00	$100.00	$100.00	$100.00	$100.00	$100.00	$3900.00
—	—	—	—	—	—	—	$3500.00
$150.00	$150.00	$150.00	$150.00	$150.00	$150.00	$150.00	$3350.00
$1500.00	—	—	—	—	—	—	$10500.00
$500.00	$500.00	$500.00	$500.00	$500.00	$500.00	$500.00	$6000.00
$4250.00	$2750.00	$2750.00	$2750.00	$2750.00	$2750.00	$2750.00	$76250.00
$100.00	$100.00	$100.00	$100.00	$100.00	$100.00	$100.00	$1300.00
$80.00	$80.00	$80.00	$80.00	$80.00	$80.00	$80.00	$1040.00
$100.00	$100.00	$100.00	$100.00	$100.00	$100.00	$100.00	$2500.00
$280.00	$280.00	$280.00	$280.00	$280.00	$280.00	$280.00	$4840.00
$250.00	—	—	$250.00	—	—	$250.00	$1500.00
—	—	—	—	—	—	—	$2500.00
$250.00	—	—	$250.00	—	—	$250.00	$4000.00
$200.00	$200.00	$200.00	$200.00	$200.00	$200.00	$200.00	$2250.00
$250.00	$250.00	$250.00	$250.00	$250.00	$250.00	$250.00	$3500.00
—	—	—	—	—	—	—	$200.00
—	—	—	—	—	—	—	$900.00
$250.00	$250.00	$250.00	$250.00	$250.00	$250.00	$250.00	$4500.00
$2375.00	$2375.00	$2375.00	$2375.00	$2375.00	$2375.00	$2375.00	$29687.50
$3333.00	$3333.00	$3333.00	$3333.00	$3333.00	$3333.00	$3333.00	$33747.00
$2000.00	$2000.00	$2000.00	$2000.00	$2000.00	$2000.00	$2000.00	$21000.00
$7708.00	$7708.00	$7708.00	$7708.00	$7708.00	$7708.00	$7708.00	$94684.50
—	—	—	—	—	—	—	$1800.00
—	—	—	—	—	—	—	$1000.00
—	—	—	—	—	—	—	$2800.00
$300.00	$300.00	$300.00	$300.00	$300.00	$300.00	$300.00	$3900.00
$200.00	$200.00	$200.00	$200.00	$200.00	$200.00	$200.00	$2200.00
$500.00	$500.00	$500.00	$500.00	$500.00	$500.00	$500.00	$6100.00
$6000.00	—	—	—	—	—	—	$36000.00
$400.00	—	—	—	—	—	—	$2300.00
$6400.00	—	—	—	—	—	—	$38300.00

Sales Projections

	Mkt Size	VCR Penetration	Mkt Share Sept. (10%)	Mkt Share Oct (15%)	Mkt Share Nov (25%)	Mkt Share Dec (25%)	Mkt Share Jan (25%)
1st Phase							
Carnegie Center	2000	1400	140	210	350	350	350
Forrestal Center	6500	5950	595	892.5	1487.5	1487.5	1487.5
Princeton Meadows	2900	2030	203	304.5	507.5	507.5	507.5
Canal Point	621	434.7	43.47	65.205	108.675	108.675	108.675
						Dec. (10%)	Jan. (15%)
2nd Phase							
Concordia	1500	1050	—	—	—	105	157.5
Rossmoor	2000	1400	—	—	—	140	210
Twin Rivers	2700	1890	—	—	—	189	283.5
Enterprise	2500	1750	—	—	—	175	262.5
Capital Complex	10000	7000	—	—	—	700	1050
Total	32721	22904.7	981.47	1472.205	2453.675	3762.675	4417.175
Rental Revenue							
Weekday @5.00	—	—	$1636.60	$2454.90	$4091.50	$6274.26	$7365.64
Weekend @7.50	—	—	$1225.61	$1838.42	$3064.03	$4698.64	$5515.95

Mkt Share Feb (25%)	Mkt Share March (25%)	Mkt Share April (25%)	Mkt Share May (25%)	Mkt Share June (25%)	Mkt Share July (25%)	Mkt Share August (25%)
350	350	350	350	350	350	350
1487.5	1487.5	1487.5	1487.5	1487.5	1487.5	1487.5
507.5	507.5	507.5	507.5	507.5	507.5	507.5
108.675	108.675	108.675	108.675	108.675	108.675	108.675
Feb. (25%)	**March** (25%)	**April** (25%)	**May** (25%)	**June** (25%)	**July** (25%)	**August** (25%)
262.5	262.5	262.5	262.5	262.5	262.5	262.5
350	350	350	350	350	350	350
472.5	472.5	472.5	472.5	472.5	472.5	472.5
437.5	437.5	437.5	437.5	437.5	437.5	437.5
1750	1750	1750	1750	1750	1750	1750
5726.175	5726.175	5726.175	5726.175	5726.175	5726.175	5726.175
$9548.40	$9548.40	$9548.40	$9548.40	$9548.40	$9548.40	$9548.40
$7150.56	$7150.56	$7150.56	$7150.56	$7150.56	$7150.56	$7150.56

Appendix A - Business Plan Template

Business Plan Template

USING THIS TEMPLATE

A business plan carefully spells out a company's projected course of action over a period of time, usually the first two to three years after the start-up. In addition, banks, lenders, and other investors examine the information and financial documentation before deciding whether or not to finance a new business venture. Therefore, a business plan is an essential tool in obtaining financing and should describe the business itself in detail as well as all important factors influencing the company, including the market, industry, competition, operations and management policies, problem solving strategies, financial resources and needs, and other vital information. The plan enables the business owner to anticipate costs, plan for difficulties, and take advantage of opportunities, as well as design and implement strategies that keep the company running as smoothly as possible.

This template has been provided as a model to help you construct your own business plan. Please keep in mind that there is no single acceptable format for a business plan, and that this template is in no way comprehensive, but serves as an example.

The business plans provided in this section are fictional and have been used by small business agencies as models for clients to use in compiling their own business plans.

GENERIC BUSINESS PLAN

Main headings included below are topics that should be covered in a comprehensive business plan. They include:

Business Summary

Purpose
Provides a brief overview of your business, succinctly highlighting the main ideas of your plan.

Includes
- Name and Type of Business
- Description of Product/Service
- Business History and Development
- Location
- Market
- Competition
- Management
- Financial Information
- Business Strengths and Weaknesses
- Business Growth

Table of Contents

Purpose

Organized in an Outline Format, the Table of Contents illustrates the selection and arrangement of information contained in your plan.

Includes

- Topic Headings and Subheadings
- Page Number References

Business History and Industry Outlook

Purpose

Examines the conception and subsequent development of your business within an industry specific context.

Includes

- Start-up Information
- Owner/Key Personnel Experience
- Location
- Development Problems and Solutions
- Investment/Funding Information
- Future Plans and Goals
- Market Trends and Statistics
- Major Competitors
- Product/Service Advantages
- National, Regional, and Local Economic Impact

Product/Service

Purpose

Introduces, defines,and details the product and/or service that inspired the information of your business.

Includes

- Unique Features
- Niche Served
- Market Comparison
- Stage of Product/Service Development
- Production
- Facilities, Equipment, and Labor
- Financial Requirements
- Product/Service Life Cycle
- Future Growth

Market Examination

Purpose
Assessment of product/service applications in relation to consumer buying cycles.

Includes

- Target Market
- Consumer Buying Habits
- Product/Service Applications
- Consumer Reactions
- Market Factors and Trends
- Penetration of the Market
- Market Share
- Research and Studies
- Cost
- Sales Volume and Goals

Competition

Purpose
Analysis of Competitors in the Marketplace.

Includes

- Competitor Information
- Product/Service Comparison
- Market Niche
- Product/Service Strengths and Weaknesses
- Future Product/Service Development

Marketing

Purpose
Identifies promotion and sales strategies for your product/service.

Includes

- Product/Service Sales Appeal
- Special and Unique Features
- Identification of Customers
- Sales and Marketing Staff
- Sales Cycles
- Type of Advertising/Promotion
- Pricing
- Competition
- Customer Services

Operations

Purpose

Traces product/service development from production/inception to the market environment.

Includes

- Cost Effective Production Methods
- Facility
- Location
- Equipment
- Labor
- Future Expansion

Administration and Management

Purpose

Offers a statement of your management philosophy with an in-depth focus on processes and procedures.

Includes

- Management Philosophy
- Structure of Organization
- Reporting System
- Methods of Communication
- Employee Skills and Training
- Employee Needs and Compensation
- Work Environment
- Management Policies and Procedures
- Roles and Responsibilities

Key Personnel

Purpose

Describes the unique backgrounds of principle employees involved in business.

Includes

- Owner(s)/Employee Education and Experience
- Positions and Roles
- Benefits and Salary
- Duties and Responsibilities
- Objectives and Goals

Potential Problems and Solutions

Purpose
Discussion of problem solving strategies that change issues into opportunities.

Includes
- Risks
- Litigation
- Future Competition
- Economic Impact
- Problem Solving Skills

Financial Information

Purpose
Secures needed funding and assistance through worksheets and projections detailing financial plans, methods of repayment, and future growth opportunities.

Includes
- Financial Statements
- Bank Loans
- Methods of Repayment
- Tax Returns
- Start-up Costs
- Projected Income (3 years)
- Projected Cash Flow (3 Years)
- Projected Balance Statements (3 years)

Appendices

Purpose
Supporting documents used to enhance your business proposal.

Includes
- Photographs of product, equipment, facilities, etc.
- Copyright/Trademark Documents
- Legal Agreements
- Marketing Materials
- Research and or Studies
- Operation Schedules
- Organizational Charts
- Job Descriptions
- Resumes
- Additional Financial Documentation

Food Distributor

FICTIONAL BUSINESS PLAN

COMMERCIAL FOODS, INC.

3003 Avondale Ave.
Knoxville, TN 37920

October 31, 1992

This plan demonstrates how a partnership can have a positive impact on a new business. It demonstrates how two individuals can carve a niche in the specialty foods market by offering gourmet foods to upscale restaurants and fine hotels. This plan is fictional and has not been used to gain funding from a bank or other lending institution.

- STATEMENT OF PURPOSE

- DESCRIPTION OF THE BUSINESS

- MANAGEMENT

- PERSONNEL

- LOCATION

- PRODUCTS AND SERVICES

- THE MARKET

- COMPETITION

- SUMMARY

- INCOME STATEMENT

- FINANCIAL STATEMENTS

STATEMENT OF PURPOSE

Commercial Food, Inc. seeks a loan of $75,000 to establish a new business. This sum together with $5,000 equity investment by the principals will be used as follows:

Merchandise inventory	$25,000
Office fixture/equipment	12,000
Warehouse equipment	14,000
One delivery truck	10,000
Working capital	39,00
Total	**$100,000**

DESCRIPTION OF THE BUSINESS

Commercial Foods, Inc. will be a distributor of specialty food service products to hotels and upscale restaurants in the geographical area in a 50 mile radius of Knoxville. Richard Roberts will direct the sales effort and John Williams will manage the warehouse operation and the office. One delivery truck will be used initially with a second truck added in the third year.

We expect to begin operation of the business within 30 days after securing the requested financing.

MANAGEMENT

A. Richard Roberts is a native of Memphis, Tennessee. He is a graduate of Memphis State University with a Bachelor's degree from the School of Business. After graduation, he worked for a major manufacturer of specialty food service products as a detail sales person for five years and for the past three years, he has served as a product sales manager for this firm.

B. John Williams is a native of Nashville, Tennessee. He holds a B.S. Degree in Food Technology from the University of Tennessee. His career includes five years as a product development chemist in gourmet food products and five years as operations manager for a food service distributor.

Both men are healthy and energetic. Their backgrounds complement each other which will ensure the success of Commercial Foods, Inc. They will set policies together and personnel decisions will be made jointly. Initial salaries for the owners will be $1,000 per month for the first few years. The spouses of both principals are successful in the business world and earn enough to support the families.

They have engaged the services of Foster Jones, CPA, and William Hale, Attorney to assist them in an advisory capacity.

PERSONNEL

The firm will employ one delivery truck driver at a wage of $8.00 per hour. One office worker will be employed at $7.50 per hour. One part-time employee will be used in the office at $5.00 per hour. The driver will load and unload his own trucks. Mr. Williams will assist in the warehouse operation as needed to assist one stock person at $7.00 per hour. An additional delivery truck and driver will be added the third year.

LOCATION

The firm will lease a 20,000 square foot building at 3003 Avondale Ave., in Knoxville, which contains warehouse and office areas equipped with two-door truck docks. The annual rental is $9,000. The building was previously used as a food service warehouse and very little modification to the building will be required.

The firm will offer specialty food service products such as soup bases, dessert mixes, sauce bases, pastry mixes, spices, and flavors, normally used by upscale restaurants and nice hotels. We are going after a niche in the market with high quality gourmet products. There is much less competition in this market than in standard run of the mill food service products. Through their work experiences, the principals have contacts with supply sources and with local chefs.

PRODUCTS AND SERVICES

We know from our market survey that there are over 200 hotels and upscale restaurants in the area we plan to serve. Customers will be attracted by a direct sales approach. We will offer samples of our products and product application data on use of our products in the finished prepared foods. We will cultivate the chefs in these establishments. The technical background of John Williams will be especially useful here.

THE MARKET

We find that we will be only distributor in the area offering a full line of gourmet food service products. Other foodservice distributors offer only a few such items in conjunction with their standard product line. Our survey shows that many of the chefs are ordering products from Atlanta and Memphis because of lack of adequate local supply.

COMPETITION

Commercial Foods, Inc. will be established as a foodservice distributor of specialty food in Knoxville. The principals, with excellent experience in the industry are seeking a $75,000 loan to establish the business. The principals are investing $25,000 as equity capital.

SUMMARY

The business will be set up as an "S" Corporation with each principal owning 50% of the common stock in the corporation.

Attached is a three year pro forma income statement we believe to be conservative. Also attached are personal financial statements of the principals and a projected cash flow statement for the first year.

	1st Year	2nd Year	3rd Year	
Gross Sales	300,000	400,000	500,000	**PRO FORMA INCOME STATEMENT**
Less Allowances	1,000	1,000	2,000	
Net Sales	299,000	399,000	498,000	
Cost of Goods Sold	179,400	239,400	298,800	
Gross Margin	119,600	159,600	199,200	
Operating Expenses				
Utilities	1,200	1,500	1,700	
Salaries	76,000	79,000	102,000	
Payroll Taxes/Benefits	9,100	9,500	13,200	
Advertising	3,000	4,500	5,000	
Office Supplies	1,500	2,000	2,500	
Insurance	1,200	1,500	1,800	
Maintenance	1,000	1,500	2,000	
Outside Services	3,000	3,000	3,000	
Whse Supplies/Trucks	6,000	7,000	10,000	
Telephone	900	1,000	1,200	
Rent	9,000	9,500	9,900	
Depreciation	2,500	2,000	3,000	
Total Expenses	114,400	122,000	155,300	
Other Expenses				
Bank Loan Payment	15,000	15,000	15,000	
Bank Loan Interest	6,000	5,000	4,000	
Total Expenses	**120,400**	**142,000**	**174,300**	
Net Profit (Loss)	**(800)**	**17,600**	**24,900**	

FINANCIAL STATEMENT I

Assets		Liabilities	
Cash	15,000		
1991 Olds	11,000	Unpaid Balance	8,000
Residence	140,000	Mortgage	105,000
Mutual Funds	12,000	Credit Cards	500
Furniture	5,000	Note Payable	4,000
Merck Stock	10,000		
	182,200		117,500
Net Worth		**64,700**	
	182,200		**182,200**

FINANCIAL STATEMENT II

Assets		Liabilities	
Cash	5,000		
1992 Buick Auto	15,000	Unpaid Balance	12,000
Residence	120,000	Mortgage	100,000
U.S. Treasury Bonds	5,000	Credit Cards	500
Home Furniture	4,000	Note Payable	2,500
AT&T Stock	3,000		
	147,000		115,000
Net Worth		**32,000**	
	147,000		**147,000**

Hardware Store

FICTIONAL BUSINESS PLAN

OSHKOSH HARDWARE, INC

123 Main St.
Oshkosh, WI 54901

June 1994

The following plan outlines how a small hardware store can survive competition from large discount chains by offering products and providing expert advice in the use of any product it sells. This plan is fictional and has not used to gain funding from a bank or other lending institution.

- EXECUTIVE SUMMARY

- THE BUSINESS

- THE MARKET

- SALES

- MANAGEMENT

- GOALS IMPLEMENTATION

- FINANCE

- JOB DESCRIPTION-GENERAL MANAGER

- QUARTERLY FORECASTED BALANCE SHEETS

- QUARTERLY FORECASTED STATEMENTS OF EARNINGS AND RETAINED EARNINGS

- QUARTERLY FORECASTED STATEMENTS OF CHANGES IN FINANCIAL POSITION

- FINANCIAL RATIO ANALYSIS

- DETAILS FOR QUARTERLY STATEMENTS OF EARNINGS

EXECUTIVE SUMMARY

Oshkosh Hardware, Inc. is a new corporation which is going to establish a retail hardware store in a strip mall in Oshkosh, Wisconsin. The store will sell hardware of all kinds, quality tools, paint and housewares. The business will make revenue and a profit by servicing its customers not only with needed hardware but also with expert advice in the use of any product it sells.

Oshkosh Hardware, Inc. will be operated by its sole shareholder, James Smith. The company will have a total of four employees. It will sell its products in the local market. Customers will buy our products because we will provide free advice on the use of all of our products and will also furnish a full refund warranty.

Oshkosh Hardware, Inc. will sell its products in the Oshkosh store staffed by three sales representatives. No additional employees will be needed to achieve its short and long range goals. The primary short range goal is to open the store by October 1, 1994. In order to achieve this goal a lease must be signed by July 1, 1994 and the complete inventory ordered by August 1, 1994.

Mr. James Smith will invest $30,000 in the business. In addition the company will have to borrow $150,000 during the first year to cover the investment in inventory, accounts receivable, and furniture and equipment. The company will be profitable after six months of operation and should be able to start repayment of the loan in the second year.

THE BUSINESS

The business will sell hardware of all kinds, quality tools, paint, and housewares. We will purchase our products from three large wholesale buying groups.

In general our customers are homeowners who do their own repair and maintenance, hobbyists, and housewives. Our business is unique in that we will have a complete line of all hardware items and will be able to get special orders by overnight delivery. The business makes revenue and profits by servicing our customers not only with needed hardware but also with expert advice in the use of any product we sell. Our major costs for bringing our products to market are cost of merchandise of 36%, salaries of $45,000, and occupancy costs of $60,000.

Oshkosh Hardware, Inc.'s retail outlet will be located at 1524 Frontage Road, which is in a newly developed retail center of Oshkosh. Our location helps facilitate accessibility from all parts of town and reduces our delivery costs. The store will occupy 7500 square feet of space. The major equipment involved in our business is counters and shelving, a computer, a paint mixing machine, and a truck.

THE MARKET

Oshkosh Hardware, Inc. will operate in the local market. There are 15,000 potential customers in this market area. We have three competitors who control approximately 98% of the market at present. We feel we can capture 25% of the market within the next four years. Our major reason for believing this is that our staff is technically competent to advise our customers in the correct use of all products we sell.

After a careful market analysis we have determined that approximately 60% of our customers are men and 40% are women. The percentage of customers that fall into the following age categories are:

> Under 16 - 0%
> 17-21 - 5%
> 22-30 - 30%
> 31-40 - 30%

41-50-20%
51-60-10%
61-70-5%
Over 70 - 0%

The reasons our customers prefer our products is our complete knowledge of their use and our full refund warranty.

We get our information about what products our customers want by talking to existing customers. There seems to be an increasing demand for our product. The demand for our product is increasing in size based on the change in population characteristics.

SALES

At Oshkosh Hardware, Inc. we will employ 3 sales people and will not need any additional personnel to achieve our sales goals. These salespeople will need several years experience in home repair and power tool usage. We expect to attract 30% of our customers from newspaper ads, 5% of our customers from local directories, 5% of our customers from the yellow pages, 10% of our customers from family and friends and 50% of our customers from current customers. The most cost effect source will be current customers. In general our industry is growing.

MANAGEMENT

We would evaluate the quality of our management staff as being excellent. Our manager is experienced and very motivated to achieve the various sales and quality assurance objectives we have set. We will use a management information system which produces key inventory, quality assurance and sales data on a weekly basis. All data is compared to previously established goals for that week and deviations are the primary focus of the management staff.

GOALS IMPLEMENTATION

The short term goals of our business are:

1. Open the store by October 1, 1994
2. Reach our breakeven point in two months
3. Have sales of $100,000 in the first six months

In order to achieve our first short term goal we must:

1. Sign the lease by July 1, 1994
2. Order a complete inventory by August 1, 1994

In order to achieve our second short term goal we must:

1. Advertise extensively in Sept. and Oct.
2. Keep expenses to a minimum

In order to achieve our third short term goal we must:

1. Promote power tool sales for the Christmas season
2. Keep good customer traffic in Jan. and Feb.

The long term goals for our business are:

1. Obtain sales volume of $600,000 in three years
2. Become the largest hardware dealer in the city
3. Open a second store in Fond du Lac

The most important thing we must do in order to achieve the long term goals for our business is to develop a highly profitable business with excellent cash flow.

FINANCE

Oshkosh Hardware, Inc. Faces some potential threats or risks to our business. They are discount house competition. We believe we can avoid or compensate for this by providing quality products complimented by quality advice on the use of every product we sell. The financial projections we have prepared are located at the end of this document.

JOB DESCRIPTION - GENERAL MANAGER

Sales

The General Manager of the business of the corporation will be the president of the corporation. He will be responsible for the complete operation of the retail hardware store which is owned by the corporation. A detailed description of his duties and responsibilities is as follows:

Train and supervise the three sales people. Develop programs to motivate and compensate these employees. Coordinate advertising and sales promotion effects to achieve sales totals as outlined in budget. Oversee purchasing function and inventory control procedures to insure adequate merchandise at all times at a reasonable cost.

Finance

Prepare monthly and annual budgets. Secure adequate line of credit from local banks. Supervise office personnel to insure timely preparation of records, statements, all government reports, control of receivables and payables and monthly financial statements.

Administration

Perform duties as required in the areas of personnel, building leasing and maintenance, licenses and permits and public relations.

QUARTERLY FORECASTED BALANCE SHEETS

	Beg Bal	1st Qtr	2nd Qtr	3rd Qtr	4th Qtr
Assets					
Cash	30,000	418	(463)	(3,574)	4,781
Accounts Receivable	0	20,000	13,333	33,333	33,333
Inventory	0	48,000	32,000	80,000	80,000
Other Current Assets	0	0	0	0	0
Total Current Assets	30,000	68,418	44,870	109,759	118,114
Land	0	0	0	0	0
Building & Improvements	0	0	0	0	0
Furniture & Equipment	0	75,000	75,000	75,000	75,000
Total Fixed Assets	0	75,000	75,000	75,000	75,000
Less Accum. Depreciation	0	1,875	3,750	5,625	7,500
Net Fixed Assets	0	73,125	71,250	69,375	67,500
Intangible Assets	0	0	0	0	0
Less Amortization	0	0	0	0	0
Net Intangible Assets	0	0	0	0	0
Other Assets	0	0	0	0	0
Total Assets	**30,000**	**141,543**	**116,120**	**179,134**	**185,614**

Liabilities and Shareholders' Equity

Short-Term Debt	0	0	0	0	0
Accounts Payable	0	12,721	10,543	17,077	17,077
Dividends Payable	0	0	0	0	0
Income Taxes Payable	0	(1,031)	(2,867)	(2,355)	(1,843)
Accured Compensation	0	1,867	1,867	1,867	1,867
Other Current Liabilities	0	0	0	0	0
Total Current Liabilities	0	13,557	9,543	16,589	17,101
Long-Term Debt	0	110,000	110,000	160,000	160,000
Other Non-Current Liabilities	0	0	0	0	0
Total Liabilities	0	123,557	119,543	176,589	177,101
Common Stock	30,000	30,000	30,000	30,000	30,000
Retained Earnings	0	(12,014)	(33,423)	(27,455)	(21,487)
Shareholders' Equity	30,000	17,986	(3,423)	2,545	8,513
Total Liabilities & Shareholders' Equity	30,000	141,543	116,120	179,134	185,614

QUARTERLY FORECASTED STATEMENTS OF EARNINGS AND RETAINED EARNINGS

	Beg Actual	1st Qtr	2nd Qtr	3rd Qtr	4th Qtr	Total
Total Sales	0	60,000	40,000	100,000	100,000	300,000
Goods/Services	0	21,600	14,400	36,000	36,000	108,000
Gross Profit	0	38,400	25,600	64,000	64,000	192,000
Operating Expenses	0	47,645	45,045	52,845	52,845	198,380
Fixed Expenses						
Interest	0	1,925	1,925	2,800	2,800	9,450
Depreciation	0	1,875	1,875	1,875	1,875	7,500
Amortization	0	0	0	0	0	0
Total Fixed Expenses	0	3,800	3,800	4,675	4,675	16,950
Operating Profit						
(Loss)	0	(13,045)	(23,245)	6,480	6,480	(23,330)
Other Income						
(Expense)	0	0	0	0	0	0

Interest Income	0	0	0	0	0	0
Earnings (Loss)						
Before Taxes	0	(13,045)	(23,245)	6,480	6,480	(23,330)
Income Taxes	0	(1,031)	(1,836)	512	512	(1,843)
Net Earnings	0	(12,014)	(21,409)	5,968	5,968	(21,487)
Retained Earnings,						
Beginning	0	0	(12,014)	(33,423)	(27,455)	0
Less Dividends	0	0	0	0	0	0
Retained Earnings,						
Ending	0	(12,014)	(33,423)	(27,455)	(21,487)	(21,487)

QUARTERLY FORECASTED STATEMENTS OF CHANGES IN FINANCIAL POSITION

	Beg Bal	1st Qtr	2nd Qtr	3rd Qtr	4th Qtr	Total
Sources (Uses) of Cash						
Net Earnings						
(Loss)	0	(12,014)	(21,409)	5,968	5,968	(21,487)
Depreciation						
& Amortization	0	1,875	1,875	1,875	1,875	7,500
Cash Provided						
by Operations	0	(10,139)	(19,534)	7,834	7,834	(13,987)
Dividends	0	0	0	0	0	0
Cash Provided by (Used For) Changes in						
Accounts Receivable	0	(20,000)	6,667	(20,000)	0	(33,333)
Inventory	0	(48,000)	16,000	(48,000)	0	(80,000)
Other Current Assets	0	0	0	0	0	0
Accounts Payable	0	12,	721	(2,178)	6,5340	17,077
Income Taxes	0	(1,031)	(1,836)	512	512	(1,843)
Accrued						
Compensation	0	1,867	0	0	0	1,867
Dividends Payable	0	0	0	0	0	0
Other Current						
Liabilities	0	0	0	0	0	0

Other Assests	0	0	0	0	0	0

Net Cash Provided by (Used For)

Operating Activities	0	(54,443)	18,653	(60,954)	512	(96,233)

Investment Transactions

Furniture &

Equipment	0	(75,000)	0	0	0	(75,000)
Land	0	0	0	0	0	0

Building &

Improvements	0	0	0	0	0	0
Intangible Assets	0	0	0	0	0	0

Net Cash From

Investment

Transactions	0	(75,000)	0	0	0	(75,000)

Financing Transactions

Short-Term Debt	0	0	0	0	0	0
Long-Term Debt	0	110,000	0	50,000	0	160,000

Other Non-Current

Liabilities	0	0	0	0	0	0

Sale of Common

Stock	30,000	0	0	0	0	0

Net Cash from Financing

Transactions	30,000	110,000	0	50,000	0	160,000

Net Increase (Decrease)

in Cash	30,000	(29,582)	(881)	(3,111)	8,355	(25,219)

Cash-Beginning

of Period	0	30,000	418	(463)	(3,574)	30,000

Cash-End

of Period	30,000	418	(463)	(3,574)	4,781	4,781

FINANCIAL RATIO ANALYSIS

	Beg Act	1st Qtr	2nd Qtr	3rd Qtr	4th Qtr
Overall Performance					
Return on Equity	0.00	(66.80)	625.45	234.50	70.10
Return on Total Assets	0.00	(8.49)	(18.44)	3.33	3.22
Operating Return	0.00	(9.22)	(20.02)	3.62	3.49
Profitability Measures					
Gross Profit Percent	0.00	64.00	64.00	64.00	64.00
Profit Margin (AIT)	0.00	(20.02)	(53.52)	5.97	5.97
Operating Income					
per Share	0.00	0.00	0.00	0.00	0.00
Earnings per Share	0.00	0.00	0.00	0.00	0.00
Test of Investment Utilization					
Asset Turnover	0.00	0.42	0.34	0.56	0.54
Equity Turnover	0.00	3.34	(11.69)	39.29	11.75
Fixed Asset Turnover	0.00	0.82	0.56	1.44	1.48
Average Collection					
Period	0.00	30.00	30.00	30.00	30.00
Days Inventory	0.00	200.00	200.00	200.00	200.00
Inventory Turnover	0.00	0.45	0.45	0.45	0.45
Working Capital Turns	0.00	1.09	1.13	1.07	0.99
Test of Financial Condition					
Current Ratio	0.00	5.05	4.70	6.62	6.91
Quick Ratio	0.00	1.51	1.35	1.79	2.23
Working Capital Ratio	1.00	0.43	0.33	0.57	0.60
Dividend Payout	0.00	0.00	0.00	0.00	0.00
Financial Leverage					
Total Assets	1.00	7.87	(33.92)	70.39	21.80

Debt/Equity	0.00	6.87	(34.92)	69.39	20.80
Debt to Total Assets	0.00	0.87	1.03	0.99	0.95

Year-End Equity History

Shares Outstanding	0	0	0	0	0
Market Price per Share	0.00	0.00	0.00	0.00	0.00
(@20x's earnings)					
Book Value per Share	0.00	0.00	0.00	0.00	0.00

Altman Analysis Ratio

1.2x(1)	1.20	0.47	0.37	0.62	0.65
1.4x(2)	0.00	(0.12)	(0.40)	(0.21)	(0.16)
3.3x(3)	0.00	(0.35)	(0.72)	0.07	0.07
0.6x(4)	0.00	0.00	0.00	0.00	0.00
1.0x(5)	0.00	0.42	0.34	0.56	0.54
Z Value	1.20	.042	(.041)	1.04	1.10

	Beg Act	1st Qtr	2nd Qtr	3rd Qtr	4th Qtr	Total	% Sales	Fixed
Sales								
Dollars Sales Forecasted								
Product 1	0	60,000	40,000	100,000	100,000	300,000		
Product 2	0	0	0	0	0	0		
Product 3	0	0	0	0	0	0		
Product 4	0	0	0	0	0	0		
Product 5	0	0	0	0	0	0		
Product 6	0	0	0	0	0	0		
Total Sales	0	60,000	40,000	100,000	100,000	300,000		

DETAILS FOR QUARTERLY STATEMENTS OF EARNINGS

DETAILS FOR QUARTERLY STATEMENTS OF EARNINGS
...continued

Cost of Sales

Dollar Cost Forecasted

Product 1	0	21,600	14,400	36,000	36,000	108,000	36.00%	0
Product 2	0	0	0	0	0	0	0.00%	0
Product 3	0	0	0	0	0	0	0.00%	0
Product 4	0	0	0	0	0	0	0.00%	0
Product 5	0	0	0	0	0	0	0.00%	0
Product 6	0	0	0	0	0	0	0.00%	0
Total Cost of Sales	0	21,600	14,400	36,000	36,000	108,000		

Operating Expenses

Payroll	0	12,000	12,000	12,000	12,000	48,000	0.00%	12,000
Paroll Taxes	0	950	950	950	950	3,800	0.00%	950
Advertising	0	4,800	3,200	8,000	8,000	24,000	8.00%	0
Automobile Expenses	0	0	0	0	0		0.00%	0
Bad Debts	0	0	0	0	0	0	0.00%	0
Commissions	0	3,000	2,000	5,000	5,000	15,000	5.00%	0
Computer Rental	0	1,200	1,200	1,200	1,200	4,800	0.00%	1,200
Computer Supplies	0	220	220	220	220	880	0.00%	220
Computer Maintenance	0	100	100	100	100	400	0.00%	100
Dealer Training	0	1,000	1,000	1,000	1,000	4,000	0.00%	1,000
Electricity	0	3,000	3,000	3,000	3,000	12,000	0.00%	3,000
Employment Ads and Fees	0	0	0	0	0	0	0.00%	0
Entertainment:								
Business	0	1,500	1,500	1,500	1,500	6,000	0.00%	1,500
General Insurance	0	800	800	800	800	32,000	0.00%	800
Health & W/C Insurance	0	0	0	0	0	0	.00%	0
Interest-LT Debt	0	2,500	2,500	2,500	2,500	10,000	0.00%	2,500
Legal & Accounting	0	1,500	1,500	1,500	1,500	6,000	0.00%	1,500
Maintenance & Repairs	0	460	460	460	460	1,840	0.00%	460

	Beg Act	1st Qtr	2nd Qtr	3rd Qtr	4th Qtr	Total	%Sales	Fixed
Office Supplies	0	270	270	270	270	1,080	0.00%	270
Postage	0	85	85	85	85	340	0.00%	85
Prof. Development	0	0	0	0	0	0	0.00%	0
Professional Fees	0	1,000	1,000	1,000	1,000	4,000	0.00%	1,000
Rent	0	8,000	8,000	8,000	8,0003	2,000	0.00%	8,000
Shows & Conferences	0	0	0	0	0	0	0.00%	0
Subscriptions & Dues	0	285	285	285	285	1,140	0.00%	285
Telephone	0	1,225	1,225	1,225	1,225	4,900	0.00%	1,225
Temporary Employees	0	0	0	0	0	0	0.00%	0
Travel Expenses	0	750	750	750	750	3,000	0.00%	750
Utilities	0	3,000	3,000	3,000	3,000	12,000	0.00%	3,000
Research & Devlpmnt.	0	0	0	0	0	0	0.00%	0
Royalties	0	0	0	0	0	0	0.00%	0
Other 1	0	0	0	0	0	0	0.00%	0
Other 2	0	0	0	0	0	0	0.00%	0
Other 3	0	0	0	0	0	0	0.00%	0

Total Operating

Expenses	0	47,645	45,045	52,845	52,845	198,380		

Percent of Sales	0.00	79.41	112.61	52.85	52.85	66.13		

DETAILS FOR QUARTERLY STATEMENT OF EARNINGS
...continued

BUSINESS PLAN TEMPLATE

Appendix - B
Organizations, Agencies and Consultants

Organizations, Agencies, & Consultants

A listing of Associations and Consultants of interest to entrepreneurs, followed by the 10 Small Business Administration Regional Offices, Small Business Development Centers, Service Corps of Retired Executives Offices, and Venture Capital & Finance Companies.

ASSOCIATIONS

This section contains a listing of associations and other agencies of interest to the small business owner. Entires are listed alphabetically by organization name.

Alliance of Minority Women for Business and Political Development
PO Box 13858
Silver Spring, Maryland 20911-3858
Phone: (301)585-8051
Brenda Alford, Pres.

American Association for Consumer Benefits
PO Box 100279
Fort Worth, Texas 76185
Phone: (800)872-8896
Fax: (817)735-1726
William D. Abbott, Contact

American Association of Franchisees and Dealers
1420 Kettner Blvd., Ste. 415
San Diego, California 92101
Phone: (619)619235-2556
Fax: (619)235-2565
Robert L. Purvin Jr., Chm.

American Business Association
292 Madison Ave., 4th Fl.
New York, New York 10017
Phone: (212)949-5900
Toll-free: (800)221-2168
Fax: (212)949-5910
Patricia Arden, Exec.Dir.

American Business Women's Association
9100 Ward Pky., PO Box 8728
Kansas City, Missouri 64114-0728
Phone: (816)816361-6621
Fax: (816)361-4991
E-mail: info@abulahq.org
Carolyn B. Elman, Exec.Dir.

American Consultants League
1290 Palm Ave.
Sarasota, Florida 34236
Phone: (941)952-9290
Fax: (941)925-6024
Hubert Bermont, Exec. Officer

American Management Association
1601 Broadway
New York, New York 10019-7420
Phone: (212)586-8100
Fax: (212)903-8168
David Fagiano, Pres. & CEO

American Small Businesses Association
1800 N. Kent St., Ste. 910
Arlington, Virginia 22209
Toll-free: (800)235-3298
Vernon Castle, Exec.Dir.

American Woman's Economic Development Corporation
71 Vanderbilt Ave., 3rd Fl.
New York, New York 10169
Phone: (212)692-9100
Fax: (212)692-9296
Suzanne Tufts, Pres. & CEO

Asian Business League of San Francisco
233 Sansome St., Ste. 515
San Francisco, California 94104
Phone: (415)788-4664
Fax: (415)788-4756
Forrest Gok, Exec.Dir.

Association of African-American Women Business Owners
Brasman Research
PO Box 13858
Silver Spring, Maryland 20911-3858
Phone: (301)585-8051
Tracy Mason, Pres.

Association of Business Products Manufacturers
PO Box 644
Millersville, Maryland 21108
Phone: (410)987-4847
John C. Vickerman, Exec.Dir.

Association of Collegiate Entrepreneurs
Center for Entrepreneurship
1845 Fairmount
Wichita, Kansas 67260-0147
Phone: (316)689-3000
Fax: (316)689-3687
Scott Schulz, Dir. of Marketing

Association for Corporate Growth
4350 DiPaolo Center, Ste. C
Dearlove Rd.
Glenview, Illinois 60025
Phone: (847)699-1331
Toll-free: (800)699-1331
Fax: (847)699-6369
E-mail: ACGHO@aol.com
Carl A. Wangman CAE, Exec.Dir.

Association of Master of Business Administration Executives
5 Summit Pl.
Branford, Connecticut 06405
Phone: (203)315-5221
Fax: (203)483-6186
Albert P. Hegyi, Pres.

Association of Small Business Development Centers
1300 Chain Bridge Rd., Ste. 201
McLean, Virginia 22101-3967
Phone: (703)448-6124
Fax: (703)448-6125
E-mail: jjohns1012@aol.com
Max Summers, Pres.

Association for University Business
and Economic Research
IBRC
801 W. Michigan, BS 4015
Indianapolis, Indiana 46202-5151
Phone: (317)274-2204
Terry Creeth, Contact

BEST Employers Association
2515 McCabe Way
Irvine, California 92714-6243
Phone: (714)756-1000
Toll-free: (800)854-7417
Fax: (714)553-0883
Donald R. Lawrenz Jr., Exec.Sec.

Booker T. Washington Foundation
4324 Georgia Ave. NW
Washington, DC 20011
Phone: (202)882-7100
Fax: (202)882-4354
Charles E. Tate, Pres.

Business Enterprise Trust
204 Junipero Serra Blvd.
Stanford, California 94305
Phone: (415)321-5100
Fax: (415)321-5774
E-mail: bet@betrust.org
Kathleen A. Meyer, Exec.Dir.

Business Market Association
4131 N. Central Expy., Ste. 720
Dallas, Texas 75204
Phone: (214)559-3900
Fax: (214)559-4143
R. Mark King, Pres.

Business for Social Responsibility
1683 Folsom St.
San Francisco, California 94103-3722
Phone: (415)865-2500
Robert H. Dunn, Pres.

Canada-United States Business
Association
100 East Jefferson
Detroit, Michigan 48226
Phone: (313)967-4422
Fax: (313)967-2565
Donald M. Vuchetich, Pres.

Center for Entrepreneurial Manage-
ment
180 Varick St., Penthouse Ste.
New York, New York 10014
Phone: (212)633-0060
Phone: (212633-0061
Fax: (212)633-0063
Joseph R. Mancuso, Pres.

Center for Family Business
PO Box 24219
Cleveland, Ohio 44124
Phone: (216)442-0800
Fax: (216)442-0178
Leon A. Danco Ph.D., Pres.

Center for International Private
Enterprise
1615 H St. NW
Washington, DC 20062
Phone: (202)463-5901
Fax: (202)887-3447
Telex: 277559 CIPE UR
E-mail: cipe@cipe.org
Willard A. Workman, VP

Chief Executives Organization
5430 Grosvenor Ln., Ste. 210
Bethesda, Maryland 20814
Phone: (301)564-9614
Fax: (301)564-0060
Windy Pangburn, Exec.Dir.

Christian Chamber of Commerce
PO Box 267
Silver Springs, Nevada 89429-0267
John P. Hansen, Founder

Coalition of Americans to Save the
Economy
1100 Connecticut Ave. NW, Ste. 1200
Washington, DC 20036-4101
Phone: (202)293-1414
Fax: (202)293-1702
Barry Maloney, Treas.

Committee of 200
625 N. Michigan Ave., Ste. 500
Chicago, Illinois 60611-3108
Phone: (312)751-3477
Fax: (312)943-9401
Lydia Lewis, Exec.Dir.

Consultants' Network
57 W. 89th St.
New York, New York 10024
Phone: (212)799-5239
Fax: (212)799-2915
E-mail: berliner@tiac.net
Stan Berliner, Dir.

Council on Employee Benefits
1144 E. Market St.
Akron, Ohio 44316
Phone: (216)796-4008
Fax: (216)824-0446
Carl S. Lazaroff, Sec.-Treas.

Deaf and Hard of Hearing Entrepre-
neurs Council
814 Thayer Ave., Ste. 301
Silver Spring, Maryland 20910-4500
Phone: (301)587-8596
Fax: (301)587-5997
Louis J. Schwarz CFP, Pres.

Dealer Management Association
239 Drakeside Rd.
Hampton, New Hampshire 03842
Phone: (603)926-8000
Toll-free: (800)370-3362
Fax: (603)926-4505
E-mail: DMA4NPI@aol.com
R. M. Caravati, Contact

EDGES Group
1 Hess Plz.
Woodbridge, New Jersey 07095
Phone: (908)750-6408
Walter Vertreace, Pres.

Entrepreneurial Leadership Center
1000 Galvin Rd. S
Bellevue, Nebraska 68005
Phone: (402)291-8100
Phone: (402)293-3743
Fax: (402293-3819
Jon B. Kayne, Dir.

The Entrepreneurship Institute
3592 Corporate Dr., Ste. 101
Columbus, Ohio 43231
Phone: (614)895-1153
Fax: (614)895-1473
Jan W. Zupnick, Pres.

Executive Leadership Council
1010 Wisconsin Ave., NW, Ste. 520
Washington, DC 20007
Phone: (202)298-8226
Ann M. Fudge, Pres.

Franchise Consultants International
Association
5147 S. Angela Rd.
Memphis, Tennessee 38117
Phone: (901)682-2951
Phone: (901)368-3361
Fax: (901368-1144
William Richey, Pres.

Home Executives National Network-
ing Association
PO Box 6223
Bloomingdale, Illinois 60108
Phone: (708)307-7130
Laura M. Vaughn, Exec.Dir.

Independent Small Business Employ-
ers of America
520 S. Pierce, Ste. 224
Mason City, Iowa 50401
Phone: (515)424-3187
Toll-free: (800)728-3187
Fax: (515)424-1673
Jim Collison, Pres.

Institute of Certified Business
Counselors
PO Box 70326
Eugene, Oregon 97401
Phone: (541)345-8064
Fax: (541)726-2402
Wally Stabbert, Pres.

The International Alliance, An
Association of Executive and
Professional Women
PO Box 1119
Baltimore, Maryland 21152-1119
Phone: (410)472-4221
Fax: (410)472-2920
E-mail: MAXX28b@Prodigy.com
Marian E. Goetze, Exec.VP

International Association of African
and American Black Business People
18900 Schoolcraft
Detroit, Michigan 48223
William Bert Johnson, Pres.

International Association of Business
701 Highlander Blvd.
Arlington, Texas 76015
Phone: (817)465-2922
Fax: (817)467-5940
Paula Rainey, Pres.

International Association of Business
Forecasting
Loyola College
Jenkins Hall, Rm. 211
4501 N. Charles St.
Baltimore, Maryland 21210-2699
Phone: (410)617-2892
Fax: (410)617-2104
E-mail: Bitnet, LFS@LOYVAX
LeRoy R. Simmons Ph.D., Pres.

International Association for Busi-
ness Organizations
PO Box 30149
Baltimore, Maryland 21270
Phone: (410)581-1373
Rudolph Lewis, Exec. Officer

International Council for Small
Business
St. Louis University
3674 Lindell Blvd.
St. Louis, Missouri 63108
Phone: (314)977-3628
Fax: (314)977-3627
E-mail: icsb@sluvca.slu.edu
William I. Dennis Jr., Pres.

International Downtown Association
915 15th St. NW, Ste. 600
Washington, DC 20005
Phone: (202)783-4963
Fax: (202)347-2161
Richard H. Bradley, Pres.

International Executive Service Corps
333 Ludlow St.
PO Box 10005
Stamford, Connecticut 06904
Phone: (203)967-6000
Fax: (203)324-2531
Hobart C. Gardiner, Pres.

International Franchise Association
1350 New York Ave. NW, Ste. 900
Washington, DC 20005
Phone: (202)628-8000
Fax: (202)628-0812
Telex: 323175
Don J. DeBolt, Pres.

International Merger and Acquisition
Professionals
600 Revere Dr., Ste. 500
Northbrook, Illinois 60062-1577
Phone: (847)480-9037
Fax: (708)480-9282
E-mail: imap@imap.com
Christine Dionne, Exec.Dir.

Interracial Council for Business
Opportunity
51 Madison Ave., Ste. 2212
New York, New York 10010
Phone: (212)779-4360
Fax: (212)779-4365
Lorraine Kelsey, Exec. Officer

Invest to Compete Alliance
1010 Pennsylvania Ave. SE
Washington, DC 20003
Phone: (202)546-4995
Fax: (202)544-7926
Garland Miller, Contact

Latin American Management
Association
419 New Jersey Ave. SE
Washington, DC 20003
Phone: (202)546-3803
Toll-free: (800)522-6623
Fax: (202)546-3807
Marina Morales Laverdy, Exec.Dir.

Latin Business Association
5400 E. Olympic Blvd., No. 3130
Los Angeles, California 90022
Phone: (213)721-4000
Fax: (213)722-5050
Diana Sanchez Roberson, Exec.Dir.

Majestic Eagles
2029 Rhode Island Ave. NE
Washington, DC 20018
Phone: (202)635-0154
Fax: (202)635-1086
John Raye, Pres.

MCAP Group
89-50 164th St., Ste. 2B
Jamaica, New York 11432
Phone: (718)657-6444
Fax: (718)523-2063
Sherman L. Brown, Pres.

Minority Business Enterprise Legal
Defense and Education Fund
900 Second St., Ste. 8
Washington, DC 20002
Phone: (202)289-1700
Fax: (202)289-1701
Anthony W. Robinson, Pres.

Mothers' Home Business Network
PO Box 423
East Meadow, New York 11554
Phone: (516)997-7394
Fax: (516)997-0839
Georganne Fiumara, Dir.

National Alliance for Fair Competition
3 Bethesda Metro Center, Ste. 1100
Bethesda, Maryland 20814
Phone: (410)235-7116
Fax: (410)235-7116
Tony Ponticelli, Exec.Dir.

National Association of Black
Women Entrepreneurs
PO Box 1375
Detroit, Michigan 48231
Phone: (313)559-9255
Fax: (313)559-9256
Marilyn French-Hubbard, Founder

National Association for Business
Organizations
PO Box 30149
Baltimore, Maryland 21270
Phone: (410)581-1373
Rudolph Lewis, Pres.

National Association for the Cottage
Industry
PO Box 14850
Chicago, Illinois 60614
Phone: (312)472-8116

National Association for Female
Executives
30 Irving Pl., 5th Fl.
New York, New York 10003
Phone: (212)477-2200
Toll-free: (800)927-6233
Fax: (212)477-8215
Rebecca Darwin, Exec.VP & COO

National Association of Home Based
Businesses
PO Box 30220
Baltimore, Maryland 21270
Phone: (410)363-3698
Rudolph Lewis, Pres.

National Association of Investment
Companies
1111 14th St. NW, Ste. 700
Washington, DC 20005
Phone: (202)289-4336
Fax: (202)289-4329
Bruce Gamble, Pres.

National Association of Minority
Women in Business
906 Grand Ave., Ste. 200
Kansas City, Missouri 64106
Phone: (816)421-3335
Fax: (816)421-3336
Inez Kaiser, Pres.

National Association of Private
Enterprise
PO Box 612147
Dallas, Texas 75261-2147
Toll-free: (800)223-6273
Fax: (817)332-4525
Heidi Williams, Acct.Exec.

National Association for the Self-
Employed
PO Box 612067
Dallas, Texas 75261-2067
Phone: (202)466-2100
Toll-free: (800)232-NASE
Fax: (800)551-4446
Bennie Thayer, Pres. & CEO

National Association of Women
Business Owners
1100 Wayne Ave., Ste. 830
Silver Spring, Maryland 20910
Caren Wilcox, Exec. Vice Pres.

National Business Association
5151 Belt Line Rd., No. 1150
Dallas, Texas 75240-7545
Phone: (214)458-0900
Toll-free: (800)456-0440
Fax: (214)960-9149
Robert G. Allen, Pres.

National Business Incubation
Association
20 E. Circle Dr., Ste. 190
Athens, Ohio 45701
Phone: (614)593-4331
Fax: (614)593-1996
Dinah Adkins, Exec.Dir.

National Business League
1511 K St. NW, Ste. 432
Washington, DC 20005
Phone: (202)737-4430
Fax: (202)466-5487
Sherman Copilin, Pres.

National Business Owners Association
1033 N. Fairfax St., Ste. 402
Alexandria, Virginia 22314
Phone: (202)737-6501
Phone: (703)838-2850
Fax: (703)838-0149
J. Drew Hiatt, Exec.VP

National Chamber of Commerce for
Women
10 Waterside Plz., Ste. 6H
New York, New York 10010
Phone: (212)685-3454
R. Wright, Exec.Dir.

National Executive Service Corps
257 Park Ave., S, 2nd Fl.
New York, New York 10010-7304
Phone: (212)529-6660
Fax: (212)228-3958
E-mail: natles@aol.com
Richard M. Clarke, Chm.

National Family Business Council
1640 W. Kennedy Rd.
Lake Forest, Illinois 60045
Phone: (708)295-1040
Fax: (708)295-1898
John E. Messervey, Dir.

National Federation of Independent
Business
53 Century Blvd., Ste. 300
Nashville, Tennessee 37214
Phone: (615)872-5800
Fax: (615)872-5899
Fred Holladay, VP & CFO

National Hispanic Corporate Council
2323 N. 3rd St., Ste. 101
Phoenix, Arizona 85004
Phone: (602)495-1988
Fax: (602)495-9085
Joanne Samora, Dir.

National Minority Business Council
235 E. 42nd St.
New York, New York 10017
Phone: (212)573-2385
Phone: (212)573-2301
Fax: (212)573-4462
John F. Robinson, CEO & Pres.

National Minority Supplier Development Council
15 W. 39th St., 9th Fl.
New York, New York 10018
Phone: (212)944-2430
Fax: (212)719-9611
Harriet Michel, Pres.

National Small Business United
1155 15th St. NW, Ste. 710
Washington, DC 20005
Phone: (202)293-8830
Toll-free: (800)345-6728
Fax: (202)872-8543
E-mail: nsbu@nsbu.org
John Paul Galles, Pres.

National Society of Hispanic MBAs
PO Box 2903
Chicago, Illinois 60690-2903
Phone: (512)472-5545
Fax: (512)316-5717
Jeanette Esquivel, Pres.

National Women's Economic
Alliance Foundation
1440 New York Ave. NW, Ste. 300
Washington, DC 20005
Phone: (202)393-5257
Fax: (202)639-8685
Telex: 756546
Patricia Harrison, Pres.

Ombudsman Association
5521 Greenville Ave., Ste. 104-265
Dallas, Texas 75206
Phone: (214)553-0043
Fax: (214)348-6621
Carole M. Trocchio, Exec. Officer

POWERLUNCH!
5 Thomar Cir. NW
Washington, DC 20005
Phone: (202)462-8004
Fax: (202)462-8448
Douglas Cook, Exec. Officer

Presidents Association
135 W. 50th St.
New York, New York 10020
Phone: (212)586-8100
Fax: (212)903-8168
Virginia L. O'Connor, Contact

The SCORE Association
Service Corps of Retired Executives
Association
409 3rd St. SW, 4th Fl.
Washington, DC 20024
Phone: (202)205-6762
Toll-free: (800)634-0245
Fax: (202)205-7636
W. Kenneth Yancey Jr., Exec.Dir.

Small Business Assistance Center
554 Main St.
PO Box 15014
Worcester, Massachusetts 01615-0014
Phone: (508)756-3513
Fax: (508)791-4709
Francis R. Carroll, Pres.

Small Business Council of America
4800 Hampden Ln., 7th Fl.
Bethesda, Maryland 20814
Phone: (301)656-7603
Fax: (301)654-7354
Paula Calimafde, Chm.

Small Business Exporters Association
4603 John Tyler Ct., Ste. 203
Annandale, Virginia 22003
Phone: (703)642-2490
Fax: (703)750-9655
E. Martin Duggan, Pres. & CEO

Small Business Foundation of
America
1155 15th St.
Washington, DC 20005
Phone: (202)223-1103
Fax: (202)476-6534
Regina Tracy, Exec.Dir.

Small Business Legislative Council
1156 15th St. NW, Ste. 510
Washington, DC 20005
Phone: (202)639-8500
Fax: (202)296-5333
John Satagaj, Pres.

Small Business Network
PO Box 30149
Baltimore, Maryland 21270
Phone: (410)581-1373
E-mail: natibb@ix.netcom.com
Rudolph Lewis, CEO

Small Business Service Bureau
554 Main St.
PO Box 15014
Worcester, Massachusetts 01615-0014
Phone: (508)756-3513
Fax: (508)791-4709
Francis R. Carroll, Pres.

Support Services Alliance
PO Box 130
Schoharie, New York 12157-0130
Phone: (518)295-7966
Toll-free: (800)322-3920
Fax: (518)295-8556
Robert M. Marquardt, Pres.

Try Us Resources
2105 Central Ave. NE
Minneapolis, Minnesota 55418
Phone: (612)781-6819
Fax: (612)781-0109
Liz Kahnk, Exec.Dir.

United States Council for International Business
1212 Ave. of the Americas, 21st Fl.
New York, New York 10036
Phone: (212)354-4480
Fax: (212)575-0327
Abraham Katz, Pres.

Washington Chinese Business
Association
7722 Keyport
Rockville, Maryland 20855
Phone: (301)208-8858
Fax: (301)208-8854
Gang Ke, Pres.

World Presidents Organization
North Bldg., Ste. 520
601 Pennsylvania Ave. NW
Washington, DC 20004-2660
Phone: (202)508-0100
Fax: (202)737-0654
Rachael M. Lowder, Exec.VP

Young Entrepreneurs Organization
1010 N. Glebe Rd., Ste. 625
Arlington, Virginia 22201
Phone: (703)527-4500
Fax: (703)527-1274
Mohamed Fathelbab, Exec.Dir.

Young Presidents' Organization
451 S. Decker, Ste. 200
Irving, Texas 75062
Phone: (214)650-4600
Fax: (214)650-4777
David E. Stahl, Exec.Dir.

CONSULTANTS

*This section contains a listing of consult-
ants specializing in small business
development. It is arranged alphabetically
by country, then by state or province, then
by city, then by firm name.*

CANADA

Alberta

Varsity Consulting Group
2-45 Faculty of Business
University of Alberta
Edmonton, Alberta T6G 2R6
Phone: (403)492-2994
Fax: (403)492-3325

Viro Hospital Consulting
42 Commonwealth Bldg.
9912 - 106 St. N.W.
Edmonton, Alberta T5K 1C5
Phone: (403)425-3871
Fax: (403)425-3871

British Columbia

Syspo Consulting
371 Delta Ave.
Burnaby, British Columbia V5B 3C7
Phone: (604)291-9545

DeBoda & DeBoda
1523 Milford Ave.
Coquitlam, British Columbia V3J 2V9
Phone: (604)936-4527
Fax: (604)936-4527

The Sage Group Ltd.
980 - 355 Burrard St.
Vancouver, British Columbia V6C 3H2
Phone: (604)669-9269
Fax: (604)681-4938

Ontario

Cynton Company
17 Massey St.
Bramalea, Ontario L6S 2V6
Phone: (905)792-7769
Fax: (905)792-8116

JPL Business Consultants
Box 1587
Niagara-on-the-Lake, Ontario L0S 1J0
Phone: (905)935-2648
Fax: (905)935-2648

The ARA Consulting Group Inc.
116 Albert St., Ste. 303
Ottawa, Ontario K1P 5G3
Phone: (613)238-7400

HST Group Ltd.
430 Gilmour St.
Ottawa, Ontario K2P 0R8
Phone: (613)236-7303
Fax: (613)236-9893

Harrison Associates
BCE Place
181 Bay Street, Ste. 3740
P.O. Box 798
Toronto, Ontario M5J 2T3
Phone: (416)364-5441
Fax: (416)364-2875

Stern International Consultants Inc.
22 College St., Ste. 307
Toronto, Ontario M5G 1K2
Phone: (416)923-7878
Fax: (416)923-8091

Ken Wyman & Associates Inc.
64B Shuter St., Ste. 200
Toronto, Ontario M5B 1B1
Phone: (416)362-2926
Fax: (416)362-3039

Douglas J. McCready
344 Craigleith Dr.
Waterloo, Ontario N2L 5B7
Phone: (519)884-2651
Fax: (519)884-0201

Quebec

The Zimmar Consulting Partnership Inc.
PO Box 95
Westmount
Montreal, Quebec H3Z 2T1
Phone: (514)484-1459
Fax: (514)484-3063

Saskatchewan

Randall Marketing Group Inc.
PO Box 197
Regina, Saskatchewan S4P 2Z6
Phone: (306)586-0870

UNITED STATES

Alabama

Business Planning Inc.
300 Office Park Dr.
Birmingham, Alabama 35223-2474
Phone: (205)870-7090
Fax: (205)870-7103

Alaska

AK Business Development Center
3335 Arctic Blvd., Ste. 203
Anchorage, Alaska 99503
Phone: (907)562-0335
Fax: (907)562-6988

Business Matters
PO Box 287
Fairbanks, Alaska 99707
Phone: (907)452-5650

Arizona

Caretree Direct Marketing Corp.
8001 E. Serene St., PO Box 3737
Carefree, Arizona 85377-3737
Phone: (602)488-4227
Fax: (602)488-2841

Thomas B. Galitski
5540 W. Glendale Ave., Ste. A101
Glendale, Arizona 85301
Phone: (602)842-0656
Fax: (602)931-3174

Arthur Aschauer & Co., Inc.
4520 E. Indian School Rd., Ste. 1
Phoenix, Arizona 85018
Phone: (602)840-0066

CMAS
1625 E. Northern, Ste. 103
Phoenix, Arizona 85020
Phone: (602)395-1001

Harvey C. Skoog
P.O. Box 26515
Prescott Valley, Arizona 86312
Phone: (602)772-1714
Fax: (602)772-2814

Advanced Consultant Technology, Inc.
5011 E. Nisbet Rd., Ste. 102
Scottsdale, Arizona 85254
Phone: (602)708-0300
Fax: (602)708-0300

Ceekay Consultants
4919 N. Granite Reef Rd.
Scottsdale, Arizona 85251-1726
Phone: (602)946-1474

Louw's Management Corp.
8711 E. Pinnacle Peak Rd.
Scottsdale, Arizona 85255-3555
Phone: (602)585-7177
Fax: (602)585-5880

Gary L. McLeod
PO Box 230
Sonoita, Arizona 85637
Phone: (602)455-5661

Trans Energy Corporation
216 S. Clark, MS103
Tempe, Arizona 85281
Phone: (602)921-0433
Fax: (602)967-6601

Van Cleve Associates
6932 E. 2nd St.
Tucson, Arizona 85710
Phone: (602)296-2587

California

Lindquist Consultants-Venture
Planning
225 Arlington
Berkeley, California 94707
Phone: (510)524-6685
Fax: (510)527-6604

Larson Associates
P.O. Box 9005
Brea, California 92621
Phone: (714)529-4121
Fax: (714)572-3606

Louis V. O'Brien, Mgmt. Consultant
1060 Whitwell Rd.
Burlingame, California 94010
Phone: (415)347-4504

Kremer Management Consulting
P.O. Box 500
Carmel, California 93921
Phone: (408)626-8311
Fax: (408)624-2663

Hunter G. Jackson Jr. - Consulting
Environmental Physicist
P.O. Drawer 880
Cupertino, California 95015-0880
Phone: (408)446-4097

JB Associates
21118 Gardena Dr.
Cupertino, California 95014
Phone: (408)257-0214
Fax: (408)257-0216

Technical Management Consultants
3624 Westfall Dr.
Encino, California 91436-4154
Phone: (818)784-0626
Fax: (818)501-5575

RAINWATER-GISH & Associates,
Business Finance & Development
317 Third St., Ste. 3
Eureka, California 95501
Phone: (707)443-0030
Fax: (707)443-5683

Burnes Consulting Group
930 Cedar St.
Fort Bragg, California 95437
Phone: (707)964-1459
Fax: (707)964-1458
Toll-free: (800)949-9021

Strategic Business Group
800 Cienaga Dr.
Fullerton, California 92635
Phone: (714)449-1040
Fax: (714)449-1040

Pioneer Business Consultants
9042 Garfield Ave., Ste. 312
Huntington Beach, California 92646
Phone: (714)964-7600
Fax: (714)962-6585

MCS Associates
18300 Von Karman, Ste. 1100
Irvine, California 92715
Phone: (714)263-8700
Fax: (714)553-0168

Kris Dean
PO Box 214
La Honda, California 94020
Phone: (415)747-0979

The Laresis Companies
P.O. Box 3284
La Jolla, California 92038
Phone: (619)452-2720
Fax: (619)452-8744

RCL & Co.
PO Box 1143
La Jolla, California 92038
Phone: (619)454-8883
Fax: (619)454-8880

General Business Services
3201 Lucas Cir.
Lafayette, California 94549
Phone: (510)283-8272

The Ribble Group
27601 Forbes Rd., Ste. 52
Laguna Niguel, California 92677
Phone: (714)582-1085
Fax: (714)582-6420

Bell Springs Publishing
Bell Springs Rd.
Box 640
Laytonville, California 95454
Phone: (707)984-6746

Norris Bernstein
9309 Marina Pacifica Dr. N
Long Beach, California 90803
Phone: (310)493-5458
Fax: (310)493-5459

Horizon Consulting Services
1315 Garthwick Dr.
Los Altos, California 94024
Phone: (415)967-0906
Fax: (415)967-0906

Brincko Associates, Inc.
1801 Ave. of the Stars
Los Angeles, California 90067
Phone: (310)553-4523
Fax: (310)553-6782

Business Expansions International
210 S. Anita Ave.
Los Angeles, California 90049
Phone: (310)476-5262
Fax: (310)478-1876

Hutchinson Consulting and Appraisals
11966 Woodbine St.
Los Angeles, California 90066
Phone: (310)391-7086
Fax: (310)391-7086

F.J. Schroeder & Associates
1926 Westholme Ave.
Los Angeles, California 90025
Phone: (310)470-2655
Fax: (310)470-6378

Western Management Associates
8351 Vicksburg Ave.
Los Angeles, California 90045-3924
Phone: (310)645-1091
Fax: (310)645-1092

Darrell Sell and Associates
Los Gatos, California 95030
Phone: (408)354-7794

Leslie J. Zambo
3355 Michael Dr.
Marina, California 93933
Phone: (408)384-7086
Fax: (408)647-4199

Marketing Services Management
PO Box 1377
Martinez, California 94553
Phone: (510)370-8527
Fax: (510)370-8527

Keck & Company Business Consultants
410 Walsh Rd.
Menlo Park, California 94027
Phone: (415)854-9588
Fax: (415)854-7240

William M. Shine Consulting Service
P.O. Box 127
Moraga, California 94556-0127
Phone: (510)376-6516

W & J Partnership
3450 Bluegrass Court, P.O. Box 1108
Morgan Hill, California 95038-1108
Phone: (408)779-1714
Fax: (408)778-1305

Palo Alto Management Group, Inc.
2672 Bayshore Pkwy., Ste. 701
Mountain View, California 94043
Phone: (415)968-4374
Fax: (415)968-4245

The Market Connection
4020 Birch St., Ste. 203
Newport Beach, California 92660
Phone: (714)731-6273
Fax: (714)833-0253

Muller Associates
PO Box 7264
Newport Beach, California 92658
Phone: (714)646-1169
Fax: (714)646-1169

NEXUS - Consultants to Management
P.O. Box 1531
Novato, California 94948
Phone: (415)897-4400
Fax: (415)898-2252

Adelphi Communications Incorporated
1300 Clay St., Ste. 600
Oakland, California 94612-1427
Phone: (510)464-8076
Fax: (510)530-3411

Creston Financial Group
1800 Harrison St., 18th Fl.
Oakland, California 94612
Phone: (510)987-8500
Fax: (510)893-1321

Intelequest Corp.
Palo Alto, California 94303
Phone: (415)968-3443
Fax: (415)493-6954

Gerber Business Development
1135 N. McDowell Blvd.
Petaluma, California 94954-1136
Phone: (707)778-2900
Fax: (707)778-2999

Management Seminars
2639 Hurricane Cove
Port Hueneme, California 93041

Business Research Consultants, Inc.
PO Box 1646
Rancho Mirage, California 92270
Phone: (619)328-3700
Fax: (619)328-2474

RECO Management Consulting
3084 Woodley Ct.
Rosamond, California 93560
Phone: (805)256-6666

Business Incubation Development
Associates
225 Broadway, Ste. 2250
San Diego, California 92101
Phone: (619)237-0559
Fax: (619)237-0521

G.R. Gordetsky Consultants Inc.
11414 Windy Summit Pl.
San Diego, California 92127
Phone: (619)487-4939
Fax: (619)487-5587

Wilson Associates
PO Box 126704
San Diego, California 92112-6704
Phone: (619)423-7772

Freeman, Sullivan & Co.
131 Steuart St., Ste. 520
San Francisco, California 94105
Phone: (415)777-0707
Fax: (415)777-2420

Ideas Unlimited
2151 California St., Ste. 7
San Francisco, California 94115
Phone: (415)931-0641
Fax: (415)931-0880

Russell Miller Inc.
300 Montgomery St., Ste. 900
San Francisco, California 94104
Phone: (415)956-7474
Fax: (415)398-0620

PKF Consulting Inc.
425 California St., Ste. 1650
San Francisco, California 94104
Phone: (415)421-5378
Fax: (415)956-7708

WEH Corporation
P.O. Box 470038
San Francisco, California 94147
Phone: (415)567-3340
Fax: (415)567-3340

Welling & Woodard, Inc.
1067 Broadway
San Francisco, California 94133
Phone: (415)776-4500
Fax: (415)776-5067

Quincy Yu
3300 Laguna St., Ste. 6
San Francisco, California 94123
Phone: (415)567-1746

Engineering Design & Business
Consultants
San Jose, California 95125
Phone: (408)279-0854

ORDIS, Inc.
6815 Trinidad Dr.
San Jose, California 95120-2056
Phone: (408)268-3321
Fax: (408)268-3582
Toll-free: (800)446-7347

Stanford Resources, Inc.
3150 Almaden Expy., Ste. 255, PO
Box 20324
San Jose, California 95160
Phone: (408)448-4440
Fax: (408)448-4445

Technology Properties Ltd., Inc.
San Jose, California 95117
Phone: (408)243-9898
Fax: (408)296-6637

Productivity Computing Services
1625 Waverly Rd.
San Marino, California 91108
Phone: (818)281-7079

Helfert Associates
1777 Borel Pl., Ste. 508
San Mateo, California 94402-3514
Phone: (415)377-0540
Fax: (415)377-0472

RB Consultants
720 9th Ave.
San Mateo, California 94402
Phone: (415)348-1619
Fax: (415)348-1619

The Information Group, Inc.
PO Box Q
Santa Clara, California 95055
Phone: (408)985-7877
Fax: (408)985-2945

Cast Management Consultants
1620 26th St., Ste. 2040N
Santa Monica, California 90404
Phone: (310)828-7511
Fax: (310)453-6831

Abrams Thompson Inc.
PO Box 14549
Santa Rosa, California 95402
Phone: (707)575-9890
Fax: (707)575-5933

Cuma Consulting Management
Box 724
Santa Rosa, California 95402
Phone: (707)785-2477
Fax: (707)785-2478

Goodrich Associates
20622 Russell Ln.
Saratoga, California 95070
Phone: (408)867-5126

Management Consultants
Sunnyvale, California 94087-4700
Phone: (408)773-0321

RJR Associates
1639 Lewiston Dr.
Sunnyvale, California 94087
Phone: (408)737-7720
Fax: (408)737-7720

Schwafel Associates
790 Lucerne Dr., Ste. 10
Sunnyvale, California 94086
Phone: (408)720-0649
Fax: (408)732-3507

Out of Your Mind...and Into the
Marketplace
13381 White Sand Dr.
Tustin, California 92680
Phone: (714)544-0248
Fax: (714)730-1414

Independent Research Services
P.O. Box 2426
Van Nuys, California 91404-2426
Phone: (818)993-3622

Ingman Company Inc.
7949 Woodley Ave., Ste. 120
Van Nuys, California 91406-1232
Phone: (818)375-5027
Fax: (818)894-5001

Innovative Technology Associates
3639 E. Harbor Blvd., Ste. 203E
Ventura, California 93001
Phone: (805)650-9353
Fax: (805)984-2979

Whittelsey Associates
180 Fox Hollow Rd.
Woodside, California 94062
Phone: (415)851-8400
Fax: (415)851-2064

J.H. Robinson & Associates
20695 Deodar Dr., Ste. 100, PO Box 351
Yorba Linda, California 92686-0351
Phone: (714)970-1279

Colorado

Janus Healthcare Consultants Inc.
210 Fifth St., Ste. A
Castle Rock, Colorado 80104
Phone: (303)660-2039
Fax: (303)688-8027

GVNW, Inc./Management
P.O. Box 25969
Colorado Springs, Colorado 80936
Phone: (719)594-5800
Fax: (719)599-0968

M-Squared, Inc.
755 San Gabriel Pl.
Colorado Springs, Colorado 80906
Phone: (719)576-2554
Fax: (719)576-2554

The Crosstern Corp.
670 Grant St.
Denver, Colorado 80203
Phone: (303)832-2546

Western Capital Holdings, Inc.
7500 E. Arapahoe Rd., Ste. 395
Englewood, Colorado 80112
Phone: (303)290-8482
Fax: (303)770-1945

Thornton Financial FNIC
1024 Centre Ave., Bldg. E
Fort Collins, Colorado 80526-1849
Phone: (303)221-2089

Tactical Technology Inc.
287 Arlington Dr.
Grand Junction, Colorado 81503
Phone: (303)241-9707
Fax: (303)245-9601

TenEyck Associates
1760 Cherryville Rd.
Greenwood Village, Colorado 80121
Phone: (303)758-6129
Fax: (303)761-8286

Associated Enterprises Ltd.
8725 W. 14th Ave., Ste. 110
Lakewood, Colorado 80215
Phone: (303)274-2783
Fax: (303)274-5429

GSI Consulting Group
28 Red Fox Ln.
Littleton, Colorado 80127
Phone: (303)979-9033
Fax: (303)979-2870

Johnson & West Management
Consultants, Inc.
7612 S. Logan Dr.

Littleton, Colorado 80122
Phone: (303)794-2060
Fax: (303)730-3219

Business Associates
PO Box 3552
Vail, Colorado 81658
Phone: (303)479-9046

Connecticut

Stratman Group Inc.
40 Tower Ln.
Avon, Connecticut 06001-4222
Phone: (203)677-2898
Fax: (203)677-8210

Cowherd Consulting Group, Inc.
106 Stephen Mather Rd.
Darien, Connecticut 06820
Phone: (203)655-2150
Fax: (203)655-6427

Greenwich Associates
8 Greenwich Office Park
Greenwich, Connecticut 06831-5149
Phone: (203)629-1200
Fax: (203)629-1229

Franchise Builders
185 Pine St., Ste. 818
Manchester, Connecticut 06040
Phone: (203)647-7542
Fax: (203)646-6544

JC Ventures, Inc.
4 Arnold St.
Old Greenwich, Connecticut 06870
Phone: (203)698-1990
Fax: (203)698-2638
Toll-free: (800)698-1997

Shoreline Business Consulting
92 Knollwood Dr.
Old Saybrook, Connecticut 06475
Phone: (203)388-9903
Fax: (203)388-9903

Charles L. Hornung
52 Ned's Mountain Rd.
Ridgefield, Connecticut 06877
Phone: (203)431-0297

Gerald S. Gilligan and Associates Inc.
One Strawberry Hill
Stamford, Connecticut 06902
Phone: (203)325-3935

Manus
100 Prospect St., S. Tower
Stamford, Connecticut 06901
Phone: (203)326-3880
Fax: (203)326-3890
Toll-free: (800)445-0942

Rhinesmith and Associates
Palmer Landing 506
123 Harbor Dr.
Stamford, Connecticut 06902
Phone: (203)327-7988
Fax: (203)327-5688

Sternbach Associates International
16 Tamarac Rd.
Westport, Connecticut 06880
Phone: (203)227-2059
Fax: (203)454-7341

Delaware

Daedalus Ventures, Ltd.
P.O. Box 1474
Hockessin, Delaware 19707
Phone: (302)239-6758
Fax: (302)234-3755
Toll-free: (800)666-6216

The Formula Group
P.O. Box 866
Hockessin, Delaware 19707
Phone: (302)456-0952
Fax: (302)456-1354

Selden Enterprises Inc.
2055 Limestone Rd., Ste. 213
Wilmington, Delaware 19808-5539
Phone: (302)999-1888
Fax: (302)999-9520

Districe of Columbia

Business Development International,
Inc.
P.O. Box 5615
Washington, DC 20016
Phone: (202)362-1765
Fax: (202)362-1765

Enterprise Consulting, Inc.
2806 36th Pl. NW, PO Box 32273
Washington, DC 20007
Phone: (202)342-7640
Fax: (703)751-9240

Bruce W. McGee and Associates
7826 Eastern Ave. NW, Ste. 300
Washington, DC 20012
Phone: (202)726-7272

McManis Associates, Inc.
2000 K St. NW, Ste. 300
Washington, DC 20006
Phone: (202)466-7680
Fax: (202)872-1898

Florida

Adams & Carbone Consulting
931 North S.R. 434, Ste. 1201
Altomonte Springs, Florida 32714
Phone: (407)620-6971
Fax: (407)277-1050

Whalen & Associates, Inc.
4255 Northwest 26 Ct.
Boca Raton, Florida 33434
Phone: (407)241-5950
Fax: (407)241-7414

H.P. Bieber and Associates
4800 Bayview Dr., PO Box 030458
Fort Lauderdale, Florida 33303
Phone: (305)771-6373

Eric Sands Consulting Services
6193 Rock Island Rd., Ste. 412
Fort Lauderdale, Florida 33319
Phone: (305)721-4767
Fax: (305)720-2815

Bridge-It
3704 Broadway, Unit 313
Fort Myers, Florida 33901
Phone: (813)278-4218
Fax: (813)936-6380

Host Media Corp.
3948 S. Third St., Ste. 191
Jacksonville Beach, Florida 32250
Phone: (904)285-3239
Fax: (904)285-5618

The Bracken Group
233 E. New Haven Ave., 2nd Fl.
Melbourne, Florida 32901
Phone: (407)725-0796
Fax: (407)724-0736

Corporate Business Computer
Services Inc.
7458 SW 48th St.
Miami, Florida 33155-4469
Phone: (305)666-2330
Fax: (305)666-2254

William V. Hall
1925 Brickell, Ste. D-701
Miami, Florida 33129
Phone: (305)856-9622
Fax: (305)856-4113

Taxplan, Inc.
Mirasol International Center
2699 Collins Ave.
Miami Beach, Florida 33140
Phone: (305)538-3303

T.C. Brown & Associates
8415 Excalibur Cir., Ste. B-1
Naples, Florida 33963
Phone: (813)594-1949
Fax: (813)594-1949

RLA International Consulting
713 Lagoon Dr.
North Palm Beach, Florida 33408
Phone: (407)626-4258
Fax: (407)626-5772

Comprehensive Franchising, Inc.
2465 Ridgecrest Ave.
Orange Park, Florida 32065
Phone: (904)272-6567
Fax: (904)272-6750
Toll-free: (800)321-6567

F.A. McGee, Inc.
2810 Ocean Shore Blvd., Ste. 8
Ormond Beach, Florida 32176
Phone: (904)441-6349

F. Newton Parks
210 El Brillo Way
Palm Beach, Florida 33480
Phone: (407)833-1727
Fax: (407)833-4541

Avery Business Development
Services
2506 St. Michel Ct.
Ponte Vedra Beach, Florida 32082
Phone: (904)285-6033
Fax: (904)285-6033

Focus Marketing
PO Box 4161
St. Petersburg, Florida 33731
Phone: (813)577-1337

Dufresne Consulting Group, Inc.
10014 N. Dale Mabry, Ste. 101
Tampa, Florida 33618-4426
Phone: (813)264-4775
Fax: (813)931-5845

Todd Organization
PO Box 552
Tampa, Florida 33601
Phone: (813)973-4909 Ext 601
Fax: (813)973-4909 Ext 222

The Apogee Group, Inc.
P.O. Box 3907
Tequesta, Florida 33469-2111
Phone: (407)575-0299
Fax: (407)575-4542

Holton Associates
50 Beach Rd., Ste. 301
Tequesta, Florida 33469
Phone: (407)744-9314

Center for Simplified Strategic
Planning, Inc.
PO Box 3324
Vero Beach, Florida 32964
Phone: (407)231-3636
Fax: (407)231-1099

Georgia

Bock, Center, Garber and Long
2 Piedmont Ctr.
Atlanta, Georgia 30305
Phone: (404)231-9011
Fax: (404)233-3756

Marketing Spectrum Inc.
990 Hammond Dr., Ste. 840
Atlanta, Georgia 30328
Phone: (404)395-7244
Fax: (404)393-4071

Nucifora Consulting Group
2859 Paces Ferry Rd., Ste. 1830
Atlanta, Georgia 30339
Phone: (404)432-1072
Fax: (404)432-3528

Richard Siedlecki Marketing &
Management
2996 Grandview Ave., Ste. 305
Atlanta, Georgia 30305-3245

Phone: (404)816-4040
J. Charles Hulsey Consulting &
Assistance Corp.
PO Box 43
Gainesville, Georgia 30503
Phone: (404)534-3142

Business Ventures Corporation
6030 Dawson Blvd., Ste. E
Norcross, Georgia 30093
Phone: (404)729-8000
Fax: (404)729-8028

E. Peter Kite, Management Consult-
ing Services
18 Coventry Close
Skidaway Island
Savannah, Georgia 31411
Phone: (912)598-1730
Fax: (912)598-0369

Illinois

TWD and Associates
431 S. Patton
Arlington Heights, Illinois 60005
Phone: (708)398-6410
Fax: (708)255-5095

Management Planning Associates, Inc.
2275 Half Day Rd., Ste. 350
Bannockburn, Illinois 60015-1277
Phone: (708)945-2421
Fax: (708)945-2425

Phil Faris Associates
86 Old Mill Ct.
Barrington, Illinois 60010

Seven Continents Technology
787 Stonebridge
Buffalo Grove, Illinois 60089
Phone: (708)577-9653
Fax: (708)870-1220

Robetta Corporation
1 Henson Pl.
Champaign, Illinois 61820
Phone: (217)359-0641
Fax: (217)359-0688

ACE Accounting Service, Inc.
3128 N. Bernard St.
Chicago, Illinois 60618
Phone: (312)463-7854
Fax: (312)463-7854 Ext 222

FMS Consultants
5801 N. Sheridan Rd., Ste. 3D
Chicago, Illinois 60660
Phone: (312)561-7362
Fax: (312)561-6274

MacDougall & Blake, Inc.
10 W. Elm St., Ste. 1402
Chicago, Illinois 60610-2744
Phone: (312)587-3330
Fax: (312)587-3699

Miller, Mason & Dickenson
123 N. Wacker Dr.
Chicago, Illinois 60606
Phone: (312)701-4800
Fax: (312)701-2347

James C. Osburn Ltd.
2701 W. Howard St.
Chicago, Illinois 60645
Phone: (312)262-4428
Fax: (312)262-6755

James B. Peterson & Associates, Inc.
3 First National Plaza
70 W. Madison St., Ste. 1400
Chicago, Illinois 60602
Phone: (312)214-3172
Fax: (312)214-3110

Tarifero & Tazewell Inc.
211 S. Clark, P.O. Box 2130
Chicago, Illinois 60690
Phone: (312)665-9714
Fax: (312)665-9716

William J. Igoe
3949 Earlston Rd.
Downers Grove, Illinois 60515
Phone: (708)960-1418

Human Energy Design Systems
620 Roosevelt Dr.
Edwardsville, Illinois 62025
Phone: (618)692-0258

The Organizational Consulting
Group, Ltd.
PO Box 54
Glenwood, Illinois 60425-0054

The Minarich Group Inc.
20940 N. Middleton Dr.
Kildeer, Illinois 60047
Phone: (708)540-9585
Fax: (708)540-9585

BioLabs, Inc.
15 Sheffield Ct.
Lincolnshire, Illinois 60069
Phone: (708)945-2767

Clyde R. Goodheart
15 Sheffield Ct.
Lincolnshire, Illinois 60069
Phone: (708)945-2767
Fax: (708)945-4382

Profit Growth, Inc.
2705 Walters Ave.
Northbrook, Illinois 60062
Phone: (708)498-9043

Smith Associates
1320 White Mountain Dr.
Northbrook, Illinois 60062
Phone: (708)480-7200
Fax: (708)480-9828

Francorp, Inc.
20200 Governors Dr.
Olympia Fields, Illinois 60461
Phone: (708)481-2900
Fax: (708)481-5885
Toll-free: (800)877-1103

Camber Business Strategy Consultants
PO Box 986
Palatine, Illinois 60078-0986
Phone: (708)705-0101
Fax: (708)705-0101

McGladrey & Pullen
1699 E. Woodfield Rd., Ste. 300
Schaumburg, Illinois 60173
Phone: (708)517-7070
Toll-free: (800)365-8353

Koch International, Inc.
1040 S. Milwaukee Ave.
Wheeling, Illinois 60090
Phone: (708)459-1100
Fax: (708)459-0471
Toll-free: (800)323-7597

A.D. Star Consulting
320 Euclid
Winnetka, Illinois 60093
Phone: (708)446-7827
Fax: (708)446-7827

Indiana

Midwest Marketing Research
P.O. Box 1077
Goshen, Indiana 46526
Phone: (219)533-0548
Fax: (219)533-0540

Crosby & Associates
5699 E. 71st, Ste. 4-A
Indianapolis, Indiana 46220
Phone: (317)841-3300
Fax: (317)841-3300

JMG Associates
4437 N. Franklin Rd., Ste. D
Indianapolis, Indiana 46226
Phone: (317)546-5780

Ketchum Consulting Group
8021 Knue Rd., Ste. 112
Indianapolis, Indiana 46250
Phone: (317)845-5411
Fax: (317)842-9941

Marketing Department Inc.
3390 W. 86th, Ste. 2-F
Indianapolis, Indiana 46268
Phone: (317)876-5780
Fax: (317)876-5770

MDI Management Consulting
1519 Park Dr.
Munster, Indiana 46321
Phone: (219)838-7909
Fax: (219)838-7909

Iowa

Management Solutions
P.O. Box 7004
Des Moines, Iowa 50311
Phone: (515)277-6408
Fax: (515)277-3506

Grandview Marketing
15 Red Bridge Dr.
Sioux City, Iowa 51104
Phone: (712)258-0065
Fax: (712)258-7578

Kansas

Strategic Planning Management
Associates, Inc.
7007 College Blvd., Ste. 420
Overland Park, Kansas 66211
Phone: (913)339-9001
Fax: (913)339-6226

Kentucky

New Horizons Planning Group, Inc.
PO Box 2616
Paducah, Kentucky 42002
Phone: (502)443-6467

Maine

Edgemont Enterprises
PO Box 8354
Portland, Maine 04104
Phone: (207)871-8964
Fax: (207)871-8964

Pan Atlantic Consultants
148 Middle St.
Portland, Maine 04101
Phone: (207)871-8622
Fax: (207)772-4842

Maryland

Imperial Group, Limited
305 Washington Ave., Ste. 501
8600 LaSalle Rd.
Baltimore, Maryland 21204-6009
Phone: (410)337-7575
Fax: (410)337-7641

Kamanitz, Uhlfelder and Permison
Professional Association
4 Reservoir Cir.
Baltimore, Maryland 21208
Phone: (410)484-8700

Burdeshaw Associates, Ltd.
4701 Sangamore Rd.
Bethesda, Maryland 20816-2508
Phone: (301)229-5800
Fax: (301)229-5045

Michael E. Cohen
5225 Pooks Hill Rd., Ste. 1119 S
Bethesda, Maryland 20814
Phone: (301)530-5738
Fax: (301)493-9147

James K. McCracken & Co.
9211 Holly Oak Dr.
Bethesda, Maryland 20817
Phone: (301)365-9188
Toll-free: (800)365-9188

World Development Group, Inc.
5101 River Rd., Ste. 1913
Bethesda, Maryland 20816-1574
Phone: (301)656-5070
Fax: (301)907-6630

Swartz Consulting
PO Box 4301
Crofton, Maryland 21114-4301
Phone: (301)262-6728

Software Solutions International
Inc.
9633 Duffer Way
Gaithersburg, Maryland 20879
Phone: (301)330-4136

Strategies, Inc.
8 Park Center Ct., Ste. 200
Owings Mills, Maryland 21117
Phone: (410)363-6669
Fax: (410)356-0602

Hammer Marketing Resources
179 Inverness Rd.
Severna Park, Maryland 21146
Phone: (410)544-9191
Fax: (410)544-9189

Andrew Sussman & Associates
13731 Kretsinger
Smithsburg, Maryland 21783
Phone: (301)824-2943
Fax: (301)824-2943

Energetics Development Inc.
109 Post Office Rd., PO Box 966
Waldorf, Maryland 20604
Phone: (301)934-8875
Toll-free: (800)377-7049

Massachusetts

Geibel Marketing Consulting
PO Box 611
Belmont, Massachusetts 02178-0005
Phone: (617)484-8285
Fax: (617)489-3567

Bain & Company, Inc.
Two Copley Pl.
Boston, Massachusetts 02117-0897
Phone: (617)572-2000
Fax: (617)572-2427

Center for Strategy Research, Inc.
101 Arch St., Ste. 1700
Boston, Massachusetts 02110
Phone: (617)345-9500
Fax: (617)345-0207

Pendergast & Co.
4 Copley Place, Box 84
Boston, Massachusetts 02116
Phone: (617)720-0400
Fax: (617)266-8341

Boston Computer Society - Consultants' and Entrepreneurs' Group
1 Kendall Sq.
Cambridge, Massachusetts 02139
Phone: (617)252-0600
Fax: (617)577-9365

Financial/Management Solutions, Inc.
180 Magazine St.
Cambridge, Massachusetts 02139
Phone: (617)876-4946
Fax: (617)547-5283

Mehr & Company
62 Kinnaird St.
Cambridge, Massachusetts 02139
Phone: (617)876-3311
Fax: (617)876-3023

Monitor Co.
25 First St.
Cambridge, Massachusetts 02141
Phone: (617)252-2000
Fax: (617)252-2100

IEEE Consultants' Network
614 Hammond St.
Chestnut Hill, Massachusetts 02167
Phone: (617)893-8379

Data and Strategies Group, Inc.
Three Speen St.
Framingham, Massachusetts 01701
Phone: (508)820-2500
Fax: (508)820-1626

Information & Research Associates
PO Box 3121
Framingham, Massachusetts 01701
Phone: (508)788-0784

Easton Consultants Inc.
252 Pond St.
Hopkinton, Massachusetts 01748
Phone: (508)435-4882
Fax: (508)435-3971

Jeffrey D. Marshall
102 Mitchell Rd.
Ipswich, Massachusetts 01938-1219
Phone: (508)356-1113
Fax: (508)356-2989

B.L. Livas Associates
620 Essex St.
Lawrence, Massachusetts 01841
Phone: (508)686-6195
Fax: (508)688-8027

Consulting Resources Corporation
6 Northbrook Park
Lexington, Massachusetts 02173
Phone: (617)863-1222
Fax: (617)863-1441

The Planning Technologies Group, Inc.
1840 Massachusetts Ave.
Lexington, Massachusetts 02173
Phone: (617)861-0999
Fax: (617)861-1099

Kalba International, Inc.
23 Sandy Pond Rd.
Lincoln, Massachusetts 01773
Phone: (617)259-9589
Fax: (617)259-1460

Coordinated Service, Inc.
531 King St.
Littleton, Massachusetts 01460
Phone: (508)486-0388
Fax: (508)486-0120

VMB Associates, Inc.
115 Ashland St.
Melrose, Massachusetts 02176
Phone: (617)665-0623

The Company Doctor
14 Pudding Stone Ln.
Mendon, Massachusetts 01756
Phone: (508)478-1747

The Enterprise Group
73 Parker Rd.
Needham, Massachusetts 02194
Phone: (617)444-6631
Fax: (617)444-6757

Practice Management Associates, Ltd.
10 Midland Ave.
Newton, Massachusetts 02158
Phone: (617)965-0055
Fax: (617)965-5152
Toll-free: (800)537-7765

Business Planning and Consulting Services
20 Beechwood Terr.
Wellesley, Massachusetts 02181
Phone: (617)237-9151
Fax: (617)237-9151

Cooper, McPhee & Associates, Inc.
70 Walnut St.
Wellesley, Massachusetts 02181

Interim Management Associates
21 Avon Rd.
Wellesley, Massachusetts 02181
Phone: (617)237-0024

Michigan

Birmingham Consultants
31625 Nixon
Birmingham, Michigan 48025
Phone: (810)644-2700

G.G.W. and Associates
1213 Hampton
Jackson, Michigan 49203
Phone: (517)782-2255
Fax: (517)784-1256

Altamar Group Ltd.
6810 S. Cedar, Ste. 2-B
Lansing, Michigan 48911
Phone: (517)694-0910
Fax: (517)694-1377
Toll-free: (800)443-2627

Sheffieck Consultants, Inc.
23610 Greening Dr.
Novi, Michigan 48375-3130
Phone: (810)347-3545
Fax: (810)347-3530

Rehmann, Robson and Company,
The Consulting Group
5800 Gratiot, P.O. Box 2025
Saginaw, Michigan 48605
Phone: (517)799-9580

Francis & Company
17200 W. Ten Mile Rd., Ste. 207
Southfield, Michigan 48075
Phone: (810)559-7600
Fax: (810)559-5249

Private Ventures, Inc.
24300 Southfield Rd., Ste. 385
Southfield, Michigan 48075
Phone: (810)569-1977
Fax: (810)569-1838
Toll-free: (800)848-7614

JGK Associates
14464 Kerner Dr.
Sterling Heights, Michigan 48313
Phone: (810)247-9055

Minnesota

Consatech Inc.
P.O. Box 1047
Burnsville, Minnesota 55337
Phone: (612)953-1088
Fax: (612)435-2870

Gieseke Management Works!
PO Box 21097
Eagan, Minnesota 55121-0097
Phone: (612)456-0757
Fax: (612)456-9138
Toll-free: (800)848-4912

Robert F. Knotek
14960 Ironwood Ct.
Eden Prairie, Minnesota 55346
Phone: (612)949-2875

Kinnon Lilligren Associates Incorpo-
rated
6211 Oakgreen Ave. S
Denmark Township
Hastings, Minnesota 55033-9469
Phone: (612)436-6530

Decker Business Consulting
6837 Booth Ave.
Inver Grove Heights, Minnesota 55076
Phone: (612)451-6600

Family Business Group - Division of
McGladrey & Pullen
800 Marquette Ave., Ste. 1300
Minneapolis, Minnesota 55402
Phone: (612)376-9376
Fax: (612)376-9876
Toll-free: (800)831-1272

Franchise Business Systems Inc.
4200 Dahlborg Dr.
Minneapolis, Minnesota 55422
Phone: (612)520-8403
Fax: (612)520-8410
Toll-free: (800)433-2540

Health Fitness Corp.
3500 W. 80th St., Ste. 200
Minneapolis, Minnesota 55431
Phone: (612)831-6830
Fax: (612)831-7264

Minnesota Cooperation Office for
Small Business & Job Creation, Inc.
5001 W. 80th St., Ste. 825
Minneapolis, Minnesota 55437
Phone: (612)830-1230
Fax: (612)830-1232

Power Systems Research
1301 Corporate Center Dr., Ste. 113
St. Paul, Minnesota 55121
Phone: (612)454-0144
Fax: (612)454-0760
Toll-free: (800)433-7746

Missouri

Business Planning and Development
Incorporated
4030 Charlotte St.
Kansas City, Missouri 64110
Phone: (816)753-0495

MedImage, Inc.
The Frances Vandivort Center
305 E. Walnut, Ste. 110LL
Springfield, Missouri 65806
Phone: (417)831-0110
Fax: (417)831-0288
Toll-free: (800)879-2357

Nebraska

Chandler & Associates Ltd.
4220 Pratt St.
Omaha, Nebraska 68111
Phone: (402)453-4560

Small Business Management
Services Inc.
10801 Pacific St., Ste. 3
Omaha, Nebraska 68154
Phone: (402)390-0456
Fax: (402)393-0629
Toll-free: (800)750-0456

Heartland Management Consulting
Group
1904 Barrington Pkwy.
Papillion, Nebraska 68128
Phone: (402)339-1319
Fax: (402)339-1319

Nevada

The DuBois Group
800 Southwood Blvd., Ste. 206
Incline Village, Nevada 89451
Phone: (702)832-0550
Fax: (702)832-0556
Toll-free: (800)375-2935

New Hampshire

Wolff Consultants
10 Buck Rd., PO Box 1003
Hanover, New Hampshire 03755
Phone: (603)643-6015

King MacRury Associates
Box 215
Rye, New Hampshire 03870
Phone: (603)439-7975

New Jersey

ConMar International, Ltd.
283 Dayton-Jamesburg Rd., PO Box 437
Dayton, New Jersey 08810
Phone: (908)274-1100
Fax: (908)274-1199

Realty Asset Services, Inc.
Meridian Center 3
6 Industrial Way W
Eatontown, New Jersey 07724
Phone: (908)531-2944
Fax: (908)517-0422

Kumar Associates, Inc.
260 Columbia Ave.
Fort Lee, New Jersey 07024
Phone: (201)224-9480
Fax: (201)585-2343

John Hall & Company, Inc.
PO Box 187
Glen Ridge, New Jersey 07028
Phone: (201)680-4449
Fax: (201)680-4449

PA Consulting Group Inc.
279 Princeton Rd.
Hightstown, New Jersey 08520
Phone: (609)426-4700
Fax: (609)426-4046

Strategic Management Group
PO Box 402
Maplewood, New Jersey 07040
Phone: (201)378-2470

Vanguard Communications Corp.
100 American Rd.
Morris Plains, New Jersey 07950
Phone: (201)605-8000
Fax: (201)605-8329

Thomas S. Adubato Associates
PO Box 89
Pequannock, New Jersey 07440
Phone: (201)835-3566
Fax: (201)835-6470

Aurora Marketing Management, Inc.
210 Carnegie Center, Ste. 101
Princeton, New Jersey 08540
Phone: (609)520-8863

HYTECH Development
PO Box 2003
Princeton, New Jersey 08543-2003

Tracelin Associates
1171 Main St., Ste. 6K
Rahway, New Jersey 07065
Phone: (908)381-3288

Schkeeper Inc.
130-6 Bodman Pl.
Red Bank, New Jersey 07701
Phone: (908)219-1965

Henry Branch Associates
2502 Harmon Cove Tower
Secaucus, New Jersey 07094
Phone: (201)866-2008
Fax: (201)601-0101

Worldwide Marketing Service, Inc.
503 E. Revere Way
Smithville, New Jersey 08201
Phone: (609)748-1983

Robert Gibbons & Co., Inc.
46 Knoll Rd.
Tenafly, New Jersey 07670-1050
Phone: (201)871-3933
Fax: (201)871-2173

PMC Management Consultants, Inc.
11 Thistle Ln. P.O. Box 332
Three Bridges, New Jersey 08887-0332
Phone: (908)788-1014
Fax: (908)806-7287

Mitchell Brian & Associates
5 Carlton Ln.
Voorhees, New Jersey 08043
Phone: (609)751-3224
Fax: (609)751-3225

R.W. Bankart & Associates
20 Valley Ave., Ste. D-2
Westwood, New Jersey 07675-3607
Phone: (201)664-7672

Albert L. Emmons
580 Jackson Ave.
Westwood, New Jersey 07675
Phone: (201)666-0225

New Mexico

Vondle & Associates, Inc.
4926 Calle de Terra NE
Albuquerque, New Mexico 87111
Phone: (505)292-8961
Fax: (505)296-2790

New York

Powers Research and Training Institute
PO Box 78
Bayville, New York 11709
Phone: (516)628-2250
Fax: (516)628-2252

Consortium House
139 Wittenberg Rd.
Bearsville, New York 12409
Phone: (914)679-8867
Fax: (914)679-9248

Progressive Finance Corporation
3549 Tiemann Ave.
Bronx, New York 10469
Phone: (718)405-9029
Toll-free: (800)225-8381

Wave Hill Associates
2621 Palisade Ave., Ste. 15-C
Riverdale
Bronx, New York 10463
Phone: (718)549-7368
Fax: (718)884-1856

Marketing Resources Group
71-58 Austin St.
Forest Hills, New York 11375
Phone: (718)261-8882

Group I Financial Services
P.O. Box 922
Highland, New York 12528
Phone: (914)883-9356
Fax: (914)883-9356

North Star Enterprises
670 N. Terrace Ave.
Mount Vernon, New York 10552
Phone: (914)668-9433

E.N. Rysso & Associates
21 Jordan Rd.
New Hartford, New York 13413-2311
Phone: (315)732-2206
Fax: (315)732-2206

Atlantic Venture International Inc.
1271 Ave. of the Americas, 4500
New York, New York 10020
Phone: (212)554-8200
Fax: (212)554-8209

Boice Dunham Group
437 Madison Ave.
New York, New York 10022
Phone: (212)752-5550
Fax: (212)752-7055

Brancato Fritsch & Co.
45 W. 60 St., Ste. 25D
New York, New York 10023
Phone: (212)315-4155
Fax: (212)315-2950

Elizabeth Capen
27 E. 95th St.
New York, New York 10128
Phone: (212)427-7654

Cypress International, Inc.
2413 Bayshore Blvd., Ste. 2102
New York, New York 10169
Phone: (212)254-0051

Dunham & Marcus International
575 Madison Ave., Ste. 1006
New York, New York 10022
Phone: (212)605-0571

Growth Dynamics, Inc.
595 Madison Ave.
New York, New York 10022
Phone: (212)758-3379
Fax: (212)753-0314

Haver Analytics
60 E. 42nd St., Ste. 620
New York, New York 10017
Phone: (212)986-9300
Fax: (212)986-5857

The Jordan, Edmiston Group, Inc.
885 3rd Ave., 25th Fl.
New York, New York 10022
Phone: (212)754-0710
Fax: (212)754-0337

Knowledge=Power, Inc.
347 Fifth Avenue, Ste. 1406
New York, New York 10016
Phone: (212)251-0470
Fax: (212)251-0472

KPMG Peat Marwick
767 5th Ave.
New York, New York 10153
Phone: (212)909-5000
Fax: (212)909-5070

Mahoney Cohen Consulting Corp.
111 W. 40th St., 12th Fl.
New York, New York 10018
Phone: (212)490-8000
Fax: (212)398-0267

Management Practice, Inc.
342 Madison Ave.
New York, New York 10173-1230
Phone: (212)867-7948
Fax: (212)972-5188

Moseley Associates, Inc.
270 Madison Ave., Ste. 1207
New York, New York 10016
Phone: (212)213-6673
Fax: (212)213-6675

Pofcher Company
43 East 63rd Street
New York, New York 10021
Phone: (212)355-1390
Fax: (212)755-3061

Practice Development Counsel
60 Sutton Pl. S
New York, New York 10022
Phone: (212)593-1549
Fax: (212)980-7940

RRA Consulting Services, Inc.
166 E. 34th St.
New York, New York 10016
Phone: (212)686-4614

Samani International Enterprises,
Marions Panyaught Consultancy
2028 Parsons
New York, New York 11357-3436
Phone: (212)287-8087
Fax: (800)873-8939

Vencon Management, Incorporated
301 W. 53rd St.
New York, New York 10019
Phone: (212)581-8787
Fax: (212)397-4126

R.A. Walsh Consultants
429 E. 52nd St.
New York, New York 10022
Phone: (212)688-6047
Fax: (212)535-4075

Werner International Inc.
111 W. 40th St.
New York, New York 10018
Phone: (212)642-6092
Fax: (212)642-6084
Toll-free: (800)333-7816

Zimmerman Business Consulting
44 E. 92nd St., Ste. 5-B
New York, New York 10128
Phone: (212)860-3107
Fax: (212)860-7730

Command Communications, Inc.
2500 Westchester Ave.
Purchase, New York 10577
Phone: (914)251-1515
Fax: (914)251-1562

David Lang Wardle
101 Birchwood Dr.
Schenectady, New York 12303-5603
Phone: (518)355-9172

ComputerEase Company
9 Hachaliah Brown Dr.
Somers, New York 10589
Phone: (914)277-5317
Fax: (914)335-7971

Executive Extra, Inc.
PO Box 6036
Syracuse, New York 13217
Phone: (315)422-2657

Innovation Management Consulting,
Inc.
209 Dewitt Rd.
Syracuse, New York 13214-2006
Phone: (315)425-5144
Fax: (315)445-8989

M. Clifford Agress
891 Fulton St.
Valley Stream, New York 11580
Phone: (516)825-8955
Fax: (516)825-8955

Destiny Kinal Marketing
Consultancy
105 Chemung St.
Waverly, New York 14892
Phone: (607)565-8317
Fax: (607)565-4083

Information Systems Planning
3 Melrose Ln.
West Nyack, New York 10994
Phone: (914)358-6546

Management Insight
96 Arlington Rd.
Williamsville, New York 14221
Phone: (716)631-3319
Fax: (716)631-0203

G.L. Michael Management Consultants
335 Evans St., Ste. A
Williamsville, New York 14221
Phone: (716)634-5091

Chester M. Malanowski
105 Turquoise Creek Dr.
Cary, North Carolina 27513
Phone: (919)460-6600

North Carolina

Ronald A. Norelli & Company
Nations Bank Corporation Center
100 N. Tyron St., Ste. 3220
Charlotte, North Carolina 28202-4000
Phone: (704)376-5484
Fax: (704)376-5485

Ohio

Transportation Technology Services
208 Harmon Rd.
Aurora, Ohio 44202
Phone: (216)562-3596

Delta Planning, Inc.
PO Box 22618
Beachwood, Ohio 44122
Phone: (216)831-2521
Fax: (216)831-7616

Empro Systems, Inc.
4777 Red Bank Expy., Ste. 1
Cincinnati, Ohio 45227-1519
Phone: (513)271-2042
Fax: (513)271-2042

Strategic Research Center
1 Corporate Exchange
25825 Science Park Dr.
Cleveland, Ohio 44122
Phone: (216)831-2410
Fax: (216)464-2308

The Adams Group
2704 Fair Ave.
Columbus, Ohio 43209
Phone: (614)231-0002
Fax: (614)231-0002

Cory Dillon Associates
111 Schreyer Pl. E
Columbus, Ohio 43214
Phone: (614)262-8211

Marketing Advisory Group
2670 Brandon Rd.
Columbus, Ohio 43221
Phone: (614)481-0033

Ransom & Associates -
COMPETITIVEdge Group
106 E. Pacemont Rd.
Columbus, Ohio 43202-1225
Phone: (614)267-7100
Fax: (614)262-7199

Herman Associates Inc.
PO Box 5351
Fairlawn, Ohio 44333
Phone: (216)836-5656
Fax: (216)836-3311
Toll-free: (800)227-3566

Young & Associates
PO Box 711
Kent, Ohio 44240
Phone: (216)678-0524
Fax: (216)678-6219
Toll-free: (800)525-9775

Robert A. Westman & Associates
359 Quarry Ln.
Warren, Ohio 44483
Phone: (216)856-4149
Fax: (216)856-2564

Oklahoma

Innovative Resources Inc.
4900 Richmond Sq., Ste. 100
Oklahoma City, Oklahoma 73118
Phone: (405)840-0033
Fax: (405)843-8359

Community & Governmental
Consultants, Inc.
Box 1121

Stillwater, Oklahoma 74076
Phone: (405)743-3048
Fax: (405)743-4459

Oregon

INTERCON - The International
Converting Institute
5200 Badger Rd.
Crooked River Ranch, Oregon 97760
Phone: (503)548-1447
Fax: (563)548-1618

Talbott ARM
HC 64, Box 120
Lakeview, Oregon 97630
Phone: (503)947-3482
Fax: (503)947-3482

Management Technology Associates,
Ltd.
1618 SW 1st Ave., Ste. 315
Portland, Oregon 97201
Phone: (503)224-5220

Nudelman & Associates
6443 SW Beaverton Hwy.
Portland, Oregon 97221
Phone: (503)292-2604
Fax: (503)292-5850

Pennsylvania

Problem Solvers for Industry
345 Park Ave.
Box 193
Chalfont, Pennsylvania 18914
Phone: (215)822-9695
Fax: (215)822-8086

Elayne Howard & Associates, Inc.
3501 Masons Mill Rd., Ste. 501
Huntingdon Valley, Pennsylvania
19006-3509
Phone: (215)657-9550

GRA, Incorporated
115 West Ave., Ste. 201
Jenkintown, Pennsylvania 19046
Phone: (215)884-7500
Fax: (215)884-1385

Mifflin County Industrial Development Corporation
Mifflin County Industrial Plaza
One Belle Ave.
Lewistown, Pennsylvania 17044
Phone: (717)242-0393
Fax: (717)242-1842

Autech Products
1289 Revere Rd.
Morrisville, Pennsylvania 19067
Phone: (215)493-3759
Fax: (215)493-3759

Advantage Associates
434 Avon Dr.
Pittsburgh, Pennsylvania 15228
Phone: (412)343-1558
Fax: (412)362-1684

Regis J. Sheehan & Associates
291 Foxcroft Rd.
Pittsburgh, Pennsylvania 15220
Phone: (412)279-1207

Egbert M. Kipp
745 Thomas St.
State College, Pennsylvania 16803
Phone: (814)231-0197

Moeller Associates
RD 3, Box 177
Towanda, Pennsylvania 18848
Phone: (717)265-6523

James W. Davidson Co., Inc.
23 Forest View Rd.
Wallingford, Pennsylvania 19086
Phone: (610)566-1462

Puerto Rico

Diego Chevere & Co.
Ste. 301, Metro Parque 7
Metro Office Park
Caparra Heights, Puerto Rico 00920
Phone: (809)782-9595
Fax: (809)782-9532

Manuel L. Porrata and Associates
898 Munoz Rivera Ave., Ste. 201
Rio Piedras, Puerto Rico 00927
Phone: (809)765-2140
Fax: (809)754-3285

Rhode Island

William L. Keefe
140 Iroquois Rd.
Cumberland, Rhode Island 02864
Phone: (401)333-1503

South Carolina

Aquafood Business Associates
P.O. Box 16190
Charleston, South Carolina 29412
Phone: (803)795-9506
Fax: (803)795-9477

Strategic Innovations International
12 Executive Court
Lake Wylie, South Carolina 29710
Phone: (803)831-1225
Fax: (803)831-2979
Minus Stage
Box 4436
Rock Hill, South Carolina 29731
Phone: (803)328-0705
Fax: (803)329-9948

Tennessee

Daniel Petchers & Associates
8820 Fernwood CV
Germantown, Tennessee 38138
Phone: (901)383-1749

Dean Winn
1114 Forest Harbor, Ste. 300
Hendersonville, Tennessee 37075
Phone: (615)822-8692
Fax: (615)822-8692
Toll-free: (800)737-8382

Growth Consultants of America
3917 Trimble Rd., PO Box 158382
Nashville, Tennessee 37215
Phone: (615)383-0550
Fax: (615)269-8940
Toll-free: (800)230-0550

Texas

Lori Williams
1000 Leslie Ct.
Arlington, Texas 76012
Phone: (817)459-3934
Fax: (817)459-3934

Erisa Adminstrative Services Inc.
12325 Haymeadow Dr., Bldg. 4
Austin, Texas 78750-1847
Phone: (512)250-9020
Fax: (512)250-9487

R. Miller Hicks & Company
1011 W. 11th St.
Austin, Texas 78703
Phone: (512)477-7000
Fax: (512)477-9697

M.A. Moses & Associates
1801 Heatherglen Ln.
Austin, Texas 78758
Phone: (512)837-2417

Market Development Services, Inc.
5350 Montrose Dr.
Dallas, Texas 75209
Phone: (214)352-7247
Fax: (214)357-1835

Peter Schaar
3515 Haynie Ave.
Dallas, Texas 75205
Phone: (214)528-7162
Fax: (214)528-7162

Jaime & Associates International Bureau of Accountants and Consultants
1731 Montana Ave.
El Paso, Texas 79902-5704
Phone: (915)532-7188

The Dowdle Poe Co.
4610 Westin Dr.
Fulshear, Texas 77441
Phone: (713)346-2560
Fax: (713)346-2558

Arnott & Associates, Inc.
PO Box 923
Grapevine, Texas 76099-0923
Phone: (817)430-1258
Fax: (817)491-4818

High Technology Associates - Division of Global Technologies, Inc.
1775 St. James Pl., Ste. 105
Houston, Texas 77056
Phone: (713)963-9300
Fax: (713)963-8341

PROTEC
4607 Linden Pl.
Pearland, Texas 77584
Phone: (713)997-9872
Fax: (713)997-9895

Industrial Distribution Consultants,
Inc.
PO Box 2530
Port Aransas, Texas 78373-2530
Phone: (512)749-7123
Fax: (512)749-7123

Business Strategy Development
Consultants
PO Box 690365
San Antonio, Texas 78269
Phone: (210)696-8000
Fax: (210)696-8000
Toll-free: (800)927-BSDC

Tom Welch Financial
6900 San Pedro Ave., Ste. 147
San Antonio, Texas 78279
Phone: (210)737-7022
Fax: (210)737-7022

Utah

CAPCON, Ltd.
8746 S. Rustler Rd.
Sandy, Utah 84093
Phone: (801)943-6339

Virginia

Elliott B. Jaffa
2530-B S. Walter Reed Dr.
Arlington, Virginia 22206
Phone: (703)931-0040

Koach Enterprises - USA
5529 N. 18th St.
Arlington, Virginia 22205
Phone: (703)241-8361
Fax: (703)241-8623

Federal Market Development
5650 Chapel Run Ct.
Centreville, Virginia 22020-3601
Phone: (703)502-8930
Fax: (703)502-8929
Toll-free: (800)821-5003

Transportation Management Sys-
tems, Inc.
11317 Beach Mill Rd.
Great Falls, Virginia 22066
Phone: (703)444-0995
Fax: (703)444-6089

Barringer, Huff & Stuart
310 Fifth St.
Lynchburg, Virginia 24504
Phone: (804)528-2356
Fax: (804)528-2357

Performance Support Systems
11835 Canon Blvd., Ste. C-101
Newport News, Virginia 23606
Phone: (804)873-3700
Fax: (804)873-3288
Toll-free: (800)488-6463

Charles Scott Pugh
4101 Pittaway Dr.
Richmond, Virginia 23235-1022
Phone: (804)560-0979

John C. Randall and Associates, Inc.
PO Box 15127
Richmond, Virginia 23227
Phone: (804)746-4450
Fax: (804)747-7426

The Dynex Group
5345 Fairfield Blvd.
Virginia Beach, Virginia 23464
Phone: (804)497-5561
Fax: (804)497-0986

Arthur L. Pepperman, II, Business/
Medical Appraiser
202 West Queens Dr.
Williamsburg, Virginia 23185
Phone: (804)229-3570
Fax: (804)229-3570

The Small Business Counselor
12423 Hedges Run Dr., Ste. 153
Woodbridge, Virginia 22192
Phone: (703)490-6755

Washington

B.A.S.I.C. Consultants, Inc.
10020 A Main St., Ste. 352
Bellevue, Washington 98004
Phone: (206)454-0341
Fax: (206)649-8809

Perry L. Smith Consulting
800 Bellevue Way NE, Ste. 400
Bellevue, Washington 98004-4208
Phone: (206)462-2072
Fax: (206)462-5638

Management Consultants, Inc.
1322 44th Ave. SW
Seattle, Washington 98116
Phone: (206)935-3388

Northwest Trade Adjustment Assis-
tance Center
900 4th Ave., Ste. 2430
Seattle, Washington 98164-1003
Phone: (206)622-2730
Fax: (206)622-1105

Spectrum West
4711 NE 50th
Seattle, Washington 98105
Phone: (206)524-5958
Fax: (206)524-7826

Business Planning Consultants
S. 3510 Ridgeview Dr.
Spokane, Washington 99206
Phone: (509)928-0332
Fax: (509)921-0842

West Virginia

MarkeTech Communications
PO Box 35
Montrose, West Virginia 26283-0035
Phone: (304)637-0805

Wisconsin

White & Associates
5349 Somerset Ln. S
Greenfield, Wisconsin 53221
Phone: (414)281-7373
Fax: (414)282-3245

SMALL BUSINESS ADMINISTRATION REGIONAL OFFICES

This section contains a listing of Small Business Administration offices arranged numerically by region. Service areas are provided. Contact the appropriate office for a referral to the nearest field office.

Region 1

U.S. Small Business Administration
10 Causeway St., Rm. 812
Boston, Massachusetts 02222
Phone: (617)565-8415
Fax: (617)565-8420
Serves Connecticut, Maine, Massachusetts, New Hampshire, Rhode Island, and Vermont.

Region 2

U.S. Small Business Administration
26 Federal Plz., Rm. 3108
New York, New York 10278
Phone: (212)264-1450
Fax: (212)264-0038
Serves New Jersey, New York, Puerto Rico, and the Virgin Islands.

Region 3

U.S. Small Business Administration
475 Allendale Rd., Ste. 201
King of Prussia, Pennsylvania 19406
Phone: (610)962-3710
Fax: (610)962-3743
Serves Delaware, the District of Columbia, Maryland, Pennsylvania, Virginia, and West Virginia.

Region 4

U.S. Small Business Administration
1375 Peachtree St. NE, Rm. 500
Atlanta, Georgia 30367-8102
Phone: (404)347-4999
Fax: (404)347-2355
Serves Alabama, Florida, Georgia, Kentucky, Mississippi, North Carolina, South Carolina, and Tennessee.

Region 5

U.S. Small Business Administration
Gateway IV Bldg., Ste. 1975 South
300 S. Riverside Plz.
Chicago, Illinois 60606-6611
Phone: (312)353-8089
Fax: (312)353-3426
Serves Illinois, Indiana, Michigan, Minnesota, Ohio, and Wisconsin.

Region 6

U.S. Small Business Administration
8625 King George Dr., Bldg. C
Dallas, Texas 75235-3391
Phone: (214)767-7611
Fax: (214)767-7870
Serves Arkansas, Louisiana, New Mexico, Oklahoma, and Texas.

Region 7

U.S. Small Business Administration
Lucas Place, Ste. 307
323 W. 8th St.
Kansas City, Missouri 64105
Phone: (816)374-6380
Fax: (816)374-6339
Serves Iowa, Kansas, Missouri, and Nebraska.

Region 8

U.S. Small Business Administration
633 17th St., 7th Fl.
Denver, Colorado 80202
Phone: (303)294-7186
Fax: (303)294-7153
Serves Colorado, Montana, North Dakota, South Dakota, Utah, and Wyoming.

Region 9

U.S. Small Business Administration
71 Stevenson St., 20th Fl.
San Francisco, California 94105
Phone: (415)744-6404
Serves American Samoa, Arizona, California, Guam, Hawaii, Nevada, and the Trust Territory of the Pacific Islands.

Region 10

U.S. Small Business Administration
1200 6th Ave., Ste. 1805
Seattle, Washington 98101-1128
Phone: (206)553-5676
Fax: (206)553-4155
Serves Alaska, Idaho, Oregon, and Washington.

SMALL BUSINESS DEVELOPMENT CENTERS

This section contains a listing of all Small Business Development Centers organized alphabetically by state/U.S. territory name, then by city, then by agency name.

Alabama

Auburn University
Small Business Development Center
108 College of Business
Auburn, Alabama 36849-5243
Phone: (334)844-4220
Fax: (334)844-4268
Pat W. Shaddix, Dir.

University of Alabama at Birmingham
Small Business Development Center
1601 11th Ave. S
Birmingham, Alabama 35294-2180
Phone: (205)934-6760
Fax: (205)934-0538
Vernon Nabors, Contact

University of North Alabama
Small Business Development Center
Box 5248, Keller Hall
Florence, Alabama 35632-0001
Phone: (205)760-4629
Fax: (205)760-4813
Kerry Gatlin, Dir.

Alabama A&M University
University of Alabama (Huntsville)
North East Alabama Regional Small Business Development Center

225 Church St. NW
PO Box 168
Huntsville, Alabama 35804-0168
Phone: (205)535-2061
Fax: (205)535-2050
Jeff Thompson, Contact
E-mail: thompsonj@email.uah.edu

Jacksonville State University
Small Business Development Center
700 Pelham Rd. N
114 Merrill Hall
Jacksonville, Alabama 36265
Phone: (205)782-5271
Fax: (205)782-5179
Paul Ganer, Dir.

Livingston University
Small Business Development Center
Station 35
Livingston, Alabama 35470
Phone: (205)652-9661
Fax: (205)652-9318
Jeff Thompson, Dir.

University of South Alabama
Small Business Development Center
College of Business, Rm. 8
Mobile, Alabama 36688
Phone: (334)460-6004
Fax: (334)460-6246
Cheryl Coleman, Dir.

Alabama State University
Small Business Development Center
915 S. Jackson St.
Montgomery, Alabama 36195
Phone: (334)293-4138
Fax: (334)269-1102
Sherrel Mitchell Price, Dir.

Troy State University
Small Business Development Center
Bibb Graves, Rm. 102
Troy, Alabama 36082-0001
Phone: (205)670-3771
Fax: (205)670-3636
Janet W. Kervin, Dir.

Alabama International Trade Center
University of Alabama
SBDC
Bidgood Hall, Rm. 201
PO Box 870396

Tuscaloosa, Alabama 35487-0396
Phone: (205)348-7621
Fax: (205)348-6974
Brian Davis, Dir.

University of Alabama
Small Business Development Center
Bidgood Hall, Rm. 250
PO Box 870397
Tuscaloosa, Alabama 35487-0397
Phone: (205)348-7011
Fax: (205)348-9644
Paavo Hanninen, Dir.
E-mail: phaninen@ua1vm.ue.edu

Alaska

University of Alaska (Fairbanks)
Small Business Development Center
510 Second Ave., Ste. 101
Fairbanks, Alaska 99701
Phone: (907)456-1701
Toll-free: (800)478-1701
Fax: (907)456-1873
Theresa Proenza, Contact

University of Alaska (Juneau)
Small Business Development Center
400 Willoughby St., Ste. 211
Juneau, Alaska 99801
Phone: (907)463-3789
Toll-free: (800)478-6655
Fax: (907)463-3929
Charles Northrop, Dir.

Kenai Peninsula Small Business
Development Center
110 S. Willow St., Ste. 106
Kenai, Alaska 99611-7744
Phone: (907)283-3335
Fax: (907)283-3913
William L. Root, Dir.

University of Alaska (Matanuska-
Susitna)
Small Business Development Center
1801 Parks Hwy., Ste. C-18
Wasilla, Alaska 99654
Phone: (907)373-7232
Fax: (907)373-2560
Marian Romano, Director

Arizona

Central Arizona College
Small Business Development Center
8470 N. Overfield Rd.
Coolidge, Arizona 85228
Phone: (520)426-4341
Fax: (520)426-4284
Donald Biggerstaff, Dir.

Coconino County Community College
Small Business Development Center
3000 N. 4th St., Ste. 25
Flagstaff, Arizona 86004
Phone: (520)526-5072
Fax: (520)526-8693
Stephen West, Dir.

Northland Pioneer College
Small Business Development Center
PO Box 610
Holbrook, Arizona 86025
Phone: (520)537-2976
Fax: (520)524-2227
Joel Eittreim, Dir.

Mohave Community College
Small Business Development Center
1971 Jagerson Ave.
Kingman, Arizona 86401
Phone: (520)757-0894
Fax: (520)757-0836
Jennee Miles, Dir.

Gateway Community College
Small Business Development Center
108 N. 40th St.
Phoenix, Arizona 85034-1795
Kathy Evans, Contact

Rio Salado Community College
Small Business Development Center
301 Roosevelt St., Ste. B
Phoenix, Arizona 85003
Phone: (602)238-9603
Fax: (602)340-1627
Marti McCorkindale, Contact

Yavapai College
Small Business Development Center
117 E. Gurley St., Ste. 206
Prescott, Arizona 86301
Phone: (520)778-3088
Fax: (520)778-3109
Richard Senopole, Contact

Eastern Arizona Community College
SBDC
1111 Thatcher Blvd.
Safford, Arizona 85546
Phone: (520)687-1904

Cochise College
Small Business Development Center
901 N. Colombo, Rm. 411
Sierra Vista, Arizona 85635
Phone: (520)515-5443
Fax: (520)515-5478
Debbie Elver, Dir.

Arizona Small Business Development
Center Network
2411 W. 14th St., Ste. 132
Tempe, Arizona 85281
Phone: (602)731-8720
Fax: (602)731-8729
Michael York, State Director
E-mail: york@maricopa.bitnet

Maricopa Community Colleges
SBDC
1414 W. Broadway, Ste. 165
Tempe, Arizona 85281
Phone: (602)966-7786
Fax: (602)966-8541
Christina Gonzalez, Director
Sonny Quinonez, Director

Eastern Arizona College
Small Business Development Center
622 College Ave.
Thatcher, Arizona 85552-0769
Phone: (520)428-8590
Fax: (520)428-8462
Greg Roers, Dir.

Pima Community College
Small Business Development Center
4905-A E. Broadway Blvd., Ste. 101
Tucson, Arizona 85709-1260
Phone: (520)748-4906
Fax: (520)748-4585
Linda Andrews, Dir.

Arizona Western College
Small Business Development Center
Century Plz., No. 152
281 W. 24th St.
Yuma, Arizona 85364
Phone: (520)341-1650
Fax: (520)726-2636
Hank Pinto, Dir.

Arkansas

Henderson State University
Small Business Development Center
1100 Henderson St.
PO Box 7624
Arkadelphia, Arkansas 71923
Phone: (501)230-5224
Fax: (501)230-5236
Bill Akin, Dir.

University of Central Arkansas
Small Business Development Center
College of Business Administration
Burdick Business Administration
Bldg., Rm. 212
201 Donaghey Ave.
Conway, Arkansas 72035-0001
Phone: (501)450-3190
Fax: (501)450-5302

Genesis Technology Incubator
SBDC Satellite Office
University of Arkansas Engineering
Research Center
Fayetteville, Arkansas 72701-1201
Phone: (501)575-7473
Fax: (501)575-7446

University of Arkansas at Fayetteville
Small Business Development Center
College of Business
BADM 1172
Fayetteville, Arkansas 72701
Phone: (501)575-5148
Fax: (501)575-4013
Jim Buckner, Dir.

University of Arkansas at Little Rock,
Regional Office (Fort Smith)
Small Business Development Center
1109 S. 16th St.
PO Box 2067
Fort Smith, Arkansas 72901
Phone: (501)785-1376
Fax: (501)785-1964
Byron Branch, Business Specialist

University of Arkansas at Little Rock,
Regional Office (Harrison)
Small Business Development Center
1818 Hwy. 62-65-412 N
PO Box 190

Harrison, Arkansas 72601
Phone: (501)741-8009
Fax: (501)741-1905
Bob Penquite, Business Specialist

University of Arkansas at Little Rock,
Regional Office (Hot Springs)
Small Business Development Center
835 Central Ave., Box 402D
Hot Springs, Arkansas 71901
Phone: (501)624-5448
Fax: (501)624-6632
Richard Evans, Business Specialist

Northeast Arkansas Regional Office
SBDC
2905 King St.
PO Box 1403
Jonesboro, Arkansas 72403
Phone: (501)932-3957
Fax: (501)932-0135
Ronny Brothers, Business Specialist

University of Arkansas Little Rock
SBDC
100 S. Main, Ste. 401
Little Rock, Arkansas 72201
Phone: (501)324-9043
Fax: (501)324-9049
John Harrison, Business Specialist

University of Arkansas at Little Rock,
Regional Office (Magnolia)
Small Business Development Center
600 Bessie
PO Box 767
Magnolia, Arkansas 71753
Phone: (501)234-4030
Fax: (501)234-0135
Lairie Kincaid, Business Specialist

University of Arkansas at Little Rock,
Regional Office (Pine Bluff)
Small Business Development Center
The Enterprise Center III
400 Main, Ste. 117
Pine Bluff, Arkansas 71601
Phone: (501)536-0654
Fax: (501)536-7713
Vonelle Vanzant, Contact

Harding University
Small Business Development Center
Mabee School of Business
Blakeny and Center Sts.

Searcy, Arkansas 72149
Phone: (501)279-4000
Fax: (501)279-4078

Arkansas State University
Small Business Development Center
PO Drawer 2650
State University, Arkansas 72467
Phone: (501)972-3517
Fax: (501)972-3868
Gerald Jones, Dir.

University of Arkansas at Little Rock,
Regional Office (Stuttgart)
Small Business Development Center
301 S. Grand, Ste. 101
PO Box 289
Stuttgart, Arkansas 72160
Phone: (501)673-8707
Fax: (501)673-8707
Larry LeFler, Business Specialist

California

Central Coast Small Business
Development Center
6500 Soquel Dr.
Aptos, California 95003
Phone: (408)479-6136
Fax: (408)479-6166
Elza Minor, Dir.

Sierra College Small Business
Development Center
560 Wall St., Ste. J
Auburn, California 95603
Phone: (916)885-5488
Fax: (916)823-4142
Mary Wolleson, Dir.

Weill Institute Small Business
Development Center
1330 22nd St., Ste. B
Bakersfield, California 93301
Phone: (805)322-5881
Fax: (805)322-8663
Jeffrey Johnson, Dir.

Butte College
Small Business Development Center
260 Cohasset Rd., Ste. A
Chico, California 95926
Phone: (916)895-9017
Fax: (916)895-9099
Kay Zimmerlee, Dir.

Southwestern College Small Business
Development and International Trade
Center
900 Otay Lakes Rd., Bldg. 1600
Chula Vista, California 91910
Phone: (619)482-6393
Fax: (619)482-6402
Mary Wylie, Dir.

Lake County Satellite Small Business
Development Center
Hilltop Professional Center, Ste. 205
15322 Lakeshore Dr.
PO Box 4550
Clearlake, California 95422-4550
Phone: (707)995-3440
Fax: (707)995-3605
Kim McKay, Admin. Asst,

Contra Costa SBDC
2425 Bisso Ln., Ste. 100
Concord, California 94520
Phone: (510)646-5517
Rita S. Hays, Interim Director

North Coast Small Business Develop-
ment Center
207 Price Mall
Crescent City, California 95531
Phone: (707)464-2168
Fax: (707)445-9652
Fran Clark, Dir.

Imperial Valley Satellite SBDC
Town & Country Shopping Center
301 N. Imperial Ave., Ste. B
El Centro, California 92243
Phone: (619)312-9800
Fax: (619)312-9838
Debbie Trujillo, Dir.

North Coast/Satellite Center
520 E. St.
Eureka, California 95501
Phone: (707)445-9720
Fax: (707)465-6008
Duff Heuttner, Bus. Counselor

Central California
Small Business Development Center
1999 Tuolumne St., Ste. 650
Fresno, California 93721
Phone: (209)237-0660
Fax: (209)237-1417
Dennis Winans, Dir.

Gavilan College Small Business
Development Center
7436 Monterey St.
Gilroy, California 95020
Phone: (408)847-0373
Fax: (408)847-0393
Peter Graff, Dir.

Accelerate Technology Assistance
Small Business Development Center
4199 Campus Dr.
University Towers, Ste. 240
Irvine, California 92715
Phone: (714)509-2990
Fax: (714)509-2997
Tiffany Haugen, Dir.

Greater San Diego Chamber of
Commerce Small Business Develop-
ment Center
4275 Executive Sq., Ste. 920
La Jolla, California 92037
Phone: (619)453-9388
Fax: (619)450-1997
Lisa Hasler, Dir.

Export SBDC of Southern California
110 E. 9th, Ste. A669
Los Angeles, California 90079
Phone: (213)892-1111
Fax: (213)892-8232
Gladys Moreau, Dir.

South Central Los Angeles/Satellite
SBDC
4060 S. Figueroa St.
Los Angeles, California 90037
Phone: (213)846-1710
Fax: (213)235-1686
David Norcross, Satellite Mgr.

Valley Sierra SBDC
Merced Satellite
1632 N St.
Merced, California 95340
Phone: (209)385-7312
Fax: (209)383-4959
Nick Starianoudakis, Satellite Mgr.

Valley Sierra Small Business Devel-
opment Center
1012 11th St., Ste. 300
Modesto, California 95354
Phone: (209)521-6177
Fax: (209)521-9373
Kelly Bearden, Dir.

Napa Valley College Small Business
Development Center
1556 First St., Ste. 103
Napa, California 94559
Phone: (707)253-3210
Fax: (707)253-3068
Michael Kauffman, Dir.

East Bay Small Business Develop-
ment Center
2201 Broadway, Ste. 701
Oakland, California 94612
Phone: (510)893-4114
Fax: (510)893-5532
Selma Taylor, Dir.

Export Satellite Center
300 Esplanade Dr., Ste. 1010
Oxnard, California 93030
Phone: (805)981-4633
Fax: (805)988-1862
Heather Wicka, Program Admin.

Coachella Valley SBDC
Palm Springs Satellite Center
501 S. Indian Canyon Dr., Ste. 222
Palm Springs, California 92264
Phone: (619)864-1311
Fax: (619)864-1319
Brad Mix, Satellite Mgr.

East Los Angeles County/Pasadena
Satellite
SBDC
2061 N. Los Robles, Ste. 101
Pasadena, California 91104
Phone: (818)398-9031
Fax: (818)398-3059
Paul Hischar, Satellite Mgr.

East Los Angeles County Small
Business Development Center
375 S. Main St., Ste. 101
Pomona, California 91766
Phone: (909)629-2247
Fax: (909)629-8310
Toni Valdez, Dir.

Superior California Economic
Development District
Cascade Small Business Develop-
ment Center
4352-A Caterpillar Rd.
Redding, California 96003

Phone: (916)241-8720
Fax: (916)241-1712
Robert Nash, Interim Director

Inland Empire Small Business
Development Center
2002 Iowa Ave., Bldg. D, Ste. 110
Riverside, California 92507
Phone: (909)781-2345
Toll-free: (800)7750-2353
Fax: (909)781-2353
Terri Corrazini Ooms, Dir.

Greater Sacramento Area SBDC
1787 Tribute Rd., Ste. A
Sacramento, California 95815
Phone: (916)263-6580
Fax: (916)263-6571

San Francisco City College
SBDC
City College of San Francisco
800 Mission St.
San Francisco, California 94103
Phone: (415)267-6504
Fax: (415)267-6536
Steven Glick, Interim Dir.

Orange County Small Business
Development Center
901 E. Santa Ana Blvd., Ste. 101
Santa Ana, California 92701
Phone: (714)647-1172
Fax: (714)835-9008
Gregory Kishel, Dir.

Silicon Valley Small Business
Development Center
c/o Silicon Valley Global Trading
Center
5201 Great America Pkwy., Ste. 429
Santa Clara, California 95054
Phone: (408)562-5704
Fax: (408)741-2190
James Hunter, Interim Dir.

Southwest Los Angeles County
Westside Satellite
SBDC
3233 Donald Douglas Loop S., Ste. C
Santa Monica, California 90405
Phone: (310)398-8883
Fax: (310)398-3024
Ken Symington, Satellite Manager

Redwood Empire SBDC
520 Mendocino Ave., Ste. 210
Santa Rosa, California 95403
Phone: (707)524-1770
Fax: (707)524-1772
Charles Robbins, Dir.

San Joaquin Delta College Small
Business Development Center
814 N. Hunter St.
Stockton, California 95202
Phone: (209)474-5089
Fax: (209)474-5605
Gillian Murphy, Dir.

Solano County Small Business
Development Center
424 Executive Court N., Ste. C
Suisun City, California 94585
Phone: (707)864-3382
Fax: (707)864-3386
Beth Pratt, Dir.

Southwest Los Angeles County Small
Business Development Center
21221 Western Ave., Ste. 110
Torrance, California 90501
Phone: (310)787-6466
Fax: (310)782-8607
Susan Hunter, Interim Dir.

North Los Angeles Small Business
Development Center
14540 Victory Blvd., Ste. 206
Van Nuys, California 91411
Phone: (818)373-7092
Fax: (818)373-7740
Lance Stevenson, Dir.

High Desert SBDC
Victorville Satellite Center
15490 Civic Dr., Ste. 102
Victorville, California 92392
Phone: (619)951-1592
Fax: (619)951-8929
Mike Roessler, Satellite Manager

Central California/Visalia Satellite
SBDC
430 W. Caldwell Ave., Ste. D
Visalia, California 93277
Phone: (209)625-3051
Fax: (209)625-3053
Randy Mason, Satellite Mgr.

Siskiyou Satellite SBDC
251 Main St.
PO Box 441
Weed, California 96094
Phone: (916)938-2658
Susan Brown, Interim Director

Colorado

Adams State College
Small Business Development Center
Business Bldg., No. 105
Alamosa, Colorado 81102
Phone: (719)589-7372
Fax: (719)589-7522
Peggy Micklich, Dir.

Aurora Small Business Management
Program
16000 E. Centretech Pky., Ste. A201
Aurora, Colorado 80011-9036
Phone: (303)360-4745

Community College of Aurora
Small Business Development Center
9905 E. Colfax
Aurora, Colorado 80010-2119
Phone: (303)341-4849
Fax: (303)361-2953
Randy Johnson, Dir.

Front Range Community College
(Boulder)
Small Business Development Center
Boulder Chamber of Commerce
2440 Pearl St.
Boulder, Colorado 80302
Phone: (303)442-1475
Fax: (303)938-8837
Joe Bell, Dir.

Pueblo Community College (Canon
City)
Small Business Development Center
402 Valley Rd.
Canon City, Colorado 81212
Phone: (719)275-5335
Fax: (719)275-4400
Elwin Boody, Dir.

Pikes Peak Community College
Small Business Development Center
Colorado Springs Chamber of
Commerce

PO Drawer B
Colorado Springs, Colorado 80901-3002
Phone: (303)471-4836
Fax: (303)635-1571

Colorado Northwestern Community
College
Small Business Development Center
50 College Dr.
Craig, Colorado 81625
Phone: (970)824-7078
Fax: (970)824-3527
Ken Farmer, Dir.

Delta Small Business Development
Center
Delta Montrose Vocational School
1765 US Hwy. 50
Delta, Colorado 81416
Phone: (970)874-8772
Fax: (970)874-8796
Steve Schrock, Dir.

Colorado Association of Commerce
and Industry (CACI)
Manager of Government Affairs
1776 Lincoln, Ste. 1200
Denver, Colorado 80203
Phone: (303)831-7411
Fax: (303)860-1439

Community College of Denver
Small Business Development Center
Greater Denver Chamber of Commerce
1445 Market St.
Denver, Colorado 80202
Phone: (303)620-8076
Fax: (303)534-3200
Tamela Lee, Dir.

Fort Lewis College
Small Business Development Center
1000 Rim Dr.
Durango, Colorado 81301
Phone: (970)247-7009
Fax: (970)247-7623
Jim Reser, Dir.
E-mail: reser-j@fortlewis.edu

Front Range Community College
(Fort Collins)
Small Business Development Center
2627 Redwing Rd., Ste. 105
Fort Collins, Colorado 80526

Phone: (970)226-0881
Fax: (970)204-0385
Frank Pryor, Dir.

Morgan Community College (Fort
Morgan)
Small Business Development Center
300 Main St.
Fort Morgan, Colorado 80701
Phone: (970)867-3351
Fax: (970)867-3352
Lori Slinn, Dir.

Colorado Mountain College
(Glenwood Springs)
Small Business Development Center
215 9th St.
Glenwood Springs, Colorado 81601
Phone: (970)928-0120
Toll-free: (800)621-6647
Fax: (970)945-1531
Russell Disberger, Dir.

Mesa State College
Small Business Development Center
304 W. Main St.
Grand Junction, Colorado 81505-1606
Phone: (970)243-5242
Fax: (970)241-0771

Greeley/Weld Chamber of Commerce
Small Business Development Center
Aims Community College
1407 8th Ave.
Greeley, Colorado 80631
Phone: (303)352-3661
Fax: (303)352-3572

Red Rocks Community College
Small Business Development Center
777 S. Wadsworth Blvd., Ste. 254
Bldg. 4
Lakewood, Colorado 80401-5398
Phone: (303)987-0710
Fax: (303)987-1331
Jayne Reiter, Acting Dir.

Lamar Community College
Small Business Development Center
2400 S. Main
Lamar, Colorado 81052
Phone: (719)336-8141
Fax: (719)336-2448
Elwood Gillis, Dir.

Arapahoe Community College SBDC
South Metro Chamber of Commerce
7901 S. Park Plz., Ste. 110
Littleton, Colorado 80120
Phone: (303)795-5855
Fax: (303)795-7520
Selma Kristel, Dir.

Pueblo Community College SBDC
900 W. Orman Ave.
Pueblo, Colorado 81004
Phone: (719)549-3224
Fax: (719)546-2413
Rita Friberg, Dir.

Morgan Community College (Stratton)
Small Business Development Center
PO Box 28
Stratton, Colorado 80836
Phone: (719)348-5596
Fax: (719)348-5887
Roni Carr, Dir.

Trinidad State Junior College SBDC
136 W. Main St.
Davis Bldg.
Trinidad, Colorado 81082
Phone: (719)846-5645
Fax: (719)846-4550
Dennis O'Connor, Dir.

Colorado Mountain College (Vail)
Small Business Development Center
1310 Westhaven Dr.
Vail, Colorado 81657
Phone: (303)476-4040
Fax: (303)479-9212

Front Range Community College
(Westminster)
Small Business and International
Development Center
3645 W. 112th Ave.
Westminster, Colorado 80030
Phone: (303)460-1032
Fax: (303)469-7143
Michael Lenzini, Dir.

Connecticut

Bridgeport Regional Business Council
Small Business Development Center
10 Middle St., 14th Fl.
Bridgeport, Connecticut 06604-4229

Phone: (203)330-4813
Fax: (203)366-0105
Juan Scott, Dir.

The Greater Danbury Chamber of
Commerce SBDC
72 West St.
Danbury, Connecticut 06810
Phone: (203)743-5565
Fax: (203)794-1439

Quinebaug Valley Community
Technical College
Small Business Development Center
742 Upper Maple St.
Danielson, Connecticut 06239
Phone: (203)774-1133
Fax: (203)774-7768
Roger Doty, Dir.

East Hartford Chamber of Commerce
SBDC
763 Burnside Ave.
East Hartford, Connecticut 06108
Phone: (203)289-0239
Fax: (203)289-0230

North Central Connecticut Chamber
of Commerce SBDC
111 Hazard Ave.
Enfield, Connecticut 06082
Phone: (203)763-2396
Fax: (203)749-1822

Glastonbury Chamber of Commerce
SBDC
2400 Main St.
Glastonbury, Connecticut 06033
Phone: (203)659-3587
Fax: (203)659-0102

University of Connecticut (Groton)
Small Business Development Center
Administration Bldg., Rm. 300
1084 Shennecossett Rd.
Groton, Connecticut 06340-6097
Phone: (860)449-1188
Fax: (860)445-3415
William Lockwood, Dir.

Hartford Enterprise Zone SBDC
10 Prospect St.
Hartford, Connecticut 06103
Phone: (203)543-8635
Fax: (203)722-6402

Middlesex Country Chamber of
Commerce
SBDC
393 Main St.
Middletown, Connecticut 06457
Phone: (860)344-2158
Fax: (860)346-1043
John Serignese

Greater New Haven Chamber of
Commerce
Small Business Development Center
195 Church St.
New Haven, Connecticut 06510-2009
Phone: (203)782-4390
Fax: (203)787-6730
Pete Rivera, Regional Dir.

Chamber of Commerce of Southeast-
ern Connecticut
SBDC
105 Huntington St.
New London, Connecticut 06320
Phone: (203)443-8332
Fax: (203)444-1529

Cooperative Extension
University of Connecticut
SBDC
562 New London Turnpike
Norwich, Connecticut 06360-7159
Phone: (203)887-1608
Fax: (203)886-1164

Old Saybrook Chamber of Commerce
SBDC
PO Box 625
Old Saybrook, Connecticut 06475
Phone: (203)388-3266
Fax: (203)388-3266

Southwestern Area Commerce and
Industry Association
Small Business Development Center
1 Landmark Sq., Ste. 230
Stamford, Connecticut 06901
Phone: (203)359-3220
Fax: (203)967-8294
George Ahl, Regional Dir.

Torrington Chamber of Commerce SBDC
PO Box 59
Torrington, Connecticut 06790
Phone: (203)482-6586
Fax: (203)489-8851

Connecticut SBDC
101 S. Main St.
Waterbury, Connecticut 06706-1042
Phone: (203)757-8937
Fax: (203)756-9077
Ilene Oppenheim

Greater Waterbury Chamber of
Commerce SBDC
83 Bank St.
Waterbury, Connecticut 06702
Phone: (203)757-0701
Fax: (203)756-3507

University of Connecticut (Greater
Hartford Campus) SBDC
1800 Asylum Ave.
West Hartford, Connecticut 06117
Phone: (860)241-4986
Fax: (860)241-4907
Zaiga Antonetti, Assoc. State Dir.

Eastern Connecticut State University
Small Business Development Center
83 Windham St.
Willimantic, Connecticut 06226-2295
Phone: (860)465-5349
Fax: (860)465-5143
Henry Reed, Dir.

Delaware

Delaware State University
School of Business and Economics
SBDC
Price Hall
1200 DuPont Hwy.
Dover, Delaware 19901
Phone: (302)678-1555
Fax: (302)739-2333
Jim Crisfield, Dir.

Delaware Technical and Community
College SBDC
PO Box 610
Georgetown, Delaware 19947
Phone: (302)856-1555
Fax: (302)856-5779
William F. Pfaff, Dir.

District of Columbia

Development Corporation of Columbia Heights SBDC
3419 14th St., NW

Washington, DC 20010
Phone: (202)483-4986
Fax: (202)806-1777
Jose Hernandez, Counselor

Gallaudet University SBDC
800 Florida Ave., NE
Washington, District of Columbia
20002-3625
Phone: (202)651-5312
Fax: (202)651-5516

George Washington University
National Law Center
Small Business Clinic
720 20th St. NW
Washington, District of Columbia 20052
Phone: (202)994-7463
Fax: (202)994-4946
Susan Jones, Dir.

George Washington University East of
the River Community Development
Corp. SBDC
3101 MLK Jr. Ave. SE, 3rd Fl.
Washington, District of Columbia 20010
Phone: (202)561-4975
Howard Johnson, Counselor

Marshall Heights Community
Development Organization
SBDC
3917 Minnesota Ave., NE
Washington, District of Columbia 20019
Phone: (202)396-1200
Terry Strong, Counselor

Ward Fice Community Development
Corp. SBDC
901 Newton St., NE, Ste. 103
Washington, DC 20017
Phone: (202)396-1200
Fax: (202)396-4106
Terry Strong

Florida

SBDC (Bartow)
600 N. Broadway, Ste. 300
PO Box 1839
Bartow, Florida 33830
Phone: (941)534-4370
Fax: (941)533-1247
Marcela Stanislaus, Vice President

Florida Atlantic University
Office of International Trade
PO Box 3091
Boca Raton, Florida 33431
Phone: (407)367-2271
Fax: (407)367-2272

Florida Atlantic University (Boca
Raton)
Small Business Development Center
PO Box 3091
Bldg. T9
Boca Raton, Florida 33431
Phone: (407)362-5620
Fax: (407)362-5623
Nancy Young, Dir.

Casselberry
Seminole Community College
SBDC
4590 S. Highway 17-92
Casselberry, Florida 32707
Phone: (407)834-4404
Fax: (407)339-1224

Brevard Community College (Cocoa)
Small Business Development Center
1519 Clearlake Rd.
Cocoa, Florida 32922
Phone: (407)951-1060
Fax: (407)634-3725

Dania SBDC
46 SW 1st Ave.
Dania, Florida 33004
Phone: (954)987-0100
William Healy, Regional Mgr.

Florida Regional SBDC
Daytona Beach Community College
1200 W. International Speedway Blvd.
Daytona Beach, Florida 32114
Phone: (904)947-3141
Fax: (904)254-4465

Stetson University SBDC
Campus Box 8417
Deland, Florida 32720
Phone: (904)822-7326
Fax: (904)822-7430

Florida Atlantic University Commercial Campus
Small Business Development Center
1515 W. Commercial Blvd., Rm. 11

Fort Lauderdale, Florida 33309
Phone: (954)771-6520
Fax: (954)776-6645
John Hudson, Regional Mgr.

Edison Community College
Small Business Development Center
8099 College Pky. SW
Fort Myers, Florida 33919
Phone: (941)489-9200
Fax: (941)489-9051
Dan Regelski, Dir.

Florida Gulf Coast University
Small Business Development Center
17595 S. Tamiami Trail, Ste. 200
Midway Ctr.
Fort Myers, Florida 33908-4500
Phone: (941)590-1053

University of South Florida (Fort Myers)
Small Business Development Center
8111 College Pkwy.
Fort Myers, Florida 33919
Phone: (813)432-5500
Fax: (813)432-5599

Indian River Community College
Small Business Development Center
3209 Virginia Ave.
Fort Pierce, Florida 34981-5599
Phone: (407)462-4756
Fax: (407)462-4796
Dan Carreno, Dir.

Okaloosa-Walton Comm. College
SBDC
1170 Martin Luther King Jr. Blvd.
Fort Walton Beach, Florida 32547
Phone: (904)863-6543
Fax: (904)863-6564
Walter Craft, Mgr.

Small Business Development Center
(Fort Walton Beach)
414 Mary Esther Cutoff
Fort Walton Beach, Florida 32548
Phone: (904)244-1036

University of North Florida
(Gainesville)
Small Business Development Center
505 NW 2nd Ave., Ste. D
Gainesville, Florida 32601-2518

Phone: (352)377-5621
Fax: (352)372-4132
Bill Stensgaard, Regional Mgr.

University of North Florida (Jacksonville)
Small Business Development Center
College of Business
4567 St. John's Bluff Rd. S
Bldg. 11, Rm. 2163
Jacksonville, Florida 32224
Phone: (904)646-2476
Fax: (904)646-2594
Lowell Salter, Dir.

Florida Keys Community College
Small Business Development Center
5901 W. College Rd.
Key West, Florida 33040
Phone: (305)296-9081

Lake City Community College
SBDC
226 N. Marlon St.
Lake City, Florida 32055
Phone: (904)646-2476
Fax: (904)646-2567
Lynn Haven

Gulf Coast Community College
SBDC
2500 Minnesota Ave.
Lynn Haven, Florida 32444
Phone: (904)271-1108
Fax: (904)271-1109
Doug Davis, Dir.

Brevard Community College
(Melbourne)
Small Business Development Center
3865 N. Wickham Rd., CM 207
Melbourne, Florida 32935
Phone: (407)632-1111
Fax: (407)232-1111
Victoria Peak, Mgr.

Florida International University
(North Miami Campus)
Small Business Development Center
Academic Bldg. No. 1, Rm. 350
NE 151 and Biscayne Blvd.
Miami, Florida 33181
Phone: (305)940-5790
Fax: (305)348-2965
Royland Jarrett, Regional Mgr.

Florida International University
(Tamiami Campus)
Small Business Development Center
Trailer TC 39 - Tamiami Campus
Miami, Florida 33199
Phone: (305)348-2272
Marvin Nesbit, Regional Dir.

Miami Dade Community College
Small Business Development Center
6300 NW 27th Ave.
Miami, Florida 33150
Phone: (305)237-1906
Fax: (305)237-1908
Frederick Bonneau, Dir.

Ocala Small Business Development
Center
110 E. Silver Springs Blvd.
PO Box 1210
Ocala, Florida 32670
Phone: (352)629-8051
Philip Geist, Regional Mgr.

University of Central Florida
Small Business Development Center
College of Business Administration, 309
PO Box 161530
Orlando, Florida 32816-1530
Phone: (407)823-5554
Fax: (407)823-3073
Al Polfer, Dir.

Valencia Community College
Small Business Development Center
PO Box 3208
Orlando, Florida 32802
Phone: (407)299-5000

Palm Beach Community College
Small Business Development Center
North Campus
3160 PGA Blvd.
Palm Beach Gardens, Florida 33410
Phone: (407)624-7222

Palm Beach Gardens
Florida Atlantic University
SBDC
Northrop Center
3970 RCA Blvd., Ste. 7323
Palm Beach Gardens, Florida 33410
Phone: (407)691-8550
Fax: (407)692-8502

Florida State University (Panama City)
Small Business Development Center
Barron Bldg.
4750 Collegiate Dr.
Panama City, Florida 32405-1099
Phone: (904)872-4655

Florida Small Business Development
Network
University of West Florida
19 W. Garden St., Ste. 300
Pensacola, Florida 32501
Phone: (904)444-2060
Fax: (904)444-2070
Jerry Cartwright, State Dir.

Procurement Technical Assistance
Program
University of West Florida
Small Business Development Center
11000 University Pky., Bldg. 8
Pensacola, Florida 32514
Phone: (904)474-2908
Fax: (904)474-2126
Martha Cobb, Dir.

St. Petersburg Community College
Small Business Development Center
3200 34th St. S
St. Petersburg, Florida 33711
Phone: (813)341-4414

University of South Florida (St.
Petersburg) SBDC
128 5th Ave. S
St. Petersburg, Florida 33701
Phone: (813)893-9529

Seminole Community College SBDC
100 Weldon Blvd., Bldg. R
Sanford, Florida 32707
Phone: (407)328-4722
Fax: (407)330-4489

Small Business Development Center
(Sarasota)
5700 N. Tamiami Trl.
Bldg. PME, Rm. 117
Sarasota, Florida 34243-2197
Phone: (813)359-4292

Florida Agricultural and Mechanical
University
Small Business Development Center
1157 E. Tennessee St.

Tallahassee, Florida 32308
Phone: (904)599-3407
Fax: (904)561-2395
Patricia McGowan, Dir.

Florida State University (Downtown
Office)
Small Business Development Center
1605 Eastwood Office Plz., Ste. 1
Tallahassee, Florida 32308
Phone: (904)644-6524

SBDC Training Center
Skipper Palms Shopping Center
1111 Westshore Blvd., Annex B
Tampa, Florida 33607
Phone: (813)974-4371

University of South Florida (Tampa)
SBDC
1111 North Westshore Blvd., Annex B
Tampa, Florida 33607
Phone: (813)554-2341
Fax: (813)554-2356
Charles Attardo, Mgr.

University of South Florida (Tampa)
Small Business Development Center
College of Business Administration
4202 E. Fowler Ave., BSN 3403
Tampa, Florida 33607-4705
Phone: (813)974-4371
Toll-free: (800)733-7232
Fax: (813)974-5020
Dick Hardesty, Mgr.

Georgia

Darton College
Southwest Georgia District Small
Business Development Center
Business and Technology Center
230 S. Jackson St., Ste. 333
Albany, Georgia 31701-2885
Phone: (912)430-4303
Fax: (912)430-3933
Organization E-mail:
sbdcalb@uga.cc.uga.edu
Sue Ford, District Dir.

Northeast Georgia District SBDC
University of Georgia
1180 E. Broad St.
Athens, Georgia 30602-5412

Phone: (706)542-7436
Fax: (706)542-6823
Gayle Rosenthal, Center Manager

Northwest Georgia District
SBDC
University of Georgia
1180 E. Broad St.
Athens, Georgia 30602-5412
Phone: (706)542-6756
Fax: (706)542-6776
Georgia State University

Small Business Development Center
Box 874
University Plz.
Atlanta, Georgia 30303-3083
Phone: (404)651-3550
Fax: (404)651-1035
Organization E-mail:
sbdcatl@uga.cc.uga.edu
Lee Quarterman, Center Mgr.

Morris Brown College
Small Business Development Center
643 Martin Luther King, Jr., Dr. NW
Atlanta, Georgia 30314
Phone: (404)220-0205
Fax: (404)688-5985
Ray Johnson, Center Mgr.

Augusta College
Small Business Development Center
1061 Katherine St.
Augusta, Georgia 30904-6105
Phone: (706)737-1790
Fax: (706)731-7937
Organization E-mail:
sbdcaug@uga.cc.uga.edu
Jeff Sanford, Center Mgr.

University of Georgia (Brunswick)
Small Business Development Center
1107 Fountain Lake Dr.
Brunswick, Georgia 31525
Phone: (912)264-7343
Organization E-mail:
sbdcrun@uga.cc.uga.edu
George Eckerd, Center Mgr.

Columbus College
Small Business Development Center
928 45th St.
North Bldg., Rm. 523

Columbus, Georgia 31904-6572
Phone: (706)649-7433
Fax: (706)649-1928
Organization E-mail:
sbdccolu@uga.cc.uga.edu
Tom Snyder, Center Mgr.

DeKalb SBDC
DeKalb Chamber of Commerce
750 Commerce Dr., Ste. 201
Decatur, Georgia 30030-2622
Phone: (404)378-8000
Fax: (404)378-3397
Eric Bonaparte, Center Mgr.

Gainesville SBDC
500 Jesse Jewell Pky., Ste. 304
Gainesville, Georgia 30501-4203
Phone: (706)531-5681
Fax: (706)531-5684
Organization E-mail:
sbdcgain@uga.cc.uga.edu
Ron Simmons, Center Mgr.

Kennesaw State College
Small Business Development Center
1000 Chastain Rd.
Kennesaw, Georgia 30144
Phone: (770)423-6480
Fax: (770)423-6564
Carlotta Roberts, Center Mgr.
E-mail: carobert@ksgmail.kennesaw.edu

Gwinnet Technical Institute
Small Business Development Center
1250 Atkinson Rd.
PO Box 1505
Lawrenceville, Georgia 30246-1505
Phone: (404)339-2287

Southeast Georgia District
SBDC
PO Box 13212
401 Cheny St., Ste. 701
Macon, Georgia 31208-3212
Phone: (912)751-6592
Fax: (912)751-6607
Organization E-mail:
sbdcmac@uga.cc.uga.edu
David Mills, District Mgr.

Clayton State College
Small Business Development Center
PO Box 285

Morrow, Georgia 30260
Phone: (404)961-3440
Fax: (404)961-3428
Organization E-mail:
sbdcmurr@uga.cc.uga.edu
Alex Ferdinand, Center Mgr.

UGA SBDC
1770 Indian Trail Rd., Ste. 410
Norcross, Georgia 30093
Phone: (770)806-2124
Robert Dixon, District Director
Robert Andoh, Center Manager

Floyd Junior College
Small Business Development Center
PO Box 1864
Rome, Georgia 30162-1864
Phone: (404)295-6326
Fax: (404)295-6732
Organization E-mail:
sbdcrome@uga.cc.uga.edu
Drew Tonsmeire, Center Mgr.

Southeast Georgia District
Small Business Development Center
450 Mall Blvd., Ste. H
Savannah, Georgia 31406-4821
Phone: (912)356-2755
Fax: (912)353-3033
Organization E-mail:
sbdcsav@uga.u.uga.edu
Harry O'Brien, Center Mgr.

University of Georgia (Statesboro)
Small Business Development Center
325 S. Main St.
Statesboro, Georgia 30460
Phone: (912)681-5194
Fax: (912)681-0648
Organization E-mail:
sbdcstat@uga.cc.uga.edu
David Lewis, Center Mgr.

Valdosta Small Business Development Center
Baytree W. Professional Offices
1205 Baytree Rd., Ste. 9
Valdosta, Georgia 31602-2782
Phone: (912)245-3738
Fax: (912)245-3741
Organization E-mail:
sbdcval@uga.cc.uga.edu
Suzanne Barnett, Center Mgr.

Warner Robins Small Business
Development Center
151 Osigian Blvd.
Warner Robins, Georgia 31088
Phone: (912)953-9356
Fax: (912)953-9376
Ronald Reaves, Center Mgr.

Guam

Guam SBDC
University of Guam
PO Box 5061
UOG Station
Mangilao, Guam 96923
Phone: (671)734-9241
Phone: (671)734-9225
Fax: (671)734-5362
Dr. Stephen L. Marder, Executive

Hawaii

Hawaii SBDC University of Hawaii at Hilo
523 W. Kawili St.
Hilo, Hawaii 96720-4091
Phone: (808)933-3515
Fax: (808)933-3683
Darryl Mleynek, State Director

Honolulu County
SBDC
130 Merchant St., Ste. 1030
Honolulu, Hawaii 96813
Phone: (808)522-8131
Fax: (808)522-8135

Manoa Innovation Center
Small Business Development Center
2800 Woodlawn Dr., Ste. 238
Honolulu, Hawaii 96822
Phone: (808)539-3800
Fax: (808)539-3799

Maui Community College
Small Business Development Center
Maui Research and Technology Center
590 Lipoa Pky.
Kihei, Hawaii 96753
Phone: (808)875-2402
Fax: (808)875-2452
Rebecca Winters, Acting Ctr.

Kauai Community College SBDC
3-1901 Kaumualii Hwy.
Lihue, Hawaii 96766-9591
Phone: (808)246-1748
Fax: (808)245-5102
Randy Gringas, Center Dir.

Idaho

Boise State University
Small Business Development Center
1910 University Dr.
Boise, Idaho 83725
Phone: (208)385-3875
Toll-free: (800)225-3815
Fax: (208)385-3877
Robert Shepard, Regional Dir.

Panhandle Area Council (Coeur d'Alene)
Small Business Development Center
11100 Airport Dr.
Hayden, Idaho 83835
Phone: (208)772-0587
Fax: (208)772-6196

Idaho State University (Idaho Falls)
Small Business Development Center
2300 N. Yellowstone
Idaho Falls, Idaho 83401
Phone: (208)523-1087
Toll-free: (800)658-3829
Fax: (208)523-1049
Betty Capps, Regional Dir.

Lewis-Clark State College SBDC
500 8th Ave.
Lewiston, Idaho 83501
Phone: (208)799-2465
Fax: (208)799-2878
Helen LeBoeuf-Binninger, Regional Dir.

Idaho State University (Pocatello)
Small Business Development Center
1651 Alvin Ricken Dr.
Pocatello, Idaho 83201
Phone: (208)232-4921
Toll-free: (800)232-4921
Fax: (208)233-0268
Paul Cox, Regional Dir.

North Idaho College
SBDC
525 W. Clearwater Loop
Post Falls, Idaho 83854

Phone: (208)769-3296
Fax: (208)769-3223
John Lynn, Regional Dir.

Panhandle Area Council (Sandpoint)
Small Business Development Center
804 Airport Way
Sandpoint, Idaho 83864
Phone: (208)263-4073
Fax: (208)263-4609

College of Southern Idaho SBDC
315 Falls Ave.
PO Box 1238
Twin Falls, Idaho 83303-1238
Phone: (208)733-9554
Fax: (208)733-9316
Cindy Bond, Regional Dir.

Illinois

Aledo Chamber of Commerce SBDC
PO Box 261
Aledo, Illinois 61231-0261
Phone: (309)582-5373

Waubonsee Community College
(Aurora Campus)
Small Business Development Center
5 E. Galena Blvd.
Aurora, Illinois 60506
Phone: (708)892-3334
Fax: (708)892-3374
Mike O'Kelley, Dir.

Spoon River College SBDC
23235 N. County 22
Canton, Illinois 61520
Phone: (309)647-4645
Fax: (309)647-6498

Southern Illinois University at
Carbondale
Small Business Development Center
College of Business Administration
Carbondale, Illinois 62901-6702
Phone: (618)536-2424
Fax: (618)453-5040
Dennis Cody, Dir.

John A. Logan College
Small Business Development Center
RR 2
Carterville, Illinois 62918

Phone: (618)985-3741
Fax: (618)985-2248
Richard Fyke, Dir.

Kaskaskia College
Small Business Development Center
27210 College Rd.
Centralia, Illinois 62801
Phone: (618)532-2049
Fax: (618)532-4983
Richard McCullum, Dir.

Parkland College
SBDC
2400 W. Bradley Ave.
Champaign, Illinois 61821-1899
Phone: (217)351-2556
Fax: (217)351-2581

University of Illinois
Small Business Development Center
428 Commerce W.
1206 S. 6th St.
Champaign, Illinois 61820
Phone: (217)244-1585
Fax: (217)333-7410
Helen Lesieur, Director

Asian American Alliance
SBDC
6246 N. Pulaski Rd., Ste. 101
Chicago, Illinois 60646
Phone: (312)202-0600
Fax: (312)202-1007
Joon H. Lee, Director

Back of the Yards Neighborhood
Council SBDC
1751 W. 47th St.
Chicago, Illinois 60609
Phone: (312)523-4419
Fax: (312)254-3525
Paul Ladniak, Dir.

Chicago Association of Neighbor-
hood Development Organization
SBDC
343 S. Dearborn St., Ste. 910
Chicago, Illinois 60604-3808
Phone: (312)939-7171
Fax: (312)939-7236

Chicago Small Business Development Center
DCCA James R. Thompson Center

100 W. Randolph, Ste. 3-400
Chicago, Illinois 60601
Phone: (312)814-6111
Fax: (312)814-2807
Carson Gallagher, Dir.

Chicago State University SBDC
9501 S. King Dr.
Chicago, Illinois 60628
Phone: (312)995-2000

Cosmopolitan Chamber of Commerce
SBDC
1326 S. Michigan Ave.
Chicago, Illinois 60605
Phone: (312)786-0212
Fax: (312)786-9079

Eighteenth Street Development Corp.
Small Business Development Center
1839 S. Carpenter
Chicago, Illinois 60608
Phone: (312)733-2287
Fax: (312)733-7315
Maria Munoz, Dir.

Greater North Pulaski Development Corp.
Small Business Development Center
4054 W. North Ave.
Chicago, Illinois 60639
Phone: (312)384-2262
Fax: (312)384-3850
Paul Peterson, Dir.

Greater Southwest Development Corp.
SBDC
2601 W. 63rd St.
Chicago, Illinois 60629
Phone: (312)436-4448
Fax: (312)471-8206

Greater Westside Development Corp.
SBDC
3555 W. Roosevelt Rd.
Chicago, Illinois 60624
Phone: (312)762-2440

Industrial Council of Northwest
Chicago
Small Business Development Center
2023 W. Carroll
Chicago, Illinois 60612
Phone: (312)421-3941
Fax: (312)421-1871
Malvin Eisland, Dir.

Latin American Chamber of Commerce
Small Business Development Center
2539 N. Kedzie, Ste. 11
Chicago, Illinois 60647
Phone: (312)252-5211
Fax: (312)252-7065
Artura Venecia, Dir.

Little Village Chamber of Commerce
SBDC
3610 W. 26th St., 2nd Fl.
Chicago, Illinois 60623
Phone: (312)521-5387
Fax: (312)521-5252

The Neighborhood Institute
SBDC
2255 E. 75th St.
Chicago, Illinois 60649
Phone: (312)933-2021
Fax: (312)933-2039

North Business and Industrial
Council (NORBIC) SBDC
2500 W. Bradley Pl.
Chicago, Illinois 60618
Phone: (312)588-5855
Fax: (312)588-0734
Tom Kamykowski, Director

North River Commission SBDC
4745 N. Kedzie
Chicago, Illinois 60625
Phone: (312)478-0202

Olive-Harvey Community College
Small Business Development Center
Heritage Pullman Bank
1000 E. 111th St., 7th Fl.
Chicago, Illinois 60628
Phone: (312)291-6296
Fax: (312)660-4847
Jerry Chambers, Contact

Richard J. Daley College
Small Business Development Center
7500 S. Pulaski Rd., Bldg. 200
Chicago, Illinois 60652
Phone: (312)838-0319
Fax: (312)838-0363
Jim Charney, Dir.

Southeast Chicago Development
Commission SBDC
9204 S. Commercial. Rm. 415

Chicago, Illinois 60617
Phone: (312)731-8755
Fax: (312)731-8618

Truman College-Economic Development
SBDC
1145 W. Wilson
Chicago, Illinois 60640

University Village Association
Small Business Development Center
925 S. Loomis St.
Chicago, Illinois 60607
Phone: (312)243-4045
Fax: (312)243-4684

Women's Business Development
Center
Small Business Development Center
8 S. Michigan, Ste. 400
Chicago, Illinois 60603
Phone: (312)853-3477
Fax: (312)853-0145
Paul Carlin, Dir.

McHenry County College
Small Business Development Center
8900 U.S. Hwy. 14
Crystal Lake, Illinois 60012-2761
Phone: (815)455-6098
Fax: (815)455-9319
Susan Whitfield, Dir.

Danville Area Community College
Small Business Development Center
28 W. North St.
Danville, Illinois 61832
Phone: (217)442-7232
Fax: (217)442-6228
Ed Adrain, Dir.

Northern Illinois University
Small Business Development Center
Department of Management
305 E. Locust
De Kalb, Illinois 60115
Phone: (815)753-1403
Joanne Rouse, Contact

Cooperative Extension Service SBDC
985 W. Pershing Rd., Ste. F-4
Decatur, Illinois 62526
Phone: (217)875-8284
Fax: (217)875-8288
Rick Russell, Director

Richland Community College
Small Business Development Center
1 College Pk.
Decatur, Illinois 62521
Phone: (217)875-7200
Fax: (217)875-6965

Sauk Valley Community College
Small Business Development Center
173 Illinois, Rte. 2
Dixon, Illinois 61021-9110
Phone: (815)288-5111
Fax: (815)288-5958
John Nelson, Dir.

Black Hawk College
Small Business Development Center
301 42nd Ave.
East Moline, Illinois 61244
Phone: (309)755-2200
Fax: (309)755-9847
Donna Scalf, Dir.

East St. Louis Small Business
Development Center
DCCA, State Office Bldg.
10 Collinsville
East St. Louis, Illinois 62201
Phone: (618)583-2272
Fax: (618)588-2274
Robert Ahart, Dir.

Southern Illinois University at
Edwardsville
Small Business Development Center
Center for Advanced Manufacturing
and Production
Campus Box 1107
Edwardsville, Illinois 62026
Phone: (618)692-2929
Fax: (618)692-2647
Alan Hauff, Dir.

Elgin Community College
Small Business Development Center
1700 Spartan Dr., Office B-15
Elgin, Illinois 60123
Phone: (847)888-7675
Fax: (847)888-7995
Craig Fowler, Dir.

Evanston Business and Technology
Center
Small Business Development Center

1840 Oak Ave.
Evanston, Illinois 60201
Phone: (847)866-1817
Fax: (847)866-1808

Highland Community College
Small Business Development Center
206 S. Galena
Freeport, Illinois 61032
Phone: (815)232-1366
Fax: (815)235-1366
Chuck Mufich, Contact

Geneseo Chamber of Commerce
SBDC
200 N. State St.
Geneseo, Illinois 61254
Phone: (309)944-2686

College of DuPage
Small Business Development Center
22nd St. & Lambert Rd.
Glen Ellyn, Illinois 60137
Phone: (708)858-2800
Fax: (708)790-1197
David Gay, Dir.

Lewis and Clark Community College
SBDC
5800 Godfrey Rd.
Godfrey, Illinois 62035
Phone: (618)466-3411
Fax: (618)466-0810
Bob Duane, Director

College of Lake County
Small Business Development Center
19351 W. Washington St.
Grayslake, Illinois 60030
Phone: (847)223-3633
Fax: (847)223-9371
Arthur Cobb Jr., Dir.

Southeastern Illinois College
Small Business Development Center
325 E. Poplar, Ste. A
Harrisburg, Illinois 62946-1528
Phone: (618)536-2424
Fax: (618)458-5040
Dennis Cody, Dir.

Rend Lake College
Small Business Development Center
Rte. 1
Ina, Illinois 62846

Phone: (618)437-5321
Fax: (618)437-5677
Lisa Payne, Dir.

Joliet Junior College SBDC
Renaissance Center, Rm. 312
214 N. Ottawa St.
Joliet, Illinois 60431
Phone: (815)727-6544
Fax: (815)722-1895
Denise Mikulski, Dir.

Kankakee Community College
Small Business Development Center
101 S. Schuyler Ave.
Kankakee, Illinois 60901
Phone: (815)933-0376
Fax: (815)933-0380
JoAnn Seggebruch, Dir.

Western Illinois University SBDC
114 Seal Hall
Macomb, Illinois 61455
Phone: (309)298-2211
Fax: (309)298-2520
Dan Voorhis, Dir.

Lake Land College
Small Business Development Center
5001 Lakeland Blvd.
South Route No. 45
Mattoon, Illinois 61938-9366
Phone: (217)234-5253
Daniel Sulsberger, Contact

Maple City Business and Technology
Center
Small Business Development Center
620 S. Main St.
Monmouth, Illinois 61462
Phone: (309)734-4664
Fax: (309)734-8579
Carol Cook, Dir.

Heartland Community College
Small Business Development Center
1226 Towanda Plz.
Normal, Illinois 61761
Phone: (217)875-7200
Fax: (217)875-6965
Maureen Ruski, Contact

Illinois Valley Community College
Small Business Development Center
815 N. Orlando Smith Ave., Bldg. 11

Oglesby, Illinois 61348
Phone: (815)223-1740
Fax: (815)224-3033
Boyd Palmer, Dir.

Illinois Eastern Community College
Small Business Development Center
401 E. Main St.
Olney, Illinois 62450
Phone: (618)395-3011
Fax: (618)395-1922
John Spitz, Dir.

William Raney-Harper College
Small Business Development Center
1200 W. Algonquin Rd.
Palatine, Illinois 60067
Phone: (708)397-3000
Fax: (708)925-6043

Moraine Valley College
Small Business Development Center
10900 S. 88th Ave.
Palos Hills, Illinois 60465
Phone: (708)974-5468
Fax: (708)974-0078
Hilary Gereg, Dir.

Bradley University
Small Business Development Center
141 N. Jobst Hall, 1st Fl.
Peoria, Illinois 61625
Phone: (309)677-2992
Fax: (309)677-3386
Roger Luman, Dir.

Illinois Central College
Small Business Development Center
124 SW Adams St., Ste. 300
Peoria, Illinois 61602
Phone: (309)676-7500
Fax: (309)676-7534
Susan Gorman, Dir.

Quincy Procurement Assistance
Center
Small Business Development Center
301 Oak St.
Quincy, Illinois 62301
Phone: (217)228-5511
Edward VanLeer, Dir.

Triton College
Small Business Development Center
2000 5th Ave.

River Grove, Illinois 60171
Phone: (708)456-0300
Fax: (708)583-3118
Meredith Roat, Dir.

Rock Valley College SBDC
1220 Rock St., Ste. 180
Rockford, Illinois 61101-1437
Phone: (815)968-4087
Fax: (815)968-4157
Beverly Kingsley, Dir.

South Suburban College SBDC
15800 S. State St.
South Holland, Illinois 60473
Phone: (708)596-2000
Toll-free: (800)248-4772
Fax: (708)596-1125

Small Business Development Center
Lincoln Land Community College
100 N. 11th St.
Springfield, Illinois 62703
Phone: (217)789-1017
Fax: (217)789-0958

Shawnee Community College SBDC
Shawnee College Rd.
Ullin, Illinois 62992
Phone: (618)634-9618
Fax: (618)634-9028
Donald Denny, Dir.

Governors State University SBDC
University Park, Illinois 60466
Phone: (708)534-4929
Fax: (708)534-8457
Christine Cochrane, Dir.

Indiana

Batesville Office of Economic
Development SBDC
132 S. Main
Batesville, Indiana 47006
Phone: (812)933-6110

Bedford Chamber of Commerce SBDC
1116 W. 16th St.
Bedford, Indiana 47421
Phone: (812)275-4493

Bloomfield Chamber of Commerce
SBDC
c/o Harrah Realty Co.

23 S. Washington St.
Bloomfield, Indiana 47424
Phone: (812)275-4493

Bloomington Area Small Business
Development Center
116 W. 6th St., No. 100
Bloomington, Indiana 47404
Phone: (812)339-8937
Fax: (812)336-0651
David Miller, Dir.

Clay Count Chamber of Commerce
SBDC
12 N. Walnut St.
Brazil, Indiana 47834
Phone: (812)448-8457

Brookville Chamber of Commerce
SBDC
PO Box 211
Brookville, Indiana 47012
Phone: (317)647-3177

Clinton Chamber of Commerce
SBDC
292 N. 9th St.
Clinton, Indiana 47842
Phone: (812)832-3844

Chamber of Commerce
SBDC
112 N. Main St.
Columbia City, Indiana 46725
Phone: (219)248-8131

Columbus Regional SBDC
4920 N. Warren Dr.
Columbus, Indiana 47203
Phone: (812)372-6480
Toll-free: (800)282-7232
Fax: (812)372-0228
Glenn Dunlap, Dir.

Connersville SBDC
504 Central
Connersville, Indiana 47331
Phone: (317)825-8328

Harrison County SBDC
The Harrison Center
405 N. Capitol, Ste. 308
Corydon, Indiana 47112
Phone: (812)738-8811

Montgomery County Chamber of
Commerce SBDC
211 S. Washington St.
Crawfordsville, Indiana 47933
Phone: (317)654-5507

Decatur Chamber of Commerce SBDC
125 E. Monroe St.
Decatur, Indiana 46733
Phone: (219)724-2604

City of Delphi Community Development
SBDC
201 S. Union
Delphi, Indiana 46923
Phone: (317)564-6692

Elkhart Chamber of Commerce SBDC
421 S. 2nd St.
Elkhart, Indiana 46515
Phone: (219)522-5453

Elwood Chamber of Commerce
SBDC
108 S. Anderson St.
Elwood, Indiana 46036
Phone: (317)552-0180

Southwestern Indiana Small Business
Development Center
100 NW 2nd St., Ste. 200
Evansville, Indiana 47708
Phone: (812)425-7232
Fax: (812)421-5883
Jeff Lake, Dir.

Northeast Indiana Small Business
Development Center
1830 Wayne Trace
Fort Wayne, Indiana 46803
Phone: (219)426-0040
Fax: (219)424-0024
A. V. Fleming, Dir.

Clinton County Chamber of Commerce
SBDC
207 S. Main St.
Frankfort, Indiana 46041
Phone: (317)654-5507

Northlake Small Business Development Center
487 Broadway, Ste. 201
Gary, Indiana 46402
Phone: (219)882-2000

Greencastle Partnership Center SBDC
2 S. Jackson St.
Greencastle, Indiana 46135
Phone: (317)653-4517

Greensburg Area Chamber of Commerce
SBDC
125 W. Main St.
Greensburg, Indiana 47240
Phone: (812)663-2832

Hammond Development Corp. SBDC
649 Conkey St.
Hammond, Indiana 46324
Phone: (219)853-6399

Hartford SBDC
PO Box 43
Hartford, Indiana 47348
Phone: (317)348-4944

Indiana Region 15 Planning Commission
SBDC
511 4th St.
Huntingburg, Indiana 47542
Phone: (812)683-5699
Phone: (812)683-4647

Indianapolis Regional Small Busi-
ness Development Center
342 N. Senate Ave.
Indianapolis, Indiana 46204-1708
Phone: (317)261-3030
Fax: (317)261-3053
Tim Tichenar, Dir.

Clark County Hoosier Falls
Private Industry Council Workforce
1613 E. 8th St.
Jeffersonville, Indiana 47130
Phone: (812)282-0456

Southern Indiana Small Business
Development Center
1613 E. 8th St.
Jeffersonville, Indiana 47130
Phone: (812)288-6451
Fax: (812)284-8314
Patricia Stroud, Dir.

Kendallville Chamber of Commerce
SBDC
228 S. Main St.
Kendallville, Indiana 46755
Phone: (219)347-1554

Kokomo-Howard County Small
Business Development Center
106 N. Washington
Kokomo, Indiana 46901
Phone: (317)457-5301
Fax: (317)452-4564
Todd Muser, Dir.

La Porte Small Business Development Center
414 Lincolnway
La Porte, Indiana 46350
Phone: (219)326-7232

Greater Lafayette Area Small Busi-
ness Development Center
122 N. 3rd
Lafayette, Indiana 47901
Phone: (317)742-2394
Fax: (317)742-6276
Susan Davis, Dir.

Dearborn County Chamber of
Commerce SBDC
213 Eads Pkwy.
Lawrenceburg, Indiana 47025
Phone: (812)537-0814
Fax: (812)537-0845

Union County Chamber of Commerce
SBDC
102 N. Main St.
Liberty, Indiana 47353-1039
Phone: (317)458-5976

Linton/Stockton Chamber of Commerce
SBDC
PO Box 208
Linton, Indiana 47441
Phone: (812)847-4846

Southeastern Indiana Small Business
Development Center
301 E. Main St.
Madison, Indiana 47250
Phone: (812)265-3127
Fax: (812)265-2923
Rose Marie Roberts, Dir.

Crawford County
Private Industry Council Workforce
SBDC
Box 224 D, R.R. 1
Marengo, Indiana 47140
Phone: (812)365-2174

Greater Martinsville Chamber of
Commerce SBDC
210 N. Marion St.
Martinsville, Indiana 46151
Phone: (317)342-8110

Lake County Public Library SBDC
1919 W. 81st Ave.
Merrillville, Indiana 46410
Phone: (219)756-7232

Northwest Indiana (Merrillville)
Small Business Development Center
8002 Utah St.
Merrillville, Indiana 46410
Phone: (219)756-7232

First Citizens Bank SBDC
515 N. Franklin Sq.
Michigan City, Indiana 46360
Phone: (219)874-9245

Mitchell Chamber of Commerce
SBDC
1st National Bank
Main Street
Mitchell, Indiana 47446
Phone: (812)849-4441

White County Industrial Foundation
SBDC
PO Box 1031
Monticello, Indiana 47960
Phone: (219)583-6557

Mount Vernon Chamber of Commerce
SBDC
405 E. 4th St.
Mt. Vernon, Indiana 47620
Phone: (812)838-3639

East Central Indiana Small Business
Development Center
401 S. High St.
PO Box 842
Muncie, Indiana 47308
Phone: (317)284-8144
Fax: (317)741-5489
Barbara Armstrong, Dir.

Brown County Chamber of Commerce
SBDC
PO Box 164
Nashville, Indiana 47448
Phone: (812)988-6647

Floyd County
Private Industry Council Workforce
3303 Plaza Dr., Ste. 2
New Albany, Indiana 47150
Phone: (812)945-2643

Henry County Economic Develop-
ment Corp.
SBDC
1325 Broad St., Ste. B
New Castle, Indiana 47362
Phone: (317)529-4635

SBDC
Jennings County Chamber of
Commerce
PO Box 340
North Vernon, Indiana 47265
Phone: (812)346-2339

Orange County
Private Industry Council Workforce
SBDC
326 B. North Gospel
Paoli, Indiana 47464
Phone: (812)723-4206

Miami Community Economic
Development Corp.
SBDC
2 N. Broadway, Ste. 202
Peru, Indiana 46970
Phone: (317)472-1923

Northwest Indiana (Portage)
Small Business Development Center
6100 Southport Rd.
Portage, Indiana 46368
Phone: (219)762-1696
Fax: (219)942-5806

Jay County Development Corp.
SBDC
121 W. Main St., Ste. A
Portland, Indiana 47371
Phone: (219)726-9311

Richmond-Wayne County Small
Business Development Center
33 S. 7th St.
Richmond, Indiana 47374
Phone: (317)962-2887
Fax: (317)966-0882
Doug Peters, Dir.

Rochester and Lake Manitou Cham-
ber of Commerce
Fulton Economic Development
Center
SBDC
617 Main St.
Rochester, Indiana 46975
Phone: (219)223-6773

Rushville Chamber of Commerce
SBDC
PO Box 156
Rushville, Indiana 47173
Phone: (317)932-2222

St. Mary-of-the-Woods College
SBDC
St. Mary-of-the-Woods, Indiana 47876
Phone: (812)535-5151

Washington County
Private Industry Council Workforce
SBDC
Hilltop Plaza
Salem, Indiana 47167
Phone: (812)883-2283

Scott County
Private Industry Council Workforce
SBDC
752 Lakeshore Dr.
Scottsburg, Indiana 47170
Phone: (812)752-3886

Seymour Chamber of Commerce
SBDC
PO Box 43
Seymour, Indiana 47274
Phone: (812)522-3681

Minority Business Development
Project Future
SBDC
401 Col
South Bend, Indiana 46634
Phone: (219)234-0051

South Bend Area Small Business
Development Center
300 N. Michigan
South Bend, Indiana 46601
Phone: (219)282-4350
Fax: (219)282-4344
Carolyn Anderson, Dir.

Economic Development Office
SBDC
46 E. Market St.
Spencer, Indiana 47460
Phone: (812)829-3245

Sullivan Chamber of Commerce
SBDC
10 S. Court St.
Sullivan, Indiana 47882
Phone: (812)268-4836

Tell City Chamber of Commerce
SBDC
Regional Federal Bldg.
645 Main St.
Tell City, Indiana 47586
Phone: (812)547-2385
Fax: (812)547-8378

Terre Haute Area Small Business
Development Center
Indiana State University
School of Business, Rm. 510
Terre Haute, Indiana 47809
Phone: (812)237-7676
Fax: (812)237-7675
William Minnis, Dir.

Tipton County Economic Development Corp.
SBDC
136 E. Jefferson
Tipton, Indiana 46072
Phone: (317)675-7300

Porter County
SBDC
911 Wall St.
Valparaiso, Indiana 46383
Phone: (219)477-5256

Vevay/Switzerland Country Foundation
SBDC
PO Box 193
Vevay, Indiana 47043
Phone: (812)427-2533

Vincennes University
SBDC
PO Box 887
Vincennes, Indiana 47591
Phone: (812)885-5749

Wabash Area Chamber of Commerce
Wabash Economic Development Corp.
SBDC
67 S. Wabash
Wabash, Indiana 46922
Phone: (219)563-1108

Washington Daviess County SBDC
1 Train Depot St.
Washington, Indiana 47501
Phone: (812)254-5262
Fax: (812)254-2550
Mark Brochin, Director

Purdue University SBDC
Business & Industrial Development
Center
1220 Potter Dr.
West Lafayette, Indiana 47906
Phone: (317)494-5858

Randolph County Economic Development Foundation
SBDC
111 S. Main St.
Winchester, Indiana 47394
Phone: (317)584-3266

Iowa

Iowa State University
Small Business Development Center
ISU Branch Office
2501 N. Loop Dr.
Bldg. 1, Ste. 608
Ames, Iowa 50010-8283
Phone: (515)296-7328
Toll-free: (800)373-7232
Fax: (515)296-9910
Steve Carter, Dir.

DMACC Small Business Development Center
Circle West Incubator
PO Box 204
Audubon, Iowa 50025
Phone: (712)563-2623
Fax: (712)563-2301
Lori Harmening-Webb, Dir.

University of Northern Iowa
Small Business Development Center
Business Bldg., Ste. 5
Cedar Falls, Iowa 50614-0120

Phone: (319)273-2696
Fax: (319)273-6830
Lyle Bowlin, Dir.

Iowa Western Community College
Small Business Development Center
2700 College Rd., Box 4C
Council Bluffs, Iowa 51502
Phone: (712)325-3260
Fax: (712)325-3408
Ronald Helms, Dir.

Southwestern Community College
Small Business Development Center
1501 W. Townline Rd.
Creston, Iowa 50801
Phone: (515)782-4161
Fax: (515)782-4164
Paul Havick, Dir.

Eastern Iowa Community College
District
Eastern Iowa Small Business Development Center
304 W. 2nd St.
Davenport, Iowa 52801
Phone: (319)322-4499
Fax: (319)322-8241
Jon Ryan, Dir.

Drake University
Small Business Development Center
Drake Business Center
2401 University
Des Moines, Iowa 50311-4505
Phone: (515)271-2655
Fax: (515)271-4540
Benjamin Swartz, Dir.

Northeast Iowa Small Business
Development Center
770 Town Clock Plz.
Dubuque, Iowa 52001
Phone: (319)588-3350
Fax: (319)557-1591
Charles Tonn, Contact

Iowa Central Community College
SBDC
900 Central Ave., Ste. 4
Fort Dodge, Iowa 50501
Phone: (515)576-0099
Fax: (515)576-0826
Todd Madson, Director

University of Iowa
Small Business Development Center
108 Papajohn Business Administration Bldg., Ste. S-160
Iowa City, Iowa 52242-1000
Phone: (319)335-3742
Toll-free: (800)253-7232
Fax: (319)353-2445
Paul Heath, Dir.
E-mail: paul-heath@uiowa.edu

Kirkwood Community College
Small Business Development Center
2901 10th Ave.
Marion, Iowa 52302
Phone: (319)377-8256
Fax: (319)377-5667
Jim Anderson, Dir.

North Iowa Area Community College
Small Business Development Center
500 College Dr.
Mason City, Iowa 50401
Phone: (515)421-4342
Fax: (515)423-0931
Richard Petersen, Dir.

Indian Hills Community College
Small Business Development Center
525 Grandview Ave.
Ottumwa, Iowa 52501
Phone: (515)683-5127
Fax: (515)683-5263
Bryan Ziegler, Dir.

Western Iowa Tech Community College
Small Business Development Center
4647 Stone Ave., Bldg. B
Box 265
Sioux City, Iowa 51102-0265
Phone: (712)274-6418
Toll-free: (800)352-4649
Fax: (712)274-6429
Dennis Bogenrief, Dir.

Iowa Lakes Community College
(Spencer)
Small Business Development Center
Gateway Center
Hwy. 71 N
Spencer, Iowa 51301
Phone: (712)262-4213
Fax: (712)262-4047
John Beneke, Dir.

Southeastern Community College
Small Business Development Center
Drawer F
West Burlington, Iowa 52655
Phone: (319)752-2731
Fax: (319)752-3407

Kansas

Cowley County Community College
Small Business Development Center
125 S. 2nd
PO Box 1147
Arkansas City, Kansas 67005
Phone: (316)442-0430
Toll-free: (800)593-2222
Fax: (316)441-5350

Benedictine College SBDC
1020 N. 2nd St.
Atchison, Kansas 66002
Phone: (913)367-5340
Fax: (913)367-6102
Don Laney, Director

Lamoille Economic Development Corp. SBDC
1020 N. 2nd St.
Atchison, Kansas 66002
Phone: (913)367-5340
Fax: (913)367-6102
Chris D'Elia, Exec. Dir.

Butler County Community College
Small Business Development Center
600 Walnut
Augusta, Kansas 67010
Phone: (316)775-1124
Dorinda Rolle, Dir.

Neosho County Community College
SBDC
1000 S. Allen
Chanute, Kansas 66720
Phone: (316)431-2820
Fax: (316)431-0082
Duane Clum, Director

Coffeyville Community College SBDC
11th and Willow Streets
Coffeyville, Kansas 67337-5064
Phone: (316)252-7007
Fax: (316)252-7098
Mark Eldridge, Director

Colby Community College SBDC
1255 S. Range
Colby, Kansas 67701
Phone: (913)462-3984
Fax: (913)462-8315
Robert Selby, Dir.

Cloud County Community College SBDC
2221 Campus Dr.
PO Box 1002
Concordia, Kansas 66901
Phone: (913)243-1435
Fax: (913)243-1459
Tony Foster, Director

Dodge City Community College
Small Business Development Center
2501 N. 14th Ave.
Dodge City, Kansas 67801
Phone: (316)227-9247
Fax: (316)227-9200
Wayne E. Shiplet, Dir.

Great Plains Development, Inc.
Small Business Development Center
Box 1116
Dodge City, Kansas 67801
Phone: (316)227-6406
Fax: (316)225-6051

Emporia State University
Small Business Development Center
207 Cremer Hall
Emporia, Kansas 66801
Phone: (316)342-7162
Fax: (316)341-5418
Lisa Brumbaugh, Dir.

Fort Scott Community College SBDC
2108 S. Horton
Fort Scott, Kansas 66701
Phone: (316)223-2700
Fax: (316)223-6530
Steve Pammenter, Director

Garden City Community College SBDC
801 Campus Dr.
Garden City, Kansas 67846
Phone: (316)276-9632
Fax: (316)276-9630
Vern Kinderknecht, Regional Director

Barton County Community College
Small Business Development Center
Rte. 3, Box 1362
Great Bend, Kansas 67530-9283
Phone: (316)792-2701
Fax: (316)792-1356

Fort Hays State University
Small Business Development Center
1301 Pine St.
Hays, Kansas 67601
Phone: (913)628-5340
Fax: (913)628-1471
Clare Gustin, Regional Dir.

Pioneer Country Development, Inc.
Small Business Development Center
Box 248
Hill City, Kansas 67642
Phone: (913)674-3488
Fax: (913)674-3496

Hutchinson Community College
Small Business Development Center
815 N. Walnut, Rm. 225
Hutchinson, Kansas 67501
Phone: (316)665-4950
Toll-free: (800)289-3501
Fax: (316)665-8354
Clark Jacobs, Dir.

Independence Community College
SBDC
College Ave. & Brookside
PO Box 708
Independence, Kansas 67301
Phone: (316)331-4100
Fax: (316)331-5344
Preston Haddan, Dir.

Allen County Community College
SBDC
1801 N. Cottonwood
Iola, Kansas 66749
Phone: (316)365-5116
Fax: (316)365-3284

Kansas City (Kansas) Community
College
Small Business Development Center
7250 State Ave.
Kansas City, Kansas 66112
Phone: (913)334-1100
Fax: (913)596-9609

University of Kansas
Small Business Development Center
734 Vermont St., Ste. 104
Lawrence, Kansas 66044
Phone: (913)843-8844
Fax: (913)865-4400
Mike O'Donnell, Regional Dir.

Seward County Community College
Small Business Development Center
1801 N. Kansas
PO Box 1137
Liberal, Kansas 67901
Phone: (316)624-1951
Fax: (316)624-0637
Tom Cornelius, Dir.

Kansas State University (Manhattan)
Small Business Development Center
College of Business Administration
2323 Anderson Ave., Ste. 100
Manhattan, Kansas 66502-2947
Phone: (913)532-2947
Fax: (913)532-5827
Fred Rice, Regional Dir.

Decatur County Economic Development
SBDC
132 S. Penn
Oberlin, Kansas 67749
Phone: (913)475-3441

Ottawa University
SBDC
College Ave., Box 70
Ottawa, Kansas 66067
Phone: (913)242-5200
Fax: (913)242-7429
Lori Kravets, Director

Johnson County Community College
Small Business Development Center
CEC Bldg., Rm. 223
Overland Park, Kansas 66210-1299
Phone: (913)469-3878
Fax: (913)469-4415
Glenda Sapp, Regional Dir.

Labette Community College SBDC
200 S. 14th
Parsons, Kansas 67357
Phone: (316)421-6700
Fax: (316)421-0921
Mark Turnbull, Director

Pittsburg State University
Small Business Development Center
Shirk Hall
Pittsburg, Kansas 66762
Phone: (316)235-4920
Fax: (316)232-6440
Kathryn Richard, Regional Dir.

Pratt Community College
Small Business Development Center
Hwy. 61
Pratt, Kansas 67124
Phone: (316)672-5641
Fax: (316)672-5288
Pat Gordon, Dir.

Kansas Institute of Technology
SBDC
131 Crompton Rd.
Salina, Kansas 67401
Phone: (913)825-0275

Kansas State University (Salina)
Small Business Development Center
2409 Scanlan Ave.
Salina, Kansas 67401
Phone: (913)826-2622
Fax: (913)826-2936
Pat Mills, Regional Dir.

Washburn University of Topeka
SBDC
School of Business
101 Henderson Learning Center
Topeka, Kansas 66621
Phone: (913)231-1010
Fax: (913)231-1063
Wayne Glass, Regional Dir.
E-mail: zzglas@acc.wuacc.edu

Wichita State University SBDC
1845 Fairmont
Wichita, Kansas 67208-0148
Phone: (316)689-3193
Fax: (316)689-3647
Chip Paul, Regional Director

Kentucky

Ashland Small Business Development Center
Morehead State University College of
Business
PO Box 830

207 15th St.
Ashland, Kentucky 41105-0830
Phone: (606)329-8011
Fax: (606)325-4607
Kimberly A. Jenkins, Dir.

Western Kentucky University
Bowling Green Small Business
Development Center
245 Grise Hall
Bowling Green, Kentucky 42101
Phone: (502)745-2901
Fax: (502)745-2902
Rick Horn, Dir.

Southeast Community College
Southeast Small Business Development Center
Chrisman Hall, Rm. 113
Cumberland, Kentucky 40823
Phone: (606)589-4514
Fax: (606)589-4941
Cortez Davis, Contact

Elizabethtown Small Business
Development Center
238 W. Dixie Ave.
Elizabethtown, Kentucky 42701
Phone: (502)765-6737
Fax: (502)769-5095
Lou Ann Allen, Dir.

Northern Kentucky University
SBDC
BEP Center 468
Highland Heights, Kentucky 41099-0506
Phone: (606)572-6524
Fax: (606)572-5566
Sutton Landry, Director

Hopkinsville Small Business Development Center
Murray State University
300 Hammond Dr.
Hopkinsville, Kentucky 42240
Phone: (502)886-8666
Fax: (502)886-3211
Mike Cartner, Dir.

Univ. of Kentucky
SBDC
c/o Downtown Public Library
140 Main St.

Lexington, Kentucky 40507-1376
Phone: (606)257-7666
Fax: (606)257-1751
Marge Berge, Program Coordinator

University of Kentucky SBDC
225 Business and Economics Bldg.
Lexington, Kentucky 40506
Phone: (606)257-7668
Fax: (606)323-1907
William Morley, Contact

Bellarmine College
Small Business Development Center
School of Business
2001 Newburg Rd.
Louisville, Kentucky 40205-0671
Phone: (502)452-8282
Fax: (502)452-8288
Thomas G. Daley, Dir.

University of Louisville
Small Business Development Centers
Center for Entrepreneurship and
Technology
Burhans Hall, Shelby Campus, Rm. 122
Louisville, Kentucky 40292
Phone: (502)588-7854
Fax: (502)588-8573
Lou Dickie, Dir.

Morehead State University SBDC
207 Downing Hall
Morehead, Kentucky 40351
Phone: (606)783-2895
Fax: (606)783-5020
Wilson Grier, District Dir.

Murray State University
West Kentucky Small Business
Development Center
College of Business and Public Affairs
Business Bldg., Rm 253
Murray, Kentucky 42071
Phone: (502)762-2856
Fax: (502)762-3049
Rosemary Miller, Dir.

Northern Kentucky University
Small Business Development Center
BEP Center, Rm. 463
Newport, Kentucky 41099-0506
Phone: (606)572-6524
Sutton Landry, Contact

Owensboro Small Business Development Center
Murray State University
3860 U.S. Hwy. 60 W
Owensboro, Kentucky 42301
Phone: (502)926-8085
Fax: (502)684-0714
Mickey Johnson, District Dir.

Pikeville Small Business Development Center
Moorehead State University
Rte. 7
110 Village St.
Pikeville, Kentucky 41501
Phone: (606)432-5848
Fax: (606)432-8924
Mike Morley, Dir.

Eastern Kentucky University SBDC
Development Center
107 W. Mt. Vernon St.
Somerset, Kentucky 42501
Phone: (606)678-5520
Fax: (606)678-8349
Donald R. Snyder, Dir.

Louisiana

Alexandria SBDC
Hibernia National Bank Bldg., Ste. 510
934 3rd St.
Alexandria, Louisiana 71301
Phone: (318)484-2123
Fax: (318)484-2126
Kathey Hunter, Consultant

Capital Small Business Development
Center
Southern University
1933 Wooddale Blvd., Ste. E
Baton Rouge, Louisiana 70806
Phone: (504)922-0998
Fax: (504)922-0999
Greg Spann, Dir.

Southeastern Louisiana University
Small Business Development Center
College of Business Administration
Box 522, SLU Sta.
Hammond, Louisiana 70402
Phone: (504)549-3831
Fax: (504)549-2127
William Joubert, Dir.

University of Southwestern Louisiana
Acadiana Small Business Development Center
Box 43732
College of Business Administration
Lafayette, Louisiana 70504
Phone: (318)262-5344
Fax: (318)262-5296
Dan Lavergne, Dir.

McNeese State University SBDC
College of Business Administration
Lake Charles, Louisiana 70609
Phone: (318)475-5529
Fax: (318)475-5012
Paul Arnold, Dir.

Louisiana Electronic Assistance
Program SBDC
NE Louisiana College of Business
Administration
Monroe, Louisiana 71209
Phone: (318)342-1215
Fax: (318)342-1209
Dr. Jerry Wall, Director

Northeast Louisiana University SBDC
College of Business Administration,
Rm. 2-57
Monroe, Louisiana 71209
Phone: (318)342-1224
Fax: (318)342-1209
Paul Dunn, Dir.

Northwestern State University
Small Business Development Center
College of Business Administration
Natchitoches, Louisiana 71497
Phone: (318)357-5611
Fax: (318)357-6810
Mary Lynn Wilkerson, Dir.

Louisiana International Trade Center
SBDC
World Trade Center, Ste. 2926
2 Canal St.
New Orleans, Louisiana 70130
Phone: (504)568-8222
Fax: (504)568-8228
Ruperto Chavarri, Director

Loyola University
Small Business Development Center
College of Business Administration

Box 134
New Orleans, Louisiana 70118
Phone: (504)865-3474
Fax: (504)865-3496
Ronald Schroeder, Dir.

Southern University—New Orleans
Small Business Development Center
College of Business Administration
New Orleans, Louisiana 70126
Phone: (504)286-5308
Fax: (504)286-3131
Jon Johnson, Dir.

University of New Orleans
Small Business Development Center
1600 Canal St., Ste. 620
New Orleans, Louisiana 70112
Phone: (504)539-9292
Fax: (504)539-9205
Norma Grace, Dir.

Louisiana Tech University
Small Business Development Center
College of Business Administration
Box 10318, Tech Sta.
Ruston, Louisiana 71271-0046
Phone: (318)257-3537
Fax: (318)257-4253

Louisiana State University at Shreveport
Small Business Development Center
College of Business Administration
1 University Pl.
Shreveport, Louisiana 71115
Phone: (318)797-5144
Fax: (318)797-5208
James O. Hicks, Dir.

Nicholls State University
Small Business Development Center
College of Business Administration
PO Box 2015
Thibodaux, Louisiana 70310
Phone: (504)448-4242
Fax: (504)448-4922
Weston Hull, Dir.

Maine

Androscoggin Valley Council of
Governments
Small Business Development Center
125 Manley Rd.

Auburn, Maine 04210
Phone: (207)783-9186
Fax: (207)780-4810
Greg Mitchell, Dir.

Coastal Enterprises Inc. SBDC
Weston Bldg.
7 N. Chestnut St.
Augusta, Maine 04330
Phone: (207)621-0245
Fax: (207)622-9739
Robert Chiozzi, Counselor

Eastern Maine Development Corp.
Small Business Development Center
1 Cumberland Pl., Ste. 300
PO Box 2579
Bangor, Maine 04402-2579
Phone: (207)942-6389
Toll-free: (800)339-6389
Fax: (207)942-3548
Ron Loyd, Dir.

Bath Chamber of Commerce SBDC
45 Front St.
Bath, Maine 04530
Phone: (207)882-4340
Fax: (207)443-9751

Waldo County Development Corp.
SBDC
67 Church St.
Belfast, Maine 04915
Phone: (207)942-6389
Phone: (207)942-6389
Fax: (800))339-6389

Biddeford-Saco Chamber of Commerce and Industry
190 Main St.
Biddeford, Maine 04005-2697
Phone: (207)282-1567
Fax: (207)282-9149
Frederick Aiello, Counselor

Brunswick Satellite SBDC
11 Cumberland St.
Brunswick, Maine 04811
Phone: (207)882-4340
Fax: (207)882-4456

Northern Maine Regional Planning
Commission
Small Business Development Center
PO Box 779

Caribou, Maine 04736
Phone: (207)498-8736
Toll-free: (800)427-8736
Fax: (207)493-3108
Rodney Thompson, Dir.

Katahdin Regional Development Corp.
SBDC
58 Main St.
East Millinocket, Maine 04430
Phone: (207)746-5338
Fax: (207)746-9535

Fort Kent Satellite SBDC
Aroostook County Registry of Deeds
Corner of Elm and Hall Streets
Fort Kent, Maine 04743
Phone: (207)498-8736
Toll-free: (800)427-8736

Houlton Satellite SBDC
Superior Ct. House
Court St.
Houlton, Maine 04730
Phone: (207)498-8736
Toll-free: (800)427-8736
Fax: (207)498-3108

Sunrise County Economic Council
(Calais Area)
SBDC
Washington County Economic
Planning Commission
63 Main St., PO Box 679
Machias, Maine 04654
Phone: (207)454-2430
Fax: (207)255-0983
Diane Tilton, Counselor

University of Maine at Machias
Small Business Development Center
Math & Science Bldg.
9 O'Brien Ave.
Machias, Maine 04654
Phone: (207)255-3313
Fax: (207)255-4864

University of Southern Maine
SBDC
15 Surrenden St.
Portland, Maine 04103
Phone: (207)780-4949
Fax: (207)780-4810
John Entwistle, Subcenter Dir.

Rockland Satellite SBDC
Key Bank of Maine
331 Main St
Rockland, Maine 04841
Phone: (207)882-4340

Southern Maine Regional Planning
Commission
Small Business Development Center
255 Main St.
PO Box Q
Sanford, Maine 04073
Phone: (207)324-0316
Fax: (207)324-2958
Joseph Vitko, Dir.

Skowhegan Satellite
SBDC
Norridgewock Ave.
Skowhegan, Maine 04976
Phone: (207)621-0245
Fax: (207)622-9739

South Paris Satellite
SBDC
166 Main St.
South Paris, Maine 04281
Phone: (207)783-9186
Fax: (207)783-5211

Thomas College
SBDC
Administrative Bldg.
180 W. River Rd.
Waterville, Maine 04976
Phone: (207)621-0245
Fax: (207)622-9739,

North Kennebec Regional Planning
Commission
Small Business Development Center
7 Benton Ave.
Winslow, Maine 04901
Phone: (207)873-0711
Fax: (207)873-5723

Coastal Enterprises, Inc. (Wiscasset)
Small Business Development Center
Water St.
PO Box 268
Wiscasset, Maine 04578
Phone: (207)882-4340
Fax: (207)882-4456
James Burbank, Dir.

York Chamber of Commerce
SBDC
449 Rte. 1
York, Maine 03909
Phone: (207)363-4422
Fax: (207)324-2958
John Entwistle, Subcenter Dir.

Maryland

Anne Arundel Office of Economic
Development
SBDC
2666 Riva Rd., Ste. 200
Annapolis, Maryland 21401
Phone: (410)224-4205
Fax: (410)222-7415
Rob Bethke, Consultant

Central Maryland
SBDC
University of Baltimore
1420 N. Charles St., Rm 142
Baltimore, Maryland 21201-5779
Phone: (410)837-4141
Fax: (410)837-4151
Barney Wilson, Executive Director

Hartford County Economic Develop-
ment Office
SBDC
220 S. Main St.
Bel Air, Maryland 21014
Phone: (410)893-3837
Fax: (410)879-8043
Maurice Brown, Consultant

University of Maryland
SBDC
Dingman Center for Entrepreneurship
College of Business and Management
College Park, Maryland 20742-1815
Phone: (301)405-2144
Fax: (301)314-9152

Howard County Economic Develop-
ment Office
SBDC
6751 Gateway Dr., Ste. 500
Columbia, Maryland 21043
Phone: (410)313-6552
Fax: (410)313-6556
Ellin Dize, Consultant

Western Region
SBDC
3 Commerce Dr.
Cumberland, Maryland 21502
Phone: (301)724-6716
Toll-free: (800)457-7232
Fax: (301)777-7504
Rubert Douglas, Exec. Dir.

Cecil County Chamber of Commerce
SBDC
135 E. Main St.
Elkton, Maryland 21921
Phone: (410)392-0597
Fax: (410)392-6225
Maurice Brown, Consultant

Frederick SBDC
5340 Spectrum Dr., Ste. K
Frederick, Maryland 21701
Phone: (301)694-4647
Fax: (301)694-4927
Mary Ann Garst, Program Dir.

Arundel Center North
SBDC
101 Crain Hwy., NW, Rm. 110B
Glen Burnie, Maryland 21601
Phone: (410)766-1910
Fax: (410)766-1911
Rob Bethke, Consultant

Community College at Saint Mary's
County
SBDC
PO Box 98, Great Mills Rd.
Great Mills, Maryland 20634
Phone: (301)868-6679
Fax: (301)868-7392
James Shepherd, Business Analyst

Hagerstown Junior College
SBDC
Technology Innovation Center
11404 Robinwood Dr.
Hagerstown, Maryland 21740
Phone: (301)797-0327
Fax: (301)777-5504
Tonya Fleming Brockett, Director

National Business League of Southern Maryland, Inc.
Small Business Development Center
9200 Basil Ct., Ste. 210

Landover, Maryland 20785
Phone: (301)772-3683
Fax: (301)772-0730

Suburban Washington Region Small
Business Development Center
1400 McCormick Dr., Ste. K
Landover, Maryland 20785
Phone: (301)883-6491
Fax: (301)883-6479

Landover SBDC
7950 New Hampshire Ave., 2nd Fl.
Langley Park, Maryland 20903
Phone: (301)445-7324
Fax: (301)883-6479
Avon Evans, Consultant

Garrett Community College
SBDC
Mosser Rd.
McHenry, Maryland 21541
Phone: (301)387-6666
Fax: (301)387-3096
Sandy Major, Business Analyst

Montgomery College (Rockville)
Small Business Development Center
Continuing Education
51 Mannakee St.
Rockville, Maryland 20850
Phone: (301)251-7940
Fax: (301)251-7937

Salisbury State University
Eastern Shore Region Small Business
Development Center
Power Professional Bldg., Ste. 400
Salisbury, Maryland 21801
Phone: (410)546-4325
Toll-free: (800)999-SBDC
Fax: (410)548-5389
John Dillard, Exec. Dir.

Baltimore County Chamber of
Commerce
SBDC
102 W. Pennsylvania Ave., Ste. 402
Towson, Maryland 21204
Phone: (410)832-5866
John Casper, Consultant

Southern Region Small Business
Development Center
235 Smallwood Village Center

Waldorf, Maryland 20602
Phone: (301)932-4155
Betsy Cooksey, Exec. Dir.

Carrol County Economic Develop-
ment Office
SBDC
125 N. Court St., Rm. 103
Westminster, Maryland 21157
Phone: (410)857-8166
Fax: (410)848-0003
Michael Fish, Consultant

Eastern Region - Upper Shore
c/o Chesapeake College
SBDC
PO Box 8
Wye Mills, Maryland 21679
Phone: (410)822-5400
Toll-free: (800)762-SBDC
Fax: (410)827-5286
Patricia Ann Marie Schaller, Consultant

Massachusetts

Boston SBDC
World Trade Center, Ste. 315
Boston, Massachusetts 02210
Phone: (617)478-4133
Fax: (617)478-4135

Minority Business Assistance Center
SBDC
University of Massachusetts
Boston College of Management, 5th Fl.
Boston, Massachusetts 02125-3393
Phone: (617)287-7750
Fax: (617)287-7725
Hank Turner, Dir.

Boston College
Metropolitan Boston Small Business
Development Center Regional Office
96 College Rd., Rahner House
Chestnut Hill, Massachusetts 02167
Phone: (617)552-4091
Fax: (617)552-2730
Jack McKiernan, Regional Dir.

Southeastern Massachusetts Small
Business Development Center
Regional Office
University of Massachusetts/
Dartmouth

200 Pocasset St.
PO Box 2785
Fall River, Massachusetts 02722
Phone: (508)673-9783
Fax: (508)674-1929
Clyde Mitchell, Regional Dir.

Salem State College
North Shore Massachusetts Small
Business Development Center
Regional Office
197 Essex St.
Salem, Massachusetts 01970
Phone: (508)741-6343
Fax: (508)741-6345
Frederick Young, Dir.

University of Massachusetts/Amherst
Western Massachusetts Small
Business Development Center
Regional Office
101 State St., Ste. 424
Springfield, Massachusetts 01103
Phone: (413)737-6712
Fax: (413)737-2312
Dianne Fuller Doherty, Dir.

Clark University
Central Massachusetts Small Busi-
ness Development Center Regional
Office
950 Main St.
Dana Commons
Worcester, Massachusetts 01610
Phone: (617)793-7615
Fax: (617)793-8890
Laurence Marsh, Dir.

Michigan

Ottawa County Economic Develop-
ment Office, Inc.
Small Business Development Center
6676 Lake Michigan Dr.
Allendale, Michigan 49401
Phone: (616)892-4120
Fax: (616)895-6670
Ken Rizzio, Dir.

Michigan Energy and Resource
Research Association
Specialty Small Business Develop-
ment Center
PO Box 130500

Ann Arbor, Michigan 48113
Phone: (313)930-0034
Fax: (313)930-6670
Mark Clevey, V. Pres.
E-mail: mark@merra.org

MMTC SBDC
2901 Hubbard Rd.
PO Box 1485
Ann Arbor, Michigan 48109
Phone: (313)769-4110
Fax: (313)769-4064
Bill Loomis
E-mail: wrl@itl.org

Center for Independent Living SBDC
2568 Packard Rd.
Ann Arbor, Michigan 48104
Phone: (313)971-0277
Fax: (313)971-0826
Roseanne Herzog, Dir.

Huron County Economic Develop-
ment Corp.
Small Business Development Center
Huron County Bldg., Rm. 303
Bad Axe, Michigan 48413
Phone: (517)269-6431
Fax: (517)269-7221
Patricia Crawford-Lewis, Dir.

Kellogg Community College
Small Business Development Center
450 North Ave.
Battle Creek, Michigan 49017-3397
Phone: (616)965-3931
Toll-free: (800)955-4KCC
Fax: (616)962-4290

Lake Michigan College Corporation
and Community Development
Small Business Development Center
2755 E. Napier
Benton Harbor, Michigan 49022-1899
Phone: (616)927-8179
Fax: (616)927-8103
Milt Richter, Dir.

Ferris State University
Small Business Development Center
330 Oak St.
West 115
Big Rapids, Michigan 49307
Phone: (616)592-3553

Fax: (616)592-3539
Lora Swenson, Dir.
E-mail: yc26@ferris.bitnet

Livingston County SBDC
131 S. Hyne
Brighton, Michigan 48116
Phone: (810)227-3556
Fax: (810)227-3080
Dennis Whitney, Dir.

Wexford-Missaukee Small Business
Development Center
222 Lake St.
Cadillac, Michigan 49601-0026
Phone: (616)775-9776
Fax: (616)775-1440
Ronald Andrews, Dir.

Tuscola County Economic Develop-
ment Corp.
Small Business Development Center
194 N. State St., Ste. 200
Caro, Michigan 48723
Phone: (517)673-2849
Fax: (517)673-2517
James McLoskey, Dir.

Detroit Economic Growth Corp.
150 W. Jefferson, Ste. 1500
Detroit, Michigan 48226
Phone: (313)963-2940
Fax: (313)963-8839

Michigan Small Business Develop-
ment Center (Detroit)
2727 2nd Ave., Rm. 107
Detroit, Michigan 48201
Phone: (313)964-1798
Fax: (313)964-4164
Ron Hall, Dir.

University of Detroit Mercy
NILAC Small Business Development
Center
4001 W. McNichols, Rm. 105
Commerce and Finance Bldg.
PO Box 19900
Detroit, Michigan 48219-0900
Phone: (313)993-1115
Fax: (313)993-1115

Wayne State University SBDC
Center for Urban Studies
3043 Faculty/Administration Bldg.

Detroit, Michigan 48202
Phone: (313)577-2788
Fax: (313)577-1274
Gary Shields, Dir.
E-mail: gshield@cms.cc.wayne.edu

Wayne State University
Procurement Technical Assistance
SBDC
2727 2nd. Ave.
Detroit, Michigan 48201
Phone: (313)577-4850
Fax: (313)577-8933
John Chichester, Dir.
E-mail: jchiche@cms.cc.wayne.edu

Wayne State University SBDC
School of Business Administration
2727 2nd. Ave., Rm. 121
Detroit, Michigan 48201
Phone: (313)577-4850
Fax: (313)577-8933
Dickran Murmurian, Dir.
E-mail: dmurmur@cms.cc.wayne.edu

Michigan State University
International Business Development
Center
7 Eppley Center
East Lansing, Michigan 48824-1022
Phone: (517)353-4336
Fax: (517)432-1009
Myron Miller, Dir.

First Step, Inc.
Small Business Development Center
228 Washington St.
Escanaba, Michigan 49829
Phone: (906)786-9234
Fax: (906)786-4442
David Gillis, Exec. Dir.

Flint Community Development Corp.
SBDC
877 E. 5th Ave., Bldg. C-1
Flint, Michigan 48503
Phone: (810)239-5847
Fax: (810)239-5575
Bobby Wells, Exec. Dir.

Genesee Economic Area Revitalization, Inc.
Small Business Development Center
412 S. Saginaw St.

Flint, Michigan 48502
Phone: (313)238-7803
Toll-free: (800)488-7803
Fax: (313)238-7866

Assn. of Commerce and Industry
SBDC
1 S. Harbor Ave.
PO Box 509
Grand Haven, Michigan 49417
Phone: (616)846-3153
Fax: (616)842-0379
Karen K. Benson, Dir.

Excell SBDC
333 Bridge St., NW, Ste. 1120
Grand Rapids, Michigan 49504
Phone: (616)458-4783
Fax: (616)774-4064
Carol Lopucki, Dir.

Grand Rapids Area Chamber of
Commerce
Small Business Development Center
111 Pearl St. NW
The Waters Bldg.
Grand Rapids, Michigan 49503-2831
Phone: (616)771-3600
Fax: (616)771-3605
Raymond DeWinkle, Dir.
E-mail: dewinkle@bizserve.com

Oceana County Economic Development Corp.
100 State St.
PO Box 168
Hart, Michigan 49420-0168
Phone: (616)873-7141
Fax: (616)873-3710
Charles Perjenaire, Dir.

Comerica Small Business Development Center
14048 Woodward
Highland Park, Michigan 48203
Phone: (313)222-2956
Fax: (313)865-8318
Dorothy Benedict, Dir.

Hillsdale County IDC
2 N. Howell St.
Hillsdale, Michigan 49242
Phone: (517)437-3200
Fax: (517)437-3735

Michigan Technological University
Small Business Development Center
Bureau of Industrial Development
1400 Townsend Dr.
Houghton, Michigan 49931
Phone: (906)487-1245
Fax: (906)487-2463
James Hainault, Program Mgr.

SBDC
Michigan Technological University
1400 Townsend Dr.
Houghton, Michigan 49931
Phone: (906)487-1245
Fax: (906)487-2463
Elsie White, Mgr.
E-mail: jmhainau@mtu.edu

Western U.P. Planning and Development Region
326 Sheldon Ave.
PO Box 365
Houghton, Michigan 49931
Phone: (906)482-7205
Fax: (906)482-9032

Livingston County Small Business
Development Center
207 M Michigan Ave.
PO Box 138
Howell, Michigan 48843
Phone: (517)546-4020
Fax: (517)546-4115
Dennis Whitney, Dir.

Greater Gratiot Development, Inc.
Small Business Center
136 Main
Ithaca, Michigan 48847
Phone: (517)875-2083
Fax: (517)875-2990

Jackson Business Development
Center
414 N. Jackson St.
Jackson, Michigan 49201
Phone: (517)787-0442
Fax: (517)787-3960
Duane K. Miller, Dir.

Kalamazoo College
Small Business Development Center
Stryker Center for Management
Studies

1327 Academy St.
Kalamazoo, Michigan 49017-3397
Phone: (616)337-7350
Fax: (616)337-7352
Carl R. Shook, Dir.

Lansing Community College
Small Business Development Center
PO Box 40010
Lansing, Michigan 48901
Phone: (517)483-1921
Fax: (517)483-1675
Deleski Smith, Dir.

Lapeer Development Corp.
Small Business Development Center
449 McCormick Dr.
Lapeer, Michigan 48446
Phone: (810)667-0080
Fax: (810)667-3541

Thumb Area Community Growth
Alliance SBDC
3270 Wilson St.
Marlette, Michigan 48453
Phone: (517)635-3561
Fax: (517)635-2230

Northern Economic Initiative Corp.
Small Business Development Center
1009 W. Ridge St.
Marquette, Michigan 49855
Phone: (906)228-5571
Fax: (906)228-5572
Todd Horton, Dir.

Midland Chamber of Commerce
SBDC
300 Rodd St.
Midland, Michigan 48640
Phone: (517)839-9522
Fax: (517)835-3701
Sam Boeke, Dir.

Genesis Centre for Entrepreneurial
Development SBDC
111 Conant Ave.
Monroe, Michigan 48161
Phone: (313)243-5947
Fax: (313)242-0009
Dani Topolski, Manager

Monroe County Community College
Monroe Small Business Center
1555 S. Raisinville Rd.

Monroe, Michigan 48161
Phone: (313)242-7300
Toll-free: (800)462-5114
Fax: (313)242-9711

Macomb County Business Assistance
Network
Small Business Development Center
115 S. Groesbeck Hwy.
Mount Clemens, Michigan 48043
Phone: (810)469-5118
Fax: (810)469-6787
Donald Morandini, Dir.

Central Michigan University SBDC
256 Applied Business Studies Complex
Mount Pleasant, Michigan 48859
Phone: (517)774-3270
Fax: (517)774-2372
Charles Fitzpatrick, Dir.

Muskegon Economic Growth Alliance
Small Business Development Center
230 Terrace Plz.
PO Box 1087
Muskegon, Michigan 49443-1087
Phone: (616)722-3751
Fax: (616)728-7251
Mert Johnson, Dir.

Oakland County Economic Develop-
ment Group
Executive Office Bldg.
1200 N. Telegraph Rd., Dept. 412
Pontiac, Michigan 48341-0412
Phone: (810)858-0783
Fax: (810)858-1080
Lillian Adams-Yanssens, Dir.

St. Clair County Community Small
Business Development Center
800 Military St., Ste. 320
Port Huron, Michigan 48060-5015
Phone: (810)982-9511
Fax: (810)982-9531
Todd Brian, Dir.

Saginaw Future, Inc.
Small Business Development Center
301 E. Genesee, 3rd Fl.
Saginaw, Michigan 48607
Phone: (517)754-8222
Fax: (517)754-1715
Matthew Hufnagel, Dir.

Washtenaw Community College
SBDC
740 Woodland
Saline, Michigan 48176
Phone: (313)944-1016
Fax: (313)944-0165
Daniel Stotz, Dir.
E-mail: dstotz@bizserve.com

West Shore Community College
Small Business Development Center
Business and Industrial Development
Institute
3000 N. Stiles Rd.
Scottville, Michigan 49454-0277
Phone: (616)845-6211
Fax: (616)845-0207
Mark Bergstrom, Dir.

Montcalm Community College
Small Business Development Center
2800 College Dr. SW
Sidney, Michigan 48885
Phone: (517)328-2111
Fax: (517)328-2950

Downriver Small Business Develop-
ment Center
15100 Northline Rd.
Southgate, Michigan 48195
Phone: (313)281-0700
Fax: (313)281-3418
Paula Buase, Dir.

Sterling Heights Area Chamber of
Commerce
Small Business Development Center
12900 Hall, Ste. 110
Sterling Heights, Michigan 48313
Phone: (810)731-5400
Fax: (810)731-3521

Greater Northwest Regional Small
Business Development Center
2200 Dendrinos Dr.
Traverse City, Michigan 49685-0506
Phone: (616)929-5000
Fax: (616)929-5012
Richard Beldin, Chief Admin. Off.

Northwestern Michigan College
Small Business Development Center
Center for Business and Industry
1701 E. Front St.

Traverse City, Michigan 49684
Phone: (616)922-1717
Fax: (616)922-1722

Northwestern Michigan Private
Industry Council
SBDC
2200 Dendrinos Dr.
Traverse City, Michigan 49685-0506
Phone: (616)929-5000
Fax: (616)929-5012

Traverse Bay Economic Development
Corp.
Small Business Development Center
202 E. Grandview Pky.
PO Box 387
Traverse City, Michigan 49685-0387
Phone: (616)946-1596
Charles Blankenship, Pres.

Traverse City Area Chamber of
Commerce
Small Business Development Center
202 E. Grandview Pky.
PO Box 387
Traverse City, Michigan 49685-0387
Phone: (616)947-5075
Fax: (616)946-2565
Matthew Meadows, V. PRES.

Michigan International Business
Development Metro Extension
Center
1300 W. Long Lake Rd., Ste. 150
Troy, Michigan 48098
Phone: (810)952-5800
Fax: (810)952-1875
Dorothy Heyart, Exec. Dir.

Saginaw Valley State University
Small Business Development Center
Business and Industrial Development
Institute
7400 Bay Rd.
University Center, Michigan 48710
Phone: (517)790-4048
Fax: (517)790-4983
Christine Greue, Dir.

Warren Chamber of Commerce
Small Business Development Center
30500 Van Dyke, Ste. 118
Warren, Michigan 48093

Phone: (810)751-3939
Fax: (810)751-3995
Janet Masi, V. PRES.

Ypsilanti Area Chamber of Commerce
Small Business Development Center
301 W. Michigan Ave., Ste. 101
Ypsilanti, Michigan 48197
Phone: (313)482-4920
Fax: (313)483-0400

Minnesota

Bemidji State University
Small Business Development Center
1500 Birchmont Dr. NE
Bemidji, Minnesota 56601
Phone: (218)755-2000

Northwest Technical College
SBDC
905 Grant Ave., SE
Bemidji, Minnesota 56601
Phone: (218)755-4286
Fax: (218)755-4289
Susan Kozojed, Dir.

Normandale Community College
(Bloomington) SBDC
9700 France Ave. S
Bloomington, Minnesota 55431
Phone: (612)832-6560
Fax: (612)832-6352
Betty Walton, Dir.

Brainerd Technical College
Small Business Development Center
300 Quince St.
Brainerd, Minnesota 56401
Phone: (218)828-5302
Fax: (218)828-5321
Pamela Thomsen, Dir.

Southwestern Technical College
(Canby Campus) SBDC
1011 1st St. W
Canby, Minnesota 56220
Phone: (507)223-7252
Toll-free: (800)658-2535
Fax: (507)223-5291

University of Minnesota at Duluth
Small Business Development Center
10 University Dr., 150 SBE

Duluth, Minnesota 55812-2496
Phone: (218)726-8758
Fax: (218)726-6338

East Grand Forks Technical Institute
Small Business Development Center
PO Box 111
Highway 220 N
East Grand Forks, Minnesota 56721
Phone: (218)773-3441
Toll-free: (800)451-3441
Fax: (218)773-4502

Normandale Community College
(Edina)
Small Business Development Center
4900 Viking Dr.
Edina, Minnesota 55435
Phone: (612)832-6221
Fax: (612)823-6352

Faribault City Hall
Small Business Development Center
208 NW 1st Ave.
Faribault, Minnesota 55021
Phone: (507)334-2222
Fax: (507)334-0124

Itasca Development Corp.
Grand Rapids Small Business
Development Center
19 NE 3rd St.
Grand Rapids, Minnesota 55744
Phone: (218)327-2241
Fax: (218)327-2242
John Damjanovich, Dir.

Hibbing Community College
Small Business Development Center
1515 E. 25th St.
Hibbing, Minnesota 55746
Phone: (218)262-6703
Fax: (218)262-6717
Allen Jackson, Dir.

Rainy River Community College
Small Business Development Center
1501 Hwy. 71
International Falls, Minnesota 56649
Phone: (218)285-2255
Fax: (218)285-2239

Southwestern Technical College
(Jackson Campus)
Small Business Development Center

401 West St.
Jackson, Minnesota 56143
Phone: (507)847-3320
Toll-free: (800)658-2522
Fax: (507)847-5383

Region Nine Development Commission
SBDC
410 Jackson St.
PO Box 3367
Mankato, Minnesota 56002-3367
Phone: (507)387-5643
Fax: (507)387-7105
Alison McKenzie, Dir.

Southwest State University
Small Business Development Center
Science and Technical Resource
Center, Ste. 105
Marshall, Minnesota 56258
Phone: (507)537-7386
Fax: (507)537-6094
Jack Hawk, Dir.

Minnesota Project Innovation
Small Business Development Center
The Mill Pl., Ste. 400
111 3rd Ave. S., Ste. 100
Minneapolis, Minnesota 55401
Phone: (612)338-3280
Fax: (612)338-3483
Randall Olson, Dir.

University of St. Thomas
SBDC
1000 La Salle Ave.
Suite MPL 100
Minneapolis, Minnesota 55403
Phone: (612)962-4500
Fax: (612)962-4410
Gregg Schneider, Dir.

Moorhead State University
Small Business Development Center
1104 7th Ave. S
PO Box 303, MSU
Moorhead, Minnesota 56563
Phone: (218)236-2289
Fax: (218)236-2280
Len Sliwoski, Dir.

Owatonna Incubator, Inc. SBDC
560 Dunnell Dr., Ste. 203
PO Box 505

Owatonna, Minnesota 55060
Phone: (507)451-0517
Fax: (507)455-2788
Lisa McGinnis, Dir.

Pine Technical College
Small Business Development Center
1100 4th St.
Pine City, Minnesota 55063
Phone: (612)629-7340
Fax: (612)629-7603
John Sparling, Dir.

Southwestern Technical College
(Pipestone Campus)
Small Business Development Center
Box 250
Pipestone, Minnesota 56164
Phone: (507)825-5471
Toll-free: (800)658-2330
Fax: (507)825-4656

Hennepin Technical College
SBDC
1820 N. Xenium Lane
Plymouth, Minnesota 55441
Phone: (612)550-7218
Fax: (612)550-7272
Danelle Wolf, Dir.

Pottery Business and Tech. Ctr.
Small Business Development Center
2000 Pottery Pl. Dr., Ste. 339
Red Wing, Minnesota 55066
Phone: (612)388-4079
Fax: (612)385-2251
Marv Bollum, Dir.

Rochester Community College
Small Business Development Center
Hwy. 14 E.
851 30th Ave. SE
Rochester, Minnesota 55904
Phone: (507)285-7536
Fax: (507)280-5502
Ellen Nelson, Dir.

Dakota County Technical College
Small Business Development Center
1300 E. 145th St.
Rosemount, Minnesota 55068
Phone: (612)423-8262
Fax: (612)322-5156
Tom Trutna, Dir.

Southeast Minnesota Development Corp.
SBDC
111 W. Jessie St.
Rushford, Minnesota 55971
Phone: (507)864-7557
Fax: (507)864-2091
Terry Erickson, Dir.

St. Cloud State University SBDC
4191 2nd St. S.
St. Cloud, Minnesota 56301-3761
Phone: (612)255-4842
Fax: (612)255-4957
Dawn Jensen-Ragnier, Dir.

University of St. Thomas
Small Business Development Center
23 Empire Dr.
St. Paul, Minnesota 55103
Phone: (612)962-4500

Thief River Falls Technical Institute
Small Business Development Center
1301 Hwy. 1 E
Thief River Falls, Minnesota 56701
Phone: (218)681-5424
Toll-free: (800)222-2884
Fax: (218)681-5519

Mesabi Community College SBDC
820-N. 9th St., Olcott Plaza, Ste. 140
Virginia, Minnesota 55792
Phone: (218)741-4251
Fax: (218)741-4249
John Freeland, Dir.

Wadena Chamber of Commerce SBDC
222 2nd St., SE
Wadena, Minnesota 56482
Phone: (218)631-1502
Fax: (218)631-2396
Paul Kinn, Dir.

Wadena Technical College SBDC
PO Box 566
Wadena, Minnesota 56482
Phone: (218)631-3530
Fax: (218)631-9207

North/East Metro Technical College
Small Business Development Center
3300 Century Ave. N
White Bear Lake, Minnesota 55110
Phone: (612)779-5764

Northeast Metro Technical College
SBDC
3300 Century Ave., N., Ste. 200-D
White Bear Lake, Minnesota 55110
Phone: (612)779-5764
Fax: (612)779-5802
Bob Rodine, Dir.

Winona State University
Small Business Development Center
Somsen Hall, Rm. 111
PO Box 5838
Winona, Minnesota 55987
Phone: (507)457-5088

Mississippi

Northeast Mississippi Community
College
SBDC
Holiday Hall, 2nd Fl.
Booneville, Mississippi 38829
Phone: (601)728-7751
Fax: (601)720-1165
Kenny Holt, Dir.

Delta State University
Small Business Development Center
PO Box 3235 DSU
Cleveland, Mississippi 38733
Phone: (601)846-4236
Fax: (601)846-4235
John Brandon, Dir.

East Central Community College
SBDC
PO Box 129
Decatur, Mississippi 39327
Phone: (601)635-2111
Fax: (601)635-2150
Ronald Westbrook, Dir.

Jones County Junior College SBDC
900 Court St.
Ellisville, Mississippi 39437
Phone: (601)477-4165
Fax: (601)477-4166

Jones County Junior College SBDC
900 Ct. St.
Ellisville, Mississippi 39437
Phone: (601)477-4165
Fax: (601)477-4152
Ken Dupre, Director

Gulf Coast Community College
SBDC
Jackson County Campus
PO Box 100
Gautier, Mississippi 39553
Phone: (601)497-9595
Fax: (601)497-9604
Dean Brown, Dir.

Mississippi Delta Community
College SBDC
PO Box 5607
Greenville, Mississippi 38704-5607
Phone: (601)378-8183
Fax: (601)378-5349
Chuck Herring, Dir.

Mississippi Contract Procurement
Center SBDC
3015 12th St.
PO Box 610
Gulfport, Mississippi 39502-0610
Phone: (601)864-2961
Fax: (601)864-2969
C. W. "Skip" Ryland, Exec. Dir.

Pearl River Community College
Small Business Development Center
5448 U.S. Hwy. 49 S.
Hattiesburg, Mississippi 39401
Phone: (601)544-0030
Fax: (601)544-0032
Heidi McDuffie, Dir.

Mississippi Valley State University
SBDC
Itta Bena, Mississippi 38941
Phone: (601)254-3601
Fax: (601)254-6704
Cliff Williams, Director

Jackson State University
Small Business Development Center
Jackson Enterprise Center, Ste. A-1
931 Hwy. 80 W
Box 43
Jackson, Mississippi 39204
Phone: (601)968-2795
Fax: (601)968-2796
Henry Thomas, Dir.

Millsaps College
Small Business Development Center
Dr. David Culpepper

Jackson, Mississippi 39210
Phone: (601)974-1000
Fax: (601)974-1260

University of Southern Mississippi
Small Business Development Center
136 Beach Park Pl.
Long Beach, Mississippi 39560
Phone: (601)865-4578
Fax: (601)865-4581
Lucy Betcher, Dir.

Alcorn State University SBDC
PO Box 90
Lorman, Mississippi 39096-9402
Phone: (601)877-6684
Fax: (601)877-6266
Sharon Witty, Dir.

Meridian Community College
Small Business Development Center
910 Hwy. 19 N
Meridian, Mississippi 39307
Phone: (601)482-7445
Fax: (601)482-5803
Kathy Braddock, Dir.

Mississippi State University
Small Business Development Center
PO Drawer 5288
Mississippi State, Mississippi 39762
Phone: (601)325-8684
Fax: (601)325-4016
Sonny Fisher, Dir.

Copiah-Lincoln Community College
Small Business Development Center
823 Hwy. 61 N.
Natchez, Mississippi 39120
Phone: (601)445-5254
Fax: (601)445-5254
Bob D. Russ, Dir.

Hinds Community College
Small Business Development Center/
International Trade Center
PO Box 1170
Raymond, Mississippi 39154
Phone: (601)857-3537
Marguerita Wall, Dir.

Holmes Community College
SBDC
412 W. Ridgeland Ave.
Ridgeland, Mississippi 39157

Phone: (601)853-0827
Fax: (601)853-0844
John Deddens, Dir.

Northwest Mississippi Community
College
SBDC
8700 Northwest Dr.
DeSoto Ctr.
Southaven, Mississippi 38671
Phone: (601)342-1570
Fax: (601)342-5686
Juely Dunning, Dir.

Southwest Mississippi Community
College
SBDC
College Dr.
Summit, Mississippi 39666
Phone: (601)276-3890
Fax: (601)276-3867
Kathryn Durham, Dir.

Itawamba Community College
Small Business Development Center
653 Eason Blvd.
Tupelo, Mississippi 38801
Phone: (601)680-8515
Fax: (601)842-6885
Rex Hollingsworth, Dir.

University of Mississippi
SBDC
Old Chemistry Bldg., Ste. 216
University, Mississippi 38677
Phone: (601)234-2120
Fax: (601)232-5650
Michael Vanderlip, Director

Missouri

Camden County
SBDC Extension Center
113 Kansas
PO Box 1405
Camdenton, Missouri 65020
Phone: (314)346-2644
Fax: (314)346-2694
Jackie Rasmussen, B&I Spec.

Missouri PAC- Southeastern
Southeastern Missouri State Univ.
SBDC
222 N. Pacific

Cape Girardeau, Missouri 63701
Phone: (314)290-5965
Fax: (314)651-5005
George Williams, Dir.

Southeast Missouri State University
Small Business Development Center
222 N. Pacific
Cape Girardeau, Missouri 63701
Phone: (314)290-5965
Fax: (314)651-5005
Frank "Buz" Sutherland, Dir.

Chillicothe City Hall SBDC
715 Washington
Chillicothe, Missouri 64601
Phone: (816)646-6920
Fax: (816)646-6811
Nanette Anderjaska, Dir.

East Central Missouri/St. Louis
County Extension Center
121 S. Meramac, Ste. 501
Clayton, Missouri 63105
Phone: (314)889-2911
Fax: (314)854-6147
Carole Leriche-Price, B&I Specialist

Boone County Extension Center
SBDC
1012 N. Hwy UU
Columbia, Missouri 65203
Phone: (314)445-9792
Fax: (314)445-9807
Casey Venters, B&I Specialist

University of Missouri-Columbia
1800 Univ. Pl.
Columbia, Missouri 65211
Phone: (314)882-3597
Fax: (314)884-4297
Morris Hudson, Dir.
E-mail:
MOPCOL@EXT.MISSOURI.EDU

University of Missouri—Columbia
Small Business Development Center
1800 University Pl.
Columbia, Missouri 65211
Phone: (314)882-7096
Fax: (314)882-6156
Organization E-mail: SBDC-
C@EXT.MISSOURI.EDU
Frank Siebert, Dir.

Hannibal Satellite Center
Hannibal, Missouri 63401
Phone: (816)385-6550
Fax: (816)385-6568

Jefferson County
Extension Center
Courthouse, Annex 203
725 Maple ST., PO Box 497
Hillsboro, Missouri 63050
Phone: (314)789-5391
Fax: (314)789-5059

Cape Girardeau County
SBDC Extension Center
815 Highway 25S
PO Box 408
Jackson, Missouri 63755
Phone: (314)243-3581
Fax: (314)243-1606
Richard Sparks, B&I Specialist

Cole County Extension Center SBDC
2436 Tanner Bridge Rd.
Jefferson City, Missouri 65101
Phone: (314)634-2824
Fax: (314)634-5463
Chris Bouchard

Missouri Southern State College SBDC
3950 Newman Rd.
107 Matthews Hall
Joplin, Missouri 64801-1595
Phone: (417)625-9313
Fax: (417)926-4588
Jim Krudwig, Dir.

Rockhurst College SBDC
1100 Rockhurst Rd.
VanAckeren Hall, Rm. 205
Kansas City, Missouri 64110-2599
Phone: (816)926-4572
Fax: (816)926-4588
Judith Burngen, Dir.

Northeast Missouri State University
Small Business Development Center
207 E. Patterson
Kirksville, Missouri 63501-4419
Phone: (816)785-4307
Fax: (816)785-4181
Organization E-mail: SBDC-
K@EXT.MISSOURI.EDU
Glen Giboney, Dir.

Thomas Hill Enterprise Center SBDC
PO Box 246
Macon, Missouri 63552
Phone: (816)385-6550
Jane Vanderham, Dir.

Northwest Missouri State University
Small Business Development Center
127 S. Buchanan
Maryville, Missouri 64468
Phone: (816)562-1701
Fax: (816)562-1900
Brad Anderson

Audrain County Extension Center
101 Jefferson
4th Fl. Courthouse
Mexico, Missouri 65265
Phone: (314)581-3231
Fax: (314)581-3232
Judy Moss, B&I Specialist

Randolph County Extension Center
417 E. Urbandale
Moberly, Missouri 65270
Phone: (816)263-3534
Fax: (816)263-1874
Ray Marshall, B&I Specialist

Mineral Area College SBDC
PO Box 1000
Park Hills, Missouri 63601-1000
Phone: (314)431-4593
Fax: (314)431-2144
Organization E-mail: SBDC-
FR@EXT.MISSOURI.EDU
Bruce Epps, Dir.

Three Rivers Community College
Small Business Development Center
Business Incubator Bldg.
3019 Fair St.
Poplar Bluff, Missouri 63901
Phone: (314)686-3499
Fax: (314)686-5467
Organization E-mail: SBDC-
PB@EXT.MISSOURI.EDU
John Bonifield, Dir.

Washington County SBDC
102 N. Missouri
Potosi, Missouri 63664
Phone: (314)438-2671
LaDonna McCuan, B&I Specialist

Center for Technology Transfer and
Economic Development
University of Missouri—Rolla
Nagogami Ter., Bldg. 1, Rm. 104
Rolla, Missouri 65401-0249
Phone: (314)341-4559
Fax: (314)346-2694
Organization E-mail: SBDC-
RT@EXT.MISSOURI.EDU
Fred Goss, Dir.

Missouri Enterprise Business Assis-
tance Center
SBDC
800 W 14th St., Ste. 111
Rolla, Missouri 65401
Phone: (314)364-8570
Fax: (314)341-6495
Organization E-mail:
MOPROLLA@EXE.MISSOURI.EDU
Rick Pugh, Dir.

Phelps County
SBDC Extension Center
Courthouse, 200 N. Main
PO Box 725
Rolla, Missouri 65401
Phone: (314)364-3147
Fax: (314)364-0436
Paul Cretin, B&I Spec.

Missouri PAC - EasternRegion
SBDC
975 Hornet Dr., Bldg. 279- Wing B
St. Louis, Missouri 63042
Phone: (314)731-3533
Organization E-mail:
MOPSTL@EXT.MISSOURI.EDU
Ken Konchel, Dir.

St. Louis Community College
SBDC
Continuing Education
3400 Pershall Rd.
St. Louis, Missouri 63135
Phone: (314)595-4219

St. Louis County
Extension Center
207 Marillac, UMSL
8001 Natural Bridge Rd.
St. Louis, Missouri 63121
Phone: (314)553-5944
John Henschke, Cont. Educ. Spec.

St. Louis University
Small Business Development Center
3750 Lindell Blvd.
St. Louis, Missouri 63108-3412
Phone: (314)977-7232
Fax: (314)977-7241
Organization E-mail: SBDC-
STL@EXT.MISSOURI.EDU
Virginia Campbell, Dir.

St. Louis County Economic Council
St. Charles County
SBDC Extension Center
260 Brown Rd.
St. Peters, Missouri 63376
Phone: (314)970-3000
Fax: (314)970-3000
Tim Wathen, B&I Specialist

Pettis County
Extension Center
1012A Thompson Blvd.
Sedalia, Missouri 65301
Phone: (816)827-0591
Fax: (816)826-8599
Betty Lorton, B&I Specialist

Southwest Missouri State University
Small Business Development Center
Center for Business Research
901 S. National
Box 88
Springfield, Missouri 65804-0089
Phone: (417)836-5685
Fax: (417)836-6337
Jane Peterson, Dir.

Franklin County
SBDC Extension Center
414 E. Main
PO Box 71
Union, Missouri 63084
Phone: (314)583-5141
Fax: (314)583-5145
Rebecca How, B&I Specialist

Central Missouri State University
Center for Technology
Grinstead, No. 75
Warrensburg, Missouri 64093-5037
Phone: (816)543-4402
Fax: (816)747-1653
Cindy Tanck, Coordinator

Central MO State Univ.
SBDC
Grinstead 75
Warrensburg, Missouri 64093-5037
Phone: (816)543-4402
Fax: (816)747-1653
Bernie Sarbaugh, Coordinator

Howell County
SBDC Extension Center
217 S. Aid Ave.
West Plains, Missouri 65775
Phone: (417)256-2391
Fax: (417)256-8569
Mick Gilliam, B&I Spec.

Montana

Billings Area Business Incubator
Small Business Development Center
Montana Tradepost Authority
115 N. Broadway, 2nd Fl.
Billings, Montana 59101
Phone: (406)256-6875
Fax: (406)256-6877
Jerry Thomas, Contact

Gallatin Development Corp.
Bozeman Small Business Development Center
321 E. Main, Ste. 413
Bozeman, Montana 59715
Phone: (406)587-3113
Fax: (406)587-9565
Darrell Berger, Contact

Rural Economic Development
Incubator
Butte Small Business Development
Center
305 W. Mercury, Ste. 211
Butte, Montana 59701
Phone: (406)782-7333
Fax: (406)782-9675
Ralph Kloser, Contact

Bear Paw Development Corp.
Havre Small Business Development
Center
PO Box 1549
Havre, Montana 59501
Phone: (406)265-9226
Fax: (406)265-3777
Randy Hanson, Contact

Flathead Valley Community College
Kalispell Small Business Development Center
777 Grandview Dr.
Kalispell, Montana 59901
Phone: (406)756-8333
Fax: (406)756-3815
Dan Manning, Contact

Missoula Business Incubator
Missoula Small Business Development Center
127 N. Higgins, 3rd Fl.
Missoula, Montana 59802
Phone: (406)728-9234
Fax: (406)721-4584
Leslie Jensen, Contact

Eastern Plains RC&D
Sidney Small Business Development
Center
123 W. Main
Sidney, Montana 59270
Phone: (406)482-5024
Fax: (406)482-5306
Dwayne Heintz, Contact

Nebraska

Chadron State College NBDC-Chadron
Administration Bldg.
Chadron, Nebraska 69337
Phone: (308)432-6282
Fax: (308)432-6430
Cliff Hanson, Dir.
E-mail: chanson@cscl.csc.edu

University of Nebraska at Kearney
NBDC-Kearney
Welch Hall
19th St. and College Dr.
Kearney, Nebraska 68849-3035
Phone: (308)865-8344
Fax: (308)865-8153
Kay Payne, Dir.

University of Nebraska at Lincoln
NBDC-Lincoln
Cornhusker Bank Bldg., Ste. 302
11th and Cornhusker Hwy.
Lincoln, Nebraska 68521
Phone: (402)472-3358
Fax: (402)472-0328
Irene Cherhoniak, Dir.

Mid-Plains Community College
NBDC-North Platte
416 N. Jeffers, Rm. 26
North Platte, Nebraska 69101
Phone: (308)534-5115
Fax: (308)534-5117
Dean Kurth, Dir.

Nebraska SBDC
University of Nebraska at Omaha
60th & Dodge St.
CBA Room 407
Omaha, Nebraska 68182
Phone: (402)554-2521
Fax: (402)554-3747
Robert Bernier, State Directo

Nebraska Small Business Development Center
Omaha Business and Technology Center
2505 N. 24 St., Ste. 101
Omaha, Nebraska 68110
Phone: (402)595-3511
Tom McCabe, Dir.

University of Nebraska at Omaha
Small Business Development Center
Peter Kiewit Conference Ctr.
1313 Farnam-on-the-Mall, Ste. 132
Omaha, Nebraska 68182-0248
Phone: (402)595-2381
Fax: (402)595-2385
Jeanne Eibes, Dir.

Peru State College NBDC-Peru
T.J. Majors Hall, Rm. 248
Peru, Nebraska 68421
Phone: (402)872-2274
Fax: (402)872-2422
David Ruenholl, Dir.

Western Nebraska Community
College
NBDC-Scottsbluff
Nebraska Public Power Bldg.
1721 Broadway, Rm. 408
Scottsbluff, Nebraska 69361
Phone: (308)635-7513
Fax: (308)635-6596
Ingrid Battershell, Dir.

Wayne State College
NBDC-Wayne
Gardner Hall

1111 Main St.
Wayne, Nebraska 68787
Phone: (402)375-7575
Fax: (402)375-7574
Loren Kucera, Dir.

Nevada

Carson City Chamber of Commerce
Small Business Development Center
1900 S. Carson St., Ste. 100
Carson City, Nevada 89701
Phone: (702)882-1565
Fax: (702)882-4179
Larry Osborne, Dir.

Great Basin College
Small Business Development Center
1500 College Pkwy.
Elko, Nevada 89801
Phone: (702)753-2245
Fax: (702)753-2242
John Pryor, Dir.

Incline Village Chamber of Commerce
SBDC
969 Tahoe Blvd.
Incline Village, Nevada 89451
Phone: (702)831-4440
Fax: (702)832-1605
Sheri Woods, Exec. Dir.

Foreign Trade Zone Office SBDC
1111 Grier Dr.
Las Vegas, Nevada 89119
Phone: (702)896-4496
Fax: (702)896-8351
Robert Holland, Bus. Dev. Specialist

University of Nevada at Las Vegas
Small Business Development Center
Box 456011
Las Vegas, Nevada 89154-6011
Phone: (702)895-0852
Fax: (702)895-4095
Sharolyn Craft, Dir.

North Las Vegas Small Business
Development Center
19 W. 4th St.
North Las Vegas, Nevada 89030
Phone: (702)399-6300
Fax: (702)399-6301
Janis Stevenson, Consultant

University of Nevada at Reno
Small Business Development Center
College of Business Administration
Mail Stop 032, Rm. 411
Reno, Nevada 89557-0100
Phone: (702)784-1717
Fax: (702)784-4337
Sam Males, Dir.

Tri-County Development Authority
Small Business Development Center
50 W. 4th St.
PO Box 820
Winnemucca, Nevada 89446
Phone: (702)623-5777
Fax: (702)623-5999
Terri Williams, Dir.

New Hampshire

First National Bank of Portsmouth
SBDC
One 3rd St., Ste. 2
Dover, New Hampshire 03820
Phone: (603)749-4264

New Hampshire Small Business
Development Center
Office of Economic Initiatives
Heidelberg-Harris Bldg.
Durham, New Hampshire 03824
Michelle Emig, Contact

University of New Hampshire SBDC
108 McConnell Hall
Durham, New Hampshire 03824-3593
Phone: (603)862-2200
Fax: (603)862-4876
Liz Lamoureaux, Dir.

Keene State College SBDC
Blake House
Keene, New Hampshire 03431
Phone: (603)358-2602
Fax: (603)358-2612
Gary Cloutier, Regional Mgr.

Small Business Development Center
120 Main St.
Littleton, New Hampshire 03561
Phone: (603)444-1053
Fax: (603)444-5463
Liz Ward, Regional Mgr.
E-mail: eaward@christa.unh.edu

Small Business Development Center
(Manchester, NH)
1000 Elm St., 14th Fl.
Manchester, New Hampshire 03101
Phone: (603)624-2000
Fax: (603)634-2449
Bob Ebberson, Regional Mgr.

Nashua Chamber of Commerce
Small Business Development Center
188 Main, Ste. 100
Nashua, New Hampshire 03060
Phone: (603)881-8333
Fax: (603)881-7323

New Hampshire Small Business
Development Center
c/o Center for Economic Development
1 Indian Head Plz., Ste. 510
Nashua, New Hampshire 03060
Phone: (603)886-1233
Fax: (603)598-1164
Bob Wilburn, Regional Mgr.
E-mail: sbdc-bw@mv.mv.com

Plymouth State College SBDC
Hyde Hall
Plymouth, New Hampshire 03264
Phone: (603)535-2523
Fax: (603)535-2611
Janice Kitchen, Regional Mgr.
E-mail: janice.kitchen@plymouth.edu

International Trade Resource Center
601 Spaulding Turnpike, Ste. 29
Portsmouth, New Hampshire 03801-2833
Phone: (603)334-6074
Fax: (603)334-6110
Barbara Garvey

MicroEnterprise Assistance Program
SBDC
PO Box 628
Portsmouth, New Hampshire 03802-0628
Phone: (603)431-2006
Fax: (603)427-1526
Jim O'Donnell

Pease Educational Training Center
Project Self-Start
601 Spaulding Tpke., Ste. 34
Portsmouth, New Hampshire 03801
Phone: (603)334-6192
Fax: (603)427-0687

New Jersey

Greater Atlantic City Chamber of
Commerce
Small Business Development Center
1301 Atlantic Ave.
Atlantic City, New Jersey 08401
Phone: (609)345-5600
Fax: (609)345-4524
William R. McGinley, Dir.

Rutgers University Schools of
Business
Small Business Development Center
Business and Science Bldg., 2nd Fl.
Camden, New Jersey 08102
Phone: (609)757-6221
Fax: (609)225-6231
Patricia Peacock, Dir.

Brookdale Community College
Small Business Development Center
Newman Springs Rd.
Lincroft, New Jersey 07738
Phone: (908)842-1900
Fax: (908)842-0203
Bill Nunnally, Dir.

Rutgers University SBDC
Ackerson Hall, 3rd Fl.
180 University Ave.
Newark, New Jersey 07102
Phone: (201)648-5950
Fax: (201)648-1110
Leroy A. Johnson, Dir.

Bergen Community College SBDC
400 Paramus Rd.
Paramus, New Jersey 07552
Phone: (201)447-7841
Fax: (201)447-7495
Melody Irvin, Dir.

Mercer County Community College
Small Business Development Center
1200 Old Trenton Rd.
Trenton, New Jersey 08690
Phone: (609)586-4800
Fax: (609)890-6338
Herb Spiegel, Dir.

Kean College
Small Business Development Center
East Campus, Rm. 242

Union, New Jersey 07083
Phone: (908)527-2956
Fax: (908)527-2960
Mira Kostak, Dir.

Warren County Community College
Small Business Development Center
Rte. 57 W.
Washington, New Jersey 07882
Phone: (908)689-9620
Fax: (908)689-7488
Robert Cerutti, Dir.

New Mexico

New Mexico State University at
Alamogordo
Small Business Development Center
1000 Madison
Alamogordo, New Mexico 88310
Phone: (505)434-5272
Fax: (505)434-5272
Dwight Harp, Dir.

Albuquerque Technical-Vocational
Institute
Small Business Development Center
525 Buena Vista SE
Albuquerque, New Mexico 87106
Phone: (505)224-4246
Fax: (505)224-4251
Roslyn Block, Dir.

South Valley
SBDC
1701 4th St. SW
Albuquerque, New Mexico 87102
Phone: (505)768-6801
Fax: (505)768-6086
Steven Becerra, Director

New Mexico State University at
Carlsbad
Small Business Development Center
PO Box 1090
Carlsbad, New Mexico 88220
Phone: (505)887-6562
Fax: (505)885-0818
Larry Coalson, Dir.

Clovis Community College
Small Business Development Center
417 Schepps Blvd.
Clovis, New Mexico 88101

Phone: (505)769-4136
Fax: (505)769-4190
Roy Miller, Dir.

Northern New Mexico Community
College SBDC
1002 N. Onate St.
Espanola, New Mexico 87532
Phone: (505)747-2236
Fax: (505)747-2180
Darien Cabral, Dir.

San Juan College
Small Business Development Center
203 W. Main St., Ste. 201
Farmington, New Mexico 87401
Phone: (505)326-4321
Fax: (505)325-1688
Brad Ryan, Dir.

University of New Mexico at Gallup
Small Business Development Center
PO Box 1395
Gallup, New Mexico 87305
Phone: (505)722-2220
Fax: (505)863-6006
Elsie Sanchez, Dir.

New Mexico State University at
Grants
Small Business Development Center
3400 S. Espina St.
Dept. 3DA, Box 30001
Grants, New Mexico 87020
Phone: (505)287-8221
Fax: (505)287-2125
Clemente Sanchez, Dir.

New Mexico Junior College
Small Business Development Center
5317 Lovington Hwy.
Hobbs, New Mexico 88240
Phone: (505)392-4510
Fax: (505)392-2526
Don Leach, Dir.

New Mexico State University—Dona
Ana Branch SBDC
3400 S. Espina St.
Dept. 3DA, Box 30001
Las Cruces, New Mexico 88003-0001
Phone: (505)527-7601
Fax: (505)527-7515
Terry Sullivan, Dir.

Luna Vocational-Technical Institute
Small Business Development Center
PO Drawer K
Las Vegas, New Mexico 87701
Phone: (505)454-2595
Fax: (505)454-2518
Michael Rivera, Dir.

University of New Mexico at Los
Alamos
Small Business Development Center
901 18th St., No. 18
Los Alamos, New Mexico 87544
Phone: (505)662-0001
Fax: (505)662-0099
Jim Greenwood, Dir.

University of New Mexico at Valencia
Small Business Development Center
280 La Entrada
Los Lunas, New Mexico 87031
Phone: (505)866-5348
Fax: (505)865-3095
Ray Garcia, Dir.

Eastern New Mexico University at
Roswell
Small Business Development Center
57 Univ. Ave.
PO Box 6000
Roswell, New Mexico 88201-6000
Phone: (505)624-7133
Fax: (505)624-7132
Eugene Simmons, Dir.

Santa Fe Community College SBDC
S. Richards Ave.
PO Box 4187
Santa Fe, New Mexico 87502-4187
Phone: (505)438-1343
Fax: (505)438-1237
Monica Montoya, Director

Western New Mexico University
Small Business Development Center
PO Box 2672
Silver City, New Mexico 88062
Phone: (505)538-6320
Fax: (505)538-6341
K. Jones, Dir.

Mesa Technical College
Small Business Development Center
PO Box 1143

Tucumcari, New Mexico 88401
Phone: (505)461-4413
Fax: (505)461-1901
Richard Spooner, Dir.

New York

SUNY at Albany
Small Business Development Center
Draper Hall, Rm. 107
135 Western Ave.
Albany, New York 12222
Phone: (518)442-5577
Fax: (518)442-5582
Peter George III, Dir.

Binghamton University
Small Business Development Center
PO Box 6000
Binghamton, New York 13902-6000
Phone: (607)777-4024
Fax: (607)777-4029
Joanne Bauman, Dir.
E-mail:
jbauman@bingvmb.cc.binghamton.edu

State University of New York
Small Business Development Center
74 N. Main St.
Brockport, New York 14420
Phone: (716)637-6660
Fax: (716)637-2102
Wilfred Bardeau, Dir.

Bronx Community College
Small Business Development Center
McCracken Hall, Rm.14
W. 181st & University Ave.
Bronx, New York 10453
Phone: (718)563-3570
Fax: (718)563-3576
Eugene Williams, Dir.

Downtown Brooklyn Outreach Center
SBDC
395 Flatbush Ave. Extension Rm.
413
Brooklyn, New York 11201
Phone: (718)260-9783
Fax: (718)260-9797

Kingsboro Community College
Small Business Development Center
2001 Oriental Blvd. Rm. 4204

Manhattan Beach
Brooklyn, New York 11235
Phone: (718)368-4619
Fax: (718)368-4629
Edward O'Brien, Dir.

State University of New York at Buffalo
Small Business Development Center
1300 Elmwood Ave.
Bacon Hall 117
Buffalo, New York 14222
Phone: (716)878-4030
Fax: (716)878-4067
Susan McCartney, Dir.

Canton Outreach Center
SBDC
Sunny Canton
Canton, New York 12617
Phone: (315)386-7312
Fax: (315)386-7945

Cobleskill Outreach Center
SBDC
State University of New York
Warner Hall, Rm. 218
Cobleskill, New York 12043
Phone: (518)234-5628
Fax: (518)234-5272

Corning Community College
Small Business Development Center
24 Denison Pky. W
Corning, New York 14830
Phone: (607)962-9461
Toll-free: (800)358-7171
Fax: (607)936-6642
Bonnie Gestwicki, Dir.

Mercy College/Westchester Outreach
Center
SBDC
555 Broadway
Dobbs Ferry, New York 10522-1189
Phone: (914)674-7485
Fax: (914)693-4996
Tom Milton, Coordinator

State University of New York at
Farmingdale
Small Business Development Center
Campus Commons Bldg.
2350 Route 110
Farmingdale, New York 11735

Phone: (516)420-2765
Fax: (516)293-5343
Joseph Schwartz, Dir.

Marist College Outreach Center
SBDC
Fishkill Extension Center
2600 Rte. 9, Unit 90
Fishkill, New York 12524-2001
Phone: (914)897-2607
Fax: (914)897-4653

State University of New York
Geneseo SBDC
1 College Circle
Geneseo, New York 14454-1485
Phone: (716)245-5429
Fax: (716)245-5430
Charles VanArsdale, Dir.

Geneva Outreach Center
SBDC
122 N. Genesee St.
Geneva, New York 14456
Phone: (315)781-1253
Fax: (716)637-2102
Sandy Bordeau, Administrative Dir.

Hempstead Outreach Center
SBDC
269 Fulton Ave.
Hempstead, New York 11550
Phone: (516)564-8672
Phone: (516)564-1895
Fax: (516)481-4938

York College/City University of New
York
Small Business Development Center
94-50 159th St.
Science Bldg. Rm. 107
Jamaica, New York 11451
Phone: (718)262-2880
Fax: (718)262-2881
James A. Heyliger

Jamestown Community College
Small Business Development Center
PO Box 20
Jamestown, New York 14702-0020
Phone: (716)665-5754
Toll-free: (800)522-7232
Fax: (716)665-6733
Kene Dobies, Dir.

Small Business Development Center
1 Development Ct.
Kingston, New York 12401
Phone: (914)339-1322
Fax: (914)339-1631
Patricia La Susa, Dir.

Baruch College
Mid-Town Outreach Center
SBDC
360 Park Ave., S., Rm. 1101
New York, New York 10010
Phone: (212)802-6620
Fax: (212)802-6613
Barrie Phillip, Coordinator

East Harlem Outreach Center
SBDC
145 E. 116th St., 3rd Fl.
New York, New York 10029
Phone: (212)346-1900
Fax: (212)534-4526
Anthony Sanchez, Coordinator

Pace University
Small Business Development Center
1 Pace Plz., Rm. W480
New York, New York 10038
Phone: (212)346-1900
Fax: (212)346-1613
Ira Davidson, Dir.

Pace University/Harlem Outreach Center
SBDC
163 W. 125th St., Rm. 1307
New York, New York 10038
Phone: (212)346-1900
Fax: (212)534-4176
Anthony Sanchez, Coordinator

SUNY Canton
SBDC
Canton
New York, New York 12617
Phone: (315)386-7312
Fax: (315)386-7945

Niagara Falls Satellite Office
SBDC
Carborundum Center
345 3rd St.
Niagara Falls, New York 14303-1117
Phone: (716)285-4793
Fax: (716)285-4797

Onondaga Community College/
Oswego Outreach Center
SBDC
44 W. Bridge St.
PO Box 4067
Oswego, New York 13126
Phone: (315)343-1545
Fax: (315)343-1546

Clinton Community College
SBDC
136 Clinton Pointe Dr.
Lake Shore Rd., Rte.95.
Plattsburgh, New York 12901
Phone: (518)564-4260
Fax: (518)563-9759
Merry Gwynn, Coordinator

Suffolk Co. Community College
Riverhead Outreach Center
SBDC
Riverhead, New York 11901
Phone: (516)369-1409
Phone: (516)369-1507
Fax: (516)369-3255

State University at Brockport
SBDC
Temple Bldg.
14 Franklin St., Ste. 200
Rochester, New York 14604
Phone: (716)232-7310
Fax: (716)637-2182

Niagara County Community College
Small Business Development Center
3111 Saunders Settlement Rd.
Sanborn, New York 14132
Phone: (716)693-1910
Fax: (716)731-3395
Richard Gork, Dir.

Long Island University at
Southhampton
SBDC
Aloney Peak, Montauk Hwy.
Southampton, New York 11968
Phone: (516)287-0059
Fax: (516)287-8287

College of Staten Island
SBDC
2800 Victory Blvd.
Staten Island, New York 10314-9806

Phone: (718)982-2560
Fax: (718)982-2038
Loretta DiCamillo, Director

State University at Stony Brook
Small Business Development Center
Harriman Hall, Rm. 109
Stony Brook, New York 11794-3775
Phone: (516)632-9070
Fax: (516)632-7176
Judith McEvoy, Dir.

Rockland Community College
Small Business Development Center
145 College Rd.
Suffern, New York 10901-3620
Phone: (914)356-0370
Fax: (914)356-0381
Thomas J. Morley, Dir.

Onondaga Community College
Small Business Development Center
4969 Onondaga Rd.
Excell Bldg., Rm. 108
Syracuse, New York 13215-1944
Phone: (315)492-3704
Fax: (315)492-3764
Robert Varney, Dir.

Manufacturing Technology Center
SBDC
Rensselaer Technology Pk.
385 Jordan Rd.
Troy, New York 12180-8347
Phone: (518)286-1014
Fax: (518)286-1006
Thomas Reynolds, Direc.

State University Institute of Technology
Small Business Development Center
PO Box 3050
Utica, New York 13504-3050
Phone: (315)792-7546
Fax: (315)792-7554
Albert Mario, Dir.

Jefferson Community College
Small Business Development Center
Coffeen St.
Watertown, New York 13601
Phone: (315)782-9262
Fax: (315)782-0901
John F. Tauner, Dir.

SBDC Outreach Small Business
Resource Center
222 Bloomingdale Rd., 3rd Fl.
White Plains, New York 10605-1500
Phone: (914)644-4116
Fax: (914)644-2184
Maria Circosta, Coordinator

SBDC Outreach Small Business
Resource Center
222 Bloomingdale Rd., 3rd Fl.
White Plains, New York 10605-1500
Phone: (914)644-4116
Fax: (914)644-2184
Maria Circosta, Coordinator

North Carolina

Asheville SBDC
34 Wall St., Ste. 707
Asheville, North Carolina 28805
Phone: (704)251-6025

Appalachian State University
Small Business and Technology
Development Center (Northwestern
Region)
Walker College of Business
2123 Raley Hall
Boone, North Carolina 28608
Phone: (704)262-2492
Fax: (704)262-2027
Bill Parrish, Regional Dir.

University of North Carolina at
Chapel Hill
Central Carolina Regional Small
Business Development Center
608 Airport Rd., Ste. B
Chapel Hill, North Carolina 27514
Phone: (919)962-0389
Fax: (919)962-3291
Dan Parks, Dir.

University of North Carolina at
Charlotte
Small Business and Technology
Development Center (Southern
Piedmont Region)
8701 Mallard Creek Rd.
Charlotte, North Carolina 28262
Phone: (704)548-1090
Fax: (704)548-9050
George McAllister, Dir.

Western Carolina University
Small Business and Technology
Development Center (Western Region)
Center for Improving Mountain
Living
Bird Bldg.
Cullowhee, North Carolina 28723
Phone: (704)227-7494
Fax: (704)227-7422
Allan Steinburg, Dir.

Elizabeth City State University
Small Business and Technology
Development Center (Northeastern
Region)
1704 Weeksville Rd.
PO Box 874
Elizabeth City, North Carolina 27909
Phone: (919)335-3247
Fax: (919)355-3648
Wauna Dooms, Dir.

Fayetteville State University
Cape Fear Small Business and
Technology Development Center
PO Box 1334
Fayetteville, North Carolina 28302
Phone: (910)486-1727
Fax: (910)486-1949
Sid Gautam, Dir.

North Carolina A&T State University
Northern Piedmont Small Business
and Technology Development Center
(Eastern Region)
C. H. Moore Agricultural Research
Center
1601 E. Market St.
PO Box D-22
Greensboro, North Carolina 27411
Phone: (910)334-7005
Fax: (910)334-7073
Cynthia Clemons, Dir.

East Carolina University
Small Business and Technology
Development Center (Eastern
Region)
Willis Bldg.
300 East 1st St.
Greenville, North Carolina 27858-4353
Phone: (919)328-6157
Fax: (919)328-6992
Walter Fitts, Dir.

Catawba Valley Region
SBDC
514 Hwy. 321 NW, Ste. A
Hickory, North Carolina 28601
Phone: (704)345-1110
Fax: (704)326-9117
Rand Riedrich, Director

Pembroke State University
Office of Economic Development and
SBTDC
SBDC
Pembroke, North Carolina 28372
Phone: (910)521-6603
Fax: (910)521-6550

North Carolina State University
Capital Region
SBDC
MCI Small Business Resource Center
800 1/2 S. Salisbury St.
Raleigh, North Carolina 27601
Phone: (919)715-0520
Fax: (919)715-0518
Gary Palin, Director

North Carolina Wesleyan College
SBDC
3400 N. Wesleyan Blvd.
Rocky Mount, North Carolina 27804
Phone: (919)985-5130
Fax: (919)977-3701

University of North Carolina at
Wilmington
Small Business and Technology
Development Center (Southeast
Region)
601 S. College Rd.
Cameron Hall, Rm. 131
Wilmington, North Carolina 28403
Phone: (910)395-3744
Fax: (910)350-3990
Mike Bradley, Dir.

Winston-Salem State University
Northern Piedmont Small Business
and Technology Center
PO Box 13025
Winston Salem, North Carolina 27110
Phone: (910)750-2030
Fax: (910)750-2031
Bill Dowa, Dir.

North Dakota

Bismarck Regional Small Business
Development Center
400 E. Broadway, Ste. 416
Bismarck, North Dakota 58501
Phone: (701)223-8583
Fax: (701)222-3843
Jan M. Peterson, Regional Dir.

Devils Lake Outreach Center
SBDC
417 5th St.
Devils Lake, North Dakota 58301
Toll-free: (800)445-7232
Gordon Synder, Regional Dir.

Dickinson Regional Center
Small Business Development Center
314 3rd Ave. W
Drawer L
Dickinson, North Dakota 58602
Phone: (701)227-2096
Fax: (701)225-5116
Bryan Vendsel, Regional Dir.

Fargo Regional Small Business
Development Center
417 Main Ave., Ste. 402
Fargo, North Dakota 58103
Phone: (701)237-0986
Fax: (701)237-9734
Jon Grinager, Regional Mgr.

Grafton Outreach Center
SBDC
PO Box 633
Grafton, North Dakota 58237
Toll-free: (800)445-7232
Gordon Snyder, Regional Dir.

Grand Forks Regional Small Business
Development Center
1407 24th Ave. S., Ste. 201
The Hemmp Center
Grand Forks, North Dakota 58201
Phone: (701)772-8502
Fax: (701)772-2772
Gordon Snyder, Regional Dir.

North Dakota Small Business
Development Center
210 10th St. SE
S.E.P.O. Box 1530

Jamestown, North Dakota 58402
Phone: (701)252-9243
Fax: (701)251-2488
Jon Grinager, Regional Dir.

Minot Regional Center
Small Business Development Center
1020 20th Ave. SW
PO Box 940
Minot, North Dakota 58702
Phone: (701)852-8861
Fax: (701)838-2488
Brian Argabright, Contact

Williston Outreach Center
Tri-County Economic Development
Association
SBDC
PO Box 2047
Williston, North Dakota 58801
Toll-free: (800)445-7232
Bryan Vendsel, Regional Dir.

Ohio

Akron Regional Development Board
Small Business Development Center
1 Cascade Plz., 8th Fl.
Akron, Ohio 44308-1192
Phone: (216)379-3170
Fax: (216)379-3164
Charles Smith, Dir.

Women's Entrepreneurial Growth
Organization
Small Business Development Center
58 W. Center St.
PO Box 544
Akron, Ohio 44309
Phone: (216)535-9346
Fax: (216)535-4523
Susan Hale, Dir.

Northwest State Community College
SBDC
22-600 ST RT 34
Archbold, Ohio 43502
Phone: (419)267-5511
Fax: (419)267-3688

Enterprise Development Corp.
SBDC
900 E. State St.
Athens, Ohio 45701

Phone: (614)592-1188
Fax: (614)593-8283
Karen Paton, Dir.

Ohio University Innovation Center
Small Business Development Center
Technical & Enterprise Bldg.
20 East Circle Dr., Ste. 153
Athens, Ohio 45701
Phone: (614)593-1797
Fax: (614)593-1795
Marianne Vermeer, Dir.
E-mail: vermeer@ouvata.cats.ohiou.edu

Ohio Hi-Point JVC SBDC
112 E. Court St.
Bellefontaine, Ohio 43311
Phone: (513)592-3585
Fax: (513)592-3683

West Central Small Business Development Center
Ohio-Point Office
2280 State Rte. 540
Bellefontaine, Ohio 43311-9594
Phone: (513)599-3010
Fax: (513)599-2318

WSOS Community Action Commission, Inc.
Wood County
SBDC
121 E. Wooster St.
PO Box 539
Bowling Green, Ohio 43402
Phone: (419)352-7469
Fax: (419)353-3291
Tom Blaha, Director

Mideast Small Business Development Center
Cambridge Office
1131 Steubenville Ave.
Cambridge, Ohio 43725
Phone: (614)439-2822
Fax: (614)439-2822

Greater Stark Development Board
Stark County Small Business Development Center
116 Cleveland Ave. NW, Ste. 600
Canton, Ohio 44702-1730
Phone: (216)453-5900
Fax: (216)453-1793

Kent State University/Stark Campus
SBDC
600 Frank Ave., NW
Canton, Ohio 44720
Phone: (216)499-9600
Fax: (216)494-6121
Amy DeGeorge, Coordinator

Wright State University—Lake Campus
Small Business Development Center
7600 State Rte. 703
Celina, Ohio 45822
Phone: (419)586-0355
Toll-free: (800)237-1477
Fax: (419)586-0358
Tum Kmayoke, Dir.

Clermont County Area
SBDC
Clermont County Chamber of Commerce
4440 Glen Este-Withamsville Rd.
Cincinnati, Ohio 45245
Phone: (513)753-7141
Fax: (513)753-7146
Dennis Begue, Director

Small Business Development Center
University of Cincinnati
IAMS Research Pk., MC189
1111 Edison Ave.
Cincinnati, Ohio 45216-2265
Phone: (513)948-2082
Fax: (513)948-2007
Bill Floretti, Dir.

Circleville/Pickway Chamber of Commerce
SBDC
135 W. Main St.
PO Box 462
Circleville, Ohio 43113
Phone: (614)474-4923
Fax: (614)477-1927

Greater Cleveland Growth Association
Small Business Development Center
200 Tower City Center
50 Public Sq.
Cleveland, Ohio 44113-2291
Fax: (216)621-4617
Danet Haar, Dir.

Northern Ohio Manufacturing
SBDC
Prospect Park Bldg.
4600 Prospect Ave.
Cleveland, Ohio 44103-4314
Phone: (216)432-5364
Fax: (216)361-2900
Gretchen Faro, Director

Columbus Area Chamber of Commerce
Small Business Development Center
Central Ohio Government Marketing
Assistance Program
77 S. High St., 28th FL.
Columbus, Ohio 43216-1001
Phone: (614)466-2711
Fax: (614)466-0829
Holly I. Schick, Dir.

Greater Columbus Area Chamber of Commerce
SBDC
37 N. High St.
Columbus, Ohio 43215-3065
Phone: (614)225-6082
Fax: (614)469-8250
Linda Steward, Dir.

Coshocton County Chamber of Commerce
Small Business Development Center
124 Chestnut St.
Coshocton, Ohio 43812
Phone: (614)622-5411
Fax: (614)622-9702

Dayton Area Chamber of Commerce
Small Business Development Center
Chamber Plz.
5th & Main Sts.
Dayton, Ohio 45402-2400
Phone: (513)226-8239
Fax: (513)226-8254
Harry Bumgarner, Dir.

Wright State University/Dayton
SBDC
Center for Small Business Assistance
College of Business, 31
0 Rike Hall
Dayton, Ohio 45435
Phone: (513)873-3503
Phone: (513)873-3545
Jeanette Davy, Director

Northwest Technical College
Small Business Development Center
1935 E. 2nd St., Ste. D
Defiance, Ohio 43512
Phone: (419)784-3777
Fax: (419)782-4649
Don Wright, Dir.

Delaware Area Chamber of Commerce
SBDC
27 W. Winter St.
Delaware, Ohio 43015
Phone: (614)369-6221
Fax: (614)369-4817

Terra Community College
Small Business Development Center
1220 Cedar St.
Fremont, Ohio 43420
Phone: (419)332-1002
Fax: (419)334-2300
Joe Wilson, Dir.

Enterprise Center
Small Business Development Center
129 E. Main St.
PO Box 756
Hillsboro, Ohio 45133
Phone: (513)393-9599
Fax: (513)393-8159
Bill Grunkemeyer, Dir.

Ashtabula County Economic Development Council, Inc.
Small Business Development Center
36 W. Walnut St.
Jefferson, Ohio 44047
Phone: (216)576-9134
Fax: (216)576-5003
Rene Keener, Dir.

Kent State University
College of Business Administration
Kent State University
College of Business Administration
302 Bowman Hall
Kent, Ohio 44242-0001
Phone: (216)672-2750
Fax: (216)672-2448
Charles Nieman, Dir.

EMTEC/Southern Area Manufacturing
SBDC
3171 Research Pk.

Kettering, Ohio 45420
Phone: (513)259-1361
Fax: (513)259-1303
James Ackley, Dir.

Lancaster/Fairfield County Chamber
of Commerce SBDC
109 N. Broad St.
Lancaster, Ohio 43130
Phone: (614)653-8251
Fax: (614)653-7074

Lima Technical College
Small Business Development Center
545 W. Market St., Ste. 305
Lima, Ohio 45801-4717
Phone: (419)229-5320
Fax: (419)229-5424
Gerald J. Bledenharn, Dir.

London Area Chamber of Commerce
SBDC
66 W. High Smith
London, Ohio 43140-1074
Phone: (614)852-2250
Fax: (614)653-7074

Lorain County Chamber of Commerce
SBDC
6100 S. Boadway
Lorain, Ohio 44053
Phone: (216)233-6500
Phone: (216)246-4050
Dennis Jones, Director

Mid-Ohio Small Business Development Center
336 E. 4th St., 4th Fl.
PO Box 1208
Mansfield, Ohio 44901
Toll-free: (800)366-7232
Fax: (419)522-6811
Tim Bowersack, Dir.

Marietta College SBDC
213 Fourth St.
Marietta, Ohio 45750
Phone: (614)376-4901
Fax: (614)376-4832
Emerson Shimp, Director

Marion Area Chamber of Commerce
SBDC
206 S. Prospect St.
Marion, Ohio 43302

Phone: (614)387-0188
Fax: (614)387-7722
Lynn Lovell, Dir.

Lake County Economic Development
Center SBDC
Lakeland Community College
750 Clocktower Dr.
Mentor, Ohio 44080
Phone: (216)951-1290
Fax: (216)951-7336
Jerry Loth, Dir.

Tuscarawas SBDC
Kent State University
300 Univ. Drive, NE
New Philadelphia, Ohio 44663-9447
Phone: (216)339-3391
Fax: (216)339-2637
Tom Farbizo, Director

Miami University
Small Business Development Center
336 Upham Hall
Oxford, Ohio 45056
Phone: (513)529-4841
Fax: (513)529-1469
Dr. Michael Broida, Dir.

Upper Valley Joint Vocational
School
Small Business Development Center
8811 Career Dr.
N. Country Rd., 25A
Piqua, Ohio 45356
Phone: (513)778-8419
Toll-free: (800)589-6963
Fax: (513)778-9237
Carol Baumhauer, Dir.

Shawnee State University SBDC
Department of Continuing Education
Portsmouth, Ohio 45662
Phone: (614)355-2471
Fax: (614)355-2598

Department of Development of the
CIC of Belmont County
Small Business Development Center
100 E. Main St.
St. Clairsville, Ohio 43950
Phone: (614)695-9678
Fax: (614)695-1536
Mike Campbell, Dir.

Kent State University/Salem Campus
SBDC
2491 State, Rte. 45 S.
Salem, Ohio 44460
Phone: (216)332-0361
Fax: (216)332-9256

Sandusky City Schools
Small Business Development Center
407 Decatur St.
Sandusky, Ohio 44870
Phone: (419)626-6940
Toll-free: (800)548-6507
Fax: (419)626-9176

Lawrence County Chamber of
Commerce SBDC
U.S. Rte. 52 & Solida Rd.
PO Box 488
South Point, Ohio 45680
Phone: (614)894-3838
Fax: (614)894-3836
Lou-Ann Walden, Dir.

Springfield Small Business Develop-
ment Center
300 E. Auburn Ave.
Springfield, Ohio 45505
Phone: (513)322-7821
Fax: (513)322-7874
Rafeal Underwood, Exec.

Greater Steubenville Chamber of
Commerce
Small Business Development Center
of Jefferson County
630 Market St.
PO Box 278
Steubenville, Ohio 43952
Phone: (614)282-6226
Fax: (614)282-6285
Jeff Castner, Dir.

Toledo Small Business Development
Center
300 Madison Ave., Ste. 200
Toledo, Ohio 43604-1575
Phone: (419)252-2700
Fax: (419)252-2724
Linda Fayerweather, Dir.

Youngstown/Warren SBDC
Region Chamber of Commerce
160 E. Market St.

Warren, Ohio 44488
Phone: (216)742-3495
Phone: (216)742-3784
Patricia Veisz, Manager

Wayne County Development Council
SBDC
1328 Dauer Rd.
Wooster, Ohio 44691
Phone: (216)264-2411
Phone: (216)264-1126

WEAV Satellite SBDC
100 Corry St.
PO Box 512
Yellow Springs, Ohio 45387
Phone: (513)767-2667
Fax: (513)767-7550

Youngstown State University
Cushwa Center for Industrial Devel-
opment
410 Wick Ave.
Youngstown, Ohio 44555-3495
Phone: (216)742-3495
Fax: (216)742-3784
Patricia Veisz, Mgr.

Zanesville Area Chamber of Com-
merce
Small Business Development Center
217 N. 5th St.
Zanesville, Ohio 43701
Phone: (614)452-4868
Fax: (614)454-2963
Bonnie J. Winnett, Dir.

Oklahoma

East Central University
Small Business Development Center
1036 E. 10th St.
Ada, Oklahoma 74820
Phone: (405)436-3190
Fax: (405)436-3190
Frank Vater

Northwestern Oklahoma State
University
Small Business Development Center
709 Oklahoma Blvd.
Alva, Oklahoma 73717
Phone: (405)327-8608
Fax: (405)327-0560

Connie Murrell, Dir.
University of Central Oklahoma
SBDC
100 N. University Blvd.
Edmond, Oklahoma 73034
Phone: (405)232-1968

Phillips University
Small Business Development Center
100 S. University Ave.
Enid, Oklahoma 73701
Phone: (405)242-7989
Fax: (405)237-1607
Bill Gregory, Coordinator

Langston University Center
Small Business Development Center
Hwy. 33 E.
Langston, Oklahoma 73050
Phone: (405)466-3256
Toll-free: (800)501-3435
Fax: (405)466-2909
Robert Allen, Dir.

Lawton Satellite
Small Business Development Center
American National Bank Bldg.
601 SW "D" Ave., Ste. 209
Lawton, Oklahoma 73501
Phone: (405)248-4946
Fax: (405)355-3560
Linda Strelecki

Miami Satellite SBDC
215 I St. NE
Miami, Oklahoma 74354
Phone: (918)540-0575
Fax: (918)540-0575
Hugh Simon

Rose State College SBDC
6420 SE 15th St.
Midwest, Oklahoma 73110
Phone: (405)733-7348
Fax: (405)733-7495
Judy Robbins, Director

Oklahoma Department of Commerce
Small Business Development Center
PO Box 26980
Oklahoma City, Oklahoma 73126-0980
Phone: (405)843-9770
Toll-free: (800)TRY-OKLA
Fax: (405)841-5199

Rose State College SBDC
6420 SE 15th
Oklahoma City, Oklahoma 73110
Phone: (405)733-7348
Fax: (405)733-7495

University of Central Oklahoma
SBDC
Bank One Building
615 N. Classen, 2nd Fl.
PO Box 1439
Oklahoma City, Oklahoma 73101-1439
Phone: (405)232-1968
Fax: (405)232-1967
Susan Urbach, Director
E-mail:
susan.urbach@oubbs.telecom.uok.nor.edu
Doris Kendrick, BDS

Carl Albert College
Small Business Development Center
1507 S. McKenna
Poteau, Oklahoma 74953
Phone: (918)647-4019
Fax: (918)647-1218
Dean Qualls, Dir.

Northeastern Oklahoma State
University
Small Business Development Center
Oklahoma Small Business Develop-
ment Center
Tahlequah, Oklahoma 74464
Phone: (918)458-0802
Fax: (918)458-2105
Danielle Coursey

Tulsa Satellite
Small Business Development Center
State Office Bldg.
440 S. Houston, Ste. 507
Tulsa, Oklahoma 74127
Phone: (918)581-2502
Fax: (918)581-2745
Jeff Horvath, Dir.

Southwestern Oklahoma State
University
Small Business Development Center
100 Campus Dr.
Weatherford, Oklahoma 73096
Phone: (405)774-1040
Fax: (405)774-7091
Chuck Felz, Dir.

Oregon

Linn-Benton Community College
Small Business Development Center
6500 SW. Pacific Blvd.
Albany, Oregon 97321
Phone: (541)917-4923
Fax: (541)917-4445
Dennis Sargent, Dir.

Southern Oregon State College/
Ashland SBDC
Regional Services Institute
Ashland, Oregon 97520
Phone: (541)482-5838
Fax: (541)482-1115
Liz Shelby, Dir.

Central Oregon Community College
Small Business Development Center
2600 NW College Way
Bend, Oregon 97701
Phone: (541)383-7290
Fax: (541)383-7503
Bob Newhart, Dir.

Southwestern Oregon Community
College
Small Business Development Center
340 Central St.
Coos Bay, Oregon 97420
Phone: (541)269-0123
Fax: (541)269-0323
Jon Richards, Dir.

Columbia Gorge Community College
Small Business Development Center
212 Washington
The Dalles, Oregon 97058
Phone: (541)298-3118
Fax: (541)298-3119
Bob Cole, Dir.

Lane Community College
Small Business Development Center
1059 Williamette St.
Eugene, Oregon 97401-3171
Phone: (541)726-2255
Fax: (541)686-0096
Jane Scheidecker, Dir.

Rogue Community College
Small Business Development Center
214 SW 4th St.

Grants Pass, Oregon 97526
Phone: (541)471-3515
Fax: (541)471-3589
Lee Merritt, Dir.

Mount Hood Community College
Small Business Development Center
323 NE Roberts St.
Gresham, Oregon 97030
Phone: (503)667-7658
Fax: (503)666-1140
Don King, Dir.

Oregon Institute of Technology
Small Business Development Center
3201 Campus Dr. South 314
Klamath Falls, Oregon 97601
Phone: (541)885-1760
Fax: (541)885-1855
Jamie Albert, Dir.

Eastern Oregon State College
Small Business Development Center
Regional Services Institute
1410 L Ave.
La Grande, Oregon 97850
Phone: (541)962-3391
Toll-free: (800)452-8639
Fax: (541)962-3668
Joni Woodwell, Dir.

Oregon Coast Community College
Small Business Development Center
4157 NW Hwy. 101, Ste. 123
PO Box 419
Lincoln City, Oregon 97367
Phone: (541)994-4166
Fax: (541)996-4958
Rose Seminary, Contact

Southern Oregon State College/
Medford
Small Business Development Center
Regional Service Institute
229 N. Bartlett
Medford, Oregon 97501
Phone: (541)772-3478
Fax: (541)776-2224
Liz Shelby, Dir.

Clackamas Community College
Small Business Development Center
7616 SE Harmony Rd.
Milwaukie, Oregon 97222

Phone: (503)656-4447
Fax: (503)652-0389
Jan Stennick, Dir.

Treasure Valley Community College
Small Business Development Center
88 SW 3rd Ave.
Ontario, Oregon 97914
Phone: (541)889-2617
Fax: (541)889-8331
Kathy Simko, Dir.

Blue Mountain Community College
Small Business Development Center
37 SE Dorion
Pendleton, Oregon 97801
Phone: (541)276-6233
Fax: (541)276-6819
Betty Udy, Contact

Portland Community College
Small Business International Trade
Program
121 SW Salmon St., Ste. 210
Portland, Oregon 97204
Phone: (503)274-7482
Fax: (503)228-6350
Tom Niland, Dir.

Portland Community College SBDC
123 NW 2nd Ave., Ste. 321
Portland, Oregon 97209
Phone: (503)414-2828
Fax: (503)294-0725
Robert Keyser, Dir.

Umpqua Community College
Small Business Development Center
744 SE Rose
Roseburg, Oregon 97470
Phone: (541)672-2535
Fax: (541)672-3679
Terry Swagerty, Dir.

Chemeketa Community College
Small Business Development Center
365 Ferry St. SE
Salem, Oregon 97301
Phone: (503)399-5181
Fax: (503)581-6017
Bobbie Clyde, Dir.

Clatsop Community College SBDC
1240 S. Holladay
Seaside, Oregon 97138

Phone: (503)738-3347
Fax: (503)738-7843
Kennetyh McCune, Dir.

Tillamook Bay Community College
Small Business Development Center
401 B Main St.
Tillamook, Oregon 97141
Phone: (503)842-2551
Fax: (503)842-2555
Mike Harris, Dir.

Pennsylvania

Lehigh University
Small Business Development Center
Ranch Business Ctr., No. 37
Bethlehem, Pennsylvania 18015
Phone: (610)758-3980
Fax: (610)758-5205
Dr. John Bonge, Dir.

Clarion University of Pennsylvania
Small Business Development Center
Dana Still Bldg., Rm. 102
Clarion, Pennsylvania 16214
Phone: (814)226-2060
Fax: (814)226-2636
Dr. Woodrow Yeaney, Dir.

Gannon University
Small Business Development Center
Carlisle Bldg., 3rd Fl.
Erie, Pennsylvania 16541
Phone: (814)871-7714
Fax: (814)871-7383
Ernie Post, Dir.

Kutztown University
Small Business Development Center
2986 N. 2nd St.
Harrisburg, Pennsylvania 17110
Phone: (717)720-4230
Fax: (717)233-3181
Katherine Wilson, Dir.

Indiana University of Pennsylvania
Robert Shaw Center
SBDC
Robert Shaw Bldg.
Indiana, Pennsylvania 15705
Phone: (412)357-7915
Fax: (412)357-4514
Mary T. McKinney, Dir.

St. Vincent College
Small Business Development Center
Alfred Hall, 4th Fl.
Latrobe, Pennsylvania 15650
Phone: (412)537-4572
Fax: (412)537-0919
Jack Fabean, Dir.

Bucknell University SBDC
126 Dana Engineering Bldg., 1st Fl.
Lewisburg, Pennsylvania 17837
Phone: (717)524-1249
Fax: (717)524-1768
Charles Coder, Dir.

St. Francis College SBDC
Business Resource Center
Loretto, Pennsylvania 15940
Phone: (814)472-3200
Fax: (814)472-3202
John A. Palko, Dir.

LaSalle University
Small Business Development Center
1900 W. Olney Ave.
Box 365
Philadelphia, Pennsylvania 19141
Phone: (215)951-1416
Fax: (215)951-1597
Andrew Lamas, Dir.

Temple University
Small Business Development Center
Rm. 6, Speakman Hall, 006-00
Philadelphia, Pennsylvania 19122
Phone: (215)204-7282
Fax: (215)204-4554
Geraldine Perkins, Dir.

University of Pennsylvania
SBDC
The Wharton School
409 Vance Hall
Philadelphia, Pennsylvania 19104
Phone: (215)898-4861
Fax: (215)898-1063
Clark Callahan, Director

Duquesne University
Small Business Development Center
Rockwell Hall, Rm. 10, Concourse
600 Forbes Ave.
Pittsburgh, Pennsylvania 15282
Phone: (412)434-6233

University of Pittsburgh
Small Business Development Center
The Joseph M. Katz Graduate School
of Business
208 Bellefield
315 S. Bellefield Ave.
Pittsburgh, Pennsylvania 15213
Phone: (412)648-1544
Fax: (412)648-1638
Ann Dugan, Dir.

University of Scranton
Small Business Development Center
St. Thomas Hall, Rm. 588
Scranton, Pennsylvania 18510
Phone: (717)941-7588
Fax: (717)941-4053
Elaine M. Tweedy, Dir.

West Chester University SBDC
319 Anderson Hall
West Chester, Pennsylvania 19383
Phone: (610)436-2162
Fax: (610)436-3170

Wilkes University
Small Business Development Center
Hollenback Hall
192 S. Franklin St.
Wilkes Barre, Pennsylvania 18766-0001
Phone: (717)831-4340
Toll-free: (800)572-4444
Fax: (717)824-2245
Kostas Mallios, Dir.

Puerto Rico

University of Puerto Rico at Humacao
Small Business Development Center
Box 10226, CUH Sta.
Humacao, Puerto Rico 00792
Phone: (809)850-2500
Fax: (809)850-2335

University of Puerto Rico SBDC
Box 5253 - College Station
Mayaguez, Puerto Rico 00681
Phone: (809)834-3590
Fax: (809)834-3790
Marian Diaz, Director

University of Puerto Rico at Ponce
Small Business Development Center
PO Box 7186

Ponce, Puerto Rico 00732
Phone: (809)841-2641
Fax: (809)844-0883
Elma Santigo, Dir.

University of Puerto Rico at Rio
Piedras
Small Business Development Center
PO Box 21417, UPR Sta.
Rio Piedras, Puerto Rico 00931
Phone: (809)763-5933
Fax: (809)763-5745
Carlos Perez, Dir.

Administration Central, U.P.R.
SBDC (Centro de Desarrolo de
Pequenas Empresas)
Officina Estatal
PO Box 364984
San Juan, Puerto Rico 00936-4984
Phone: (809)250-2072
Fax: (809)282-6882
Jorge Hernandez, State Director

Interamerican University
Small Business Development Center
PO Box 191293
San Juan, Puerto Rico 00919-1293
Phone: (809)765-2335
Fax: (809)756-6929

Rhode Island

University of Rhode Island SBDC
24 Woodward Hall
Kingston, Rhode Island 02881
Phone: (401)792-2451
Fax: (401)792-4017

Aquidneck Island Small Business
Development Center
26 Jacome Way
Middletown, Rhode Island 02840
Phone: (401)849-6900
Fax: (401)849-0815
Sam Carr, Contact

Galilee Resource Center SBDC
355 Great Island Road
PO Box 178
Narragansett, Rhode Island 02882
Phone: (401)783-2466
Fax: (401)783-2466
Sue Barker, Asst. State Dir.

Arthur T. Koph, Program Manager
Salve Regina University
East Bay SBDC
Miley Hall, Rm. 006
Newport, Rhode Island 02840
Phone: (401)849-6900
Fax: (401)847-5490
Sam Carr, Case Mgr.

SBDC (North Kingstown)
35 Belver Ave. Rm. 217
North Kingstown, Rhode Island
02852-7522
Phone: (401)294-1227
Fax: (401)294-6897

Bryant College
Small Business Development Center
7 Jackson Walkway
Providence, Rhode Island 02903
Phone: (401)831-1330
Fax: (401)274-5410
Erwin Robinson, Program Mgr.

Community College of Rhode Island
(Providence Campus)
Small Business Development Center
1 Hilton St.
Providence, Rhode Island 02905
Phone: (401)455-6042
Fax: (401)455-6047

Rhode Island/DOT
SBDC
Supportive Services Program
2 Capitol Hill, Rm. 106
Providence, Rhode Island 02903
Phone: (401)277-4576
Fax: (401)277-6168
O. J. Silas, Program Mgr.

Bryant College
Export Assistance Center
SBDC
1150 Douglas Pike
Smithfield, Rhode Island 02917
Phone: (401)232-6111
Fax: (401)232-6416
Douglas Jobling, Dir.

Rhode Island Small Business Devel-
opment Center
Export Assistance Ctr.
Bryant College

1150 Douglas Pke.
Smithfield, Rhode Island 02917
Phone: (401)232-6407
Fax: (401)232-6416
Raymond Fogarty, Dir.

Community College of Rhode Island
(Warwick)
Small Business Development Center
400 East Ave.
Warwick, Rhode Island 02886
Phone: (401)825-1000

South Carolina

Aiken Small Business Development
Center
171 University Pky., Ste. 100
Aiken, South Carolina 29801
Phone: (803)641-3646
Fax: (803)641-3647
Jackie Moore, Area Mgr.

University of South Carolina at
Beaufort
Small Business Development Center
800 Carteret St.
Beaufort, South Carolina 29902
Phone: (803)521-4143
Fax: (803)521-4142
Martin Goodman, Area Mgr.

University of South Carolina
Small Business Development Center
PO Box 20339
Charleston, South Carolina 29413-0339
Phone: (803)727-2020

Clemson University
Small Business Development Center
College of Commerce and Industry
425 Sirrine Hall
Box 341392
Clemson, South Carolina 29634-1392
Phone: (803)656-3227
Fax: (803)656-4869
Becky Hobart, Regional Dir.

USC Regional Small Business
Development Center
University of South Carolina
College of Business Administration
Columbia, South Carolina 29208
Phone: (803)777-5118

Fax: (803)777-4403
James Brazell, Dir.
E-mail:
brazell@univscvm.csd.scarolina.edu

Coastal Carolina College
Small Business Development Center
School of Business Administration
PO Box 1954
Conway, South Carolina 29526
Phone: (803)349-2170
Fax: (803)349-2455
Tim Lowery, Area Mgr.

Florence-Darlington Technical
College
Small Business Development Center
PO Box 100548
Florence, South Carolina 29501-0548
Phone: (803)661-8256
Fax: (803)661-8041
David Raines, Area Mgr.

Greenville Chamber of Commerce
Small Business Development Center
24 Cleveland St.
Greenville, South Carolina 29601
Phone: (803)271-4259
Fax: (803)282-8549

SBDC Manufacturing Field Office
53 E. Antrim Dr.
Greenville, South Carolina 29607
Phone: (803)271-3005

Upper Savannah Council of Government
Small Business Development Center
Exchange Building
222 Phoenix St., Ste. 200
SBDC Exchange Bldg.
PO Box 1366
Greenwood, South Carolina 29648
Phone: (803)941-8071
Fax: (803)941-8090
George Long, Area Mgr.

University of South Carolina at
Hilton Head SBDC
Kiawah Bldg., Ste. 300
10 Office Park Rd.
Hilton Head, South Carolina 29928
Phone: (803)785-3995
Fax: (803)777-0333
Jim DeMartin, Consultant

North Augusta Small Business
Development Center
Triangle Plz.
215-B Edgefield Rd.
North Augusta, South Carolina 29841
Phone: (803)442-3670
Fax: (803)641-3445

Charleston SBDC
5900 Core Dr., Ste. 104
North Charleston, South Carolina 29406
Phone: (803)740-6160
Fax: (803)740-1607
Merry Boone, Area Mrg.

South Carolina State College SBDC
School of Business Administration
300 College Ave.
Orangeburg, South Carolina 29117
Phone: (803)536-8445
Fax: (803)536-8066
John Gradson, Regional Dir.

Winthrop College SBDC
School of Business Administration
119 Thurman Bldg.
Rock Hill, South Carolina 29733
Phone: (803)323-2283
Fax: (803)323-4281
Nate Barber, Dir.

Spartanburg Chamber of Commerce
Small Business Development Center
105 Pine St.
PO Box 1636
Spartanburg, South Carolina 29304
Phone: (803)594-5080
Fax: (803)594-5055
John Keagle, Area Mgr.

South Dakota

Aberdeen Small Business Develop-
ment Center
226 Citizens Bldg.
Aberdeen, South Dakota 57401
Phone: (605)626-2252
Fax: (605)626-2667
Bryce Anderson, Dir.

Pierre Small Business Development
Center
105 S. Euclid, Ste. C
Pierre, South Dakota 57501

Phone: (605)773-5941
Fax: (605)773-5942
Greg Sunt, Dir.

Rapid City SBDC
444 N. Mount Rushmore Rd., Rm. 208
Rapid City, South Dakota 57701
Phone: (605)394-5311
Fax: (605)394-6140
Matthew Johnson, Dir.

Sioux Falls Region SBDC
200 N. Phillips, Rm. 302
Sioux Falls, South Dakota 57102
Phone: (605)367-5757
Fax: (605)367-5755
Wayne Flemmer, Dir.

Sioux Falls Small Business Development Center
200 N. Phillips, Ste. L103
Sioux Falls, South Dakota 57102
Phone: (605)330-6011
Fax: (605)330-6010
Nancy Straw, Contact

Univeristy of South Dakota
SBDC
414 E. Clark
Vermillion, South Dakota 57069
Phone: (605)367-5757
Fax: (605)677-5272
Jeffrey Heisinger, Director

Tennessee

Chattanooga State Technical Community College
SBDC
4501 Amnicola Hwy.
Chattanooga, Tennessee 37406-1097
Phone: (615)697-4410
Fax: (615)698-5653
Alan Artress

Southeast Tennessee Development District
Small Business Development Center
PO Box 4757
Chattanooga, Tennessee 37405
Phone: (615)266-5781
Fax: (615)267-7705
Vann Cunningham, Dir.

Austin Peay State University SBDC
College of Business
Clarksville, Tennessee 37044
Phone: (615)648-7674
Fax: (615)648-5985
John Volker, Dir.

Cleveland State Community College
Small Business Development Center
Adkisson Dr.
PO Box 3570
Cleveland, Tennessee 37320
Phone: (615)478-6247
Fax: (615)478-6251
Don Green, Dir.

SBDC (Columbia)
Memorial Bldg., Rm. 205
308 W. 7th St.
Columbia, Tennessee 38401
Phone: (615)388-5674
Fax: (615)388-5474
Richard Prince, Senior Specialist

Tennessee Technological Univ. SBDC
College of Business Administration
PO Box 5023
Cookeville, Tennessee 38505
Phone: (615)372-6634
Fax: (615)372-6249

Dyersburg State Community College
Small Business Development Center
1510 Lake Rd.
Dyersburg, Tennessee 38024
Phone: (901)286-3201
Fax: (901)286-3271
Bob Wylie

Four Lakes Regional Industrial
Development Authority SBDC
PO Box 63
Hartsville, Tennessee 37074-0063
Phone: (615)374-9521
Fax: (615)374-4608
Dorothy Vaden, SB Specialist

Jackson State Community College
Small Business Development Center
2046 N. Parkway St.
Jackson, Tennessee 38305
Phone: (901)424-5389
Fax: (901)425-2647
David L. Brown

Lambuth University
SBDC
705 Lambuth Blvd.
Jackson, Tennessee 38301
Phone: (901)425-3326
Fax: (901)425-3327
Phillip Ramsey, SB Specialist

East Tennessee State University
Small Business Development Center
College of Business
PO Box 70698
Johnson City, Tennessee 37614
Phone: (615)929-5630
Fax: (615)461-7080
Bob Justice, Dir.

East Tennessee State University
SBDC
Kingsport University Center
1501 University Blvd.
Kingsport, Tennessee 37660
Phone: (615)392-8017
Fax: (615)392-8017
Rob Lytle, Business Counselor

International Trade Center
SBDC
301 E. Church Ave.
Knoxville, Tennessee 37915
Phone: (615)637-4283
Fax: (615)523-2071
Richard Vogler, IT Specialist

Pellissippi State Technical Community College
Small Business Development Center
301 East Church Ave.
Knoxville, Tennessee 37915
Phone: (615)525-0277
Fax: (615)971-4439

University of Memphis
International Trade Center SBDC
Memphis, Tennessee 38152
Phone: (901)678-4174
Fax: (901)678-4072
Philip Johnson, Director

University of Memphis SBDC
Memphis, Tennessee 38152
Phone: (901)678-2500
Fax: (901)678-4072
Kenneth J. Burns, Dir.

University of Memphis
SBDC
320 S. Dudley St.
Memphis, Tennessee 38104-3206
Phone: (901)527-1041
Fax: (901)527-1047
Earnest Lacey, Director

Walters State Community College
Tennessee Small Business Development Center
500 S. Davy Crockett Pky.
Morristown, Tennessee 37813
Phone: (615)585-2675
Fax: (615)585-2679
Jack Tucker, Dir.
E-mail: jtucker@wscc.cc.tn.us

Middle Tennessee State University
Small Business Development Center
School of Business
PO Box 487
Murfreesboro, Tennessee 37132
Phone: (615)898-2745
Fax: (615)898-2681
Patrick Geho, Dir.

Tennessee State University
Small Business Development Center
College of Business
330 10th Ave. N.
Nashville, Tennessee 37203-3401
Phone: (615)963-7179
Fax: (615)963-7160
Billy E. Lowe, Dir.

Texas

Abilene Christian University
Small Business Development Center
College of Business Administration
648 E. Hwy. 80
Abilene, Texas 79699
Phone: (915)670-0300
Fax: (915)670-0311
Judy Wilhelm, Dir.

Sul Ross State University
Big Bend SBDC Satellite
PO Box C-35, Rm. 315
Alpine, Texas 79832
Phone: (915)837-8694
Fax: (915)837-8104
Michael Levine, Director

Alvin Community College
Small Business Development Center
3110 Mustang Rd.
Alvin, Texas 77511-4898
Phone: (713)388-4686
Fax: (713)388-4903
Gina Mattei, Dir.

West Texas State University
Small Business Development Center
T. Boone Pickens School of Business
1800 S. Washington, Ste. 209
Amarillo, Texas 79102
Phone: (806)372-5151
Fax: (806)372-5261

Trinity Valley Community College
Small Business Development Center
500 S. Prairieville
Athens, Texas 75751
Phone: (903)675-7403
Toll-free: (800)335-7232
Fax: (903)675-5199
Judy Loden, Dir.

Lower Colorado River Authority
Small Business Development Center
3701 Lake Austin Blvd.
PO Box 220
Austin, Texas 78741
Phone: (512)473-3510
Fax: (512)473-4094
Larry Lucero, Dir.

Lee College
Small Business Development Center
PO Box 818
Rundell Hall
Baytown, Texas 77522-0818
Phone: (713)425-6309
Fax: (713)425-6307
Kenneth Voytek, Contact

John Gray Institute/Lamar University
Small Business Development Center
855 Florida Ave.
Beaumont, Texas 77705
Phone: (409)880-2367
Fax: (409)880-2201
Roy Huckaby, Contact/Dir.

Bonham Satellite
Chamber of Commerce
SBDC

110 W. 1st
Bonham, Texas 75418
Phone: (903)583-4811
Fax: (903)583-6706
Darroll Martin, Coordinator

Bonham Small Business Development Center
Sam Rayburn Library
Bonham, Texas 75418
Blinn College
Small Business Development Center
902 College Ave.
Brenham, Texas 77833
Phone: (409)830-4137
Fax: (409)830-4135
Phillis Nelson, Dir.

Brazos Valley
SBDC
4001 E. 29th St., Ste. 175
Bryan, Texas 77802
Phone: (409)260-5222
Fax: (409)260-5208
Sam Harwell, Dir.

Bryan/College Station Chamber of Commerce
Small Business Development Center
PO Box 3695
Bryan, Texas 77805
Phone: (409)823-3034
Fax: (409)822-4818
Sam Harwell, Contact

American National Bank—Corpus Christi
Small Business Development Center
PO Box 6469
Corpus Christi, Texas 78466
R.J. Sandoval, Contact

Corpus Christi Chamber of Commerce
Small Business Development Center
1201 N. Shoreline
Corpus Christi, Texas 78403
Phone: (512)881-1888
Fax: (512)882-4256
Kathy Elliot, Dir.

Corsicana Small Business Development Center
120 N. 12th St.

Corsicana, Texas 75110
Phone: (903)874-0658
Toll-free: (800)320-7232
Fax: (903)874-4187
Leon Allard, Dir.

International Trade Center
SBDC
World Trade Center, Ste. 150
2050 Stemmons Fwy.
PO Box 58299
Dallas, Texas 75258
Phone: (214)747-1300
Toll-free: (800)337-7232
Fax: (214)748-5774
Beth Huddleston, Director

Bill J. Priest Institute for Economic
Development
North Texas-Dallas Small Business
Development Center
1402 Corinth St.
Dallas, Texas 75215
Phone: (214)860-5831
Toll-free: (800)350-7232
Fax: (214)860-5813
Elizabeth Klimback, Regional Dir.

Texas Center for Government
Contracting
Small Business Development Center
1402 Corinth
Dallas, Texas 75215
Phone: (214)565-5850
Fax: (214)565-5857
Al Sabado, Dir.

Grayson County College
Small Business Development Center
6101 Grayson Dr.
Denison, Texas 75020
Phone: (903)786-3551
Toll-free: (800)316-7232
Fax: (903)463-5284
Cynthia Flowers-Whitfield, Dir.

Denton Small Business Development
Center
PO Drawer P
Denton, Texas 76202
Phone: (817)380-1849
Fax: (817)382-0040
Carolyn Birkhead, Coordinator

Best Southwest SBDC
214 S, Main, Ste. 102A
Duncanville, Texas 75116
Phone: (214)709-5878
Toll-free: (800)317-7232
Fax: (214)709-6089
Herb Kamm, Dir.

DeSoto Small Business Development
Center
2145 Main, Ste. 101-D
Duncanville, Texas 75116
Phone: (214)709-5878
Toll-free: (800)717-7232

University of Texas—Pan American
Small Business Development Center
1201 W. University Dr.
Center for Entrepreneurship &
Economic Development
Edinburg, Texas 78539
Phone: (512)381-3361
Fax: (512)381-2322
Irene Sanchez-Casas, Contact
David Armstrong, Acting Dir.

El Paso Community College
Small Business Development Center
103 Montana Ave., Ste. 202
El Paso, Texas 79902
Phone: (915)534-3410
Fax: (915)534-3420
Rogue Segura, Contact/Dir.

Automation and Robotics Research
Institute SBDC
7300 Jack Newell Blvd., S.
Fort Worth, Texas 76118
Phone: (817)794-5900
Fax: (817)794-5952
Don Liles, Director

Tarrant County Junior College
Small Business Development Center
Mary Owen Center
1500 Houston St., Rm. 163
Fort Worth, Texas 76102
Phone: (817)244-7158
Fax: (817)244-0627
Truitt Leake, Dir.

Cooke County Community College
Small Business Development Center
1525 W. California

Gainesville, Texas 76240
Phone: (817)668-4220
Toll-free: (800)351-7232
Fax: (817)668-6049
Cathy Keeler, Dir.

Galveston College
Small Business Development Center
4015 Avenue Q
Galveston, Texas 77550
Phone: (409)740-7380
Fax: (409)740-7381
Joe Harper, Contact/Dir.

Western Bank and Trust Satellite
SBDC
PO Box 461545
Garland, Texas 75046
Phone: (214)860-5850
Fax: (214)860-5857
Al Salgado, Director

Grand Prairie Satellite
SBDC
Chamber of Commerce
900 Conover Dr.
Grand Prairie, Texas 75053
Phone: (214)860-5850
Fax: (214)860-5857
Al Salgado, Director

Hillsboro Small Business Develop-
ment Center
SOS Bldg.
PO Box 619
Hillsboro, Texas 76645
Phone: (817)582-2555
Fax: (817)582-7591

Houston International Trade Center
Small Business Development
Center
1100 Louisiana, Ste. 500
Houston, Texas 77002
Phone: (713)752-8404
Fax: (713)756-1500
Carlos Lopez, Dir.

Houston Small Business Develop-
ment Center
2700 W. W. Thorne Dr., Ste. A-127
Houston, Texas 77073
Phone: (713)443-5477
Fax: (713)443-5402

North Harris Montgomery CC District
Small Business Development Center
250 N. Sam Houston Pky.
Houston, Texas 77060
Phone: (713)591-9320
Fax: (713)591-3513
Ray Laughter, Contact

Texas Information Procurement
Service SBDC
1100 Louisiana, Ste. 500
Houston, Texas 77002
Phone: (713)752-8477
Toll-free: (800)252-7232
Fax: (713)756-1515
Jacqueline Taylor, Dir.

Texas International Trade Center
Small Business Development Center
1100 Louisiana, Ste. 500
Houston, Texas 77002
Luis Saldarriaga, Contact

Texas Product Development Center
Small Business Development Center
1100 Louisiana, Ste. 500
Houston, Texas 77002
Phone: (713)752-8440
Fax: (713)756-1515
Susan Macy, Contact

University of Houston SBDC
1100 Louisiana, Ste. 500
Houston, Texas 77002
Phone: (713)752-8400
Fax: (713)752-1500
Mike Young, Dir.

Sam Houston State University
Small Business Development Center
College of Business Administration
PO Box 2058
Huntsville, Texas 77341-2058
Phone: (409)294-3737
Fax: (409)294-3738
Bob Barragan, Contact/Dir.

Kingsville Chamber of Commerce
Small Business Development Center
635 E. King
Kingsville, Texas 78363
Phone: (512)595-5088
Fax: (512)592-0866
Gilbert Elizabeth, Contact

Brazosport College
Small Business Development Center
500 College Dr.
Lake Jackson, Texas 77566
Phone: (409)266-3380
Fax: (409)265-7208
Patricia Leyendecker, Dir.

Laredo Development Foundation
Small Business Development Center
Division of Business Administration
616 Leal St.
Laredo, Texas 78041
Phone: (210)722-0563
Fax: (210)722-6247
David Puig, Contact

Longview
SBDC
110 Triple Creek Dr., Ste. 70
Longview, Texas 75601
Phone: (903)757-5857
Toll-free: (800)338-7232
Fax: (903)753-7920
Brad Bunt, Dir.

Northwest Texas
Small Business Development Center
2579 S. Loop 289, Ste. 114
Lubbock, Texas 79423
Phone: (806)745-1637
Fax: (806)745-6207
Craig Bean, Reg. Dir.

Angelina Community College
Small Business Development Center
PO Box 1768
Lufkin, Texas 75902
Phone: (409)639-1887
Fax: (409)639-1887
Chuck Stemple, Dir.

Midlothian Satellite
SBDC
330 N. 8th St., Ste. 203
Midlothian, Texas 76065-0609
Phone: (214)775-4336
Fax: (214)775-4337

Northeast Texas Community College
Small Business Development Center
PO Box 1307
Mount Pleasant, Texas 75456
Phone: (903)572-1911

Toll-free: (800)357-7232
Fax: (903)572-0598
Bob Wall, Dir.

University of Texas—Permian Basin
Small Business Development Center
College of Management
4901 E. University
Odessa, Texas 79762
Phone: (915)552-2455
Fax: (915)552-2433
Karl Painter, Dir.

Paris Junior College
Small Business Development Center
2400 Clarksville St.
Paris, Texas 75460
Phone: (903)784-1802
Fax: (903)784-1801
Pat Bell, Dir.

Collin SBDC
4800 Preston Park Blvd., Ste. A126
Box 15
Plano, Texas 75093
Phone: (214)985-3770
Fax: (214)985-3775
Chris Jones, Dir.

Collin County Community College
Small Business Development Center
Piano Market Sq.
2000 E. Spring Creek Pky., No. 109
Plano, Texas 75074
Phone: (214)881-0506
Fax: (214)985-3775

Angelo State University
Small Business Development Center
2610 West Ave. N.
Campus Box 10910
San Angelo, Texas 76909
Phone: (915)942-2098
Fax: (915)942-2096
Patty Warrington, Dir.

South Texas Border Small Business
Development Center
University of Texas, San Antonio
1222 N. Main St., Ste. 450
San Antonio, Texas 78212
Phone: (210)558-2458
Fax: (210)558-2464
Judith Ingalls, Dir.

The University of Texas at San
Antonio
Regional Office/Technology Center
SBDC
UTSA Downtown
1222 N. Main Ave., Ste. 450
San Antonio, Texas 78212
Phone: (210)558-2450
Phone: (210)558-2464
Robert McKinley, Regional Dir.

University of Texas at San Antonio
South Texas Border Small Business
Development Center
1222 N. Main St., Ste. 450
San Antonio, Texas 78212
Phone: (210)558-2460
Fax: (210)558-2464
Morrison Woods, Dir.

UTSA International Small Business
Development Center
801 S. Bowie St.
San Antonio, Texas 78205
Phone: (210)227-2997
Fax: (210)222-9834
Sara Jackson, Dir.

Houston Community College System
Small Business Development Center
13600 Murphy Rd.
Stafford, Texas 77477
Phone: (713)499-4870
Fax: (713)499-8194
Ted Charlesworth, Acting Dir.

Tarleton State University
Small Business Development Center
School of Business Administration
Box T-0650
Stephenville, Texas 76402
Phone: (817)968-9330
Fax: (817)968-9329
Rusty Freed, Dir.

College of the Mainland
Small Business Development Center
8419 Emmett F. Lowry Expy.
Texas City, Texas 77591
Phone: (409)938-7578
Toll-free: (800)246-7232
Fax: (409)935-5186
Elizabeth Boudreau, Dir.

Tyler Junior College
Small Business Development Center
1530 South SW Loop 323, Ste. 100
Tyler, Texas 75701
Phone: (903)510-2975
Fax: (903)510-2978
Frank Viso, Dir.

Middle Rio Grande Development
Council
Small Business Development Center
209 N. Getty St.
Uvalde, Texas 78801
Phone: (210)278-2527
Fax: (210)278-2929
Mario Riojas, Dir.

University of Houston—Victoria
Small Business Development Center
700 Main Center, Ste. 102
Victoria, Texas 77901
Phone: (512)575-8944
Fax: (512)575-8852
Carol Parks, Contact/Dir.

McLennan Community College SBDC
4601 N. 19th, Ste. A-15
Waco, Texas 76708
Phone: (817)750-3600
Toll-free: (800)349-7232
Fax: (817)756-3620
Lu Billings, Dir.

Wharton County Junior College SBDC
Administration Bldg., Rm. 102
911 Boling Hwy.
Wharton, Texas 77488-0080
Phone: (409)532-0604
Fax: (409)532-2410
Lynn Polson, Dir.

Midwestern State University SBDC
Division of Business Administration
3400 Taft Blvd.
Wichita Falls, Texas 76308
Phone: (817)689-4373
Fax: (817)689-4374
Tim Thomas, Dir.

Utah

Southern Utah University
Small Business Development Center
351 W. Center

Cedar City, Utah 84720
Phone: (801)586-5400
Fax: (801)586-5493
Greg Powell, Contact

Snow College
Small Business Development Center
345 West 1st North
Ephraim, Utah 84627
Phone: (801)283-4021
Fax: (801)283-6913
Russell Johnson, Dir.

Utah State University
Small Business Development Center
E. Campus Bldg., Rm. 24
Logan, Utah 84322-8330
Phone: (801)797-2277
Fax: (801)797-3317
Franklin C. Prante, Contact

Weber State University
Small Business Development Center
College of Business and Economics
Ogden, Utah 84408-3806
Phone: (801)626-7232
Fax: (801)626-7423
Bruce Davis, Contact

Utah Valley State College
Utah Small Business Development
Center
800 West 1200 South
Orem, Utah 84058
Phone: (801)222-8230
Fax: (801)225-1229
Michael Finnerty, Contact

College of Eastern Utah SBDC
451 East 400 North
Price, Utah 84501
Phone: (801)637-1995
Fax: (801)637-4102
Patrick Glenn, Dir.

Brigham Young University
Small Business Development Center
Graduate School of Management
790 Tanner Bldg.
Provo, Utah 84602
Phone: (801)378-4636

Utah Basin Applied Technology
Center
Small Business Development Center

1100 E. Lagoon, 124-5
Roosevelt, Utah 84066
Phone: (801)722-4523
Fax: (800))722-5804
Scott Bigler, Contact

Dixie College
Small Business Development Center
225 South 700 East
St. George, Utah 84770
Phone: (801)673-4811
Fax: (801)673-8552
Keldon Bauer, Director

University of Utah
SBDC
102 W. 500 S., No. 315
Salt Lake City, Utah 84101
Phone: (801)581-7905
Fax: (801)581-7814
Jeff Syphus, Director

Vermont

Brattleboro Development Credit Corp.
SBDC
PO Box 1177
Brattleboro, Vermont 05301-1177
Phone: (802)257-7731
Fax: (802)258-3886
William McGrath, Exec. V. P.

Northwestern Vermont Small Business Development Center
Greater Burlington Industrial Corp
PO Box 786
Burlington, Vermont 05402-0786
Phone: (802)862-5726
Fax: (802)860-1899
William A. Farr, Contact

Roger Kilburn
Addison County Economic Development Corp.
SBDC
2 Court St.
Middlebury, Vermont 05753
Phone: (802)388-7953
Fax: (802)388-8066
William Kenerson, Exec. Director

Central Vermont Economic Development Center
SBDC

PO Box 1439
Montpelier, Vermont 05601-1439
Phone: (802)223-4654
Fax: (802)223-4655
Donald Rowan, Exec. Director

Bennington County Industrial Corp.
SBDC
PO Box 357
North Bennington, Vermont 05257-0357
Phone: (802)442-8975
Fax: (802)442-1101
Chris Hunsinger, Exec. Director

Lake Champlain Island Chamber of Commerce SBDC
PO Box 213
North Hero, Vermont 05474-0213
Phone: (802)372-5683
Fax: (802)372-6104
Barbara Mooney, Exec. Dir.

Vermont Technical College
Small Business Development Center
PO Box 422
Randolph, Vermont 05060
Phone: (802)728-9101
Fax: (802)728-3026
Donald L. Kelpinski, Contact

Southwestern Vermont Small Business Development Center
Rutland Industrial Development Corp.
256 North Main Street
Rutland, Vermont 05701-0039
Phone: (802)773-9147
Fax: (802)773-2772
James B. Stewart, Contact

Franklin County Industrial Development Corporation SBDC
PO Box 1099
St. Albans, Vermont 05478-1099
Phone: (802)524-2194
Fax: (802)527-5258
Timothy J. Soule, Executive Director

Northeastern Vermont Small Business Development Center
PO Box 630
St. Johnsbury, Vermont 05819-0640
Phone: (802)748-1014
Fax: (802)748-1223
Charles E. Carter, Exec. Dir.

Southeastern Vermont Small Business Development Center
Springfield Development Corp.
PO Box 58
Springfield, Vermont 05156-0058
Phone: (802)885-2071
Fax: (802)885-3027
Al Moulton, Contact

Green Mountain Economic Development Corporation
SBDC
PO Box 246
White River Jct., Vermont 05001-0246
Phone: (802)295-3710
Fax: (802)295-3779
Lenne Quillen-Blume, SBDC Specialist
Peter Markou, Executive Director

Virgin Islands

University of the Virgin Islands (Charlotte Amalie)
Small Business Development Center
8000 Nisky Center, Ste. 202
Charlotte Amalie, Virgin Islands 00802
Phone: (809)776-3206
Fax: (809)775-3756
Ian Hodge

University of the Virgin Islands
Small Business Development Center
Sunshine Mall
No.1 Estate Cane, Ste. 104
Frederiksted, Virgin Islands 00840
Phone: (809)778-8270
Fax: (809)778-7629
Chester Williams, State Dir.

Fredriksted Small Business Revolving Loan Fund
Small Business Development Agency
Box 6400
St. Thomas, Virgin Islands 00804
Phone: (809)774-8784
Fax: (809)774-4390

Virgin Islands Small Business Development Agency
Box 6400
St. Thomas, Virgin Islands 00804
Phone: (809)774-8784
Fax: (809)774-4390

Virginia

Virginia Highlands SBDC
PO Box 828
Abingdon, Virginia 24212
Phone: (703)676-5615
Fax: (703)628-7576
Jim Tilley, Director

Arlington Small Business Development Center
George Mason University, Arlington Campus
3401 N. Fairfax Dr.
Arlington, Virginia 22201
Phone: (703)993-8128
Fax: (703)993-8130
Paul Hall, Contact

Eastern Shore Office
SBDC
PO Box 395
Belle Haven, Virginia 23306
Phone: (804)442-7181

Mount Empire Community College
Southwest Small Business Development Center
Drawer 700, Rte. 23, S.
Big Stone Gap, Virginia 24219
Phone: (703)523-6529
Fax: (703)523-8139
Tim Blankenbeder, Contact

Western Virginia Small Business Development Center Consortium
New River Valley Small Business Development Center
234 Donaldson Brown Center
Blacksburg, Virginia 24061-0548
Phone: (703)231-4004
Fax: (703)231-8850
David Shanks, Contact

Western Virginia Small Business Development Center Consortium
VPI & SU
Economic Development Assistance Center
404 Clay St.
Blacksburg, Virginia 24061-0539
Phone: (703)231-5278
Phone: (703)231-8850
Michael Hensley, Contact

Central Virginia Small Business Development Center
918 Emmet St., Ste. 200
Charlottesville, Virginia 22903-4878
Phone: (804)295-8198
Fax: (804)295-7066
Charles Kulp, Contact

Northern Virginia Small Business Development Center
George Mason University
4031 Univ. Drive, Ste. 200
Fairfax, Virginia 22030
Phone: (703)993-2131
Phone: (703)993-2130
Fax: (703)993-2126
Michael Kehoe

Longwood College (Farmville)
Small Business Development Center
515 Main St.
Farmville, Virginia 23901
Phone: (804)395-2086
Fax: (804)395-2539
Gerald L. Hughes, Contact

Rappahannock Region Small Business Development Center
1301 College Ave.
Seacobeck Hall
Fredericksburg, Virginia 22401
Phone: (703)899-4076
Fax: (703)899-4373
Jeffrey R. Sneddon, Contact

Small Business Development Center of Hampton Roads, Inc. (Hampton)
Thomas Nelson Community College
PO Box 9407
Hampton, Virginia 23670
Phone: (804)825-2957
Fax: (804)825-2960

James Madison University SBDC
JMU College of Business
Zane Showker Hall, Rm. 523
Harrisonburg, Virginia 22807
Phone: (703)568-3227
Fax: (703)568-3299
Karen Wigginton, Contact

Lynchburg Regional Small Business Development Center
147 Mill Ridge Rd.

Lynchburg, Virginia 24502-4341
Phone: (804)582-6170
Toll-free: (800)876-7232
Fax: (804)582-6106
Barry Lyons, Contact

Dr. William E. S. Flory Small Business Development Center
10311 Sudley Manor Dr.
Manassas, Virginia 22110
Phone: (703)335-2500
Phone: (703)335-1700
Laura Decker, Contact

Lord Fairfax Community College
SBDC
PO Box 47
Skirmisher Ln.
Middletown, Virginia 22645
Phone: (703)869-6649
Fax: (703)868-7002
Robert Crosen, Director

Small Business Development Center of Hampton Roads, Inc. (Norfolk)
420 Bank St.
PO Box 327
Norfolk, Virginia 23501
Phone: (804)825-2957
Fax: (804)825-3552
William J. Holloran Jr., Contact

New River Valley SBDC
New River Valley Planning District Commission Office
1612 Wadsworth St.
PO Box 3726
Radford, Virginia 24143
Phone: (703)731-9546
Fax: (703)831-6093

Southwest Virginia Community College
Southwest Small Business Development Center
PO Box SVCC
Richlands, Virginia 24641
Phone: (703)964-7345
Fax: (703)964-5788
R. Victor Brungart, Contact

Capital Area Small Business Development Center
403 E. Grace St.

Richmond, Virginia 23219
Toll-free: (800)646-SBDC
Fax: (804)648-7849
Taylor Cousins, Contact

Micro Business Program
SBDC
403 E. Grace St.
Richmond, Virginia 23219
Phone: (804)648-7113
Fax: (804)648-7849
Larry Roberts, Mgr.

Virginia Small Business Development Center
1021 E. Cary St., 11th Fl.
Richmond, Virginia 23219

Blue Ridge Small Business Development Center
Western Virginia SBDC Consortium
310 1st St., SW Mezzanine
Roanoke, Virginia 24011
Phone: (703)933-0717
Fax: (703)983-0723
John Jennings, Contact

Longwood
Small Business Development Center
South Boston Branch
515 Broad St.
PO Box 1116
South Boston, Virginia 24592
Phone: (804)575-0444
Vincent Decker, Bus. Analyst

South Boston SBDC
515 Broad St.
PO Box 1116
South Boston, Virginia 24592
Phone: (804)575-0444
Fax: (804)572-4087

Loudoun County Small Business Development Center
21515 Ridge Top Cir., Ste. 220
Sterling, Virginia 20166
Phone: (703)430-7222
Fax: (703)430-9562
Joseph Messina, Dir.

Warsaw Small Business Development Center
106 W. Richmond Rd.
PO Box 490

Warsaw, Virginia 22572
Phone: (804)333-0286
Fax: (804)333-0187
John Clickener, Dir.

Wytheville Small Business Development Center
Wytheville Community College
1000 E. Main St.
Wytheville, Virginia 24382
Phone: (703)223-4798
Toll-free: (800)468-1195
Fax: (703)223-4850
Rob Edwards, Contact

Washington

Grays Harbor College SBDC
1602 Edward P. Smith Dr.
Aberdeen, Washington 98520
Phone: (206)538-4021

Bellevue Small Business Development Center
Bellevue Community College
3000 Landerholm Circle SE
Bellevue, Washington 98007-6484
Phone: (206)643-2888
Fax: (206)649-3113
Bill Huenefeld, Contact

Western Washington University
Small Business Development Center
308 Parks Hall
Bellingham, Washington 98225-9073
Phone: (360)650-3899
Fax: (360)650-4844
Lynn Trzynka, Contact

Whatcom Community College SBDC
237 W. Kellogg Rd.
Bellingham, Washington 98226
Phone: (206)676-2170

Centralia Community College
Small Business Development Center
600 W. Locust St.
Centralia, Washington 98531
Phone: (206)736-9391
Fax: (206)753-3404
Don Hayes, Contact

Washington Small Business Development Center (Colville)
347 W. 2nd, Ste. A

Colville, Washington 99114
Phone: (509)684-4571
Fax: (509)684-4788

Columbia Basin College—TRIDEC
Small Business Development Center
901 N. Colorado
Kennewick, Washington 99336
Phone: (509)735-6222
Fax: (509)735-6609
Glynn Lamberson, Contact

Edmonds Community College
Small Business Development Center
2000 68th Ave. W
Lynnwood, Washington 98036
Phone: (206)640-1435
Fax: (206)640-1532
Jack Wicks, Contact

Big Bend Community College
Small Business Development Center
7662 Chanute St., Bldg. 1500
Moses Lake, Washington 98837-3299
Phone: (509)762-6289
Fax: (509)762-6329
Ed Baroch, Contact

Skagit Valley College
Small Business Development Center
2405 College Way
Mount Vernon, Washington 98273
Phone: (360)428-1282
Fax: (360)386-6116
Peter Stroosma, Contact

Okanogan County Council for Economic Development (OCCED)
SBDC
Box 741
Okanogan, Washington 98840
Phone: (509)826-5107
Fax: (509)826-1812
Ron Neilsen

DTED, Business Assistance Center
SBDC
PO Box 42516
Olympia, Washington 98504-2516
Phone: (206)586-4854

Washington State University (Olympia)
Small Business Development Center
721 Columbia St. SW
Olympia, Washington 98501

Phone: (360)753-5616
Fax: (360)586-5493
Douglas Hammel, Contact

Wenatchee Valley College
Small Business Development Center
PO Box 741
Omak, Washington 98841
Phone: (509)826-5107
Fax: (509)826-1812

Port Angeles
SBDC
PO Box 1085
Port Angeles, Washington 98362
Phone: (206)457-7793
Fax: (206)452-9618

Washington State University (Pullman)
Small Business Development Center
Kruegle Hall, Ste. 135
Pullman, Washington 99164-4727
Phone: (509)335-1576
Fax: (509)335-0949
Lyle M. Anderson, Contact

Duwamish Industrial Education
Center
Small Business Development Center
6770 E. Marginal Way S
Seattle, Washington 98108-1499
Phone: (206)764-5375
Ruth Ann Halford, Contact

International Trade Institute
North Seattle Community College
Small Business Development Center
9600 College Way N
Seattle, Washington 98103-3599
Phone: (206)527-3733
Fax: (206)527-3734
Ann Tamura, Contact

South Seattle Community College
Community College District 6
SBDC
6000 16th Ave. SW
Seattle, Washington 98108
Phone: (206)764-5375
Fax: (206)764-5838

South Seattle Community College
SBDC
Duwamish Industrial Educational
Center

6770 E. Marginal Way S.
Seattle, Washington 98108-3405
Phone: (206)764-5375
Fax: (206)764-5838
Ruth Ann Halford, BDS

Washington Management Advisory
Services SBDC
2401 4th Ave., 3rd Fl.
Seattle, Washington 98121-1436
Conrad Rosing, Contact

Washington Small Business Development Center (Seattle)
180 Nickerson, Ste. 207
Seattle, Washington 98109
Phone: (206)464-5450
Fax: (206)464-6357
Bill Jacobs, Contact

Washington State University (Spokane)
Small Business Development Center
665 North Riverpoint Blvd.
Spokane, Washington 99204-0399
Phone: (509)358-2051
Fax: (509)358-2059
Terry Chambers, Contact

Pierce College SBDC
9401 Farwest Dr. SW
Tacoma, Washington 98498
Phone: (206)964-6500
Fax: (206)964-6746

Washington Small Business Development Center (Tacoma)
950 Pacific Ave., Ste. 300
PO Box 1933
Tacoma, Washington 98401-1933
Phone: (206)272-7232
Fax: (206)597-7305
Neil Delisanti, Contact

Columbia River Economic Development Council
Small Business Development Center
100 E. Columbia Way
Vancouver, Washington 98660-3156
Phone: (206)737-2021
Fax: (206)696-6431
Dennis Hanslits, Contact

Columbia River Economic Development Council
SBDC

100 E. Columbia Way
Vancouver, Washington 98660-3156
Phone: (360)693-2555
Fax: (360)694-9927
Janet Harte, BDS

Port of Walla Walla SBDC
500 Tausick Way
Walla Walla, Washington 99362
Phone: (509)527-4681
Fax: (509)525-3101
Rich Monacelli, BDS

Wenatchee Small Business Development Center
327 East Penny Rd.
Industrial Building No. 2, Ste. D.
Wenatchee, Washington 98801
Phone: (509)662-8016
Fax: (509)663-0455
Charles DeJong, Contact

Yakima Valley College
Small Business Development Center
PO Box 1647
Yakima, Washington 98907
Phone: (509)454-3608
Fax: (509)454-4155
Corey Hansen, Contact

West Virginia

College of West Virginia
SBDC
PO Box AG
Beckley, West Virginia 25802
Phone: (304)255-4022
Fax: (304)255-4022
Ken Peters, Program Manager

Charleston Subcenter
Governor's Office of Community and
Industrial Development SBDC
950 Kanawha Blvd.
Charleston, West Virginia 25301
Phone: (304)558-2960
Fax: (304)558-0127
Wanda Chenoweth, Program Mgr.

West Virginia Small Development
Center
950 Kanawha Blvd. East
E. Capitol Complex
Charleston, West Virginia 25301

Phone: (304)558-2960
Fax: (304)348-0127
Hazel Kroesser, Contact/State Dir.

Elkins Satellite
SBDC
10 Eleventh St., Ste. 1
Elkins, West Virginia 26241
Phone: (304)637-7205
Fax: (304)637-4902
James Martin, Business Analyst

Fairmont State College
SBDC
Fairmont, West Virginia 26554
Phone: (304)367-4125
Fax: (304)366-4870
Dale Bradley, Program Manager

Fairmont State College
Small Business Development Center
Locust Ave.
Fairmont, West Virginia 26554
Phone: (304)367-4125
Fax: (304)366-4870

Marshall University SBDC
1050 4th Ave.
Huntington, West Virginia 25755-2126
Phone: (304)696-6789
Fax: (304)696-6277
Edna McClain, Contact

West Virginia Institute of Technology
Small Business Development Center
Engineering Bldg., Rm. 102
Montgomery, West Virginia 25136
Phone: (304)442-5501
Fax: (304)442-3307
James Epling, Program Mgr.

West Virginia University SBDC
PO Box 6025
Morgantown, West Virginia 26506-6025
Phone: (304)293-5839
Fax: (304)293-7061
Stan Kloc, Program Mgr.

West Virginia University
(Parkersburg) SBDC
Rte. 5, Box 167-A
Parkersburg, West Virginia 26101-9577
Phone: (304)424-8277
Fax: (304)424-8315
Greg Hill, Program Mgr.

Shepherd College SBDC
120 N. Princess St.
Shepherdstown, West Virginia 25443
Phone: (304)876-5261
Toll-free: (800)344-5231
Fax: (304)876-5117
Fred Baer, Program Mgr.

West Virginia Northern Community
College SBDC
1701 Market St.
College Sq.
Wheeling, West Virginia 26003
Phone: (304)233-5900
Fax: (304)232-9065
Ed Huttenhower, Program Mgr.

West Virginia Northern Community
College SBDC
College Sq.
Wheeling, West Virginia 26003
Phone: (304)233-5900
Fax: (304)232-9065
Ed Huttenhower, Program Manager

Wisconsin

University of Wisconsin—Eau Claire
Small Business Development Center
PO Box 4004
Eau Claire, Wisconsin 54702
Phone: (715)836-5811
Fax: (715)836-5263
Fred Waedt, Dir.

University of Wisconsin—Green Bay
Small Business Development Center
Wood Hall, Ste. 460
Green Bay, Wisconsin 54301
Phone: (414)465-2089
Fax: (414)465-2660
Jim Holly, Contact

University of Wisconsin—Parkside
Small Business Development Center
284, Tallent Hall
Kenosha, Wisconsin 53141-2000
Phone: (414)595-2189
Fax: (414)595-2513
Patricia Deutsch, Contact

University of Wisconsin—La Crosse
Small Business Development Center
120 N. Hall

La Crosse, Wisconsin 54601
Phone: (608)785-8782
Fax: (608)785-6919
Jan Gallagher, Dir.

University of Wisconsin—Madison
Small Business Development Center
975 University Ave., Rm. 3260
Grainger Hall
Madison, Wisconsin 53706
Phone: (608)263-2221
Fax: (608)263-0818
Joan Gillman, Contact

University of Wisconsin—Milwaukee
Small Business Development Center
161 W. Wisconsin Ave., Ste. 600
Milwaukee, Wisconsin 53203
Phone: (414)227-3240
Fax: (414)227-3142
Sara Murray, Dir.

University of Wisconsin—Oshkosh
Small Business Development Center
157 Clow Faculty Bldg., 800 Algoma
Blvd.
Oshkosh, Wisconsin 54901
Phone: (414)424-1453
Fax: (414)424-7413
John Mozingo, Contact

University of Wisconsin—Stevens
Point SBDC
Lower Level Main Bldg.
Stevens Point, Wisconsin 54481
Phone: (715)346-2004
Fax: (715)346-4045
Mark Stover, Contact

University of Wisconsin—Superior
Small Business Development Center
29 Sundquist Hall
Superior, Wisconsin 54880
Phone: (715)394-8351
Fax: (715)394-8454
Neil Hensrud, Dir.

University of Wisconsin—Whitewater
Small Business Development Center
Carlson Bldg., No. 2000
Whitewater, Wisconsin 53190
Phone: (414)472-3217
Fax: (414)472-4863
Carla Lenk, Contact

Wisconsin Innovation Service Center
SBDC
University of Wisconsin at
Whitewater
402 McCutchan Hall
Whitewater, Wisconsin 53190
Phone: (414)472-1365
Fax: (414)472-1600
Debra Malewicki, Director

Wisconsin Technology Access Center
SBDC
University of Wisconsin at
Whitewater
416 McCutchen HaLL
Whitewater, Wisconsin 53190
Phone: (414)472-1365
Fax: (414)472-1600
Debra Malewicki, Director
E-mail: malewicd@uwwvax.uww.edu

Wyoming

Casper Small Business Development
Center
111 W. 2nd St., Ste. 502
Casper, Wyoming 82601
Phone: (307)234-6683
Toll-free: (800)348-5207
Fax: (307)577-7014
Leonard Holler, Dir.

Laramie County Enterprise Center
1400 E. College Dr.
Cheyenne, Wyoming 82007
Phone: (307)632-6141
Toll-free: (800)348-5208
Fax: (307)632-6061

Eastern Wyoming Community College
Small Business Development Center
Douglas Branch
203 S. 6th St.
Douglas, Wyoming 82633
Phone: (307)358-5622
Fax: (307)358-5625

Northern Wyoming Community
College District
Business and Industry Center
1001 Plaza, Ste. 110
Gillette, Wyoming 82716
Phone: (307)686-0297
Fax: (307)682-7927

State Office
Wyoming Small Business Develop-
ment Center
University of Wyoming
PO Box 3622
Laramie, Wyoming 82071-3275
Phone: (307)766-3505
Toll-free: (800)348-5194
Fax: (307)766-3406
Drane Wolverton, State Dir.

Northwest Community College
Small Business Development Center
Northwest College
John Dewitt Student Center
Powell, Wyoming 82435
Phone: (307)754-6067
Toll-free: (800)348-5203
Fax: (307)754-6069
Dwane Heintz, Dir.

Rock Springs Small Business
Development Center
PO Box 1168
Rock Springs, Wyoming 82902
Phone: (307)352-6894
Toll-free: (800)348-5205
Fax: (307)352-6876

SERVICE CORPS OF RETIRED EXECUTIVES (SCORE) OFFICES

*This section contains a listing of all
SCORE offices organized alphabetically by
state/U.S. territory name, then by city, then
by agency name.*

Alabama

SCORE Office (Anniston)
c/o Calhoun County Chamber of
Commerce
PO Box 1087
Anniston, Alabama 36202
Phone: (205)237-3536

SCORE Office (North Alabama)
1601 11th Ave. S
Birmingham, Alabama 35294-4552
Phone: (205)934-6868

SCORE Office (Fairhope)
c/o Fairhope Chamber of Commerce
327 Fairhope Ave.
Fairhope, Alabama 36532
Phone: (334)928-8799

SCORE Office (Florence)
104 S. Pine St.
Florence, Alabama 35630
Phone: (205)764-4661
Fax: (205)766-9017

SCORE Office (Foley)
c/o Foley Chamber of Commerce
PO Box 1117
Foley, Alabama 36536
Phone: (334)943-3291
Fax: (334)943-6810

SCORE Office (Mobile)
c/o Mobile Area Chamber of Com-
merce
PO Box 2187
Mobile, Alabama 36652
Phone: (334)433-6951

SCORE Office (Alabama Capitol
City)
c/o Montgomery Area Chamber of
Commerce
41 Commerce St.
PO Box 79
Montgomery, Alabama 36101-1114
Phone: (334)240-9295

SCORE Office (Tuscaloosa)
2200 University Blvd.
PO Box 020410
Tuscaloosa, Alabama 35402
Phone: (205)758-7588

Alaska

SCORE Office (Anchorage)
c/o U.S. Small Business Administration
222 W. 8th Ave., No. 67
Anchorage, Alaska 99513-7559
Phone: (907)271-4022

Arizona

SCORE Office (Casa Grande)
Chamber of Commerce
575 N. Marshall
Casa Grande, Arizona 85222
Phone: (520)836-2125
Toll-free: (800)916-1515
Fax: (520)836-3623

SCORE Office (Cottonwood)
1010 S. Main St.
Cottonwood, Arizona 86326
Phone: (520)634-7593
Fax: (520)634-7594

SCORE Office (Flagstaff)
1 E. Rte. 66
Flagstaff, Arizona 86001
Phone: (520)556-7333

SCORE Office (Glendale)
7105 N. 59th Ave.
Glendale, Arizona 85311
Phone: (602)937-4754
Toll-free: (800)ID-SUNNY
Fax: (602)937-3333

SCORE Office (Green Valley)
W. Continental Rd.
PO Box 270
Green Valley, Arizona 85614
Phone: (602)625-7575
Toll-free: (800)858-5872
Fax: (602)648-6154

SCORE Office (Holbrook)
100 E. Arizona St.
Holbrook, Arizona 86025
Phone: (520)524-6558
Toll-free: (800)524-2459
Fax: (602)524-1719

SCORE Office (Kingman)
c/o Bill Murie
1070 Palo Verde
Kingman, Arizona 86401
Phone: (520)753-6106

SCORE Office (Lake Havasu)
Mohave Community College
1977 W. Acoma Blvd.
Lake Havasu City, Arizona 86403
Phone: (520)855-7812

SCORE Office (Pinetop)
592 W. White Mountain Blvd.
Lakeside, Arizona 85929
Phone: (602)367-4290

SCORE Office (East Valley)
Federal Bldg., Rm. 104
26 N. MacDonald St.
Mesa, Arizona 85201
Phone: (602)379-3100

SCORE Office (Payson)
PO Box 1380
Payson, Arizona 85547
Phone: (520)474-4515
Toll-free: (800)6-PAYSON
Fax: (520)474-8812

SCORE Office (Phoenix)
2828 N. Central Ave., No. 800
Phoenix, Arizona 85004
Phone: (602)640-2329

SCORE Office (Northern Arizona)
Post Office Bldg., Ste. 307
101 W. Goodwin St.
Prescott, Arizona 86303
Phone: (520)778-7438

SCORE Office (St. Johns)
PO Box 178
St. Johns, Arizona 85936
Phone: (520)337-2000

SCORE Office (Sedona)
Forest & 89th Ave.
PO Box 478
Sedona, Arizona 86339
Phone: (520)282-7722

SCORE Office (Show Low)
PO Box 1083
Show Low, Arizona 85901
Phone: (520)537-2326
Fax: (520)537-2326

SCORE Office (Snowflake)
PO Box 776
Snowflake, Arizona 85937
Phone: (520)536-4331

SCORE Office (Springerville)
PO Box 31
Springerville, Arizona 85938
Phone: (520)333-2123
Fax: (520)333-5690

SCORE Office (Tucson)
c/o Tucson Art Council
240 N. Stone
Tucson, Arizona 85701
Phone: (520)884-9602

Arkansas

SCORE Office (South Central)
PO Box 1271
El Dorado, Arkansas 71731
Phone: (501)863-6113

SCORE Office (Ozark)
c/o Margaret B. Parrish
1141 Eastwood Dr.
Fayetteville, Arkansas 72701
Phone: (501)442-7619

SCORE Office (Northwest Arkansas)
Glenn Haven Dr., No. 4
Fort Smith, Arkansas 72901
Phone: (501)783-3556

SCORE Office (Garland County)
330 Kleinshore, No. 32
Hot Springs Village, Arkansas 71913
Phone: (501)922-0020

SCORE Office (Little Rock)
U.S. Small Business Administration
2120 Riverfront Dr., Rm. 100
Little Rock, Arkansas 72202-1747
Phone: (501)324-5893

SCORE Office (Southeast Arkansas)
PO Box 6866
Pine Bluff, Arkansas 71611
Phone: (501)535-7189

California

SCORE Office (Agoura)
5935 Kanan Rd.
Agoura Hills, California 91301
Phone: (818)889-3150
Fax: (818)889-3366

SCORE Office (Angels Camp)
1211 S. Main St.
Box 637
Angels Camp, California 95222
Phone: (209)736-0049
Toll-free: (800)225-3764
Fax: (209)736-9124

SCORE Office (Arroyo Grande)
800 W. Branch, Ste. A
Arroyo Grande, California 93420
Phone: (805)489-1488
Fax: (805)489-2239

SCORE Office (Atascadero)
6550 El Camino Real
Atascadero, California 93422
Phone: (805)466-2044
Fax: (805)466-9218

SCORE Office (Golden Empire)
1033 Truxton Ave.
PO Box 1947
Bakersfield, California 93301
Phone: (805)327-4421

SCORE Office (Kernville)
c/o Kernville Chamber of Commerce
1330 22nd St., Ste. B
Bakersfield, California 93301
Phone: (805)322-5849
Phone: (805)327-4421

SCORE Office (Bellflower)
9729 E. Flower St.
Bellflower, California 90706
Phone: (310)867-1744
Fax: (310)866-7545

SCORE Office (Brawley)
204 S. Empirial
Brawley, California 92227
Phone: (619)344-3160
Fax: (619)344-7611

SCORE Office (Burbank)
200 W. Magnolia Blvd.
Burbank, California 91502
Phone: (818)846-3111
Fax: (818)846-0109

SCORE Office (Calexico)
PO Box 948
Calexico, California 92231
Phone: (619)357-1166
Fax: (619)357-9043

SCORE Office (California City)
c/o California City Chamber of
Commerce
8048 California City Blvd.
PO Box 8001
California City, California 93504
Phone: (619)373-8676

SCORE Office (Camarillo)
c/o Camarillo Chamber of Commerce
632 Las Posas Rd.
Camarillo, California 93010
Phone: (805)484-4383
Phone: (805)484-1395

SCORE Office (Cambria)
c/o Cambria Chamber of Commerce
767 Main St.
Cambria, California 93428
Phone: (805)927-3624
Fax: (805)927-9426

SCORE Office (Canoga Park)
7248 Owensmouth Ave.
Canoga Park, California 91303
Phone: (818)884-4222

SCORE Office (Capitola)
621B Capitola Ave.
Capitola, California 95010
Phone: (408)475-6522
Toll-free: (800)474-6522
Fax: (408)475-6530

SCORE Office (Carlsbad)
PO Box 10605
Carlsbad, California 92018
Phone: (619)931-8400
Fax: (619)931-9153

SCORE Office (Carpinteria)
PO Box 956
Carpinteria, California 93014
Phone: (805)684-5479
Fax: (805)684-3477

SCORE Office (Greater Chico Area)
1324 Mangrove St., Ste. 114
Chico, California 95926
Phone: (916)342-8932

SCORE Office (Chino)
13134 Central Ave.
Chino, California 91710
Phone: (909)627-6177
Fax: (909)627-4180

SCORE Office (Chula Vista)
233 4th Ave.
Chula Vista, California 91910
Phone: (619)420-6602
Fax: (619)420-1269

SCORE Office (Claremont)
205 Yale Ave.
Claremont, California 91711
Phone: (909)624-1681
Fax: (909)624-6629

SCORE Office (Clearlake)
PO Box 629
Clearlake, California 95422
Phone: (707)994-3600
Fax: (707)994-6410

SCORE Office (Colton)
620 N. Lacadena Dr.
Colton, California 92324
Phone: (909)825-2222
Fax: (909)824-1630

SCORE Office (Concord)
2151-A Salvio St., Ste. B
Concord, California 94520
Phone: (510)685-1181
Fax: (510)685-5623

SCORE Office (Covina)
935 W. Badillo St.
Covina, California 91723
Phone: (818)967-4191
Fax: (818)966-9660

SCORE Office (Rancho Cucamonga)
8280 Utica, Ste. 160
Cucamonga, California 91730
Phone: (909)987-1012
Fax: (909)987-5917

SCORE Office (Culver City)
PO Box 707
Culver City, California 90232-0707
Phone: (310)287-3850
Fax: (310)287-1350

SCORE Office (Danville)
380 Diablo Rd., Ste. 103
Danville, California 94526
Phone: (510)837-4400

SCORE Office (Downey)
11131 Brookshire Ave.
Downey, California 90241
Phone: (310)923-2191
Fax: (310)864-0461

SCORE Office (El Cajon)
109 Rea Ave.
El Cajon, California 92020
Phone: (619)444-1327
Fax: (619)440-6164

SCORE Office (El Centro)
1100 Main St.
El Centro, California 92243
Phone: (619)352-3681
Fax: (619)352-3246

SCORE Office (Escondido)
720 N. Broadway
Escondido, California 92025
Phone: (619)745-2125
Fax: (619)745-1183

SCORE Office (Fairfield)
1111 Webster St.
Fairfield, California 94533
Phone: (707)425-4625
Fax: (707)425-0826

SCORE Office (Fontana)
17009 Valley Blvd., Ste. B
Fontana, California 92335
Phone: (909)822-4433
Fax: (909)822-6238

SCORE Office (Foster City)
1125 E. Hillsdale Blvd.
Foster City, California 94404
Phone: (415)573-7600
Fax: (415)573-5201

SCORE Office (Fremont)
2201 Walnut Ave., Ste. 110
Fremont, California 94538
Phone: (510)795-2244
Fax: (510)795-2240

SCORE Office (Central California)
2719 N. Air Fresno Dr., Ste. 107
Fresno, California 93727-1547
Phone: (209)487-5605

SCORE Office (Gardena)
1204 W. Gardena Blvd.
Gardena, California 90247
Phone: (310)532-9905
Fax: (310)515-4893

SCORE Office (Glendale)
330 N. Brand Blvd., Ste. 190
Glendale, California 91203-2304
Phone: (818)552-3206

SCORE Office (Glendale)
330 N. Brand Blvd., Rm. 190
Glendale, California 91203
Phone: (818)552-3206

SCORE Office (Lompoc)
c/o Lompoc Chamber of Commerce
330 N. Brand Blvd., Ste. 190
Glendale, California 91203-2304
Phone: (818)552-3206
Fax: (818)552-3260

SCORE Office (Glendora)
131 E. Foothill Blvd.
Glendora, California 91741
Phone: (818)963-4128
Fax: (818)914-4822

SCORE Office (Grover Beach)
177 S. 8th St.
Grover Beach, California 93433
Phone: (805)489-9091
Fax: (805)489-9091

SCORE Office (Hawthorne)
12477 Hawthorne Blvd.
Hawthorne, California 90250
Phone: (310)676-1163
Fax: (310)676-7661

SCORE Office (Hayward)
22300 Foothill Blvd., Ste. 303
Hayward, California 94541
Phone: (510)537-2424

SCORE Office (Hemet)
1700 E. Florida Ave.
Hemet, California 92544
Phone: (909)652-4390

SCORE Office (Hesperia)
16367 Main St.
PO Box 403656
Hesperia, California 92340
Phone: (619)244-2135
Phone: (619)244-1333

SCORE Office (Hollister)
c/o Hollister Small Business Development Center
321 San Felipe Rd., No. 11
Hollister, California 95023

SCORE Office (Hollywood)
7018 Hollywood Blvd.
Hollywood, California 90028
Phone: (213)469-8311
Fax: (213)469-2805

SCORE Office (Indio)
82503 Hwy. 111
PO Drawer TTT
Indio, California 92202
Phone: (619)347-0676

SCORE Office (Inglewood)
330 Queen St.
Inglewood, California 90301
Phone: (818)552-3206

SCORE Office (La Puente)
218 N. Grendanda St. D.
La Puente, California 91744
Phone: (818)330-3216
Fax: (818)330-9524

SCORE Office (La Verne)
2078 Bonita Ave.
La Verne, California 91570
Phone: (909)593-5265
Phone: (909)652-4390
Fax: (714)929-8475

SCORE Office (Lake Elsinore)
132 W. Graham Ave.
Lake Elsinore, California 92530
Phone: (909)674-2577

SCORE Office (Lakeport)
PO Box 295
Lakeport, California 95453
Phone: (707)263-5092

SCORE Office (Lakewood)
5445 E. Del Amo Blvd., Ste. 2
Lakewood, California 90714
Phone: (213)920-7737

SCORE Office (Antelope Valley)
c/o Bruce Finlayson, Chair
747 E. Ave. K-7
Lancaster, California 93535
Phone: (805)948-4518

SCORE Office (Long Beach)
1 World Trade Center
Long Beach, California 90831

SCORE Office (Los Alamitos)
901 W. Civic Center Dr., Ste. 160
Los Alamitos, California 90720

SCORE Office (Los Altos)
c/o Los Altos Chamber of Commerce
321 University Ave.
Los Altos, California 94022
Phone: (415)948-1455

SCORE Office (Los Angeles)
404 S. Bixel
Los Angeles, California 90071

SCORE Office (Manhattan Beach)
PO Box 3007
Manhattan Beach, California 90266
Phone: (310)545-5313
Fax: (310)545-7203

SCORE Office (Merced)
1632 N. St.
Merced, California 95340
Phone: (209)725-3800
Fax: (209)383-4959

SCORE Office (Milpitas)
75 S. Milpitas Blvd., Ste. 205
Milpitas, California 95035
Phone: (408)262-2613
Fax: (408)262-2823

SCORE Office (Yosemite)
c/o Stanislaus County Economic
Development Corp.
1012 11th St., Ste. 300
Modesto, California 95354
Phone: (209)521-9333

SCORE Office (Montclair)
5220 Benito Ave.
Montclair, California 91763

SCORE Office (Monterey)
Monterey Peninsula Chamber of
Commerce
380 Alvarado St.
Monterey, California 93940-1770
Phone: (408)649-1770

SCORE Office (Moreno Valley)
25480 Alessandro
Moreno Valley, California 92553

SCORE Office (Morgan Hill)
Morgan Hill Chamber of Commerce
25 W. 1st St.
PO Box 786
Morgan Hill, California 95038
Phone: (408)779-9444
Fax: (408)778-1786

SCORE Office (Morro Bay)
Morro Bay Chamber of Commerce
880 Main St.
Morro Bay, California 93442
Phone: (805)772-4467

SCORE Office (Mountain View)
580 Castro St.
Mountain View, California 94041
Phone: (415)968-8378
Fax: (415)968-5668

SCORE Office (Napa)
1556 1st St.
Napa, California 94559
Phone: (707)226-7455
Fax: (707)226-1171

SCORE Office (North Hollywood)
5019 Lankershim Blvd.
North Hollywood, California 91601
Phone: (818)552-3206

SCORE Office (Northridge)
8801 Reseda Blvd.
Northridge, California 91324
Phone: (818)349-5676

SCORE Office (Novato)
807 De Long Ave.
Novato, California 94945
Phone: (415)897-1164
Fax: (415)898-9097

SCORE Office (East Bay)
2201 Broadway, Ste. 701
Oakland, California 94612
Phone: (510)273-6611

SCORE Office (Oceanside)
928 N. Coast Hwy.
Oceanside, California 92054
Phone: (619)722-1534

SCORE Office (Ontario)
121 West B. St.
Ontario, California 91762
Fax: (714)984-6439

SCORE Office (Oxnard)
PO Box 867
Oxnard, California 93032
Phone: (805)385-8860
Fax: (805)487-1763

SCORE Office (Pacifica)
450 Dundee Way, Ste. 2
Pacifica, California 94044
Phone: (415)355-4122

SCORE Office (Palm Desert)
72990 Hwy. 111
Palm Desert, California 92260
Phone: (619)346-6111
Fax: (619)346-3463

SCORE Office (Palm Springs)
555 S. Palm Canyon, Rm. A206
Palm Springs, California 92264
Phone: (619)320-6682

SCORE Office (Lakeside)
c/o Paul Heindel
2150 Low Tree
Palmdale, California 93551
Phone: (805)948-4518
Fax: (805)949-1212

SCORE Office (Palo Alto)
Thoits/Love, Hershaberger, Inc.
325 Forest Ave.
Palo Alto, California 94301
Phone: (415)324-3121
Fax: (415)324-1215

SCORE Office (Pasadena)
117 E. Colorado Blvd., Ste. 100
Pasadena, California 91105
Phone: (818)795-3355
Fax: (818)795-5663

SCORE Office (Paso Robles)
c/o Paso Robles Chamber of Commerce
1225 Park St.
Paso Robles, California 93446-2234
Phone: (805)238-0506
Fax: (805)238-0527

SCORE Office (Petaluma)
799 Baywood Dr., Ste. 3
Petaluma, California 94954
Phone: (707)762-2785
Fax: (707)762-4721

SCORE Office (Pico Rivera)
9122 E. Washington Blvd.
Pico Rivera, California 90660

SCORE Office (Pittsburg)
2700 E. Leland Rd.
Pittsburg, California 94565
Phone: (510)439-2181
Fax: (510)427-1599

SCORE Office (Pleasanton)
777 Peters Ave.
Pleasanton, California 94566
Phone: (510)846-9697

SCORE Office (Monterey Park)
485 N. Garey
Pomona, California 91769

SCORE Office (Pomona)
c/o Pomona Chamber of Commerce
485 N. Garey Ave.
PO Box 1457
Pomona, California 91769-1457
Phone: (909)622-1256

SCORE Office (Shasta)
c/o Shasta Chamber of Commerce
747 Auditorium Dr.
Redding, California 96099
Phone: (916)225-4433

SCORE Office (Redwood City)
1675 Broadway
Redwood City, California 94063
Phone: (415)364-1722
Fax: (415)364-1729

SCORE Office (Richmond)
3925 MacDonald Ave.
Richmond, California 94805

SCORE Office (Ridgecrest)
c/o Ridgecrest Chamber of Commerce
PO Box 771
Ridgecrest, California 93555
Phone: (619)375-8331
Fax: (619)375-0365

SCORE Office (Riverside)
3685 Main St., Ste. 350
Riverside, California 92501
Phone: (909)683-7100

SCORE Office (Sacramento)
660 J St., Ste. 215
Sacramento, California 95814-2413
Phone: (916)498-6420

SCORE Office (Salinas)
PO Box 1170
Salinas, California 93902
Phone: (408)424-7611
Fax: (408)424-8639

SCORE Office (Inland Empire)
777 E. Rialto Ave.
San Bernardino, California 92415-0760
Phone: (909)386-8278

SCORE Office (Inland Empire)
San Bernardino Chamber of Commerce
PO Box 658
San Bernardino, California 92402
Phone: (909)885-7515

SCORE Office (San Carlos)
San Carlos Chamber of Commerce
PO Box 1086
San Carlos, California 94070
Phone: (415)593-1068
Fax: (415)593-9108

SCORE Office (Encinitas)
550 W. C St., Ste. 550
San Diego, California 92101-3540
Phone: (619)557-7272
Fax: (619)557-5894

SCORE Office (San Diego)
c/o U..S. Small Business Administration
550 West C. St., Ste. 550
San Diego, California 92101-3540
Phone: (619)557-7272

SCORE Office (Menlo Park)
1100 Merrill St.
San Francisco, California 94105
Phone: (415)325-2818
Phone: (415)744-6827
Fax: (415)325-0920

SCORE Office (San Francisco)
c/o U..S. Small Business Administration
211 Main St., 4th Fl.
San Francisco, California 94105
Phone: (415)744-6827

SCORE Office (San Gabriel)
401 W. Las Tunas Dr.
San Gabriel, California 91776
Phone: (818)576-2525
Fax: (818)289-2901

SCORE Office (San Jose)
Small Business Institute
Deanza College
201 S. 1st. St., Ste. 137
San Jose, California 95113
Phone: (408)288-8479

SCORE Office (Santa Clara County)
280 S. 1st St., Rm. 137
San Jose, California 95113
Phone: (408)288-8479

SCORE Office (San Luis Obispo)
3566 S. Higuera
San Luis Obispo, California 93401
Phone: (805)547-0779

SCORE Office (San Mateo)
1021 S. El Camino, 2nd Fl.
San Mateo, California 94402
Phone: (415)341-5679
Phone: (415)341-0674

SCORE Office (San Pedro)
390 W. 7th St.
San Pedro, California 90731
Phone: (310)832-7272

SCORE Office (Orange County)
200 W. Santa Anna Blvd., Ste. 700
Santa Ana, California 92701
Phone: (714)550-7369

SCORE Office (Santa Barbara)
PO Box 30291
Santa Barbara, California 93130
Phone: (805)563-0084

SCORE Office (Central Coast)
1650 E. Clark Ave., No. 252
Santa Maria, California 93455
Phone: (805)934-2620

SCORE Office (Santa Maria)
Santa Maria Chamber of Commerce
614 S. Broadway
Santa Maria, California 93454-5111
Phone: (805)925-2403
Fax: (805)928-7559

SCORE Office (Santa Monica)
501 Colorado, Ste. 150
Santa Monica, California 90401
Phone: (310)393-9825
Fax: (310)394-1868

SCORE Office (Santa Rosa)
777 Sonoma Ave., Rm. 115E
Santa Rosa, California 95404
Phone: (707)571-8342

SCORE Office (Scotts Valley)
c/o Scotts Valley Chamber of Commerce
4 Camp Evers Ln.
Scotts Valley, California 95066
Phone: (408)438-1010
Fax: (408)438-6544

SCORE Office (Simi Valley)
c/o Simi Valley Chamber of Commerce
40 W. Cochran St., Ste. 100
Simi Valley, California 93065
Phone: (805)526-3900
Fax: (805)526-6234

SCORE Office (Sonoma)
453 1st St. E
Sonoma, California 95476
Phone: (707)996-1033

SCORE Office (Los Banos)
222 S. Shepard St.
Sonora, California 95370
Phone: (209)532-4212

SCORE Office (Tuolumne County)
c/o Tuolumne County Chamber of
Commerce
222 S. Shepherd St.
Sonora, California 95370
Phone: (209)532-4212

SCORE Office (South San Francisco)
c/o Chamber of Commerce
PO Box 469
South San Francisco, California
94080
Phone: (415)588-1911
Fax: (415)588-1529

SCORE Office (Stockton)
401 N. San Joaquin St., Rm. 215
Stockton, California 95202
Phone: (209)946-6293

SCORE Office (Taft)
314 4th St.
Taft, California 93268
Phone: (805)765-2165
Fax: (805)765-6639

SCORE Office (Conejo Valley)
c/o Conejo Valley Chamber of
Commerce
625 W. Hillcrest Dr.
Thousand Oaks, California 91360
Phone: (805)499-1993
Fax: (805)498-7264

SCORE Office (Torrance)
Torrance Chamber of Commerce
3400 Torrance Blvd., Ste. 100
Torrance, California 90503
Phone: (310)540-5858
Fax: (310)540-7662

SCORE Office (Truckee)
PO Box 2757
Truckee, California 96160
Phone: (916)587-2757
Fax: (916)587-2439

SCORE Office (Visalia)
c/o Tulare County E.D.C.
113 S. M St,
Tulare, California 93274
Phone: (209)627-0766
Toll-free: (800)718-2332
Fax: (209)627-8149

SCORE Office (Upland)
c/o Upland Chamber of Commerce
433 N. 2nd Ave.
Upland, California 91786
Phone: (909)931-4108

SCORE Office (Vallejo)
2 Florida St.
Vallejo, California 94590
Phone: (707)644-5551
Fax: (707)644-5590

SCORE Office (Van Nuys)
14540 Victory Blvd.
Van Nuys, California 91411
Phone: (818)989-0300
Fax: (818)989-3836

SCORE Office (Ventura)
Gold Coast Small Business Development Center
5700 Ralston St., Ste. 310
Ventura, California 93003
Phone: (818)552-3210

SCORE Office (Vista)
201 E. Washington St.
Vista, California 92084
Phone: (619)726-1122
Fax: (619)226-8654

SCORE Office (Watsonville)
PO Box 1748
Watsonville, California 95077
Phone: (408)724-3849
Fax: (408)728-5300

SCORE Office (West Covina)
811 S. Sunset Ave.
West Covina, California 91790
Phone: (818)338-8496
Fax: (818)960-0511

SCORE Office (Westlake)
30893 Thousand Oaks Blvd.
Westlake Village, California 91362
Phone: (805)496-5630
Fax: (818)991-1754

Colorado

SCORE Office (Colorado Springs)
2 N. Cascade Ave., Ste. 110
Colorado Springs, Colorado 80903
Phone: (719)636-3074

SCORE Office (Denver)
US Custom's House, 4th Fl.
721 19th St.
Denver, Colorado 80201-0660
Phone: (303)844-3985

SCORE Office (Tri-River)
1102 Grand Ave.
Glenwood Springs, Colorado 81601
Phone: (970)945-6589

SCORE Office (Grand Junction)
c/o Grand Junction Chamber of
Commerce
360 Grand Ave.
Grand Junction, Colorado 81501
Phone: (303)242-3214

SCORE Office (Gunnison)
c/o Russ Gregg
608 N. 11th
Gunnison, Colorado 81230
Phone: (303)641-4422

SCORE Office (Montrose)
1214 Peppertree Dr.
Montrose, Colorado 81401
Phone: (970)249-6080

SCORE Office (Pagosa Springs)
c/o Will Cotton
PO Box 4381
Pagosa Springs, Colorado 81157
Phone: (970)731-4890

SCORE Office (Rifle)
0854 W. Battlement Pky., Apt. C106
Parachute, Colorado 81635
Phone: (970)285-9390

SCORE Office (Pueblo)
302 N. Santa Fe
Pueblo, Colorado 81003
Phone: (719)542-1704

SCORE Office (Ridgway)
c/o Ken Hanson
143 Poplar Pl.
Ridgway, Colorado 81432

SCORE Office (Silverton)
c/o EF Homann
PO Box 480
Silverton, Colorado 81433
Phone: (303)387-5430

SCORE Office (Minturn)
PO Box 2066
Vail, Colorado 81658
Phone: (970)476-1224

Connecticut

SCORE Office (Greater Bridgeport)
10 Middle St., 14th Fl.
PO Box 999
Bridgeport, Connecticut 06601-0999
Phone: (203)335-3800

SCORE Office (Bristol)
10 Main St. 1st. Fl.
Bristol, Connecticut 06010
Phone: (203)584-4718
Fax: (203)584-4722

SCORE Office (Greater Danbury)
100 Mill Plain Rd.
Danbury, Connecticut 06811
Phone: (203)791-3804

SCORE Office (Eastern Connecticut)
University of Connecticut
Administration Bldg., Rm. 313
PO 625
61 Main St. (Chapter 579)
Groton, Connecticut 06475
Phone: (203)388-9508

SCORE Office (Greater Hartford
County)
330 Main St.
Hartford, Connecticut 06106
Phone: (203)240-4640

SCORE Office (Manchester)
c/o Manchester Chamber of Commerce
20 Hartford Rd.
Manchester, Connecticut 06040
Phone: (203)646-2223
Fax: (203)646-5871

SCORE Office (New Britain)
185 Main St.,Ste. 431
New Britain, Connecticut 06051
Phone: (203)827-4492
Fax: (203)827-4480

SCORE Office (New Haven)
25 Science Pk., Bldg. 25, Rm. 366
New Haven, Connecticut 06511
Phone: (203)865-7645

SCORE Office (Fairfield County)
24 Beldon Ave., 5th Fl.
Norwalk, Connecticut 06850
Phone: (203)847-7348

SCORE Office (Old Saybrook)
c/o Old Saybrook Chamber of Commerce
146 Main St.
PO Box 625
Old Saybrook, Connecticut 06475
Phone: (203)388-9508

SCORE Office (Simsbury)
Simsbury Chamber of Commerce
Box 244
Simsbury, Connecticut 06070
Phone: (203)651-7307
Fax: (203)651-1933

SCORE Office (Torrington)
Northwest Chamber of Commerce
23 North Rd.
Torrington, Connecticut 06791
Phone: (203)482-6586

Delaware

SCORE Office (Dover)
Treadway Towers
P.O. Box 576
Dover, Delaware 19903
Phone: (302)678-0892
Fax: (302)678-0189

SCORE Office (Lewes)
PO Box 1
Lewes, Delaware 19958
Phone: (302)645-8073
Fax: (302)645-8412

SCORE Office (Milford)
Milford Chamber of Commerce
204 NE Front St.
Milford, Delaware 19963
Phone: (302)422-3301

SCORE Office (Wilmington)
824 Market St., Ste. 610
Wilmington, Delaware 19801
Phone: (302)573-6552
Fax: (302)573-6060

District of Columbia

SCORE Office (George Mason
University)
409 3rd St. SW, 4th Fl.
Washington, District of Columbia 20024
Toll-free: (800)634-0245

SCORE Office (Washington DC)
1110 Vermont Ave. NW, 9th Fl.
PO Box 34346
Washington, District of Columbia 20043
Phone: (202)606-4000

Florida

SCORE Office (Desota County
Chamber of Commerce)
16 South Velucia Ave.
Arcadia, Florida 34266
Phone: (941)494-4033
Phone: (941)494-3312

SCORE Office (Suncoast/Pinellas)
Airport Business Ctr.
4707 - 140th Ave. N, No. 311
Clearwater, Florida 34622
Phone: (813)532-6800

SCORE Office (Dade)
1320 S. Dixie Hwy., Ste. 501
Coral Gables, Florida 33146
Phone: (305)536-5521

SCORE Office (Daytona Beach)
First Union Bldg., Ste. 365
444 Seabreeze Blvd.
Daytona Beach, Florida 32118
Phone: (904)255-6889

SCORE Office (DeLand)
336 N. Woodland Blvd.
DeLand, Florida 32720
Phone: (904)734-4331
Fax: (904)734-4333

SCORE Office (South Palm Beach)
1050 S. Federal Hwy., Ste. 132
Delray Beach, Florida 33483
Phone: (407)278-7752

SCORE Office (Ft. Lauderdale)
Federal Bldg., Ste. 123
299 E. Broward Blvd.
Ft. Lauderdale, Florida 33301
Phone: (305)356-7263

SCORE Office (Southwest Florida)
The Renaissance
8695 College Pky., Ste. 345 & 346
Fort Myers, Florida 33919
Phone: (813)489-2935

SCORE Office (Indian River)
Treasure Coast Professional Center, Ste. 2
3229 S. US No. 1
Fort Pierce, Florida 34982
Phone: (407)489-0548

SCORE Office (Gainesville)
101 SE 2nd Pl., Ste. 104
Gainesville, Florida 32601
Phone: (904)375-8278

SCORE Office (Hialeah Dade Chamber)
59 W. 5th St.
Hialeah, Florida 33010
Phone: (305)887-1515
Fax: (305)887-2453

SCORE Office (South Broward)
3475 Sheridan St., Ste. 203
Hollywood, Florida 33021
Phone: (305)966-8415

SCORE Office (Jacksonville)
7825 Baymeadows Way, Ste. 100-B
Jacksonville, Florida 32256-7504
Phone: (904)443-1911

SCORE Office (Jacksonville Satellite)
c/o Jacksonville Chamber of Commerce
3 Independent Dr.
Jacksonville, Florida 32202
Phone: (904)366-6600
Fax: (904)632-0617

SCORE Office (Central Florida)
404 N. Ingraham Ave.
Lakeland, Florida 33801
Phone: (813)688-4060

SCORE Office (Lakeland)
Lakeland Public Library
100 Lake Morton Dr.
Lakeland, Florida 33801
Phone: (941)686-2168

SCORE Office (St. Petersburg)
800 W. Bay Dr., No. 505
Largo, Florida 33712
Phone: (813)585-4571
Phone: (904)327-7207

SCORE Office (Leesburg)
Lake Sumter Community College
9501 US Hwy. 441
Leesburg, Florida 34788-8751
Phone: (352)365-3556
Fax: (352)365-3501

SCORE Office (BCC/Space Coast)
Space Coast
Melbourne Professional Complex
1600 Sarno, Ste. 205
Melbourne, Florida 32935
Phone: (407)254-2288

SCORE Office (Cocoa)
1600 Farno Rd., Unit 205
Melbourne, Florida 32935
Phone: (407)254-2288

SCORE Office (Melbourne)
Space Coast
Melbourne Professional Complex
1600 Samo, Ste. 205
Melbourne, Florida 32935
Phone: (407)254-2288

SCORE Office (Merritt Island)
1600 Farno Rd., Unit 205
Melbourne, Florida 32935
Phone: (407)254-2288

SCORE Office (Naples of Collier)
Sun Bank Naples
3301 Danis Blvd.
PO Box 413002
Naples, Florida 33941-3002
Phone: (941)643-0333

SCORE Office (Pasco County)
6014 US Hwy. 19, Ste. 302
New Port Richey, Florida 34652
Phone: (813)842-4638

SCORE Office (Southeast Volusia)
Chamber of Commerce
115 Canal St.
New Smyrna Beach, Florida 32168
Phone: (904)428-2449
Fax: (904)423-3512

SCORE Office (Ocala)
PO Box 1210
Ocala, Florida 34478
Phone: (904)629-5959

Clay County SCORE Office
Clay County Chamber of Commerce
1734 Kingsdey Ave.
PO Box 1441
Orange Park, Florida 32073
Phone: (904)264-2651
Fax: (904)269-0363

SCORE Office (Orlando)
Federal Bldg., Rm. 455
80 N. Hughey Ave.
Orlando, Florida 32801
Phone: (407)648-6476

SCORE Office (Emerald Coast)
19 W. Garden St., No. 325
Pensacola, Florida 32501
Phone: (904)444-2060
Fax: (904)444-2070

SCORE Office (Charlotte County)
Punta Gorda Professional Center
201 W. Marion Ave., Ste. 211
Punta Gorda, Florida 33950
Phone: (813)575-1818

SCORE Office (St. Augustine)
c/o St. Augustine Chamber of
Commerce
1 Riberia St.
St. Augustine, Florida 32084
Phone: (904)829-5681
Fax: (904)829-6477

SCORE Office (Bradenton)
2801 Fruitville, Ste. 280
Sarasota, Florida 34237
Phone: (813)955-1029

SCORE Office (Manasota)
2801 Fruitville Rd., Ste. 280
Sarasota, Florida 34237
Phone: (813)955-1029

SCORE Office (Tallahassee)
c/o Leon County Library
200 W. Park Ave.
Tallahassee, Florida 32302
Phone: (904)487-2665

SCORE Office (Hillsborough)
4732 Dale Mabry Hwy. N, Ste. 400
Tampa, Florida 33614-6509
Phone: (813)870-0125

SCORE Office (Lake Sumter)
First Union National Bank
122 E. Main St.
Tavares, Florida 32778
Phone: (904)365-3556

SCORE Office (Titusville)
2000 S. Washington Ave.
Titusville, Florida 32780
Phone: (407)267-3036
Fax: (407)264-0127

SCORE Office (Venice)
257 N. Tamiami Trl.
Venice, Florida 34285
Phone: (941)488-2236
Fax: (941)484-5903

SCORE Office (Palm Beach)
500 Australian Ave. S, Ste. 100
West Palm Beach, Florida 33401
Phone: (407)833-1672

SCORE Office (Wildwood)
Sumter County Small Business Services
103 N. Webster St.
Wildwood, Florida 34785

Georgia

SCORE Office (Atlanta)
1720 Peachtree Rd. NW, 6th Fl.
Atlanta, Georgia 30309
Phone: (404)347-2442

SCORE Office (Augusta)
3126 Oxford Rd.
Augusta, Georgia 30909
Phone: (706)869-9100

SCORE Office (Columbus)
School Bldg.
P.O. Box 40
Columbus, Georgia 31901
Phone: (706)327-3654

SCORE Office (Dalton-Whitfield)
PO Box 1941
Dalton, Georgia 30722-1941
Phone: (706)279-3383

SCORE Office (Gainesville)
Chamber of Commerce
PO Box 374
Gainesville, Georgia 30503
Phone: (770)532-6206
Fax: (770)535-8419

SCORE Office (Macon)
711 Grand Bldg.
Macon, Georgia 31201
Phone: (912)751-6160

SCORE Office (Brunswick)
4 Glen Ave.
St. Simons Island, Georgia 31520
Phone: (912)265-0620
Fax: (912)265-0629

SCORE Office (Savannah)
33 Bull St., Ste. 580
Savannah, Georgia 31401
Phone: (912)652-4335

Guam

SCORE Office (Guam)
Pacific News Bldg., Rm. 103
238 Archbishop Flores St.
Agana, Guam 96910-5100
Phone: (671)472-7308

Hawaii

SCORE Office (Honolulu)
300 Ala Moana Blvd., No. 2213
PO Box 50207
Honolulu, Hawaii 96850-3212
Phone: (808)541-2977

SCORE Office (Kahului)
c/o Chamber of Commerce
250 Alamaha, Unit N16A
Kahului, Hawaii 96732
Phone: (808)871-7711

Idaho

SCORE Office (Treasure Valley)
1020 Main St., No. 290
Boise, Idaho 83702
Phone: (208)334-1780

SCORE Office (Eastern Idaho)
2300 N. Yellowstone, Ste. 119
Idaho Falls, Idaho 83401
Phone: (208)523-1022

Illinois

SCORE Office (Fox Valley)
Greater Aurora Chamber of Commerce
40 W. Downer Pl.

PO Box 277
Aurora, Illinois 60507
Phone: (708)897-9214

SCORE Office (Greater Belvidere)
Greater Belvidere Chamber of Commerce
419 S. State St.
Belvidere, Illinois 61008
Phone: (815)544-4357
Fax: (815)547-7654

SCORE Office (Bensenville)
Greater O'Hare Association
1050 Busse Hwy. Suite 100
Bensenville, Illinois 60106
Phone: (708)350-2944
Fax: (708)350-2979

SCORE Office (Southern Illinois)
150 E. Pleasant Hill Rd.
Box 1
Carbondale, Illinois 62901
Phone: (618)453-6654

SCORE Office (Chicago)
Oliver Harvey College
Small Business Development Center
Pullman Bldg.
1000 E. 11th St., 7th Fl.
Chicago, Illinois 60628
Fax: (312)468-8086

SCORE Office (Chicago)
Northwest Atrium Center
500 W. Madison St., No. 1250
Chicago, Illinois 60661
Phone: (312)353-7724

SCORE Office (Danville)
28 W. N. Street
Danville, Illinois 61832
Phone: (217)442-7232
Phone: (217)442-1887
Fax: (217)442-6228

SCORE Office (Decatur)
Millikin University
1184 W. Main St.
Decatur, Illinois 62522
Phone: (217)424-6297

.SCORE Office (Downers Grove)
Downers Grove Chamber of Commerce
925 Curtis
Downers Grove, Illinois 60515
Phone: (708)968-4050
Fax: (708)968-8368

SCORE Office (Elgin)
Elgin Area Chamber of Commerce
24 E. Chicago, 3rd Fl.
PO Box 648
Elgin, Illinois 60120
Phone: (847)741-5660
Fax: (847)741-5677

SCORE Office (Freeport Area)
Freeport Area Chamber of Commerce
26 S. Galena Ave.
Freeport, Illinois 61032
Phone: (815)233-1350
Fax: (815)235-4038

.SCORE Office (Galesburg)
Galesburg Area Chamber of Commerce
292 E. Simmons St.
PO Box 749
Galesburg, Illinois 61401
Phone: (309)343-1194
Fax: (309)343-1195

SCORE Office (Glen Ellyn)
Glen Ellyn Chamber of Commerce
500 Pennsylvania
Glen Ellyn, Illinois 60137
Phone: (708)469-0907
Fax: (708)469-0426

SCORE Office (Alton)
Lewis & Clark Community College
Alden Hall
5800 Godfrey Rd.
Godfrey, Illinois 62035-2466
Phone: (618)467-2280

SCORE Office (Grayslake)
College of Lake County
19351 W. Washington St.
Grayslake, Illinois 60030
Phone: (708)223-3633
Fax: (708)223-9371

SCORE Office (Harrisburg)
Ec. Devel. Services Center
303 S. Commercial
Harrisburg, Illinois 62946-1528
Phone: (618)252-8528
Fax: (618)252-0210

SCORE Office (Joliet)
Joliet Region Chamber of Commerce
100 N. Chicago
Joliet, Illinois 60432
Phone: (815)727-5371
Fax: (815)727-5374

SCORE Office (Kankakee)
Kankakee Small Business Development Center
101 S. Schuyler Ave.
Kankakee, Illinois 60901
Phone: (815)933-0376
Fax: (815)933-0380

SCORE Office (Macomb)
Western Illinois University
216 Seal Hall, Rm. 214
Macomb, Illinois 61455
Phone: (309)298-1128
Fax: (309)298-2520

SCORE Office (Matteson)
Prairie State College
210 Lincoln Mall
Matteson, Illinois 60443
Phone: (708)709-3750
Fax: (708)503-9322

SCORE Office (Mattoon)
Mattoon Association of Commerce
1701 Wabash Ave.
Mattoon, Illinois 61938
Phone: (217)235-5661
Fax: (217)234-6544

SCORE Office (Quad City)
Quad City Chamber of Commerce
622 19th St.
Moline, Illinois 61265
Phone: (309)797-0082

SCORE Office (Naperville)
Naperville Area Chamber of Commerce
131 W. Jefferson Ave.
Naperville, Illinois 60540
Phone: (708)355-4141
Fax: (708)355-8355

SCORE Office (Northbrook)
Northbrook Chamber of Commerce
2002 Walters Ave.
Northbrook, Illinois 60062
Phone: (847)498-5555
Fax: (847)498-5510

SCORE Office (Palos Hills)
Moraine Valley Community College
Small Business Development Center
10900 S. 88th Ave.
Palos Hills, Illinois 60465
Phone: (847)974-5468
Fax: (847)974-0078

SCORE Office (Peoria)
c/o Peoria Chamber of Commerce
124 SW Adams, Ste. 300
Peoria, Illinois 61602
Phone: (309)676-0755

SCORE Office (Prospect Heights)
Harper College, Northeast Center
1375 Wolf Rd.
Prospect Heights, Illinois 60070
Phone: (847)537-8660
Fax: (847)537-7138

SCORE Office (Quincy Tri-State)
Quincy Chamber of Commerce
300 Civic Center Plz., Ste. 245
Quincy, Illinois 62301
Phone: (217)222-8093

SCORE Office (River Grove)
Triton College
2000 5th Ave.
River Grove, Illinois 60171
Phone: (708)456-0300
Fax: (708)583-3121

SCORE Office (Northern Illinois)
Rockford Illinois Chamber of Commerce
515 N. Court St.
Rockford, Illinois 61103
Phone: (815)962-0122

SCORE Office (St. Charles)
St. Charles Chamber of Commerce
103 N. 1st Ave.
St. Charles, Illinois 60174-1982
Phone: (847)584-8384
Fax: (847)584-6065

SCORE Office (Springfield)
U.S. Small Business Administration
511 W. Capitol Ave., Ste. 302
Springfield, Illinois 62704
Phone: (217)492-4416
Fax: (217)492-4867

SCORE Office (Springfield)
NORBIC
511 West Capitol Ave., Ste. 302
Springfield, Illinois 62704
Phone: (217)492-4416

SCORE Office (Sycamore)
Greater Sycamore Chamber of Commerce
112 Somunak St.
Sycamore, Illinois 60178
Phone: (815)895-3456
Fax: (815)895-0125

SCORE Office (University)
Governors State University
Hwy. 50 & Stuenkel Rd. Ste. C3305
University Park, Illinois 60466
Phone: (708)534-5000
Fax: (708)534-8457

Indiana

SCORE Office (Anderson)
c/o Anderson Chamber of Commerce
205 W. 11th St.
PO Box 469
Anderson, Indiana 46015
Phone: (317)642-0264

SCORE Office (Bloomington)
c/o Bloomington Chamber of
Commerce
400 W. 7th St., Ste. 102
Bloomington, Indiana 47404
Phone: (812)336-6381

SCORE Office (Southeast)
c/o Columbus Chamber of Commerce
500 Franklin St.
Box 29
Columbus, Indiana 47201
Phone: (812)379-4457

SCORE Office (Corydon)
310 N. Elm St.
Corydon, Indiana 47112
Phone: (812)738-2137
Fax: (812)738-6438

SCORE Office (Crown Point)
Old Courthouse Sq. Ste. 206
P.O. Box 43
Crown Point, Indiana 46307
Phone: (219)663-1800
Phone: (219)663-1989

SCORE Office (Elkhart)
418 S. Main St.
P.O. Box 428
Elkhart, Indiana 46515
Phone: (219)293-1531

SCORE Office (Evansville)
Old Post Office Pl.
100 NW 2nd St., No. 300
Evansville, Indiana 47708
Phone: (812)421-5879

SCORE Office (Fort Wayne)
1300 S. Harrison St.
Fort Wayne, Indiana 46802
Phone: (219)422-2601

SCORE Office (Gary)
973 W. 6th Ave., Rm. 326
Gary, Indiana 46402
Phone: (219)882-3918

SCORE Office (Hammond)
7034 Indianapolis Blvd.
Hammond, Indiana 46324
Phone: (219)931-1000
Fax: (219)845-9548

SCORE Office (Indianapolis)
429 N. Pennsylvania St., Ste. 100
Indianapolis, Indiana 46204-1873
Phone: (317)226-7264

SCORE Office (Jasper)
PO Box 307
Jasper, Indiana 47547-0307
Phone: (812)482-6866

SCORE Office (Kokomo/Howard
Counties)
106 N. Washington
PO Box 731
Kokomo, Indiana 46903-0731
Phone: (317)457-5301
Fax: (317)452-4564

SCORE Office (Logansport)
Logansport Chamber of Commerce
300 E. Broadway, Ste. 103
Logansport, Indiana 46947
Phone: (219)753-6388

SCORE Office (Madison)
301 E. Main St.
Madison, Indiana 47250
Phone: (812)265-3135
Fax: (812)265-2923

SCORE Office (Marengo)
c/o Marengo Chamber of Commerce
Rte. 1 Box 224D
Marengo, Indiana 47140
Fax: (812)365-2793

SCORE Office (Marion/Grant Counties)
215 S. Adams
Marion, Indiana 46952
Phone: (317)664-5107

SCORE Office (Merrillville)
255 W. 80th Pl.
Merrillville, Indiana 46410
Phone: (219)769-8180
Fax: (219)736-6223

SCORE Office (Michigan City)
200 E. Michigan Blvd.
Michigan City, Indiana 46360
Phone: (219)874-6221
Fax: (219)873-1204

SCORE Office (South Central
Indiana)
1702 E. Spring St.
PO Box 653
New Albany, Indiana 47150
Phone: (812)945-0054

SCORE Office (Rensselaer)
104 W. Washington
Rensselaer, Indiana 47978

SCORE Office (Salem)
c/o Salem Chamber of Commerce
210 N. Main St.
Salem, Indiana 47167
Phone: (812)883-4303
Fax: (812)883-1467

SCORE Office (South Bend)
300 N. Michigan St.
South Bend, Indiana 46601
Phone: (219)282-4350

SCORE Office (Valparaiso)
150 Lincolnway
Valparaiso, Indiana 46383
Phone: (219)462-1105
Fax: (219)469-5710

SCORE Office (Vincennes)
Vincennes Chamber of Commerce
27 N. 3rd
P.O. Box 553
Vincennes, Indiana 47591
Phone: (812)882-6440
Fax: (812)882-6441

SCORE Office (Wabash)
PO Box 371
Wabash, Indiana 46992
Phone: (219)563-1168
Fax: (219)563-6920

Iowa

SCORE Office (Burlington)
Federal Bldg.
300 N. Main St.
Burlington, Iowa 52601
Phone: (319)752-2967

SCORE Office (Cedar Rapids)
Lattner Building, Ste. 200
215-4th Avenue, SE
Cedar Rapids, Iowa 52401-1806
Phone: (319)362-6405
Fax: (319)362-7861

SCORE Office (Southwest Iowa)
700 W. Clark
Clarinda, Iowa 51632
Phone: (712)542-2906

SCORE Office (Illowa)
River City Chamber of Commerce
333 4th Ave. S
Clinton, Iowa 52732
Phone: (319)242-5702

SCORE Office (Council Bluffs)
Council Bluffs Chamber of Commerce
P.O. Box 1565
Council Bluffs, Iowa 51502-1565
Phone: (712)325-1000

SCORE Office (Northeast Iowa)
3404 285th St.
Cresco, Iowa 52136
Phone: (319)547-3377

SCORE Office (Des Moines)
Federal Bldg., Rm. 749
210 Walnut St.
Des Moines, Iowa 50309-2186
Phone: (515)284-4760

SCORE Office (Fort Dodge)
Federal Bldg., Rm. 436
205 S. 8th St.
Fort Dodge, Iowa 50501
Phone: (515)955-2622

SCORE Office (Independence)
Independence Area Chamber of
Commerce
110 1st. St. east
Independence, Iowa 50644
Phone: (319)334-7178
Fax: (319)334-7179

SCORE Office (Iowa City)
210 Federal Bldg.
PO Box 1853
Iowa City, Iowa 52240-1853
Phone: (319)338-1662

SCORE Office (Keokuk)
Keokuk Area Chamber of Commerce
Pierce Bldg., No. 1
401 Main St.
Keokuk, Iowa 52632
Phone: (319)524-5055

SCORE Office (Central Iowa)
Fisher Community Center
709 S. Center
Marshalltown, Iowa 50158
Phone: (515)753-6645

SCORE Office (River City)
15 West State St.
P.O. Box 1128
Mason City, Iowa 50401
Phone: (515)423-5724

SCORE Office (South Central)
c/o Indian Hills Community College
525 Grandview Ave.
Ottumwa, Iowa 52501
Phone: (515)683-5127
Fax: (515)683-5263

SCORE Office (Dubuque)
Northeast Iowa Community College
10250 Sundown Road
Peosta, Iowa 52068
Phone: (319)556-5110

SCORE Office (Southwest Iowa)
Chamber of Commerce
403 W. Sheridan
Shenandoah, Iowa 51601
Phone: (712)542-2906

SCORE Office (Sioux City)
c/o Sioux City Federal Bldg.
320 6th St.
Sioux City, Iowa 51101
Phone: (712)277-2325

SCORE Office (Iowa Lakes)
21 W. 5th St., Rm. 5
PO Box 7026
Spencer, Iowa 51301-3059
Phone: (712)262-3059

SCORE Office (Vista)
Storm Lake Chamber of Commerce
119 W. 6th St.
Storm Lake, Iowa 50588
Phone: (712)732-3780

SCORE Office (Waterloo)
Waterloo Chamber of Commerce
215 E. 4th
Waterloo, Iowa 50703
Phone: (319)233-8431

Kansas

SCORE Office (Southwest Kansas)
Dodge City Area Chamber of Com-
merce
PO Box 939
Dodge City, Kansas 67801
Phone: (316)227-3119

SCORE Office (Emporia)
Emporia Chamber of Commerce
427 Commercial
Emporia, Kansas 66801
Phone: (316)342-1600

SCORE Office (Golden Belt)
Chamber of Commerce
1307 Williams
Great Bend, Kansas 67530
Phone: (316)792-2401

SCORE Office (Hays)
c/o Empire Bank
PO Box 400
Hays, Kansas 67601
Phone: (913)625-6595

SCORE Office (Hutchinson)
One E. 9th St.
Hutchinson, Kansas 67501
Phone: (316)665-8468

SCORE Office (Southeast Kansas)
404 Westminster Pl.
PO Box 886
Independence, Kansas 67301-0886
Phone: (316)331-4741

SCORE Office (McPherson)
McPherson Chamber of Commerce
306 N. Main
McPherson, Kansas 67460
Phone: (316)241-3303

SCORE Office (Salina)
PO Box 586
Salina, Kansas 67401
Phone: (913)827-9301

SCORE Office (Topeka)
1700 College
Topeka, Kansas 66621
Phone: (913)231-1010
Phone: (913)231-1305

SCORE Office (Wichita)
U.S. Small Business Administration
100 E. English, Ste. 510
Wichita, Kansas 67202
Phone: (316)269-6273

SCORE Office (Ark Valley)
Box 314
Winfield, Kansas 67156
Phone: (316)221-1617

Kentucky

SCORE Office (Ashland)
PO Box 830
Ashland, Kentucky 41105
Phone: (606)329-8011
Fax: (606)325-4607

SCORE Office (Bowling Green)
Bowling Green-Warren Chamber of
Commerce
812 State St.
P.O. Box 51
Bowling Green, Kentucky 42101
Phone: (502)781-3200
Fax: (502)843-0458

SCORE Office (Tri-Lakes)
508 Barbee Way
Danville, Kentucky 40422-1548
Phone: (606)231-9902

SCORE Office (Glasgow)
301 W. Main St.
Glasgow, Kentucky 42141
Phone: (502)651-3161
Fax: (502)651-3122

SCORE Office (Hazard)
B & I Technical Center
100 Airport Gardens Rd.
Hazard, Kentucky 41701
Phone: (606)439-5856
Fax: (606)439-1808

SCORE Office (Lexington)
1460 Newton Pke., Ste. A
Lexington, Kentucky 40511
Phone: (606)231-9902

SCORE Office (Louisville)
188 Federal Office Bldg.
600 Dr. Martin L. King Jr. Pl.
Louisville, Kentucky 40202
Phone: (502)582-5976

SCORE Office (Madisonville)
257 N. Main
Madisonville, Kentucky 42431
Phone: (502)825-1399
Fax: (502)825-1396

SCORE Office (Paducah)
Federal Office Bldg.
501 Broadway, Rm. B-36
Paducah, Kentucky 42001
Phone: (502)442-5685

Louisiana

SCORE Office (Central Louisiana)
802 3rd St.
PO Box 992
Alexandria, Louisiana 71309
Phone: (318)442-6671

SCORE Office (Baton Rouge)
564 Laurel St.
PO Box 3217
Baton Rouge, Louisiana 70801
Phone: (504)381-7125

SCORE Office (North Shore)
PO Box 1458
Hammond, Louisiana 70404
Phone: (504)345-4457

SCORE Office (Lafayette)
Lafayette Chamber of Commerce
804 St. Mary Blvd.
PO Drawer 51307
Lafayette, Louisiana 70505-1307
Phone: (318)233-2705

SCORE Office (Lake Charles)
120 W. Pujo
Lake Charles, Louisiana 70601
Phone: (318)433-3632

SCORE Office (New Orleans)
365 Canal St., Ste. 2250
New Orleans, Louisiana 70130
Phone: (504)589-2356

SCORE Office (Shreveport)
400 Edwards St.
Shreveport, Louisiana 71101
Phone: (318)677-2509

Maine

SCORE Office (Augusta)
40 Western Ave.
Augusta, Maine 04330
Phone: (207)622-8509

SCORE Office (Bangor)
Husson College
Peabody Hall, Rm. 229
One College Cir.
Bangor, Maine 04401
Phone: (207)941-9707

SCORE Office (Central & Northern
Arrostock)
111 High St.
PO Box 357
Caribou, Maine 04736
Phone: (207)498-6156

SCORE Office (Penquis)
Chamber of Commerce
South St.
Dover Foxcroft, Maine 04426
Phone: (207)564-7021

SCORE Office (Maine Coastal)
Federal Bldg.
Main & Water St.
Box 1105
Ellsworth, Maine 04605
Phone: (207)667-5800

SCORE Office (Lewiston-Auburn)
c/o Chamber of Commerce
179 Lisbon St.
Lewiston, Maine 04240
Phone: (207)782-3708

SCORE Office (Portland)
66 Pearl St., Rm. 210
Portland, Maine 04101
Phone: (207)772-1147

SCORE Office (Western Mountains)
c/o Fleet Bank
108 Congress St.
PO Box 400
Rumford, Maine 04276
Phone: (207)364-3733

SCORE Office (Oxford Hills)
166 Main St.
South Paris, Maine 04281
Phone: (207)743-0499
Fax: (207)743-5917

Maryland

SCORE Office (Southern Maryland)
2525 Riva Rd., Ste. 110
Annapolis, Maryland 21401
Phone: (410)267-6206

SCORE Office (Baltimore)
The City Crescent Bldg., 6th Fl.
10 S. Howard St.
Baltimore, Maryland 21201
Phone: (410)962-2233
Fax: (410)962-1805

SCORE Office (Dundalk)
Eastern Baltimore Chamber of
Commerce
2200 Broening Hwy. Ste. 102
Baltimore, Maryland 21224
Phone: (410)282-9100
Fax: (410)631-9099

SCORE Office (Bel Air)
Bel Air Chamber of Commerce
108 S. Bond St.
Bel Air, Maryland 21014
Phone: (410)838-2020
Fax: (410)893-4715

SCORE Office (Bethesda)
7910 Woodmont Ave., Ste. 1204
Bethesda, Maryland 20814
Phone: (301)652-4900
Fax: (301)657-1973

SCORE Office (Bowie)
6670 Race Track Rd.
Bowie, Maryland 20715
Phone: (301)262-0920
Fax: (301)262-0921

SCORE Office (Dorchester County)
c/o Chamber of Commerce
203 Sunburst Hwy.
Cambridge, Maryland 21613
Phone: (410)228-3575

SCORE Office (Upper Shore)
c/o Talbout County Chamber of
Commerce
PO Box 1366
Easton, Maryland 21601
Phone: (410)822-4606
Fax: (410)822-7922

SCORE Office (Frederick County)
43A S. Market St.
Frederick, Maryland 21701
Phone: (301)662-4164

SCORE Office (Gaithersburg)
9 Park Ave.
Gaithersburg, Maryland 20877
Phone: (301)840-1400
Fax: (301)963-3918

SCORE Office (Glen Burnie)
Glen Burnie Chamber of Commerce
103 Crain Hwy. SE
Glen Burnie, Maryland 21061
Phone: (410)766-8282
Fax: (410)766-9722

SCORE Office (Hagerstown)
111 W. Washington St.
Hagerstown, Maryland 21740
Phone: (301)739-2015

SCORE Office (Laurel)
7901 Sandy Spring Rd. Ste. 501
Laurel, Maryland 20707
Phone: (301)725-4000
Fax: (301)725-0776

SCORE Office (Salisbury)
c/o Salisbury Chamber of Commerce
300 E. Main St.
Salisbury, Maryland 21801
Phone: (410)749-0185

Massachusetts

SCORE Office (Boston)
10 Causeway St., Rm. 265
Boston, Massachusetts 02222
Phone: (617)565-5591
Fax: (617)565-5598

SCORE Office (Southeastern)
60 School St.
Brockton, Massachusetts 02401
Phone: (508)587-2673

SCORE Office (North Adams)
Northern Berkshire Development Corp.
820 N. State Rd.
Cheshire, Massachusetts 01225
Phone: (413)743-5100

SCORE Office (Clinton Satellite)
c/o Clinton Chamber of Commerce
1 Green St.
Clinton, Massachusetts 01510
Fax: (508)368-7689

SCORE Office (Northeastern Massa-
chusetts)
Danvers Savings Bank
1 Conant St.
Danvers, Massachusetts 01923
Phone: (508)777-2200

SCORE Office (Bristol/Plymouth
Counties)
Fall River Area Chamber of Com-
merce and Industry
PO Box 1871
Fall River, Massachusetts 02722-1871
Phone: (508)676-8226

SCORE Office (Greenfield)
PO Box 898
Greenfield, Massachusetts 01302
Phone: (413)773-5463
Fax: (413)773-7008

SCORE Office (Haverhill)
Haverhill Chamber
87 Winter St.
Haverhill, Massachusetts 01830
Phone: (508)373-5663
Fax: (508)373-8060

SCORE Office (Hudson Satellite)
c/o Hudson Chamber of Commerce
PO Box 578
Hudson, Massachusetts 01749
Phone: (508)568-0360
Fax: (508)568-0360

SCORE Office (Cape Cod)
Independence Pk., Ste. 5B
270 Communications Way
Hyannis, Massachusetts 02601
Phone: (508)775-4884

SCORE Office (Lawrence)
264 Essex St.
Lawrence, Massachusetts 01840
Phone: (508)686-0900
Fax: (508)794-9953

SCORE Office (Leominster Satellite)
c/o Leominster Chamber of Commerce
110 Erdman Way
Leominster, Massachusetts 01453
Phone: (508)840-4300
Fax: (508)840-4896

SCORE Office (Newburyport)
29 State St.
Newburyport, Massachusetts 01950
Phone: (617)462-6680

SCORE Office (Pittsfield)
Central Berkshire Chamber
66 West St.
Pittsfield, Massachusetts 01201
Phone: (413)499-2485

SCORE Office (Haverhill)
32 Derby Sq.
Salem, Massachusetts 01970
Phone: (508)745-0330
Fax: (508)745-3855

SCORE Office (Springfield)
1550 Main St., Ste. 212
Springfield, Massachusetts 01103
Phone: (413)785-0314

SCORE Office (Carver)
12 Taunton Green, Ste. 201
Taunton, Massachusetts 02780
Phone: (508)824-4068
Fax: (508)824-4069

SCORE Office (Cape Cod)
c/o Martha's Vineyard Chamber of Commerce
Beach Rd.
PO Box 1698
Vineyard Haven, Massachusetts 02568
Phone: (508)693-0085

SCORE Office (Worcester)
33 Waldo St.
Worcester, Massachusetts 01608
Phone: (508)753-2924

Michigan

SCORE Office (Allegan)
c/o Allegan Chamber of Commerce
PO Box 338
Allegan, Michigan 49010
Phone: (616)673-2479

SCORE Office (Ann Arbor)
425 S. Main St., Ste. 103
Ann Arbor, Michigan 48104
Phone: (313)665-4433

SCORE Office (Battle Creek)
c/o Battle Creek Chamber of Commerce
34 W. Jackson Ste. 4A
Battle Creek, Michigan 49017-3505
Phone: (616)962-4076
Fax: (616)962-6309

SCORE Office (Cadillac)
c/o Cadillac Chamber of Commerce
222 Lake St.
Cadillac, Michigan 49601
Phone: (616)775-9776
Fax: (616)775-1440

SCORE Office (Detroit)
477 Michigan Ave., Rm. 515
Detroit, Michigan 48226
Phone: (313)226-7947

SCORE Office (Flint)
Mott Community College
708 Root Rd., Rm. 308
Flint, Michigan 48503
Phone: (810)233-6846

SCORE Office (Grand Rapids)
110 Michigan Ave.
Grand Rapids, Michigan 49503
Phone: (616)771-0305

SCORE Office (Holland)
c/o Holland Chamber of Commerce
480 State St.
Holland, Michigan 49423
Phone: (616)396-9472

SCORE Office (Jackson)
Jackson Chamber of Commerce
209 East Washington
PO Box 80
Jackson, Michigan 49204
Phone: (517)782-8221
Fax: (517)782-0061

SCORE Office (Kalamazoo)
128 N. Kalamazoo Mall
Kalamazoo, Michigan 49007
Phone: (616)381-5382

SCORE Office (Lansing)
117 E. Allegan
PO Box 14030
Lansing, Michigan 48901
Phone: (517)487-6340
Fax: (517)484-6910

SCORE Office (Livonia)
Livonia Chamber of Commerce
15401 Farmington Rd.
Livonia, Michigan 48154
Phone: (313)427-2122
Fax: (313)427-6055

SCORE Office (Madison Heights)
26345 John R
Madison Heights, Michigan 48071
Phone: (810)542-5010
Fax: (810)542-6821

SCORE Office (Monroe)
Monroe Chamber of Commerce
111 E. 1st
Monroe, Michigan 48161
Phone: (313)242-3366
Fax: (313)242-7253

SCORE Office (Mount Clemens)
Macomb County Chamber of Commerce
58 S/B Gratiot
Mount Clemens, Michigan 48043
Phone: (810)463-1528
Fax: (810)463-6541

SCORE Office (Muskegon)
c/o Muskegon Chamber of Commerce
PO Box 1087
230 Terrace Plz.
Muskegon, Michigan 49443
Phone: (616)722-3751
Fax: (616)728-7251

SCORE Office (Petoskey)
c/o Petoskey Chamber of Commerce
401 E. Mitchell St.
Petoskey, Michigan 49770-9961
Phone: (616)347-4150

SCORE Office (Pontiac)
Pontiac Chamber of Commerce
PO Box 430025
Pontiac, Michigan 48343
Phone: (810)335-9600

SCORE Office (Pontiac)
Oakland County Economic Development Group
Executive Office Bldg.
1200 N. Telegraph Rd.
Pontiac, Michigan 48341
Phone: (810)975-9555

SCORE Office (Port Huron)
920 Pinegrove Ave.
Port Huron, Michigan 48060
Phone: (810)985-7101

SCORE Office (Rochester)
Rochester Chamber of Commerce
71 Walnut Ste. 110
Rochester, Michigan 48307
Phone: (810)651-6700
Fax: (810)651-5270

SCORE Office (Saginaw)
901 S. Washington Ave.
Saginaw, Michigan 48601
Phone: (517)752-7161
Fax: (517)752-9055

SCORE Office (Upper Peninsula)
c/o Chamber of Commerce
2581 I-75 Business Spur
Sault Sainte Marie, Michigan 49783
Phone: (906)632-3301

SCORE Office (Southfield)
21000 W. 10 Mile Rd.
Southfield, Michigan 48075
Phone: (810)204-3050
Fax: (810)204-3099

SCORE Office (Traverse City)
202 E. Grandview Pkwy.
PO Box 387
Traverse City, Michigan 49685
Phone: (616)947-5075

SCORE Office (Warren)
Warren Chamber of Commerce
30500 Van Dyke, Ste. 118
Warren, Michigan 48093
Phone: (810)751-3939

Minnesota

SCORE Office (Aitkin)
c/o Donald F. Gode
Aitkin, Minnesota 56431
Phone: (218)741-3906

SCORE Office (Albert Lea)
Albert Lea Chamber of Commerce
202 N. Broadway Ave.
Albert Lea, Minnesota 56007
Phone: (507)373-7487

SCORE Office (Austin)
PO Box 864
Austin, Minnesota 55912
Phone: (507)437-4561
Fax: (507)437-4869

SCORE Office (South Metro)
Burnsville Chamber of Commerce
101 W. Burnsville Pkwy., No. 150
Burnsville, Minnesota 55337
Phone: (612)435-6000
Phone: (612)898-5645

SCORE Office (Fairmont)
c/o Fairmont Chamber of Commerce
PO Box 826
Fairmont, Minnesota 56031
Phone: (507)235-5547
Fax: (507)235-8411

SCORE Office (Southwest Minnesota)
112 Riverfront St.
Box 999
Mankato, Minnesota 56001
Phone: (507)345-4519

SCORE Office (Minneapolis)
North Plaza Bldg., Ste. 51
5217 Wayzata Blvd.
Minneapolis, Minnesota 55416
Phone: (612)591-0539

SCORE Office (Owatonna)
PO Box 331
Owatonna, Minnesota 55060
Phone: (507)451-7970
Fax: (507)451-7972

SCORE Office (Red Wing)
2000 W. Main St., Ste. 324
Red Wing, Minnesota 55066
Phone: (612)388-4079

SCORE Office (Southeastern Minnesota)
Mashall Chamber of Commerce
220 S. Broadway, Ste. 100
Rochester, Minnesota 55904
Phone: (507)288-1122
Fax: (507)282-8960

SCORE Office (Brainerd)
Brainerd Chamber of Commerce
St. Cloud, Minnesota 56301
Phone: (612)255-4955
Fax: (612)255-4957

SCORE Office (Central Area)
4191 2nd St. S
St. Cloud, Minnesota 56301-3600
Phone: (612)255-4955

SCORE Office (St. Paul)
St. Paul Chamber of Commerce
55 5th St. E, No. 101
St. Paul, Minnesota 55101-1713
Phone: (612)223-5010

SCORE Office (Winona)
Box 870
Winona, Minnesota 55987
Phone: (507)452-2272
Fax: (507)454-8814

SCORE Office (Worthington)
Worthington Chamber of Commerce
1121 3rd Ave.
Worthington, Minnesota 56187
Phone: (507)372-2919
Fax: (507)372-2827

Mississippi

SCORE Office (Delta)
Greenville Chamber of Commerce
915 Washington Ave.
PO Box 933
Greenville, Mississippi 38701
Phone: (601)378-3141
Fax: (601)378-3143

SCORE Office (Gulfcoast)
c/o Small Business Administration
Hancock Plz., Ste. 1001
Gulfport, Mississippi 39501-7758
Phone: (601)863-4449

SCORE Office (Jackson)
1st Jackson Center, Ste. 400
101 W. Capitol St.
Jackson, Mississippi 39201
Phone: (601)965-5533

SCORE Office (Meridian)
5220 16th Ave.
Meridian, Mississippi 39305
Phone: (601)482-4412

Missouri

SCORE Office (Lake Ozark)
University Extension
113 Kansas St.
PO Box 1405
Camdenton, Missouri 65020
Phone: (314)346-2644
Fax: (314)346-2694

SCORE Office (Cape Girardeau)
c/o Chamber of Commerce
PO Box 98
Cape Girardeau, Missouri 63702-0098
Phone: (314)335-3312

SCORE Office (Mid-Missouri)
c/o Milo Dahl
1705 Halstead Ct.
Columbia, Missouri 65203
Phone: (314)874-1132

SCORE Office (Ozark-Gateway)
101 E. Washington St.
Cuba, Missouri 65453-1826
Phone: (314)885-4954

SCORE Office (Kansas City)
323 W. 8th St., Ste. 104
Kansas City, Missouri 64105
Phone: (816)374-6675
Fax: (816)374-6759

SCORE Office (Sedalia)
c/o State Fair Community College
Lucas Place
323 W. 8th St., Ste.104
Kansas City, Missouri 64105
Phone: (816)374-6675
Phone: (816)374-6759

SCORE Office (Tri-Lakes)
HCR1 Box 85
Lampe, Missouri 65681
Phone: (417)858-6798

SCORE Office (South East Missouri)
c/o Carl Trautman
505 Lalor Dr.
Manchester, Missouri 63011
Phone: (314)256-3331

SCORE Office (Mexico)
Mexico Chamber of Commerce
111 N. Washington St.
Mexico, Missouri 65265
Phone: (314)581-2765

SCORE Office (Poplar Bluff Area)
c/o James W. Carson, Chair
Rte. 1, Box 280
Neelyville, Missouri 63954
Phone: (314)785-4727

SCORE Office (St. Joseph)
3418 W. Colony Sq.
St. Joseph, Missouri 64506
Phone: (816)232-9793

SCORE Office (St. Louis)
815 Olive St., Rm. 242
St. Louis, Missouri 63101-1569
Phone: (314)539-6600
Fax: (314)889-7687

SCORE Office (Lewis & Clark)
425 Spencer Rd.
St. Peters, Missouri 63376
Phone: (314)928-2900

SCORE Office (Springfield)
620 S. Glenstone, Ste. 110
Springfield, Missouri 65802-3200
Phone: (417)864-7670

SCORE Office (Springfield)
C/o Small Business Administration
620 S. Glenstone, Ste. 110
Springfield, Missouri 65802-3200
Phone: (417)864-7670
Fax: (417)864-4108

Montana

SCORE Office (Billings)
815 S. 27th St.
Billings, Montana 59101
Phone: (406)245-4111

SCORE Office (Bozeman)
1205 E. Main St.
Bozeman, Montana 59715
Phone: (406)586-5421
Fax: (406)586-8286

SCORE Office (Butte)
2950 Harrison Ave.
Butte, Montana 59701
Phone: (406)494-5595
Phone: (406)494-8165

SCORE Office (Great Falls)
815 2nd St. S.
Great Falls, Montana 59405
Phone: (406)761-4434

SCORE Office (Helena)
Federal Bldg.
301 S. Park
Drawer 10054
Helena, Montana 59626-0054
Phone: (406)449-5381
Fax: (406)449-5474

SCORE Office (Kalispell)
2 Main St.
Kalispell, Montana 59901
Phone: (406)756-5271
Fax: (406)752-6665

SCORE Office (Missoula)
802 Normans Ln.
Missoula, Montana 59803
Phone: (406)543-6623

Nebraska

SCORE Office (Columbus)
1823 27th St.
Columbus, Nebraska 68601
Phone: (402)564-2769
Phone: (402)564-5379
Phone: (402)564-0401

SCORE Office (North Platte)
414 E. 16th St.
Cozad, Nebraska 69130
Phone: (308)784-2690

SCORE Office (Fremont)
PO Box 325
Freemont Chamber of Commerce
92 W. 5th St.
Fremont, Nebraska 68025
Phone: (402)721-2641

SCORE Office (Hastings)
Box 42
Kearney, Nebraska 68848
Phone: (308)234-9647

SCORE Office (Lincoln)
8800 East O St.
Lincoln, Nebraska 68520
Phone: (402)437-2409

SCORE Office (Norfolk)
504 Pierce St.
Norfolk, Nebraska 68701
Phone: (402)371-0940

SCORE Office (Nebraska Small
Business Development Center)
11145 Mill Valley Rd.
Omaha, Nebraska 68154
Phone: (402)221-3604

SCORE Office (Panhandle)
11145 Mill Valley Rd.
Omaha, Nebraska 68154
Phone: (402)221-3604

Nevada

SCORE Office (Incline Village)
c/o Incline Village Chamber of
Commerce
969 Tahoe Blvd.
Incline Village, Nevada 89451
Phone: (702)831-7327
Fax: (702)832-1605

SCORE Office (Carson City)
301 E. Stewart
PO Box 7527
Las Vegas, Nevada 89125
Phone: (702)388-6104

SCORE Office (Las Vegas)
301 E. Stewart
Box 7527
Las Vegas, Nevada 89125
Phone: (702)388-6104

SCORE Office (Northern Nevada)
50 S. Virginia St., No. 233
PO Box 3216
Reno, Nevada 89505-3216
Phone: (702)784-5477

New Hampshire

SCORE Office (North Country)
PO Box 34
Berlin, New Hampshire 03570
Phone: (603)752-1090

SCORE Office (Concord)
PO Box 1258
Concord, New Hampshire 03302-1258
Phone: (603)225-7763

SCORE Office (Dover)
299 Central Ave.
Dover, New Hampshire 03820
Phone: (603)742-2218
Fax: (603)749-6317

SCORE Office (Monadnock)
34 Mechanic St.
Keene, New Hampshire 03431-3421
Phone: (603)352-0320

SCORE Office (Lakes Region)
67 Water St., Ste. 105
Laconia, New Hampshire 03246
Phone: (603)524-9168

SCORE Office (Upper Valley)
First New Hampshire Bank Bldg.
316 First
Lebanon, New Hampshire 03766
Phone: (603)448-3491

SCORE Office (Merrimack Valley)
275 Chestnut St., Rm. 618
Manchester, New Hampshire 03103
Phone: (603)666-7561

SCORE Office (Seacoast)
195 Commerce Way, Unit-A
Portsmouth, New Hampshire 03801-3251
Phone: (603)433-0576

New Jersey

SCORE Office (Chester)
c/o John C. Apelian, Chair
5 Old Mill Rd.
Chester, New Jersey 07930
Phone: (908)879-7080

SCORE Office (Greater Princeton)
4 A George Washington Dr.
Cranbury, New Jersey 08512
Phone: (609)520-1776

SCORE Office (Freehold)
Western Monmouth Chamber of
Commerce
36 W. Main St.
Freehold, New Jersey 07728
Phone: (908)462-3030
Fax: (908)462-2123

SCORE Office (Monmouth)
Brookdale Community College
Career Services
765 Newman Springs Rd.
Lincroft, New Jersey 07738
Phone: (908)224-2573

SCORE Office (Manalapan)
Monmough Library
125 Symmes Dr.
Manalapan, New Jersey 07726
Phone: (908)431-7220

SCORE Office (Jersey City)
2 Gateway Ctr., 4th Fl.
Newark, New Jersey 07102
Phone: (201)645-3982
Fax: (201)645-6265

SCORE Office (Newark)
2 Gateway Center, 4th Fl.
Newark, New Jersey 07102-5553
Phone: (201)645-3982

SCORE Office (Bergen County)
327 E. Ridgewood Ave.
Paramus, New Jersey 07652
Phone: (201)599-6090

SCORE Office (Pennsauken)
United Jersey Bank
4900 Rte. 70
Pennsauken, New Jersey 08109
Phone: (609)486-3421

SCORE Office (Southern New Jersey)
c/o United Jersey Bank
4900 Rte. 70
Pennsauken, New Jersey 08109
Phone: (609)486-3421

SCORE Office (Shrewsbury)
Monmouth County Library
Hwy. 35
Shrewsbury, New Jersey 07702
Phone: (908)842-5995
Fax: (908)219-6140

SCORE Office (Somerset)
Paritan Valley Community College
PO Box 3300
Somerville, New Jersey 08876
Phone: (908)218-8874

SCORE Office (Ocean County)
33 Washington St.
Toms River, New Jersey 08754
Phone: (908)505-6033

SCORE Office (Wall)
Wall Library
2700 Allaire Rd.
Wall, New Jersey 07719
Phone: (908)449-8877

SCORE Office (Wayne)
2055 Hamburg Tpke.
Wayne, New Jersey 07470
Phone: (201)831-7788
Fax: (201)831-9112

New Mexico

SCORE Office (Albuquerque)
Silver Sq., Ste. 330
625 Silver Ave., SW
Albuquerque, New Mexico 87102
Phone: (505)766-1900

SCORE Office (Las Cruces)
Loretto Towne Center
505 S. Main St., Ste. 125
Las Cruces, New Mexico 88001
Phone: (505)523-5627

SCORE Office (Roswell)
Federal Bldg., Rm. 237
Roswell, New Mexico 88201
Phone: (505)625-2112

SCORE Office (Santa Fe)
Montoya Federal Bldg.
120 Federal Place, Rm. 307
Santa Fe, New Mexico 87501
Phone: (505)988-6302

New York

SCORE Office (Northeast)
Lee O'Brien Office Bldg., Rm. 815
Pearl & Clinton Aves.
Albany, New York 12207
Phone: (518)472-6300

SCORE Office (Auburn)
c/o Auburn Chamber of Commerce
30 South St.
PO Box 675
Auburn, New York 13021
Phone: (315)252-7291

SCORE Office (South Tier Binghamton)
Metro Center, 2nd Fl.
49 Court St.
PO Box 995
Binghamton, New York 13902
Phone: (607)772-8860

SCORE Office (Queens County City)
12055 Queens Blvd., Rm. 333
Borough Hall, New York 11424
Phone: (718)263-8961

SCORE Office (Buffalo)
Federal Bldg., Rm. 1311
111 W. Huron St.
Buffalo, New York 14202
Phone: (716)846-4301

SCORE Office (Canandaigua)
Chamber of Commerce Bldg.
113 S. Main St.
Canandaigua, New York 14424
Phone: (716)394-4400
Fax: (716)394-4546

SCORE Office (Chemung)
c/o Small Business Administration, 4th Fl.
333 E. Water St.
Elmira, New York 14901
Phone: (607)734-3358

SCORE Office (Geneva)
Chamber of Commerce Bldg.
PO Box 587
Geneva, New York 14456
Phone: (315)789-1776
Fax: (315)789-3993

SCORE Office (Glens Falls)
Adirondack Region Chamber of Commerce
84 Broad St.
Glens Falls, New York 12801
Phone: (518)798-8463
Fax: (518)745-1433

SCORE Office (Orange County)
Orange County Chamber of Commerce
40 Matthews St.
Goshen, New York 10924
Phone: (914)294-8080
Toll-free: (800)294-8181
Fax: (914)294-6121

SCORE Office (Huntington Area)
c/o Huntington Chamber of Commerce
151 W. Carver St.
Huntington, New York 11743
Phone: (516)423-6100

SCORE Office (Tompkins County)
c/o Tompkins County Chamber of Commerce
904 E. Shore Dr.
Ithaca, New York 14850
Phone: (607)273-7080

SCORE Office (Long Island City)
120-55 Queens Blvd.
Jamaica, New York 11424
Phone: (718)263-8961
Fax: (718)263-9032

SCORE Office (Chatauqua)
c/o Chatauqua Chamber of Commerce
101 W. 5th St.
Jamestown, New York 14701
Phone: (716)484-1103

SCORE Office (Queens County City)
120-55 Queens Blvd., Rm. 333
Queens Borough Hall
Kew Gardens, New York 11424
Phone: (718)263-8961

SCORE Office (Brookhaven)
Dept. of Economic Development
3233 Rte. 112
Medford, New York 11763
Phone: (516)451-6563
Phone: (516)751-3886

SCORE Office (Melville)
35 Pinelawn Rd., Rm. 207-W
Melville, New York 11747
Phone: (516)454-0771

SCORE Office (Nassau County)
400 County Seat Dr., No. 140
Mineola, New York 11501
Phone: (516)571-3304
Phone: (516)571-3341

SCORE Office (Mount Vernon)
c/o Mount Vernon Chamber of Commerce
4 N. 7th Ave.
Mount Vernon, New York 10550
Phone: (914)667-7500

SCORE Office (New York)
26 Federal Plz., Rm. 3100
New York, New York 10278
Phone: (212)264-4507

SCORE Office (Newburgh)
47 Grand St.
Newburgh, New York 12550
Phone: (914)562-5100

SCORE Office (Owego)
Tioga County Chamber of Commerce
188 Front St.
Owego, New York 13827
Phone: (607)687-2020

SCORE Office (Peekskill)
c/o Peekskill Chamber of Commerce
1 S. Division St.
Peekskill, New York 10566
Phone: (914)737-3600
Fax: (914)737-0541

SCORE Office (Penn Yan)
Penn Yan Chamber of Commerce
2375 Rte. 14A
Penn Yan, New York 14527
Phone: (315)536-3111

SCORE Office (Dutchess)
c/o Chamber of Commerce
110 Main St.
Poughkeepsie, New York 12601
Phone: (914)454-1700

SCORE Office (Rochester)
601 Keating Federal Bldg., Rm. 410
100 State St.
Rochester, New York 14614
Phone: (716)263-6473

SCORE Office (Saranac Lake)
30 Main St.
Saranac Lake, New York 12983
Phone: (315)448-0415

SCORE Office (Suffolk)
286 Main St.
Setauket, New York 11733
Phone: (516)751-3886

SCORE Office (Staten Island)
c/o Staten Island Chamber of Commerce
130 Bay St.
Staten Island, New York 10301
Phone: (718)727-1221

SCORE Office (Ulster)
Ulster County Community College
Clinton Bldg., Rm. 107
Stone Ridge, New York 12484
Phone: (914)687-5035

SCORE Office (Syracuse)
100 S. Clinton St., Rm. 1073
Syracuse, New York 13260
Phone: (315)448-0422

SCORE Office (Oneida)
SUNY Institute of Technology
PO Box 3050
Utica, New York 13504-3050
Phone: (315)792-7553

SCORE Office (Watertown)
CAPC Office
518 Davidson St.
PO Box 899
Watertown, New York 13601
Phone: (315)788-1200

SCORE Office (Westchester)
350 Main St.
White Plains, New York 10601
Phone: (914)948-3907

SCORE Office (Yonkers)
c/o Yonkers Chamber of Commerce
540 Nepperhan Ave., Ste.200
Yonkers, New York 10701
Phone: (914)963-0332

North Carolina

SCORE Office (Asheville)
Federal Bldg., Rm. 259
151 Patton
Asheville, North Carolina 28801
Phone: (704)271-4786

SCORE Office (Chapel Hill)
c/o Chapel Hill/Carrboro Chamber of
Commerce
104 S. Estes Dr.
PO Box 2897
Chapel Hill, North Carolina 27514
Phone: (919)967-7075

SCORE Office (Coastal Plains)
PO Box 2897
Chapel Hill, North Carolina 27515
Phone: (919)967-7075
Fax: (919)968-6874

SCORE Office (Charlotte)
200 N. College St., Ste. A-2015
Charlotte, North Carolina 28202
Phone: (704)344-6576

SCORE Office (Durham)
3411 Chapel Hill Blvd.
Durham, North Carolina 27707
Phone: (919)541-2171

SCORE Office (Gastonia)
c/o Gastonia Chamber of Commerce
PO Box 2168
Gastonia, North Carolina 28053
Phone: (704)864-2621
Fax: (704)854-8723

SCORE Office (Greensboro)
400 W. Market St., Ste. 410
Greensboro, North Carolina 27401-2241
Phone: (919)333-5399

SCORE Office (Henderson)
PO Box 917
Henderson, North Carolina 27536
Phone: (919)492-2061
Fax: (919)430-0460

SCORE Office (Hendersonville)
Federal Bldg., Rm. 108
W. 4th Ave. & Church St.
Hendersonville, North Carolina 28792
Phone: (704)693-8702

SCORE Office (Unifour)
c/o Catawba County Chamber of
Commerce
PO Box 1828
Hickory, North Carolina 28603
Phone: (704)328-6111

SCORE Office (High Point)
c/o High Point Chamber of Commerce
1101 N. Main St.
High Point, North Carolina 27262
Phone: (910)882-8625

SCORE Office (Outer Banks)
c/o Outer Banks Chamber of Commerce
PO Box 1757
Kill Devil Hills, North Carolina
27948
Phone: (919)441-8144

SCORE Office (Down East)
PO Box 14294
New Bern, North Carolina 28561
Phone: (919)633-6688

SCORE Office (Kinston)
PO Box 14294
New Bern, North Carolina 28561
Phone: (919)633-6688

SCORE Office (Raleigh)
Century Post Office Bldg., Ste. 306
PO Box 406
Raleigh, North Carolina 27602
Phone: (919)856-4739

SCORE Office (Sanford)
Small Business Assistance Center
1801 Nash St.
Sanford, North Carolina 27330
Phone: (919)774-6442
Fax: (919)776-8739

SCORE Office (Sandhills Area)
c/o Sand Area Chamber of Commerce
1480 Hwy. 15-501
PO Box 458
Southern Pines, North Carolina 28387
Phone: (910)692-3926

SCORE Office (Wilmington)
Alton Lennon Federal Bldg.
2 Princess St., Ste. 103
Wilmington, North Carolina 28401-3958
Phone: (919)343-4576

North Dakota

SCORE Office (Bismarck-Mandan)
418 E. Broadway Ave.
PO Box 1912
Bismarck, North Dakota 58501-1912
Phone: (701)250-4303

SCORE Office (Fargo)
657 2nd Ave., Rm. 225
PO Box 3086
Fargo, North Dakota 58108-3083
Phone: (701)239-5677

SCORE Office (Upper Red River)
202 N. 3rd St.
Grand Forks, North Dakota 58203
Phone: (701)772-7271

SCORE Office (Minot)
PO Box 507
Minot, North Dakota 58701-0507
Phone: (701)852-6883

Ohio

SCORE Office (Akron)
c/o Akron Regional Development
Board
One Cascade Plz., 7th Fl.
Akron, Ohio 44308
Phone: (216)379-3163

SCORE Office (Ashland)
Ashland University
Gill Center
47 W. Main St.
Ashland, Ohio 44805
Phone: (419)281-4584

SCORE Office (Canton)
116 Cleveland Ave. NW, Ste. 601
Canton, Ohio 44702-1720
Phone: (216)453-6047

SCORE Office (Chillicothe)
165 S. Paint St.
Chillicothe, Ohio 45601
Phone: (614)772-4530

SCORE Office (Cincinnati)
Ameritrust Bldg., Rm. 850
525 Vine St.
Cincinnati, Ohio 45202
Phone: (513)684-2812

SCORE Office (Cincinnati)
525 Vine St.
Ameritrust Bldg., Rm. 850
Cincinnati, Ohio 45202
Phone: (513)684-2812

SCORE Office (Cleveland)
Eaton Center, Ste. 620
1100 Superior Ave.
Cleveland, Ohio 44114-2507
Phone: (216)522-4194

SCORE Office (Columbus)
2 Nationwide Plz., Ste. 1400
Columbus, Ohio 43215-2542
Phone: (614)469-2357

SCORE Office (Dayton)
200 W. 2nd St.
Federal Bldg., Rm. 505
Dayton, Ohio 45402
Phone: (513)225-2887

SCORE Office (Dayton)
Dayton Federal Bldg., Rm. 505
201 W. Second St.
Dayton, Ohio 45402-1430
Phone: (513)225-2887

SCORE Office (Defiance)
Defiance Chamber of Commerce
615 W. 3rd St.
PO Box 130
Defiance, Ohio 43512
Phone: (419)782-7946

SCORE Office (Findlay)
Findlay Chamber of Commerce
123 E. Main Cross St.
PO Box 923
Findlay, Ohio 45840
Phone: (419)422-3314

SCORE Office (Lima)
147 N. Main St.
Lima, Ohio 45801
Phone: (419)222-6045
Fax: (419)229-0266

SCORE Office (Mansfield)
Mansfield Chamber of Commerce
55 N. Mulberry St.
Mansfield, Ohio 44902
Phone: (419)522-3211

SCORE Office (Marietta)
Marietta College
Thomas Hall
Marietta, Ohio 45750
Phone: (614)373-0268

SCORE Office (Medina)
County Administrative Bldg.
144 N. Broadway
Medina, Ohio 44256
Phone: (216)764-8650

SCORE Office (Licking County)
50 W. Locust St.
Newark, Ohio 43055
Phone: (614)345-7458

SCORE Office (Salem)
2491 State Rte. 45 S
Salem, Ohio 44460
Phone: (216)332-0361
Phone: (216)332-9256

SCORE Office (Tiffin)
Tiffin Chamber of Commerce
62 S. Washington St.
Tiffin, Ohio 44883
Phone: (419)447-4141
Fax: (419)447-5141

SCORE Office (Toledo)
1946 N. 13th St., Rm. 352
Toledo, Ohio 43624
Phone: (419)259-7598

SCORE Office (Wooster)
377 W. Liberty St.
Wooster, Ohio 44691
Phone: (216)262-5735

SCORE Office (Youngstown)
Youngstown University
306 Williamson Hall
Youngstown, Ohio 44555
Phone: (216)746-2687

Oklahoma

SCORE Office (Anadarko)
PO Box 366
Anadarko, Oklahoma 73005
Phone: (405)247-6651
Phone: (405)247-6652

SCORE Office (Ardmore)
PO Box 1585
Ardmore, Oklahoma 73402
Phone: (405)223-7765

SCORE Office (Northeast Oklahoma)
Bank of Oklahoma Bldg.
210 S. Main
Grove, Oklahoma 74344
Phone: (918)786-4729

SCORE Office (Lawton)
Federal Bldg., Rm. 107
431 East Ave.
Lawton, Oklahoma 73501
Phone: (405)353-8726

SCORE Office (Oklahoma City)
c/o SBA, Oklahoma Tower Bldg.
210 Park Ave., No. 1300
Oklahoma City, Oklahoma 73102
Phone: (405)231-5163

SCORE Office (Stillwater)
Stillwater Chamber of Commerce
439 S. Main
Stillwater, Oklahoma 74074
Phone: (405)372-5573
Fax: (405)372-4316

SCORE Office (Tulsa)
Tulsa Chamber of Commerce
616 S. Boston, Ste. 406
Tulsa, Oklahoma 74119
Phone: (918)581-7462

Oregon

SCORE Office (Bend)
c/o Bend Chamber of Commerce
63085 N. Hwy. 97
Bend, Oregon 97701
Phone: (503)382-3221

SCORE Office (Willamette)
1401 Willamette St.
PO Box 1107
Eugene, Oregon 97401-4003
Phone: (503)484-5485

SCORE Office (Florence)
c/o Lane Community College
3149 Oak St.
Florence, Oregon 97439
Phone: (503)997-8444
Fax: (503)997-8448

SCORE Office (Southern Oregon)
132 W. Main St.
Medford, Oregon 97501
Phone: (503)776-4220

SCORE Office (Portland)
222 SW Columbia, Ste. 500
Portland, Oregon 97201
Phone: (503)326-3441

SCORE Office (Salem)
PO Box 4024
Salem, Oregon 97302-1024
Phone: (503)370-2896

Pennsylvania

SCORE Office (Altoona-Blair)
c/o Altoona-Blair Chamber of Commerce
1212 12th Ave.
Altoona, Pennsylvania 16601-3493
Phone: (814)943-8151

SCORE Office (Lehigh Valley)
Lehigh University
Rauch Bldg. 37
621 Taylor St.
Bethlehem, Pennsylvania 18015
Phone: (610)758-4496
Butler County Chamber of Commerce

SCORE Office
100 N. Main St.
PO Box 1082
Butler, Pennsylvania 16003
Phone: (412)283-2222
Fax: (412)283-0224

SCORE Office (Cumberland Valley)
Chambersburg Chamber of Commerce
75 S. 2nd St.
Chambersburg, Pennsylvania 17201
Phone: (717)264-4496

SCORE Office (Monroe County-
Stroudsburg)
556 Main St.
East Stroudsburg, Pennsylvania 18301
Phone: (717)421-4433

SCORE Office (Erie)
120 W. 9th St.
Erie, Pennsylvania 16501
Phone: (814)871-5650

SCORE Office (Bucks County)
c/o Bucks County Chamber of
Commerce
409 Hood Blvd.
Fairless Hills, Pennsylvania 19030
Phone: (215)943-8850
Hanover Chamber of Commerce

SCORE Office
146 Broadway
Hanover, Pennsylvania 17331
Phone: (717)637-6130
Fax: (717)637-9127

SCORE Office (Harrisburg)
100 Chestnut, Ste. 309
Harrisburg, Pennsylvania 17101
Phone: (717)782-3874

SCORE Office (Montgomery County)
Baederwood Shopping Center
1653 The Fairways, Ste. 204
Jenkintown, Pennsylvania 19046
Phone: (215)885-3027

SCORE Office (Kittanning)
c/o Kittanning Chamber of Commerce
2 Butler Rd.
Kittanning, Pennsylvania 16201
Phone: (412)543-1305
Fax: (412)543-6206

SCORE Office (Lancaster)
118 W. Chestnut St.
Lancaster, Pennsylvania 17603
Phone: (717)397-3092

SCORE Office (Westmoreland
County)
St. Vincent College
Latrobe, Pennsylvania 15650
Phone: (412)539-7505

SCORE Office (Lebanon)
Lebanon Chamber of Commerce
252 N. 8th St.
PO Box 899
Lebanon, Pennsylvania 17042-0899
Phone: (717)273-3727
Fax: (717)273-7940

SCORE Office (Lewistown)
Lewistown Chamber of Commerce
3 W. Monument Sq., Ste. 204
Lewistown, Pennsylvania 17044
Phone: (717)248-6713
Fax: (717)248-6714

SCORE Office (Delaware County)
Delaware County Chamber of Commerce
602 E. Baltimore Pike
Media, Pennsylvania 19063
Phone: (610)565-3677
Fax: (610)565-1606

SCORE Office (Milton)
Milton Area Chamber of Commerce
112 S. Front St.
Milton, Pennsylvania 17847
Phone: (717)742-7341
Fax: (717)792-2008

SCORE Office (Mon-Valley)
435 Donner Ave.
Monessen, Pennsylvania 15062
Phone: (412)684-4277
Monroeville Chamber of Commerce

SCORE Office
William Penn Plaza
2790 Mosside Blvd., Ste. 295
Monroeville, Pennsylvania 15146
Phone: (412)856-0622
Fax: (412)856-1030

SCORE Office (Airport Area)
Chamber of Commerce
986 Brodhead Rd.
Moon Twp, Pennsylvania 15108-2398
Phone: (412)264-6270
Fax: (412)264-1575

SCORE Office (Northeast)
8601 E. Roosevelt Blvd.
Philadelphia, Pennsylvania 19152
Phone: (215)332-3400
Fax: (215)332-6050

SCORE Office (Philadelphia)
3535 Market St., Rm. 4480
Philadelphia, Pennsylvania 19104
Phone: (215)596-5077

SCORE Office (Pittsburgh)
960 Penn Ave., 5th Fl.
Pittsburgh, Pennsylvania 15222
Phone: (412)644-5447

SCORE Office (Pittsburgh Satellite)
960 Penn Ave., 5th Fl.
Pittsburgh, Pennsylvania 15222
Phone: (412)644-5447
Fax: (412)644-5446

SCORE Office (Tri-County)
238 High St.
Pottstown, Pennsylvania 19464
Phone: (610)327-2673

SCORE Office (Reading)
c/o Reading Chamber of Commerce
645 Penn St.
Reading, Pennsylvania 19601
Phone: (610)376-6766

SCORE Office (Scranton)
Federal Bldg., Rm. 104
Washington Ave. & Linden
Scranton, Pennsylvania 18503
Phone: (717)347-4611

SCORE Office (Central Pennsylvania)
200 Innovation Blvd., Ste. 242-B
State College, Pennsylvania 16803
Phone: (814)234-9415

SCORE Office (Uniontown)
Federal Bldg.
Pittsburg St.
PO Box 2065 DTS
Uniontown, Pennsylvania 15401
Phone: (412)437-4222

SCORE Office (Warren County)
Warren County Chamber of Commerce
315 2nd Ave.
PO Box 942
Warren, Pennsylvania 16365
Phone: (814)723-9017

SCORE Office (Waynesboro)
323 E. Main St.
Waynesboro, Pennsylvania 17268
Phone: (717)762-7123
Fax: (717)962-7124

SCORE Office (Chester County)
Government Service Center, Ste. 281
601 Westtown Rd.
West Chester, Pennsylvania 19382-4538
Phone: (610)344-6910

SCORE Office (Wilkes-Barre)
20 N. Pennsylvania Ave.
Wilkes Barre, Pennsylvania 18702
Phone: (717)826-6502

SCORE Office (North Central Pennsylvania)
240 W. 3rd St., Rm. 304
PO Box 725
Williamsport, Pennsylvania 17703
Phone: (717)322-3720

SCORE Office (York)
Cyber Center
1600 Pennsylvania Ave.
York, Pennsylvania 17404
Phone: (717)845-8830

Puerto Rico

SCORE Office (Puerto Rico)
Citibank Towers Plaza, 2nd Fl.
252 Ponce de Leon Ave.
San Juan, Puerto Rico 00918-2041
Phone: (809)766-5001

Rhode Island

SCORE Office (Barrington)
Barrington Public Library
281 County Rd.
Barrington, Rhode Island 02806
Phone: (401)247-1920
Fax: (401)247-3763

SCORE Office (Woonsocket)
640 Washington Hwy.
Lincoln, Rhode Island 02865
Phone: (401)334-1000
Fax: (401)334-1009

SCORE Office (Wickford)
8045 Post Rd.
North Kingstown, Rhode Island 02852
Phone: (401)295-5566
Fax: (401)295-8987

SCORE Office (J.G.E. Knight)
380 Westminster St.
Providence, Rhode Island 02903
Phone: (401)528-4571

SCORE Office (Warwick)
3288 Post Rd.
Warwick, Rhode Island 02886
Phone: (401)732-1100
Fax: (401)732-1101

SCORE Office (Westerly)
74 Post Rd.
Westerly, Rhode Island 02891
Phone: (401)596-7761
Toll-free: (800)732-7636
Fax: (401)596-2190

South Carolina

SCORE Office (Aiken)
Aiken Chamber of Commerce
P.O. Box 892
Aiken, South Carolina 29802
Phone: (803)641-1111
Toll-free: (800)542-4536
Fax: (803)641-4174

SCORE Office (Anderson)
Tri-County Technical College
Anderson Mall
3130 N. Main St.
Anderson, South Carolina 29621
Phone: (864)224-0453

SCORE Office (Coastal)
284 King St.
Charleston, South Carolina 29401
Phone: (803)727-4778

SCORE Office (Midlands)
Strom Thurmond Bldg., Rm. 358
1835 Assembly St.
Columbia, South Carolina 29201
Phone: (803)765-5131

SCORE Office (Piedmont)
Federal Bldg., Rm. B-02
300 E. Washington St.
Greenville, South Carolina 29601
Phone: (803)271-3638

SCORE Office (Greenwood)
Piedmont Technical College
PO Drawer 1467
Greenwood, South Carolina 29648
Phone: (864)223-8357

SCORE Office (Hilton Head)
Hilton Head Chamber of Commerce
PO Box 5647
Hilton Head, South Carolina 29938
Phone: (803)785-3673
Fax: (803)785-7110

SCORE Office (Grand Strand)
48th Executive Ct., Ste. 211
1109 48th Ave. N
Myrtle Beach, South Carolina 29577
Phone: (803)449-8538

SCORE Office (Spartanburg)
c/o Vernon Wyant Chamber of
Commerce
P.O. Box 1636
Spartanburg, South Carolina 29304
Phone: (864)594-5000
Fax: (864)594-5055

South Dakota

SCORE Office (Rapid City)
444 Mount Rushmore Rd., No. 209
Rapid City, South Dakota 57701
Phone: (605)394-5311

SCORE Office (Sioux Falls)
First Financial Center, No. 200
110 S. Phillips Ave.
Sioux Falls, South Dakota 57102-1109
Phone: (605)330-4231

Tennessee

SCORE Office (Chattanooga)
Federal Bldg., Rm. 26
900 Georgia Ave.
Chattanooga, Tennessee 37402
Phone: (423)752-5190

SCORE Office (Cleveland)
Cleveland Chamber of Commerce
P.O. Box 2275
Cleveland, Tennessee 37320
Phone: (423)472-6587
Fax: (423)472-2019

SCORE Office (Upper Cumberland
Center)
1225 S. Willow Ave.
Cookeville, Tennessee 38501
Phone: (615)432-4111
Fax: (615)432-6010

SCORE Office (Unicoi County)
c/o Chamber of Commerce
PO Box 713
Erwin, Tennessee 37650
Phone: (423)743-3000
Fax: (423)743-0942

SCORE Office (Greeneville)
Greeneville Chamber of Commerce
115 Academy St.
Greeneville, Tennessee 37743
Phone: (423)638-4111
Fax: (423)638-5345

SCORE Office (Jackson)
c/o Jackson Chamber of Commerce
197 Auditorium St.
PO Box 1904
Jackson, Tennessee 38302
Phone: (901)423-2200

SCORE Office (Northeast Tennessee)
c/o Chamber of Commerce
2710 S. Roan St.
Johnson City, Tennessee 37601
Phone: (423)929-7686
Fax: (423)461-8052

SCORE Office (Kingsport)
c/o Kingsport Chamber of Commerce
151 E. Main St.
Kingsport, Tennessee 37662
Phone: (423)392-8805

SCORE Office (Greater Knoxville)
Farragot Bldg., Ste. 224
530 S. Gay St.
Knoxville, Tennessee 37902
Phone: (423)545-4203

SCORE Office (Maryville)
Blount County Chamber of Com-
merce
201 S. Washington St.
Maryville, Tennessee 37804-5728
Phone: (423)983-2241
Toll-free: (800)525-6834
Fax: (423)984-1386

SCORE Office (Memphis)
Federal Bldg., Ste. 148
167 N. Main St.
Memphis, Tennessee 38103
Phone: (901)544-3588

SCORE Office (Nashville)
50 Vantage Way, Ste. 201
Nashville, Tennessee 37228-1500
Phone: (615)736-7621

Texas

SCORE Office (Abilene)
2106 Federal Post Office and Court
Bldg.
Abilene, Texas 79601
Phone: (915)677-1857

SCORE Office (Austin)
300 E. 8th St., Rm. 572
Austin, Texas 78701
Phone: (512)482-5112

SCORE Office (Golden Triangle)
c/o Community Bank
700 Calder, Ste. 101
Beaumont, Texas 77701
Phone: (409)838-6581

SCORE Office (Brownsville)
3505 Boca Chica Blvd., No. 305
Brownsville, Texas 78521
Phone: (210)541-4508

SCORE Office (Brazos Valley)
Victoria Bank & Trust
3000 Briarcrest, Ste. 302
Bryan, Texas 77802
Phone: (409)776-8876

SCORE Office (Cleburne)
Watergarden Pl., 9th Fl., Ste. 400
Cleburne, Texas 76031
Phone: (817)871-6002

SCORE Office (Corpus Christi)
c/o Robert Martens
606 N. Carancahua, Ste. 1200
Corpus Christi, Texas 78476
Phone: (512)888-3306
Fax: (512)888-3418

SCORE Office (Dallas)
17218 Preston Road, No. 3202
Dallas, Texas 75252
Phone: (214)733-0189
Phone: (214)733-3953

SCORE Office (El Paso)
10737 Gateway W, Ste. 320
El Paso, Texas 79935
Phone: (915)540-5155

SCORE Office (Bedford)
100 E. 15th St., Ste. 400
Fort Worth, Texas 76102
Phone: (817)871-6002

SCORE Office (Fort Worth)
100 E. 15th St., No. 24
Fort Worth, Texas 76102
Phone: (817)871-6002

SCORE Office (Garland)
2734 W. Kingsley Rd.
Garland, Texas 75041
Phone: (214)271-9224

SCORE Office (Granbury Chamber of
Commerce)
416 S. Morgan
Granbury, Texas 76048
Phone: (817)573-1622
Fax: (817)573-0805

SCORE Office (Rio Grande Valley)
222 E. Van Buren, Ste. 500
Harlingen, Texas 78550
Phone: (210)427-8533

SCORE Office (Houston)
9301 Southwest Fwy., Ste. 550
Houston, Texas 77074
Phone: (713)773-6565

SCORE Office (Irving)
c/o Irving Chamber of Commerce
3333 N. MacArthur Blvd., Ste. 100
Irving, Texas 75062
Phone: (214)252-8484
Fax: (214)252-6710

SCORE Office (Lubbock)
1611 10th St., Ste. 200
Lubbock, Texas 79401
Phone: (806)743-7462

SCORE Office (Midland)
Post Office Annex
200 E. Wall St., Rm. P121
Midland, Texas 79701
Phone: (915)687-2649

SCORE Office (Orange)
c/o Orange Chamber of Commerce
1012 Green Ave.
Orange, Texas 77630-5620
Phone: (409)883-3536
Toll-free: (800)528-4906
Fax: (409)886-3247

SCORE Office (Plano)
c/o Plano Chamber of Commerce
1200 E. 15th St.
P.O. Drawer 940287

Plano, Texas 75094-0287
Phone: (214)424-7547
Fax: (214)422-5182

SCORE Office (Port Arthur)
c/o Port Arthur Chamber of Commerce
4749 Twin City Hwy., Ste. 300
Port Arthur, Texas 77642
Phone: (409)963-1107
Fax: (409)963-3322

SCORE Office (Richardson)
c/o Richardson Chamber of Com-
merce
411 Belle Grove
Richardson, Texas 75080
Phone: (214))234-4141
Toll-free: (800)777-8001
Fax: (214)680-9103

SCORE Office (San Antonio)
c/o SBA, Federal Bldg., Rm. A527
727 E. Durango
San Antonio, Texas 78206
Phone: (210)229-5931
Phone: (210)229-5900

SCORE Office (Texarkana State College)
819 State Line Ave.
PO Box 1468
Texarkana, Texas 75501
Phone: (903)792-7191

SCORE Office (East Texas)
1530 SW Loop 323, Ste. 100
Tyler, Texas 75701
Phone: (903)510-2975

SCORE Office (Waco)
Business Resource Center
4601 N. 19th St.
Waco, Texas 76708
Phone: (817)754-8898

SCORE Office (Wichita Falls)
Hamilton Bldg.
PO Box 1860
Wichita Falls, Texas 76307
Phone: (817)766-1602

Utah

SCORE Office (Ogden)
324 25th St., Ste. 6104
Ogden, Utah 84401
Phone: (801)625-5712

SCORE Office (Central Utah)
Old County Court House
51 S. University Ave.
Provo, Utah 84601
Phone: (801)379-2444

SCORE Office (Southern Utah)
c/o Dixie College Small Business
Development Center
225 South 700 East
St. George, Utah 84770
Phone: (801)673-4811

SCORE Office (Salt Lake)
125 S. State St., Rm. 2237
Salt Lake City, Utah 84138
Phone: (801)524-3211

Vermont

SCORE Office (Champlain Valley)
Winston Prouty Federal Bldg.
11 Lincoln St., Room 106
Essex Junction, Vermont 05452
Phone: (802)951-6762

SCORE Office (Montpelier)
c/o U.S. Small Business Administration
87 State St., Rm. 205
PO Box 605
Montpelier, Vermont 05601
Phone: (802)828-4422

SCORE Office (Marble Valley)
Rutland Industrial Development
Corp.
256 N. Main St.
Rutland, Vermont 05701-2413
Phone: (802)773-9147

SCORE Office (Northeast Kingdom)
c/o NCIC
20 Main St.
PO Box 904
St. Johnsbury, Vermont 05819
Phone: (802)748-5101

Virgin Islands

SCORE Office (St. Croix)
United Plaza Shopping Center
PO Box 4010, Christiansted
St. Croix, Virgin Islands 00822
Phone: (809)778-5380

SCORE Office (St. Thomas-St. John)
Federal Bldg., Rm. 21
Veterans Dr.
St. Thomas, Virgin Islands 00801
Phone: (809)774-8530

Virginia

SCORE Office (Arlington)
2009 N. 14th St., Ste. 111
Arlington, Virginia 22201
Phone: (703)525-2400

SCORE Office (Blacksburg)
141 Jackson St.
Blacksburg, Virginia 24060
Phone: (540)552-4061

SCORE Office (Bristol)
20 Volunteer Pkwy.
PO Box 519
Bristol, Virginia 24203
Phone: (540)968-4399

SCORE Office (Central Virginia)
918 Emmet St. N, Ste. 200
Charlottesville, Virginia 22903-4878
Phone: (804)295-6712

SCORE Office (Alleghany Satellite)
c/o Chamber of Commerce
241 W. Main St.
Covington, Virginia 24426
Phone: (540)962-2178
Fax: (540)962-2179

SCORE Office (Central Fairfax)
3975 University Dr., Ste. 350
Fairfax, Virginia 22030
Phone: (703)591-2450

SCORE Office (Falls Church)
P.O. Box 491
Falls Church, Virginia 22040
Phone: (703)532-1050
Fax: (703)237-7904

SCORE Office (Glenns)
c/o Rappahannock Community
College
Glenns Campus
Box 287
Glenns, Virginia 23149
Phone: (804)693-9650

SCORE Office (Peninsula)
c/o Peninsula Chamber of Commerce
6 Manhattan Sq.
PO Box 7269
Hampton, Virginia 23666
Phone: (804)766-2000

SCORE Office (Tri-Cities)
c/o Chamber of Commerce
108 N. Main St.
Hopewell, Virginia 23860
Phone: (804)458-5536

SCORE Office (Lynchburg)
Federal Bldg.
1100 Main St.
Lynchburg, Virginia 24504-1714
Phone: (804)846-3235

SCORE Office (Danville)
c/o Martinsville Chamber of Commerce
115 Broad St.
PO Box 709
Martinsville, Virginia 24112-0709
Phone: (540)632-6401

SCORE Office (Eastern Shore)
c/o Eastern Shore Chamber of
Commerce
Federal Bldg.
200 Grandby St.
Norfolk, Virginia 23510
Phone: (804)441-3733

SCORE Office (Norfolk)
Federal Bldg., Rm. 737
200 Granby St.
Norfolk, Virginia 23510
Phone: (804)441-3733

SCORE Office (Virginia Beach)
Virginia Beach Office of Hampton
Roads
Chamber of Commerce
200 Grandby St., Rm 737
Norfolk, Virginia 23510
Phone: (804)441-3733

SCORE Office (Greater Prince
William)
Prince William Chamber of Commerce
4320 Ridgewood Center Dr.
Prince William, Virginia 22192
Phone: (703)590-5000

SCORE Office (Radford)
Radford Chamber of Commerce
1126 Norwood St.
Radford, Virginia 24141
Phone: (540)639-2202

SCORE Office (Richmond)
Dale Bldg., Ste. 200
1504 Santa Rosa Rd.
Richmond, Virginia 23229
Phone: (804)771-2400

SCORE Office (Roanoke)
Federal Bldg.
PO Box 1366, Rm. 716
Roanoke, Virginia 24007
Phone: (540)857-2834

SCORE Office (Fairfax)
8391 Old Courthouse Rd., Ste. 300
Vienna, Virginia 22182
Phone: (703)749-0400

SCORE Office (Greater Vienna)
513 Maple Ave. West
Vienna, Virginia 22180
Phone: (703)281-1333
Fax: (703)242-1482

SCORE Office (Shenandoah Valley)
c/o Waynesboro Chamber of Commerce
301 W. Main St.
Waynesboro, Virginia 22980
Phone: (540)949-8203

SCORE Office (Williamsburg)
c/o Williamsburg Chamber of
Commerce
201 Penniman Rd.
Williamsburg, Virginia 23185
Phone: (804)229-6511

SCORE Office (Northern Virginia)
c/o Winchester-Frederick Chamber of
Commerce
1360 S. Pleasant Valley Rd.
Winchester, Virginia 22601
Phone: (540)662-4118

Washington

SCORE Office (Gray's Harbor)
c/o Gray's Harbor Chamber of
Commerce
506 Duffy St.

Aberdeen, Washington 98520
Phone: (360)532-1924
Fax: (360)533-7945

SCORE Office (Bellingham)
Fourth Corner, Economic Development Group
PO Box 2803
1203 Cornwall Ave.
Bellingham, Washington 98227
Phone: (360)676-4255

SCORE Office (Everett)
Everett Public Library
2702 Hoyt Ave.
Everett, Washington 98201-3556
Phone: (206)259-8000

SCORE Office (Gig Harbor)
c/o Gig Harbor Chamber of Commerce
3125 Judson St.
Gig Harbor, Washington 98335
Phone: (206)851-6865
Phone: (206)851-6881

SCORE Office (Kennewick)
Kennewick Chamber of Commerce
PO Box 6986
Kennewick, Washington 99336
Phone: (509)736-0510

SCORE Office (Puyallup)
Puyallup Chamber of Commerce
322 2nd St. SW
PO Box 1298
Puyallup, Washington 98371
Phone: (206)845-6755
Fax: (206)848-6164

SCORE Office (Seattle)
1200 6th Ave., Ste. 1700
Seattle, Washington 98174
Phone: (206)553-7311

SCORE Office (Spokane)
601 1st Ave. W, 10th Fl.
Spokane, Washington 99204-0317
Phone: (509)353-2820

SCORE Office (Clover Park)
PO Box 1933
Tacoma, Washington 98401-1933
Phone: (206)627-2175

SCORE Office (Tacoma)
950 Pacific Ave., No. 300
Tacoma, Washington 98402
Phone: (206)627-2175

SCORE Office (Fort Vancouver)
1200 Fort Vancouver Way
Box 8900
Vancouver, Washington 98668
Phone: (360)699-3241

SCORE Office (Walla Walla)
Walla Walla Small Business Center
500 Tausick Way
Walla Walla, Washington 99362
Phone: (509)527-4681

SCORE Office (Mid-Columbia)
c/o Yakima Chamber of Commerce
PO Box 1490
Yakima, Washington 98907
Phone: (509)248-2021

West Virginia

SCORE Office (Charleston)
1116 Smith St.
Charleston, West Virginia 25301
Phone: (304)347-5463

SCORE Office (Virginia Street)
1116 Smith St., Ste. 302
Charleston, West Virginia 25301
Phone: (304)347-5463

SCORE Office (Marion County)
PO Box 208
Fairmont, West Virginia 26555-0208
Phone: (304)363-0486

SCORE Office (Upper Monongahela Valley)
200 Fairmont Ave., Ste. 100
Fairmont, West Virginia 26554
Phone: (304)363-0486

SCORE Office (Huntington)
1101 6th Ave., Ste. 220
Huntington, West Virginia 25701-2309
Phone: (304)523-4092

SCORE Office (Wheeling)
1310 Market St.
Wheeling, West Virginia 26003
Phone: (304)233-2575

Wisconsin

SCORE Office (Fox Cities)
227 S. Walnut St.
Box 1855
Appleton, Wisconsin 54915
Phone: (414)734-7101

SCORE Office (Beloit)
136 W. Grand Ave., Ste. 100
PO Box 717
Beloit, Wisconsin 53511
Phone: (608)365-8835
Fax: (608)365-9170

SCORE Office (Eau Claire)
Federal Bldg., Rm. B11
510 S. Barstow St.
Eau Claire, Wisconsin 54701
Phone: (715)834-1573

SCORE Office (Fond Du Lac)
c/o Fond Du Lac Chamber of Commerce
207 N. Main St.
Fond Du Lac, Wisconsin 54935
Phone: (414)921-9500
Fax: (414)921-9559

SCORE Office (Green Bay)
835 Potts Ave.
Green Bay, Wisconsin 54305
Phone: (414)496-8930

SCORE Office (Janesville)
20 S. Main St., Ste. 11
PO Box 8008
Janesville, Wisconsin 53547
Phone: (608)757-3160
Fax: (608)757-3170

SCORE Office (La Crosse)
712 Main St.
PO Box 219
La Crosse, Wisconsin 54602-0219
Phone: (608)784-4880

SCORE Office (Madison)
4406 Somerset Lake
Madison, Wisconsin 53711
Phone: (608)831-5464

SCORE Office (Manitowoc)
Manitowoc Chamber of Commerce
1515 Memorial Dr.
PO Box 903
Manitowoc, Wisconsin 54221-0903
Phone: (414)684-5575
Toll-free: (800262-7892
Fax: (414)684-1915

SCORE Office (Madison)
c/o M&I Bank
7448 Hubbard Ave.
Middleton, Wisconsin 53562
Phone: (608)831-5464

SCORE Office (Milwaukee)
310 W. Wisconsin Ave., Ste. 425
Milwaukee, Wisconsin 53203
Phone: (414)297-3942

SCORE Office (Central Wisconsin)
c/o Chapter Chairperson
1224 Lindbergh Ave.
Stevens Point, Wisconsin 54481
Phone: (715)344-7729

SCORE Office (Superior)
305 Harborview Pkwy.
Superior, Wisconsin 54880
Phone: (715)394-7716

SCORE Office (Waukesha)
c/o Waukesha Chamber of Commerce
223 Wisconsin Ave.
Waukesha, Wisconsin 53186-4926
Phone: (414)542-4249
Phone: (414)542-8068

SCORE Office (Wausau)
300 3rd St.
PO Box 6190
Wausau, Wisconsin 54402-6190
Phone: (715)845-6231

SCORE Office (Central Wisconsin)
2240 Kingston Rd.
Wisconsin Rapids, Wisconsin 54494
Phone: (715)423-1830
Phone: (715)421-3900

Wyoming

SCORE Office (Casper)
Federal Bldg., No. 2215
100 East B St.
Casper, Wyoming 82602
Phone: (307)261-6529

VENTURE CAPITAL & FINANCING COMPANIES

This section contains a listing of financing and loan companies in the United States and Canada. These listings are arranged alphabetically by country, then by state/territory/province, then by city, then by organization name.

CANADA

Manitoba

Manitoba Industry, Trade and Tourism
Small Business Services Entrepreneurial Development
Business Start Program
155 Carlton St., 5th Fl., Rm. 525
Winnipeg, Manitoba R3C 3H8
Phone: (204)945-7719
Toll-free: (800)282-8069
Fax: (204)945-2804

A matching loan guarantee program that will promote the success of new business start-ups by ensuring that entrepreneurs have a comprehensive business plan, by offering business training and counseling, and by providing access to funding up to $10,000 via a loan guarantee through a number of existing financial institutions.

Ontario

Industry and Science Canada
Small Business Loans Administration Branch
235 Queen St., 8th Fl., E.
Ottawa, Ontario K1A 0H5
Phone: (613)954-5540
Fax: (613)952-0290

Quebec

Societe de Developpement Industriel du Quebec
Small Business Revival Program
1126, Chemin Saint-Louis, 5th Fl.

Bureau 500
Sillery, Quebec G1S 1E5
Phone: (418)643-5172
Toll-free: (800)461-AIDE
Fax: (418)528-2063

Allows businesses facing temporary difficulties to obtain financial assistance aimed at reinforcing their financial structures.

Saskatchewan

Saskatchewan Department of Economic Development
Investment Programs Branch
Labour-Sponsored Venture Capital Program
1919 Saskatchewan Dr., 5th Fl.
Regina, Saskatchewan S4P 3V7
Phone: (306)787-2252
Fax: (306)787-3872

Promotes the formation of venture capital corporations by employees of a small business, to provide equity capital for the expansion of existing facilities or establishment of new businesses. Federal and provincial tax credits are available to the investor.

UNITED STATES

Alabama

Alabama Small Business Investment Co.
1732 5th Ave. N
Birmingham, Alabama 35203
Phone: (205)324-5231
Fax: (205)324-5234

A minority enterprise small business investment company. Diversified industry preference.

Jefferson County Community
Development
Planning and Community Development
805 N. 22nd St.
Birmingham, Alabama 35203
Phone: (205)325-5761
Fax: (205)325-5095

Provides loans for purchasing real estate, construction, working capital, or machinery and equipment.

FJC Growth Capital Corp.
200 W. Court Sq., Ste. 750
Huntsville, Alabama 35801
Phone: (205)922-2918
Fax: (205)922-2909

A minority enterprise small business investment company. Diversified industry preference.

Hickory Venture Capital Corp.
200 W. Court Sq., Ste. 100
Huntsville, Alabama 35801
Phone: (205)539-1931
Fax: (205)539-5130

A small business investment corporation. Prefers to invest in later-stage companies. Will not consider oil and gas, or real estate investments.

Alabama Capital Corp.
16 Midtown Park E.
Mobile, Alabama 36606
Phone: (334)476-0700
Fax: (334)476-0026
David C. DeLaney, President

Preferred Investment Size: $400,000. Investment Policies: Asset based loans with equity. Investment Types: Seed, early, expansion, later stages. Industry Preferences: Diversified. Geographic Preferences: Southeast.

First SBIC of Alabama
16 Midtown Park E.
Mobile, Alabama 36606
Phone: (334)476-0700
Fax: (334)476-0026
David C. DeLaney, President

Preferred Investment Size: $400,000. Investment Policies: Asset based loans with equity. Investment Types: Seed, early, expansion, later stages. Industry Preferences: Diversified. Geographic Preferences: Southeast.

Southern Development Council
4101 C Wall St.
Montgomery, Alabama 36106
Phone: (205)244-1801
Fax: (334)244-1421

Statewide nonprofit financial packaging corporation. Helps small businesses arrange financing.

Alaska

Alaska Department of Commerce and Economic Development (Anchorage)
Division of Investments
3601 C St., Ste. 724
Anchorage, Alaska 99503
Phone: (907)269-8150
Fax: (907)562-5941

Offers a program that assists purchasers to assume existing small business loans.

Alaska Department of Commerce and Economic Development (Anchorage)
Industrial Development and Export Authority
480 W. Tudor Rd.
Anchorage, Alaska 99503-6690
Phone: (907)269-3000
Fax: (907)269-3044

Assists businesses in securing long-term financing for capital investments, such as the acquisition of equipment or the construction of a new plant, at moderate interest rates.

Calista Business Investment Corp.
601 W. 5th Ave., Ste. 200
Anchorage, Alaska 99501-2225
Phone: (907)279-5516
Fax: (907)272-5060

A minority enterprise small business investment corporation. No industry preference.

Alaska Department of Commerce and Economic Development (Juneau)
Division of Investments
PO Box 34159
Juneau, Alaska 99803-4159
Phone: (907)465-2510
Toll-free: (800)478-LOAN
Fax: (907)465-2103

Offers a program that assists purchasers to assume existing small business loans.

Alaska Department of Natural Resources
Division of Agriculture
Agricultural Revolving Loan Fund
PO Box 949
Palmer, Alaska 99645-0949

Phone: (907)745-7200
Toll-free: (800)770-3276
Fax: (907)745-7112

Provides loans for farm development, general farm operations, chattel, and land clearing.

Arizona

First Interstate Equity Corp.
100 W. Washington St.
Phoenix, Arizona 85003
Phone: (602)528-6447
Fax: (602)440-1320

A small business investment company. Diversified industry preference.

Rocky Mountain Equity Corp.
2525 E. Camelback Rd., Ste. 275
Phoenix, Arizona 85016
Phone: (602)955-6100
Fax: (602)956-5909

A small business investment corporation. No industry preference.

Sundance Venture Partners, L.P.
(Phoenix)
400 E. Van Buren, Ste. 750
Phoenix, Arizona 85004
Phone: (602)259-3441
Fax: (602)259-1450

A small business investment company.

Arizona Growth Partners
6155 Scottsdale, Ste. 100
Scottsdale, Arizona 85258
Phone: (602)661-6600
Fax: (602)661-6262

Venture capital firm. Industry preferences include high technology, medical, biotechnology, and computer industries.

First Commerce & Loan LP
5620 N. Kolb, No. 260
Tucson, Arizona 85715
Phone: (602)298-2500
Fax: (602)745-6112

A small business investment company. Diversified industry preference.

Arkansas

Southern Ventures, Inc.
605 Main St., Ste. 202
Arkadelphia, Arkansas 71923
Phone: (501)246-9627
Fax: (501)246-2182

A small business investment company. Diversified industry preference.

Arkansas Development Finance Authority
PO Box 8023
Little Rock, Arkansas 72203-8023
Phone: (501)682-5900
Fax: (501)682-5939

Provides bond financing to small borrowers, who may otherwise be excluded from the bond market due to high costs, by using umbrella bond issues. Can provide interim financing for approved projects awaiting a bond issuance.

Capital Management Services, Inc.
1910 N. Grant St., Ste.200
Little Rock, Arkansas 72207-4427
Phone: (501)664-8613

A minority enterprise small business investment corporation. No industry preference.

Small Business Investment Capital, Inc.
12103 Interstate 30
P.O. Box 3627
Little Rock, Arkansas 72203
Phone: (501)455-6599
Fax: (501)455-6556
Charles E. Toland, President

Preferred Investment Size: Up to $230,000. Investment Policies: Loans. Investment Types: Start-ups and debt consolidation. Industry Preferences: Supermarkets. Geographic Preferences: Arkansas, Oklahoma, Texas, Louisiana.

Power Ventures Inc.
PO Box 518
Malvern, Arkansas 72104-0518
Phone: (501)332-3695
Fax: (501)337-4393

California

Calsafe Capital Corp.
245 E. Main St., Ste. 107
Alhambra, California 91801
Phone: (818)289-3400
Fax: (818)300-8025

A minority enterprise small business investment company. Diversified industry preference.

Ritter Partners
150 Isabella Ave.
Atherton, California 94027
Phone: (415)854-1555
Fax: (415)854-5015
William C. Edwards, President

Ally Finance Corp.
9100 Wilshire Blvd., Ste. 408
Beverly Hills, California 90212
Phone: (310)550-8100
Fax: (310)550-6136

A small business investment corporation. No industry preference.

Comdisco Venture Group
770 Tamalais Dr., Ste. 300
Corte Madera, California 94925-1737
Phone: (415)927-6777
Fax: (415)927-6767

Prefers start-up businesses in fields of semiconductors, computer hardware and software, computer services and systems, telecommunications, and medical and biotechnology. Investments range from $500,000 to $5 million.

BankAmerica Capital Corp.
3233 Park Center Dr.
Costa Mesa, California 92626
Phone: (714)973-8495

Venture capital firm preferring investments of $1 million-$3 million. Diversified industry preference.

Domain Associates
650 Town Center Dr., Ste. 1830
Costa Mesa, California 92626
Phone: (714)434-6227
Fax: (714)434-6088

Venture capital firm providing early stage financing. Areas of interest include life sciences and biotechnology companies (biopharmaceuticals, medical devices, diagnostics, and new materials).

Fairfield Venture Partners
650 Town Center Dr., Ste. 810
Costa Mesa, California 92626
Phone: (714)754-5717
Fax: (714)754-6802

First SBIC of California (Costa Mesa)
3029 Harbor Blvd.
Costa Mesa, California 92626
Phone: (714)668-6099
Fax: (714)668-6099

A small business investment corporation and venture capital company. No industry preference.

Pearl Capital, Inc.
575 Anton Blvd., Ste. 300
Costa Mesa, California 92626
Phone: (714)432-6301
Fax: (714)497-2560

Venture capital firm providing late stage and mezzanine investments of $1 million to $10 million. Prefers investments of $2 million. Areas of interest include diversified industries and computer technology.

Westar Capital (Costa Mesa)
950 S. Coast Dr., Ste. 165
Costa Mesa, California 92626
Phone: (714)434-5160
Fax: (714)434-5166

Venture capital firm providing management financing and corporate buyouts. Areas of interest include information, computer and business services, health care, food processing, and defense/aerospace.

Fulcrum Venture Capital Corp.
300 Corp. Pl.,Suite 380
Culver City, California 90230
Phone: (310)645-1271
Fax: (310)645-1272

A minority enterprise small business investment corporation. Noindustry preference.

Bay Partners
10600 N. De Anza Blvd., Ste. 100
Cupertino, California 95014
Phone: (408)725-2444
Fax: (408)446-4502

Venture capital supplier. Provides start-up financing primarily to West Coast technology companies that have highly qualified management teams. Initial investments range from $100,000 to $800,000. Where large investments are required, the company will act as lead investor to bring in additional qualified venture investors.

El Dorado Ventures (Cupertino)
20300 Stevens Creek Blvd., Ste. 395
Cupertino, California 95014
Phone: (408)725-2474
Fax: (408)252-2762

Grace Ventures Corp./Horn Venture Partners
20300 Stevens Creek Blvd., Ste. 330
Cupertino, California 95014
Phone: (408)725-0774
Fax: (408)725-0327

Areas of interest include information technology, life sciences, specialty retail and consumer products, restaurant, and biotechnology industries.

Novus Ventures, L.P.
20111 Stevens Creek Blvd., Ste. 130
Cupertino, California 95014
Phone: (408)252-3900
Fax: (408)252-1713
Daniel D. Tompkins, Manager

Preferred Investment Size: $400,000 to $1 Million. Investment Policies: Convertible debt, Convertible stock. Industry Preferences: Information technology. Geographic Preferences: Western U.S.

Sundance Venture Partners, L.P.
10600 N. DeAnza Blvd., Ste. 215
Cupertino, California 95014
Phone: (408)257-8100
Fax: (408)257-8111

A small business investment company. Diversified industry preference.

Chemical Venture Partners
840 Apollo St., Ste. 223 Chase Capitol
El Segundo, California 90245
Phone: (310)335-1955
Fax: (310)335-1965

Venture capital firm providing later stage financing. Areas of interest include health, environmental, service, distribution, manufacturing, information services, and education. Exclusions are real estate and high technology.

Pacific Mezzanine Fund, L.P.
2200 Powell St., Ste. 1250
Emeryville, California 94608
Phone: (510)595-9800
Fax: (510)595-9801
David C. Woodward, General Partner

Preferred Investment Size: $2 to $5 Million. Investment Policies: Loans with equity features. Investment Types: Expansion, later stage. Industry Preferences: Diversified. Geographic Preferences: Western US.

BankAmerica Ventures
950 Tower Ln., Ste. 700
Foster City, California 94404
Phone: (415)378-6000
Fax: (415)378-6040
Robert L Boswell, Senior Vice President

First American Capital Funding, Inc.
10840 Warner Ave., Ste. 202
Fountain Valley, California 92708
Phone: (714)965-7190
Fax: (714)965-7193

A minority enterprise small business investment corporation. No industry preference.

Opportunity Capital Corp.
2201 Walnut Ave., Ste. 210
Fremont, California 94538-2261
Phone: (510)795-7000
Fax: (510)494-5439

A minority enterprise small business
investment corporation. No industry
preference.

Opportunity Capital Partners II, LP
2201 Walnut Ave., Ste. 210
Fremont, California 94538
Phone: (510)795-7000
Fax: (510)494-5439

A minority enterprise small business
investment company. Diversified
industry preference.

R and D Funding Corp.
440 Mission Ct., Ste. 250
Fremont, California 94539
Phone: (510)656-1949
Fax: (510)656-1949

Venture capital firm. Invests in high-
growth businesses. Direct investment
in research and development.

San Joaquin Business Investment
Group, Inc.
1900 Mariposa Mall, Ste. 100
Fresno, California 93721
Phone: (209)233-3580
Fax: (209)233-3709

A minority enterprise small business
investment company. Diversified
industry preference.

Magna Pacific Investments
330 N. Brand Blvd., Ste. 670
Glendale, California 91203
Phone: (818)547-0809
Fax: (818)547-9303

A minority enterprise small business
investment company. Diversified
industry preference.

Asian American Capital Corp.
1251 W. Tennyson Rd., Ste. 4
Hayward, California 94544-4423
Phone: (510)887-6888

A minority enterprise small business
investment corporation. Diversified
industry preferences.

Brentwood Associates (Irvine)
1920 Main St., Ste. 820
Irvine, California 92714
Phone: (714)251-1010

Prefers to invest in the electronics and
health care industries.

Crosspoint Venture Partners (Irvine)
18552 MacArthur, No. 400
Irvine, California 92715
Phone: (714)852-1611
Fax: (714)852-9804

Venture capital firm investing in
medical, software, and telecommunications.

Ventana Growth Fund L.P. (Irvine)
18881 Von Karman Ave., Ste. 350,
Tower 17
Irvine, California 92715
Phone: (714)476-2204
Fax: (714)833-8962

South Bay Capital Corporation
5325 E. Pacific Coast Hwy.
Long Beach, California 90804
Phone: (310)597-3285
Fax: (310)498-7167
John Wang, Manager

Aspen Ventures West II, L.P.
1000 Fremont Ave., Ste. V
Los Altos, California 94024
Phone: (415)917-5670
Fax: (415)917-5677
Alexander Cilento, Mgr.
David Crocket, Mgr.

Preferred Investment Size: $500,000
to $2,5 million. Investment Policies:
Equity. Investment Types: Early
stage. Industry Preferences: Information technology. Geographic Preferences: Western U.S.

AVI Capital, L.P.
1 1st St., Ste. 12
Los Altos, California 94022

Phone: (415)949-9862
Fax: (415)949-8510
P. Wolken, Mgr.
B. Weinman, Mgr.

Preferred Investment Size:
$1,000,000. Investment Policies:
Equity Only. Investment Types: Seed,
early stage. Industry Preferences:
High technology and electronic deals
only. Geographic Preferences: West
coast, California.

Crosspoint Venture Partners (Los
Altos)
1 1st St., Ste. 2
Los Altos, California 94022
Phone: (415)948-8300
Fax: (415)948-6172

Venture capital partnership. Seeks to
invest start-up capital in unique
products, services, and/or market
opportunities in high-technology and
biotechnology industries located in
the western United States.

HMS Group
1 1st St., Ste. 16
Los Altos, California 94022
Phone: (415)917-0390
Fax: (415)917-0394

Prefers communications industries.

MBW Management, Inc. (Los Altos)
350 2nd St., Ste. 7
Los Altos, California 94022
Phone: (415)941-2392
Fax: (415)941-2865

Best Finance Corp.
4929 W. Wilshire Blvd., Ste. 407
Los Angeles, California 90010
Phone: (213)937-1636
Fax: (213)937-6393
Vincent Lee, General Manager

Preferred Investment Size: $50,000.
Investment Policies: Loans and/or
equity. Investment Types: Purchase,
seed, expansion. Industry Preferences:
Diversified. Geographic Preferences:
California.

Brentwood Associates (Los Angeles)
11150 Santa Monica Blvd., Ste. 1200
Los Angeles, California 90025-3314
Phone: (310)477-6611
Fax: (310)477-1011

Venture capital supplier. Provides start-up and expansion financing to technology-based enterprises specializing in computing and data processing, electronics, communications, materials, energy, industrial automation, and bioengineering and medical equipment. Investments generally range from $1 million to $3 million.

BT Capital Corp. (Los Angeles)
300 S. Grand Ave.
Los Angeles, California 90071

A small business investment company.

Charterway Investment Corp.
One Wilshire Bldg., No.1600
Los Angeles, California 90017-3317
Phone: (213)689-9107
Fax: (213)890-1968

A minority enterprise small business investment corporation. No industry preference.

Developers Equity Capital Corp.
1880 Century Pk. E, Ste. 218
Los Angeles, California 90067
Phone: (310)277-0330
Fax: (310)277-4271

A small business investment corporation. Real estate preferred.

Far East Capital Corp.
977 N. Broadway, Ste.401
Los Angeles, California 90012
Phone: (213)687-1361
Fax: (213)626-7497

A minority enterprise small business investment company. Diversified industry preference.

Imperial Ventures, Inc.
PO Box 92991
Los Angeles, California 90009

Phone: (310)417-5710
Fax: (310)338-2611

A small business investment company. Diversified industry preference.

Kline Hawkes California SBIC, LP
11726 San Vicente Blvd., Ste. 300
Los Angeles, California 90049
Phone: (310)442-4700
Fax: (310)442-4707
Frank R Kline, Manager

Peregrine Ventures
12400 Wilshire Blvd Ste. 230
Los Angeles, California 90025
Phone: (310)458-1441

Venture capital firm providing start-up, first stage, and leveraged buyout financing. Areas of interest include communications and health.

Riordan Lewis & Haden
300 S. Grand Ave., 29th Fl.
Los Angeles, California 90071
Phone: (213)229-8500
Fax: (213)229-8597

Venture capital firm providing all types of financing, including management buyouts and turn-arounds. Areas of interest include food and service.

The Seideler Companies, Inc.
515 S. Figueroa St., 11th Fl.
Los Angeles, California 90071-3396
Phone: (213)624-4232
Fax: (213)688-7848

Union Venture Corp.
445 S. Figueroa St.
Los Angeles, California 90071
Phone: (213)236-5658
Fax: (213)688-0101

A small business investment company. Diversified industry preference.

Advanced Technology Ventures (Menlo Park)
485 Ramona St., Ste. 200

Menlo Park, California 94028
Phone: (415)321-8601
Fax: (415)321-0934

Bessemer Venture Partners (Menlo Park)
3000 Sand Hill Rd., Bldg. 3, Ste. 225
Menlo Park, California 94025
Phone: (415)854-2200
Fax: (415)854-7415

Brentwood Associates (Menlo Park)
2730 Sandhill Rd. Ste. 250
Menlo Park, California 94025-7020
Phone: (415)854-7691
Fax: (415)854-9513

Canaan Partners
2884 Sand Hill Rd., Ste. 115
Menlo Park, California 94025-7022
Phone: (415)854-8092
Fax: (415)854-8127

Venture capital firm providing start-up, second and third stage, and buyout financing. Areas of interest include information industry products and services, medical technology, and health care services.

Comdisco Venture Group (Menlo Park)
3000 Sand Hill Rd., Bldg. 1 Ste. 290
Menlo Park, California 94025-7141
Phone: (415)854-9484
Fax: (415)854-4026

Prefers start-up businesses in fields of semiconductors, computer hardware and software, computer services and systems, telecommunications, and medical and biotechnology. Investments range from $500,000 to $5 million.

Glenwood Management
3000 Sand Hill Rd., Bldg. 4, Ste. 230
Menlo Park, California 94025
Phone: (415)854-8070
Fax: (415)854-4961

Venture capital supplier. Areas of interest include high technology and biomedical industries.

Institutional Venture Partners
3000 Sand Hill Rd., Bldg. 2, Ste. 290
Menlo Park, California 94025
Phone: (415)854-0132
Fax: (415)854-5762

Venture capital fund. Invests in early stage ventures with significant market potential in the computer, information sciences, communications, and life sciences fields.

Interwest Partners (Menlo Park)
3000 Sand Hill Rd., Bldg. 3, Ste. 255
Menlo Park, California 94025
Phone: (415)854-8585
Fax: (415)854-4706

Venture capital fund. Both high-tech and low- or non-technology companies are considered. No oil, gas, real estate, or construction projects.

Kleiner Perkins Caufield & Byers (Menlo Park)
2750 Sand Hill Rd.
Menlo Park, California 94025
Phone: (415)233-2750
Fax: (415)233-0300

Provides seed, start-up, second and third-round, and bridge financing to companies on the West Coast. Preferred industries of investment include electronics, computers, software, telecommunications, biotechnology, medical devices, and pharmaceuticals.

Matrix Partners
2500 Sand Hill Rd., Ste. 113
Menlo Park, California 94025-7016
Phone: (415)854-3131
Fax: (415)854-3296

Private venture capital partnership. Investments range from $500,000 to $1 million.

Mayfield Fund
2800 Sand Hill Rd., Ste. 250
Menlo Park, California 94025
Phone: (415)854-5560
Fax: (415)854-5712

Venture capital partnership. Prefers high-technology and biomedical industries.

McCown De Leeuw and Co. (Menlo Park)
3000 Sand Hill Rd., Bldg. 3, Ste. 290
Menlo Park, California 94025
Phone: (415)854-6000
Fax: (415)854-0853

A venture capital firm. Preferences include the mortgage servicing, building materials, printing, and office products industries.

Menlo Ventures
3000 Sand Hill Rd., Bldg. 4, Ste. 100
Menlo Park, California 94025
Phone: (415)854-8540
Fax: (415)854-7059

Venture capital supplier. Provides start-up and expansion financing to companies with experienced management teams, distinctive product lines, and large growing markets. Primary interest is in technology-oriented, service, consumer products, and distributioncompanies. Investments range from $500,000 to $3 million; also provides capital for leveraged buy outs.

Merrill Pickard Anderson & Eyre I
2480 Sand Hill Rd., Ste. 200
Menlo Park, California 94025
Phone: (415)854-8600
Fax: (415)854-0345
Steven Merrill, President

New Enterprise Associates (Menlo Park)
2490 Sand Hill Road
Menlo Park, California 94025
Phone: (415)854-9499
Fax: (415)854-9397

Venture capital supplier.

New Enterprise Associates (San Francisco)
2490 Sand Hill Road
Menlo Park, California 94025

Phone: (415)854-9499
Fax: (415)854-9397

Venture capital supplier. Concentrates in technology-based industries that have the potential for product innovation, rapid growth, and high profit margins.

Norwest Equity Partners IV (Menlo Park)
3000 Sand Hill Rd., Bldg. 3, Ste. 245
Menlo Park, California 94025
Phone: (415)223-6622

A small business investment company.

Norwest Venture Partners
3000 Sand Hill Rd., Bldg. 3., Ste. 105
Menlo Park, California 94025
Phone: (415)854-6366
Fax: (415)854-6652

A small business investment corporation. No industry preference.

Paragon Venture Partners
3000 Sand Hill Rd., Bldg. 1, Ste. 275
Menlo Park, California 94025
Phone: (415)854-8000
Fax: (415)854-7260

Venture capital firm. Areas of interest include high technology and life sciences with an emphasis on data communications, networking, software, medical devices, biotechnology, and health care services industries.

Pathfinder Venture Capital Funds (Menlo Park)
3000 Sand Hill Rd., Bldg. 3, Ste. 255
Menlo Park, California 94025
Phone: (415)854-0650
Fax: (415)854-4706

Venture capital supplier. Provides start-up and early-stage financing to emerging companies in the medical, computer, pharmaceuticals, and data communications industries. Emphasis is on companies with proprietary technology or market positions and with substantial potential for revenue growth.

Sequoia Capital
3000 Sand Hill Rd., Bldg. 4, Ste. 280
Menlo Park, California 94025
Phone: (415)854-3927
Fax: (415)854-2977

Private venture capital partnership with $300 million under management. Provides financing for all stages of development of well-managed companies with exceptional growth prospects in fast-growth industries. Past investments have been made in computers and peripherals, communications, health care, biotechnology, and medical instruments and devices. Investments range from $350,000 for early stage companies to $4 million for late stage accelerates.

Sierra Ventures
3000 Sand Hill Rd., Bldg. 4, Ste. 210
Menlo Park, California 94025
Phone: (415)854-1000
Fax: (415)854-5593

Venture capital partnership.

Sigma Partners
2884 Sand Hill Rd., Ste. 121
Menlo Park, California 94025-7022
Phone: (415)854-1300
Fax: (415)854-1323

Independent venture capital partnership. Prefers to invest in the following areas: communications, computer hardware, computer software, manufacturing, medical equipment, and semiconductor capital equipment. Avoids investing in construction, hotels, leasing, motion pictures, and natural resources. Minimum initial commitment is $500,000.

Sprout Group (Menlo Park)
3000 Sand Hill Rd., Bldg. 4, Ste. 270
Menlo Park, California 94025
Phone: (415)854-1550
Fax: (415)854-8779

Technology Venture Investors
2480 Sand Hill Rd., Ste. 101
Menlo Park, California 94025
Phone: (415)854-7472
Fax: (415)854-4187

Private venture capital partnership. Primary interest is in technology companies with minimum investment of $1 million.

U.S. Venture Partners
2180 Sand Hill Rd., Ste. 300
Menlo Park, California 94025
Phone: (415)854-9080
Fax: (415)854-3018

Venture capital partnership. Prefers the specialty retail, consumer products, technology, and biomedical industries.

USVP-Schlein Marketing Fund
2180 Sand Hill Rd., Ste. 300
Menlo Park, California 94025
Phone: (415)854-9080
Fax: (415)854-3018

Venture capital fund. Prefers specialty retailing/consumer products companies.

Hall, Morris & Drufva II, L.P.
26161 Lopoz St., Ste. E
Mission Viejo, California 92691
Phone: (714)707-5096
Fax: (714)707-5121

A small business investment corporation. No industry preference. Provides capital for small and medium-sized companies through participation in private placements of subordinated debt, preferred, and common stock. Offers growth-acquisition and later-stage venture capital.

ABC Capital Corp.
917 Whittier Blvd.
Montebello, California 90640
Phone: (213)725-7890
Fax: (213)725-7115

A minority enterprise small business investment corporation. No industry preference.

Allied Business Investors, Inc.
428 S. Atlantic Blvd., Ste. 201
Monterey Park, California 91754
Phone: (818)289-0186
Fax: (818)289-2369
Jack Hong, President

Preferred Investment Size: $50,000.
Investment Policies: Loans only.
Investment Types: Early stage.
Industry Preferences: Diversified.
Geographic Preferences: Los Angeles.

LaiLai Capital Corp.
223 E. Garvey Ave., Ste. 228
Monterey Park, California 91754
Phone: (818)288-0704
Fax: (818)288-4101

A minority enterprise small business investment company. Diversified industry preference.

Myriad Capital, Inc.
701 S. Atlantic Blvd., Ste. 302
Monterey Park, California 91754-3242
Phone: (818)570-4548
Fax: (818)570-9570

A minority enterprise small business investment corporation. Prefers investing in production and manufacturing industries.

DSV Partners (Newport Beach)
620 Newport Center Dr., Ste. 990
Newport Beach, California 92660
Phone: (714)759-5657
Fax: (714)760-6947

Venture capital firm. Prefers to invest in software, medical, biotechnical, environmental, and other high-growth technology companies.

Enterprise Partners
5000 Birch St., Ste. 6200
Newport Beach, California 92660
Phone: (714)833-3650
Fax: (714)833-3652

Venture capital fund. Prefers to invest in medical or high-technology industries in California.

Marwit Capital Corp.
180 Newport Center Dr., Ste. 200
Newport Beach, California 92660
Phone: (714)640-6234
Fax: (714)759-1363

A small business investment corporation. Provides financing for leveraged
buyouts, mergers, acquisitions, and
expansion stages. Investments are in
the $100,000 to $4 million range.
Does not provide financing for start-
ups or real estate ventures.

Inman and Bowman
4 Orinda Way, Bldg. D, Ste. 150
Orinda, California 94563
Phone: (510)253-1611
Fax: (510)253-9037

Asset Management Co.
2275 E. Bayshore, Ste. 150
Palo Alto, California 94303
Phone: (415)494-7400
Fax: (415)856-1826

Venture capital firm. High-technol-
ogy industries preferred.
BankAmerica Ventures (Palo Alto)
5 Palo Alto Sq., Ste. 938
Palo Alto, California 94306
Phone: (415)424-8011
Fax: (415)424-6830

Campbell Venture Management
375 California St.
Palo Alto, California 94308
Phone: (415)853-0766
Fax: (415)857-0303

Citicorp Venture Capital, Ltd.
2 Embarcadero Pl.
2200 Geny Rd., Ste. 203
Palo Alto, California 94303
Phone: (415)424-8000

A small business investment company.

Greylock Management Corp.
755 Page Mill Rd., Ste. A-100
Palo Alto, California 94304-1018
Phone: (415)493-5525
Fax: (415)493-5575

Venture capital firm providing all
stages of financing. Areas of interest
include computer software, communications, health, biotechnology,
publishing, and specialty retail.

MK Global Ventures
2471 E. Bayshore Rd., Ste. 520
Palo Alto, California 94303
Phone: (415)424-0151
Fax: (415)494-2753

Oak Investment Partners (Menlo Park)
525 University Avenue, Ste. 1300
Palo Alto, California 94301
Phone: (415)614-3700
Fax: (415)328-6345

Small business investment corporation. Areas of interest include
communications, computer hardware
and software, high technology,
manufacturing, medical equipment
and instrumentation, pharmaceuticals, and retail.

Patricof & Co. Ventures, Inc.
1 Embarcadero Pl.
2100 Geng Rd., Ste. 220
Palo Alto, California 94303
Phone: (415)494-9944
Fax: (415)494-6751

Venture capital firm providing equity
investments, diversified by markets
and stage of company. Prefers to fund
growth.

Summit Partners (Newport Beach)
499 Hamilton Ave., Ste. 200
Palo Alto, California 94301
Phone: (415)321-1166
Fax: (415)321-1188

Venture capital firm providing
investments in the $2 million-$20
million range. Areas of interest
include technology, health care, and
financial services.

Sutter Hill Ventures
755 Page Mill Rd., Ste. A-200
Palo Alto, California 94304-1005
Phone: (415)493-5600
Fax: (415)858-1854

Venture capital partnership providing
start-up financing for high technology businesses.

TA Associates (Palo Alto)
435 Tasso St.
Palo Alto, California 94301
Phone: (415)328-1210
Fax: (415)326-4933

Private venture capital firm. Prefers
technology companies and leveraged
buy outs. Provides from $1 to $20
million in investments.

Venrock Associates
755 Page Mill, A-230
Palo Alto, California 94304
Phone: (415)493-5577
Fax: (415)493-6443

Private venture capital supplier.
Prefers high-technology start-up
equity investments.

BankAmerica Ventures (Pasadena)
155 N. Lake Ave., Ste. 1010
Pasadena, California 91109
Phone: (818)304-3451
Fax: (818)440-9931

First SBIC of California (Pasadena)
155 N. Lake Ave., Ste. 1010
Pasadena, California 91109
Phone: (818)304-3451
Fax: (818)440-9931

A small business investment company.

The Money Store Investment Corp.
3301 "C" St., Ste. 130
Sacramento, California 95816
Phone: (916)446-5000
Toll-free: (800)639-1102
Fax: (916)488-1868

Non-bank lender providing start-up
and expansion financing.

AMF Financial, Inc.
4330 La Jolla Village Dr., Ste. 110
San Diego, California 92122-1233
Phone: (619)546-0167
Fax: (619)455-0868

A small business investment company. Diversified industry preference.

Forward Ventures
10975 Torreyana Rd., No. 230
San Diego, California 92121
Phone: (619)677-6077
Fax: (619)452-8799

Venture capital firm preferring investments of $100,000-$500,000. Areas of interest include biotechnology and health care.

Idanta Partners Ltd.
4660 La Jolla Village Dr., Ste. 775
San Diego, California 92122-4606
Phone: (619)452-9690
Fax: (619)452-2013

Venture capital partnership. Minimum investment is $500,000.

New West Partners II
4350 Executive Dr., Ste. 206
San Diego, California 92121
Phone: (619)457-0722
Fax: (619)457-0829

A small business investment corporation.

Sorrento Growth Partners I, L.P.
4225 Executive Sq., Ste. 1450
San Diego, California 92137
Phone: (619)452-6400
Fax: (619)452-7607
Robert Jaffe, Manager

Preferred Investment Size: $750,000 to $2 Million. Investment Policies: Equity only. Investment Types: Seed, early, expansion, later stages. Industry Preferences: Medicine, health, communications, electronics, special retail. Geographic Preferences: Southern California.

Ventana Growth Fund L.P.
Rio Vista Tower, Ste. 500
8880 Rio San Diego Dr.
San Diego, California 92108
Phone: (619)291-2757
Fax: (619)295-0189

Venture capital firm.

Accel Partners (San Francisco)
1 Embarcadero Center, Ste. 3820
San Francisco, California 94111
Phone: (415)989-5656
Fax: (415)989-5554

Venture capital firm providing start-up financing. Areas of interest include health care, information technology, software, and telecommunications.

American Realty and Construction
1489 Webster St., Ste. 218
San Francisco, California 94115-3767
Phone: (415)928-6600
Fax: (415)928-6363

A minority enterprise small business investment corporation. No industry preference.

BANEXI Corp.
555 California St., Ste. 2600
San Francisco, California 94104
Phone: (415)693-3345
Toll-free: (800)766-3863
Fax: (415)433-7326

Venture capital firm preferring late stage investments. Areas of interest include biotechnology, health care products/services, industrial and environmental services, electronic technology and information services, communications, business services, and specialty retailing.

Bentley Capital
592 Vallejo St. Ste. 2
San Francisco, California 94133
Phone: (415)362-2868
Fax: (415)398-8209

A minority enterprise small business investment company. Diversified industry preference.

Bryan and Edwards Partnership
600 Montgomery St., 35th Fl.
San Francisco, California 94111-2854
Phone: (415)421-9990
Fax: (415)421-0471

A small business investment corporation. No industry preference.

Burr, Egan, Deleage, and Co. (San Francisco)
1 Embarcadero Center, Ste. 4050
San Francisco, California 94111-3729
Phone: (415)362-4022
Fax: (415)362-6178

Private venture capital supplier. Invests start-up, expansion, and acquisitions capital nationwide. Principal concerns are strength of the management team; large, rapidly expanding markets; and unique products for services. Past investments have been made in the fields of biotechnology and pharmaceuticals, cable TV, chemicals/plastics, communications, software, computer systems and peripherals, distributorships, radio common carriers, electronics and electrical components, environmental control, health services, medical devices and instrumentation, and radio and cellular telecommunications. Primarily interested in medical, electronics, and media industries.

Dillon Read Venture Capital
555 California St., No. 4950
San Francisco, California 94104-1714
Phone: (415)296-7900
Fax: (415)296-8956

A venture capital firm. Provides early-stage financing to companies in the biomedical field and the information systems industry.

Dominion Ventures, Inc.
44 Montgomery St., Ste. 4200
San Francisco, California 94104
Phone: (415)362-4890
Fax: (415)394-9245

Venture capital firm providing seed, start-up, second and third stage, and buyout financing. Areas of interest include biotechnology, health care, telecommunications, software, and financial services.

First Century Partners (San Bruno)
101 California St., Ste. 3160
San Francisco, California 94111
Phone: (415)433-4200
Fax: (415)433-4250

Venture capital firm. Health care, software, technology-based service, and specialty retailing industries preferred.

G C and H Partners
1 Maritime Plz., 20th Fl.
San Francisco, California 94111
Phone: (415)693-2000
Fax: (415)951-3699

A small business investment corporation. No industry preference.

Hambrecht and Quist (San Francisco)
1 Bush St.
San Francisco, California 94104
Phone: (415)576-3300
Toll-free: (800)227-3958
Fax: (415)576-3621

Prefers to invest in computer technology, environmental technology, and biotechnology. Investments range from $500,000 to $5,000,000.

Heller First Capital Corp.
650 California St., 23rd Fl.
San Francisco, California 94108
Phone: (415)274-5700
Fax: (415)274-5744

Non-bank lender providing start-up and expansion financing.

Jafco America Ventures, Inc.
555 California St., Ste. 4380
San Francisco, California 94104
Phone: (415)788-0706
Fax: (415)765-4976

Venture capital firm. Provides middle- to later-stage investments. Avoids investments in real estate, natural resources, entertainment, motion pictures, oil and gas, construction, and non-technical industries.

Jupiter Partners
600 Montgomery St., 35th Fl.
San Francisco, California 94111
Phone: (415)421-9990
Fax: (415)421-0471

A small business investment company. Prefers to invest in electronic manufacturing industry.

Montgomery Securities
600 Montgomery St., 21st Fl.
San Francisco, California 94111-2702
Phone: (415)627-2454
Fax: (415)249-5516

Private venture capital and investment banking firm. Diversified, but will not invest in real estate or energy-related industries. Involved in both start-up and later-stage financing.

Morgan Stanley Venture Capital Fund L.P.
555 California St., Ste. 2200
San Francisco, California 94104
Phone: (415)576-2345
Fax: (415)576-2099

Venture capital firm providing second and third stage and buyout financing. Areas of interest include information technology andhealth care products/services.

Positive Enterprises, Inc.
1489 Webster St., Ste. 228
San Francisco, California 94115
Phone: (415)885-6600
Fax: (415)928-6363

A minority enterprise small business investment company. Diversified industry preference.

Quest Ventures (San Francisco)
555 California St., Ste. 2955
San Francisco, California 94104
Phone: (415)546-7118
Fax: (415)243-8514

Independent venture capital partnership. Diversified industry preference.

Robertson-Stephens Co.
555 California St., Ste. 2600
San Francisco, California 94104
Phone: (415)781-9700
Fax: (415)781-0278

Investment banking firm. Considers investments in any attractive merg-

ing-growth area, including product and service companies. Key preferences include health care, hazardous waste services and technology, biotechnology, software, and information services. Maximum investment is $5 million.

Round Table Capital Corp.
655 Montgomery St., Ste. 700
San Francisco, California 94111
Phone: (415)392-7500
Fax: (415)362-7967

A small business investment corporation. No industry preference.

Taylor and Turner
220 Montgomery Penthouse 10
San Francisco, California 94104
Phone: (415)398-6325
Fax: (415)398-3220

A venture capital firm. Industry preferences include the biotechnology, education, medical, and electronics industries.

VenAd Administrative Services
657 Mission Street Ste. 601
San Francisco, California 94105
Phone: (415)543-4448
Fax: (415)541-7775

Private venture capital supplier. Provides all stages of financing.

VK Capital Co.
600 California St., Ste. 1700
San Francisco, California 94108
Phone: (415)391-5600
Fax: (415)397-2744

A small business investment company. Diversified industry preference.

Volpe, Welty and Co.
1 Maritime Plz., 11th Fl.
San Francisco, California 94111
Phone: (415)956-8120
Fax: (415)986-6754

Prefers investing with companies involved in entertainment, multimedia, computer-aided software engineering, gaming, software tools, biotechnology, and health care industries.

Walden Capital Partners
750 Battery St., 7th Fl., Ste. 700
San Francisco, California 94111
Phone: (415)391-7225
Fax: (415)391-7262

Walden Group of Venture Capital Funds
750 Battery St., Ste. 700
San Francisco, California 94111
Phone: (415)391-7225
Fax: (415)391-7262

Venture capital firm providing seed, start-up, and second and third stage financing. Areas of interest include high technology, consumer products, health-related industries, hardware, software, EDP, environmental, communications, and education.

Weiss, Peck and Greer Venture Partners L.P. (San Francisco)
555 California St., Ste. 4760
San Francisco, California 94104
Phone: (415)622-6864
Fax: (415)989-5108

Dougery & Wilder (San Mateo)
155 Bovet Rd., Ste. 350
San Mateo, California 94402-3113
Phone: (415)358-8701
Fax: (415)358-8706

Venture capital supplier. Areas of interest include computers systems and software, communications, and medical/biotechnology industries.

Drysdale Enterprises
177 Bovet Rd., Ste. 600
San Mateo, California 94402
Phone: (415)341-6336
Fax: (415)341-1329

Venture capital firm preferring investments of $250,000-$2 million. Areas of interest include food processing, health care, and communications.

Technology Funding
2000 Alameda de las Pulgas, Ste. 250
San Mateo, California 94403
Phone: (415)345-2200
Toll-free: (800)821-5323
Fax: (415)341-1400

Small business investment corporation. Provides primarily late first-stage and early second-stage equity financing. Also offers secured debt with equity participation to venture capital backed companies. Investments range from $500,000 to $1 million.

Trinity Ventures Ltd.
155 Bovet Rd., Ste. 660
San Mateo, California 94402
Phone: (415)358-9700
Fax: (415)358-9785

Private venture capital firm investing in computer software, consumer products, and health care industries.

Phoenix Growth Capital Corp.
2401 Kerner Blvd.
San Rafael, California 94901
Phone: (415)485-4655
Toll-free: (800)227-2626
Fax: (415)485-4663

Small business investment corporation providing start-up, second and third stage, and buyout financing. Areas of interest include secured debt for high technology, biotechnology, computers and peripherals, and service industries. (All must be equity venture capital based.)

InterVen II L.P.
301 Arizona Ave., Ste 306
Santa Monica, California 90401
Phone: (310)587-3550
Fax: (310)587-3440

A small business investment corporation. Currently making only follow-on investments in existing portfolio companies.

InterVen Partners (Santa Monica)
301 Arizona Ave., No. 306
Santa Monica, California 90401-1305

Phone: (310)587-3550
Fax: (310)587-3440

Venture capital fund. Diversified industry preferences; geographicpreference is the West Coast.

DSC Ventures II, LP
12050 Saratoga Ave. Ste.,B
Saratoga, California 95070
Phone: (408)252-3800
Fax: (408)252-0757

A small business investment company. Diversified industry preference.

Western General Capital Corp.
13701 Riverside Dr., Ste. 610
Sherman Oaks, California 91423
Phone: (818)986-5038
Fax: (818)905-9220

A minority enterprise small business investment company. Diversified industry preference.

Astar Capital Corp.
9537 E. Gidley St.
Temple City, California 91780
Phone: (818)350-1211
Fax: (818)443-5874
George Hsu, President

Spectra Enterprise Associates
PO Box 7688
Thousand Oaks, California 91359-7688
Phone: (818)865-0213
Fax: (818)865-1309

Venture capital partnership. Areas of interest include information, computer, semiconductor, software, life sciences, and wireless industries.

National Investment Management, Inc.
2601 Airport Drive., Ste.210
Torrance, California 90505
Phone: (310)784-7600
Fax: (310)784-7605

Venture capital firm providing leveraged buyout financing. Areas of interest include general manufacturing and distribution.

Colorado

Hill, Carman, and Washing
885 Arapahoe
Boulder, Colorado 80302
Phone: (303)442-5151
Fax: (303)442-8525

Weiss, Peck and Greer Venture
Partners L.P. (Boulder)
1113 Spruce St., Ste. 300
Boulder, Colorado 80302
Phone: (303)443-1023
Fax: (303)443-0986

Capital Health Management
2084 S. Milwaukee St.
Denver, Colorado 80210
Phone: (303)692-8600
Fax: (303)692-9656

The Centennial Funds
1999 Broadway, Ste. 2100
Denver, Colorado 80202
Phone: (303)298-9066
Fax: (303)292-3512

Venture capital fund. Prefers to invest
in early stage companies in the
Rocky Mountain region.

Colorado Housing and Finance
Authority
1981 Blake St.
Denver, Colorado 80202-1272
Phone: (303)297-2432
Fax: (303)297-2615

Operates financing programs for small
and minority businesses.

Colorado Office of Business Development
1625 Broadway, Ste. 1710
Denver, Colorado 80202
Phone: (303)892-3840
Fax: (303)892-3848

Provides loans to new and expanding
businesses.

UBD Capital, Inc.
1700 Broadway
Denver, Colorado 80274

Phone: (303)863-6329

A small business investment company. Diversified industry preference.

Columbine Ventures
5460 S. Quebec St., Ste. 270
Englewood, Colorado 80111-1917
Phone: (303)694-3222
Fax: (303)694-9007

Venture capital firm interested in
biotechnology, medical, computer,
electronics, and advanced materials
industries.

Connecticut

First Connecticut SBIC
1000 Lafayette St.
Bridgeport, Connecticut 06604
Phone: (203)366-4726
Toll-free: (800)401-3222

A small business investment corporation.

AB SBIC, Inc.
275 School House Rd.
Cheshire, Connecticut 06410
Phone: (203)272-0203
Fax: (203)272-9978

A small business investment company. Prefers to invest in grocery
stores.

Financial Opportunities, Inc.
1 Vision Dr.
Enfield, Connecticut 06082
Phone: (203)741-4444
Fax: (860)741-4494

A small business investment corporation. Prefers full franchise convenience stores.

Consumer Venture Partners
3 Pickwick Plz.
Greenwich, Connecticut 06830
Phone: (203)629-8800
Fax: (203)629-2019

Prefers consumer and expansion-stage
investments.

First New England Capital, LP
100 Pearl St.
Hartford, Connecticut 06103
Phone: (203)293-3333
Fax: (203)549-2528

A small business investment company. Diversified industry preference.

FRE Capital Partners, LP
36 Grove St.
New Canaan, Connecticut 06840
Phone: (203)966-2800
Fax: (203)966-3109

A small business investment company. Diversified industry preference.

RFE Investment Partners V, L.P.
36 Grove St.
New Canaan, Connecticut 06840
Phone: (203)966-2800
Fax: (203)966-3109
James A. Parsons, General Partner

Preferred Investment Size: $5 - $9
Million. Investment Policies: Prefer
equity investments. Investment
Types: Later stage, expansion,
acquisitions. Industry Preferences:
Manufacturing & services. Geographic Preferences: National, eastern
U.S.

The Vista Group
36 Grove St.
New Canaan, Connecticut 06840
Phone: (203)972-3400
Fax: (203)966-0844

Venture capital supplier. Provides
start-up and second-stage financing
to technology-related businesses that
seek to become major participants in
high-growth markets of at least $100
million in annual sales. Areas of
investment interest include information systems, communications,
computer peripherals, medical
products and services, retailing,
agrigenetics, biotechnology, low
technology, no technology, instrumentation, and genetic engineering.

All State Venture Capital Corp.
The Bishop House
32 Elm St.
PO Box 1629
New Haven, Connecticut 06506
Phone: (203)787-5029
Fax: (203)785-0018

A small business investment company. Diversified industry preference.

Nova Tech-Eicon
142 Temple St., 2nd Fl.
New Haven, Connecticut 06510
Phone: (203)789-1260
Fax: (203)789-8261

DCS Growth Fund (Old Greenwich)
PO Box 740
Old Greenwich, Connecticut 06870-0740
Phone: (203)637-1704
Fax: (203)637-1705

Canaan Partners
105 Rowayton Ave.
Rowayton, Connecticut 06853
Phone: (203)855-0400
Fax: (203)854-9117

Venture capital supplier.

Marcon Capital Corp.
10 John St.
Southport, Connecticut 06490-1437
Phone: (203)259-7233
Fax: (203)259-9428

A small business investment corporation; secured lending preferred.

Central Texas SBI Corporation
1 Canterbury Green
201 Broad St., 2nd Fl.
Stamford, Connecticut 06901
Phone: (203)352-4056
Fax: (203)352-4184
David E. Erb, Contact Person

James B. Kobak and Co.
2701 Summer St., Ste. 200
Stamford, Connecticut 06905
Phone: (203)363-2221
Fax: (203)363-2218

Venture capital supplier and consultant. Provides assistance to new ventures in the communications field through conceptualization, planning, organization, raising money, and control of actual operations. Special interest is in magazine publishing.

Saugatuck Capital Co.
1 Canterbury Green
Stamford, Connecticut 06901
Phone: (203)348-6669
Fax: (203)324-6995

Private investment partnership. Seeks to invest in various industries not dependent on technology, including health care, telecommunications, insurance, financial services, manufacturing, and consumer products. Prefers leveraged buy out situations, but will consider start-up financing. Investments range from $3 to $5 million.

Schroder Ventures
1055 Washington Blvd. 5th Fl.
Stamford, Connecticut 06901
Phone: (203)324-7700
Fax: (203)324-3636

TSG Ventures, Inc.
177 Broad St.,12th Fl.
Stamford, Connecticut 06901
Phone: (203)363-5344
Fax: (203)406-1590

A minority enterprise small business investment company. Diversified industry preference.

J. H. Whitney and Co. (New York)
177 Broad St.
Stamford, Connecticut 06901
Phone: (203)973-1400
Fax: (203)973-1422

Xerox Venture Capital (Stamford)
Headquarters
800 Long Ridge Rd.
Stamford, Connecticut 06904
Phone: (203)968-3000

Venture capital subsidiary of operating company. Prefers to invest in document processing industries.

The SBIC of Connecticut, Inc.
2 Corporate Rd., Ste. 203
Trumbull, Connecticut 06611
Phone: (203)261-0011
Fax: (203)459-1563

A small business investment corporation. No industry preference.

Capital Resource Company of Connecticut, LP
2558 Albany Ave.
West Hartford, Connecticut 06117
Phone: (203)236-4336
Fax: (860)232-8161

A small business investment corporation. No industry preference.

Marketcorp Venture Associates
285 Riverside Ave.
Westport, Connecticut 06880
Phone: (203)222-1000
Toll-free: (800)243-5077
Fax: (203)222-5829

Venture capital firm. Prefers to invest in consumer-market businesses, including the packaged goods, specialty retailing, communications, and consumer electronics industries.

Oak Investment Partners (Westport)
1 Gorham Island
Westport, Connecticut 06880
Phone: (203)226-8346
Fax: (203)227-0372

Oxford Bioscience Partners
315 Post Rd. W.
Westport, Connecticut 06880
Phone: (203)341-3300
Fax: (203)341-3309

Independent venture capital partnership. Areas of interest include biotechnology, medical devices/ services, and health care services. Initial investments range from $500,000 to $1.5 million; up to $3 million over several later rounds of financing.

Prince Ventures (Westport)
25 Ford Rd.
Westport, Connecticut 06880
Phone: (203)227-8332
Fax: (203)226-5302

Provides early stage financing for medical and life sciencesventures.

Delaware

Delaware Economic Development Authority
99 Kings Hwy.
PO Box 1401
Dover, Delaware 19903-1401
Phone: (302)739-4271
Toll-free: (800)441-8846
Fax: (302)739-5749

Provides financing to new and expanding businesses at interest rates below the prime rate by issuing industrial revenue bonds (IRBs). Manufacturing and agricultural projects are eligible.

PNC Capital Corp.
300 Delaware Ave., Ste. 304
Wilmington, Delaware 19801
Phone: (302)427-5895
Fax: (302)427-5810
Gary J. Zentner, President

Preferred Investment Size: $2 to $8 million. Investment Policies: Loans and/or equity. Investment Types: Expansion, later stage. Industry Preferences: No real estate or tax-oriented investments. Geographic Preferences: Northeast.

District of Columbia

Allied Capital Commercial Corp.
1666 K St. NW, 9th Fl.
Washington, District of Columbia 20006
Phone: (202)331-1112
Fax: (202)659-2053

Real estate investment trust managed by Allied Capital Advisers, Inc. Investments range from $500,000 to $7.5 million. Prefers to purchase small business loans secured by real estate that are owner-operated or small business controlled. Areas of property interest include convenience stores, hotel/motel establishments, offices, medical facilities and nursing homes, industrial and retail properties, service stations, RV and mobile home parks, office condominiums, mini-storage facilities, and restaurants.

Allied Capital Corp.
1666 K St. NW, 9th Fl.
Washington, District of Columbia 20006
Phone: (202)331-1112
Fax: (202)659-2053

Venture capital fund managed by Allied Capital Advisers, Inc. Investments range from $500,000 to $6 million. Prefers later-stage companies that have been in business for at least one year, but gives consideration to early-stage companies and turnaroundsituations. Geographical preferences include the Northeast, Mid-Atlantic, and Southeast. Areas of interest include communications, computer hardware and software, consumer products, educational products, electronics, environmental, energy, franchising, industrial products and equipment, manufacturing, media, medical/health, publishing, recreation/tourism, restaurant, retail, service, transportation, and wholesale distribution industries.

Allied Capital Corp. II
1666 K St. NW, 9th Fl.
Washington, District of Columbia 20006
Phone: (202)331-1112
Fax: (202)659-2053

Venture capital fund managed by Allied Capital Advisers, Inc. Investments range from $500,000 to $1 million. Prefers later-stage companies that have been in business for at least one year, but gives consideration to early-stage companies and turnaround situations. Geographical preferences include the Northeast,
Mid-Atlantic, and Southeast. Areas of interest include communications, computer hardware and software, consumer products, educational products, electronics, environmental, energy, franchising, industrial products and equipment, manufacturing, media, medical/health, publishing, recreation/tourism, restaurant, retail, service, transportation, and wholesale distribution industries.

Allied Capital Lending Corp.
1666 K St. NW, 9th Fl.
Washington, District of Columbia 20006
Phone: (202)331-1112
Fax: (202)659-2053

Management investment company managed by Allied Capital Advisers, Inc. Investments range from $200,000 to $1 million. Prefers to provide small, privately owned businesses with SBA-guaranteed loans. Areas of interest include manufacturing, hotel/motel, consumer products, retail shops/convenience stores, service stations, laundries and dry cleaning, home furnishings, printing, real estate, recreation/tourism, restaurant, and service industries.

Allied Financial Corp.
1666 K St. NW, 9th Fl.
Washington, District of Columbia 20006
Phone: (202)331-1112
Fax: (202)659-2053

A minority enterprise small business investment corporation. Diversified industry preference, excluding startups, turnarounds,real estate development, natural resources, and foreign companies.

Broadcast Capital, Inc.
1771 N St. NW
Washington, District of Columbia 20036
Phone: (202)429-5393
Fax: (202)775-2991

A minority enterprise small business investment corporation. Invests only in radio and TV stations. Investments lie in the $300,000-$400,000 range.

Fulcrum Venture Capital Corp
2021 K St. NW, Ste. 210
Washington, District of Columbia 20006
Phone: (202)785-4253

Helio Capital, Inc.
666 11th St., NW, Ste. 900
Washington, District of Columbia 20001
Phone: (202)272-3617
Fax: (202)504-2247

A minority enterprise small business
investment corporation. No industry
preference.

Minority Broadcast Investment Corp.
1000 Connecticut NW, Ste. 622
Washington, District of Columbia 20036
Phone: (202)293-1166
Fax: (202)872-1669

A minority enterprise small business
investment corporation. Communications industry preferred.

Zaitech Capital Corp.
SBA, Receiver for Zaitech Capital Corp.
666 11th St. NW Ste.900
Washington, District of Columbia 20001
Phone: (202)504-2245
Fax: (202)504-2247

A minority enterprise small business
investment company. Diversified
industry preference.

Florida

North American Fund, II
312 SE 17th St., Ste.300
Fort Lauderdale, Florida 33316
Phone: (305)463-0681
Fax: (305)527-0904

A small business investment corporation. No industry preference. Prefers
controlling interest investments and
acquisitions of established businesses
with a history of profitability.

Quantum Capital Partners, Ltd.
4400 NE 25th Ave.
Fort Lauderdale, Florida 33308
Phone: (305)776-1133

Fax: (305)938-9406

A small business investment company. Diversified industry preference.

Pro-Med Investment Corp.
Presidential Circle
4000 Hollywood Blvd., Ste.435 S.
Hollywood, Florida 33021-6754
Phone: (305)966-8868
Toll-free: (800)954-3617
Fax: (305)969-3223

A minority enterprise small business
investment company.

Venture First Associates
1901 S. Harbor City Blvd., Ste. 501
Melbourne, Florida 32901
Phone: (407)952-7750
Fax: (407)952-5787

Venture capital firm providing seed,
start-up and first stage financing.
Areas of interest include health care,
advanced chemicals, computer
software and hardware, industrial
equipment, electronics, and communications.

BAC Investment Corp.
600 NW 27th Ave.
Miami, Florida 33147
Phone: (305)693-5919
Fax: (305)693-7450

A minority enterprise small business
investment company. Diversified
industry preference.

J and D Capital Corp.
12747 Biscayne Blvd.
North Miami, Florida 33181
Phone: (305)893-0303
Fax: (305)891-2338

A small business investment corporation. No industry preference.

PMC Investment Corp.
AmeriFirst Bank Bldg., 2nd Fl. S
18301 Biscayne Blvd.

North Miami Beach, Florida 33160
Phone: (305)933-5858
Fax: (305)931-3054

Western Financial Capital Corp.
(North Miami Beach)
AmeriFirst Bank Bldg., 2nd Fl. S
18301 Biscayne Blvd.
North Miami Beach, Florida 33160
Phone: (305)933-5858
Fax: (305)931-3054

A small business investment company.

Florida High Technology and
Industry Council
Collins Bldg.
107 W. Gaines St., Rm. 315
Tallahassee, Florida 32399-2000
Phone: (904)487-3136
Fax: (904)487-3014

Provides financing for research and
development for high-tech businesses.

Florida Capital Ventures, Ltd.
880 Riverside Plz.
100 W. Kennedy Blvd.
Tampa, Florida 33602
Phone: (813)229-2294
Fax: (813)229-2028

A small business investment company. Diversified industry preference.

Market Capital Corp.
1102 N. 28th St.
PO Box 31667
Tampa, Florida 33631
Phone: (813)247-1357
Fax: (813)248-6679

A small business investment corporation. Grocery industry preferred.

South Atlantic Venture Fund
614 W. Bay St., Ste. 200
Tampa, Florida 33606-2704
Phone: (813)253-2500
Fax: (813)253-2360

A minority enterprise small business
investment corporation. Provides
expansion capital for privately

owned, rapidly growing companies located in the southeastern United States and Texas. Prefers to invest in communications, computer services, consumer, electronic components and instrumentation, medical/health-related services, medical products, finance, and insurance industries. Will not consider real estate or oil and gas investments.

Allied Financial Services Corp. (Vero Beach)
Executive Office Center, Ste. 303
2770 N. Indian River Blvd.
Vero Beach, Florida 32960
Phone: (407)778-5556
Fax: (407)569-9303

A minority enterprise small business investment company.

Allied Investment Corp. (Vero Beach)
Executive Office Center, Ste.305
2770 N. Indian River Blvd.
Vero Beach, Florida 32960
Phone: (407)778-5556
Fax: (407)569-9303

A small business investment company.

Georgia

Advanced Technology Development Fund
1000 Abernathy Rd., Ste. 1420
Atlanta, Georgia 30328
Phone: (770)668-2333
Fax: (770)668-2330

Venture capital firm providing start-up, first stage, second stage expansion, purchase or secondary positions, and buyout or acquisition financing. Areas of interest include information processing, health care and specialized mobile radio.

Arete Ventures, Inc./Utech Venture Capital Funds
115 Perimeter Center Pl. NE, No. 1140
Atlanta, Georgia 30346-1282
Phone: (404)399-1660

Venture capital firm providing start-up, first stage, second stage expansion and late stage expansion financing. Areas of interest include utility-related industries.

Cordova Capital Partners, L.P.
3350 Cumberland Cir., Ste. 970
Atlanta, Georgia 30339
Phone: (770)951-1542
Fax: (770)955-7610
Paul DiBella, Manager
Ralph Wright, Manager

Preferred Investment Size: $1 to $3 million. Investment Policies: Equity and/or debt. Investment Types: Early stage, expansion, later stage. Industry Preferences: Diversified. Geographic Preferences: Southeast.

Cravey, Green & Wahlen, Inc./CGW Southeast Partners
12 Piedmont Center, Ste. 210
Atlanta, Georgia 30305-4805
Phone: (404)816-3255
Toll-free: (800)249-6669
Fax: (404)816-3258

Venture capital firm providing buyout or acquisition financing. Areas of interest include manufacturing, distribution, and serviceindustries. Does not provide start-up financing or investments in high technology and medical industries.

EGL Holdings, Inc.
6600 Peachtree-Dunwoody Rd.
300 Embassy Row, Ste. 630
Atlanta, Georgia 30328
Phone: (770)399-5633
Fax: (770)393-4825

Venture capital firm providing late stage expansion, purchase or secondary positions, and buyout or acquisition financing. Areas of interest include information technology, medical/health care, industrial automation, electronic components

and instrumentation for venture capital deals, and all industries for buyouts.

Equity South
1790 The Lenox Bldg.
3399 Peachtree Rd., Ste. 1790
Atlanta, Georgia 30326
Phone: (404)237-6222
Fax: (404)261-1578

Venture capital firm providing second stage expansion, late stage expansion, purchase or secondary positions, and buyout or acquisition financing.

Georgia Department of Community Affairs
Government Information Division
1200 Equitable Bldg.
100 Peachtree St. NW
Atlanta, Georgia 30303
Phone: (404)656-5526
Fax: (404)656-9792

Central source for information on Georgia's people, economy, and local governments, including information on federal and state funding sources.

Georgia Department of Community Affairs
Community and Economic Development Division
1200 Equitable Bldg.
100 Peachtree St. NW
Atlanta, Georgia 30303
Phone: (404)656-3836
Fax: (404)656-9792

Provides assistance in applying for state and federal grants.

Green Capital Investors L.P.
3343 Peachtree Rd., Ste. 1420
Atlanta, Georgia 30326
Phone: (404)261-1187
Fax: (404)266-8677

Venture capital firm providing purchase or secondary positions and buyout or acquisition financing.

Investor's Equity, Inc.
1355 Peachtree
Atlanta, Georgia 30309
Phone: (404)897-1910

A small business investment corporation.

Noro-Moseley Partners
4200 Northside Pky., Bldg. 9
Atlanta, Georgia 30327
Phone: (404)233-1966
Fax: (404)239-9280

Venture capital partnership. Prefers to invest in private, diversified small and medium-sized growth companies located in the southeastern United States.

Premier HealthCare
3414 Peachtree Rd., Ste. 238
Atlanta, Georgia 30326
Phone: (404)816-0049
Fax: (404)816-0248

Venture capital firm providing start-up, first stage, second stage expansion, late stage expansion, purchase or secondary positions, and buyout or acquisition financing. Areas of interest include health care.

Renaissance Capital Corp.
34 Peachtree St. NW, Ste. 2230
Atlanta, Georgia 30303
Phone: (404)658-9061
Fax: (404)658-9064

A minority enterprise small business investment company. Diversified industry preference.

River Capital, Inc.
1360 Peachtree St. NE, Ste. 1430
Atlanta, Georgia 30309
Phone: (404)873-2166
Fax: (404)873-2158

Venture capital firm providing second stage expansion, late stage expansion, purchase or secondary positions, and buyout or acquisition financing. Areas of interest include light manufacturing and distribution companies with annual revenues exceeding $20 million.

Seaboard Management Corp.
3400 Peachtree Rd. NE, Ste. 741
Atlanta, Georgia 30326
Phone: (404)239-6270
Fax: (404)239-6284

Venture capital firm providing first stage and second stage expansion financing. Areas of interest include manufacturing and telecommunications.

First Growth Capital, Inc.
Best Western Plz.
PO Box 815
Forsyth, Georgia 31029
Phone: (912)994-9260
Toll-free: (800)447-3241
Fax: (912)994-9260

A minority enterprise small business investment company. Diversified industry preference.

North Riverside Capital Corp.
50 Technology Pk./Atlanta
Norcross, Georgia 30092
Phone: (770)446-5556
Fax: (770)446-8627

A small business investment corporation. No industry preference.

Hawaii

Bancorp Hawaii SBIC
130 Merchant St.
Honolulu, Hawaii 96813
Phone: (808)521-6411
Fax: (808)537-8557

A small business investment corporation. No industry preference.

Hawaii Agriculture Department
PO Box 22159
Honolulu, Hawaii 96823-2159
Phone: (808)973-9600
Fax: (808)973-9613

Provides information and advice in such areas as marketing, production, and labeling. Administers loan programs, including the New Farmer Loan Program, the Emergency Loan Program, and the Aquaculture Loan Program.

Hawaii Department of Business, Economic Development, and Tourism
Financial Assistance Branch
Grosvenor Center, Mauka Tower
737 Bishop St., Ste. 1900
PO Box 2359
Honolulu, Hawaii 96813
Phone: (808)586-2576
Fax: (808)587-3832

Provides loans to small businesses, including the Hawaii Capital Loan Program and the Hawaii Innovation Development Loan Program.

Pacific Venture Capital Ltd.
222 S. Vineyard St., No. PH-1
Honolulu, Hawaii 96813-2445
Phone: (808)521-6502
Toll-free: (800)455-1888
Fax: (808)521-6541

A minority enterprise small business investment corporation.

Illinois

ABN AMRO Capital (USA) Inc.
135 S. La Salle St.
Chicago, Illinois 60603
Phone: (312)904-6445
Phone: (312)904-6376
Joseph Rizzi, Chairman

Alpha Capital Venture Partners
3 1st National Plz.-Ste. 1400
Chicago, Illinois 60602
Phone: (312)214-3440
Fax: (312)214-3376

A small business investment corporation providing expansion or later stage financing in the Midwest. No industry preference; however, no real estate, oil and gas, or start-up ventures are considered.

Ameritech Development Corp.
225 W. Randolph, 18th C Fl.
Chicago, Illinois 60606
Phone: (312)750-5000
Fax: (312)609-0244

Venture capital supplier. Prefers to

invest in telecommunications and information services.

Batterson, Johnson and Wang
Venture Partners
303 W. Madison St., Ste. 1110
Chicago, Illinois 60606-3300
Phone: (312)269-0300
Fax: (312)269-0021

William Blair and Co. (Chicago)
222 W. Adams St.
Chicago, Illinois 60606-5312
Phone: (312)364-8250
Fax: (312)236-1042

A small business investment corporation. Areas of interest include cable,
media, communications, consumer
products, retail, health care services,
technology and information services,
and other service industries.

Brinson Partners, Inc.
209 S. LaSalle, 12th Fl.
Chicago, Illinois 60604-1295
Phone: (312)220-7100
Fax: (312)220-7199

Business Ventures, Inc.
20 N. Wacker Dr., Ste. 1741
Chicago, Illinois 60606-2904
Phone: (312)346-1580
Fax: (312)346-6693

A small business investment corporation. No industry preference; considers only ventures in the Chicago area.

Capital Health Venture Partners
122 S. Michigan, Ste. 1320
Chicago, Illinois 60603
Phone: (312)427-1227
Fax: (312)691-0124

Investments limited to early stage
medical, biotech, and health care
related companies.

The Combined Fund, Inc.
915 E. Hyde Park Blvd.
Chicago, Illinois 60615
Phone: (312)363-0300
Fax: (312)363-6816

A minority enterprise small business
investment company. Diversified
industry preference.

Continental Illinois Venture Corp.
231 S. LaSalle St.
Chicago, Illinois 60697
Phone: (312)828-8023
Fax: (312)987-0763

A small business investment corporation. Provides start-up and early stage
financing to growth-oriented companies with capable management teams,
proprietary products, and expanding
markets.

Essex Venture Partners
190 S. LaSalle St., Ste. 2800
Chicago, Illinois 60603
Phone: (312)444-6040
Fax: (312)444-6034

Prefers to invest in health care
companies.

First Analysis Corp.
c/o Bret Maxwell
233 S. Wacker Dr., Ste. 9500
Chicago, Illinois 60606
Phone: (312)258-1400
Toll-free: (800)866-3272
Fax: (312)258-0334

Small business investment corporation providing first and second stage,
mezzanine, and leveraged buyout
financing in the $100,000 to $3
million range. Will act as deal
originator or investor in deals created
by others. Areas of interest include
environmental, infrastructure, special
chemicals/materials, repetitive
revenue service, telecommunications,
software, consumer/specialty retail,
and health care companies.

First Capital Corp. of Chicago
3 1st National Plz., Ste. 1330
Chicago, Illinois 60602
Phone: (312)732-5400
Fax: (312)732-4098

A small business investment corporation. No industry preference.

First Chicago Venture Capital
3 1st National Plz., Ste. 1330
Chicago, Illinois 60602
Phone: (312)732-5400
Fax: (312)732-4098

Venture capital supplier. Invests a
minimum of $1 million in early stage
situations to a maximum of $25
million in mature growth or buy out
situations. Emphasis is placed on a
strong management team and unique
market opportunity.

Frontenac Co.
135 S. LaSalle St., Ste. 1900
Chicago, Illinois 60603
Phone: (312)368-0044
Fax: (312)368-9520

A small business investment corporation. No industry preference.

Golder, Thoma, Cressey, Rauner, Inc.
6100 Sears Tower
233 S. Wacker
Chicago, Illinois 60606
Phone: (312)382-2200
Fax: (312)382-2201

Private venture capital firm. Diversified industry preference, but does not
invest in high technology or real
estate industries.

Heller Equity Capital Corp.
500 W. Monroe St.
Chicago, Illinois 60661
Phone: (312)441-7200
Fax: (312)441-7378

A small business investment company. Diversified industry preference.

IEG Venture Management, Inc.
70 West Madison, Ste. 1400
Chicago, Illinois 60602
Phone: (312)644-0890
Fax: (312)454-0369

Venture capital supplier. Provides
start-up financing primarily to
technology-based companies located
in the Midwest.

Illinois Development Finance Authority
Sears Tower
233 S. Wacker Dr., Ste. 5310
Chicago, Illinois 60606
Phone: (312)793-5586
Fax: (312)793-6347

Provides bond, venture capital, and
direct loan programs.

Mesirow Capital Partners SBIC, Ltd.
350 N. Clark St., 3rd Fl.
Chicago, Illinois 60610
Phone: (312)595-6000
Fax: (312)595-7208

A small business investment corporation providing later stage growth
financing and acquisition financing
of non-high-technology companies.
Does not provide start-up and
turnaround financing.

The Neighborhood Fund, Inc.
1950 E. 71st St., Jeffery's Blvd.
Chicago, Illinois 60649-2030
Phone: (312)753-5670
Fax: (312)493-6609

A minority enterprise small business
investment company. Diversified
industry preference.

Neighborhood Fund, Inc. (The)
25 E. Washington Blvd., Ste. 2015
Chicago, Illinois 60602
Phone: (312)726-6084
Fax: (312)726-0167
Derrick Collins, President

Preferred Investment Size: $100,000
to $300,000. Investment Policies:
Equity and loans. Industry Preferences: Manufacturing, technology,
product based. Geographic Preferences: Midwest.

Peterson Finance and Investment Co.
3300 W. Peterson Ave., Ste. A
Chicago, Illinois 60659
Phone: (312)539-0502
Fax: (312)267-8846

A minority enterprise small business
investment company. Diversified
industry preference.

Polestar Capital, Inc.
180 N. Michigan Ave., Ste. 1905
Chicago, Illinois 60601
Phone: (312)984-9875
Fax: (312)984-9877
Wallace Lennox, President

Preferred Investment Size: $350,000
to $700,000. Investment Policies:.
Primarily equity. Investment Types:
Early to later stages.

Prince Ventures (Chicago)
10 S. Wacker Dr., Ste. 2575
Chicago, Illinois 60606
Phone: (312)454-1408
Fax: (312)454-9125

Shorebank Capital Incorp.
7936 S. Cottage Grove
Chicago, Illinois 60619
Phone: (312)371-7030
Fax: (312)371-7035

A minority enterprise small business
investment corporation providing second
stage, buyout, and acquisition financing
to companies in the Midwest. Diversified
industry preference.

Tower Ventures, Inc.
Sears Tower, BSC 23-27
33333 Beverly Holtman, Ste. AC254A
Chicago, Illinois 60179
Phone: (708)286-0571
Fax: (312)906-0164

A minority enterprise small business
investment company. Diversified
industry preference.

Walnut Capital Corp. (Chicago)
2 N. LaSalle St., Ste.2410
Chicago, Illinois 60602
Phone: (312)269-0126
Fax: (312)346-2231

A small business investment corporation. Diversified industry preference.

Wind Point Partners (Chicago)
676 N. Michigan Ave., No. 3300
Chicago, Illinois 60611-2804
Phone: (312)649-4000
Fax: (312)649-9644

Marquette Venture Partners
520 Lake Cook Rd., Ste. 450
Deerfield, Illinois 60015
Phone: (708)940-1700
Fax: (708)940-1724

Seidman, Fisher and Co.
1603 Orrington Ave. Ste. 2050
Evanston, Illinois 60201-5910
Phone: (708)492-1812
Fax: (708)864-9692

Private venture capital supplier.

The Cerulean Fund
1701 E. Lake Ave., Ste. 170
Glenview, Illinois 60025
Phone: (847)657-8002
Fax: (847)657-8168

Providers of equity investment.
Allstate Venture Capital
3075 Sanders Rd., Ste. G5D
Northbrook, Illinois 60062-7127
Phone: (708)402-5681
Fax: (708)402-0880

Venture capital supplier. Investments
are not limited to particular industries
or geographical locations. Interest is
in unique products or services that
address large potential markets and
offer great economic benefits;
strength of management team is also
important. Investments range from
$500,000 to $5 million.

Caterpillar Venture Capital, Inc.
100 NE Adams St.
Peoria, Illinois 61629
Phone: (309)675-1000
Fax: (309)675-4457

Venture capital subsidiary of operating firm.

Cilcorp Ventures, Inc.
300 Hamilton Blvd., Ste. 300
Peoria, Illinois 61602
Phone: (309)675-8850
Fax: (309)675-8800

Invests in environmental services
only.

Comdisco Venture Group (Rosemont)
6111 N. River Rd.
Rosemont, Illinois 60018
Phone: (708)698-3000
Toll-free: (800)336-6000
Fax: (847)518-5440

Venture capital subsidiary of operating firm.

Indiana

Cambridge Ventures, LP
8440 Woodfield Crossing, No. 315
Indianapolis, Indiana 46240
Phone: (317)469-9704
Fax: (317)469-3926

A small business investment company. Diversified industry preference.

Circle Ventures, Inc.
26 N. Arsenal Ave.
Indianapolis, Indiana 46201-3808
Phone: (317)636-7242
Fax: (317)637-7581

A small business investment corporation. Prefers second-stage, leveraged buy out, and growth financings. Geographical preference is Indianapolis.

Heritage Venture Partners
135 N. Pennsylvania St., Ste. 2380
Indianapolis, Indiana 46204
Phone: (317)635-5696
Fax: (317)635-5699

Venture capital fund. Prefers radio broadcast properties in mid-sized radio markets wherein major universities are located.

Indiana Business Modernization and Technology Corp.
1 N. Capitol Ave., Ste. 925
Indianapolis, Indiana 46204
Phone: (317)635-3058
Toll-free: (800)877-5182
Fax: (317)231-7095

Invests in and counsels applied research ventures.

Indiana Development Finance Authority
1 N. Capitol Ave., Ste. 320
Indianapolis, Indiana 46204
Phone: (317)233-4332
Phone: (317)232-6786
Fax: (317)232-6786

Administers the Ag Finance, Export Finance, Loan Guarantee, and Industrial Development Bond Financing Programs.

First Source Capital Corp.
PO Box 1602
South Bend, Indiana 46634
Phone: (219)235-2180
Fax: (219)235-2227

A small business investment corporation. No industry preference.

Iowa

Allsop Venture Partners (Cedar Rapids)
2750 1st Ave. NE, Ste. 210
Cedar Rapids, Iowa 52402
Phone: (319)363-8971
Fax: (319)363-9519

InvestAmerica Venture Group, Inc. (Cedar Rapids)
101 2nd St. SE, Ste. 800
Cedar Rapids, Iowa 52401
Phone: (319)363-8249
Fax: (319)363-9683

A small business investment corporation. Invests in later stage manufacturing and service businesses.

MorAmerica Capital Corp. (Cedar Rapids)
101 2nd St. SE, Ste. 800
Cedar Rapids, Iowa 52401
Phone: (319)363-8249
Fax: (319)363-9683

A small business investment company. Diversified industry preference.

Iowa Department of Economic Development
Iowa Seed Capitol Corp.

200 E. Grand Ave., Ste. 160
Des Moines, Iowa 50309
Phone: (515)242-4860
Phone: (515)242-4722

Provides risk capital to ventures that have new-job potential in Iowa. Profits are reinvested in other Iowa businesses and products.

Iowa Dept. of Economic Development
International Division
Export Finance Program
200 E. Grand Ave.
Des Moines, Iowa 50309
Phone: (515)242-4742
Fax: (515)242-4918

Provides funding to qualified exporters of Iowa-manufactured and processed products.

Iowa Department of Economic Development
Iowa New Jobs Training Program
150 Des Moines St.
Des Moines, Iowa 50309
Phone: (515)281-9028
Fax: (515)281-9033

Reimburses new or expanding companies for up to 50 percent of new employees' salaries and benefits for up to one year of on-the-job training. Coordinated through the state's 15 community colleges.

Iowa Department of Economic Development
Bureau of Business Finance
Self-Employment Loan Program
Iowa Dept. of Economic Development
200 E. Grand Ave.
Des Moines, Iowa 50309
Phone: (515)242-4793
Phone: (515)242-4749

Provides low-interest loans for low-income entrepreneurs who are expanding or starting a new business.

Iowa Department of Economic Development
Division of Financial Assistance

Community Development Block Grants
200 E. Grand Ave.
Des Moines, Iowa 50309
Phone: (515)242-4825
Fax: (515)242-4809

Bestows grants from the U.S. Department of Housing and Urban Development to help finance community improvements and job-generating expansions. Funds are primarily awarded on a competitive basis.

Iowa Finance Authority
100 E. Grand Ave., Ste. 250
Des Moines, Iowa 50309
Phone: (515)242-4990
Fax: (515)242-4957

Provides loans to new and expanding small businesses. Funds may be used to purchase land, construction, building improvements, or equipment; loans cannot be used for working capital, inventory, or operations.

Kansas

Allsop Venture Partners (Overland Park)
7400 College Blvd., Ste. 302
Overland Park, Kansas 66210
Phone: (913)338-0820
Fax: (913)649-2125

Kansas Venture Capital, Inc. (Overland Park)
6700 Antioch Plz., Ste. 460
Overland Park, Kansas 66204-1200
Phone: (913)262-7117
Fax: (913)262-3509

A small business investment corporation. Prefers to invest in wholesale or distribution, high technology, and service businesses.

Kansas City Equity Partners
4200 Somerset Dr., Ste. 101
Prairie Village, Kansas 66208
Phone: (913)649-1771
Fax: (913)649-2125
Paul H. Henson, Manager

Preferred Investment Size: $500,000 to $2 million. Investment Policies: Equity. Investment Types: Seed, early stage, expansion. Industry Preferences: Diversified. Geographic Preferences: Midwest.

Kansas Development Finance Authority
700 SW Jackson
Jayhawk Tower, Ste. 1000
Topeka, Kansas 66603
Phone: (913)296-6747
Fax: (913)296-6810

Dedicated to improving access to capital financing to business enterprises through the issuance of bonds.

Kansas Housing and Commerce Department
Division of Community Development
700 SW Harrison, Ste. 1300
Topeka, Kansas 66603-3712
Phone: (913)296-3485
Fax: (913)296-0186

Administers Community Development Block Grants and the enterprise zone program, in which businesses receive tax credits and exemptions for locating in targeted areas.

Kentucky

Kentucky Cabinet for Economic Development
Financial Incentives Department
Capitol Plaza Tower
500 Mero St.
Frankfort, Kentucky 40601
Phone: (502)564-4554
Fax: (502)564-3256

Provides loans to supplement private financing. Offers two major programs: issuance of industrial revenue bonds; and second mortgage loans to private firms in participation with other lenders. Also has a Crafts Guaranteed Loan Program providing loans up to $20,000 to qualified craftspersons, and a Commonwealth Venture

Capital Program, encouraging the establishment or expansion of small business and industry.

Kentucky Cabinet for Economic Development
Commonwealth Small Business Development Corp.
2300 Capitol Plaza Tower
Frankfort, Kentucky 40601
Phone: (502)564-4320
Fax: (502)564-3256

Provides loans of up to 40 percent of the costs of expansion to qualified small businesses unable to obtain financing without government aid.

Mountain Ventures, Inc.
362 Old Whitley Rd.
PO Box 1738
London, Kentucky 40743-1738
Phone: (606)864-5175
Fax: (606)864-5194

A small business investment corporation. No industry preference; geographic area limited to southeast Kentucky.

Equal Opportunity Finance, Inc.
420 S. Hurstbourne Pky., Ste. 201
Louisville, Kentucky 40222-8002
Phone: (502)423-1943
Fax: (502)423-1945

A minority enterprise small business investment corporation. No industry preference; geographic areas limited to Indiana, Kentucky, Ohio, and West Virginia.

Louisiana

Louisiana Department of Economic Development
Economic Development Corp.
PO Box 94185
Baton Rouge, Louisiana 70804-9185
Phone: (504)342-3000
Fax: (504)342-5389

Premier Venture Capital Corp.
451 Florida St.
Baton Rouge, Louisiana 70801

Phone: (504)332-4421
Fax: (504)332-7929

A small business investment corporation. No industry preference.

S.C.D.F. Investment Corp., Inc.
PO Box 3885
Lafayette, Louisiana 70502
Phone: (318)232-7672
Fax: (318)232-5094

A minority enterprise small business investment corporation. No industry preference.

First Commerce Capital, Inc.
201 St. Charles Ave., 16th Fl.
PO Box 60279
New Orleans, Louisiana 70160
Phone: (504)623-1600
Fax: (504)623-1779
William Harper, Manager

Preferred Investment Size: $1 to $2 million. Investment Policies: Loans, equity. Investment Types: Later stage, acquisition, buyouts.Industry Preferences: Manufacturing healthcare, retail, wholesale/distribution. Geographic Preferences: Gulf South region.

Maine

Finance Authority of Maine
83 Western Ave.
PO Box 949
Augusta, Maine 04332-0949
Phone: (207)623-3263
Phone: (207)623-0095
Fax: (800)623-0095

Assists business development and job creation through direct loans, loan guarantee programs, and project grants.

Maine Capital Corp.
70 Center St.
Portland, Maine 04101
Phone: (207)772-1001
Fax: (207)772-3257

A small business investment corporation. No industry preference.

Maryland

ABS Ventures Limited Partnerships (Baltimore)
135 E. Baltimore St.
Baltimore, Maryland 21202
Phone: (410)727-1700
Toll-free: (800)638-2596
Fax: (410)234-3699

Invests in the computer software, health care, and biotechnology industries.

American Security Capital Corp., Inc.
100 S. Charles St., 5th Fl.
Baltimore, Maryland 21201
Phone: (410)547-4205
Fax: (410)547-4990

A small business investment company. Diversified industry preference.

Anthem Capital, L.P.
16 S. Calvert St., Ste. 800
Baltimore, Maryland 21202
Phone: (410)625-1510
Fax: (410)625-1735
William M. Gust II, Manager

Broventure Capital Management
16 W. Madison St.
Baltimore, Maryland 21201
Phone: (410)727-4520
Fax: (410)727-1436

Venture capital partnership. Provides start-up capital to early stage companies, expansion capital to companies experiencing rapid growth, and capital for acquisitions. Initial investments range from $400,000 to $750,000.

Maryland Department of Economic and Employment Development Financing Programs Division Industrial Development Financing Authority
217 E. Redwood St.
Baltimore, Maryland 21202-3316
Phone: (410)767-6300
Fax: (410)333-8628

Insures up to 80 percent of loans or obligations. Also provides tax-exempt revenue bonds for the financing of fixed assets.

Maryland Department of Economic and Employment Development Financing Programs Division Small Business Development Center
217 E. Redwood St., 10th Fl.
Baltimore, Maryland 21202-3316
Phone: (410)767-0095
Toll-free: (800)333-6995
Fax: (410)333-1836

Provides short-term financing for government contracts and long-term financing for equipment and working capital. Also operates a surety bond guarantee program for small businesses and an equity participation investment program for potential minority franchises.

Maryland Department of Economic and Employment Development Financing Programs Division Community Financing Group
111 N. Utah St.
Baltimore, Maryland 21201-3316
Phone: (410)333-4304
Phone: (410)767-2000
Fax: (410)333-6931

New Enterprise Associates
1119 St. Paul St.
Baltimore, Maryland 21202
Phone: (410)244-0115
Fax: (410)752-7721

Private free-standing venture capital partnership providing seed and start-up financing. Prefers information technology and medical and life science industries.

T. Rowe Price
100 E. Pratt St.
Baltimore, Maryland 21202
Phone: (410)547-2000
Toll-free: (800)638-7890

Venture capital supplier. Offers specialized investment services to meet the needs of companies in various stages of growth.

Triad Investor's Corp.
300 E. Joppa, Ste. 1111
Baltimore, Maryland 21204
Phone: (410)828-6497
Fax: (410)337-7312

Venture capital firm providing seed and early stage financing. Areas of interest include communications, computer-related, medical/health-related, genetic engineering, and electronic components and instrumentation industries.

Calvert Social Venture Partners
7201 Wisconsin Ave., Ste. 310
Bethesda, Maryland 20814
Phone: (301)718-4272
Fax: (301)656-4421

Private venture capital partnership focusing on Mid-Atlantic companies involved in socially or environmentally beneficial products or services.

Security Financial and Investment Corp.
7720 Wisconsin Ave., Ste. 207
Bethesda, Maryland 20814
Phone: (301)951-4288
Fax: (301)951-9282

A minority enterprise small business investment corporation. No industry preference.

Greater Washington Investments, Inc.
5454 Wisconsin Ave.
Chevy Chase, Maryland 20815
Phone: (301)656-0626
Fax: (301)656-4053

A small business investment company. Diversified industry preference.

Jupiter National, Inc.
5454 Wisconsin Ave.
Chevy Chase, Maryland 20815
Phone: (301)656-0626
Fax: (301)656-4053

A small business investment corporation. Prefers low to medium technology and subordinated debt investments.

Greater Washington Investments, Inc.
39 W. Montgomery Ave.
Rockville, Maryland 20850
Phone: (301)738-3939
Fax: (301)738-7949
Haywood Miller, Manager

Preferred Investment Size: $1,000,000. Investment Policies: Subordinated debt with warrant. Investment Types: Expansion, later stage. Industry Preferences: Diversified. Geographic Preferences: National.

Syncom Capital Corp.
8401 Coalville Rd., Ste. 300
Silver Spring, Maryland 20910
Phone: (301)608-3203
Fax: (301)608-3307

A minority enterprise small business investment corporation. Areas of interest include telecommunications and media.

Grotech Capital Group
9690 Deereco Rd., Ste. 800
Timonium, Maryland 21093
Phone: (410)560-2000
Fax: (410)560-1910

Massachusetts

Advanced Technology Ventures (Boston)
10 Post Office Sq. Ste 970
Boston, Massachusetts 02109
Phone: (617)423-4050
Fax: (617)423-4573

Private venture capital firm. Prefers early stage financing in high-technology industries.

Advent Atlantic Capital Co. LP
75 State St., Ste. 2500
Boston, Massachusetts 02109

Phone: (617)345-7200
Fax: (617)345-7201

Venture capital fund. Communications industry preferred.

Advent V Capital Co.
75 State St., Ste. 2500
Boston, Massachusetts 02109
Phone: (617)345-7200
Fax: (617)345-7201

Venture capital fund. Communications industry preferred.

Advent IV Capital Co.
75 State St., Ste. 2500
Boston, Massachusetts 02109
Phone: (617)345-7200
Fax: (617)345-7201

Venture capital fund. Communications industry preferred.

Advent Industrial Capital Co. LP
75 State St., Ste. 2500
Boston, Massachusetts 02109
Phone: (617)345-7200
Fax: (617)345-7201

Venture capital fund. Communications industry preferred.

Advent International Corp.
101 Federal St.
Boston, Massachusetts 02110
Phone: (617)951-9400
Fax: (617)951-0566

Venture capital firm. Invests in all stages, from start-up technology-based companies to well-established companies in rapid growth or mature industries; no retail clothing or real estate.

American Research and Development
45 Milk St., 4th Fl.
Boston, Massachusetts 02109
Phone: (617)423-7500
Fax: (617)423-9655

Independent private venture capital partnership. All stages of financing; no minimum or maximum investment.

Aspen Ventures (Boston)
1 Post Office Square, Ste. 3320
Boston, Massachusetts 02109
Phone: (617)426-2151
Fax: (617)426-2181

Venture capital supplier. Provides
start-up and early stage financing to
companies in high-growth industries
such as biotechnology, communications, electronics, and health care.

Atlas Venture
222 Berkeley
Boston, Massachusetts 02116
Phone: (617)859-9290
Fax: (617)859-9292

Bain Capital Fund (Boston)
2 Copley Pl.
Boston, Massachusetts 02116
Phone: (617)572-3000
Fax: (617)572-3274

Private venture capital firm. No
industry preference, but avoids
investing in high-tech industries.
Minimum investment is $500,000.

BancBoston Ventures, Inc.
100 Federal St., 32nd Fl.
PO Box 2016
Boston, Massachusetts 02110
Phone: (617)434-2442
Fax: (617)434-1153

A small business investment corporation. Minimum investment is $1
million.

Battery Ventures (Boston)
200 Portland St.
Boston, Massachusetts 02114
Phone: (617)367-1011
Fax: (617)367-1070

Venture capital firm providing
financing to early and emerging
software and communications
companies. Average investments are
from $1 million to $5 million.

Boston Capital Ventures
Old City Hall
45 School St.

Boston, Massachusetts 02108
Phone: (617)227-6550
Fax: (617)227-3847

Venture capital firm.

Burr, Egan, Deleage, and Co.
1 Post Office Sq., Ste. 3800
Boston, Massachusetts 02109
Phone: (617)482-8020
Toll-free: (800)756-2877
Fax: (617)482-1944

Private venture capital supplier.
Invests start-up, expansion, and
acquisitions capital nationwide.
Principal concerns are strength of the
management team; large, rapidly
expanding markets; and unique
products or services. Past investments
have been made in the fields of
electronics, health, and communications. Investments range from
$750,000 to $5 million.

Charles River Ventures
10 Post Office Sq., Ste. 1330
Boston, Massachusetts 02109
Phone: (617)292-7717
Fax: (617)292-7718

Venture capital partnership providing
early stage financing. Areas of
interest include communications,
software, environmental, and specialty financial service industries.

Chestnut Street Partners, Inc.
75 State St., Ste. 2500
Boston, Massachusetts 02109
Phone: (617)345-7220
Fax: (617)345-7201

A small business investment company. Diversified industrypreference.

Claflin Capital Management, Inc.
77 Franklin St.
Boston, Massachusetts 02110
Phone: (617)426-6505
Fax: (617)482-0016

Private venture capital firm investing
its own capital. No industry preference but prefers early stage companies.

Commonwealth Enterprise Fund, Inc.
10 Post Office Sq., Ste. 1090
Boston, Massachusetts 02109
Phone: (617)482-1881
Fax: (617)482-9141

A minority enterprise small business
investment corporation. No industry
preference, but clients must be
located in Massachusetts.

Copley Venture Partners
600 Atlantic Ave., 13th Fl.
Boston, Massachusetts 02210
Phone: (617)722-6030
Fax: (617)523-7739

Eastech Management Co.
45 Milk St., 4th Fl.
Boston, Massachusetts 02109
Phone: (617)423-7500
Fax: (617)423-9655

Private venture capital supplier.
Provides start-up and first- and
second-stage financing to companies
in the following industries: communications, computer-related electronic
components and instrumentation, and
industrial products and equipment.
Will not consider real estate, agriculture, forestry, fishing, finance and
insurance, transportation, oil and gas,
publishing, entertainment, natural
resources, or retail.

Fidelity Venture Associates, Inc.
Fidelity Investments
82 Devonshire St., Mail Zone R25C
Boston, Massachusetts 02109
Phone: (617)563-7000
Fax: (617)728-6755

Privately-held investment management firm providing financing to
young companies at various stages of
development. Areas of interest
include financial services, publishing, specialty retailing, health care,
transportation, computer systems and
software, and telecommunications
industries.

Greylock Management Corp. (Boston)
1 Federal St.
Boston, Massachusetts 02110
Phone: (617)423-5525
Fax: (617)482-0059

Private venture capital partnership. Minimum investment of $250,000; preferred investment size of over $1 million. Will function either as deal originator or investor in deals created by others.

Harvard Management Co., Inc.
600 Atlantic Ave.
Boston, Massachusetts 02210
Phone: (617)523-4400
Toll-free: (800)723-0044
Fax: (617)523-1283

Diversified venture capital firm. Minimum investment is $1 million.

Highland Capital Partners
2 International Pl.
Boston, Massachusetts 02110
Phone: (617)330-8765
Fax: (617)531-1550

Industry preferences include health care, software, and telecommunications.

John Hancock Venture Partners, Inc.
1 Financial Center, 44th Fl.
Boston, Massachusetts 02111
Phone: (617)348-3707
Fax: (617)350-0305

Venture capital supplier. Diversified investments.

Liberty Ventures Corp.
1 Liberty Sq.
Boston, Massachusetts 02109
Phone: (617)423-1765
Toll-free: (800)423-1766
Fax: (617)338-4362

Venture capital partnership. Provides start-up, early stage, and expansion financing to companies that are pioneering applications of proven technology; also will consider nontechnology-based companies

with strong management teams and plans for expansion. Investments range from $500,000 to $1 million, with a $6 million maximum.

Massachusetts Business Development Corp.
1 Liberty Sq.
Boston, Massachusetts 02109
Phone: (617)350-8877
Fax: (617)350-0052

Provides assistance to businesses and individuals attempting toutilize federal, state, and local loan finance programs.

Massachusetts Community Development Finance Corp.
10 Post Office Sq., Ste. 1090
Boston, Massachusetts 02109
Phone: (617)482-9141
Fax: (617)482-9141

Provides financing for small businesses and for commercial, industrial, and residential business developments through community development corporations (CDCs) in depressed areas of Massachusetts. Three investment programs are offered: the Venture Capital Investment Program, the Community Development Program, and the Small Loan Guarantee Program.

Massachusetts Industrial Finance Agency
75 Federal St.
Boston, Massachusetts 02110
Phone: (617)451-2477
Toll-free: (800)445-8030
Fax: (617)451-3429

Promotes expansion, renovation, and modernization of small businesses through the use of investment incentives.

Massachusetts Minority Enterprise Investment Corp.
100 Franklin St.
Boston, Massachusetts 02110
Phone: (617)338-0425
Fax: (617)338-0481

Minority enterprise small business investment corporation. Involved with community development. Loans range from $25,000 to $250,000.

Massachusetts Technology Development Corp. (MTDC)
148 State St., 9th Fl.
Boston, Massachusetts 02109-2506
Phone: (617)723-4920
Fax: (617)723-5983

Makes investments in start-up or early stage expansion technology-based businesses within the Commonwealth of Massachusetts only.

MC PARTNERS
75 State St., Ste. 2500
Boston, Massachusetts 02109
Phone: (617)345-7200
Fax: (617)345-7201

Venture capital fund. Communications industry preferred.

Mezzanine Capital Corp.
75 State St., Ste. 2500
Boston, Massachusetts 02109
Phone: (617)345-7200
Fax: (617)345-7201

A small business investment company. Diversified industry preference.

Northeast Small Business Investment Corp.
130 New Market Square
Boston, Massachusetts 02118
Phone: (617)445-2100
Fax: (617)442-1013

A small business investment corporation. No industry preference.

P. R. Venture Partners, L.P.
100 Federal St., 37th Fl.
Boston, Massachusetts 02110
Phone: (617)357-9600
Fax: (617)357-9601

Venture capital firm providing early stage financing. Areas of interest include health care, information, and food.

Pioneer Ventures Limited Partnership
60 State St.
Boston, Massachusetts 02109
Phone: (617)742-7825
Fax: (617)742-7315

A small business investment company. Diversified industry preference.

Private Equity Management
75 State St., Ste. 2220
Boston, Massachusetts 02109
Phone: (617)345-9440
Fax: (617)345-9878

Summit Partners
600 Atlantic Ave.
Boston, Massachusetts 02210-2227
Phone: (617)742-5500
Fax: (617)824-1100

Venture capital firm. Prefers to invest in emerging, profitable, growth companies in the electronic technology, environmental services, and health care industries. Investments range from $1 million to $4 million.

TA Associates (Boston)
125 High St., Ste. 2500
Boston, Massachusetts 02110-2720
Phone: (617)338-0800
Fax: (617)574-6728

Private venture capital partnership. Technology companies, media communications companies, and leveraged buy outs preferred. Will provide from $1 million to $20 million in investments.

Transportation Capital Corp. (Boston)
45 Newbury St., Rm. 207
Boston, Massachusetts 02116
Phone: (617)536-0344
Fax: (617)536-5750

A minority enterprise small business investment corporation. Specializes in taxicabs and taxicab medallion loans.

TVM Techno Venture Management
101 Arch St., Ste. 1950
Boston, Massachusetts 02110

Phone: (617)345-9320
Toll-free: (800)345-2093
Fax: (617)345-9377

Venture capital firm providing early stage financing. Areas of interest include high technology such as software, communications, medical, and biotechnology industries. Preferred investment size is $1 million.

UST Capital Corp.
30-40 Court St.
Boston, Massachusetts 02108
Phone: (617)726-7000
Toll-free: (800)441-8782
Fax: (617)723-9414

A small business investment company. Diversified industry preference.

Venture Capital Fund of New England II
160 Federal St., 23rd Fl.
Boston, Massachusetts 02110
Phone: (617)439-4646
Fax: (617)439-4652

Venture capital fund. Prefers New England high-technology companies that have a commercial prototype or initial product sales. Will provide up to $500,000 in first-round financing.

First Capital Corp. of Chicago (Boston)
Bank Of Boston
1380 Mass Ave.
Cambridge, Massachusetts 02111
Phone: (617)434-2500
Fax: (617)434-2506

A small business investment company.

MDT Advisers, Inc.
25 Acorn Pk.
Cambridge, Massachusetts 02140
Phone: (617)498-5000
Toll-free: (800)677-3000
Fax: (617)498-7200

Zero Stage Capital V, L.P.
Kendall Sq.
1010 Main St., 17th Fl.
Cambridge, Massachusetts 02142
Phone: (617)876-5355
Fax: (617)876-1248
Paul Kelley, Manager

Preferred Investment Size: $50,000 to $500,000. Investment Types: Equity, debit with equity features. Industry Preferences: Biotech, computer hardware and software, energy. Geographic Preferences: Northeast.

Boston College Capital Formation Service
96 College Rd.
Rahner House
Chestnut Hill, Massachusetts 02167
Phone: (617)552-4091
Fax: (617)552-2730

Capital Formation Service
Boston College
96 College Rd., Rahner House
Chestnut Hill, Massachusetts 02167
Phone: (617)552-4091
Fax: (617)552-2730

Provides assistance to clients requiring financing from nonconventional sources, such as quasi-public financing programs; state, federal, and local programs; venture capital; and private investors.

Seacoast Capital Partners, L.P.
55 Ferncroft Rd.
Danvers, Massachusetts 01923
Phone: (508)777-3866
Fax: (508)750-1301
Eben Moulton, Manager

Preferred Investment Size: $1 to $6 million. Investment Policies: Loans and equity investments. Investment Types: Expansion, later stage. Industry Preferences: Diversified. Geographic Preferences: National.

Argonauts MESBIC Corp.
929 Worcester Rd.
Framingham, Massachusetts 01701
Phone: (508)820-3430

A minority enterprise small business investment company. Diversified industry preference.

Applied Technology Partners
1 Cranberry Hill
Lexington, Massachusetts 02173-7397
Phone: (617)862-8622
Fax: (617)862-8367

Venture capital firm providing early stage investment. Areas of interest include hardware technologies, electronics, software, communications, and information services.

Venture Founders Corp.
1 Cranberry Hill
Lexington, Massachusetts 02173
Phone: (617)862-8622
Fax: (617)862-8367

Venture capital fund. Preferred geographical area is the New England states. Required initial investment size is between $50,000 and $400,000.

Business Achievement Corp.
1172 Beacon St., Ste. 202
Newton, Massachusetts 02161
Phone: (617)965-0550
Fax: (617)969-2671

A small business investment corporation. No industry preference.

LRF Capital, Limited Partnership
189 Wells Ave., Ste. 4
Newton, Massachusetts 02159
Phone: (617)964-0049
Fax: (617)965-4100

A small business investment company. Diversified industry preference.

Comdisco Venture Group (Newton)
2221 Washington 3rd Fl.
Newton Lower Falls, Massachusetts 02162
Phone: (617)244-6622
Toll-free: (800)321-1111
Fax: (617)630-5599

New England MESBIC Inc.
530 Turnpike St.
North Andover, Massachusetts 01845-5812
Phone: (508)688-4326

Analog Devices, Inc.
1 Technology Way
PO Box 9106
Norwood, Massachusetts 02062-9106
Phone: (617)329-4700
Toll-free: (800)262-5643
Fax: (617)326-8703

Venture capital supplier. Prefers to invest in industries involved in analog devices.

ABS Ventures Limited Partnerships (Boston)
404 Wymin St. Ste. 365
Waltham, Massachusetts 02154
Phone: (617)290-0004
Fax: (617)290-0999

Hambro International Equity Partners (Boston)
404 Wyman, Ste. 365
Waltham, Massachusetts 02154
Phone: (617)523-7767
Fax: (617)290-0999

Private venture firm. Seeks to invest in software, electronics and instrumentation, biotechnology, retailing, direct marketing of consumer goods, and environmental industries.

Matrix Partners III
1000 Winter St., Ste.4500
Waltham, Massachusetts 02154
Phone: (617)890-2244
Fax: (617)890-2288

Private venture capital partnership. Industry preference includes high technology, communications, and software.

Ampersand Ventures
55 William St., Ste. 240
Wellesley, Massachusetts 02181
Phone: (617)239-0700
Toll-free: (800)239-0706
Fax: (617)239-0824

Venture capital supplier. Provides start-up and early stage financing to technology-based companies. Investments range from $500,000 to $1 million.

Geneva Middle Market Investors, L.P.
70 Walnut St.
Wellesley, Massachusetts 02181
Phone: (617)239-8230
Fax: (617)239-8064
James J. Goodman, Manager

Northwest Venture Partners
40 William St., Ste. 305
Wellesley, Massachusetts 02181
Phone: (617)237-5870
Fax: (617)237-6270

Norwest Equity Partners IV
40 William St., Ste. 305
Wellesley, Massachusetts 02181
Phone: (617)237-5870
Fax: (617)237-6270

Norwest Growth Fund, Inc.
40 William St., Ste. 305
Wellesley, Massachusetts 02181
Phone: (617)237-5870
Fax: (617)237-6270

Bessemer Venture Partners
83 Walnut St.
Wellesley Hills, Massachusetts 02181
Phone: (617)237-6050
Fax: (617)235-7068

Palmer Partners L.P.
300 Unicorn Park Dr.
Woburn, Massachusetts 01801
Phone: (617)933-5445
Fax: (617)933-0698

Venture capital partnership. Provides early stage, commercialization, and second and third stage financing.

Michigan

White Pines Capital Corp.
2929 Plymouth Rd., Ste. 210
Ann Arbor, Michigan 48105

Phone: (313)747-9401
Fax: (313)747-9704

A small business investment company. Diversified industry preference.

Thomas Lowe Ventures
805 Wolfe Ave.
PO Box 248
Cassopolis, Michigan 49031-0248
Phone: (616)445-2413
Fax: (616)445-8772

Venture capital firm preferring to invest in the toy industry.

Dearborn Capital Corp.
American Rd.
Dearborn, Michigan 48126-2701
Phone: (313)337-8577
Fax: (313)845-6124

A minority enterprise small business investment corporation. Loans to minority-owned, operated, and controlled suppliers to Ford Motor Company, Dearborn Capital Corporation's parent.

Motor Enterprises, Inc.
3044 W. Grand Blvd.
Detroit, Michigan 48202
Phone: (313)556-4273
Fax: (313)974-4854

A minority enterprise small business investment corporation. Prefers automotive-related industries.

Metro-Detroit Investment Co.
30777 Northwestern Hwy., Ste. 300
Farmington Hills, Michigan 48334-2549
Phone: (810)851-6300
Fax: (810)851-9551

A minority enterprise small business investment corporation. Food store industry preferred.

Demery Seed Capital Fund
3707 W. Maple Rd.
Franklin, Michigan 48025
Phone: (810)433-1722
Fax: (810)644-4526

Invests in start-up companies in Michigan.

The Capital Fund
6412 Centurion Dr., Ste. 150
Lansing, Michigan 48917
Phone: (517)323-7772
Fax: (517)323-1999

A small business investment company. Provides expansion financing.

State Treasurer's Office
Alternative Investments Division
PO Box 15128
Lansing, Michigan 48901
Phone: (517)373-4330
Fax: (517)335-3668

Minnesota

Control Data Corp
8100 34th Ave. S
Bloomington, Minnesota 55425-1640
Phone: (612)853-8100

Northland Capital Venture Partnership
613 Missabe Bldg.
Duluth, Minnesota 55802
Phone: (218)722-0545
Fax: (218)722-7241

A small business investment corporation. No industry preference.

Altair Ventures, Inc.
7550 France Ave. S, Ste. 201
Minneapolis, Minnesota 55435
Phone: (612)449-0250
Fax: (612)896-4909

Venture capital firm providing acquisitions and leveraged buyout financing. Diversified industry preference.

Artesian Capital Limited Partnership
821 Marquette Ave., Ste. 1700
Minneapolis, Minnesota 55402-2905
Phone: (612)334-5600
Fax: (612)334-5600

Venture capital firm providing seed and start-up financing in the upper Midwest. Areas of interest include medical, communications, and environmental industries.

Capital Dimensions Ventures Fund, Inc.
2 Appletree Sq., Ste. 335
Minneapolis, Minnesota 55425
Phone: (612)854-3007

A minority enterprise small business investment corporation. No industry preference.

Cherry Tree Investment Co.
1400 Northland Plz.
3800 W. 80th St., Ste. 1400
Minneapolis, Minnesota 55431
Phone: (612)893-9012
Fax: (612)893-9036

Venture capital supplier. Provides start-up and early stage financing. Fields of interest include information/software, retail, education, and publishing industries located in the Midwest. There are no minimum or maximum investment limitations.

Coral Group, Inc.
60 6th St., Ste 3510
Minneapolis, Minnesota 55402
Phone: (612)335-8666
Fax: (612)335-8668

Venture capital firm providing all types of financing. Areas of interest include communications, computer products, electronics, medical/health, genetic engineering, industrial products, transportation and diversified.

Crawford Capital Corp.
1150 Interchange Tower
600 S. Hwy. 169
Minneapolis, Minnesota 55426
Phone: (612)544-2221
Toll-free: (800)457-1543
Fax: (612)544-5885

Venture capital firm providing financing for firm's own venturefund limited partnerships. Areas of interest include medical, software, and technology industries.

FBS SBIC, Limited Partnership
601 2nd Ave. S
Minneapolis, Minnesota 55402-4302

Phone: (612)973-0988
Fax: (612)973-0203

A small business investment corporation. Generally invests in high-technology companies, although they are not necessarily preferred.

FBS SBIC, Ltd. Partnership
1st Bank Place
601 2nd Ave. S., 16th Fl.
Minneapolis, Minnesota 55402
Phone: (612)973-0988
Fax: (612)973-0203
Richard Rinkoff, Manager

Investment Policies: Loans, loans with warrants. Investment Types: Expansion, early stage. Industry Preferences: Diversified. Geographic Preferences: National.

Milestone Growth Fund, Inc.
75 S. 5th St., Ste.705
Minneapolis, Minnesota 55402
Phone: (612)338-0090
Fax: (612)338-1172

Minority enterprise small business investment corporation providing financing for expansion of existing companies. Diversified industry preference.

Northwest Venture Partners
2800 Piper Jaffray Tower
222 S. 9th St.
Minneapolis, Minnesota 55402
Phone: (612)339-9322
Fax: (612)337-8017

A small business investment company. Diversified industry preference.

Norwest Equity Partners IV
2800 Piper Jaffray Tower
222 S. 9th St.
Minneapolis, Minnesota 55402-3388
Phone: (612)667-1650
Fax: (612)667-1660

Small business investment company. Invests in all industries except real estate.

Norwest Equity Partners V, L.P.
2800 Piper Jaffrey Tower
Minneapolis, Minnesota 55402
Phone: (612)667-1667
Fax: (612)667-1660
John F. Whaley, Manager

Preferred Investment Size: $3 to $15 million. Investment Policies: Equity. Investment Types: Start-up, expansion, later stage. Industry Preferences: Diversified. Geographic Preferences: National.

Norwest Growth Fund, Inc.
2800 Piper Jaffray Tower
222 S. 9th St.
Minneapolis, Minnesota 55402
Phone: (612)339-9322
Fax: (612)337-8017

A small business investment company. Diversified industry preference.

Oak Investment Partners (Minneapolis)
4550 Norwest Center
90 S. 2nd St., Ste. 4550
Minneapolis, Minnesota 55402
Phone: (612)339-9322
Fax: (612)337-8017

Prefers to invest in retail industries.

Pathfinder Venture Capital Funds (Minneapolis)
7300 Metro Blvd., Ste. 585
Minneapolis, Minnesota 55439
Phone: (612)835-1121
Fax: (612)835-8389

Venture capital supplier providing early stage financing. Areas of interest include medical, pharmaceutical, and health care service; and computer and computer-related industries in the Upper Midwest and West.

Peterson-Spencer-Fansler Co.
821 Marquette , Ste. 1900
Minneapolis, Minnesota 55402
Phone: (612)904-2305
Fax: (612)546-4844

Venture capital firm providing seed, research and development, start-up, first stage, and bridge financing. Areas of interest include medical technology and health care service industries.

Piper Jaffray Ventures, Inc.
Piper Jaffray Tower
222 S. 9th St.
Minneapolis, Minnesota 55402
Phone: (612)339-9322
Fax: (612)337-8017

University Technology Center, Inc.
1313 5th St. SE
Minneapolis, Minnesota 55414
Phone: (612)379-3800
Fax: (612)379-3875

Venture capital firm providing start-up, first stage, initial expansion and acquisition financing. Areas of interest include environment, consumer products, industrial products, transportation and diversified industry.

Wellspring Corp.
4530 IDS Center
Minneapolis, Minnesota 55402
Phone: (612)338-0704
Fax: (612)338-0744

Venture capital firm providing acquisition and leveraged buyout financing. Areas of interest include marine transportation equipment and weighing and measuring equipment manufacturing.

Food Fund
5720 Smatana Dr., Ste. 300
Minnetonka, Minnesota 55343
Phone: (612)939-3944
Fax: (612)939-8106

Venture capital firm providing expansion, management buyouts, early stage and acquisition financing. Areas of interest include food products, food equipment, food packaging, and food distribution.

Medical Innovation Partners, Inc.
Opus Center, Ste. 421
9900 Bren Rd. E
Minnetonka, Minnesota 55343
Phone: (612)931-0154
Fax: (612)931-0003

St. Paul Growth Ventures
1450 Energy Park Dr., Ste. 110-D
St. Paul, Minnesota 55108-1013
Phone: (612)641-1667
Fax: (612)641-1147

Venture capital firm providing early stage ventures, product development, product launch and early organizational development. Prefers software companies in the Minneapolis/St. Paul area.

Quest Venture Partners
730 E. Lake St.
Wayzata, Minnesota 55391-1769
Phone: (612)473-8367
Fax: (612)473-4702

Venture capital firm providing second stage and bridge financing. Areas of interest include communications, computer products and medical/health care.

Threshold Ventures, Inc.
15500 Wayzata Blvd., Ste.819
Wayzata, Minnesota 55391-1418
Phone: (612)473-2051

A small business investment corporation. No industry preference.

Mississippi

Sun-Delta Capital Access Center, Inc.
819 Main St.
Greenville, Mississippi 38701
Phone: (601)335-5291
Fax: (601)335-5295

A minority enterprise small business investment corporation. No industry preference.

Mississippi Department of Economic and Community Development

Mississippi Business Finance Corp.
1200 Walter Sillers Bldg.
PO Box 849
Jackson, Mississippi 39205
Phone: (601)359-3552
Fax: (601)359-2832

Administers the SBA(503) Loan and the Mississippi Small Business Loan Guarantee.

Vicksburg SBIC
PO Box 821568
Vicksburg, Mississippi 39182
Phone: (601)636-4762
Fax: (601)636-9476

A small business investment corporation. No industry preference.

Missouri

Bankers Capital Corp.
3100 Gillham Rd.
Kansas City, Missouri 64109
Phone: (816)531-1600
Fax: (816)531-1334

A small business investment corporation. No industry preference.

Capital for Business, Inc. (Kansas City)
1000 Walnut St., 18th Fl.
Kansas City, Missouri 64106-2123
Phone: (816)234-2357
Fax: (816)234-2333

A small business investment corporation. No industry preference.

CFB Venture Fund II, Inc.
1000 Walnut St., 18th Fl.
Kansas City, Missouri 64106
Phone: (816)234-2357
Fax: (816)234-2333

A small business investment company. Diversified industry preference.

InvestAmerica Venture Group, Inc. (Kansas City)
Commerce Tower Bldg.
911 Main St., Ste. 2424
Kansas City, Missouri 64105

Phone: (816)842-0114
Fax: (816)471-7339

A small business investment corporation. No industry preference.

MorAmerica Capital Corp. (Kansas City, MO)
911 Main St., Ste. 2424
Kansas City, Missouri 64105
Phone: (816)842-0114
Fax: (816)471-7339

A small business investment company.

United Missouri Capital Corp.
PO Box 419226
Kansas City, Missouri 64141
Phone: (816)860-7333
Fax: (816)556-7143

A small business investment corporation. No industry preference.

Midland Bank
740 NW Blue Pky.
Lees Summit, Missouri 64086
Phone: (816)524-8000
Fax: (816)524-3093

A small business investment company. Diversified industry preference.

Allsop Venture Partners (St. Louis)
55 W. Port Plz., Ste. 575
St. Louis, Missouri 63146
Phone: (314)434-1688
Fax: (314)434-6560

Capital for Business, Inc. (St. Louis)
11 S. Meramec, Ste. 1430
St. Louis, Missouri 63105
Phone: (314)746-7427
Fax: (314)746-8739

A small business investment corporation. Focuses primarily on later-stage expansion and acquisition in the manufacturing anddistribution industries.

CFB Venture Fund I, Inc.
11 S. Meramec, Ste. 1436
St. Louis, Missouri 63105

Phone: (314)746-7427
Fax: (314)746-8739

A small business investment company. Diversified industry preference.

Gateway Associates L.P.
8000 Maryland Ave., Ste. 1190
St. Louis, Missouri 63105
Phone: (314)721-5707
Fax: (314)721-5135

ITT Small Business Finance Corp.
635 Maryville Center Dr., Ste. 120
St. Louis, Missouri 63141
Phone: (314)205-3500
Toll-free: (800)447-2025
Fax: (314)205-3699

Non-bank lender providing start-up and expansion financing.

Montana

Montana Board of Investments
Office of Development Finance
Capitol Sta.
555 Fuller Ave.
Helena, Montana 59620-0125
Phone: (406)444-0001
Fax: (406)449-6579

Provides investments to businesses that will bring long-term benefits to the Montana economy.

Montana Department of Commerce
Economic Development Division
Finance Technical Assistance
1424 9th Ave.
Helena, Montana 59620-0401
Phone: (406)444-4780
Phone: (406)444-1872

Provides financial analysis, financial planning, loan packaging, industrial revenue bonding, state and private capital sources, and business tax incentives.

Nebraska

Nebraska Investment Finance
Authority
1230 "O" St., Ste. 200

Lincoln, Nebraska 68508
Phone: (402)434-3900
Toll-free: (800)204-6432
Fax: (402)434-3921

Provides lower cost financing for manufacturing facilities, certain farm property, and health care and residential development. Also established a Small Industrial Development Bond Program to help small Nebraska-based companies (those with fewer than 100 employees or less than $2.5 million in gross salaries).

United Financial Resources Corp.
PO Box 1131
Omaha, Nebraska 68101
Phone: (402)339-7300
Fax: (402)734-0650

A small business investment corporation. Only interests include the grocery industry.

Nevada

Nevada Department of Business and
Industry
Bond Division
1665 Hot Springs Rd.
Carson City, Nevada 89710
Phone: (702)687-4250
Fax: (702)687-4266

Issues up to $100 million in bonds to fund venture capital projects in Nevada; helps companies expand or build new facilities through the use of tax-exempt financing.

Atlanta Investment Co., Inc.
601 Fairview Blvd.
Incline Village, Nevada 89451
Phone: (702)833-1836
Fax: (702)833-1890
L. Mark Newman, Chairman of the Board

Preferred Investment Size: $2,000,000. Investment Policies: Equity. Investment Types: Expansion, later stage. Industry Preferences: Technology. Geographic Preferences: National.

New Hampshire

Business Finance Authority of the
State of New Hampshire
4 Park St., Ste. 302
Concord, New Hampshire 03301-6313
Phone: (603)271-2391
Fax: (603)271-2396

Works to foster economic development and promote the creation of employment in the state of New Hampshire. Provides guarantees on loans to businesses made by banks and local development organizations; guarantees on portions of loans guaranteed in part by the U.S. Small Business Administration; cash reserves on loans made by state banks to businesses with annual revenues less than or equal to $5,000,000; and opportunities for local development organizations to acquire additional funds for the purpose of promoting and developing business within the state.

New Jersey

MidMark Capital, L.P.
466 Southern Blvd.
Chatham, New Jersey 07928
Phone: (201)822-2999
Fax: (201)822-8911
Denis Newman, Manager

Preferred Investment Size: $5,000,000. Investment Policies: Equity. Investment Types: Expansion, later stage. Industry Preferences: Diversified, communication, manufacturing, retail/service. Geographic Preferences: East, Midwest.

Transpac Capital Corp.
1037 Rte. 46 E
Clifton, New Jersey 07013
Phone: (201)470-8855
Fax: (201)470-8827

A minority enterprise small business investment company. Diversified industry preference.

Monmouth Capital Corp.
125 Wyckoff Rd.
Midland National Bank Bldg.
PO Box 335
Eatontown, New Jersey 07724
Phone: (908)542-4927

A small business investment corporation. No industry preference.

Capital Circulation Corp.
2035 Lemoine Ave., 2nd Fl.
Fort Lee, New Jersey 07024
Phone: (201)947-8637
Fax: (201)585-1965

A minority enterprise small business investment company. Diversified industry preference.

Japanese American Capital Corp.
716 Jersey Ave.
Jersey City, New Jersey 07310-1306
Phone: (201)798-5000
Fax: (201)798-4362

Taroco Capital Corp.
716 Jersey Ave.
Jersey City, New Jersey 07310-1306
Phone: (201)798-5000
Fax: (201)798-4322

A minority enterprise small business investment corporation. Focuses on Chinese-Americans.

Edison Venture Fund
997 Lenox Dr., Ste. 3
Lawrenceville, New Jersey 08648
Phone: (609)896-1900
Fax: (609)896-0066

Private venture capital firm. No industry preference.

Tappan Zee Capital Corp. (New Jersey)
201 Lower Notch Rd.
PO Box 416
Little Falls, New Jersey 07424
Phone: (201)256-8280
Fax: (201)256-2841

A small business investment company. Diversified industry preference.

CIT Group/Venture Capital, Inc.
650 CIT Dr.
Livingston, New Jersey 07039
Phone: (201)740-5429
Fax: (201)740-5555

A small business investment company. Diversified industry preference.

ESLO Capital Corp.
212 Wright St.
Newark, New Jersey 07114
Phone: (201)242-4488
Fax: (201)643-6062
Leo Katz, President

Preferred Investment Size: $100,000. Investment Policies: Loans. Investment Types: Start-ups, early stage. Industry Preferences: Business services, manufacturing. Geographic Preferences: Northeast.

Rutgers Minority Investment Co.
180 University Ave., 3rd Fl.
Newark, New Jersey 07102-1803
Phone: (201)648-5627

A minority enterprise small business investment corporation. No industry preference.

Accel Partners (Princeton)
1 Palmer Sq.
Princeton, New Jersey 08542
Phone: (609)683-4500
Fax: (609)683-0384

Venture capital firm. Telecommunications, software, and health careindustries preferred.

Carnegie Hill Co.
202 Carnegie Center, Ste. 103
Princeton, New Jersey 08540
Phone: (609)520-0500
Fax: (609)520-1160

Domain Associates
1 Palmer Sq.
Princeton, New Jersey 08542
Phone: (609)683-4500
Fax: (609)683-0384

DSV Partners (Princeton)
221 Nassau St.
Princeton, New Jersey 08542
Phone: (609)924-6420
Fax: (609)683-0174

Provides financing for the growth of companies in the biotechnology/health care, environmental, and software industries. Also provides capital to facilitate consolidation of fragmented industries.

Johnston Associates, Inc.
181 Cherry Valley Rd.
Princeton, New Jersey 08540
Phone: (609)924-3131
Fax: (609)683-7524

Venture capital supplier providing seed and start-up financing. Areas of interest include pharmaceutical research, biotechnology, and bioremediation of toxic waste.

Bishop Capital, L.P.
500 Morris Ave.
Springfield, New Jersey 07081
Phone: (201)376-0345
Fax: (201)376-6527

A small business investment company. Diversified industry preference.

BCI Advisors, Inc.
Glenpointe Center W
Teaneck, New Jersey 07666
Phone: (201)836-3900
Fax: (201)836-6368

Venture capital firm providing mezzanine financing for growth companies with revenues of $25 million to $200 million. Diversified industry preference.

Demuth, Folger and Terhune
300 Frank W. Burr, 5th Floor
Teaneck, New Jersey 07666
Phone: (201)836-6000
Fax: (201)836-5666

Venture capital firm with preferences for technology, services, and health care investments.

DFW Capital Partners, L.P.
Glenpointe Center E., 5th Fl.
300 Frank W. Burr Blvd.
Teaneck, New Jersey 07666
Phone: (201)836-2233
Fax: (201)836-5666
Donald F. DeMuth, Manager

Preferred Investment Size:
$4,000,000. Investment Policies:
Equity. Investment Types: Early
through later stage. Industry Preferences: Healthcare, services, diversified. Geographic Preferences:
National.

New Jersey Commission on Science
and Technology
28 W. State St., CN 832
Trenton, New Jersey 08625-0832
Phone: (609)984-1671
Fax: (609)292-5920

Awards bridge grants to small
companies that have received seed
money under the Federal State
Business Innovation Research
programs and works to improve the
scientific and technical research
capabilities within the state. Also
provides management and technical
assistance and other services to small,
technology-oriented companies.

New Jersey Department of Agriculture
Division of Rural Resources
John Fitch Plz., CN 330
Trenton, New Jersey 08625
Phone: (609)292-5532
Fax: (609)633-7229

Fosters the agricultural economic
development of rural areas of the state
through financial assistance for
farmers and agribusinesses.

New Jersey Economic Development
Authority
200 S. Orange St.
Trenton, New Jersey 08625
Phone: (609)292-1800
Fax: (609)292-0368

Arranges low-interest, long-term
financing for manufacturing facilities,

land acquisition, and business
equipment and machinery purchases.
Also issues taxable bonds to provide
financing for manufacturing, distribution, warehousing, research, commercial, office, and service uses.

Edelson Technology Partners
Whiteweld Ctr.
300 Tice Blvd.
Woodcliff Lake, New Jersey 07675
Phone: (201)930-9898
Fax: (201)930-8899

Venture capital partnership interested
in high technology investment,
including medical, biotechnology,
and computer industries.

New Mexico

Albuquerque Investment Co.
P.O. Box 487
Albuquerque, New Mexico 87103-3132
Phone: (505)247-0145
Fax: (505)843-6912

A small business investment corporation. No industry preference.

Associated Southwest Investors, Inc.
1650 University NE, Ste.200
Albuquerque, New Mexico 87102
Phone: (505)247-4050
Fax: (505)247-4050

A minority enterprise small business
investment corporation. No industry
preference.

Industrial Development Corp. of Lea
County
PO Box 1376
Hobbs, New Mexico 88240
Phone: (505)397-2039
Toll-free: (800)443-2236
Fax: (505)392-2300

Certified development company.

Ads Capital Corp.
1302 Osage Ave.
Santa Fe, New Mexico 87505
Phone: (505)983-1769
Fax: (505)983-2887

Venture capital supplier. Prefers to
invest in manufacturing or distribution companies.

New Mexico Economic Development
Department
Economic Development Division
1100 St. Francis Dr.
Santa Fe, New Mexico 87503
Phone: (505)827-0300
Toll-free: (800)374-3061
Fax: (505)827-0438

Provides start-up or expansion loans
for businesses that areestablished in
or are new to New Mexico.

New Mexico Economic Development
Department
Technology Enterprise Division
1100 St. Francis Dr.
Santa Fe, New Mexico 87503
Phone: (505)827-0265
Fax: (505)827-0588

Provides state funds to advanced-
technology business ventures that are
close to the commercial stage.

New Mexico Labor Department
Job Training Division
Aspen Plz.
1596 Pacheco St.
PO Box 4218
Santa Fe, New Mexico 87502
Phone: (505)827-6827
Fax: (505)827-6812

Provides new and expanding industries with state-sponsored funds to
train a New Mexican workforce.

New York

Fleet Bank
69 St.
Albany, New York 12201
Phone: (518)447-4115
Fax: (518)447-4043

Venture capital supplier. No industry
preference. Typical investment is
between $500,000 and $1 million.

NYBDC Capital Corp.
41 State St.
PO Box 738
Albany, New York 12201
Phone: (518)463-2268
Fax: (518)463-0240

A small business investment corporation.

Vega Capital Corp.
80 Business Park Dr., Ste. 201
Armonk, New York 10504-1701
Phone: (914)273-1025
Fax: (914)273-1028

A small business investment corporation. Diversified industry preferences.

Triad Capital Corp. of New York
960 Southern Blvd.
Bronx, New York 10459-3402
Phone: (718)589-5000
Fax: (718)589-4744

A minority enterprise small business investment corporation. No industry preference.

Avdon Capital Corp.
1322 Avenue J
Brooklyn, New York 11230
Phone: (718)692-0950
Toll-free: (800)888-5280
Fax: (718)253-0383

A minority enterprise small business investment corporation. No industry preference.

First New York Management Co.
1 Metrotech Center N, 11th Fl.
Brooklyn, New York 11201
Phone: (718)797-5990
Fax: (718)722-3533

A small business investment corporation. No industry preference.

M & T Capital Corporation
1 Fountain Plz., 9th Fl.
Buffalo, New York 14203-1495
Phone: (716)848-3800
Fax: (716)848-3131

A small business investment corporation providing equity financing for

small to mid-size companies for expansion activities, acquisitions, recapitalizations, and buyouts. Initial investments range from $500,000 - $2 million. Prefers businesses located in the Northeast and Midwest.

Rand SBIC, Inc.
1300 Rand Bldg.
Buffalo, New York 14203
Phone: (716)853-0802
Fax: (716)854-8480

A small business investment corporation. Prefers to invest in communications, computer-related, consumer, distributor, and electronic components and instrumentation industries.

Fifty-Third Street Ventures, L.P.
155 Main St.
Cold Spring, New York 10516
Phone: (914)265-4244
Fax: (914)265-4158

A small business investment company. Diversified industry preference.

Tessler and Cloherty, Inc.
155 Main St.
Cold Spring, New York 10516
Phone: (914)265-4244
Fax: (914)265-4158

A small business investment corporation. No industry preference.

Esquire Capital Corp.
69 Veterans Memorial Hwy.
Commack, New York 11725
Phone: (516)462-6946
Fax: (516)864-8152

A minority enterprise small business investment company. Diversified industry preference.

Pan Pac Capital Corp.
121 E. Industry Ct.
Deer Park, New York 11729
Phone: (516)586-7653
Fax: (516)586-7505

A minority enterprise small business investment corporation. No industry preference.

First County Capital, Inc.
135-14 Northern Blvd., 2nd Fl.
Flushing, New York 11354
Phone: (718)461-1778
Fax: (718)461-1835

A minority enterprise small business investment company. Diversified industry preference.

Flushing Capital Corp.
39-06 Union St., Rm.202
Flushing, New York 11354
Phone: (718)886-5866
Fax: (718)939-7761

A minority enterprise small business investment company. Diversified industry preference.

Sterling Commercial Capital, Inc.
175 Great Neck Rd., Ste. 408
Great Neck, New York 11021
Phone: (516)482-7374
Fax: (516)487-0781

A small business investment company. Diversified industry preference.

CEDC Inc.
134 Jackson St.
Hempstead, New York 11550-2418
Phone: (516)292-9710

Situation Ventures Corp.
56-20 59th St.
Maspeth, New York 11378
Phone: (718)894-2000
Fax: (718)326-4642
Sam Hollander, President

Preferred Investment Size: $100,000. Investment Policies: Loans and/or equity. Industry Preferences: Manufacturing, service, retail. Geographic Preferences: New York metro area.

KOCO Capital Co., L.P.
111 Radio Cir.
Mount Kisco, New York 10549
Phone: (914)242-2324
Fax: (914)241-7476
Albert Pastino, President

Preferred Investment Size: $2 to $3 million. Investment Policies: Equity and debt with warrants. Investment Types: Expansion. Industry Preferences: Healthcare, media, basic manufacturing. Geographic Preferences: Mid-Atlantic.

Tappan Zee Capital Corp. (New York)
120 N. Main St.
New City, New York 10956
Phone: (914)634-8890

A small business investment company.

American Asian Capital Corp.
130 Water St., Ste. 6-L
New York, New York 10005
Phone: (212)422-6880
Howard H. Lin, President

Argentum Capital Partners, LP
405 Lexington Ave., 54th Fl.
New York, New York 10174
Phone: (212)949-8272
Fax: (212)949-8294

A small business investment company. Diversified industry preference.

ASEA—Harvest Partners II
767 3rd Ave.
New York, New York 10017
Phone: (212)838-7776
Fax: (212)593-0734

A small business investment corporation. No industry preference.

Barclays Capital Investors Corp.
222 Broadway, 11th Fl.
New York, New York 10038
Phone: (212)412-3937
Fax: (212)412-5662

A small business investment company. Diversified industrypreference.

Bradford Ventures Ltd.
1212 Avenue of the Americas, Ste. 1802
New York, New York 10036
Phone: (212)221-4620
Fax: (212)764-3467

Venture capital firm. No industry preference.

BT Capital Corp.
130 Liberty St., M S 2255
New York, New York 10006
Phone: (212)250-8082
Fax: (212)454-2421

A small business investment corporation. No industry preference.

The Business Loan Center
919 3rd Ave., 17th Fl.
New York, New York 10022-1902
Phone: (212)751-5626
Fax: (212)751-9345

A small business loan company.

Capital Investors and Management Corp.
210 Canal St., Ste. 611
New York, New York 10013-4155
Phone: (212)964-2480
Fax: (212)349-9160

A minority enterprise small business investment corporation. No industry preference.

CB Investors, Inc.
560 Lexington Ave., 20th Fl.
New York, New York 10022
Phone: (212)207-6119
Fax: (212)207-6095

A small business investment company. Diversified industry preference.

CBIC Woody Gundy Ventures, Inc.
425 Lexington Ave., 9th Fl.
New York, New York 10017
Phone: (212)856-3713
Fax: (212)697-1554

A small business investment company. Diversified industry preference.

Chase Manhattan Capital Corp.
1 Chase Plz., 8th Fl.
New York, New York 10081
Phone: (212)552-6275
Fax: (212)552-1159

A small business investment corporation.

Chemical Venture Capital Associates
270 Park Ave., 5th Fl.
New York, New York 10017-2070

Phone: (212)270-3220
Fax: (212)270-2327

A small business investment corporation. Areas of interest include health care, specialty retail, media and telecommunications, natural resources, consumer products, and environmental industries.

Chemical Venture Partners
270 Park Ave., 5th Fl.
New York, New York 10017
Phone: (212)270-3220
Fax: (212)270-2327

Venture capital and leveraged buy out firm. Invests in leveraged buy outs and growth equity.

Citicorp Venture Capital Ltd. (New York City)
399 Park Ave., 14th Fl./Zone 4
New York, New York 10043
Phone: (212)559-1127
Fax: (212)888-2946

A small business investment corporation. Invests in the fields of information processing and telecommunications, transportation and energy, and health care; provides financing to companies in all stages of development. Also provides capital for leveraged buy out situations.

CMNY Capital II, LP
135 E. 57th St., 26th Fl.
New York, New York 10022
Phone: (212)909-8432
Fax: (212)980-2630

A small business investment company. Diversified industry preference.

Concord Partners
535 Madison Ave.
New York, New York 10022
Phone: (212)906-7000
Fax: (212)888-0649

Venture capital partnership. Diversified in terms of stage of development, industry classification, and geographic location. Areas of special interest include computer software, electronics, environmental services, biopharmaceuticals, health care, and oil and gas.

Creditanstalt SBIC
245 Park Ave., 27th Fl.
New York, New York 10167
Phone: (212)856-1248
Fax: (212)856-1699
Dennis O'Dowd, President

CW Group
1041 3rd Ave.
New York, New York 10021
Phone: (212)308-5266
Fax: (212)644-0354

Venture capital supplier. Interest is in the health care field, including diagnostic and therapeutic products, services, and biotechnology. Invests in companies at developing and early stages.

DAEDHIE
1261 Broadway, Rm. 405
New York, New York 10001
Phone: (212)684-6411
Fax: (212)684-6474

A minority enterprise small business investment company. Diversified industry preference.

DnC Capital Group
55 5th Ave., 15th Fl.
New York, New York 10003
Phone: (212)206-6041
Fax: (212)727-0563

Small business investment corporation interested in financing acquisitions in the real estate industry.

East Coast Venture Capital, Inc.
313 W. 53rd St., 3rd Fl.
New York, New York 10019
Phone: (212)245-6460
Fax: (212)265-2962

A minority enterprise small business investment company. Diversified industry preference.

Edwards Capital Co.
2 Park Ave., 20th Fl.
New York, New York 10016
Phone: (212)686-5449
Fax: (212)213-6234

A small business investment corporation. Transportation industry preferred.

Elf Aquitain, Inc.
280 Park Ave., 36th Fl. W
New York, New York 10017-1216
Phone: (212)922-3000
Toll-free: (800)922-0027
Fax: (212)922-3001

Elk Associates Funding Corp.
747 3rd Ave., 7th Fl.
New York, New York 10017
Phone: (212)421-2111
Fax: (212)421-3488

A minority enterprise small business investment corporation. Transportation industry preferred.

Elron Technologies, Inc.
850 3rd Ave., 10th Fl.
New York, New York 10022
Phone: (212)935-3110
Fax: (212)935-3882

Venture capital supplier. Provides incubation and start-up financing to high-technology companies.

Empire State Capital Corp.
170 Broadway, Ste. 1200
New York, New York 10038
Phone: (212)513-1799
Toll-free: (800)569-9630
Fax: (212)513-1892

A minority enterprise small business investment company. Diversified industry preference.

Eos Partners SBIC, L.P.
520 Madison Ave., 42nd Fl.
New York, New York 10022
Phone: (212)832-5814
Fax: (212)832-5805
Marc H. Michel, Manager

Preferred Investment Size: $1 - $3 Million. Investment Policies: Equity and equity-oriented Debt. Investment Types: Expansion, later stage. Industry Preferences: Diversified, telecommunications, info-processing, data services. Geographic Preferences: National.

Euclid Partners Corp.
50 Rockefeller Plz., Ste. 1022
New York, New York 10020
Phone: (212)489-1770
Fax: (212)757-1686

Venture capital firm. Prefers early stage health care and information processing industries.

Exeter Equity Partners, L.P.
10 E. 53rd St.
New York, New York 10022
Phone: (212)872-1170
Fax: (212)872-1198
Keith Fox
Timothy Bradley

Preferred Investment Size: $3,000,000. Investment Policies: Equity investments. Investment Types: Expansion, later stage. Industry Preferences: Diversified. Geographic Preferences: National.

Exeter Venture Lenders, L.P.
10 E. 53rd St.
New York, New York 10022
Phone: (212)872-1170
Fax: (212)872-1198
Keith Fox, Manager

Preferred Investment Size: $3,000,000. Investment Policies: Loans and equity investments. Investment Types: Expansion, later stage. Industry Preferences: Diversified. Geographic Preferences: National.

Exim Capital Corp.
241 5th Ave., 3rd Fl.
New York, New York 10016-8703
Phone: (212)683-3375
Fax: (212)689-4118

A minority enterprise small business investment corporation. No industry preference.

Fair Capital Corp.
212 Canal St., Ste. 611
New York, New York 10013
Phone: (212)964-2480
Fax: (212)349-9160

A minority enterprise small business investment corporation. No industry preference.

First Boston Corp.
Park Ave. Plaza 55 E. 52nd St.
New York, New York 10055
Phone: (212)909-2000
Fax: (212)318-1187

Investment banker. Provides financing to the oil and gas pipeline, hydroelectric, medical technology, consumer products, electronics, aerospace, and telecommunications industries. Supplies capital for leveraged buy outs.

First Wall Street SBIC, LP
26 Broadway, Ste. 1320
New York, New York 10004
Phone: (212)742-3770
Fax: (212)742-3776

A small business investment company. Diversified industry preference.

Franklin Corp.
450 Park Ave.
G.M. Bldg. 23rd Fl.
New York, New York 10022
Phone: (212)486-2323
Fax: (212)755-5451

A small business investment corporation. No industry preference; no start-ups.

Fredericks Michael and Co.
2 Wall St., 4th Fl.
New York, New York 10005
Phone: (212)732-1600
Fax: (212)732-1872

Private venture capital supplier.

Provides start-up and early stage financing, and supplies capital for buy outs and acquisitions.

Fresh Start Venture Capital Corp.
313 W. 53rd St., 3rd Fl.
New York, New York 10019
Phone: (212)265-2249
Fax: (212)265-2962

A minority enterprise small business investment corporation. No industry preference.

Furman Selz SBIC, L.P.
230 Park Ave.
New York, New York 10169
Phone: (212)309-8200
Fax: (212)692-9608
Brian Friedman, Manager

Preferred Investment Size: $2 to $6 million. Investment Policies: Equity. Investment Types: Expansion, later stage, no start-ups. Industry Preferences: Diversified. Geographic Preferences: National.

Hambro International Equity Partners (New York)
650 Madison Ave., 21st Floor
New York, New York 10022
Phone: (212)223-7400
Fax: (212)223-0305

Venture capital supplier. Seeks to invest in mature companies as well as in high-technology areas from start-ups to leveraged buy outs.

Hanam Capital Corp.
38 W.32nd St., Rm. 1512
New York, New York 10001
Phone: (212)564-5225
Fax: (212)564-5307

A minority enterprise small business investment company. Diversified industry preference.

Harvest Partners, Inc. (New York)
767 3rd Ave.
New York, New York 10017
Phone: (212)838-7776
Fax: (212)593-0734

Private venture capital supplier. Prefers to invest in high-technology, growth-oriented companies with proprietary technology, large market potential, and strong management teams.

Holding Capital Management Corp.
685 5th Ave., 14th Fl.
New York, New York 10022
Phone: (212)486-6670
Fax: (212)483-0843

A small business investment corporation. No industry preference. Prefers to purchase well-managed middle market companies with a minimum of $1 million cash flow.

IBJS Capital Corp.
1 State St., 8th Fl.
New York, New York 10004
Phone: (212)858-2000
Fax: (212)425-0542

A small business investment company. Diversified industry preference.

InterEquity Capital Partners, L.P.
220 5th Ave., 10th Fl.
New York, New York 10001
Phone: (212)779-2022
Fax: (212)779-2103

A small business investment company. Diversified industry preference.

Investor International (U.S.), Inc.
15 W. 54th St., 1st Fl.
New York, New York 10019
Phone: (212)957-3232
Fax: (212)957-9866

Jafco America Ventures, Inc. (New York)
2 World Financial Center, Bldg. B, 17th Fl.
225 Liberty St.
New York, New York 10281-1196
Phone: (212)667-9001
Fax: (212)667-1004

Venture capital firm. Provides middle- to later-stage financing to technology-oriented companies.

Jardine Capital Corp.
105 Lafayette St., Unit 204
New York, New York 10013
Phone: (212)941-0993
Fax: (212)941-0998
Lawrence Wong, President

Preferred Investment Size: $360,000.
Investment Policies: Loans and/or
equity. Investment Types: Expansion.
Industry Preferences: Diversified.
Geographic Preferences: North/South.

Josephberg, Grosz and Co., Inc.
810 7th Ave.
New York, New York 10170
Phone: (212)370-4564
Fax: (310)397-5832

Venture capital firm. Invests in companies having a minimum of $2.5 million in
sales, significant growth potential, and a
strong management base.

J.P. Morgan Investment Corp.
60 Wall St.
New York, New York 10260
Phone: (212)483-2323

A small business investment company. Diversified industry preference.

Kwiat Capital Corp.
579 5th Ave.
New York, New York 10017
Phone: (212)223-1111
Fax: (212)223-2796

A small business investment corporation. No industry preference.

Lambda Fund Management, Inc.
115 E. 69th
New York, New York 10021
Phone: (212)794-6060
Fax: (212)794-6169

Venture capital partnership.

Lawrence, Tyrrell, Ortale, and Smith
(New York)
515 Madison Ave., 29th Fl.
New York, New York 10022
Phone: (212)826-9080
Fax: (212)759-2561

Venture capital firm. Prefers to invest
in health care, software, and fragmented industries that grow by
acquisition.

McCown, De Leeuw and Co.
101 E. 52nd St., 31st Fl.
New York, New York 10022-6018
Phone: (212)355-5500
Fax: (212)355-6283

Medallion Funding Corp.
205 E. 42nd St., Ste. 2020
New York, New York 10017-5706
Phone: (212)682-3300
Fax: (212)983-0351

A minority enterprise small business
investment corporation. Transportation industry preferred.

Mercury Capital, L.P.
650 Madison Ave.
New York, New York 10022
Phone: (212)838-0888
Fax: (212)838-7598
David W. Elenowitz, Manager

Monsey Capital Corp.
9 E. 40th St., 4th Fl.
New York, New York 10016
Phone: (212)689-2700
Fax: (212)683-7300

A minority enterprise small business
investment corporation. No industry
preference.

Morgan Stanley Venture Capital
(New York)
c/o M. Fazle Husain
1251 Avenue of the Americas, 33rd Fl.
New York, New York 10020
Phone: (212)703-6981
Toll-free: (800)223-2440
Fax: (212)703-8957

Venture capital firm providing later stage
financing. Areas of interest include high
technology and health care.

NatWest USA Capital Corp.
175 Water St., 27th Fl.
New York, New York 10038

Phone: (212)602-1200
Fax: (212)602-3393

A small business investment company. Diversified industry preference.

Nazem and Co.
645 Madison Ave., 12th Fl.
New York, New York 10022
Phone: (212)371-7900
Fax: (212)751-2150

Venture capital fund. Electronics and
medical industries preferred. Will
provide seed and first- and second-
round financing.

Needham Capital SBIC, L.P.
400 Park Ave.
New York, New York 10022
Phone: (212)705-0291
Fax: (212)371-8418
John Michaelson, Manager

Preferred Investment Size: $500,000
to $1 Million. Investment Policies:
Equity. Industry Preferences: Technology. Geographic Preferences:
National.

New York Job Development Author-
ity
630 3rd Ave.
New York, New York 10158
Phone: (212)818-1700
Fax: (212)682-1476

Assists companies in New York or
those moving to New York wishing to
expand or build new facilities,
thereby retaining existing jobs or
creating new employment opportunities. Provides loans and loan guarantees.

New York State Urban Development
Corp.
633 3rd Ave.
New York, New York 10017
Phone: (212)803-3100

Participates in a broad range of
initiatives. Addresses the needs of the
state in six areas, including downtown development, industrial
development, minority business

development, university research and development, and planning and special projects.

Norwood Venture Corp.
1430 Broadway, Ste. 1607
New York, New York 10018
Phone: (212)869-5075
Fax: (212)869-5331

A small business investment company. Diversified industry preference.

Paribas Principal, Inc.
787 7th Ave., 33rd Fl.
New York, New York 10019
Phone: (212)841-2000
Fax: (212)841-2146

A small business investment company. Diversified industry preference.

Patricof & Co. Ventures, Inc. (New York)
445 Park Ave., 11th Fl.
New York, New York 10022
Phone: (212)753-6300
Fax: (212)319-6155

Venture capital firm.

Pierre Funding Corp.
805 3rd Ave., 6th Fl.
New York, New York 10022
Phone: (212)888-1515
Fax: (212)688-4252

A minority enterprise small business investment corporation. No industry preference.

Prospect Street NYC Discovery Fund, L.P.
250 Park Ave., 17th Fl.
New York, New York 10177
Phone: (212)490-0480
Fax: (212)490-1566
Richard E. Omohundro, CEO

Prudential Equity Investors
717 5th Ave., Ste. 1100
New York, New York 10022
Phone: (212)753-0901
Fax: (212)826-6798

Venture capital fund. Specialty retailing, medical and health services, communications, and technology companies preferred. Will provide $3 to $7 million in equity financing for later-stage growth companies.

Pyramid Ventures, Inc.
130 Liberty St., 25th Fl.
New York, New York 10006
Phone: (212)250-9571
Fax: (212)250-7651

A small business investment company. Diversified industry preference.

Questech Capital Corp.
600 Madison Ave., 21st Fl.
New York, New York 10022
Phone: (954)583-2960

A small business investment corporation. No industry preference.

R and R Financial Corp.
1370 Broadway
New York, New York 10018
Phone: (212)356-1400
Toll-free: (800)999-4800
Fax: (212)356-0900

A small business investment corporation. No industry preference.

Rothschild Ventures, Inc.
1251 Avenue of the Americas
New York, New York 10020
Toll-free: (800)753-5151
Fax: (212)403-3500

Private venture capital firm. Prefers seed and all later-stage financing.

767 Limited Partnership
767 3rd Ave.
New York, New York 10017
Phone: (212)838-7776
Fax: (212)593-0734

A small business investment corporation. No industry preference.

Sixty Wall Street SBIC Fund, L.P.
60 Wall St.
New York, New York 10260

Phone: (212)648-7778
Fax: (212)648-5032
David Cromwell
Seth Cunningham

Spectra International Mgmt. Group
140 E. 44th St.
Box 776
New York, New York 10017
Phone: (212)986-6030

Venture capital firm providing all stages of financing. Areas of interest include all industries, excluding oil and gas.

Sprout Group (New York City)
277 Park Ave.
New York, New York 10172
Phone: (212)892-3600
Fax: (212)892-3444

Venture capital supplier.

TCW Capital
200 Park Ave., Ste. 2200
New York, New York 10166
Phone: (212)297-4055
Fax: (212)297-4024

Venture capital fund. Companies with sales of $25 to $100 million preferred. Will provide up to $20 million in later-stage financing for recapitalizations, restructuring management buy outs, and general corporate purposes.

399 Venture Partners
399 Park Ave., 14th Fl./ Zone 4
New York, New York 10043
Phone: (212)559-1127
Fax: (212)888-2940

A small business investment company. Diversified industrypreference.

Transportation Capital Corp.
60 E. 42nd St., Ste. 3115
New York, New York 10165-0006
Phone: (212)697-4885

Transportation Capital Corp.
315 Park Ave. S, 10th Fl.
New York, New York 10010

Phone: (212)598-3225
Fax: (212)598-3102

A minority enterprise small business
investment company. Diversified
industry preference.

Trusty Capital, Inc.
350 5th Ave., Ste. 2026
New York, New York 10118
Phone: (212)736-7653
Fax: (212)629-3019

A minority enterprise small business
investment company. Diversified
industry preference.

UBS Partners, Inc.
299 Park Ave.
New York, New York 10171
Phone: (212)821-6490
Fax: (212)821-6333
Justin S. Maccarone, President

United Capital Investment Corp.
60 E. 42nd St., Ste. 1515
New York, New York 10165
Phone: (212)682-7210
Fax: (212)573-6352

A minority enterprise small business
investment company. Diversified
industry preference.

Venture Capital Fund of America, Inc.
509 Madison Ave., Ste. 812
New York, New York 10022
Phone: (212)838-5577
Fax: (212)838-7614

Venture Opportunities Corp.
150 E. 59th St., 16th Fl.
New York, New York 10022-1304
Phone: (212)832-3737

A minority enterprise small business
investment corporation. Areas of
interest include radio, cable, television, telecommunications, real estate
development, medical consumer
products, and service and manufacturing businesses. Second- or third-stage
for expansion,mergers, or acquisitions. No start-up or seed capital
investments.

Warburg Pincus Ventures, Inc.
466 Lexington Ave., 10th Fl.
New York, New York 10017-3147
Phone: (212)878-0600
Toll-free: (800)888-3697
Fax: (212)878-9351

Venture capital firm providing all
stages of financing. Areas of interest
include all industries, excluding
gaming, real estate, and investments
in South Africa.

Weiss, Peck and Greer Venture
Partners L.P. (New York)
1 New York Plz.
New York, New York 10004
Phone: (212)908-9500
Fax: (212)908-9652

Welsh, Carson, Anderson, & Stowe
200 Liberty Ste. 3601
New York, New York 10281
Phone: (212)945-2000
Fax: (212)945-2016

Venture capital partnership.

Wolfensohn Associates, L.P. (New
York)
599 Lexington Ave., 39th Fl.
New York, New York 10022
Phone: (212)909-8100
Fax: (212)446-1307

First Century Partners (New York)
1 Palmer Sq. Ste. 425
Princton, New York 12056
Phone: (609)683-8848
Fax: (609)683 8848

Private venture capital firm. Minimum investment is $1.5 million.
Prefers specialty retailing and
consumer products industries.

International Paper Capital Forma-
tion, Inc. (Purchase)
2 Manhattanville Rd.
Purchase, New York 10577-2196
Phone: (914)397-1500
Fax: (914)397-1909

A minority enterprise small business
investment company.

Genesee Funding, Inc.
100 Corporate Woods
Rochester, New York 14623
Phone: (716)272-2332
Toll-free: (800)933-7739
Fax: (716)272-2396

A small business investment company. Diversified industry preference.

Ibero-American Investors Corp.
104 Scio St.
Rochester, New York 14604-2552
Phone: (716)262-3440
Fax: (716)262-3441

A minority enterprise small business
investment corporation. No industry
preference.

Square Deal Venture Capital Corp.
766 N. Main St.
Spring Valley, New York 10977-1903
Phone: (914)354-4100

A minority enterprise small business
investment company. Diversified
industry preference.

Northwood Ventures
485 Underhill Blvd., Ste. 205
Syosset, New York 11791
Phone: (516)364-5544
Fax: (516)364-0879

Venture capital firm providing
leveraged buyout financing, between
$500,000 - $1 million. Diversified
industry preference.

TLC Funding Corp.
660 White Plains Rd.
Tarrytown, New York 10591
Phone: (914)332-5200
Fax: (914)332-5660

A small business investment corporation. No industry preference.

Bessemer Venture Partners
(Westbury)
1025 Old Country Rd., Ste. 205
Westbury, New York 11590
Phone: (516)997-2300
Fax: (516)997-2371

Venture capital partnership. No industry preference.

Winfield Capital Corp.
237 Mamaroneck Ave.
White Plains, New York 10605
Phone: (914)949-2600
Fax: (914)949-7195

A small business investment corporation. No industry preference.

North Carolina

First Union Capital Partners, Inc.
1 1st Union Center, 18th Fl.
301 S. College St.
Charlotte, North Carolina 28288-0732
Phone: (704)374-6487
Fax: (704)374-6711

A small business investment company. Diversified industry preference.

Kitty Hawk Capital Ltd.
2700 Coltsgate Rd., Ste. 202
Charlotte, North Carolina 28211
Phone: (704)362-3909
Fax: (704)362-2774

Venture capital firm. Geographical preference is the southeast. Investment policy is liberal, but does not invest in real estate, natural resources, and single store retail businesses and does not provide invention development financing.

NationsBanc Capital Corp.
100 N. Tryon St., 10th Fl.
Charlotte, North Carolina 28255
Phone: (704)386-8063
Fax: (704)386-6432
Walter W. Walker Jr., President

Preferred Investment Size: $3 to $25 million. Investment Policies: Equity, sub debt with warrants. Investment Types: Later stage, expansion. Industry Preferences: Diversified. Geographic Preferences: National.

Southgate Venture Partners
528 E. Blvd.

Charlotte, North Carolina 28203
Phone: (704)373-0051
Fax: (704)343-0170

Private venture capital firm. Diversified industry preference.

Springdale Venture Partners, LP
2039 Queens Rd., E.
Charlotte, North Carolina 28207
Phone: (704)344-8290
Fax: (704)386-6695
S. Epes Robinson, General Partner

Center for Community Self-Help
North Carolina's Development Bank
PO Box 3619
Durham, North Carolina 27702-3619
Phone: (919)956-4400
Toll-free: (800)476-7428
Fax: (919)688-3615

Statewide, private-sector financial institution providing technical assistance and financing to small businesses, non-profit organizations, and low-income homebuyers in North Carolina.

Atlantic Venture Partners (Winston Salem)
380 Knollwood St., No. 410
Winston Salem, North Carolina 27103
Phone: (910)721-1800
Fax: (910)748-1208

Private venture capital partnership. Prefers to invest in manufacturing, distribution, and service industries.

North Dakota

Bank of North Dakota
Small Business Loan Program
700 E. Main Ave.
Box 5509
Bismarck, North Dakota 58506-5504
Phone: (701)328-5600
Toll-free: (800)472-2166
Fax: (701)328-5632

Assists new and existing businesses in securing competitive financing with reasonable terms and conditions.

Fargo Cass County Economic Development Corp.
406 Main Ave., Ste. 404
Fargo, North Dakota 58103
Phone: (701)237-6132
Fax: (701)293-7819

Certified development company that lends to small and medium-sized businesses at fixed rates.

North Dakota SBIC, L.P.
417 Main Ave., Ste. 401
Fargo, North Dakota 58103
Phone: (701)237-6132
Fax: (701)293-7819

North Dakota Small Business Loan Services
406 Main Ave., Ste.404
Fargo, North Dakota 58103
Phone: (701)235-7885
Fax: (701)235-6706

Administers the 504 Loan Program.

Ohio

River Capital Corp. (Cleveland)
2544 Chamberlain Rd.
Akron, Ohio 44333
Phone: (216)781-3655
Fax: (216)781-2821

A small business investment corporation. No industry preference.

River Cities Capital Fund L.P.
221 E. 4th St., Ste. 2250
Cincinnati, Ohio 45202
Phone: (513)621-9700
Fax: (513)579-8939
R. Glen Mayfield, Manager

Preferred Investment Size: $750,000 to $1.5 Million. Investment Policies: Equity investments. Investment Types: Early stage, expansion, later stage. Industry Preferences: Diversified. Geographic Preferences: Ohio, Kentucky, Indiana.

Brantley Venture Partners, L.P.
20600 Chagrin Blvd., Ste. 1150

Cleveland, Ohio 44122
Phone: (216)283-4800
Fax: (216)283-5324

Venture capital firm. Areas of interest include computer and electronics, medical/health care, biotechnology, computer software, telecommunications, traditional manufacturing, information processing, and environmental industries.

Clarion Capital Corp.
Ohio Savings Plz., Ste. 510
1801 E. 9th St.
Cleveland, Ohio 44114
Phone: (216)687-1096
Fax: (216)694-3545

Small business investment corporation. Interested in manufacturing, computer software, natural resources/natural gas, and health care.

Gries Investment Co.
1801 E. 9th St., Ste. 16
Cleveland, Ohio 44114-3110
Phone: (216)861-1146
Fax: (216)861-0106

A small business investment corporation.

Key Equity Capital Corp.
127 Public Sq., 6th Fl.
Cleveland, Ohio 44114
Phone: (216)689-5776
Fax: (216)689-3204
Raymond Lancaster, President

Preferred Investment Size: $2.000,000. Investment Policies: Willing to make equity investments. Industry Preferences: Diversified. Geographic Preferences: National.

Morgenthaler Ventures
629 Euclid Ave., Ste. 1700
Cleveland, Ohio 44111
Phone: (216)621-3070
Fax: (216)621-2817

Private venture capital firm providing start-up and later-stage financing to all types of business in North America; prefers not to invest in real estate and oil and gas.

National City Capital Corp.
1965 E. 6th St., Ste.400
Cleveland, Ohio 44114
Phone: (216)575-2491
Fax: (216)575-9965

A small business investment corporation. Provides equity for expansion programs, recapitalizations, acquisitions, and management buyouts. Seeks investment opportunities ranging from $1 million to $5 million. Diversified industry preference.

Primus Venture Partners
1 Cleveland Center, Ste. 2700
1375 E. 9th St.
Cleveland, Ohio 44114
Phone: (216)621-2185
Fax: (216)621-4543

Venture capital partnership. Provides seed, early stage, and expansion financing to companies located in Ohio and the Midwest. Does not engage in gas, oil, or real estate investments.

Society Venture Capital Corp.
127 Public Sq. 6th Fl.
Cleveland, Ohio 44114
Phone: (216)689-5776
Fax: (216)689-3204

A small business investment corporation. Prefers to invest in manufacturing and service industries.

Tomlinson Industries
13700 Broadway Ave.
Cleveland, Ohio 44125-1992
Phone: (216)587-3400
Toll-free: (800)526-9634
Fax: (216)587-0733

A small business investment corporation. Miniature supermarket industry preferred.

Banc One Capital Partners Corp. (Columbus)
10 W. Broad St., Ste. 400
Columbus, Ohio 43215
Phone: (614)224-6900

Toll-free: (800)837-5100
Fax: (614)227-7787

A small business investment corporation. No industry preference.

Scientific Advances, Inc.
601 W. 5th Ave.
Columbus, Ohio 43201
Phone: (614)424-7005
Fax: (614)424-4874

Venture capital partnership interested in natural gas related industries.

Center City MESBIC, Inc.
8 N. Maine St.
Miami Valley Tur, Ste. 1400
Dayton, Ohio 45402
Phone: (513)461-6164
Fax: (513)222-7035

A minority enterprise small business investment corporation. Diversified industries.

Seed One
Park Pl.
10 W. Streetsboro St.
Hudson, Ohio 44236
Phone: (216)650-2338
Fax: (216)650-4946

Private venture capital firm. No industry preference. Equity financing only.

Fifth Third Bank of Northwestern Ohio, N.A.
606 Madison Ave.
Toledo, Ohio 43604
Phone: (419)259-7141
Fax: (419)259-7134

A small business investment corporation. No industry preference.

Lubrizol Performance Products Co.
29400 Lakeland Blvd.
Wickliffe, Ohio 44092
Phone: (216)943-4200
Fax: (216)943-5337

Venture capital supplier. Provides seed capital and later-stage expansion financing to emerging companies in the biological, chemical, and material sciences whose technology is applicable to and related to the production and marketing of specialty and fine chemicals.

Cactus Capital Co.
6660 High St., Office 1-B
Worthington, Ohio 43085
Phone: (614)436-4060
Fax: (614)436-4060

A minority enterprise small business investment company. Diversified industry preference.

Oklahoma

Southwestern Oklahoma Development Authority
PO Box 569
Burns Flat, Oklahoma 73624
Phone: (405)562-4884
Toll-free: (800)627-4882
Fax: (405)462-4880

Langston University
Minority Business Assistance Center
Hwy. 37 E.
PO Box 667
Langston, Oklahoma 73050
Phone: (405)466-3256
Toll-free: (800)879-6552
Fax: (405)841-5142

BancFirst Investment Corp.
1101 N. Broadway
Oklahoma City, Oklahoma 73126
Phone: (405)270-1000
Fax: (405)270-1089
T. Kent Faison, Manager

Preferred Investment Size: Up to $500,000. Investment Policies: Loans and/or equity. Investment Types: Early stage, expansion. Industry Preferences: Diversified. Geographic Preferences: Oklahoma.

Oklahoma Department of Commerce
Business Development Division
PO Box 26980
Oklahoma City, Oklahoma 73126-0980
Phone: (405)843-9770

Helps companies gain access to capital needed for growth. Provides financial specialists to help businesses analyze their financing needs and to work closely with local economic development staff to help package proposals for their companies. Also responsible for assisting in the development of new loan and investment programs.

Oklahoma Development Finance Authority
301 NW 63rd St., Ste. 225
Oklahoma City, Oklahoma 73116
Phone: (405)848-9761
Fax: (405)848-3314

Issues tax-exempt industrial development bonds for manufacturing firms.

Oklahoma Industrial Finance Authority
301 NW 63rd. Ste. 225
Oklahoma City, Oklahoma 73116-7904
Phone: (405)842-1145
Fax: (405)898-3314

Provides financing for manufacturing projects involving the purchase of land, buildings, and stationary equipment.

Oklahoma State Treasurer's Office
Agriculture/Small Business Linked Deposit Programs
217 State Capitol
Oklahoma City, Oklahoma 73105
Phone: (405)521-3191
Fax: (405)521-4994

Provides reduced loan rates for Oklahoma's farming, ranching, and small business communities.

Rees/Source Ventures, Inc.
3001 United Founders Blvd.
Oklahoma City, Oklahoma 73112
Phone: (405)843-8049
Fax: (405)843-8068

Venture capital firm providing seed, start-up, first-stage, and second-stage financing. Prefers to make investments in the $250,000 to $500,000 range to companies within a three-mile radius of Oklahoma City. Areas

of interest include recreation and leisure, environmental products and services, packaging machinery and materials, energy-related technologies, printing and publishing, manufacturing and automation, information processing and software, and specialty chemicals industries. Will not consider the following industries: oil, gas, or mineral exploration; real estate; motion pictures; and consulting services.

Alliance Business Investment Co. (Tulsa)
320 South Boston Ste. 1000
Tulsa, Oklahoma 74103-3703
Phone: (918)584-3581
Fax: (918)582-3403

A small business investment corporation. Provides later-stage financing for basic industries.

Davis Venture Partners (Tulsa)
320 S. Boston Ste.,1000
Tulsa, Oklahoma 74103-3703
Phone: (918)584-7272
Fax: (918)582-3403

Venture capital firm. Provides later-stage financing for basic industries.

Rubottom, Dudash and Associates, Inc.
4870 S. Lewis, Ste. 180
Tulsa, Oklahoma 74105
Phone: (918)742-3031
Fax: (918)742-3059

Management and investment consultants. Emphasis on retail, wholesale, and light fabrication.

Oregon

Olympic Venture Partners II (Lake Oswego)
340 Oswego Pointe Dr., No. 204
Lake Oswego, Oregon 97034-3230
Phone: (503)697-8766
Fax: (503)697-8863

Invests in early stage high technology, biotechnology, and communications businesses.

Orien Ventures
4550 SW Cruse Way Ste. 245
Lake Oswego, Oregon 97035-2580
Phone: (503)699-1680
Fax: (503)699-1681

Venture capital firm interested in all types of investment.

Northern Pacific Capital Corp.
PO Box 1658
Portland, Oregon 97207
Phone: (503)241-1255
Fax: (503)299-6653

A small business investment company. Diversified industry preference.

Northwest Capital Network
PO Box 6650
Portland, Oregon 97228-6650
Phone: (503)796-3321
Fax: (503)280-6080

Nonprofit business/investor referral service that brings together entrepreneurs requiring capital with investors seeking specific venture opportunities, through means of a confidential database of investment opportunity profiles and investment interest profiles.

Oregon Resource and Technology Development Fund
4370 NE Halsey
Portland, Oregon 97213
Phone: (503)282-4462
Fax: (503)282-2976

Provides investment capital for early stage business finance and applied research and development projects that leads to commercially viable products.

Shaw Venture Partners
400 SW 6th Ave., Ste. 1100
Portland, Oregon 97204-1636
Phone: (503)228-4884
Fax: (503)227-2471

Small business investment corporation interested in computers, retail, medical/biotechnology, consumer products and international trade investment.

U.S. Bancorp Capital Corp.
P.O. Box 4412
Portland, Oregon 97208
Phone: (503)275-6111
Fax: (503)275-7565

A small business investment company. Diversified industry preference.

Oregon Economic Development Department
Business Finance Section
Oregon Business Development Fund
775 Summer St. NE
Salem, Oregon 97310
Phone: (503)986-0160
Fax: (503)581-5115

Structures and issues loans to manufacturing, processing, and tourism-related small businesses.

Oregon Economic Development Department
Business Finance Section
SBA Loans Program
775 Summer St. NE
Salem, Oregon 97310
Phone: (503)986-0160
Toll-free: (800)233-3306
Fax: (503)581-5115

A state-wide company providing Small Business Administration 504 and 7(A) financing to eligible small businesses; works closely with local certified development companies.

Tektronix Development Co.
PO Box 1000, Mail Sta. 63-862
Wilsonville, Oregon 97070
Phone: (503)685-4233
Fax: (503)685-3754

Venture capital firm interested in high tech, opto electronics and measurement systems investment.

Pennsylvania

NEPA Venture Fund LP
125 Goodman Dr.
Bethlehem, Pennsylvania 18015
Phone: (610)865-6550

Private venture capital partnership providing seed and start-up financing.

Erie SBIC
32 W. 8th St., Ste. 615
Erie, Pennsylvania 16501
Phone: (814)453-7964

A small business investment corporation. No industry preference. Prefers investments ranging from $100,000 - $200,000.

Pennsylvania Department of Commerce
Bureau of Bonds
Revenue Bond and Mortgage Program
466 Forum Bldg.
Harrisburg, Pennsylvania 17120
Phone: (717)783-1109
Fax: (717)234-4560

Financing for projects approved through the Program are borrowed from private sources, and can be used to acquire land, buildings, machinery, and equipment. Borrowers must create a minimum number of new jobs within three years of the loan's closing.

Pennsylvania Department of Commerce
Governor's Response Team
439 Forum Bldg.
Harrisburg, Pennsylvania 17120
Phone: (717)787-8199
Phone: (717)234-4560
Fax: (717)772-5419

Works with individual companies to find buildings or sites for start-up or expansion projects; contacts manufacturers to make them aware of financial and technical assistance available, to assist with difficulties, and to learn of future plans for expansions or cutbacks.

Pennsylvania Department of Commerce
Bureau of Bonds
Employee Ownership Assistance Program
Office of Program Management

466 Forum Bldg.
Harrisburg, Pennsylvania 17120
Phone: (717)783-1109

Fax: (717)234-4560Preserves existing jobs and creates new jobs by assisting and promoting employee ownership in existing enterprises which are experiencing layoffs or would otherwise close.

Pennsylvania Department of Energy
Energy Development Authority
P.O. Box 8772 13th Fl.
Rachael Carson State Official
Harrisburg, Pennsylvania 17105-8772
Phone: (717)783-9981
Fax: (717)783-2703

Finances research and development of energy technology projects.

Hillman Medical Ventures, Inc. (Berwyn)
2 Walnut Grove Dr., Ste. 130
Horsham, Pennsylvania 19044-2255
Phone: (215)443-5531
Fax: (215)443-5970

Venture capital firm that invests in early-stage medical technology companies.

Enterprise Venture Capital Corp. of Pennsylvania
111 Market St.
Johnstown, Pennsylvania 15901
Phone: (814)535-7597
Fax: (814)535-8677

A small business investment corporation. No industry preference. Geographic preference is two-hour driving radius of Johnstown, Pennsylvania.

Foster Management Co.
1016 W. 9th Ave.
King of Prussia, Pennsylvania 19406
Phone: (610)992-7650
Fax: (610)992-3390

Private venture capital supplier. Not restricted to specific industries or geographic locations; diversified

with investments in the health care, transportation, broadcasting, communications, energy, and home furnishings industries. Investments range from $2 million to $15 million.

CIP Capital, LP
20 Valley Stream Pky., Ste.265
Malvern, Pennsylvania 19355
Phone: (610)695-8380
Fax: (215)695-8388

A small business investment company. Diversified industry preference.

Ben Franklin Technology Center of Southeastern Pennsylvania
University City Science Center
3624 Market St.
Philadelphia, Pennsylvania 19104
Phone: (215)382-0380
Fax: (215)387-6050

Public venture capital fund interested in technology industries.

Core States Enterprise Fund
1345 Chestnut St., F.C. 1-8-12-1
Philadelphia, Pennsylvania 19107
Phone: (215)973-6519
Fax: (215)973-6900

Venture capital supplier. Invests with any industry except real estate or construction. Minimum investment is $1 million.

Fidelcor Capital Corp.
Fidelity Bldg., 11th Fl.
123 S. Broad St.
Philadelphia, Pennsylvania 19109
Phone: (215)985-3722
Fax: (215)985-7282

A small business investment company. Diversified industry preference.

Genesis Seed Fund
c/o Howard, Lawson and Co.
2 Penn Center Plz.
Philadelphia, Pennsylvania 19102
Phone: (215)988-0010
Fax: (215)568-0029

Venture capital fund.

Keystone Venture Capital Management Co.
1601 Market St., Ste.2500
Philadelphia, Pennsylvania 19103
Phone: (215)241-1200
Phone: (215)241-1200
Fax: (215)241-1211

Private venture capital partnership. Provides later-stage investments in the telecommunications, health care, manufacturing, media, software, and franchise industries, primarily in the mid-Atlantic states.

Penn Janney Fund, Inc.
1801 Market St.
Philadelphia, Pennsylvania 19103
Phone: (215)665-6193
Fax: (215)665-6197

Private venture capital limited partnership.

Philadelphia Ventures
200 S. Broad St., 8th Fl.
Philadelphia, Pennsylvania 19102
Phone: (215)732-4445
Fax: (215)732-4644

A small business investment corporation. Provides financing to companies offering products or services based on technology or other proprietary capabilities. Industries of particular interest are information processing equipment and services, medical products and services, data communications, and industrial automation.

PNC Corporate Finance
100 S. Broad St., 6th Fl.
Philadelphia, Pennsylvania 19101
Phone: (215)585-6282
Fax: (215)585-5525

Small business investment company.

Fostin Capital Corp.
681 Andersen Dr.
Pittsburgh, Pennsylvania 15220
Phone: (412)928-1400
Phone: (412)928-1413
Fax: (412)928-9635

Venture capital corporation.

Loyalhanna Venture Fund
PO Box 81927
Pittsburgh, Pennsylvania 15217
Phone: (412)687-9027
Fax: (412)681-0960

Venture capital firm. No industry
preference.

PNC Capital Corp.
One PNC Plaza 19th Fl.
249 5th Ave.
Pittsburgh, Pennsylvania 15222
Phone: (412)762-7035
Fax: (412)762-6233

A small business investment corporation.
Prefers to invest in later-stage and
leveraged buy out situations. Will not
consider real estate, coal, or gas ventures.

APA/Fostin Pennsylvania Venture
Capital Fund
100 Matsonford Rd., Bldg. 5, Ste. 470
Radnor, Pennsylvania 19087
Phone: (610)687-3030
Fax: (610)687-8520

Private venture capital limited partnership providing mid- and later stage
financing.

Meridian Venture Partners
The Fidelity Court Bldg., Ste. 140
259 Radnor-Chester Rd.
Radnor, Pennsylvania 19087
Phone: (610)254-2999

Venture capital firm.

Patricof & Co. Ventures, Inc. (Radnor)
100 Matsonford Rd., Bldg. 5, Ste. 470
Radnor, Pennsylvania 19087
Phone: (610)687-3030
Fax: (610)687-8520

Venture capital firm providing mid-
to later stage financing.

Meridian Capital Corp.
601 Plum St.
Reading, Pennsylvania 19603
Phone: (215)655-2924
Fax: (215)655-1908

Small business investment corporation.

TDH
1 Rosemont Business Campus, Ste.
301
919 Conestoga Rd.
Rosemont, Pennsylvania 19010
Phone: (610)526-9970
Fax: (610)526-9971

Private venture capital fund. No
industry preferences.

BankAmerica Ventures (Washington,
PA)
PO Box 512
Washington, Pennsylvania 15301
Phone: (412)223-0707
Fax: (412)546-8021
Daniel A. Dye, Contact

First SBIC of California (Washington,
PA)
PO Box 512
Washington, Pennsylvania 15301
Phone: (412)223-0707
Fax: (412)223-8290

A small business investment company.

S. R. One Ltd.
565 E. Swedesford Rd., Ste. 315
Wayne, Pennsylvania 19087
Phone: (610)293-3400
Fax: (610)293-3419

Sandhurst Co. LP
351 E. Constoga Rd.
Wayne, Pennsylvania 19087
Phone: (610)254-8900
Fax: (610)254-8958

Private venture capital fund.

Technology Leaders LP
800 The Safeguard Bldg.
435 Devon Park Dr.
Wayne, Pennsylvania 19087
Phone: (610)293-0600
Fax: (610)293-0601

Private venture capital fund. Areas of
interest includebiotechnology, health
care, information services, and high
technology industries.

Zero Stage Capital Co., Inc.
1562 Mcdaniel Dr.
West Chester, Pennsylvania 19380
Phone: (610)430-8853
Fax: (610)430-8857

Venture capital firm. Industry
preferences include high-technology
start-up companies located in the
northeastern U.S.

Puerto Rico

North America Investment Corp.
P.O. Box 191831
San Juan, Puerto Rico 00919-1813
Phone: (809)754-6177
Fax: (809)754-6181

A minority enterprise small business
investment corporation. Diversified
industry preference.

Rhode Island

Domestic Capital Corp.
815 Reservoir Ave.
Cranston, Rhode Island 02910
Phone: (401)946-3310
Fax: (401)943-6708

A small business investment corporation. No industry preference.

Fairway Capital Corp.
285 Governor St.
Providence, Rhode Island 02906
Phone: (401)454-7500
Fax: (401)455-3636

A small business investment company. Diversified industry preference.

Fleet Equity Partners (Providence)
111 Westminster St., 4th Fl.
Providence, Rhode Island 02903
Phone: (401)278-6770
Fax: (401)278-6387

Venture capital firm specializing in
acquisitions and recapitalizations.

Fleet Venture Resources, Inc.
111 Westminster St., 4th Fl.
Providence, Rhode Island 02903

Phone: (401)278-6770
Fax: (401)278-6387
Robert M. Van Degna, President

Preferred Investment Size: $5 to $125 million. Investment Policies:Equity. Investment Types: Leverage buyouts, expansion. Industry Preferences: Media/communications, healthcare, printing, manufacturing. Geographic Preferences: National.

Moneta Capital Corp.
285 Governor St.
Providence, Rhode Island 02906-4314
Phone: (401)454-7500
Fax: (401)455-3636

A small business investment corporation. No industry preference.

NYSTRS/NV Capital, Limited Partnership
111 Westminster St.
Providence, Rhode Island 02903
Phone: (401)276-5597
Fax: (401)278-6387

A small business investment company. Diversified industry preference.

Rhode Island Department of Economic Development
Rhode Island Port Operations Division
1 W. Exchange
Providence, Rhode Island 02903
Phone: (401)277-2601
Fax: (401)277-2102

Provides financing through tax-exempt revenue bonds.

Rhode Island Department of Economic Development
Rhode Island Industrial-Recreational Building Authority
1 W. Exchange
Providence, Rhode Island 02903
Phone: (401)277-2601
Fax: (401)277-2102

Issues mortgage insurance on financing obtained through other financial institutions.

Rhode Island Department of Economic Development
Rhode Island Partnership for Science and Technology
1 W. Exchange
Providence, Rhode Island 02903
Phone: (401)277-2601
Fax: (401)277-2102

Offers grants to businesses for applied research with a potential for profitable commercialization. Research must be conducted in conjunction with universities, colleges, or hospitals. Also has a program which provides consulting services and grants to applicants of the Federal Small Business Innovation Research Program.

Rhode Island Department of Economic Development
Ocean State Business Development Authority
1 W. Exchange
Providence, Rhode Island 02903
Phone: (401)277-2601
Fax: (401)277-2102

Private, nonprofit corporation certified by the Small Business Administration to administer the SBA(504) loan program.

Rhode Island Office of the General Treasurer
Business Investment Fund
40 Fountain St., 8th Fl.
Providence, Rhode Island 02903-1855
Phone: (401)277-2287
Toll-free: (800)752-8088
Fax: (401)277-6141

Provides fixed-rate loans in cooperation with the U.S. Small Business Administration and local banks.

Richmond Square Capital Corp.
1 Richmond Sq.
Providence, Rhode Island 02906
Phone: (401)521-3000
Fax: (401)751-8997

A small business investment company. Diversified industry preference.

Wallace Capital Corp.
170 Westminster St., Ste. 1200
Providence, Rhode Island 02903
Phone: (401)273-9191
Fax: (401)273-9648

A small business investment company. Diversified industry preference.

South Carolina

Charleston Capital Corp.
111 Church St.
PO Box 328
Charleston, South Carolina 29402
Phone: (803)723-6464
Fax: (803)723-1228

Small business investment corporation preferring secured loans. Assists the southeastern U.S. only.

Lowcountry Investment Corp.
4401 Piggly Wiggly Dr.
PO Box 18047
Charleston, South Carolina 29405
Phone: (803)554-9880
Fax: (803)745-2730

A small business investment corporation. Diversified industry preference.

Floco Investment Co., Inc.
PO Box 1629
Lake City, South Carolina 29560
Phone: (803)389-2731
Fax: (803)389-4199

A small business investment corporation. Invests only in grocery stores.

South Dakota

South Dakota Department of Agriculture
Office of Rural Development
Agricultural Loan Participation Program
Foss Bldg., 523 E. Capitol
Pierre, South Dakota 57501-3182
Phone: (605)773-3375
Toll-free: (800)228-5254
Fax: (605)773-5926

Provides loans, administered and serviced through local lenders, that are intended to supplement existing credit.

South Dakota Development Corp.
SBA 504 Loan Program
711 E. Wells Ave.
Pierre, South Dakota 57501-3369
Toll-free: (800)872-6190
Fax: (605)773-3256

Offers subordinated mortgage financing to healthy and expanding small businesses.

South Dakota Governor's Office of Economic Development
Economic Development Finance Authority
711 E. Wells Ave.
Pierre, South Dakota 57501-3369
Toll-free: (800)872-6190

Pools tax-exempt or taxable development bonds to construct any site, structure, facility, service, or utility for the storage, distribution, or manufacture of industrial, agricultural, or nonagricultural products, machinery, or equipment.

South Dakota Governor's Office of Economic Development
Revolving Economic Development and Initiative Fund
711 E. Wells Ave.
Pierre, South Dakota 57501-3369
Toll-free: (800)872-6190

Provides low-interest revolving loans for the creation of primary jobs, capital investment, and the diversification of the state's economy. Costs eligible for participation include land and the associated site improvements; construction, acquisition, andrenovation of buildings; fees, services and other costs associated with construction; the purchase and installation of machinery and equipment; and trade receivables, inventory, and work-in-progress inventory.

Tennessee

Valley Capital Corp.
100 W. Martin L. King Blvd., Ste. 212
Chattanooga, Tennessee 37402

Phone: (423)265-1557
Fax: (423)265-1588

A minority enterprise small business investment corporation. Diversified industry preferences. Limited to the Southeast, preferably four-hour driving radius.

Franklin Venture Capital, Inc.
237 2nd Ave. S
Franklin, Tennessee 37064
Phone: (615)791-9462
Fax: (615)791-9636

A small business investment corporation. Prefers to invest in the health care and biotechnology industries.

Chickasaw Capital Corp.
6200 Poplar Ave.
PO Box 387
Memphis, Tennessee 38147
Phone: (901)383-6000
Fax: (901)383-6141

A minority enterprise small business investment corporation. No industry preference.

Flemming Companies
1991 Corporate Ave.
Memphis, Tennessee 38132
Phone: (901)395-8000
Fax: (901)395-8595

A small business investment corporation.

Gulf Pacific
5100 Poplar Ave., No. 427
Memphis, Tennessee 38137-0401
Phone: (901)767-3400
Toll-free: (800)456-1867
Fax: (901)680-7033

A minority enterprise small business investment corporation.

International Paper Capital Formation, Inc.
6400 Poplar Ave.
Tower 2, 4th Fl., Rm. 130
Memphis, Tennessee 38197
Phone: (901)763-6217
Fax: (901)763-7278

A minority enterprise small business investment corporation. Diversified industry preference. Involvement includes expansion, refinancing, and acquisitions, but no start-up projects. Requires a minimum investment of $50,000 to $300,000.

Leader Capital Corp.
PO Box 275
158 Madison Ave.
Memphis, Tennessee 38103-0708
Phone: (901)578-2405
Toll-free: (800)821-9979

A small business investment corporation.

West Tennessee Venture Capital Corp.
5 N. 3rd St.
Memphis, Tennessee 38103-2610
Phone: (901)523-1884
Fax: (901)527-6091

A minority enterprise small business investment corporation.

Lawrence, Tyrrell, Ortale, and Smith (Nashville)
3100 W. End Ave., Ste. 400
Nashville, Tennessee 37203
Phone: (615)383-0982
Fax: (615)269-0463

Private venture capital firm. Prefers to invest in health care industries.

L.P. Equitas
2000 Glen Echo Rd., Ste 100
PO Box 158838
Nashville, Tennessee 37215
Phone: (615)383-8673
Fax: (615)383-8693
D. Shannon LeRoy, President

Massey Burch Investment Group
310 25th Ave. N, Ste. 103
Nashville, Tennessee 37203
Phone: (615)329-9448
Fax: (615)329-9237

Venture capital firm providing investments ranging from $1 to $3 million. Areas of interest include health care services, information services, environmental services, privatization, systems integration, and telecommunications.

Sirrom Capital, LP
500 Church St., Ste. 200
Nashville, Tennessee 37219
Phone: (615)256-0701
Fax: (615)726-1208

A small business investment company. Diversified industry preference.

Tennessee Department of Economic and Community Development
Grants Program Management Section
Rachel Jackson Bldg.
320 6th Ave. N.
Nashville, Tennessee 37243-0405
Phone: (615)741-6201
Toll-free: (800)342-8470
Fax: (615)741-5070

Administers grant money for the community development block grant program, the Appalachian Regional Commission, and the Economic Development Administration.

Tennessee Equity Capital Corp.
1102 Stonewall Jackson Ct.
Nashville, Tennessee 37220-1705

A minority enterprise small business investment corporation.

Texas

Austin Ventures L.P.
1300 Norwood Tower, Ste. 1300
114 W. 7th St.
Austin, Texas 78701
Phone: (512)479-0055
Fax: (512)476-3952

Administers investments through two funds, Austin Ventures L.P. and Rust Ventures L.P., in the $1 million to $4 million range. Prefers to invest in start-up/emerging growth companies located in the southwest, and in special situations such as buy outs, acquisitions, and mature companies.

No geographic limitations are placed on later-stage investments. Past investments have been made in media, data communications, telecommunications, software, environmental services, and general manufacturing.

Forum Financial
600 Congress Ave., No. 1630
Austin, Texas 78701-3236
Phone: (512)476-7800
Fax: (512)476-3850

Venture capital firm providing second stage, acquisitions and leveraged buyout financing. Areas of interest include mining, oil and gas, real estate development, and project financing.

Huber Capital Ventures
11917 Oak Knoll, Ste. G
Austin, Texas 78759
Phone: (512)258-8668
Fax: (512)258-9091

Venture capital firm providing short-term working capital funding for specific projects. Areas of interest include small capitalization companies in manufacturing, wholesaling, and technical services.

Texas Department of Commerce
Finance Office
PO Box 12728
Austin, Texas 78711
Phone: (512)936-0281
Fax: (512)936-0520

Administers several programs that benefit small businesses, including those authorized under the Industrial Development Corporation Act of 1979 and the Rural Development Act, as well as the state industrial revenue bond program.

Triad Ventures Ltd.
4901 Spicewood Springs Rd., Ste. 200
Austin, Texas 78759
Phone: (512)343-8087
Fax: (512)343-1802

Venture capital firm providing second stage, acquisitions, mezzanine and leveraged buyout financing. Areas of interest include Texas-based companies.

Alliance Enterprise Corp.
N. Central Plz. 1, Ste. 710
12655 N. Central Expy.
Dallas, Texas 75243
Phone: (214)991-1597
Fax: (214)991-1647

A minority enterprise small business investment company. Diversified industry preference.

AMT Capital, Ltd.
8204 Elmbrook Dr., Ste. 101
Dallas, Texas 75247
Phone: (214)905-9760
Fax: (214)905-9761
Tom H. Delimitros, CGP

Preferred Investment Size: $200,000 to $500,000. Investment Policies: Loan or equity. Investment Types: Early stage, expansion. Industry Preferences: Advanced materials & products. Geographic Preferences: National.

Banc One Capital Partners Corp. (Dallas)
300 Crescent Ct., Ste. 1600
Dallas, Texas 75201
Phone: (214)979-4375
Fax: (214)979-4355

A small business investment corporation. Specializes in later-stage investments for traditional businesses with revenues in excess of $15 million annually. Areas of interest include manufacturing, distribution, and health care industries.

Brittany Capital Co.
9400 N. Central Expressway, Ste. 1311
Dallas, Texas 75231
Phone: (214)363-1541

A small business investment corporation. No industry preference.

Capital Southwest Corp.
12900 Preston Rd., Ste. 700
Dallas, Texas 75230
Phone: (214)233-8242
Fax: (214)233-7362

Venture capital firm. Provides first
stage and expansion financing.

Citicorp Venture Capital, Ltd.
(Dallas)
2001 Ross Ave.
1400 Tramalcrowe Center
Dallas, Texas 75201
Phone: (214)953-3800
Fax: (214)953-1495

A small business investment company.

Davis Venture Partners (Dallas)
2121 San Jacinto St., Ste. 975
Dallas, Texas 75201
Phone: (214)954-1822
Fax: (214)969-0256

Venture capital firm interested in
diversified industries, excluding oil,
gas, and real estate.

Diamond A. Ford Corp.
Zoo Crescent Court, Ste. 1350
Dallas, Texas 75201
Phone: (214)871-5177
Fax: (214)871-5199

A small business investment company. Diversified industry preference.

Erickson Capital Group, Inc.
5950 Berkshire Lane, Ste. 1100
Dallas, Texas 75225
Phone: (214)365-6060
Fax: (214)365-6001

Venture capital firm providing seed,
start-up, first and second stage, and
expansion financing. Areas of interest
include health care.

Hook Partners
13760 Noel Rd., Ste. 805
Dallas, Texas 75240-4360
Phone: (214)991-5457

Venture capital firm providing seed,
start-up and first stage financing.

Areas of interest include high
technology industries.

Interwest Partners (Dallas)
1 Galleria Tower
13355 Noel Rd., Ste. 1375/LB 65
Dallas, Texas 75240
Phone: (214)392-7279
Fax: (214)490-6348

Kahala Investments, Inc.
8214 Westchester Dr., Ste. 715
Dallas, Texas 75225
Phone: (214)987-0077

Venture capital firm providing
financing for all stages including
expansion capital, leveraged buyouts,
and management buyouts. Areas of
interest include a wide variety of
industries.

Mapleleaf Capital, Ltd.
3 Forest Plz., Ste.935
12221 Merit Dr.
Dallas, Texas 75251
Phone: (214)239-5650
Fax: (214)701-0024

A small business investment company. Diversified industry preference.

May Financial Corp.
8333 Douglas Ave., Ste. 400
Lock Box 82
Dallas, Texas 75225
Phone: (214)987-5200
Toll-free: (800)767-4397
Fax: (214)987-1994

Brokerage firm working with a
venture capital firm. Prefers food, oil
and gas, and electronics industries.

Merchant Banking Group Ltd.
700 N. Pearl, Ste. 1910 NT, LB 321
Dallas, Texas 75201
Phone: (214)777-6466
Fax: (214)777-6475

Venture capital firm providing
leveraged buyout financing. Areas
ofinterest include basic manufacturing and distribution.

MESBIC Ventures, Inc.
12655 N. Central Expy., Ste. 710
Dallas, Texas 75243-1739
Phone: (214)991-1597
Fax: (214)991-1647

A minority enterprise small business
investment corporation. Diversified
industry preference.

MESBIC Ventures, Inc.
N. Central Plaza 1, Ste. 710
12655 N. Central Expy.
Dallas, Texas 75243
Phone: (214)991-1597
Fax: (214)991-1647
Donald R. Lawhorne, President

Preferred Investment Size: Up to
$1,000,000. Investment Policies: Loans
and/or equity. Investment Types: early
stage, expansion, later stage. Industry
Preferences: Diversified. Geographic
Preferences: Mostly Southwest.

MSI Capital Investments
6500 Greenville Ave., Ste. 720
Dallas, Texas 75206-1012
Phone: (214)265-1801
Fax: (214)265-1804

No industry preference.

Nations Bank Venture Capital
901 Maine St., Ste. 664
Dallas, Texas 75202-2911
Phone: (214)508-0988
Fax: (214)508-0604

A small business investment company. Diversified industry preference.

NationsBanc Capital Corp.
1401 Elm St., Ste. 4764
Dallas, Texas 75202
Phone: (214)508-6262
Fax: (214)508-5060

Venture capital firm providing
second stage, mezzanine and leveraged buyout financing. Areas of
interest include communications,
medical, environmental, specialty
retail, transportation and energy
services.

NCNB Texas Venture Group, Inc.
1401 Elm St., Ste. 4764
Dallas, Texas 75202
Phone: (214)508-6262

Venture capital firm providing expansion and leveraged buyout financing. Areas of interest include medical products and services, energy service, environmental, specialty retail, transportation, general manufacturing, and communications.

North Texas MESBIC, Inc.
12770 Coit Rd., Ste.240
Dallas, Texas 75251
Phone: (214)991-8060
Fax: (214)991-8061

A minority enterprise small business investment company. Diversified industry preference.

Performance Properties Corp.
4131 N. Central Expy., Ste. 900
Dallas, Texas 75204
Phone: (214)528-8883
Fax: (214)528-8058

Venture capital firm providing acquisition, start-up, and leverage equity financing. Areas of interest include real estate.

Phillips-Smith Specialty Retail Group
5080 Spectrum Dr., Ste. 700 W
Dallas, Texas 75248
Phone: (214)387-0725
Fax: (214)458-2560

Prefers specialty retail industry investments, including the restaurant industry.

PMC Capital, Inc.
Attn: Andy Rosemore
17290 Preston Rd., 3rd Fl.
Dallas, Texas 75252-5618
Phone: (214)380-0044
Toll-free: (800)486-3223
Fax: (214)380-1371

A small business investment corporation, minority enterprise small business investment corporation, and SBA guaranteed lender. No industry preferred.

Pro-Med Investment Corp.
17290 Preston Rd., Ste. 300
Dallas, Texas 75252
Phone: (214)380-0044
Fax: (214)380-1371

A minority enterprise small business investment company. Diversified industry preference.

Sevin Rosen Funds
13455 Noel Rd., Ste. 1670
Dallas, Texas 75240
Phone: (214)702-1100
Fax: (214)702-1103

Venture capital firm providing start-up and first stage financing. Industry preferences include information sciences and electronic sciences.

Southwest Enterprise Associates
14457 Gillis Rd.
Dallas, Texas 75244
Phone: (214)450-3894
Fax: (214)450-3899

Venture capital supplier. Concentrates on technology-based industries that have the potential for product innovation, rapid growth, and high profit margins. Investments range from $250,000 to $1.5 million. Past investments have been made in the following industries: computer software, medical and life sciences, computers and peripherals, communications, semiconductors, and defense electronics. Management must demonstrate intimate knowledge of its marketplace and have a well-defined strategy for achieving strong market penetration.

Stratford Capital Partners, L.P.
200 Crescent Ct., Ste. 1650
Dallas, Texas 75201
Phone: (214)740-7377
Fax: (214)740-7340
Michael D. Brown, President

Preferred Investment Size: $3 to $9 million. Investment Policies: Equity, sub debt with equity. Investment Types: Expansion, later stage,

acquisition. Industry Preferences: Manufacturing, distribution, diversified. Geographic Preferences: National.

Sullivan Enterprises
9130 Markville Dr.
PO Box 743803
Dallas, Texas 75374-3803
Phone: (214)414-5690

Venture capital firm providing refinancings and expansion, mezzanine, and leveraged buyouts financing. Areas of interest include manufacturing, service, retailing, wholesale and distribution.

Sunwestern Capital Corp.
12221 Merit Dr., Ste. 1300
Dallas, Texas 75251-2248
Phone: (214)239-5650
Fax: (214)701-0024

Small business investment corporation providing start-up, first stage, second stage, third stage and leveraged buyout financing.Areas of interest include computer peripherals, software, information services, biotechnology and telecommunications.

Tower Ventures, Inc.
N. Central Plaza 1, Ste. 710
12655 N. Central Expy.
Dallas, Texas 75243
Phone: (214)991-1597
Phone: (214)991-1647
Donald R. Lawhorne, President

Preferred Investment Size: Up to $500,000. Investment Policies: Loans and/or equity. Investment Types: Early stage, expansion, later stage.

Western Financial Capital Corp.
17290 Preston Rd., Ste. 300
Dallas, Texas 75252
Phone: (214)380-0044
Fax: (214)380-1371

A small business investment company. Provides financing to the medical industry.

Wingate Partners
750 N. St. Paul St., Ste. 1200
Dallas, Texas 75201
Phone: (214)720-1313
Fax: (214)871-8799

Venture capital firm providing mature stage financing. Areas of interest include manufacturing and distribution.

HCT Capital Corp.
4916 Camp Bowie Blvd., Ste. 200
Fort Worth, Texas 76107
Phone: (817)763-8706
Fax: (817)377-8049

A small business investment company. Diversified industry preference.

SBIC Partners, L.P.
201 Main St., Ste. 2302
Fort Worth, Texas 76102
Phone: (817)729-3222
Fax: (817)729-3226
Gregory Forrest, Manager
Jeffrey Brown, Manager

Preferred Investment Size: $2 to $5 million. Investment Policies: Equity. Investment Types: Expansion, later stage. Industry Preferences: Diversified. Geographic Preferences: National.

Acorn Ventures, Inc.
520 Post Oak Blvd., Ste. 130
Houston, Texas 77027
Phone: (713)622-9595

No industry preference.

Alliance Business Investment Co.
(Houston)
1221 McKinney Ste.3100
Houston, Texas 77010
Phone: (713)659-3131
Fax: (713)659-8070

A small business investment corporation.

Aspen Capital Ltd.
55 Waugh, Ste. 710
Houston, Texas 77007
Phone: (713)880-4494

A small business investment corporation. No industry preference.

The Catalyst Fund, Ltd.
3 Riverway, Ste. 770
Houston, Texas 77056
Phone: (713)623-8133
Fax: (713)623-0473

A small business investment company. Diversified industry preference.

Charter Venture Group, Inc.
2600 Citadel Plaza Dr., Ste. 600
PO Box 4525
Houston, Texas 77210-4525
Phone: (713)622-7500
Fax: (713)552-8446

A small business investment corporation. No industry preference.

Chen's Financial Group, Inc.
10101 Southwest Fwy., Ste. 370
Houston, Texas 77074
Phone: (713)772-8868
Fax: (713)772-2168

A minority enterprise small business investment corporation. Areas of interest include real estate, franchise restaurants, banking, and import/export industries.

Criterion Ventures
5 Post Oak Pk., Ste. 2650
Houston, Texas 77027
Phone: (713)627-9200
Fax: (713)627-9292

Venture capital fund. Raises venture capital. Interested in companies headquartered in the Sunbelt region. Areas of interest include telecommunications, biomedical, and specialty retail.

Cureton & Co., Inc.
1100 Louisiana, Ste. 3250
Houston, Texas 77002
Phone: (713)658-9806
Fax: (713)658-0476

Prefers oilfield service, environmental, electronics, manufacturing, and distribution.

Energy Assets, Inc.
4900 Republic Bank Center
700 Louisiana, Ste. 5000

Houston, Texas 77002
Phone: (713)236-9999
Toll-free: (800)933-5508

A small business investment corporation. Specializes in oil and gas energy industries.

High Technology Associates
1775 St. James Pl., Ste. 105
Houston, Texas 77056
Phone: (713)963-9300
Fax: (713)963-8341

Venture capital firm providing second stage and expansion financing. Areas of interest include biotechnology, chemicals, food processing and food processing machinery. Particularly interested in companies willing to establish operations in the Northern Netherlands.

Houston Partners, SBIC
Capital Center Penthouse, 8th Fl.
401 Louisiana
Houston, Texas 77002
Phone: (713)222-8600
Fax: (713)222-8932

A small business investment company. Diversified industry preference.

MESBIC Financial Corp.
401 Studewood Ste.201
Houston, Texas 77007
Phone: (713)869-8595
Fax: (713)869-4462

A minority enterprise small business investment corporation. Diversified industry preference, excluding real estate. Limited geographically to Houston.

MESBIC Financial Corp. of Houston
401 Studewood, Ste. 200
Houston, Texas 77007
Phone: (713)869-4061
Fax: (713)869-4462
Atillio Galli, President

Preferred Investment Size: $100,000 to $1 million. Investment Policies: Loans and equity investments.

Investment Types: Consolidated debt & preferred stock with warrants. Industry Preferences: Diversified - no real estate or gas and oil. Geographic Preferences: Houston.

Payne Webber, Inc.
700 Louisiana St., Ste.3700
Houston, Texas 77002
Phone: (713)236-3180
Fax: (713)236-3303

Penzoil
PO Box 2967
Houston, Texas 77252
Phone: (713)546-8910
Fax: (713)546-4154

A small business investment company. Diversified industry preference.

SBI Capital Corp.
PO Box 570368
Houston, Texas 77257-0368
Phone: (713)975-1188

A small business investment corporation. No industry preference; Texas businesses only.

Southern Orient Capital Corp.
2419 Fannin, Ste. 200
Houston, Texas 77002-9181
Phone: (713)225-3369

A minority enterprise small business investment corporation. No industry preference.

Tenneco Ventures, Inc.
PO Box 2511
Houston, Texas 77252
Phone: (713)757-8229
Fax: (713)651-1666

Venture capital supplier. Provides financing to small, early stage growth companies. Areas of interest include energy-related technologies, factory automation, biotechnology, and health care services. Prefers to invest in Texas-based companies, but will consider investments elsewhere within the United States. Investments range from $250,000 to $1 million;

will commit additional funds over several rounds of financing, and will work with other investors to provide larger financing.

Texas Commerce Investment Co.
Texas Commerce Bank Bldg., 30th Fl.
712 Main St.
Houston, Texas 77002
Phone: (713)236-4719

A small business investment corporation. No industry preference.

UNCO Ventures, Inc.
520 Post Oak Blvd., Ste. 130
Houston, Texas 77027
Phone: (713)622-9595
Fax: (713)622-9007

A small business investment company. Diversified industry preference.

United Oriental Capital Corp.
908 Town and Country Blvd., Ste. 310
Houston, Texas 77024-2207
Phone: (713)461-3909
Fax: (713)465-7559

A minority enterprise small business investment corporation. No industry preference.

Ventex Partners, Ltd.
1001 Fannin St., Ste. 1095
Houston, Texas 77002
Phone: (713)659-7860
Fax: (713)659-7855

A small business investment partnership providing later stage financing.

Capital Marketing Corp.
P.O. Box 1177
Keller, Texas 76244
Phone: (817)431-5767

A small business investment corporation.

Southwest Venture Partnerships
16414 St. Pedro, Ste. 1345
San Antonio, Texas 78232
Phone: (210)402-1200
Toll-free: (800)725-0867
Fax: (210)402-1221

Venture capital partnership. Invests in maturing companies located primarily in the southwest. Average investment is $1 million.

Victoria Capital Corp. (San Antonio)
First Capital Group of Texas
PO Box 15616
San Antonio, Texas 78212-8816
Phone: (210)736-4233
Fax: (210)736-5449

A small business investment corporation. No industry preference, but does not invest in oil, gas, and real estate industries.

Victoria Capital Corp. (Victoria)
1 O'Connor Plz.
Victoria, Texas 77902
Phone: (512)573-5151
Fax: (512)574-5236

A small business investment company. Diversified industry preference.

Woodlands Venture Partners L.P.
2170 Buckthome Pl., Ste. 170
The Woodlands, Texas 77380
Phone: (713)367-9999
Fax: (713)298-1295

Venture capital firm providing start-up, first stage, second stage and seed financing. Areas of interest include medical/biotechnology only.

Utah

Deseret Certified Development Corp.
7050 Union Park Center, No. 570
Midvale, Utah 84047
Phone: (801)566-1163
Fax: (801)566-1532

Maintains an SBA(504) loan program, designed for community development and job creation, and an intermediary loan program, through Farmer's Home Administration.

Deseret Certified Development Corp.
907 S. Orem Blvd.
Orem, Utah 84058-5011

Phone: (801)221-7772
Fax: (801)221-7775

Maintains an SBA(504) loan program, designed for community development and job creation, and an intermediary loan program, through Farmer's Home Administration.

First Security Business Investment Corp.
79 S. Main St., Ste. 800
Salt Lake City, Utah 84111
Phone: (801)246-5737
Fax: (801)246-5424
Louis D. Alder, Manager

Preferred Investment Size: $500,000 to $1 million. Investment Policies: Loans and/or equity. Investment Types: Expansion, later stage. Industry Preferences: Diversified. Geographic Preferences: West/Midwest.

Utah Technology Finance Corp.
177 E., 100 S.
Salt Lake City, Utah 84111
Phone: (801)364-4346
Fax: (801)364-4361

Assists the start-up and growth of emerging technology-based businesses and products.

Utah Ventures
419 Wakara Way, Ste. 206
Salt Lake City, Utah 84108
Phone: (801)583-5922
Fax: (801)583-4105

Invests in the life sciences at an early stage.

Wasatch Venture Corp.
1 S. Main St., Ste. 1000
Salt Lake City, Utah 84133
Phone: (801)524-8939
Fax: (801)524-8941
W. David Hemingway, Manager

Preferred Investment Size: $500,000. Investment Policies: Equity and debt. Investment Types: Early stage. Industry Preferences: High technology. Geographic Preferences: West, Midwest, Rocky.

Vermont

Queneska Capital Corp.
123 Church St.
Burlington, Vermont 05401
Phone: (802)865-1806
Fax: (802)865-1891

A small business investment company. Diversified industry preference.

Vermont Economic Development Authority
56 E. State St.
Montpelier, Vermont 05602
Phone: (802)223-7226
Fax: (802)223-4205

Several financial programs to assist small and medium-sized manufacturing firms in the state.

Vermont Economic Development Authority
Vermont Job Start
56 E. State St.
Montpelier, Vermont 05602
Phone: (802)229-5627
Fax: (802)223-4205

A state-funded economic opportunity program aimed at increasing self-employment by low-income Vermonters.

Green Mountain Capital, L.P.
RR 1 Box 1503
Waterbury, Vermont 05676
Phone: (802)244-8981
Fax: (802)244-8990

A small business investment company. Diversified industry preference.

Virgin Islands

Tri-Island Economic Development Council, Inc.
Box 838
St. Thomas, Virgin Islands 00804
Phone: (809)774-7215

Provides counseling, information, referrals, and management and technical assistance to help

strengthen existing businesses and expand the rate of development of new businesses.

Virginia

Metropolitan Capital Corp.
2550 Huntington Ave.
Alexandria, Virginia 22303
Phone: (703)550-0747

A small business investment corporation. Equity or loans with equity features. Does not invest in retail or real estate.

Continental SBIC
4141 N. Henderson Rd., Ste. 8
Arlington, Virginia 22203
Phone: (703)527-5200
Fax: (703)527-3700

A minority enterprise small business investment company. Diversified industry preference.

East West United Investment Co. (Falls Church)
200 Park Ave.
Falls Church, Virginia 22046-3107
Phone: (703)536-0268
Fax: (703)536-0619

A minority enterprise small business investment company. Diversified industry preference.

Rural America Fund, Inc.
Attention: Richard Balman
2201 Cooperative Way
Herndon, Virginia 22071
Phone: (703)709-6750
Fax: (703)709-6774

A small business investment company. Diversified industry preference.

East West United Investment Co. (Mc Lean)
1568 Spring Hill Rd., Ste. 100
Mc Lean, Virginia 22102
Phone: (703)442-0150
Fax: (703)442-0156
Dung Bui, President

Ewing, Monroe & Co.
901 E. Cary St., Ste. 1410
Richmond, Virginia 23219
Phone: (804)780-1900
Fax: (804)780-1901

A small business investment corporation. No industry preference.

Virginia Small Business Financing Authority
PO Box 798
Richmond, Virginia 23218
Phone: (804)371-8254
Fax: (804)225-3384

Assists small businesses in obtaining financing for development and expansion.

Walnut Capital Corp. (Vienna)
8000 Towers Crescent Dr., Ste. 1070
Vienna, Virginia 22182-2700
Phone: (703)448-3771
Fax: (703)448-7751

A small business investment corporation. No industry preference.

Washington

Cable and Howse Ventures (Bellevue)
777 108th Ave. NE, Ste. 2300
Bellevue, Washington 98004
Phone: (206)646-3030
Fax: (206)646-3041

Venture capital investor. Provides start-up and early stage financing to enterprises in the western United States, although a national perspective is maintained. Interests lie in proprietary or patentable technology. Investments range from $50,000 to $2 million.

Pacific Northwest Partners SBIC, L.P.
Ste. 800, Koll Center Bellevue
500 - 108th Ave., NE
Bellevue, Washington 98004
Phone: (206)646-7357
Fax: (206)646-7356
Theodore M Wight, Manager

Preferred Investment Size: $1,000,000. Investment Policies: Private equity investments. Invest-

ment Types: Seed Through later stage. Industry Preferences: Diversified, retail, healthcare, technology. Geographic Preferences: Pacific Northwest.

Materia Venture Associates, L.P.
3435 Carillon Pointe
Kirkland, Washington 98033
Phone: (206)822-4100
Fax: (206)827-4086

Prefers investing in advanced materials and related technologies.

Olympic Venture Partners (Kirkland)
2420 Carillon Pt.
Kirkland, Washington 98033-7353
Phone: (206)889-9192
Fax: (206)889-0152

Prefers to fund early stage, technology companies in the West.

Washington Department of Community Development
Community Development Finance (CDF) Program
900 Columbia St. SW
PO Box 8300
Olympia, Washington 98504-3800
Phone: (360)753-5630
Fax: (360)753-5630

Helps businesses and industries secure needed financing by combining private financial loans with federal and state loans.

Washington Department of Community Trade & Economic Development
Development Loan Fund
906 Columbia St. SW
PO Box 48300
Olympia, Washington 98504-8300
Phone: (360)753-5630
Fax: (360)586-2424

Provides capital for businesses in distressed areas to create new jobs, particularly for low and moderate income persons.

The Phoenix Partners
1000 2nd Ave., Ste. 3600
Seattle, Washington 98104

Phone: (206)624-8968
Fax: (206)624-1907

Prefers to invest in companies involved in biotechnology, health care, medical devices, computer software, semiconductors, and telecommunications.

Washington State Department of Community, Trade, and Economic Development
Industrial Revenue Bonds
2001 6th Ave., Ste. 2600
Seattle, Washington 98121
Phone: (360)464-7350
Fax: (360)464-7222

Issued to finance the acquisition, construction, enlargement, orimprovement of industrial development facilities.

West Virginia

Anker Capital Corp.
208 Capital St., Ste. 300
Charleston, West Virginia 25301
Phone: (304)344-1794
Fax: (304)344-1798
Thomas Loehr, Manager

Preferred Investment Size: $500,000. Investment Policies: Combination of debt and equity. Investment Types: Expansion, early stage, spin-off. Industry Preferences: Wood products, computer industry, manufacturing. Geographic Preferences: West Virginia, Ohio, Pennsylvania, Virginia, Maryland.

Shenandoah Venture Capital L.P.
208 Capital St., Ste. 300
Charleston, West Virginia 25301
Phone: (304)344-1796
Fax: (304)344-1798
Thomas E. Loehr, President

West Virginia Development Office
West Virginia Economic Development Authority
State Capitol Complex, Bldg. 6, Rm. 525
1018 Kanawha Blvd., E., Ste. 501

Charleston, West Virginia 25301-2827
Phone: (304)558-3650
Fax: (304)558-0206

Provides low-interest loans for land or building acquisition, building construction, and equipment purchases.

West Virginia Development Office
West Virginia SBA
504 Certified Development Corp.
State Capitol Complex, Bldg 6, Rm. 525
1018 Kanawha Blvd., Ste. 501
Charleston, West Virginia 25305
Phone: (304)558-3650
Fax: (304)558-0206

Provides long-term, fixed-rate loans for small and medium-sized firms.

WestVen Ltd. Partnership
208 Capitol St., Ste. 300
Charleston, West Virginia 25301
Phone: (304)344-1794
Fax: (304)344-1798
Thomas E. Loehr, President

Preferred Investment Size: $500,000. Investment Policies:Combination of debt and equity. Investment Types: Expansion, early stage, spin-off. Industry Preferences: Wood products, computer industry, manufacturing. Geographic Preferences: West Virginia, Ohio, Pennsylvania, Virginia, Maryland.

Wisconsin

Impact Seven, Inc.
651 Darvfield
Almena, Wisconsin 54805
Phone: (715)357-3334
Fax: (715)635-6233

Provides equity investment.

Bando-McGlocklin SBIC
13555 Bishops Ct., Ste. 205
Brookfield, Wisconsin 53005
Phone: (414)784-9010
Fax: (414)784-3426
George Schonath, Chief Executive Officer

Preferred Investment Size: $3,000,000. Investment Policies: Loans. Investment Types: Early stage, expansion, later stage. Industry Preferences: Diversified. Geographic Preferences: Midwest.

Polaris Capital Corp.
2525 N. 124th St., Ste.200
Brookfield, Wisconsin 53005-4614
Phone: (414)789-5780
Fax: (414)789-5799

A small business investment corporation. Prefers equity-type investments of up to $500,000, expansion stage companies, seasoned companies, and management buyouts. Diversified industry preference, including industrial, electronic products/equipment, and consumer and business products/services in Wisconsin and northern Illinois.

Madison Development Corp.
550 W. Washington Ave.
Madison, Wisconsin 53703
Phone: (608)256-2799
Fax: (608)256-1560

Provides loans of up to $150,000 to eligible businesses in Dane County for working capital, inventory, equipment, leasehold improvements, and business real estate.

Venture Investors of Wisconsin, Inc. (Madison)
565 Science Dr., Ste. A
Madison, Wisconsin 53711
Phone: (608)233-3070
Fax: (608)238-5120

Venture capital firm providing early-stage financing to Wisconsin-based companies with strong management teams. Areas of interest include biotechnology, software, analytical instruments, medical products, consumer products, and publishing industries.

Venture Investors of Wisconsin, Inc. (Milwaukee)
565 Science Dr., Ste. A

Madison, Wisconsin 53711
Phone: (414)298-3070

Providers of equity financing.

Wisconsin Business Development Finance Corp.
PO Box 2717
Madison, Wisconsin 53701
Phone: (608)258-8830
Fax: (608)258-1664

Provides small business financing for the purchase of land, buildings, machinery, equipment, and the construction and modernization of facilities.

Wisconsin Department of Development
Wisconsin Development Fund
123 W. Washington Ave.
PO Box 7970
Madison, Wisconsin 53707
Phone: (608)266-2742
Toll-free: (800)HELP-BUS
Fax: (608)264-6151

Wisconsin Housing and Economic Development Authority
Venture Capital Fund
Economic Development Analyst
1 S. Pinckney St., No. 500
PO Box 1728
Madison, Wisconsin 53701
Phone: (608)266-7884
Toll-free: (800)334-6873
Fax: (608)267-1099

Invests in new and existing businesses that are developing new products.

Wisconsin Innovation Network Foundation
PO Box 71
Madison, Wisconsin 53701-0071
Phone: (608)256-8348
Fax: (608)256-0333

Seeks to join people with marketing and sales ideas to those willing to finance them. Acts as a resource center for financing information; offers networking opportunities for business professionals, entrepreneurs, and small business owners at regular monthly meetings.

Capital Investment, Inc.
1009 W. Glen Oaks Ln., Ste. 103
Mequon, Wisconsin 53092
Phone: (414)241-0303
Fax: (414)241-8451
James R. Sanger, President

Preferred Investment Size: $500,000 to $1 million. Investment Policies: Subordinated debt with warrant. Investment Types: Expansion, later stage. Industry Preferences: Manufacturing and value-added distributors. Geographic Preferences: Midwest, national.

Banc One Venture Corp. (Milwaukee)
111 E. Wisconsin Ave.
Milwaukee, Wisconsin 53202
H. Wayne Foreman, President

Preferred Investment Size: $1 to $10 million. Investment Types: Later stage, expansion, LBO, MBO. Industry Preferences: Publishing, distribution, manufacturing, mail-order. Geographic Preferences: National.

Capital Investments, Inc.
700 N. Water St., Ste.235
Milwaukee, Wisconsin 53202
Phone: (414)278-7744
Toll-free: (800)345-6462
Fax: (414)278-8403

A small business investment corporation. Prefers later-stage companies located in the Midwest, involved in manufacturing and specialty distribution.

Future Value Venture, Inc.
330 G. Kilbourn Ave., Ste.711
Milwaukee, Wisconsin 53202
Phone: (414)278-0377
Fax: (414)278-7321

A minority enterprise small business investment corporation. Diversified industry preference. Minimum initial investment is $100,000.

Horizon Partners, Ltd.
225 E. Mason St., Ste. 600
Milwaukee, Wisconsin 53202
Phone: (414)271-2200
Fax: (414)271-4016

Providers of equity financing for low-to-medium technology industries.

InvestAmerica Venture Group, Inc. (Milwaukee)
600 E. Mason St., Ste.304
Milwaukee, Wisconsin 53202
Phone: (414)276-3839
Fax: (414)276-1885

A small business investment corporation. Prefers later-stage and acquisition financings of $1,000,000 to $3,000,000 with equity participation. Will not consider real estate investments.

Lubar and Co., Inc.
3380 Firstar Center
777 E. Wisconsin, Ste. 3380
Milwaukee, Wisconsin 53202
Phone: (414)291-9000
Fax: (414)291-9000

Private investment and management firm.

M & I Ventures Corp.
770 N. Water St.
Milwaukee, Wisconsin 53202
Phone: (414)765-7910
Toll-free: (800)342-2265
Fax: (414)765-7850

A small business investment corporation. Areas of interest include manufacturing, technology, electronics, health care, publishing, and communications industries. Average investment is from $1 million to $3 million.

MorAmerican Capital Corp. (Milwaukee)
600 E. Mason St., Ste. 304
Milwaukee, Wisconsin 53202
Phone: (414)276-3839
Fax: (414)276-1885

A small business investment company.

Wisconsin Venture Capital Fund
777 E. Wisconsin Ave., Ste. 3380
Milwaukee, Wisconsin 53202
Phone: (414)291-9000
Fax: (414)291-9061

WITECH Corp., Inc.
231 W. Michigan St.
PO Box 2949
Milwaukee, Wisconsin 53201
Phone: (414)347-1550
Fax: (414)221-4668

Venture capital firm.

Wind Point Partners (Racine)
420 3 Mile , Apt. B4
Racine, Wisconsin 53402
Phone: (414)639-3113
Fax: (414)632-5660

Venture capital firm.

Wyoming

Frontier Certified Development Co.
PO Box 3599
Casper, Wyoming 82602
Phone: (307)234-5351
Toll-free: (800)934-5351
Fax: (307)234-0501

Created by the Wyoming Industrial Development Corporation to provide expansion financing for Wyoming business.

Wyoming Industrial Development Corp.
PO Box 3599
Casper, Wyoming 82602
Phone: (307)234-5351
Toll-free: (800)934-5351
Fax: (307)234-0501

Administers SBA 7(A) and SBA(502) programs. Purchases the guaranteed portion of U.S. Small Business Administration and Farmers Home Administration Loans to small businesses to pool into a common fund that enables small businesses to obtain loans at more reasonable rates and terms.

Wyoming Department of Commerce
Economic and Community Development Division
New Business Retention and Financing
Barrett Bldg.
6109 Yellowstone
Cheyenne, Wyoming 82002
Phone: (307)777-6418
Fax: (307)777-6005

Appendix C - Glossary of Small Business Terms

Glossary of Small Business Terms

Absolute liability
Liability that is incurred due to product defects or negligent actions. Manufacturers or retail establishments are held responsible, even though the defect or action may not have been intentional or negligent.

ACE
See Active Corps of Executives

Accident and health benefits
Benefits offered to employees and their families in order to offset the costs associated with accidental death, accidental injury, or sickness.

Account statement
A record of transactions, including payments, new debt, and deposits, incurred during a defined period of time.

Accounting system
System capturing the costs of all employees and/or machinery included in business expenses.

Accounts payable
See Trade credit

Accounts receivable
Unpaid accounts which arise from unsettled claims and transactions from the sale of a company's products or services to its customers.

Active Corps of Executives (ACE)
(See also Service Corps of Retired Executives)
A group of volunteers for a management assistance program of the U.S. Small Business Administration; volunteers provide one-on-one counseling and teach workshops and seminars for small firms.

ADA
See Americans with Disabilities Act

Adaptation
The process whereby an invention is modified to meet the needs of users.

Adaptive engineering
The process whereby an invention is modified to meet the manufacturing and commercial requirements of a targeted market.

Adverse selection
The tendency for higher-risk individuals to purchase health care and more comprehensive plans, resulting in increased costs.

Advertising
A marketing tool used to capture public attention and influence purchasing decisions for a product or service. Utilizes various forms of media to generate consumer response, such as flyers, magazines, newspapers, radio, and television.

Age discrimination
The denial of the rights and privileges of employment based solely on the age of an individual.

Agency costs
Costs incurred to insure that the lender or investor maintains control over assets while allowing the borrower or entrepreneur to use them. Monitoring and information costs are the two major types of agency costs.

Agribusiness
The production and sale of commodities and products from the commercial farming industry.

America Online
(See also Prodigy)
An online service which is accessible by computer modem. The service features Internet access, bulletin boards, online periodicals, electronic mail, and other services for subscribers.

Americans with Disabilities Act (ADA)
Law designed to ensure equal access and opportunity to handicapped persons.

Annual report
(See also Securities and Exchange Commission)
Yearly financial report prepared by a business that adheres to the requirements set forth by the Securities and Exchange Commission (SEC).

Antitrust immunity
(See also Collective ratemaking)
Exemption from prosecution under antitrust laws. In the transportation industry, firms with antitrust immunity are

permitted—under certain conditions—to set schedules and sometimes prices for the public benefit.

Applied research
Scientific study targeted for use in a product or process.

Asians
A minority category used by the U.S. Bureau of the Census to represent a diverse group that includes Aleuts, Eskimos, American Indians, Asian Indians, Chinese, Japanese, Koreans, Vietnamese, Filipinos, Hawaiians, and other Pacific Islanders.

Assets
Anything of value owned by a company.

Audit
The verification of accounting records and business procedures conducted by an outside accounting service.

Average cost
Total production costs divided by the quantity produced.

Balance Sheet
A financial statement listing the total assets and liabilities of a company at a given time.

Bankruptcy
(See also Chapter 7 of the 1978 Bankruptcy Act; Chapter 11 of the 1978 Bankruptcy Act)
The condition in which a business cannot meet its debt obligations and petitions a federal district court either for reorganization of its debts (Chapter 11) or for liquidation of its assets (Chapter 7).

Basic research
Theoretical scientific exploration not targeted to application.

Basket clause
A provision specifying the amount of public pension funds that may be placed in investments not included on a state's legal list (see separate citation).

BBS
See Bulletin Board Service

BDC
See Business development corporation

Benefit
Various services, such health care, flextime, day care, insurance, and vacation, offered to employees as part of a hiring package. Typically subsidized in whole or in part by the business.

BIDCO
See Business and industrial development company

Billing cycle
A system designed to evenly distribute customer billing throughout the month, preventing clerical backlogs.

Birth
See Business birth

Blue chip security
A low-risk, low-yield security representing an interest in a very stable company.

Blue sky laws
A general term that denotes various states' laws regulating securities.

Bond
(See also General obligation bond; Taxable bonds; Treasury bonds)
A written instrument executed by a bidder or contractor (the principal) and a second party (the surety or sureties) to assure fulfillment of the principal's obligations to a third party (the obligee or government) identified in the bond. If the principal's obligations are not met, the bond assures payment to the extent stipulated of any loss sustained by the obligee.

Bonding requirements
Terms contained in a bond (see separate citation).

Bonus
An amount of money paid to an employee as a reward for achieving certain business goals or objectives.

Brainstorming
A group session where employees contribute their ideas for solving a problem or meeting a company objective without fear of retribution or ridicule.

Brand name
The part of a brand, trademark, or service mark that can be spoken. It can be a word, letter, or group of words or letters.

Bridge financing
A short-term loan made in expectation of intermediate-term or long-term financing. Can be used when a company plans to go public in the near future.

Broker
One who matches resources available for innovation with those who need them.

Budget
An estimate of the spending necessary to complete a project or offer a service in comparison to cash-on-hand and expected earnings for the coming year, with an emphasis on cost control.

Bulletin Board Service (BBS)
An online service enabling users to communicate with each other about specific topics.

Business birth
The formation of a new establishment or enterprise. The appearance of a new establishment or enterprise in the Small Business Data Base (see separate citation).

Business conditions
Outside factors that can affect the financial performance of a business.

Business contractions
The number of establishments that have decreased in employment during a specified time.

Business cycle
A period of economic recession and recovery. These cycles vary in duration.

Business death
The voluntary or involuntary closure of a firm or establishment. The disappearance of an establishment or enterprise from the Small Business Data Base (see separate citation).

Business development corporation (BDC)
A business financing agency, usually composed of the financial institutions in an area or state, organized to assist in financing businesses unable to obtain assistance through normal channels; the risk is spread among various members of the business development corporation, and interest rates may vary somewhat from those charged by member institutions. A venture capital firm in which shares of ownership are publicly held and to which the Investment Act of 1940 applies.

Business dissolution
For enumeration purposes, the absence of a business that was present in the prior time period from any current record.

Business entry
See Business birth

Business ethics
Moral values and principles espoused by members of the business community as a guide to fair and honest business practices.

Business exit
See Business death

Business expansions
The number of establishments that added employees during a specified time.

Business failure
Closure of a business causing a loss to at least one creditor.

Business format franchising
(See also Franchising)
The purchase of the name, trademark, and an ongoing business plan of the parent corporation or franchisor by the franchisee.

Business and industrial development company (BIDCO)
A private, for-profit financing corporation chartered by the state to provide both equity and long-term debt capital to small business owners (see separate citations for equity and debt capital).

Business license
A legal authorization issued by municipal and state governments and required for business operations.

Business name
(See also Business license; Trademark)
Enterprises must register their business names with local governments usually on a "doing business as" (DBA) form. (This name is sometimes referred to as a "fictional name.") The procedure is part of the business licensing process and prevents any other business from using that same name for a similar business in the same locality.

Business norms
See Financial ratios

Business permit
See Business license

Business plan
A document that spells out a company's expected course of action for a specified period, usually including a detailed listing and analysis of risks and uncertainties. For the small business, it should examine the proposed products, the market, the industry, the management policies, the marketing policies, production needs, and financial needs. Frequently, it is used as a prospectus for potential investors and lenders.

Business proposal
See Business plan

Business service firm
An establishment primarily engaged in rendering services to other business organizations on a fee or contract basis.

Business start
For enumeration purposes, a business with a name or similar designation that did not exist in a prior time period.

Cafeteria plan
See Flexible benefit plan

Capacity
Level of a firm's, industry's, or nation's output corresponding to full practical utilization of available resources.

Capital
Assets less liabilities, representing the ownership interest in a business. A stock of accumulated goods, especially at a specified time and in contrast to income received during a specified time period. Accumulated goods devoted to production. Accumulated possessions calculated to bring income.

Capital expenditure
Expenses incurred by a business for improvements that will depreciate over time.

Capital gain
The monetary difference between the purchase price and the selling price of capital. Capital gains are taxed at a rate of 28% by the federal government.

Capital intensity
(See also Debt capital; Equity midrisk venture capital; Informal capital; Internal capital; Owner's capital; Secondhand capital; Seed capital; Venture capital)
The relative importance of capital in the production process, usually expressed as the ratio of capital to labor but also sometimes as the ratio of capital to output.

Capital resource
The equipment, facilities and labor used to create products and services.

Caribbean Basin Initiative
An interdisciplinary program to support commerce among the businesses in the nations of the Caribbean Basin and the United States. Agencies involved include: the Agency for International Development, the U.S. Small Business Administration, the International Trade Administration of the U.S. Department of Commerce, and various private sector groups.

Catastrophic care
Medical and other services for acute and long-term illnesses that cost more than insurance coverage limits or that cost the amount most families may be expected to pay with their own resources.

CDC
See Certified development corporation

CD-ROM
Compact disc with read-only memory used to store large amounts of digitized data.

Certified development corporation (CDC)
A local area or statewide corporation or authority (for profit or nonprofit) that packages U.S. Small Business Administration (SBA), bank, state, and/or private money into financial assistance for existing business capital improvements. The SBA holds the second lien on its maximum share of 40 percent involvement. Each state has at least one certified development corporation. This program is called the SBA 504 Program.

Certified lenders
Banks that participate in the SBA guaranteed loan program (see separate citation). Such banks must have a good track record with the U.S. Small Business Administration (SBA) and must agree to certain conditions set forth by the agency. In return, the SBA agrees to process any guaranteed loan application within three business days.

Champion
An advocate for the development of an innovation.

Channel of distribution
The means used to transport merchandise from the manufacturer to the consumer.

Chapter 7 of the 1978 Bankruptcy Act
Provides for a court-appointed trustee who is responsible for liquidating a company's assets in order to settle outstanding debts.

Chapter 11 of the 1978 Bankruptcy Act
Allows the business owners to retain control of the company while working with their creditors to reorganize their finances and establish better business practices to prevent liquidation of assets.

Closely held corporation
A corporation in which the shares are held by a few persons, usually officers, employees, or others close to the management; these shares are rarely offered to the public.

Code of Federal Regulations
Codification of general and permanent rules of the federal government published in the Federal Register.

Code sharing
See Computer code sharing

Coinsurance
(See also Cost sharing)
Upon meeting the deductible payment, health insurance participants may be required to make additional health care cost-sharing payments. Coinsurance is a payment of a fixed percentage of the cost of each service; copayment is usually a fixed amount to be paid with each service.

Collateral
Securities, evidence of deposit, or other property pledged by a borrower to secure repayment of a loan.

Collective ratemaking
(See also Antitrust immunity)
The establishment of uniform charges for services by a group of businesses in the same industry.

Commercial insurance plan
See Underwriting

Commercial loans
Short-term renewable loans used to finance specific capital needs of a business.

Commercialization
The final stage of the innovation process, including production and distribution.

Common stock
The most frequently used instrument for purchasing ownership in private or public companies. Common stock generally carries the right to vote on certain corporate actions and may pay dividends, although it rarely does in venture investments. In liquidation, common stockholders are the last to share in the proceeds from the sale of a corporation's assets; bondholders and preferred shareholders have priority. Common stock is often used in first-round start-up financing.

Community development corporation
A corporation established to develop economic programs for a community and, in most cases, to provide financial support for such development.

Competitor
A business whose product or service is marketed for the same purpose/use and to the same consumer group as the product or service of another.

Computer code sharing
An arrangement whereby flights of a regional airline are identified by the two-letter code of a major carrier in the computer reservation system to help direct passengers to new regional carriers.

Consignment
A merchandising agreement, usually referring to second-hand shops, where the dealer pays the owner of an item a percentage of the profit when the item is sold.

Consortium
A coalition of organizations such as banks and corporations for ventures requiring large capital resources.

Consultant
An individual that is paid by a business to provide advice and expertise in a particular area.

Consumer price index
A measure of the fluctuation in prices between two points in time.

Consumer research
Research conducted by a business to obtain information about existing or potential consumer markets.

Continuation coverage
Health coverage offered for a specified period of time to employees who leave their jobs and to their widows, divorced spouses, or dependents.

Contractions
See Business contractions

Convertible preferred stock
A class of stock that pays a reasonable dividend and is convertible into common stock (see separate citation). Generally the convertible feature may only be exercised after being held for a stated period of time. This arrangement is usually considered second-round financing when a company needs equity to maintain its cash flow.

Convertible securities
A feature of certain bonds, debentures, or preferred stocks that allows them to be exchanged by the owner for another class of securities at a future date and in accordance with any other terms of the issue.

Copayment
See Coinsurance

Copyright
A legal form of protection available to creators and authors to safeguard their works from unlawful use or

claim of ownership by others. Copyrights may be acquired for works of art, sculpture, music, and published or unpublished manuscripts. All copyrights should be registered at the Copyright Office of the Library of Congress.

Corporate financial ratios
(See also Industry financial ratios)
The relationship between key figures found in a company's financial statement expressed as a numeric value. Used to evaluate risk and company performance. Also known as Financial averages, Operating ratios, and Business ratios.

Corporation
A legal entity, chartered by a state or the federal government, recognized as a separate entity having its own rights, privileges, and liabilities distinct from those of its members.

Cost containment
Actions taken by employers and insurers to curtail rising health care costs; for example, increasing employee cost sharing (see separate citation), requiring second opinions, or preadmission screening.

Cost sharing
The requirement that health care consumers contribute to their own medical care costs through deductibles and coinsurance (see separate citations). Cost sharing does not include the amounts paid in premiums. It is used to control utilization of services; for example, requiring a fixed amount to be paid with each health care service.

Cottage industry
(See also Home-based business)
Businesses based in the home in which the family members are the labor force and family-owned equipment is used to process the goods.

Credit Rating
A letter or number calculated by an organization (such as Dun & Bradstreet) to represent the ability and disposition of a business to meet its financial obligations.

Customer service
Various techniques used to ensure the satisfaction of a customer.

Cyclical peak
The upper turning point in a business cycle.

Cyclical trough
The lower turning point in a business cycle.

DBA
See Business name

Death
See Business death

Debenture
A certificate given as acknowledgment of a debt (see separate citation) secured by the general credit of the issuing corporation. A bond, usually without security, issued by a corporation and sometimes convertible to common stock.

Debt
(See also Long-term debt; Mid-term debt; Securitized debt; Short-term debt)
Something owed by one person to another. Financing in which a company receives capital that must be repaid; no ownership is transferred.

Debt capital
Business financing that normally requires periodic interest payments and repayment of the principal within a specified time.

Debt financing
See Debt capital

Debt securities
Loans such as bonds and notes that provide a specified rate of return for a specified period of time.

Deductible
A set amount that an individual must pay before any benefits are received.

Demand shock absorbers
A term used to describe the role that some small firms play by expanding their output levels to accommodate a transient surge in demand.

Demographics
Statistics on various markets, including age, income, and education, used to target specific products or services to appropriate consumer groups.

Demonstration
Showing that a product or process has been modified sufficiently to meet the needs of users.

Deregulation
The lifting of government restrictions; for example, the lifting of government restrictions on the entry of new businesses, the expansion of services, and the setting of prices in particular industries.

Desktop Publishing
Using personal computers and specialized software to produce camera-ready copy for publications.

Disaster loans
Various types of physical and economic assistance available to individuals and businesses through the U.S. Small Business Administration (SBA). This is the only SBA loan program available for residential purposes.

Discrimination
The denial of the rights and privileges of employment based on factors such as age, race, religion, or gender.

Diseconomies of scale
The condition in which the costs of production increase faster than the volume of production.

Dissolution
See Business dissolution

Distribution
Delivering a product or process to the user.

Distributor
One who delivers merchandise to the user.

Diversified company
A company whose products and services are used by several different markets.

Doing business as (DBA)
See Business name

Dow Jones
An information services company that publishes the Wall Street Journal and other sources of financial information.

Dow Jones Industrial Average
An indicator of stock market performance.

Earned income
A tax term that refers to wages and salaries earned by the recipient, as opposed to monies earned through interest and dividends.

Economic efficiency
The use of productive resources to the fullest practical extent in the provision of the set of goods and services that is most preferred by purchasers in the economy.

Economic indicators
Statistics used to express the state of the economy. These include the length of the average work week, the rate of unemployment, and stock prices.

Economically disadvantaged
See Socially and economically disadvantaged

Economies of scale
See Scale economies

EEOC
See Equal Employment Opportunity Commission

8(a) Program
A program authorized by the Small Business Act that directs federal contracts to small businesses owned and operated by socially and economically disadvantaged individuals.

Electronic mail (e-mail)
The electronic transmission of mail via phone lines.

E-mail
See Electronic mail

Employee leasing.
A contract by which employers arrange to have their workers hired by a leasing company and then leased back to them for a management fee. The leasing company typically assumes the administrative burden of payroll and provides a benefit package to the workers.

Employee tenure
The length of time an employee works for a particular employer.

Employer identification number
The business equivalent of a social security number. Assigned by the U.S. Internal Revenue Service.

Enterprise
An aggregation of all establishments owned by a parent company. An enterprise may consist of a single, independent establishment or include subsidiaries and other branches under the same ownership and control.

Enterprise zone
A designated area, usually found in inner cities and other areas with significant unemployment, where businesses receive tax credits and other incentives to entice them to establish operations there.

Entrepreneur
A person who takes the risk of organizing and operating a new business venture.

Entry
See Business entry

Equal Employment Opportunity Commission (EEOC)
A federal agency that ensures nondiscrimination in the hiring and firing practices of a business.

Equal opportunity employer
An employer who adheres to the standards set by the Equal Employment Opportunity Commission (see separate citation).

Equity
(See also Common Stock; Equity midrisk venture capital)
The ownership interest. Financing in which partial or total ownership of a company is surrendered in exchange for capital. An investor's financial return comes from dividend payments and from growth in the net worth of the business.

Equity capital
See Equity; Equity midrisk venture capital

Equity financing
See Equity; Equity midrisk venture capital

Equity midrisk venture capital
An unsecured investment in a company. Usually a purchase of ownership interest in a company that occurs in the later stages of a company's development.

Equity partnership
A limited partnership arrangement for providing start-up and seed capital to businesses.

Equity securities
See Equity

Equity-type
Debt financing subordinated to conventional debt.

Establishment
A single-location business unit that may be independent (a single-establishment enterprise) or owned by a parent enterprise.

Establishment and Enterprise Microdata File
See U.S. Establishment and Enterprise Microdata File

Establishment birth
See Business birth

Establishment Longitudinal Microdata File
See U.S. Establishment Longitudinal Microdata File

Ethics
See Business ethics

Evaluation
Determining the potential success of translating an invention into a product or process.

Exit
See Business exit

Experience rating
See Underwriting *Export*
A product sold outside of the country.

Export license
A general or specific license granted by the U.S. Department of Commerce required of anyone wishing to export goods. Some restricted articles need approval from the U.S. Departments of State, Defense, or Energy.

Failure
See Business failure

Fair share agreement
(See also Franchising)
An agreement reached between a franchisor and a minority business organization to extend business ownership to minorities by either reducing the amount of capital required or by setting aside certain marketing areas for minority business owners.

Feasibility study
A study to determine the likelihood that a proposed product or development will fulfill the objectives of a particular investor.

Federal Trade Commission (FTC)
Federal agency that promotes free enterprise and competition within the U.S.

Federal Trade Mark Act of 1946
See Lanham Act

Fictional name
See Business name

Fiduciary
An individual or group that hold assets in trust for a beneficiary.

Financial analysis
The techniques used to determine money needs in a business. Techniques include ratio analysis, calculation of return on investment, guides for measuring profitability, and break-even analysis to determine ultimate success.

Financial intermediary

A financial institution that acts as the intermediary between borrowers and lenders. Banks, savings and loan associations, finance companies, and venture capital companies are major financial intermediaries in the United States.

Financial ratios

See Corporate financial ratios; Industry financial ratios

Financial statement

A written record of business finances, including balance sheets and profit and loss statements.

Financing

See First-stage financing; Second-stage financing; Third-stage financing

First-stage financing

(See also Second-stage financing; Third-stage financing) Financing provided to companies that have expended their initial capital, and require funds to start full-scale manufacturing and sales. Also known as First-round financing.

Fiscal year

Any twelve-month period used by businesses for accounting purposes.

504 Program

See Certified development corporation

Flexible benefit plan

A plan that offers a choice among cash and/or qualified benefits such as group term life insurance, accident and health insurance, group legal services, dependent care assistance, and vacations.

FOB

See Free on board

Format franchising

See Business format franchising; Franchising

401(k) plan

A financial plan where employees contribute a percentage of their earnings to a fund that is invested in stocks, bonds, or money markets for the purpose of saving money for retirement.

Four Ps

Marketing terms referring to Product, Price, Place, and Promotion.

Franchising

A form of licensing by which the owner—the franchisor—distributes or markets a product, method, or service through affiliated dealers called franchisees. The product, method, or service being marketed is identified by a brand name, and the franchisor maintains control over the marketing methods employed. The franchisee is often given exclusive access to a defined geographic area.

Free on board (FOB)

A pricing term indicating that the quoted price includes the cost of loading goods into transport vessels at a specified place.

Frictional unemployment

See Unemployment

FTC

See Federal Trade Commission

Fulfillment

The systems necessary for accurate delivery of an ordered item, including subscriptions and direct marketing.

Full-time workers

Generally, those who work a regular schedule of more than 35 hours per week.

Garment registration number

A number that must appear on every garment sold in the U.S. to indicate the manufacturer of the garment, which may or may not be the same as the label under which the garment is sold. The U.S. Federal Trade Commission assigns and regulates garment registration numbers.

Gatekeeper

A key contact point for entry into a network.

GDP

See Gross domestic product

General obligation bond

A municipal bond secured by the taxing power of the municipality. The Tax Reform Act of 1986 limits the purposes for which such bonds may be issued and establishes volume limits on the extent of their issuance.

GNP

See Gross national product

Good Housekeeping Seal

Seal appearing on products that signifies the fulfillment of the standards set by the Good Housekeeping Institute to protect consumer interests.

Goods sector
All businesses producing tangible goods, including agriculture, mining, construction, and manufacturing businesses.

GPO
See Gross product originating

Gross domestic product (GDP)
The part of the nation's gross national product (see separate citation) generated by private business using resources from within the country.

Gross national product (GNP)
The most comprehensive single measure of aggregate economic output. Represents the market value of the total output of goods and services produced by a nation's economy.

Gross product originating (GPO)
A measure of business output estimated from the income or production side using employee compensation, profit income, net interest, capital consumption, and indirect business taxes.

HAL
See Handicapped assistance loan program

Handicapped assistance loan program (HAL)
Low-interest direct loan program through the U.S. Small Business Administration (SBA) for handicapped persons. The SBA requires that these persons demonstrate that their disability is such that it is impossible for them to secure employment, thus making it necessary to go into their own business to make a living.

Health maintenance organization (HMO)
Organization of physicians and other health care professionals that provides health services to subscribers and their dependents on a prepaid basis.

Health provider
An individual or institution that gives medical care. Under Medicare, an institutional provider is a hospital, skilled nursing facility, home health agency, or provider of certain physical therapy services.

Hispanic
A person of Cuban, Mexican, Puerto Rican, Latin American (Central or South American), European Spanish, or other Spanish-speaking origin or ancestry.

HMO
See Health maintenance organization

Home-based business
(See also Cottage industry)
A business with an operating address that is also a residential address (usually the residential address of the proprietor).

Hub-and-spoke system
A system in which flights of an airline from many different cities (the spokes) converge at a single airport (the hub). After allowing passengers sufficient time to make connections, planes then depart for different cities.

Human Resources Management
A business program designed to oversee recruiting, pay, benefits, and other issues related to the company's work force, including planning to determine the optimal use of labor to increase production, thereby increasing profit.

Idea
An original concept for a new product or process.

Import
Products produced outside the country in which they are consumed.

Income
Money or its equivalent, earned or accrued, resulting from the sale of goods and services.

Income statement
A financial statement that lists the profits and losses of a company at a given time.

Incorporation
The filing of a certificate of incorporation with a state's secretary of state, thereby limiting the business owner's liability.

Incubator
A facility designed to encourage entrepreneurship and minimize obstacles to new business formation and growth, particularly for high-technology firms, by housing a number of fledgling enterprises that share an array of services, such as meeting areas, secretarial services, accounting, research library, on-site financial and management counseling, and word processing facilities.

Independent contractor
An individual considered self-employed (see separate citation) and responsible for paying Social Security taxes and income taxes on earnings.

Indirect health coverage
Health insurance obtained through another individual's health care plan; for example, a spouse's employer-sponsored plan.

Industrial development authority
The financial arm of a state or other political subdivision established for the purpose of financing economic development in an area, usually through loans to non-profit organizations, which in turn provide facilities for manufacturing and other industrial operations.

Industry financial ratios
(See also Corporate financial ratios)
Corporate financial ratios averaged for a specified industry. These are used for comparison purposes and reveal industry trends and identify differences between the performance of a specific company and the performance of its industry. Also known as Industrial averages, Industry ratios, Financial averages, and Business or Industrial norms.

Inflation
Increases in volume of currency and credit, generally resulting in a sharp and continuing rise in price levels.

Informal capital
Financing from informal, unorganized sources; includes informal debt capital such as trade credit or loans from friends and relatives and equity capital from informal investors.

Initial public offering (IPO)
A corporation's first offering of stock to the public.

Innovation
The introduction of a new idea into the marketplace in the form of a new product or service or an improvement in organization or process.

Intellectual property
Any idea or work that can be considered proprietary in nature and is thus protected from infringement by others.

Internal capital
Debt or equity financing obtained from the owner or through retained business earnings.

Internet
A government-designed computer network that contains large amounts of information and is accessible through various vendors for a fee.

Intrapreneurship
The state of employing entrepreneurial principles to nonentrepreneurial situations.

Invention
The tangible form of a technological idea, which could include a laboratory prototype, drawings, formulas, etc.

IPO
See Initial public offering

Job description
The duties and responsibilities required in a particular position.

Job tenure
A period of time during which an individual is continuously employed in the same job.

Joint marketing agreements
Agreements between regional and major airlines, often involving the coordination of flight schedules, fares, and baggage transfer. These agreements help regional carriers operate at lower cost.

Joint venture
Venture in which two or more people combine efforts in a particular business enterprise, usually a single transaction or a limited activity, and agree to share the profits and losses jointly or in proportion to their contributions.

Keogh plan
Designed for self-employed persons and unincorporated businesses as a tax-deferred pension account.

Labor force
Civilians considered eligible for employment who are also willing and able to work.

Labor force participation rate
The civilian labor force as a percentage of the civilian population.

Labor intensity
(See also Capital intensity)
The relative importance of labor in the production process, usually measured as the capital-labor ratio; i.e., the ratio of units of capital (typically, dollars of tangible assets) to the number of employees. The higher the capital-labor ratio exhibited by a firm or industry, the lower the capital intensity of that firm or industry is said to be.

Labor surplus area
An area in which there exists a high unemployment rate. In procurement (see separate citation), extra points are given to firms in counties that are designated a labor surplus area; this information is requested on procurement bid sheets.

Labor union
An organization of similarly-skilled workers who collectively bargain with management over the conditions of employment.

Laboratory prototype
See Prototype

LAN
See Local Area Network

Lanham Act
Refers to the Federal Trade Mark Act of 1946. Protects registered trademarks, trade names, and other service marks used in commerce.

Large business-dominated industry
Industry in which a minimum of 60 percent of employment or sales is in firms with more than 500 workers.

LBO
See Leveraged buy-out

Leader pricing
A reduction in the price of a good or service in order to generate more sales of that good or service.

Legal list
A list of securities selected by a state in which certain institutions and fiduciaries (such as pension funds, insurance companies, and banks) may invest. Securities not on the list are not eligible for investment. Legal lists typically restrict investments to high quality securities meeting certain specifications. Generally, investment is limited to U.S. securities and investment-grade blue chip securities (see separate citation).

Leveraged buy-out (LBO)
The purchase of a business or a division of a corporation through a highly leveraged financing package.

Liability
An obligation or duty to perform a service or an act. Also defined as money owed.

License
(See also Business license)
A legal agreement granting to another the right to use a technological innovation.

Limited partnerships
See Venture capital limited partnerships

Liquidity
The ability to convert a security into cash promptly.

Loans
See Commercial loans; Disaster loans; SBA direct loans; SBA guaranteed loans; SBA special lending institution categories

Local Area Network (LAN)
Computer networks contained within a single building or small area; used to facilitate the sharing of information.

Local development corporation
An organization, usually made up of local citizens of a community, designed to improve the economy of the area by inducing business and industry to locate and expand there. A local development corporation establishes a capability to finance local growth.

Long-haul rates
Rates charged by a transporter in which the distance traveled is more than 800 miles.

Long-term debt
An obligation that matures in a period that exceeds five years.

Low-grade bond
A corporate bond that is rated below investment grade by the major rating agencies (Standard and Poor's, Moody's).

Macro-efficiency
(See also Economic efficiency)
Efficiency as it pertains to the operation of markets and market systems.

Managed care
A cost-effective health care program initiated by employers whereby low-cost health care is made available to the employees in return for exclusive patronage to program doctors.

Management and technical assistance
A term used by many programs to mean business (as opposed to technological) assistance.

Management Assistance Programs
See SBA Management Assistance Programs

Mandated benefits
Specific treatments, providers, or individuals required by law to be included in commercial health plans.

Market evaluation
The use of market information to determine the sales potential of a specific product or process.

Market failure
The situation in which the workings of a competitive market do not produce the best results from the point of view of the entire society.

Market information
Data of any type that can be used for market evaluation, which could include demographic data, technology forecasting, regulatory changes, etc.

Market research
A systematic collection, analysis, and reporting of data about the market and its preferences, opinions, trends, and plans; used for corporate decision-making.

Market share
In a particular market, the percentage of sales of a specific product.

Marketing
Promotion of goods or services through various media.

Master Establishment List (MEL)
A list of firms in the United States developed by the U.S. Small Business Administration; firms can be selected by industry, region, state, standard metropolitan statistical area (see separate citation), county, and zip code.

Maturity
(See also Term)
The date upon which the principal or stated value of a bond or other indebtedness becomes due and payable.

Medicaid (Title XIX)
A federally aided, state-operated and administered program that provides medical benefits for certain low-income persons in need of health and medical care who are eligible for one of the government's welfare cash payment programs, including the aged, the blind, the disabled, and members of families with dependent children where one parent is absent, incapacitated, or unemployed.

Medicare (Title XVIII)
A nationwide health insurance program for disabled and aged persons. Health insurance is available to insured persons without regard to income. Monies from payroll taxes cover hospital insurance and monies from general revenues and beneficiary premiums pay for supplementary medical insurance.

MEL
See Master Establishment List

MESBIC
See Minority enterprise small business investment corporation

MET
See Multiple employer trust

Metropolitan statistical area (MSA)
A means used by the government to define large population centers that may transverse different governmental jurisdictions. For example, the Washington, D.C. MSA includes the District of Columbia and contiguous parts of Maryland and Virginia because all of these geopolitical areas comprise one population and economic operating unit.

Mezzanine financing
See Third-stage financing

Micro-efficiency
(See also Economic efficiency)
Efficiency as it pertains to the operation of individual firms.

Microdata
Information on the characteristics of an individual business firm.

Mid-term debt
An obligation that matures within one to five years.

Midrisk venture capital
See Equity midrisk venture capital

Minimum premium plan
A combination approach to funding an insurance plan aimed primarily at premium tax savings. The employer self-funds a fixed percentage of estimated monthly claims and the insurance company insures the excess.

Minimum wage
The lowest hourly wage allowed by the federal government.

Minority Business Development Agency
Contracts with private firms throughout the nation to sponsor Minority Business Development Centers which provide minority firms with advice and technical assistance on a fee basis.

Minority Enterprise Small Business Investment Corporation (MESBIC)
A federally funded private venture capital firm licensed by the U.S. Small Business Administration to provide capital to minority-owned businesses (see separate citation).

Minority-owned business
Businesses owned by those who are socially or economically disadvantaged (see separate citation).

Mom and Pop business
A small store or enterprise having limited capital, principally employing family members.

Moonlighter
A wage-and-salary worker with a side business.

MSA
See Metropolitan statistical area

Multi-employer plan
A health plan to which more than one employer is required to contribute and that may be maintained through a collective bargaining agreement and required to meet standards prescribed by the U.S. Department of Labor.

Multimedia
The use of several types of media to promote a product or service. Also, refers to the use of several different types of media (sight, sound, pictures, text) in a CD-ROM (see separate citation) product.

Multiple employer trust (MET)
A self-funded benefit plan generally geared toward small employers sharing a common interest.

NAFTA
See North American Free Trade Agreement

NASDAQ
See National Association of Securities Dealers Automated Quotations

National Association of Securities Dealers Automated Quotations
Provides price quotes on over-the-counter securities as well as securities listed on the New York Stock Exchange.

National income
Aggregate earnings of labor and property arising from the production of goods and services in a nation's economy.

Net assets
See Net worth

Net income
The amount remaining from earnings and profits after all expenses and costs have been met or deducted. Also known as Net earnings.

Net profit
Money earned after production and overhead expenses (see separate citations) have been deducted.

Net worth
(See also Capital)
The difference between a company's total assets and its total liabilities.

Network
A chain of interconnected individuals or organizations sharing information and/or services.

New York Stock Exchange (NYSE)
The oldest stock exchange in the U.S. Allows for trading in stocks, bonds, warrants, options, and rights that meet listing requirements.

Niche
A career or business for which a person is well-suited. Also, a product which fulfills one need of a particular market segment, often with little or no competition.

Nodes
One workstation in a network, either local area or wide area (see separate citations).

Nonbank bank
A bank that either accepts deposits or makes loans, but not both. Used to create many new branch banks.

Noncompetitive awards
A method of contracting whereby the federal government negotiates with only one contractor to supply a product or service.

Nonmember bank
A state-regulated bank that does not belong to the federal bank system.

Nonprofit
An organization that has no shareholders, does not distribute profits, and is without federal and state tax liabilities.

Norms
See Financial ratios

North American Free Trade Agreement (NAFTA)
Passed in 1993, NAFTA eliminates trade barriers among businesses in the U.S., Canada, and Mexico.

NYSE
See New York Stock Exchange

Occupational Safety & Health Administration (OSHA)
Federal agency that regulates health and safety standards within the workplace.

Optimal firm size
The business size at which the production cost per unit of output (average cost) is, in the long run, at its minimum.

Organizational chart
A hierarchical chart tracking the chain of command within an organization.

OSHA
See Occupational Safety & Health Administration

Overhead
Expenses, such as employee benefits and building utilities, incurred by a business that are unrelated to the actual product or service sold.

Owner's capital
Debt or equity funds provided by the owner(s) of a business; sources of owner's capital are personal savings, sales of assets, or loans from financial institutions.

P & L
See Profit and loss statement

Part-time workers
Normally, those who work less than 35 hours per week. The Tax Reform Act indicated that part-time workers who work less than 17.5 hours per week may be excluded from health plans for purposes of complying with federal nondiscrimination rules.

Part-year workers
Those who work less than 50 weeks per year.

Partnership
Two or more parties who enter into a legal relationship to conduct business for profit. Defined by the U.S. Internal Revenue Code as joint ventures, syndicates, groups, pools, and other associations of two or more persons organized for profit that are not specifically classified in the IRS code as corporations or proprietorships.

Patent
A grant made by the government assuring an inventor the sole right to make, use, and sell an invention for a period of 17 years.

PC
See Professional corporation

Peak
See Cyclical peak

Pension
A series of payments made monthly, semiannually, annually, or at other specified intervals during the lifetime of the pensioner for distribution upon retirement. The term is sometimes used to denote the portion of the retirement allowance financed by the employer's contributions.

Pension fund
A fund established to provide for the payment of pension benefits; the collective contributions made by all of the parties to the pension plan.

Performance appraisal
An established set of objective criteria, based on job description and requirements, that is used to evaluate the performance of an employee in a specific job.

Permit
See Business license

Plan
See Business plan

Pooling
An arrangement for employers to achieve efficiencies and lower health costs by joining together to purchase group health insurance or self-insurance.

PPO
See Preferred provider organization

Preferred lenders program
See SBA special lending institution categories

Preferred provider organization (PPO)
A contractual arrangement with a health care services organization that agrees to discount its health care rates in return for faster payment and/or a patient base.

Premiums
The amount of money paid to an insurer for health insurance under a policy. The premium is generally paid periodically (e.g., monthly), and often is split between the employer and the employee. Unlike deductibles and coinsurance or copayments, premiums are paid for coverage whether or not benefits are actually used.

Prime-age workers
Employees 25 to 54 years of age.

Prime contract
A contract awarded directly by the U.S. Federal Government.

Private company
See Closely held corporation

Private placement
A method of raising capital by offering for sale an investment or business to a small group of investors (generally avoiding registration with the Securities and Exchange Commission or state securities registration agencies). Also known as Private financing or Private offering.

Pro forma
The use of hypothetical figures in financial statements to represent future expenditures, debts, and other potential financial expenses.

Proactive
Taking the initiative to solve problems and anticipate future events before they happen, instead of reacting to an already existing problem or waiting for a difficult situation to occur.

Procurement
(See also 8(a) Program; Small business set asides)
A contract from an agency of the federal government for goods or services from a small business.

Prodigy
(See also America Online)
An online service which is accessible by computer modem. The service features Internet access, bulletin boards, online periodicals, electronic mail, and other services for subscribers.

Product development
The stage of the innovation process where research is translated into a product or process through evaluation, adaptation, and demonstration.

Product franchising
An arrangement for a franchisee to use the name and to produce the product line of the franchisor or parent corporation.

Production
The manufacture of a product.

Production prototype
See Prototype

Productivity
A measurement of the number of goods produced during a specific amount of time.

Professional corporation (PC)
Organized by members of a profession such as medicine, dentistry, or law for the purpose of conducting their professional activities as a corporation. Liability of a member or shareholder is limited in the same manner as in a business corporation.

Profit and loss statement (P & L)
The summary of the incomes (total revenues) and costs of a company's operation during a specific period of time. Also known as Income and expense statement.

Proposal
See Business plan

Proprietorship
The most common legal form of business ownership; about 85 percent of all small businesses are proprietorships. The liability of the owner is unlimited in this form of ownership.

Prospective payment system
A cost-containment measure included in the Social Security Amendments of 1983 whereby Medicare payments to hospitals are based on established prices, rather than on cost reimbursement.

Prototype
A model that demonstrates the validity of the concept of an invention (laboratory prototype); a model that meets the needs of the manufacturing process and the user (production prototype).

Prudent investor rule or standard
A legal doctrine that requires fiduciaries to make investments using the prudence, diligence, and intelligence that would be used by a prudent person in making similar investments. Because fiduciaries make investments on behalf of third-party beneficiaries, the standard results in very conservative investments. Until recently, most state regulations required the fiduciary to apply this standard to each investment. Newer, more progressive regulations permit fiduciaries to apply this standard to the portfolio taken as a whole, thereby allowing a fiduciary to balance a portfolio with higher-yield, higher-risk investments. In states with more progressive regulations, practically every type of security is eligible for inclusion in the portfolio of investments made by a fiduciary, provided that the portfolio investments, in their totality, are those of a prudent person.

Public equity markets
Organized markets for trading in equity shares such as common stocks, preferred stocks, and warrants. Includes markets for both regularly traded and nonregularly traded securities.

Public offering
General solicitation for participation in an investment opportunity. Interstate public offerings are supervised by the U.S. Securities and Exchange Commission (see separate citation).

Quality control
The process by which a product is checked and tested to ensure consistent standards of high quality.

Rate of return
(See also Yield)
The yield obtained on a security or other investment based on its purchase price or its current market price. The total rate of return is current income plus or minus capital appreciation or depreciation.

Real property
Includes the land and all that is contained on it.

Realignment
See Resource realignment

Recession
Contraction of economic activity occurring between the peak and trough (see separate citations) of a business cycle.

Regulated market
A market in which the government controls the forces of supply and demand, such as who may enter and what price may be charged.

Regulation D
A vehicle by which small businesses make small offerings and private placements of securities with limited disclosure requirements. It was designed to ease the burdens imposed on small businesses utilizing this method of capital formation.

Regulatory Flexibility Act
An act requiring federal agencies to evaluate the impact of their regulations on small businesses before the regulations are issued and to consider less burdensome alternatives.

Research
The initial stage of the innovation process, which includes idea generation and invention.

Research and development financing
A tax-advantaged partnership set up to finance product development for start-ups as well as more mature companies.

Resource mobility
The ease with which labor and capital move from firm to firm or from industry to industry.

Resource realignment
The adjustment of productive resources to interindustry changes in demand.

Resources
The sources of support or help in the innovation process, including sources of financing, technical evaluation, market evaluation, management and business assistance, etc.

Retained business earnings
Business profits that are retained by the business rather than being distributed to the shareholders as dividends.

Revolving credit
An agreement with a lending institution for an amount of money, which cannot exceed a set maximum, over a specified period of time. Each time the borrower repays a portion of the loan, the amount of the repayment may be borrowed yet again.

Risk capital
See Venture capital

Risk management
The act of identifying potential sources of financial loss and taking action to minimize their negative impact.

Routing
The sequence of steps necessary to complete a product during production.

S corporations
See Sub chapter S corporations

SBA
See Small Business Administration

SBA direct loans
Loans made directly by the U.S. Small Business Administration (SBA); monies come from funds appropriated specifically for this purpose. In general, SBA direct loans carry interest rates slightly lower than those in the private financial markets and are available only to applicants unable to secure private financing or an SBA guaranteed loan.

SBA 504 Program
See Certified development corporation

SBA guaranteed loans
Loans made by lending institutions in which the U.S. Small Business Administration (SBA) will pay a prior agreed-upon percentage of the outstanding principal in the event the borrower of the loan defaults. The terms of the loan and the interest rate are negotiated between the borrower and the lending institution, within set parameters.

SBA loans
See Disaster loans; SBA direct loans; SBA guaranteed loans; SBA special lending institution categories

SBA Management Assistance Programs
(See also Active Corps of Executives; Service Corps of Retired Executives; Small business institutes program)
Classes, workshops, counseling, and publications offered by the U.S. Small Business Administration.

SBA special lending institution categories.
U.S. Small Business Administration (SBA) loan program in which the SBA promises certified banks a 72-hour turnaround period in giving its approval for a loan, and in which preferred lenders in a pilot program are allowed to write SBA loans without seeking prior SBA approval.

SBDB
See Small Business Data Base

SBDC
See Small business development centers

SBI
See Small business institutes program

SBIC
See Small business investment corporation

SBIR Program
See Small Business Innovation Development Act of 1982

Scale economies
The decline of the production cost per unit of output (average cost) as the volume of output increases.

Scale efficiency
The reduction in unit cost available to a firm when producing at a higher output volume.

SCORE
See Service Corps of Retired Executives

SEC
See Securities and Exchange Commission

SECA
See Self-Employment Contributions Act

Second-stage financing
(See also First-stage financing; Third-stage financing)
Working capital for the initial expansion of a company that is producing, shipping, and has growing accounts receivable and inventories. Also known as Second-round financing.

Secondary market
A market established for the purchase and sale of outstanding securities following their initial distribution.

Secondary worker
Any worker in a family other than the person who is the primary source of income for the family.

Secondhand capital
Previously used and subsequently resold capital equipment (e.g., buildings and machinery).

Securities and Exchange Commission (SEC)
Federal agency charged with regulating the trade of securities to prevent unethical practices in the investor market.

Securitized debt
A marketing technique that converts long-term loans to marketable securities.

Seed capital
Venture financing provided in the early stages of the innovation process, usually during product development.

Self-employed person
One who works for a profit or fees in his or her own business, profession, or trade, or who operates a farm.

Self-Employment Contributions Act (SECA)
Federal law that governs the self-employment tax (see separate citation).

Self-employment income
Income covered by Social Security if a business earns a net income of at least $400.00 during the year. Taxes are paid on earnings that exceed $400.00.

Self-employment retirement plan
See Keogh plan

Self-employment tax
Required tax imposed on self-employed individuals for the provision of Social Security and Medicare. The tax must be paid quarterly with estimated income tax statements.

Self-funding

A health benefit plan in which a firm uses its own funds to pay claims, rather than transferring the financial risks of paying claims to an outside insurer in exchange for premium payments.

Service Corps of Retired Executives (SCORE)

(See also Active Corps of Executives)

Volunteers for the SBA Management Assistance Program who provide one-on-one counseling and teach workshops and seminars for small firms.

Service firm

See Business service firm

Service sector

Broadly defined, all U.S. industries that produce intangibles, including the five major industry divisions of transportation, communications, and utilities; wholesale trade; retail trade; finance, insurance, and real estate; and services.

Set asides

See Small business set asides

Short-haul service

A type of transportation service in which the transporter supplies service between cities where the maximum distance is no more than 200 miles.

Short-term debt

An obligation that matures in one year.

SIC codes

See Standard Industrial Classification codes

Single-establishment enterprise

See Establishment

Small business

An enterprise that is independently owned and operated, is not dominant in its field, and employs fewer than 500 people. For SBA purposes, the U.S. Small Business Administration (SBA) considers various other factors (such as gross annual sales) in determining size of a business.

Small Business Administration (SBA)

An independent federal agency that provides assistance with loans, management, and advocating interests before other federal agencies.

Small Business Data Base

(See also U.S. Establishment and Enterprise Microdata File; U.S. Establishment Longitudinal Microdata File)

A collection of microdata (see separate citation) files on individual firms developed and maintained by the U.S. Small Business Administration.

Small business development centers (SBDC)

Centers that provide support services to small businesses, such as individual counseling, SBA advice, seminars and conferences, and other learning center activities. Most services are free of charge, or available at minimal cost.

Small business development corporation

See Certified development corporation

Small business-dominated industry

Industry in which a minimum of 60 percent of employment or sales is in firms with fewer than 500 employees.

Small Business Innovation Development Act of 1982

Federal statute requiring federal agencies with large extramural research and development budgets to allocate a certain percentage of these funds to small research and development firms. The program, called the Small Business Innovation Research (SBIR) Program, is designed to stimulate technological innovation and make greater use of small businesses in meeting national innovation needs.

Small business institutes (SBI) program

Cooperative arrangements made by U.S. Small Business Administration district offices and local colleges and universities to provide small business firms with graduate students to counsel them without charge.

Small business investment corporation (SBIC)

A privately owned company licensed and funded through the U.S. Small Business Administration and private sector sources to provide equity or debt capital to small businesses.

Small business set asides

Procurement (see separate citation) opportunities required by law to be on all contracts under $10,000 or a certain percentage of an agency's total procurement expenditure.

Smaller firms

For U.S. Department of Commerce purposes, those firms not included in the Fortune 1000.

SMSA

See Metropolitan statistical area

Socially and economically disadvantaged

Individuals who have been subjected to racial or ethnic prejudice or cultural bias without regard to their qualities as individuals, and whose abilities to compete are impaired because of diminished opportunities to obtain capital and credit.

Sole proprietorship
An unincorporated, one-owner business, farm, or professional practice.

Special lending institution categories
See SBA special lending institution categories

Standard Industrial Classification (SIC) codes
Four-digit codes established by the U.S. Federal Government to categorize businesses by type of economic activity; the first two digits correspond to major groups such as construction and manufacturing, while the last two digits correspond to subgroups such as home construction or highway construction.

Standard metropolitan statistical area (SMSA)
See Metropolitan statistical area

Start-up
A new business, at the earliest stages of development and financing.

Start-up costs
Costs incurred before a business can commence operations.

Start-up financing
Financing provided to companies that have either completed product development and initial marketing or have been in business for less than one year but have not yet sold their product commercially.

Stock
(See also Common stock; Convertible preferred stock)
A certificate of equity ownership in a business.

Stop-loss coverage
Insurance for a self-insured plan that reimburses the company for any losses it might incur in its health claims beyond a specified amount.

Strategic planning
Projected growth and development of a business to establish a guiding direction for the future. Also used to determine which market segments to explore for optimal sales of products or services.

Structural unemployment
See Unemployment

Sub chapter S corporations
Corporations that are considered noncorporate for tax purposes but legally remain corporations.

Subcontract
A contract between a prime contractor and a subcontractor, or between subcontractors, to furnish supplies or services for performance of a prime contract (see separate citation) or a subcontract.

Surety bonds
Bonds providing reimbursement to an individual, company, or the government if a firm fails to complete a contract. The U.S. Small Business Administration guarantees surety bonds in a program much like the SBA guaranteed loan program (see separate citation).

Swing loan
See Bridge financing

Target market
The clients or customers sought for a business' product or service.

Targeted Jobs Tax Credit
Federal legislation enacted in 1978 that provides a tax credit to an employer who hires structurally unemployed individuals.

Tax number
(See also Employer identification number)
A number assigned to a business by a state revenue department that enables the business to buy goods without paying sales tax.

Taxable bonds
An interest-bearing certificate of public or private indebtedness. Bonds are issued by public agencies to finance economic development.

Technical assistance
See Management and technical assistance

Technical evaluation
Assessment of technological feasibility.

Technology
The method in which a firm combines and utilizes labor and capital resources to produce goods or services; the application of science for commercial or industrial purposes.

Technology transfer
The movement of information about a technology or intellectual property from one party to another for use.

Tenure
See Employee tenure

Term
(See also Maturity)
The length of time for which a loan is made.

Terms of a note
The conditions or limits of a note; includes the interest rate per annum, the due date, and transferability and convertibility features, if any.

Third-party administrator
An outside company responsible for handling claims and performing administrative tasks associated with health insurance plan maintenance.

Third-stage financing
(See also First-stage financing; Second-stage financing)
Financing provided for the major expansion of a company whose sales volume is increasing and that is breaking even or profitable. These funds are used for further plant expansion, marketing, working capital, or development of an improved product. Also known as Third-round or Mezzanine financing.

Time deposit
A bank deposit that cannot be withdrawn before a specified future time.

Time management
Skills and scheduling techniques used to maximize productivity.

Trade credit
Credit extended by suppliers of raw materials or finished products. In an accounting statement, trade credit is referred to as "accounts payable."

Trade name
The name under which a company conducts business, or by which its business, goods, or services are identified. It may or may not be registered as a trademark.

Trade periodical
A publication with a specific focus on one or more aspects of business and industry.

Trade secret
Competitive advantage gained by a business through the use of a unique manufacturing process or formula.

Trade show
An exhibition of goods or services used in a particular industry. Typically held in exhibition centers where exhibitors rent space to display their merchandise.

Trademark
A graphic symbol, device, or slogan that identifies a business. A business has property rights to its trademark from the inception of its use, but it is still prudent to register all trademarks with the Trademark Office of the U.S. Department of Commerce.

Translation
See Product development

Treasury bills
Investment tender issued by the Federal Reserve Bank in amounts of $10,000 that mature in 91 to 182 days.

Treasury bonds
Long-term notes with maturity dates of not less than seven and not more than twenty-five years.

Treasury notes
Short-term notes maturing in less than seven years.

Trend
A statistical measurement used to track changes that occur over time.

Trough
See Cyclical trough

UCC
See Uniform Commercial Code

UL
See Underwriters Laboratories

Underwriters Laboratories (UL)
One of several private firms that tests products and processes to determine their safety. Although various firms can provide this kind of testing service, many local and insurance codes specify UL certification.

Underwriting
A process by which an insurer determines whether or not and on what basis it will accept an application for insurance. In an experience-rated plan, premiums are based on a firm's or group's past claims; factors other than prior claims are used for community-rated or manually rated plans.

Unfair competition
Refers to business practices, usually unethical, such as using unlicensed products, pirating merchandise, or misleading the public through false advertising, which give the offending business an unequitable advantage over others.

Unfunded accrued liability
The excess of total liabilities, both present and prospective, over present and prospective assets.

Unemployment
The joblessness of individuals who are willing to work, who are legally and physically able to work, and who are seeking work. Unemployment may represent the temporary joblessness of a worker between jobs (frictional unemployment) or the joblessness of a worker whose skills are not suitable for jobs available in the labor market (structural unemployment).

Uniform Commercial Code (UCC)
A code of laws governing commercial transactions across the U.S., except Louisiana. Their purpose is to bring uniformity to financial transactions.

Uniform product code (UPC symbol)
A computer-readable label comprised of ten digits and stripes that encodes what a product is and how much it costs. The first five digits are assigned by the Uniform Product Code Council, and the last five digits by the individual manufacturer.

Unit cost
See Average cost

UPC symbol
See Uniform product code

U.S. Establishment and Enterprise Microdata (USEEM) File
A cross-sectional database containing information on employment, sales, and location for individual enterprises and establishments with employees that have a Dun & Bradstreet credit rating.

U.S. Establishment Longitudinal Microdata (USELM) File
A database containing longitudinally linked sample microdata on establishments drawn from the U.S. Establishment and Enterprise Microdata file (see separate citation).

U.S. Small Business Administration 504 Program
See Certified development corporation

USEEM
See U.S. Establishment and Enterprise Microdata File

USELM
See U.S. Establishment Longitudinal Microdata File

VCN
See Venture capital network

Venture capital
(See also Equity; Equity midrisk venture capital)
Money used to support new or unusual business ventures that exhibit above-average growth rates, significant potential for market expansion, and are in need of additional financing to sustain growth or further research and development; equity or equity-type financing traditionally provided at the commercialization stage, increasingly available prior to commercialization.

Venture capital company
A company organized to provide seed capital to a business in its formation stage, or in its first or second stage of expansion. Funding is obtained through public or private pension funds, commercial banks and bank holding companies, small business investment corporations licensed by the U.S. Small Business Administration, private venture capital firms, insurance companies, investment management companies, bank trust departments, industrial companies seeking to diversify their investment, and investment bankers acting as intermediaries for other investors or directly investing on their own behalf.

Venture capital limited partnerships
Designed for business development, these partnerships are an institutional mechanism for providing capital for young, technology-oriented businesses. The investors' money is pooled and invested in money market assets until venture investments have been selected. The general partners are experienced investment managers who select and invest the equity and debt securities of firms with high growth potential and the ability to go public in the near future.

Venture capital network (VCN)
A computer database that matches investors with entrepreneurs.

WAN
See Wide Area Network

Wide Area Network (WAN)
Computer networks linking systems throughout a state or around the world in order to facilitate the sharing of information.

Withholding
Federal, state, social security, and unemployment taxes withheld by the employer from employees' wages; employers are liable for these taxes and the corporate umbrella and bankruptcy will not exonerate an employer

from paying back payroll withholding. Employers should escrow these funds in a separate account and disperse them quarterly to withholding authorities.

Workers' compensation

A state-mandated form of insurance covering workers injured in job-related accidents. In some states, the state is the insurer; in other states, insurance must be acquired from commercial insurance firms. Insurance rates are based on a number of factors, including salaries, firm history, and risk of occupation.

Working capital

Refers to a firm's short-term investment of current assets, including cash, short-term securities, accounts receivable, and inventories.

Yield

(See also Rate of return)
The rate of income returned on an investment, expressed as a percentage. Income yield is obtained by dividing the current dollar income by the current market price of the security. Net yield or yield to maturity is the current income yield minus any premium above par or plus any discount from par in purchase price, with the adjustment spread over the period from the date of purchase to the date of maturity.

Appendix D - Bibliography

Bibliography

Bibliography citations are listed alphabetically by title under appropriate subject subheadings, which also appear alphabetically (in bold).

Accounting/Budgets and Budgeting

"Account Yourself" in *Business Start-Ups* (Vol. 7, No. 8, August 1995, p. 79).

"Accountant Wanted" in *Business Start-ups* (October 1994, pp. 20-23). By Gloria Gibbs Marullo.

Accounting for Business. Newton, MA: Butterworth-Heinemann, 1991. By Peter Atrill, David Harvey, and Edward McLaney.

Accounting the Business Environment. Philadelphia, PA: Trans-Atlantic Publications, Inc., 1995. By John Watts.

The Accounting Cycle. Menlo Park, CA: Crisp Publications. By Jay Jacquet and William C. Miller, Jr.

An Accounting Primer. New York, NY: Mentor, revised edition, 1992. By Elwin W. Midgett.

Accounting Services for Small Service Firms. Denver, CO: U.S. Small Business Administration (SBA).

Accounting Software Guide. San Jose, CA: Anderson McLean, Inc., annual, summer. By Ray London, Editor.

Activity-Based Costing for Small and Mid-sized Businesses: An Implementation Guide. Somerset, NJ: John Wiley & Sons, Inc., 1992. By Douglas T. Hicks.

Analyze Your Records to Reduce Costs. Denver, CO: U.S. Small Business Administration (SBA).

"Audit Tip Sheet" in *Inc.* (Vol. 16, No. 4, April 1994, pp. 118). By Jill Andresky Fraser.

"Balancing Act" *Entrepreneur* (Vol. 23, No. 3, March 1995, pp. 56, 58- 59, 61). By Bob Weinstein.

Basic Accounting. Albany, NY: Delmar Publishers, 1997.

Basic Accounting for the Small Business: Simple, Foolproof Techniques for Keeping Your Books Straight and Staying Out of Trouble. Bellingham, WA: Self-Counsel Press, Inc., fourth edition, 1992. By Clive G. Cornish.

Basic Budgets for Profit Planning. Denver, CO: U.S. Small Business Administration (SBA).

"Bill Auditing" in *Small Business Opportunities* (Vol. 8, No. 2, March 1996, pp. 20). By Terry Schwartz.

"Bill of Wrongs" in *Entrepreneur* (Vol. 23, No. 5, May 1995, pp. 166, 168, 170-171). By David R. Honodel.

"Bookkeeper in a Box" in *Inc. Technology* (Vol. 15, No. 13, pp. 98). By Phaedra Hise.

Bookkeeping Service Directory. Omaha, NE: American Business Directories, Inc., annual.

Budgeting for a Small Business. Menlo Park, CA: Crisp Publications, Inc., 1993. By Terry Dickey.

Budgeting in a Small Service Firm. Denver, CO: U.S. Small Business Administration (SBA).

Business, Accounting and Finance Problem Solver. Piscataway, NJ: Research & Education Association, revised edition, 1994.

Business Owner's Guide to Accounting & Bookkeeping. Grants Pass, OR: Oasis Press, 1991. By Oliver Placencia and Welge staff.

The Cash Flow Control Guide: Methods to Understand and Control the Small Business's Number One Problem. Dover, NH: Upstart Publishing Co., Inc., 1989. By David H. Bangs, Jr.

Cash Traps: Small Business Secrets for Reducing Costs and Improving Cash Flow. Somerset, NJ: John Wiley & Sons, Inc., 1992. By Jeffrey P. Davidson and Charles W. Dean.

College Accounting: A Small Business Approach. Burr Ridge, IL: Richard D. Irwin, 1994. By Eleanor Schrader.

"Count On It" in *Entrepreneur* (Vol. 23, No. 8, August 1995, pp. 30, 32- 33). By Cheryl J. Goldberg.

"Counting On Profit" in *Small Business Opportunities* (Vol. 7, No. 3, May 1995, pp. 42-43, 82). By Martin Waterman.

"Cut Rates" in *Business Start-Ups* (Vol. 7, No. 9, September 1995).

"Database Husbandry" in *Inc. Technology* (Vol. 16, No. 13, pp. 100). By Phaedra Hise.

"Dream Accountant" in *Income Opportunities* (Vol. 30, No. 1, January 1995, pp. 108, 110). By Peg Byron.

Employee Benefits for Small Business. Englewood Cliffs, NJ: Prentice Hall, second edition, 1993. By Jane White.

"The Employee-Run Budget Work Sheet" in *Inc*. (Vol. 17, No. 2, pp. 81-83). By Stephanie Gruner.

"Fast Cash" in *Income Opportunities* (Vol. 31, No. 4, April 1996, pp. 38, 40). By Diana G. Lasseter.

"Fax Attack" in *Entrepreneur* (Vol. 23, No. 4, April 1995, pp. 26). By Heather Page.

Finance & Accounting. Dubuque, IA: Kendall Hunt Publishing Co., 1995. By Henry Beam.

Financial Accounting: Guide. Dubuque, IA: Kendall Hunt Publishing Co., 1995. By Mohamed Ibrahim.

Financial Accounting & Reporting. Cincinnati, OH: South-Western Publishing Co., 1995.

Financial Essentials for Small Business Success: Accounting, Planning & Recordkeeping Techniques for a Healthy Bottom Line. Dover, NH: Upstart Publishing Company, Inc., 1994. By Joe Tabet.

The Financial Planning Organizer: A Complete Budgeting Resource. Chicago, IL: Moody Press, 1991. By Larry Burkett.

"Firing Line" in *Entrepreneur* (Vol. 23, No. 12, November 1995, pp. 56, 59). By David R. Evanson.

"Five Strategies for Cutting Your Company's Costs" in *Working Woman* (Vol. 20, No. 7, July 1995, pp. 57-58). By Laura Teller.

"Food for Thought" in *Small Business Opportunities* (Vol. 8, No. 3, May 1996, pp. 72, 74). By Dannah Yurkosky.

"For the Record" in *Business Start-Ups* (Vol. 7, No. 5, May 1995, pp. 78, 80-81). By Cynthia E. Griffin.

"Free Exchange" in *Income Opportunities* (Vol. 30, No. 10, October 1995, pp. 50, 52). By Julie Monahan

"A Healthy Profit" in *Business Start-Ups* (Vol. 8, No. 3, March 1996, pp. 68, 70-72). By Haidee Jezek.

"How to Save Money on a Grand Scale" in *Crain's Small Business* (October 1995, p. 17). By Bob Ruby.

"How to Survive an IRS Audit" in *Nation's Business* (Vol. 82, No. 4, April 1994, pp. 42-43). By Joan C. Szabo.

"Hunting for an Accountant" in *Pennsylvania CPA Journal* (Vol. 63, No. 4, Summer 1993, pp. 10-13). By Gerald J. Rosenthal.

"It Adds Up" in *Income Opportunities* (Vol. 31, No. 1, January 1996, pp. 32, 34, 38). By Debra D'Agostino.

Keeping the Books: Basic Recordkeeping and Accounting for the Small Business. Dover, NH: Upstart Publishing Co., Inc., second edition, 1993. By Linda Pinson and Jerry Jinnett.

"Making The Cut" in *Entrepreneur* (Vol. 23, No. 5, May 1995, pp. 50, 52-53). By Bob Weinstein.

Managing by the Numbers: Financial Essentials for the Growing Business. Dover, NH: Upstart Publishing Co., Inc., 1992. By David H. Bangs, Jr.

McGraw-Hill Small Business Tax Advisor. New York, NY: McGraw-Hill, Inc., second edition, 1992. By Cliff Roberson.

"The Numbers Speak Volumes" in *Small Business Reports* (Vol. 19, No. 7, July 1994, pp. 39-43). By Lamont Change.

"Out With The Old?" in *Entrepreneur* (Vol. 23, No. 4, April 1995, pp. 54, 56-57). By Bob Weinstein.

"Please, Mr. Postman" in *Entrepreneur* (Vol. 23, No. 8, August 1995, pp. 62-63). By Jacquelyn Lynn.

Powerful Budgeting for Better Planning and Management. New York, NY: AMACOM, 1993. By Robert G. Finney.

"Pricing by the Numbers" in *Inc. Technology* (Vol. 16, No. 13, pp. 101). By Phaedra Hise.

"Pruning Postage Costs" in *Income Opportunities* (Vol. 30, No. 1, January 1995, pp. 76, 78). By Kathryn A. Clark.

Ready-to-Use Business Forms: A Complete Package for the Small Business. Bellingham, WA: Self-Counsel Press, Inc., second edition, 1992.

Record Keeping in a Small Business. Denver, CO: U.S. Small Business Administration (SBA).

Record Keeping for Small Rural Businesses. Amherst, MA: University of Massachusetts. By Eligia Murcia.

"Reduce Your Rates" in *Income Opportunities* (Vol. 30, No. 9, September 1995, pp. 40, 42, 44). By Sheila Gibson.

The Shoebox Syndrome (Record-Keeping). Hyde Park, MA: Nikmal Publishing. By Selma H. Lamkin.

Simple Break-Even Analysis for Small Stores. Denver, CO: U.S. Small Business Administration (SBA).

Simplified Small Business Accounting. Carbondale, IL: Nova Publishing Co., 1995. By Daniel Sitarz.

Small Business Accountant. Cincinnati, OH: South-Western Publishing Co., 1994. By Hamilton.

"Small Business Controller" in *Management Accounting* (Vol. 76, No. 5, November 1994, pp. 38-41). By Bonnie D. Labrack.

Sound Cash Management and Borrowing. Denver, CO: U.S. Small Business Administration (SBA).

Step-by-Step Bookkeeping: The Complete Handbook for the Small Business. New York, NY: Sterling Publishing Co., Inc., revised edition, 1992. By Robert C. Ragan.

Tax Planning & Preparation Made Easy for the Self-Employed. New York, NY: John Wiley & Sons, 1995. By Gregory L. Dent.

"To the Rescue" in *Business Start-Ups* (Vol. 7, No. 5, May 1995, pp. 68, 70-71). By Sue Clayton.

"What's the Best $500 You Ever Spent, and Why?" in *Business Start-Ups* (Vol. 8, February 1996, p. 8). By Gloria Gibbs Marullo.

"You May Need the 'C' in CPA" in *Inc.* (Vol. 16, No. 9, September 1994, pp. 126). By Jill Andresky Fraser.

Business Growth & Statistics

Action Plans for the Small Business: Growth Strategies for Businesses Wondering Where to Go Next. New York, NY: DBM Publishing, 1995. By Shailendra Vyakarnam.

America's 25 Hottest Businesses. Irvine, CA: Entrepreneur, Inc.

"And Still We Rise" in *Black Enterprise* (Vol. 26, No. 9, April 1996, p. 18). By Cliff Hocker.

"Are You Ready to Go Public?" in *Nation's Business* (Vol. 83, No. 1, January 1995, pp. 30-32). By Roberta Maynard.

"At the Brink" in *Inc.* (Vol. 17, No. 16, November 1995, pp. 21-22). By Rick McCloskey.

Basic Business Statistics. Englewood Cliffs, NJ: Prentice Hall, 1995.

"Branching Out" in *Nation's Business* (Vol. 82, No. 11, November 1994, pp. 53). By Roberta Maynard.

"Brave New World" in *Income Opportunities* (Vol. 30, No. 4, April 1995, pp. 30-32, 34-36, 38, 40, 42, 44). By Dale D. Buss.

"Brighter Days" in *Entrepreneur* (Vol. 23, No. 7, July 1995, pp. 16). By Janean Chun.

"Bringing Up Business" in *Entrepreneur* (vol. 23, No. 1, January 1995, pp. 124-128). By Erika Kotite.

"Building Companies to Last" in *Inc.* (Special Issue: The State of Small Business, February 1996, pp. 83-84, 87-88). By James C. Collins.

"Business Finally Invests Some Trust in Bank Lending" in *Crain's Small Business* (October 1995, p. 8). By Jeffrey McCracken.

"Business Must Refocus Once It Outgrows Entrepreneur's Control" in *Crain's Small Business* (October 1995, p. 16). By Jon Greenawalt.

Business Statistics. Saint Louis, MO: Mosby-Year Book, 1996.

Business Statistics of the United States. Lanham, MD: Bernan Press, 1995. By Courtenay M. Slater.

"Capital Steps" in *Inc.* (Vol. 18, No. 2, February 1996, pp. 42-44, 47). By Jill Andresky Fraser.

The Complete Demographic Reference Guide. Marina del Rey, CA: Urban Decision Systems, 1992.

Dun & Bradstreet State Sales Guide. New Providence, NJ: Dun & Bradstreet Inc., quarterly, January, March, July, September.

The Entrepreneur's Guide to Growing Up: Taking Your Small Company to the Next Level. Bellingham, WA: Self-Counsel Press, Inc., 1993. By Edna Sheedy.

"The Fast Trackers" in *Working Woman* (March 1995, pp. 44-48, 86). By Louise Washer.

"A Field Guide to Your Local Economy" in *Inc.* (Special Issue: The State of Small Business, February 1996, pp. 51-54). By Joel Garreau.

"Financial Ratios in Large Public and Small Private Firms" in *Journal of Small Business Management* (Vol. 30, No. 3, July 1992, pp. 35). By Jerome Osteryoung and Richard L. Constand and Donald Nast.

"Fueling the Growth of Black Companies" in *Black Enterprise* (Vol. 25, No. 4, November 1994, pp. 158-159, 162, 164). By Gracian Mack.

Go for Growth: Five People-Centered Ways to Re-Energize. Essex Junction, VT: Oliver Wight Publications, 1995. By Robert M. Tomasko.

"Growing Companies Gain from University Relationships" in *Income Opportunities* (Vol. 30, No. 4, April 1995, pp. 3). By Patricia Hamilton.

"Growing with the Flow" in *Inc.* (Vol. 16, No. 11, 1994, pp. 88-90). By Martha E. Mangelsdorf.

"A Growing Year for Small Business" in *Income Opportunities* (Vol. 30, No. 10, October 1995, pp. 3). By Heath F. Eiden.

"Growing Your Consulting Business" in *Black Enterprise* (Vol. 25, No. 4, November 1994, pp. 108-116). By Margie Markarian.

"Growth in a Developing Market" in *Inc. 500* (Vol. 16, No. 11, 1994, pp. 92, 94, 96, 98-99). By Martha E. Mangelsdorf.

"Hitting the Wall" in *Inc.* (Vol. 17, No. 10, July 1995, pp. 21-22). By James L. Bildner.

"The Hottest Industries for New Business Opportunities" in *Black Enterprise* (Vol. 25, No. 8, March 1995). By Carolyn M. Brown, Yolanda Gault, Lloyd Gite, Adrienne Harris, Eric Houston, Dasha Jones and Valencia Roner.

Introduction to Business Statistics. Orlando, FL: Harcourt Brace College Publishers, 1996.

"Is Bigger Better?" in *Working Woman* (March 1995, pp. 39-40, 42, 90). By Louise Washer.

"It Cuts Both Ways" in *Crain's Detroit Business* (Vol. 10, No. 41, October 10-16, 1994, pp. 9). By Marilyn Sambrano.

"The Knockout Lesson" in *Inc.* (Vol. 17, No. 8, June 1995, pp. 21-22). By Amy Miller.

The McGraw-Hill Guide to Managing Growth in Your Emerging Business. New York, NY: McGraw-Hill, Inc., 1994. By Stephen C. Harper.

"Mistakes Your Growing Company Needs To Avoid" in *Money: Money Guide Supplement* (Vol. , No. , 1994, pp. 76-81). By Mary Rowland.

Modern Business Statistics. Belmont, CA: Wadsworth Publishing Co., 1995. By George C. Canova.

"Networking Works" in *Business Start-Ups* (Vol. 7, No. 10, October 1995, p. 10). By Leann Anderson.

"A New Loan Option to Bank, Venture Capital" in *Crain's Small Business* (February 1996, p. 9-10). By Jeffrey McCracken.

"One-Hit Wonders" in *Entrepreneur* (Vol. 23, No. 1, January 1995, pp. 258-260, 262, 264). By Mark Henricks.

"The 100 Fastest-Growing Companies: Under Control" in *Hispanic Business* (Vol. 17, No. 8, August 1995, pp. 22). By Maria Zate.

"The Six Secrets of Strategic Growth" in *Working Woman* (March 1995, pp. 50-51, 78). By Rhonda M. Abrams.

"Small Biz Can Give Input, Vital Data Via Web Site" in *Crain's Small Business* (March 1996, p. 3). By Jeffrey McCracken.

"Small Businesses are Thriving" in *Income Opportunities* (Vol. 30, No. 1, January 1995, pp. 2). By Eric Barnes.

"Small Is Beautiful! Big Is Best!" in *Inc.* (Special Issue: The State of Small Business, February 1996, pp. 39-44, 46, 48-49). By George Gendron.

"Small World" in *Entrepreneur* (Vol. 23, No. 8, August 1995, pp. 17). By Heather Page.

"Sounding Board" in *Income Opportunities* (Vol. 30, No. 6, June 1995, pp. 114, 116). By Richard J. Maturi.

"A Strategy For Growth" in *Black Enterprise* (Vol. 25, No. 4, November 1994). By Joan Delaney.

"Striking the Faustian Bargain" in *Corporate Detroit* (Vol. 12, No. 11, November 1994, pp. 38-39). By Gary Hoffman.

"The Survival Factor" in *Hispanic Business* (Vol. 17, No. 8, August 1995, pp. 44-46). By Rick Mendosa.

"A Sweet Deal" in *Black Enterprise* (Vol. 25, No. 2, September 1994, pp. 30-32). By Ann Brown.

"There Are No Simple Businesses Anymore" in *Inc.* (Special Issue: The State of Small Business, February 1996, pp. 66-79). By Edward O. Welles.

"To Advance, Try a Retreat" in *Crain's Small Business* (January 1996, p. 17). By Jim Brady.

Where to Make Money: A Rating Guide to Opportunities in America's Metro Areas. Amherst, NY: Prometheus Books, 1993. By G. Scott Thomas.

"The Wonderland Economy" in *Inc.* (Special Issue: The State of Small Business, February 1996, pp. 14-16, 18-20, 23-24, 26-27, 29). By John Case.

Business Law

"Adequacy, Availability & Quality of Legal Services for Small Businesses" in *South Dakota Business Review* (Vol. 53, No. 2, December 1994, pp. 1, 4). By Bruce E. May.

"Ads For Your Biz" in *Small Business Opportunities* (Vol. 6, No. 5, September 1994, pp. 10). By Marie Sherlock.

"At Lagerheads" in *Inc.* (Vol. 16, No. 3, March 1994, pp. 36). By Alessandra Bianchi.

The Attorney's Handbook on Small Business Reorganization Under Chapter 11. Lakewood, CO: Argyle Publishing Company, 1992. By John H. Williamson.

Bankruptcy Basics for Small Business. New York, NY: Clark Boardman Callaghan, 1994. By S. Suzanne Walsh.

The Barclays Guide to Law for the Small Business. Cambridge, MA: Blackwell Publishers, 1991. By Stephen Lloyd.

Basic Legal Forms for Business. Somerset, NJ: John Wiley & Sons, Inc., 1993. By Morris A. Nunes.

Business Law. Orlando, FL: Dryden Press, 1992. By John R. Allison and Robert A. Prentice.

Business Law Made Simple. New York, NY: Doubleday & Co., 1995. By Stephen G. Christianson.

The Complete Book of Business Forms and Agreements. New York, NY: McGraw-Hill, Inc., 1993. By Cliff Roberson.

The Complete Book of Small Business Legal Forms. Carbondale, IL: Nova Publishing Co., 1995, second edition. By Daniel Sitarz.

The Complete Guide to Business Agreements. Chicago, IL: Financial Publishing, 1992. By Ted Nicholas.

"Confidential Financials" in *Business Start-Ups* (Vol. 8, No. 2, February 1996, p. 12).

Contemporary Business Law. Saint Paul, MN: West Publishing Co., 1995. By Richard A. Mann.

Corporation & Business Associations, Statutes, Rules, Materials, & Forms. Westbury, NY: Foundation Press, Inc., 1995. By Melvin A. Eisenberg.

"Court TV Offers Biz Legal Aid on the Net" in *Crain's Small Business* (March 1996, p. 6). By Jeffrey McCracken.

"Decide and Conquer" in *Business Start-Ups* (Vol. 7, No. 11, November 1995, p. 7). By Lauren Fischbein.

"Defining Your Workers" in *Income Opportunities* (Vol. 30, No. 10, October 1995, pp. 44, 46, 48). By Heath F. Eiden.

The Essential Corporation Handbook. Grants Pass, OR: The Oasis Press, 1992. By Carl R. Sniffen.

Essentials of Business Law II. Piscataway, NJ: Research & Education Association, revised edition, 1994.

Every Manager's Legal Guide to Hiring. Burr Ridge, IL: Irwin Professional Publishing, 1989. By August Bequai.

"Finding a Lawyer for Your Business" in *Nation's Business* (Vol. 82, No. 4, April 1994, pp. 34-35). By Kenneth A. Ehrman.

"Getting Briefed On-line" in *Working Woman* (March 1996, pp. 51). By Judith Broadhurst.

A Guide to Marketing Law: What Every Seller Should Know. San Diego, CA: Harcourt Brace & Co. By Richard M. Steuer.

How and When to Be Your Own Lawyer: A Step-by-Step Guide to Effectively Using Our Legal System. Garden City Park, NY: Avery Publishing Group, 1993. By Robert V. Schachner, with Marvin Quittner.

Inc. Yourself: How to Profit by Setting Up Your Own Corporation. New York, NY: Harper Business, 1995, eighth edition. By Judith H. McQuown.

Incorporating Form Samples or Information for the Fifty States. Denver, CO: Data Notes Publishing Co., 1997. By A. C. Doyle, Editor.

The Law (in Plain English) for Small Businesses. Somerset, NJ: John Wiley & Sons, Inc., Second edition, 1991. By Leonard D. DuBoff.

Law for the Small Business Owner. Dobbs Ferry, NY: Oceana Publications, Inc., 1994. By Margaret C. Jasper.

"Legal Aid" in *Business Start-Ups* (Vol. 7, No. 2, February 1995, pp. 78, 80-81). By Sue Clayton.

Legal & Corporate Forms for Small Business. New York, NY: Prentice Hall General Reference & Travel, 1994. By J. K. Lasser Staff.

"Legal Eagles" in *Entrepreneur* (Vol. 23, No. 7, July 1995, pp. 26, 28-29). By Cheryl J. Goldberg.

A Legal Guide for Small Business. Menlo Park, CA: Crisp Publications, 1995. By Charles P. Lickson.

The Legal Guide for Starting and Running a Small Business. Berkeley, CA: Nolo Press, 1994. By Fred S. Steingold.

Legal Handbook for Small Business. New York, NY: AMACOM, revised edition, 1989. By Marc J. Lane.

Legal Power for Small Business Owners and Managers. Kenner, LA: A Granite Publishers, 1991. By Raymond J. Munna.

Legal Requirements for Business Records: State Requirements. Englewood, CO: Information Requirements Clearinghouse, 1990. By Donald S. Skupsky.

"Looney Laws" in *Entrepreneur* (Vol. 23, No. 4, April 1995, pp. 17). By Cynthia E. Griffin.

"Meeting the Wrongful Discharge Challenge" in *Journal of Small Business Management* (Vol. 30, No. 4, October 1992, pp. 96-105). By Glenn M. Gomes and James F. Morgan.

"PC Pirates" in *Entrepreneur* (Vol. 23, No. 12, November 1995, pp. 30). By Jacquelyn Lynn.

SBC's One Hundred & One Laws—and Perhaps More. Scotts Valley, CA: Small Businessman's Clinic (SBC), second edition, 1991. By Austin M. Elliott.

"See You In Court" in *Entrepreneur* (Vol. 23, No. 4, April 1995, pp. 70, 72-74). By Jane Easter Bahls.

Selecting the Legal Structure for Your Business. Denver, CO: U.S. Small Business Administration (SBA).

The Small Business Legal Guide. Chicago, IL: Dearborn Trade, 1993. By Robert Friedman.

Standard Legal Forms and Agreements for Small Business. Bellingham, WA: Self-Counsel Press, Inc., 1990. By Steve Sanderson.

What Do You Know About Business Law. Syosset, NY: National Learning Corp., 1994. By Jack Rudman.

"Workplace Privacy: Setting Boundaries in the Information Age" in *HR Focus* (Vol. 71, No. 12, December 1994, pp. 1). By Donald J. McNerney.

Business Plans

"Best Laid Plans" in *Business Start-Ups* (Vol. 7, No. 11, November 1995, p. 7). By Lynn Norquist.

"The Best Laid Plans" in *Entrepreneurial Woman* (September 1990, pp. 74-79). By Edward C. Rybka.

"Building a Better Business Plan" in *Home Office-Computing* (February 1990, p. 30). By Charles H. Gajeway.

Building Your Business Plan: A Step-By-Step Approach. Somerset, NJ: John Wiley & Sons, Inc., 1985. By Harold J. McLaughlin.

"Business Busters" in *Black Enterprise* (Vol. 23, No. 4, November 1992, pp. 75-85). By Caryne Brown..

"Business Plan" in *Business Start-Ups* (Vol. 7, No. 12, December 1995, pp. 8, 10-11). By Charles Fuller.

Business Plan Handbook. Leverett, MA: Rector Press, Ltd., 1995.

"A Business-Plan Outline" in *Crain's Small Business* (December 1995, p. 11). By Jeffrey McCracken.

"Business Plan Stumbling Blocks" in *Working Woman* (October 1994, pp. 45-48). By Rhonda M. Abrams.

The Business Plan Workbook. Englewood Cliffs, NJ: Prentice Hall, 1989. By Gary A. Cooper.

The Business Planner: A Complete Guide to Raising Finances for Your Business. Newton, MA: Butterworth-Heinemann, 1992. By Iain Maitland.

Business Planning: An Approach to Strategic Management. Philadelphia, PA: Trans-Atlantic Publications, Inc., 1992. By Bill Richardson and Roy Richardson.

Business Planning for the Entrepreneur. Lancaster, OH: Tangent Publishing, 1990. By Andrew J. Batchelor, Jr.

Business Planning in Four Steps & a Leap. Marquette, MI: Northern Economic Initiatives Corp., 1995. By Scott Sporte.

The Business Planning Guide: Creating a Plan for Success in Your Own Business. Dover, NH: Upstart Publishing Co., Inc., sixth edition, 1992. By David H. Bangs, Jr.

Business Plans to Manage Day-to-Day Operations: Real-life Results for Small Business Owners and Operators. Somerset, NJ: John Wiley & Sons, Inc., 1993. By Christopher R. Malburg.

Business Plans That Win Venture Capital. Somerset, NJ: John Wiley & Sons, Inc., 1989. By Terrence B. McGarty.

"Change of Plans" in *Business Start-Ups* (Vol. 7, No. 6, June 1995, p. 9). By Erika Kotite.

The Complete Book of Business Plans: Simple Steps to Writing a Powerful Business Plan. Naperville, IL: Sourcebooks, Inc., 1994. By Joseph A. Covello and Brian J. Hazelgreen.

"The Complete New-Business Survival Guide" in *Inc.* (Vol. 14, No. 7, July 1992, pp. 48-66). By Susan Greco.

Computer Applications for Business Planning: A Practical Hands-On Text. Lancaster, OH: Tangent Publishing, 1995. By Andrew J. Batchelor.

Crafting the Successful Business Plan. Englewood Cliffs, NJ: Prentice Hall, 1992. By Erik Hyypia.

Develop Your Business Plan. Detroit, MI: Small Business Development Center.

Developing a Strategic Business Plan. Denver, CO: U.S. Small Business Administration (SBA).

Developing a Successful Business Plan. Irvine, CA: Entrepreneur, Inc.

"Do Business Plans Matter?" in *Inc.* (Vol. 18, No. 2, February 1996, pp. 21). By Mary Baechler.

"Do You Have a Plan?" in *In Business* (April 1990, pp. 12-14). By David M. Freedman.

"The Do's and Don'ts of Writing A Winning Business Plan" in *Black Enterprise* (Vol. 26, No. 9, April 1996, pp. 114-116, 120, 122). By Carolyn M. Brown.

The Entrepreneur's Guide to Building a Better Business Plan: A Step-By-Step Approach. Somerset, NJ: John Wiley & Sons, Inc., 1992. By Harold J. McLaughlin.

The Entrepreneur's Guide to Developing a Basic Business Plan. Northbrook, IL: S. K. Brown Publishing, 1991. By Chris Stevens.

The Entrepreneur's Guide to Preparing a Winning Business Plan and Raising Venture Capital. Englewood Cliffs, NJ: Prentice Hall, 1990. By Keith W. Schilit.

The Ernst and Young Business Plan Guide. Somerset, NJ: John Wiley & Sons, Inc., second edition, 1993.

"Facing an Uphill Battle" in *Black Enterprise* (Vol. 22, No. 4, November 1991, pp. 51-57). By Kevin D. Thompson.

"A Factor Analytic Study of the Perceived Causes of Small Business Failure" in *Journal of Small Business Management* (Vol. 31, No. 4, October 1993, pp. 18-31). By LuAnn Ricketts Gaskill and Howard E. Van Auken and Ronald A. Manning.

"Financial Ratios in Large Public and Small Private Firms" in *Journal of Small Business Management* (Vol. 30, No. 3, July 1992, pp. 35). By Jerome Osteryoung and Richard L. Constand and Donald Nast.

"Fools Rush In? The Institutional Context of Industry Creation" in *Academy of Management Review* (Vol. 19, No. 4, October 1994, pp. 645). By Howard E. Aldrich and Marlene C. Fiol.

"Game Plan" in *Entrepreneur* (Vol. 23, No. 8, August 1995, pp. 38-41). By David R. Evanson.

Getting Ready. Bellingham, WA: Self-Counsel Press, 1991. By Dan Kennedy.

Growth Company Starter Kit. New York, NY: Coopers & Lybrand.

How to Make a Business Plan That Works!. Teaneck, NJ: NAPL. By Lyman Henderson.

How to Prepare and Present a Business Plan. New York, NY: Simon & Schuster Trade, 1992. By Joseph R. Mancuso.

How to Prepare a Results-Driven Business Plan. New York, NY: AMACOM, 1993. By Gregory J. Massarella, Patrick D. Zorsch, Daniel D. Jacobson, and Marc J. Rittenhouse.

How to Really Create a Successful Business Plan. Boston, MA: Inc. Publishing, 1994, revised edition. By David E. Gumpert.

"How To Start an Inc. 500 Company" in *Inc. 500* (Vol. 16, No. 11, 1994, pp. 51-52, 54, 57-58, 60, 63-65). By Leslie Brokaw.

How to Write a Business Plan. Berkeley, CA: Nolo Press, fourth edition, 1992. By Mike McKeever.

"How to Write a Business Plan" in *Nation's Business* (Vol. 81, No. 2, February 1993, pp. 29-30). By J. Tol Broome, Jr.

How to Write a Successful Business Plan. New York, NY: AMACOM, 1986. By Julie K. Brooks and Barry A. Stevens.

How to Write a Successful Business Plan: Step-by-Step Guide to Business Success. Interlochen, MI: Lewis & Renn Associates, 1995. By Jerre G. Lewis.

How to Write a Winning Business Plan. Englewood Cliffs, NJ: Prentice Hall, 1990. By Joseph Mancuso.

"It's All In The Plan" in *Small Business Reports* (Vol. 19, No. 6, June 1994, pp. 38-43). By Alan W. Jackson.

"Keys to Success? For Starters, Here Are 15" in *Contractor* (Vol. 41, No. 11, November 1994, pp. 12). By Jeff Ferenc.

Launching New Ventures. Dover, NH: Upstart Publishing Co., 1995.

"The Money Is Out There...How To Get It" in *Agency Sales Magazine* (Vol. 24, No. 2, February 1994, pp. 15-17). By Jeff Fromberg.

"The Numbers Speak Volumes" in *Small Business Reports* (Vol. 19, No. 7, July 1994, pp. 39-43). By Lamont Change.

"Opening a New Store...Reasonable Goals and Careful Planning" in *Stores* (Vol. 76, No. 10, October 1994, pp. 101-102). By Bill Pearson.

"Plan of Action" in *Income Opportunities* (Vol. 30, No. 7, July 1995, pp. 96, 98, 100). By Toni Reinhold.

"Plan of Attack" in *Entrepreneur* (Vol. 23, No. 8, August 1995, pp. 150, 152-157).

"Plan of Attack" in *Inc.* (Vol. 18, No. 1, January 1996, pp. 41-44). By Martha E. Mangelsdorf.

Planning and Goal Setting for Small Business. Denver, CO: U.S. Small Business Administration (SBA).

"Planning for Projects" in *Income Opportunities* (Vol. 29, No. 7, July 1994, pp. 44). By Carol More.

"Planning for Success" in *Business Start-Ups* (Vol. 8, No. 3, March 1996, pp. 50, 52-53). By Lynn L. Norquist.

"Poor Planning Plagues Small Business" in *Income Opportunities* (Vol. 30, No. 4, April 1995, pp. 2). By Patricia Hamilton.

Preparing a Successful Business Plan: A Practical Guide for Small Business. Bellingham, WA: Self-Counsel Press, Inc., second edition, 1993. By Rodger Touchie.

The Process of Business Planning: A Practical Hands-on Text. Lancaster, OH: Tangent Publishing, 1994. By Andrew J. Batchelor Sr.

Raising Capital: How to Write a Financing Proposal to Raise Venture Capital. Grants Pass, OR: The Oasis Press, 1994. By Lawrence Flanagan.

"SCORE Points to Success" in *Black Enterprise* (Vol. 25, No. 6, January 1995, pp. 38). By Christina F. Watts.

Small Business Planning Workbook. New York, NY: Clark Boardman Callaghan, 1990. By John C. Wisdom.

"Start with Strategic Fundamentals" in *Crain's Small Business* (September 1995, p. 9). By Jim Brady.

The Start-up Business Plan. Englewood Cliffs, NJ: Prentice Hall, 1991. By William M. Luther.

"Staying Alive " in *Black Enterprise* (Vol. 25, No. 4, November 1994, pp. 90-92, 95-96). By Rhonda Reynolds.

Strategic Planning for the New & Small Business. Dover, NH: Upstart Publishing Co., Inc., 1995. By Fred L. Fry.

Strategic Planning for the Small Business: Situations, Weapons, Objectives & Tactics. Holbrook, MA: Adams Publishing, 1990. By Craig Rice.

The Successful Business Plan: Secrets and Strategies. Grants Pass, OR: PSI Research, 1993. By Rhonda M. Abrams.

Successful Manager's Guide to Business: Seven Practical Steps to Producing Your Best Ever Business Plan. New York, NY: McGraw-Hill, Incorporated, 1994. By David Freemantle.

"Ten Steps to Creating Your Business Plan" in *Income Opportunities* (December/January 1991, pp. 55-56). By Ruth Anne King.

The Total Business Plan: How to Write, Rewrite, and Revise. New York, NY: John Wiley & Sons, Inc., 1994, second edition. By Patrick D. O'Hara.

Total Business Planning: A Step-By-Step Guide with Forms. New York, NY: John Wiley & Sons, Inc., 1991. By E. James Burton and W. Blan McBride.

Trademark: How to Name Your Business and Product. Berkeley, CA: Nolo Press, 1992. By Stephen Elias and Kate McGrath.

"When Your Banker Says No" in *Income Opportunities* (Vol. 30, No. 11, November 1995, pp. 24-28). By Randall Kirkpatrick.

"Why My Business Failed" in *Black Enterprise* (Vol. 24, No. 11, June 1994, pp. 236-242). By Charles Jamison.

Writing Business Plans That Get Results: A Step-by-Step Guide. Chicago, IL: Contemporary Books, Inc., 1991. By Michael O'Donnell.

Writing a Convincing Business Plan. Hauppauge, NY: Barron's Educational Series, 1995. By Art DeThomas.

Writing Effective Business Plans. Irvine, CA: Entrepreneur, Inc.

Your Business Plan. Eugene, OR: Oregon Small Business Development Center Network, revised edition, 1990. By Dennis J. Sargent.

Your First Business Plan: Learn the Critical Steps to Writing a Winning Business Plan. Naperville, IL: Sourcebooks Inc., 1995. By Joseph A. Covello.

Business Vision & Goals

"Added Attraction " in *Entrepreneur: Buyer's Guide to Franchise and Business Opportunities* (Vol. 22, No. 11, 1995, pp. 36, 38-40). By Guen Sublette.

"Back To The Future" in *Entrepreneur* (Vol. 23, No. 1, January 1995, pp. 238-242, 245). By Robert McGarvey.

Benchmarking for Best Practices: How to Define, Locate, and Emulate the Best in the Business. New York, NY: McGraw-Hill, Inc., 1995. By Christopher E. Bogan and Michael M. English.

"The Best Of Times" in *Entrepreneur* (Vol. 24, No. 4, April 1996, pp. 139-142). By Mark Henricks.

"Bright Ideas" in *Business Start-Ups* (Vol. 7, No. 8, August 1995, pp. 50, 52-54, 57). By Bob Weinstein.

"Building Companies to Last" in *Inc.* (Special Issue: The State of Small Business, February 1996, pp. 83-84, 87-88). By James C. Collins.

"Business Must Refocus Once It Outgrows Entrepreneur's Control" in *Crain's Small Business* (October 1995, p. 16). By Jon Greenawalt.

"Essential Books for Start-ups" in *Working Woman* (February 1995, pp. 54). By Jane Applegate.

"Everything According to Plan" in *Inc.* (Vol. 17, No. 3, March 1995, pp. 79-85). By Jay Finegan.

Goals and Goal Setting. Menlo Park, CA: Crisp Publications. By Larrie Rouillard.

"Inventor's Workshop" in *Business Start-ups* (October 1994, pp. 26-29). By Jacquelyn Lynn Denali.

"Just Their Luck" in *Entrepreneur* (Vol. 23, No. 2, February 1995, pp. 120, 122-25). By Gayle Sato Stodder.

"A Nation of Owners" in *Inc.* (Special Issue: The State of Small Business, February 1996, pp. 89-91). By William Bridges.

"Opening a New Store...Reasonable Goals and Careful Planning" in *Stores* (Vol. 76, No. 10, October 1994, pp. 101-102). By Bill Pearson.

"Say When" in *Inc.* (Vol. 17, No. 2, February 1995, pp. 19-20). By Steven L. Marks.

"A Smaller, Smarter World: Excerpted from The Road Ahead" in *Working Woman* (January 1996, pp. 34-41). By Bill Gates.

"Sounding Board" in *Income Opportunities* (Vol. 30, No. 6, June 1995, pp. 114, 116). By Richard J. Maturi.

"Staying Alive" in *Entrepreneur* (Vol. 23, No. 3, March 1995, pp. 114-118). By Robert McGarvey.

"Tomorrow Land" in *Entrepreneur* (Vol. 24, No. 2, February 1996, pp. 135-138). By Robert McGarvey.

Vision: How Leaders Develop It, Share It, & Sustain It. New York, NY: McGraw-Hill, Inc., 1993. By Joseph V. Quigley.

"What Does Business Really Want from Governments?" in *Inc.* (Special Issue: The State of Small Business, February 1996, pp. 92-103). By Tom Richman.

Buying a Business

"Am I Going to Mind Sweeping the Floors?" in *Forbes* (Vol. 152, No. 11, November 8, 1994, pp. 142-148). By Fleming Meeks and Nancy Rotenier.

"Appetizing Acquisitions" in *Income Opportunities* (Vol. 30, No. 10, October 1995, pp. 2). By Heath F. Eiden.

"Auctioning the Airways" in *Income Opportunities* (Vol. 29, No. 9, September 1994, pp. 84-90). By Edmond M. Rosenthal.

"Bad Company" in *Business Start-Ups* (Vol. 7, No. 5, May 1995, pp. 84-87). By Charles E. Davis.

"The Best Way to Start A Business" in *Working Woman* (March 1996, pp. 33-34, 74). By Mitchell Stern.

"Beyond the Basics" in *Income Opportunities* (Vol. 29, No. 7, July 1994, pp. 24, 26). By Robert L. Perry.

Business Brokerage Business Guide. Irvine, CA: Entrepreneur, Inc.

Business Buying Basics. Poway, CA: Robert Erdmann Publishing, 1992. By Martin Bloom.

"Business Opportunity 500" in *Entrepreneur* (Vol. 23, No. 7, July 1995, pp. 134-169). By Shannon Hill.

"Buy Now—Avoid the Rush" in *Inc.* (February 1991, pp. 36-45). By John Case.

Buy the Right Business—At the Right Price: The Guide to Small Business Acquisition. Dover, NH: Upstart Publishing Co., Inc. By Brian Knight.

"Buyer Beware" in *Business Start-Up* (Vol. 7, No. 8, August 1995, p. 8). By Jacquelyn Lynn.

Buying a Business. Menlo Park, CA: Crisp Publications, Inc., 1993. By Ronald J. McGregor.

"The Buying Game" in *Entrepreneur* (Vol. 23, No. 3, March 1995, pp. 132-137). By David R. Evanson.

Buying In: A Complete Guide to Acquiring a Business or Professional Practice. New York, NY: McGraw-Hill, Inc., 1991. By Lawrence W. Tuller.

Buying and Selling a Business: A Step-by-Step Guide. Somerset, NJ: John Wiley & Sons, Inc., 1988. By Robert F. Klueger.

Buying and Selling a Business Successfully: A Proven Guide for Entrepreneurs. Homewood, IL: Dow Jones-Irwin, 1990. By Arnold S. Goldstein.

Buying and Selling Private Companies and Businesses. Charlottesville, VA: MICHIE, fourth edition, 1992. By Humphrey Wine and Simon Beswick.

Buying & Selling Small Business. Bellingham, WA: Self-Counsel Press, Inc., 1994. By Michael M. Coltman.

Buying Your Own Business. Holbrook, MA: Adams Publishing, 1995. By Russell Robb.

"Caveat Emptor" in *Income Opportunities* (Vol. 30, No. 3, March 1995, pp. 76-78, 80). By Robert L. Perry.

"Choosing A Dance Partner Ain't Easy" in *Computer Reseller News* (No. 576, May 2, 1994, pp. 16). By Robert C. DeMarzo.

"Company for Sale" in *Working Woman* (Vol. 17, No. 6, June 1992, pp. 38-40). By Jane Applegate.

The Complete Guide to Selling Your Business. Dover, NH: Upstart Publishing Co., Inc. By Paul S. Sperry and Beatrice H. Mitchell.

"CPR Owner Sees the Benefits of Age" in *Crain's Small Business* (December 1995, p. 16). By Michelle Krebs.

"Forward Spin" in *Black Enterprise* (Vol. 25, No. 9, April 1995, pp. 17). By Hiawatha Bray.

Getting Out: A Step-by-Step Guide to Selling a Business or Professional Practice. Blue Ridge Summit, PA: TAB Books, Inc., 1990. By Lawerence W. Tuller.

"Golden Opportunity" in *Entrepreneur* (Vol. 23, No. 7, July 1995, pp. 122-126, 128-130, 132-133). By Andrew A. Caffey.

"Good Buy?" in *Entrepreneur* (Vol. 23, No. 5, May 1995, pp. 74, 76-77). By Patricia Schiff Estess.

Guide to Buying & Selling A Business, Vol. 1. Fort Worth, TX: Practitioners Publishing Co., 1995. By William R. Bischoff.

Guide to Buying & Selling a Business, Vol. 2. Fort Worth, TX: Practitioners Publishing Co., 1995. By William R. Bischoff.

How to Buy a Business in the Country. New York, NY: Gordon Press, Publishers, 1991.

How to Buy a Business with No Money Down: The Complete Guide to Finding, & Buying, the Business You Want. Rockville Centre, NY: International Wealth Success, 1996.

How to Buy a Great Business With No Cash Down. Somerset, NJ: John Wiley & Sons, Inc., 1991. By Arnold S. Goldstein.

How to Buy or Sell a Business. Denver, CO: U.S. Small Business Administration (SBA).

How to Buy a Small Business. Babylon, NY: Pilot Books, revised edition, 1987. By M. A. Mangold.

How to Find Financial Information About Companies. West Nyack, NY: Todd Publications.

How Much Is Your Business Worth? How to Value a Small Business. Seattle, WA: Law Forum Press, 1988. By Don Berry.

How to Sell Your Business for the Best Price (With the Least Worry). Burr Ridge, IL: Probus Publishing Company, Inc., 1990. By Vaughn Cox.

How to Start, Expand and Sell a Business: The Complete Guide for Entrepreneurs. Santa Barbara, CA: Venture Perspective Press, third edition, 1991. By James C. Comiskey.

"Instant Success: Buy an Existing Business" in *Income Opportunities* (December/January 1991, p. 66). By Holly A. Miller.

Legal Handbook for Small Business. New York, NY: AMACOM, revised edition, 1989. By Marc J. Lane.

Mergers and Acquisitions: The Human Factor. Newton, MA: Butterworth-Heinemann, 1992. By Sue Cartwright.

Negotiating the Purchase or Sale of a Business. Grants Pass, OR: PSI Research.

"A New Chapter" in *Entrepreneur* (April 1991, pp. 163-169). By Mark Henricks.

"One Person's Experience: How to Buy an Existing Business or Franchise" in *Crain's Small Business* (December 1995, p. 16). By Michelle Krebs.

"Performance of Acquisitions of Distressed Firms" in *Academy of Management Journal* (Vol. 37, No. 4, August 1994, pp. 972-989). By Farry D. Bruton, Benjamin M. Oviatt and Margaret A. White.

"The Pros & Cons of Buying a Business" in *Black Enterprise* (Vol. 25, No. 4, November 1994, pp. 143-153). By Courtney Price.

Purchase and Sale of Small Businesses: Tax and Legal Aspects. New York, NY: John Wiley & Sons, Inc., second edition, 1991. By Marc J. Lane.

Research Guide to Corporate Acquisitions, Mergers, and Other Restructuring. Westport, CT: Greenwood Publishing Group, Inc., 1992. By Michael Halperin.

The Right Fit: The Entrepreneur's Guide to Finding the Perfect Business. Blue Ridge Summit, PA: TAB Books, Inc., 1988. By Halloran.

Smart Way to Buy a Business: An Entrepreneur's Guide to Questions That Must Be Asked. Irving, TX: Woodland Publishers, 1986. By John C. Kohl, Sr.

"So, You Want to Buy a Business?" in *Black Enterprise* (April 1991, pp. 47-56). By Michelle L. Singletary and Kevin D. Thompson.

Suggestions for Starting a Business From Businesses That Are Going Out of Business. Denver, CO: Center for Self-Sufficiency Publishing, revised edition, 1992.

"Trading Up" in *Entrepreneur* (Vol. 23, No. 2, February 1995, pp. 170-171). By Laura Radloff.

"Traps To Avoid When Purchasing a Business" in *Journal of Financial Planning* (Vol. 7, No. 1, January 1994, pp. 38-41). By Gene H. Johnson, Rudolph S. Lindbeck, and Winston N. McVea, Jr.

"Understanding Business Protocol" in *Black Enterprise* (Vol. 25, No. 9, April 1995, pp. 36). By Wiley M. Woodard.

"When Up Means Down" in *Crain's Detroit Business* (Vol. 11, No. 4, January 23-29, 1995, pp. 38-39). By Matt Roush.

"Where Sellers Can Spot Buyers" in *Inc.* (Vol. 15, No. 8, August 1993, pp. 32). By Bruce G. Posner.

Customer Service

Achieving Excellence Through Customer Service. Englewood Cliffs, NJ: Prentice Hall, 1991. By John Tschohl with Steve Franzmeier.

AMA Customer Satisfaction Research. Lincolnwood, IL: NTC Publishing Group, 1994. By Alan Dutka.

"At Your Service" in *Business Start-Ups* (Vol. 7, No. 5, May 1995, pp. 72, 74). By Lin Grensing-Pophal.

"At Your Service" in *Entrepreneur* (Vol. 23, No. 3, March 1995, pp. 222). By Stephen Barlas.

Benchmarking Customer Service. Philadelphia, PA: Trans-Atlantic Publications, 1995. By Glen Peters.

Beyond Customer Service. Menlo Park, CA: Crisp Publications. By Richard F. Gerson.

Building Bridges to Customers. Portland, OR: Productivity Press, 1995. By Gerald A. Michaelson.

"Capture the Future" in *Success* (Vol. 40, No. 10, December 1993, pp. 63-70). By Katherine Callan.

"Child's Play" in *Entrepreneur* (Vol. 23, No. 12, November 1995, pp. 32). By Lynn Beresford.

"Companies Greet E-mail Nation" in *Inc.* (Vol. 17, No. 6, May 1995, pp. 133). By Susan Greco.

The Complete Customer Service Letter Book. New York, NY: McGraw-Hill, Inc., 1995. By Edward W. Werz.

The Complete Guide to Customer Service. Somerset, NJ: John Wiley & Sons, Inc., 1989. By Linda M. Lash.

Creating a Customer Focused Company: 25 Proven Customer Service Strategies. Philadelphia, PA: Trans-Atlantic Publications, 1995. By Ian Linton.

Creating Customer Value: The Path to Sustainable Competitive Advantage. Cincinnati, OH: South-Western Publishing Co., 1995. By Earl Naumann.

Creating Customers for Life. Portland, OR: Productivity Press, 1995. By Eberhard E. Scheuing.

Creating Values for Customers: Designing and Implementing a Total Corporate Strategy. Somerset, NJ: John Wiley & Sons, Inc., 1991. By William A. Band.

The Customer Comes Second: And Other Secrets of Exceptional Service. New York, NY: William Morrow & Co., Inc., 1994. By Hal F. Rosenbluth.

Customer Driven Growth. Reading, MA: Addison-Wesley Publishing, 1996. By Richard Whiteley.

Customer Driven Strategy: Winning Through Operational Excellence. New York, NY: John Wiley and Sons, 1995. By Thomas E. Wallace.

The Customer Is Key: Gaining an Unbeatable Advantage Through Customer Satisfaction. Somerset, NJ: John Wiley & Sons, Inc., 1991. By Milind M. Lele and Jagdish N. Sheth.

Customer Service: A Practical Approach. Englewood Cliffs, NJ: Prentice Hall, 1996. By Elaine K. Harris.

Customer Service for Dummies. Indianapolis, IN: I D G Books Worldwide, 1995. By Karen Dunn.

The Customer Service Rep's Survival Guide: How to Keep Your Customers Coming Back. Chicago, IL: Dartnell Corp., 1989. By David Dee.

Customer Service: Skills and Concepts for Business. Burr Ridge, IL: Irwin Professional Publishing, 1995. By Robert W. Lucas.

"Customers" in *Business Start-Ups* (Vol. 7, No. 12, December 1995, pp. 12, 14). By Jacquelyn Lynn.

"Customers For Keeps" in *Selling Power* (Vol. 16, No. 3, April 1996, pp. 50-51). By John Graham.

Delivering Customer Value: It's Everyone's Job. Portland, OR: Productivity Press, 1995. By Karl Albrecht.

Delivering Knock Your Socks off Service. New York, NY: AMACOM, 1991. By Kristin Anderson and Ron Zemke.

The Dynamics of Service: Reflections on the Changing Nature of Customer-Provider Interactions. San Francisco, CA: Jossey-Bass, 1995. By Barbara A. Gutek.

Employee Incentive Contests: For Improved Marketing, Customer Service, and Morale. Chapel Hill, NC: Silverpoint Press, 1995. By Dave Marley.

"Engineering Customer Experiences" in *Marketing Management* (Vol. 3, No. 3, Winter 1994, pp. 8-19). By Lewis P. Carbone and Stephan H. Haeckel.

"Entreprenuerism + Customer Service = Success" in *Management Review* (Vol. 82, No. 11, November 1993, pp. 38-44). By Lori Stones and Kelly O. Lynn.

"Fax Forward" in *Entrepreneur* (Vol. 23, No. 7, July 1995, pp. 56). By Jacquelyn Lynn.

"First Impressions" in *Business Start-Ups* (Vol. 8, No. 1, January 1996, p. 10). By Jonathan Leer.

"Five Things Customers Don't Need" in *ABA Banking Journal* (Vol. 86, No. 1, January 1994, pp. 55-57). By John R. Graham.

40 Activities for Improving Customer Service. Brookfield, VT: Ashgate Publishing Co., 1996. By Ian Linton.

Front-Line Customer Service: 15 Keys for Customer Satisfaction. Somerset, NJ: John Wiley & Sons, Inc., 1990. By Clay Carr.

Great Customer Service on the Telephone. New York, NY: AMACOM, 1992. By Kristin Anderson.

Great Customer Service for Your Small Business, 1995. By Richard F. Gerson.

"Guaranteed Growth" in *Inc.* (Vol. 17, No. 12, September 1995, pp. 69-70, 72, 75, 76, 78). By Joshua Hyatt.

"How to Make Your Ex-Boss Your Client" in *Black Enterprise* (Vol. 24, No. 9, April 1994, pp. 92-96). By Caryne Brown.

How to Turn Customer Service Into Customer Sales. Lincolnwood, IL: NTC Business Books, 1989. By Bernard Katz.

"In the Customer's Shoes" in *Inc.* (Vol. 17, No. 6, May 1995, pp. 45-46, 48-53). By Jay Finegan.

"An Independent Point of View" in *Stores* (Vol. 76, No. 3, March 1994, pp. 57-58). By Bill Pearson.

"The Informers" in *Inc.* (Vol. 17, No. 3, March 1995, pp. 50-52, 54, 56, 59, 61). By John Kerr.

The Kaizen Way to Successful Customer Service. Lanham, MD: National Book Network, 1995. By Europe-Japan Center Staff.

"Keep Cash Flowing During Down Times" in *Nation's Business* (Vol. 81, No. 4, April 1993, pp. 10). By Bradford McKee.

Keeping Customers Happy. Bellingham, WA: Self-Counsel Press, Inc., third edition, 1994. By Jacqueline Dunckel and Brian Taylor.

"Lip Service" in *Business Start-Ups* (Vol. 8, No. 2, February 1996, p. 78, 80). By Lynn L. Norquist.

Lip Service vs. Customer Service: Making Customer Cents for Customer Sense. Dubuque, IA: Kendall Hunt Publishing Co., 1995. By Lynda Jeppesen.

"Long Live The Customer" in *Selling Power* (Vol. 16, NO. 3, April 1996, pp. 56-57). By Tim Becker.

"Make Your Customers' Dreams Come Alive" in *STN* (Vol. 18, No. 3, January 1994, pp. 20). By Thomas Richards.

"Make Your Service Fail-Safe" in *Sloan Management Review* (Vol. 35, No. 3, Spring 1994, pp. 35-44). By Richard B. Chase and Douglas M. Stewart.

Managing to Keep the Customer: How to Achieve and Maintain Superior Customer Service Throughout the Organization. San Francisco, CA: Jossey-Bass, Inc., Publishers, revised edition, 1993. By Robert L. Desatnick and Denis H. Detzel.

Managing Knock Your Socks Off Service. San Diego, CA: Pfeiffer & Co. By Chip R. Bell and Ron Zemke.

Managing Quality Customer Service. Menlo Park, CA: Crisp Publications. By William B. Martin.

"Marketing's Colors: Al's GasTown" in *Marketing Management* (Vol. 3, No. 2, pp. 16-24). By Thomas Bonoma.

Measuring Customer Satisfaction. Menlo Park, CA: Crisp Publications. By Richard F. Gerson.

Meeting Customer Needs. Newton, MA: Butterworth-Heinemann, 1994. By Ian Smith.

Multicultural Customer Service. Burr Ridge, IL: Irwin Professional Publishing, 1995. By Leslie Aguilar.

"The Personal Touch" in *Income Opportunities* (Vol. 30, No. 7, July 1995, pp. 80-81). By Richard J. Maturi.

Quality Customer Service. Menlo Park, CA: Crisp Publications. By William B. Martin.

The Quest for Quality: Prescriptions for Service Excellence. New York, NY: Saint Martin's Press, 1996. By Phillip S. Wexler.

Raving Fans: A Revolutionary Approach to Customer Service. New York, NY: William Morrow & Co., Inc., 1993. By Ken Blanchard and Sheldon Bowles.

Real-World Customer Service: Tried and True Techniques for Giving Your Customers Superior Service Every Time. Naperville, IL: Sourcebooks Inc., 1995. By Bernice B. Johnston.

"Repeat Business" in *Income Opportunities* (Vol. 31, No. 4, April 1996, pp. 48, 50, 52). By Sheila Gibson.

"Sales Tales" in *Entrepreneur* (Vol. 23, No. 8, August 1995, pp. 180, 182, 184). By Jeffrey Gitomer.

The Service Edge: 101 Companies That Profit From Customer Care. New York, NY: Plume. By Ron Zemke and Dick Schaaf.

"Service Savvy" in *Business Start-Ups* (Vol. 8, No. 1, January 1996, pp. 48-50, 52). By Paul Hughes.

Service, Service, Service...The Key to Winning and Keeping Customers for Life. Overland Park, KS: National Press Publications, 1992. By Marian Thomas.

"Shopping Spy" in *Income Opportunities* (Vol. 30, No. 12, December 1995, pp. 92, 94, 96). By Laurel Berger.

Strategic Customer Alliances: How to Win, Manage & Develop Key Account Business in the 1990s. Burr Ridge, IL: Irwin Professional Publishing, 1994. By Ken Burnett.

"Success Insured Via Customer Service" in *Crain's Small Business* (October 1995, p. 23). By Jeffrey McCracken.

"Survey Says..." in *Entrepreneur* (Vol. 23, No. 5, May 1995, pp. 60-61). By Jacquelyn Lynn.

Sustaining Knock Your Socks Off Service. New York, NY: AMACOM, 1993. By Ron Zemke and Thomas K. Connellan.

"Take Careful Aim to 'Bullet-Proof' Profits" in *Crain's Detroit Business* (Vol. 10, No. 48, November 28-December 4, 1994). By John Groustra.

Telephone Terrific! Facts, Fun and 103 "How-To" Tips for Phone Success. Chicago, IL: Dartnell Corporation, 1994. By David Dee.

"Tough Customers" in *Entrepreneur* (Vol. 23, No. 2, February 1995, pp. 58-59). By Gayle Sato Stodder.

"Turn Customer Service into Customer Profitability" in *Management Review* (Vol. 83, No. 7, July 1994, pp. 22-24). By Robert E. Wayland

Twenty-Five Tips for Customer Service: An Action Plan for Service Success. Philadelphia, PA: Trans-Atlantic Publications, Inc., 1995. By Ian Linton.

Twenty Ways to Improve Customer Service. Menlo Park, CA: Crisp Publications. By Lloyd Finch.

Value Added Customer Service: The Employees Guide to Creating Satisfied Customer. Chicago, IL: Contemporary Books, 1996. By Tom Reilly.

"Waxing Customer Service and Cars" in *Management Review* (Vol. 83, No. 7, July 1994, pp. 25-28). By Jo-Ann Johnston.

"Where Did We Go Wrong?" in *Inc.* (Vol. 17, No. 10, July 1995, pp. 91). By Susan Greco.

"Working the Night Shift" in *Income Opportunities* (Vol. 31, No. 2, February 1996, pp. 18-21). By Dale D. Buss.

"Working Successfully With the Difficult Client" in *Trusts & Estates* (Vol. 134, No. 2, February 1995, pp. 8-33). By Roy Adams, Charles Fox, Debra Stetter and John Utley.

"You Sell Merchandise, But Customer Buys Service" in *Crain's Small Business* (March 1996, p. 18). By Ken Guoin.

"Your Secret Weapon" in *Success* (Vol. 42, No. 1, February 1995, pp. 48A-48H). By Thomas J. Winninger.

Entrepreneurial Traits/Skills

"Beyond Work" in *Inc.* (The Inc. 500: Special Issue, Vol. 17, No. 15, October 1995, pp. 155, 152). By Christopher Caggiano.

"The Big Lie" in *Inc.* (Vol. 18, No. 3, March 1996, pp. 70-71, 73, 75). By Steven Berglas.

"Born To Be Wild" in *Entrepreneur* (Vol. 24, No. 4, April 1996, pp. 13). By Lynn Beresford.

The Brass Tacks Entrepreneur. New York, NY: Henry Holt & Company, Inc., 1993. By Jim Schell.

"Character Study" in *Entrepreneur* (Vol. 24, No. 2, February 1996, pp. 30). By Jacquelyn Lynn.

Contemporary Entrepreneurs. Detroit, MI: Omnigraphics Inc., 1992. By Craig E. Aronoff, Editor.

"Do or Die" in *Business Start-Ups* (Vol. 7, No. 11, November 1995, pp. 22-24, 26). By Jacquelyn Lynn.

"Dream On" in *Business Start-Ups* (Vol. 7, No. 6, June 1995, p. 9).

E Is for Ethics: Essentials for Entrepreneurs. Boulder, CO: Lifelong Learning Options, 1995. By Lorraine M. Zinn.

The Entrepreneur Small Business Advisor and Desk Reference. New York, NY: John Wiley & Sons, 1995. By Entrepreneur Magazine Staff.

The Entrepreneurial Mind: Winning Strategies for Starting, Renewing, & Harvesting. Amherst, NH: Brick House Publishing Co., Inc., 1994. By Jeffry A. Timmons.

Hail Entrepreneur!: An Encyclopedia of Basic Survival Skills. Pittsburgh, PA: Dorrance Publishing Co., 1994. By Edward Lowe.

"Hoop Dreams" in *Business Start-Ups* (Vol. 7, No. 6, June 1995, pp. 58, 60, 62, 64-65). By Jacquelyn Lynn.

How to Think Like an Entrepreneur. New York, NY: Bret Publishing Limited Partnership, 1994. By Michael B. Shane.

"I'm Mary, and I'm a Workaholic" in *Inc.* (Vol. 18, No. 5, April 1996, pp. 29-30). By Mary Baechler.

"The Joy Of Business" in *Entrepreneur* (Vol. 23, No. 8, August 1995, pp. 144, 146-148). By Debra Phillips.

"Learning Curve" in *Income Opportunities* (Vol. 30, No. 1, January 1995, pp. 98, 100). By Robert L. Perry.

Mind Your Own Business: Getting Started As an Entrepreneur. Indianapolis, IN: JIST Works, 1994. By LaVerne Ludden.

"New Frontiers" in *Entrepreneur* (Vol. 23, No. 5, May 1995, pp. 158, 160-165). By Bob Weinstein.

"A Perfect World?" in *Small Business Opportunities* (Vol. 8, No. 3, May 1996, pp. 20, 40). By Anne Hart.

"Reality Check" in *Entrepreneur* (Vol. 23, No. 8, August 1995, pp. 166-170). By Erika Kotite.

Secrets of a Successful Entrepreneur: How to Start & Succeed at Running Your Own Business. Pleasanton, CA: K & A Publications, 1993. By Gene Dailey.

Small Business Management Guide: Advice from the Brass-Tacks Entrepreneur. New York, NY: Henry Holt & Company, Inc., 1994. By Jim Schell.

"Soul Man" in *Entrepreneur* (Vol. 23, No. 11, October 1995, pp. 144-149). By Robert McGarvey.

"Step 1: Choosing Your Business" in *Business Start-Ups* (Vol. 8, No. 5, May 1996, pp. 12, 14). By Kylo-Patrick Hart.

Street Smarts: Real Life Lessons from a Successful Entrepreneur. Evanston, IL: Evanston Publishing, Inc., 1994. By John Fernandez.

"Studying the Entrepreneurial Process" in *Income Opportunities* (Vol. 31, No. 3, March 1996, pp. 4-5). By Michele Marrinan.

"Success Secrets" in *Business Start-Ups* (Vol. 7, No. 8, August 1995, pp. 46-47). By Bob Weinstein.

A Survival Guide for the Novice Entrepreneur: Crucial Things You Need to Know-If You Wanted to Survive & Succeed. Charlottesville, VA: Hampton Roads Publishing Co., 1993. By Joan M. Burge.

"Take a Break" in *Business Start-Ups* (Vol. 7, No. 6, June 1995, pp. 66, 68-69). By Guen Sublette.

Target Success: How You Can Become a Successful Entrepreneur-Regardless of Your Background. Holbrook, MA: Adams Publishing, 1993. By Don Dwyer.

"Thanks for the Memory" in *Business Start-Ups* (Vol. 7, No. 2, February 1995, p. 13). By Erika Kotite.

"The Thrill Is On" in *Entrepreneur* (Vol. 23, No. 1, January 1995, pp. 274-276, 279-280). By Leah Ingram.

"Top Dogs" in *Entrepreneur* (Vol. 23, No. 1, January 1995, pp. 11). By Janean Huber and Debra Phillips.

"Turning Points" in *Income Opportunities* (Vol. 31, No. 4, April 1996, pp. 12-17). By Malinda Reinke.

What's Stopping You?: Attitude Adjustment for the About-to-Be Entrepreneur. Point Richmond, CA: Know How Now, 1995. By William A. Remas.

"Workaholics Anonymous" in *Entrepreneur* (Vol. 23, No. 8, August 1995, pp. 13). By Lynn Beresford.

Working Without a Net: The Realities of Going Into Business for Yourself. Huntington, NY: Vocational Video, 1995. By Daniel J. Fardella.

Young Entrepreneur's Guide to Creating What Matters Most: Building Attitudes, Behaviors & an Action Plan for Success in Your Own Business. Forest Grove, OR: Courage Press, 1994. By Mary S. Moore.

"Zeal" in *Business Start-Ups* (Vol. 7, No. 12, December 1995, p. 78). By Jacquelyn Lynn.

"Zen-trepreneurs" in *Entrepreneur* (Vol. 23, No. 4, April 1995, pp. 58-59). By Mark Henricks.

Financial Management

ABC's of Borrowing. Denver, CO: U.S. Small Business Administration (SBA).

Account for Your Own Success: Everything You Need to Manage Your Own Business and Personal Finances. Alexandria, VA: Management Communications Systems, Inc. (MCS), 1993. By Dan Meyer.

American Bank Directory. Skokie, IL: Thomson Financial Publishing Inc., semiannual, April and October. By Elizabeth F. Swann, Editor.

American Banker—Top Commercial Banks by Assets, Deposits. New York, NY: American Banker-Bond Buyer, semiannual, March and September. By Dave Branch.

Analysis for Financial Management. Burr Ridge, IL: Richard D. Irwin, Inc., fourth edition, 1994. By Robert C. Higgins.

"The Art of Financial Mapping" in *Black Enterprise* (October 1994, pp. 83-84, 86, 89-90). By Gracian Mack.

"At the Brink" in *Inc.* (Vol. 17, No. 16, November 1995, pp. 21-22). By Rick McCloskey.

"Balancing Act" *Entrepreneur* (Vol. 23, No. 3, March 1995, pp. 56, 58- 59, 61). By Bob Weinstein.

The Barclays Guide to Financial Management for the Small Business. Cambridge, MA: Blackwell Publishers, 1990. By Peter Wilson.

"Barter Power" in *Business Start-Ups* (Vol. 8, No. 3, March 1996, pp. 12, 14). By Carla Goodman.

"By the Numbers" in *Business Start-Ups* (Vol. 8, No. 5, May 1996, pp. 66, 68-70). By Jacquelyn Lynn.

"Can Your Bank Do This?" in *Inc.* (Vol. 18, No. 3, March 1996, pp. 29-30, 33-36, 38). By Robert A. Mamis.

"Capital Steps" in *Inc.* (Vol. 18, No. 2, February 1996, pp. 42-44, 47). By Jill Andresky Fraser.

"Capitalists on a Mission" in *Black Enterprise* (Vol. 25, No. 4, November 1994, pp. 166-167, 170-171). By Mark Lowery.

The Cash Flow Control Guide: Methods to Understand and Control the Small Business's Number One Problem. Dover, NH: Upstart Publishing Co., Inc., 1989. By David H. Bangs, Jr.

"The Cash-Flow Crunch" in *Income Opportunities* (Vol. 30, No. 5, May 1995, pp. 77-78). By Richard J. Maturi.

Cash Traps: Small Business Secrets for Reducing Costs and Improving Cash Flow. Somerset, NJ: John Wiley & Sons, Inc., 1992. By Jeffrey P. Davidson and Charles W. Dean.

Changing Roles of Financial Management. Morristown, NJ: Financial Executives Research Foundation, 1990. By Patrick J. Keating and Stephen F. Jablonsky.

"The Cobbler's Shoes" in *Inc.* (Vol. 18, No. 1, January 1996, pp. 21-22). By Roxanne Coady.

Collection Agency Directory. Warren, MI: First Detroit Corporation, 1995. By Albert W. Scace.

Controller's and Treasurer's Desk Reference. New York, NY: McGraw-Hill, Inc., 1995. By Christopher R. Malburg.

Corporate Liquidity: A Guide to Managing Working Capital. San Rafael, CA: Professional Publishing, 1993. By Kenneth L. Parkinson and Jarl G. Kallberg.

"Cost Controls" in *Income Opportunities* (Vol. 30, No. 5, May 1995, pp. 8). By Lana Sanderson.

"A Costly Start-Up's Wise Moves" in *Inc.* (Vol. 16, No. 9, September 1994, pp. 125). By Jill Andresky Fraser.

Directory of the Savings & Community Bankers of America. Washington, DC: Savings & Community Bankers of America, annual, July.

"Dream Accountant" in *Income Opportunities* (Vol. 30, No. 1, January 1995, pp. 108, 110). By Peg Byron.

Entrepreneurial Finance: Taking Control of Your Financial Decision Making. Dana Point, CA: Lord Publishing, Inc., 1988. By Robert C. Ronstadt.

"Entrepreneurial Problem Solver; Finding a Financial Mentor" in *Executive Female* (Vol. 17, No. 4, July-August 1994, pp. 28). By Joan Delaney.

"Family Business Consulting" in *Tax Advisor* (Vol. 24, No. 1, January 1994, pp. 3-16). By Gary A. Zwick.

"Finance for Small and Medium-Sized Enterprises" in *International Journal of Bank Marketing* (Vol. 12, No. 6, 1994, pp. 3-9). By Pamela Edwards, Peter Turnbull.

Financial Basics of Small Business Success: Deciding Which Reports to Read and Understand. Menlo Park, CA: Crisp Publications, Inc., 1994. By James O. Gill.

Financial Essentials for Small Business Success: Accounting, Planning & Recordkeeping Techniques for a Healthy Bottom Line. Dover, NH: Upstart Publishing Company, Inc., 1994. By Joe Tabet.

"Financial Forecast" in *Entrepreneur* (Vol. 22, No. 13, December 1994, pp. 97-100). By Cynthia E. Griffin.

Financial Letters for the Small Business. Somerset, NJ: John Wiley & Sons, Inc., 1992. By Thomas Morton.

Financial Management. New York, NY: Routledge Inc., 1995. By Leslie Chadwick.

Financial Management. Cincinnati, OH: South-Western Publishing Co., 1997.

Financial Management. Hauppauge, NY: Barron's Educational Series, Inc., 1991. By Joel G. Siegel.

Financial Management: How to Make a Go of Your Business. New York, NY: Gordon Press Publishers, 1995.

Financial Management: How to Make a Go of Your Business. Washington, DC: U.S. Government Printing Office, 1986.

Financial Management of the Small Firm. Englewood Cliffs, NJ: Prentice Hall, second edition, 1986. By Ernest W. Walker and J. Petty.

Financial Management Techniques for Small Business. Grants Pass, OR: Oasis Press. By Art R. De Thomas.

Financial Planning for New Businesses. Somerset, NJ: John Wiley & Sons, Inc., 1985. By V. Durkacz.

"Financial Statement Serves as Foundation for Growth" in *Crain's Small Business* (October 1995, p. 20). By Jim Brady.

Financial Structure in Small Business. New York, NY: Springer-Verlag New York, Inc., 1988. By D. Van der Wijst.

Financial Troubleshooting: An Action Plan for Money Management in the Small Business. Dover, NH: Upstart Publishing Co., Inc., 1992. By David H. Bangs, Jr.

"Fiscal Fix-Up" in *Independent Business* (Vol. 7, No. 2, March/April 1996, pp. 26-30, 32). By David Honodel.

"Five Strategies for Cutting Your Company's Costs" in *Working Woman* (Vol. 20, No. 7, July 1995, pp. 57-58). By Laura Teller.

"Gimme Shelter" in *Entrepreneur* (Vol. 23, No. 7, July 1995, pp. 43-45). By Lorayne C. Fiorillo.

The Global Directory of Financial Information Vendors. Burr Ridge, IL: Irwin Professional Publishing, 1993. By James Essinger, Editor.

"Golden Goose Mathematics" in *Nation's Business* (Vol. 83, No. 1, January 1995, pp. 54-55). By Craig E. Aronoff and John L. Ward.

Guide to Business Credit for Women, Minorities, and Small Businesses. New York, NY: Gordon Press, Publishers, 1992.

The Guide to Understanding Financial Statements. New York, NY: McGraw-Hill, Inc., second edition, 1995. By S.B. Costales and Geza Szurovy.

Hands-On Financial Controls for Your Small Business. Blue Ridge Summit, PA: TAB Books, Inc., 1991. By Cecil J. Bond.

"The House Business House Built" in *Crain's Small Business* (December 1995, p. 8). By Amy Lane.

"How to Figure Your Break-Even Point" in *Business Start-Ups* (Vol. 8, No. 2, February 1996, p. 12). By Carolyn Lawrence.

"Hunting for an Accountant" in *Pennsylvania CPA Journal* (Vol. 63, No. 4, Summer 1993, pp. 10-13). By Gerald J. Rosenthal.

"In Search of the Perfect Portfolio" in *Inc.* (Vol. 17, No. 16, pp. 26-28, 32, 35). By Neal Ochsner.

Introduction to Financial Management. Burr Ridge, IL: Richard D. Irwin, Inc., 1991. By C. P. Jones.

"Job One: Find Money" in *Success Magazine* (Vol. 41, No. 10, December 1994, pp. 23-33). By Jenny C. McCune.

Keeping the Books: Basic Recordkeeping and Accounting for the Small Business. Dover, NH: Upstart Publishing Co., Inc., second edition, 1993. By Linda Pinson and Jerry Jinnett.

"Keeping Track of Your Cashflow" in *Black Enterprise* (October 1994, pp. 93-94, 96). By Gracian Mack.

"Listing Your Company on a Stock Exchange" in *D & B Reports* (Vol. 40, No. 2, March/April 1992, pp. 62-63). By Mark Stevens.

"The Logic of Profit" in *Inc.* (Vol. 18, No. 3, March 1996, pp. 17). By Jack Stack.

Management Accounts: How to Use Them To Control Your Business. Brookfield, VT: Ashgate Publishing Co., 1995. By Tony Skone.

Managing by the Numbers: Financial Essentials for the Growing Business. Dover, NH: Upstart Publishing Co., Inc., 1992. By David H. Bangs, Jr.

"Managing Your Cash Flow" in *Black Enterprise* (Vol. 25, No. 10, May 1995, p. 38). By Ann Brown.

The McGraw-Hill Thirty-Six Hour Course in Finance for Nonfinancial Managers. New York, NY: McGraw-Hill, Inc., 1995. By Robert A. Cooke.

"Me & My Banker" in *Inc.* (Vol. 17, No. 3, March 1995, pp. 43-45, 48). By Robert A. Mamis.

"A New Year's Guide for CEOs" in *Inc.* (Vol. 18, No. 1, January 1996, pp. 30-37). By Martha E. Mangelsdorf.

"The Numbers Speak Volumes" in *Small Business Reports* (Vol. 19, No. 7, July 1994, pp. 39-43). By Lamont Change.

"On The Money" in *Entrepreneur* (Vol. 32, No. 4, April 1995, pp. 117-121). By David R. Evanson.

"Pay Bonuses for Profits" in *Inc.* (Vol. 17, No. 2, February 1995, pp. 107). By Susan Greco.

Polk Financial Institutions Directory. Nashville, TN: R. L. Polk & Co., semiannual. By Barbara Blake, Editor.

"Price Pointers" in *Business Start-Ups* (Vol. 6, No. 9, September 1994, pp. 102, 104-105). By Gloria Gibbs Marullo.

A Pricing Checklist for Small Retailers. Denver, CO: U.S. Small Business Administration (SBA).

Pricing Your Products and Services Profitably. Denver, CO: U.S. Small Business Administration (SBA).

"Put it in Writing" in *Business Start-Ups* (Vol. 7, No. 2, February 1995, pp. 26, 28-29). By Gloria Gibbs Marullo.

"Record-Keeping" in *Business Start-Ups* (Vol. 7, No. 12, December 1995, pp. 62-63). By Johanna S. Billings.

Saving Your Business: How to Survive Chapter 11 Bankruptcy and Successfully Reorganize Your Company. Englewood Cliffs, NJ: Prentice Hall, 1992. By Suzanne Caplan.

"Seizing an Opportunity: Do the Dollars Add Up?" in *Crain's Small Business* (December 1995, pp. 10-11). By Jeffrey McCracken.

"The Six Best Ways to Raise Cash" in *Money: Money Guide Supplement* (Vol. , No. , 1994, pp. 34-39). By Vanessa O'Connell.

The Small Business Financial Planner. New York, NY: John Wiley & Sons, Inc., 1989. By Gregory R. Glau.

The Small Business Survival Guide to Debits, Credits, and Cash: What Every Growing Business Needs to Know About Accounting & Finance. Burr Ridge, IL: Probus Publishing Company, Inc., 1993. By Rose Marie L. Bukics.

The Small Business Survival Guide: How to Manage Your Cash, Profits, and Taxes. Naperville, IL: Sourcebooks, Inc., 1992. By Robert E. Fleury.

"Stock Marketing" in *Entrepreneur* (Vol. 23, No. 4, April 1995, pp. 42, 44-45). By David R. Evanson.

"Super CPAs" in *Entrepreneur* (Vol. 23, No. 1, January 1995, pp. 43- 45). By David R. Evanson.

Taking Money Out of Your Corporation: Perfectly Legal Methods to Maximize Your Income. New York, NY: John Wiley & Sons, Inc., 1993. By M. John Storey.

"Taking Your Pulse" in *Business Start-Ups* (Vol. 8, No. 1, January 1996, p. 72). By Richard Maturi.

Ten Keys to Sales & Financial Success for Small Business. Alexandria, VA: Wave Communications, Inc., 1994. By Ron Torrence.

"Then and Now" in *Inc.* (Vol. 16, No. 9, September 1994, pp. 69-70, 75-77). By Leslie Brokaw and David Whitford.

Think Like an Investor. Irvine, CA: Entrepreneur Media Inc. By Nancy L. Scarlato.

Thomson Bank Directory. Skokie, IL: Thomson Financial Publishing, semiannual, May and November.

"Treasure Hunt" in *Business Start-ups* (October 1994, pp. 80-84). By Gustav Berle.

Understanding Cash Flow. Denver, CO: U.S. Small Business Administration (SBA).

Understanding Financial Statements. Menlo Park, CA: Crisp Publications. By James O. Gill.

Understanding and Managing Financial Information: The Non-financial Manager's Guide. Bellingham, WA: Self-Counsel Press, 1993. By Michael M. Coltman.

"Venturing Into Business" in *Black Enterprise* (Vol. 25, No. 9, April 1995, pp. 38). By Tania Pagett.

"Volumes of Bank Bashing" in *Detroit Free Press Business Monday* (February 20, 1995, Section F).

"Will Power" in *Entrepreneur* (Vol. 23, No. 12, November 1995, pp. 60, 62). By Lorayne C. Fiorillo.

"Your '96 Personal Finance Calendar" in *Working Woman* (January 1996, pp. 46-47).

Zero Cash Success Techniques Kit. Rockville Centre, NY: International Wealth Success, Inc., sixth edition, 1993. By Tyler G. Hicks.

Franchising

"About Face" in *Entrepreneur* (Vol. 23, No. 2, February 1995, pp. 166). By Janean Huber.

"Affordable Fast Food" in *Income Opportunities* (Vol. 29, No. 8, August 1994, pp. 22, 24, 26, 28, 30-31). By Robert L. Perry.

"All Talk, No Action" in *Black Enterprise* (Vol. 26, No. 2, September 1996, pp. 60-64). By Carolyn M. Brown.

"At Your Service" in *Income Opportunities* (Vol. 30, No. 6, June 1995, pp. 20-22, 24-25). By Robert L. Perry.

"Attention, Franchise Shoppers" in *Entrepreneur* (January 1991, pp. 94-99). By Irwin W. Fisk.

"B. E. Franchise 50 Report: Tapping into Low-Cost Franchising" in *Black Enterprise* (Vol. 23, No. 2, Sept. 1992, pp. 66-72). By Shelly Branch.

"The B. E. Franchise Start-Up Guide" in *Black Enterprise* (September 1990, pp. 73-75). By Alfred Edmond.

"Back In The Saddle" in *Entrepreneur* (Vol. 23, No. 11, October 1995, pp. 110). By Janean Chun.

Best Home-Based Franchises. New York, NY: Doubleday & Company Inc., 1992. Compiled by Philip Lief Group, Inc., staff.

The Best Nonfranchise Business Opportunities: The Smart Entrepreneur's Guide to Dealerships, License Agreements, Distributors, and More. New York, NY: Henry Holt & Company, Inc., 1993. By Andrew J. Sherman and Donna T. Cavanagh.

"Better Together: Perspectives" in *Franchising World* (Vol. 27, No. 1, January/February 1995, pp. 12-23).

"Beyond the Basics" in *Income Opportunities* (Vol. 29, No. 7, July 1994, pp. 24, 26). By Robert L. Perry.

"Black Franchise Hopefuls Beware" in *Black Enterprise* (Vol. 26, No. 2, September 1995, pp. 81-82, 84, 86).

The Blueprint for Franchising a Business. Somerset, NJ: John Wiley & Sons, Inc., 1987. By Steven S. Raab and Gregory Matusky.

Bond's Franchise Guide. Oakland, CA: Source Book Publications, 1996. By Bond Staff.

"Breaking Ground" in *Entrepreneur* (Vol. 23, No. 7, July 1995, pp. 222, 224-225). By Janean Chun.

Buying Your First Franchise. Menlo Park, CA: Crisp Publications, 1994. By Rebecca Luhn.

"By The Book?" in *Entrepreneur* (Vol. 23, No. 5, May 1995, pp. 202, 204-205). By Janean Huber.

"Cable Vision" in *Crain's Detroit Business* (Vol. 11, No. 9, February 27-March 5, 1995, pp. 38-39). By Michael Goodin.

"Can This Business Be Franchised" in *Success* (Vol. 41, No. 5, June 1994, pp. 73-75).

"Capture the Future" in *Success* (Vol. 40, No. 10, December 1993, pp. 63-70). By Katherine Callan.

"Cashing In On Coupons" in *Small Business Opportunities* (Vol. 6, No. 5, September 1994, pp. 26-28, 90).

"Catch the High-Tech Wave" in *Income Opportunities* (Vol. 29, No. 7, July 1994, pp. 16, 18, 20, 22). By Robert L. Perry.

"Caveat Emptor" in *Income Opportunities* (Vol. 30, No. 3, March 1995, pp. 76-78, 80). By Robert L. Perry.

"Cease & Desist" in *Income Opportunities* (Vol. 29, No. 9, September 1994, pp. 48-56). By Robert L. Perry.

"Changing Times" in *Entrepreneur* (Vol. 23, No. 1, January 1995, pp. 84-90). By Janean Huber.

"Choosing a Franchise" in *Journal of Small Business Management* (Vol. 31, No. 2, April 1993, pp. 91-104). By David A. Baucus and Melissa S. Baucus and Sherrie E. Human.

"A Closer Look" in *Entrepreneur: Buyer's Guide to Franchise and Business Opportunities* (Vol. 22, No. 11, 1995, pp. 20, 22, 24-27). By Andrew A Caffey.

"Co-operation" in *Business Start-Ups* (Vol. 8, No. 2, February 1996, pp. 10, 12). By Janean Chun.

"Code of Honor?" in *Entrepreneur* (Vol. 22, No. 9, September 1994, pp. 216-218). By Janean Huber.

"The Collectively Bargained Franchise Agreement" In *Inc.* (Vol. 17, No. 16, November 1995, pp. 73-75). By Christopher Caggiano.

"Common Ground" in *Entrepreneur* (Vol. 23, No. 11, October 1995, pp. 168, 170, 172). By Lynn Beresford.

The Complete Franchise Book: What You Must Know & Are Rarely Told About Buying or Starting Your Own Franchise. Rocklin, CA: Prima Publishing & Communications, 1989. By Dennis L. Foster.

"Contract Renewal Can Be a Rude Awakening" in *Crain's Small Business* (February 1996, p. 14). By Julie Bennett.

"Corporate Castaways" in *Income Opportunities* (Vol. 30, No. 5, May 1995, pp. 18-22, 24, 26-27). By Robert L. Perry.

Directory of Franchising Organizations. Babylon, NY: Pilot Books, annual, January. By Samuel Small, Editor.

"Down To Business" in *Income Opportunities* (Vol. 31, No. 2, February 1996, pp. 52-60). By Robert L. Perry.

The Encyclopedia of Franchises and Franchising. New York, NY: Facts on File, Inc., 1989. By Dennis L. Foster.

Entrepreneur Magazine—Franchise 500 Survey Issue. Irvine, CA: Entrepreneur, Inc., annual, January. By Maria Anton, Editor.

Entrepreneur's Buyer's Guide to Franchise and Business Opportunities. Irvine, CA: Entrepreneur, Inc., annual, September. By Rieva Lesensky, Editor.

Evaluating Franchise Opportunities. Denver, CO: U.S. Small Business Administration (SBA).

"Exclusive Franchise Report: Cease & Desist" in *Income Opportunities* (Vol. 30, No. 2, February 1995, pp. 64-72). By Robert L. Perry.

"False Promises" in *Income Opportunities* (Vol. 29, No. 11, November 1994, pp. 36-40). By Robert L. Perry.

"Fast Cash In Fast Food" in *Small Business Opportunities* (Vol. 6, No. 5, September 1994, pp. 46).

The Fifty Best Low-Investment, High-Profit Franchises. Englewood Cliffs, NJ: Prentice Hall, 1994. By Robert L. Perry.

Financing Your Franchise. New York, NY: McGraw-Hill, Inc., 1993. By Andrew J. Sherman, Ripley Hotch, and Meg Whittemore.

"The Foreign Invasion" in *Income Opportunities* (Vol. 30, No. 7, July 1995, pp. 22-26, 82, 84). By Robert L. Perry.

"Four Paths to Franchising" in *Nation's Business* (October 1989, pp. 75-85). By Meg Whittemore.

Franchise. New York, NY: Little, Brown and Co., 1995.

Franchise. Mankato, MN: Creative Education, Inc., 1989. By Isaac Asimov.

"Franchise Advantage" in *Entrepreneur* (Vol. 23, No. 2, February 1995, pp. 132, 134-137). By Jacqueline Lynn.

Franchise Annual. Coral Springs, FL: B. Klein Publications, 1995.

Franchise Annual. West Nyack, NY: Todd Publications.

The Franchise Annual Directory, 1995: The Original Franchise Handbook and Directory. Lewiston, NY: Info Press, 1995. By Edward L. Dixon.

Franchise Bible: How to Buy a Franchise or Franchise Your Own Business. Grants Pass, OR: Oasis Press, 1994. By Erwin J. Keup.

"Franchise & Business Opportunities" in *Entrepreneur*: Buyer's Guide to Franchise & Business Opportunities (Vol. 22, No. 11, 1995, pp. 53). By Shannon Hill, et al.

"Franchise Finds" in *Small Business Opportunities* (Vol. 7, No. 1, January 1995, pp. 88).

"Franchise Fundamentals" in *New Business Opportunities* (November 1990, pp. 36-42). By Lynn Allison.

Franchise Handbook. Milwaukee, WI: Enterprise Magazines, Inc., quarterly. By Michael McDermott, Editor.

Franchise Kit: A Nuts & Bolts Guide to Owning & Running a Franchise Business. New York, NY: McGraw-Hill Co., 1995.

Franchise Opportunities. New York, NY: Sterling Publishing Co., 1995.

Franchise Opportunities Handbook. Washington, DC: Superintendent of Documents, 1991.

Franchise Opportunity Handbook. Indianapolis, IN: JIST Works, Inc., 1995. By LaVerne Ludden.

The Franchise Option: A Legal Guide. New York, NY: Elsevier Science, 1989. By Mark Abell.

"Franchise Outlook" in *Entrepreneur: Buyer's Guide to Franchise and Business Opportunities* (Vol. 22, No. 11, 1995, pp. 42-48). By Erika Kotite.

Franchise Riches Success Kit. Rockville Centre, NY: International Wealth Success, 1996. By Tyler G. Hicks.

The Franchise Survival Guide: Real-World Solutions for Turning Your Investment Into a Money-Making Business. Burr Ridge, IL: Probus Publishing Company, Inc., 1993. By Carol B. Green.

Franchises: Dollars & Sense—A Guide for Evaluating Franchises and Projecting Franchise Earnings. Dubuque, IA: Kendall/Hunt Publishing Co., 1993. By Warren L. Lewis.

"Franchises That Capitalize On Solving Our Problems" in *Inc.* (Vol. 16, No. 9, September 1994, pp. 106-109). By Echo Montgomery Garrett.

Franchises You Can Run From Home. Somerset, NJ: John Wiley & Sons, Inc., 1990. By Lynie Arden.

Franchising. Cincinnati, OH: South-Western Publishing Co., 1988. By Robert T. Justis and Richard J. Judd.

Franchising: A Case-Study Approach. Brookfield, VT: Ashgate Publishing Co., Inc., 1992. By Antony Dnes.

"The Franchising of Accounting and Tax Services" in *Practical Accountant* (Vol. 27, No. 8, August 1994, pp. 40-43). By Paul Clolery.

Franchising in America: The Development of a Business Method, 1840-1980. Chapel Hill, NC: University of North Carolina Press, 1992. By Thomas S. Dicke.

BIBLIOGRAPHY

"Franchising: American Business in High Gear" in *Franchising World* (Vol. 27, No. 1, January/February 1995, pp. 7-10). By Ed Rensi.

Franchising: An Accounting, Auditing, and Income Tax Guide: Somerset, NJ: John Wiley & Sons, Inc., 1993. By Ross A. McCallum.

"Franchising Beats the Recession" in *Nation's Business* (Vol. 80, No. 3, March 1992, pp. 55-64). By Meg Whittemore.

Franchising in Canada: Pros & Cons. Bellingham, WA: Self-Counsel Press, Inc., 1995. By Michael M. Coltman.

Franchising: Contemporary Issues & Research. Binghamton, NY: Haworth Press, Inc., 1995. By Patrick J. Kaufmann.

"Franchising Databases" in *Database* (Vol. 17, No. 3, June 1994, pp. 92-94). By Marydee Ojala.

Franchising for Free: Owning Your Own Business Without Investing Your Own Cash. Somerset, NJ: John Wiley & Sons, Inc., 1988. By Dennis L. Foster.

The Franchising Handbook. New York, NY: AMACOM, 1993. By Andrew J. Sherman, editor.

Franchising and Licensing: Two Ways to Build Your Business. New York, NY: AMACOM, 1991. By Andrew J. Sherman.

Franchising 1992: Business and Legal Issues. New York, NY: Practising Law Institute, 1992.

"Franchising as a Strategic Partnership" in *International Small Business Journal* (Vol. 10, No. 3, April-June 1992, pp. 40-52). By Cecilia M. Falbe and Thomas C. Dandridge.

Franchising: The Business Strategy That Changed the World. Englewood Cliffs, NJ: Prentice Hall, 1993. By Carrie Shook and Robert L. Shook.

Franchising: The How-To Book. Englewood Cliffs, NJ: Prentice Hall, 1986. By Lloyd T. Tarbutton.

Franchising: The Inside Story. New York, NY: HarperCollins Publishers, Inc., 1986. By John P. Hayes.

Franchising in the U.S.: Pros & Cons. Bellingham, WA: Self-Counsel Press, Inc., 1988. By Michael M. Coltman.

"Franchisors Aren't Using Aid and Incentives" in *Crain's Small Business* (February 1996, p. 15). By Julie Bennett.

"The Fund Zone" in *Entrepreneur* (Vol. 23, No. 1, January 1995, pp. 113-117). By Jacquelyn Lynn.

"The Future of Franchising...Today!" in *Business Start-Ups* (Vol. 8, No. 2, February 1996, pp. 34, 36-39). By Andrew A. Caffey.

"The Future Is...Wow" in *Crain's Small Business* (February 1995, pp. 1, 21). By H. Lee Murphy.

"Gatzaros' Projects" in *Crain's Detroit Business* (Vol. 11, No. 9, February 27-March 5, 1995, pp. 38-39). By Michael Goodin.

"Get Rich in '95" in *Small Business Opportunities* (Vol. 7, No. 1, January 1995, pp. 20, 22, 24, 26, 28, 30, 32, 34, 36, 38-40, 42-45). By Cheryl Rogers, et al.

"Global Warming" in *Entrepreneur* (Vol. 23, No. 1, January 1995, pp. 118-123). By Cynthia E. Griffin.

"Golden Opportunity" in *Entrepreneur* (Vol. 23, No. 7, July 1995, pp. 122-126, 128-130, 132-133). By Andrew A. Caffey.

"Golden Rule?" in *Entrepreneur* (Vol. 24, No. 4, April 1996, pp. 160, 162). By Janean Chun.

"Grow Or Die" in *Success* (Vol. 41, No. 6, July/August 1994, pp. 65). By Carol Steinberg.

Handbook of Successful Franchising. Blue Ridge Summit, PA: TAB Books, Inc., third edition, 1989. By Friedlander and Gurney.

"Happy New Year" in *Entrepreneur* (Vol. 24, No. 2, February 1996, pp. 170-171). By Janean Chun.

"The Hard Facts About Franchising" in *D & B Reports* (Vol. 42, No. 5, September/October 1993, pp. 36-38). By Kevin McDermott.

"Have Calculator, Will Franchise" in *CFO: The Magazine for Senior Financial Executives* (Vol. 10, No. 11, November 1994, pp. 21). By John P. Mello.

"Home-Based Franchises" in *Income Opportunities* (Mid-March 1990, pp. 51-52). By Lynie Arden.

How to Be a Franchisor. Washington, DC: International Franchise Association (IFA), 1989. By Robert E. Kushell and Carl E. Zwisler.

How to Buy and Manage a Franchise. New York, NY: Simon & Schuster Trade, 1993. By Joseph R. Mancuso and Donald Boroian.

"How to Fight Your Franchisor and Win" in *Money: Money Guide Supplement* (1994, pp. 28-32).

How to Franchise Your Business. Babylon, NY: Pilot Books, third edition, 1990. By Mack O. Lewis.

How to Open a Franchise Business. New York, NY: Avon Books, 1995. By Michael Powers.

International Franchise Association—Franchise Opportunities Guide. Washington, DC: International Franchise Association (IFA), Semiannual, October and April. By John Reynolds, Editor.

International Franchising Law. New York, NY: Matthew Bender & Co., Inc., 1993. By Dennis Campbell, editor.

"Interview With The Franchisee" in *Inc.* (Vol. 16, No. 12, November 1994, pp. 148-152, 154). By Echo Montgomery Garrett.

Investigate Before Investing: Guidance for Prospective Franchises. Washington, DC: International Franchise Association (IFA), 1992. By H. Bret Lowell and Lewis G. Rudnick.

"Is Franchising For You?" in *Entrepreneur: Buyer's Guide to Franchise and Business Opportunities* (Vol. 22, No. 11, 1995, pp. 14, 16-18). By Erika Kotite.

"Is Franchising For You?" in *Income Opportunities* (Vol. 31, No. 3, March 1996, pp. 38-40, 42). By Pamela Rohland.

Is Franchising for You?. Washington, DC: International Franchise Association (IFA), 1985. By Robert K. McIntosh.

"It's Not So Elementary, Watson" in *Entrepreneur* (January 1990, pp. 69-73). By Geraldine M. Strozier.

"It's Show Time" in *Entrepreneur* (Vol. 23, No. 4, April 1995, pp. 151-157). By Andrew A. Caffey and Janean Huber.

"It's Showtime" in *Entrepreneur* (Vol. 24, No. 2, February 1996, pp. 146, 148-149). By Andrew A. Caffey.

"The Kiddie Corner" in *Income Opportunities* (Vol. 30, No. 11, November 1995, pp. 58-64, 66). By Robert L. Perry.

"Learning Curve" in *Income Opportunities* (Vol. 30, No. 1, January 1995, pp. 98, 100). By Robert L. Perry.

"Less a Parent, More a Partner" in *Nation's Business* (Vol. 82, No. 3, March 1994, pp. 49-57). By Meg Whittemore.

Licensing—A Strategy for Profits: Useful Business Strategies. Chapel Hill, NC: KEW Licensing Press, 1990.

"Look Before You Leap" in *Inc.* (Vol. 17, No. 10, July 1995, pp. 23-24). By Timothy Bates.

"The Low Down" in *Income Opportunities* (Vol. 30, No. 10, October 1995, pp. 58-60, 62-63, 65-66). By Robert L. Perry.

"Low-Risk, High-Growth Franchises" in *Working Woman* (Vol. 21, No. 4, April 1996, pp. 51-52, 54-55). By Janet Bamford.

Mancuso's Small Business Basics: Start, Buy or Franchise Your Way to a Successful Business. Naperville, IL: Sourcebooks, Inc., 1995. By Joseph R. Mancuso.

"McSchool Days" in *Entrepreneur* (Vol. 23, No. 8, August 1995, pp. 200, 202, 205). By Lynn Beresford.

"Meet Your Match" in *Business Start-Ups* (Vol. 7, No. 2, February 1995, p. 12). By Janean Huber.

"Money from Home" in *Income Opportunities* (Vol. 29, No. 11, November 1994, pp. 28-34). By Robert L. Perry.

"New Attitude" in *Entrepreneur* (Vol. 23, No. 3, March 1995, pp. 194-195). By Heather Page.

"New Directions in Franchising" in *Nation's Business* (Vol. 83, No. 1, January 1995, pp. 45-52). By Meg Whittemore.

"New & Noteworthy" in *Income Opportunities* (Vol. 29, No. 9, September 1994, pp. 40-46). By Robert L. Perry.

"New Study Predicts Unsurpassed Growth in Franchising" in *Franchising World* (April 1990, pp. 20-25). By Joyce Endoso.

"9 Steps To Franchise Success" in *Small Business Opportunities* (Vol. 7, No. 1, January 1995, pp. 72, 90). By Leone Ackerly.

"No Hang-Out Booths Here" in *Restaurant Hospitality* (Vol. 75, No. 12, December 1991, pp. 122-128). By David Farkas.

North American Directory of Fast Food & Quick Service Restaurant Franchises. Yorktown Heights, NY: Limulus Inc. By Joseph Katz, Editor.

"O Pioneers!" in *Entrepreneur* (Vol. 22, No. 9, September 1994, pp. 138-143). By Karen Sulkis.

"On The Home Front" in *Income Opportunities* (Vol. 31, No. 4, April 1996, pp. 54-60, 62, 64-65, 72). By Robert L. Perry.

"Opportunities" in *Business Start-Ups* (Vol. 7, No. 12, December 1995, pp. 54, 56-57). By Andrew A. Caffey.

Opportunities in Franchising Careers. Lincolnwood, IL: NTC Publishing Group, 1995. By Kent B. Banning.

"Opportunity Abounds in Computers" in *Crain's Small Business* (October 1995, p. 19). By Len Strazewski.

"Opportunity Overhaul" in *Entrepreneur* (Vol. 23, No. 4, April 1995, pp. 196, 198). By Janean Huber.

Owning Your Own Franchise. Englewood Cliffs, NJ: Prentice Hall, 1991. By Herbert Rust.

"Planning for Projects" in *Income Opportunities* (Vol. 29, No. 7, July 1994, pp. 44). By Carol More.

"The Platinum 200" in *Income Opportunities* (Vol. 31, No. 3, March 1996, pp. 13-20, 22-32, 34-37). By Robert L. Perry.

"The Platinum Zoo: This Year's Best Franchises" in *Income Opportunities* (Vol. 30, No. 2, February 1995, pp. 20-21). By Robert L. Perry.

"Protection for Potential Buyer" in *Crain's Small Business* (February 1996, p. 13). By Geoffrey Stebbins.

"Quality Check: What Franchisors are Looking for" in *Business Start-Ups* (Vol. 7, No. 8, September 1995, p. 7). By Will Collins.

Rating Guide to Franchises. New York, NY: Facts on File, Inc., Revised edition, 1991. By Dennis L. Foster.

"The Real Money in Franchising" in *Inc.* (Vol. 16, No. 9, September 1994, pp. 110-114). By Gregory Matusky.

"Resources on Franchising" in *Nation's Business* (Vol. 81, No. 4, April 1993, pp. 54-55).

Restaurant Franchising. New York, NY: Van Nostrand Reinhold, 1995.

"The Retail Route" in *Income Opportunities* (Vol. 30, No. 7, July 1995, pp. 45-47). By Edmond M. Rosenthal.

"Reversal of Fortune" in *Income Opportunities* (Vol. 30, No. 2, February 1995, pp. 54-55, 58-62). By Edmond M. Rosenthal.

"The Right Stuff" in *Entrepreneur* (Vol. 23, No. 8, August 1995, pp. 158-162, 164). By Lynn Beresford.

"The Road Ahead" in *Entrepreneur: Buyer's Guide to Franchise and Business Opportunities* (Vol. 22, No. 11, 1995, pp. 6-8, 10-13). By Janean Huber.

"Roll of the Dice" in *Business Start-Ups* (Vol. 7, No. 11, November 1995, pp. 86, 88-89). By Karin Moeller and Maura Hudson Pomije.

"Room To Grow" in *Entrepreneur* (Vol. 23, No. 3, March 1995, pp. 234, 236-237). By Janean Huber.

"The Second Generation" in *Nation's Business* (Vol. 82, No. 6, June 1994, pp. 57-64). By Meg Whittemore.

"Seeing Double" in *Entrepreneur* (Vol. 23, No. 11, October 1995, pp. 164, 166-167). By Lynn Beresford.

"Should You Franchise Your Business?" in *Income Opportunities* (Vol. 30, No. 2, February 1995, pp. 42-43, 44, 46, 48, 50, 52). By Nancy Kennedy.

"A Side Order of Success?" in *Hispanic Business* (Vol. 17, No. 8, August 1995, pp. 48, 50). By Rick Mendosa.

"6 Steps to Franchising Success" in *Crain's Small Business* (December 1995, p. 17).

Small Business Franchise Made Simple. New York, NY: Doubleday & Company Inc., 1994. By William Lasher.

"The Smartest Franchisees in America" in *Inc.* (Vol. 17, No. 16, November 1995, pp. 48-50, 52-54, 57-58). By Jay Finegan.

"So You Want to Be a Franchisor?" in *Black Enterprise* (Vol. 26, No. 2, February 1996, pp. 88-91). By Tonia L. Shakespeare.

"Something's Brewing" in *Entrepreneur* (Vol. 23, No. 3, March 1995, pp. 198). By Heather Page.

"The Son Also Rises" in *Entrepreneur* (Vol. 23, No. 3, March 1995, pp. 200-204). By Leah Ingram.

The Sourcebook of Franchise Opportunities. Burr Ridge, IL: Irwin Professional Publishing, Annual, November. By Robert E. Bond, Editor.

"Start Your Engines" in *Income Opportunities* (Vol. 31, No. 1, January 1996, pp. 58-65). By Robert L. Perry.

Starting a Franchise. Nashville, TN: Business of Your Own, 1988. Compiled by Business of Your Own staff.

"Terms of Agreement" in *Income Opportunities* (Vol. 30, No. 8, August 1995, pp. 104-109). By Robert L. Perry.

"Thrill Seekers" in *Entrepreneur* (Vol. 23, No. 5, May 1995, pp. 128-134). By Janean Huber.

"Turning Points" in *Income Opportunities* (Vol. 31, No. 4, April 1996, pp. 12-17). By Malinda Reinke.

"Twenty-five Years of Blacks in Financing" in *Black Enterprise* (Vol. 25, No. 3, October 1994, pp. 146-149). By Matthew S. Scott, Rhonda Reynolds and Cassandra Hayes.

"20 Great Service Businesses To Get Into—Now!" in *Small Business Opportunities* (Vol. 7, No. 3, May 1995, pp. 22).

The Two Hundred Twenty Best Franchises to Buy. New York, NY: Bantam Books, Inc., Revised edition, 1993. Compiled by Philip Lief Group, Inc. staff.

"Two's A Crowd?" in *Entrepreneur* (Vol. 24, No. 2, February 1996, pp. 156, 158-159). By Janean Chun.

"Understanding The UFOC" in *Entrepreneur* (Vol. 23, No. 1, January 1995, pp. 106, 108-111). By Andrew A. Caffey.

"Up and Comers: How Can You Tell a Good Deal?" in *Inc.* (Vol. 16, No. 9, September 1994, pp. 100-103, 105). By Echo Montgomery Garrett.

"Upper Crust" in *Entrepreneur* (Vol. 23, No. 1, January 1995, pp. 131-133). By Erika Kotite.

"Wanna-be Owners Put Eyes on Franchise" in *Crain's Detroit Business* (Vol. 10, No. 41, October 10-16, 1994, pp. 9-10). By Chris Mead.

"Watch Your Step" in *Entrepreneur* (Vol. 23, No. 1, January 1995, pp. 100-103, 105). By Andrew A. Caffey.

"A Welcome Addition" in *Entrepreneur* (January 1990, p. 211). By Kevin McLaughlin.

"What's Next?" in *Entrepreneur* (Vol. 22, No. 9, September 1994, pp. 144-151). By Janean Huber.

"Where the Riches Are" in *Success* (November 1989, pp. 57-72).

"Who Makes the Perfect Franchisee?" in *Inc.* (Vol. 16, No. 12, November 1994, pp. 142-144, 146-147). By Echo Montgomery Garrett.

"Wish List" in *Entrepreneur* (Vol. 23, No. 1, January 1995, pp. 92, 94, 97-98). By Debra Phillips.

"Worth Sinking Your Teeth Into" in *Black Enterprise* (Vol. 25, No. 8, March 1995, pp. 40). By Lloyd Gite.

"You Can Go Home Again" in *Business Start-Ups* (Vol. 7, No. 5, May 1995, pp. 28, 30-34, 36-38). By Carol Steinberg.

Government Assistance

The Action Guide to Government Grants, Loans, & Giveaways. New York, NY: Berkeley Publishing Group, 1993. By George Chelekis.

"Alphabet Soup" in *Inc.* (Vol. 16, No. 12, November 1994, pp. 31-32). By Heather E. Stone.

"Business Empowers Cities" in *Income Opportunities* (Vol. 31, No. 2, February 1996, pp. 14-16). By Michele Marrinan.

Catalog of Federal Domestic Assistance. Washington, DC: Superintendent of Documents.

"A Directory of Export Services: The Trade Information Center One-Stop Shop" in *Business America* (Vol. 113, No. 9, 1992, pp. 8-13).

Doing Business with the Government: Federal, State, Local and Foreign Purchasing Practices for Every Business and Public Institution. New York, NY: Paragon House Publishers, 1992. By Susan A. MacManus.

Economic Development Assistance Programs in State Government. Upland, PA: Diane Publishing Co., 1994. By Wendy Umino.

"Entrepreneurs Get a Hand" in *Crain's Small Business* (September 1995, p. E-7). By Larry Perl.

Exporter's Guide to Federal Resources for Small Business. New York, NY: Gordon Press Publishers, 1995.

"Fighting Chance" in *Entrepreneur* (Vol. 23, No. 12, November 1995, pp. 106). By Philip Lader.

"Franchisors Aren't Using Aid and Incentives" in *Crain's Small Business* (February 1996, p. 15). By Julie Bennett.

Free Dollars From the Federal Government. New York, NY: Prentice Hall General Reference and Travel, 1991. By Laurie Blum.

Free Help from Uncle Sam to Start Your Own Business (or Expand the One You Have). Santa Maria, CA: Puma Publishing, 1996. By William M. Alarid, Editor.

Free Money from the Federal Government for Small Businesses & Entrepreneurs. Somerset, NJ: John Wiley & Sons, Inc., 1993. By Laurie Blum.

"Global Got Ahead with Help From the SBA" in *South Florida Business Journal* (Vol. 14, No. 36, April 29, 1994, pp. 17A). By Alison Turner.

Government Assistance Almanac, 1994-95: The Guide to All Federal Financial & Other Domestic Programs. Detroit, MI: Omnigraphics, Inc., 1994. By J. Robert Domouchel.

"Government" in *Business Start-Ups* (Vol. 7, No. 12, December 1995, pp. 24, 26). By Karin Moeller.

"Government Trade Loans" in *Black Enterprise* (Vol. 25, No. 7, February 1995, pp. 42). By Rhonda Reynolds.

"Green and Growing" in *Business Start-Ups* (Vol. 7, No. 2, February 1995, p. 14). By Cynthia E. Griffin.

"Hard To Get" in *Entrepreneur* (Vol. 23, No. 8, August 1995, pp. 186, 188, 190). By Stephen Barlas.

"Helping Small- and Medium-Sized Businesses" in *Business America* (Vol. 115, No. 9, September 1994, pp. 40-51).

"High Score" in *Entrepreneur* (Vol. 24, No. 2, February 1996, pp. 35). By Janean Chun.

"How to Get Started" in *Inc.* (Vol. 17, No. 6, May 1995, pp. 31-32). By Paul Reynolds.

"In Living Color" in *Entrepreneur* (Vol. 23, No. 3, March 1995, pp. 32). By Erika Kotite and Heather Page.

Insider's Guide to Small Business Loans. Grants Pass, OR: Oasis Press, 1995. By Dan M. Koehler.

"It's Your SCORE!" in *Independent Business* (Vol. 7, No. 2, March/April 1996, pp. 16-19). By Maryann Hammers.

Leadership Directories on CD-ROM. New York, NY: Monitor Publishing Co., Quarterly, or semiannually.

"Leveling the Field" in *Black Enterprise* (Vol. 25, No. 1, August 1994, pp. 33). By Carolyn M. Brown and Cassandra Hayes.

"More SBA Loans Going to Firms in Detroit" in *Crain's Small Business* (January 1996, p. 3). By Jeffrey McCracken.

"Need R & D Funds? Check with the Government" in *Research & Development* (Vol. 28, June 1986, pp. 68). By C. L. Propst and H. N. Hoppes.

"The New Deal" in *Entrepreneur* (Vol. 23, No. 7, July 1995, pp. 10-11). By Debra Phillips.

"No-cost (and Low-cost) Consulting" in *Occupational Hazards* (Vol. 57, No. 1, January 1995, pp. 59-63). By Mark S. Kuhar.

"On A Mission" in *Entrepreneur* (Vol. 23, No. 7, July 1995, pp. 78, 81). By Erika Kotite.

"Quick Fix" in *Income Opportunities* (Vol. 30, No. 3, March 1995, pp. 88, 90). By Peg Byron.

"Resource Guide: Small-Business Help From the Government" in *Entrepreneur* (April 1990, pp. 218-223). By Iris Lorenz-Fife.

"SBA: A Paint-By-Numbers Portrait" in *Crain's Small Business* (October 1995, pp. 1, 12-13). By Jeffrey McCracken.

"SBA Loans: Tales from the Front" in *Commercial Lending Review* (Vol. 9, No. 4, Fall 1994, pp. 83-86). By Paul S. Nadler.

"SBA Reaches Out by Speeding Loan Approval" in *Crain's Small Business* (October 1995, p. 3). By Jeffrey McCracken.

"SBA Streamlines Women's Loan Program" in *Business First-Columbus* (Vol. 10, No. 48, August 1, 1994, pp. 15). By Christine B. O'Malley.

"SBA Treasure Chest" in *Business Start-Ups* (Vol. 8, No. 1, January 1996, pp. 38, 40-41). By Cynthia E. Griffin.

State Executive Directory Annual. West Nyack, NY: Todd Publications, Annual.

The States and Small Business: A Directory of Programs and Activities. Washington, DC: Office of Advocacy, March 1993. By John Ward, Editor.

"Tech It Away" in *Entrepreneur* (Vol. 23, No. 3, March 1995, pp. 218, 220-221). By Stephen Barlas.

"To The Rescue" in *Entrepreneur* (Vol. 23, No. 1, January 1995, pp. 304). By Bernard Kulik.

"Turning to the Government" in *Practical Accountant* (Vol. 27, No. 6, June 1994, pp. 37-44). By John Cosgriff and Leonard Sliwoski.

"The U.S. Chamber of Commerce: The Voice of Business" in *Business America* (Vol. 113, No. 23, November 16, 1992, pp. 18-20). By Mark Van Fleet.

The United States Government Manual. Washington, DC: Superintendent of Documents, Annual.

"What's The BIC Idea?" in *Entrepreneur* (Vol. 23, No. 5, May 1995, pp. 194). By Philip Lader.

"Where to Get Export Assistance" in *Business America* (World Trade Week Supplement, April 1994, pp. 11-29).

"Where to Get Export Counseling" in *Business America* (Vol. 114, No. 9, 1993, pp. 8-11).

Who Knows. West Nyack, NY: Todd Publications.

Winning Government Grants and Contracts for Your Small Business. New York, NY: McGraw-Hill, Inc., 1992. By Mark Rowh.

Incubators

"Al Geiger Aiming to Help Small Businesses Grow" in *The Business Journal* (Vol. 11, No. 26, September 19, 1994, pp. 16). By Ray Dussault.

"Alphabet Soup" in *Inc.* (Vol. 16, No. 12, November 1994, pp. 31-32). By Heather E. Stone.

"Blastoff" in *Forbes* (Vol. 154, No. 5, August 29, 1994, pp. 154). By James M. Clash.

"A Boost for Start-Ups" in *Nation's Business* (Vol. 80, No. 8, August 1992, pp. 40). By Bradford McKee.

"Business Incubation" in *California Business* (Vol. 29, No. 5, September 1994, pp. 10). By Claudia Viek.

"Cash Infusion to Incubator Nurtures Small Businesses" in *The Business Journal Serving Greater Sacramento* (Vol. 11, No. 18, July 25, 1994, pp. 2). By Mike McCarthy.

"Company Coach" in *The Kansas City Business Journal* (Vol. 12, No. 17, January 14, 1994, pp. 3). By Barry Henderson.

Directory of Business Incubators and University Research & Science Parks. Stamford, CT: International Venture Capital Institute, Inc. (IVCI), Annual. By Carroll A. Greathouse, Editor.

"Fledgling Business Incubator Hatches 13 New Enterprises" in *The Business Journal* (Vol. 12, No. 31, October 31, 1994, pp. 13). By Michele Hostetler.

"Growing Places" in *Entrepreneur* (Vol. 23, No. 2, February 1995, pp. 108, 110-113). By Cynthia E. Griffin.

"Hatching a New Venture" in *EDN* (Vol. 39, No. 17, August 18, 1994, pp. 51).

"How to Hatch New Businesses" in *D & B Reports* (Vol. 39, No. 4, July/August 1991, pp. 54-55). By Bill Hogan.

"Incubator Boosts LI's High Tech" in *Long Island Business News* (No. 6, February 7, 1994, pp. 3T). By Christopher Hord.

"Incubator Roundup" in *Entrepreneur* (Vol. 23, No. 11, October 1995, pp. 188). By Cynthia E. Griffin.

"Incubators Nurture Start-Up Firms: Do Incubators Really Work?" in *Computerworld* (Vol. 25, No. 37, September 16, 1991, pp. 105, 112). By Johanna Ambrosio.

NBIA Directory of Business Incubators and Members. Athens, OH: National Business Incubation Association (NBIA), Annual. By Dinah Adkins, Editor.

"New Product Incubator: Pilot Plant Helps Processors Develop New Products" in *Dairy Foods* (Vol. 95, No. 9, September 1994, pp. 139).

Regional Economic Analysis of Innovation & Incubation. Brookfield, VT: Ashgate Publishing Company, 1991. By E.J. Davelaar.

"Tech Incubator Growing Up" in *Denver Business Journal* (Vol. 46, No. 15, December 23, 1994, pp. 1B). By Tom Locke.

"Trapped in the Nest? Start-Up Firms Try to Fly" in *Baltimore Business Journal* (Vol. 12, No. 9, July 22, 1994, pp. 1). By Greg Abel.

"VC Incubators Are Hatching New Companies Again" in *Electronic Business Buyer* (Vol. 20, No. 1, January 1994, pp. 90). By Stephen W. Quickel.

"What the Incubators Have Hatched" in *Planning* (Vol. 58, No. 5, May 1992, pp. 28-30). By Richard Steffens.

"Yellow Brick Road Winds into Florida" in *Orlando Business Journal* (Vol. 10, No. 35, February 4, 1994, pp. 16). By Danialle Weaver.

Insurance

"Accidents Happen" in *Entrepreneur* (Vol. 23, No. 7, July 1995, pp. 93-97, 99). By Cynthia E. Griffin.

"Big Savings for Small Companies" in *Business & Health* (Vol. 13, No. 1, January 1995, pp. 38-42). By Geoffrey Leavenworth.

Business Insurance—Agent/Broker Profiles Issue. Chicago, IL: Crain Communications, Inc., Annual, July. By Sandra L. Budde, Editor.

Buyer's Guide to Business Insurance. Grants Pass, OR: Oasis Press, 1994. By Don Bury.

"Contesting Unemployment Claims" in *Small Business Reports* (Vol. 19, No. 7, July 1994, pp. 37).

"Cover Charge" in *Entrepreneur* (Vol. 24, No. 2, February 1996, pp. 140, 142, 144). By Cynthia E. Griffin.

"Crime Insurance: Protect People First" in *Nation's Business* (Vol. 82, No. 3, March 1994, pp. 24). By John S. DeMott.

"Forfeit the Game" in *Business Start-Ups* (Vol. 7, No. 8, August 1995, P. 75). By Joseph S. Gall.

"Get Ready for Elder Care" in *Inc.* (Vol. 17, No. 12, September 1995, pp. 101). By Donna Fenn.

"A Healthcare Sampler" in *Small Business Reports* (Vol. 17, No. 3, March 1992, pp. 57-61). By Elizabeth J. Sampson.

"Healthy Workers Cost Less" in *Inc.* (Vol. 17, No. 6, May 1995, pp. 137). By Susan Greco.

"How to Control Workers' Comp" in *Small Business Reports* (Vol. 17, No. 8, August 1992, pp. 29-39). By Eileen Davis.

How to Insure a Business: Solving the Business Insurance Puzzle. Santa Barbara, CA: Venture Publications, Revised edition, 1988. By Finn A. Sundheim.

"An Insurance Consultant May Benefit Your Bottom Line" in *Air Conditioning, Heating & Refrigeration News* (Vol. 193, No. 5, October 3, 1994, pp. 22). By Joseph Arkin.

"Insurance: Easy Rider" in *Business Start-Ups* (Vol. 7, No. 6, June 1995, p. 18). By Janean Huber.

"Insurers Tap Into Small Employer 401(k) Market" in *National Underwriter* (Vol. 99, No. 2, January 9, 1995, pp. 2). By Colleen Mulcahy.

"IRS May Reclassify Independent Contractors" in *San Diego Business Journal* (Vol. 15, No. 6, February 7, 1994, pp. 6A). By James R. Urquhart III.

"The Last Hurdle" in *Inc.* (Vol. 16, No. 1, January 1994, pp. 50). By Phaedra Hise.

"Leasing Workers" in *Nation's Business* (Vol. 80, No. 11, November 1992, pp. 20-28). By Rosalind Resnick.

"Look Out for These Symptoms" in *Crain's Small Business* (January 1996, p. 11). By Joel Garfield.

"Mastering Disaster" in *Business Start-Ups* (Vol. 8, No. 2, February 1996, pp. 54, 56-58). By Carla Goodman.

"Medical Self-Defense" in *Small Business Reports* (Vol. 17, No. 6, June 1992, pp. 60-64). By Robert L. Turell.

"On Small Business Benefits, Conventional Thinking is Wrong" in *Business & Health* (Vol. 12, No. 7, July 1994, pp. 10).

"Out of the Ashes" in *Entrepreneur* (Vol. 23, No. 7, July 1995, pp. 181-184, 186-187). By Marta McCave.

"Paying More for Less" in *Business & Health* (Vol. 12, No. 7, July 1994, pp. 29-33). By Norma Harris and Steven Findlay.

"Personnel Safety" in *Entrepreneur* (Vol. 23, No. 1, January 1995, pp. 11). By Janean Huber and Debra Phillips.

"Premium Insurance" in *Business Start-Ups* (Vol. 8, No. 4, April 1996, pp. 8, 10). By Carla Goodman.

Small Business Risk Management Guide. Denver, CO: U.S. Small Business Administration (SBA).

"Small Employers and the Health Insurance Market" in *Health Affairs* (Vol. 13, No. 5, Winter 1994, pp. 149-161). By Michael A. Morrisey, Gail A. Jensen, and Robert J. Morlock.

"Under Cover" in *Business Start-Ups* (Vol. 7, No. 3, March 1995, pp. 58-62). By Sue Clayton.

Workers Compensation Insurance: Profiles of the State Systems. Schaumburg, IL: Alliance of American Insurers, 1995. By Alliance of American Insurers Staff.

Worker's Compensation Insurance: The Survival Guide for Business. Charlottesville, VA: MICHIE, 1992. By Joseph P. Bacarro.

Loans

"All in the Family" in *Black Enterprise* (Vol. 26, No. 7, February 1996, p. 34). By Rhonda Reynolds.

"All in the Family" in *Business Start-Ups* (Vol. 8, No. 2, February 1996, p. 10). By Gloria Gibbs Marullo.

Bank Directory of South Carolina. Nashville, TN: R. L. Polk & Co., Annual. By B. Gordon Cunningham, Editor.

Bank Directory of South Dakota. Nashville, TN: R. L. Polk & Co., Annual. By B. Gordon Cunningham, Editor.

Bank Directory of Tennessee. Nashville, TN: R. L. Polk & Co., Annual. By B. Gordon Cunningham, Editor.

Bank Directory of Virginia. Nashville, TN: R. L. Polk & Co., Annual. By B. Gordon Cunningham, Editor.

Bank Directory of West Virginia. Nashville, TN: R. L. Polk & Co., Annual. By B. Gordon Cunningham, Editor.

"Banks, Businesses Give SBA Higher Marks" in *Crain's Small Business* (October 1995, p. 14). By Jeffrey McCracken.

"Begin Quest for Cash by Following 10 Steps" in *Crain's Small Business* (January 1996, p. 9). By Elaine McMahon.

"Borrowing Money from Loved Ones" in *Nation's Business* (Vol. 82, No. 11, November 1994, pp. 40). By Joan C. Szabo.

"Buddy System" in *Entrepreneur* (Vol. 23, No. 7, July 1995, pp. 62, 64-65). By Bob Weinstein.

"Building a Bank Alliance" in *Black Enterprise* (Vol. 26, No. 9, April 1996, p. 34). By Joan Delaney.

Business Borrowers Complete Success Kit. Rockville Centre, NY: International Wealth Success, 1996. By Tyler G. Hicks.

"Business Finally Invests Some Trust in Bank Lending" in *Crain's Small Business* (October 1995, p. 8). By Jeffrey McCracken.

"Business Microloans" in *Black Enterprise* (Vol. 26, No. 3, October 1995, p. 38). By Rhonda Reynolds.

California Savings Institutions Directory. Nashville, TN: R. L. Polk & Co., Annual. By B. Gordon Cunningham, Editor.

Cash for Your Business. Deerfield Beach, FL: Garrett Publishing, 1995.

"Chamber of Commerce" in *Income Opportunities* (Vol. 31, No. 3, March 1996, pp. 4). By Michele Marrinan.

"Currency Events" in *Entrepreneur* (Vol. 24, No. 4, April 1996, pp. 124, 126-130). By Cynthia E. Griffin.

Doing Business with Banks. Lakewood, CO: dba USA Press, Incorporated, 1991. By Gibson Heath.

"Easier Money" in *Business Start-Ups* (Vol. 7, No. 2, February 1995, p. 13). By Cynthia E. Griffin.

"Eating, Drinking Places Among Most Appetizing" in *Crain's Small Business* (October 1995, p. 13). By Jeffrey McCracken.

"Export Bank Can Do Biz World of Good" in *Crain's Small Business* (October 1995, p. 4). By Jeffrey McCracken.

"Family Ties" in *Income Opportunities* (Vol. 31, No. 1, January 1996, pp. 50, 52). By Michele Marrinan.

The Financial Institutions Directory of Nevada. Nashville, TN: R. L. Polk & Co., Annual. By B. Gordon Cunningham, Editor.

Georgia Financial Institutions Directory & Fact Book. Nashville, TN: R. L. Polk & Co., Annual. By B. Gordon Cunningham, Editor.

"Get Cash Now!" in *Success* (Vol. 38, No. 10, December 1991, pp. 26-32). By Ronit Addis Rose.

"Get Personal" in *Business Start-Ups* (Vol. 7, No. 6, June 1995, p. 85). By Gloria Gibbs Marullo.

Getting Money. Bellingham, WA: Self-Counsel Press, 1991. By Dan Kennedy.

"Government Trade Loans" in *Black Enterprise* (Vol. 25, No. 7, February 1995, pp. 42). By Rhonda Reynolds.

"How to Borrow from Family and Friends" in *Inc.* (Vol. 17, No. 10, July 1995, pp. 99). By Jill Andresky Fraser.

How to Get a Loan or Line of Credit for Your Business. Naperville, IL: Sourcebooks, Incorporated, 1993. By Bryan E. Milling.

"How to Obtain Export Capital" in *Nation's Business* (Vol. 82, No. 5, May 1994, pp. 24).

The Illinois Financial Institutions Directory & Fact Book. Nashville, TN: R. L. Polk & Co., Annual. By B. Gordon Cunningham, Editor.

Insider's Guide to Small Business Loans. Grants Pass, OR: Oasis Press, 1995. By Dan M. Koehler.

"Investing Dollars and Sense in a Friend's Business" in *Black Enterprise* (Vol. 24, No. 9, April 1994, pp. 46). By Debra Wishik Englander.

"Investments Designed for Economic Growth" in *Income Opportunities* (Vol. 31, No. 2, February 1996, pp. 5). By Michele Marrinan.

"It Pays to Learn How to Talk with Your Loan Officer" in *Crain's Small Business* (January 1996, p. 8). By Lawrence Garner.

Kentucky Financial Institutions Directory. Nashville, TN: R. L. Polk & Co., Annual. By B. Gordon Cunningham, Editor.

"Kid Venture Capital" in *Black Enterprise* (Vol. 25, No. 5, December 1994, pp. 34). By Tonia L. Shakespeare.

"Legal Tips for Relationship Loans" in *Inc.* (Vol. 17, No. 10, July 1995, pp. 99). By Jill Andresky Fraser.

"Lending Some Loan Insight" in *Crain's Small Business* (March 1996, p. 4). By David Guilford.

"Leveling the Field" in *Black Enterprise* (Vol. 25, No. 1, August 1994, pp. 33). By Carolyn M. Brown and Cassandra Hayes.

Loan Broker—Annual Directory. Owosso, MI: Ben Campbell, Publisher, Annual, February. By Ben Campbell, Editor.

"Loan Defaults: Failure Rates Higher — But So Is Risk" in *Crain's Small Business* (October 1995, p. 13). By Jeffrey McCracken.

"Loan Fraud" in *Income Opportunities* (Vol. 30, No. 1, January 1995, pp. 3). By Eric Barnes.

"A Loan at Last" in *Income Opportunities* (Vol. 30, No. 5, May 1995, pp. 122, 124-125). By Peg Byron.

"A Loan at Last?" in *Nation's Business* (Vol. 82, No. 8, August 1994, pp. 40-43). By J. Tol Broome, Jr.

"Loan Negotiations Should Begin with a Blueprint" in *Crain's Small Business* (February 1996, p. 10-11). By Lawrence Gardner.

"Loan Stars" in *Entrepreneur* (Vol. 23, No. 4, April 1995, pp. 95-107). By Cynthia E. Griffin.

Loans Directory. Omaha, NE: American Business Directories, Inc., Annual.

"Local Heroes" in *Entrepreneur* (Vol. 24, No. 2, February 1996, pp. 13). By Cynthia E. Griffin.

"Look at Every Option—And Beyond" in *Nation's Business* (Vol. 79, No. 7, July 1991, pp. 9). By Thomas Hierl.

"Low-Interest Loans For Small Companies" in *Entrepreneur* (Vol. 22, No. 13, December 1994, pp. 18). By Cynthia E. Griffin.

"The Magnificent 7(a)" in *Business Start-Ups* (Vol. 7, No. 5, May 1995, p. 10). By Cynthia E. Griffin.

Minnesota Bank Directory. Nashville, TN: R. L. Polk & Co., Annual. By B. Gordon Cunningham, Editor.

"The Money Is Out There...How To Get It" in *Agency Sales Magazine* (Vol. 24, No. 2, February 1994, pp. 15-17). By Jeff Fromberg.

"Money Rules" in *Business Start-Ups* (Vol. 7, No. 7, July 1995, p. 79). By Steve Marshall Cohen.

"Never Give Up" in *Business Start-Ups* (Vol. 7, No. 7, July 1995, p. 77). By Nancy L. Scarlato.

New Mexico Bank Directory. Nashville, TN: R. L. Polk & Co., Annual. By B. Gordon Cunningham, Editor.

The New York Financial Institutions Directory & Fact Book. Nashville, TN: R. L. Polk & Co., Annual. By B. Gordon Cunningham, Editor.

"Next Up, Scrutiny of Small-Business Lending" in *ABA Banking Journal* (Vol. 87, No. 2, February 1995, pp. 34-40). By Jo Ann S. Barefoot.

The North Dakota Financial Institutions Directory. Nashville, TN: R. L. Polk & Co., Annual. By B. Gordon Cunningham, Editor.

"The Numbers Speak Volumes" in *Small Business Reports* (Vol. 19, No. 7, July 1994, pp. 39-43). By Lamont Change.

The Ohio Financial Institutions Directory & Fact Book. Nashville, TN: R. L. Polk & Co., Annual. By B. Gordon Cunningham, Editor.

"The Paper Chase" in *Income Opportunities* (Vol. 30, No. 6, June 1995, pp. 86, 88). By Toni Reinhold.

The Pennsylvania Financial Institutions Directory & Fact Book. Nashville, TN: R. L. Polk & Co., Annual. By B. Gordon Cunningham, Editor.

Polk World Bank Directory. Nashville, TN: R. L. Polk & Co., Annual. By B. Gordon Cunningham, Editor.

"Put Away the Bootstraps" in *Hispanic Business* (Vol. 17, No. 7, July 1995, pp. 38-42). By Maria Zate.

"Quest for Success Starts at Right Bank" in *Crain's Small Business* (October 1995, p. 14). By Jeffrey McCracken.

"Quick Change" in *Entrepreneur* (Vol. 22, No. 9, September 1994, pp. 208). By Erksine Bowles.

"Quick Fix" in *Income Opportunities* (Vol. 30, No. 3, March 1995, pp. 88, 90). By Peg Byron.

The Registry of Michigan Financial Institutions. Nashville, TN: R. L. Polk & Co., Annual. By B. Gordon Cunningham, Editor.

Registry of Utah Financial Institutions. Nashville, TN: R. L. Polk & Co., Annual. By B. Gordon Cunningham, Editor.

"Restructure for Profitability" in *Bank Management* (Vol. 70, No. 6, November/December 1994, pp. 78-82). By Beth Raphael.

"SBA Loans: Tales from the Front" in *Commercial Lending Review* (Vol. 9, No. 4, Fall 1994, pp. 83-86). By Paul S. Nadler.

"SBA Reaches Out by Speeding Loan Approval" in *Crain's Small Business* (October 1995, p. 3). By Jeffrey McCracken.

"SBA Streamlines Women's Loan Program" in *Business First-Columbus* (Vol. 10, No. 48, August 1, 1994, pp. 15). By Christine B. O'Malley.

"SBA Treasure Chest" in *Business Start-Ups* (Vol. 8, No. 1, January 1996, pp. 38, 40-41). By Cynthia E. Griffin.

"The Secrets of Bootstrapping" in *Inc.* (Vol. 13, No. 9, September 1991, pp. 52-70). By Robert A. Mamis.

"Show And Tell" in *Entrepreneur* (Vol. 23, No. 12, November 1995, pp. 72-73). By Jacquelyn Lynn.

"The Six Best Ways to Raise Cash" in *Money: Money Guide Supplement* (Vol. , No. , 1994, pp. 34-39). By Vanessa O'Connell.

"Small Banks Top State Rankings" in *Crain's Small Business* (April 1996, p. 3). By Jeffrey McCracken.

"Small Business: Funding Women's Ventures" in *Working Woman* (Vol. 19, No. 6, June 1994, pp. 17). By Holly Yeager.

"Small Loans, Big Dreams" in *Working Woman* (Vol. 20, No. 2, February 1995, pp. 46-49, 72-73, 77). By Elizabeth Kadetsky.

The Texas Financial Institutions Directory & Fact Book. Nashville, TN: R. L. Polk & Co., Annual. By B. Gordon Cunningham, Editor.

Think Like an Investor. Irvine, CA: Entrepreneur Media Inc. By Nancy L. Scarlato.

"Treasure Hunt" in *Business Start-Ups* (Vol. 7, No. 7, July 1995, 56-58, 60-61). By Gloria Gibbs Marullo.

"Turning to the Government" in *Practical Accountant* (Vol. 27, No. 6, June 1994, pp. 37-44). By John Cosgriff and Leonard Sliwoski.

"Venturing into Business" in *Black Enterprise* (Vol. 25, No. 9, April 1995, pp. 38). By Tania Padgett.

"When Your Banker Says No" in *Income Opportunities* (Vol. 30, No. 11, November 1995, pp. 24-28). By Randall Kirkpatrick.

"Where Are All the Wanda Buffets?" in *Money* (Vol. 23, No. 11, November 1994, pp. 116-117). By Nancy J. Perry.

"Where to Look for Money Now" in *Working Woman* (Vol. 19, No. 10, October 1994, pp. 56-62). By Ilyce R. Glink.

World Bank Lending for Small & Medium Enterprises: Fifteen Years of Experience. Washington, DC: World Bank, The Office of the Publisher, 1991. By Leila Webster.

Management

"Absenteeism Control" in *International Journal of Bank Marketing* (Vol. 10, No. 6, 1992, pp. 19-22). By Thomas C. Cole and Brian H. Kleiner.

"Ad It Up" in *Entrepreneur* (Vol. 22, No. 13, December 1994, pp. 47). By Jane Easter Bahls.

Adapting to Change: Making It Work for You. Menlo Park, CA: Crisp Publications, Inc., 1993. By Carol K. Goman.

"After the Covers: What Are They Up to Now?" in *Chain Store Age Executive* (Vol. 70, No. 7, July 1994, pp. 19-33).

Assertiveness for Managers: Learning Effective Skills for Managing People. Bellingham, WA: Self-Counsel Press, 1992, third edition. By Diana Cawood.

Be an Even Better Manager: Improve Performance, Profits, and Productivity. Bellingham, WA: Self-Counsel Press, 1990, second edition. By Michael Armstrong.

"Been There, Doing That" in *Inc.* (Vol. 18, No. 3, March 1996, pp. 21-22). By Joline Godfrey.

"Before and After" in *Inc.* (Vol. 17, No. 8, June 1995, pp. 44-48, 50). By David Whitford.

"Benefiting from Workforce Diversity" in *Healthcare Forum* (Vol. 35, No. 1, January/February 1992, pp. 23-26). By Sue Shea and Ruby K. Okada.

Beyond Entrepreneurship: Turning Your Business Into an Enduring Great Company. Englewood Cliffs, NJ: Prentice Hall, 1992. By James C. Collins and William C. Lazier.

"Book Value" in *Inc.* (Vol. 18, No. 1, January 1996, pp. 23-24). By Jim Collins.

Bradford's Directory of Marketing Research Agencies and Management Consultants in the United States and the World. Centreville, VA: Management Consultants, Biennial, January of even years. By Douglas Ford, Editor.

"Brain Power" in *Entrepreneur* (Vol. 23, No. 2, February 1995, pp. 54-55). By Mark Henricks.

"Building the Creative Organization" in *Organizational Dynamics* (Vol. 22, No. 4, Spring 1994, pp. 22-37). By Lisa K. Gundry and Charles W. Prather and Jill R. Kickul.

"Business Busters" in *Black Enterprise* (Vol. 23, No. 4, November 1992, pp. 75-85). By Caryne Brown.

Business Forms for Managing a Small Business. New York, NY: Prentice Hall General Reference & Travel, 1994. By J.K. Lasser Staff.

Business: Gaining the Competitive Edge. Needham Heights, MA: Allyn & Bacon, Inc., 1992. By Norman M. Scarborough.

"Capture the Future" in *Success* (Vol. 40, No. 10, December 1993, pp. 63-70). By Katherine Callan.

"A Case For Planning and Merchandise Management" in *Stores* (Vol. 75, No. 3, March 1993, pp. 53-54). By Bill Pearson.

Cases in Small Business Management: A Strategic Problems Approach. Dover, NH: Upstart Publishing Co., Third edition, 1994. By John DeYoung.

"Change is Big Even for a Little Guy" in *Business Quarterly* (Vol. 59, No. 2, Winter 1994, pp. 21-27). By Nan Napier.

Change from Within: People Make the Difference. Washington, DC: CEEPress Books, 1995. By Robert Reid and Howard Scott.

"The Changing Face of Leadership" in *Nation's Business* (Vol. 83, No. 1, January 1995, pp. 41-42). By Michael Brown.

Coaching Through Effective Feedback: Successful Communication. San Diego, CA: Pfeiffer & Co. By Paul J. Jerome.

"The Color-Coded Priority Setter" in *Inc.* (Vol. 17, No. 8, June 1995, pp. 69-71). By Christopher Caggiano.

"Confessions of a Reengineered Manager" in *Working Woman* (Vol. 20, No. 8, August 1995, pp. 19, 22-23). By Jacky Seyegorf.

"Covering Your Assets" in *Inc.* (Vol. 17, No. 12, September 1995, pp. 102). By Donna Fenn.

"Cutting Down on Absenteeism" in *Black Enterprise* (Vol. 25, No. 8, March 1995, pp. 39). By Joan Delaney.

"Damage Control" in *Entrepreneur* (Vol. 22, No. 13, December 1994, pp. 40). By Gayle Sato Stodder.

"Deadly Force" in *Entrepreneur* (Vol. 23, No. 12, November 1995, pp. 79-81). By Robert McGarvey.

Directory of Management Consultants. Fitzwilliam, NH: Kennedy Publications, Biennial. By James H. Kennedy, Editor.

"The Discomfort Zone" in *Inc.* (vol. 17, No. 16, November 1995, pp. 19-20). By Barry Diller.

"Does Size Matter?" in *Economist* (Vol. 331, No. 7867, June 11, 1994, pp. 66).

"Doing More with Less" in *Small Business Reports* (Vol. 19, No. 3, March 1994, pp. 22-30).

"Double Duty" in *Entrepreneur* (Vol. 23, No. 3, March 1995, pp. 74, 76-77). By Jane Easter Bahls.

"Effective Business Decision Making" in *Small Business Reports* (Vol. 17, No. 3, March 1992, pp. 68-71). By William F. O'Dell.

Effective Small Business Management. Old Tappan, NJ: Macmillan Publishing Co., Inc. By Thomas W. Zimmerer.

Effective Small Business Management. Fort Worth, TX: Dryden Press. By Richard Hodgetts.

Effective Small Business Management. Englewood Cliffs, NJ: Prentice Hall, 1995. By Norman M. Scarborough.

"80/20 Vision" in *Entrepreneur* (Vol. 24, No. 4, April 1996, pp. 68, 70-71). By Mark Henricks.

"An Empirical Investigation of the Organizational Life Cycle Model..." in *Journal of Small Business Management* (Vol. 30, No. 1, January 1992, pp. 27-37). By Robert H. Dodge and John E. Robbins.

"Employee Crime: The Cost and Some Control Measures" in *Review of Business* (Vol. 16, No. 2, Winter 1994, pp. 9-14). By Randall M. Hogsett III and William J. Radig.

"The Enneagram: Management's New Numbers Game" in *Working Woman* (Vol. 20, No. 11, November 1995, pp. 16, 21). By Nancy K. Austin.

Entrepreneur and Small Business Problem Solver. Somerset, NJ: John Wiley & Sons, Inc., 1990. By William A. Cohen.

"Entrepreneurial Problem Solver: Who to Hire? How to Delegate?" in *Executive Female* (Vol. 17, No. 1, January-February 1994, pp. 28). By Joan Delaney.

Entrepreneurial Systems for the 1990s: Their Creation, Structure, and Management. Westport, CT: Greenwood Publishing Group, Inc., 1989. By John E. Tropman and Gersh Morningstar.

Entrepreneurship: A Contemporary Approach. Fort Worth, TX: Dryden Press, 1992. By Donald F. Kuratko and Richard M. Hodgetts.

"Entrepreneurship: The Role of the Individual in Small Business Development" in *IBAR* (Vol. 15, 1994, pp. 62-75). By Stan Cromie.

The Essentials of Small Business Management. Old Tappan, NJ: Macmillan Publishing Company, Incorporated, 1994. By Thomas W. Zimmerer.

"Ethical Aspects of Japanese Leadership Style" in *Journal of Business Ethics* (Vol. 13, No. 2, February 1994, pp. 135-148). By Iwao Taka and Wanda D. Foglia.

Excellence in Management. Menlo Park, CA: Crisp Publications. By Rick Conlow.

Expanding Leadership Impact: Managing People and Processes. San Diego, CA: Pfeiffer & Co. By Kevin R. Kehoe.

"A Factor Analytic Study of the Perceived Causes of Small Business Failure" in *Journal of Small Business Management* (Vol. 31, No. 4, October 1993, pp. 18-31). By LuAnn Ricketts Gaskill and Howard E. Van Auken and Ronald A. Manning.

Fail-Safe Strategies for Small Businesses. Somerset, NJ: John Wiley & Sons, Inc., 1994. By Ron Tepper.

Fast Track to Quality: A 12-Month Program for Small- to Mid-Sized Businesses. New York, NY: McGraw-Hill, Inc., 1992. By Roger Tunks.

"Fighting Back" in *Entrepreneur* (Vol. 24, No. 2, February 1996, pp. 84). By Jacquelyn Lynn.

"Fighting Fraud" in *Income Opportunities* (Vol. 29, No. 11, November 1994, pp. 114, 116). By Richard J. Maturi.

"First Steps" in *Inc.* (Vol. 17, No. 6, May 1995, pp. 27-28). By Mary Baechler.

The First-Time Manager: A Survival Guide. Bellingham, WA: Self-Counsel Press, 1992 (print); 1995 (audiocassette). By Theodore G. Tyssen.

"Five Little Words" in *Successful Meetings* (Vol. 43, No. 2, February 1994, pp. 28). By Harvey Mackay.

"A Flexible Style of Management" in *Nation's Business* (Vol. 82, No. 12, December 1993, pp. 24-31). By Sharon Nelton.

Gambling on Growth: How to Manage the Small High-Tech Firm. Somerset, NJ: John Wiley & Sons, Inc., 1992. By Stuart Slatter.

"The Gender Gap" in *Entrepreneur* (Vol. 23, No. 5, May 1995, pp. 108-113). By Debra Phillips.

Getting Business to Come to You. New York, NY: Jeremy P. Tarcher Inc., 1991. By Paul Edwards.

"Gone Fishing" in *Entrepreneur* (Vol. 23, No. 2, February 1995, pp. 60-61). By Gayle Sato Stodder.

"Good Advice" in *Income Opportunities* (Vol. 30, No. 4, April 1995, pp. 116-117). By Richard J. Maturi.

Guide to Small Business Management. Cincinnati, OH: South-Western Publishing Co., 1997.

Handbook on Building a Profitable Business: An Expert's Step-by-Step Presentation on How to Make Money in Business. Seattle, WA: Entrepreneurial Workshops Publications, 1990. By Fred Klein.

The Healthy Company. Teaneck, NJ: NAPL. By R. H. Rosen.

Honest Business: A Superior Strategy for Starting & Maintaining Your Own Business. Boston, MA: Shambhala Publications, Inc., 1996. By Michael Phillips.

"Hot Commodity" in *Inc.* (Vol. 18, No. 2, February 1996, pp. 50-52, 54, 57-58, 60-61). By Joshua Hyatt.

How to Be the Life of the Podium: Openers, Closers & Everything in Between to Keep Them Listening. New York, NY: AMACOM, 1993. By Sylvia Simmons.

"How Better People Management Adds to the Bottom Line" in *Working Woman* (March 1996, pp. 18). By Harris Collingswood.

How to Make the Transition from an Entrepreneurship to a Professionally Managed Firm. Ann Arbor, MI: Books on Demand. By Eric G. Flamholtz.

How to Run a Small Business. New York, NY: McGraw-Hill, Inc., 1993. Compiled by the J. K. Lasser Tax Institute Staff.

How to Start, Finance, and Manage Your Own Small Business: Featuring Andrew Tobias' Managing Your Money Software. New York, NY: Random House, Inc., 1993. By Joseph R. Mancuso.

"Identity Crisis" in *Entrepreneur* (Vol. 24, No. 4, April 1996, pp. 74-76). By Robert McGarvey.

Innovation & Small Firms. Cambridge, MA: MIT Press, 1990. By Zoltan Acs.

The ISO 9000 Almanac, 1994-1995 Edition. Burr Ridge, IL: Irwin Professional Publishing, 1994-1995 edition. By Timeplace, Inc.

"ISO 9000: The Inside Advantage" in *Inc.* (Vol. 17, No. 12, September 1995, pp. 102). By Donna Fenn.

Just Promoted: How to Survive and Thrive in Your First 12 Months as a Manager. New York, NY: McGraw Hill, Inc., 1992. By Edward Betof.

"Keeping In Touch" in *Small Business Opportunities* (Vol. 8, No. 2, March 1996, pp. 58-60). By Martin P. Waterman.

"Keeping Tabs" in *Entrepreneur (Vol.* 22, No. 13, December 1994, pp. 43). By Erika Kotite.

"The Kiddie Zone" in *Income Opportunities* (Vol. 30, No. 10, October 1995, pp. 32, 34, 36). By Pamela Rohland.

"The Killer Within" in *Entrepreneur* (Vol. 23, No. 12, November 1995, pp. 148, 150-153). By Robert McGarvey.

Kuehl, Small Business: Planning & Management. Fort Worth, TX: Dryden Press, 1994. By Raymond C. Shea.

"A League of Their Own" in *Small Business Reports* (Vol. 19, No. 4, April 1994, pp. 35-42). By Robert F. Lynch and Thomas J. Werner.

Learning Leadership. Chicago, IL: Bonus Books, Inc., 1992. By Abraham Zaleznik.

"Lighten Your Load" in *Selling Power* (Vol. 16, NO. 3, April 1996, pp. 48). By Pete Radigan.

"Loves Me, Loves Me Not" in *Inc.* (Vol. 17, No. 12, September 1995, pp. 19-20). By Mary Baechler.

"Make Your Service Fail-Safe" in *Sloan Management Review* (Vol. 35, No. 3, Spring 1994, pp. 35-44). By Richard B. Chase and Douglas M. Stewart.

Management. Boston, MA: Houghton Mifflin Co., 1992.

"Managing Cultural Diversity: Implications for Organizational" in *Competitiveness* (Vol. 5, No. 3, August 1991, pp. 45-56). By Taylor H. Cox, Jr. and Stacy Blake.

Managing the Growing Firm. Englewood Cliffs, NJ: Prentice Hall, 1992. By Lorraine U. Hendrickson.

Managing to Have Profits: The Secret Japan Learned but the U.S. Forgot. Cambridge, MA: CashFlow Books, 1992. By Arnold J. Olenick.

Managing People: A Practical Guide. Grants Pass, OR: PSI Research.

Managing People and Organizations. New York, NY: McGraw-Hill, Inc., 1992. By John Gabarro.

Managing for Results: Economic Tasks and Risk-Taking Decisions. New York, NY: Harper Business, 1993. By Peter F. Drucker.

Managing the Small Business: Insights and Readings. Englewood Cliffs, NJ: Prentice Hall, 1989. By Cynthia C. Ryans.

Managing Small Businesses. St. Paul, MN: West Publishing Co., 1993. By Robert L. Anderson.

Managing the Small to Mid-Sized Company: Concepts & Cases. Burr Ridge, IL: Richard D. Irwin Incorporated, 1994. By James C. Collins.

"Managing Technology When You're Not a Techie" in *Working Woman* (Vol. 20, No. 10, October 1995, pp. 24-25, 98). By Bronwyn Fryer.

"Managing Temporary Workers: A Permanent HRM Challenge" in *Organizational Dynamics* (Vol. 23, No. 2, Autumn 1994, pp. 49-63). By Daniel Feldman, Helen Doerpinghaus and William Turnley.

Mastering the Business Cycle: How to Keep Your Company on Track in Times of Economic Change. Burr Ridge, IL: Probus Publishing Company, Inc., 1990. By Albert N. Link.

Mastering Change Management: Turning Obstacles Into Opportunities. San Diego, CA: Pfeiffer & Co. By Richard Y. Chang.

"Military Style Yields to Leader" in *Crain's Small Business* (March 1996, p. 17). By Jim Brady.

"Minute by Minute" in *Entrepreneur* (Vol. 23, No. 4, April 1995, pp. 65). By Gayle Sato Stodder.

"Mistakes That Three Out of Four Businesses Make" in *National Public Accountant* (Vol. 40, No. 1, January 1995, pp. 12). By Louis A. Orlando.

"Mistakes Your Growing Company Needs To Avoid" in *Money: Money Guide Supplement* (Vol. , No. , 1994, pp. 76-81). By Mary Rowland.

Monitoring and Evaluating Small Business Projects: A Step by Step Guide for Private Development Organizations. New York, NY: PACT, Inc., 1987. By Shirley Buzzard, editor.

"Myth of the Gunslinger" in *Success* (Vol. 41, No. 2, March 1994, pp. 34-40). By Ingrid Abramovitch.

New Venture Strategies. Englewood Cliffs, NJ: Prentice Hall, 1980. By Karl H. Vesper.

"A New Year's Guide for CEOs" in *Inc.* (Vol. 18, No. 1, January 1996, pp. 30-37). By Martha E. Mangelsdorf.

"On the Edge" in *Entrepreneur* (Vol. 23, No. 8, August 1995, pp. 76, 78-79). By Robert McGarvey.

"On Hold" in *Entrepreneur* (Vol. 22, No. 9, September 1994, pp. 76-78). By Charlotte Taylor.

On-the-Job Training and Orientation: Enhanced Performance. San Diego, CA: Pfeiffer & Co. By Larry R. Smalley.

101 Simple Things to Improve Your Business. Menlo Park, CA: Crisp Publications, 1995. By Dottie and Lilly Walters.

"The Open Book Revolution" in *Inc.* (Vol. 17, No. 8, June 1995, pp. 26-30, 32, 34, 36, 38-43).

"The Open Corporation" in *Small Business Reports* (Vol. 19, No. 7, July 1994, pp. 31). By Jenny C. McCune.

"Open House" in *Entrepreneur* (Vol. 23, No. 5, May 1995, pp. 54-55). By Mark Henricks.

Opportunity Management: Strategic Planning for Small Business. Englewood Cliffs, NJ: Prentice Hall, 1985. By Omer Carey and D. Olson.

"Out Of Bounds" in *Entrepreneur* (Vol. 23, No. 12, November 1995, pp. 74, 76, 78). By Mark Henricks.

"Pairing Up" in *Entrepreneur* (Vol. 22, No. 9, September 1994, pp. 60-62). By Cynthia E. Griffin.

"Paradox Found" in *Entrepreneur* (Vol. 24, No. 2, February 1996, pp. 69-72). By Mark Henricks.

Performance Improvement Resources and Membership Directory. Washington, DC: International Society for Performance Improvement.

"Pizza De Resistance" in *Entrepreneur* (Vol. 22, No. 13, December 1994, pp. 50). By Charlotte Taylor.

Prentice Hall Small Business Management Handbook. Englewood Cliffs, NJ: Prentice Hall, 1996.

"The Preventive Corrective-Action Report" in *Inc.* (Vol. 18, No. 1, January 1996, pp. 67-69). By Donna Fenn.

"Problem-Solving Approach Works Best for Small Professional Firms" in *Marketing News* (Vol. 28, No. 6, March 14, 1994, pp. 15). By Vicki Clift.

Quality Management & the Small Business. Englewood Cliffs, NJ: Prentice Hall, 1994. By Lionel Stebbing.

"Quality Time" in *Entrepreneur* (Vol. 23, No. 11, October 1995, pp. 156, 158-162). By Loretta Ownes and Mark Henricks.

"A Question Of Privacy" in *Entrepreneur* (Vol. 23, No. 3, March 1995, pp. 24). By Janean Huber and Debra Phillips.

Real World of the Small Business Owner. New York, NY: Routledge, Chapman & Hall, Inc., 1987. By Richard Scase.

Reengineering the Corporation: A Manifesto for Business Revolution. New York, NY: Harper Business. By Michael Hammer and James Champy.

"Relationship of Structure to Entrepreneurial & Innovative Success" in *Marketing Intelligence & Planning* (Vol. 12, No. 9, 1994, pp. 37). By Paul Herbig and James E. Golden and Steven Dunphy.

"Run Your Company Smarter" in *Money* (Vol. 23, No. 11, November 1994, pp. 136-140). By Marlys J. Harris.

Running a One-Person Business. Berkeley, CA: Ten Speed Press, 1994. By Claude Whitmyer.

Running Things: The Art of Making Things Happen. New York, NY: McGraw-Hill, Inc. By Philip B. Crosby.

The Save Your Business Book: A Business Survival Handbook for the 1990s and Beyond. New York, NY: The Free Press, 1993. By John D. Goldhammer.

Secrets of Entrepreneurial Leadership: Building Top Performance Through Trust & Teamwork. Chicago, IL: Dearborn Financial Publishing, Inc., 1992. By Ted Nicholas.

Simple Case Books for Small Businesses. Woodstock, NY: Beekman Publishers, Inc., 1990. By Paul D. Ordidge.

"The Skill Every Manager Must Master" in *Working Woman* (vol 20, No. 5, May 1995, pp. 29-30). By Nancy K. Austin.

Small Business Barriers & Battlefields: Adding Reality to the American Dream. Saint Charles, IL: Matahari Publishing. By Robert E. Fleury.

Small Business Basics. Dubuque, IA: Kendall/Hunt Publishing Co., 1991. By Benedetto.

Small Business Decision Making. Denver, CO: U.S. Small Business Administration (SBA).

Small Business Fundamentals. Old Tappan, NJ: Merrill Publishing Co., 1988. By Thomas Zimmerer and Norman Scarborough.

The Small Business Guide to the Malcolm Baldridge National Quality Award: Proven Strategies for Building Quality into Your Organization. Burr Ridge, IL: Irwin Professional Publishing, 1995. By John O. Brown.

The Small Business Handbook. New York, NY: Simon & Schuster Trade, 1989. By Irving Burstiner.

The Small Business Information Handbook. New York, NY: John Wiley & Sons, Inc., 1990. By Gustave Berle.

Small Business Management. Albany, NY: Delmar Publishers, Fourth edition, 1989. By William D. Hailes, Jr.

Small Business Management. New York, NY: John Wiley & Sons, Inc., Fifth edition, 1990. By Hal B. Pickle and Royce L. Abrahamson.

Small Business Management. Boston, MA: Houghton Mifflin Co., Fourth edition, 1990. By Siropolis.

Small Business Management. Cincinnati, OH: South-Western Publishing Company, 1996. By Longnecker.

Small Business Management: A Planning Approach. Burr Ridge, IL: Irwin Professional Publishing, 1995. By Joel Corman.

Small Business Management: An Entrepreneur's Guide to Success. Homewood, IL: Richard D. Irwin, Inc., 1993. By William L. Megginson.

Small Business Management Fundamentals. New York, NY: McGraw-Hill, Inc., Sixth edition, 1993. By Dan Steinhoff.

Small Business Management Guide: Advice from the Brass-Tacks Entrepreneur. New York, NY: Henry Holt & Company, Inc., 1994. By Jim Schell.

Small Business: Planning and Management. Fort Worth, TX: Dryden Press, Second edition, 1990. By Charles Kuehl.

The Small Business Survival Guide: How to Manage Your Cash, Profits, and Taxes. Naperville, IL: Sourcebooks, Inc., 1992. By Robert E. Fleury.

"Smooth Moves" in *Entrepreneur* (Vol. 23, No. 1, January 1995, pp. 58). By Gayle Sato Stodder.

"Sounding Board" in *Income Opportunities* (Vol. 30, No. 6, June 1995, pp. 114, 116). By Richard J. Maturi.

"Speed Reading" in *Entrepreneur* (Vol. 23, No. 3, March 1995, pp. 177-183). By Deborah W. Flores.

"Starting an Appraisal Firm" in *Real Estate Appraiser* (Vol. 58, No. 1, April 1992, pp. 16-20). By Terrence L. Love.

BIBLIOGRAPHY

"Staying Alive" in *Entrepreneur* (Vol. 23, No. 3, March 1995, pp. 114-118). By Robert McGarvey.

Strategic Planning in Small Business. Cincinnati, OH: South-Western Publishing Co., 1987. By Charles R. Stoner.

Street Smarts: New Ideas for Small Companies. East Lansing, MI: Michigan State University Press, 1990. By William H. Franklin.

Success in Managing a Small Business. Brookfield, VT: Ashgate Publishing Company, 1994. By Henry Kyambalesa.

Successful Small Business Management. Burr Ridge, IL: Richard D. Irwin, Inc., 1990. By Leon C. Megginson, Charles R. Scott, Lyle R. Trueblood, and William C. Megginson.

Successful Training Practice: A Manager's Guide to Personnel Development. Cambridge, MA: Blackwell Publishers, 1993. By Alan H. Anderson.

Supervisor's Infobank: 1000 Quick Answers to Your Toughest Problems. New York, NY: McGraw-Hill, Inc., 1995. By Arthur R. Pell.

Survival Handbook for Small Business. Denver, CO: Prosperity & Profits Unlimited, Distribution Services, Revised edition, 1992. By Frieda Carrol.

"Taking the Fall" in *Inc.* (Vol. 17, No. 12, September 1995, pp. 81-83, 85-86). By Anne Murphy.

"Taming the Beast" in *Inc.* (Vol. 18, No. 5, April 1996, pp. 35-36, 39, 42, 44, 47). By David Whitford.

"Tax Driver" in *Entrepreneur* (Vol. 22, No. 13, December 1994, pp. 32). By Mark Henricks.

"The Team-Building Peer Review" in *Inc.* (Vol. 17, No. 10, July 1995, pp. 63-65). By Stephanie Gruner.

Team Entrepreneurship. Thousand Oaks, CA: Sage Publications, Inc., 1989. By Alex Stewart.

Techniques for Problem Solving. Denver, CO: U.S. Small Business Administration (SBA).

"Terms of Agreement" in *Entrepreneur* (Vol. 22, No. 9, September 1994, pp. 72-75). By Jane Easter Bahls.

"Time Out" in *Entrepreneur* (Vol. 23, No. 11, October 1995, pp. 70, 72-74). By Mark Henricks.

"Tips on People Management" in *D&B Reports* (Vol. 43, No. 2, March/April 1994, pp. 60).

"To Thine Own Self Be True" in *Inc.* (Volume 16, No. 8, August 1994, pp. 50-56). By Ronald E. Merrill and Henry D. Sedgewick.

Total Improvement Management: How to Coordinate Diverse Improvement Efforts for Maximum Gain. New York, NY: McGraw-Hill, Inc., 1995. By H. James Harrington.

The Total Quality Handbook for the Small Business. Holbrook, MA: Adams Publishing, 1995. By John Woods.

The TQM Almanac, 1994-1995 Edition. Burr Ridge, IL: Irwin Professional Publishing, 1994-1995 edition. By Timeplace, Inc.

The Ultimate No B.S., No Holds Barred, Kick Butt, Take No Prisoners, and Make Tons of Money Business Success Book. Bellingham, WA: Self-Counsel Press, 1993. By Dan Kennedy.

Untold Facts About the Small Business Game: How to Be Competent in Business. Berkeley, CA: Blagrove Publications, 1988. By Luanna C. Blagrove.

Value-Added Sales Management: A Guide for Salespeople and Their Managers. Chicago, IL: Contemporary Books, Inc., 1993. By Tom Reilly.

"What to Do with a Lousy Business" in *Management Review* (Vol. 83, No. 6, June 1994, pp. 40-43). By Dan Thomas.

"When Employees Lie, Steal, or Cheat" in *Working Woman* (January 1995). By Wilma Randle.

"When to Go Pro" in *Inc.* (The Inc. 500: Special Issue, Vol. 17, No. 15, October 1995, pp. 72). By Donna Fenn.

Why Entrepreneurs Fail: Avoid the 20 Fatal Pitfalls of Running Your Business. Blue Ridge Summit, PA: TAB Books, Inc., 1991. By James W. Halloran.

"Why Take Sides?" in *Inc.* (Vol. 17, No. 3, March 1995, pp. 29). By Jeffrey Mount.

Winning With the Power of Persuasion: Mancuso's Secrets for Small Business Success. Chicago, IL: Dearborn Financial Publishing, Inc., 1993. By Joseph Mancuso.

"Women As Managers: Not Just Different—Better" in *Working Woman* (Vol. 20, No. 11, November 1995, pp. 14). By Harris Collingwood.

Your Small Business Made Simple. New York, NY: Doubleday & Company Inc., 1989. By Richard R. Gallagher.

"Zen-trepreneurs" in *Entrepreneur* (Vol. 23, No. 4, April 1995, pp. 58-59). By Mark Henricks.

Nontraditional Financing

"A Capital Idea Helps Nurture Small Firms in Wayne County" in *Crain's Small Business* (October 1995, p. 21). By Pam Woodside.

"Cards May Be Ticket to Survive Cash-Flow Crunch" in *Crain's Small Business* (March 1996, p. 14). By Lawrence Gardner.

"Found Money" in *Entrepreneur* (Vol. 23, No. 4, April 1995, pp. 108-110, 112-115). By David R. Evanson.

"Get Cash Now!" in *Success* (Vol. 38, No. 10, December 1991, pp. 26-32). By Ronit Addis Rose.

Getting Money. Bellingham, WA: Self-Counsel Press, 1991. By Dan Kennedy.

Guerrilla Financing: Alternative Techniques to Finance Any Small Business. Boston, MA: Houghton Mifflin Co., 1992. By Bruce J. Blechman and Jay C. Levinson.

"Hatching Uncle Sam's Entrepreneurs" in *Management Today* (November 1993, pp. 54-56). By John Thackray.

"How to Obtain Export Capital" in *Nation's Business* (Vol. 82, No. 5, May 1994, pp. 24).

"Kid Venture Capital" in *Black Enterprise* (Vol. 25, No. 5, December 1994, pp. 34). By Tonia L. Shakespeare.

"LEAF Me a Loan" in *Business Start-Ups* (Vol. 8, No. 1, January 1996, pp. 74-75).

"Leasing Lessons" in *Business Start-Ups* (Vol. 8, No. 2, February 1996, p. 72). By Eric J. Adams.

"Look at Every Option—And Beyond" in *Nation's Business* (Vol. 79, No. 7, July 1991, pp. 9). By Thomas Hierl.

"The Money Is Out There...How To Get It" in *Agency Sales Magazine* (Vol. 24, No. 2, February 1994, pp. 15-17). By Jeff Fromberg.

Money Sources for Small Business: How You Can Find Private, State, Federal & Corporate Financing. Santa Maria, CA: Puma Publishing Company, 1991. By William M. Alarid.

"A New Loan Option to Bank, Venture Capital" in *Crain's Small Business* (February 1996, p. 9-10). By Jeffrey McCracken.

"19 Sources of Capital for Your Start-Up" in *Income Opportunities* (Vol. 31, No. 2, February 1996, pp. 26-30). By Terri Cullen.

"Northern Exposure" in *Entrepreneur* (Vol. 23, No. 5, May 1995, pp. 15). By Cynthia E. Griffin.

"The Numbers Speak Volumes" in *Small Business Reports* (Vol. 19, No. 7, July 1994, pp. 39-43). By Lamont Change.

"Peer Power" in *Entrepreneur* (Vol. 23, No. 4, April 1995, pp. 15). By Heather Page.

"Play Misty for Me" in *Business Start-Ups* (Vol. 7, No. 9, September 1995, p. 114). By Eric J. Adams.

"Program Gives Small Businesses A Financial Boost" in *Entrepreneur* (Vol. 32, No. 7, July 1995, pp. 17). By Cynthia E. Griffin.

"The Secrets of Bootstrapping" in *Inc.* (Vol. 13, No. 9, September 1991, pp. 52-70). By Robert A. Mamis.

"The Six Best Ways to Raise Cash" in *Money: Money Guide Supplement* (Vol. , No. , 1994, pp. 34-39). By Vanessa O'Connell.

"Small Loans, Big Dreams" in *Working Woman* (Vol. 20, No. 2, February 1995, pp. 46-49, 72-73, 77). By Elizabeth Kadetsky.

"Treasure Hunt" in *Business Start-Ups* (Vol. 7, No. 7, July 1995, 56-58, 60-61). By Gloria Gibbs Marullo.

"Where Are All the Wanda Buffets?" in *Money* (Vol. 23, No. 11, November 1994, pp. 116-117). By Nancy J. Perry.

"Where to Look for Money Now" in *Working Woman* (Vol. 19, No. 10, October 1994, pp. 56-62). By Ilyce R. Glink.

Outfitting the Office

"A Bike Shop in Harlem: Part IV of a Special Series" in *Income Opportunities* (Vol. 30, No. 1, January 1995, pp. 70, 72, 74). By Maureen Nevin Duffy.

"A Bike Shop in Harlem: Part IX of a Special Series" in *Income Opportunities* (Vol. 30, No. 6, June 1995, pp. 52, 54, 56, 58). By Maureen Nevin Duffy.

"Comfort Zone" in *Entrepreneur* (Vol. 23, No. 11, October 1995, pp. 34, 36-37). By Cheryl J. Goldberg.

Complete Guide to Building & Outfitting an Office in Your Home. Cincinnati, OH: Betterway Books, 1994. By Jerry Germer.

Directory of Store Planners, Interior Designers & Architects. Plantation, FL: National Association of Store Fixture Manufacturers, Annual, September.

Home Office - Small Office Quick Planner. Bridgeton, MO: Gardeners' Guide, 1995.

"Ideal Setting" in *Entrepreneur* (Vol. 23, No. 1, January 1995, pp. 14). By Gayle Sato Stodder.

Increasing Productivity and Profit in the Workplace: A Guide to Office Planning and Design. Somerset, NJ: John Wiley & Sons, Inc., 1992. By M. Glynn Shumake.

Office Design. New York, NY: Watson-Guptill Publicatons, Inc., 1992.

Office Design That Really Works. Lincolnwood, IL: N T C Publishing Group, 1995. By Kathleen Allen.

Office Design That Really Works! Design for the 90s. Los Angeles, CA: Affinity Publishing, 1995. By Kathleen R. Allen.

Office Space Planning and Management: A Manager's Guide to Techniques and Standards. Westport, CT: Greenwood Publishing Group, Inc., 1986. By Donald B. Tweedy.

"The Reorganized Executive" in *Working Woman* (January 1996, pp. 66-68). By Anne Armbuster.

"Setting Up Shop" in *Income Opportunities* (Vol. 31, No. 1, January 1996, pp. 40, 42, 44). By Dora Johnson.

Store Fixtures—Wholesale Directory. Omaha, NE: American Business Directories, Inc.

Store Fronts Directory. Omaha, NE: American Business Directories, Inc., Annual.

"Workspace" in *Business Start-Ups* (Vol. 7, No. 12, December 1995, p. 72). By Lisa Kanarek.

Publicity

"Advertising" in *Business Start-Ups* (Vol. 7, No. 12, December 1995, pp. 6-7). By Sue Clayton.

The Advertising Handbook for Small Business. Bellingham, WA: Self-Counsel Press, 1994, second edition. By Dell Dennison.

"Be Your Own Publicist" in *Business Start-Ups* (Vol. 8, No. 1, January 1996, pp. 58, 60-61). By Sue Clayton.

Big Ideas for Small Service Businesses: How to Successfully Advertise, Publicize, and Maximize Your Business or Professional Practice. Buena Vista, CO: Communication Creativity, 1994. By Marilyn Ross and Tom Ross.

"A Bike Shop in Harlem: Part VII of a Special Series" in *Income Opportunities* (Vol. 30, No. 4, April 1995, pp. 68, 70, 72, 74, 76). By Maureen Nevin Duffy.

"Bootstrapping on the Web" in *Inc.* (Vol. 18, No. 1, January 1996, pp. 93). By Phaedra Hise.

"Brochure Cure" in *Business Start-Ups* (Vol. 7, No. 6, June 1995, pp. 70-73). By Charles W. Crawford.

Bulletproof News Releases: Help at Last for the Publicity Deficient. Marietta, GA: Franklin-Sarrett Publishers, 1994. By Kay Borden.

"Butter Up!" in *Entrepreneur* (Vol. 23, No. 4, April 1995, pp. 180, 182). By Jerry Fisher. Jerry

Buttons—Advertising Directory. Omaha, NE: American Business Directories, Inc.

"Co-Opportunities in Advertising" in *Business Start-Ups* (Vol. 8, No. 2, February 1996, pp. 60, 62-63). Lin Grensing-Pophal.

"A Comparison of Major Advertising Media" in *Business Start-Ups* (Vol. 8, No. 1, January 1996, p. 10). By Dr. Robert B. Woodruff.

"Desktop 101" in *Entrepreneur* (Vol. 23, No. 12, November 1995, pp. 34, 36-37). By Cheryl J. Goldberg.

Directory of Print Media Advertising Resources. Santa Barbara, CA: Richler & Co., 1992.

Do-It-Yourself Business Promotions Kit. Englewood Cliffs, NJ: Prentice Hall, 1994. By Jack Griffin.

"Door Prizes" in *Entrepreneur* (Vol. 24, No. 4, April 1996, pp. 88, 90-91). By Jerry Fisher.

"The Envelope, Please" in *Entrepreneur* (Vol. 23, No. 8, August 1995, pp. 86, 88-89). By Jerry Fisher.

Getting Publicity: A Do-It-Yourself Guide for Small Business and Non-Profit Groups. Bellingham, WA: Self-Counsel Press, 1990. By Tana Fletcher and Julia Rockler.

Getting Publicity: The Very Best Book for Your Small Business. Bellingham, WA: Self-Counsel Press, 1995. By Tana Fletcher.

"Giving It Away" in *Income Opportunities* (Vol. 31, No. 4, April 1996, pp. 44, 46). By Maureen Nevin Duffy.

"Glory Days" in *Income Opportunities* (Vol. 29, No. 11, November 1994, pp. 62-64). By Penelope Patsuris.

"Going Home Page" in *Crain's Small Business* (October 1995, p. T-14 of Supplement). By Hiawatha Bray.

Guerrilla Advertising: Cost-Effective Tactics for Small Business Success. Boston, MA: Houghton Mifflin Company, 1994. By Jay C. Levinson.

"Handsome Prints" in *Business Start-Ups* (Vol. 7, No. 10, October 1995, pp. 30, 32-33). By Sue Clayton.

How to Work with the Media in Promoting Your Business or Organization. Dallas, TX: Shay Publications, 1994. By Kevin J. Shay.

"Instant Image" in *Business Start-Ups* (Vol. 7, No. 10, October 1995, p. 76). By Eric J. Adams.

"Journalists" in *Business Start-Ups* (Vol. 7, No. 12, December 1995, pp. 34, 36-37). By Jacquelyn Lynn.

"Just Imagine!" in *Direct Marketing* (Vol. 56, No. 12, April 1994, pp. 38-40). By Ray Jutkins.

"Lights, Camera, Interaction" in *Entrepreneur* (Vol. 23, No. 11, October 1995, pp. 28). By Lynn Beresford.

"Lip Service" in *Business Start-Ups* (Vol. 8, No. 2, February 1996, p. 78, 80). By Lynn L. Norquist.

"Local Exposure" in *Income Opportunities* (Vol. 30, No. 5, May 1995, pp. 112, 114). By Maureen Nevin Duffy.

Logos of America's Fastest Growing Corporations. Austin, TX: Reference Press, Inc. By David E. Carter, Editor.

"Making Headlines" in *Business Start-Ups* (Vol. 7, No. 9, September 1995, pp. 86, 88, 91). By Sue Clayton.

"Mellow Yellow" in *Income Opportunities* (Vol. 30, No. 4, April 1995, pp. 104, 108). By Maureen Nevin Duffy.

"Name Dropping" in *Entrepreneur* (Vol. 22, No. 9, September 1994, pp. 200-202). By Jerry Fisher.

"Naming Your Business" in *Business Start-Ups* (Vol. 7, No. 12, December 1995, pp. 52-53). By Dennis Whittington.

The New Publicity Kit. New York, NY: John Wiley & Sons, 1995. By Jeanette Smith.

"News Flash" in *Entrepreneur* (Vol. 23, No. 7, July 1995, pp. 226-227). By Laura Radloff.

"Nose for News" in *Business Start-Ups* (Vol. 7, No. 11, November 1995, p. 10). By Loreene Maurer.

"On the Air" in *Entrepreneur* (Vol. 32, No. 4, April 1995, pp. 128, 130-135). By Heather Page.

"On the Radio" in *Income Opportunities* (Vol. 30, No. 8, August 1995, pp. 100, 102). By Maureen Nevin Duffy.

101 Big Ideas for Promoting a Business on a Small Budget. Phoenix, AZ: Marketing Methods Press, 1989. By Barbara Lambesis.

"Order Now!" in *Income Opportunities* (Vol. 29, No. 7, July 1994, pp. 28, 30). By Stew Caverly.

Perfect Sales Piece: A Complete Do-It-Yourself Guide to Creating Brochures, Catalogs, Fliers. New York, NY: John Wiley & Sons, Incorporated, 1994. By Robert W. Bly.

"Playing the Telecard Hand" in *Inc.* (Vol. 18, No. 1, January 1996, pp. 84). By Stephanie Gruner.

"Prime Time" in *Entrepreneur* (Vol. 24, No. 2, February 1996, pp. 32). By Lynn Beresford.

"Profiting on the Internet" in *Income Opportunities* (Vol. 30, No. 4, April 1995, pp. 24-29). By Reed Berkowitz.

Publicity Club of Chicago—Media/Membership Directory. Chicago, IL: Publicity Club of Chicago (PCC), 1995. By David Brimm, Editor.

The Publicity Kit: A Complete Guide for Entrepreneurs, Small Businesses, and Non-Profit Organizations. New York, NY: John Wiley & Sons, Inc., 1991. By Jeanette Smith.

Publicity Power: A Practical Guide to Effective Promotion. Menlo Park, CA: Crisp Publications. By Charles Mallory.

"Pump It Up!" in *Business Start-Ups* (Vol. 7, No. 9, September 1995, p. 102). By Theresa A. Hamilton.

"Reeling Them In" in *Entrepreneur* (Vol. 23, No. 12, November 1995, pp. 32). By Lynn Beresford.

"Reviving the Dying Store" in *Direct Marketing* (Vol. 56, No. 7, November 1993, pp. 20-21). By Murray Raphel.

Sales Promotion, Advertising & PR. Old Tappan, NJ: Macmillan Publishing Co., Inc., 1991. By R. Bagehot.

"Screen Stars" in *Entrepreneur* (Vol. 23, No. 3, March 1995, pp. 32). By Erika Kotite and Heather Page.

"Screen Test" in *Entrepreneur* (Vol. 23, No. 4, April 1995, pp. 132). By Heather Page.

"The Searchers" in *Business Start-Ups* (Vol. 7, No. 8, September 1995, pp. 82, 84-85). By Lynn H. Colwell.

"Second That Emotion" in *Entrepreneur* (Vol. 23, No. 7, July 1995, pp. 198, 200). By Jerry Fisher.

"Show And Tell" in *Entrepreneur* (Vol. 23, No. 11, October 1995, pp. 28). By Lynn Beresford.

"Sign Language" in *Business Start-Ups* (Vol. 7, No. 11, November 1995, p. 8).

"Talk of the Town" in *Entrepreneur* (Vol. 23, No. 7, July 1995, pp. 116, 118-121). By Brian Ruberry.

"Truth or Dare" in *Entrepreneur* (Vol. 23, No. 5, May 1995, pp. 66, 68-69). By Jane Easter Bahls.

"What's in a Logo?" in *Small Business Opportunities* (Vol. 7, No. 3, May 1995, pp. 12, 82). By Arlene Evans.

"Your Company: On TV" in *Inc.* (Vol. 17, No. 10, July 1995, pp. 91). By Robina A. Gangemi.

Site Selection

"Against the Odds" in *Income Opportunities* (Vol. 31, No. 2, February 1996, pp. 12-16). By Malinda Reinke.

"And Stay Out!" in *Entrepreneur* (Vol. 22, No. 9, September 1994, pp. 54). By Gayle Sato Stodder.

Black's Office Leasing Guide: Washington/Baltimore. Gaithersburg, MD: Black's Guide, Inc., Semiannual. By Susan Dudley, Editor.

"Branching Out" in *Nation's Business* (Vol. 82, No. 11, November 1994, pp. 53). By Roberta Maynard.

Business Facilities—Site Seekers' Guide. Red Bank, NJ: Group C. Communications, Inc., Annual, January. By Eric Peterson, Editor.

Commercial Space Directory. Albuquerque, NM: New Mexico Chapter, Annual, summer.

Facility Layout and Location: An Analytical Approach. Englewood Cliffs, NJ: Prentice Hall, Second edition, 1991. By Richard L. Francis, Jr.

"A Field Guide to Your Local Economy" in *Inc.* (Special Issue: The State of Small Business, February 1996, pp. 51-54). By Joel Garreau.

A Guide to Site Planning & Landscape Construction. New York, NY: John Wiley & Sons, 1996. By Harvey M. Rubenstein.

"Hot Spots" in *Inc. 500* (Vol. 16, No. 11, 1994, pp. 37-40, 42, 44, 46). By Anne Murphy.

"House Hunting" in *Entrepreneur* (Vol. 23, No. 4, April 1995, pp. 84, 86-87). By Cynthia E. Griffin.

Industrial Location: Principles and Policies. Cambridge, MA: Blackwell Publishers, Second edition, 1991. By Keith Chapman and David F. Walker.

"Interior Design" in *Business Start-Ups* (Vol. 7, No. 7, July 1995, p. 18). By Wendy Neuman.

"Key Factors in Selecting the Best Location for Your Company" in *Telemarketing Magazine* (Vol. 12, No. 8, February 1994, pp. 44-45). By Bob Cooper.

"Love Thy Neighbor?" in *Entrepreneur* (Vol. 23, No. 7, July 1995, pp. 6, 68-69). By Jane Easter Bahls.

"Paradise Found" in *Entrepreneur* (Vol. 23, No. 7, July 1995, pp. 172-176, 178-179). By Jacquelyn Lynn.

"The Rise of the Urban Entrepreneur" in *Inc.* (Special Issue: The State of Small Business, February 1996, pp. 104-119). By Michael E. Porter.

"St. Louis: Bringing Minorities into the Mainstream" in *Black Enterprise* (Vol. 24, No. 10, May 1994, pp. 64). By Gregory Freeman.

"Select a Business Site" in *Income Opportunities* (October 1991, pp. 64, 74). By Sandra Holland.

"Setting Your Sites" in *Business Start-Ups* (Vol. 7, No. 9, September 1995, pp. 6-7). By Lynn Beresford.

"Shopping Malls Attract Small Firms" in *Nation's Business* (Vol. 80, No. 12, December 1992, pp. 53-56). By Meg Whittemore.

"Site Seeing" in *Business Start-ups* (October 1994, pp. 54-58). By Cynthia E. Griffin.

Site Selection: Finding and Developing Your Best Location. Blue Ridge Summit, PA: TAB Books, Inc., 1989. By Kay Whitehouse.

Site Selection and Industrial Development—Work Force Issue. Norcross, GA: Conway Data, Inc., Annual, December. By Jack Lyne,

Site Selection and Investigation. Brookfield, VT: Ashgate Publishing Co., Inc., 1991. By Dan Lampert.

"The Ten Best Cities for Women Entrepreneurs" in *Working Woman* (Vol. 19, No. 3, March 1994, pp. 37-43). By Laurel Touby.

"30 Best Cities for Small Business" in *Entrepreneur* (Vol. 23, No. 8, August 1995, pp. 122-143). By Cynthia E. Griffin, Lynn Beresford, Heather Page, and Debra Phillips.

"Top 10 Cities for International Companies" in *World Trade* (Vol. 5, No. 8, October 1992, pp. 32-44). By Robin Soslow, Daniel J. McConville, Ben Warner and Patrice D. Raia.

"The Twenty Top Spots for Entrepreneurs" in *Money* (Vol. 23, No. 11, November 1994, pp. 126-34). By Mark Bautz.

"Xtra Cost-Cutting Tips" in *Business Start-Ups* (Vol. 7, No. 12, December 1995, p. 74). By Karin Moeller.

Small Business Development

The ABC's of Starting a Business. New York, NY: Publicity Plus, 1990. By Valerie White.

"After the Covers: What Are They Up to Now?" in *Chain Store Age Executive* (Vol. 70, No. 7, July 1994, pp. 19-33).

"Alphabet Soup" in *Inc.* (Vol. 16, No. 12, November 1994, pp. 31-32). By Heather E. Stone.

American Companies. Austin, TX: Reference Press, Inc., Biennial, Fall.

Anatomy of a Start-Up: Why Some New Businesses Succeed and Others Fail. Boston, MA: Inc. Publishing, 1991. By Elizabeth K. Longsworth, editor.

Avoiding Mistakes in Your Small Business. Menlo Park, CA: Crisp Publications. By David Karlson.

Avoiding the Pitfalls of Starting Your Own Business. New York, NY: Shapolsky Publishers, Inc., 1990. By Jeffrey P. Davidson.

Beating the Odds: Ten Smart Steps to Small Business Success. New York, NY: AMACOM, 1992. By Scott A. Clark.

"Betting on the Future" in *D&B Reports* (Vol. 40, No. 6, Nov./Dec. 1992, pp. 44). By Robert J. Klein.

Beyond Entrepreneurship: Turning Your Business Into an Enduring Great Company. Englewood Cliffs, NJ: Prentice Hall, 1992. By James C. Collins and William C. Lazier.

"Big Ideas for Your Small Business" in *Changing Times* (November 1989, pp. 57-60).

The Brass Tacks Entrepreneur. New York, NY: Henry Holt & Company, Inc., 1993. By Jim Schell.

"Bright Ideas" in *Business Start-Ups* (Vol. 7, No. 8, August 1995, pp. 50, 52-54, 57). By Bob Weinstein.

"Building a Better Burger" in *Business Start-Ups* (Vol. 8, No. 3, March 1996, pp. 21-22, 24-25). By Bob Weinstein.

Building a Profitable Business: A Proven Step-by-Step Guide to Starting and Running Your Own Business. Holbrook, MA: Bob Adams, Inc., Second edition, 1994. By Charles Chickadel and Greg Straughn.

The Business Forms on File Collection. New York, NY: Facts on File, Inc., 1995.

Business Operations Guidebook: The How-to Guide for Start-up Entrepreneurs. Poughquag, NY: Info Devils Press, 1993. By Robert Haiber.

Business Opportunities in the United States: The Complete Reference Guide to Practices and Procedures. Burr Ridge, IL: Irwin Professional Publishing, 1992. By Robert F. Cushman and R. Lawrence Soares, editors.

"Capture the Future" in *Success* (Vol. 40, No. 10, December 1993, pp. 63-70). By Katherine Callan.

Checklist for Going into Business. Denver, CO: U.S. Small Business Administration (SBA).

"A Checklist for Starting a Business" in *Crain's Small Business* (December 1995, p. 30).

The Competitive Edge: Essential Business Skills for Entrepreneurs. New York, NY: NAL/Dutton, 1991. By Fran Tarkenton and Joseph H. Boyett.

Complete Handbook for the Entrepreneur. Englewood Cliffs, NJ: Prentice Hall, 1990. By Gary Brenner, Joe Ewan, and Henry Custer.

The Coopers and Lybrand Guide to Growing Your Business. Somerset, NJ: John Wiley & Sons, Inc., 1988. By Seymour Jones, M. Bruce Cohen, and Victor V. Coppola.

"Could You Succeed in Small Business" in *Business Horizons* (September/October 1989, pp. 65-69).

"Dare to Be Different" in *Entrepreneur* (Vol. 23, No. 4, April 1995, pp. 122, 124-127). By Gayle Sato Stodder.

"The Deal Maker" in *Inc.* (Vol. 15, No. 13, December 1993, pp. 129-130). By Phaedra Hise.

Directory of Business Incubators and University Research & Science Parks. Stamford, CT: International Venture Capital Institute, Inc. (IVCI), Annual. By Carroll A. Greathouse, Editor.

The Do-It-Yourself Business Book. Somerset, NJ: John Wiley & Sons, Inc., 1989. By Gustav Berle.

Entrepreneur Magazine's The Secrets of Starting Your Own Business. Irvine, CA: Entrepreneur, Inc.

"Entrepreneurial Fables" in *Entrepreneur* (Vol. 23, No. 8, August 1995, pp. 120, 122-124, 127). By Gayle Sato Stodder.

The Entrepreneurial Mind: Winning Strategies for Starting, Renewing, & Harvesting. Amherst, NH: Brick House Publishing Co., Inc., 1994. By Jeffry A. Timmons.

The Entrepreneurial PC. Blue Ridge Summit, PA: TAB Books, Inc., 1991. By Bernard J. David.

Entrepreneurially Yours: A Compilation of Articles About Starting and Managing a Small Business. Nashville, TN: Business of Your Own, 1990. By Millicent G. Lownes.

The Entrepreneur's Guide to Growing Up: Taking Your Small Company to the Next Level. Bellingham, WA: Self-Counsel Press, Inc., 1993. By Edna Sheedy.

Entrepreneur's Guide to Starting a Successful Business. New York, NY: McGraw-Hill, Inc., Second edition, 1992. By James W. Halloran.

Entrepreneur's Road Map to Business Success. Alexandria, VA: Saxtons River Publications, Inc., Revised edition, 1992. By Lyle R. Maul and Dianne Craig Mayfield.

Entrepreneurship. Homewood, IL: Irwin Professional Publishing, 1989. By Robert D. Hisrich and Michael Peters.

Entrepreneurship. New York, NY: McGraw-Hill, Inc., 1989. By Vivian K. Ely, R. G. Berys, Debbie L. Popo and R. L. Lynch.

Entrepreneurship: Creating and Managing New Ventures. New York, NY: Elsevier Science, 1989. By Bruce Lloyd, editor.

Entrepreneurship: Creativity and Growth. Old Tappan, NJ: Macmillan Publishing Co., Inc., 1991. By Donald L. Sexton.

Entrepreneurship for the Nineties. Englewood Cliffs, NJ: Prentice Hall, 1990. By Gordon B. Baty.

"Entrepreneurship: The Role of the Individual in Small Business Development" in *IBAR* (Vol. 15, 1994, pp. 62-75). By Stan Cromie.

The Essence of Small Business. New York, NY: Prentice Hall General Reference & Travel, 1993. By Colin Barrow.

Evaluate Your Business: Small Business Baseline Evaluation Workbook. Fresno, CA: Willow Tree, Inc., 1992. By J. W. Irwin.

"Experience" in *Business Start-Ups* (Vol. 7, No. 12, December 1995, p. 20). By Jacquelyn Lynn.

Family Businesses, Small Businesses, Home Businesses & General Business Possibilities Encyclopedia. Denver, CO: Prosperity & Profits Unlimited, Distribution Services, 1991.

"Fifteen Start-Up Mistakes" in *Business Start-Ups* (Vol. 7, No. 12, December 1995, p. 22). By Mel Mandell.

501 Business Leads. New York, NY: Citadel Press, 1994.

"Focus on: Small Business" in *Journal of Accountancy* (Vol. 177, No. 5, May 1994, pp. 41). By Jacqueline L. Babicky and Larry Field and Norman C. Pricher.

"Fools Rush In? The Institutional Context of Industry Creation" in *Academy of Management Review* (Vol. 19, No. 4, October 1994, pp. 645). By Howard E. Aldrich and Marlene C. Fiol.

Forget Starting a Business. New York, NY: Simon & Schuster Trade, 1990. By Stephen Pollan.

Free Help from Uncle Sam to Start Your Own Business (or Expand the One You Have). Santa Maria, CA: Puma Publishing, 1996. By William M. Alarid, Editor.

From Concept to Market. Somerset, NJ: John Wiley & Sons, Inc., 1989. By Gary S. Lynn.

From Executive to Entrepreneur: Making the Transition. New York, NY: AMACOM, 1991. By Gilbert G. Zoghlin.

Getting-Into-Business Guides. Bellingham, WA: Self-Counsel Press, Inc., 1991. By Dan Kennedy.

Getting Started. Bellingham, WA: Self-Counsel Press, 1991. By Dan Kennedy.

"Going Solo" in *Income Opportunities* (Vol. 30, No. 11, November 1995, pp. 30, 32, 34). By Pamela Rohland.

"Group Therapy" in *Crain's Small Business* (September 1995, pp. 1, 12-13). By Kimberly Lifton.

Growing Your Small Business Made Simple. New York, NY: Doubleday & Company Inc., 1993. By Wilbur Cross.

The Growth Challenge: How to Build Your Business Profitably. Chicago, IL: Dearborn Trade, 1993. By Stephen A. Stumpf.

Have You Got What It Takes?. Bellingham, WA: Self-Counsel Press, 1993, third edition. By Douglas A. Gray.

"Help Getting Started" in *Business Start-Ups* (Vol. 7, No. 12, December 1995, pp. 28-29). By Sue Clayton.

The Home Office and Small Business Answer Book: Solutions to the Most Frequently Asked Questions About Starting and Running Home Offices. New York, NY: Henry Holt & Company, Inc., 1993. By Janet Attard.

"Hot Areas for Small Business" in *Black Enterprise* (Vol. 24, No. 4, November 1993, pp. 54).

"The Hottest Entrepreneurs in America" in *Inc.* (Vol. 14, No. 13, December 1992, pp. 88-103). By Martha E. Mangelsdorf.

How to Be in Business for Yourself. New York, NY: Gordon Press, Publishers, 1992.

How to Find Information About Companies. West Nyack, NY: Todd Publications.

How to Leave Your Job and Buy a Business of Your Own. New York, NY: McGraw-Hill, Inc., 1992. By C. D. Peterson.

"How to Make Your Ex-Boss Your Client" in *Black Enterprise* (Vol. 24, No. 9, April 1994, pp. 92-96). By Caryne Brown.

How to Organize and Operate a Small Business. Englewood Cliffs, NJ: Prentice Hall, Eighth edition, 1988. By Clifford M. Baumback.

How to Set Up Your Own Small Business. Minneapolis, MN: American Institute of Small Business (AISB), 1993. By Max Fallek.

How to Start a Business on a Shoestring. New York, NY: Gordon Press, Publishers, 1992.

How to Start a Business Without Quitting Your Job: The Moonlight Entrepreneur's Guide. Berkeley, CA: Ten Speed Press, 1992. By Philip Holland.

How to Start, Expand and Sell a Business: The Complete Guide for Entrepreneurs. Santa Barbara, CA: Venture Perspective Press, Third edition, 1991. By James C. Comiskey.

How to Start and Manage Your Own Business: A Practical Way to Start Your Own Business. Interlochen, MI: Lewis & Renn Associates, Inc., 1991. By Jerre G. Lewis and Leslie D. Renn.

How to Start, Run, and Stay in Business. Somerset, NJ: John Wiley & Sons, Inc., Second edition, 1993. By Gregory F. Kishel and Patricia G. Kishel. Price

How to Start and Run Your Own Business. Norwell, MA: Kluwer Academic Publishers, 1989. By Mike Mogano.

How to Start Your Business the Smart Way: 20 Common Mistakes to Avoid. Palm City, FL: You Can Do It!, 1989. By Susan H. Littauer.

How to Start Your Own Business—and Succeed. New York, NY: McGraw-Hill, Inc., Second edition, 1992. By Arthur H. Kuriloff.

How to Start Your Own Business on a Shoestring and Make Up to $500,000 a Year. Rocklin, CA: Prima Publishing & Communications, Revised edition, 1994. By Tyler G. Hicks.

How to Start Your Own Business Without Losing Your Shirt: Secrets of the Artful Entrepreneur. New York, NY: Macmillan Publishing Co., 1988. By Mortimer Levitt.

"How to Succeed in 4 Easy Steps" in *Inc.* (Vol. 17, No. 10, July 1995, pp. 30-32, 34, 36-40, 42). By Bo Burlingham.

How to Think Small Business for Big Profits. Saginaw, MI: Confectionery World, Inc., 1987. By Reynold J. Anschuetz.

In Business for Yourself. Lanham, MD: Madison Books, 1991. By Bruce Williams and Warren Sloat.

"Is the Price Right?" in *Income Opportunities* (Vol. 29, No. 9, September 1994, pp. 102-104). By Jo Frohbieter-Mueller.

Jane Applegate's Strategies for Small Business Success. New York, NY: NAL Dutton, 1995. By Jane Applegate. Price: $12.95.

"Jimmy's Top Ten List" in *Business Start-Ups* (Vol. 7, No. 8, August 1995, p. 7).

"Keeping Small Businesses Healthy" in *Franchising World* (Vol. 27, No. 1, January/February 1995, pp. 56-57). By Cindy Murphy.

Keys to Starting a Small Business. Hauppauge, NY: Barron's Educational Series, Inc., 1991. By Joel G. Siegel and Jae K. Shim.

"Keys to Success? For Starters, Here Are 15" in *Contractor* (Vol. 41, No. 11, November 1994, pp. 12). By Jeff Ferenc.

"Knowledge" in *Business Start-Ups* (Vol. 7, No. 12, December 1995, p. 38). By Carolyn Lawrence.

Make Money With Your PC!. Berkeley, CA: Ten Speed Press, 1994. By Lynn Waldorf.

Making It on Your Own: What to Know Before You Start Your Own Business. Austell, GA: Acropolis Books, Revised edition, 1991. By S. Norman Feingold.

Making Your Small Business a Success: More Expert Advice From the U.S. Small Business Administration. Blue Ridge Summit, PA: TAB Books, Inc., 1991. By Poteet.

McGraw-Hill Guide to Starting Your Own Business: A Step-by-Step Blueprint. New York, NY: McGraw-Hill, Inc., 1992. By Stephen C. Harper.

"Mentoring Helps Grow Emerging Businesses" in *Puget Sound Business Journal* (Vol. 12, No. 18, September 23, 1991, pp. 24). By Linda Lang.

The Mid-Career Entrepreneur: How to Start a Business and Be Your Own Boss. Chicago, IL: Dearborn Financial Publishing, Inc., 1993. By Joseph R. Mancuso.

The Millionaire's Bible: How to Start Your Own Business. Ft. Myers Beach, FL: Island Press Publishers, Revised edition, 1987. By Monroe C. Babcock.

"Mind Power" in *Entrepreneur* (Vol. 23, No. 5, May 1995, pp. 100, 102-106). By Robert McGarvey.

Mind Your Own Mini-Business!: How to Start Your Own "Mini-Biz" with 10 to 1,000 Dollars and Make All the Money You Need. Raleigh, NC: Success Team, 1991. By Will Davis.

BIBLIOGRAPHY

Minority Small Business & Capital Ownership Development Program. New York, NY: Gordon Press Publishers, 1995.

"Myth of the Gunslinger" in *Success* (Vol. 41, No. 2, March 1994, pp. 34-40). By Ingrid Abramovitch.

Network of Small Businesses—Membership Directory. Lyndhurst, OH: Network of Small Businesses (NSB), 1995. By Irwin Friedman, Editor.

"New Beginnings" in *Business Start-Ups* (Vol. 8, No. 1, January 1996, p. 96). By Joann K. Jones.

New Business Ventures and the Entrepreneur. Burr Ridge, IL: Richard D. Irwin, 1989. By Howard H. Stevenson.

The New Small Business Survival Guide. New York, NY: W. W. Norton & Co., Inc., 1991. By Bob Coleman.

"1995 Small Business Tax Guide" in *Income Opportunities* (Vol. 30, No. 1, January 1995, pp. 48-60). By Randall Kirkpatrick and Meg North.

Nobody Gets Rich Working for Somebody Else: An Entrepreneur's Guide. Menlo Park, CA: Crisp Publications, Inc., 1993. By Roger Fritz.

"On Your Mark..." in *Business Start-Ups* (Vol. 7, No. 2, February 1995, pp. 37-44). By Gustav Berle and Jacquelyn Lynn.

Operating a Really Small Business. Menlo Park, CA: Crisp Publications. By Betty Bivins.

"Out of the Blue" in *Inc.* (Vol. 17, No. 10, July 1995, pp. 68-72). By Tom Ehrenfeld.

"Out on a Limb and on Their Own" in *Nation's Business* (Vol. 82, No. 3, March 1994, pp. 33-34). By John S. DeMott.

Out of Work? Get Into Business!: Shifting Gears and Turning Job Loss into Success. Bellingham, WA: Self-Counsel Press, 1994, first edition. By Don Doman.

"A Perfect Fit" in *Business Start-Ups* (Vol. 7, No. 9, September 1995, pp. 78, 80-81). By Jacquelyn Lynn.

The Prentice Hall Small Business Survival Guide: A Blueprint for Success. Englewood Cliffs, NJ: Prentice Hall, 1993. Compiled by Prentice Hall editorial staff.

"Quitting" in *Business Start-Ups* (Vol. 7, No. 12, December 1995, pp. 60-61). By Sue Clayton.

Racing Failure: What It Takes to Become an Entrepreneur...and Make It. Cedar Falls, IA: Freiberg Publishing Co., 1989. By Bill D. Freiberg.

"Run Your Company Smarter" in *Money* (Vol. 23, No. 11, November 1994, pp. 136-140). By Marlys J. Harris.

"Say When" in *Inc.* (Vol. 17, No. 2, February 1995, pp. 19-20). By Steven L. Marks.

"Saying Goodbye to Corporate America" in *Black Enterprise* (Vol. 22, No. 11, June 1992, pp. 312-318). By Shawn Kennedy.

SBA Hotline Answer Book. New York, NY: John Wiley & Sons, Inc., 1991. By Gustav Berle.

"SCORE Points to Success" in *Black Enterprise* (Vol. 25, No. 6, January 1995, pp. 38). By Christina F. Watts.

Searching for the Spirit of Enterprise. New York, NY: NAL/Dutton, 1994. By Larry C. Farrell.

Second Coming of the Wooly Mammoth: An Entrepreneur's Bible. Berkeley, CA: Ten Speed Press, 1991. By Ted Frost.

Secrets to Running a Successful Business. 1994. By Jeanette L. Rosenberg.

"Setting Up Shop (in SOHO)" in *Working Woman* (October 1994, pp. 65-69). By Jeff Ubois.

The Small Business Bible: The Make-or-Break Factors for Survival and Success. New York, NY: John Wiley & Sons, Inc., 1988. By Paul Resnik.

The Small Business Directory. Pueblo, CO: U.S. Government Printing Office, 1992.

Small Business Encyclopedia. Irvine, CA: Entrepreneur, Inc.

The Small Business Survival Guide to Debits, Credits, and Cash: What Every Growing Business Needs to Know About Accounting & Finance. Burr Ridge, IL: Probus Publishing Company, Inc., 1993. By Rose Marie L. Bukics.

The Small Business Test. Berkeley, CA: Ten Speed Press, 1990. By Colin Ingram.

Small Firms and Economic Growth. Brookfield, VT: Ashgate Publishing, 1995. By Zoltan J. Acs.

Small Firms and the Modern Economy. Cambridge, MA: Blackwell Publishers, 1996. By P. H. Admiraal.

"Start with Strategic Fundamentals" in *Crain's Small Business* (September 1995, p. 9). By Jim Brady.

The Start-Up Entrepreneur: How You Can Succeed in Building Your Own Company Into a Major Enterprise Starting From Scratch. New York, NY: Harper Collins Publishers, Inc., 1987. By James R. Cook.

The Start-Up Guide: A One-Year Plan for Entrepreneurs. Dover, NH: Upstart Publishing Co., Inc., 1994. By David H. Bangs, Jr.

Start Your Own Business After 50—or 60—or 70!. San Leandro, CA: Bristol Publishing Enterprises, Inc., 1990. By Lauraine Snelling.

"Starting an Appraisal Firm" in *Real Estate Appraiser* (Vol. 58, No. 1, April 1992, pp. 16-20). By Terrence L. Love.

Starting a Business After Fifty. Babylon, NY: Pilot Books, Revised edition, 1990. By Samuel Small.

Starting and Managing the Small Business. New York, NY: McGraw-Hill, Inc., 1992. By Arthur H. Kuriloff and John M. Hemphill.

Starting Millionaire Success Kit. Rockville Centre, NY: International Wealth Success, Inc., Sixth edition, 1993. By Tyler G. Hicks.

Starting a Mini-Business: A Guidebook for Seniors. Sunnyvale, CA: Fair Oaks Publishing Co., Revised edition, 1988. By Nancy Olson.

Starting and Operating a Business. Grants Pass, OR: The Oasis Press, 1992. By Michael D. Jenkins.

Starting and Operating a Business in Alabama: A Step-by-Step Guide. Grants Pass, OR: PSI Research, Revised edition, 1992. By Michael D. Jenkins.

Starting and Operating a Business in Alaska: A Step-by-Step Guide. Grants Pass, OR: PSI Research, Revised edition, 1992. By Michael D. Jenkins.

Starting and Operating a Business in Arizona: A Step-by-Step Guide. Grants Pass, OR: PSI Research, Revised edition, 1992. By Michael D. Jenkins.

Starting and Operating a Business in Arkansas: A Step-by-Step Guide. Grants Pass, OR: PSI Research, Revised edition, 1992. By Michael D. Jenkins.

Starting and Operating a Business in California: A Step-by-Step Guide. Grants Pass, OR: PSI Research, Revised edition, 1992. By Michael D. Jenkins.

Starting and Operating a Business in Colorado: A Step-by-Step Guide. Grants Pass, OR: PSI Research, Revised edition, 1992. By Michael D. Jenkins.

Starting and Operating a Business in Connecticut: A Step-by-Step Guide. Grants Pass, OR: PSI Research, Revised edition, 1992. By Michael D. Jenkins.

Starting and Operating a Business in Delaware: A Step-by-Step Guide. Grants Pass, OR: PSI Research, Revised edition, 1992. By Michael D. Jenkins.

Starting and Operating a Business in District of Columbia: A Step-by-Step Guide. Grants Pass, OR: PSI Research, Revised edition, 1992. By Michael D. Jenkins.

Starting and Operating a Business in Florida: A Step-by-Step Guide. Grants Pass, OR: PSI Research, Revised edition, 1992. By Michael D. Jenkins.

Starting and Operating a Business in Georgia: A Step-by-Step Guide. Grants Pass, OR: PSI Research, Revised edition, 1992. By Michael D. Jenkins.

Starting and Operating a Business in Hawaii: A Step-by-Step Guide. Grants Pass, OR: PSI Research, Revised edition, 1992. By Michael D. Jenkins.

Starting and Operating a Business in Idaho: A Step-by-Step Guide. Grants Pass, OR: PSI Research, Revised edition, 1992. By Michael D. Jenkins.

Starting and Operating a Business in Illinois: A Step-by-Step Guide. Grants Pass, OR: PSI Research, Revised edition, 1992. By Michael D. Jenkins.

Starting and Operating a Business in Indiana: A Step-by-Step Guide. Grants Pass, OR: PSI Research, Revised edition, 1992. By Michael D. Jenkins.

Starting and Operating a Business in Iowa: A Step-by-Step Guide. Grants Pass, OR: PSI Research, Revised edition, 1992. By Michael D. Jenkins.

Starting and Operating a Business in Kansas: A Step-by-Step Guide. Grants Pass, OR: PSI Research, Revised edition, 1992. By Michael D. Jenkins.

Starting and Operating a Business in Kentucky: A Step-by-Step Guide. Grants Pass, OR: PSI Research, Revised edition, 1992. By Michael D. Jenkins.

Starting and Operating a Business in Louisiana: A Step-by-Step Guide. Grants Pass, OR: PSI Research, Revised edition, 1992. By Michael D. Jenkins.

Starting and Operating a Business in Maine: A Step-by-Step Guide. Grants Pass, OR: PSI Research, Revised edition, 1992. By Michael D. Jenkins.

Starting and Operating a Business in Maryland: A Step-by-Step Guide. Grants Pass, OR: PSI Research, Revised edition, 1992. By Michael D. Jenkins.

Starting and Operating a Business in Massachusetts: A Step-by-Step Guide. Grants Pass, OR: PSI Research, Revised edition, 1992. By Michael D. Jenkins.

Starting and Operating a Business in Michigan: A Step-by-Step Guide. Grants Pass, OR: PSI Research, Revised edition, 1992. By Michael D. Jenkins.

Starting and Operating a Business in Minnesota: A Step-by-Step Guide. Grants Pass, OR: PSI Research, Revised edition, 1992. By Michael D. Jenkins.

Starting and Operating a Business in Mississippi: A Step-by-Step Guide. Grants Pass, OR: PSI Research, Revised edition, 1992. By Carl R. Sniffen and Michael D. Jenkins.

Starting and Operating a Business in Missouri: A Step-by-Step Guide. Grants Pass, OR: PSI Research, Revised edition, 1992. By Michael D. Jenkins.

Starting and Operating a Business in Montana: A Step-by-Step Guide. Grants Pass, OR: PSI Research, Revised edition, 1992. By Michael D. Jenkins

Starting and Operating a Business in Nebraska: A Step-by-Step Guide. Grants Pass, OR: PSI Research, Revised edition, 1992. By Michael D. Jenkins.

Starting and Operating a Business in Nevada: A Step-by-Step Guide. Grants Pass, OR: PSI Research, Revised edition, 1992. By Michael D. Jenkins.

Starting and Operating a Business in New Hampshire: A Step-by-Step Guide. Grants Pass, OR: PSI Research, Revised edition, 1992. By Michael D. Jenkins.

Starting and Operating a Business in New Jersey: A Step-by-Step Guide. Grants Pass, OR: PSI Research, Revised edition, 1992. By Michael D. Jenkins.

Starting and Operating a Business in New Mexico: A Step-by-Step Guide. Grants Pass, OR: PSI Research, Revised edition, 1992. By Michael D. Jenkins.

Starting and Operating a Business in New York: A Step-by-Step Guide. Grants Pass, OR: PSI Research, Revised edition, 1992. By Michael D. Jenkins.

Starting and Operating a Business in North Carolina: A Step-by-Step Guide. Grants Pass, OR: PSI Research, Revised edition, 1992. By Michael D. Jenkins.

Starting and Operating a Business in North Dakota: A Step-by-Step Guide. Grants Pass, OR: PSI Research, Revised edition, 1992. By Michael D. Jenkins.

Starting and Operating a Business in Ohio: A Step-by-Step Guide. Grants Pass, OR: PSI Research, Revised edition, 1992. By Michael D. Jenkins.

Starting and Operating a Business in Oklahoma: A Step-by-Step Guide. Grants Pass, OR: PSI Research, Revised edition, 1992. By Michael D. Jenkins.

Starting and Operating a Business in Oregon: A Step-by-Step Guide. Grants Pass, OR: PSI Research, Revised edition, 1992. By Michael D. Jenkins.

Starting and Operating a Business in Pennsylvania: A Step-by-Step Guide. Grants Pass, OR: PSI Research, Revised edition, 1992. By Michael D. Jenkins.

Starting and Operating a Business in Rhode Island: A Step-by-Step Guide. Grants Pass, OR: PSI Research, Revised edition, 1992. By Michael D. Jenkins.

Starting and Operating a Business in South Carolina: A Step-by-Step Guide. Grants Pass, OR: PSI Research, Revised edition, 1992. By Michael D. Jenkins.

Starting and Operating a Business in South Dakota: A Step-by-Step Guide. Grants Pass, OR: PSI Research, Revised edition, 1992. By Michael D. Jenkins.

Starting and Operating a Business in Tennessee: A Step-by-Step Guide. Grants Pass, OR: PSI Research, Revised edition, 1992. By Michael D. Jenkins.

Starting and Operating a Business in Texas: A Step-by-Step Guide. Grants Pass, OR: PSI Research, Revised edition, 1992. By Michael D. Jenkins.

Starting and Operating a Business in Utah: A Step-by-Step Guide. Grants Pass, OR: PSI Research, Revised edition, 1992. By Michael D. Jenkins.

Starting and Operating a Business in Vermont: A Step-by-Step Guide. Grants Pass, OR: PSI Research, Revised edition, 1992. By Michael D. Jenkins.

Starting and Operating a Business in Virginia: A Step-by-Step Guide. Grants Pass, OR: PSI Research, Revised edition, 1992. By Michael D. Jenkins.

Starting and Operating a Business in Washington: A Step-by-Step Guide. Grants Pass, OR: PSI Research, Revised edition, 1992. By Michael D. Jenkins.

Starting and Operating a Business in West Virginia: A Step-by-Step Guide. Grants Pass, OR: PSI Research, Revised edition, 1992. By Michael D. Jenkins.

Starting and Operating a Business in Wisconsin: A Step-by-Step Guide. Grants Pass, OR: PSI Research, Revised edition, 1992. By Michael D. Jenkins.

Starting and Operating a Business in Wyoming: A Step-by-Step Guide. Grants Pass, OR: PSI Research, Revised edition, 1992. By Michael D. Jenkins.

"Starting Over" in *Business Start-Ups* (Vol. 7, No. 8, August 1995, p. 6). By Lynn H. Colwell.

Starting on a Shoestring: Building a Business Without a Bankroll. New York, NY: John Wiley & Sons, Inc., Third edition, 1995. By Arnold S. Goldstein.

"Starting on a Shoestring" in *New Business Opportunities* (March 1990, pp. 26-28).

Starting a Small Business Handbook: How to Start and Operate Your Own Small Business. Plano, TX: Data-Lynn Book Co., Second edition, 1992. By Andrew J. Lynn.

Starting a Small Business of Your Own—With "No" Money. Milton, MA: The Empire Publishing, Inc., 1990. By David F. Cox.

Starting a Successful Business on the West Coast. Bellingham, WA: Self-Counsel Press, Inc., Third edition, 1992. By Douglas L. Clark.

Starting Up. Philadelphia, PA: Trans-Atlantic Publications, Inc., 1990. By Gary Jones.

Starting Up Your Own Business: Expert Advice From the U.S. Small Business Administration. Blue Ridge Summit, PA: TAB Books, Inc., 1990. By G. Howard Poteet.

Starting Your New Business: A Guide for Entrepreneurs. Menlo Park, CA: Crisp Publications, Inc., Revised edition, 1992. By Charles L. Martin.

Starting Your Own Business: No Money Down. New York, NY: John Wiley & Sons, Inc., 1988. By M. John Storey.

Steps to Small Business Start-Up: Everything You Need to Know to Turn Your Idea Into a Successful Business. Dover, NH: Upstart Publishing Co., Inc., 1993. By Linda Pinson and Jerry Hinnett.

Succeeding in Small Business: The 101 Toughest Problems and How to Solve Them. New York, NY: NAL/Dutton, 1992. By Jane Applegate.

"Support System" in *Entrepreneur* (Vol. 23, No. 4, April 1995, pp. 136-142). By Bob Weinstein.

Surviving the Start-up Years in Your Own Business. Evansville, IN: F & W Publishing, 1991. By Joyce S. Marder.

"The 10 Best Businesses to Start in 1996" in *Income Opportunities* (Vol. 31, No. 1, January 1996, pp. 12-16, 72, 79-80). By Jack Rosenberger.

"The Three Criteria for a Successful New Business" in *Inc.* (Vol. 18, No. 5, April 1996, pp. 21-22). By Norm Brodsky.

"The Truth About Start-Ups" in *Inc.* (Vol. 17, No. 2, February 1995, pp. 23-24). By Paul Reynolds.

"The 12 Biggest Mistakes Made By New Businesses" in *Income Opportunities* (Vol. 31, No. 4, April 1996, pp. 18-21). By Pamela Rohland.

Twenty-Three Principles to Being a Successful Entrepreneur: The Block Buster. Detroit, MI: Multi Business Concepts, 1989. By Anthony Bragdon.

The Ultimate No B.S., No Holds Barred, Kick Butt, Take No Prisoners, and Make Tons of Money Business Success Book. Bellingham, WA: Self-Counsel Press, 1993. By Dan Kennedy.

Ultrapreneuring: Taking a Venture from Start-Up to Harvest in Three Years or Less. New York, NY: McGraw-Hill, Inc., 1993. By James B. Arkebauer.

"Use Your Head" in *Business Start-Ups* (Vol. 7, No. 7, July 1995, pp. 44, 46-49). By Bob Weinstein.

We Own It: Starting & Managing Cooperatives & Employee-Owned Businesses. Laytonville, CA: Bell Springs Publishing Co., Revised edition, 1991. By Peter Honigsberg, Bernard Kamoroff and Jim Beatty.

The Wealth Creators: An Entrepreneurial History of the United States. New York, NY: NAL Dutton, 1990. By Gerald Gunderson.

"What to Do with a Lousy Business" in *Management Review* (Vol. 83, No. 6, June 1994, pp. 40-43). By Dan Thomas.

"What's the Big Idea?" in *Small Business Opportunities* (Vol. 7, No. 5, September 1995, pp. 17). By Carla Goodman.

Winning With the Power of Persuasion: Mancuso's Secrets for Small Business Success. Chicago, IL: Dearborn Financial Publishing, Inc., 1993. By Joseph Mancuso.

Working Knowledge: What You Need to Know Before Opening a Business. Houston, TX: Echelon Publishing, 1994. By William A. Walls.

World Class: Thriving Locally in the Global Economy. New York, NY: Simon & Schuster Trade, 1995. By Rosabeth M. Kanter.

World Databases in Business. New Providence, NJ: National Register Publishing. By C.J. Armstrong, Editor.

"The Wrong Question" in *Inc.* (Vol. 17, No. 3, March 1995, pp. 27). By Henry Kressel and Bruce Guile.

"The Year of Living Dangerously" in *Business Start-Ups* (Vol. 7, No. 6, June 1995, pp. 74, 76-77). By Jeannie Pearce.

"Year One" in *Business Start-Ups* (Vol. 7, No. 12, December 1995, pp. 76-77). By Jacquelyn Lynn.

"Yes, You Can Create Your Own Job" in *Public Relations Journal* (Vol. 50, No. 6, June/July 1994, pp. 18-20). By Betty Hall.

Your New Business: A Personal Plan for Success. Menlo Park, CA: Crisp Publications, Inc., 1993. By Charles Martin.

Sole Proprietorships

"Dealing with Government: What to Expect" in *Crain's Small Business* (December 1995, p. 8). By Jeffrey McCracken.

"Last-Minute Tax Tips" in *Business Start-Ups* (Vol. 8, No. 3, March 1996, pp. 74, 76). By Gloria Gibbs Marullo.

The Law of Corporations, Partnerships, & Sole Proprietorships Instructor's Guide. Albany, NY: Delmar Publishers, 1993. By Angela Schneeman.

PPC Tax Planning Guide: S Corporations. Fort Worth, TX: Practitioners Publishing Co., Revised edition, 1993. By Andrew R. Bield.

"PR Company Straightens the 'S' Curve to Thrive as a 'C'" in *Crain's Small Business* (December 1995, pp. 19-20). By Michelle Krebs.

S Corporation Manual: A Special Tax Break for Small Business Corporations. Englewood Cliffs, NJ: Prentice Hall, 1988. By Peter L. Faber.

"Selecting a Form of Business" in *Crain's Small Business* (December 1995, P. 21).

Selecting the Legal Structure for Your Business. Denver, CO: U.S. Small Business Administration (SBA).

Taxation

"Are You Self-Employed? Here's How to Meet Your Tax Requirements" in *Crain's Small Business* (December 1995, p. 30).

"Audit Angst" in *Entrepreneur* (Vol. 23, No. 8, August 1995, pp. 53-55). By David R. Evanson.

"Audit Tip Sheet" in *Inc.* (Vol. 16, No. 4, April 1994, pp. 118). By Jill Andresky Fraser.

"Avoiding an Audit" in *Income Opportunities* (Vol. 31, No. 1, January 1996, pp. 18-21). By Janine S. Pouliot.

"Brilliant Deductions" in *Entrepreneur* (Vol. 24, No. 4, April 1996, pp. 54). By Cynthia E. Griffin.

"Business and Pleasure" in *Business Start-Ups* (Vol. 7, No. 11, November 1995, p. 94). By Nancy L. Scarlato.

"Change Sought in Alternative-Profits Tax" in *Crain's Small Business* (October 1995, p. 7). By Amy Lane.

"Choose Your Poison" in *Entrepreneur* (Vol. 23, No. 3, March 1995, pp. 48, 50). By David R. Evanson.

Corporations: Tax Choices for Business Planning— Explanation, Law & Regulations, Legislative History, Cases & Rulings, Indexes. Englewood Cliffs, NJ: Prentice Hall. Compiled by Prentice Hall Editorial staff.

"CPA Versus CPU" in *Business Start-Ups* (Vol. 8, No. 4, April 1996, pp. 12, 14, 16). By Glen Weisman.

"A Crummey Idea" in *Small Business Opportunities* (Vol. 7, No. 5, September 1995, pp. 20). By Joseph F. Blum.

"Dealing with Downshifters" in *Working Woman* (December 1995, pp. 19-20, 75). By Martine Costello.

"Declaration Of Independents" in *Entrepreneur* (Vol. 24, No. 2, February 1996, pp. 56, 58-59). By David R. Evanson.

"Details, Details" in *Business Start-Ups* (Vol. 7, No. 10, October 1995, pp. 48, 50, 52). By Johanna S. Billings.

"Earners, Keepers" in *Business Start-Ups* (Vol. 8, No. 4, April 1996, p. 4). By Karin Moeller.

The Ernst & Young Tax Guide 1995. Somerset, NJ: John Wiley & Sons, Inc., 1995. Compiled by Ernst & Young.

Federal Taxation of Business Enterprises. New York, NY: Clark Boardman Callaghan, 1990. By Samuel C. Thompson, Jr., Paul R. Wysocki, Robert R. Pluth, Jr. and Catherine A. Jacobsen.

"Get a (Tax) Break from Your Kids" in *Crain's Small Business* (January 1996, p. 7). By Stanfield Hill.

"Head Start" in *Business Start-Ups* (Vol. 6, No. 8, September 1994, pp. 78, 80, 82). By Mark Henricks.

"How to Survive an IRS Audit" in *Nation's Business* (Vol. 82, No. 4, April 1994, pp. 42-43). By Joan C. Szabo.

"In Your Best Interest" in *Business Start-Ups* (Vol. 7, No. 3, March 1995, pp. 24-27). By Gloria Gibbs Marullo.

"IRS May Reclassify Independent Contractors" in *San Diego Business Journal* (Vol. 15, No. 6, February 7, 1994, pp. 6A). By James R. Urquhart III.

"IRS May Reduce Paperwork for Small Businesses" in *Income Opportunities* (Vol. 31, No. 3, March 1996, pp. 4). By Michele Marrinan.

"The IRS Wages War on the Self-Employed" in *Insight* (Vol. 10, No. 4, January 24, 1994, pp. 6). By James Bovard.

"Last-Minute Tax Tips" in *Business Start-Ups* (Vol. 8, No. 3, March 1996, pp. 74, 76). By Gloria Gibbs Marullo.

"Many Sides Push Reform of Single Business Tax" in *Crain's Small Business* (Vol. 3, No. 1, January 1995, pp. 9). By Amy Lane.

McGraw-Hill Small Business Tax Advisor. New York, NY: McGraw-Hill, Inc., Second edition, 1992. By Cliff Roberson.

"New Office Reviews Penalty Disputes" in *Crain's Small Business* (September 1995, p. 5). By Amy Lane.

"Paper Weight" in *Income Opportunities* (Vol. 30, No. 9, September 1995, pp. 46, 48). By Janine S. Pouliot.

"Paying Your Date" in *Income Opportunities* (Vol. 31, No. 2, February 1996, pp. 40, 42). By Janine S. Pouliot.

"Planning Can Help You Pass on Wealth to Family" in *Crain's Small Business* (October 1995, p. 11). By Richard Balamucki.

"Play It Again, Sam" in *Entrepreneur* (Vol. 23, No. 8, August 1995, pp. 43-45). By David R. Evanson.

"PR Company Straightens the 'S' Curve to Thrive as a 'C'" in *Crain's Small Business* (December 1995, pp. 19-20). By Michelle Krebs.

"Reasonable Deductions" in *Income Opportunities* (Vol. 30, No. 10, October 1995, pp. 54, 56). By Janine S. Pouliot.

"Reasons for Preparer Usage by Small Business Owners" in *National Public Accountant* (Vol. 37, No. 2, February 1992, pp. 20-26). By Peggy A. Hite and Toby Stock and Bryan C. Cloyd.

"Refund? We Fund!" in *Income Opportunities* (Vol. 30, No. 1, January 1995, pp. 82-84, 86). By Richard Marini.

"Self-employment Tax: Maximizing Benefits, Minimizing Costs" in *National Public Accountant* (Vol. 40, No. 2, February 1995, pp. 28-32). By Joseph R. Oliver.

"The Shared Foreign Sales Corporation" in *National Public Accountant* (Vol. 39, No. 12, December 1994, pp. 24). By Richard W. Sherman.

Small Business Tax Guide: Guide to Small Business Tax. Plano, TX: Data-Lynn Book Co., 1992. By Andrew J. Lynn.

Small Business Tax Handbook: Guide to Understanding Business Taxes. Plano, TX: Data-Lynn Book Co., 1990. By William C. Kennard.

Small Business Tax Survival Handbook. Berkeley, CA: Nolo Press, 1994. By Frederick W. Daily.

"Some Get to Avoid It and Many Pay Less" in *Crain's Small Business* (February 1996, p. 3). By Amy Lane.

"State Efforts: Small Business" in *National Public Accountant* (Vol. 37, No. 2, February 1992, pp. 38-41). By Harley T. Duncan and Verenda C. Smith.

"Stupid Tax Tricks" in *Entrepreneur* (Vol. 23, No. 4, April 1995, pp. 46, 48-49). By David R. Evanson.

"Take Steps Now to Pay Less Taxes for 1996" in *Crain's Small Business* (January 1996, p. 7). By Dan Lockman and Karl Fava.

"Tax Advantages of Statutory Employees" in *Agency Sales Magazine* (Vol. 24, No. 3, March 1994, pp. 6-11). By John Sandmeier.

"Tax Countdown" in *Independent Business* (Vol. 7, No. 2, March/April 1996, pp. 24-25). By Stephen Kunkel.

"Tax Credits" in *Small Business Opportunities* (Vol. 7, No. 3, May 1995, pp. 10). By John Kellmayer.

"Tax Driver" in *Entrepreneur* (Vol. 22, No. 13, December 1994, pp. 22). By Cheryl J. Goldberg.

Tax Tricks. York, NY: Concept Publishing, 1995. By David Coleman.

Taxation & Business Decisions. Cincinnati, OH: South-Western Publishing Co., 1996.

Taxation & Small Businesses. Washington, DC: Organization for Economic Cooperation & Development, 1994. By OECD Staff.

The Taxation of Sole Proprietors. Orlando, FL: Unicorn Research Corporation, 1995. By James A. Fellows.

"Taxes" in *Business Start-Ups* (Vol. 7, No. 12, December 1995, pp. 66-67). By Nancy L. Scarlato.

Taxes and Business Strategy: A Planning Approach. Englewood Cliffs, NJ: Prentice Hall, 1991. By Myron S. Scholes and M. Wolfson.

"A Taxing Headache" in *Business Start-Ups* (Vol. 7, No. 11, November 1995, p. 96).

"Taxing Matters" in *Business Start-Ups* (Vol. 7, No. 5, May 1995, pp. 18, 20). By Gloria Gibbs Marullo.

"Taxing Times" in *Small Business Opportunities* (Vol. 8, No. 3, May 1996, pp. 10, 40). By Richard G. Ensman, Jr.

"They've Got Your Number" in *Entrepreneur* (Vol. 23, No. 5, May 1995, pp. 42, 44-45). By David R. Evanson.

"The Three Tax Changes You Can't Afford to Miss" in *Working Woman* (January 1996, pp. 30). By Clint Willis.

"Timely Ways to Cut Your Taxes" in *Money: Money Guide Supplement* (1994, pp. 68). By Mary L. Sprouse.

"To the Rescue" in *Business Start-Ups* (Vol. 7, No. 5, May 1995, pp. 68, 70-71). By Sue Clayton.

Top Tax Saving Ideas for Today's Small Business. Grants Pass, OR: The Oasis Press, 1994. By Thomas J. Stemmy.

"Year in Review" in *Entrepreneur* (Vol. 23, No. 7, July 1995, pp. 39-41). By David R. Evanson.

Venture Capital/Other Funding

"Angel Networks" in *Black Enterprise* (Vol. 25, No. 12, July 1995, p. 38). By Carolyn M. Brown.

"Balancing Act" in *Entrepreneur* (Vol. 24, No. 2, February 1996, pp. 52, 54-55). By David R. Evanson.

"Bank On It!" in *Entrepreneur* (May 1993, pp. 85-88). By Elizabeth Wallace.

"A Bike Shop in Harlem: Part VIII of a Special Series" in *Income Opportunities* (Vol. 30, No. 5, May 1995, pp. 58, 60, 62-63, 66). By Maureen Nevin Duffy.

"Borrowing Against Collateral You May Not Know You Have" in *Money* (Vol. 23, No. 11, November 1994, pp. 114-116). By Nancy J. Perry.

Borrowing for Your Business: Winning the Battle for the Banker's "Yes". Dover, NH: Upstart Publishing Co., Inc. By George M. Dawson.

"Breaking the Bank" in *Entrepreneur* (May 1993, pp. 78, 80-82). By Stephanie Barlow.

"Breaking the Bank" in *Entrepreneurial Woman* (November 1990, pp. 60-63). By Kim Remesch.

Business Capital Sources. Rockville Centre, NY: International Wealth Success, Inc., 1994. By Tyler G. Hicks.

"Business Owners Dip into Capital" in *Black Enterprise* (Vol. 26, No. 9, April 1996, p. 29). By Carolyn M. Brown.

The Business Planner: A Complete Guide to Raising Finances for Your Business. Newton, MA: Butterworth-Heinemann, 1992. By Iain Maitland.

"Calculated Risk" in *Business Start-Ups* (Vol. 8, No. 1, January 1996, pp. 75-76). By Steve Marshall Cohen.

"Capitalists on a Mission" in *Black Enterprise* (Vol. 25, No. 4, November 1994, pp. 166-167, 170-171). By Mark Lowery.

"The Card File" in *Business Start-Ups* (Vol. 7, No. 11, November 1995, p. 98). By Karin Moeller.

"Charge It" in *Business Start-Ups* (Vol. 8, No. 1, January 1996, pp. 62-63). By Gerri Detweiler.

Classified Advertising Sources: Where to Find or Place Ads Pertaining to Surplus, Travel or Business Capital Funding Workbook. Houston, TX: Nunciata Publishing, 1992.

The Complete Book of Raising Capital. New York, NY: McGraw-Hill, Inc., 1993. By Lawrence W. Tuller.

"Criteria Used by Venture Capitalists" in *International Small Business Journal* (Vol. 13, No. 1, October/December 1994, pp. 26-37). By Russell M. Knight.

"Dialing For Dollars" in *Entrepreneur* (Vol. 23, o. 12, November 1995, pp. 52, 54-55). By David R. Evanson.

Directory of Operating Small Business Investment Companies. Washington, DC: Investment Division, Semiannual, April and October. By John R. Wilmeth, Editor.

Doing Business with Banks. Lakewood, CO: dba USA Press, Incorporated, 1991. By Gibson Heath.

The Entrepreneur's Guide to Preparing a Winning Business Plan and Raising Venture Capital. Englewood Cliffs, NJ: Prentice Hall, 1990. By Keith W. Schilit.

Entrepreneurship, Small Business and Venture Capital. Chapel Hill, NC: Eno River Press, Inc., 1990. By Richard Schwindt, editor.

The Ernst and Young Guide to Raising Capital. Somerset, NJ: John Wiley & Sons, Inc., 1991. By Daniel R. Garner.

The Evans One Thousand Venture Capital Directory. Los Angeles, CA: Community People Press, 1995. By Mervin L. Evans.

"Factors to Consider" in *Small Business Opportunities* (Vol. 7, No. 3, May 1995, pp. 20, 74). By Robert Kassebaum.

"A Fair to Remember" in *Entrepreneur* (Vol. 23, No. 2, February 1995, pp. 38-39). By Davis R. Evanson.

"Finance for Small and Medium-Sized Enterprises" in *International Journal of Bank Marketing* (Vol. 12, No. 6, 1994, pp. 3-9). By Pamela Edwards, Peter Turnbull.

Financing the Small Business. New York, NY: Prentice Hall General Reference and Travel, 1991. By Lawrence W. Tuller.

Financing Sources for Business. New York, NY: Gordon Press, Publishers, 1992.

"Financing Your Franchise" in *Business Start-Ups* (Vol. 8, No. 1, January 1996, pp. 68, 70-71). By Jacquelyn Lynn.

Financing Your Small Business: Techniques for Planning, Acquiring, and Managing Debt. Grants Pass, OR: Oasis Press, 1992. By Art DeThomas.

"Find Financing" in *Income Opportunities* (December/January 1991, p. 57). By D. Frederick Riggs.

A Firm Foundation: How to Secure Venture Capital. Grants Pass, OR: The Oasis Press, 1995. By Wyman Bravard.

Fitzroy Dearborn Directory of Venture Capital Funds. Chicago, IL: Fitzroy Dearborn Publishers, Inc., 1994. By A. David Silver.

"For What It's Worth" in *Entrepreneur* (Vol. 23, No. 5, May 1995, pp. 40-41). By David R. Evanson.

43 Proven Ways to Raise Capital for Your Small Business. Chicago, IL: Dearborn Financial Publishing, Inc., 1991. By Ted Nicholas.

Free Help From Uncle Sam to Start Your Own Business (or Expand the One You Have). Santa Maria, CA: Puma Publishing Co., Third edition, 1992. By William M. Alarid and Gustav Berle.

Free Money: For Small Businesses and Entrepreneurs. Somerset, NJ: John Wiley & Sons, Inc., Third edition, 1992. By Laurie Blum.

"Get Cash Now!" in *Success* (Vol. 38, No. 10, December 1991, pp. 26-32). By Ronit Addis Rose.

Getting a Business Loan. New York, NY: Gordon Press, Publishers, 1992.

Getting a Business Loan: Your Step-by-Step Guide. Menlo Park, CA: Crisp Publications, Inc., 1993. By Orlando J. Antonini.

Getting Money. Bellingham, WA: Self-Counsel Press, 1991. By Dan Kennedy.

Getting the Money: How to Successfully Borrow the Cash Your Business Needs. San Antonio, TX: Jefferson Publishing, 1990. By John Stonecipher.

"Going for Broke" in *Inc.* (September 1990, pp. 34-44).

Guerrilla Financing: Alternative Techniques to Finance Any Small Business. Boston, MA: Houghton Mifflin Co., 1992. By Bruce J. Blechman and Jay C. Levinson.

Guide to Business Credit for Women, Minorities, and Small Businesses. New York, NY: Gordon Press, Publishers, 1992.

"Hatching Uncle Sam's Entrepreneurs" in *Management Today* (November 1993, pp. 54-56). By John Thackray.

"Heaven Cent" in *Entrepreneur* (Vol. 24, No. 2, February 1996, pp. 29). By Cynthia E. Griffin.

"How to Finance Anything" in *Inc.* (February 1993, pp. 54, 56-58, 62, 64, 66, 68). By Bruce G. Posner.

How to Get a Loan or Line of Credit for Your Business. Naperville, IL: Sourcebooks, Incorporated, 1993. By Bryan E. Milling.

"How to Obtain Export Capital" in *Nation's Business* (Vol. 82, No. 5, May 1994, pp. 24).

How to Prepare and Present a Venture Capital Funding Request!. Los Angeles, CA: Community People Press, 1995. By Mervin Evans.

"Inatome Made It, Now He Wants To Help Others" in *Crain's Small Business* (March 1996, p. 11). By Jeffrey McCracken.

Instant Money Ideas for Finding Business and Real Estate Capital Today. Rockville Centre, NY: International Wealth Success, Inc., Fifth edition, 1992. By Tyler G. Hicks.

"Investors Look for Businesses Likely to Hit a Home Run'" in *Crain's Small Business* (March 1996, p. 11). By Jeffrey McCracken.

"An Investor's View" in *In Business* (January/February 1990, pp. 32-33). By Abbie C. Page.

"It's Who You Know" in *Entrepreneur* (Vol. 23, No. 11, October 1995, pp. 48, 51). By David R. Evanson.

IVCI Directory of Venture Networking Groups (Clubs) and Other Resources. Stamford, CT: International Venture Capital Institute (IVCI). By Carroll A. Greathouse, Editor.

"Job One: Find Money" in *Success* (Vol. 41, No. 10, December 1994, pp. 23-33). By Jenny C. McCune.

"Kid Venture Capital" in *Black Enterprise* (Vol. 25, No. 5, December 1994, pp. 34). By Tonia L. Shakespeare.

The Lender Liability Deskbook. Burr Ridge, IL: Irwin Professional Publishing, 1992. By Peter M. Edelstein.

"Listing Your Company on a Stock Exchange" in *D & B Reports* (Vol. 40, No. 2, March/April 1992, pp. 62-63). By Mark Stevens.

The Loan Package. Grants Pass, OR: Oasis Press. By Emmett Ramey.

"Look at Every Option—And Beyond" in *Nation's Business* (Vol. 79, No. 7, July 1991, pp. 9). By Thomas Hierl.

"Making a Statement" in *Entrepreneur* (Vol. 23, No. 7, July 1995, pp. 34-37). By David R. Evanson.

"A Match Made in Fiber Optics" in *Hispanic Business* (Vol. 16, No. 9, September 1994, pp. 24, 26). By Rick Mendosa.

"Money" in *Business Start-Ups* (Vol. 7, No. 12, December 1995, pp. 50-51). By Nancy Scarlato.

Money Connection: Where & How to Apply for Business Loans & Venture Capital. Grants Pass, OR: The Oasis Press, 1994. By Lawrence Flanagan.

"Money Guide" in *Crain's Small Business* (Vol. 3, No. 1, January 1995, pp. 4-6). By Dorothy Heyart and Gail Popyk.

"The Money Is Out There...How To Get It" in *Agency Sales Magazine* (Vol. 24, No. 2, February 1994, pp. 15-17). By Jeff Fromberg.

"Money Now" in *Success* (December 1990, pp. 29-36). By Ronit Addis Rose.

The Money Source Book. Dallas, TX: Business Information Network, Inc., Annual, spring. By Greg Hanson, Editor.

Money Sources for Small Business—How You Can Find Private, State, Federal, and Corporate Financing. Santa Maria, CA: Puma Publishing, 1991.

The Money Trail: Funding for Women, & Minorities & Disabled Entrepreneurs. Grants Pass, OR: The Oasis Press, 1995. By Trevor Pearson.

"Name Your Price" in *Business Start-Ups* (Vol. 7, No. 11, November 1995, pp. 96-97). By Steve Marshall Cohen.

National Association of Investment Companies—Membership Directory. Washington, DC: National Association of Investment Companies, Annual, June.

National Venture Capital Association—Membership Directory. Arlington, VA: National Venture Capital Association, Annual, November. By Molly M. Myers, Editor.

"New Enterprise Forum" in *Crain's Small Business* (December 1995, p. 31). By William Beardsley,

New Venture Creation: Entrepreneurship in the 1990s. Burr Ridge, IL: Richard D. Irwin, Inc., Third edition, 1990. By Jeffry A. Timmons.

"A New Way to Get Funding for Your Business" in *Successful Opportunities* (April 1990, pp. 36-38). By David Brainer.

"Nothing Ventured" in *Crain's Small Business* (March 1996, pp. 1, 10). By Jeffrey McCracken.

"Nothing Ventured, Nothing Gained" in *Entrepreneur* (Vol. 23, No. 4, April 1995, pp. 110). By David R. Evanson.

"The Numbers Speak Volumes" in *Small Business Reports* (Vol. 19, No. 7, July 1994, pp. 39-43). By Lamont Change.

Obtaining Venture Financing: Principles & Practices. New York, NY: The Free Press, 1991. By James W. Henderson.

Outcome Funding—A New Approach to Public-Sector Grant Making. Rensselaerville, NY: Rensselaerville Institute, 1991. By Harold S. William.

Planning and Financing the New Venture. Amherst, NH: Brick House Publishing Co., 1990. By Jeffrey A. Timmons.

Pratt's Guide to Venture Capital Sources. Phoenix, AZ: Oryx Press. By Dan Bokser, Editor.

Proposal Planning and Writing. Phoenix, AZ: Oryx Press, 1993. By Lynn E. Miner and Jerry Griffith.

"Quick Fix" in *Income Opportunities* (Vol. 30, No. 3, March 1995, pp. 88, 90). By Peg Byron.

The Radical New Road to Wealth: How to Raise Venture Capital for a New Business. Rockville Centre, NY: International Wealth Success, Inc., 1996. By David A Silver.

Raising Capital: How to Write a Financing Proposal to Raise Venture Capital. Grants Pass, OR: The Oasis Press, 1994. By Lawrence Flanagan.

Raising Money From Grants and Other Sources Kit. Rockville Centre, NY: International Wealth Success, Inc., 1993. By Tyler G. Hicks.

"Raising Money From Your Bank" in *In Business* (April 1990, pp. 21-23). By Allen C. Finley and Robert W. Pricer.

"Report Seeks to Show How State Should Venture Forth" in *Crain's Small Business* (March 1996, p. 13). By Jeffrey McCracken.

"Reservations Accepted" in *Entrepreneur* (Vol. 23, No. 3, March 1995, pp. 46-47). By David R. Evanson.

"SBA Lends a Hand" in *New Business Opportunities* (April 1990, pp. 10-15). By Iris Lorenz-Fife.

SBA Loan Guide. Irvine, CA: Entrepreneur, Inc.

SBA Loans: A Step-by-Step Guide. New York, NY: John Wiley & Sons, Inc., 1994, second edition. By Patrick D. O'Hara.

"The Secrets of Bootstrapping" in *Inc.* (Vol. 13, No. 9, September 1991, pp. 52-70). By Robert A. Mamis.

"The Six Best Ways to Raise Cash" in *Money: Money Guide Supplement* (Vol. , No. , 1994, pp. 34-39). By Vanessa O'Connell.

"Small Offerings" in *Entrepreneur* (Vol. 23, No. 1, January 1995, pp. 40-41). By David R. Evanson.

"Something Ventured" in *Entrepreneur* (Vol. 23, No. 11, October 1995, pp. 24). By David R. Evanson.

"Start-up Funding: Consider the Sources" in *Inc.* (Vol. 6, No. 8, August 1994, pp. 32). By Martha E. Mangelsdorf.

Starting Your Own Big Business with Venture Capital. Reno, NV: Western Book Journal Press, 1995. By William A. Gilmartin.

"Three Sources to Finance a Small Business" in *Crain's Small Business* (December 1995, p. 15). By Jeffrey McCracken.

"Turning to the Government" in *Practical Accountant* (Vol. 27, No. 6, June 1994, pp. 37-44). By John Cosgriff and Leonard Sliwoski.

Vankirk's Venture Capital Directory. Arlington, VA: Online Publishing, Inc., 1993. By Clarke V. Simmons, editor.

"Venture Capital" in *Business Start-Ups* (Vol. 7, No. 12, December 1995, p. 70). By Nancy Scarlato.

Venture Capital Directory. Centerport, NY: Forum Publishing Co., Annual, February. By Raymond Lawrence, Editor.

Venture Capital: Law, Business Strategies, and Investment Planning. New York, NY: John Wiley & Sons, Inc., 1988; 1992, supplement. By Joseph W. Bartlett.

Venture Capital Made Easy! Los Angeles, CA: Community People Press, 1995. By Mervin L. Evans.

Venture Capital Primer for Small Business. Denver, CO: U.S. Small Business Administration (SBA).

Venture Capital and Small Business Financings. New York, NY: Clark Boardman Callaghan, 5 vols. 1984; revised annually. By Robert J. Haft.

Venture Capital Sourcebook: The Definitive Guide to Finding Start-Up Funds & Growth Capital. Burr Ridge, IL: Probus Publishing Company, Inc., 1994. By A. David Silver.

Venture Capital: Where to Find It. Alexandria, VA: National Association of Small Business Investment Companies (NASBIC), Annual, September. By Jeanette D. Paschal, Editor.

Western Association of Venture Capitalists—Directory of Members. Menlo Park, CA: Western Association of Venture Capitalists, Annual, March.

When the Bank Says No!: Creative Financing for Closely Held Businesses. Blue Ridge Summit, PA: TAB Books, Inc., 1991. By Lawrence W. Tuller.

"Where Are All the Wanda Buffets?" in *Money* (Vol. 23, No. 11, November 1994, pp. 116-117). By Nancy J. Perry.

Where to Find Venture Capital: A Resource Guide. Highland City, FL: Rainbow Books, Inc., 1995. By Philip C. Paul.

Where to Get the Money & Management Help for New Business Start-Ups & Small Business Growth: Middle Atlantic Region. Willow Grove, PA: Special Reports, Incorporated, 1994. By Richard S. Guyer.

"Where to Look for Money Now" in *Working Woman* (Vol. 19, No. 10, October 1994, pp. 56-62). By Ilyce R. Glink.

"You Can't Start Too Soon" in *Inc.* (Vol. 17, No. 6, May 1995, pp. 144). By Susan Greco.